Library and Book Trade Almanac™

formerly The Bowker Annual

2013 | 58th Edition

Library and Book Trade Almanac™

formerly **The Bowker Annual**

2013 | 58th Edition

Editor Dave Bogart
Consultant Betty J. Turock

 **Information Today, Inc.**

Published by Information Today, Inc.
Copyright © 2013 Information Today, Inc.
All rights reserved

International Standard Book Number 978-1-57387-468-7
International Standard Serial Number 2150-5446
Library of Congress Catalog Card Number 55-12434

Information Today, Inc.
143 Old Marlton Pike
Medford, NJ 08055-8750
Phone: 800-300-9868 (customer service)
         800-409-4929 (editorial queries)
Fax: 609-654-4309
E-mail (orders): custserv@infotoday.com
Web Site: http://www.infotoday.com

Printed and bound in the United States of America

Contents

Part 2
Legislation, Funding, and Grants

Part 3
Library/Information Science Education, Placement, and Salaries

Part 4
Research and Statistics

Book Trade Research and Statistics

Part 5
Reference Information

Bibliographies

Ready Reference

Distinguished Books

Part 6
Directory of Organizations

Directory of Library and Related Organizations

Directory of Book Trade and Related Organizations

Preface

This 58th edition of the *Library and Book Trade Almanac* once again presents informed analysis and practical information of interest to librarians, publishers, and others in the evolving information world.

A striking feature of the past year has been the steadily progressing "digital revolution," which has required new ways of thinking in publishing and librarianship. The resulting changes are seen everywhere in the industry as challenges continue to arise in the way information is handled and made available to the public.

This edition's Special Reports focus on four topics of current interest.

- Sari Feldman, Carrie Russell, and Robert Wolven look in detail at the various business models libraries and publishers can follow in dealing with e-books.
- Peter Brantley discusses the e-book phenomenon itself and speculates on its far-reaching effects.
- Nicole A. Cooke examines developments in library education in the growing world of distance education and online learning.
- Winston Tabb and Brian J. Shields of Johns Hopkins University tell the story of the planning and creation of their institution's new Brody Learning Commons, an example of the evolution of library facilities.

Part 1 continues with reports on the activities of federal libraries, federal agencies, and national and international library, publishing, and bookselling organizations.

Legislation affecting libraries and publishers is featured in Part 2, together with the programs of two major grant-making agencies.

Part 3 offers a wealth of professional information for librarians, including salary studies, job-seeking tips, and a listing of the year's library scholarship and award winners.

Part 4 contains our useful statistics and research section, which offers detailed data on many aspects of the library and publishing worlds, from library acquisition expenditures to a close examination of U.S. world trade in books and a review of a year of many changes in the publishing industry.

Reference information fills Part 5, including a roster of major literary award winners and lists of notable books and other resources for all ages.

Part 6 is our directory of library and publishing organizations at the state, national, and international levels, and also includes a calendar of upcoming information industry events.

The *Library and Book Trade Almanac* is the work of many hands, and we are grateful to everyone who supplied reports, assembled statistics, and responded to our many requests for information. Very particular thanks are due to Consultant Editor Betty J. Turock, Contributing Editor Catherine Barr, and to Christine Weisel McNaull for her invaluable skill in making it all turn into a book.

We believe you will use this reference work frequently, and, as always, we welcome your comments and suggestions for future editions.

Dave Bogart
Editor

Part 1
Reports from the Field

Special Reports

E-Book Business Models for Public Libraries: A Response to Publisher-Library Differences

Sari Feldman
Carrie Russell
Robert Wolven

In March 2011 HarperCollins Publishing announced a new licensing arrangement for e-book sales to libraries—igniting a deeper and broader conversation about e-book business models for public libraries. Under the new plan, libraries could license access to an e-book for 26 loans, after which time the library would lose access to the e-book (unless it decided to renew the license). The news was met with outrage from librarians and media observers. Publishers were "shooting themselves in the foot," on track to make the same mistakes as the recording industry, demanding more money for a product that costs less to produce. Meanwhile, public libraries were experiencing some of the biggest budget cuts in history. In spite of the public demand for e-book lending, libraries would be unable to meet the needs of the public. A "Boycott HarperCollins" website and campaign were born and hundreds of libraries joined the cause.

HarperCollins responded in an open letter to libraries: "We are striving to find the best model for all parties," the company said. "Guiding our decisions is our goal to make sure that all of our sales channels, in both print and digital formats, remain viable, not just today but in the future. Ensuring broad distribution through booksellers and libraries provides the greatest choice for readers and the greatest opportunity for authors' books to be discovered."

Fortunately, HarperCollins and one other trade book publisher—Random House—did at least sell e-books to libraries. They just couldn't figure out the best way to do so. Random House chose to sell e-books to libraries at highly inflated prices—sometimes more than three times the price of e-books sold in the consumer market—but again, something is better than nothing. Four of the other Big Six trade publishers had different solutions (or not). Penguin and Hachette made a limited collection of e-books available to libraries. Macmillan and Simon & Schuster chose not to sell e-book titles to libraries.[1]

Sari Feldman is executive director of Cuyahoga County (Ohio) Public Libraries; Carrie Russell is director of the Program on Public Access to Information in the Washington Office of the American Library Association (ALA); Robert Wolven is associate university librarian for bibliographic services and collection development at Columbia University. Wolven is also co-chair of the Business Models subgroup of the ALA Digital Content and Libraries Working Group, and Russell is its ALA staff liaison.

Selling e-books to libraries was just one of many publisher concerns. The marketplace for print books was changing dramatically. Bookstores across the country were closing. Print book sales were down. More sophisticated and lower cost e-readers were being manufactured and sold, drawing more readers to the e-book format. Moreover, online retailers like Amazon made significant headway in the market for e-books and could sell e-books at greatly reduced prices. Consumers grew to expect that e-books would be priced much lower than print books. While expenditures for manufacturing and distributing e-books were less than print books, up-front costs remained the same. Publishers still had to discover worthy authors, nurture their development, review and edit content, promote authors and their books, and retain bestselling authors. Publishers also noted that publishing is a risky business. For every successful author, there are a number of authors whose work never pans out or fails to become popular with the public. Trade publishers banked their futures on bestsellers.

For public librarians, commitment to providing access to information to serve their communities was unchanging. Library lending was the key way to connect people, regardless of circumstance, to reading through books. Libraries pointed out the value they bring to the market for books. Libraries expose people to new authors, topics, and genres. Libraries buy a wide selection of books, many not available in the local bookstore. Librarians are in a key position to build literacy and digital literacy skills and to develop new readers with the necessary skills to navigate in the digital marketplace. Current e-book business models did not work for libraries and the high costs could not be sustained, ultimately threatening the mission of libraries. Prudent publishers should understand that selling e-books to libraries would be in their best interests. Furthermore, libraries were more than willing to work with publishers to develop mutually beneficial business models. Libraries and publishers needed to work together and better understand each other's concerns.

Friction

A basic concern for some publishers and other rights holders was the whole idea of library lending. Library lending of any kind, it was reasoned, cut into book sales. A library book would be borrowed many times over its shelf life—didn't at least some of that sharing account for missed sales? Furthermore, the United States does not have a public lending right in its copyright law. Under many other nations' copyright laws, libraries are required to pay additional fees for lending books to compensate the rights holders. This issue is so critical to U.S. publishers and other rights holders that legislation proposing its implementation in United States was introduced in 1973, 1983, and 1985. Congress ultimately took no action on these bills.

As free book-lending continued unabated, publishers thought that at least there was sufficient friction in the library lending process to mitigate some of the market harm. After all, library users had to be willing to exert some effort to obtain the book that they wanted to borrow. Library users had to travel to the library and be present when the desired book was available. If the book was already checked out, they had to place a hold on it in hope of borrowing it at a later date. When their name made the top of the wait list, the library held the book for them, but they still had to go the library to check it out. When their loan period was up, they had to go back to the library to return the book. The hope was that if library book borrowing was burdensome, at least some library users would just give up and buy the book.

Unlike book borrowing, e-book borrowing was frictionless, at least in principle. Downloading e-books from any location at any time surely diverted more sales, some publishers argued. The supposed ease of library e-book borrowing was a big reason why some publishers refused to sell to libraries under any conditions. In reality, library e-book lending is hampered by clunky interfaces and usually bound by highly constrained geographical service areas. So one library e-book does not equal unlimited access to everyone in the nation, as was suggested in some early conversations with publishers.

American Library Association Response

Librarians turned to the American Library Association (ALA), convinced that ALA would it make possible for the publishers to sell e-books to libraries under the same conditions they had always been able to purchase print books. Conversations between ALA and the publishers began, although making significant headway was difficult, in part because of the antitrust concerns of the publishers. More importantly, for both publishers and libraries, continuous change in the book marketplace was bewildering. It was difficult to track and fully comprehend digital advances. No one knew the best course of action, leading parties to be defensive, often clinging to old thinking and models of doing business.

To address the immediate problem of public library access to e-books, and more fundamentally consider how libraries could now, and in the future, respond to digital content opportunities and issues from both a policy and practical perspective, ALA 2011–2012 President Molly Raphael appointed a task force—the Digital Content and Libraries Working Group. A key priority was the consideration of e-book business models and licenses to acquire access to e-books. This priority resulted in the establishment of the Business Model/Licensing subgroup,[2] which analyzed existing e-book business models and created a report that explained how these models might play out in public libraries in both positive and negative ways.[3] The concern was not only to figure out a way to help public libraries acquire e-books from unwilling publishers but also to understand how models might, in the long term, advance or diminish the mission of public libraries to provide access to information for all people. To be clear, the business model subgroup was not expected to recommend a model suitable for all public libraries or meet publishers at the negotiating table with a preferred model.

In this report, we describe aspects of e-book business models that—when combined in different ways—might be winning formulas, or at least tolerable, to both publishers and libraries. This consideration of business models is not exhaustive and continues to shift among the participants and in their relationships to one another. Self-publishing continues to grow. The number of distributors and the services they offer is expanding. Many libraries are experimenting with the development of their own licensing schemes, some already entering into agreements with independent publishers and self-publishing groups. This report focuses on the kinds of licensing terms we see generally in the e-book industry at this time, and the kinds of variables libraries should consider when bargaining with publishers. Libraries may also use this information when they determine that they want to develop their own business models, as some proactive libraries already have done. Moreover, advancement of digital technologies and networks will have an impact on the business models we encounter in the future.

Business Models

Pulling apart the intricate practice of selling e-books to libraries, and really examining all of the components was the first step in understanding e-book business models. At the time, the dominant model for doing e-book business with libraries involved several players, some of them working behind the scenes, making decisions that the library as end user knows nothing about. When publishers did not hold the rights to produce and sell a digital copy of a previously print book, they had to work with the authors to license rights. That alone is an arduous process. The book contract between authors and trade publishers is a dissection of exclusive copyrights and other terms. Authors may reserve certain rights, split them up geographically or provide for only a limited term or for a specific purpose, like the first print publication of a book. Some authors refuse to clear the digital rights. Some publishers say that they already had the rights. While the book contract was the first process of developing a business model, it was not a concern of the business model subgroup.[4]

Once rights are cleared, the publisher is able to license the book to an intermediary. The intermediary, much like the book jobber, acquires as many titles as possible to sell to libraries. The intermediary can only provide access to the e-book under the individual publisher's business model (pay-per-use, perpetual access, time limited, and so forth). On top of these terms, the intermediary imposes additional terms for the library—such as agreement that digital rights management systems will be used, that the e-book is available to only one user at a time, and the intermediary's agreement to maintain the server where the e-books are stored for a certain annual fee. In simple terms, the intermediary implements the business terms that the publisher has set. Thus, when talking about business models, the business model subgroup assumed a business deal with the publisher, even though there was an intermediary in between that transaction.

For our purposes, a business model assumes a license or other agreement, not a direct sale. Licenses can be a less desirable way to acquire content and inferior to outright purchase of information resources. This is because certain library use rights and privileges familiar to us under federal copyright law—such as preservation, replacement, and interlibrary loan—are not necessarily included. By licensing content, libraries have access to the content *under the terms of the license* unless libraries have the opportunity and wherewithal to negotiate. The Harper-Collins 26-loan model brought home the fact that terms of use could require that e-books be purchased more than once, and if payment was not delivered content previously purchased would disappear. Much of the outrage directed at Harper-Collins by libraries was due to the fact that HarperCollins was the first publisher to implement a business model without perpetual access.

The HarperCollins decision rekindled opposition to licenses in general. Many librarians thought that business models should promote full ownership of e-books by libraries via direct sale. The subgroup agreed, but reasoned that the only way to achieve ownership at this time was through licensing agreements. Licenses were unavoidable in the short term—nearly all digital content purchased by libraries is licensed. Some believed that the U.S. copyright law should be amended to enable digital first sale. This would be an amendment to Section 109, the exception to the exclusive right of distribution (first sale). This was the idea that once a buyer purchased a lawfully made copyright-protected work, the rights holder had exhausted his distribution right to that copy. First sale allows owners of copies the right to lend, rent, sell, or otherwise dispose of their copies. First sale allows libraries to lend books that they buy without the authority of the rights holder. Adding digital first sale to Section 109 would mean that the first sale exception would be extended to digital files—once you paid for a lawfully made digital file, you could lend it without authorization. Once the loan occurred, the original buyer of the file would lose access to the file, ensuring that only one copy of the file existed.

For a number of reasons, it was doubtful that copyright law could be amended in a timely fashion to enable digital first sale. Congress would not consider digital first sale legislation given the other priorities it faced. Lobbying for such legislation would be quite risky. Amending copyright law is highly contentious. Rights holders always have the upper hand in financial wherewithal to lobby, and if they even agreed that digital first sale was realistic, the quid pro quo could be disastrous for libraries. Furthermore, the U.S. Copyright Office already had issued a report to Congress that digital first sale should not to be included in the copyright law. The business model subgroup also reflected on ways that academic libraries were successful in crafting license agreements with publishers that included contract terms that enabled full ownership and all of the rights associated with it. Admittedly, academic and school library markets are substantially different from the public library market because they hold primary market share. Public library purchases of trade books made a somewhat smaller dent in the overall market for trade publications. Ultimately, the subgroup's goal was encouraging publishers to sell e-books to libraries. The mechanism by which this was realized was not critical. If via a license agreement, contract terms would enable the desired aspects of ownership, including library lending.

Process

The business model subgroup began its work by considering what librarians would prefer to see in a business model and what conditions they would refuse to accept. Guaranteed perpetual access (as discussed above) to the e-book was a top priority. If the library could not purchase the e-book outright as a sale, licensing agreements would have to include language that allowed the library to retain the e-book file permanently. This would address concerns regarding retaining and maintaining the e-book, the ability to move e-book files from one platform to another, and censorship. Integration of e-book files into the library online catalog for easy discovery and use also was highly desirable as was the ability to purchase any titles publishers made available in the e-book format.

Other "must-haves" included:[5]

- Accessibility for people with print or other disabilities
- Choice in business models

- Cooperative purchasing
- Discounts
- Fair and flexible pricing models
- Interlibrary loan
- Price consistency
- Reader privacy
- Remote access
- Revenue sharing
- Simultaneous access
- Simultaneous release of content to library and consumer market

This was the "pie in the sky" list of desirables, some of which would not be acceptable to publishers.

The undesirables list was less clear in the subgroup's minds because there was less of a consensus among librarians. Depending on values and circumstances, some libraries might be willing to accept embargo periods, or even charging library users an additional fee for e-book loans. But clearly libraries would not accept the condition that library users must be present in the library in order to download.

Desirables and undesirables lists also were considered from the publisher perspective.

The publisher desirables included:

- Ability to change subscription/license depending on market needs
- Demand driven acquisition (a number of holds on an e-book automatically would trigger another library sale)
- Patron driven acquisition (particularly good for backlist or older titles)
- Enhanced discovery
- Embargoes of frontlist titles
- Friction
- Higher prices for e-books
- Library borrowers must be in the library in order to download
- Limited user community has access
- One user/one copy
- Price discrimination

Publisher undesirables included simultaneous access and inclusion of their full catalog of e-books, including frontlist and bestsellers.

The subgroup speculated on additional factors that might encourage publishers to sell to libraries.

- Free promotion of e-books to library users
- Promotion of reading and literacy
- Continued purchase of print books

- Potential purchase of backlist titles in e-book format
- Ability for readers to buy e-books from the library website
- Library data on circulation, acquisitions budget projections, library best-sellers, and so on
- Evidence that friction did exist with e-book lending as shown by the very long wait lists for desired titles

This process clarified that aspects of business models could be combined in any number of ways. Some formulas would be favorable to some librarians and publishers, and others would not. For example, smaller libraries might be willing to accept pay-per-use—a publisher "desirable"—while larger libraries might be less inclined. Depending on the circulation and the per-use cost, smaller libraries likely would end up paying less for the same e-book than a larger library paid. The variables could be placed on a matrix for libraries to pick and choose from as desired or appropriate. Yet the mix of available variables had to be realistic, without compromising too much to the publisher desirables.

Assumptions

It was helpful for the subgroup to consider some assumptions or suppositions about the models we would develop, both for ourselves and for the librarians seeking to understand our rationale. It ended up being a long list:

Any successful business strategy will depend on concessions from both publishers and libraries.

The business models proposed include some terms that are favorable to publishers. Our assumption is that we must have some publisher-friendly terms for negotiation purposes. However, we are not going to negotiate models unfavorable to libraries.

The business models only pertain to public libraries and trade e-books.

We have no intention of negotiating a business model on behalf of all public libraries. Our expectation is that the business models will provide the publishers with new ways of thinking about selling e-books to libraries.

The proposed business models are not etched in stone. They provide an idea of what a business model *could* look like, not what it *should* look like.

While the business models promote full access to all titles in the publisher catalog, we think that discussions around the backlist may be helpful and could be a primary factor in any business model proposed.

Any duration or per-use business model leads to perpetual access to e-book titles as one of its features.

All models assume one copy/one user at a given time, but multiple copies could be purchased to improve wait time or enable simultaneous access.

We recognize that negotiations with publishers will be a process of stops and starts. There may be a time when we walk away from negotiations because proposed solutions are not acceptable to libraries, and pursue advocacy through the media, governmental channels, and/or grassroots campaigns.

We acknowledge that some business model characteristics will not be popular with all librarians, for example, the direct sale of e-books to library users from the library website.

Testing out business models with willing libraries is preferred by the publishers rather than diving in headfirst, with the potential for bad publicity or the need to withdraw from libraries when business models proved unsuccessful.

Steps forward should be viewed as pilots. We cannot anticipate future developments, and recalibration of strategies likely will be necessary.

Any model could include revenue sharing, price discrimination, and/or embargo periods for the library.

Any embargo period that we accept would be no longer than 28 days and preferably reflect existing business models.

None of the models require that the library user must be physically in the library to access e-books (that is non-negotiable).

Communication

By the time the business model subgroup was ready to release its work to the library world, its knowledge about the marketplace was much improved. It also had adopted publisher lingo after being steeped in the process. Since the subgroup wanted the report to be transparent to librarians, we issued the background paper found in the Addendum following this report.

The Final Cut

The subgroup ultimately developed five business models for public library acquisition of e-books. When publishing the final five, the assumptions document proved valuable by reflecting all of the subgroup's caveats. We specifically pulled out the following assumptions about the five models we developed.

- All models assume one copy/one user at a given time, but multiple copies could be purchased to improve wait time or enable simultaneous access.
- Any model could include revenue sharing, price discrimination, and/or embargo periods for the library. (There is one model that would allow embargo for the library but not the library user purchasing the book from the library.)
- Any embargo that we accept would be short term (e.g., 14 to 30 days) and preferably reflect existing business models, such as the first release DVD model.
- Any model eventually leads to perpetual access to e-book titles as one of its features.
- All models do not require that the user is physically in the library (that is non-negotiable).

The Store Front

Under this model, libraries display a publisher's full catalog of books (or those titles available in e-book format) on their websites, enhancing discovery. All titles could be purchased by a library user. Titles available in the library but on the hold list also would be available for sale, allowing library users the choice of immediate satisfaction, addressing patron frustration with e-book wait time. The library would share revenue generated by sales as a *requirement* of this model.

Variables

Sales generated by the library could earn the library discounts on future purchases; e.g., library sells five e-books, gets one free.

Sales generated for titles (not owned by the library) could trigger a sale.

Library users would have access to all titles, including embargoed titles, that the library might not be able to purchase. Library user purchases of embargoed titles could reduce the duration of the embargo period for the library.

The library serves as a partner and creates an additional revenue stream for publishers.

HarperCollins Model with Defined Limits

Under this model, libraries pay for a certain number of uses. If uses are not depleted within a year or other fixed period of time, the library obtains perpetual access to the e-book. If uses are depleted, the library can choose to re-buy the title at a discounted price *taking along the already depleted uses*. This model would only generate the re-purchase of an e-book if it were circulated more than a certain number of times within a certain period.

Examples

In this example, libraries pay for 30 loans that, if not expended by year two, triggers the provision that the library has perpetual access to the e-book.

Library X buys an e-book with 30 loans, then uses all loans before or by the end of the two-year deadline. It then decides to repurchase the e-book (at a discounted price) in order to have perpetual access. Library X no longer needs to repurchase the book.

Library Y buys the same e-book under the same conditions. By the end of the two-year period, Library Y only expends six loans. Library Y continues to have access to the e-book without having to repurchase it because the two-year point has lapsed and Library Y has not used all of its 30 loans.

Variables

The publisher could choose to embargo particular titles, with the assumption that the embargo period would be short and reflect existing industry practices.

The publisher could vary number of loans for premium titles, facilitating repurchase of the book. For example, bestsellers could have a lower number of loans, forcing the library to repurchase if it wanted to maintain access.

The library could make a decision to provide simultaneous access with one copy by using its "uses" at the same time. A very popular title might have to be purchased more than once, but library users would not have to wait on the "hold" list. The costs would be prohibitive if an e-book was extremely popular, but might be something the library occasionally did to draw user traffic.

When the library holds reach a certain number, purchase of an additional copy automatically could be available, easing library-user dissatisfaction. With this variable, libraries would lose some control over budget, because the decision to repurchase the book is automatically triggered.

The long tail (the principle of collecting books on all topics, not just bestsellers) is enabled because even books borrowed once are in the collection.

Libraries are able to build their collections of e-books over time.

Short Embargo with Premium Pricing Available

Under this model, publishers could implement an embargo period for any title, potentially at any time. If a backlist book becomes popular again—for instance, because of the release of a movie based on the book—publishers could set an embargo for a time period to allow for more direct sales to consumers for new library purchases. (Libraries that had already purchased the e-book would be unaffected.) For first-release titles, the assumption is that the embargo period would be short and reflect existing industry practices.

Variables

Libraries could purchase embargoed books at a higher price.

A publisher's full catalog of e-books could be made available for library users to purchase.

Embargo with Discounts

The date a book is released to the public determines price and availability of bestsellers. First-run books could be embargoed and not available for sale as determined by the publisher. Alternatively, the publisher could make all books available to the library at the same time, but popular books would have a higher price. After the embargo period, regardless of whether the library purchased a popular book or not, it could purchase the same book for a discounted price. In general, the price of a title decreases over time, and the library would pay only once for perpetual access to the e-book.

Examples

During the embargo period, the library can buy a popular book for $55 but chooses not to purchase it. After the embargo, the library can purchase the same book for $20. (Note: the library does not repurchase the book year after year. Instead, if it waits to buy the book when it is less popular, the library increases purchase power and/or saves money.) This model dictates that embargoes can only occur when a book is first released to the public for sale.

Preview Model

The library user has access to a large catalog of books for preview purposes (the library does not own the preview books). After previewing, if the user decides to read the entire book, a loan is generated and the library pays a loan fee. Alternatively, the user buys the book.

Variables

If selecting the pay-per-use model, the library could cap loans and/or buy the book.

Per-use fees could count toward final sale price. For example: Per-use fee is $1. The e-book costs $20. Six pay-per-uses are generated by library users in a short time period. The library decides to turn off pay-per-use and buy the book for $14.

The preview option could be turned "off" once a book is purchased or "on" for titles not held by the library.

The library could purchase one copy and have a second copy for pay-per-use.

Embargo would still be an option for the publisher.

Discovery would be enhanced if the collection of preview books were substantial.

Conclusion

While a few publishers continue to deliberate about selling e-books to libraries, acceptance of certain aspects of e-book licensing once abhorred by libraries have gained traction with some. For instance, the need to have access to an e-book in perpetuity is waning. Some librarians are reconsidering whether they require permanent access to *every* book in their collection while larger libraries may be willing to pay a higher price for the guarantee of long-term access. Smaller libraries may find that pay-per-use models are most effective in maximizing their budgets. Others are beginning to advocate for a central source for e-book preservation where all preserved titles could be held. Some libraries already are participating in revenue-generating models where libraries get a percentage of the sale.

Today, looking at the maze of possibilities that exist for acquiring e-books may be daunting, but public libraries are already finding that having a variety of business models to choose from is in their best interest.

Fast forward just one year after HarperCollins announced its 26-loan model and you'll discover that librarians are beginning to *like* the once-unappealing business model. "We have had no problems to date—smooth sailing," said Robin Nesbitt, technical services director at Columbus (Ohio) Metropolitan Library. "I'm not sure we've even hit the cap—so for all of the hand-wringing out there, we have been just fine."

New options no doubt will develop over time, changing how libraries acquire digital books and other resources. Additional e-book intermediaries have entered the market, encouraging more competition. A small group of libraries have already cut out the middle man at least to some extent and maintain their own e-book servers. The rapid growth of self-publishing is bound to have some impact on library collections. The perception that self-publishing is merely vanity press under a different name is quickly eroding. New reader opportunities already are being developed by innovative entrepreneurs. By next year, we may be talking about the demise of the e-book—it having been replaced by some more-advanced technology that savvy readers will come to expect. Reading and technological advances associated with digital reading will move ahead at a breakneck pace. One must accept unceasing change and be prepared to run with eyes wide open.

Notes

1. Later in 2012 Hachette and Penguin conducted pilots at a limited number of libraries to test various business models and to work with new intermediary vendors who had entered the market. Macmillan announced a pilot program to begin in 2013.
2. Rod Gauvin, Ric Hasenyeager, Eric Hellman, M. Kathleen Kern, Erika Linke (co-chair), Rob Maier, Vailey Oehlke, Carrie Russell (ALA staff liaison), Brian E. C. Schottleander, Robert Wolven (co-chair), Junko Yokota, and Holly Yu are members of the Business Models subgroup.
3. This report was released in August 2012: http://americanlibrariesmagazine.org/e-content/ala-releases-ebook-business-models-public-libraries.
4. However, ALA is interested in author-publisher relationships insofar as they are important to the health of the publishing ecosystem overall.
5. These attributes are described in some detail in the addendum that follows.

Additional Sources

Kelley, M. "One Year Later, HarperCollins Sticking to 26-Loan Cap, and Some Librarians Rethink Opposition," *The Digital Shift,* February 17, 2012. http://www.thedigitalshift.com/2012/02/ebooks/one-year-later-harpercollins-sticking-to-26-loan-cap-and-some-librarians-rethink-opposition.

Library Journal. Patron Profiles: Public Library Edition. "Library Patrons and the Changing Ebook Landscape," Vol. 2, No. 1, October 2012.

Marwell, J. "Open Letter to Librarians," March 3, 2011. http://www.harpercollins.com/footer/release.aspx?id=938&b=&year=2011.

Schneck, J. M. "Closing the Book on the Public Lending Right," 63 *N.Y.U. Law Review* 878 (1988).

U.S. Copyright Office. "DMCA Section 104 Report," http://www.copyright.gov/reports/studies/dmca/sec-104-report-vol-1.pdf.

Zickuhr, K., et al. *Libraries, Patrons, and E-books,* Pew Research Center, Pew Internet and American Life, released June 22, 2012. http://www.pewinternet.org/Media-Mentions/2012/EBook-Reading-Is-Up-Study-Says.asp.

Addendum

This explanatory statement was authored by the Digital Content and Libraries Working Group, ALA, and published online only on the ALA Econtent Blog on August 8, 2012, at http://americanlibrariesmagazine.org/sites/default/files/EbookBusinessModelsPublicLibs_ALA.pdf.

E-Book Business Models for Public Libraries

In response to urgent member concerns, the Digital Content and Libraries Working Group of the American Library Association (ALA), in close collaboration with ALA's president and executive director, has focused on influencing the Big 6 trade publishers to sell to libraries on reasonable terms. During the past months, the Working Group has developed considerable knowledge about the e-book market, publishers, and various aspects of library lending to inform its discussions with publishers and distributors. However, the Working Group is well aware that information about this topic is highly sought in the library community generally, and so this report was prepared to share some of what we have learned.

Libraries and the E-book Marketplace

E-book publishing is expanding and evolving rapidly, and the terms under which e-books are made available to libraries show wide variation and frequent change. Some major trade publishers will not sell e-books to libraries under any terms; others do so only at inflated prices or with severe restrictions. Some publishers have scaled back their initial offerings, but are beginning to explore new business models under pilot programs of limited duration or in selected regions. Other publishers seem to be making little or no headway in dealing with libraries.

In this volatile period of experimentation, no single business model will offer the best terms for all libraries or be adopted by all publishers or distributors. This report describes model terms libraries should look for in their dealings with e-book publishers and distributors, as well as conditions libraries should avoid. While business models will continue to evolve, models that are explored in the year ahead may well pave the way to the models of the future. It is therefore important that libraries negotiate aggressively for the most favorable and flexible terms possible.

General Features and Attributes

Replicating the Print Model: Unlike a printed book, a single copy of an e-book could potentially be read by many users simultaneously, from any location. Thus, a major concern of publishers is that e-book borrowing from libraries will be so easy as to erode consumer sales. To counter this opinion, many publishers insist on terms that replicate aspects of print book lending. Some of these terms may be necessary and tolerable, at least temporarily, to offset perceived risks in selling e-books to libraries. Others, such as requiring patrons to come to the library to check out e-books, will be onerous to patrons, [contradicting] a fundamental benefit of e-book technology, and [damaging perceptions] of library service. In any case, innovative models that test new and alternative potentials offered by e-books should be encouraged, rather than slavishly imposing restrictions based on the characteristics of print.

Trade-offs: Many publishers offer e-books to libraries only under conditions less favorable than those for print. For example, new publications may be offered only after an embargo period, or the number of circulations may be limited. In such cases, when libraries are asked to give up some rights they have always had, it is reasonable and fair to expect some other benefit in return. Possibilities are discussed in more detail below, but they include discounted prices for certain titles, a share of the revenues generated from sales to patrons made through the library's website, and limited free access to selected titles.

Essential Features: Three basic attributes are desirable under any business model for e-books. While it may not be feasible to realize all of these immediately, and a library may elect to do without one or more in return for more favorable terms in other areas, at least temporarily, these features are ultimately essential to the library's public role:

- Inclusion of all titles: All e-book titles available for sale to the public should also be available to libraries. Libraries may choose not to purchase some titles if restrictions or prices are deemed unacceptable, but withholding titles under any terms removes the library's ability to provide the services its patrons need and expect.
- Enduring rights: Libraries should have an option to effectively own the e-books they purchase, including the right to transfer them to another delivery platform and to continue to lend them indefinitely. Libraries may choose more limited options for some titles or copies, or in return for lower pricing, but they should have some option that allows for permanent, enduring access.
- Integration: Libraries try to provide coherent access across all of the services they offer. To do this effectively, they need access to metadata and management tools provided by publishers or distributors to enhance the discovery of e-books. Separate, stand-alone offerings of e-books are likely to be marginalized, or to diminish awareness of other library offerings. Mechanisms that allow e-books to be discovered within the library's catalog and checked out or reserved without undue complexity are basic needs.

Characteristics of Business Models: Constraints and Restrictions

To enable library and retail distribution channels for e-books to coexist, most business models currently offered to libraries include constraints on how e-books can be used.

Single User: By replicating the print model, loans are limited to one user at a time for each e-book license purchased. This constraint often results in long waiting lists for popular titles, and is currently found in almost all publisher models.

While the single-user constraint is generally accepted, alternatives might be considered and sought, e.g., the ability to allow two or more simultaneous users for a higher price; the ability to combine multiple simultaneous users with a limited-number-of-loans model.

Limited Number of Loans: The library must repurchase the same title after a defined number of loans. (In theory, this is to offset the fact that e-books don't wear out, get lost or stolen, have coffee spilled on them, etc.) While this model violates the principle of ownership, it may be an acceptable way of achieving lower pricing if the defined number of loans is high enough.

Ideally, this model could be combined with a sunset provision, providing for permanent ownership after a period of years. At minimum, the library should have permanent access if the e-book title is no longer offered for sale when the loan limit is reached.

Paying a set price for a limited number of loans is, in effect, a rental. Librarians may seek to apply a similar fee to current titles: a cost-per-circulation that replaces or augments purchased titles. Under this model, the library will never have enduring access to the title, unless the fee schedule is maintained. A lease-to-own arrangement[1] may be more prudent. Another option might be to seek the right to sell those materials that did not circulate well at a discount to the community. In this case, the library might share some percentage of the sale with the publisher.

Variable Pricing: E-book prices for libraries vary widely, with some titles well above the print price and others offered at a discount. While libraries will always want to seek the best terms possible, the maximum price that is considered acceptable depends on other terms of the sale. One example of this might be a "platform" fee—a merging of a sale with database-like annual subscriptions.

Delayed Sale: Publishers may delay sales of e-books to libraries for a period after the title is released for public sale. This embargo period or "window" may last anywhere from a few weeks to several months or more. While any delayed sale violates the principle of inclusion of all titles, a brief delay may be acceptable, especially if titles are then offered at a discount. Embargoed titles are less valuable, and their price should reflect that. Conversely, libraries may be willing to pay a premium for immediate access to the most popular titles.

In-Library Checkout: Publishers may insist that patrons come to the library in order to check out e-books. Although this is often seen as a way of adding "friction" to the transaction, it is also presented as a guard against "shopping" for library privileges in desirable districts, or to counter the perceived risk that patrons will forgo buying e-books while traveling if borrowing is simpler. In the absence of hard evidence that these risks are real, few libraries will find this model acceptable. The requirement for in-library check-out will make no sense to users, but may be seen as a barrier needlessly imposed by the library. If unavoidable, an alternative may be to allow check-out only by patrons who are physically present within the geographic boundaries of the library's service area.

Restrictions on Consortial or Interlibrary Loans: Publishers may attempt to forbid through license agreements the sharing of titles among more than one institution. In essence, this is no different than a library restricting circulation to some subset of its branches. With the one-use-at-a-time model, these restrictions should be avoided.

Digital-Native Business Models: Libraries will need to consider business models that take advantage of the digital nature of e-books to go beyond what has existed for print. These models will have unique advantages and drawbacks that should be carefully considered. For example, subscription models may provide unlimited or metered access to broad collections. Open-Access models, in which access to content is unrestricted, can provide global benefits when libraries act together to provide funding. Finally, libraries should give more emphasis to the use of public domain and open license e-books.

Characteristics of Business Models: Advantages to Publishers

Because of the fundamental shift facing trade publishing including the entry of retail companies who currently dominate the e-book market, publishers and authors have much to gain from enabling libraries to distribute e-books. There is compelling evidence that during periods of technological, social and economic change, people use libraries more. With many bricks-and-mortar bookstores closing, publishers need new ways to "showroom" their titles. Publishers may be willing to offer more favorable terms and lower prices in exchange for specific accommodations (described below).

Enhanced Discovery: Library readers are also heavy book buyers, and publishers value the role libraries play in connecting readers with authors. Libraries might offer to provide access to a publisher's entire catalog (including books not yet purchased) as a way of connecting readers with additional offerings which they may buy or request the library purchase. This would also enhance integration. (In addition, by refusing to load titles excluded from library sales, libraries may gain leverage in reducing or eliminating embargoes.)

Sales Channel: By adding a "buy it" link in the library catalog, libraries can generate additional sales for the publisher. In return, libraries may negotiate for a share of the revenues generated through this channel, either as a direct payment or as a discount on future purchases.

Readers Advisory: Librarians stimulate interest in books through their recommendations. By expanding this service in the e-book realm, libraries will strengthen their role of connecting readers with authors and books they might otherwise miss. Libraries may also enhance publisher offerings through reader and staff reviews incorporated into the catalog, and/or local recommendation engines.

Summary

With today's rapidly changing business environment for e-books, the choices that libraries make today can have profound impact on the direction taken by the entire reading ecosystem. It is thus of utmost importance that these choices be made with careful consideration of the needs of both present and future users. Decisions are best made in the context of an informed community and never in isolation or with passivity.

1. As an example, a library would pay a fixed fee for each loan. After a pre-defined number of loans is reached, the library will have purchase rights to the title.

Books Going Digital: Betwixt and Between

Peter Brantley

Director of Scholarly Communication, Hypothes.is

In terms of technical transitions, it is not too much of a stretch to suggest that e-books are living through their 19th century. What our age's digital industrial revolution will bring to literature is not clear. Our captains of industry currently are found in Apple, Amazon, and Google; whether we will ever see a return to higher-tech local-crafts-based manufacturing is uncertain. As in every era of great change, early choices and patterns leave their marks far into the future, arguably transforming publishers, booksellers, and libraries from the dawn of the digital age.

There are times when the road stretching into the future seems preordained. For ground transportation this must have been the case in the 1950s and 1960s: the car was ascendant, and urban science focused on what kind of roads to build, and where. There are equally times when the path into the future is obscure. In 1861, not quite understanding what cars were about, the English restricted "road locomotives" to a maximum speed of 2 mph and required a crew of three, one person walking ahead of the vehicle with a red flag to warn carriages and pedestrians (Locomotive Acts 2013). The speed limit was raised to 14 mph in 1896, and the requirement for a crew of three was eliminated. With e-books, we are living in 1896.

The early nature of our epoch can be seen in the frustrations we face. I recently spoke with a friend who was expressing difficulties with reading an e-book on a tablet; accustomed to zooming and pinching Web pages and other text displays, he was exercising his digits to no avail in an attempt to zoom a map of a Civil War battle to a size where his eyes could see something beyond squiggles. But the map, which had limited scalability and no interactivity, zoomed only so large and then just sat there, silently mocking his efforts.

Such "dumbness" in digital information is a reflection of the limited level of innovation that has emerged from traditional publishing. How did we get here?

Print Books, Digitized

In the automation of any industrial endeavor, the first transition is a straightforward translation of historical practices to digital equivalents. When mainframes made corporate data processing attractive, initially improvements were limited to back-end functions such as payroll. The first user-facing screens on mainframes with real-time, interactive operating systems were limited in their ability to present anything but simple text on the screen; it was a mark of high accomplishment

Peter Brantley is the convener of the Books in Browsers conference, a summit for software developers and UX designers creating new forms of storytelling. He is a contributing editor to *Publishers Weekly* on libraries and publishing, and speaks widely on transformations in media and information access. He has served on the board of the International Digital Publishing Forum, the standards-setting body for digital books, and was previously executive director of the Digital Library Federation and director of the BookServer Project at the Internet Archive, a not-for-profit digital library.

to mirror a complex paper-based data entry form as a digital surrogate. It took familiarity with translations of existing procedures to project new means of conducting business that could take advantage of digital affordances.

Yet even in the 1960s and 1970s antecedents to modern networked computing were apparent to those seeking them. The PLATO computer system, funded in part by the United States' National Science Foundation, was an international educational network of computers from Control Data Corporation, designed to support experimentation with online learning systems (PLATO [computer system] 2013). PLATO introduced some of the first multiplayer games and collaboration spaces, much akin to blogs and wikis. Yet arguably it would take a visual rewrite of the underlying network through the development of the World Wide Web and its accompanying protocols and standards before we were able to wholly reconceive how we communicated and shared information.

We are only now emerging from our mainframe era for digital books. The first examples of e-books found only modest commercial success, with the Rocket e-Book of the 1990s and Peanut Press, which was adopted by Palm for its hand-held devices. There were other proprietary text-based systems on expensive mobile equipment, usually in logistics, medical, or military applications. These early efforts failed to achieve widespread consumer adoption for a range of reasons, including inexperience with mobile computing, the lack of integrated media stores, and the absence of an extensive catalog of digital content.

E-books began to mature with the emergence in the late 1990s of the Open eBook Forum (OeBF), now known as the International Digital Publishing Forum (IDPF), as an industry standards body. The early Open eBook format was based on a subset of the hypertext markup language (HTML), with book contents clumsily separated into three separate physical files stitched together via a zip archive. The specification gave rise to the Mobipocket format, eventually acquired by and adopted as Amazon's proprietary standard. OeBF's succeeding EPUB format, created and supported by IDPF, has become the dominant e-book standard. It is itself currently deprecated in favor of the successor format, EPUB3, which incorporates a subset of the World Wide Web Consortium's (W3C's) newer Web markup language, HTML5, along with the extended family of associated Web standards (Comparison of E-Book Formats 2013).

The complex genealogies of technical standards are convoluted, but one of the distinguishing characteristics of this work emerges from the fact that e-book standards all embody a conception of a book as a *file* instead of a website. This critical presumption means that digital books are a packaged construct that can be moved from place to place, sold or given away, and protected through digital rights management systems that operate only under the presumption they are protecting discrete digital objects.

The genesis of e-books as files is rooted in their development in a pre-Web world. During the 1990s the dominant graphical desktop was Microsoft Windows, and the first enterprise-capable edition of Windows 2000—itself based on Digital Equipment Corporation's VMS minicomputer operating system—emerged at the tail end of the 20th century. The only way to soberly conceive of producing and consuming content was through a file-based system; to develop a commercial electronic book platform on the Web in 2000 would have been brazen. Indeed, it is only the rise of modern mobile interface systems from Google, in its Android operating system, and Apple, with its iOS, that computer platforms are beginning to effectively disguise the legacy file-restricted nature of e-books and other media through self-contained content management systems such as iTunes and Google Play.

Falling from Print to Digital

Representing e-books as files provided direct benefits for publishing companies, who were already working with text-processing tools on minicomputer-based office automation systems, and then later through desktop operating systems. Although a "save as" function for EPUB has been a long time coming, it has been customary for book content to be created in word-processing programs by the author, and subsequently managed in more professional layout engines by the publisher. Although this does not mitigate the burden of print-based workflows, having a workable digital file meant that an intermediary format was accessible for translation into a retail package either by a conversion house or by internal digital production teams.

Although it's rarely obvious, the fact that e-books did not wind up as websites, but rather utilized subsets of the Web's markup language in an e-book file format that was divorced from the Web's heritage as server-based content retrieval, meant that publishers had a relatively easy transition to production of new kinds of book objects. That publishers encountered difficulties transitioning to digital workflows speaks primarily to the entrenched nature of book production systems that had been defined in a pre-automated age, not to cataclysmic change in the underlying *gestalt* of the book.

Another not inconsequential factor in the development of e-books, one that was not as ultimately benign for publishers, was that the threshold for putting up a website and commercially distributing content—even for individual consumers—is fairly low. Large numbers of organizations established corporate websites in the early 2000s, and a wide range of new, viable businesses were formed on the Internet, surviving periodic over-exuberant bursts of investment in large part because the value proposition was so attractive. Once established on the Web, the business of selling e-books would unfold along a trajectory that would take it way outside boundaries familiar to publishers.

The file-based nature of e-books determined *how* they became commercialized. Because e-books were files, reading was not based on live streaming content—an advantage for readers, who could have books on hand even when they were not connected to the network. Early explorations in browser caching and distributed Web annotations that would have forced some reconsideration of this approach were not pursued ("Why Andreessen-Horowitz Is Investing . . ." 2012). Additionally, the non-transient nature of e-books suggested the advisability of technical protection measures such as digital rights management to prevent users from redistributing e-books without hindrance.

Far more critically, online distributors of e-books were forced to create fairly sophisticated Internet-based retailing and distribution systems. A Web-based commerce system requires user accounts and a record of what content has been purchased by whom. But much more additional engineering is required to store files, make them available for download, and create a compelling end-user experience.

Books are unique cultural products, demanding a physical intimacy with a reader that computers cannot easily provide. The early efforts of Rocket, Palm, and other players all pointed to the need for some kind of small device that would serve as a surrogate for a bound book.

The existence of books as files meant that a retailer could not pull together a collection of links to e-books across publisher websites and put up a pay wall, but instead had to negotiate with publishers for the right to obtain e-books and sell them to consumers. Theoretically this provided a significant negotiating advantage for publishers, which could extract attractive terms and conditions, and potentially exert pricing influence. However, it also implied that publishers were forsaking the creation of direct customer relationships with readers—something they had also lacked in the print book space, where they served as distributors, not retailers. Continuing this hands-off approach inadvertently created an opportunity for retailers to become far more important than publishers.

Once books went digital, some new kind of retailing operation had to enter the market to present a compelling, unified catalog. For print books, it was enough for a bookstore—irrespective of its status as a small independent store or part of a national chain—to acquire an inventory attractive enough for the local book market to support a sustainable level of sales. For e-books, as for print, it made no sense for that function to be filled by publishers, which not only lacked technical expertise but also were unable to imagine an effective and legal collaboration that would create a common online storefront spanning imprints—a crucial artifice as consumers have very little connection with publishers as brands.

When viewed holistically as a market for goods and not simply as a book filling inventory, one can perceive how stressful the transition to digital books was for publishers. Despite being able to modify production workflows to convert books into digital file formats, they lacked the wherewithal to create a unified digital bookstore; lacked the technical expertise to mount a serious digital retailing operation; and did not possess the kind of engineering expertise needed to create a compelling, intimate reading experience. Most importantly of all, they couldn't tie these pieces together.

The Rise of the Tech Companies

But Amazon—one of the pioneering Internet commerce companies—could assemble these components. It already had put together a compelling trans-publisher, comprehensive catalog of books. When Amazon unveiled the Kindle e-reader in November 2007, it introduced a package of services that not only re-birthed the e-book industry but also propelled it on a takeoff trajectory. This handheld gadget was far from elegant but "good enough," with an adequate catalog of frontlist e-books, an easy-to-use discovery system, a means of delivering purchased content to the e-reader, and a satisfactory reading experience. The initial inventory of the first-generation Kindle sold out within five and a half hours (Amazon Kindle).

In the last five years, all of the technology giants—Apple, Amazon, and Google—have reprised and improved on this model, their approaches informed by their priorities and competencies. Apple created a new mobile operating system, iOS, and launched the iPhone and then a tablet, the iPad, that redefined consumer expectations for portable computing. Google, responding to Apple's success, acquired the Android mobile operating system. Its encouragement of Android's adoption by independent mobile phone and tablet developers ensured that it would rapidly become Apple's primary mobile competitor. Not having its own mobile platform, Amazon adapted a forked Android build for its line of Kindle e-Ink readers and Kindle Fire tablets, and was expected to introduce a Kindle mobile phone in 2013.

Each of these firms was able to build or modify existing e-retailing sites on the Web to accommodate a rapid accumulation of digital content, including e-books. Amazon built support for e-books directly within its commerce site with relatively little modification. Apple constructed the pathbreaking iTunes store for music, movies, and eventually e-books. Google rummaged through several iterations of storefronts but eventually settled on an iTunes-like Google Play service that combines Android apps, music, movies, books, and magazines. Behind all of these stores are contractual agreements with media companies, large and small, that enable these technology companies to sell—or, more accurately, license—content to consumers.

These technology giants are creating enclosed walled gardens for consumer experiences, pipelined from mobile operating systems to devices, to storefronts, to content delivery, and finally to various applications for reading, listening, and watching. Seamlessly knitting together a chain of proprietary, consumer-facing media services, they are creating the digital equivalent of shopping malls with stores, food courts, and long-term parking. They are efficient and well enough thought through to actually abstract away the file-based delivery of content. E-book readers, movie watchers, and music listeners would in most cases be hard pressed to actually find the media files they have purchased on their mobile devices or computers (Brantley, P. 2012a). The file system has become buried under thick layers of user interface that hide the guts of our computers, just as car hoods and engine covers disguise the complexity of motors and transmissions.

We live in a new media world wholly beyond the capacity of book publishers, and even content megafirms, to sell books, music, and movies. The need to create a full-service media consumption environment is what alienates publishers from their ability to retain their position within staid organizational networks that just a few short years ago ensured their pivotal presence in the value chain of content production and distribution. Financially, the technology companies would all survive if no more books were ever written, or ever sold. There would be movies and music and games enough to continue to fill their coffers. Publishers have been relegated to secondary roles by forces well beyond their control.

This is the strength of the Internet. Once media turned into digital files, it could eliminate all historical barriers to the selling and distribution of content. It would require no trucks; no airplanes; no printing paper; no pressing of CDs, DVDs, or Blu-Rays; no tape or film to wind onto reels; no buildings to lease, rent, or buy to store books and music; no clerks to hire; no parking lots to keep paved. All of that would be gone.

The world in which publishers find themselves is unlike anything they have encountered before. If, for example, they were in the automotive industry, they might face the challenge of a more efficient engine. That kind of innovation could be met with a response. Rather, it is as if it suddenly were possible to 3D-print personal flying machines and the plans for them were being sold on Amazon. This is a level of disruption wholly beyond the event horizon of automotive manufacturers, beyond their ability to respond competitively. This is the challenge Amazon poses to Random House.

Living on the Network

Once media traffic moves onto the network, technical evolution rapidly moves beyond the strict translation services that are characteristic of first-generation automation.

We live in a unique moment, on the cusp of reimagining how to communicate and share stories. Books, only a few hundred years old, were a preindustrial packaging of information in bound volumes whose production benefitted from the standardization and mechanization of the Industrial Revolution. In printed form, books fell into a small range of sizes, thicknesses, and weights. Their contents became increasingly uniformly presented; texts with easy-to-read fonts, gutters, margins, and other essential elements all made for a common experience. With the invention of moveable mechanized type printing, book production in Europe increased to 20 million copies by the end of the 15th century and nearly 1 billion copies at the close of the 18th century (Buringh and van Zanden 2009).

In a digital age, some of the value of self-bounded information is retained because it coheres with our limited human capacity for intellectual engagement. Yet it is not inviolate, and the presentation of information, the potential for user interaction, and the porosity of narrative are open to experimentation. Wholly self-contained "apps" can be optimized to exploit low-level tablet and phone functionality to deliver an immersive and satisfying experience; at the other extreme, websites possess the innate reach of a globally distributed network.

The networked world is a community—not one of solitary readers curled into comfortable chairs in living rooms, but a world in which each of us is one among many, leaving a trail of digital footsteps behind us. Books need not stand alone and apart from each other; they can be made aware of each other. Startups like MobNotate and SmallDemons are applying concept maps across books, mining texts for terms, and deriving information of value to reader and retailer alike. Sophisticated recommendation engines push readers from one title to another, even across genres, based on historical purchasing patterns captured in Web server logs. Reading applications can record what we read, when, and where, through geolocation.

Technical experimentation using simple, lightweight tools and scripting languages is now beginning to push at the historical edges of how we define books. They are now being reimagined as fully fledged network objects—books that live on the Web. The tools and applications being developed around books are the tools being used to create new Web applications, and new forms of publishing are emerging rapidly as a result. A straightforward example is Pressbooks, an e-book authoring program capable of outputting EPUB and Mobi files, built on top of Wordpress, and recently released in open source (McGuire 2012).

Tipping points come unexpectedly. For the past three years, I have run a small publishing conference called "Books in Browsers" (BiB) for the Internet Archive (Brantley 2012b). BiB has tracked the evolution of e-book developments on the Web, but 2012 represented a clear rupture in the application of network design and engineering to e-book development. Software engineers from Safari Books demonstrated a voice-recognition-powered collaborative editing tool using the GitHub software repository; Mozilla demonstrated macro-like HTML "X-tags" for automating in-browser formatting of books, magazines, and similar content; Mozilla also demonstrated methods of editing and producing new video narratives using transcript copy and paste functions in the Popcorn Maker video tool. Poetica from Blaine Cook (the original technical architect of Twitter) and Maureen Evans presented a visual symphony of collaborative editing. These tools, combined with a design ethos stressing simplicity and ease of use, reflect a design sensibility that reshapes the narratives we create.

In December 2012 the *New York Times* launched an eye-opening multimedia project on the Web, "Snowfall: The Avalanche at Tunnel Creek" (Branch 2012). As the *Economist*'s "Lean Back 2.0" blog wrote, "John Branch's article . . . has been turned into a beautiful reading experience through the use of a clean layout, interactive maps, inlaid videos and graphics that move as your [*sic*] scroll. The result is an online reading experience like no other" (Gardner 2012). In a single blow, the *Times* reset the bar for interactive online narratives. Executive Editor Jill Abramson wrote a letter to the staff in which she said, "[r]arely have we been able to create a compelling destination outside the home page that was so engaging in such a short period of time on the Web" (Romenesko 2012).

For book lovers, the future presents a growing cornucopia of representations of how we communicate with others, but they will not be books. Like "Snowfall," they trend in new directions. The new journalism project MATTER, launched in November 2012, noted that it "isn't quite a website, it's not really a magazine and it's not exactly a book publisher either" (Mod 2012). In a December 2012 interview with television host Charlie Rose, publishing pioneer Tim O'Reilly remarked, "I don't really [care] if literary novels go away." O'Reilly's remarks were in the context of observing that "no one owes [publishers] continuation of the current players and business model," and that we will find ways of using the technology we have at hand to tell stories to each other in the most compelling ways we can imagine (Anderson 2012). Inevitably, much of the old world of print books will be left behind. How quickly this will change, and how much it will matter to readers and authors, is not yet knowable.

Whatever the eventual nature of books, the companies that put the Web into the hands of users around the planet—Apple, Amazon, Google, and possibly others—will inevitably see benefit from these transitions. Whether they are selling access to websites or downloadable e-books, controlling the platform translates into control of the reading experience. But as we transform our stories, so will we also transform our understanding of what it means to be a publisher, and the roles that older organizations have played in producing, acquiring, and distributing content will inevitably shift.

With the conception of e-books as files, publishers lost control of the distribution of books because they lacked the wherewithal to imagine and develop the broad platforms capable of exploiting network scale. As books themselves finally take advantage of Web technologies to turn into new narratives that evolve far beyond websites as we know them today, publishers will have lost control even of the act of publishing. And then, finally, books will have entered their post-industrial age.

Consequences for Libraries

In a networked, digital environment, every library, in a sense, occupies the same niche as a bricks-and-mortar bookstore. The last five years have seen a dramatic diminishment of the large national bookstore chains that emerged in the 1990s to consolidate book purchasing and distribution. Borders is gone from the United States, and many question the long-term viability of Barnes & Noble, which is turning its retail stores into general toy and merchandise outlets as fast as it can. Although print sales have been steady, distribution of books through Amazon is far more efficient; the online catalog knows very few limits and delivery is close to same-day. The erosion of even a small part of the print business, coupled with the growing digital market, ruthlessly squeezes the profitability out of bookstores. Even Barnes & Noble's digital arm, Nook Media, has needed shoring investments from Microsoft and Pearson.

Libraries face many of the same pressures. Their inventory is lacking compared with Amazon's comprehensiveness; although all carry the hottest frontlist books, libraries cannot fill consumer demand with limited inventory, a constraint not faced by online retailers. Although print books are not always cheap, market trends have encouraged the ascendance of trade paperbacks over hardbacks, with the windowing of delayed paper releases generally being reduced or eliminated. The barriers for readers who have been library book borrowers to enter the commercial market have been reduced, so proportionately more transactions are likely to be culminated through an online retailer than was the case a decade ago.

More critical still is the emergence of the digital book market. As with publishers, any given public library—excepting only the very largest—faces great challenges in creating its own server infrastructure for lending e-books. It would be forced to operate as efficiently as online retailers, acquiring content from publishers or distributors, applying any industry standard DRM, controlling access to registered users, and assisting in the end user's consumption of the content. But, like publishers, and unlike technology companies, libraries have no direct ability to manage the reading experience because they are reliant on Apple, Amazon, and Google for the software, and often the hardware, required to enjoy the e-books they provide.

Scaling works against individual libraries as it does for other supply chain actors in the book business. Technically there need only be one lending library for e-books, in the same way that theoretically—antitrust issues aside—Amazon could meet the needs of the e-book marketplace worldwide. Once an infrastructure is created to manage the hosting and distribution of e-book files for borrowers, that infrastructure can be scaled up to meet a demand that spans any number of communities. Although it might be possible to help create e-library-in-a-box turnkey server systems, there is no compulsion for that to happen aside from local control and policy imperatives. Even localized acquisition and special needs communities could be ably managed from a single large digital library. For these reasons, the nascent Digital Public Library of America could conceivably serve this need on behalf of the public library system, although other priorities may claim precedence.

One of the primary library-based barriers to the creation of a national e-book lending infrastructure is the challenge posed by coordinating unaffiliated and highly heterogeneous public library systems whose financial support is overwhelmingly locally determined. With the exception of the Urban Libraries Council, there are few organization-based library associations in the United States; the American Library Association (ALA) is based on an individual librarian membership model, and is ill equipped to orchestrate or pool library resources. Furthermore, ALA's membership diffuses strategic focus by drawing from the diversity of public, academic, and special libraries. Even more debilitating, most public libraries have possessed few staff with technical design or software engineering skills, limiting their ability to construct shared, nativist solutions (Brantley 2013).

In the absence of library initiatives, commercial e-book distributors provide the technical infrastructure for e-books, with partial integration into library catalogs for discovery. The largest and most prominent of these in the public library market, OverDrive, fills a variety of retail distribution needs both in the United States and other markets, primarily in Europe and Commonwealth countries. It has scrambled to develop and integrate into its delivery systems its own reading applications for mobile devices, but pending the maturation of its platform, the hodgepodge nature of e-book acquisition and reading systems has resulted in a discouraging experience for e-book borrowers. OverDrive's primary competitors, 3M and Baker & Taylor, have little international presence, and their innovation in lending platforms has been minute; both 3M and Baker & Taylor introduced features that serve largely to differentiate, rather than disrupt, the market.

What libraries need is their own cross-library open source discovery service married to an e-book file hosting and management platform that can replace Over-Drive with a less intrusive, open source, interoperable system that can relieve libraries from per-loan fees and excessive setup costs. Unfortunately, this is a tall order.

Legal Parameters

Publishers have never fully acknowledged the roles that libraries have played in fostering reading, long believing that lending books eroded sales. However, the U.S. "first sale doctrine," which exhausts the copyright-holder's rights to control follow-on distribution of their works once they have been legitimately acquired, permits libraries to use books as they see fit, thus making it possible for libraries to lend books free of charge. Even involving physical goods, first sale rights remain under threat, with an important case soon to be decided by the Supreme Court involving importation.

For digital goods, the ability to impose licensing agreements that trump first sale ownership rights is highly alluring to publishers. The digital rights group Electronic Frontier Foundation recently commented that "Not only does big content deny that first sale doctrine applies to digital goods, but they are also trying to undermine the first sale rights we do have by forcing users to license items they would rather buy." Licensing so often trumps permitted copyright exceptions and limitations that the United Kingdom's Intellectual Property Office is amending British copyright law to prohibit such contravention.

As an unpublished 2012 report commissioned by the International Federation of Library Associations and Institutions (IFLA) observes, "The current models that provide access to digital content to libraries have for the most part been designed to support, safeguard and reflect the commercial interests of publishers, online retailers and rights holders" (Simon and Sturges 2012). Although it is clear in retailers' legal language that e-book consumers are only renting books, and not purchasing them, that has been less obvious to consumers. However, from the perspective of copyright holders, there is very little incentive to permit libraries to lend books to patrons for free when retailers are effectively renting those same titles under the guise of a permanent purchase. The possibility that nascent subscription models could be developed for e-books—much as Spotify works in music, providing access to a large catalog of titles for a modest monthly fee—makes libraries even less attractive (Brantley 2012a).

Retailers intuit that the library community is a perfect market for new content services; in 2012 Amazon launched its Kindle Lending Library, available to those customers who own a Kindle reader and retain Amazon Prime membership ("Literary Labors Lent" 2012). It is also easy to speculate that online sites with large, engaged social communities such as Goodreads might enter the e-book market, although they presently lack an integrating device and e-reader (Greenfield 2013). The more retailers enter the e-book market, arguably the less desirable libraries appear to the publishers with which they must do business.

Whether ownership of digital books is truly necessary, or whether liberal licensing conventions might afford advantages that ownership could not deliver, is a worthwhile question. If licensing frameworks endorse content portability and interoperability, how necessary is ownership beyond the national library network, where a real preservation need exists? From another perspective, what is the bundle of rights that libraries require, and are they optimally obtained via licensing or ownership? A dual track could theoretically be pursued, accepting liberalized licensing under current copyright models, but pursuing significant copyright reform that would include more-explicit exceptions and limitations that modernize lending.

No Haven on Earth

The denial to libraries of access to digital titles is a transnational problem. Canada, which has a small number of domestic publishers, represents the most successful alliance between libraries and publishers. Two years of negotiations with the Association of Canadian Publishers resulted in a landmark draft proposal for licensing a bundle of e-books with terms loosely based on the HarperCollins model, but good for 40 loans, with each library paying out over five years. The initiative is receiving some initial government support, but it is intended ultimately to be self-funding with an outsourced platform delivery subsequent to request for proposal evaluation and vendor selection. However, few large international publishers are expected to participate.

Many countries have seen years of negotiations break down in futile stalemate. Relations between Swedish libraries and publishers soured to such a point that libraries are now engaging in a public relations campaign that paints their country's "next librarian" as a suit-clad fat cat publisher. The United States, Sweden, Denmark, Germany, and Australia can all share accounts with similar tales of woe.

The Danish case is particularly interesting, involving a joint agreement by Danish publishers and libraries to expand access to e-books—then quite immature in the domestic market—via digital lending using a white-labeled e-reader application. The libraries paid publishers about two euros per loan, and 100,000 individuals took advantage of the trial with more than 600,000 loans within the first year—an astounding level for a small country. The experiment was such a success that the largest publishers halted the trial after the consequent surge of e-book acceptance and readership, citing lost sales revenues. Notably, the project continues with smaller publishers and lending activity remains high.

In Germany, large publishers and libraries were also unable to come to terms, with publishers such as Bertelsmann predictably asserting that loans substituted for book sales. In a partial accommodation, publishers rent access to e-books via commercial lending, but at very high prices that often bring in greater profits than a direct sale. German publisher manipulation of fixed book-pricing laws puts them in a bind: the publishers association says that e-books are substitutes for books, and therefore susceptible to fixed-price laws; however, they reiterate the differences between e-books and print for licensing and lending.

The continued tales of large international publishers asserting lost revenues and refraining from e-book provision to libraries, with smaller presses and independent distributors continuing to demonstrate more willingness to negotiate, suggests that libraries might be well advised to abandon or de-emphasize negotiations with the largest international publishers. However, for many library systems, such a recommendation may seem unrealistic as the bulk of borrowing demand persists in bestsellers predominantly sold by these publishers.

Other correctives might be more structural. In many European countries, government funds flow to national publishers to support domestic language and literature. Conceivably legislatures could require that these funds cycle back to the public by permitting libraries to acquire and lend books, through formal exceptions when necessary. The possibility of noting that there is a market failure in access to digital content by libraries is also conceivable, necessitating legislative intervention for a special needs exception, along the lines of support for the reading impaired via the United States' Chafee Amendment. This idea is currently under international treaty discussion at the World Intellectual Property Organization (WIPO).

Publishing consultant Brian O'Leary delivers a well-reasoned argument that libraries fill the market need where the price is zero—that "libraries are the first, best defense against piracy" and in their absence, a true market failure would arise that would trigger a truly undesirable consumer response (O'Leary 2012). Arguably, libraries are the last footholds that publishers and authors have for connecting with readers in their communities, with more than 230,000 public library buildings across the world. Public libraries possess unparalleled opportunities for the collection and development of community literature and the promulgation of its history. Everyone should be able to celebrate a world where libraries use technology to bring people and their communities closer together.

But there are powerful smartphones and tablets everywhere, and more each day. Ultimately the most serious threat for libraries is not publishers but e-book and digital media retailers such as Amazon, Apple, and Google. Despite protests that libraries are not in the business of contending with such companies—the best in the world at management and market disruption—libraries are indeed in such competition. If public libraries can't be better than Amazon *at something,* then libraries will certainly cede their relevance in the future of books. Absent near-immediate innovation, libraries will be unable to address the expectations of their patrons.

That would be a great loss. But it is likely an inevitable one. The future lies elsewhere for libraries.

References

"Amazon Kindle." 2013. Wikipedia. Retrieved Jan. 18, 2013, from http://en. wikipedia.org/wiki/Amazon_Kindle.

Anderson, P. 2012. "No More Predictions." "Writing On the Ether." Retrieved Jan. 6, 2013, from http://janefriedman.com/2012/12/27/writing-on-the-ether-70/#1.

Branch, J. 2012. "Snowfall: The Avalanche at Tunnel Creek." *New York Times* Retrieved Jan. 20, 2013, from http://www.nytimes.com/projects/2012/snow-fall.

Brantley, P. 2012a. "Hey, Dad, What's a File?" *Publishers Weekly.* Retrieved Jan. 7, 2013, from http://blogs.publishersweekly.com/blogs/PWxyz/2012/08/03/hey-dad-whats-a-file.

Brantley, P. 2012b. "BiB 2012: Program." Internet Archive. Retrieved Jan. 19, 2013, from http://bib.archive.org/2012/07/12/bib-2012-program.

Brantley, P. 2012c. "Unsubscribing to the Library." *Publishers Weekly.* http://blogs. publishersweekly.com/blogs/PWxyz/2012/12/14/unsubscribing-to-th-library.

Brantley, P. 2013. "Design for Communities." *Publishers Weekly.* Retrieved Jan. 8, 2013, from http://blogs.publishersweekly.com/blogs/PWxyz/2013/01/02/united-steps-big-impact.

Buringh, E., and Luiten J. van Zanden. 2009. "Charting the 'Rise of the West': Manuscripts and Printed Books in Europe, a Long-Term Perspective from the Sixth Through Eighteenth Centuries. *Journal of Economic History* 69(2): 409–445.

"Comparison of E-Book Formats." 2013. Wikipedia. Retrieved Jan. 7, 2013, from http://en.wikipedia.org/wiki/Comparison_of_e-book_formats.

Gardner, E. 2012. "The New York Times Pushes the Limits of Online Storytelling." "Lean Back 2.0." Retrieved Jan. 8, 2013 from http://www.economist-group.com/leanback/lean-back-reading/the-new-york-times-pushes-the-limits-of-online-storytelling.

Greenfield, J. 2013. "The Predictions for Book Publishing in 2013." *Forbes.* Retrieved from http://www.forbes.co/sites/jeremygreenfield/2012/12/21/three-predictions-for-book-publishing-in-2013.

"Literary Labors Lent." 2012. The *Economist* (July 28, 2012). Retrieved Jan. 8, 2013, from http://www.economist.com/node/21559654.

"Locomotive Acts." 2013. Wikipedia. Retrieved Jan. 7, 2013 from http://en.wikipedia.org/wiki/Locomotive_Acts.

McGuire, H. 2012. "Pressbooks Going Open Source." Pressbooks Blog. Retrieved Jan. 19, 2013, from http://blog.pressbooks.com/?p=167.

Mod, C. 2012. "Subcompact Publishing." @CraigMod. Retrieved Jan. 8, 2013, from http://craigmod.com/journal/subcompact_publishing.

O'Leary, B. 2012. "The First, Best Defense." Magellan Media (2012). Retrieved Jan. 6, 2013, from http://www.magellanmediapartners.com/index.php/mmcp/article/the_first_best_defense.

"PLATO (computer system)." 2013. Wikipedia. Retrieved Jan. 7, 2013 from http://en.wikipedia.org/wiki/PLATO_(computer_system).

Romenesko, J. 2012. "More Than 3.5 Million Page Views for New York Times' 'Snow Fall' Feature." Retrieved from http://jimromenesko.com/2012/12/27/more-than-3-5-million-page-views-for-nyts-snow-fall.

Simon, D., and P. Sturges. 2012. "Libraries, e-Lending and the Future of Public Access to Digital Content." Paper given at IFLA, November 2012. Unpublished.

"Why Andreessen-Horowitz Is Investing in Rap Genius." 2012. Retrieved Jan. 19, 2013, from http://rapgenius.com/Marc-andreessen-why-andreessen-horowitz-is-investing-in-rap-genius-lyrics.

Library Education in the World of Online Learning

Nicole A. Cooke

As online education continues to expand and infiltrate multiple educational opportunities and innovations, scholars and practitioners endeavor to further identify how library and information science (LIS) students interact and learn online. Because of the technological, proximal, and often asynchronous uniqueness of online education, learners face challenges not native to face-to-face education.

Challenges notwithstanding, online learners should have access to the same quality curriculum and student services extended to on-campus learners. With entire degrees now available online, and with the emergence of massively open online courses (MOOCs) and other new online learning opportunities such as m-learning (mobile learning), the library profession continues and expands efforts to recruit, retain, and optimally serve the new generation of learners and librarians.

Online Learning in Higher Education

Students select distance education for the flexibility and convenience afforded by this mode of delivery, which enables them to maintain jobs and accommodate family and other obligations (Huang 2002). Among those who engage in distance learning are traditional-age college students (ages 18 to 22) who enjoy the convenience and scheduling of online courses; "Learners can arrange their learning around their everyday lives without being constrained by time and place" (Huang 2002, p. 28). Regardless of age, distance learners may have access to courses not otherwise available in a traditional on-ground program and to subject experts around the world. Students may also enjoy the anonymity and psychological space promoted by this mode of educational delivery.

With the benefits of distance education come drawbacks; for example, the lack of shared physical and psychological space can be problematic. Online classes require a different approach to instructional design, pedagogy, and knowledge construction, particularly if course delivery is asynchronous (Moller 1998).

Distance education in its current iteration—user-centered, Web-based learning through course management systems (CMS)—is referred to as New Millennium, Fifth Generation distance education, or e-learning (Bates 2003; Downes 2005; Garrison and Anderson 2003; Taylor 2001; Wenger, White, and Smith 2009). It is overcoming difficulties relating to time and geography, reaching populations around the world and students of all ages and abilities, as well as having tangible benefits in both finance and prestige for higher education. Higher education organizations, traditional and for-profit colleges and universities, are increas-

Nicole A. Cooke is an assistant professor in the Graduate School of Library and Information Science at the University of Illinois, Urbana-Champaign. She holds a Ph.D. in Communication, Information, and Library Studies, as well as an MLS, from Rutgers University, and a master's degree in Adult Education from Penn State. Her research interests include LIS distance education and instruction; human information behavior in online settings; the retention and mentoring of minority librarians and LIS doctoral students; and leadership, organizational development, and communication in libraries.

ing online offerings and marketing efforts, training faculty and staff to meet the growing need for distance learning, and accommodating students that this type of learning attracts.

> Online learning has become popular because of its potential for providing more *flexible access to content and instruction at any time, from any place.* Frequently, the focus entails: (a) increasing the availability of learning experiences for learners who cannot or choose not to attend traditional face-to-face offerings, (b) assembling and disseminating instructional content more cost-efficiently, or (c) enabling instructors to handle more students while maintaining learning outcome quality that is equivalent to that of comparable face-to-face instruction (Means et al. 2010, p. 1).

Evolution of Distance Education

Teaching and learning from a distance has a long and diverse history that can be traced back to 1840 when correspondence courses first began in the United Kingdom. Distance education is defined as:

> planned learning that normally occurs in a different place from teaching and as a result requires special techniques of course design, special instruction techniques, special methods of communication by electric and other technology, as well as special organization and administrative arrangements (Moore and Kearsley 1996, p. 2).

Distance education continues to gain in popularity and effectiveness and to make great strides through advances in technology and high scholarship standards.

Cooke (2004, p. 49) traces the development of distance education since 1840, and notes the following milestones:

- Passage of the Morrill Act in 1862, which enabled land-grant colleges to offer extension programs to rural areas
- Establishment of the first university-level correspondence teaching department at the University of Chicago in the late 1800s
- Issuance of radio licenses in 1921 to universities in Utah, Wisconsin, and Minnesota to permit educational radio
- Establishment of the National Home Study Council in 1926 to improve and oversee correspondence courses
- The first televised course at the State University of Iowa in 1933
- Establishment of the FCC's [Federal Communications Commission's] Television Fixed Service Program in 1963, which granted colleges and universities licensed television frequencies to broadcast courses
- The first audio conference via telephone in 1965
- The creation of the Corporation for Public Broadcasting in 1967, authorized by President Lyndon B. Johnson
- The establishment of the British Open University in 1969
- The first online undergraduate course, offered in 1984 by the New Jersey Institute of Technology

Distance education has evolved from correspondence courses, traveling instructors, and satellite television and radio broadcasts; teleconferencing, audio conferencing, and computer conferencing have improved steadily. The trend continued in the 1990s and 2000s as the Internet and related technologies became popular and accessible to mainstream society. The U.S. Department of Education reported that the number of institutions offering distance learning programs increased 72 percent between 1995 and 1998 (Goodson 2001), and by 2001 there were more than 3 million enrollments in distance learning programs (National Center for Education Statistics 2003). By the 2007–2008 academic year, 20 percent of all U.S. undergraduates (out of a total of 4.3 million students) took at least one distance education course, with 4 percent of them taking their entire course of study online (Radford 2011). It is expected that these totals will continue to rise steeply over time.

E-learning programs are also making steady progress in K–12 education; high school students are taking classes online (Means et al. 2010) and Internet-based initiatives such as the Khan Academy are becoming a welcome presence in traditional elementary and secondary school classrooms. Similar sites appearing on the distance learning landscape include YouTube EDU, PBS (Public Broadcasting Service) Teachers, iTunes U, Connexions, and Google Code University.

The latest advancement, or trend, in e-learning is the proliferation of MOOCs and their derivatives. Championed by such companies as Coursera, Udacity, and edX, MOOC courses are run through partner higher education institutions and are freely offered to thousands of people at once. Classes range in topic and structure (i.e., self-paced or modeled on a standard semester-based timetable) and feature a do-it-yourself model of learning where the onus is on the student because sheer class size makes interaction with the instructor unlikely. As a result, students enrolled in MOOCs must make arrangements to meet with classmates in another online venue, or even offline, if some level of interaction is desired. This is not unlike the initiative that students would have to show when taking correspondence courses by postal mail. Education trade publications, such as the *Chronicle of Higher Education,* devote entire sections and publish almost daily on MOOCs and their potential consequences for higher education—namely how MOOCs will affect credentialing and the proposed sale of student information to recruiters. The future and impact of MOOCs remain to be seen, but they have taken e-learning in yet another direction and expanded its reach even further.

LIS and Distance Education

Distance learning programs in LIS are influencing graduate study in academic institutions. The role of distance education in higher learning is substantial and dates back to 1888 and correspondence study under the direction of Melvil Dewey (Barron 2003). Paralleling the development of distance learning in education as a whole, LIS education has made great use of distance learning technologies and their corresponding opportunities (Barron 2003). *Benchmarks in Distance Education: The LIS Experience* (Barron 2003) provides a wealth of information about the LIS programs engaged in this mode of content delivery. At the time of publication 28 library and information science programs were offering distance learning options in some fashion and detailing their experiences.

For example, the University of Oklahoma began offering LIS courses via satellite locations as early as 1957; Indiana University used two-way video services in 1995; Rutgers University offered asynchronous online courses in 1996; and, also in 1996, the University of Illinois, Urbana-Champaign initiated its LEEP program, which featured synchronous online classes and multiple on-campus residencies. (A residency refers to a required campus visit during which a distance student physically attends his or her LIS school to complete coursework or other related tasks. Residency requirements vary by program.)

This trend continues, with LIS programs continually implementing more and expanded online offerings into their curricula. As of 2012, of the 58 American Library Association- (ALA-) accredited programs in LIS, 24 offered some classes online, 13 provided significant portions of their degree program online, and 23 offered the entire master's degree in an online format (ALA 2012). These programs may or may not include residencies, and feature synchronous and asynchronous modes of content delivery.

Adding to the LIS community's commitment to e-learning is the Web-based Information Science Education (WISE) Consortium. A collective of LIS programs, WISE routinely offers seats in its online classes for students at other institutions that may or may not engage in distance learning. This cooperation enables students to enroll in specialized classes and perhaps take part in a mode of e-learning not offered by their home institution.

Once librarians complete their formal education, they find that continuous learning is still necessary; to that end, there are numerous online education offerings and professional development opportunities. These opportunities range from free professional blogs and wikis to active professional information sharing on Twitter and Facebook, membership-based community forums (such as WebJunction), fee-based for-credit classes offered by ALA and other professional organizations, and full-on conferences offered online such as the Library 2.0 Conference (http://www.library20.com).

The distance education literature, as it specifically pertains to LIS, addresses community development among online learners, especially as made available through computer-mediated communication (Haythornthwaite and Hagar 2005; Haythornthwaite et al. 2000; Kazmer 2006; Kazmer 2000). Because online learners do not have physical access to their instructors and fellow students, they must be purposeful in their interactions and efforts to make contact with one another. Socializing becomes a function facilitated by technology (Kazmer, 2000). Kazmer states that forming community is an important coping skill for distance students:

> They are in a new and unfamiliar learning environment, without physical classrooms and with limited face-to-face contact. They face a variety of problems, social and technological, that students in more traditional programs do not. As students enter this new learning environment, they need support to help them gain entry to the community and to begin their interaction with others (Kazmer 2000, p. 2).

Haythornthwaite and colleagues (2000) suggest that not only is community building important for distance learners; community maintenance is vital as well. Technology facilitates community building, but concerted effort by students to maintain and nurture the initial bonds formed is needed. Disengaging and not maintaining the social bonds and connections is referred to as "fading back" (p.

12). "Those who fail to make such connections feel isolated and more stressed than those who are more active in the community" (p. 2). Palloff and Pratt (2001) concur, stating that "Successful learners in the online environment need to be active, creative and engage in the learning process" (p. 14).

Palloff and Pratt (2001) state that "It is always important to remember that in the online environment, we present ourselves in text. Because it is a flat medium, we need to make an extra effort to humanize the environment" (p. 18). In the online classroom, students may interact exclusively via text, e-mail, journals, assignments, and threaded discussions. In this less interactive environment, it is important to promote social presence (Biocca et al. 2003; Gunawardena and Zittle 1997; Kehrwald 2008; Rettie 2003; Richardson and Swan 2003; Stein and Wanstreet 2003; Tu 2000; Tu and McIsaac 2002). Social presence is defined as ". . . the degree of salience of the other person in the (mediated) interaction and the consequent salience of the interpersonal relationship. This is interpreted as the degree to which a person is perceived as 'real' in mediated communication" (Richardson and Swan 2003, p. 70). This realness can be thought of as ". . . the degree to which a user feels access to the intelligence, intentions and sensory impression" of the other members of the online environment (Tu 2000, p. 28). Social presence needs to be cultivated, varies from group to group, depends on the particular technologies available to the learners, and the culture of the group in question (Gunawardena and Zittle 1997). Social presence is an important element in an online learning environment because of the lack of nonverbal and other interpersonal cues that are fundamental to face-to-face classrooms. Online cues and interactions are how learners overcome transactional distance, get to know one another, and form the basis for community that may result in the online environment. ("Transactional distance" is defined as the ". . . psychological and communications space to be crossed, a space of potential misunderstandings." These spaces occur between students and instructors, and between learners themselves [Moore, 1993, p. 22]).

The importance of nonverbal cues is especially evident when considering Internet-based asynchronous learner communities, or asynchronous learning networks (ALNs) (Rovai 2000; Rovai 2001; Rovai 2002a; Rovai 2002b; Rovai 2003; Rovai 2007; Rovai and Jordan 2004; Rovai and Wighting 2005; Wegerif 1998). One of several models employed in distance education and virtual communities, ALNs involve learners and instructors who are separated not only by space but also by time. Students in such courses, or communities, ". . . interact with each other mostly through the use of discussion boards, without the requirements to be online at the same time" (Rovai 2001, p. 33). These learners are the most at-risk for alienation, boredom, and lack of engagement with other students and course content (Rovai and Wighting 2005) and run a higher risk of dropping out or removing themselves from the online environment. Asynchronous learners have the greatest challenge to surmount in building a sense of community due to the lack of same-time interactions and of physical and verbal cues, but may benefit the most from community formation.

Haythornthwaite and Hagar (2005) suggest that there are barriers to forming communities through mediated means. Because technology is so pervasive and plentiful, care must be taken to use the right tools—those capable of accommodating various hardware and software requirements and learners' varying levels of technological skill. Technological tools should be used in meaningful ways so that learners feel they are connecting with others and engaging in personal relationships and networks (Haythornthwaite et al. 2000), as opposed to simply using electronic tools to complete academic requirements.

Social Constructivism in Teaching and Learning

In partial response to the aforementioned concerns about teaching and learning in the online environment, effective pedagogy is necessary. The pedagogy employed in a face-to-face classroom is not efficient or appropriate in an online setting. Social constructivism is a beneficial approach to online pedagogy because it removes the instructor as the center of the education process, makes the environment learner-centered, and suggests that learners and instructors work together to construct knowledge and co-create the online learning environment (Anagnostopoulos et al. 2005; Brandt 1997; Chen 1997; Huang 2002; Jonassen 1994; Jonassen 2000; Kearsley 1998; Lock 2002; Moller 1998; Petraglia 1998; Rogoff 1994; Tu and Corry 2002). In the spirit of educational theories such as those of Piaget (1950) and Vygotsky (1978), collaboration and discovery are emphasized in the online learning environment. The teacher acts as a facilitator (Anagnostopoulos et al. 2005; Moller 1998) and ". . . as a guide rather than a director," so that learning allows more "creative interaction with the teacher than outcome-based teaching" (Huang 2002, p. 29). The constructivist role of the teacher is to provide feedback and guidance and to prompt dialogue and reflection (Moller 1998, p. 118). The learning environment is socially constructed, provides a venue for information dissemination, and allows learners to apply course content to their ". . . real life problems" (Huang 2002, p. 29).

In the construction of the online learning environment, a prominent feature is technology. Online courses are typically delivered via a CMS and employ such features as bulletin or discussion boards, listservs, e-mail, podcasting, videos, conferencing, chats, and other interactive tools. The use of technology facilitates social constructivism in the online classroom by encouraging interaction and collaboration, promoting hands-on learning, and allowing students to ". . . search actively and discover rich resources to solve problems or construct his or her own knowledge" (Huang 2002, p. 30).

Jonassen (2000) suggests that online students can use technology as an educational and intellectual partner (not unlike the partnership with the instructor) in order to ". . . articulate what they know, reflect on what they have learned, support the internal negotiation of meaning making, construct personal representations of meaning and support intentional, mindful thinking" (p. 24). However, the literature cautions that distance learning environments are for both information exchange and social reinforcement (Moller 1998, p. 116) and that " . . . technology and social context are equally important for distance learning" (Kearsley 1998, p. 49). Technology is a tool, and should not be used as a crutch or as a substitute for creating social, meaningful, and personal learning environments. While useful, the CMS environment can isolate distance learners and remove the human element from the learning process (Huang 2002, p. 31). Jonassen concurs, stating that technology should be used in conjunction with the other components of a constructivist classroom to create ". . . a social negotiation environment" that ". . . can foster reflective response and support collaborative construction" (p. 33).

A truly constructivist online classroom can serve as an interpersonally and intellectually supportive community that facilitates learners' critical thinking and ". . . cognitive development through argument construction, communication of ideas, and critical analysis of new ideas" (Moller 1998, p. 119). In such a community, students can capitalize on new information and incorporate it into their lives.

Toward More-Effective Online Pedagogy

Online learning in the LIS landscape needs to be continually developed, expanded, and customized, as does LIS education as a whole. ALA (http://www.ala.org) and other accrediting bodies, such as the Middle States Commission on Higher Education (http://www.msche.org), are issuing increasingly high standards and expectations for online learning, providing guidelines for LIS programs in an effort to help ensure that high-quality content is consistently offered to online learners. Courses delivered online must be of the same quality and rigor as those offered in a physical classroom. Online offerings also benefit practicing librarians who want to increase their knowledge and continue LIS study, and LIS schools that wish to expand their reach to alumni and the broader professional community. Evidence in the literature suggests that many factors contribute to the successful development and implementation of effective online pedagogy. These factors include instructor immediacy, group learning, community building, user-centered learning, and instructional design.

Instructor Immediacy, Group Learning, Community Building

Participation in a constructivist environment enables learners to engage in critical thinking and collaborative learning. Although these assertions are not unfounded, they are not automatic. Research has also suggested that the instructor's role in the online class is imperative and probably the most important component to its success. The instructor's role of providing structure and dialogue for an online class from a transactional distance is referred to as social presence or immediacy in the online classroom. Instructor immediacy includes such elements as these:

- How often does the professor participate in threaded discussion?
- Does the professor provide timely feedback for assignments?
- Does the professor design collaborative learning opportunities?
- Does the professor possess adequate group facilitation skills? (Rovai 2001)

Instructor immediacy is key (Bliss and Lawrence 2009), and consistent, motivating, interactive, interaction-based, and blended course design is critical (Liu et al. 2007; Rovai 2001; Rovai 2004; Rovai 2007). Course design and instructor immediacy facilitate interaction in the online classroom, which in turn increases students' perceived sense of community and learning (Chayko 2002; Rovai 2002c; Shen et al. 2008). Immediacy is a contributing factor to fostering students' social presence, defined in the literature as "person-to-person awareness" (Dow 2008, p. 231). Social presence is inextricably tied to students' affective information behavior and communication, and depends upon user-centered course design; transparency; ease-of-use of the environment; online communication and interactivity; and self-reflection (Finlay and Willoughby 2008).

Social presence and participation enable students to learn better in groups, such as the group present in the online classroom. Learners in groups or cohorts share a communal space, co-create knowledge, collaborate in learning processes, and engage in experiential learning and knowing. The literature suggests that cohort learning is beneficial and enhances student learning. The literature characterizes cohorts as formal groupings of students who progress together over time, perhaps years, as an academic program is completed. The literature highlights benefits of the group learning, which include sense of identity, community, persistence, cooperation, collaboration, decreased competition, and critical thinking skills (Imel 2002, p. 3; Lawrence 2002, p. 86).

Student and instructor perceptions of community are also paramount to the success of an online class. If course participants do not believe a course can, or needs to, facilitate a sense of community, that community will not form no matter how well designed the course. However, a community is not always desired, and trying to force one to form is likely detrimental. As a result, no one party (students or instructor) can ensure the success of an online class precisely because it is truly a collaborative effort. Forging connection and creating community in an online environment can be difficult to accomplish because of the anonymity, asynchronicity, and lack of personal interaction and visual cues. Forming relationships in this environment is more challenging than doing so in a face-to-face environment and requires effort, risk-taking, and a willingness to trust (Finlay and Willoughby 2008). Developing and maintaining social presence in an online learning environment is an emotionally strenuous but essential factor for learner satisfaction (Dow 2008).

Developing and supporting cooperative learning groups is a major challenge, since the participants are asked to engage in more personal risk-taking behavior than in typical courses. Creating online groups of any form tacitly requires finding ways to support the social processes that would be typical of face-to-face groups (Kling and Courtright 2003, p. 226).

With these pieces in place, students are in a position to socially construct their online learning environments.

User-Centered Learning

Online learning environments are not composed of any one major component, but multiple components. These include discussion forums; social presence; instructor immediacy; cognitive and affective communication and information interaction; group work and cohort learning; and social roles. Yet the sum is greater than its parts. The social construction of an online learning environment can no longer simply be referred to as distance education; this holistic view of the online learning environment supersedes it and is now referred to as *e-learning*. This represents a paradigm shift away from the teacher-centered instruction of distance education to student-centered and student-led learning (Wenger et al. 2009). The change from basic learning to "communal constructivism" is described by Holmes and Gardner (2006 p. 76):

Communal constructivism, which like the notion of communities of practice, deals with "a process in which individuals not only learn socially but contribute their learning to the creation of a communal knowledge base for other learners." Online learning affords them the linked community, the knowledge bases, the knowledge-creation tools and the facility to provide their learning for others.

Instructional Design

The discussion of the constructivist and social learning components can enhance and advance the understanding of LIS distance education. Incorporating these elements into the proactive instructional design of LIS online learning environments can lead to more productive pedagogies in online classes. "Productive pedagogies" refers to the classroom infrastructures needed for in-depth learning by students. Discussed in the teacher education literature, productive pedagogies are suitable for training future librarians and information specialists, as well as learners in other disciplines. The goal of productive pedagogies is to create learning environments that emphasize process over substance, hands-on learning, knowledge integration, higher-order thinking, learner engagement, and cultural inclusivity (Gore, Griffiths, and Ladwig 2004; McFadden and Mums 2002). Productive pedagogies speak to the important role of the instructor in the creation of effective online learning environments. Instructor involvement and immediacy set the tone for the learning environment and facilitate the construction of knowledge and exchange of information that occur in successful online classes.

Distance education is not just about delivering course content in an online format, but rather is a way to put learners first in the course-design process by considering how they learn best and facilitating the development of learning communities.

References

American Library Association. 2012. ALA Accredited Programs. Retrieved from http://www.ala.org/accreditedprograms.

Anagnostopoulos, D., K. G. Basmadjian, and R. McCrory. 2005. "The decentered teacher and the construction of social space in the virtual classroom." *Teachers College Record* 107(8), 1699–1729.

Barron, D. D. (ed.). 2003. *Benchmarks in Distance Education: The LIS Experience.* Libraries Unlimited.

Bates, A. W. 2003. *Technology, E-Learning and Distance Education* (2nd ed.). Routledge.

Biocca, F., C. Harms, and J. K. Burgoon. 2003. "Criteria for a Theory and Measure of Social Presence." *Presence: Teleoperators and Virtual Environments* 12(5), 456–480.

Bliss, C. A., and B. Lawrence. 2009. "From Posts to Patterns: A Metric to Characterize Discussion Board Activity in Online Courses." *Journal of Asynchronous Learning Networks* 13(2), 15–32.

Brandt, D. S. 1997. "Constructivism: Teaching for Understanding of the Internet." *Communications of the ACM* 40(10), 112–117.

Chayko, M. 2002. *Connecting: How We Form Social Bonds and Communities in the Internet Age.* SUNY Press.

Chen, L. L. 1997. "Distance Delivery Systems in Terms of Pedagogical Considerations: A Re-evaluation." *Educational Technology,* 37(4), 34–37.

Cooke, N. A. 2004. "The Role of Libraries in Web-Based Distance Education: An Account and an Analysis of the Impact of Web Technology on Distance Learning—What Remains Unchanged, What Is Changing." *Journal of Library and Information Services in Distance Learning* 1(4), 47–57.

Dow, M. J. 2008. "Implications of Social Presence for Online Learning: A Case Study of MLS Students." *Journal of Education for Library and Information Science* 29(4), 231–242.

Downes, S. 2005. E-Learning 2.0. *eLearn Magazine. Education and Technology in Perspective.* Available at http://www.elearnmag.org/subpage.cfm?section=articles&article=29-1.

Finlay, J., and L. Willoughby. 2008. "Exploring Online Learning Relationships: A Case Study in Higher Education." In S. Holland (ed.), *Remote Relationships in a Small World* (pp. 53–73). Peter Lang.

Garrison, D. R., and T. Anderson. 2003. *E-Learning in the 21st Century: A Framework for Research and Practice.* Routledge.

Goodson, C. 2001. *Providing Library Services for Distance Learning Students.* Neal-Schuman.

Gore, J. M., T. Griffiths, and J. G. Ladwig. 2004. "Towards Better Teaching: Productive Pedagogy as a Framework for Teacher Education." *Teaching and Teacher Education* 20, 375–387.

Gunawardena, C. N., and F. J. Zittle. 1997. "Social Presence as a Predictor of Satisfaction Within a Computer-Mediated Conferencing Environment." *American Journal of Distance Education* 11(3), 8–26.

Haythornthwaite, C., and C. Hagar. 2005. "The Social Worlds of the Web." *Annual Review of Information Science and Technology* 39, 311–346.

Haythornthwaite, C., M. M. Kazmer, J. Robins, and S. Shoemaker. 2000. "Community Development Among Distance Learners: Temporal and Technological Dimensions." *Journal of Computer-Mediated Communication* 6(1). Retrieved from http://jcmc.indiana.edu/vol6/issue1/haythornthwaite.html.

Holmes, B., and J. Gardner. 2006. *E-learning: Concepts and practice.* Sage.

Huang, H. M. 2002. "Toward Constructivism for Adult Learners in Online Learning Environments." *British Journal of Educational Technology* 33(1), 27–37.

Imel, S. 1999. *Distance Learning Myths and Realities.* ERIC Clearinghouse on Adult, Career, and Vocational Education. (ERIC Document Reproduction Service No. ED 426 213).

Imel, S. 2002. *Adult Learning in Cohort Groups.* ERIC Clearinghouse on Adult, Career, and Vocational Education. (ERIC Document Reproduction Service No. ED 472 604).

Jonassen, D. H. 1994. "Thinking Technology: Toward a Constructivist Design Model." *Educational Technology Research and Development* 34(4), 34–37.

Jonassen, D. H. 2000. "Toward a Design Theory of Problem Solving." *Educational Technology Research and Development,* 48(4), 63–85.

Kazmer, M. M. 2000. "Coping in a Distance Environment: Sitcoms, Chocolate Cake, and Dinner with a Friend." *First Monday* 5(9). Electronic journal, no pagination. Retrieved from http://firstmonday.org/htbin/cgiwrap/bin/ojs/index. php/fm/article/view/791/700.

Kazmer, M. M. 2006. "Creation and Loss of Sociotechnical Capital Among Information Professionals Educated Online." *Library and Information Science Research* 28(2), 172–191.

Kearsley, G. 1998. "Educational Technology: A Critique." *Educational Technology* 38(2), 47–51.

Kehrwald, B. 2008. "Understanding Social Presence in Text-Based Online Learning Environments." *Distance Education* 29(1), 89–106.

Kling, R., and C. Courtright. 2003. "Group Behavior and Learning in Electronic Forums: A Sociotechnical Approach. *The Information Society* 19(3), 221–235.

Lawrence, R. L. 2002. "A Small Circle of Friends: Cohort Groups as Learning Communities." *New Directions for Adult and Continuing Education* 95, 83–92.

Liu, X., R. J. Magjuka, C. J. Bonk, and S. Lee. 2007. "Does Sense of Community Matter?" *Quarterly Review of Distance Education* 8(1), 9–24.

Lock, J. V. 2002. "Laying the Groundwork for the Development of Learning Communities Within Online Courses." *Quarterly Review of Distance Education* 3(4), 395–408.

McFadden, M., and G. Munns. 2002. "Engagement and the Social Relations of Pedagogy." *British Journal of Sociology of Education* 23(3), 357–366.

Means, B., Y. Toyama, R. Murphy, M. Bakia, and K. Jones. 2010. *Evaluation of evidence-based practices in online learning: A meta-analysis and review of online learning studies.* U.S. Department of Education, Office of Planning, Evaluation, and Policy Development.

Moller, L. 1998. "Designing Communities of Learners for Asynchronous Distance Education." *Educational Technology Research and Development* 46(4), 115–122.

Moore, M. G. 1993. "Theory of Transactional Distance." In D. Keegan (ed.) *Theoretical Principles of Distance Education* (pp. 22–38). Routledge.

Moore, M. G. and Kearsley, G. 1996. *Distance Education: A Systems View.* Wadsworth.

National Center for Education Statistics (NCES). 2003. *Distance Learning at Degree Granting Postsecondary Institutions: 2000–2001.*

Palloff, R. M., and K. Pratt. 2001. *Lessons from the Cyberspace Classroom: The Realities of Online Teaching.* Jossey-Bass.

Petraglia, J. 1998. "The Real World on a Short Leash: The (Mis)application of Constructivism to the Design of Educational Technology." *Educational Technology Research and Development* 46(3), 53–65.

Radford, A. W. 2011. *Learning at a Distance: Undergraduate Enrollment in Distance Education Courses and Degree Programs.* National Center for Education Statistics, Institute of Education Sciences.

Rettie, R. 2003. "Connectedness, Awareness and Social Presence." *PRESENCE 2003, 6th Annual International Workshop on Presence.* Aalborg, Denmark. Retrieved from http://citeseerx.ist.psu.edu/viewdoc/download?doi=10.1.1.10 1.9820&rep=rep1&type=pdf.

Richardson, J. C., and K. Swan. 2003. "Examining Social Presence in Online Courses in Relation to Students' Perceived Learning and Satisfaction." *Journal of Asynchronous Learning Networks* 7(1), 68–88.

Rogoff, B. 1994. "Developing Understanding of the Idea of Communities of Learners." *Mind, Culture, and Activity* (1)4, 209–229.

Rovai, A. P. 2000. "Building and Sustaining Community in Asynchronous Learning Networks." *Internet and Higher Education* 3(4), 285–297.

Rovai, A. P. 2001. "Building Classroom Community at a Distance: A Case Study." *Educational Technology Research and Development* 49(4), 33–48.

Rovai, A. P. 2002a. "Development of an Instrument to Measure Classroom Community." *Internet and Higher Education* 5, 197–211.

Rovai, A. P. 2002b. CCS Test Booklet. Unpublished document received from the author.

Rovai, A. P. 2002c. "A Preliminary Look at the Structural Differences of Higher Education Classroom Communities in Traditional and ALN Courses." *Journal of Asynchronous Learning Networks* 6(1), 41–56.

Rovai, A. P. 2003. "The Relationships of Communicator Style, Personality-Based Learning Style, and Classroom Community Among Online Graduate Students." *The Internet and Higher Education* 6(4), 347–363.

Rovai, A. P. 2004. "A Constructivist Approach to Online College Learning. *Internet and Higher Education* 7(2), 79–93.

Rovai, A. P. (2007). "Facilitating Online Discussions Effectively." *Internet and Higher Education* 10(1), 77–88.

Rovai, A. P., and H. Jordan. 2004. "Blended Learning and Sense of Community: A Comparative Analysis with Traditional and Fully Online Graduate Courses." *International Review of Research in Open and Distance Learning* 5(2). Electronic journal, no pagination. Retrieved from http://www.irrodl.org/index.php/irrodl/article/view/192/274.

Rovai, A. P., and M. J. Wighting. 2005. "Feelings of Alienation and Community Among Higher Education Students in a Virtual Classroom." *Internet and Higher Education* 8(2), 97–110.

Sher, D., P. Nuankhieo, X. Huang, C. Amelung, and J. Laffey. 2008. "Using Social Network Analysis to Understand Sense of Community in an Online Learning Environment." *Journal of Educational Computing Research* 39(1), 17–36.

Stein, D., and C. Wanstreet. 2003. "Role of Social Presence, Choice of Online or Face-to-Face Group Format, and Satisfaction with Perceived Knowledge Gained in a Distance Learning Environment." *2003 Midwest Research-to-Practice Conference in Adult, Continuing, and Community Education*

193–198. Retrieved from https://scholarworks.iupui.edu/bitstream/handle/1805/358/Stein%20&%20Wanstreet.pdf?sequence=1.

Taylor, J. 2001. "Fifth Generation Distance Education." Keynote address presented at the 20th ICDE World Conference, Dusseldorf, Germany.

Tu, C. H. 2000. "On-Line Learning Migration: From Social Learning Theory to Social Presence Theory in a CMC Environment." *Journal of Network and Computer Applications* 23(1), 27–37.

Tu, C. H., and M. McIsaac. 2002. "The Relationship of Social Presence and Interaction in Online Classes." *American Journal of Distance Education* 16(3), 131–150.

Tu, C. H., and M. Corry. 2002. "eLearning Communities." *Quarterly Review of Distance Education* 3(2), 207–218.

Wegerif, R. 1998. "The Social Dimension of Asynchronous Learning Networks." *Journal of Asynchronous Learning Networks* 2(1), 34–49.

Wenger, E., N. White, and J. D. Smith. 2009. *Digital Habitats: Stewarding Technology for Communities.* CPsquare.

Learning With and From Each Other: The Brody Learning Commons at Johns Hopkins University

Winston Tabb

Dean of University Libraries and Museums

Brian J. Shields

Director of Communications and Marketing, Libraries and University Museums

Johns Hopkins University

Both/And

As researchers continue to push libraries in different but often complementary directions, the "both/and" model of library use is becoming the norm. At Johns Hopkins, we know from recent LibQUAL+[1] results that our scholars greatly value the library as a physical place in which to work, study, and even socialize. But their feedback and user behavior also tell us that their work requires an ever-more-robust arsenal of online resources with which to accomplish their aims. Use of the university's vast collections can be much higher than the size of our population (15,511 full-time-equivalent [FTE]) would suggest. In 2011 faculty and students downloaded more than 8 million full-text articles. When we examine our consortial use statistics, the download numbers are always closer to those of an institution that has four times the number of FTE students.

The vast majority of student users—and a growing number of faculty—are digital natives. Yet we see from the gate count that the library as a physical place remains essential. Our gate count—which is not a tally of unique visitors but a sum of visits—for the period since opening the Brody Learning Commons (BLC) in 2012 and the corresponding period in the previous year shows an increase of more than 120,000 visits.[2] Whether seeking group study rooms for collaborative work or the proverbial "clean, well-lighted place" for silent study, our users don't simply appreciate the variety of spaces we provide; they depend on them.

On August 13, 2012, we opened the doors to BLC, a space open 24 hours a day and seven days a week that connects on all floors to the Milton S. Eisenhower Library, the university's main research library and home to its legacy collections. The commons comprises 42,000 square feet and more than 500 seats, increasing the library's seating capacity by almost a third. The building includes:

Sixteen flexible group study rooms

- The walls of group study rooms are covered in "idea paint" to allow them to serve as white boards or projection screens.
- Rooms can be reserved online for four-hour blocks up to 24 hours in advance.

Six teaching and seminar rooms

Robust technology throughout

- TeamSpot in various locations allows students to collaborate from individual laptops using a shared screen.
- Short-throw projectors enable students to write on walls with interactive pens and save the resulting documents to their laptops or flash drives.
- Group study rooms outfitted with equipment allow students to record themselves practicing presentations.
- Video teleconferencing enables distance education or teleconferenced meetings.
- A pod-based learning classroom facilitates interactive group learning opportunities.
- Group study rooms outfitted with LifeCam cameras and Skype permit groups to work with colleagues remotely.

100-seat quiet reading room

Commissioned art installation in the quiet reading room

- "An Archaeology of Knowledge" by artist Mark Dion is a true *Wunderkammer,* a cabinet or wall of wonders with more than 700 objects that span millennia and include everything from ancient Roman inscriptions and an early university library card catalog to glass pipettes, miniature books, and a sculpture of the university's founder and namesake, philanthropist Johns Hopkins. The cabinet holds items from all corners of the Hopkins universe and represents a history of the university shown through objects.

Visualization Wall

- A 12-foot by 7-foot interactive video display wall, part of a joint research initiative between the Whiting School of Engineering and the Sheridan Libraries, is designed to explore human-computer interactions and engage students in the creative process of designing applications.
- The wall contains interactive games that students can play to relieve stress along with thousands of images from the libraries' collections.
- Library programmers worked side by side with computer science students to build the wall and develop and write the code that runs it. Programmers continue to work with students to develop new games, programs, and other visual tools.

75-seat café

Teaching and research space for the Department of Special Collections

- Curators and faculty teach classes, both undergraduate and graduate, using the unique and rare materials in the libraries' special collections.

Laboratory space for the Department of Conservation and Preservation

- The department is home to the Heritage Science for Conservation project, a Mellon-funded initiative that sponsors original research conducted by postgrads in such areas as chemistry and materials science to discover novel approaches to conserving paper-based collections.

The data we have so far lead us to believe that we have succeeded in our attempt to provide the Johns Hopkins University community with a new kind of library building—one built to match the way students and faculty work. In the months and years to come, we will be testing this belief through the efforts of our User Experience team and through tools like LibQUAL+.

What follows is the story of why and how we built the commons. In a very short period of time, the building has become a second home for students who have not only christened it "BroCo" but also started a Tumblr[3] dedicated to it. Already BLC is one of the most utilized buildings on Homewood campus.

The Libraries at Johns Hopkins, a Brief History

The Sheridan Libraries, named to honor the generosity of philanthropists Champ and Debbie Sheridan, are located in several places around the city of Baltimore. The five libraries—the Brody Learning Commons, the Milton S. Eisenhower Library, the Albert D. Hutzler Reading Room, the John Work Garrett Library, and the George Peabody Library—serve campus and community populations and are indispensable to the university's twin missions of teaching and research.

Johns Hopkins University was nearly 90 years old before one central library for the university was proposed on the Homewood campus. Prior to construction of what would become the Milton S. Eisenhower Library (honoring the university's eighth president and a champion of the project), collections were scattered among departmental libraries. This divided structure had served researchers' needs in the past but became increasingly untenable as interdisciplinary research increased in popularity in the 1960s.

Four design principles guided the architects' work on the Eisenhower Library:

- Bring together 11 libraries and accommodate 1 million books
- Be the heart of the university
- Include a computing center connected to Welch Medical Library and the Applied Physics Laboratory (APL)[4] for academic research and to automate library processes
- Be flexible to allow easy expansion up to 4 million volumes

The second principle, "Be the heart of the university," has become, in the nearly half century since the Eisenhower Library opened, something of a first principle for the students and faculty of Johns Hopkins. For reasons relating to the community—such as a populace composed of driven, high-achieving individuals; the library's central location on the campus; and the absence of a student union building—the Eisenhower Library truly became the heart of the university and the center of the student experience on the Homewood campus.

It also became very crowded. By the late 1990s the library was routinely forced to rent folding chairs to meet seating needs during such high-volume periods as midterms and finals. Users continued to appreciate the services they received and the resources to which they had access, but the lack of space and natural light—Eisenhower rests mostly below ground—kept coming to the fore as faculty and students responded to surveys about library use and satisfaction.

As we were outgrowing our space, other libraries were expanding theirs through the addition of information commons. Starting in the early 1990s, schools including the University of Southern California and the University of Iowa designed spaces that combined collaborative work areas, lots of computers, and service desks staffed by librarians, information technologists, and other student services staff (Lippincott 2012). The literature on information commons is voluminous, on topics ranging from practical to highly theoretical (Beagle 2010). It shares one thing: As the century drew to a close, articles began to stress the need for libraries to move beyond seeing these spaces as another way to support learning, and instead looked at ways they could organize resources to actively further learning initiatives and learning outcomes. That is, rather than simply functioning as a service point that delivered the tools for learning, they became "integrated centers for research, teaching and learning" (Bailey and Tierney 2002). The Sheridan Libraries embraced this emphasis on integration as a natural reflection of the university's mission to "educate its students and cultivate their capacity for lifelong learning, to foster independent and original research, and to bring the benefits of discovery to the world" (Johns Hopkins University mission statement 2013).

As a late-adaptor of the commons concept, Johns Hopkins ultimately benefited from others' work. We made a conscious decision to avoid building a glorified computer lab and instead installed a robust wireless network that could combine with software to let students easily collaborate using their own laptops. In a very real sense, the Brody Learning Commons supports collaborative research, not just collaborative learning.

Planning

Concepts for a learning commons were explored over a five-year period through the Eisenhower Library Expansion Feasibility Study, which was conducted by architectural firm Shepley Bulfinch in March 2003, updated by that firm in 2009, and affirmed in the university's 2008 master plan update.

The following, taken from the architectural firm's project summary definition document (Bulfinch 2009), offered guidance on what we hoped to offer students both physically and programmatically. In the years that followed, we would work with our user community to ensure the vision transcended the document and to refine, where needed, to best meet user needs.

> The [Brody Learning Commons] is envisioned as a student-focused building that furthers the library's role as the intellectual, social, and physical heart of the Homewood campus, enhances the user experience in Milton S. Eisenhower Library (MSEL), and is a portal to the

physical and virtual resources of the Sheridan library system . . . The program established for Brody will contain teaching, learning, and collaboration spaces, including group study spaces, reading rooms, seminar rooms, and technology laboratories . . . Placing an atrium as a transition between Brody and the south end of MSEL allows natural light to continue to reach the lower levels of the south end of MSEL while providing a civic space for the library community.

User-Driven, User-Designed

After the project received approval from the university's board of trustees but before it was publicly announced, we began a multi-year user outreach effort. The first survey, conducted in April 2008, asked users about their library use (including inquiries on resources used, hours spent in the library, and typical time of day for visits) and invited them to rate the importance of specific features—for instance, group study rooms and individual carrels. The survey also included an open-ended question about what should be included in a new library space. (The project was not named at this stage and no additional details were given to allow respondents to provide responses uninhibited by a sense of meeting or matching an existing design concept.)

As the design program began in earnest the following fall, conversations within the library and across the university continued. We also gained input from all stakeholders through a series of focus groups with faculty and liaison librarians with a particular interest in how the library instruction spaces would be designed. With input from staff at our Center for Educational Resources, we arrived at the concept of flexible learning spaces that would allow us to divide students into smaller pods for group-work. Understanding that active learners retain more information (Holderied 2011), we felt that spaces that included moveable furniture, white boards, smart projectors, and software for collaboration would enhance the learning experience.

The project was officially announced in December 2008. The following spring we began a series of student initiatives, one per semester, designed to engage students with the project. This was a particular challenge with upperclassmen who would graduate before it opened, as was encouraging feedback to ensure that the building would truly meet the needs of its users.

For each initiative, we used both traditional and social media channels, including the libraries' Facebook page, Twitter feed, and Flickr page, and a blog with a live cam showing the construction. These efforts were complemented with outreach to the student newspaper for interviews with the dean and project managers, once-per-semester hard-hat tours for student reporters/photographers, and ongoing consultation with the library's Student Advisory Committee, the Student Government Association (SGA), and the Graduate Representative Organization (GRO).

Because the library remained open throughout construction, care was taken to provide as much information about the construction process as possible, using social media to make users aware of progress and inconveniences (such as anticipated noise and scheduled outages) and to quickly respond to problems or questions. The following provides an overview of our activities during a three-year period, including the two years of construction.

2009

During the spring semester, the BLC project was introduced with a communications campaign designed to inform the university community about the building and to elicit feedback on specific topics or ideas concerning space needs and amenities. For six weeks input was solicited from students, faculty, and staff. The primary vehicle was the UserVoice forum (http://brodylearningcommons.uservoice.com/forums/15044-brody-learning-commons-input-forum), a Web-based voting site that provides voters a specific number of votes to cast for specific topics and also affords users the opportunity to add their own suggestions. Prior to opening voting, we populated the forum with 16 topics (drawn from the 2008 survey) for voting and commentary. The forum was promoted via print and electronic media and was visited by 479 voters who cast 4,355 votes for 62 topics, 46 of which were added by the respondents. UserVoice does not require that voters establish an account or sign in, but it does update in real time and displays all results. Some users chose to sign in, but the option of anonymity and the transparent nature of the voting process combined to generate some thoughtful submissions and a significant amount of good will from the campus community about their stake in the project. We were careful to communicate to students that a top vote-getter was not guaranteed for the final design. This can be seen in the vote tally (Figure 1), where the top vote recipient at the cut-off date reflected a concerted effort on the part of graduate students to secure separate space in the building, a desire that did not become part of the plans.

Figure 1 / Top Ten Topics by Votes Received[5]

Graduate student-specific workspace (472)
Natural light (407)
More food options, i.e., more cafés (344)
Quiet study space that is separate and enforced (261)
Internet that works (204)
Reading room with a variety of comfortable seating types (196)
Designated space for graduate students to hold office hours (171)
Later café operating hours (160)
Art and exhibit displays/space throughout the building (148)
Designated social space (141)

The dynamic nature of the online forum allowed for conversations to occur through the comment function between students and between students and library staff, and offered students the opportunity to provide links to suggestions, e.g., library spaces or specific items they felt strongly about.

Issues relating to social space and food received a great deal of attention, confirming our view of the library as an essential social space for the Johns Hopkins community. At the same time, there was evidence of a desire that the new building include spaces that are well-lit and quiet for study. Planners were surprised that the inclusion of art and exhibition space ranked as highly as it did, but this helped inform the ultimate design of the building's iconic quiet reading room and continues to inform our planning for renovation of the Eisenhower Library.

Attendant to this online effort was a five-day initiative asking students to respond on a brown paper "idea wall" in the Eisenhower Library to topics that appeared to generate significant interest on the UserVoice forum. This effort was less successful in drawing substantive responses, which may have been due to timing as the wall was posted for a week right before reading period and finals.

The importance of additional group study space was established in the 2008 survey and several suggestions for specific technologies and amenities were received via the UserVoice forum. In the fall of 2009, a design contest was launched in which students were invited to submit designs for their ideal group study space. The premise was simple: The best ideas for what is needed in a group study room will come from those who are already using group study spaces. We left the contest open to any medium from Google SketchUp to cocktail napkin and asked only that the contestants adhere to the following guidelines: The room designed should be between 150 and 300 square feet and should include specific technologies, furniture types, and amenities, and the suggestions should be backed by an explanatory essay. First prize was $250 and a plaque in the new building indicating which design inspired the group study room. We partnered with the university's Digital Media Center to offer an introductory session for using Google SketchUp. The Friends of the Johns Hopkins University Libraries sponsored the contest, awarding cash prizes to the winners. A panel of judges, which included university administrators, students, and an architect from the firm designing the building, reviewed all submissions and judged them on creativity, sustainability, effectiveness, and the flexibility of the space.

2010

Contest winners were announced and the first-place design was displayed on the libraries' blog and in the student newspaper. The judges felt all of the submissions were strong, and they were excited at the different approaches the students took in deciding what was required for an ideal group study room. Indeed, while the room inspired by the winning design can be seen on the Quad (or Q) level of the building, features from technology to seating styles from each of the submissions can be seen in the various study rooms and throughout the building.

With groundbreaking scheduled for June, after the conclusion of the spring semester, we produced a video (http://you.tube/GFIRli8ABq8) to engage students, particularly graduating seniors, in a project that focused on the importance of the library to life at Johns Hopkins. The shoot was unscripted and consisted entirely of interviews conducted in spots outside the Eisenhower Library with students and staff. The video was shown to donors and alumni at the groundbreaking event in attendance and shared with the university community via YouTube.

The following fall, when students returned to campus to find the "big dig" under way, the campus community was invited to test more than two dozen chairs and tables under consideration for use in the commons. The furniture was placed on the main level of the Eisenhower Library, and paper ballots were provided as well as an online voting site to allow library users to vote and comment on the offerings. Selections varied according to function—for example, task chair for group study, lounge chair, café chair. Several choices were available for each. As with previous efforts, engagement was a key part of the initiative, and the exercise was fun but also functional. It made manifest a good-faith effort on the part of the library to be inclusive and involve students in the process of selecting furnishings for the building. And it yielded real results; the students selected each style and type of furniture in the various spaces of the commons.

2011

As construction proceeded and the building rose, the effort to minimize inconveniences continued, scheduling noisy or at least noisier work in the early mornings, our lightest usage time, and during term breaks. Near the end of the spring semester, there was a "topping off" ceremony (http://www.youtube.com/watch?v=uKHSLMck9Rk) for the campus community. For a week prior to the event, a period that overlapped with reunion weekend, students, friends, and alumni were invited to stop by the patio outside the Eisenhower Library to sign their names on a beam that would be the last placed in the roof structure. As with the furniture selection, the goal of the event was to involve students, including those who would be graduating, in the building process and to encourage them to consider it theirs. The following fall, with the building truly taking shape, we began offering hard-hat tours to student groups, including the Student Advisory Committee and members of SGA and GRO.

2012

As construction neared completion, we continued to provide meaningful experiences for students. The last of these initiatives was one of the most popular; it focused on choosing a vendor for the new café. A student committee was formed to review prospective vendors and help inform selection of the finalist. Invitations for participation were broadcast to the student community, and approximately 20 students from the Sheridan Libraries Student Advisory Committee, student employees at the Eisenhower Library, and members of SGA and GRO worked with staff to review proposed offerings and business models, including sustainability plans, student employment policies, and prices. Students also attended vendor presentations, sampled foods and beverages, and visited vendors' business sites.

Participants continue to be involved with the café. There has been a consistent stream of feedback throughout the first semester of the café's operation. The vendor has appreciated the open communication and in several instances has made adjustments as a result of student requests, creating a sense of good will and community engagement. This was most evident at the end of the semester when the café worked with SGA to extend hours during final exams and to sponsor complimentary coffee for night owls busy at work in the building past the café's normal hours of operation.

Looking Ahead

The opening of the Brody Learning Commons—named in honor of retiring university President William R. Brody and his wife Wendy—was not only a major event for the Johns Hopkins community; it was also a diagnostic point from which future assessments will take place. Future work to understand the effects of the commons, including successes and areas for improvement, will be informed by established pre-commons baselines, especially regarding user perceptions of the libraries. This was the core assumption behind the spring 2012 implementation of LibQUAL+, the library services perception tool made available by the Association of Research Libraries.

The first implementation of LibQUAL+ occurred in the fall of 2012 at Johns Hopkins with the survey of users across all university libraries. It included feedback from 771 Sheridan Libraries users. The majority of respondents to this survey were graduate students, and what was confirmed was the assumption that library users sought improvements in the area of "library as a place." Most notably, this section of the survey saw users express desire for "Library space that inspires study and learning" and "A comfortable and inviting location."

The spring 2012 implementation of LibQUAL+ reached a broader audience of 2,585 respondents. It was the final pre-commons assessment activity undertaken. Again, library users expressed desire for improvements in the areas of "library as a place," and notably, relatively even expectations for improvement across all five components, which concerned the library as a place that inspires study and learning, a quiet space, a comfortable and inviting place, a getaway space for academic activities, and community space for group learning. Respondents often provided comments at the end of the survey that, in sum, went even further to put into words what the library meant as a place in the community and the amount of anticipation that was shared for the opening of the commons. A total of 180 comments specifically referenced needs for improvement of library spaces, and another 53 expressed anticipation for the opening of the building.

The results of the spring 2012 implementation of LibQUAL+ were reaffirming in many ways. The importance of the relatively large number of respondents should prove a powerful assessment tool moving forward. A spring 2014 implementation of the survey is planned that will offer an opportunity to understand how the opening of the commons, along with other library initiatives, has fared in the eyes of library users. Alongside this and other assessment efforts, the libraries' commitment to success is benchmarked by high expectations of users and even higher expectations of staff, who still view the commons as a process in the making. Increasingly sophisticated understandings of use, user behavior, and user perception will continue to inform development and iterations of spaces and services to support users in the new learning commons.

References

Bailey, R., and B. Tierney (2002). "Information Commons Redux: Concept, Evolution and Transcending the Tragedy of the Commons," *Journal of Academic Librarianship* 28(5): 277–286.

Beagle, D. (2010). "The Emergent Information Commons: Philosophy, Models and 21st Century Learning Paradigms," *Journal of Library Administration* 50(1): 10–16.

Bulfinch, S. (2009). "Project Definition Summary, Brody Learning Commons," July 2009.

Holderied, A. C. (2011). "Instructional Design for the Active: Employing Inter-active Technologies and Active Learning Exercises to Enhance Information Literacy," *Journal of Information Literacy* 5(1), 23–32.

Johns Hopkins University mission statement. Retrieved January 22, 2013, from http://webapps.jhu.edu/jhuniverse/information_about_hopkins/about_jhu/mission_statement.

Lippincott, J. K. (2012). "Information Commons: Meeting Millennials' Needs," *Journal of Library Administration* 52(6/7): 538–548.

Notes

1. LibQUAL+ is a suite of services that libraries use to solicit, track, understand, and act upon users' opinions of service quality. These services are offered to the library community by the Association of Research Libraries. The program's centerpiece is a rigorously tested Web-based survey bundled with training that helps libraries assess and improve library services.

2. Aug. 13–Dec. 31, 2011: 449,872; Aug. 13–Dec. 31, 2012: 570,607.

3. Tumblr is a Web-based service that allows users to create blogs and post "text, photos, quotes, links, music, and videos." Tumblr.com.

4. Welch Medical Library serves the East Baltimore medical campus, including the School of Medicine, the School of Nursing, the Bloomberg School of Public Health, and Johns Hopkins Hospital. APL is the Applied Physics Laboratory, a non-degree-granting division of the university.

5. "Needs a student center like ones at other schools," a topic added by a respondent, was the fifth most popular by vote tally (235). It was removed from this list, as it did not relate to the Brody Learning Commons. Several other topics unconnected to the commons were added and received support/commentary—data that may be useful to other Johns Hopkins University departments.

Federal Agency and Federal Library Reports

Library of Congress

10 First St. S.E., Washington, DC 20540
202-707-5000
World Wide Web http://www.loc.gov

James H. Billington
Librarian of Congress

Founded in 1800, the Library of Congress is the nation's oldest federal cultural institution and the largest library in the world, with more than 155 million items in various languages, disciplines, and formats. As the world's largest repository of knowledge and creativity, the library's mission is to support Congress in fulfilling its constitutional duties and to further the progress of knowledge and creativity for the benefit of the American people.

The library's collections are housed in its three buildings on Capitol Hill, and in special climate-controlled facilities for books at Fort Meade, Maryland, and for audiovisual materials at the Packard Campus for Audio Visual Conservation in Culpeper, Virginia. The library also provides global access to its resources through its award-winning website, http://www.loc.gov.

Legislative Support to Congress

Serving Congress is the library's highest priority, particularly in the area of legislative support. It provides legislative support to Congress through the Congressional Research Service (CRS), the Law Library, and the U.S. Copyright Office.

During the past year CRS supported Congress with policy analyses as it considered increasingly complex legislative domestic issues such as national security, economic stimulus and job creation, employment and training, unemployment compensation, food safety, transportation, and judicial nominations. CRS responded to more than 700,000 congressional reference requests and members of Congress accessed CRS products and services more than 1 million times.

The Law Library is the world's largest, comprising 2.8 million volumes. During the year it provided Congress with comprehensive international, comparative, and foreign law research based on the most current information available. Law Library staff prepared more than 300 legal research reports, special studies, and

Report compiled by Audrey Fischer, Public Affairs Specialist, Library of Congress memoranda in response to congressional inquiries. Foreign-law specialists provided foreign and comparative law reports relating to U.S. legislative issues including international trade and tariffs, immigration reform, welfare reform, environmental protection, nuclear power, and alternative military service.

The Global Legal Information Network (GLIN) provided Congress and other participating parliamentary bodies with more than 210,000 laws, judicial decisions, and related legal materials contributed by 28 member nations and international organizations. As a consortium, the members of the network share responsibility for its management. During 2012 preparations were made for the transfer of GLIN Central functions from the Library of Congress to a successor institution.

The U.S. Copyright Office provided policy advice and technical assistance to Congress on important copyright laws and related issues. At the request of Congress, the Copyright Office initiated a study to explore ways to resolve copyright infringement claims of relatively small value without the burden and expense of traditional federal litigation. During the year, the office solicited stakeholder input and received public comments. It expects to issue a report in October 2013.

Congress also asked the Copyright Office to study how copyright law affects visual artists and how a federal resale royalty right for visual artists might affect groups or individuals who create, license, sell, exhibit, disseminate, and preserve works of visual art. An artist resale royalty would allow artists to benefit from increases in the value of their works over time by granting them a percentage of the proceeds from the resale of their original works.

Bringing together its combination of technical expertise and knowledge of the congressional process, the library introduced several new information services during the year. Working with other legislative branch data partners, it launched a *Congressional Record* app on January 16, 2012, and on September 19 it debuted Congress.gov, a new public beta site for accessing legislative information. The library also coordinated with the House Recording Studio to launch the House Committee Streaming Video Project to broadcast House committee hearings. The first hearing was broadcast on January 17, 2012.

Security

The library's Office of Security and Emergency Preparedness continued to work to improve security at the library's Capitol Hill buildings and outlying facilities, implementing additional physical security controls to protect the collections, enhancing the emergency preparedness program, and strengthening personnel security programs. Work continued to improve emergency readiness by conducting preparedness briefings, training classes, and no-notice evacuation drills. This included re-emphasizing the proper response procedures for safe egress of persons with mobility impairments. The library's *Employee Emergency Action Guide,* an all-hazards emergency manual for staff, was updated to reflect enhanced procedures for earthquakes and other emergency situations.

The library continued to improve the electronic and physical security controls that protect collections and assets in all library buildings. It implemented additional security measures in order to strengthen access controls for special-format collections areas. A major initiative strengthened security through a 100-percent ID badge reissuance for staff and contractors.

The Information Technology Services Office (ITS) ensures that the library's mission-critical systems are reliable and secure and that the technology infrastructure that supports these systems is uncompromised. ITS continued to work to ensure continuity of operations in the event of a pandemic or other emergency, including enhancing the Alternate Computing Facility and remote access. Throughout the year ITS ensured that the library's infrastructure and the services it provides continued to adapt to new technology and respond to other changes and requirements. The library's IT infrastructure includes data centers in four building locations: the Packard Campus for Audio Visual Conservation in Virginia; the National Library for the Blind and Physically Handicapped on Taylor Street in Northeast Washington, D.C.; the Alternative Computing Facility; and two centers in the James Madison building on Capitol Hill. The data centers support more than 650 physical servers, 300 virtual servers, 250 enterprise systems and applications, 5.8 petabytes (PB) of disk storage and 8.5 PB of backup and archive data on tape. The IT infrastructure also includes a wide-area network, a metropolitan-area network and local-area networks that comprise 350 network devices. ITS also supports more than 8,600 voice connections, 14,700 network connections, and 5,300 workstations.

Strategic Planning

The library made significant progress during the year in implementing its Strategic Plan for fiscal year (FY) 2011 through FY 2016 and the related planning and budgeting framework. The plan describes the library's goals and strategies for serving Congress and the people and demonstrates the organization's commitment to the Government Performance and Results Act. The framework integrates planning and budgeting processes, adds rigor to the library's planning and budgeting activities, and enhances the organization's ability to measure progress toward achieving the plan's outcomes and goals. In 2012 newly appointed Deputy Librarian Robert Dizard, Jr., facilitated regular performance meetings to track and measure progress, establishing clear lines of accountability for achieving results called for in the Strategic Plan.

Budget

On December 23, 2011, the president signed the Consolidated Appropriations Act, 2012 (P.L. 112-74), which provided an FY 2012 appropriation for the library of $629.2 million, including authority to spend up to $41.9 million in offsetting receipts.

Development

During FY 2012 the library's fund-raising activities brought in a total of $9.98 million, representing 796 gifts from 573 donors. Those gifts, including $3.35 million in cash gifts, $5.23 million in new pledges, $425,000 in in-kind gifts, and $966,000 received through planned gifts, were made to support 75 library initiatives. The library forged partnerships with 222 first-time donors; they gave $1.29 million, representing 13 percent of the gifts received during the year. Private gifts supported a variety of new and continuing initiatives throughout the library, including exhibitions, acquisitions, and scholarly programs.

Gifts from the James Madison Council—the library's private-sector advisory group—totaled more than $5.49 million in FY 2012. Council gifts supported the World Digital Library, the Junior Fellows Program, an exhibition featuring the library's Armenian collections, and the Madisonian Awards, given to library staff members in recognition of distinguished service.

Target Corp., Wells Fargo, AT&T, the Institute of Museum and Library Services, and a number of additional donors gave more than $1.3 million to support the 2012 National Book Festival. David M. Rubenstein, Madison Council member and co-chair of the National Book Festival board, donated $1 million to the festival as part of his $5 million pledge, in 2010, to support the festival for five years.

Educational Outreach

The library's Educational Outreach Office makes its online resources accessible to teachers and students through the Teachers Page website (http://www.loc.gov/teachers) and through its Teaching with Primary Sources Program (TPS). In 2012 the program provided professional development to more than 27,000 teachers throughout the country. The 28 educational institutions that make up the TPS Educational Consortium served educators in 17 states. Through the TPS Regional Program, 152 organizations delivered TPS programming to teachers in 36 states and the District of Columbia.

The library offered five week-long Summer Teacher Institutes to 129 educators from 33 states. The Educational Outreach Office continued its collaboration with PBS TeacherLine, a provider of online professional development courses. Working together, they provided a 45-hour online course titled "Teaching with Primary Sources from the Library of Congress" for nearly 200 teachers.

Educational Outreach continued to manage the Teachers Page, a library service providing teacher resources. It expanded the teacher blog, "Teaching with the Library of Congress," which promotes practical strategies for the effective use of the library's online collections. During the year 100 new posts were published on a wide range of K–12-related topics.

Literacy Promotion

The Library of Congress promotes reading and literacy through the Center for the Book, the National Book Festival, collaborative public service advertising campaigns, the appointment of a National Ambassador for Young People's Literature, and through its popular literacy promotion website, http://www.Read.gov. In 2012 the library launched a multiyear Celebration of the Book.

The Center for the Book, with its network of affiliates in all 50 states and more than 80 organizational partners, continued to lead reading promotion efforts.

The Center for the Book also provided oversight for the Read.gov website. Read.gov is supported by an advertising campaign directed by the library's Public Affairs Office in cooperation with the nonprofit Advertising Council. In July a free, interactive version of *Aesop's Fables* was made available on the Read.gov site, along with a free app for the iPhone, iPad, and Android platforms. The interactive book is adapted from the 1919 book *The Aesop for Children: With Pictures by Milo Winter,* which is housed in the library's Rare Book and Special Collections Division. [For more on the center's activities, see the following article, "Center for the Book"—*Ed.*]

Celebration of the Book

Calling books "the cornerstones of American culture and democracy," Librarian of Congress James H. Billington declared 2012 the start of a multiyear "Celebration of the Book." The celebration includes exhibitions, symposia, and other special events that explore the important ways in which books have affected people, politics, culture, and history.

In June 2012 the library hosted a conference titled "Creating a Dynamic, Knowledge-based Democracy." The conference explored the legacy of three key events that profoundly shaped the nation: the founding of more than 1,600 free libraries by steel magnate Andrew Carnegie, the establishment of land-grant universities under legislation introduced by U.S. Rep. Justin S. Morrill of Vermont in 1857, and the founding of the National Academy of Sciences.

The library also celebrated the book at its 12th Annual National Book Festival on September 22–23, which featured more than 125 authors and illustrators discussing their works.

On December 6–7 the library hosted the first International Summit of the Book—a gathering of leaders in academia, libraries, culture, and technology—to debate and discuss the book as a powerful and crucial form of information transmittal. At the summit, David Rubenstein, a co-founder of the Carlyle Group and major donor to the Library of Congress, announced that he would contribute $1.5 million to fund three new Library of Congress annual literacy awards over five years. The three annual awards are the David M. Rubenstein Prize for a groundbreaking contribution to the sustained advancement of literacy by any individual or entity worldwide; the American Prize, honoring a project developed and deployed in the United States during the preceding decade with special emphasis on combating aliteracy; and the International Prize, which would honor the outstanding work of an individual, a nation, or a non-governmental organization (NGO) working in a specific country or region.

Books That Shaped America

On June 25, 2012, the library opened an exhibition, "Books That Shaped America," that featured 88 titles published over a 250-year period (see list below).

Curators and experts from throughout the library contributed their choices for the list and there was much debate about cutting worthy titles from a much larger list in order to accommodate the physical restrictions of the exhibition space. Some of the titles on display have been the source of great controversy, even derision, in U.S. history. Nevertheless, they shaped Americans' views of their world and the world's views of America. The initial selection of titles was not meant to be definitive, but rather to spark a national conversation on books that have influenced Americans' lives.

Bloggers and critics across America wrote commentary about the selections throughout the summer. The public commented through a survey on the library's National Book Festival website at http://www.loc.gov/bookfest. More than 10,000 people have responded, many listing their own nominations. Additions to the original list of 88 titles will be announced in 2013. The 2012 list follows:

Experiments and Observations on Electricity, Benjamin Franklin, 1751

Poor Richard Improved and *The Way to Wealth,* Benjamin Franklin, 1758

Common Sense, Thomas Paine, 1776

A Grammatical Institute of the English Language, Noah Webster, 1783

The Federalist, anonymous, 1787

A Curious Hieroglyphick Bible, anonymous, 1788

A Survey of the Roads of the United States of America, Christopher Colles, 1789

The Private Life of the Late Benjamin Franklin, LL.D., Benjamin Franklin, 1793

American Cookery, Amelia Simmons, 1796

New England Primer, anonymous, 1803

Meriwether Lewis, History of the Expedition Under the Command of the Captains Lewis and Clark, 1814

The Legend of Sleepy Hollow, Washington Irving, 1820

McGuffey's Newly Revised Eclectic Primer, William Holmes McGuffey, 1836

Peter Parley's Universal History, Samuel Goodrich, 1837

The Narrative of the Life of Frederick Douglass, Frederick Douglass, 1845

The Scarlet Letter, Nathaniel Hawthorne, 1850

Moby-Dick; or, The Whale, Herman Melville, 1851

Uncle Tom's Cabin, Harriet Beecher Stowe, 1852

Walden; or, Life in the Woods, Henry David Thoreau, 1854

Leaves of Grass, Walt Whitman, 1855

Little Women, or, Meg, Jo, Beth and Amy, Louisa May Alcott, 1868

Mark, the Match Boy, Horatio Alger, Jr., 1869

The American Woman's Home, Catharine E. Beecher and Harriet Beecher Stowe, 1869

Adventures of Huckleberry Finn, Mark Twain, 1884

Poems, Emily Dickinson, 1890

How the Other Half Lives, Jacob Riis, 1890

The Red Badge of Courage, Stephen Crane, 1895

The Wonderful Wizard of Oz, L. Frank Baum, 1900

Harriet, the Moses of Her People, Sarah H. Bradford, 1901

The Call of the Wild, Jack London, 1903

The Souls of Black Folk, W. E. B. Du Bois, 1903

The History of Standard Oil, Ida Tarbell, 1904

The Jungle, Upton Sinclair, 1906

The Education of Henry Adams, Henry Adams, 1907

Pragmatism, William James, 1907
Riders of the Purple Sage, Zane Grey, 1912
Tarzan of the Apes, Edgar Rice Burroughs, 1914
Family Limitation, Margaret Sanger, 1914
Spring and All, William Carlos Williams, 1923
New Hampshire, Robert Frost, 1923
The Great Gatsby, F. Scott Fitzgerald, 1925
The Weary Blues, Langston Hughes, 1925
The Sound and the Fury, William Faulkner, 1929
Red Harvest, Dashiell Hammett, 1929
Joy of Cooking, Irma Rombauer, 1931
Gone with the Wind, Margaret Mitchell, 1936
How to Win Friends and Influence People, Dale Carnegie, 1936
Their Eyes Were Watching God, Zora Neale Hurston, 1937
Idaho: A Guide in Word and Pictures, Federal Writers' Project, 1937
Our Town: A Play, Thornton Wilder, 1938
Alcoholics Anonymous, anonymous, 1939
The Grapes of Wrath, John Steinbeck, 1939
For Whom the Bell Tolls, Ernest Hemingway, 1940
Native Son, Richard Wright, 1940
A Tree Grows in Brooklyn, Betty Smith, 1943
A Treasury of American Folklore, Benjamin A. Botkin, 1944
A Street in Bronzeville, Gwendolyn Brooks, 1945
The Common Sense Book of Baby and Child Care, Benjamin Spock, 1946
The Iceman Cometh, Eugene O'Neill, 1946
Goodnight Moon, Margaret Wise Brown, 1947
A Streetcar Named Desire, Tennessee Williams, 1947
Sexual Behavior in the Human Male, Alfred C. Kinsey, 1948
The Catcher in the Rye, J. D. Salinger, 1951
Invisible Man, Ralph Ellison, 1952
Charlotte's Web, E. B. White, 1952
Fahrenheit 451, Ray Bradbury, 1953
Howl, Allen Ginsberg, 1956
Atlas Shrugged, Ayn Rand, 1957
The Cat in the Hat, Dr. Seuss, 1957
On the Road, Jack Kerouac, 1957
To Kill a Mockingbird, Harper Lee, 1960
Catch-22, Joseph Heller, 1961
Stranger in a Strange Land, Robert A. Heinlein, 1961
The Snowy Day, Ezra Jack Keats, 1962
Silent Spring, Rachel Carson, 1962

Where the Wild Things Are, Maurice Sendak, 1963
The Fire Next Time, James Baldwin, 1963
The Feminine Mystique, Betty Friedan, 1963
The Autobiography of Malcolm X, Malcolm X and Alex Haley, 1965
Unsafe at Any Speed, Ralph Nader, 1965
In Cold Blood, Truman Capote, 1966
The Double Helix, James D. Watson, 1968
Bury My Heart at Wounded Knee, Dee Brown, 1970
Our Bodies, Ourselves, Boston Women's Health Book Collective, 1971
Cosmos, Carl Sagan, 1980
Beloved, Toni Morrison, 1987
And the Band Played On, Randy Shilts, 1987
The Words of César Chávez, César Chávez, 2002

Collections

During 2012 the size of the library's collections grew to nearly 155.4 million items, an increase of more than 3.5 million over the previous year. This figure included more than 35 million cataloged books and other print materials, 68 million manuscripts, 16.7 million microforms, 5.5 million maps, 6.5 million pieces of sheet music, 15.7 million visual materials (photographs, posters, moving images, prints, and drawings), 3.6 million audio materials, and more than 1 million items in miscellaneous formats.

In April 2012 the library established a Collection Development Office to supports its goal to acquire and maintain a universal collection of knowledge and a mint record of American creativity to meet the needs of Congress, scholars, and the public.

Important Acquisitions

The Library of Congress receives millions of items each year from copyright deposits, federal agencies, and purchases, exchanges, and gifts.

In 2012 the Copyright Office forwarded more than 636,000 copies of works with a net value estimated at $30.5 million to the library. About half were received from publishers under the mandatory-deposit provisions of the copyright law. The library also received more than 1,000 electronic serial issues through the eDeposit program that provides for the receipt of electronic serials demanded under copyright law.

The Madison Council funded the library's acquisition of a 40-volume set of Rudolph Ackermann's *Repository of the Arts* (1809–1829), a letter written by First Lady Mary Todd Lincoln in 1862, and the first Russian celestial atlas from 1829.

The library also acquired many significant items and collections by gift or purchase. The following were among them:

- The Law Library acquired *Speculum Conjugiorum,* printed in Mexico in 1556 by Juan Pablos, believed to be the first printer in the Americas.

- The Manuscript Division acquired the papers of former Speaker of the House Nancy Pelosi; astronomer Carl Sagan (1934–1996); actor/director Lee Strasberg (1901–1982); and Edwin J. Feulner, founding trustee and long-time president of the Heritage Foundation; and Federal Judge Harry T. Edwards.
- The Motion Picture, Broadcasting, and Recorded Sound Division acquired the Joe Smith Collection, a total of 238 hours of interviews with music industry icons, recorded by the former president of Capitol Records/EMI.
- The Music Division acquired the papers of composer George Crumb (1929–), dancer and choreographer Pearl Lang (1921–2009), and playwright/director Arthur Laurents (1918–2011).
- The Prints and Photographs Division received the photographic archives of *Congressional Quarterly* and *Roll Call*, which merged in 2009.
- The Rare Book and Special Collections Division acquired a Latin version of *Sur la Figure de la Terre*, written by 18th century French mathematician and philosopher Pierre-Louis Moreau de Maupertuis. The item, which originally belonged to Thomas Jefferson, was donated by the U.S. Naval Observatory to aid the library in its effort to reconstruct Jefferson's library.
- The Serial and Government Publications Division purchased at auction rare issues of historic newspapers from the Civil War era that include coverage of the first Vicksburg campaign and the Battle of Gettysburg from a Southern perspective.

Cataloging

The library provides cataloging records to the nation's 122,000 public, school, academic, and research libraries and other institutions that rely on its bibliographic data. In 2012 the library cataloged in its Voyager system 350,201 new works on 330,621 separate bibliographic records. Production of full- and standard-level original cataloging totaled 212,332 bibliographic records. The library and other member institutions of the international Program for Cooperative Cataloging created 312,346 name and series authority records, and 3,950 subject authorities. The library served as secretariat for the program and created 91,321 of the name and series authority records and 1,437 of the subject authorities. Dewey Decimal Classification numbers were assigned to 92,099 titles as a service to other libraries throughout the world that use that system to organize their collections.

Bibliographic Control and Standards

The Library of Congress, along with the National Library of Medicine and the National Agricultural Library, agreed to implement the new cataloging standard Resource Description and Access (RDA) in March 2013. Implementation of RDA was conditional on additional rewording of RDA and continued progress on transforming the metadata infrastructure for bibliographic data. To address the latter, work began on the development of a new bibliographic framework, along with final preparations for RDA implementation. Preparations include extensive training of more than 400 library staff members, comprising 36 hours of classroom instruction followed by review and desk-side coaching. During 2012 trained staff in the Acquisitions and Bibliographic Access Directorate produced 24,103 bibliographic records using RDA. At the end of the fiscal year, all conditions were being met for nationwide implementation of RDA on March 31, 2013.

Reference Services

In addition to serving Congress, the Library of Congress provides reference services to the public in its reading rooms and through its website. During the year library staff handled more than 540,000 reference requests received in person, on the telephone, and through written and electronic correspondence. The library's digital reference staff also responded to more than 16,500 questions posed by patrons using the Ask a Librarian feature on the library's website. Nearly 1 million items were circulated for use within the library.

A total of 37,216 new patrons were registered in the Automated Reader Registration System, bringing the total to more than 142,000 since its inception in April 2009. Patrons continued to register in person for the library-issued user card. The Automated Call Slip system was upgraded in 2012 to allow patrons in the library's reading rooms to request library materials from the general collections through the library's online public-access catalog rather than by using paper call slips.

During the year, the library added 74 new encoded archival description (EAD) finding aids online. The system offers approximately 1,700 Web-accessible finding aids to more than 43 million archival items in library divisions including Manuscript; Music; American Folklife Center; Prints and Photographs; and Motion Picture, Broadcasting, and Recorded Sound; and other Library of Congress research centers.

Online Resources

Through its National Digital Library program and digitization efforts by its various divisions, the library has been adding high-quality digital content to its award-winning website at http://www.loc.gov. During 2012, 6.2 million new digital files were added, bringing the total to 37.6 million. This figure includes files from the National Digital Newspaper Program and other online collections.

Consistently recognized as one of the top federal sites, the library's website recorded 87 million visits and 545 million page-views in 2012. The website provides access to the institution's unparalleled resources such as its online catalog, selected collections in various formats, copyright and legislative information, webcasts and podcasts of library events, and other resources.

Accessible on the website, the public legislative information system known as THOMAS received more than 11.5 million visits during the year. The Law Library implemented numerous improvements to THOMAS, making it significantly easier to find and access legislative information. The legacy system, which was launched in 1995, will be replaced by Congress.gov following full content migration.

By subscribing to the library's RSS feeds and e-mail update service, users can stay up to date about areas of the website that interest them. To sign up for either service, visit http:/www.loc.gov/rss.

The library continued to promote its activities by producing podcasts and making them accessible on its website at http://www.loc.gov/podcasts. The podcasts include interviews conducted with authors participating in the National Book Festival. Webcasts of selected lectures, readings, conferences, and symposia held at the library were also added to the website at http://www.loc.gov/webcasts.

Social Media

To develop new communication channels and new relationships, to reach new audiences, and to experiment with and explore new technologies, the Library of Congress continued to participate in media-sharing and social-networking sites such as Flickr, YouTube, iTunes U, Facebook, and Twitter. In 2012 the library added more than 3,000 new photos to its Flickr account, bringing the total to 17,000. The site has received more than 62.8 million page views since its debut in 2008. New videos added to the library's YouTube channel included those featuring the 2012 National Book Festival. The site has provided more than 4 million video views since its launch in 2009. New educational content on the library's iTunes U site includes the 2012 National Book Festival, presentations from the Kluge Center, concerts, and an RDA training series for librarians.

In addition to its main Facebook site, the library offers Facebook pages for the Law Library, the American Folklife Center, and the National Digital Information Infrastructure and Preservation Program. The library's Twitter presence includes feeds for the World Digital Library, the digital preservation program, the Congressional Research Service, copyright issues, and maps. A live Twitterfall could be viewed by attendees of the 2012 National Book Festival.

The library's main blog at http://blogs.loc.gov—among the first federal blogs at the time of its launch in April 2007—has since been joined by blogs generated by the Law Library; the National Digital Preservation Program; the Music, Prints, and Photographs Division; the Science, Technology, and Business Division; and the Educational Outreach Office. In 2012 new blogs were introduced by the Copyright Office and the Poetry and Literature Center.

Global Access

The Library of Congress acquires global resources through cooperative agreements and exchanges with other nations, through its overseas offices, and via the World Digital Library initiative. The overseas offices collect and catalog materials from 86 countries in some 150 languages and 25 scripts, from Africa, Asia, Latin America, and the Middle East. These items are accessible in the library's area studies reading rooms. Selected items have been digitized—many through cooperative digitizing projects—and are accessible on the library's website.

Overseas Offices

The library's six overseas offices (in Rio de Janeiro, Cairo, New Delhi, Jakarta, Nairobi, and Islamabad) acquired, cataloged, and preserved materials from parts of the world where the book and information industries are not well developed.

Those offices brought in and distributed 259,840 items and, on a cost-recovery basis, provided 374,498 items to other U.S. libraries.

During 2012 the library continued the West Africa Acquisitions Pilot Project, a collaboration that began in 2011 with the Council of American Overseas Research Centers (CAORC) to select, purchase, and provide bibliographic services for materials from West African countries. In its second year of operation, the project yielded 3,025 titles for cataloging.

World Digital Library

Launched in April 2009, the World Digital Library (WDL) website makes significant primary source materials, in various formats from cultures around the world, available on the Internet, free of charge and in multilingual format. During the year WDL recorded 5,175,381 visits, accounting for 29,937,438 page views.

The content of the WDL website more than doubled during the year to 6,330 items, comprising more than 295,000 images. Noteworthy content added to the site from partner institutions included a papyrus fragment from *Orestes* by Euripides (200 B.C.) from the Austrian National Library; the *Kiev Missal* (circa 800–1000 A.D.), one of the oldest examples of the ancient Slavic written language, from the V. I. Vernadsky National Library of Ukraine; the *Poem of the Cid* (circa 1300–1400), the only surviving copy of this epic Castilian poem, from the National Library of Spain; *Babylonian Talmud* (circa 1342), from the Bavarian State Library; the *Bible of Borso d'Este* (circa 1455), from Italy's Estense Library; *Marquesado del Valle Codex* (circa 1550–1600), 28 petitions protesting seizures by conqueror Hernán Cortés, from the General Archive of the Nation of Mexico; and Mozart's original score for *The Magic Flute* (1791), from the Berlin State Library.

A key objective of the WDL project is to build digital library capabilities in the developing world. In support of this, WDL continued to operate three digital-conversion centers around the world: at the National Library and Archives of Egypt in Cairo; at the Iraqi National Library and Archives in Baghdad; and at the National Library of Uganda in Kampala. Established with private funding, these centers contribute to the capacity-building mission of WDL and are digitizing rare and at-risk material that otherwise would be inaccessible.

Preservation

Preserving its unparalleled collections—from cuneiform tablets to born-digital items—is one of the library's major activities.

During the year, nearly 6 million items from the library's collections were bound, repaired, mass-deacidified, or microfilmed or otherwise reformatted. The Preservation Directorate surveyed the preservation needs of nearly 585,000 items from the general and special collections, including books, photographs, maps, audiovisual materials, and other formats. Of these, more than 100,000 items were housed in protective containers.

Books

During the year the library transferred 130,082 items to its climate-controlled off-site storage facility at Fort Meade, Maryland, bringing the total to more than 4 million collection items stored at the facility. Additions to the facility in 2012 included 70,614 books and 59,468 containers of special-format materials, such as 1,800 cases of maps and 3,733 containers of rare folio volumes. With storage space at Fort Meade Modules 1 and 2 at capacity, compatible shelving was erected at the Landover Center Annex in Bays 3 and 4 to accommodate approximately 750,000 to 800,000 volumes from the general and Area Studies collections. The pallet racking storage aid system in Bay 2 was redesigned to increase the overall capacity. To address overcrowding in the bookstacks of the Thomas Jefferson and John Adams Buildings on Capitol Hill, plans were made to expand the library's use of the National Archives and Records Administration's records depository center in Valmeyer, Illinois. Plans were also under way to explore an interim measure—fixed-location shelving for portions of the general collection.

The library continued to sustain the book-digitization program that was initially created in 2008 with a grant of $2 million from the Alfred P. Sloan Foundation to address at-risk "brittle books" in the library's public-domain general collection. The program's scanning facilities are shared by the library with other federal libraries through a FEDLINK master contract. The scanned materials are accessible for reading online or for downloading on the Internet Archive's website. As of September 30, 2012, a total of 122,000 volumes comprising 25 million images had been scanned since the project's inception.

During 2012 the library joined research library partners as a member of the HathiTrust digital repository for the books scanned by U.S. libraries. The library submitted more than 89,000 digitized volumes to this shared online collection. All of these works are pre-1923 American imprints, thus in the public domain and freely available on the Internet. The library has participated in the establishment of governance and planning for HathiTrust as it has grown in size and significance in the research community. At year's end the HathiTrust digital archive comprised more than 10 million digital volumes.

Newspapers

In partnership with the National Endowment for the Humanities (NEH), the library sponsors the National Digital Newspaper Program (NDNP), a project to digitize and provide free and public access to U.S. newspapers that are in the public domain. During 2012 the number of state projects contributing digitized content grew to 32. At year's end the project reached a milestone when the 5 millionth newspaper page was scanned and posted online. Since March 2007 the library has been making this material accessible on the Chronicling America website, a free, national, searchable database of 800 American newspapers published between 1836 and 1922. The popular site hosted more than 2.5 million page views a month during the year.

Maps

The library's online maps include some of the world's great cartographic treasures, such as the 1507 Waldseemüller world map—the first map to show the word "America"—and the Abel Buell map (1783), the first map to depict the boundaries of the new American nation at the end of the American Revolution. In fiscal 2012 the Preservation Directorate undertook the task of evaluating the performance of the existing anoxic encasement that houses library treasures. The directorate also worked with the library's Interpretive Programs Office and the National Institute for Standards and Technology to develop an oxygen-free encasement and external display case for the Buell map, allowing it to be displayed indefinitely without deterioration.

Audiovisual Collections

The library's state-of-the-art Packard Campus for Audio Visual Conservation in Culpeper, Virginia, houses its sound, film, and video collections—the world's largest and most comprehensive. During 2012 the Packard Campus Film Laboratory processed 1,718 original reels of nitrate film. Of these, 963 reels were digitized and 755 received photochemical processing. Each reel of original nitrate film was inspected, cleaned, and hand-repaired prior to transfer to safety-preservation copies. More than 10,600 recorded sound and 23,000 video collection items were digitally preserved in the audio and video preservation laboratories. The library continued its collaboration with physicists at the Lawrence Berkeley National Laboratory to further develop imaging technology (IRENE for "Image, Reconstruct, Erase Noise, Etc.") that provides noninvasive preservation and access to endangered recorded-sound collections.

Films

It is estimated that half of the films produced before 1950 and 80 percent to 90 percent of those made before 1920 have disappeared forever. The library is working with many organizations to prevent such losses and to preserve motion pictures through the National Film Registry. Under the terms of the National Film Preservation Act of 1988, the Librarian of Congress—with advice from the National Film Preservation Board—began selecting 25 films annually for the National Film Registry to be preserved for all time. The films are chosen based on whether they are "culturally, historically, or aesthetically significant." The Library of Congress works to ensure that registry films are preserved by its staff or through collaboration with other archives, motion picture studios, and independent filmmakers.

In December the library announced the following additions to the registry, which brought the total to 600.

3:10 to Yuma (1957)

Anatomy of a Murder (1959)

The Augustas (1930s–1950s)

Born Yesterday (1950)

Breakfast at Tiffany's (1961)

A Christmas Story (1983)

The Corbett-Fitzsimmons Title Fight (1897)

Dirty Harry (1971)

Hours for Jerome: Parts 1 and 2 (1980–1982)

The Kidnappers Foil (1930s–1950s)

Kodachrome Color Motion Picture Tests (1922)

A League of Their Own (1992)

The Matrix (1999)
The Middleton Family at the New York World's Fair (1939)
One Survivor Remembers (1995)
Parable (1964)
Samsara: Death and Rebirth in Cambodia (1990)
Slacker (1991)
Sons of the Desert (1933)
The Spook Who Sat by the Door (1973)
They Call It Pro Football (1966)
The Times of Harvey Milk (1984)
Two-Lane Blacktop (1971)
Uncle Tom's Cabin (1914)
The Wishing Ring; An Idyll of Old England (1914)

Sound Recordings

The National Recording Preservation Act of 2000 tasks the Librarian of Congress with annually choosing recordings that are "culturally, historically, or aesthetically significant." In May 2012 the following 25 sound recordings were added to the National Recording Registry, bringing the total to 350.

Edison Talking Doll cylinder (1888)
"Come Down Ma Evenin' Star," Lillian Russell (1912)
"Ten Cents a Dance," Ruth Etting (1930)
"Voices from the Days of Slavery," Various speakers (1932–1941 interviews; 2002 compilation)
"I Want to Be a Cowboy's Sweetheart," Patsy Montana (1935)
"Fascinating Rhythm," Sol Hoopii and his Novelty Five (1938)
"Artistry in Rhythm," Stan Kenton and his Orchestra (1943)
Debut performance with the New York Philharmonic, Leonard Bernstein (November 14, 1943)
"International Sweethearts of Rhythm: Hottest Women's Band of the 1940s" (1944–1946)
"The Indians for Indians Hour" (March 25, 1947)
"Hula Medley," Gabby Pahinui (1947)
"I Can Hear It Now," Fred W. Friendly and Edward R. Murrow (1948)
"Let's Go Out to the Programs," The Dixie Hummingbirds (1953)
"Also Sprach Zarathustra," Fritz Reiner and the Chicago Symphony Orchestra (1954, 1958)
"Bo Diddley" and "I'm a Man," Bo Diddley (1955)
"Green Onions," Booker T. and the M.G.'s (1962)
"Forever Changes," Love (1967)
"The Continental Harmony: Music of William Billings," Gregg Smith Singers (1969)

"A Charlie Brown Christmas," Vince Guaraldi Trio (1970)
"Coat of Many Colors," Dolly Parton (1971)
"Mothership Connection," Parliament (1975)
Barton Hall concert by the Grateful Dead (May 8, 1977)
"I Feel Love," Donna Summer (1977)
"Rapper's Delight," Sugarhill Gang (1979)
"Purple Rain," Prince and the Revolution (1984)

Oral History

The American Folklife Center continued its mandate to preserve and present American folklife through a number of outreach and oral-history programs such as the Veterans History Project and StoryCorps.

Established by Congress in 2000, the Veterans History Project is a major program of the Folklife Center. The program has preserved the memories of both those who have served in the armed services and others who were part of the national wartime experience in the 20th and early 21st centuries.

In 2012 the project collected nearly 5,500 personal recollections, bringing the total to more than 83,000. To commemorate the 50th anniversary of the Vietnam War, the Veterans History Project featured on its website a series of collections from that era titled "Vietnam War: Looking Back." Selected content from the website is also accessible on iTunes U.

StoryCorps, launched in 2003 by MacArthur Fellow Dave Isay and his award-winning documentary company, Sound Portraits Productions, is one of the nation's largest oral narrative projects. Isay was inspired by the Works Progress Administration's (WPA's) Federal Writers' Project of the 1930s, which recorded oral history interviews with everyday Americans across the country. During 2012 more than 2,537 audio files of interviews were added to the StoryCorps collection, bringing the total to more than 42,000. The collection, housed at the American Folklife Center, also includes some 98,000 digital photographs of the participants. In addition to weekly broadcasts on National Public Radio's (NPR's) "Morning Edition," selected interviews are available as downloadable podcasts from NPR and on the Storycorps website.

The Civil Rights History Project Act of 2009 (P.L. 111-19) directs the Library of Congress and the Smithsonian Institution's National Museum of African American History and Culture to conduct a survey of existing oral history collections with relevance to the civil rights movement, and to record new interviews with people who participated in the movement. In 2012 the library maintained the Civil Rights History Project website, which was launched in August 2011. This Web portal provides public access to the oral-history interviews with participants in the civil rights movement that are housed in more than 1,200 archives, libraries, museums, and other repositories. More than 50 new interviews were added during the year and plans are under way to augment the site with materials from the library's civil rights collections. During the year the American Folklife Center developed and launched an innovative Web-based collaborative cataloging tool and database that allows its partners to provide descriptive information on the new interview recordings from off-site locations.

Digital Preservation and Management

The National Digital Information Infrastructure and Preservation Program (NDIIPP) is a strategic initiative mandated by Congress in 2000 to collect and preserve at-risk digital content of cultural and historical importance. Under the auspices of the library's Office of Strategic Initiatives, NDIIPP has grown to a distributed network of 200 national and international partners in 47 states and 39 countries with stewardship for more than 150 billion digital items comprising 29 petabytes of data. These partners are seeking to preserve a wide range of born-digital records, including public and commercial content, and are working collaboratively to establish standards for digital preservation.

A highlight of 2012 was the Digital Science Meeting in June, made possible with support from the Alfred P. Sloan Foundation. The meeting convened an expert session of 35 scientists, librarians, and historians of science. The exchange of ideas resulted in a set of proposed projects to preserve scientific ephemera such as blogs, websites, and crowd-sourced data sets. The final report is available online at http://www.digitalpreservation.gov/meetings/scienceonline_2012.html.

The National Digital Stewardship Alliance is working to identify digital content at risk of loss, develop and adopt digital preservation standards, share tools and services, support innovation of practice and research, and promote national outreach for digital preservation. The alliance—comprising 133 organizations—met in July to present project results, share expertise, and conduct working group meetings.

In addition to the content from the original collecting partners, NDIIPP collaborated with state, archival, and private-sector organizations, thereby reflecting the growing diversity of content and expertise in the network, including standards development and Web archiving. Major accomplishments in 2012 included the following:

State Records

Most states lack the resources to ensure the preservation of the information they produce in digital form only, such as legislative records, court case files, and executive agency records. As a result, much state government digital information—including content useful to policymakers—is at risk. In 2012 the four projects composing the NDIIPP Preserving State Government Information initiative were completed. The projects represent a geographically and thematically diverse body of important state government digital information in 35 states.

Standards

The Federal Agency Digitization Guidelines Working Group under NDIIPP is a collaborative effort by nearly 20 federal agencies to define common guidelines, methods, and practices to digitize historical content. Two main working groups—still images and audiovisual—continued their work of developing guidelines and tools that can be broadly applied. The still image group recommended the "Minimal Descriptive Embedded Metadata in Digital Still Images" guideline from the Smithsonian Institution. The group also updated the Digital Image Conformance Environment (DICE) software used for analyzing scanner performance and reviewed research conducted by library staff to evaluate image compression and

JPEG 2000 file configuration. The audiovisual working group continued development of a Material Exchange Format (MXF) standard for video preservation. The group also published its revised guideline for Broadcast WAVE file (BWF) metadata, a file header for audio files that is used by the European Broadcast Union.

Web Archiving

The library's Web Archiving team in the Office of Strategic Initiatives provided project management and technical support for a growing number of Web archive collections, and continued to develop tools and strengthen the library's infrastructure for long-term storage and preservation of Web archive content. The team managed 21 collections, which included more than 4,300 nominated websites. At year's end, the library's Web archives comprised more than 6.9 billion Web documents or 374 terabytes of data. The team worked with the Law Library and Library Services, including the overseas offices in Pakistan, Indonesia, India, Egypt, and Brazil, to archive sites on a variety of subjects such as the Civil War's sesquicentennial, the 2012 Olympics, the U.S. national elections, and elections in Burma/Myanmar, Egypt, Laos, Malaysia, Thailand, Timor-Leste, and Vietnam.

U.S. Copyright Office

The U.S. Copyright Office administers U.S. copyright law, under which authors of creative works register claims to protect their intellectual property. Congress enacted the first copyright law in May 1790; in 1870 it centralized the national copyright function in the Library of Congress. The collections of the library have been created largely through the copyright deposit system.

During the year the Copyright Office registered 511,539 copyright claims. The office continued its multiyear project to make historical copyright records created between 1870 and 1977 searchable and available online. In 2012 the office digitized 10.5 million cards for copyright registrations and assignments from 1955 to 1977, bringing the total cards scanned to nearly 23 million. The office completed the project to digitize all 667 volumes of the Catalog of Copyright Entries. To engage copyright constituents on issues of records digitization and access, the office launched a blog titled "Copyright Matters: Digitization and Public Access."

The Copyright Royalty Judges (CRJ) administer the provisions of Chapter 8 of Title 17 of the Copyright Act, which relates to setting royalty rates and terms as well as determining the distribution of royalties for certain copyright statutory licenses. In 2012 the Copyright Royalty Judges approved a record distribution of more than $835 million to copyright owners.

National Library Service for the Blind and Physically Handicapped

During the year the National Library Service for the Blind and Physically Handicapped (NLS) circulated more than 25 million copies of Braille and recorded books and magazines to some 800,000 reader accounts through a network of 103 cooperating libraries. NLS also honored a growing number of centenarians with membership in the 10^2 Talking-Book Club.

Through its digital talking-book program, NLS distributes digital players and audiobooks on flash-memory cartridges in specially designed mailing containers to libraries nationwide.

Approximately 265,000 users are enjoying digital talking-book players and books. They may select from more than 8,500 titles available on cartridges. Administered by the network of cooperating libraries, the Braille and Audio Reading Download (BARD) website offers more than 27,000 titles to more than 50,000 registered users. At year's end BARD was being upgraded to incorporate Web-Braille holdings such as music materials and to add foreign-language materials and network-produced materials.

John W. Kluge Center

The John W. Kluge Center was established in 2000 with a gift of $60 million from the late John W. Kluge, Metromedia president and founding chairman of the James Madison Council, the library's private sector advisory group. Located within the library's Office of Scholarly Programs, the center's goal is to bring the world's best thinkers to the library to use its unparalleled resources and interact with policymakers in Washington.

During the year the Kluge Center brought to Washington 125 scholars in the humanities. Senior scholars, post- and pre-doctoral fellows, and interns researched topics of historical and contemporary significance in the fields of humanities, social sciences, foreign policy, and law. These ranged from medieval customs and ancient graffiti to the impact of stress on contemporary humanity and the shape of social movements in the Internet Age. The Kluge Center managed the first competition for the Baruch S. Blumberg NASA/Library of Congress Chair in Astrobiology. President Felipe Calderón of Mexico delivered the sixth Kissinger Lecture at a private event held at the library on April 23. For more information about the Kluge Center, visit http://www.loc.gov/kluge.

Publications

Each year, the library publishes books, calendars, and other printed products featuring its vast content. All told, 200 Library of Congress publications currently are in print and can be ordered in bookstores nationwide and from the Library Shop.

Among the titles published in 2012 were several volumes drawn from the collections of the Prints and Photographs Division. *Gardens for a Beautiful America, 1895–1935* by Sam Watters features the work of photographer Frances Benjamin Johnston, and *Presidential Campaign Posters* spotlights the library's collection of presidential campaign art from Andrew Jackson to Barack Obama.

A companion volume to the library's Armenian exhibition, *To Know Wisdom and Instruction: A Visual Survey of the Armenian Literary Tradition from the Library of Congress* was compiled by the curator, Levon Avdoyan. *Perspectives on the Hebraic Book: The Myron M. Weinstein Memorial Lectures at the Library of Congress* was published in conjunction with a new exhibition marking the centennial of the library's Hebraic collection.

Two of the library's cartographic treasures are the subject of *Seeing the World Anew: The Radical Vision of Martin Waldseemüller's 1507 and 1516 World Maps* by John W. Hessler and Chet Van Duzer.

The work of American folklorist Alan Lomax is highlighted in *The Southern Journey of Alan Lomax: Words, Photographs, and Music* and "America's sweetheart" is the subject of *Mary Pickford: Queen of the Movies.*

Exhibitions

In addition to the exhibitions described above, others marked historical milestones, including the sesquicentennial of the start of the Civil War ("The Civil War in America"), and the centennial of Japan's gift of Washington, D.C.'s flowering cherry trees ("Sakura: Cherry Blossoms as Living Symbols of Friendship").

Displays in the Performing Arts Reading Room foyer featured the library's dance collections ("Politics and the Dancing Body") and the work of Irish-American composer/conductor Victor Herbert ("The Musical Worlds of Victor Herbert").

The Herblock Gallery celebrates the work of editorial cartoonist Herbert L. Block, better known by his pen name "Herblock," who donated his body of work to the library. The 2012 rotation "Down to Earth" focused on Herblock's take on the environment.

From pre-Columbian artifacts to rare 15th century Bibles, from America's founding documents to Thomas Jefferson's personal library and the art and architecture of the library building named for him, continuing exhibitions offer a variety of attractions. The exhibitions can be viewed online at http://www.loc.gov/exhibits.

Special Events

During 2012 the library presented hundreds of public events such as poetry and literary programs, concerts, lectures, and symposia, many of which were broadcast live or archived on the library's website at http://www.loc.gov/webcasts. For a list of upcoming events, visit http://www.loc.gov/loc/events. For concert information, go to www.loc.gov/concerts.

Literary Events

Book lovers of all ages gathered on the National Mall for the 12th Annual National Book Festival September 22 and 23. The festival was organized by the Library of Congress, with President Barack Obama and First Lady Michelle Obama serving as honorary chairs. The event featured more than 120 authors and illustrators discussing their works before record crowds estimated at about 200,000. [For more on the festival, see the following article, "Center for the Book"—*Ed.*]

During the year the Poetry and Literature Center sponsored a number of programs featuring new and renowned poets reading from their works. The center also sponsored programs that celebrated the birthdays of Walt Whitman, Langston Hughes, Gwendolyn Brooks, Ralph Ellison, Tennessee Williams, and William Shakespeare.

Philip Levine served as the 18th Poet Laureate Consultant in Poetry during 2011–2012. Born in Detroit, Levine is the author of 20 collections of poems, including his most recent work, *News of the World*. Levine won a 1995 Pulitzer Prize for *The Simple Truth* and the National Book Award in 1991 for *What Work Is*. The former chancellor of the Academy of American Poets (2000–2006), Levine is professor emeritus at California State University, Fresno. On May 3, 2012, Levine closed the literary season at the library with a reading from his works. On June 7 the Librarian of Congress announced the appointment of Natasha Trethewey as the 19th Poet Laureate Consultant in Poetry, for 2012–2013. She delivered her inaugural reading on September 13.

Concerts

Since 1925 the library's Coolidge Auditorium has provided a venue for world-class performers and world premieres of commissioned works. Sponsored by the Music Division, the annual concert series reflects the nation's diversity of music and features many music genres.

The 86th season of concerts presented a 30-event roster of classical, jazz, pop, country, folk, and world music performances, along with films and noontime lectures by notable scholars. All concerts were presented free of charge in the library's 500-seat Coolidge Auditorium.

The noontime folklife concert series known as "Homegrown: The Music of America" featured diverse musical traditions from around the nation. Presented by the American Folklife Center and the Music Division in cooperation with the Kennedy Center Millennium Stage, the eight-concert series presented such attractions as Mexican music from Texas, Paraguayan music from Nevada, and fiddle music from New Hampshire, West Virginia, and Missouri.

Symposia and Lectures

Various library divisions sponsored programs and lectures on a wide range of topics during the year, providing opportunities to share ideas, celebrate diversity, and showcase the library's collections. A symposium titled "Jung and Aging: Bringing to Life the Possibilities and Potentials for Vital Aging," explored the work of the Swiss psychiatrist Carl Gustav Jung (1875–1961) and its meaning to an aging population. Hosted jointly by the Library of Congress and the Jung Society of Washington, the event was made possible by the American Association of Retired People (AARP).

The library's Kluge Center sponsored numerous public programs during the year, including "The Profound Impact of Stress: Human Biology and Social Implications for the Individual and Society."

In April, in conjunction with the "Sakura: Cherry Blossoms as Living Symbols of Friendship" exhibition, the Interpretive Programs Office presented several lectures relating to the significance of cherry blossoms in American and Japanese culture. These included "Japanese Culture Day," an event for children and families, and a workshop for teachers to learn strategies for exploring 20th century Japanese and United States relations.

On May 1, in recognition of Law Day 2012, the Library of Congress welcomed actor Richard Dreyfuss for a discussion focused on the Dreyfuss Initiative, a nonprofit organization that aims to revitalize civics education in public schools.

The Geography and Map Division sponsored a two-day conference, May 19 and 20, 2012, devoted to mapping the nation's capital. It covered the period from Pierre-Charles L'Enfant's 1791 "Plan of the City of Washington" to the present. Former District of Columbia Mayor Anthony Williams delivered the keynote address.

In September the American Folklife Center presented a symposium on Yiddish radio in America to mark the center's recent acquisition of the Henry Sapoznik Collection of more than 1,000 historic Yiddish radio broadcasts from the 1920s through the 1950s.

Film Screenings

The library's Packard Campus Theater in Culpeper, Virginia, continued its popular film screenings that showcase the library's film, television, radio, and recorded sound collections. The theater is one of only five in the country equipped to show original classic film prints on nitrate film stock as they would have been screened in theaters before 1950. The theater also features a custom-made organ that provides live musical accompaniment for silent movies to enhance the cinematic experience. During the year the theater offered 139 public screenings of more than 240 titles, attended by more than 13,500 people.

Honors and Awards

Gershwin Prize for Popular Song

In May Grammy- and Academy Award-winning songwriters Burt Bacharach and Hal David were awarded the library's Gershwin Prize for Popular Song. They were honored May 8, 2012, with a tribute concert at the library. The following day, President Obama presented the Gershwin Prize at a concert in the East Room of the White House. The Gershwin Prize commemorates the songwriting team of brothers George and Ira Gershwin, whose extensive manuscript collection resides in the library. The prize is awarded to musicians whose lifetime contributions in the field of popular song exemplify the standard of excellence associated with the Gershwins. Previous recipients are Paul Simon, Stevie Wonder, and Paul McCartney.

John W. Kluge Prize

Fernando Henrique Cardoso, a leading scholar and practitioner of political economy in recent Latin American history, was awarded the $1 million 2012 Kluge Prize for lifetime achievement in the study of humanity. His scholarly analysis of the social structures of government, the economy, and race relations in Brazil laid the intellectual groundwork for his leadership as president in the transformation of Brazil from a military dictatorship with high inflation into a vibrant, more-inclusive democracy with strong economic growth. The $1 million award, which was presented by the Librarian of Congress on July 10, was established by the late John W. Kluge.

Creative Achievement Award

Pulitzer Prize-winning novelist Philip Roth received the National Book Festival Creative Achievement Award at the 2012 National Book Festival.

Additional Sources of Information

Library of Congress telephone numbers for public information:

Main switchboard (with menu)	202-707-5000
Reading room hours and locations	202-707-6400
General reference	202-707-3399
	TTY 202-707-4210
Visitor information	202-707-8000
	TTY 202-707-6200
Exhibition hours	202-707-4604
Copyright information	202-707-3000
Copyright hotline (to order forms)	202-707-9100
Library of Congress Shop (credit card orders)	888-682-3557

Center for the Book

Library of Congress, Washington, DC 20540
World Wide Web http://www.Read.gov, http://www.loc.gov/cfbook

John Y. Cole
Director

Congress established the Center for the Book in the Library of Congress by statute (Public Law 95-129) in 1977. The center's purpose was to use the resources and prestige of the Library of Congress to stimulate public interest in books and reading. Through the years, the center's mission has expanded to include literacy and library promotion and encouraging the historical study of books, reading, libraries, and print culture. A network of affiliated state centers was inaugurated in 1984, and in 1987 the center started to develop a partnership program that included both nonprofit organizations and interested government agencies. Both of these national reading and literacy promotion networks met for their annual "idea exchanges" at the Library of Congress in 2012.

The Center for the Book is an early example of a successful public-private partnership. The library supports its five staff positions; all of its activities must be supported by private contributions.

Highlights of 2012

During 2012 the Center for the Book

- Completed its third year of administering the Library of Congress Young Readers Center in the library's Jefferson Building, the first space in the institution's history devoted to the reading interests of young people under the age of 16
- Played key roles in the planning and organization of "Books That Shaped America," an educational program and popular exhibit in the Jefferson Building May 25–September 29, and the first International Summit of the Book, held at the Library of Congress on December 6–7
- Participated in the organization and program development of the 2012 National Book Festival, which attracted approximately 200,000 people to the National Mall September 22–23
- Presented more than 30 public programs at the Library of Congress, many of them author book talks and book signings in its "Books and Beyond" series
- In December undertook the management of the new Library of Congress Literacy Awards, funded by philanthropist David M. Rubenstein

Young Readers Center

Opened in 2009, the Young Readers Center is increasingly seen by families as a major reason for visiting the Library of Congress, making available current and classic books for browsing and reading aloud as well as media and Internet resources. The center is open to readers under 16 provided they are accompanied by an adult. In 2012 it attracted more than 40,000 visitors, an increase of 11,000 over 2011. Programs were shaped in cooperation with organizations such as the Library of Congress Asian Division and the Kids Euro Festival, an annual fall festival organized by the nations of the European Union. Its collection grew to more than 4,000 volumes, all donated by publishers or individuals or obtained from Library of Congress surplus book collections.

National Ambassador

Award-winning author Walter Dean Myers completed his first year as National Ambassador for Young People's Literature, a program developed with the Children's Book Council to promote the importance of literature for young audiences. He spoke nationwide about his theme, "Reading Is Not Optional," in many different settings, including the opening of Children's Book Week in New York, the National Book Festival in September, and visits to nearly a dozen correctional institutions where he talked to young inmates about the importance of books and reading in his own life as he grew up in Harlem.

Letters About Literature

The six national winners of the 2011–2012 Letters About Literature reading and writing contest were announced in April, along with the national honors winners and state winners. To enter, a young (grades 4 through 12) reader writes a personal letter to an author, living or dead, from any genre—fiction or nonfiction, contemporary or classic—explaining how that author's work changed the student's way of thinking about the world or himself or herself. For the third straight year, more than 70,000 letters were submitted. The contest is sponsored by the Center for the Book, its state centers, and the Target store chain, which donated gift cards to all winners, $10,000 to a library designated by each of the six national winners, and $1,000 to a library designated by each of the 12 honorable mention winners.

River of Words

Since its inception in 1995 under the leadership of U.S. Poet Laureate Robert Hass, the Center for the Book has cosponsored River of Words, an annual environmental poetry and art competition for students ages 5 to 19. Several affiliated state centers also participate. The contest was suspended during 2011 until a new funding sponsor was secured: the Center for Environmental Literacy at St. Mary's College in Moraga, California. The River of Words awards ceremony, hosted by Hass, returned to the Library of Congress with great success on April 23, 2012. More than 200 people attended the event.

National Collegiate Book Collecting Contest

On October 19 the center hosted its third annual awards ceremony for the National Collegiate Book Collecting Contest. Its partners were the Library of Congress Rare Book and Special Collections Division, the Antiquarian Booksellers' Association of America, and the Fellowship of American Bibliophilic Societies; additional support came from the Jay I. Kislak Foundation. Established in 2005 by *Fine Books and Collections* magazine to recognize outstanding book-collecting efforts by college and university students, the contest aims to encourage young collectors to become accomplished lifetime bibliophiles. In 2009 contest organizers turned its leadership over to the new collaboration of institutional sponsors.

The winners honored on October 19 were: (first prize) Jordan Haug, University of Californian, San Diego, for his collection on "Mormon Fundamentalism and Polygamy"; (second prize) Jessica Anne Kahan, University of Michigan, for "Romance Novels in DJ, 1925–1935"; (third prize) Andrew Ferguson, University of Virginia, for "Bibliography and the Puzzle of R. A. Lafferty." The essay prize was awarded to Kevin Baggot Roberts for his essay about his collection, "Cheap Thrills: Sex in American Publishing, 1924–1970."

Online Resources

A new multimedia website overseen by the Center for the Book, http://www.Read.gov, was launched in September 2009 to centralize Library of Congress resources aimed at stimulating interest in books and reading for all age groups. The Center for the Book's website, http://www.loc.gov/cfbook, is part of the site. Read.gov is one of the few sites on http://www.loc.gov that offers contemporary programming relating to reading and to current books and authors. It comprises four subsites tailored to children, teens, adults, and educators and parents. A National Ambassador for Young People's Literature subsite was added in 2010. The site was upgraded in 2011 with the addition of many more digitized public domain books, most of them for young people. The books are presented in a page-turning format that emulates the experience of reading a physical book.

Major enhancements during 2012 resulted in 2,283,254 page views—a fourfold increase over 2011. These enhancements included a reintroduction of the successful "Exquisite Corpse" serialized story and the introduction of an online version and an app version of *Aesop's Fables*. In December a subsite was added for the new Library of Congress Literacy Awards.

The Center for the Book website includes links to more than 200 organizations, including affiliated state centers and national reading promotion partners, that share the center's interest in promoting books and reading and encouraging the study of books, libraries, and print culture.

National Book Festival

As it has done since 2001, the Center for the Book took the lead in organizing the author program and the Pavilion of the States at the annual National Book Festival, held September 22–23. More than 120 authors, illustrators, and poets participated—a record number—and the crowd matched the 2011 record of approximately 100,000 each day. In addition to the author presentation pavilions—Children, Teens, Contemporary Life, Poetry and Prose, Fiction and Mystery, History and Biography—and the Family Storytelling Stage, on Sunday there was a pavilion featuring "Sci Fi, Fantasy and Graphic Novels" plus special presentations about classic books and their authors and presentations by student poets and the winners of the student "A Book That Shaped Me" summer reading contest.

Featured writers at the 2012 festival included T. C. Boyle, Geraldine Brooks, Robert Caro, Stephen L. Carter, Michael Connelly, Patricia Cornwell, Junot Diaz, Joy Harjo, Charlaine Harris, Stephen Millhauser, Marilynne Robinson, Mario Vargas Llosa, and Colson Whitehead; poets Nikky Finney, Laura Kasischke, and Philip Levine; and popular writers of books for young people John Green, Lois Lowry, Mary Pope Osborne, Christopher Paolini, and R. L. Stine. Novelist Philip Roth won the Library of Congress National Book Festival Creative Achievement Award.

The most popular attraction at the festival, the Pavilion of the States, was organized by the Center for the Book and staffed by representatives from affiliated state centers for the book, state libraries, state humanities councils, and affiliates from various U.S. territories. They provided handouts and information about their states' writers, libraries, book festivals, book awards, and reading promotion activities. In addition, several festival authors and illustrators made scheduled visits to their state's table to greet fans and sign autographs.

An especially popular Pavilion of the State feature among young readers and their families was "Discover Great Places Through Reading," a free map of the United States that visitors presented at each table for an appropriate state sticker or stamp. The map included "52 Great Reads About Great Places," a reading list of books for young people recommended by each state and territory.

Reading Promotion Networks

The center's partnership program, Reading Promotion Networks, which includes more than 80 national nonprofit and governmental organizations, strengthens and supports the center's reading and literacy projects nationwide. At its annual idea exchange at the Library of Congress, partners introduce themselves and their projects and look for new partners.

The state affiliates of the Center for the Book must renew their partnerships with the national center every three years. The purpose of the network is to link reading promotion resources and ideas from the Library of Congress with related projects and interests at the state and local level. The annual idea exchange meeting is an important way in which representatives of the state centers can gather to learn how their peers around the country promote reading, literacy, and libraries. Prominent state center for the book projects include book awards, literary maps, databases about local authors, book festivals, and participation in Letters About Literature and River of Words.

National Agricultural Library

U.S. Department of Agriculture, Abraham Lincoln Bldg.,
10301 Baltimore Ave., Beltsville, MD 20705-2351
E-mail agref@nal.usda.gov
World Wide Web http://www.nal.usda.gov

Jennifer Gilbert
Special Assistant to the Director

The U.S. Department of Agriculture's National Agricultural Library (NAL) is one of the world's largest and most accessible agricultural research libraries, offering service directly to the public via its website, http://www.nal.usda.gov.

The library was instituted in 1862 at the same time as the U.S. Department of Agriculture (USDA). It became a national library in 1962 when Congress established it as the primary agricultural information resource of the United States (7 USCS § 3125a). Congress assigned to the library the responsibilities to

- Acquire, preserve, and manage information resources relating to agriculture and allied sciences
- Organize agricultural information products and services and provide them within the United States and internationally
- Plan, coordinate, and evaluate information and library needs relating to agricultural research and education
- Cooperate with and coordinate efforts toward development of a comprehensive agricultural library and information network
- Coordinate the development of specialized subject information services among the agricultural and library information communities.

NAL is located in Beltsville, Maryland, near Washington, D.C., on the grounds of USDA's Henry A. Wallace Beltsville Agricultural Research Center. Its 15-story Abraham Lincoln Building is named in honor of the president who created the Department of Agriculture and signed several of the major U.S. laws affecting agriculture.

The library employs about 100 librarians, information specialists, computer specialists, administrators, and clerical personnel, supplemented by about 50 volunteers, contract staff, and cooperators from NAL partnering organizations.

In 2012 NAL reorganized to better align its functions with its overall strategic plan, which includes simplified access to all NAL content, expansion of digital content, and the integration of scientific data sets and discovery tools.

NAL's reputation as one of the world's foremost agricultural libraries is supported and burnished by its expert staff, ongoing leadership in delivering information services, expanding collaborations with other U.S. and international agricultural research and information organizations, and its extensive collection of agricultural information, searchable through AGRICOLA (AGRICultural On-Line Access), the library's bibliographic database.

The Collection

The NAL collection dates to the congressionally approved 1839 purchase of books for the Agricultural Division of the Patent Office, predating the 1862 establishment of USDA itself. Today NAL provides access to billions of pages of agricultural information—an immense collection of scientific books, journals, audiovisuals, reports, theses, artifacts, and images—and to a widening array of digital media, as well as databases and other information resources germane to the broad reach of agriculture-related sciences.

The library's collection contains nearly 3.6 million items, dating from the 16th century to the present, including the most complete repository of USDA publications and the world's most extensive set of materials on the history of U.S. agriculture.

Building the Collection

NAL has primary responsibility for collecting and retaining publications of USDA and its agencies, and it is the only U.S. national library with a legislated mandate to collect in the following disciplines: plant and animal health, welfare, and production; agricultural economics, products, and education; aquaculture; forestry; rural sociology and rural life; family and consumer science; and food science, safety, and nutrition. In addition to collecting as comprehensively as possible in these core subject areas, NAL collects extensively in many related subjects, such as biology, bioinformatics, biochemistry, chemistry, entomology, environmental science, genetics, invasive species, meteorology, natural resources, physics, soil science, sustainability, water quality, and zoology.

In general, NAL's acquisition program and collection development policy are based upon its responsibility to provide service to the staff of the Department of Agriculture, U.S. land-grant universities, and the general public in all subjects pertaining to agriculture. The NAL Collection Development Policy (http://www. nal.usda.gov/about/policy/coll_dev_toc.shtml) outlines the scope of subjects collected and the degree of coverage for each subject. NAL collection policies also reflect and differentiate the collecting responsibilities of the National Library of Medicine and the Library of Congress. Together, these three national libraries have developed cooperative collection development policy statements for the subject areas of biotechnology, human nutrition and food, and veterinary sciences.

During 2012 NAL announced a shift in collection development emphasis to digital items. The library will no longer purchase printed monographs, but will concentrate its resources on commercially available digital content and the digitization of items in the existing collection.

Rare and Special Collections

The NAL Rare and Special Collections program emphasizes access to and preservation of rare and unique materials documenting the history of agriculture and related sciences. Items in the library's special collections include rare books, manuscripts, nursery and seed trade catalogs, posters, objects, photographs, and other rare materials documenting agricultural subjects. Materials date from the 1500s to the late 1900s and include many international sources. Detailed information about these special collections is available on the NAL website at http://specialcollections. nal.usda.gov.

Special collections of note include the following:

- The U.S. Department of Agriculture History Collection (http://www.nal. usda.gov/speccoll/collect/history), assembled over 80 years by USDA historians, includes letters, memoranda, reports, and papers of USDA officials, as well as photographs, oral histories, and clippings covering the activities of the department from its founding through the early 1990s.

- The U.S. Department of Agriculture Pomological Watercolor Collection includes more than 7,000 detailed, botanically accurate watercolor illustrations of fruit and nut varieties developed by growers or introduced by USDA plant explorers. Created between 1880 and the 1940s, the watercolors served as official documentation of the work of the Office of the Pomologist and were used to create chromolithographs in publications distributed widely by the department. Although created for scientific accuracy, the works are artistic treasures in their own right. The full collection has been digitized and is available online at http://usdawatercolors.nal.usda.gov.

- The Henry G. Gilbert Nursery and Seed Trade Catalog Collection (http:// www.nal.usda.gov/speccoll/collectionsguide/nurserycatalogs.shtml), begun in 1904 by USDA economic botanist Percy L. Ricker, has grown to comprise more than 200,000 American and foreign catalogs. The earliest items date from the late 1700s, but the collection is strongest from the 1890s to the present. Researchers commonly use the collection to document the introduction of plants to the United States, study economic trends, and illustrate early developments in American landscape design.

- The Rare Book Collection (http://specialcollections.nal.usda.gov/guide-collections/rare-book-collection) highlights agriculture's printed historical record. It covers a wide variety of subjects but is particularly strong in botany, natural history, zoology, and entomology. International in scope, the collection documents early agricultural practices in Britain and Europe, as well as the Americas. Of particular note are the more than 300 books by or about Carl Linnaeus, the "father of taxonomy," including a rare first edition of his 1735 work *Systema Naturae*.

- Manuscript collections, now numbering more than 400, document the story of American agriculture and its influence on the world. The collections guide is at http://specialcollections.nal.usda.gov/guide-collections/index-manuscript-collections.

NAL continues to digitize these and other unique materials to share them broadly via its website and has published detailed indexes to the content of many manuscript collections to improve discovery. AGRICOLA, NAL's catalog, includes bibliographic entries for special collection items, manuscripts, and rare books. The library provides in-house research and reference services for its special collections and offers fee-based duplication services.

Preservation/Digitization

NAL is committed to the preservation of its print and nonprint collections. It continues to monitor and improve the environmental quality of its stacks to extend the longevity of all materials in the collection. The library has instituted a long-term strategy to ensure the growing body of agricultural information is systematically identified, preserved, and archived.

NAL's digital conversion program has resulted in a growing digital collection of USDA publications and many non-USDA historical materials not restricted by copyright. These materials are now part of the expanding NAL Digital Collections.

NAL Digital Collections

NAL has undertaken several projects to digitize, store, and provide online access to nearly 1 million pages of historic print documents and images, primarily from USDA. In an effort to unify all digital content, the library launched an interface for the NAL Digital Collections (http://naldc.nal.usda.gov) accompanied by policies for collecting, storing, and making publicly available federally funded research outcomes published by USDA scientists and researchers. Long-range plans include collecting, maintaining, and providing access to a broad range of agricultural information in a wide variety of digital formats. The result will be a perpetual, reliable, publicly accessible collection of digital documents, data sets, images, and other items relating to agriculture.

AGRICOLA

AGRICOLA catalogs and indexes NAL collections and delivers worldwide access to agricultural information through its searchable Web interface (http://agricola.nal.usda.gov). Alternatively, users can access AGRICOLA on a fee basis through several commercial vendors, or they can subscribe to the complete AGRICOLA file, also on a fee basis, from the National Technical Information Service (NTIS) within the U.S. Department of Commerce.

The AGRICOLA database covers materials in all formats, including printed works from the 16th century onward. The records describe publications and resources encompassing all aspects of agriculture and allied disciplines. AGRICOLA, which is updated daily, comprises the following two components:

- NAL Public Access Catalog, containing more than 1 million citations to books, audiovisual materials, serial titles, and other materials in the NAL collection. (The catalog also contains some bibliographic records for items cataloged by other libraries but not held in the NAL collection.)
- NAL Article Citation Database, consisting of more than 3 million citations to serial articles, book chapters, reports, and reprints.

LCA Digital Commons

NAL has launched the LCA Digital Commons, a life cycle inventory database, to address a lack of information resources regarding the life cycle of agricultural products. The LCA Digital Commons provides, through a fully searchable Web interface (http://www.lcacommons.gov), peer-reviewed crop production data sets for nine commodity crops measuring the material and energy flows to and from the environment. A planned expansion will include data sets from other industries.

Information Management and Information Technology

Over the past quarter century NAL has applied increasingly sophisticated information technology to support the ever more complex and demanding information needs of researchers, practitioners, policymakers, and the general public. Technological developments spearheaded by the library date back to the 1940s and 1950s, when NAL Director Ralph Shaw invented "electronic machines" such as the photo charger, rapid selector, and photo clerk. Over the years NAL has made numerous technological improvements, from automating collections information to delivering full-text and image collections digitally on the Internet.

NAL has fully implemented the Voyager integrated library management system from Ex Libris, Ltd. The system supports ordering, receiving, and invoice processing for purchases; creating and maintaining indexing and cataloging records for AGRICOLA; circulating print holdings; and providing a Web-based online catalog for public searching and browsing of the collection. In addition, the system is fully integrated with an automated interlibrary loan and document delivery system by Relais International that streamlines services and provides desktop delivery of needed materials.

English-Spanish Agricultural Thesaurus and Glossary

NAL is known for its expertise in developing and using a thesaurus, or controlled vocabulary, a critical component of effective digital information systems. The NAL Agricultural Thesaurus (NALT) (http://agclass.nal.usda.gov/agt.shtml) is a hierarchical vocabulary of agricultural and biological terms, organized according to 17 subject categories. It comprises primarily biological nomenclature, with additional terminology supporting the physical and social sciences.

In January 2013 NAL released the 12th edition of NALT, which has grown to approximately 91,000 terms. This edition includes updates in the areas of aquaculture and fisheries terminology. Taxonomic terms were expanded this edition, including more than 900 new animal species and 100 new plant species, along with their common names. In addition, more than 300 new virus names were added to the thesaurus.

NALT continues to be available as Linked Open Data, which translates information into a form both readable and *understandable* by computers, a shift that makes it possible to provide integrated access to data, virtually eliminating data silos. NAL can now connect its vocabulary to other linked data vocabularies, which, in turn, will connect the NALT to the larger semantic Web. Such interconnections will help programmers create meaningful relationships that will make it easier to locate related content.

Associated with NALT, the NAL Glossary provides definitions of agricultural terms. The 2013 edition contains 3,492 definitions ranging across agriculture and its many ancillary subjects, an increase of 190 definitions (in both Spanish and English) over the previous year. Most definitions are composed by NALT staff. (Suggestions for new terms or definitions can be sent by e-mail to agref@ars.usda.gov.)

NAL publishes Spanish-language versions of the thesaurus and glossary, which carry the names *Tesauro Agrícola* and *Glosario,* respectively. Both are updated concurrently with the annual release of the English-language version. The 2013 edition of the Spanish-language version of NALT contains more than 78,000 terms.

The thesaurus and glossary are primarily used for indexing and for improving the retrieval of agricultural information, but they can also be used by students (from fifth grade up), teachers, writers, and others who are seeking precise definitions of words from the agricultural sciences. Users can download all four publications—English and Spanish thesaurus and glossary—in both machine-readable (MARC 21, RDF-SKOS, and XML) and human-readable (doc, pdf) formats at http://agclass.nal.usda.gov/download.shtml.

Library Services

NAL serves the agricultural information needs of customers through a combination of Web-based and traditional library services, including reference, document delivery, and information center services. The NAL website offers access to a wide variety of full-text resources, as well as online access to reference and document delivery services. In 2012 the library delivered more than 107 million direct customer service transactions throughout the world via its website and other Internet-based services.

The main reading room in the library's Beltsville facility features a walk-up service desk, access to an array of digital information resources (including full-text scientific journals), current periodicals, and an on-site request service for materials from NAL's collection. NAL also operates a walk-in reference and digital services center at USDA headquarters in downtown Washington, D.C. Services at both facilities are available 8:30 A.M. to 4:30 P.M. Monday through Friday, except federal holidays.

NAL's reference services are accessible online using the Ask a Question form on the NAL Web pages; by use of email addressed to agref@ars.usda.gov; by telephone at 301-504-5755; or by mail to Reference Research Services, National Agricultural Library ARS/USDA, 10301 Baltimore Avenue, Beltsville, MD 20705. Requesters receive assistance from Reference Research Services staff in all areas and aspects of agriculture, but staff particularly answer questions, provide research guidance, and make presentations on topics not addressed by the seven subject-focused information centers of the library.

NAL's seven information centers are reliable sources of comprehensive, science-based information on key aspects of U.S. agriculture, providing timely, accurate, and in-depth coverage of their specialized subject areas. Their expert staff offer extensive Web-based information resources and advanced reference services. Each NAL information center has its own website and is a partner in AgNIC (see heading AgNIC later in this report).

- The Alternative Farming Systems Information Center (AFSIC) (http://afsic.nal.usda.gov) specializes in identifying and accessing information relating to farming methods that maintain the health and productivity of the entire farming enterprise, including the world's natural resources. This focus includes sustainable and alternative agricultural systems, crops, and livestock.
- The Animal Welfare Information Center (AWIC) (http://awic.nal.usda.gov) provides scientific information and referrals to help ensure the proper care and treatment of animals used in biomedical research, testing, teaching, and exhibitions, and by animal dealers. Among its varied outreach activities, the center conducts workshops for researchers on meeting the information requirements of the Animal Welfare Act.
- The Food and Nutrition Information Center (FNIC) (http://fnic.nal.usda.gov) provides credible, accurate, and practical resources for nutrition and health professionals, educators, government personnel, and consumers. FNIC maintains a staff of registered dietitians who can answer questions on food and human nutrition.
- The Food Safety Research Information Office (FSRIO) (http://fsrio.nal.usda.gov) delivers information on publicly funded—and, to the extent possible, privately funded—food safety research initiatives. Its Research Projects Database, with more than 7,000 projects cited, provides ready access to the largest searchable collection of food safety research being conducted within U.S. and international governmental agencies.
- The National Invasive Species Information Center (NISIC) (http://www.invasivespeciesinfo.gov) delivers accessible, accurate, referenced, up-to-date, and comprehensive information on invasive species drawn from federal, state, local, and international sources.
- The Rural Information Center (RIC) (http://ric.nal.usda.gov) assists local officials, organizations, businesses, and rural residents working to maintain the vitality of rural areas. It collects and disseminates information on such diverse topics as community economic development, small business development, health care, finance, housing, environment, quality of life, community leadership, and education.
- The Water Quality Information Center (WQIC) (http://wqic.nal.usda.gov) collects, organizes, and communicates scientific findings, educational methodologies, and public policy issues relating to water quality and agriculture.

In addition to these information centers, NAL manages the popular Nutrition.gov website (http://www.nutrition.gov) in collaboration with other USDA agencies and the Department of Health and Human Services. This site provides vetted, science-based nutrition information for the general consumer and highlights the latest in nutrition news and tools from across federal government agencies. The site is an important tool for disseminating the work of multiple federal agencies in a national obesity prevention effort. A team of registered dietitians at NAL's Food and Nutrition Information Center maintains Nutrition.gov and answers questions on food and nutrition issues.

Web-Based Products and Services

In 2012 the NAL websites, which encompass nearly all the content and services described here, collectively received an average of 8.2 million page views per month from people seeking agricultural information.

NAL has had growing success using Twitter to disseminate information about agriculture to a broad audience. Through 2012 the eight NAL Twitter feeds—a general NAL account and seven subject-specific streams—have together acquired more than 95,000 followers; the figure for 2011 was 59,000.

DigiTop

DigiTop, USDA's Digital Desktop Library, delivers the full text of thousands of journals and hundreds of newspapers worldwide, provides 11 agriculturally significant citation databases, supplies a range of digital reference resources, and offers focused, personalized services. DigiTop is available to the entire USDA work force worldwide—more than 100,000 people—around the clock. NAL staff provides help desk and reference services, continuous user education, and training for DigiTop users. During fiscal year 2012 more than 1,200,000 articles were downloaded through DigiTop.

Document Delivery Services

NAL's document delivery operation responds to thousands of requests each year from USDA employees and from libraries and organizations around the world. NAL uses the Relais Enterprise document request and delivery system to support document delivery. With Relais fully integrated with the Voyager library system, with DigiTop, and with other Open-URL and ISO ILL compliant systems, NAL customers can request materials or check on the status of their requests via the Web, and the needed materials can be easily delivered electronically. Document requests can also be submitted via OCLC (NAL's symbol is AGL) and DOCLINE (NAL's libid is MDUNAL). Visit http://www.nal.usda.gov/services/request.shtml for details.

Networks of Cooperation

The NAL collection and information resources are supplemented by networks of cooperation with other institutions, including arrangements with agricultural libraries at U.S. land-grant universities, other U.S. national libraries, agricultural libraries in other countries, and libraries of the United Nations and other international organizations.

AgNIC

The library serves as secretariat for the Agriculture Network Information Center (AgNIC) Alliance, a voluntary, collaborative partnership that hosts a distributed network of discipline-specific agricultural information websites at http://www.agnic.org. AgNIC provides access to high-quality agricultural information selected by its 48 partner members, which include land-grant universities, NAL, and other institutions globally. Together they offer 71 subject-specific sites and reference services, with additional sites and resources regularly added.

During 2012 AgNIC partners continued to build full-text content through a variety of projects. One project, metadata harvesting, uses the Open Archives Initiative protocols to harvest metadata for full-text resources from targeted institutional repositories and collections. Once the metadata is harvested, AgNIC delivers it through a single point of access with the bibliographic citations linked to another service to help users find items in nearby libraries. The AgNIC system now links to more than 5 million full-text and bibliographic items.

AGLINET

Through the Agricultural Libraries Network (AGLINET), NAL serves as the U.S. node of an international agricultural information system that brings together agricultural libraries with strong regional or country coverage and other specialized collections. NAL functions as a gateway to U.S. agricultural libraries and resources, fulfilling requests for information via reciprocal agreements with several other libraries, information centers, and consortia. As an AGLINET member, NAL agrees to provide low-cost interlibrary loan and photocopy service to other AGLINET libraries. Most materials requested through AGLINET are delivered digitally, although reproductions via fiche or photocopy are used when appropriate. AGLINET is administered by the Food and Agriculture Organization of the United Nations.

National Library of Medicine

8600 Rockville Pike, Bethesda, MD 20894
301-496-6308, 888-346-3656, fax 301-496-4450
E-mail publicinfo@nlm.nih.gov
World Wide Web http://www.nlm.nih.gov

Kathleen Cravedi
Director, Office of Communications and Public Liaison

Melanie Modlin
Deputy Director, Office of Communications and Public Liaison

The National Library of Medicine (NLM), a component of the National Institutes of Health (NIH), was founded in 1836 as the Library of the Surgeon General of the Army. It has been a hub of information innovation ever since. NLM

* Produces electronic information resources that are searched billions of times by millions of people each year
* Supports and conducts research, development, and training in biomedical informatics and health information technology
* Is the world's largest biomedical library and coordinator of the 6,000-member National Network of Libraries of Medicine that promotes and provides access to health information in communities with significant health disparities across the United States

Through advanced information systems, a cutting-edge informatics research portfolio, and extensive partnerships, NLM plays a pivotal role in catalyzing and supporting the translation of basic science into new treatments, improved practice, useful decision support for health professionals and patients, and effective disaster and emergency preparedness and response.

NLM's advanced information systems disseminate an enormous range of information, including: genetic, genomic, chemical, toxicology, and clinical research data; images; published and unpublished research results; decision support resources; standards for scientific and health data and publications; informatics tools for system developers; and quality health information for the public. The library describes and organizes information produced by, and available from, government agencies, NIH-funded scientists, universities, nonprofit organizations, commercial publishers, and the nation's libraries. Scientists, health professionals, and the public can search or download much of this information directly from an NLM website, find it via an Internet search engine, or use an externally developed app that provides value-added access to NLM data. Thousands of commercial and nonprofit system developers regularly use the applications programming interfaces (APIs) that NLM provides to promote innovation and facilitate use of its high-quality information in products and services produced by others.

NLM's large and rapidly expanding stores of electronic scientific data, research results, and high-quality health information—coupled with the growing availability of stores of standardized electronic health records—provide extraordinary scientific opportunities to increase understanding of disease onset and progression, to identify new therapeutic avenues, and to speed the translation of such discoveries into improved health and health care.

In 2012 NLM continued to expand and refine its current information services, focusing on improved access to these services in underserved communities and on support for research, development, and education that will help to take advantage of new opportunities to advance biomedical research, health care, and public health.

Some of the major themes and activities of the past year follow.

Delivering reliable, high-quality biomedical and health information services
At the heart of NLM are the world's largest, continually expanding collection of biomedical literature and a broad array of authoritative databases for health professionals, scientists, and for the public and the librarians and information specialists who serve them. NLM develops and uses sophisticated information systems to support the complex, high-volume operations necessary to acquire, describe, index, and provide rapid access to materials in its collections and to build and refine electronic databases and services for many different audiences.

In 2012 NLM greatly increased the quantity and range of information it has readily available. Major advances included

- Expansion of the National Center for Biotechnology Information's (NCBI's) Entrez system, an integrated collection of some 40 databases and 570 million records of molecular and genomic data
- Coordination with NIH Institutes for deposition of high-throughput sequencing data from projects they fund
- Development of dbVar, the database of genomic structural variation, and other new resources that house the growing body of data relating to genetic variation
- Continued support for PubChem, the archive of chemical and biological data from the NIH Molecular Libraries Roadmap initiative, which now contains more than 30 million unique chemical structures and half a million bioassays
- A significant increase in the number of full-text articles in PubMed Central, which now provides public access to more than 2.3 million research articles, including those produced by NIH-funded researchers
- Improved public access to the results of clinical effectiveness research and systematic reviews
- Maintenance of @medlineplus on Twitter, a companion to NLM's popular and respected consumer health website, MedlinePlus.gov, as one of several initiatives to use social media to reach new audiences that can benefit from high-quality health information
- Continued expansion of ClinicalTrials.gov to encompass summary results and adverse event information from a growing number of clinical trials of FDA-regulated products
- Development of new information services on the impact of the Gulf Oil Spill, the earthquake in Haiti, women's health issues, disaster preparation and response, and other important topics

Mobile applications and social media were also used to disseminate many of these resources.

Promoting public awareness and access to information
NLM has extensive outreach programs to enhance awareness of its diverse information services among biomedical researchers, health professionals, librarians, patients, and the public. To improve access to health information, NLM utilizes its National Network of Libraries of Medicine as well as formal partnerships such as Partners in Information Access for the Public Health Workforce and the Environmental Health Information Partnership with Historically Black Colleges and Universities, tribal colleges, and other minorities-serving institutions. NLM also fosters informal community partnerships and uses exhibitions, the media, and new technologies in its efforts to reach underserved populations and to promote young people's interest in careers in science, medicine, and technology. NLM has mounted a major new exhibition, "Native Voices: Native Peoples' Concepts of Health and Illness," as part of its outreach efforts to populations that suffer from serious health disparities and in response to congressional interest in ensuring the documentation of traditional Native Hawaiian healing practices. NLM continues to expand its successful traveling exhibitions program as another means of enhancing access to the library's services and promoting interest in careers in science and medicine. Examples include the highly popular "Harry Potter's World: Renaissance Science, Magic, and Medicine," and "Life and Limb: The Toll of the Civil War." A traveling version of "Native Voices" is currently in development.

As part of its outreach efforts, NLM also continually solicits feedback from users on how existing resources can be improved. In 2012 dozens of community-based projects were funded across the nation to enhance awareness and access to health information, using a combination of high-tech and "high-touch" approaches. With assistance from other NIH components and outside partners, NLM continues to increase the distribution of the NIH *MedlinePlus* magazine. The magazine, which is also available online in Spanish and English, is distributed to doctors' offices, health science libraries, Congress, the media, federally supported community health centers, select hospital emergency and waiting rooms, and other locations where the public receives health services nationwide. During the past year NLM and NIH continued to partner with the National Hispanic Medical Association, the American Diabetes Association, and the Peripheral Arterial Disease Coalition, among others, to extend the distribution of the magazine. Depending on partners for each issue, between 300,000 and 600,000 copies of the quarterly magazine are distributed and reach more than 5 million readers.

Developing advanced information systems, standards, and research tools
NLM's advanced information services have long benefited from its intramural research and research and development (R&D) programs. The library has two organizations that conduct advanced R&D on different aspects of biomedical communication—the Lister Hill National Center for Biomedical Communications (LHC) and NCBI.

Established in 1968, LHC conducts and supports research in such areas as the development and dissemination of health information technology standards; the dissemination, processing, and use of high-quality imagery; medical language processing; high-speed access to biomedical information; and advanced technology for emergency and disaster management. Imaging tools developed by LHC, for example in colposcopy, are integral to training and testing proficiency in medical schools and residency programs nationwide. In addition to its groundbreaking research in natural language processing and medical image processing, LHC has also made advances that will facilitate health information exchange and meaningful use of electronic health records (EHRs). LHC researchers used frequency data from multiple healthcare organizations to produce more useful, manageable subsets of large standard clinical vocabularies; worked with other U.S. Department of Health and Human Services (HHS) agencies to assist two states in testing NLM-developed guidance for standardizing newborn screening data; and established partnerships to test the use and impact of personal health records.

NCBI, created in 1988, conducts R&D on the representation, integration, and retrieval of molecular biology data and biomedical literature; provides an integrated, genomic information resource for biomedical researchers at NIH and around the world; and conducts basic research in computational biology. NCBI continues to expand its resources, which include more than 40 integrated biomedical databases, to support the accelerated pace of research made possible by new technologies such as next-generation DNA sequencing, microarrays, and small molecule screening. NCBI is one of the world's largest repositories of DNA sequence information, ranging from data on microorganisms to analyses of human genomes. Access to these data and data from associated NCBI databases, such dbGaP, PubChem, and numerous other protein and gene databases, all of which are linked to the scientific literature, provide the foundation for researchers to accelerate the rate of discovery and facilitate the translation of basic science into new diagnostics and treatments.

Through its intramural and extramural programs, NLM has been a leader in natural language understanding and biomedical text-mining research over the past two decades, developing and sharing innovative algorithms, resources, and tools, including the Unified Medical Language System (UMLS), MetaMap, Medical Text Indexer (MTI), and SemRep. This research has been applied to indexing, information retrieval, question answering, and literature-based discovery. For example, MTI plays a crucial role in indexing MEDLINE citations at NLM, and the output of SemRep is used in the development of clinical guidelines.

There is growing evidence of the utility of text-mining techniques in the clinical domain. Application of text-mining techniques developed by NLM-funded researchers and applied in the eMERGE Network (supported by NIH's National Human Genome Research Institute [NHGRI]) has recently demonstrated that combining genotype information with phenotype information extracted from electronic medical records is not only a viable way to study the relationship between genome-wide genetic variation and common human traits, but is also 100 times more cost-effective than the traditional genome-wide association studies (GWAS).

In conclusion, NLM and its grantees continue to bring many threads together—genomic data, standardized electronic health records, natural language understanding applied to clinical text and published knowledge, low-cost parallel processing, a prized print collection, and a world-class suite of electronic databases and mobile platforms—to make the right health and medical information available when and where it is needed, free of charge, in the proper format, to persons in the United States and around the globe for the benefit of the public health.

Administration

The director of the library, Donald A. B. Lindberg, M.D., is guided in matters of policy by a Board of Regents consisting of 10 appointed and 11 ex officio members.

Table 1 / Selected NLM Statistics*

Library Operations	Volume
Collection (book and non-book)	20,869,244
Items cataloged	19,656
Serial titles received	19,184
Articles indexed for MEDLINE	760,903
Circulation requests processed	316,644
For interlibrary loan	234,662
For on-site users	74,993
MEDLINE/PubMed Searches	2,204,710,177
Budget Authority	$383,605,000
Staff	800

*For the year ending September 30, 2012

United States Government Printing Office

732 North Capitol St. N.W., Washington, DC 20401
World Wide Web http://www.gpo.gov

Gary Somerset

Media and Public Relations Manager
202-512-1957, e-mail gsomerset@gpo.gov

The U.S. Government Printing Office (GPO) was created when President James Buchanan signed Joint Resolution 25 on June 23, 1860. GPO opened its doors for business nine months later on March 4, 1861, the same day Abraham Lincoln took the oath of office to become the 16th president of the United States. On that day GPO began operation in buildings purchased by Congress, at the same address it occupies today.

Under Title 44 of the United States Code, GPO is responsible for the production and distribution of information products for all three branches of the federal government. These include the official publications of Congress, federal agencies, and the courts. Today GPO provides products in print and a variety of digital forms, all of which are born digital. In addition, GPO produces passports for the Department of State and secure credentials for many government agencies. As the federal government's official, digital, secure resource for gathering, producing, cataloging, providing access to, and preserving published information in all forms, GPO has disseminated millions of publications to the public.

GPO's Superintendent of Documents and its Library Services and Content Management (LSCM) organizations administer and manage the four programs described in Title 44, U.S. Code:

* The Federal Depository Library Program (FDLP)
* Cataloging and indexing (C&I)
* Distributing publications to the International Exchange Service
* Distribution of certain government publications to members of Congress and other government agencies, as mandated by law (the By-Law program)

FDLP dates back to 1813 when Congress first authorized legislation to ensure the provision of certain congressional documents to selected universities, historical societies, and state libraries. At that time, the secretary of state was responsible for distributing publications. In 1857 the secretary of the interior assumed oversight of printing and the designation of depositories. In the Printing Act of 1895 the governance of the depository program was transferred to the Office of the Superintendent of Documents at GPO. Fast forward to 1993, when Public Law 103-40, the Government Printing Office Electronic Information Access Enhancement Act, amended GPO's duties to provide public access not only to printed publications but to Internet-accessible publications as well. Nearly 200 years after the start of FDLP, the program continues to serve a vital public need through its partnership with federal depository libraries located in almost every congressional district.

Today's GPO is obviously a much different agency than it was 150 years ago, but its mission has remained the same. FDLP and GPO's information dissemination programs are examples of its longstanding commitment: permanent public access to U.S. government information.

Collaboration

Digital Partnerships with Federal Depository Libraries

Since 1997 GPO has been developing digital partnerships with federal depository libraries and other federal agencies to increase access to electronic federal information. With an increasing amount of federal information available electronically, partnerships ensure permanent public access to electronic content and provide services to assist depositories in providing access to electronic material and in managing their depository collections. These partnerships also allow GPO to take advantage of the expertise of federal depository librarians and the services they have developed in the depository collections.

Partnership Updates

GPO currently maintains partnerships with 15 depository libraries and nine agencies. During fiscal year (FY) 2012 LSCM renewed three partnerships:

- The Enhanced Shipping List Service with the University at Buffalo, a tool that assists depositories in processing their depository shipments
- Government Information Online—Ask a Librarian with the University of Illinois at Chicago; staffed by members of the library's depository staff, this service provides e-mail and chat reference assistance on government information
- The Federal Agency Directory, a guide to government Internet sites, with the Louisiana State University, which provides a quick and easy way to locate federal agencies' websites

A partnership with the University of Florida was expanded to include digitization of content and bibliographic records from four additional federal agencies—the Depression-era National Recovery Administration; the National Commission on Libraries and Information Science (NCLIS), which existed from 1970 to 2008; the Institute of Museum Services, which existed from 1976 to 1996; and the Institute of Museum and Library Services—and to allow sharing bibliographic records with LSCM for House and Senate hearings that are cataloged by the university.

Finally, LSCM developed a pilot project with the Treasury Department to test GPO's Federal Digital System (FDsys) standard collection ingest processing and increase public access to digitized Treasury Department content. The first installment of treasury content, Treasury Reporting Rates of Exchange for the years 1956–2005, was released on FDsys in October 2012.

Partnerships with Outside Groups

During 2012 LSCM staff participated and collaborated with a number of outside groups relevant to the FDLP community, including the American Association of Law Libraries; the Legal Information Preservation Alliance; the Cartographers Users Advisory Council; CENDI and the CENDI Policy Working Group (CENDI is an interagency working group of senior scientific and technical information [STI] managers representing 13 U.S. federal agencies); the CENDI Digitization Specification Working Group; the End of Term Harvest of Government Websites Group; Ex Libris Users of North America; the Federal Agencies Digitization Guidelines Initiative; the Audiovisual Working Group; the Still Image Digitization Working Group; the Still Image File Format Working Group; the Federal Library and Information Center Committee (now known as FEDLINK); the Preservation Working Group, the Federal Library and Information Network; the Federal Library Shared Collection; Imaging Science and Technology Archiving; the International Internet Preservation Consortium; the National Digital Strategy Advisory Board; the National Federation of Advanced Information Services; the National Information Standards Organization (NISO); the North American Serials Interest Group; and the Science.gov Alliance.

In 2011 GPO worked with the Administrative Office of the U.S. Courts to launch a pilot project to increase public access to federal court opinions. The United States Courts Opinions collection in FDsys contains opinions from federal appellate, district, and bankruptcy courts, with the majority of the content dating back to April 2004. The pilot featured 29 courts, and the number of accesses and downloads has been heavy; the collection numbers some 600,000 opinions, and more than 40 million opinions were downloaded in FY 2012. In September 2012 the Judicial Conference of the United States approved the national implementation of access to all lower-level federal court opinions through FDsys. This means that in FY 2013 opinions of ten additional appellate courts, 75 additional district courts, and 87 additional bankruptcy courts will be added to the United States Courts Opinions collection in FDsys.

FY 2012 LSCM Events

Interagency Depository Seminar

GPO hosted the 25th annual Interagency Depository Seminar at GPO headquarters in Washington, D.C., July 30–August 3. The seminar focused on federal government agencies and their information products and services and included a number of speakers from federal agencies. Speakers made presentations, led hands-on training sessions, and facilitated on-site tours in the general vicinity of GPO. The seminar, sometimes referred to as a "boot camp" for government information professionals, was a busy five days with experts from ten federal agencies giving presentations to 29 attendees.

Key GPO Tools

Federal Digital System

GPO's Federal Digital System (FDsys) (http://www.fdsys.gov) is a one-stop site for online access to authentic published information. This system automates the collection and dissemination of electronic information for all three branches of the federal government. Information is submitted directly into FDsys, permanently available in electronic format, authenticated and versioned, and publicly accessible for searching and downloading. FDsys is a content management system; it securely controls digital content throughout its life cycle to ensure content integrity and authenticity. It is a preservation repository that follows archival system standards to ensure long-term preservation and access of digital content.

GPO is charged with cataloging a comprehensive index of public documents issued or published by the federal government that are not confidential in character. The goal of the Cataloging and Indexing Program is to develop a comprehensive and authoritative national bibliography of U.S. government publications to increase the visibility and use of government information products, and to develop a premier destination for information searchers. This undertaking serves libraries and the public nationwide and enables people to locate desired government publications in all formats. The main public interface for the access of cataloging records is the *Catalog of U.S. Government Publications (CGP)*, accessible at http://catalog.gpo.gov.

GPO's goal is to expand to a more comprehensive online index of public documents, both historic and current, to increase the visibility and use of government information products. Electronic information dissemination and access have greatly expanded the number of publications that require cataloging and indexing.

Enhancement/Progression/Innovation

FDsys Accomplishments

During FY 2012 GPO's Federal Digital System (FDsys) achieved a significant milestone: more than 300 million retrievals since its launch in 2009. LSCM continued focusing on identifying additional content to gain via partnerships to increase free, authentic, and authoritative online access to federal government information.

FDLP and FDsys Promotion

To assist federal depository libraries in promoting their depositories and FDLP, LSCM launched several new promotional strategies in FY 2012. A promotional campaign was created: "Government Information at your Fingertips: Federal Depository Libraries." GPO also released three promotional brochures, for the Federal Digital System, the Federal Depository Library Program, and *CGP*.

LSCM also developed a complete FDLP promotion plan, with additional FDLP and FDsys promotional items, set to release during FY 2013.

Upcoming promotional items include posters for FDLP and FDsys, door decals and table tents for FDLP, bookmarks for FDLP and FDsys, and computer screensavers for FDLP, FDsys, and *CGP*.

LSCM also will launch a nationwide media campaign for FDLP and FDsys through news articles and public service announcements during FY 2013.

Cataloging Record Distribution Project

In October 2009 GPO contracted with MARCIVE, Inc. to use that company's existing MARC record distribution infrastructure to deliver cataloging records to participating depository libraries. Based on the success of the pilot project, GPO has continued providing this service.

In March 2012 GPO surveyed participating libraries and received overwhelming positive feedback. Highlighted benefits for Cataloging Record Distribution Program (CRDP) participants include customizable output profiles, automatic updates to project selection profiles, a straightforward process to retrieve records, and hands-on customer service provided by the contracting company. Ultimately, CRDP reduces the amount of time participating libraries must spend cataloging and provides improved access to federal government information.

Currently 80 libraries are participating in the receipt of MARCIVE records. Through this program, GPO is better able to assess long-term solutions for bibliographic record distribution.

Integrated Library System

In FY 2012 the Integrated Library System (ILS) saw the creation of a new logical base, or "Catalogs to Search" for serials and for historic shelflist publications. This allows targeted searching in those subsets of *CGP*. Additionally, the *CGP* interface was refreshed with the shutdown of GPO Access. LSCM staff also stood up the Aleph acquisitions module, transferred tasks to it from the legacy ACSIS system, and implemented Aleph minor release 20.2.2, which contained elements to accommodate the new RDA (resource description and access) standard in the catalog.

National Bibliographic Records Inventory

Work began in FY 2012 to establish a comprehensive plan to create and make available online a complete National Bibliographic Records Inventory for FDLP and C&I materials. This project includes converting bibliographic publication information currently available only in local historical paper record files. In addition, GPO is identifying and adding materials for which LSCM has no record, with the help of FDLP partner libraries. *CGP* will serve as the authority tool and delivery mechanism for making this bibliographic inventory available to FDLP libraries and the public. *CGP* will utilize a format and platform that allows for easy data and record exchange. With a comprehensive inventory available in *CGP*, new reference tools, research tools, and helper applications can be developed later to enhance the use of this information.

LSCM projects that fall under this initiative are historic shelflist transcription; historic MoCat cataloging, beginning with the transcription of 1895 and 1898 volumes in FY 2013; historic item card/number transcription; cooperative cataloging projects (in Montana and Florida); LSCM internal manual records conversion; and congressional serial set.

Pre-1976 Shelflist Conversion Project

GPO's shelflist contains bibliographic information on publications dating from the 1870s to the shelflist's closure in 1992. The more than 1 million cards are arranged in Superintendent of Documents (SuDoc) classification order and are still used by GPO staff to verify the creation of new SuDoc numbers.

While not a complete inventory of all publications distributed through FDLP, the shelflist contains information on publications in all formats (monographs, serials, maps, integrating resources, and microfiche) as well as publications distributed directly to depositories by the publishing agency. The cards were also used by GPO staff to record information about how to obtain copies of a title, information discovered about publication history, and contact information for staff at the publishing agencies.

Two projects were initiated to make the information included in the shelflist more accessible to both GPO staff and the depository community.

Shelflist Transcription

Since January 2010 a team of contract staff from the LAC Group has been at work transcribing the cards into MARC21 records using the GPO ILS. GPO does not have the publications in hand to consult, so the bibliographic information is being transcribed as it is found on the cards. In FY 2012 progress with the transcription continued. As of the end of the fiscal year there were 142,441 shelflist records available through *CGP.*

Shelflist Digitization

As part of its records management requirement, GPO has been planning for the eventual transfer of the tangible shelflist to the National Archives and Records Administration (NARA) for long-term preservation and archiving. The cards date back to the 19th century, and their condition is beginning to deteriorate. In April 2012 scanning and digitization of the historic shelflist cards was completed. More than 686,300 shelflist cards were scanned and digitized to ensure quality images. These records must remain accessible to GPO staff after the tangible shelflist is transferred to NARA.

GPO Access Transition

On December 20, 2010, FDsys was released as GPO's official system of record for online government information, and on that date the countdown to the shutdown of GPO Access began. With more than 15 years of service, GPO Access is a well-respected and heavily accessed resource for users throughout the world. In order to ensure continuity of access from GPO Access to FDsys, a plan was developed to provide a seamless transition to FDsys for federal depository libraries, Congress, federal agencies, and the general public. The plan divided the shutdown into three phases: the system-of-record phase, the archive phase, and the shutdown phase.

The system-of-record phase began with the announcement that FDsys was officially GPO's system of record, and it continued through October 2011. This phase focused on introducing GPO Access users to FDsys while GPO Access and FDsys were maintained in tandem. Users were notified of the official release of FDsys and given a link to the site via a pop-up banner on strategic GPO Access Web pages.

In early November 2011 the pop-up banner was modified to announce the implementation of the archive phase of GPO Access. Starting on November 5 that year, FDsys became GPO's only site for both current and historical information from all three branches of the federal government. GPO Access remained accessible. but exclusively as a reference archive.

On March 16, 2012, in the final phase of the shutdown, GPO Access was decommissioned. The URL redirects searchers to the FDsys equivalent of GPO Access resources.

FDsys Training Initiative

In response to repeated requests from the FDLP community, LSCM staff developed a training curriculum for FDsys in FY 2011. Training included curriculum guides, developing lesson plans, class handouts, talking points for trainers, and class exercises. The initial target audiences for educational sessions on FDsys included federal depository library staff, federal agency staff members, and congressional staff.

The live classroom training sessions began in FY 2012. Between November 2011 and the end of FY 2012 (11 months), 46 live sessions were conducted, with approximately 300 participants. In addition, LSCM staff began teaching FDsys virtual webinars in April 2012. In 22 webinars taught during the fiscal year, more than 1,500 people received FDsys instruction. Additionally, between June and September 2012 the archived webinars were viewed for more than 20,000 minutes.

The 2012 Interagency Depository Seminar included a live classroom FDsys training session at GPO that was also broadcast as a webinar for those unable to attend. Altogether, 61 attendees participated in inter-agency virtual FDsys training.

Also in FY 2012, LSCM staff created scripts for 32 FDsys educational videos. The first and longest video, on FDsys Basic Searching and how to work with search results, was launched on gpo.gov and fdlp.gov in July 2012. Other videos were to be launched in FY 2013.

During 2012 LSCM began a FDsys Training Analysis project to assess the resources devoted to the training initiative. Evaluating costs, staff time/effort, and tools will help LSCM plan staff and project training resources for FY 2013 and beyond.

Harvesting Initiative

GPO has undertaken an initiative to modernize its Web harvesting program. Because federal agencies are publishing less in print and producing more information on the Web, the scope has increased to include entire websites rather than single publications. For the automated pilot project, LSCM is exploring automated harvesting of websites and outsourced hosting of Web content for public access via the Internet Archive's "Archive-It" automated Web harvester. Harvested content is hosted and publicly accessible on the Internet Archive's Wayback Machine. GPO is one of 228 agencies worldwide using Archive-It.

Depository Library Spotlight

Each month GPO Depository Library Spotlight highlights a federal depository library and describes the library and the unique services it offers. The feature appears on the GPO website and in the *FDLP Connection* newsletter. The following depositories were highlighted in FY 2012: University of Central Florida Library; Des Moines Public Library; Fondren Library Center at Southern Methodist University; Ottenheimer Library at the University of Arkansas at Little Rock; University of Colorado–Boulder Library; Elmer Ellis Library at the University of Missouri–Columbia; Robert L. Carothers Library, University of Rhode Island; Bierce Library, University of Akron; Hawaii State Library; Marriott Library, University of Utah; Newark (New Jersey) Public Library; and Indiana University–Kokomo Library.

Metrics

Notable LSCM metrics for FY 2012:

New titles acquired (online and tangible)	19,798
Searches of the *Catalog of U.S. Government Publications*	18,739,250
Total titles cataloged	21,958
Total PURLs created	15,160
Total titles distributed	6,029
Total copies distributed	1,455,988
Number of federal depository libraries	1,196

Public Access Assessment

A Public Access Assessment (PAA) is a review by GPO staff of an individual library's federal depository operations and services. GPO has the responsibility, pursuant to 44 U.S.C. 19, to ensure that the resources it distributes to federal depository libraries are made accessible to the public and that participating libraries comply with the requirements and regulations of FDLP.

Each assessment is intended to be supportive of each individual depository library and involves sharing of best practices and recognition of notable achievements that will help each library continue to enhance its operations and services. The PAA is organized according to the same categories found in *Legal Requirements and Program Regulations of the Federal Depository Library Program*. In FY 2012 PAAs were completed in 14 states: Colorado, Delaware, Idaho, Maine, Mississippi, New Jersey, Nevada, New York, North Dakota, Rhode Island, Tennessee, Utah, Vermont, and West Virginia.

Serials Management Plan

During FY 2012 LSCM continued working on several multiyear serials projects. These projects were identified in the Serials Management Plan for FDLP and the C&I Program initially formulated and published in FY 2011. They were undertaken to increase access to serial information through *CGP*, because previously the majority of information about individual issues of serials was not available to the public or libraries, but kept only in internal GPO databases. These projects will serve to capture serial issue and holdings information for each serial issue in GPO's ILS.

Several key serials projects, including the transcription of historic shelflist serial issues, check-in of serial issues from LSCM manual files, and check-in of newly acquired tangible serial issues, continued with the help of contracted staff. In FY 2012 a total of 138,362 issues were checked into *CGP*. In addition more than 400 publication patterns were created for new serial titles. Creating these serial patterns enabled the check-in of individual issues in *CGP*. The Serials Management Plan also called for the creation of new serial bibliographic records for newly published U.S. government serial titles. This work is part of the day-to-day activities of LSCM's Bibliographic Control Section. In FY 2012 a total of 1,535 new serial titles were identified, and new bibliographic records were created for these titles in *CGP.*

RDA Compliance Project

Staff members in LSCM's Library Technical Information Services have been making preparations for the implementation of resource description and access (RDA). The cataloging team has been training in RDA via reading, webinars, tests, and training records since February 2011. The ILS interface was updated to reflect labels for the new RDA MARC fields (336, 337, and 338). Several RDA records were created in ILS and were made available to the public. A GPO Cataloging Policy on RDA capitalization rules was prepared and released on the FDLP Desktop.

In FY 2012 GPO continued to monitor developments announced by the Joint Steering Committee for the Development of RDA. Testing the new MARC-based standard was completed in 2012. The U.S. RDA Test Coordinating Committee recommended that libraries implement the new standards no earlier than January 2013. Based on this recommendation, GPO established an RDA Implementation Team and created a tentative timeline for RDA implementation for 2013.

GPO continued training its Bibliographic Control and Library Technical Services staff on the new RDA standards during the fiscal year. In addition, test records were created for inclusion in *CGP.* Sample test records were made available to GPO cataloging record customers and to the FDLP library community for review and comment. Staff made necessary modifications to *CGP* to accommodate new and modified MARC fields required by the new standard. Throughout the process, GPO reviewed internal procedures and established several local practice options for RDA government documents records. In late FY 2012 LSCM staff received RDA training for the creation of name authorities for the Name Authority Cooperative Project (NACO) by staff at the Library of Congress.

Selling Government Information

GPO's Sales Program currently offers for sale approximately 4,000 individual government titles on a broad array of subjects. These are sold principally via the Internet, e-mail, telephone, fax, mail, and through the GPO main bookstore. The program operates on a cost-recovery basis. Publications for sale include books, e-books, forms, posters, pamphlets, and CD-ROMs. Subscription services for both dated periodicals and basic-and-supplement services (involving an initial volume and supplemental issues) also are offered.

GPO's U.S. Government Online Bookstore (http://bookstore.gpo.gov) is the prime source of information on its sales inventory. The bookstore includes a searchable database of all in-print publications. It also includes a broad spectrum of special publication collections featuring new and popular titles and key product lines. GPO uses Pay.gov, a secure government-wide financial management transaction portal available around the clock to provide timely and efficient processing of online orders. Free shipping is included. The online bookstore also gives customers the options of expedited shipping, an improved shopping cart, order confirmation e-mails, and expanded ordering options for international customers.

Express service, which includes priority handling and expedited delivery, is available for orders placed by telephone for domestic delivery. Orders placed before noon (eastern time) for in-stock publications and single-copy subscriptions will be delivered within two working days. For more information, call the GPO Contact Center toll-free at 866-512-1800 (or at 202-512-1800 in the Washington, D.C., area). The Contact Center is open from 8 A.M. to 5:30 P.M.

GPO also offers publications for sale through the main bookstore, which is located at 710 North Capitol St. N.W., in Washington, which has recently undergone a major renovation. Hours of operation are 8 A.M. to 4 P.M. eastern time. The bookstore is available by telephone at 202-512-0132 or by e-mail at mainbks@gpo.gov.

Consumer-oriented publications also are either sold or distributed at no charge through the Federal Citizen Information Center in Pueblo, Colorado, which GPO operates on behalf of the General Services Administration.

Interested parties can register to receive e-mail updates free of charge when new publications become available for sale through GPO's New Titles by Topic e-mail alert service, which can be accessed at http://bookstore.gpo.gov/alertservice.jsp.

Standing order service is available to ensure automatic receipt of many of GPO's most popular recurring and series publications. Standing order customers receive each new edition automatically as soon as it is published. This service can be set up using a MasterCard, American Express, or Discover credit card, or through a Superintendent of Documents deposit account. For more information on how to set up a standing order for recurring or series publications, e-mail contactcenter@gpo.gov or call 866-512-1800 (toll free) or 202-512-1800 in the Washington area.

The GPO sales program has begun using print-on-demand technology to increase the long-term availability of publications. The program also has brought its bibliographic practices more in line with those of the commercial publishing sector by utilizing ONIX (Online Information Exchange), the publishing industry's standard electronic format for sharing product data with wholesale and retail booksellers, other publishers, library buyers, and anyone else involved in the sale of books. ONIX enables GPO to have government publications listed, promoted, and sold by commercial book dealers worldwide. In 2010 GPO began Government Book Talk (http://govbooktalk.gpo.gov), a blog that reviews government publications past and present. In its first year and a half, the new blog received more than 210,000 page views and added more than 1,760 subscribers.

To learn more about GPO, visit http://www.gpo.gov or connect with GPO through social media on Facebook, Pinterest, Twitter, and YouTube.

National Technical Information Service

U.S. Department of Commerce, Alexandria, VA 22312
800-553-NTIS (6847) or 703-605-6000
World Wide Web http://www.ntis.gov

Wayne Strickland
Manager, Office of Product and Program Management

The National Technical Information Service (NTIS) is the nation's largest and most comprehensive source of government-funded scientific, technical, engineering, and business information produced or sponsored by U.S. and international government sources. NTIS is a federal agency within the U.S. Department of Commerce.

Since 1945 the NTIS mission has been to operate a central U.S. government access point for scientific and technical information useful to American industry and government. NTIS maintains a permanent archive of this declassified information for researchers, businesses, and the public to access quickly and easily. Release of the information is intended to promote U.S. economic growth and development and to increase U.S. competitiveness in the world market.

The NTIS collection of more than 2.5 million titles contains products available in various formats. Such information includes reports describing research conducted or sponsored by federal agencies and their contractors; statistical and business information; multimedia training programs; databases developed by federal agencies; and technical reports prepared by research organizations worldwide. NTIS maintains a permanent repository of its information products.

More than 200 U.S. government agencies contribute to the NTIS collection, including the National Aeronautics and Space Administration; the Environmental Protection Agency; the departments of Agriculture, Commerce, Defense, Energy, Health and Human Services, Homeland Security, Interior, Labor, Treasury, Veterans Affairs, Housing and Urban Development, Education, and Transportation; and numerous other agencies. International contributors include Canada, Japan, Britain, and several European countries.

NTIS on the Web

NTIS offers Web-based access to information on government scientific and technical research products. Visitors to http://www.ntis.gov can search the entire collection dating back to 1964 free of charge. NTIS provides many of the technical reports for purchase on CD, paper copies, or downloaded pdf files. RSS feeds of recently catalogued materials are available in 39 major subject categories at http://www.ntis.gov/rss/RSSNTISCategoryList.aspx.

NTIS Database

The NTIS Database offers unparalleled bibliographic coverage of U.S. government and worldwide government-sponsored research information products acquired by NTIS since 1964. Its contents represent hundreds of billions of research dollars and cover a range of topics including agriculture, biotechnology, business, communication, energy, engineering, the environment, health and safety, medicine, research and development, science, space, technology, and transportation.

The NTIS Database can be leased directly from NTIS and can also be accessed through several commercial services. For a list of organizations offering NTIS Database products, see http://www.ntis.gov/products/commercial.aspx.

To lease the NTIS Database directly from NTIS, contact the NTIS Office of Product Management at 703-605-6515. For more information, see http://www.ntis.gov/products/ntisdb.aspx.

NTIS National Technical Reports Library

The National Technical Reports Library (NTRL) enhances accessibility to the NTIS technical reports collection. Subscription rates are based on institutional FTE levels. NTRL operates on a system interface that allows users to do queries on the large NTIS bibliographic database. The intent is to broadly expand and improve access to more than 2.5 million bibliographic records (pre-1960 to the present) and more than 700,000 full-text documents in pdf format that are directly linked to that bibliographic database. For more information, visit http://www.ntis.gov/products/ntrl.aspx.

Other Databases Available from NTIS

NTIS offers several valuable research-oriented database products. To find out more about accessing the databases, visit http://www.ntis.gov/products/data.aspx.

AGRICOLA

As one of the most comprehensive sources of U.S. agricultural and life sciences information, the AGRICOLA (Agricultural Online Access) Database contains bibliographic records for documents acquired by the U.S. Department of Agriculture's National Agricultural Library. To access an updated list of organizations offering AGRICOLA Database products, see http://www.ntis.gov/products/agricola.aspx.

AGRIS

The International Information System for the Agricultural Science and Technology (AGRIS) Database is a cooperative system for collecting and disseminating information on the world's agricultural literature. More than 100 national and multinational centers take part in the system. References to citations for U.S. publications given coverage in the AGRICOLA Database are not included in AGRIS. To access an updated list of organizations offering AGRIS Database products, see http://www.ntis.gov/products/agris.aspx.

Energy Science and Technology

The Energy Science and Technology Database (EDB) is a multidisciplinary file containing worldwide references to basic and applied scientific and technical research literature. The information is collected for use by government managers, researchers at the national laboratories, and other research efforts sponsored by the U.S. Department of Energy, and the results of this research are transferred to the public. To access an updated list of organizations offering EDB products, see http://www.ntis.gov/products/engsci.aspx.

FEDRIP

The Federal Research in Progress Database (FEDRIP) provides access to information about ongoing federally funded projects in such fields as the physical sciences, engineering, and life sciences. To access an updated list of organizations offering FEDRIP Database products, see http://www.ntis.gov/products/fedrip.aspx.

Online Subscriptions

NTIS offers quick, convenient online access, on a subscription basis, to the following resources:

World News Connection

World News Connection (WNC) is an NTIS online news service accessible only via the World Wide Web. WNC makes available English-language translations of time-sensitive news and information from thousands of non-U.S. media. Particularly effective in its coverage of local media, WNC provides the power to identify what is happening in a specific country or region. The information is obtained from speeches, television and radio broadcasts, newspaper articles, periodicals, and books. The subject matter focuses on socioeconomic, political, scientific, technical, and environmental issues and events.

The information in WNC is provided to NTIS by the Open Source Center (OSC), a U.S. government agency. For more than 60 years, analysts from OSC's domestic and overseas bureaus have monitored timely and pertinent open source material, including gray literature. Uniquely, WNC allows subscribers to take advantage of the intelligence-gathering experience of OSC. WNC is updated every government business day. New information is added hourly.

Access to WNC is available through Dialog Corporation. To use the service, complete the WNC form at http://www.dialog.com/contacts/forms/wnc.shtml.

U.S. Export Administration Regulations

U.S. Export Administration Regulations (EAR) provides the latest rules controlling the export of U.S. dual-use commodities, technology, and software. Step by step, EAR explains when an export license is necessary and when it is not, how to obtain an export license, policy changes as they are issued, new restrictions on exports to certain countries and of certain types of items, and where to obtain further help.

This information is available through NTIS in looseleaf form, on CD-ROM, and online. An e-mail update notification service is also available. For more information, see http://www.ntis.gov/products/export-regs.aspx.

Special Subscription Services

NTIS eAlerts

More than 1,000 new titles are added to the NTIS collection every week. NTIS prepares a list of search criteria that is run against all new studies and research and development reports in 16 subject areas. An NTIS eAlert provides a twice-monthly information briefing service, by e-mail, covering a wide range of technology topics.

For more information, call the NTIS Subscriptions Department at 703-605-6060 or see http://www.ntis.gov/products/alerts.aspx.

NTIS Selected Research Service

NTIS Selected Research Service (SRS) is a tailored information service that delivers complete electronic copies of government publications based on your needs, automatically, within a few weeks of announcement by NTIS. SRS includes the full bibliographic information in XML and HTML formats. Customers choose between Standard SRS (selecting one or more of the 320 existing subject areas) or Custom SRS, which creates a new subject area to meet their particular needs. Custom SRS requires a one-time fee to cover the cost of strategy development and computer programming to set up a profile. Except for this fee, the cost of Custom SRS is the same as the Standard SRS. Through this ongoing subscription service, customers download copies of new reports pertaining to their field(s) of interest as NTIS obtains the reports.

For more information, see http://www.ntis.gov/products/srs.aspx. To place an order, call 800-363-2068 or 703-605-6060.

This service is also available in CD-ROM format as Science and Technology on CD, which delivers the documents digitized and stored in pdf format.

For more information on SRS, see http://www.ntis.gov/products/SRS.aspx. For more information on Science and Technology on CD, see http://www.ntis.gov/products/STonCD.aspx.

Federal Science Repository Service

Collections of scientific and technical documents, images, videos, and other content represent the mission and work of an agency or other institution. To help preserve these collections, NTIS formed a joint venture with Information International Associates, Inc. of Oak Ridge, Tennessee, to develop for federal agencies a searchable, digital Federal Science Repository Service (FSRS). FSRS provides a supporting infrastructure, long-term storage, security, interface design, and content management and operational expertise. An agency can utilize this entire service or select components, resulting in the design of an agency-specific repository that serves as a distinct gateway to its content.

NTIS Customer Service

NTIS's automated systems keep it at the forefront when it comes to customer service. Shopping online at NTIS is safe and secure; its secure socket layer (SSL) software is among the best available.

Electronic document storage is fully integrated with NTIS's order-taking process, allowing it to provide rapid reproduction for the most recent additions to the NTIS document collection. Most orders for shipment are filled and delivered anywhere in the United States in five to seven business days. Rush service is available for an additional fee.

Key NTIS Contacts for Ordering

Order by Phone

Sales Desk   800-553-6847 or 703-605-6000
8:30 A.M.–5:00 P.M. Eastern time, Monday–Friday

Subscriptions   800-363-2068 or 703-605-6060
8:30 A.M.–5:00 P.M. Eastern time, Monday–Friday
TDD (hearing impaired only)   703-487-4639
8:30 A.M.–5:00 P.M. Eastern time, Monday–Friday

Order by Fax

24 hours a day, seven days a week   703-605-6900

To verify receipt of fax, call 703-605-6090, 7:00 A.M.–5:00 P.M. Eastern time
Monday–Friday

Order by Mail

National Technical Information Service
5301 Shawnee Rd.
Alexandria, VA 22312

RUSH Service (available for an additional fee)   800-553-6847 or 703-605-6000
Note: If requesting RUSH Service, please do not mail your order

Order Online

Direct and secure online ordering   http://www.ntis.gov

National Archives and Records Administration

700 Pennsylvania Ave. N.W., Washington, DC 20408
202-357-5000
World Wide Web http://www.archives.gov

The National Archives and Records Administration (NARA), an independent federal agency, is the nation's record keeper. NARA safeguards and preserves the important records of all three branches of the federal government so that the people can discover, use, and learn from this documentary heritage. NARA ensures continuing access to records that document the rights of American citizens and the actions of their government.

NARA carries out its mission through a national network of archives and records centers stretching from Boston to California and Atlanta to Alaska, in addition to 13 presidential libraries documenting administrations back to that of Herbert Hoover—a total of 44 locations.

NARA also assists federal agencies, the courts, and Congress in documenting their activities by providing records storage, offering reference service, administering records management programs, scheduling records, and retiring non-current records to federal records centers. NARA also provides training, advice, and guidance on many issues relating to records management.

The agency also assists the National Historical Publications and Records Commission (NHPRC) in its grants program; the Office of the Federal Register, which publishes the official records of the actions of the government; the Information Security Oversight Office (ISOO), which oversees the government's classification programs; the National Declassification Center (NDC), which is streamlining the declassification process; and the Office of Government Information Services (OGIS), which reviews agencies' Freedom of Information Act (FOIA) administration and practices.

NARA constituents include educators and their students at all levels, a historyminded public, family historians, the media, the archival community, and a broad spectrum of professional associations and researchers in such fields as history, political science, law, library and information services, and genealogy.

The size and breadth of NARA's holdings are staggering. Together, NARA's facilities hold approximately 4.5 million cubic feet (equivalent to more than 11 billion pieces of paper) of original textual and nontextual materials from the executive, legislative, and judicial branches of the federal government.

The holdings also include some 25 million still pictures and graphics; 300,000 reels of motion picture film and 400,000 sound and video recordings; 12 million maps. charts, and architectural and engineering plans; more than 27 million aerial photographs; and about 515 terabytes of federal (including the census), presidential, and congressional records.

In addition, a network of 18 Federal Records Centers (FRCs) provides storage for about 71 billion pages of non-current records for 400 federal government agencies.

Records and Access

Information Security Oversight Office

The Information Security Oversight Office (ISOO) is responsible to the president for policy and oversight of the government-wide security classification system, the National Industrial Security Program and the emerging federal policy on "controlled unclassified" information. ISOO receives policy and program guidance from the National Security Staff in the Executive Office of the President.

ISOO oversees the security classification programs (classification, safeguarding, and declassification) in both government and industry. It is also responsible for exercising NARA's authorities and responsibilities as the executive agent for controlled unclassified information. ISOO contributes materially to the effective implementation of the government-wide security classification program and has a direct impact on the performance of thousands of government employees and contract personnel who work with classified national security information. For more information on ISOO, visit http://www.archives.gov/isoo.

National Declassification Center

In December 2009 President Barack Obama directed an overhaul of the way documents created by the federal government are classified and declassified. This initiative is aimed at promoting transparency and accountability of government. The president also directed the creation of the National Declassification Center (NDC), now located within NARA.

NDC is leading the streamlining of the declassification process throughout the federal government. In particular, it is accelerating the processing of historically valuable classified records in which more than one federal agency has an interest. It oversees the development of common declassification processes among agencies, and it is prioritizing declassification based on public interest and the likelihood of declassification. For more information about NDC, go to http://www.archives.gov/declassification.

Office of Government Information Services

Congress refers to the Office of Government Information Services (OGIS) as "the Federal FOIA (Freedom of Information Act) ombudsman." OGIS serves as a bridge between requesters and agencies, particularly in situations where clear, direct communication has been lacking.

OGIS was created within NARA when the Open Government Act of 2007 amended FOIA. Its key responsibilities include reviewing compliance by federal agencies and proposing any changes in FOIA to Congress; mediating disputes between persons making FOIA requests and agencies; and serving as ombudsman for the agencies and the public regarding the administration of FOIA and to improve communications between agencies and requesters.

OGIS also provides dispute resolution training for the FOIA staff of federal agencies, and works closely with key FOIA stakeholders, including the requester community and open government advocates. For more information about OGIS, visit http://ogis.archives.gov.

In cooperation with the Environmental Protection Agency and the Department of Commerce, OGIS developed and established a Web portal, FOIAonline, at https://foiaonline.regulations.gov. The public can submit FOIA requests, track their progress, communicate with the participating agency, file appeals, and find records that have been released to the public under FOIA. Six federal agencies including NARA are now partners in this new shared-services system.

Electronic Records Archives

The Electronic Records Archives (ERA) system captures electronic records and information, regardless of format, saves them permanently, and provides access to them. ERA development was completed at the end of fiscal year (FY) 2011 and ERA moved to an operations and maintenance phase at the beginning of FY 2012.

The focus then shifted to increasing the use of ERA by federal departments and agencies in anticipation of ERA becoming mandatory by the end of 2012 for federal agency use in scheduling and transferring permanent electronic records to NARA. The adoption of ERA by federal agencies has led to the transfer of increasing volumes of electronic records to NARA for preservation and eventual access.

In 2013 NARA plans to make several improvements to meet the needs of all stakeholders that rely on the ERA system to schedule, transfer, preserve, and provide access to the permanently valuable digital heritage of the federal government. For more information about ERA, see http://www.archives.gov/era.

Applied Research Division

NARA's Applied Research Division—formerly known as the Center for Advanced Systems and Technologies—serves as the agency's premier center for advanced and applied research capabilities in the fields of computer science, engineering, and archival science. The division's staff conducts research on new technologies, both to be aware of new types of electronic records that will need to be preserved, and to evaluate new technologies that might be incorporated into the ERA system or other systems to increase their value. The staff also helps NARA managers and employees acquire the knowledge and skills they need to function effectively in e-government. For more information, visit http://www.archives.gov/applied-research.

Online Research Catalog

Today anyone with a computer connected to the Internet can search descriptions of more than 80 percent of NARA's nationwide holdings and view digital copies of some of its most popular documents through NARA's Online Public Access portal. Because of the vast amount of NARA holdings, it will take several more years to fully populate the catalog. At present the catalog contains more than 6.4 million descriptions of archival holdings. Included in the catalog are more than 1,125,000 digital copies of high-interest documents, representing many of the holdings highlighted in the Public Vaults, NARA's permanent interactive exhibition. The catalog is available on the Internet at http://www.archives.gov/research.

NARA's Website

Newly designed in late 2010, NARA's award-winning website (http://www.archives.gov) provides the most widely available means of electronic access to information about and services available from the agency. Feedback from visitors to the website, as well as from visitors to the National Archives Building in Washington, D.C., led to task-oriented portals designed to support the particular needs of researchers. These include veterans and their families, educators and students, and the general public—as well as records managers, journalists, information security specialists, members of Congress, and federal employees.

Since the redesigned website launched in December 2010, the Citizen Archivist Dashboard was developed and is where researchers and other members of the public can tag, transcribe, edit articles, upload, and share images. The Citizen Archivist Dashboard was used to index the 1940 Census, which was released, in digital format only, on April 2, 2012 (http://1940census.archives.gov).

Under the dashboard, NARA launched a Transcription Pilot Project where 300 documents totaling 1,000 pages were transcribed completely or partially within the first two weeks. NARA released the open-source module (developed in Drupal) to make it available to other agencies and cultural institutions interested in crowdsource transcription. The site includes

- Directions on how to contact NARA and do research at its facilities
- Descriptions of holdings in an online catalog at http://www.archives.gov/research/search
- Direct access to certain archived electronic records at http://www.archives.gov/aad
- Digital copies of selected archived documents
- An Web form, at http://www.archives.gov/contact/inquire-form.html, for customer questions, reference requests, comments, and complaints
- Electronic versions of *Federal Register* publications
- Online exhibits
- Classroom resources for students and teachers
- Online tools, such as eVetRecs (http://www.archives.gov/veterans/military-service-records), which allows veterans and their next-of-kin to complete and print, for mail-in submission, requests for their military service records

Copies of military pension records from the American Revolution through World War I, census pages, land files, court records, and microfilm publications can be ordered online as well as books, apparel, and accessories at http://www.archives.gov/shop. Researchers can also submit reference questions about various research topics online.

Digitization Projects

Within its recently created Office of Innovation, NARA is working to digitize its traditional (paper) holdings to preserve them and provide greater access to them. The Office of Innovation will accelerate NARA's innovation activities and culture, support innovation in public access delivery, and demonstrate leadership in the archival and information access field.

While NARA's online catalog gives users the ability to identify the archival holdings it has attached to descriptions and made available through the catalog, the amount of material digitized and fully made available online is limited.

Most of NARA's holdings currently are available only from the archival facility in which they are stored. Through a series of digitization projects, NARA is working to vastly increase online public access to more of its holdings. In 2008 the agency created a strategy to deal with digitization efforts, which includes working with partners in the private sector. NARA added 868,000 digital copies created by its Digitization Services Branch or accessioned from other government agencies to its online catalog in 2012.

Also, for the first time, in 2012 NARA released the 3.8 million pages of the 1940 census to the public digitally and provided free online access to it at http://1940census.archives.gov. The first 247,000 digital images created by NARA's digitization partners are being added to the online catalog in 2013, and NARA anticipates adding millions of additional images created by its partners to the catalog in the future. More information about the digitization partnerships is available at http://www.archives.gov/digitization/index.html.

Social Media

The National Archives has embraced the use of social media for open government. The main goals are to increase awareness about archival holdings and programs and to enrich the relationship with the public through conversations about its services and holdings. The hope is that by learning more about NARA and its holdings online, citizens will make a first-time or repeat visit to one of its locations nationwide.

Social media also lets NARA's researchers, friends, and the general public become "citizen archivists" at the National Archives by tagging, sharing, and transcribing documents. Explore the dashboard at http://www.archives.gov/citizen-archivist.

The National Archives has more than a dozen blogs, including one by the Archivist of the United States. It shares historical videos from its holdings and recent public events on its YouTube channel. It also shares photographs and documents from its collections through Flickr Commons.

In addition to blogs and wikis, visitors to NARA's website can interact with NARA staff through a wide variety of social media including Facebook, Twitter, Foursquare, GitHub, HistoryPin, Pinterest, Tumblr, Storify, and Ustream, as well as obtaining Really Simple Syndication (RSS) feeds of the "Document for Today" feature, NARA news, and press releases. Several mobile apps have been developed and are available for free in the iTunes store and Android Market for Today's Document, DocsTeach, and the 2012 exhibit "To the Brink: JFK and the Cuban Missile Crisis."

More information about NARA's Web 2.0 projects is available at http://www.archives.gov/social-media.

National Archives Experience

The National Archives Experience, a set of interconnected resources made possible by a public-private partnership between NARA and the Foundation for the National Archives, provides a variety of ways to explore the power and importance of the nation's records.

The Rotunda for the Charters of Freedom at the National Archives Building in Washington is the cornerstone of the National Archives Experience. On display are the Declaration of Independence, the Constitution, and the Bill of Rights—known collectively as the Charters of Freedom. The Public Vaults is a 9,000-square-foot permanent exhibition that conveys the feeling of going beyond the walls of the rotunda and into the stacks and vaults of the working archives. Dozens of individual exhibits, many of them interactive, reveal the breadth and variety of NARA's holdings.

Complementing the Public Vaults, the Lawrence F. O'Brien Gallery hosts a changing array of topical exhibits based on National Archives records. The 290-seat William G. McGowan Theater is a showplace for NARA's audiovisual holdings and serves as a forum for lectures and discussion. It also is home to the Charles Guggenheim Center for the Documentary Film at the National Archives.

An expanded museum shop opened in late 2012, and a new exhibition gallery and visitor orientation plaza are scheduled to open in late 2013. The David M. Rubinstein Gallery will house a new permanent interactive exhibit, "Records of Rights," which documents the struggles and debates over civil rights and liberties throughout American history. The Rubinstein Gallery will also be the new home for a 1297 copy of the Magna Carta, owned by Rubinstein.

Inside the Boeing Learning Center, the ReSource Room is an access point for teachers and parents to explore documents found in the exhibits and to use NARA records as teaching tools. The center's "Constitution-in-Action" Learning Lab is designed to provide an intense field trip adventure for middle and high school students that links to curriculum in the classroom.

DocsTeach (http://www.docsteach.org) is an education website designed to provide instruction to teachers in the best practices of teaching with primary sources. Using documents in NARA's holdings as teachable resources, DocsTeach strongly supports the goal to promote civic literacy. This tool provides all teachers with access to primary sources, instruction in best practices, and opportunities to interact with teachers across the nation. When developing the site, the agency established an online community that served as a virtual meeting place for NARA's education team and colleagues from schools, institutions, and organizations nationwide to collaborate and share innovative ideas and best practices for this online resource.

NARA launched two e-books in 2012 in commemoration of two landmark documents. In September it published *225th Anniversary of the Constitution,* highlighting that document's history, and in December it launched *The Meaning and Making of the Emancipation Proclamation,* highlighting the proclamation's 150th anniversary.

The National Archives Experience has expanded to the National Archives in New York City, which has relocated to the Alexander Hamilton U.S. Custom House at the southern tip of Manhattan. There NARA has not only a new research area but a Learning Center for education and public programs and a Welcome Center with exhibit space. The new Learning Center incorporates many of the resources and activities found in the Washington, D.C., location. This new expansion into New York gives NARA further incentive to consider establishing learning centers at other regional facilities.

A set of Web pages now makes the entire National Archives Experience available anywhere. An illustrated history of the Charters of Freedom can be found, as well as information on educational programs, special events, and exhibits currently at the National Archives. Those traveling to Washington can bypass the public line during peak tourist season by making online reservations at http://www.recreation.gov. For more information, see "The National Archives Experience" at http://www.archives.gov/national-archives-experience.

NARA also provided informative public programs at its various facilities for nearly 15,000 people. More than a million visited the National Archives Experience in Washington, and exhibits in the presidential library museums were visited by more than 2.4 million.

Research Services

Few records repositories serve as many customers as NARA. In FY 2012 there were nearly 123,000 researcher visits to NARA facilities nationwide, including archives, presidential libraries, and federal records centers. Well over a million people requested information in writing.

National Archives Research Centers

At the Robert M. Warner Research Center in the National Archives Building in Washington and the Steny Hoyer Research Center at the National Archives at College Park, Maryland, researchers can consult with staff experts on federal records held in each building and submit requests to examine original documents.

The Warner Research Center holds approximately 275,000 rolls of microfilmed records, documenting military service prior to World War I, immigration into the United States, the federal census, the U.S. Congress, federal courts in the District of Columbia, the Bureau of Indian Affairs, and the Freedmen's Bureau. The center also contains an extensive, ever-expanding system of reference reports, helping researchers conduct research in federal documents. Executive branch records housed in the National Archives Building include those of the Bureau of Indian Affairs and of civilian agencies responsible for maritime affairs. Military records in this building include records of the Army before World War I and the Navy and Marine Corps before World War II. In addition there are many records relating to the federal government's interaction with individuals that are often consulted for genealogical research.

The Hoyer Research Center in College Park holds textual records of civilian agencies from 1789, investigative records and military holdings that include records from the Army and Army Air Forces dating from World War I and Navy, Marine Corps, intelligence, defense-related, and seized enemy records dating from World War II. In addition to textual records, special media records include motion pictures, still photographs and posters, sound recordings, maps, architectural drawings, aerial photographs and electronic records. A research room for accessioned microfilm holds records of the Department of State's Berlin Document Center and other World War II-era captured documents.

Regional Archives

NARA has 13 regional archives where the public can do research. They are located in or near Boston, New York, Philadelphia, Atlanta, Chicago, St. Louis, Kansas City, Fort Worth, Denver, Riverside and San Francisco, Seattle, and Anchorage.

Archived records of regional significance, as well as, in some locations, immigration records, are available for use by the public in these regional archives.

Presidential Libraries

NARA operates the libraries and museums of the 13 most recent U.S. presidents, beginning with Herbert Hoover, whose library is in West Branch, Iowa. The others are Franklin D. Roosevelt, Hyde Park, New York; Harry S. Truman, Independence, Missouri; Dwight D. Eisenhower, Abilene, Kansas; John F. Kennedy, Boston; Lyndon B. Johnson, Austin; Richard Nixon, Yorba Linda, California; Gerald R. Ford, Ann Arbor (library) and Grand Rapids (museum), Michigan; Jimmy Carter, Atlanta; Ronald Reagan, Simi Valley, California; George H. W. Bush, College Station, Texas; William J. Clinton, Little Rock; George W. Bush, Dallas.

In FY 2012 nearly 2 million people visited exhibits in the presidential library museums; the libraries had more than 10,000 researcher visits. At http://www. archives.gov/presidential-libraries visitors can link to individual presidential library websites to learn about the lives of the presidents and the times in which they served.

Federal Records Centers

NARA also serves federal agencies, the courts, and Congress by providing records storage, reference service, training, advice, and guidance on many issues relating to records management.

A network of 18 Federal Records Centers (FRCs) stores 28.5 million cubic feet (about 71 billion pages) of non-current records for 400 agencies. In FY 2012 these records centers replied to more than 8.2 million requests for information and records, including more than 1.5 million requests for information regarding military and civilian service records provided by the National Personnel Records Center in St. Louis.

In addition to the military and civilian divisions of the National Personnel Records Center in St. Louis, NARA has records centers in or near Atlanta; Boston; Chicago; Dayton; Denver; Fort Worth; Kansas City; Kingsridge, Ohio; Lee's Summit, Missouri; Lenexa, Kansas; Philadelphia; Pittsfield, Massachusetts; Riverside, California; San Francisco; Seattle; and Suitland, Maryland.

Archives Library Information Center

The Archives Library Information Center (ALIC) provides access to information on American history and government, archival administration, information management, and government documents. ALIC is located in the National Archives at College Park. Customers also can visit ALIC on the Internet at http://www. archives.gov/research/alic, where they will find "Reference at Your Desk" Internet links, staff-compiled bibliographies and publications, and an online library catalog. ALIC can be reached by telephone at 301-837-3415 in College Park.

Government Documents

Government publications are generally available to researchers at many of the 1,250 congressionally designated federal depository libraries throughout the

United States. A record set of these publications also is part of NARA's archival holdings. Publications of the U.S. Government (Record Group 287) is a collection of selected publications of government agencies, arranged by the SuDoc classification system devised by the Office of the Superintendent of Documents, U.S. Government Printing Office (GPO).

The core of the collection is a library established in 1895 by GPO's Public Documents Division. By 1972, when NARA acquired the library, it included official publications dating from the early years of the federal government and selected publications produced for and by federal government agencies. Since 1972 the 25,000-cubic-foot collection has been augmented periodically with accessions of government publications selected by the Office of the Superintendent of Documents as a byproduct of its cataloging activity. As with the federal depository library collections, the holdings in NARA's Record Group 287 comprise only a portion of all U.S. government publications.

NARA Publications

Historically NARA has published guides and indexes to various portions of its archival holdings; many of these are still in print, though the most up-to-date information about NARA holdings now is available almost exclusively through online searches at http://www.archives.gov. The agency also publishes informational leaflets and brochures and NARA's flagship publication, *Prologue,* a scholarly magazine published quarterly. Some publications appear on NARA's website, at http://www.archives.gov/publications/online.html, and many are available from NARA's Customer Service Center in College Park, by calling 800-234-8861 or 866-272-6272 (in the Washington, D.C., area, 301-837-2000) or faxing 301-837-0483. The NARA website's publications homepage, http://www.archives.gov/publications, provides more detailed information about available publications and ordering.

General-interest books about NARA and its holdings that will appeal to anyone with an interest in U.S. history, exhibition catalogs, and facsimiles of certain documents are published by the Foundation for the National Archives and are available for sale at the National Archives Shop in Washington and on the NARA website's eStore page, http://www.archives.gov.shop.

Federal Register

The *Federal Register* is the daily gazette of the U.S. government, containing presidential documents, proposed and final federal regulations, and public notices of federal agencies. It is published by the Office of the Federal Register and printed and distributed by GPO. The two agencies collaborate in the same way to produce the annual revisions of the *Code of Federal Regulations (CFR).* Free access to the full text of the electronic version of the *Federal Register* and *CFR* and to an unofficial, daily-updated electronic *CFR* (the *e-CFR*), is available via http://www.fdsys.gov. Federal Register documents scheduled for future publication are available for public inspection at the Office of the Federal Register (800 North Capitol St. N.W., Washington, DC 20002) or online at the electronic Public Inspection Desk (http://www.federalregister.gov/public-inspection). Access to rules published in the *Fed-*

eral Register and open for public comment and a means to provide comments is provided through http://www.federalregister.gov or through the multiagency website http://www.regulations.gov.

The full catalog of other Federal Register publications is posted at http://www. ofr.gov and includes the *Compilation of Presidential Documents, Public Papers of the President,* slip laws, *U.S. Statutes at Large,* and the *United States Government Manual.* Printed or microfiche editions of Federal Register publications also are maintained at federal depository libraries (http://www.gpo.gov/libraries). The Public Law Electronic Notification Service (PENS) is a free subscription e-mail service available for notification of recently enacted public laws. Varied subscriptions to the daily *Federal Register* are available from http://www.federalregister. gov. Additional information about Federal Register programs appears on Facebook (http://www.facebook.com/federalregister) and Twitter (@FedRegister).

The Office of the Federal Register also publishes information about its ministerial responsibilities associated with the operation of the Electoral College and ratification of constitutional amendments and provides access to related records. Publication information concerning laws, regulations, and presidential documents and services is available from the Office of the Federal Register (telephone 202-741-6070). Information on Federal Register finding aids, the Electoral College, and constitutional amendments is available through http://www.archives.gov/federal-register.

Publications can be ordered by contacting GPO at http://bookstore.gpo.gov, or by toll-free telephone at 866-512-1800. To submit orders by fax or by mail, see http://bookstore.gpo.gov/help/index.jsp.

Grants

The National Historical Publications and Records Commission (NHPRC) is the grantmaking affiliate of NARA's national grants program. The Archivist of the United States chairs the commission and makes grants on its recommendation. NHPRC's 14 other members represent the president (two appointees), the Supreme Court, the Senate and House of Representatives, the departments of State and Defense, the Librarian of Congress, the American Association for State and Local History, the American Historical Association, the Association for Documentary Editing, the National Association of Government Archives and Records Administrators, the Organization of American Historians, and the Society of American Archivists.

The commission carries out a statutory mission to ensure understanding of the nation's past by promoting nationwide the preservation and use of essential historical documents. The commission supports the creation and publication of documentary editions and research in the management and preservation of authentic electronic records, and it works in partnership with a national network of state archives and state historical records advisory boards to develop a national archival infrastructure. NHPRC grants help state and local governments, and archives, universities, historical societies, professional organizations, and other nonprofit organizations establish or strengthen archival programs, improve training and techniques, preserve and process records collections, and provide access to them through finding aids, digitization of collections, and documentary editions of the papers of significant historical figures and movements in American history. For more information about the commission, visit http://www.archives.gov/nhprc. For more information about the projects it supports, go to http://www.facebook.com/nhprc.

Customer Service

Few records repositories serve as many customers as NARA. In FY 2012 there were about 123,000 researcher visits to NARA facilities nationwide, including archives, presidential libraries, and federal records centers. At the same time, well over a million customers requested information in writing.

NARA also provided informative public programs at its various facilities for nearly 15,000 people. More than a million visited the National Archives Experience in Washington, and exhibits in the presidential library museums were visited by more than 2.4 million.

NARA also maintains an Internet form (http://www.archives.gov/contact/inquire-form.html) to facilitate continuous feedback from customers about what is most important to them and what NARA might do better to meet their needs.

Administration

The head of NARA is David S. Ferriero, who was appointed Archivist of the United States in late 2009 by President Obama. As of FY 2012 the agency employed approximately 3,380 people, of whom about 2,670 were full-time permanent staff members working at 44 locations.

Federal Library Information Network (FEDLINK)

Blane K. Dessy
Executive Director

During fiscal year (FY) 2012 the Federal Library Information and Information Center Committee (FLICC) made systemic revisions to the organization's bylaws. The newly adopted bylaws create a single organization, authorized by the FEDLINK statute, which performs the tasks of FEDLINK (FLICC's cooperative network) as well as incorporating the FLICC responsibilities. The bylaws streamline the organization's governance structure, create a more transparent organization, encourage greater membership participation, and create a single "brand" for the organization.

Now called simply FEDLINK, the organization's new mission is a merger of the FLICC and FEDLINK missions, goals, and objectives into four distinct responsibilities: improve utilization of federal library and information resources; provide the most cost-effective and efficient way to procure necessary services and materials for federal libraries and information centers; serve as a forum for learning and discussion about federal library and information policies, programs and procedures; and help inform Congress, federal agencies, and others concerned with libraries and information centers.

The bylaws then created the FEDLINK Advisory Board (FAB) to propose program policies, objectives, and plans; recommend an annual budget; establish committees, working groups, and advisory councils; and keep the federal library community apprised of issues relating to FEDLINK programs, services, policies, and objectives, and recommend solutions for settling disputes and interpret matters relating to all FEDLINK business. FAB replaces both the FLICC Executive Board and the FEDLINK Advisory Committee and serves as a governing body for the entire FEDLINK program.

Throughout FY 2012 FAB focused bimonthly meetings on a variety of broad federal information issues including the Federal Library Shared Collection Management Program, FEDLINK Research Agenda, Federal Science Repository Service, Library of Congress area studies collection research, health information collection research, and the development of Native American Tribal Libraries.

The new FEDLINK bylaws also redefined the roles of working groups by delineating those that function as administrative standing committees and those that are mission-supportive and ongoing. New to the FEDLINK structure are task- and/or objective-driven ad hoc committees that disband when their mission is complete. All of these committees, working groups, and ad hoc committees completed an ambitious agenda in FY 2012. Notably, the FEDGrey working group achieved a great deal in its first year. The working group sponsored a speaker from NIST (the National Institute of Standards and Technology) on the "Research Library's Role in Publishing and Disseminating NIST's Gray Literature" and developed a prototype website that focuses on Cold War era gray literature to promote access to related collections.

The Awards Committee announced the following awards: 2011 Federal Library/Information Center of the Year, large library/information center (staff of 11 or more): Woodworth Consolidated Library, DFMWR, Recreation Division and

TRADOC, Fort Gordon, Georgia; small library/information center (staff of ten or fewer employees): Eglin Air Force Base Library, Florida; 2011 Federal Librarian of the Year: MaryLynn Francisco, GEOINT Research Center, National Geospatial-Intelligence Agency, Springfield, Virginia; 2011 Federal Library Technician of the Year: Leanna Bush, U.S. Army Medical Research Institute of Chemical Defense, Aberdeen Proving Ground, Maryland.

The Education Working Group sponsored a variety of programs for members of the federal library and information center community. These programs focused on such topics as preservation, searching the invisible Web, the future of the 1410 employment series, gray literature, and "big data." A special five-day institute for federal library technicians focused on developing technology competencies.

The new interagency Health Information Technology Advisory Committee launched a three-part series that explores the value that library and information science (LIS) professionals bring to health care in the areas of clinical care, public health, and the overall reduction of costs. The first study looks at the roles and partnerships in which LIS professionals engage to support clinical care.

The Human Resources Working Group initiated a series of discussions, workshops, and forums to engage the library community on the future of the 1410 series. The working group surveyed the federal library community and commissioned the Federal Research Division (FRD) to analyze the results of that survey, as well as historical discussions, and deliver a final report.

The NewFeds working group hosted its second annual library conference and training on desktop research tools. The NewFeds were also featured in an article on *Library Journal*'s website, "New Feds Working Group Supports Librarians in Government." The co-chairs also collaborated on an article, "Growing the NewFeds: A Brief History of the New Community of LIS Professionals," for *Best Practices for Government Libraries: Pushing Boundaries.*

The Preservation Working Group focused on providing a number of educational programs featuring events from its Safety Net program, studying emergency response and mitigation techniques to stabilize paper- and film-based materials, along with digital disaster planning. It also sponsored two programs presented as part of the first FEDLINK Spring Exposition on the role of preservation in federal collections and available preservation services for federal libraries.

In conjunction with the working groups, FEDLINK offered 30 seminars, workshops, brokered conferences, and lunchtime discussions to more than 1,700 members of the federal library and information center community. Under the new bylaws requirements, FEDLINK also launched a semiannual exposition series. The first exposition, "Brave New World for Federal Librarians," in May 2012, featured programming around the major trends FEDLINK identified in its environmental scan. The new series, plus enhanced webcasting of both larger and smaller programs, extended the outreach to and the participation of the federal information professional community.

Another outgrowth of the environmental scan was the development of the FEDLINK research agenda. In response to the trends identified in the development of its business plan, FEDLINK further defined six research areas as priorities for innovative investment. In fall 2012 FEDLINK hosted its first "brainstorming dialogue" to investigate research priorities and posted a draft research agenda on its website for public comment. Participants in the dialogue shared their thoughts in facilitated roundtable discussions. Participants identified important issues and proposed areas for future work and collaboration with FEDLINK. The dialogue influenced the future directions of the FEDLINK research agenda, ensuring that the needs and interests of the community were reflected in the proposed program areas, and more importantly garnered support for FEDLINK's leadership role in research initiatives across the federal information community.

FEDLINK continued to enhance its fiscal operations while providing its members with $80.3 million in transfer-pay services, $7 million in direct-pay services, and an estimated $61.7 million in "direct express" services, saving federal agencies more than $29 million in vendor volume discounts and approximately $43 million more in cost avoidance.

FEDLINK also completed work with the Office of Management and Budget (OMB) and the General Services Administration (GSA) to be designated the lead agent for strategic sourcing of information resources procurement for federal agencies. FEDLINK, which serves all three branches of the federal government as well as the District of Columbia, is the first non-GSA agency to receive such a designation. FEDLINK formed two commodity councils to concentrate on specific subject areas first, one for legal information resources and the other for resources focusing on science, technology, engineering, and mathematics (STEM) subjects.

To further its work toward shared collection management across the federal government, FEDLINK sponsored analysis done at the Library of Congress comparing federal library collections. Use of a tool provided by OCLC gave some preliminary information, such as the percentage of unique items individual federal libraries have identified in OCLC's WorldCat network of library content and services as held in their collections. A pilot group of libraries shared their OPAC records with the Library of Congress for more in-depth analysis in FY 2013.

FEDLINK gave federal agencies cost-effective access to automated information retrieval services for online research, cataloging, and resource sharing. FEDLINK members procured print serials, electronic journals, books and other publications, document delivery, online language-learning systems, digitization, preservation, and other library support services via Library of Congress/FEDLINK contracts with approximately 150 companies. The program obtained further discounts through consortia and enterprise-wide licenses for journals, aggregated information retrieval services, and electronic books.

FEDLINK awarded contracts for an integrated library system for one agency, two staffing contracts for another agency, and cataloging contracts for two agencies. It renewed a contract with Information International Associates to support CENDI, the interagency working group of senior scientific and technical information managers from 14 federal agencies. FEDLINK established an interagency agreement with the Office of Science and Technology Information at the Department of Energy to support Science.gov, a Web portal integrating access to federal science and technology information, and another interagency agreement with the National Archives and Records Administration (NARA) for remote storage of federal collections. FEDLINK also awarded 16 contracts to support preservation, conservation, and digitization services.

FEDLINK's budgeting efforts projected both costs and revenue for FY 2013, looking at both private sector and historic costs based on vendor and GAO predictions. After examining FEDLINK program growth and realized savings through program management and program reserves, FEDLINK's governing bodies recommended that fees remain the same in FY 2013.

Five-Year FEDLINK Business Plan

FEDLINK published its newest five-year business plan in FY 2012. After a thorough environmental scan and an analysis of constituent surveys combined with efforts to define the federal information market, FEDLINK established a new approach to its business planning and committed to the "balanced score card" methodology. Below are the results for FY 2012.

Goal 1—Coordinate cooperative activities and services among federal libraries, information centers, and other information users

Outcomes and Results Statements

- Redefine the membership of the federal information community to include all providers, users, and suppliers of information and data. Both the Library of Congress and FAB approved the new FEDLINK bylaws in FY 2012. The bylaws expand membership and representation in the FLICC community to all federal agencies. FEDLINK now defines membership as any agency with an interest in libraries and information.

- Combine the unique expertise of the Library of Congress and federal libraries and information centers, professional associations, and information organizations. Libraries across the federal government often have unique expertise or develop groundbreaking programs or services, not only for themselves but also for other libraries and the public. This federal creativity has not been sufficiently studied or coordinated in the past to promote significant change. As one of its tasks, FEDLINK has begun to look at the federal libraries and information centers as a single enterprise that can work together to achieve greater results and greater visibility for libraries in the government and nationally.

- Create a flexible intergovernmental infrastructure to take advantage of the changing needs for information and information environments within the federal government. The information services profession is changing rapidly because of a number of circumstances, including technology, publisher consolidation, new audiences, and new areas of information services. To respond to this, FEDLINK must operate in a flexible, responsive manner to the needs of its members as well as external circumstances that require adaptation. With the development of the new bylaws and expanded membership, the formation of new FEDLINK working groups, commodity councils, and advisory boards, the creation of a research agenda, and new government-wide studies, FEDLINK began to position itself to have the flexible intergovernmental infrastructure it needs to respond to challenges and opportunities. To this end, FEDLINK began partnering with FRD and with GSA, OMB, and the Small Business Administration to create new programs and flexibilities.

- Provide professional expertise to facilitate research, analysis, consultation, reference, resource sharing, organization of knowledge, and management of information services within the federal government. By leveraging the resources in its network, FEDLINK continued its work with FRD on the study of the federal information marketplace; with OMB and GSA to conduct analysis and planning for federal information acquisitions; with the office of the Library of Congress's assistant librarian for library services for collection management and planning; with the Department of the Interior on Native American libraries; with the National Information Standards Organization (NISO) on metadata issues, and many other efforts. FEDLINK members also collaborated on the various FEDLINK standing and ad hoc working groups, committees, commodity councils, and advisory boards, and used professional association meetings and electronic communication tools such as FEDLIB to exchange information and share resources.

- Create communities of practice to support the various roles of information professionals. Since their beginning, FLICC and FEDLINK have created communities of practice in a variety of areas including library technology, human resources, education, and marketing. In FY 2012 FEDLINK created two new working groups: the Library Technicians Working Group and the Federal Depository Library Program Working Group. Additionally, FEDLINK created two commodity councils, in Legal Resources and Science/Technology/Engineering/Medical (STEM) Resources, to plan for the improved acquisition of electronic information retrieval services. FEDLINK continued to promote and support federal participation in wider communities of practice in library and other information-related organizations.

Finally, in response to member concerns about membership inclusion, FEDLINK began use of a new distance learning and collaboration platform—iCohere. This platform permitted greater participation from federal libraries regardless of geographic location, and pilot projects suggest it can provide a foundation for expanding Web-based communities of practice.

Strategies

- Implement new FEDLINK bylaws. Throughout FY 2012 FEDLINK staff continued to seek approval for the new bylaws from the Library of Congress administration and membership. Both of these efforts were successful, and the new bylaws became effective on October 1

- Coordinate annual planning of working groups. The FEDLINK working groups comprise an important part of the ongoing work of the organization. At the beginning of FY 2012 FEDLINK convened multiple working groups to develop individual plans as well as look at collaborative opportunities for work and products.

- Develop a program approach for two membership expositions each year. FY 2012 was the first year for the newly established FEDLINK expositions. FEDLINK staff, led by the Publications and Education Office, planned the event, including programs, speakers, logistics, and publicity. The first exposition, in May 2012, was successful and work began immediately for the fall exposition in November.

- Expand the universe of potential FEDLINK users (i.e., procurement officials, general counsels, content creators, financial officers, vendors) through increased market penetration. As the newly designated "Executive Agent for Information Resources in the Federal Government," FEDLINK contacted current and potential new constituencies. In an effort to expand its vendor portfolio, staff contacted new vendors in the data analytic and mobile application sectors, engaged the general business community through the publication of a FEDLINK Vendor Communication Plan and survey in FedBizOpps.gov—a government website advertising federal business opportunities—and began planning a training program for procurement officers of information resources. FEDLINK also offered vendor sessions at the FEDLINK expositions and exhibited at the annual Special Libraries Association conference and the National Contract Managers Association annual meeting in Washington, D.C.

- Increase outreach to FEDLINK affiliate groups. FEDLINK strives to serve as a focal point for the various groups and associations that involve federal libraries. To that end, it created a space on its website for various affiliate groups as well as extending invitations to multiple library and information associations to appoint liaisons to the FEDLINK Advisory Board. The goal of the liaison program is to enhance information sharing and planning at FAB meetings.

- Manage virtual federal library census. The virtual federal library census is a vital tool in FEDLINK's planning and working with the many federal libraries around the world. Feedback from the member and vendor communities suggests that they consider it a valuable tool. Throughout FY 2012 FEDLINK and FRD updated the latest directory as more federal libraries offered their data for inclusion.

- Offer marketing, research, analysis, and consultation assistance to members. FEDLINK began an extensive research agenda project, focusing initially on the nexus of health information technology and librarianship, the analysis of prices paid for information resources across the federal government, and the comparison of federal library collections, beginning with selected science and technology libraries. FEDLINK staff members in both the network office and fiscal services also worked regularly with members on both programmatic and financial issues over the year. These issues include analysis and planning for new solicitations, consultation on ongoing projects in preservation, digitization, and use of the Web, and financial analysis and reconciliation tasks.

- Demonstrate federal information community uses of new technologies as a part of educational programs. As part of the FEDLINK expositions, staff and members have presented programs on new information technologies used in federal libraries and information centers. Staff members visited various federal libraries to learn more about innovative uses of technology and facilitated sharing such information among libraries. FEDLINK also increased its use of distance learning technology, not only to disseminate FEDLINK programming but also to encourage members to use this new learning technology in their own planning.

- Issue a federal shared collection management plan. Work began in FY 2012 on a long-term project to compare federal library collections with a goal of being able to issue a shared collection management plan in FY 2016. FED-LINK investigated use of an OCLC tool from which it learned some basic contours of federal collections and how they compare to collections among federal libraries and around the world. This led to a determination to work more deeply to analyze collections using off-the-shelf tools and by collecting data directly from federal libraries. During FY 2012 staff identified appropriate software, developed appropriate and reliable algorithms, and began analysis with the intake of approximately 20 million bibliographic records from selected science and technology libraries. Initial analysis of these bibliographic records has produced useful results. As FEDLINK continues to expand its bibliographic database and to conduct further analysis, it will be possible to construct a portrait of federal library collections and to develop from that the beginnings of a shared collection management plan.

Goal 2: Serve as a forum to consider and make recommendations to the federal information community

Outcomes and Results Statements

- Create research agenda for the federal information community. By the end of FY 2012 FEDLINK had developed its federal research agenda based upon the FEDLINK Business Plan and Environmental Scan. FEDLINK proposed a set of broad research themes and vetted the themes with a group of FEDLINK staff, members, and liaisons for input.

- Conduct research and report on issues and policies that affect the federal information community. FEDLINK continued its examination during FY 2012 of the federal information marketplace with the collaboration of FRD. Four quarterly reports were compiled and published on the federal government's expenditure on information resources. This is the only publication that tracks federal spending on information content, and FEDLINK has become the de facto "analyst" for this marketplace. In addition FEDLINK has conducted research on the government's employment series 1410 and the future of the library profession in the federal government, the intersection of new health information technology and information professionals, federal library collections, and other topics.

- Identify, prioritize, and recommend solutions to meet the challenges of providing information services to the federal government. FEDLINK built on an environmental scan of the information ecosystem that identified seven major trends expected to affect current and future information services. This scan formed the basis for the strategic planning and ongoing work of the FEDLINK Advisory Board, the FEDLINK working groups, research activity, and new information products and services for FEDLINK members. Based on consultation with members, FEDLINK identified, prioritized, and recommended solutions.

- Establish FEDLINK as the library and information science authority of the federal government. FEDLINK undertook several initiatives during FY 2012 to become the library and information science authority in the federal government. First it revised its bylaws to become a more inclusive and more transparent agency. It applied to both OMB and GSA to become the executive agent for information resources in the federal government, and received this designation in June 2012. FEDLINK convened two commodity councils, increased vendor engagement, began work on a major new procurement vehicle for electronic information retrieval products, improved its distance learning capacity, and began to develop a research capacity.

Strategies

- Issue policy and administrative reports on issues affecting the federal information community and specialized topics in federal content management. To further its work toward shared collection management across the federal government, FEDLINK sponsored analysis done at the Library of Congress comparing federal library collections. Use of a tool provided by OCLC gave some preliminary information such as the percentage of unique items individual federal libraries have identified in OCLC WorldCat as held in their collections. A pilot group of libraries shared their OPAC records with the library for more in-depth analysis in FY 2013. FEDLINK issued a report analyzing the cost benefits of use of its procurement vehicles compared with other acquisition resources. The report provides a transparent framework under which agencies can benchmark their costs against a generalized standard.

- Conduct formal research on the information market, the federal library and information center community, and the profession. FEDLINK commissioned FRD to research and report on the "current landscape of the federal marketplace regarding the acquisition of information goods and services, including electronic databases, books, and serials." The report analyzed data from the first quarter of FY 1979 through the third quarter of FY 2012 on the amount federal agencies spent on products and services. FRD issued four quarterly reports on this data throughout FY 2012.

- Maximize opportunities for augmenting information resources, and research capacity across the federal government. FEDLINK gave federal agencies cost-effective access to automated information retrieval services for online research, cataloging, and resource sharing. FEDLINK members procured print serials, electronic journals, books and other publications, document delivery, online language-learning systems, digitization, preservation, and other library support services via Library of Congress/ FEDLINK contracts with approximately 150 companies. The program obtained further discounts through consortia and enterprise-wide licenses for journals, aggregated information retrieval services, and electronic books. FEDLINK renewed a contract with Information International Associates to support CENDI, the interagency working group of senior scientific and technical information managers from 14 federal agencies. It established an interagency agreement with the Office of Science and Technology Information at the Department of Energy to support Science.gov, a Web portal integrating access to federal science and technology information, and another interagency agreement with NARA for remote storage of federal collections. FEDLINK also awarded 16 contracts to support preservation, conservation, and digitization services. It assisted contracting officers and members in gathering evaluations of vendor performance and successfully resolving potential performance problems. FEDLINK also investigated two new opportunities for information resources in data analytics and in mobile applications for information resources. In addition, in FY 2012 FEDLINK began work on the development and implementation of a research agenda based upon its environmental scan of the information ecosystem.

- Expand participation in information conferences and with the federal procurement community. FEDLINK exhibited at the Military Libraries Workshop, the American Library Association Annual Conference, and the Special Libraries Association conference as well as other national conferences.

Goal 3: Encourage and promote development of librarians and information professionals

Outcomes and Results Statements

- Strengthen management and services of federal libraries and information centers. FEDLINK has worked to strengthen management and services of federal libraries and information centers through continuous educational offerings including the new FEDLINK expositions, the management of approximately 150 vendor contracts and modifications, research into significant information issues, and engagement with librarians and information professionals globally. In addition FEDLINK has worked collaboratively with other organizations to expand training and awareness of management and information issues.

- Serve as a steward of federal information resources. FEDLINK firmly believes in the proper stewardship of federal information resources and, to that end, has established contracts with more than 30 preservation and digitization vendors for services. FEDLINK also sponsored multiple training programs regarding resource preservation, both in traditional formats and digital content. FEDLINK worked collaboratively with the Library of Congress to educate federal information professionals about current issues and to encourage them to develop emergency plans and procedures for potential disasters. In FY 2012 FEDLINK entered into a cooperative agreement with NARA for the remote storage of little-used federal library materials, thus ensuring their preservation for future generations.

- Encourage effective use of information resources through expert assistance to end-users. FEDLINK's Network Office and Fiscal Office provides ongoing assistance to members on a variety of topics ranging from procurement planning, development and review of solicitations, contract awards, and account management. FEDLINK has expertise both in the programmatic and financial issues surrounding information resources. FEDLINK staff members have been available for single or group consultations or training, presentations, and advice.

- Support the sharing of information resources and the transition to new formats and media. FEDLINK conducted many events for members in FY 2012 to support the sharing of information about resources and services. It hosted 29 vendor demonstrations for 153 members and investigated adding two new product categories into FEDLINK: data analytics and mobile applications.

Strategies

- Make programs and services more readily available to professionals in diverse communities and locations. FEDLINK increased its distance learning offerings by using Web conferencing software for a number of its free events, and routinely incorporated electronic versions of PowerPoint and other presentation materials to enhance access to the resources available at educational programs. To make the discussions and presentations available for members in remote locations, staff used Web conferencing services to offer interactive attendance and to record sessions for later use.
- Provide information resource portfolio management training for federal acquisition professionals. With its designation as the executive agent for information resources, FEDLINK began to develop plans for a training package for vendor portfolio management. This training is for information and acquisitions professionals to help them perform more knowledgeable and more efficient information procurements. The basis for strategic sourcing of information products and services is an established body of knowledge and practices that lead to successful conclusions.
- Offer relevant and diverse educational opportunities that support the development of professional competencies. In conjunction with the working groups, FEDLINK offered a total of 30 seminars, workshops, brokered conferences, and lunchtime discussions to members of the federal library and information center community. Institutes and workshops looked at preservation, searching the invisible Web, the future of the 1410 series, gray literature, and "big data" to more than 1,700 attendees. A special five-day Institute for Federal Library Technicians focused on developing technology competencies. The ongoing FLICC Great Escapes series returned in FY 2012 with library tours at the Brookings Institution, the Institute of Peace, the Daughters of the American Revolution, the National Portrait Gallery, the Government Printing Office, and NASA Goddard Space Flight Center.

Goal 4: Support procurement efforts to centralize and streamline options to provide efficient and cost-effective use of federal library and information resources and services

Outcomes and Results Statements

- Use strategic sourcing methods to create a fact-based and analytical process to optimize federal information procurement. Throughout FY 2012 FEDLINK used strategic sourcing methods to optimize federal information procurement. FEDLINK first identified the commodity (information resources), conducted thorough and ongoing research into the federal government's spending by agency and vendor, created projections for future government spending and possible savings, and developed a plan to reach agencies and vendors for implementation in FY 2013 and to report to the Federal Strategic Sourcing Initiatives dashboard. FEDLINK established two commodity councils that assisted in developing the framework for a data call to be implemented in early FY 2013 to collect more-detailed information about procurement of information resources, and provided input on terms and conditions for contracts that will result in more effective and less costly use of information resources. This methodology is consistent with GSA's practices in strategic sourcing.

- Assist federal agencies with information resource audits to ensure effective and efficient use of resources while reducing total costs. In response to FRD's research into individual agency spending and vendor sales research, FEDLINK remains committed to communicating frequently and constructively with industry early in the acquisition process to gain market/industry information to ensure a more successful outcome; ensuring that small businesses are included in communications about agency requirements through agency postings and vendor outreach efforts; engaging in timely, constructive, and professional information exchanges with the vendor community, with an emphasis on high-dollar, complex procurements; reducing unnecessary barriers to attract new vendors and enhance competition, especially where there is a pattern of receiving only one quotation or proposal; protecting proprietary information contained in proposals and other information obtained during the source selection process, including preventing inadvertent release through the Freedom of Information Act (FOIA) process or divulging vendors' confidential information or source selection information to those without a legitimate need to know; identifying requirements likely to involve opportunity for additional communication with industry and publicizing communication engagement opportunities on the Federal Business Opportunities website, including pre-solicitation and/or pre-proposal conferences for high-dollar, high-risk, or complex programs, or those that fail to attract new vendors during re-competitions; developing detailed profiles of information commodities including spend profiles and specifications.

- Conduct market analysis to identify supply and demand levers, new suppliers, and buyer advantage. FEDLINK combined its approach to both of these strategies in collaboration with FRD. It has developed a detailed profile of both federal agency spending and vendor sales spanning multiple years and published this research on a quarterly basis. At the same time, FEDLINK has worked with its two new commodity councils to identify contract and licensing issues. FEDLINK has also been conducting research into other consortial practices as well as engaging vendors to determine ways to maximize federal savings and enhance access to information resources.

- Develop and issue contract requests based on sourcing strategy. Throughout FY 2012 FEDLINK worked with its two commodity councils to prepare for new solicitations in FY 2013. Sourcing strategy calls for the involvement of knowledgeable commodity councils to assist staff in preparing solicitations. Analysis identified areas for potential cost savings and terms and conditions that would promote more effective federal access to information resources. Additionally, sourcing strategy calls for vendor engagement and, to that end, FEDLINK conducted a series of vendor meetings, published a vendor communication plan on FedBizOpps, and conducted a survey to gather information from vendors about conducting more successful solicitations and contract management tasks.
- Conduct negotiations, evaluate proposals, and award contracts. FY 2012 was a year of contract renewals for FEDLINK with some small, specialized new procurements for FEDLINK members. However, in preparation for FY 2013, FEDLINK planned its acquisitions and its sourcing strategies for electronic information retrieval, some specialized library support contracts, digital preservation, data analytics, and possibly mobile applications.
- Establish and use structured metrics and periodic review of contractor performance. FEDLINK has been studying the most effective metrics used with information contractors to incorporate strong metrics and periodic review of contractor performance into new solicitations. It has also been studying ways to ensure that contractors provide consistent, reliable metrics on a regular basis to both FEDLINK and its members. Finally, as part of the larger federal government strategic sourcing effort, FEDLINK will be gathering metrics in three primary areas: money saved by the federal government, the percentage of federal spending under FEDLINK vehicles, and the amount of small business involvement in federal contracting in information resources.
- Offer new and competitively priced goods and services to reach new federal clients and balance sources of revenue. FY 2012 was a planning year for FEDLINK as it assumed its role as GSA's executive agent for information resources.

Strategies

- Work collaboratively with OMB and GSA on strategic sourcing initiative. FEDLINK started the single solicitation process in FY 2013 for electronic information retrieval services that include the legal and STEM resources.
- Cultivate a dynamic menu of consultative services targeted to federal information professionals. FEDLINK continued to conduct market research as the basis for planning and developing successful acquisitions, and shared results with federal customers as well as using results to inform its activities.
- Improve acquisition planning by identifying product and services offerings for 2012–2016 and 2017–2021. For the duration of FEDLINK's current

business plan, staff members will continue to monitor trends and collaborate with GSA to develop a larger and more robust product-offering portfolio. FEDLINK's first initiative in this strategy has been the investigation of opportunities for both data analytics and mobile applications. Staff continued to broaden their experience and knowledge of further markets through acquiring goods and services for individual agencies, e.g., integrated library systems, library Web and database development, staffing, and special projects.

- Engage FAB as a primary commodity council. FAB, the FEDLINK Advisory Board, serves as the major policy and planning body for FEDLINK and, as such, is serving as the primary commodity council for FEDLINK. It provided input on pricing issues and on license and contract terms and conditions and assisted in recruiting members to the subject-specialized commodity councils. As FEDLINK undergoes more transition in FY 2013 and beyond, FAB will continue to provide guidance to FEDLINK staff.
- Improve acquisition workflow. As the executive agent for information resources, FEDLINK has begun to plan strategically to develop a more sophisticated acquisition-planning model.
- Monitor federal information market on a quarterly basis. FEDLINK initiated its work with FRD and published this research on its website four times in FY 2012.
- Identify future service areas/investigate offering library function contracts (e.g., technical processing, temporary staffing). In addition to the traditional categories of information resources, FEDLINK staff also began in FY 2012 to explore the possibility of adding staffing and training contracts to its vendor portfolio, and continued to explore the market for library support software.

Goal: 5: Manage proactively to achieve results

Outcomes and Results Statements

- Gather feedback from customers and vendors annually and longitudinally. FEDLINK published its Vendor Communication Plan on FedBizOpps and shortly thereafter released a survey asking vendors about contracting difficulties, contract licensing terms, pricing, small business involvement, and metrics. As of the time this report was prepared, FEDLINK had received 66 responses to the ongoing survey.
- Develop metrics to establish performance standards and create a balanced scorecard and dashboard mechanisms. Throughout FY 2012 FEDLINK researched and began preliminary work on both its performance standards and the criteria for its balanced scorecard dashboard. By the end of the year staff members had established all criteria and began developing measurement tools for each discrete item.

Strategies

- Employ consistent business practices and ensure timely and efficient work-flows. In FY 2012 FEDLINK took preliminary steps to establish a contract to study FEDLINK's acquisition planning, management, and contracting functions.
- Train staff to keep pace with new skills needed in their work. FEDLINK staff members are encouraged to pursue training to keep them apprised of new developments and up to date with new duties and technologies.
- Develop long-term strategy for reserve account development and use. While FEDLINK must maintain at least two fiscal quarters of FEDLINK operating expenses, there are limitations to the reserves on account. To respond to these requirements, FEDLINK staff began planning how best to use any excess funds.
- Implement e-invoicing. FEDLINK continued planning in FY 2012 for e-invoicing implementation, studying options under its projected new fiscal systems.
- Ensure successful internal audits. FEDLINK passed its internal audits.
- Ensure appropriate staff training and certifications. FEDLINK staff began in FY 2012 to refresh, or initiated required contracting representative training to maintain, their continued COR designations.
- Successfully implement SYMIN II and FEDLINK Customer Account Management System (FCAM) modules. Extensive work was completed through FY 2012 to prepare FEDLINK for the transition to the SYMIN II system and the new FEDLINK Customer Account Management System.
- Update and validate the methodology used to calculate cost avoidance and cost savings for members. FEDLINK updated its cost savings and cost avoidance study during the fiscal year. Based on the new calculations, the study found that the full-service FEDLINK strategic sourcing model replicates the strategic sourcing savings at the higher end with an anticipated 20 percent rate reduction.

FEDLINK Fiscal Operations

FEDLINK continued to enhance its fiscal operations while providing its members with $80.3 million in transfer-pay services, $7 million in direct-pay services, and an estimated $61.7 million in the "direct express" services, saving federal agencies more than $29 million in vendor volume discounts and approximately $43 million more in cost avoidance.

FEDLINK Budget and Finance Committee

In the spring quarter the FEDLINK Budget and Finance Committee developed the FY 2013 budget and fee structure. The group reviewed survey results from FED-

LINK members and used the results to verify assumptions for the FY 2013 budget. The final budget held membership fees steady for transfer-pay customers at 6 percent on amounts exceeding $100,000; fees remain 6.75 percent below $100,000 and 4 percent on amounts exceeding $1 million. Direct-pay fees remained at FY 2009 levels, as did "direct express" fees of 0.75 percent for all participating commercial online information services vendors.

Transfer Pay Accounts Payable Services

Staff processed vendor 38,202 invoices and earned $13,368 in discounts in excess of interest payment penalties levied for the late payment of invoices to FEDLINK vendors. FEDLINK continued to maintain open accounts for three prior years to pay publications service invoices for members using books and serials services. FEDLINK completed the closing of FY 2007. A total of 75,043 statements are issued to members for the current year and prior years.

Direct Express Services

The FEDLINK Direct Express Program now includes more than 70 vendors offering database retrieval services. The program is set up to provide procurement and payment options similar to those of GSA in which the vendors pay a quarterly service fee to FEDLINK based on customer billings for usage.

National Center for Education Statistics Library Statistics Program

U.S. Department of Education, Institute of Education Sciences
Elementary/Secondary and Libraries Studies Division
1990 K St. N.W., Washington, DC 20006

Tai A. Phan
Program Director

In an effort to collect and disseminate more complete statistical information about libraries, the National Center for Education Statistics (NCES) initiated a formal library statistics program in 1989 that included surveys on academic libraries, school library media centers, public libraries, and state libraries.* At the end of December 2006, the Public Libraries Survey and the State Library Agencies Survey were officially transferred to the Institute of Museum and Library Services (IMLS). The Academic Libraries Survey and the School Library Media Centers Survey continue to be administered and funded by NCES, under the leadership of Tai A. Phan, program director, Library Statistics Program. [For detailed information on the surveys now being handled by IMLS, see "Institute of Museum and Library Services Library Programs" in Part 2 and "Highlights of IMLS Surveys" in Part 4—*Ed.*]

The library surveys conducted by NCES are designed to provide comprehensive nationwide data on the status of libraries. Federal, state, and local officials, professional associations, and local practitioners use these surveys for planning, evaluating, and making policy. These data are also available to researchers and educators.

The Library Statistics Program's Web site, http://nces.ed.gov/surveys/libraries, provides links to data search tools, data files, survey definitions, and survey designs for each survey. The two library surveys are described below.

Academic Libraries

The Academic Libraries Survey (ALS) provides descriptive statistics from more than 3,600 academic libraries in the 50 states, the District of Columbia, and the outlying areas of the United States. NCES surveyed academic libraries on a three-year cycle between 1966 and 1988. From 1988 to 1998, the ALS was a component of the Integrated Postsecondary Education Data System (IPEDS), and was on a two-year cycle. Since fiscal year 2000, the survey has no longer been a component of IPEDS, but remains on a two-year cycle. IPEDS and ALS data can still be linked by the identification codes of the postsecondary education institutions. In aggregate, these data provide an overview of the status of academic libraries nationally and by state. The survey collects data on libraries in the entire universe of degree-granting postsecondary institutions, using a Web-based data collection system.

*The authorization for the National Center for Education Statistics (NCES) to collect library statistics is included in the Education Sciences Reform Act of 2002 (PL 107-279), under Title I, Part C.

The ALS has an established working group composed of representatives of the academic library community. Its mission is to improve data quality and the timeliness of data collection, processing, and release. NCES also works cooperatively with the American Library Association (ALA), the Association of Research Libraries, the Association of College and Research Libraries, and academic libraries.

The survey collects data on the number of academic libraries, operating expenditures, full-time-equivalent library staff, number of service outlets, collection size, circulation, interlibrary loans, number of public service hours, gate count, information services to individuals, library visits, consortia services, number of presentations, attendance at presentations, electronic services, information literacy, and virtual reference. Academic libraries are also asked whether they provide reference services by e-mail or the Internet, have technology for patrons with disabilities, and whether documents are digitized by library staff.

An NCES First Look report "Academic Libraries, 2010" (NCES 2012-365) was released on the NCES Web site in December 2011, as were the final data file and documentation for the 2010 ALS public use data file (NCES 2011-367). NCES has developed a Web-based peer analysis tool for the ALS called "Compare Academic Libraries." This tool currently uses the ALS 2010 data.

Additional information on academic library statistics can be obtained from Tai A. Phan, Elementary/Secondary and Libraries Studies Division, telephone 202-502-7431, e-mail tai.phan@ed.gov.

School Library Media Centers

National surveys of school library media centers in elementary and secondary schools in the United States were conducted in 1958, 1962, 1974, 1978, and 1986, 1993–1994, 1999–2000, and 2003–2004. The 2007–2008 data was available in summer 2009.

NCES, with the assistance of the U.S. Bureau of the Census, conducts the School Library Media Centers Survey as part of the Schools and Staffing Survey (SASS). SASS is the nation's largest sample survey of teachers, schools, and principals in K–12 public and private schools. Data from the school library media center questionnaire provide a national picture of public school library staffing, collections, expenditures, technology, and services. Results from the 2007–2008 survey can be found in *Public and Bureau of Indian Education Elementary and Secondary School Library Media Centers in the United States: 2007–08 Schools and Staffing Survey* (NCES 2009-322).

NCES also published a historical report about school libraries entitled *Fifty Years of Supporting Children's Learning: A History of Public School Libraries and Federal Legislation from 1953–2000*. Drawn from more than 50 sources, this report presents descriptive data about public school libraries since 1953. Along with key characteristics of school libraries, the report also presents national and regional standards, and federal legislation affecting school library media centers. Data from sample surveys are presented at the national, regional, and school levels, and by state.

NCES has included some library-oriented questions relevant to the library usage and skills of the parent and the teacher instruments of the new Early Childhood Longitudinal Study (ECLS). For additional information, visit http://nces.

ed.gov/ecls. Library items also appear in National Household Education Survey (NHES) instruments. For more information about that survey, visit http://nces.ed.gov/nhes.

NCES also included a questionnaire about high school library media centers in the Education Longitudinal Study of 2002 (ELS: 2002). This survey collected data from tenth graders about their schools, their school library media centers, their communities, and their home life. The report, *School Library Media Centers: Selected Results from the Education Longitudinal Study of 2002 (ELS: 2002)* (NCES 2005-302), is available on the NCES Web site. For more information about this survey, visit http://nces.ed.gov/surveys/els2002.

Additional information on school library media center statistics may be obtained from Tai A. Phan, National Center for Education Statistics, telephone 202-502-7431, e-mail tai.phan@ed.gov.

How to Obtain Printed and Electronic Products

Reports are currently published in the First Look format. First Look reports consist of a short collection of tables presenting state and national totals, a survey description, and data highlights. NCES also publishes separate, more in-depth studies analyzing these data.

Internet Access

Many NCES publications (including out-of-print publications) and edited raw data files from the library surveys are available for viewing or downloading at no charge through the Electronic Catalog on the NCES Web site at http://nces.ed.gov/pubsearch.

Ordering Printed Products

Many NCES publications are also available in printed format. To order one free copy of recent NCES reports, contact the Education Publications Center (ED Pubs) at: http://www.edpubs.org, by e-mail at edpubs@edpubs.ed.gov, by toll-free telephone at 877-4-ED-PUBS (1-877-433-7827) or TTY/TDD 877-576-7734, by fax at 703-605-6794, or by mail at ED Pubs, P.O. Box 22207, Alexandria, VA 22304.

Many publications are available through the Educational Resources Information Clearinghouse (ERIC) system. For more information on services and products, visit the EDRS Web site at http://www.eric.ed.gov.

Out-of-print publications and data files may be available through the NCES Electronic Catalog on the NCES Web site at http://nces.ed.gov/pubsearch or through one of the 1,250 federal depository libraries throughout the United States (see http://catalog.gpo.gov/fdlpdir/FDLPdir.jsp). Use the NCES publication number included in the citations for publications and data files to quickly locate items in the NCES Electronic Catalog. Use the GPO number to locate items in a federal depository library.

Defense Technical Information Center

Fort Belvoir, VA 22060
World Wide Web http://www.dtic.mil

Sandy Schwalb
Public Affairs Officer

The Defense Technical Information Center (DTIC) was formed in 1945 to collect and catalog scientific and technical documents from World War II. In the 21st century DTIC continues to serve as a vital link in the transfer of information within the defense community.

The center offers engineers, researchers, scientists, information professionals, and those in laboratories, universities, and the acquisition field access to more than 2 million publications.

DTIC's mission is "to provide essential, technical, research, development, testing, and evaluation information rapidly, accurately, and reliably to support our customers' needs." A Department of Defense (DoD) "field activity," DTIC is in the Office of the Under Secretary of Defense for Acquisition, Technology, and Logistics and reports to the assistant secretary of defense, research, and engineering.

Transition

Christopher Thomas was named administrator of DTIC in March 2012. Thomas had served as acting administrator since December 2010 and as chief technology officer. He also was director of DTIC's information technology directorate and oversaw the development and hosting of more than 70 DoD websites.

During 2012 DTIC leadership began looking at moving the organization from a static repository of information focused on capture, preservation, and paper dissemination to a more technology-focused organization committed to accelerating the flow of information within the DoD community.

Secretary of Defense Award

DTIC was recognized by the secretary of defense in 2012 for its work in the employment of individuals with disabilities and participation in the Workforce Recruitment Program (WRP). A Department of Labor program, WRP connects federal agencies with college students or recent graduates who have disabilities. DTIC has participated in the program since 2008 and has hired 12 WRP summer interns.

In 2010 DTIC began to work with Operation Warfighter (OWF), a DoD program that places wounded, injured, or ill service members in internships with federal government agencies to provide a positive work setting while they recuperate. Eight wounded service members, all of whom had served in Iraq or Afghanistan, have worked as DTIC interns since 2010.

For more information about WRP, visit https://wrp.gov/AboutPre.do. OWF information can be found at http://warriorcare.dodlive.mil/wounded-warrior-resources/operation-warfighter.

Reaching Customers

DTIC offers its suite of services to a diverse population of the defense community. Because of the nature of the information it handles, individuals must be eligible to register with DTIC. By registering, one can take advantage of value-added services, for instance having research performed by trained information professionals and having access to limited (not publicly available) information. More information about who is eligible to register with DTIC can be found at http://www.dtic.mil/dtic/registration.

In addition to individuals in DoD and federal sectors, DTIC's registered customers can be found in academia, the intelligence community, foreign governments (there are negotiated agreements with Australia, Canada, France, Germany, the Netherlands, the Republic of Korea, and the United Kingdom), military school students, and taxpayers.

Among DTIC's more than 25,000 registered users are:

- Acquisition instructors
- Active duty military personnel
- Congressional staff
- DoD contractors
- Faculty and students at military schools
- Historians
- Information professionals/librarians
- Logistics management specialists
- Small business owners
- Security managers
- Software engineers and developers

Creating Tools for DoD

DTIC has been playing a key role within DoD by producing collaboration tools (often not available to the public) to help DoD research and engineering communities work in a secure environment. In order to gain access to many of the organization sites, individuals must be registered with DTIC.

The culture of DoD has encouraged communities to keep their projects closely held. But, in a more networked world, the defense work force needs tools that will help them create, share, and reuse knowledge developed both within DoD and its external partners (in industry and academia, for example). DTIC has made strides in creating and hosting sites aimed at enhancing the ability of DoD to connect internally and externally.

DoDTechipedia

DTIC designed DoDTechipedia, one of the first DoD scientific and technical wikis, in 2008. A secure online system, it facilitates the sharing of knowledge throughout the defense community. A collaborative tool, DoDTechipedia ensures greater transparency and communication among DoD scientists, engineers, and program managers. It helps members of the DoD community collaborate and identify solutions for technology challenges. Among its numerous features are a live forum and interest-area pages for DoD personnel and DoD contractors to work together on challenges and solutions.

DoDTechSpace

A relatively new venture for DTIC, DoDTechSpace is a social business tool. A place for DTIC customers to collaborate, share, find, and post information, DoDTechSpace is a secure application, not publicly available. It connects the defense research and engineering community, DoD laboratories, and other DoD agencies and personnel, while providing current and next-generation researchers with advanced Web 2.0 tools. Offering real-time discussions on capability needs and solutions, events and people, this collaborative environment can support community activities, social networking, discussions, and a way to share lessons learned.

As of late 2012 the site was in its pilot stage and being used, on a limited scale, for discussion and collaboration by people within the defense community. DoDTechSpace was expected to be unveiled for wider DoD use in mid-2013.

Defense Innovation Marketplace

The Defense Innovation Marketplace was launched in late 2011 and was widely used in 2012 as an online resource (in part limited-access) for the purpose of "connecting industry with government customers." Creation of this site was a direct result of the "Better Buying Power" initiative within DoD, calling for the department to deliver better value to the taxpayer and the military by improving the way it was doing business. In short, industry submits information about defense-related ideas and projects, which helps DoD to see more easily what industry is working on. This can help the department to plan future acquisitions and see what gaps are being encountered in research.

DTIC Online Access Controlled

The secure site DTIC Online Access Controlled offers a gateway to DoD unclassified (but not public) science, technology, research, and engineering information. Users can get congressional budget information, DoD science and technology planning documents, the Biomedical Research Database, more than 2 million technical reports, research summaries of work in progress, and numerous other resources, all free of charge.

New Look for Public Site

DTIC's public website, DTIC Online (http://www.dtic.mil), had a new look in 2012. The site offers such features as DTIC News Wire, which provides information about DoD scientific and technical priorities; news from the more than 65 DoD laboratories located across the United States, and an easier-to-read home page.

Web Hosting Expertise

DTIC has been hosting DoD websites since 1994 and currently hosts more than 70. Customers include organizations reporting to the Secretary of Defense, military service headquarters organizations, and several defense agencies, such as the Joint Chiefs of Staff and Defense Prisoner of War/Mission Personnel Office. As a leader in information storage and retrieval, DTIC has been able to advise DoD components concerning policy, law, best practices, and security strategies that relate to the transmission and use of all types of information. This is an effective support program for senior-level planners and other users of information resources. The shared infrastructure allows many organizations to obtain technologies and resources that no single organization could afford on its own.

As the nation geared up for the 2012 presidential election, DTIC staff worked on the Federal Voter's Assistance Program (FVAP) website, http://www.fvap.gov. This high-profile site is heavily used by active-duty members of the armed forces, merchant marine, public health service, and the National Oceanic and Atmospheric Administration and their family members, in addition to U.S. citizens living outside the United States for work, school, or other reasons. DTIC ensured that the site and its applications were up and running so that eligible U.S. voters anywhere in the world could cast their ballots.

DoD Instruction 5230.24 Signed

A priority of DTIC in handling information is to safeguard national security, export control, and intellectual property rights. While there is much publicly accessible material in the DTIC collection, some information is restricted by security classifications. DoD's scientific and technical information is always categorized (or "marked") by the office that originates the document. This marking determines how, and to whom, the information can be disseminated.

DTIC was instrumental in getting a DoD instruction (DoDI 5230.24) approved relating to the marking of information. DoD instructions establish or implement policy. This particular instruction is an important policy document for the operation of DTIC. "Distribution Statements on Technical Documents" establishes DoD policies and defines responsibilities for marking and managing technical DoD-related documents. How a document is marked determines who can see the information, such as the public at large or just the DoD community. Documents in question might include research, engineering, and logistics information. The instruction was initially submitted for internal coordination in December 2010 and was finally approved in August 2012.

Resources

DTIC's holdings include technical reports on completed research; research summaries of planned, ongoing, and completed work; independent research and development summaries; defense technology transfer agreements; DoD planning documents; DoD directives and instructions; conference proceedings; security classification guides; command histories; and special collections that date back to World War II. DoD-funded researchers are required to search DTIC's collections to ensure that they do not "reinvent the wheel" and undertake unnecessary or redundant research.

Information Sources

DTIC information is derived from many sources, including DoD organizations (civilian and military) and DoD contractors; U.S. government organizations and their contractors; nonprofit organizations working on DoD scientific, research, and engineering activities; academia; and foreign governments. DTIC accepts information in print, nonprint (CDs and DVDs), and electronically over the Web. DTIC gets information from the defense community, for the defense community, about defense and more. Having a full range of science and technology and research and development information within the DTIC collection ensures that technological innovations are linked to defense development and acquisition efforts. New research projects can begin with the highest level of information available. This avoids duplication of effort, maximizing the use of DoD project dollars.

Information Analysis Centers (IACs)

Information Analysis Centers (IACs) are research and analysis organizations established by DoD and managed by DTIC to help researchers, engineers, scientists, and program managers use existing scientific and technical information. IACs identify, analyze, and use scientific and technical information in specific technology areas and develop information and analysis products for the defense science and engineering communities. Staffed by experienced technical area scientists, engineers, and information specialists, they help users locate and analyze scientific and technical information.

Many of the products and services produced by IACs are free of charge and include announcements of reports relevant to the particular IAC's field of interest, authoritative bibliographic search reports, the latest scientific and engineering information on specific technical subjects, consultation with or referral to world-recognized technical experts, and the status of current technologies.

During 2012 the program began a major restructuring, reducing the number of IACs by combining responsibilities and looking for more small-business support. In summer 2012 DTIC announced the awarding of the newest IAC, Cyber Security and Information Systems (CSIAC), to a small business. CSIAC took over the operations of the Data and Analysis Center for Software (DACS), the Information Assurance IAC (IATAC), and the Modeling and Simulation IAC (MSIAC). The CSIAC award marks an important step for the IAC program in executing the most significant transformation in the program's history of more than 65 years. More program changes are being made in 2013. For more information, visit http://iac.dtic.mil.

DTIC Annual Conference

DTIC held its 2012 annual conference March 27–28 at Fort Belvoir, Virginia, as well as virtually on Defense Connect Online (DCO). More than 200 individuals registered to attend in person and nearly 100 via DCO. Zachary J. Lemnios, assistant secretary of defense for research and engineering, the keynote speaker, told his audience that DTIC was the largest central resource for government-funded science, technical, engineering, and business-related information available. Other speakers included senior science and technology officials at the Pentagon. Capt. Alvin E. Shell, Jr., an Army retiree, provided "Recollections of a Wounded Warrior." The conference theme was "DTIC: Connecting Lab Research with the Warfighter."

The 2013 DTIC conference is scheduled for August 19–23. The conference will again be both an on-site and virtual event; its theme is "Connecting People and Information."

Free Training Opportunities

"DTIC Boot Camp: S&T Resources for Labs" offers hands-on training, including sessions about DTIC Online Access Controlled, DoDTechipedia, and Aristotle (a Web-based DTIC professional networking tool), as well as instruction on how to submit documents. This one-day, interactive workshop is held monthly for customers to learn how to maximize DTIC's suite of services to meet their information needs. The boot camp model has proven to be effective, and demand for training is on the increase. DTIC users have requested additional training sessions both at Fort Belvoir and at their own locations.

Another facet of DTIC's free training consists of DoDTechipedia 101 webinars—a way to provide information about the DoD wiki without the expense of traveling. DTIC has also produced online tutorials to help individuals learn how to use the wiki's key features.

DoD Scientific and Technical Information (STINFO) training can help attendees gain a better understanding of this program. Training can be held at DTIC or off-site, and provides instruction on the management and conduct of an organizational STINFO program. For more information, visit http://www.dtic.mil/dtic/customer/training/training.html.

DTIC is a registered service mark of the Defense Technical Information Center.

National Library of Education

Knowledge Utilization Division
National Center for Education Evaluation and Regional Assistance
Institute of Education Sciences, U.S. Department of Education
400 Maryland Ave. S.W., Washington, DC 20202
World Wide Web http://ies.ed.gov/ncee/projects/nat_ed_library.asp

Ruth Curran Neild
Acting Director, National Library of Education
202-208-1200, e-mail ruth.neild@ed.gov

The U.S. Department of Education's National Library of Education (NLE), created in 1994, is the primary resource center for education information in the federal government, serving the research needs of the education community through the Education Resources Information Center (ERIC) and the department's Research Library. NLE resides in the National Center for Education Evaluation and Regional Assistance, Institute of Education Sciences.

The National Library of Education was created by Public Law 103-227, the Educational Research, Development, Dissemination, and Improvement Act of 1994, and reauthorized under Public Law 107-279, the Education Sciences Reform Act of 2002. The act outlines four primary functions of NLE:

- Collect and archive information, including products and publications developed through, or supported by, the Institute of Education Sciences; and other relevant and useful education-related research, statistics, and evaluation materials and other information, projects, and publications that are consistent with scientifically valid research or the priorities and mission of the institute, and developed by the department, other federal agencies, or entities
- Provide a central location within the federal government for information about education
- Provide comprehensive reference services on matters relating to education to employees of the Department of Education and its contractors and grantees, other federal employees, and members of the public
- Promote greater cooperation and resource sharing among providers and repositories of education information in the United States

NLE's programs—ERIC and the Research Library—share these functions by complementing and supporting one another. ERIC collects and archives information and provides a central location within the federal government for information about education, while the Research Library offers comprehensive reference services.

ERIC was established in 1966 and became part of NLE in 1994. ERIC is responsible for providing a comprehensive, easy-to-use, searchable, Internet-based bibliographic and full-text database of education research and information for educators, researchers, and the general public. ERIC's digital library is centered around a collection of more than 1.4 million bibliographic records of education resources, including journal articles, books, research syntheses, conference papers, technical reports, policy papers, and other education-related materials, including more than 350,000 full-text documents. In 2012 ERIC users conducted more than 220 million searches through the ERIC website (http://www.eric.ed.gov). Because ERIC serves as the major public program and outreach arm of NLE, it is covered separately. [See the following article, "Education Resources Information Center"—*Ed.*]

Research Library

The primary responsibility of NLE is to provide information services to agency staff and contractors, the general public, other government agencies, and other libraries. Located in the agency's headquarters building in Washington, D.C., the Research Library houses current and historical collections and archives of information on education issues, research, statistics, and policy; there is a special emphasis on agency publications and contractor reports, as well as current and historical federal education legislation. The library strongly supports Institute of Education Sciences (IES) programs by collecting journals indexed in the ERIC database, and through information discovery and literature searches supporting the What Works Clearinghouse and the Regional Educational Laboratories.

NLE gives agency staff desktop access to scholarly research on education, psychology, sociology, public policy, and law. To promote its information services, manage customer requests, and increase its own internal information resources, the library employs virtual reference technology to provide reference services to department staff and contractors and to support the activities of the IES Regional Educational Laboratories' (RELs') Ask-A-REL Program. The library continues to deliver the great majority of its products and services in digital formats. Promoting and improving services remains a primary consideration in achieving its objectives.

With a staff of 11—three full-time federal staff and eight contract librarians— NLE has two units: Technical Services and Reference and Information Services. Staffing and organizational structure are kept flexible to support changing needs and to allow for fast, competent response to customer requests, institutional initiatives, and advances in technology. NLE's primary customer base includes about 5,000 department staff nationwide; department contractors performing research; education organizations and media; and academic, special, and government libraries. All services are supported by NLE's budget, which in fiscal year 2012 was approximately $2 million.

Use of NLE

NLE receives about 18,700 requests a year. In 2012 department staff and contractors working for the department made about 7,125 requests for information, including interlibrary loans and database searches, representing about 38 percent of the total number of information requests. Complex and large-scale requests were made by the contractors for the What Works Clearinghouse. NLE also invested considerable effort and resources in support of the Regional Educational Laboratories.

About 7,000 requests were made by members of the public during 2012, representing about 37 percent of the total requests to the library. Requests were made by K–12 educators, students in institutions of higher education, researchers, parents, and others. The majority of these customers contacted the library by telephone, e-mail, or a visit to the facility.

Academic, government, and special libraries compose NLE's third-largest user group; together they generated slightly more than 4,700 requests (25 percent of total requests). Outreach to academic libraries included interlibrary loan and a gift books program that has become increasingly popular in recent years with more than 200 libraries participating in 2012.

Collections

NLE's collection focus has remained the same since its creation: education issues, with an emphasis on research and policy; and related topics including law, public policy, economics, urban affairs, sociology, history, philosophy, psychology, and cognitive development.

NLE has maintained special collections of historical documents associated with its parent agency, the U.S. Department of Education, having a complete collection of ERIC microfiche; research reports reviewed by the What Works Clearinghouse and special panels; and publications of or relating to the department's predecessor agencies, including the National Institute of Education and the U.S. Office of Education in the Department of Health, Education, and Welfare. These collections include reports, studies, manuals, statistical publications, speeches, and policy papers. NLE also serves as a federal depository library under the U.S. Government Printing Office program.

Services

NLE provides reference and other information services, including legislative reference and statistical information services, to department staff and contractors, to the education community at large, and to the general public, as well as providing document delivery services to department staff and contractors and interlibrary loan services to other libraries and government agencies. Through its involvement in the Regional Education Laboratories Ask-A-REL program, the library provides resources and reference services to education practitioners.

Contact Information

The U.S. Department of Education Research Library can be contacted by e-mail at askalibrarian@ed.gov. The library's reference desk is available by telephone at 800-424-1616 (toll free) or 202-205-5015, and by fax at 202-401-0547. For the hearing impaired, the number for the Federal Relay Service is 800-877-8339.

Located in the Department's headquarters building at 400 Maryland Ave. S.W., it is open from 9 A.M. to 5 P.M. weekdays, except federal holidays.

Education Resources Information Center

National Library of Education
National Center for Education Evaluation and Regional Assistance
Institute of Education Sciences, U.S. Department of Education
400 Maryland Ave. S.W., Washington, DC 20202
World Wide Web http://www.eric.ed.gov

Erin Pollard
Program Officer, ERIC
202-219-3400, e-mail erin.pollard@ed.gov

The Education Resources Information Center (ERIC) is the world's largest and most frequently used digital library of education resources. It is composed of more than 1.4 million bibliographic records and more than 350,000 full-text materials indexed from 1966 to the present. Each ERIC bibliographic record contains an abstract of a journal article or non-journal document (e.g., technical report, conference paper), along with indexed information such as author, title, and publication date.

Background

ERIC has served the information needs of schools, institutions of higher education, educators, parents, administrators, policymakers, researchers, and public and private entities for decades, through a variety of library services and formats—first in paper copy, then in microfiche, and today exclusively in electronic format. ERIC provides service directly to the public via its website, http://www.eric.ed.gov.

With a 45-year history of public service, ERIC is one of the oldest programs in the U.S. Department of Education. As the world's largest education resource, it is distinguished by two hallmarks: free dissemination of bibliographic records and the collection of gray literature such as research conference papers and government contractor reports.

The authorizing legislation for ERIC is part of the Education Sciences Reform Act of 2002, Public Law 107-279. This legislation envisioned ERIC subject areas or topics (previously covered by the ERIC Clearinghouses) as part of the totality of enhanced information dissemination to be conducted by the Institute of Education Sciences. In addition, information dissemination includes material on closing the achievement gap and on educational practices that improve academic achievement and promote learning.

ERIC Mission

The mission of ERIC is to provide a comprehensive, easy-to-use, searchable, Internet-based bibliographic and full-text database of education research and information for educators, researchers, and the general public. Terms defining the ERIC mission are as follows:

- *Comprehensive*: The ERIC digital library consists of journal articles and non-journal materials, including materials not published by commercial publishers that are directly related to education and education research.
- *Easy-to-use and searchable*: ERIC users—including students, educators, researchers, and the general public—will be able to find the education information they need quickly and efficiently.
- *Electronic*: ERIC is an entirely electronic system comprising the ERIC website and the digital library. It links to libraries, publishers, and commercial sources of journal articles, and is made available to commercial database vendors through authorization agreements.
- *Bibliographic and full-text*: Bibliographic records convey the information users need in a simple and straightforward manner, and, whenever possible, full-text journal articles and non-journal materials are included free of charge in the digital library. Other full-text articles and materials, whenever possible, will be immediately available for purchase through an online link to the publisher's website.

Selection Standards

The broad selection standard provides that all materials added to the ERIC database are directly related to the field of education. The majority of the journals indexed in ERIC are peer-reviewed, and the peer-reviewed status is indicated for all journals indexed since 2004, when this data began to be documented by the ERIC system. The collection scope includes early childhood education through higher education, vocational education, and special education; it includes teacher education, education administration, assessment and evaluation, counseling, information technology, and the academic areas of reading, mathematics, science, environmental education, languages, and social studies.

To be considered for selection, all submissions must be in digital format and accompanied by author permission for dissemination. For individual document submissions, authors (copyright holders) register through the ERIC website feature "My ERIC"; follow the steps to enter bibliographic information, abstract, and document file; and submit the electronic document release form authorizing ERIC to disseminate the materials. Journal publishers, associations, and other entities with multiple documents also submit electronic content following guidance and instructions consistent with provider agreements from ERIC. Once publishers have signed an ERIC agreement, files can be submitted by e-mail or disk or by upload to ERIC's ftp site.

ERIC Collection

In addition to being the largest education library, ERIC is one of the few collections to index non-journal materials as well as journal literature. The largest share of the collection consists of citations to journal articles (953,604 records), and a smaller portion consists of non-journal materials (523,804 records). The non-journal materials are frequently called gray literature, materials that are not easy to find and are not produced by commercial publishers. In ERIC, the gray literature consists of research syntheses, dissertations, conference proceedings, and such selected papers as keynote speeches, technical reports, policy papers, literature reviews, bibliographies, congressional hearings and reports, reports on federal and state standards, testing and regulations, U.S. Department of Education contractor reports (such as the What Works Clearinghouse and the National Center for Education Statistics), and working papers for established research and policy organizations.

To support consistency and reliability in content coverage, most education journals are indexed comprehensively so that all articles in each issue are included. ERIC currently indexes a total of 1,143 journals; 1,046 journals comprehensively and 97 selectively. Articles from selectively covered journals are acquired by ERIC subject specialists, who identify individual documents for the ERIC database according to the ERIC selection policy.

The complete list of journals indexed in ERIC, including the years of coverage and the number of articles indexed, is a tool on the ERIC website enabling users to identify more easily specific journal literature. There is also a non-journal source list of more than 800 organizations producing education-related materials providing content to ERIC. Another convenience for users that is designed to streamline the process of obtaining full text is the "Find in a Library" feature, which leverages the Open URL Gateway and WorldCat to provide a link from ERIC records to electronic and print resources available in libraries. For all journals currently indexed in ERIC, there are links to publishers' websites if users choose to purchase full-text articles.

To facilitate electronic access to more archived materials, ERIC launched a microfiche digitization project in 2006; this project was concluded in 2009. The project scope was to digitize and archive microfiche full-text documents containing an estimated 43 million pages and to provide copyright due diligence by seeking permission from the copyright holders to make the electronic version available to users.

Approximately 340,000 full-text documents, indexed 1966–1992, were converted from microfiche to digital image files, and more than 65 percent of these documents were added to the ERIC digital library. The ERIC website provides various lists for librarians to manage microfiche collections in their institutions based on what is now available in pdf format on the ERIC website.

In 2010 ERIC established a partnership with ProQuest to begin indexing education-related doctoral dissertations from 700 academic institutions worldwide. More than 10,350 recent records from the ProQuest Dissertations and Thesis Database have been added to the ERIC collection. As the project expands, records will reach back to 1997, the year digital copies of dissertations were first acquired.

ERIC Website

Recent enhancements to ERIC focus on increased access for special audiences and new search features. For example, the home page provides links with information for publishers and authors, librarians, and licensors of the ERIC database. Searchers can mark records for placement in a temporary workspace called "My Clipboard." This feature permits users to print, e-mail, or export records, or save them to a "My ERIC" account. Additional website improvements include search-term highlighting so that users see where and how frequently their search terms occur in the results set; a metadata field indicating peer-reviewed articles for records acquired 2004 to the present; and quicker loading of search results. Search facets are a new feature, allowing users to narrow searches by author, descriptor, date, audience, source, education level, and publication type, with each category offering the most frequently occurring names or terms in the results set.

Automated systems for acquisition and processing help to reduce the total time required to produce a database record, and most records are processed in fewer than 30 days. New content is added to the ERIC database every day, and ERIC publishes approximately 4,000 new records to the ERIC digital library each month. Commercial vendors receive updates to the database monthly.

RSS feeds enable users to keep up to date with new content from several sources. For example, users can receive regular updates from specific U.S. Department of Education programs: the Regional Educational Laboratories, the What Works Clearinghouse, and the National Assessment of Educational Progress (NAEP). Moreover, any ERIC search can become an RSS feed, or users can click to one of several education topics including community colleges, financial aid for college, and teacher effectiveness.

Tutorials provide added support for users searching the ERIC collection, helping searchers take advantage of website features. Tutorials include author search using full name, citation management, field code search, refining a search, and many more titles found under the ERIC "Help" section.

While the ERIC database has traditionally used narrative abstracts to describe full-text documents, database contributors now have the option of writing structured abstracts for their research papers and conference presentations. Structured abstracts present important details about research studies and their outcomes under predefined headings or elements such as research design types and study samples.

The website also provides links to find ERIC on Facebook and Twitter. This feature provides frequent news updates, links, and downloadable materials, with the goal of broadening ERIC outreach.

ERIC Access

Use of ERIC continues to grow. There are now approximately 13 million searches of ERIC each month—adding up to more than 150 million a year. In addition to the government-sponsored website at http://www.eric.ed.gov, ERIC is carried by search engines, including Google and Google Scholar, MSN, and Yahoo!, and by commercial database providers, including EBSCO, OCLC, OVID, ProQuest, SilverPlatter, and Dialog. ERIC is also available through statewide networks in Ohio, Texas, Kentucky, and North Carolina.

The ERIC digital library can be reached toll-free by telephone in the United States, Canada, and Puerto Rico at 800-LET-ERIC (800-538-3742), Monday through Friday, 8 A.M. to 8 P.M. eastern time. Questions can also be transmitted via the message box on the "Contact Us" page on the ERIC website.

National Association and Organization Reports

American Library Association

50 E. Huron St., Chicago, IL 60611
800-545-2433
World Wide Web http://www.ala.org

Maureen Sullivan
President

The American Library Association (ALA)—the world's oldest, largest, and most influential library association—was founded in 1876 in Philadelphia and later chartered in the Commonwealth of Massachusetts. ALA has about 50,000 members, including librarians, library trustees, and other interested people from every state and many nations. The association serves public, state, school, and academic libraries, as well as special libraries for people working in government, commerce and industry, the arts, and the armed services or in hospitals, prisons, and other institutions.

ALA's mission is "to provide leadership for the development, promotion, and improvement of library and information services and the profession of librarianship in order to enhance learning and ensure access to information for all."

ALA is governed by an elected council, which is its policy making body, and an executive board, which acts for the council in the administration of established policies and programs. In this context, the executive board is the body that manages the affairs of the association, delegating management of the association's day-to-day operation to the executive director. ALA also has 37 standing committees, designated as committees of the association or of the council. ALA operations are directed by the executive director and implemented by staff through a structure of programmatic offices and support units.

ALA is home to 11 membership divisions, each focused on a type of library or library function. They are the American Association of School Librarians (AASL), the Association for Library Collections and Technical Services (ALCTS), the Association for Library Service to Children (ALSC), the Association of College and Research Libraries (ACRL), United for Libraries: Association of Library Trustees, Advocates, Friends, and Foundations (ALTAFF), the Association of Specialized and Cooperative Library Agencies (ASCLA), the Library and Information Technology Association (LITA), the Library Leadership and Management Association (LLAMA), the Public Library Association (PLA), the Reference and User

Services Association (RUSA), and the Young Adult Library Services Association (YALSA).

ALA also hosts 18 round tables for members who share interests that lie outside the scope of any of the divisions. A network of affiliates, chapters, and other organizations enables ALA to reach a broad audience.

Key action areas include diversity, equitable access to information and library services, education and lifelong learning, intellectual freedom, advocacy for libraries and the profession, literacy, and organizational excellence.

ALA offices address the broad interests and issues of concern to ALA members; they track issues and provide information, services, and products for members and the general public. Current ALA offices are the Chapter Relations Office, the Development Office, the Governance Office, the International Relations Office, the Office for Accreditation, the Office for Diversity, the Office of Government Relations (OGR), the Office for Human Resource Development and Recruitment, the Office for Information Technology Policy (OITP), the Office for Intellectual Freedom (OIF), the Office for Library Advocacy, the Office for Literacy and Outreach Services, the Office for Research and Statistics, the Public Information Office (PIO), the Public Programs Office (PPO), and the Washington Office.

ALA's headquarters is in Chicago; OGR and OITP are housed at ALA's Washington Office. ALA also has an editorial office for *Choice,* a review journal for academic libraries, in Middletown, Connecticut.

ALA is a 501(c)(3) charitable and educational organization.

Presidential Focus

Maureen Sullivan, 2012–2013 ALA president, is an organization development consultant to libraries and a professor of practice in the Managerial Leadership in the Information Professions doctoral program of the Graduate School of Library and Information Science at Simmons College in Boston. In her presidential year, Sullivan highlighted two areas of need: preparing leaders for what will be different in the digital world and creating an ALA leadership development institute.

During her campaign for the ALA presidency, Sullivan noted a number of areas of professional concern, including competition from publishers and other vendors of information access that believe they can bypass libraries and sell information products directly to the publics that libraries serve; challenges to and erosion of libraries' principles and values, especially intellectual freedom, privacy, and access to information; and the difficulty those whom libraries serve have in achieving information and media literacy as the complex world of information greatly expands in a socially networked environment.

"We must continue to provide free and open access to information," Sullivan said. "We must increase our efforts to defend and foster our principles and values locally, nationally, and globally. Our ability to make the case for the value of libraries in community development, lifelong learning, and education is essential to our democracy. Continued collaboration with our international colleagues is critical to advocacy for the value of libraries and the work of librarians and library staff throughout the world. ALA and the ALA Allied Professional Association must be at the forefront of this work."

Among her goals were to develop an ALA-wide leadership development initiative, identify sustainable ways to promote synergies between local government and libraries, and explore ways to strengthen and extend international activities.

At her inauguration at the 2012 Annual Conference in Anaheim, Sullivan noted that ALA's strategic plan, ALA 2015, provides "an excellent framework to engage all of us in fulfilling the overarching goal to build 'a world where libraries, both physical and virtual, are central to lifelong discovery and learning and where everyone is a library user.' This invites us to focus our collective attention on our communities—to understand the needs, interests, challenges, expectations, and opportunities of the diverse and changing constituencies we serve."

Barbara Stripling, assistant professor of practice at Syracuse University, is serving as president-elect for the 2012–2013 term and will be inaugurated as ALA president at the 2013 Annual Conference in Chicago. Stripling said she looks forward to continuing the work begun by her predecessors in transforming libraries into virtual and face-to-face community centers of conversation, equitable access to information, lifelong learning, and civic engagement.

Three ALA Executive Board members were elected at the 2012 ALA Midwinter Meeting in Dallas: Robert Banks, chief operating officer of the Topeka and Shawnee County (Kansas) Public Library; Alexia Hudson-Ward, reference and instruction librarian at Pennsylvania State University's Abington College; and John Moorman, director of the Williamsburg (Virginia) Regional Library. They are serving three-year terms that conclude in June 2015.

Highlights of the Year

U.S. public libraries continue to connect and transform communities, providing essential resources for job-seekers, support for critical e-government services, and programs to promote financial literacy—all in the context of deep economic uncertainty. And ALA continues to lead the way in the transformation of libraries and library services in an increasingly global digital information environment.

According to the 2011–2012 Public Library Funding and Technology Access Study (PLFTAS) funded by the Bill and Melinda Gates Foundation, more than 62 percent of libraries report offering the only free Internet access in their community. More than 90 percent of public libraries now offer formal or informal technology training. In addition, more than three-quarters of libraries (76.3 percent) offer access to e-books, a significant increase (9.1 percent) from the previous year, while e-book readers are available for checkout at 39.1 percent of public libraries.

ALA also took an aggressive stance on library access to e-books. In August 2012 it released "E-Book Business Models for Public Libraries," a report created by the ALA Digital Content and Libraries Working Group. And in September ALA released an open letter from its president to publishers denouncing the refusal of several large trade publishers to sell e-books to libraries. In September President Sullivan led an ALA delegation to New York City to meet with publishers to discuss the many concerns of the library community about e-book publishing.

School Library Funding

In 2011 U.S. Sen. Jack Reed (D-R.I.) recognized that school libraries needed a direct funding source in the federal budget and, through report language in the fiscal year (FY) 2012 Appropriations Bill, directed money to the U.S. Department of Education for the Innovative Approaches to Literacy program. In FY 2012 $28.6 million was appropriated for this program. By law, at least half this money ($14.3 million) must be allocated to a competitive grant program for underserved school libraries. The remaining funds are allocated to competitive grants for national nonprofit organizations that work to improve childhood literacy.

National Library Legislative Day

More than 350 librarians and library supporters convened in Washington, D.C., April 22–24, 2012, to participate in National Library Legislative Day. Activities began with preconference sessions, also known as "new participant training," hosted by United for Libraries (ALTAFF) and ALA's Washington Office. Advocacy Associates representative Stephanie Vance facilitated the session with ALA Grassroots Coordinator Ted Wegner and OGR Director Lynne Bradley. More than 50 attendees learned tips on the right things to say and do in meetings with members of Congress and strategies to build and maintain advocacy efforts at home.

Text Message Advocacy Service

ALA launched Mobile Commons, a new advocacy tool that will allow library supporters to receive text message alerts from OGR. Advocates can sign up for the text alerts to receive the most up-to-date information on advocacy alerts and events by texting "library" to 877877. The opt-in service will allow ALA to communicate advocacy messages in a quick and effective fashion using an innovative texting and calling feature. Advocacy subscribers have the option to call legislators toll-free through Mobile Commons to discuss particular issues. The text messages will provide subscribers with talking points on issues before automatically transferring the advocates to the offices of their legislators.

Membership Demographic Study

More than 40,776 current ALA members have participated in a voluntary, self-selected membership demographics survey.

Baby boomers—born from 1946 to 1964—represent 46.9 percent of the ALA membership responding as of the March 2012 analysis of the ALA Member Demographic Survey. Members already at retirement age (older than 65) represent 7.5 percent (2,940) of those who provided a date of birth in their response. If retirement age is said to start at age 62, then approximately 14.7 percent of members reporting their date of birth fall into that range (5,735 respondents).

Basic membership demographics remain largely unchanged since ALA began collecting these characteristics. Much like the library profession overall, ALA members are predominantly female (80.7 percent), predominantly white (88.7 percent), and hold an MLS or other master's degrees (63.8 percent and 26.5 percent, respectively).

Library Card Sign-Up Month

As honorary chair of Library Card Sign-Up Month, Baseball Hall of Famer and author Cal Ripken donated his image to a print public service announcement

(PSA) that appeared in national publications including *Time* magazine, with place-ments totaling almost $500,000. Library Card Sign-Up Month, held annually in September, is a time to remind parents that a library card is the most important school supply of all.

National Library Week

Bestselling author Brad Meltzer was honorary chair of National Library Week 2012, held April 8–14. A full-page PSA of the author and host of the History Channel's "Decoded" appeared in *Time* and other publications with national reach. The total circulation for the publications was 5.4 million, and the donated ad value was more than $400,000.

Money Smart Week

Libraries from Maine to Hawaii helped members of their communities become "money smart" during Money Smart Week @ your library, held April 21–28, 2012. The program is a partnership initiative between ALA and the Federal Reserve Bank of Chicago to expand Money Smart Week—a public awareness campaign designed to help consumers better manage their personal finances—to libraries across the country. More than 250 libraries in 39 states presented programs for all ages relating to personal financial literacy. Libraries partnered with community groups, financial institutions, government agencies, educational organizations, and other financial experts in the effort.

Campaign for the World's Libraries

Library associations around the world expanded their @ your library programs in 2012.

In March the Library and Information Association of South Africa (LIASA) developed its latest South African Library Week campaign, Develop @ your li-brary. The theme reminded users that libraries create programs that focus on skills development, providing access to information, granting access to computers and online tools, and enabling users to develop their computer skills, as well as provid-ing tools that allow them to write résumés and search for jobs. Posters featuring the theme were sent out to all LIASA member libraries, along with downloadable bookmarks, T-shirt designs, and customizable graphics.

The Library and Information Association of Jamaica launched its own @ your library campaign in partnership with the Jamaica Library Service, the Public Library Network, and the School Library Network to provide reading activities under the theme Learn to Read—Read to Learn @ your library. The objectives of the partnership included developing lifelong voluntary readers and promoting the role of libraries and librarians.

The Campaign for the World's Libraries was developed by ALA and the Inter-national Federation of Library Associations and Institutions (IFLA) to showcase the unique and vital roles played by public, school, academic, and special libraries worldwide.

Programs and Partners

Campaign for America's Libraries

The Campaign for America's Libraries continued to work with partners to generate public awareness about the value of libraries and librarians.

Season seven of the Step Up to the Plate @ your library program, developed by ALA and the National Baseball Hall of Fame and Museum, concluded with a grand-prize drawing at the Hall of Fame in Cooperstown, New York. The winner was Stuart Wolf of Wilmette, Illinois. The program promotes libraries and important information centers. Fans of all ages used the print and electronic resources at their libraries to answer a series of baseball trivia questions developed by the library and research staff at the hall of fame.

Another program, Connect with your kids @ your library, continued to position the library as the place for high-quality family time. With content for parents online at atyourlibrary.org/connectwithyourkids, the program promotes the library as a trusted place offering free programs for parents and their children and teens. Each week, the Connect with your kids @ your library blog features new content for parents.

A digital supplement to ALA's *American Libraries* magazine in 2012 featured highlights from the second round of the American Dream Starts @ your library program. The supplement tells the story of how libraries expanded their print and digital ESL (English as a second language) collections, added new technologies, increased outreach and bookmobile services, built community partnerships, and engaged the media to promote library resources. In the second round, the Dollar General Literacy Foundation provided 73 public libraries in 23 states $5,000 grants to build innovative literacy services for adult English language learners living in their communities. A third round was launched in early 2013.

On the Road with PPO

The ALA Public Programs Office toured 11 traveling exhibitions to 306 public, academic, and special libraries, reaching an estimated audience of more than 255,000 library patrons through related programs. The exhibitions that continued their tours in 2012 were "John Adams Unbound"; "Lewis and Clark and the Indian Country"; "Lincoln: The Constitution and the Civil War"; "Manifold Greatness: The Creation and Afterlife of the King James Bible"; the Nextbook, Inc.-sponsored series of exhibitions on Jewish artists, including "In a Nutshell: The Worlds of Maurice Sendak," "Emma Lazarus: Voice of Liberty, Voice of Conscience," and "A Fine Romance: Jewish Songwriters, American Songs, 1910–1965"; "Pride and Passion: The African American Baseball Experience"; and "Visions of the Universe: Four Centuries of Discovery."

During the year PPO also began two new traveling exhibitions in partnership with the National Center for Interactive Learning at Space Science Institute, the Lunar and Planetary Institute, and the National Girls Collaborative Project. Ten libraries were selected to host "Discover Earth: A Century of Change" from January 2012 to December 2013. The exhibition focuses on local earth science topics— such as weather, water cycle, and ecosystem changes—as well as a global view of a changing planet. "Discover Tech: Engineers Make a World of Difference" will be hosted by eight public libraries through June 2014. The traveling exhibition was developed to raise awareness that engineers, through a creative and collaborative design process, arrive at practical solutions to help solve society's problems.

Understanding Louisa May Alcott

A series of five reading, viewing, and discussion programs featuring the video documentary *Louisa May Alcott: The Woman Behind Little Women* and the companion biography of the same name were hosted by 30 libraries. The library outreach program is a collaboration among the National Endowment for the Humanities (NEH), the ALA Public Programs Office, and Nancy Porter and Harriet Reisen for Filmmakers Collaborative. The film, biography, and library programs reintroduce audiences to Alcott by presenting a story full of fresh insights, startling discoveries about the author, and a new understanding of American culture during her lifetime.

Talking About the Civil War

"Let's Talk About It: Making Sense of the American Civil War" follows the popular Let's Talk About It model, which engages participants in discussion of a set of common texts selected by a nationally known scholar for their relevance to a larger, overarching theme. Sixty-five public and academic college libraries hosted "Let's Talk About It: Making Sense of the American Civil War" reading and discussion programs. The selected libraries each received a $3,500 cash grant from PPO and NEH to support program expenses. Grant recipients also received program support materials, including 30 copies of three titles, promotional materials, and training for the local project director and scholar.

A total of 37 state humanities councils were also given "Making Sense of the Civil War" grants, which included $10,000 program support stipends and 100 copies each of three titles in the series. Each state council selected a minimum of four libraries to receive the collection of books and host a five-part reading and discussion series. An additional 148 libraries hosted programs during 2012 with state council support.

Build Common Ground Through Discussion

"Building Common Ground: Discussions of Community, Civility, and Compassion," a multiformat discussion program for public audiences funded by the Fetzer Institute, brings adults together in libraries for programs and events that include reading, viewing, reflection, discussion, and civic engagement initiatives. This programming initiative supports public libraries as they strive to enhance the quality of life and learning in their communities.

PPO Celebrates American Music

"America's Music: A Film History of Our Popular Music from Blues to Bluegrass to Broadway" is a six-week series of public programs created by Tribeca Film Institute in partnership with PPO and NEH and in consultation with the Society for American Music. The programs feature documentary screenings and scholar-led discussions of 20th century American popular music. Libraries will host the series of six viewing and discussion programs through December 31, 2013.

Bringing Science to Girls

"Astro4Girls and Their Families" is a collaboration between PPO and NASA-funded astrophysics education and public outreach. The project is designed to offer participants an opportunity to celebrate women in science, learn about the universe through hands-on activities, and empower girls to explore the role of science in life and in their careers. The nine participating libraries were chosen from libraries that had hosted the traveling exhibition "Visions of the Universe: Four Centuries of Discovery."

Exploring Muslim Culture Through Books

PPO partnered with NEH to develop the "Bridging Cultures: Muslim Worlds Bookshelf." In the pilot program, six libraries hosted programs designed to help public audiences in the United States become more familiar with the people, places, history, faith, and cultures of Muslims around the world, through book discussion. In 2013 the program was to be expanded to up to 1,000 libraries and state humanities councils.

Teen Tech Week

More than 1,400 libraries registered to participate in the fifth annual Teen Tech Week in March 2012. The theme was "Geek Out @ your library." The week-long initiative encourages teens to explore the nonprint resources available at their libraries, including DVDs, databases, audiobooks, and electronic games, while urging them to learn how to navigate these new technologies safely and properly. Promotional partners include ALA Graphics, Audio Publishers Association, AudioGo, Figment, Hackasaurus, Peachtree Publishers, and Tutor.com.

Conferences and Workshops

2012 Annual Conference

The 2012 ALA Annual Conference, held June 21–26 in Anaheim, saw a unanimous resolution in support of the value of school libraries passed by the ALA Council, as well as discussions about e-books, privacy, library advocacy, and other critical issues.

Coinciding with the conference was the release of a report from the Pew Internet and American Life Project. "Libraries, Patrons, and E-Books" demonstrates the crucial role libraries play in the shifting digital terrain as e-reading, tablet computers, and e-book readers become more popular. Pew's Lee Rainie discussed the survey findings in a session titled "The Rise of E-Reading" and then on a panel on "Access to Digital Content: Diverse Approaches."

One of the programs, "The E-Book Elephant in the Room," featured a panel that included librarian Sue Polanka of Wright State University in Dayton, Ohio. Polanka demonstrated how the consortium OhioLINKS negotiated with such major publishers as ABC-CLIO, Gale, Oxford University Press, Sage, and Springer to buy each year's entire front list rather than individual books. By locally uploading the books using eXtensible Text Framework (XTF), they were able to make available a collection offering more books than Project Gutenberg.

ALA's Washington Office, in its update, provided a sobering overview of library funding issues and emphasized the crucial need for vigilance in the area of library advocacy.

The Washington Office also introduced the new advocacy tool Mobile Commons and paired it with presentations from speakers representing the Federal Communications Commission (FCC), the Electronic Frontier Foundation, and OpenTheGovernment.org.

Patrice McDermott of OpenTheGovernment.org said the organization was created because "there were groups working on similar issues, but they weren't talking to one another, and we needed to find a bridge between these groups." Through OpenTheGovernment.org, concerned citizens can give their input on such issues as the increasing restrictions on Freedom of Information Act requests, privacy concerns, and national security.

Also at the Washington Office update session, Jordan Usdan, director of public-private initiatives at FCC, said 66 million Americans do not use the Internet and encouraged libraries to help more people become "connected" and bridge the digital divide. He said a Literacy Finder App is being developed to help people find free local training opportunities by pointing to libraries and other groups participating in the program.

The first recipients of the Andrew Carnegie Medals for Excellence in Fiction and Nonfiction, funded by a grant from Carnegie Corporation of New York and sponsored by RUSA and *Booklist*, were announced. Anne Enright's *The Forgotten Waltz* received the medal for fiction and Robert K. Massie's *Catherine the Great: Portrait of a Woman* won the nonfiction prize.

"In many ways, librarians are the first book critics many readers come into contact with, and hence we are deeply thankful for their insight and guidance," said Vartan Gregorian, president of Carnegie Corporation of New York and a former president of the New York Public Library. "The Andrew Carnegie Medals for Excellence in Fiction and Nonfiction take that notion one step further and place the librarians' seal of approval on these wonderful books."

Rebecca MacKinnon, author of *Consent of the Networked*, who works on global Internet policy as a Schwartz Senior Fellow, was keynote speaker at the Opening General Session. MacKinnon warned about the lack of privacy in the age of the Internet. Giving examples of government intrusion, ranging from Chinese citizens blocked from access to certain websites to Egypt's Mubarak government collecting surveillance data, MacKinnon said similar kinds of activities also have occurred in the United States.

MacKinnon was part of a distinguished roster of speakers that included those who spoke as part of the Auditorium Speaker Series. Among them was author John Irving, whose 13th book, *In One Person*, has been described as his most political work since *The Cider House Rules*. The book's bisexual protagonist Billy Dean lives in 1950s small-town Vermont, where he becomes infatuated with a transgender librarian. Irving told the audience that he often portrayed "sexual outsiders." He said, "Writers are attracted to outsiders because that is who we think we are."

The ALA President's Program featured a conversation between ALA President Raphael and bestselling author Jodi Picoult and her daughter Samantha Van Leer. The mother-daughter author team appeared as part of their tour for the launch of *Between the Lines*.

When Van Leer was asked by a young girl from the audience about where the idea for *Between the Lines* had come from, she admitted to conceiving of the book while daydreaming in French class—and then quickly advised the girl that she should pay attention in class. From there, Van Leer's idea traveled to her mother, who was stuck in Los Angeles traffic but who was excited about the novel's concept, which involves an "incredibly handsome prince" who turns out to be more than a one-dimensional character in a book. "Who among us has not had a literary crush?" she asked.

Other popular speakers included author and actor Chris Colfer, broadcaster Dan Rather, psychology professor and author Dan Ariely, and actor Henry Winkler.

The Closing General Session featured "Dancing with the Stars" winner and Iraq war veteran J. R. Martinez, who, less than a month after being deployed to Iraq in 2003, was critically injured when his Humvee ran over a landmine. Martinez was trapped inside the burning vehicle, where he suffered smoke inhalation and severe burns to more than 40 percent of his body. After 34 months of recovery and 33 surgeries, Martinez began using his experience to help others, and he soon became a sought-after motivational speaker.

Several authors, including Stephen King, Amy Tan, Scott Turow, and Matt Groening, let their hair down by performing as the rock band the Rock Bottom Remainders during the ALA/ProQuest Scholarship Bash. They were joined by rock legend Roger McGuinn of the Byrds.

The annual LLAMA President's Program "Leading at All Levels: Taking Charge of Your Career Growth While Mentoring Others" featured Heather Krasna, director of career services at the Evans School of Public Affairs at the University of Washington and author of *Jobs That Matter: Find a Stable, Fulfilling Career in Public Service.* Krasna spoke about career development to both new librarians and seasoned leaders and managers.

The PLA President's Program and Awards Presentation recognized the PLA 2012 award winners and hosted keynote speaker author Sherman Alexie. PLA also cosponsored "Consultants Giving Back," an opportunity for attendees to meet one-on-one with nationally recognized library consultants for complimentary half-hour sessions. More than 15 consultants participated.

ALSC and YALSA teamed up to present "The Digital Lives of Tweens and Young Teens." The collaborative event featured two speakers, Stephen Abram and Michelle Poris, followed by a video presentation. Abram, author of ALA Editions' bestselling *Out Front with Stephen Abram,* was named by *Library Journal* as one of the top 50 people influencing the future of libraries. Poris has nearly 20 years of research experience with youth and families, including more than 12 years of designing and executing business building research for many of the world's largest corporations.

YALSA also hosted two half-day preconferences in Anaheim: "Books We'll Still Be Talking About 45 Years from Now" and "Source Code: Digital Youth Participation."

In addition, YALSA honored its award winners at the Edwards Luncheon on June 23 and the Printz Reception and Program on June 25. YALSA again hosted its YA Coffee Klatch event, where hundreds of attendees met authors who had appeared on YALSA's selected booklists in a speed-dating format.

The Freedom to Read Foundation hosted a sneak preview of the film *The Perks of Being a Wallflower.* The author on whose book it is based, Steven Chbosky, appeared to answer questions and sign books.

A packed room heard Duane Bray, a partner at IDEO, a global innovation and design consulting firm where he heads global digital business, talk about his vision for the future of the book at the joint ALCTS/ACRL President's Program. Bray's presentation, "Future of the Book: Innovation in Traditional Industries," presented the challenges traditional industries often face when experiencing disruptive change.

It was standing room only as United for Libraries President Donna McDonald welcomed award-winning journalist and author Dan Rather as part of the Auditorium Speaker's Series. Rather spoke about his experience and his new book *Rather Outspoken: My Life in the News*; afterward, hundreds stood in line to meet him and receive a signed copy of his book donated by Hachette Book Group.

Total attendance for the Anaheim conference was 20,021.

2013 Midwinter Meeting

Librarians and library supporters—including 6,694 attendees and 4,037 exhibitors—gathered at the 2013 ALA Midwinter Meeting in Seattle Jan. 25–29 to discuss ways libraries can engage and transform their communities as well as keep current on issues facing public, school, academic, and special libraries. Those topics included e-book lending, increasing technological change, and the rapid growth of social media.

During the meeting, ALA President Sullivan announced a new partnership between ALA and the Harwood Institute of Public Innovation. "The Promise of Libraries Transforming Communities" is a multiphase initiative funded through an Institute of Museum and Library Services (IMLS) grant that gives librarians the tools and training they need to lead communities in finding innovative solutions by advancing library-led community engagement and innovation.

"This initiative offers a means to build upon the strengths and assets of our libraries and to engage with our communities in deeper, meaningful ways," Sullivan said in a press conference.

Sullivan also welcomed a new report from the Pew Research Center's Internet and American Life Project on "Library Services in the Digital Age." Among the findings: 91 percent of people age 16 and older surveyed said libraries are important to them, and more than a quarter of people 16 and older said they used the computer or wifi at the library to go online. In addition, the report found that libraries continue to innovate and evolve in ways that bring value to communities, with 70 percent of public libraries offering digital/virtual reference and information services to answer patron questions.

The ALA Washington Office provided an update on the current political scene, including commentary from *Cook Political Report* Senior Editor Jennifer Duffy. "Every election teaches us something," Duffy said, "and the 2012 election taught us a whole lot." Among the lessons, she said, were the superior use of technology by the Obama campaign and the trend of nonwhite voters occupying a greater share of the electorate.

ACRL provided an update on the Value of Academic Libraries Initiative, including information on ACRL's new IMLS grant "Assessment in Action: Academic Libraries and Student Success."

E-book lending in libraries was also a popular topic. The ALA Digital Content Working Group held a session on "E-Books and Libraries: Where Do We Stand and Where Are We Going?" moderated by working group member Sari Feldman, executive director of the Cuyahoga County (Ohio) Public Library. ALA President Sullivan praised the decision by publisher Macmillan for its e-book lending library pilot program, which offered more than 1,200 backlist titles to libraries nationwide.

The Martin Luther King, Jr. Sunrise Celebration featured Jeanne Theoharis, professor of political science at Brooklyn College of the City University of New York, delivering the keynote address. Theoharis's latest book, *The Rebellious Mrs. Rosa Parks,* offers a new look at the civil rights figure.

National Library Week 2013 Honorary Chair Caroline Kennedy was a featured speaker during the Auditorium Speaker Series, moderated by ALA President-Elect Barbara Stripling, who engaged Kennedy in a question-and-answer session.

"I'm descended from a long line of bookworms and librarians," said Kennedy, who has worked to improve New York City public school libraries as vice chair of the New York City Fund for Public Schools and served on the board of New Visions for Public Schools and the John F. Kennedy Library Foundation. "They would be very proud of me for being here with you." Kennedy talked about her family's love of poetry, noting that her uncle, the late Senator Edward Kennedy, could recite "The Midnight Ride of Paul Revere" in its entirety—and would even do so at book signings.

During the ALA President's Program, author and consultant Peter Block discussed how libraries play a central role in bringing people together and empowering change.

Authors Terry Brooks, Ivan Doig, Greg Olsen, and Ruth Ozeki were featured in the popular Exhibits Round Table/*Booklist* Author Forum. Moderator Brad Hooper explored the subject of whether the novel was "alive and well."

Bestselling author Steven Johnson spoke on the connection between science, technology, and personal experience. "We like to tell the story of the 'eureka moment,' when the apple falls from the tree," Johnson said, "but most of the world's great ideas and breakthroughs do not actually begin that way . . . rather they occur over time with the 'slow hunch.'" And libraries, he said, "are wonderful curators of slow hunches."

Neuroscientist Lisa Genova, author of *Love Anthony,* presented the 15th annual Arthur Curley Memorial Lecture.

The annual Youth Media Awards—heavily attended both in person and through social media—announced the top books, videos, and audiobooks for children and young adults.

Author Jamaica Kincaid praised librarians during the Freedom to Read Foundation Banned/Challenged Author event at Town Hall Seattle. "You are the gatekeepers between reader and writer," she said. "For someone like me, you have no idea how beautiful your existence is."

Librarians got a variety of tips for enhancing their public relations efforts on Facebook in an ALA Masters Series session featuring Ben Bizzle, director of technology at Crowley Ridge Regional Library in Jonesboro, Arkansas, and David Lee King, digital services director at Topeka and Shawnee County (Kansas) Public Library.

Bizzle developed a case study with seven libraries over 28 days to demonstrate how a $10 Google ad increased the libraries' Facebook audiences. The libraries, which included small and large urban systems, all found at least 100 percent increases in their Facebook fans, and one library saw a more than 400 percent increase in Facebook fans after 28 days, he said.

More than half of all Americans over the age of 13 are on Facebook, King said, and librarians can reach that public free of charge on Facebook.

PLA Conference

The 2012 PLA Conference March 13–17 in Philadelphia drew more than 8,700 library staff, supporters, exhibitors, and authors. The conference included nearly 200 educational programs, special events, and tours, along with some 400 exhibitors representing everything from large library vendors to ALA divisions.

Programming focused on key public library issues of advocacy, technology, literacy, and serving adults and youth. At the forefront were emerging technologies, e-books, and digital rights management.

The conference opened with a welcome from Deborah Jacobs, director of the Global Libraries Initiative, Bill and Melinda Gates Foundation; an update on association-wide efforts to resolve e-book challenges from Sari Feldman, co-chair of the Digital Content and Libraries Working Group; and a keynote address by environmental business leader, advocate, and author Robert F. Kennedy, Jr. The conference also hosted a series of entertaining author events featuring best-selling adult, young adult, and children's authors David Baldacci (*Absolute Power*), Ally Carter (Gallagher Girls series), Joyce Carol Oates, and Jerry Pinkney. The closing keynote speaker was actor and comedian Betty White.

ALA Virtual Membership Meeting

Nearly 550 ALA members from around the world participated in the first-ever ALA Virtual Membership Meeting June 6, 2012. Members were able to participate directly in the discussions through chat and voiceover Internet protocol (voiceover IP), asking questions of ALA leaders while sharing information and insights from their own libraries. Under the leadership of the ALA Committee on Membership Meetings, the virtual event was held to provide new access to association information and business while allowing more participation by members who do not attend conferences regularly.

2012 ALSC National Institute

The ALSC National Institute in Indianapolis September 20–22 featured award-winning authors Peter Brown, Denise Fleming, Kevin Henkes, Eric Rohmann, Gary Paulsen, Bryan Collier, Doreen Rappaport, and April Pulley Sayre, with 20 educational programs spread over two days. Programs delved into some of the most important topics in library service to children, such as using technology in programming, what's hot in children's spaces, working with underserved populations, putting Every Child Ready to Read into practice, and using local partnerships to improve programming. Special events included a celebration of the 75th anniversary of the Caldecott Medal, a reception at Indiana University–Purdue University Indianapolis, and a tour of the infoZone and Children's Museum of Indianapolis.

ALA Publishing

Booklist Publications

Two major events marked 2012 for Booklist Publications—the introduction of a new subscription model offering a combination of print and online access, and *Booklist*'s cosponsor role (with RUSA) in the launch of the Andrew Carnegie Medals for Excellence in Fiction and Nonfiction.

Booklist regained ground and exceeded pre-recession revenue.

The annual Andrew Carnegie Medals for Excellence in Fiction and Nonfiction were established in 2012 to recognize the best fiction and nonfiction books for adult readers published in the United States the previous year. The seven-member selection committee includes three *Booklist* editors or contributors. A shortlist will be announced each May from a list of up to 50 titles drawn from the previous year's Booklist Editors' Choice and RUSA Notable Books lists.

The new *Booklist* subscription model, with the tagline "Feel like print? Want online too? Get both with the new *Booklist*!" includes the added benefit of around-the-clock password-access to *Booklist Online*. The combination offers libraries an added way to streamline collection development and readers' advisory workflows.

The current multiplatform suite of 11 products includes the 22 print issues of *Booklist* and four of *Book Links; Booklist Online* (now serving 1.25 million pages per month); six revenue-generating e-newsletters (some with exclusive sponsorships, some selling advertising on an issue-by-issue basis); *Booklist* webinars (sponsor-supported online programs, free to registrants); and Booklist Delivers (an e-blast service delivering sponsors' HTML promotions to the *Booklist* audience).

ALA Editions

ALA Editions, which already included ALA TechSource, grew in FY 2012 with the acquisition of Neal-Schuman Publishers, which specializes in professional books for librarians and archivists, and the launch of the trade imprint Huron Street Press, in addition to producing and disseminating more than 130 new products, including books, serial publications, and online learning opportunities.

Huron Street Press launched in spring 2012 with an immediate bestseller— *Read with Me: Best Books for Preschoolers* by ALA editor Stephanie Zvirin. The book was well reviewed in major parenting and educational publications. *Build Your Own App for Fun and Profit* by Scott La Counte followed, and a list of up to five titles is planned for each season going forward. In line with ALA's mission to enhance learning and ensure access to information for all, Huron Street Press titles are designed to appeal to a broad consumer and library market, harnessing the expertise of the association while encouraging library use. Huron titles are distributed by the Independent Publishers Group (iPg) and are stocked in traditional retail outlets as well as being widely available as e-books.

Despite the focus on the Neal-Schuman acquisition and launching Huron Street Press, ALA Editions and ALA TechSource produced and disseminated a record 137 new products. The catalog was redesigned to accommodate the developing range of types of content and formats. The emphasis continued to be on maximizing the content created by expert authors, in formats ranging from print books to print/online periodicals such as *Library Technology Reports* and *Smart Libraries Newsletter, and from combined print/e-book bundles to multipart online workshops. American Libraries* magazine also increased its use of content by ALA Editions and TechSource authors.

Standouts among the new publications included *College Libraries and Student Culture: What We Now Know,* edited by Lynda M. Duke and Andrew D. Ashe, which was well publicized in the general market (including substantial articles in *Inside Higher Education* and *USA Today*), and the highly anticipated Tech Set 11-20, published in collaboration with LITA.

Workshops, E-Courses Grow in Scope

ALA TechSource and ALA Editions workshops and online offerings grew significantly in FY 2012, with 34 distinct workshop events (50 sessions total) that attracted 6,000 attendees and 21 e-courses with more than 1,300 registrations, many of which included groups. Workshops and e-courses have become an increasingly important source of revenue for ALA Editions, and cover a growing range of topics, some built on content from new or bestselling backlist books and *Library Technology Reports* topics such as electronic resource management and the mobile Web.

ALA Graphics

Celebrities, book characters, tie-ins in with movies adapted from books, and event-related themes all continued to inspire ALA Graphics products, resulting in a strong year.

Collaborating with units across ALA to create new posters, bookmarks, digital files, and other products for library-related events continued to be a major part of ALA Graphics' work. These included National Library Week and Library Card Sign-Up Month in April, Banned Books Week in September, and Choose Privacy Week in May; Teen Read Week in October and Teen Tech Week in March; School Library Month in April; *El Día de los Niños/El Día de los Libros* in April; and National Friends of Libraries Week in October.

Hugo, the movie based on Brian Selznick's Caldecott-winning *The Invention of Hugo Cabret,* was highlighted on a poster and bookmark, as was *The Hunger Games.* Celebrity READ poster scores of the year included Oprah Winfrey in a landmark third appearance, and actress Lily Collins.

Picture-book favorites appearing on posters and bookmarks included Mo Willems's pals Elephant, Piggie, and Pigeon; Ladybug Girl; Ezra Jack Keats (in time for the 50th anniversary of *The Snowy Day*); and Clifford the Big Red Dog. Young readers were drawn to posters and bookmarks featuring characters from popu-

lar book and cartoon series such as Captain Underpants, Frankie Pickle, Goose-
bumps, Origami Yoda, and Avatar: The Last Airbender.

ALA JobLIST

ALA JobLIST, the association's library jobs site, continued to support the pro-
fession as a valued source of job search and career advice. Shared through its
Facebook and Twitter presences, as well as a growing presence on Google+, ALA
JobLIST is cited in the 25,000-strong ALA LinkedIn group as a valuable resource.
Now in its second year of publication, the biweekly *ALA JobLIST Direct* e-news-
letter has attracted more than 7,000 opt-in subscribers.

This joint project of the ACRL's *C&RL News* magazine, *American Libraries,*
and ALA's Office for Human Resource Development and Recruitment listed more
than 1,800 open positions during FY 2012 and increased its online banner advertising significantly. Enhancements are regularly made to increase ease of use and
effectiveness for both employers and job-seekers.

American Libraries had an eventful year, adding key staff and offering added
content in more channels, as well as increasing its social media presence. It has
evolved from being a monthly print magazine to serving news and other information to readers daily through a suite of products that includes print and multiple
digital options. Laurie D. Borman joined *American Libraries* in December 2011
as editor and publisher.

In conjunction with ALA's wider digital content initiative, the weekly e-newsletter *AL Direct* expanded its coverage of electronic trends in librarianship by creating a regular "E-Content" section. A new *American Libraries* blog, "E-Content"
by Christopher Harris launched in early October to complement the work of the
ALA Working Group on Digital Content and Libraries.

Special digital supplements were delivered throughout the year in a mobile-
friendly format for iPads and smartphones, posted on Facebook and Twitter, and
archived on the *American Libraries* website.

Topics included online learning/digital content, the annual "State of America's Libraries" report produced in collaboration with ALA's Public Information
Office, Library Design Showcase, the American Dream Starts @ your library, e-
books, and research.

RDA Implementation

The Library of Congress announced in late February 2012 that it would fully implement RDA: Resource Description and Access on March 31, 2013, citing the significant progress that has been made toward addressing the June 2011 recommendations of the U.S. RDA Test Coordinating Committee and the need for sufficient
lead time to prepare staff for the switch to RDA cataloging. Other national libraries were targeting their own implementation in the first quarter of 2013. This announcement set the framework for ALA Digital Reference's ongoing work on the
product itself and in helping prepare catalogers and other users for implementation.

Grants and Contributions

Gates Foundation Benchmarks Project

OITP, with PLA, continues its work as a member of the Public Access Technology Benchmarks coalition. OITP and PLA joined with other library and government leaders to develop a series of public-access technology benchmarks for public libraries. With $2.8 million in funding from the Bill and Melinda Gates Foundation and with the Urban Libraries Council as project lead and facilitator, the coalition will develop guidelines that define high-quality technology services at libraries.

Dollar General Expands Support

The Dollar General Literacy Foundation renewed its commitment to AASL and school libraries by dedicating an additional $435,000 in grants to Beyond Words: The Dollar General School Library Relief Fund. This donation brings the foundation's support of rebuilding school libraries affected by natural disaster to a total of $1.6 million. In addition, a new round of grants offers two annual awards and an increase in grant amounts. Previous grants ranged from $5,000 to $15,000; they now range from $10,000 to $20,000.

A grant of $50,000 will be awarded to two schools that meet the "beyond words" eligibility requirements and receive the highest application evaluation scores. Additional requirements are outlined on the AASL website.

OITP, PLA, COSLA Partner on Digital Literacy

IMLS awarded PLA a $291,000 grant to develop an online collection of digital literacy resources that will be accessible to libraries, patrons, and community-based organizations. The grant will include handouts, the development of training curricula in English and Spanish and library patron skills assessments. PLA will partner with OITP and Chief Officers of State Library Agencies (COSLA) to generate the online digital literacy resource collection.

Grant Funds Summer Reading Program

PLA received a planning grant of $50,000 from IMLS in May 2012 to support the research and design of a national digital summer reading (NDSR) program website application. PLA will partner with Influx Library User Experience to manage the project and plan development of the app. Expected to be built on the Digital Public Library of America platform, the app will be available to all U.S. libraries and will enable children and teens to interact with public libraries and summer reading content in numerous ways, including reading, listening, watching, playing, writing, reviewing, drawing, and recording.

News Know-How Project

OIF received a two-year grant from Open Society Foundations to design, market, and deliver a media literacy training program to high school students, using libraries and librarians as the information literacy hubs. In the first year OIF delivered the program to more than 10 libraries and more than 50 students. Libraries held summer schools for students, who learned about their "news neighborhoods" and studied examples of fact-checking press stories. With a focus of projects involving the 2012 national elections, some students reported that the program broadened the scope of their career choices and changed the way they look at the news.

Major Awards and Honors

Honorary Membership

ALA paid tribute to two new Honorary Members at the 2012 Annual Conference, bestowing ALA's highest honor on Betty J. Turock and U.S. Sen. Jack Reed (D-R.I.).

Turock, professor and dean emerita of the School of Communication and Information at Rutgers University and a past ALA president, was nominated in recognition of her outstanding commitment and achievement in the field of library and information science and as a practitioner, educator, advocate, and philanthropist. Her efforts have increased the emphasis of ALA and the field on diversity, innovation, leadership, and access for all.

Reed was nominated for his continuing, unwavering, and effective support of libraries in Congress. Throughout his career, he has supported education and libraries, statewide and nationally. He sponsored every major piece of library legislation as a member of the House of Representatives from 1990 to 1996 and as a Senator since 1997.

James Madison Award

Rep. Zoe Lofgren (D-Calif.) received the James Madison Award during the 2012 National Freedom of Information Day Conference, conducted by a partnership of ALA, the Reporters Committee for Freedom of the Press, OMB Watch, Open-TheGovernment.org, and the National Security Archive at George Washington University; and in cooperation with the annual "Sunshine Week" initiative sponsored by the American Society of News Editors. Lofgren was recognized for her fight against the Stop Online Piracy Act (SOPA), which would require Internet service providers to police users' activities in an attempt to combat online infringement overseas. Recognizing the potential harm that SOPA could have on First Amendment rights, intellectual freedom and privacy, Lofgren fought tirelessly to oppose the bill.

American Booksellers Association

333 Westchester Ave., White Plains, NY 10604
914-406-7500
World Wide Web http://www.bookweb.org

The year 2012 was one of sustained growth and development for the American Booksellers Association (ABA) and its more than 1,900 independent bookstore locations. Member stores recorded solid growth in year-over-year sales, and, once again, ABA saw a modest growth in the number of new members.

For much of the year ABA member bookstores saw double-digit sales growth over 2011, based on the unit sales of approximately 500 bookstores reporting to the association's Indie Bestseller Lists. Given the strong holiday season of 2011, ABA had projected that 2012's robust numbers would come down a little as the year progressed; however, at year's end the association reported that sales had grown almost 8 percent over 2011. In a letter to the membership, ABA CEO Oren Teicher noted that "The very healthy year-end number clearly demonstrates the vitality of independent bookstores," adding that the association doesn't "for one second underestimate the myriad challenges we continue to face—and I appreciate that the increases in sales did not happen in every store—but the fact is that 2012 was a good year for independent bookstores in the United States. As you and I know and appreciate, these sales are the result of careful planning and countless hours of hard work, and, importantly, they are also a testament to the unique role that indies play in helping book buyers discover new titles and experience firsthand a deeper connection with authors, great writing, and their own community."

Further evidence of strong sales in the indie bookstore channel came from a post-holiday Independent Business Survey conducted by the Institute for Local Self-Reliance in partnership with ABA and other independent business organizations. The survey found that independent businesses experienced solid revenue growth in 2012, buoyed in part by "buy local first" initiatives and growing public interest in supporting locally owned businesses.

These were among the study's key findings:

- Survey respondents reported revenue growth of 6.8 percent on average. More than two-thirds experienced revenue growth in 2012—a larger share than in the 2011 and 2010 post-holiday surveys.
- Independent businesses in communities with an active "buy local first" initiative run by a local business organization reported average revenue growth of 8.6 percent in 2012, compared with 3.4 percent for those in areas without such an initiative.
- Among survey respondents in cities with a "buy local first" initiative, 75 percent reported that the initiative had had a positive impact on their business.
- "Showrooming" (the term for customers examining products and seeking information in local stores and then buying online) was identified by independent retailers as one of their biggest challenges. More than 80 percent said showrooming was affecting their business, with 47 percent describing the impact as "moderate" or "significant."

- Lack of financing was also a challenge, with 23 percent of businesses sur-veyed reporting that they had been unable to secure a needed bank loan for their business in the last two years.

A heartening sign of growing consumer commitment to the shop local/"local first" movement was the success of American Express's annual "AmEx Small Business Saturday," held November 24 in 2012. ABA heard firsthand from scores of members that Small Business Saturday was one of their busiest days of the year, and after the event American Express reported that nationwide an estimated $5.5 billion was spent that day in independent businesses. For a number of years, inde-pendent bookstores have been leaders in their communities' independent business alliances, and that work has shown dividends as it continues to reshape the way millions of Americans are shopping.

Membership Growth Continues

ABA welcomed 43 indie bookstores that opened in 2012 in 25 states. This was the third year in a row that the association's bookstore membership numbers in-creased. Among the new member stores were six branches of existing businesses and seven selling primarily used books. California is home to seven new stores; New York, five; Florida and Texas, three each; and Kansas, Minnesota, Pennsylva-nia, and South Carolina, two each.

In a presentation in February 2013 at the O'Reilly Tools of Change for Pub-lishing Conference, ABA's Teicher talked about some of the factors of what he characterized as "a renaissance of indie bookselling." These included independent booksellers actively adopting and implementing appropriate technology; the fact that the localism/shop local movement had reached a tipping point with consum-ers; the introduction of appropriate nonbook items into the overall inventory of successful indie bookstores; a focus on children's books; and a full calendar of unique store events.

However, Teicher underscored that "the most important element . . . is the fact that physical bookstores offer a unique and unparalleled experience for readers and book buyers to discover a wide range of new titles." Though the indies' overall market share remains modest, that one data point doesn't tell the full story, he said. "Our channel's positive sales numbers highlight that bricks-and-mortar indepen-dent bookstores continue to offer book buyers a unique and essential browsing and discovery experience" that is fueling sales in other channels as well.

Association and Governance Activity

In May 2012 ABA announced the results of the association's 2012 board of direc-tors election. Elected by ABA's bookstore members to serve three-year terms as directors were Betsy Burton of the King's English Bookshop in Salt Lake City, Valerie Koehler of Blue Willow Bookshop in Houston, and Jonathon Welch of Talking Leaves . . . Books in Buffalo.

Burton started her second three-year term as an ABA board member in June; for Koehler and Welch, this was their first full three-year term. Koehler had been appointed earlier to the board to fill the vacancy created by a March 2011 ABA bylaws amendment that made the presidency a separate and distinct position from the board of directors. Welch was filling the seat vacated by Beth Puffer, who retired in April 2012 from New York's Bank Street Bookstore.

In June 2012 Becky Anderson of Anderson's Bookshops in Naperville and Downers Grove, Illinois, and Steve Bercu of BookPeople in Austin, Texas, began the second year of their two-year terms as ABA president and vice president, respectively.

Also continuing on the board were Sarah Bagby of Watermark Books & Café in Wichita; Tom Campbell of the Regulator Bookshop in Durham, North Carolina; John Evans of "Diesel, a Bookstore" in Brentwood, Malibu, and Oakland, California; Matt Norcross of McLean & Eakin Booksellers in Petoskey, Michigan; and Ken White of the San Francisco State University Bookstore.

Book Awards

BookExpo America (BEA), ABA's major trade show, was the site of the presentation of the 2012 Indies Choice Book Awards and the E. B. White Read-Aloud Awards, chosen by a record-breaking number of owners and staff at member stores.

The 2012 Indies Choice Book Award winners were (adult fiction) *The Marriage Plot* by Jeffrey Eugenides (Farrar, Straus & Giroux); (adult nonfiction) *Blood, Bones and Butter: The Inadvertent Education of a Reluctant Chef* by Gabrielle Hamilton (Random); (adult debut book) *The Tiger's Wife* by Téa Obreht (Random); and (young adult) *Between Shades of Gray* by Ruta Sepetys (Philomel).

The E. B. White Read-Aloud Awards (formerly offered by the Association of Booksellers for Children, which merged with ABA in 2010) reflect the universal appeal to a wide range of ages typified by E. B. White's books. The winner in the picture book category was *I Want My Hat Back* by Jon Klassen (Candlewick). For middle readers, there was a tie between books by brother-and-sister authors: *The Apothecary* by Maile Meloy and Ian Schoenherr, illustrator (Putnam), and *Wildwood* by Colin Meloy and Carson Ellis, illustrator (Balzer + Bray).

ABA members also chose bestselling author and fellow indie bookseller Ann Patchett as Most Engaging Author for 2012. Patchett was recognized for her exceptional involvement and responsiveness during in-store appearances and for having a strong sense of the importance of independent booksellers to their local communities.

In addition, booksellers inducted three of their all-time favorite books into the Indies Choice Book Awards Picture Book Hall of Fame: *Curious George* by H. A. Rey (Houghton Mifflin Harcourt); *The Little Engine That Could* by Watty Piper (Grosset & Dunlap/Philomel); and *Miss Rumphius* by Barbara Cooney (Viking Juvenile/Puffin).

The winners and finalists in all categories, with the exception of Most Engaging Author and Picture Book Hall of Fame, were chosen from titles appearing on ABA's Indie Next Lists in 2011, with additional titles for the E. B. White Read-Aloud Awards nominated by bookseller members of the ABC Group at ABA.

ABA Personnel Changes

The association announced in May 2012 that Neil Strandberg, a longtime staff member at Denver's Tattered Cover Book Store, would be joining the association in the newly created position of director of member technology.

Strandberg began his career in independent bookselling in 1988 at A Clean Well-Lighted Place for Books at Larkspur Landing in Marin County, California. A year later he returned home to Denver and started what turned into a 23-year career, encompassing a number of positions, at Tattered Cover. For the last several years he had been the store's manager of operations.

In December ABA's offices moved from Tarrytown to White Plains, New York.

Member Education

Despite a record-breaking snowstorm that shut the Kansas City airport a day before its opening, the eighth annual ABA Winter Institute (Wi8) opened on time and presented its full slate of educational sessions, plenary speakers, and author events. The three-day program, which ran February 22–25, 2013, provided members with a mix of relevant information, best practices, expert insights, and networking opportunities with colleagues from across the country and, for the first time, representatives of publishing houses. The institute's programming covered an array of topics, including selling high-end sidelines, working with self-published authors, nonfiction buying with core curriculum in mind, and addressing the special needs market for children. The event's lead sponsor is the Ingram Content Group.

Wi8 was co-scheduled with the National Association of College Stores' CAMEX (Campus Market Expo), and institute programming included a field trip for bookseller attendees to the CAMEX trade floor.

Concurrent with the Winter Institute, ABA offered a free, full-day "Introduction to Retail Bookselling" seminar. The workshop was facilitated by Donna Paz Kaufman and Mark Kaufman of the bookstore training group Paz & Associates.

The 2014 Winter Institute is scheduled for Seattle January 21–24.

ABA also held three one-day specialty institutes during 2012—two for the first time: the Children's Specialty Institute (held June 6 during BookExpo America) and the Events Specialty Institute (on October 3, just prior to the Heartland Regional Trade Show)—and the second IndieCommerce Institute (held September 13 at ABA's new headquarters in White Plains).

ABA also continued to offer members free education seminars and panels in conjunction with the nine regional trade shows organized by the industry's regional booksellers' associations, and a series of ABA forums, also organized with the regional trade associations.

ABA again published its annual financial survey of participating independent bookstores, the ABACUS report. Stores participating in the ABACUS project received a customized report that analyzes their financial results, including comparisons with other businesses based on multiple criteria (such as sales level, store size, and community type) in addition to year-to-year trending information.

ABACUS helps participants benchmark key economic indicators and create a roadmap for growth and profitability. ABACUS data is used in aggregate by ABA to create timely education for member stores.

ABA/Kobo Partnership, IndieCommerce

In August ABA and Kobo, a leader in e-books and digital reading devices with more than 10 million registered users worldwide, announced a partnership designed to bring Kobo's e-reading platform to independent bookstores.

Under the agreement, all ABA members can now offer their customers a full line of e-readers, accessories, and e-books from Kobo's catalog of nearly 3 million titles. Participating ABA members will retain their customer relationships and share in the revenue on every sale. The program includes training for booksellers and in-store merchandising, as well as marketing, sales, and logistics support. By partnering with ABA, Kobo continues its strategy of working with booksellers, and ABA member bookstores increase their ability to offer customers easy and convenient online shopping opportunities.

"We are very excited to work with the ABA and independent booksellers across America to bring an indie alternative to the e-reading market," said Kobo CEO Mike Serbinis. "With this partnership, we are confident that independents will have a world-class offering for their loyal customers and a voice in the digital transformation."

ABA CEO Oren Teicher said, "We are pleased to offer our ABA members a competitive e-book retailing solution uniquely crafted to meet the needs of independent booksellers and their customers. Through this partnership, indie bookstore customers will have access to a broad and diverse inventory of e-books. Today's readers want a first-class shopping experience, both in-store and online, and this new partnership allows indie booksellers to meet the ever-changing needs of shoppers in a dynamic marketplace."

ABA continued in 2012 to introduce enhancements and new features to IndieCommerce, its e-commerce business solution for member stores, and the bookstore user base for IndieCommerce continued to grow. For the 420 bookstores now using the IndieCommerce platform, online sales grew by 28 percent during the year.

Advocacy

ABA continued its advocacy efforts on behalf of member bookstores during 2012. The fight for sales tax equity was a key focus of energy and resources, as ABA worked with member bookstores and allies for sales tax fairness, advocating on the national level for the passage of federal legislation and on the state level in support of booksellers in states considering the passage of legislation that would ensure a fair and sensible enforcement of sales tax collection for online sales. Efforts included grassroots outreach, visits to state and federal elected officials, member education and lobbying support, and working with an active alliance of trade associations and organizations.

Early in November ABA joined with 19 retailers and trade groups, including the National Association of College Stores and the National Retail Federation, to petition a federal court for rejection of a proposed class action settlement of a federal antitrust lawsuit over increasing Visa and MasterCard credit card swipe fees.

In a brief submitted to the U.S. District Court for the Eastern District of New York, the groups argued that the proposed settlement would fail to bring the swipe fees charged by Visa and MasterCard under control and did not give retailers opposing the settlement an adequate mechanism to opt out.

On November 9 U.S. District Court Judge John Gleeson granted preliminary approval to the proposed class action settlement of the federal antitrust lawsuit. The decision to grant preliminary approval came after hearing oral arguments from both opponents and proponents of the settlement. On December 3 a majority of named class plaintiffs filed a notice of appeal to challenge the ruling. The group will ask the U.S. Court of Appeals for the Second Circuit to deny preliminary approval due to the legal defects in the proposed settlement.

In another case, on September 6 Federal Judge Denise Cote issued an order entering as a final judgment the Department of Justice's proposed settlement agreement with three publishers—Hachette, HarperCollins, and Simon & Schuster—in a matter involving e-books antitrust litigation. Under the ruling, the three settling publishers are required to terminate all of their agency agreements and any agreement that restricts an e-book retailer's discretion over pricing as soon as allowed under contract; typically, on 30 days' notice. The settling publishers are also prevented from adopting new agency-type agreements for two years. Apple, Macmillan, and Penguin did not choose to settle, and their case was scheduled to go to trial in June 2013.

Independent booksellers had vigorously argued against the settlement agreement. Hundreds of booksellers wrote the U.S. Department of Justice to oppose it, arguing that the settlement would unfairly hurt bricks-and-mortar retailers, greatly limit consumer options, facilitate below-cost pricing, and, ultimately, very likely lead to a monopoly.

ABA joined booksellers—as well as publishers, authors, and literary agents—in submitting comments to the Justice Department. In a June 14 letter to the department, ABA's Teicher wrote, "We believe that elimination of the agency model will radically change the current e-book distribution system, will significantly discourage new entry, and will lead to the departure from the market of a sizable number of the independent bookstores that are currently selling e-books."

Strongly underscoring ABA's support for the agency model and its positive effects for readers and book buyers, the letter noted that "The agency model is pro-competitive and enhances consumer choice. It is a perfectly legitimate mode of business. Indeed, it is a completely appropriate response to aggressive pricing strategies that include the sales of e-books below the cost at which those books were acquired from publishers."

In addition, the court approved a request by ABA and Barnes & Noble to submit a joint friends-of-the-court brief in regard to the settlement.

Supporting Booksellers and Readers

In fall 2012 ABA rolled out its first multi-publisher promotion for participating member bookstores, "Thanks for Shopping Indie."

The program, which began on November 24, Small Business Saturday, gave booksellers the opportunity to offer an "extra" to customers on a broad range of 2012 Indie Next List titles, and it included a shortlist of more than 60 titles chosen by an experienced group of independent booksellers and approved by participating ABA publisher partners. ABA produced a number of marketing and collateral materials for booksellers to use in their stores and online to promote "Thanks for Shopping Indie," and booksellers reported a number of in-store successes with the promotion. Additional multi-publisher promotions are planned.

Association of Research Libraries

21 Dupont Circle N.W., Washington, DC 20036
202-296-2296, e-mail arlhq@arl.org
World Wide Web http://www.arl.org

Lee Anne George
Publications Program Officer

The Association of Research Libraries (ARL) is a nonprofit organization of 125 research libraries in the United States and Canada. Its mission is to influence the changing environment of scholarly communication and the public policies that affect research libraries and the diverse communities they serve. ARL pursues this mission by advancing the goals of its member research libraries, providing leadership in public and information policy to the scholarly and higher education communities, fostering the exchange of ideas and expertise, facilitating the emergence of new roles for research libraries, and shaping a future environment that leverages its interests with those of allied organizations.

ARL and its member libraries addressed a number of strategic issues in 2012. Key areas included content management and collections in 21st century research libraries; services to patrons with print disabilities; skills for 21st century library staff; organizational strategies for work force transformation; and owners' rights, first sale doctrine, and other copyright issues. The association's diversity and leadership initiatives continue to expand the capacity of libraries to reflect society's diversity in staffing, collections, leadership, and programs. Ongoing and new assessment activities continue to support research libraries' ability to effectively measure their performance. Following are highlights of the association's programs and activities in 2012.

Influencing Public Policies

A primary goal of the ARL Influencing Public Policies program is to encourage federal legislative and executive branch action that is favorable to the research library and higher education communities. To achieve this goal, the program helps ARL members keep abreast of the legislative landscape and of rapidly changing issues, players, regulations, and community priorities. The program analyzes, responds to, and seeks to influence public initiatives on information, intellectual property, and telecommunications policies, among others. In addition, the program promotes funding for numerous agencies and national institutions and advances ARL members' interests on these issues. The program also monitors Canadian information policies, in such areas as copyright and intellectual property and access to government information, through the Canadian Association of Research Libraries (CARL).

Copyright and Intellectual Property

In late January 2012 ARL released the *Code of Best Practices in Fair Use for Academic and Research Libraries,* an easy-to-use statement of fair and reasonable approaches to fair use developed by and for librarians who support academic inquiry and higher education. The code was developed in partnership with the Center for Social Media and the Washington College of Law at American University, and the effort was supported by a grant from the Andrew W. Mellon Foundation. Staff from the partnership spent 2012 traveling around the country promoting it and educating library staff on its contents. In late November five directors of ARL member libraries reflected in a set of video interviews on the success they'd had using the code. The videos featured David Carlson (Texas A&M), Susan Gibbons (Yale), Tom Leonard (California, Berkeley), Judy Russell (University of Florida), and Gary Strong (UCLA). The interviews are part of an ongoing effort to highlight successes and good practices using the code to encourage libraries to take full advantage of their fair use rights. The "ARL Policy Notes" blog is also highlighting success stories in an ongoing series called "Code Stories" (http://policynotes. arl.org/tagged/code-stories). A downloadable pdf of the code, a calendar of code-related events, FAQs, videos, slideshows, and briefings are available on the ARL website.

ARL worked with the other members of the Library Copyright Alliance (LCA)—the American Library Association (ALA) and the Association of College and Research Libraries (ACRL)—during early 2012 in opposing the proposed Stop Online Piracy Act (SOPA) and the PROTECT IP Act (PIPA).

In February ARL released "A New Day for Website Archiving 2.0," an updated analysis of the legal arguments available to support website archiving by research libraries, written by copyright expert Jonathan Band (http://www.policy bandwidth.com). Band's analysis focuses on the fair use doctrine and takes account of key developments in case law, as well as a helpful memo by the U.S. Patent and Trademark Office and the recently released *Code of Best Practices in Fair Use for Academic and Research Libraries.*

In May 2012 the ARL Board of Directors enthusiastically endorsed the Visual Resources Association's Statement on the Fair Use of Images for Teaching, Research, and Study. The statement is a concise guide to best practices around a medium that can seem especially intimidating for educational users, written by professionals who work with images every day and vetted by experts in the field of copyright. ARL believes that the association's recommendations will help libraries better serve their educational mission by informing library practices and policies with the values of educators, scholars, and students. The ARL board also noted that the practices described in the statement are fully consistent with the Code of Best Practices in Fair Use.

In early June Band testified in a U.S. Copyright Office hearing on behalf of LCA in favor of renewing selected exemptions to Section 1201 of the Digital Millennium Copyright Act (DMCA). In particular, he called for the renewal of the exemption for the creation of film-clip compilations for classroom and educational use by all college and university faculty, regardless of academic discipline. In October the Copyright Office released its latest iteration of rules describing exemptions and renewed those that LCA requested.

During the year ARL joined the new Owners' Rights Initiative (ORI) (http:// ownersrightsinitiative.org), which represents a diverse set of retailers, libraries, educators, Internet companies, and associations to protect "first-sale" rights in the United States. ORI is committed to ensuring the right to re-sell legitimate goods, regardless of where they were manufactured. The first-sale doctrine is the provision in the Copyright Act that allows any purchaser of a legal copy of a book or other copyrighted work to sell or lend that copy. ARL Associate Executive Director Prue Adler is a member of the ORI steering committee.

Court Cases and Related Activities

ARL filed or participated in nine amicus (friend-of-the-court) briefs in 2012, including one regarding affirmative action.

Capitol Records v. *Jammie Thomas-Rasset*

ARL joined other organizations in a brief in a highly publicized file-sharing case, *Capitol Records* v. *Jammie Thomas-Rasset*. The brief supported the trial court's decision to greatly reduce a damages award for copyright infringement. It warned that such exorbitant damage awards were inconsistent with the purpose of copyright and could have a chilling effect on legitimate uses, especially fair use. The brief is available at https://www.eff.org/sites/default/files/filenode/ThomasRasset Brief.pdf.

Authors Guild v. *HathiTrust*

In April, in an amicus brief prepared by Band, LCA warned against a radical misinterpretation of the Copyright Act put forth by the Authors Guild in its lawsuit against HathiTrust—a collaborative repository of digital content from research libraries—and several partner libraries. In its brief, LCA pointed out that this view was inconsistent with the purpose and history of both Section 107 and Section 108 of the Copyright Act, as well as the plain text of Section 108, which includes an explicit savings clause to preserve libraries' fair use rights. On July 6 LCA and the Electronic Frontier Foundation (EFF) filed a second amicus brief in the case, urging a federal court to find that the fair use doctrine permitted the creation of a valuable digital library. On October 10 Judge Harold Baer, Jr., of the District Court for the Southern District of New York ruled in favor of HathiTrust Digital Library and the National Federation of the Blind in the suit brought by the Authors Guild.

Georgia State Decision

In May Judge Orinda Evans of the U.S. District Court for the North District of Georgia released a 350-page opinion in a copyright infringement lawsuit against Georgia State University (GSU). The case concerns the use at GSU of electronic course reserves and electronic course sites to make excerpts from academic books available online to students enrolled in particular courses. The named plaintiffs are three academic publishers (Oxford University Press, Cambridge University Press, and Sage), but an early filing in the case confirmed that the lawsuit was being funded equally by the Copyright Clearance Center (CCC) and the Association of American Publishers (AAP). The plaintiffs argued that the unlicensed posting of digital excerpts for student access almost always exceeded fair use and should require a license. Judge Evans's opinion represents a significant victory for GSU individually, a major defeat for the plaintiffs, and overall a positive development for libraries generally. The substance of the opinion is not ideal, but it is far more generous than the publishers had sought; it establishes a comfortable safe harbor for fair use of books on e-reserve, and libraries remain free to take more progressive steps. On May 15, 2012, ARL released an Issue Brief prepared by Brandon Butler summarizing the GSU decision and its implications for libraries. At the end of May ARL hosted a webcast detailing what the GSU decision means for libraries.

Kirtsaeng v. Wiley & Sons

In July ARL joined the other members of LCA in filing an amicus brief with the U.S. Supreme Court in support of petitioner Supap Kirtsaeng in *Kirtsaeng* v. *Wiley & Sons* (http://www.librarycopyrightalliance.org/bm~doc/lca-kirtsaeng-brief-3july 2012.pdf). LCA asked the court to reverse the Second Circuit ruling and apply the first sale doctrine to all copies manufactured with the lawful authorization of the holder of a work's U.S. copyright. The high court's eventual decision in *Kirtsaeng* v. *Wiley* could have profound effects for libraries because the case calls into question whether materials printed abroad can circulate legally in the United States. On October 16 ARL hosted a webcast to discuss the case, the first sale doctrine, and what's at stake for libraries and others.

Authors Guild v. Google, Inc.

In August LCA and EFF filed a "friend of the court" brief in *Authors Guild* v. *Google, Inc.* The brief defends Google Book Search (GBS) as permissible under the doctrine of fair use and argues that GBS is beneficial to the public, that this public benefit tilts the analysis firmly in favor of fair use, that a legislative "fix" is both unnecessary and unworkable, and that the Authors Guild should not be permitted to shut down GBS after years of encouraging public reliance on the tool. In November LCA filed an amicus brief with the Second Circuit Court of Appeals asking that the court not allow the Authors Guild and several individual authors to represent all authors in a class action copyright lawsuit against Google over its GBS program. The brief argues three main points: that class certification in this case threatens to undermine the public interest; that the case presents no common issue of law or fact; and that using subclasses to determine fair use is an unworkable solution to the problems inherent in litigating this dispute as a class action. The brief was prepared by Stefan Mintzer of the law firm White & Case.

International Copyright Activities

In February 2012 ARL joined other members of the open-government community in requesting that President Barack Obama increase the transparency of the Trans-Pacific Partnership (TPP) Free Trade Agreement negotiating process (http://www. openthegovernment.org/node/3377). In August LCA sent a letter to Ambassador Ron Kirk, U.S. Trade Representative, concerning the agreement. On behalf of LCA, ARL Associate Executive Director Adler noted LCA's appreciation for the "U.S. proposal for copyright exceptions and limitations" in the agreement. In the letter to Kirk, LCA welcomed inclusion of this language in the TPP agreement and noted that the U.S. Trade Representative "should encourage the other Parties to agree to make the entire draft IP chapter text publicly available for review and discussion." The letter is at http://www.librarycopyrightalliance.org/bm~doc/lt_kirktpp14aug12.pdf.

In July, at the World Intellectual Property Organization (WIPO) 24th Copyright and Related Rights Standing Committee session, LCA was represented by international copyright advocate and librarian Lori Driscoll. She carried the message that copyright exceptions for libraries ensure a vibrant arena for the creation and use of creative works as well as the advancement of learning. Because U.S. copyright law is one of the world's most flexible, member nations of WIPO were eager to hear from U.S. libraries about their experiences. Throughout the year, LCA responded to draft treaty language and worked with the U.S. delegation. For more information, see http://www.librarycopyrightalliance.org/submissions/international/wipo.shtml.

In November WIPO met in Geneva to further consider an international treaty concerning access to copyrighted works by individuals with print disabilities. Jonathan Band represented LCA at the meeting. Following up on those discussions, Adler, ARL, and Carrie Russell of ALA sent a letter on behalf of LCA to the Under Secretary of State for Economic Growth, Energy, and the Environment and the director of the Institute of Museum and Library Services (IMLS) expressing support for a treaty and detailing continuing concerns with existing language in the international instrument. On December 18 the WIPO General Assembly decided to convene a diplomatic conference in 2013 to complete negotiations on the treaty. For details, see http://www.librarycopyrightalliance.org/submissions/international/wipo.shtml.

Public Access Policies

Open Access and Public Access Policies

In January 2012 ARL submitted responses to two requests for information (RFIs) from the White House on public access to the results of federally funded research, one pertaining to scholarly publications and the other to digital data. ARL collaborated with the Johns Hopkins University (JHU) Libraries and SPARC on the digital data RFI. ARL's response to the scholarly publications RFI and the JHU/ARL/SPARC response to the digital data RFI are available on the ARL website.

Later in January ARL joined nine organizations in a letter to members of the U.S. House of Representatives that signaled strong opposition to the Research Works Act (H.R. 3699). In February ARL and 89 universities and organizations wrote to members of the House expressing deep concerns with the legislation. The Association of Public and Land-grant Universities and the Association of American Universities, as well as more than 30 organizations of the open government community, also wrote in opposition to the act. Soon afterward the cosponsors of the act said they would not take legislative action on the bill.

Also in February the Federal Research Public Access Act (FRPAA, S. 2096 and H.R. 4004) was introduced in the House of Representatives and the Senate. These companion bills would ensure free, timely, online access to the published results of research funded by 11 federal agencies. The legislation seeks to extend and expand access to these federally funded research resources and, importantly, spur and accelerate scientific discovery. ARL, with nine organizations, wrote to Congress in support of FRPAA.

In May Access2Research, a group of advocates for open access, posted the "We the People" White House petition for public access to federally funded research. A broad range of open access supporters, including ARL and SPARC, spread the word about the petition using e-mail, blogs, Twitter, Facebook, and YouTube.

Open Government

In April 2012 ARL joined EFF and OpenTheGovernment.org in endorsing comments by Public.Resource.Org to the U.S. Office of Management and Budget (OMB) on the incorporation of rulemaking standards by reference. ARL, EFF, and OpenTheGovernment.org noted that "all material incorporated by reference—regardless of the stage in the regulatory process, the subject matter of the regulation, or the identity of the regulated entity—should be made freely available, with no purported copyright restrictions and downloadable on a government agency's website."

In May ARL and other open government allies urged the Senate to reject a decision by the House of Representatives to defund the U.S. Census Bureau's American Community Survey (ACS) and to include sufficient funding for the survey in fiscal year 2013. ACS is an annual survey that provides data on the social and economic needs of local communities. ACS's rich data set on such neighborhood characteristics as income, education, and occupational skills is used by retailers to decide where they should open new locations and by manufacturers and service sector firms to identify the occupational skills of local labor markets.

In July ARL joined many open government groups in support of the Congressional Research Service Electronic Accessibility Resolution of 2012 (H.R. 727). U.S. Reps. Mike Quigley (D-Ill.) and Leonard Lance (R-N.J.) introduced this legislation to increase transparency and access to Congressional Research Service (CRS) reports. The resolution calls for the reports—which are routinely cited by members of Congress, the media and others—to be publicly available on a website maintained by the House Clerk. For more information, see the Sunlight Foundation's blog post about the bill (http://sunlightfoundation.com/blog/2012/07/10/new-bill-would-open-crs-reports-to-public).

In September ARL joined other organizations, including OpenTheGovernment org, to release a progress report to mark the one-year anniversary of the Obama administration's release of the Open Government Partnership U.S. National Action Plan (http://www.openthegovernment.org/sites/default/files/NAP-ProgressReportFinal.pdf). The action plan includes a variety of commitments aimed to further public participation and government transparency, and to improve citizen access to government information.

Throughout the year, ARL joined open government advocates in promoting legislation for whistleblower protection, which became law, and legislation regarding Freedom of Information Act (FOIA).

Privacy and Civil Liberties Issues

In April 2012 ARL joined more than 30 organizations in a letter to Congress noting serious concerns with H.R. 3523, the Cyber Intelligence Sharing and Protection Act of 2011 (CISPA). ARL also joined with 40 members of the FOIA community in identifying significant flaws in the legislation. Following the passage of CISPA in the House, the Senate considered two cybersecurity bills. ARL participated in a series of bipartisan letters to the Senate expressing concerns about the Cyber Security Act of 2012 (S. 2105) and the SECURE IT Act (S. 2151). For more information, see http://www.openthegovernment.org/node/3446 and http://www.constitutionproject.org/pdf/51012_senatecybersecuritys2105coalitionletter.pdf.

In June ARL joined a variety of civil liberties groups in demanding that reauthorization of the FISA Amendments Act of 2008 (FAA) be conditioned on tighter protections for privacy. Several civil liberties groups raised concerns about the bill, urging key congressional leaders to institute stronger safeguards for privacy. For details, see https://www.cdt.org/files/pdfs/fisa_amendact_signon_ltr.pdf.

In September ARL joined a diverse group of stakeholders in a letter to U.S. Senator Patrick Leahy (D-Vt.) applauding his introduction of an amendment that would make important updates to the Electronic Communications Privacy Act (ECPA) (http://www.educause.edu/ir/library/pdf/EPO1212.pdf). Among other things, the amendment would require a warrant for access to e-mail and other private electronic communications, which are currently available without a warrant in some circumstances. The U.S. Court of Appeals for the Sixth Circuit has declared that access to e-mail without a warrant is unconstitutional, adding to the need for an update. The update will bring the law's protections, which have not been changed since they were originally passed in 1986, into line with 21st century technology and expectations of privacy.

In November ARL issued a press statement applauding a bipartisan majority of the Senate Judiciary Committee, which endorsed a bill including provisions proposed by Leahy that would provide vital privacy protection to e-mail and cloud storage. The proposal that passed the committee would require a warrant for access to these materials across the board, no matter where they are stored or for how long.

Federal Funding

Deficit Reduction

In July ARL joined nearly 3,000 organizations and institutions in a letter urging policymakers to avoid sequestration and find a balanced approach to deficit reduction that includes no further cuts to the nondefense discretionary (NDD) portion of the federal budget. Signatories to the letter noted that "NDD programs support our economy, drive our global competitiveness, and provide an environment where all Americans may lead healthy, productive lives. Only a balanced approach to deficit reduction can restore fiscal stability, and NDD has done its part."

Fiscal Cliff

In December ARL, the American Association for the Advancement of Science, and 125 partner organizations representing U.S. science, engineering, higher education, and businesses sent a letter to President Obama and congressional leaders urging them to reach a balanced compromise on the looming "fiscal cliff" to avoid harming critical research efforts (http://www.aaas.org/news/releases/2012/media/ AAAS Interorganizational Sequestration Letter 12-07-2012_2.pdf).

Student Loan Cap

ARL joined the American Council on Education (ACE) and more than 40 higher-education-related organizations in letters to Congress supporting legislation to maintain the current Stafford student loan interest rate at 3.4 percent. Writing on behalf of these organizations, ACE President Molly Corbett Broad commented that "we are very encouraged by the bipartisan interest in preventing the rate from rising to 6.8 percent in just over two months time. With interest rates on many consumer loans available at rates below 3.4 percent, raising student loan interest rates to 6.8 percent in this environment makes little sense and would create considerable hardship for students and their families."

Other Public Policy Issues

In May 2012 ARL formed the Joint Task Force on Services to Patrons with Print Disabilities to expand upon the ongoing work of the Library Copyright Alliance in support of an international instrument for the print disabled that is under active consideration by WIPO. In November ARL published a report that contains nine recommendations for research libraries to better align their services with the mission to make information accessible to their full range of diverse users equitably. See http://www.arl.org/focus-areas/accessibility.

In August ARL joined ACE and 38 other higher education associations in an amicus brief to the Supreme Court in *Fisher* v. *University of Texas at Austin,* supporting the university in a case concerning affirmative action. ACE urged the court to reaffirm the constitutionality of the university's use of race and ethnicity in its admissions process. For more information, see http://www.acenet.edu/news-room/Pages/Amicus-Brief-Supreme-Court-Fisher-v-UT.aspx.

In October ARL published a 15-page issue brief, "Massive Open Online Courses: Legal and Policy Issues for Research Libraries," prepared by Brandon Butler. The paper describes some of the ways in which research libraries are supporting university engagement with these courses (known as MOOCs), the legal issues with which libraries may be asked to wrestle in these roles, and the policy questions and priorities that may be raised by MOOC teaching. For more information and to view the brief, see the "ARL Policy Notes" blog entry http://policy notes.arl.org/post/34106531376/arl-issue-brief-moocs-libraries.

Advancing Scholarly Communication

In an environment that is increasingly global, the ARL Scholarly Communication program encourages the advancement of effective, extensible, sustainable, and economically viable models of scholarly communication that provide barrier-free access to high-quality information. The program's strategic plan was updated in 2012 and now has the following components:

- To analyze and characterize the dynamic and diverse system of scholarly communication and ensure a continuing dialogue among its many stakeholders
- To support selected new models and tools of scholarly communication
- To aggressively develop and pursue new strategies to advance fair pricing and the terms and conditions under which content is made available and preserved, including openness and transparency in contract agreements

Licensing Initiative

ARL actively began an overall licensing initiative in 2011 by establishing an agreement with the library consortium LYRASIS to serve as the agent to negotiate licenses for online content on behalf of interested ARL member libraries. The goals of the licensing initiative are to influence the marketplace regarding licensing rights, technical specifications, and business terms that meet the needs of research libraries in the emerging e-book market. Moreover, the license is available to other academic libraries with which ARL members have established consortial relations. Several agreements that adhered to the principles ARL expressed in its requirements were reached in 2012. Offerings made available to ARL members included Project MUSE/UPCC e-book collections for 2012 and 2013, a 2013 University Press Scholarship Online offer from Oxford University Press, and a 2013 Harvard University Press content offer through De Gruyter Online.

New Publishing Models

Information on new publishing models is shared by ARL with its members and the broader library community.

The SCOAP[3] project, which works toward open access publishing in particle physics, made significant progress as publishing partners were identified through a tender process. The governance model was established and processes to reconcile subscription fee reductions and redirection of subscription money were being developed at the end of 2012. ARL provided information on the project and helped to identify member contacts to ensure the broadest participation.

In order to encourage positive open access policies and publishing models, the ARL Advancing Scholarly Communication Committee established a process in 2012 to acknowledge adoption of open access policies by scholarly societies and funding and research organizations.

ARL raised awareness about library publishing activities by promoting best practices and sharing information about business cases for new service development.

Transforming Research Libraries

The transformation of research libraries mirrors the ongoing evolution of research institutions and the practices of research and scholarship. ARL's Transforming Research Libraries strategic direction focuses on articulating, promoting, and facilitating new and expanding roles for ARL libraries that support, enable, and enrich the transformations affecting research and research-intensive education.

Research Library Collections Task Force

In January 2011 ARL launched the 21st Century Research Library Collections Task Force, which was charged to "articulate an action plan on 21st century research library collections and some of the emerging functions related to content managed by research libraries in a digital age." In May 2012 the task force released a briefing paper for research library directors titled *21st-Century Collections: Calibration of Investment and Collaborative Action.* The paper notes that, in the 21st century, collections are still a core asset for research libraries, but the context and strategies for decisions and investments are changing. The task force was co-chaired by Deborah Jakubs of Duke University and Thomas Leonard of the University of California, Berkeley. Christine Avery of Penn State University was the ARL Visiting Program Officer supporting the task force.

E-Science Institute

ARL and the Council on Library and Information Resources/Digital Library Federation (CLIR/DLF) jointly developed an E-Science Institute in 2011 to support member libraries seeking to build or enhance the library's capacity to advance e-science. The institute took small teams from participating research libraries through experiences that strengthen and advance their e-science support role. The development and delivery of the institute was funded by sponsoring libraries that are members of ARL and CLIR/DLF.

The first of the three ARL/DLF E-Science Institute capstone events took place in Atlanta in November 2011, and the institute held its final two capstone events in Phoenix and in Dallas in January 2012. Nearly 70 ARL institutions participated in the institute and drafted strategic agendas for the development of e-science and e-research services and infrastructure on their campuses.

ARL and DLF asked DuraSpace to host a new e-science institute in the 2012–2013 academic year. This institute is offered to any academic and research library audiences seeking opportunities to boost institutional support of e-research and the management and preservation of the scientific and scholarly record. The new institute includes ongoing communication with the ARL/CLIR Connect E-Science/E-Research Community—an interactive website for ESI participants to maintain contact with one another, the ESI faculty, and experts and professionals in the fields of information and library science to build a community of emerging practice. ARL and DLF worked with DuraSpace to shape the new institute, building on the earlier successful program of creating a valuable learning experience and ongoing community collaboration among academic and research libraries.

Sustainability of Digitized Special Collections

In late 2010 ARL and Ithaka S+R partnered in a two-year study, funded by the Institute for Museum and Library Services, of how libraries, archives, and museums are sustaining digitized special collections. In November 2011 Ithaka S+R and ARL led a webcast, "Sustainability of Digitized Special Collections: A Participant's Guide," for more than 70 attendees from ARL libraries. In March 2012 ARL and Ithaka S+R launched a three-part survey of the ARL membership to collect information critical to understanding the financial and organizational basis for sustaining digitized special collections. Part I asked ARL deans and directors for a brief institutional perspective on the role of digitized special collections within the organization. Part II surveyed each organization's activities, costs, and revenues associated with sustaining digitized special collections in the aggregate. Part III asked each organization for more details about a specific collection or project representing significant institutional investment. A report of the survey findings will be published in 2013.

Services to Patrons with Print Disabilities

ARL formed the Joint Task Force on Services to Patrons with Print Disabilities in May 2012 to expand upon the ongoing work of LCA in support of an international instrument for the print disabled that is under active consideration by WIPO. Print disabilities—visual, physical, perceptual, developmental, cognitive, or learning disabilities—prevent those affected from effectively reading print information resources. In November 2012 ARL published a report that contains nine recommendations for research libraries to better align their services with the mission to make information accessible to their full range of diverse users equitably. In particular, the report focuses on critical partnerships necessary to fully exploit the opportunities of digital information resources to open an unprecedented quantity of information to print-disabled patrons. See http://www.arl.org/focus-areas/accessibility.

Special Collections, Archives in the Digital Age

Research Library Issues no. 279 (June 2012) was devoted to legal concerns and evolving professional practices around digitizing special collections and archival materials. The issue included a model digitization contract, model "deeds of gift" that can secure permission to make donated material accessible on the Internet, and an essay by Kevin L. Smith on a new way of thinking about copyright and risk management. The issue is available from ARL Digital Publications; see http://publications.arl.org/rli279.

ARL-ACRL Human Resources Symposium

In November more than 90 human resources professionals and library leaders gathered in Washington, D.C., for a two-day Human Resources Symposium sponsored by ARL in partnership with the ACRL Personnel Administrators and Staff Development Officers Discussion Group. The symposium featured three keynote speakers: Christopher Collins, associate professor of human resource management and director of the Center for Advanced Human Resource Studies, ILR School, Cornell University; James Neal, vice president for information services and university librarian, Columbia University; and Stanley Wilder, university librarian, University of North Carolina at Charlotte. Keynote presentation topics included strategic human resources, 21st century academic librarian skills, and changing demographics of the ARL library work force.

Research Library Services for Graduate Students

In December ARL released the second report in the "New Roles for New Times" series. The report, written by Lucinda Covert-Vail and Scott Collard of New York University Libraries, presents findings from interviews and other research into the current state of graduate student programming in primarily ARL libraries. The authors provide several recommendations for serving graduate students more effectively in a changing higher education landscape.

Diversity, Professional Work Force, and Leadership Development

ARL works closely with member libraries, graduate library and information science programs, and other libraries and library associations to promote awareness of career opportunities in research libraries and to support the success of library professionals from racial and ethnic groups currently underrepresented in the profession. ARL's Diversity Programs support member libraries as they strive to reflect society's diversity in their staffing, collections, leadership, and programs. Central to the diversity agenda are programs that facilitate the recruitment, preparation, and advancement of librarians into leadership positions in research libraries. The themes and curricula of these programs introduce participants to major trends affecting research libraries and the communities they serve: the changing nature of scholarly communication, the influence of information and other public policies, and new and expanding library roles in support of research and scholarship.

Leadership Institute

More than 30 master of library and information science (MLIS) students attended the Eighth Annual ARL Leadership Symposium held in Dallas January 19–22, 2012. Program participants included ARL Career Enhancement Program Fellows, ARL Diversity Scholars, and other MLIS students and new professionals from throughout the country. Presentations by ARL staff covered the major strategic areas of the association, as well as strategies for transitioning into the professional research library work force. A highlight of the event was a panel presentation on "emerging professional roles" in research libraries. Ameet Doshi (Georgia Tech), Marianne Stowell Bracke (Purdue), Sarah Shreeves (Illinois at Urbana-Champaign), and Alison Regan (Utah) spoke to symposium participants on user experience, integrating data services in subject liaison work, and trends and services in digital scholarship. The symposium included a job-search skills workshop led by Brian Keith (Florida). The event was underwritten by IMLS, Innovative Interfaces, OCLC, EBSCO, and ARL member libraries.

Initiative to Recruit a Diverse Workforce

The ARL Initiative to Recruit a Diverse Workforce (IRDW) reflects the commitment of ARL members to create a diverse academic and research library community that will better meet the challenges of changing demographics in higher education and the emphasis on global perspectives in the academy. It offers numerous financial benefits, leadership development provided through the annual ARL Leadership Symposium, a formal mentor program, career placement assistance, and a research library visit. The program is funded by IMLS and by contributions from 52 ARL member libraries.

The library visit introduces the Diversity Scholars to the advanced operations of a research library, with the goals of raising the students' awareness of issues facing such libraries and increasing their interest in working in these organizations. For the eighth year, Purdue University Libraries hosted an IRDW visit in April that included sessions on scholarly communication, archives and special collections, e-science, and Purdue University Learning Initiatives.

In July the ARL Committee on Diversity and Leadership selected 14 MLIS students to participate in the 2012–2014 IRDW as ARL Diversity Scholars.

Leadership and Career Development

Since 2007 ARL has offered the Leadership and Career Development Program (LCDP), an 18-month fellowship experience designed to help prepare mid-career librarians from underrepresented racial and ethnic groups to take on increasingly demanding leadership roles in research libraries.

LCDP convened in Houston March 20–23, 2012, for the Institute on Transforming Research Library Roles and Scholarly Communication. The program included a one-day site visit to the University of Houston Libraries hosted by Dean of Libraries Dana Rooks. The institute faculty included ARL program officers; University of Houston President Ranu Khator; Lorraine Stewart, archives director at the Houston Museum of Fine Arts; and Mark McFarland, head of the Texas Digital Libraries.

In December the Committee on Diversity and Leadership selected 21 fellows to participate in the 2013–2014 program.

Career Enhancement Program

Beginning in January five ARL institutions hosted MLIS students from traditionally underrepresented racial and ethnic groups as part of the ARL Career Enhancement Program (CEP). This competitive fellowship program, funded by IMLS and ARL member libraries, gives MLIS students a robust fellowship experience that includes a paid internship in an ARL member library, a mentor program, and support to attend the annual ARL Leadership Symposium held during the ALA Midwinter Meeting. CEP reflects the commitment of ARL members to create a diverse research library community that will better meet the challenges of changing demographics in higher education and the emphasis on global perspectives in the academy.

In June the ARL Diversity Programs were awarded a $481,751 grant by IMLS to support CEP from 2012 to 2015. CEP will partner with eight ARL member libraries to provide each program participant with a six- to twelve-week paid internship, a formal mentoring program, opportunities for leadership development, and career placement assistance. In December the CEP coordinating committee selected ten fellows to participate in the 2013 program.

Research Library Leadership Fellows

The Research Library Leadership Fellows (RLLF) executive leadership development program seeks to meet increasing demands for succession planning for research libraries by preparing the next generation of deans and directors. The fourth offering of the RLLF program concluded its 18-month schedule during 2012. The program is designed and sponsored by seven ARL member libraries.

In February 2012 the fellows attended their final Strategic Issues Institute, which was hosted by the University of Miami in Coral Gables, Florida. During the institute, on "The Politics of Technology," they met with senior university administrators, including the faculty senate chair, the provost, and University President Donna Shalala.

The fellows also participated in three optional site visits. In March a visit to the University of Colorado at Boulder focused on leadership within the context of librarians as tenure-track faculty. The program agenda included discussions with the library's management team, a visit to the National Center for Atmospheric Research (NCAR), presentations by NCAR senior managers and Chancellor Phil DiStefano, and an informal meeting with academic deans. A site visit hosted by the University of Illinois at Chicago and Northwestern University in May focused on "Leadership Approaches to Strategic Facilities Planning" and gave the fellows an opportunity to spend a day on each campus and interact with library and campus leaders. The July visit to the Dartmouth College Library focused on institutional planning and featured several sessions on such topics as the library's role in campus-wide strategic planning, budget planning and investment, and innovation and change. A highlight of the visit was a session presented by Ron Adner, professor of strategy and entrepreneurship at the Tuck School of Business at Dartmouth, who exposed the fellows to new models for approaching innovation in the library context.

ARL/MLA Diversity and Inclusion Initiative

The ARL/Music Library Association (MLA) Diversity and Inclusion Initiative (DII) scholarship program, funded by IMLS and ARL member libraries, offers minority candidates an opportunity to pursue an MLIS degree while gaining hands-on experience in a large academic music library. The total award package for DII is in excess of $20,000 and includes a tuition stipend of up to $10,000 in support of MLIS education; a paid internship in a partner music/performing arts library for a period not to exceed one year (compensation is $11,880 a year); financial assistance for relocation ($1,000) to the area of the MLIS program into which the participant has been accepted; paid student membership in MLA and ALA for one year; and support for travel to and attendance at an annual MLA Annual Meeting. MLA will develop and host a career development workshop that will address strategies for job searching, skills development, résumé writing, interviewing skills, and other topics relating to job placement. In September ARL announced the selection of two MLIS students to participate in the Initiative.

Synergy: News from ARL Diversity Programs

The ARL Diversity Programs released issue 8 of *Synergy: News from ARL Diversity Programs* in January 2012. The issue featured three articles by former ARL diversity program participants who offered their reflections on transitioning from one setting to another within the library and information profession, and how their experiences in ARL programs informed their thinking and behaviors as they made those transitions.

Issue 9, released in August, focused on science and technology. Three articles discussed issues germane to scientific and technological constituencies in research-intensive environments, and to the work of managing information and resources in libraries.

Statistics and Assessment

The ARL Statistics and Assessment program focuses on describing and measuring the performance of research libraries and their contributions to research, scholarship, and teaching. ARL serves a leadership role in the development, testing, and application of academic library performance measures, statistics, and management tools. The program provides analysis and reports of quantitative and qualitative indicators of library collections, personnel, and services by using a variety of evidence-gathering mechanisms and tools. The program hosts the StatsQUAL (Statistics and Service Quality) suite of services that focus on developing new approaches for describing and evaluating library service effectiveness, value and return on investment, digital library services, the impact of networked electronic services, diversity, leadership, and organizational climate, among others. StatsQUAL tools include LibQUAL+, ClimateQUAL, MINES for Libraries, and ARL Statistics. More information is available at http://www.arl.org/focus-areas/ statistics-assessment.

Webcast Series

The 2012 ARL Statistics and Assessment Webcast Series was a set of free workshops designed to provide potential and current participants with information on the StatsQUAL tools. Each workshop covered a variety of topics including the strategic aspects of a specific tool, the tool's development, objectives and goals for its implementation, promoting its purpose, analyzing results, and creating improvement strategies. The series highlights the impact of these tools in individual libraries as well as the tools' transformative agency in an environment where libraries are asked to demonstrate their value in new and innovative ways.

LibQUAL+ and LibQUAL+ Lite

In 2012 a total of 171 institutions registered for the LibQUAL+ survey and library users completed over 215,500 surveys. The optional LibQUAL+ Lite protocol garnered higher response rates and shortened response times compared with the longer version of the survey. In September the LibQUAL+ team began offering User Subgroup Custom Analysis notebooks. This new analysis can be performed for each of three different user groups: undergraduate, graduate, and faculty. For example, an Undergraduate User Subgroup Custom Analysis notebook will drill down into the undergraduate data and provide analysis for first-year, second-year, third-year, fourth-year, fifth-year and above, and non-degree students.

In February 2012 three libraries were selected to receive in-kind grants to facilitate their participation in the 2012 LibQUAL+ survey. The selection of grantees was based on financial need, contribution to the growth of LibQUAL+, and potential for surfacing best practices in the area of library service improvements.

ClimateQUAL

The centerpiece of the ClimateQUAL: Organizational Climate and Diversity Assessment project is an online survey of staff perceptions of an organization's commitment to the principles of diversity, organizational policies and procedures, and staff attitudes. The survey addresses such issues as diversity, teamwork, learning, fairness, current managerial practices, and staff attitudes and beliefs. ARL, in partnership with the University of Maryland Industrial/Organizational Psychology Program, offers this protocol to the library community.

With the entire ClimateQUAL service—survey administration, data collection, and results reporting—newly housed within the StatsQUAL platform in 2012, the service has the ability to deliver data analysis with a more robust set of tools. The new standard report that participating libraries now receive upon completing a ClimateQUAL survey provides additional analysis to complement the existing inferential statistics, and presents the data and analysis in a more visually appealing way. During the year 14 academic libraries administered the ClimateQUAL survey, including four from the United Kingdom that administered a survey adapted to fit their culture. To learn more about ClimateQUAL, visit http://climatequal.org/home.

Library Assessment Forum

A Library Assessment Forum, held in Dallas in early 2012, featured several presentations about the Lib-Value project as well as an update on the Library Assessment Conference. Pdfs from the presentations are on the Library Assessment blog at http://libraryassessment.info/?p=895. The summer Library Assessment Forum, held in Anaheim in June, featured two presentations on the Lib-Value project as well as an update on the upcoming Library Assessment Conference in Charlottesville, Virginia. Pdfs from the presentations are available at http://libraryassessment.info/?p=1016.

'Share Fair' in Sweden

The Library Assessment Seminar and LibQUAL+ Share Fair, held at Lund University in Sweden in September 2012, featured speakers from the United States and the United Kingdom who discussed the contributions of LibQUAL+ to library assessment activities in libraries. An informal, science-fair style gathering featured brief presentations and poster sessions by current and past LibQUAL+ survey participants highlighting examples of quantitative and qualitative analysis and marketing ideas, as well as strategy plans from participating libraries and their relation to metrics. Presentations and posters from the event are available at http://www.libqual.org/about/share_fair.

Library Assessment Conference 2012

Hurricane Sandy made attending the 2012 Library Assessment Conference in Charlottesville, Virginia, a challenging task. More than 580 participants made it to the conference, which culminated with a Halloween celebration on the University of Virginia lawn. The conference website includes all slides used in the presentations (http://libraryassessment.org/schedule/index.shtml). The full text of the articles will be published in 2013 in the proceedings. Among the highlights of the conference was the Library Assessment Career Achievement Awards ceremony, honoring four notable colleagues: Karin De Jager (South Africa), Sam Kalb (Canada), Don King (United States), and Joan Rapp (South Africa). Their achievements are highlighted in a press release at http://www.arl.org/news/pr/LACA-Awards-23oct12.shtml.

Balanced Scorecard

In December ARL hosted a webinar covering the strategic aspects of the Balanced Scorecard, the tool's development, objectives and goals for its implementation, promoting its purpose, analyzing results, and creating improvement strategies. An archive of the webinar is available on ARL's YouTube Channel at http://www.youtube.com/watch?v=1PXT_QubQ7o&feature=youtu.be.

Statistics Review Task Force

ARL formed a task force during 2011 to review and implement changes in the annual statistical surveys. The task force gathered feedback from the ARL survey coordinators and SPEC liaisons, the ACRL Personnel Administrators and Staff Development Officers discussion group, the Preservation Administrators Forum, and ARL member representatives. At the ARL Membership Meetings, the ARL Statistics and Assessment Committee discussed recommendations from stakeholders on revisions to the annual surveys. Revised surveys were mailed to members in summer 2012.

Publications

Annual electronic and print publications produced by the program describe salary compensation and collection, staffing, expenditures, and service trends for research libraries. The series includes the *ARL Annual Salary Survey, ARL Statistics, ARL Academic Law Library Statistics,* and *ARL Academic Health Sciences Library Statistics.* Online access to these publications from 2006 to the present is available through ARL Digital Publications (http://publications.arl.org).

SPEC Surveys and Kits

The SPEC survey program gathers information on current research library operating practices and policies on topics relevant to ARL's strategic directions and publishes the SPEC Kit series as guides for libraries as they face ever-changing management issues. Six SPEC Kits were published in 2012—*SPEC Kit 328: Collaborative Teaching and Learning Tools; SPEC Kit 329: Managing Born-Digital Special Collections and Archival Materials; SPEC Kit 330: Library Contribution to Accreditation; SPEC Kit 331: Changing Role of Senior Administrators; SPEC*

Kit 332: Organization of Scholarly Communication Services; and *SPEC Kit 333: Art and Artifact Management*. Links to free pdfs of the tables of contents and executive summaries of SPEC Kits from 2006 to the present are available at http://publications.arl.org/SPEC_Kits; pdfs of complete SPEC Kits from 1977 through 2005 are available through Google Books (http://books.google.com) and HathiTrust (http://www.hathitrust.org). Online access to complete SPEC Kits from 2006 to the present is available for purchase through ARL Digital Publications (http://publications.arl.org).

Workshops and Other Events

The Statistics and Assessment program offers various other workshops on related topics such as XML development. Presentations at research conferences on topics relating to the value of libraries, analytics, and library assessment also took place throughout the year.

Communications

Using electronic and print media as well as direct outreach, ARL's communications capability disseminates information and sparks conversations about ARL and strategic issues relating to research libraries. The primary audiences are ARL member libraries and the broader higher education and scholarly communities, particularly decision-makers.

During 2012 ARL signed a contract with the PICnet Web development firm, which uses open source software to help nonprofits implement creative technology solutions. The website redesign team solicited input from ARL member representatives and staff during the redesign process to develop a more user-friendly and visually appealing website. The new website was scheduled to launch in 2013.

ARL publishes a full range of timely and informative resources to assist library and higher education communities in their efforts to improve the delivery of scholarly communication. Many of these resources are available via the ARL website; some are available in excerpted form for preview before purchase, and others are available in their entirety. See http://www.arl.org/publications-resources/ for more information.

News Feeds

News about ARL activities and publications is available through several public e-mail lists that reach a large audience in the library and higher education communities. To subscribe, visit http://www.arl.org/news.

ARL is also active on social networks, including Twitter (http://twitter.com/ARLnews and http://twitter.com/ARLpolicy); Google+ (http://plus.google.com/116038873630463451082); LinkedIn (http://www.linkedin.com/company/association-of-research-libraries); YouTube (http://www.youtube.com/ARLvideo); and Flickr (http://www.flickr.com/photos/arl-pix).

In addition, the "ARL Policy Notes" blog (http://policynotes.arl.org) deals with public policy issues that affect the research library community, and the "Library Assessment" blog (http://libraryassessment.info) offers a discussion of library service assessment, evaluation, and improvement.

ARL Digital Publications Website

The ARL Digital Publications website provides online access to collections of ARL publications from 2006 to the present, including the *ARL Annual Salary Survey*, *ARL Statistics*, *Research Library Issues*, and SPEC Kits. *Research Library Issues* is freely available. Access to the ARL Statistics collection and the ARL Annual Salary Survey collection is free to ARL members; individual issues or an annual subscription are available to others. Access to the SPEC Kit collection is available by annual subscription. Access to individual SPEC Kits can also be purchased. For more information, visit http://publications.arl.org.

ARL partners with the CLOCKSS ("Controlled LOCKSS") Archive to preserve flagship digital publications in its geographically and geopolitically distributed network of redundant archive nodes located at 12 major research libraries around the world.

Governance and Membership Meetings

2012 Spring Membership Meeting

The 160th ARL Membership Meeting was held in Chicago May 2–4. ARL President Winston Tabb (Johns Hopkins) welcomed members and guests. Program sessions were held on the Code of Best Practices in Fair Use, open scholarship, scenario planning, Balanced Scorecard, and the Digital Preservation Network. Other programs highlighted the recently completed E-Science Institute and the issue paper on 21st century research library collections. Mark A. Puente, ARL director of diversity and leadership programs, presented an overview of ARL's diversity programs and their impact over the previous 12 years.

During the ARL Business Meeting on May 4, committee chairs provided updates on projects and issues committees are addressing, including legislation on orphan works, reform of Section 108 of the Copyright Act, organizational design, strategy and alignment of the library work force, and revisions to the ARL suite of statistics.

Elliott Shore Named Executive Director

In September Elliott Shore was appointed executive director of ARL, effective January 1, 2013. Shore was at that time the chief information officer, Constance A. Jones director of libraries, and professor of history at Bryn Mawr College.

Fall Membership Meeting and Forum

The 161st ARL Membership Meeting was held October 10–11 in Washington, D.C. A total of 117 ARL member library representatives participated in sessions about services to the print disabled, 21st century scholar and research services, data governance, and data mining for library operations. Staff from Penn State Public Broadcasting presented a video trailer for a new project, "Treasures of the Special Collections" (http://pspb.org/public-service-media/treasures-of-the-special-collections.html).

At the business meeting, member library representatives ratified the ARL Board of Directors' election of Carol Pitts Diedrichs (Ohio State) as ARL vice president/president-elect and elected four new board members: Larry Alford (Toronto), Connie Vinita Dowell (Vanderbilt), Thomas Hickerson (Calgary), and Olivia M. A. Madison (Iowa State). Wendy Pradt Lougee (Minnesota) began her term as ARL president.

The ARL Fall Forum, "Library Workforce for 21st Century Research Libraries," was held October 11–12 in Washington, immediately following the ARL Membership Meeting. The forum examined such issues as demographic trends and their impact, staffing priorities for transformation, changing the collective mindset, strategies for deep change, and new roles for the 21st century.

SPARC—The Scholarly Publishing and Academic Resources Coalition

Heather Joseph

Executive Director

21 Dupont Circle, Suite 800, Washington, DC 20036
202-296-2296, fax 202-872-0884, e-mail sparc@arl.org
World Wide Web http://www.arl.org/sparc

Background and Mission

SPARC (the Scholarly Publishing and Academic Resources Coalition) is a global organization that promotes expanded sharing of scholarship in the networked digital environment. It believes that faster and wider sharing of outputs of the research process increases the impact of research, fuels the advancement of knowledge, and increases the return on research investments.

Established in 1997, SPARC was launched by the Association of Research Libraries to act on library concern that the promise of the Internet to improve scholarly communication was inhibited by pricing and access barriers in the journals marketplace. SPARC has been an innovative leader in the rapidly expanding international movement to make scholarly communication more responsive to the needs of researchers, students, the academic enterprise, funders, and the public.

SPARC is a catalyst for action. Its pragmatic agenda focuses on collaborating with other stakeholders to stimulate the emergence of new scholarly communication norms, practices, and policies that leverage the networked digital environment to support research, expand the dissemination of research findings, and reduce financial pressures on libraries.

As support for and conversations about "open access" have emerged at ever higher levels, SPARC has had increasing opportunities to participate and contribute to policy-making in multiple arenas.

The growth of SPARC's influence parallels that of the open access movement, which is expanding in scale and becoming more global. Open access is now a factor in the valuation of companies and a considerable force gaining power.

Today SPARC is supported by a membership of more than 225 academic and research libraries and works in cooperation with affiliates in Europe and Japan. Together, SPARC and SPARC Japan represent more than 800 libraries worldwide.

Strategy

SPARC's strategy focuses on reducing barriers to the access, sharing, and use of scholarship. SPARC's highest priority is advancing the understanding and implementation of policies and practices that ensure open access to scholarly research outputs. While much of SPARC's focus to date has been on journal literature, its evolving strategy reflects an increasing focus on open access to research outputs and digital data of all kinds, in all subject areas. SPARC's role in stimulating change centers on three key program areas:

- Educating stakeholders about the problems facing scholarly communication and the opportunities for them to play a role in achieving positive change
- Advocating policy changes that advance scholarly communication and explicitly recognize that dissemination of scholarship is an essential, inseparable component of the research process
- Incubating demonstrations of new publishing and sustainability models that benefit scholarship and academe

Priorities

SPARC activities will advance acceptance and long-term sustainability of an open system for scholarly communication, with a primary focus on advancing open access models for publishing and archiving the results of scholarly research. SPARC will promote changes in both the infrastructure and culture needed to make open access the norm in scholarly communication.

Key program priorities for 2012 included the following:

Professionalize advocacy campaign—Refine strategy, communications, messaging, and resource portfolio to position the organization to operate more effectively on national and international levels.

Convene discussions on evaluation, tenure, and promotion practices—Partner with key stakeholders to discuss the changing nature of scholarly communications and its potential impact on faculty/researcher evaluation, tenure, and promotion.

Implement international reorganization—Fully implement reorganization of SPARC's European program activities according to a plan developed and approved in 2011.

Explore opportunities to build internal capacity—Explore scenarios that would enable SPARC to consider adding an additional professional staff position.

Activities and Outcomes for 2012

Advocacy and Policy Front

During 2012 SPARC continued high-level open access advocacy, working with the White House, Congress, and federal agencies in the development of new federal public access policies.

Early in the year SPARC actively opposed the Research Works Act, proposed legislation that attempted to repeal the requirement that research by the National Institutes of Health (NIH) be published in the online open access PubMed Central. The bill was withdrawn by its sponsors in late February.

Also in early 2012 the Federal Research Public Access Act (FRPAA) was reintroduced. The legislation would require that 11 U.S. government agencies with annual extramural research expenditures of more than $100 million make manuscripts of journal articles stemming from research funded by that agency publicly available via the Internet. The manuscripts would be maintained and preserved in a digital archive maintained by the agency or in another suitable repository that permits free public access, interoperability, and long-term preservation.

The White House continued active consideration of the issue as well, and convened an interagency working group that was expected to make recommendations in 2013. To help demonstrate public support for public access to all federally funded research, SPARC helped to coordinate a petition on the White House's "We the People" website, which in less than two weeks garnered the 25,000 signatures needed to be considered for action by the Obama administration.

SPARC continued to lead the work of the U.S.-based Open Access Working Group (OAWG), an alliance of leading organizations that support open access, and served as the organizational focal point for the Alliance for Taxpayer Access (ATA). SPARC also maintained its ties with the "open science" and "open educational resource" communities.

SPARC participated in the Berlin 10 open access conference in Stellenbosch, South Africa, November 6–8. Presenters at the conference from SPARC included Heather Joseph, SPARC executive director; Lars Bjørnshauge, director of European library relations; and Nick Shockey, director of the SPARC-sponsored student Right to Research Coalition.

Through its website, SPARC highlighted the work of open access champions. In March 2012 a profile was posted about the efforts of Tyler Neylon and Tim Gowers to organize a boycott, by researchers, of journals published by Elsevier, the preeminent publisher of academic journals. Heather Piwowar was featured in May for her work at the University of British Columbia to advocate for better access to digital articles to enable computational technologies such as text mining. SPARC also profiled Jenica Rogers, director of libraries on the Potsdam campus of the State University of New York, and her campaign to highlight high journal prices and their impact on academic libraries.

SPARC continued to support campus-based policy action in conjunction with a panel of experts to promote resources that support data-driven, community-engaging, and successful open access policy development. SPARC provides Web and administrative support for the Coalition of Open Access Policy Institutions (COAPI), a group that has grown to include 44 U.S. and Canadian institutions that have implemented campus-based open access policies.

In response to media requests for information on public access issues, SPARC provided materials to reporters and expert sources for interviews. Its staff also authored articles for various publications. For examples of SPARC in the press, see http://www.arl.org/sparc/media/inthenews/index.html.

SPARC continued work with the Committee for Economic Development (CED), a Washington-based think tank whose board of trustees includes several dozen university and college presidents, as well as leaders in private industry. CED and the Kauffman Foundation provided support and funding for a well-received paper that explored the impact of the NIH public access policy and made policy recommendations to other agencies.

SPARC collaborated with partners in its global network including Bjørnshauge and Alma Swan, director of European advocacy.

Campus Education

In partnership with several organizations in the United States and internationally, SPARC once again sponsored International Open Access Week in October 2012 to spread the word and highlight the research community's deep commitment to open access. Thousands of students and scholars observed the week worldwide with the theme "Set the Default to Open Access." Open Access Week began with a global webcast and live panel discussion hosted by the World Bank on October 22 centering on the theme of the week.

On college and university campuses, SPARC continued to encourage and aid libraries' grassroots advocacy efforts to support open access with presentations, consulting, and new or enhanced resources. During 2012 SPARC staff met with faculty members, department heads, deans, and campus administrators to discuss campus advocacy and other scholarly communication issues. SPARC's guide to campus open access funds continues to be heavily used as a resource by college-based advocates.

During the year SPARC continued support of Peter Suber's bimonthly *SPARC Open Access Newsletter* and the "Open Access News" blog. SPARC offered programs to connect directors with thought leaders in scholarly communication.

SPARC-ACRL Forums

A major component of SPARC's community outreach occurs at meetings of the American Library Association (ALA) when SPARC works with the Association of College and Research Libraries, an ALA division, and its scholarly communication committee to bring current issues to the attention of the community.

In January 2012 the SPARC-ACRL forum "Getting the Rights Right for the Future of Scholarly Communication" was held in Chicago. In June a second forum, "Sustaining Open Access: The Latest on Campus-based Open Access Journal Funds," took place in California.

Student Campaign

SPARC continued to expand its partnership with student groups and educate the next generation of academics on issues relating to scholarly communication. The student Right to Research Coalition expanded to include international student groups, with 63 member institutions now representing students in 100 countries, and in July the coalition hosted its first general assembly in Budapest.

Governance

SPARC is guided by a steering committee. Members of the 2012 committee were Jun Adachi, Japanese National Institute of Informatics (for SPARC Japan); Lorraine Haricombe, University of Kansas; Lee Van Orsdel, Grand Valley State University; Rosann Bazirjian, University of North Carolina at Greensboro; Gerald Beasley, Concordia University; Richard Clement, Utah State University; Kevin Smith, Duke University; Deborah Jenkins, Duke University; Martha Whitehead, Queen's University; Mary Case, University of Illinois at Chicago; Barbara I. Dewey, Pennsylvania State University, Mary Marlino, National Center for Atmospheric Research, and Alma Swan, SPARC Europe.

Council on Library and Information Resources

1707 L St. N.W., Suite 650, Washington, DC 20036
202-939-4754
World Wide Web http://www.clir.org

Kathlin Smith
Director of Communications

The Council on Library and Information Resources (CLIR) is an independent, nonprofit organization that forges strategies to enhance research, teaching, and learning environments in collaboration with libraries, cultural institutions, and communities of higher learning. Its staff of ten is led by its president, Charles Henry.

CLIR is supported by fees from sponsoring institutions, grants from public and private foundations, contracts with federal agencies, and donations from individuals. CLIR's board of directors establishes policy, oversees the investment of funds, sets goals, and approves strategies for their achievement. In 2012 the board appointed new members Kurt De Belder, university librarian and director of the Leiden University Libraries and Leiden University Press in the Netherlands; Kathleen Fitzpatrick, director of scholarly communication at the Modern Language Association; and Michael Keller, Ida M. Green University Librarian at Stanford University, founder and publisher of HighWire Press, and publisher of Stanford University Press. A full listing of CLIR board members is available at http://www.clir.org/about/governance.

G. Sayeed Choudhury and Elliott Shore continued their affiliations with CLIR as senior presidential fellows in 2012. Choudhury is associate dean for research data management and Hodson Director of the Digital Research and Curation Center at the Sheridan Libraries, Johns Hopkins University. Shore is executive director of the Association of Research Libraries (ARL) and professor of history at Bryn Mawr College.

Activities

CLIR seeks to identify models of collaboration that could redefine the research library and produce more cost-effective services and programs to improve support of research and teaching. The components of the scholarly communication cycle—discovering, reconstituting, publishing, and sharing knowledge, and keeping its various manifestations preserved and accessible—are increasingly interrelated and interdependent.

To fulfill this goal, CLIR launched four new projects in 2012, described in the following sections, with a review of continuing CLIR programs.

Committee on Coherence at Scale

Among the most significant developments in 2012 was formation of the Committee on Coherence at Scale for Higher Education. Established by CLIR in partnership with Vanderbilt University, the committee's charge is to examine emerging national-scale digital projects and their potential to help transform higher education in terms of scholarly productivity, teaching, cost-efficiency, and sustainability.

The committee comprises college and university presidents and provosts, deans, university librarians, and association heads. A list of members is available at http://www.clir.org/initiatives-partnerships/coherenceatscale. The committee will focus on research and analysis of the large projects and their correlation; initial costs, operating costs, and business plans for sustainability; governance; and benefits and transformational aspects. Examples of these projects include the HathiTrust Digital Library, the Digital Public Library of America, the Digital Preservation Network, and data curation centers.

The committee held its first meeting in March 2013. Results of the committee's work will be publicized as they become available.

Anvil Academic Publishing

In February 2012 CLIR and the National Institute for Technology in Liberal Education (NITLE), in partnership with a group of colleges and universities, launched Anvil Academic, a digital publisher for the humanities. Anvil Academic focuses on publishing new forms of scholarship that cannot be adequately conveyed in the traditional monograph and serves as a test bed for alternate business models for scholarly publishing.

Anvil is developing a production system for use by other institutions, each of which will have the opportunity to publish under its own imprint. NITLE and CLIR will enlist additional publishers, scholarly societies, librarians, administrators, and faculty to participate in planning and developing Anvil-forged college and university publishing enterprises.

In November 2012 Anvil announced its "Built Upon" initiative and issued a call for proposals. The Built Upon series aims to be an incubator and an accelerator of humanities innovation. It encourages authors to investigate and invigorate existing digital tools and collections in developing their own scholarly arguments or pedagogical projects.

Fred Moody serves as editor of Anvil Academic. In June 2012 Lisa Spiro, coordinator of NITLE's Innovation Studio and director of NITLE Labs, was named program manager. That same month, Korey Jackson, American Council of Learned Societies public fellow and former CLIR postdoctoral fellow, was named program coordinator and analyst.

Anvil Academic Publishing received startup funding from the Brown Foundation. In addition, Stanford University, the University of Virginia, Washington University in St. Louis, Bryn Mawr College, Amherst College, Middlebury College, and Southwestern University provide funds and staffing.

Leading Change Institute

A third significant development of 2012 was the autumn launch of the Leading Change Institute (LCI), successor to the Frye Leadership Institute. LCI is driven by the same goals that inspired the first Frye Institute in 2000: to prepare and develop the next generation of leaders in libraries, information services, and higher education by engaging those who seek to further develop their skills for the benefit of higher education. The name change, however, reflects a new focus and curriculum.

LCI's curriculum is based on three guiding principles:

- Participants learn how to be part of a collaborative community that takes leadership on critical issues to develop a platform for collective action.
- Participants develop the skills to build public will, set an agenda for change, and advocate for the policies that need to be adopted to bring about change.
- Participants learn by doing through collaborative engagement.

The inaugural LCI was scheduled for June 2–7, 2013, in Washington, D.C.

Postdoctoral Fellowships in Data Curation

The fourth new development in 2012 was creation of the CLIR Postdoctoral Fellowships in Data Curation. The fellowships are an expansion of the Postdoctoral Fellowships in Academic Libraries program, initiated nearly a decade ago to offer recent Ph.D. graduates an opportunity to work on projects that forge and strengthen connections among library collections, educational technologies, and current research. The data curation fellowships respond to a growing recognition within the professional community that research data management poses particular challenges to libraries and other departments serving today's researchers. CLIR seeks to help its host institutions establish staffing models, policies, resources, and services relating to research data curation by matching those institutions with recent Ph.D.'s with expertise relevant to their needs.

Two types of data curation fellowships are available. The first, launched in spring 2012 with support from the Alfred P. Sloan Foundation, is the CLIR/Digital Library Federation (DLF) Postdoctoral Fellowship in Data Curation for the Sciences and Social Sciences. In its pilot cycle (2012–2014), CLIR is cohosting seven fellows with its partner institutions—Indiana University, Lehigh University, McMaster University, Purdue University, UCLA, and the University of Michigan.

The second new program, launched in the fall of 2012, is the CLIR/DLF Postdoctoral Fellowship in Data Curation for Medieval Studies. Established with funding from the Andrew W. Mellon Foundation, the program provides five fully funded fellowships to recent Ph.D.'s with relevant expertise in medieval studies.

Working together with CLIR's Postdoctoral Fellows in Academic Libraries, data curation fellows will share information and experiences with one another, gaining a broad understanding of the importance of data and information management to the emerging research environment while becoming a cohort of highly skilled and deeply knowledgeable specialists.

Continuing Programs

Digital Library Federation Program (DLF). CLIR's DLF program focuses on the technological aspects of developing, sustaining, and aggregating digital resources; promoting standards, protocols, and best practices; and supporting digital architectures that are open source, extensible, and interoperable. Highlights of 2012 include the following:

- DLF Forum. The forum is an important venue for the exchange of information that will lead to a better understanding of the elements and complexity of digital library evolution, as well as for collaboration on practical work. The 2012 Fall Forum was held November 3–6 in Denver.

- ARL/DLF E-Science Institute. In 2012 CLIR/DLF partnered with ARL and DuraSpace to host a second E-Science Institute. The institute, first offered by ARL and DLF last year, was created to give participants the tools and knowledge needed to develop a sound strategic approach to exploring and supporting e-science within their organizations. Sixty-seven institutions and 180 people participated in the first institute, which culminated in three capstone events in late 2011 and early 2012. Eighty-eight individuals from 28 institutions are participating in this year's institute.

- Digital Public Library of America (DPLA). DPLA is envisioned as a large-scale digital public library that will make the cultural and scientific record available to all. The DPLA planning initiative grew out of a meeting at the Radcliffe Institute for Advanced Study in late 2010, and the Berkman Center for Internet and Society at Harvard University has since served as secretariat. The work of DPLA is currently organized by six workstreams that are defined and coordinated through a steering committee. One of the workstreams, Content and Scope, is led by DLF Program Director Rachel Frick. The staff of the workstream held a meeting in February 2012 that focused on discussing and formulating phase one of the DPLA Collection Development Strategic Plan: metadata aggregation of open cultural heritage objects. A DPLA Think Tank meeting was held June 15, 2012, to discuss technical architecture plans in the context of expected DPLA content. In July 2012 CLIR published a report that it had commissioned to review research on the management of large-scale collections and practical efforts to aggregate them. *Core Infrastructure Considerations for Large Digital Libraries* by Geneva Henry examines basic functional aspects of large digital libraries and draws on examples of existing digital libraries to illustrate their varying approaches to storage and content delivery, metadata approaches and harvesting, search and discovery, services and applications, and system sustainability.

Workshops on Participatory Design in Academic Libraries. Led by Nancy Fried Foster, director of anthropological research at the University of Rochester's River Campus Libraries, the workshops on participatory design in academic libraries provide an overview of the participatory design process and strategies for including faculty members, graduate students, undergraduates, and library staff in the design process. The first workshop was held in 2007, and as of November 30, 2012, more than 300 people had participated.

In May 2012 the first CLIR "Seminar on Issues of Participatory Design in Academic Libraries" was held at the University of Maryland. It was an opportunity for previous participants of participatory design workshops to present projects that they have conducted using the techniques they learned. Teams from 12 sponsoring institutions gave presentations on a range of topics that are described in an online report available at http://www.clir.org/pubs/reports/pub155. A second seminar was planned for June 2013.

An Ethnographic Research User Group was formed shortly after the seminar. Composed of alumni from the participatory design workshops and other interested constituents, it is a resource for librarians and academic technologists in higher education who aspire to build community, collaborate, network, and share information. The group advances its mission by organizing regular online meetings and meeting informally at events where multiple members are in one place.

Cataloging Hidden Special Collections and Archives. Launched in 2008 with the support of the Andrew W. Mellon Foundation, CLIR's Cataloging Hidden Special Collections and Archives Program supports efforts to expose unknown or underutilized cultural materials to communities of scholars, students, and other users who need them for their work. In 2012 CLIR issued the program's fifth call for proposals. A review panel met on September 14 and recommended funding 22 projects for approximately $3.73 million.

In late June 2012 CLIR launched its Registry of Hidden Special Collections and Archives, a Web-based, browsable registry of hidden materials compiled from data submitted by grant applicants. The registry is available at http://www.clir.org/hiddencollections/registry.

Mellon Dissertation Fellowships. Seventeen graduate students were selected during 2012 to receive Mellon Dissertation Fellowships. The fellowship program, initiated in 2002, is intended to help graduate students in the humanities and related social science fields pursue doctoral research using original sources and gain skill and creativity in using primary source materials in libraries, archives, museums, and related repositories. The program has so far supported 143 graduate students who have carried out their dissertation research in public and private libraries and archives worldwide.

Chief Information Officers Group. CLIR's Chief Information Officers Group is composed of 33 directors of organizations that have merged their library and technology units on liberal arts college campuses. The group met twice in 2012 to discuss common concerns and to exchange ideas about possible solutions for organizational and policy problems. They explored such topics as open access; the effect of the recession on their organizational structure, technology, business strategies, and attitudes; cloud computing; portals versus Web 2.0; strategies for measuring the use and effectiveness of services; and ideas for prioritizing services. Throughout the year, members exchange ideas and solutions through a listserv.

A. R. Zipf Fellowship in Information Management. Jodi Schneider, a Ph.D. candidate in the Digital Enterprise Research Institute at the National University of Ireland in Galway, was selected to receive the A. R. Zipf Fellowship in Information Management for 2012. Her research focuses on information management and knowledge representation of contested information from social media.

Rovelstad Scholarship in International Librarianship. Molly Schwartz, a library science student at the University of Maryland at College Park, was awarded the 2012 Rovelstad Scholarship. Schwartz is creating her own specialization in international archives by combining courses in archives, international librarianship, and e-government.

Publications and Communications

New CLIR Website

In February 2012 CLIR launched a new website at http://www.clir.org. In addition to the full range of publications, news, and award information featured on its previous website, new functionality was included for CLIR sponsors and DLF members. The most important of these is CLIR Connect, an area where sponsors and members can sign in to do such things as initiate or join discussions, post resources, connect with other members of the sponsor community, and share blogs.

In June 2012 CLIR launched a weekly blog series, titled "Re: Thinking," which features perspectives from a variety of contributors on topics relating to the emerging digital environment, research, and higher education.

Publications

One Culture: Computationally Intensive Research in the Humanities and Social Sciences by Christa Williford and Charles Henry (June 2012). Available at http://www.clir.org/pubs/reports/pub151. In January 2010 CLIR entered a cooperative agreement with the National Endowment for the Humanities (NEH) Office of Digital Humanities to provide a strategic assessment of the Digging Into Data Challenge. The challenge was launched to better understand how "big data" changes the research landscape for the humanities and social sciences, and to discover what new computationally based research methods might be applied to these sources.

In its first year, the challenge made awards to eight teams of scholars, librarians, and computer and information scientists. Over the following two years, CLIR staff members Williford and Henry conducted site visits, interviews, and focus groups to understand how these complex international projects were being managed, what challenges they faced, and what project teams were learning from the experience. This report presents their findings, along with a series of recommendations for researchers, administrators, scholarly societies, academic publishers, research libraries, and funding agencies.

Core Infrastructure Considerations for Large Digital Libraries by Geneva Henry (July 2012). Available at http://www.clir.org/pubs/reports/pub153. This study examines basic functional aspects of large digital libraries and draws on examples of existing digital libraries to illustrate their varying approaches to storage and content delivery, metadata approaches and harvesting, search and discovery, services and applications, and system sustainability. The author stresses that scalability is of fundamental importance to enable long-term growth of the system, and recommends a modular system, following SOA (service-oriented architecture) principles used in software development to enable flexibility, code reusability, and stronger system sustainability.

The Problem of Data by Lori Jahnke, Andrew Asher, and Spencer D. C. Keralis, with an introduction by Charles Henry (August 2012). Available at http://www.clir.org/pubs/reports/pub154. This volume points out the urgent need for a reliable and more sophisticated professional cohort to support data-intensive research in the academy. It includes findings from two studies commissioned in the fall of 2011. The first study examines data curation practices among scholars at five institutions of higher education. The second study is an environmental scan of professional development needs and of education and training opportunities for digital curation in the academy.

Participatory Design in Academic Libraries: Methods, Findings, and Implementations with an introduction by Nancy Fried Foster (October 2012). Available at http://www.clir.org/pubs/reports/pub155. This volume of project reports, adapted from presentations at a May 2012 seminar, provides candid accounts of the methods, findings, successes, and challenges faced by project teams at 12 institutions as they sought to learn what students and faculty most want from the library, and how they would redesign library space if they could.

CLIR Annual Report, 2011–2012 (November 2012). Available at http://www.clir. org/pubs/annual.

Association for Library and Information Science Education

ALISE Headquarters, 65 E. Wacker Place, Suite 1900, Chicago, IL 60601-7246
312-795-0996, fax 312-419-8950, e-mail contact@alise.org
World Wide Web http://www.alise.org

Melissa Gross
President 2012–2013

The Association for Library and Information Science Education (ALISE) is an independent, nonprofit professional association. Its mission is to promote excellence in research, teaching, and service for library and information science (LIS) education through leadership, collaboration, advocacy, and dissemination of research. The association was founded in 1915 as the Association of American Library Schools (AALS). In 1983 it changed its name to its present form to reflect more accurately the mission, goals, and membership of the association.

Membership

Membership categories are personal and institutional. Personal members can include anyone who has an interest in the objectives of the association, with categories including full-time (faculty member, administrator, librarian, researcher, or other interested individual); part-time/adjunct (retired or part-time faculty member); and doctoral student. At the 2013 ALISE Annual Conference, categories under personal membership were expanded to include a "new professional" category for members making the transition from doctoral studies to a professional position. Membership under the doctoral student category will now be limited to six years. Institutional members include schools with programs accredited by the American Library Association (ALA) and other U.S. and Canadian schools that offer a graduate degree in library and information science or a cognate field. International affiliate institutional membership is open to any school outside the United States or Canada that offers a program of education for the practice of librarianship or other information work at the professional level as defined or accepted by the country in which the school is located.

Structure and Governance

Operational groups within ALISE are the board of directors; committees; council of deans, directors, and program chairs; school representatives; and special interest groups. Since 2006 the Medical Library Association has managed ALISE, with Kathleen Combs serving as ALISE executive director.

The board of directors is composed of seven elected officers serving three-year terms. Officers for 2012–2013 were Melissa Gross (Florida State University), president; Eileen Abels (Drexel University), vice president/president-elect; Lynne Howarth (University of Toronto), past president; Steven McCall (University of Alabama), secretary/treasurer; Ann Carlson Weeks (University of Maryland), director for membership services; Louise Spiteri (Dalhousie University), director for external relations; and Kathleen DeLong (University of Alberta), director for special interest groups. At the end of the January 2013 Annual Conference, Lynne Howarth, Ann Carlson Weeks, and Kathleen DeLong concluded their terms of service on the board and newly elected officers joined the board. The new officers are Clara Chu (University of North Carolina, Greensboro), vice-president/president-elect; Laurie Bonnici (University of Alabama), director for membership services; and Don Latham (Florida State University), director for special interest groups. The board establishes policy, sets goals and strategic directions, and provides oversight for the management of the association. Face-to-face meetings are held in January in conjunction with the Annual Conference and in April and September to focus on strategic planning. For the remainder of the year, business is conducted through teleconferences and e-mail.

Committees have important roles in carrying out the work of the association. Since fall 2008, an open call for volunteers to serve on committees has been used to ensure broader participation in committee service, with members for the coming year appointed by the vice president/president-elect. Principal areas of activity include awards, budget and finance, conference program planning, governance, membership, nominations, publications, research competitions, and tellers (see http://www.alise.org/mc/page.do?sitePageId=86452 for a full list). Each committee is given an ongoing term of reference to guide its work as well as the specific charges for the year. Task forces can be charged to carry out tasks outside the scope of the existing standing committees. For example, in 2012 the Diversity Task Force, chaired by Chu, developed an ALISE diversity statement proposal that was unanimously approved by the voting membership in early 2013.

The ALISE Council of Deans, Directors, and Program Chairs consists of the chief executive officers of each ALISE institutional member school. The group convenes at the Annual Conference and can discuss issues via e-mail in the interim. Stephen Bajjaly (Wayne State University) and Mary Stansbury (University of Denver) were co-chairs for 2012, since succeeded by Clara Chu (University of North Carolina at Greensboro), Ling Hwey Jeng (Texas Woman's University), and Susan Roman (Dominican University).

Within each institutional member school, a school representative is named to serve as a direct link between the membership and the ALISE Board of Directors. These individuals communicate to the faculty of their school about ALISE and the association's events and initiatives and provide input on membership issues to the ALISE board.

Special interest groups (SIGs) enable members with shared interests to communicate and collaborate, with a particular emphasis on programs at the Annual Conference. New SIGs are established as new areas of interest emerge among ALISE members. For example, two new SIGs have been proposed and are in the process of forming—the Development and Fundraising SIG and the Student Services SIG. Ongoing SIGs, grouped by broad theme, are:

- *Roles and Responsibilities*: Assistant/Associate Deans and Directors, Doctoral Students, New Faculty, Part-time and Adjunct Faculty
- *Teaching and Learning*: Curriculum, Distance Education, Teaching Methods

- *Topics and Courses*: Archival/Preservation Education; Gender Issues; Historical Perspectives; Information Ethics; Information Policy; International Library Education; Multicultural, Ethnic, and Humanistic Concerns; Research; School Library Media; Technical Services Education, Youth Services

At the 2013 conference a special session was presented by the ALISE Diversity Statement Task Force and Multicultural, Ethnic, and Humanistic Concerns special interest group called "What of Diversity? (Always the Beautiful, and Essential, Question): An Ignite Session on Ideas You Can Use to Advance Diversity." The Annual Conference also has an active placement service and facilitates support for job candidates through résumé and portfolio reviews and scheduled interviews.

Publications

The ALISE publications program has four components:

- The *Journal of Education for Library and Information Science* (*JELIS*) is a peer-reviewed quarterly journal edited by Kathleen Burnett and Michelle Kazmer of Florida State University. Under their leadership, *JELIS* has published a number of research articles, brief communications and discussions of research in progress, and the ALISE 2012 Best Conference Papers. The journal continues to showcase outstanding contributed papers presented at each Annual Conference. The editors manage and update the companion website for *JELIS* at http://jelis.org. The goal is to raise the visibility of the journal and to create an interactive website that engages the ALISE membership and others interested in LIS education in scholarly conversation. The ALISE 2012 Best Conference Papers appeared in Volume 53, no. 4, published in fall 2012.
- The *ALISE Directory of LIS Programs and Faculty in the United States and Canada* is published annually. It is now made available to members only in electronic form through the ALISE website. Listings of faculty for each school include indications of teaching and research areas, using codes from the LIS Research Areas Classification Scheme that ALISE maintains.
- The *ALISE Library and Information Science Education Statistical Report* publishes data collected from its institutional members. It is an annual compilation of statistical data on curriculum, faculty, students, income and expenditures, and continuing professional education. Since his appointment as ALISE statistical data manager in 2008, Danny Wallace (University of Alabama) has worked to bring publication of the annual volumes up to date and to enhance the database designed to support production of the statistical report. As a result of improvements to the reporting process, the 2012 report was published ahead of schedule. Enhancements to the database continue with the goal of further simplifying data entry and providing members with the ability to produce on-demand reports. Members can gain access to existing reports by logging in on the members-only site.

- The ALISE website keeps members informed with posting of updates on association activities. Information compiled from each Annual Conference and made available on the website includes abstracts of papers and posters presented and the president's report. The website is used to highlight awards and other member news. ALISE has an established presence on social media including Facebook, LinkedIn, and Twitter.

Annual Conference

The ALISE Annual Conference is held immediately before the ALA Midwinter Meeting. The 2013 conference drew 433 attendees to Seattle January 22–25 to explore the theme "Always the Beautiful Question: Inquiry to Support Teaching, Research, and Professional Practice." The program co-chairs, Heidi Julien (University of Alabama) and Don Latham (Florida State University), put together a rich array of program sessions, including the keynote speech by Ann Curry, professor, Graduate Program in Communication and Technology, University of Alberta, whose presentation was "'Always the beautiful answer who asks a more beautiful question': e. e. cummings and LIS education." Two poster sessions, Work-in-Progress and the Doctoral Student Research Poster Session, offered opportunities to discuss a wide range of research. The Birds-of-a-Feather brown-bag lunch fostered discussion of teaching various content areas. Scheduled sessions included presentation of papers, panel discussions, a special program on diversity, and SIG-sponsored programs. The first day of the conference was devoted to continuing professional development, with a workshop on online pedagogy sponsored by WISE, the Web-based Information Science Education consortium, and the ALISE Academy sponsored by the H. W. Wilson Foundation. The ALISE Academy is in its fifth year and provides a continuing education opportunity designed to support and inspire members at all stages of their careers. The concentration for the 2013 conference was on qualitative research methods. John Budd (University of Missouri) worked with workshop leaders Lisa Given (Charles Sturt University), Diane Neal (Western University), and Marie Radford (Rutgers University) to design the "Quality Behind Qualitative Research" ALISE Academy.

Grants and Awards

ALISE seeks to stimulate research and recognize accomplishments through its grants and awards programs. Research competitions include the ALISE Research Grant Competition, the ALISE/Bohdan S. Wynar Research Paper Competition, the ALISE/Dialog Methodology Paper Competition, the ALISE/Eugene Garfield Doctoral Dissertation Competition, the ALISE/Linworth Youth Services Paper Award, and the OCLC/ALISE Library and Information Science Research Grant Competition. Support for conference participation is provided by the University of Washington Information School Youth Services Graduate Student Travel Award and the Doctoral Student to ALISE Award. This year two additional Doctoral Students to ALISE Awards were supported by John Bertot (University of Maryland). Awards recognizing outstanding accomplishments include the ALISE/Norman Horrocks Leadership Award (for early-career leadership), the ALISE/Pratt-Severn

Faculty Innovation Award, the ALISE Service Award, the ALISE Award for Teaching Excellence, and the ALISE Award for Professional Contribution. Winners are recognized at an awards reception at the Annual Conference. [For a list of award winners, see "Library Scholarship and Award Recipients, 2012" in Part 3—*Ed.*]

Collaboration with Other Organizations

ALISE seeks to collaborate with other organizations on activities of mutual interest. The association is represented on the ALA Committee on Education (COE) by Director for External Relations Louise Spiteri, who has also been actively engaged, on behalf of ALISE, with the ALA COE Diversity Working Group. Several ALISE institutional members collaborate on staffing an ALISE booth anchoring the LIS Education Pavilion area of the exhibit hall at the ALA Annual Conference each summer. This year, for the first time, a subset of refereed presentations at ALISE were showcased at ALA Midwinter in a session called ALISE@ALA.

Lorna Peterson (University of Buffalo), a past president of ALISE, serves as a member of the Coalition on the Academic Workforce. The Coalition listserv keeps ALISE members apprised of developments relating to the academic workplace and work force.

ALISE is seeking to build more international connections. At the 2012 IFLA World Library and Information Congress in Finland in August, Executive Director Kathleen Combs again organized a dinner for ALISE members. ALISE continues to seek opportunities to partner with the IFLA Sections on Education and Training (SET) and Library Theory and Research (LTR).

Conclusion

As ALISE looks ahead to celebrating its 100th anniversary in 2015, the board of directors has appointed a committee, chaired by Elizabeth Aversa (University of Alabama), to launch a campaign to raise significant funding for the ALISE endowment. Concurrently, a centennial celebration committee, chaired by Michele Cloonan (Simmons College), is planning activities and events to showcase the association and the accomplishments of its members over the past century. The ALISE archives, housed at the University of Illinois, will be invaluable resources in this endeavor. Through its programs, the work of its personal and institutional members, and its focus on outreach to cognate disciplines, and to international affiliates, ALISE is well positioned to provide leadership for library and information science research and education in the 21st century.

International Reports

International Federation of Library Associations and Institutions

P.O. Box 95312, 2509 CH The Hague, Netherlands
Tel. 31-70-314-0884, fax 31-70-383-4827, e-mail ifla@ifla.org
World Wide Web http://www.ifla.org

Beacher Wiggins

Director for Acquisitions and Bibliographic Access, Library of Congress
American Library Association Representative to the Standing Committee on Government
Libraries, 2011–2013

The International Federation of Library Associations and Institutions (IFLA) is the preeminent international organization representing librarians, other information professionals, and library users. Like many other nonprofit and international organizations, in 2012 IFLA was challenged by worldwide economic constraints, political upheaval, and natural disasters. Nevertheless, IFLA promoted high standards of provision and delivery of library and information services; encouraged widespread understanding of the value of good library and information services; and represented the interests of its members throughout the world. Throughout the year, IFLA promoted an understanding of libraries as cultural heritage resources that are the patrimony of every nation.

World Library and Information Congress

The World Library and Information Congress (WLIC)/78th IFLA General Conference and Council attracted nearly 4,000 attendees from 114 countries to Helsinki, Finland, August 11–17, 2012. There were 2,486 registered full participants, a slight increase over the 2,418 who registered for the 2011 WLIC in San Juan, Puerto Rico, but nearly 25 percent lower than the 3,236 registered participants at the 2010 WLIC in Gothenburg, Sweden, and nearly one-third lower than the 3,568 who registered at the WLIC in Milan, Italy, in 2009. The decrease in registrations in 2011 and 2012 reflected the continuing weakness of the global economy and financial constraints on many libraries that restricted travel to a relatively expensive city such as Helsinki. In addition to registered full participants, the conference had 277 volunteers who worked at the Helsinki Exhibition and Convention Centre, 99 accompanying persons, and 1,113 attendees who registered for only one day of the conference. Of the nearly 4,000 attendees, 1,378 were attending their first IFLA

General Conference, an encouraging sign for a profession that is concerned about its rapidly aging membership.

The 2012 conference theme, "Libraries Now: Inspiring, Surprising, Empowering," beckoned participants to learn more about their profession and the many ways in which libraries foster technological, economic, and cultural progress around the world. The conference in Helsinki, which was celebrating its 200th anniversary as the capital of Finland, highlighted the importance of libraries to prosperous and literate societies. Helsinki Mayor Jussi Pajunen stated in his welcome to conference attendees, "It is impossible to overestimate the significance of the library system in the Nordic welfare model." Conference participants saw the truth of this statement as they were invited to visit the Helsinki City Library, National Library of Finland, and dozens of libraries in Finland, Estonia, and Russia. Current IFLA President Ingrid Parent, university librarian at the University of British Columbia, stressed the values of inclusion, transformation, innovation, and convergence of resources and initiatives in her opening address. The congress keynote speaker was Helena Ranta, professor at the University of Helsinki, a forensic dentist who provided evidence of massacres in Kosovo in the 1990s and in other international conflicts. Ranta spoke on genocide and destruction of cultural heritage, weaving together cultural and scientific themes.

Seventeen satellite meetings in various Finnish locales, the Netherlands, Estonia, Latvia, and Lithuania permitted in-depth exploration of current topics in librarianship. The furthest-flung satellite meeting, "Bibliography in the Digital Age," was held at the National Library of Poland (Biblioteka Narodawa) in Warsaw, and cosponsored by IFLA's Bibliography and Cataloguing sections. Other satellite meetings explored "The Future of Health Information," "Art Now!", "Let's Read: Reading and Print Disabilities in Young People," and such classic topics as metadata, library management, and information literacy.

The 2013 World Library and Information Congress will take place in Singapore August 17–23. Under the current IFLA WLIC conference planning guidelines, the conference cities are selected three years in advance, and at each WLIC the IFLA Governing Board announces the specific location of the conference that will take place two years later. The 2014 conference will take place in Lyon, France, to be followed by conferences in Africa (2015), North America (2016), Europe (2017), Latin America or the Caribbean region (2018), and again in Europe (2019). The IFLA Governing Board is committed to continuously improving both the conference experience for participants and the financial security of the organization. The WLIC in Helsinki enjoyed sponsorship by its platinum sponsor, OCLC, Inc.; silver sponsor, Infor; bronze sponsors, Gale Cengage Learning, Axiell, and Open Edition; and associate sponsors, InterSystems and LM Information Delivery, in addition to subsidies by local civic and tourism bodies. Although the exhibitor fees and registration are higher than for most conferences in the library community, WLIC does not make money for IFLA, and the custom of convening all registered participants in opening and closing ceremonies limits the number of cities that can host the conference to those with conference halls seating at least 3,000 people. Furthermore, member organizations have reported that the scheduling requirements make it difficult to send representatives to both the general conference and the numerous specialized satellite meetings. The current seven-year planning cycle and conference model were adopted after a consultation in early 2010 that Pleiade Management and Consultancy of Amsterdam conducted for IFLA among four major stakeholder groups: delegates and members who were represented at recent conferences; IFLA Section Standing Committees, special interest groups, and core activities; former national conference committee members; and conference sponsors and exhibitors. In the resulting model, each IFLA conference is organized around three to five tracks or themes. In both San Juan and Helsinki, the five tracks were: open access and digital resources; policy, strategy, and advocacy; users driving access and services; tools and techniques; and ideas, innovation, and anticipating the new. Through its governing board, IFLA retains overall ownership of each conference, and the IFLA Governing Board, IFLA Headquarters, and the conference National Committee (the local organizing committee) are responsible for each conference overall. Program content is guided by the IFLA Professional Committee. Actual conference planning and services are contracted to a "provider of conference organization," or event management company. In San Juan the contractor was CongrexUK; in Helsinki the conference was managed by the K.I.T. Group of Berlin. A more extensive review of conference governance, the host city selection process, the planning cycle, and financial management is planned for 2015/2016, after the site of the 2018 conference is announced and all of IFLA's regions have hosted at least one recent conference.

Five Key Initiatives

In 2010 IFLA's Governing Board adopted a new Strategic Plan for the years 2010–2105. The plan, grounded in IFLA's four core values, sets forth four strategic directions: empowering libraries to enable their user communities to have equitable access to information; building the strategic capacity of IFLA and that of its members; transforming the profile and standing of the library profession; and representing the interests of IFLA's members and their users throughout the world. The five key initiatives for 2010–2015 are the digital content program, international librarianship leadership development, outreach for advocacy and advancement of the profession, cultural heritage disaster reconstruction, and the multilingualism program. The governing board determines priority activities every two years under the strategic plan.

Digital Content Program

In its digital content program, IFLA is advocating vigorously for open access to digital content and for the right of libraries to benefit from fair use and exemptions from copyright restrictions. The federation's position is that the current framework of copyright exceptions is not adequate for the digital era. Through participation in the World Intellectual Property Organization's (WIPO's) Standing Committee on Copyright and Related Rights, IFLA is seeking a binding international instrument on copyright limitations and exceptions that will enable the world's libraries to continue their historic mission of providing universal access to knowledge and information. With the International Council on Archives, Electronic Information for Libraries (EIFL), and Corporación Innovarte, IFLA's Committee on Copyright and Other Legal Matters has proposed the Treaty Proposal on Copyright Limitations and Exceptions for Libraries and Archives (TLIB). It would protect libraries in the areas of preservation, right of reproduction and supply of copies, legal deposit, library lending, parallel importation, cross-border uses, orphan works, retracted and withdrawn works, liability of libraries and archives, technological measures of protection, contracts, and the right to translate works.

International Leadership and Advocacy Programs

Planning for this key initiative essentially began at the Helsinki WLIC in 2012. It will be carried out through IFLA's existing Action for Development through Libraries program. The program for Advocacy and Advancement of the Profession will basically advise the IFLA Governing Board on best use of limited resources in executing the 2010–2015 strategic plan.

Cultural Heritage Disaster Reconstruction Program

Since 1996 IFLA has been a founding member of the International Committee of the Blue Shield (ICBS) to protect cultural property in the event of natural and human disasters. Its current partners in ICBS are the International Council on Archives, the International Council on Monuments and Sites, the International Council of Museums, and the Coordinating Council of Audiovisual Archives Associations. In 2012 ICBS continued its concern for the preservation of cultural heritage in the ongoing aftermath of earlier wars and natural disasters. The IFLA North American regional center for preservation and conservation, hosted at the Library of Congress, continued to develop a network of colleague institutions to provide a safety net for library collections during emergencies.

In April 2012 the IFLA Governing Board endorsed principles of engagement for cultural heritage recovery, spurred by IFLA's support of cultural reconstruction in Haiti after the massive earthquake of January 2010. The principles will guide IFLA and its members in deciding when and how to provide assistance in natural disasters that threaten libraries and cultural heritage objects. The IFLA Preservation and Conservation Section undertook to create an online registry of at-risk areas where cultural heritage may be jeopardized by war or natural disaster.

Multilingualism Program

Recognizing that the Internet is becoming a prevalent means of communication and resource sharing, IFLA has undertaken to make its website at http://www.ifla. org multilingual, adding French and Spanish content in 2012 and endorsing the goal of making key content available in all seven official IFLA languages by the end of 2014.

Grants and Awards

The federation continues to work with corporate partners and national libraries to maintain programs and opportunities that would otherwise not be possible, especially for librarians and libraries in developing countries. The Jay Jordan IFLA/ OCLC Early Career Development Fellowships provide four weeks of intensive experience, based in OCLC headquarters in Dublin, Ohio, for library and information science professionals from countries with developing economies who are in the early stages of their careers. The fellows for 2012 were from Bangladesh, Ghana, Kenya, Nigeria, and Pakistan. As announced in Helsinki, the fellows for 2013 will be from Jamaica, Kenya, Nigeria, Macedonia, and the Philippines. The American Theological Library Association is the third sponsor of the program, and one of the fellows must be a theological librarian. Since its inception in 2001, the program has supported 65 librarians from 34 developing countries.

The Frederic Thorpe Awards, established in 2003, are administered by the IFLA Libraries Serving Persons with Print Disabilities Section and the Ulverscroft Foundation of Leicester, England, which Thorpe founded to support visually impaired people. The Ulverscroft Foundation renewed the program as the Ulverscroft/IFLA Best Practice Awards (Frederic Thorpe Awards) in 2006, 2007, 2008, 2010, and 2011, with no award in 2009 or 2012. The Ulverscroft Foundation intended to continue the awards in 2013.

The Bill and Melinda Gates Foundation Access to Learning Award in 2012 was presented at the Helsinki conference to the Dominican Republic's Community Technology Centers, which make technology and training available to traditionally underserved populations. This annual award presents up to $1 million to libraries, library agencies, or comparable organizations outside the United States that have been innovative in providing free public access to information. In addition to the cash award, Microsoft, Inc., announced that it would donate approximately $18 million in software to the community technology centers.

Numerous awards and grants encourage travel to the annual IFLA conferences. For the 2010 conference in Gothenburg, De Gruyter Saur Publishers provided grants for travelers from the Pacific Region; the Swedish Library Association and the Stichting IFLA Foundation made €60,000 available to support participation from developing countries; and Axiell Library Group provided €16,000 for travel grants. The IFLA International Marketing Award includes a stipend and travel to the conference. In 2002, 2003, and 2004, IFLA and 3M Library Systems cosponsored the marketing awards. After a hiatus in 2005, IFLA cosponsored the awards with SirsiDynix in 2006 and 2007. The Emerald Group has sponsored the award since 2008. In 2012 the first-place winner was the Tsinghua University Library of Beijing for its program "Falling in Love with the Library." The Council on Library and Information Resources (CLIR) sponsors the Rovelstad Scholarship that brings one international library science student to IFLA conference each year. The 2012 Rovelstad Scholar was Molly Schwartz, a graduate student at the University of Maryland. The Dr. Shawky Salem Conference Grant supports conference attendance from an Arab country. While many national library professional associations subsidize travel to the IFLA conference, the Comité français IFLA supports travelers from any francophone country. The newest travel award is the Aspire Award, established to support travel to conferences of IFLA and of CILIP, the Chartered Institute of Library and Information Professionals (United Kingdom). The Aspire Award honors the memory of Bob McKee (1950–2010), chief executive of CILIP. In 2011 and 2012 the Aspire Award supported travel to the IFLA WLIC by librarians from Ukraine.

The De Gruyter/Saur Research Paper Award consists of €1,000 and travel support to attend the IFLA conference. In 2012 the winner was Adam Girard, a doctoral candidate at the School of Information and Library Studies, University College Dublin, for his paper "E-Books Are Not Books: The Challenges and

Chances in the New Media Context." The IFLA Academic and Research Libraries Section instituted an annual essay contest, awarding conference registration for three contestants from Africa, Latin America, and the Asia/Pacific region. The Section on Education and Training sponsors a Student Paper Award for library science students.

The Guust van Wesemael Literacy Prize was awarded biennially to a school or public library in a country with a developing economy from 1993 to 2009.

The IFLA Honorary Fellowships, the IFLA Medal, and the IFLA Scroll of Appreciation recognize service to IFLA by individuals. At the Helsinki conference in 2012, Ellen Tise, library director at Stellenbosch University, South Africa, and president of IFLA from 2009 through 2011, and Winston Tabb, Sheridan Dean of Libraries and Museums at Johns Hopkins University and chair of IFLA's Committee on Copyright and other Legal Matters (CLM) from 2007 through 2011, were named honorary fellows, the highest award IFLA bestows. The IFLA Medal was awarded to Helena Asamoah-Hassan, University Librarian, Kwame Nkrumah University of Science and Technology, Ghana Jay Jordan, president and chief executive officer of OCLC, Inc.; and Eeva Kristiina Murtomaa, librarian of the National Library of Finland. Three IFLA Scrolls of Appreciation were presented to the National Committee for the Helsinki WLIC; Michael Heaney, executive secretary, the Bodleian Libraries, University of Oxford; and Magda Bouwens, office manager at IFLA headquarters. Jérôme Fronty, of the Bibliothèque de l'Hôtel de Ville, Paris, France, was the IFLA Communicator of the Year for 2012. He was the third person to be so honored; Sebastian Wilke and Dierk Eichel were named Communicators of the Year in 2011 to honor their work for the IFLA New Professional Special Interest Group.

Membership and Finances

IFLA has more than 1,500 members in 150 countries. Initially established at a conference in Edinburgh, Scotland, in 1927, it has been registered in the Netherlands since 1971 and has headquarters facilities at the Koninklijke Bibliotheek (Royal Library) in The Hague. Although IFLA did not hold a General Conference outside Europe and North America until 1980, there has since been steadily increasing participation from Asia, Africa, South America, and Australia. The federation now maintains regional offices for Africa (in Pretoria, South Africa); for Asia and Oceania (in Singapore); and for Latin America and the Caribbean (moved from Rio de Janeiro to Mexico City in 2011). The organization has seven official working languages—Arabic, Chinese, English, French, German, Russian, and Spanish. It offers a range of membership categories: international library associations, national library associations, other associations (generally regional or special library associations), institutions, institutional sub-units, one-person libraries, school libraries, association affiliates, personal affiliates, student affiliates, new graduate members, and nonsalaried personal members. Association and institution members have voting rights in the IFLA General Council and IFLA elections and may nominate candidates for IFLA offices. Institutional sub-units, one-person libraries, and school libraries have limited voting rights for section elections; affiliates and personal members do not have voting rights but may submit nominations for any IFLA office and individuals may run for office themselves. Except for affiliates, membership fees are keyed to the UNESCO Scale of Assessment and the United Nations List of Least Developed Countries, to encourage participation regardless of economic circumstances. The IFLA Core Activity Fund is supported by national libraries worldwide.

UNESCO has given IFLA formal associate relations status, the highest level of relationship accorded to non-governmental organizations by UNESCO. In addition, IFLA has observer status with the United Nations, WIPO, the International Organization for Standardization, and the World Trade Organization, and associate status with the International Council of Scientific Unions. The federation continues joint activities with the World Summit on the Information Society, including its Forum in Geneva held in May 2012.

More than two dozen corporations in the information industry have formed working relationships with IFLA as corporate partners, providing financial and in-kind support. Gold Corporate Partners in 2012 were OCLC, De Gruyter Saur, Elsevier, Emerald, NBD Biblion, Sabinet, and Sage. The current corporate partnership program is being reviewed with the aim of tailoring it more closely to the needs of both IFLA and corporate sponsors.

The IFLA Foundation (Stichting IFLA) was established in 2007. The foundation accepts private donations and also is funded by other IFLA income. It gives funding priority to proposals and projects that promise to have a long-term impact in developing and strengthening IFLA; are clearly related to at least one of IFLA's three pillars; and are not likely to be funded by other bodies.

IFLA's Three Pillars: Society, Members, and Profession

The operational model for IFLA is based on the three pillars of society, membership, and professional matters. All of the federation's core functions relate to three strategic factors: the societal contexts in which libraries and information services operate; the membership of the federation; and the library profession.

Although the three pillars and the infrastructure of IFLA are interdependent, they can be roughly analyzed as follows: The Society Pillar focuses on the role and impact of libraries and information services in society. Activities supported by the Society Pillar include FAIFE (Committee on Freedom of Access to Information and Free Expression), CLM, Blue Shield, IFLA's presence at the World Summit on the Information Society, and the advocacy office at IFLA headquarters—all activities that preserve memory, feed development, enable education and research, and support international understanding and community well-being. The Profession Pillar focuses on IFLA's role as the global voice for libraries and information services. The Members Pillar includes IFLA's member services, conferences, and publications.

The federation's operational infrastructure—consisting of IFLA Headquarters, the IFLA website, and the IFLA governance structure—support and receive strategic direction from the three pillars. The three pillars enable IFLA to promote its four core values: freedom of access to information and expression, as stated in Article 19 of the Universal Declaration of Human Rights; the belief that such access must be universal and equitable access to support human well-being; delivery of high-quality library and information services in support of that access; and the commitment to enabling all members of IFLA to participate without regard to citizenship, disability, ethnic origin, gender, geographical location, political philosophy, race, or religion.

Personnel, Structure, and Governance

The secretary general of IFLA is Jennefer Nicholson, former executive director of the Australian Library and Information Association. Joanne Yeomans joined IFLA headquarters as professional support officer in September 2011. Julia Brungs is the new policy and projects officer, while Andrea Beccalli is projects manager. Stuart Hamilton continues as director for policy and advocacy, also a headquarters position. The editor of the quarterly *IFLA Journal* is J. Stephen Parker. IFLA's communications staff includes communications officers Susan Schaepman and Louis Takács and webmaster Simon Lemstra. The manager for conference and business relations is Josche Ouwerkerk.

After IFLA's biennial elections in spring 2011, new officers and board members took office at the close of the Puerto Rico conference. President Ingrid Parent, university librarian, University of British Columbia, Vancouver, succeeded Ellen R. Tise of the University of Stellenbosch, South Africa. The president-elect of IFLA is Sinikka Sipilä, president of the Finnish Library Association, who will become president at the close of the 2013 conference in Singapore. The treasurer is Donna Scheeder of the Congressional Research Service, Library of Congress.

Under the revised 2008 IFLA Statutes, the 19 members of the IFLA Governing Board (plus the secretary general, ex officio) are responsible for the federation's general policies, management, and finance. Additionally, the board represents the federation in legal and other formal proceedings. The board is composed of the president, president-elect, ten directly elected members, the chair of the Professional Committee, the chairs of each IFLA division, and the chair of the Standing Committee of the Management of Library Associations Section, currently Gerald Leitner, secretary general of the Austrian Library Association. Current members, in addition to Parent, Sipilä, Scheeder, Nicholson, and Leitner, are Kent Skov Andreasen (Denmark), Frédéric Blin (France), Ingrid Bon (Netherlands), Genevieve Clavel-Merrin (Switzerland), Barbara Lison (Germany), Inga Lundén (Sweden), Christine Mackenzie (Australia), Buhle Mbambo-Thata (South Africa), and Paul Whitney (Canada), plus the chairs of the Professional Committee and divisions, named below.

The Governing Board delegates responsibility for overseeing the direction of IFLA between board meetings, within the policies established by the board, to the IFLA Executive Committee, which includes the president, president-elect, treasurer, chair of the Professional Committee, two members of the governing board (elected every two years by members of the board from among its elected members), and IFLA's secretary general, ex officio. The current elected Governing Board members of the executive committee are Mbambo-Thata and Whitney.

The IFLA Professional Committee monitors the planning and programming of professional activities carried out by IFLA's two types of bodies: professional groups—5 divisions, 43 sections, and discussion groups—and core activities (formerly called core programs). The Professional Committee is composed of one elected officer from each division, plus a chair elected by the outgoing committee; the president, the president-elect, and the professional support officer, who serves as secretary; the chairs of the CLM and FAIFE committees, and two elected members of the Governing Board, currently Skov Andreasen and Clavel-Merrin. Ann Okerson, special adviser on electronic strategies, Center for Research Libraries (New Haven, Connecticut), chairs the committee.

The five divisions of IFLA and their representatives on the Professional Committee are: Library Types (Lynne M. Rudasill, USA); Library Collections (Russell S. Lynch, USA); Library Services (Tone Eli Moseid, Norway); Support of the Profession (Anna Maria Tammaro, Italy); and Regions (Filiberto Felipe Martínez-Arellano, Mexico). The new chair of the Copyright and Legal Matters Committee is Victoria Owen (Canada). The chair of the Freedom of Access to Information and Freedom of Expression Committee is Kai Ekholm (Finland). The 43 sections focus on topical interests, such as statistics and evaluation, library theory and research, and management and marketing, or on particular types of libraries or parts of the world.

The five core activities are Action for Development through Libraries (ALP, formerly Advancement of Librarianship); Preservation and Conservation (PAC); IFLA UNIMARC Core Activity, which maintains and develops the Universal MARC Format, UNIMARC; Free Access to Information and Freedom of Expression (FAIFE); and Copyright and Other Legal Matters (CLM). The IFLA-CDNL Alliance for Digital Strategies (ICADS) core activity ceased at the end of 2011 as its work has been absorbed by numerous IFLA sections. Two other longstanding IFLA projects are the IFLA World Wide Web site and the IFLA Voucher Scheme, which replaced the IFLA Office for International Lending. The voucher scheme enables libraries to pay for international interlibrary loan requests using vouchers purchased from IFLA rather than actual currency or credit accounts. By eliminating bank charges and invoices for each transaction, the voucher scheme reduces the administrative costs of international library loans and allows libraries to plan budgets with less regard to short-term fluctuations in the value of different national currencies. The voucher scheme has also encouraged participating libraries to voluntarily standardize their charges for loans at the rate of one voucher for up to fifteen pages.

To ensure an arena within IFLA for discussion of new social, professional, or cultural issues, the Professional Committee approves the formation of special interest groups for a limited time period. There currently are discussion groups for Access to Information Network/Africa (ATINA); Agricultural Libraries; E-Learning; E-Metrics; Environmental Sustainability and Libraries; Indigenous Matters; Library and Information Science Education in Developing Countries; Library History; National Information and Library Policy; National Organizations and International Relations; New Professionals; Religious Libraries in Dialogue; RFID; Semantic Web; and Women, Information, and Libraries.

Canadian Library Association

1150 Morrison Drive, Suite 400, Ottawa, ON K2H 8S9
613-232-9625, fax 613-563-9895
E-mail info@cla.ca
World Wide Web http://www.cla.ca

Kelly Moore
Executive Director

The Canadian Library Association/Association Canadienne des Bibliothèques (CLA) is Canada's major national professional association for the library and information community. It is predominantly English-language, with selected activities also in French. Its mission states: "CLA is the national voice for Canada's library communities. We champion library values and the value of libraries. We influence public policy impacting libraries. We inspire and support member learning. We collaborate to strengthen the library community."

Founded in 1946, CLA is a federally incorporated not-for-profit organization. It is governed by a six-person executive council, which is advised by appointed advisory and standing committees and as-needed task forces.

Membership includes both individuals (librarians, library staff, other information professionals, and library board trustees) and institutions (mainly libraries, but also suppliers to the library and information community).

There are CLA student chapters at six English-language library and information science postgraduate programs in Canada, and there is a student chapter at one library technician program.

To facilitate sharing of information in specific areas of interest, CLA currently has 22 "networks" focusing on topics as diverse as accessible collections and services, evidence-based library and information practice, human resources, library history, government library and information management professionals, and voices for school libraries. New networks are forming regularly.

Governance

In January 2013 the role of CLA president was assumed by Pilar Martinez, executive director of public services at Edmonton Public Library. She succeeded Karen Adams, director of libraries, University of Manitoba, who had served as president since May 2011.

Others serving as officers for 2013 are Vice President/President-Elect Marie DeYoung, Treasurer Mary-Jo Romaniuk, and Executive Director Kelly Moore.

Major Activities

CLA continues to lead a variety of national advocacy initiatives and to offer professional development opportunities. Major activities have focused on these two elements, with federal advocacy taking a predominant role.

Advocacy and Public Awareness

Canada Post has maintained the Library Book Rate for 2013 with only a slight increase in costs. CLA continues to support Conservative MP Merv Tweed (Brandon-Souris) on his private member's bill (C-321) to create legislation supporting the rate. The bill has the support of the government and all opposition parties, and at the time this report was prepared was awaiting final approval from the Senate.

During 2012 CLA met with members of parliament and officials and staff in federal government ministries to raise awareness of key issues. National and international developments in the area of copyright and related rights were a major focus. CLA was pleased that the federal government passed new copyright legislation. However, concern was expressed at federal government budget cuts to federal libraries.

CLA continues to track intellectual freedom issues in Canada through its annual survey of challenges to library materials and policies. The survey, conducted in English and French, captures details of challenges from libraries of all types across the country.

The association also spearheads Canadian Library Month/Le Mois Canadien des Bibliothèques, partnering with provincial, regional, and territorial library associations and governments. Under the theme "Libraries Connect/Bibliothèques branchées," this collection of events helped raise awareness during 2012 of all types of libraries—public, academic, school, and special—and their roles for Canadians of all ages.

Professional Development

CLA's major contribution to continuing professional development continues to be its annual National Conference. The 2012 National Conference and Trade Show was held in Ottawa May 30–June 2, and the 2013 conference was set for Winnipeg, Manitoba, May 29–June 1.

International Activities

CLA maintains strong contact with the international library community, mainly through its involvement with the International Federation of Library Associations and Institutions (IFLA). CLA Executive Director Kelly Moore attended the 2012 IFLA Congress in Helsinki, along with a large Canadian delegation. The Canadian library community supports Ingrid Parent, university librarian at the University of British Columbia, as Canada's first IFLA president. She assumed presidency of the federation in August 2011 for a two-year term. CLA also maintains observer status with the World Intellectual Property Organization's (WIPO's) Standing Committee on Copyright and Related Rights.

Communications

As information professionals, Canadian librarians depend on timely and attractive publications and other resources from their professional association, and those outside the community look to the major national association as a significant source of information.

CLA's bimonthly publication, *Feliciter,* published since 1956, explores core themes in the library community. In 2012 CLA transitioned *Feliciter* from a print publication to an online magazine. A second publication, *CLA Digest,* is a bi-weekly e-newsletter for members, with links to in-depth news items.

Awards and Honors

CLA continued in 2012 to recognize individuals from the library and information community with awards and honors.

The association's most significant award is for Outstanding Service to Librarianship. It is presented only in years when there is a candidate deemed worthy to receive it. In 2012 CLA presented the award to Ken Roberts of the Hamilton (Ontario) Public Library.

The CLA Award for the Advancement of Intellectual Freedom was presented to the Calgary Freedom to Read Committee. Since 1988 the award has recognized outstanding contributions to intellectual freedom of individuals and groups, both in and outside the library community.

The CLA/Ken Haycock Award—established in honor of educator, administrator, advocate, and former CLA President Ken Haycock—honors an individual for demonstrating exceptional success in enhancing public recognition and appreciation of librarianship. The 2012 recipient was Pilar Martinez, Edmonton Public Library.

The CLA/OCLC Award for Innovative Technology went to the Windsor (Ontario) Public Library. The award is given in recognition of innovative use of technology to foster community awareness and engagement in the political process.

The 29th annual student article award was won by Nicole Dalmer for "Women in Archives: Present Contexts and Future Implications."

[For additional CLA awards, see "Library Scholarships and Awards" in Part 3—*Ed.*]

Conclusion

CLA is constantly adapting to meet the needs of its members and the broader library community in Canada. The association achieved tangible success with government on some key files, and efforts continued to advance issues such as copyright and the library book rate. Promoting public awareness of the role and importance of libraries and literacies remains a key CLA function.

Special Libraries Association

331 South Patrick St., Alexandria, VA 22314
703-647-4900, fax 703-647-4901
E-mail membership@sla.org
World Wide Web http://www.sla.org

Janice R. Lachance
Chief Executive Officer

Founded in 1909 and headquartered in Alexandria, Virginia, the Special Libraries Association (SLA) is a global organization for information professionals and their strategic partners. As an international professional association, SLA represents thousands of information experts and knowledge managers in 85 countries who collect, analyze, evaluate, package, and disseminate information to facilitate strategic decision making. SLA members are known for finding innovative ways to contribute to the overall goals of their organizations, regardless of industry.

SLA's 9,000 members work in a range of sectors including financial services, legal. biomedical, engineering, petroleum, academic, government, military, nonprofit, and more. SLA promotes and strengthens its members through learning, advocacy, and networking initiatives.

History

SLA was founded in 1909 by John Cotton Dana and a group of librarians who believed that libraries serving business, government, social agencies, and the academic community were very different from other libraries. Dana recognized a need for unity within the special librarian profession, and his initial goal was to provide numerous and continuous opportunities for special librarians to come together and achieve that unity. The association still identifies with this initial goal more than 100 years later. The founders believed that these libraries operate using a different philosophy and more-diverse resources than the typical public or school library.

These "special"—or, more aptly, "specialized"—libraries at first were distinguished by being subject collections with a specialized clientele, but gradually it was recognized that their chief characteristic was that they existed to serve the organization of which they were a part. Their purpose was not education per se, but the delivery of practical, focused, and decision-ready information to the executives and other clients within their organizations. Specialist librarians, commonly referred to today as "information professionals," are unique in their relationship with their users and customers, and are proactive partners in information and knowledge management.

SLA members are focused on providing access to the most reliable information in the most efficient manner. This information can relate to a wide range of fields. such as financial research, social data, market research, copyright protection, commodities, materials, private and public companies, Web 2.0 tools, training methods, consumer healthcare, and publications.

Information professionals contribute to a diverse variety of industries, but their expertise can be classified into a few broad categories.

- Corporate information professionals synthesize and analyze information to help executives make sound business decisions that contribute to short-term and long-term growth.
- Government information professionals organize and deliver information for congressional, parliamentary, judicial, and executive leaders to make policy decisions at the local, state, and federal levels.
- Academic librarians organize, digitize, and deliver research information so that faculty can effectively relay knowledge to students, and students can utilize efficient methods of gathering information for research projects and dissertations.
- Legal librarians contribute case research, package that research in ways that is acceptable in civil and criminal courts, and conduct patent research for publishing firms and other organizations that are responsible for and use intellectual property and protected materials.
- Medical librarians conduct research to support hospitals, medical practices, and pharmaceutical companies pursuing patents, issuing papers and reports to their communities, and serving their constituents through medicine and medical equipment and facilities.

SLA empowers its members by focusing on three crucial areas: learning, networking, and advocacy. These underpinnings prompted the information pioneers of 1909 to come together in a cooperative association, and they are still the fundamental benefits SLA provides to information professionals today.

The association's core values are

Leadership—Strengthening members' strategic roles within their organizations and on behalf of their clients and stakeholders

Service—Proactively responding to clients' needs by adding qualitative and quantitative value to their information services

Continuous learning—Embracing innovative solutions for the enhancement of services and intellectual advancement within the profession

Results and accountability—Delivering measurable results in the information economy and members' organizations; the association and its members are expected to operate with the highest level of ethics and honesty

Collaboration and partnering—Providing opportunities and a consistent platform, both online and in-person, to meet, communicate, collaborate, and partner within the information industry and the business community

Strategic Agenda

In 2012 the association adopted a strategic agenda to prioritize key areas of focus through 2014. These areas include the SLA Annual Conference, professional development, communications and member engagement, creating new markets through collaboration, and researching future required skills.

Chapters, Divisions, Caucuses

SLA chapter membership provides a network of information professionals for members in their geographic community or region, while SLA division membership links them to information professionals within their topical area of expertise. SLA membership includes membership in one chapter and one division. For a small fee, members can join additional chapters, divisions, and caucuses.

SLA is organized into 55 regional chapters in the United States, Canada, Europe, Asia, and the Middle East; 27 divisions representing a variety of industries; and ten special-interest caucuses.

SLA's regional chapters elect officers, issue bulletins or e-newsletters, hold three to nine program meetings a year, hold niche conferences, and manage blogs. Members may affiliate with the chapter nearest to their own preferred mailing address (either business or residence).

SLA divisions represent the fields to which SLA members contribute their expertise and information services. Each division elects officers, publishes a newsletter, manages a website, and holds meetings (both in-person and virtually) to discuss current trends and connect with corporate partners. They also conduct sessions, panels, and in some cases, continuing education courses during the association's annual conferences. The association added an Academic Division in 2008 and a Taxonomy Division in 2009. The largest divisions are Business and Finance and Legal.

A caucus is an informal network of members gathered to discuss a specific topic or discipline, not necessarily related to their individual day-to-day work. Examples of SLA caucuses include the Futurist Caucus (using science fiction films and stories to find parallels to where the profession is headed in the digital age), the User-Experience Caucus (SLA's newest caucus, examining how users interact with libraries and information centers, and how this interaction can be made more efficient and valuable), and the Baseball Caucus (discussing everything from current events in the baseball community to methods of organizing and analyzing baseball statistics).

Governance

SLA is governed by a board of directors elected by the membership. The board and the association both operate on a calendar year, with newly elected officers, as well as chapter and division leaders, taking office in January. SLA's president in 2013 is Deb Hunt, principal of InformationEdge. Janice R. Lachance is the association's chief executive officer. [Additional officers are listed in SLA's directory entry in Part 6 of this volume—*Ed.*].

Programs and Services

Click University

SLA's Click University (Click U), launched in 2005, is an online learning community focusing on continuing education for information professionals. Click U produces ongoing learning opportunities in partnership with industry thought leaders. Courses on such topics as copyright laws and issues, leadership, information architecture, competitive intelligence, knowledge management, uses of new Web 2.0 tools, and social media enhance the skills acquired through traditional library and information science education. Click U and its programs are available to SLA members and nonmembers. The majority of the webinars offered through Click U are free of charge as SLA membership benefits, and are available to members only. The offerings that carry an additional fee are designated as "Click U Premium," including Click U at Annual Conference and Click U Certificate Programs that help members improve their résumés and skill sets.

Click U also allows SLA members to gain public speaking experience as course presenters and instructors.

Click U Certificate Programs (Premium)

Thirteen Certificate in Copyright Management (CCM) and Certificate in Knowledge Management (CKM) programs are offered in 2013, including two full-day courses at the 2013 Annual Conference in San Diego June 9–11.

Continuing Education at Annual Conference

SLA offers in-person training and continuing education at the Annual Conference. Workshops (half day) or Learning Forums (full day) are designed to educate and inspire participants to make an impact in their organizations. The 2013 conference in San Diego scheduled the following courses: "The Accidental Systems Librarian," "Chemistry for the Non-Chemist Librarian," "Preparing for, Planning, and Managing a Sales Call," "Thinking Strategically and Building the Future," "Information Is Beautiful: Using Design to Enhance Your Narrative," "Introduction to Taxonomies," "Patent Research: The Next Level," "Chemical Information Sources," "The Road to Successful CI: From Novice to Expert," and "Social Media Techniques for Info Pros."

Advocacy

SLA advocates publicly on the value of the information profession. Its activities range from communicating with executives and hiring professionals on the important role information professionals play to sharing the membership's views and opinions with government officials worldwide.

Public Policy Program

Government bodies and related international organizations play a critical role in establishing the legal and social framework within which SLA members conduct information services. Because of the importance of governments and international organizations to its membership, SLA maintains an active public policy program. SLA staff and the association's Public Policy Advisory Council monitor and proactively work to shape legislation and regulatory proposals that affect SLA's membership.

SLA supports government policies that

- Strike a fair and equitable balance among the rights and interests of all parties in the creation, distribution, and use of information and other intellectual property

- Strengthen the library and information management operations of government agencies
- Promote access to government public information through the application of modern technologies and sound information management practices
- Encourage the development and application of new information and communications technologies to improve library services, information services, and information management
- Protect intellectual freedom and the confidentiality of library records, safeguard freedom of expression, and oppose government censorship
- Foster international exchange of information

With regard to the actions of government bodies and related international organizations in the policy areas listed above, the association will

- Monitor executive, legislative, and judicial actions and initiatives at the national and international level, and to the extent practical at various local levels
- Educate key decision-makers on the concerns of SLA's members, and highlight the importance of these concerns
- Provide timely updates to the membership on critical issues and actions
- Encourage and empower members to influence actions by expressing their opinions
- Develop cooperative relationships with other like-minded organizations to expand SLA's visibility and impact

SLA recently joined the Medical Library Association, the American Association of Law Libraries, and the Copyright Office of the United States in proposing solutions to issues surrounding the mass digitization of "orphan works," copyrighted works for which the copyright owner cannot be contacted. For more information, visit the SLA Blog (http://slablogger.typepad.com) and select the Public Policy category.

Employment and Career Services

SLA's online Career Center provides a variety of services to meet its members' career needs, including career coaching, articles and resources such as podcasts, and career disruption assistance mentoring. It includes a job board where employers publicize current information and library job opportunities to an audience of professionals with master's degrees in library and information science. SLA members and nonmembers have access to the listings on the job board, but only members are able to utilize the resources such as career coaching articles.

SLA Career Connections is the in-person educational component of SLA's career services, and takes place at its Annual Conference. An expanded program of Career Connections courses in 2013 includes workshops led by a leading recruitment firm.

SLA invites universities specializing in library and information science higher education to partner with it in providing student members with information on the job market, job search strategies, and relevant positions.

New Association Website

SLA launched a redesigned website, http://www.sla.org, in March, providing more-efficient access to resources, online education, communication tools, and industry news.

Professional and Student Networks

SLA's student groups are affiliated with accredited graduate schools of library and information science. Student members enjoy all the benefits of SLA membership at a lower cost. They become part of a network of peers, gain professional advice from like-minded professionals, and make industry contacts well in advance of officially starting their careers.

Publications, Blogs, and Newsletters

Information Outlook

SLA's semi-monthly magazine went digital in 2013 and remains a member benefit. Approximately 400 subscribing institutions also access the magazine, which covers industry topics and trends, such as new developments in research tools and applications of research in such areas as venture capitalism and marketing, and provides examples of information professionals shaping and supporting the strategies of their institutions.

SLA Blog

The SLA Blog (http://slablogger.typepad.com) provides a platform for interactive, professionally relevant discussions among readers and ongoing updates on the association's activities, initiatives, and product launches.

SLA Connections

SLA's bi-monthly e-newsletter covers information industry news and SLA's ongoing events and stories. The e-newsletter includes content from the SLA Blog.

Unit Blogs, Industry Outreach Blogs, Division Newsletters

Aside from the blogs administrated on the association level, many SLA chapters and divisions actively write their own blogs to keep their members and the rest of the association community informed on their recent activities. Many divisions publish a monthly bulletin or newsletter, featuring current industry information as it relates to new technologies.

Social Media and Web 2.0

SLA has a presence on various social media networking sites, including Twitter, LinkedIn, and Facebook. Each provides members with an opportunity to build community when physical meetings aren't possible. SLA hosts Twitter chats to allow members to network and participate in useful and educational virtual discussions with their peers.

SLA also has a podcast, "My SLA," which is an avenue for member-to-member discussions about the value of networking and active involvement within professional associations. In 2012 and 2013 new episodes were added to the podcast featuring testimonies from employers on the information professionals they have on staff. To access the podcast, go to http://my.sla.org.

SLA Awards and Honors

The SLA awards and honors program was created in 1948 to honor exceptional individuals, achievements, and contributions to the association and the information profession. The program's purpose is to bring attention to the important work of special librarians and information professionals within the corporate and academic setting.

SLA's highest honor is named after its founder, John Cotton Dana, and is granted to professionals to recognize a lifetime of professional achievement and contribution to the association. For a full list of past and current award recipients, visit the "Awards and Honors" page on SLA's website, http://www.sla.org. [The major SLA awards are included in "Library Scholarship and Award Recipients, 2012" in Part 3—*Ed.*]

Fund Raising

SLA's Loyalty Club, launched in 2012, will help the association provide international networking opportunities at annual conferences, deliver Click University webinars free of charge to association members, and publish salary surveys, all of which carry costs that are not covered by annual membership dues. Donations will support other existing programs and services or fund the development and delivery of new ones. For more information, visit http://www.sla.org/content/SLA/donate/index.cfm.

Research

SLA funds surveys and projects, endowment fund grants, and research studies relating to all aspects of information management.

Grants

SLA offers grants on a rolling basis for research projects for the advancement of library sciences; the support of programs developed by SLA chapters, divisions, or committees; and the support of the association's expanding international agenda. Additionally, grants, scholarships, and stipends are offered separately by many of SLA's chapters and divisions. The program has been temporarily suspended, but the association plans to re-launch it in the coming year.

Events and Conferences

SLA's Annual Conference and Info-Expo brings together thousands of information professionals and provides a forum for discussion of issues shaping the information industry. The conference offers more than 400 events, programs, panel discussions, and seminars, and includes an exhibit hall with more than 200 participating companies.

The 2013 conference in San Diego features keynote speaker Mike Walsh, author of the bestselling book *Futuretainment: Yesterday the World Changed, Now It's Your Turn*. Walsh is CEO of the innovation research lab Tomorrow and an authority on emerging technologies and markets.

The theme of the conference is "Connect. Collaborate. Strategize." Sessions and panels address the current need to enhance search skills, adopt new technologies and tools, connect with new service and solution providers, and strengthen relationships with existing providers.

Part 2
Legislation, Funding, and Grants

Legislation

Legislation and Regulations Affecting Libraries in 2012

Emily Sheketoff
Executive Director

Jazzy Wright
Press Officer

Washington Office, American Library Association

Overall, the 112th Congress proved to be a waiting game across the board for library supporters and others following federal legislation. According to the U.S. House Clerk's Office, by the end of the session it had passed just 238 public laws—the lowest total since the 80th Congress of 1947–1948.

Congress did manage to make cuts to discretionary spending in the Budget Control Act and scheduled another trillion in spending cuts through an automatic sequester. At the end of 2012 it passed, and the president signed into law, H.R. 8, the American Taxpayer Relief Act of 2012. The bill extended tax cuts for all individuals making less than $400,000 and married couples making less than $450,000 and delayed sequestration for two months. But in March 2013 sequestration went into effect after Congress failed to reach an agreement on a deficit reduction plan. [Sequestration is a fiscal policy procedure designed to force cutbacks in spending on government programs and to use the resulting funds to pay down the national deficit. It was part of the deal made to avoid the "fiscal cliff" in January 2013—*Ed.*]

Sequestration will have an impact on all libraries served by their state library agencies.

Funding for the Institute of Museum and Library Services (IMLS) has been cut by $12 million, which includes $7.86 million in cuts to the Library Services and Technology Act (LSTA). Overall, state programs will be cut, and each state will decide how the reduced budgets will affect the services delivered to the public. Possible adjustments include the reduction of summer reading programs, database subscriptions, work force development programs including employment skills and job searching, and services to people with disabilities. Future grant program budgets will also be slashed, though grants already awarded will not be affected by sequestration.

The funding situation had not been resolved at the time this report was prepared; it was unclear what course Congress would take in late March, when action would be taken on a continuing resolution to fund the government.

Library Appropriations Changes

From 2002 to 2010, the Improving Literacy through School Libraries program under the U.S. Department of Education was the primary source for federal funding for school library materials. However, in recent years, the president and Congress have either consolidated or zero-funded this program to the point that it was not funded at all in fiscal year (FY) 2011 or FY 2012. In 2011 Sen. Jack Reed (D-R.I.) recognized that school libraries needed a direct funding source in the federal budget, and redirected the money—through report language in the FY 2012 Appropriations Bill—to the U.S. Department of Education for the Innovative Approaches to Literacy program.

In FY 2012, which was the first year of this redirected money, the Innovative Approaches to Literacy program was funded $28.6 million. By law, at least half of this money ($14.3 million) must be allocated to a competitive grant program for underserved school libraries. The remaining money is allocated to competitive grants for national nonprofit organizations that work to improve childhood literacy. The first-year grants from this program were announced in late September.

Earlier, on March 20, 2012, two "Dear Colleague" letters were sent to the House Appropriations Committee. One of these letters, sponsored by Reps. Raul Grijalva (D-Ariz.) and Rush Holt (D-N.J.) and including 45 other signatures from members of Congress, asked for the committee to fund LSTA at $184.7 million for FY 2013. Another letter was sent to the appropriations committee with 120 signatures, sponsored by Reps. James McGovern (D-Mass.) and Don Young (R-Alaska), as well as Holt and Grijalva. This letter asked the committee to appropriate $28.6 million for Innovative Approaches to Literacy.

National Library Legislative Day

In late April 2012 more than 350 librarians and library supporters gathered in Washington, D.C., to take part in National Library Legislative Day. Activities began with preconference sessions. Also known as "newbie training," these were hosted by the American Library Association's (ALA's) United for Libraries division (formerly ALTAFF, the Association of Library Trustees, Advocates, Friends and Foundations) and the ALA Washington Office. Stephanie Vance, the "Advocacy Guru" of Advocacy Associates, which describes itself as an "advocacy communications firm catering to the association market," facilitated the session with ALA Grassroots Coordinator Ted Wegner and ALA Office of Government Relations (OGR) Director Lynne Bradley.

More than 50 attendees heard tips on the right things to say and do in meetings with a member of Congress and on strategies to build and maintain advocacy efforts at home. Sen. Reed was given ALA Honorary Membership for his efforts as a strong library champion, and United for Libraries presented its 2012 Public Service Award to Rep. Holt.

Susan Hildreth, IMLS director, and Yvette Sanchez Fuentes, director of the Office of Head Start, Administration for Children and Families, Department of Health and Human Services, met to sign an information memorandum between the two federal agencies. The memorandum creates a natural partnership and encourages collaboration efforts between federally funded early child care programs, such as Head Start, and public libraries throughout the country.

Copyright

Overall, 2012 was a very busy year for copyright issues. In January grassroots advocates effectively stopped two congressional bills—the Protect IP Act (PIPA) and the Stop Online Piracy Act (SOPA). ALA went on record taking a strong stance in opposition to these bills, and OGR constructed the *PIPA, SOPA and OPEN Act Quick Reference Guide*. On January 18, 2012, on a day designated Internet Blackout Day, several popular websites—including Google, Wikipedia, and Flickr—protested the two bills by holding a day-long protest during which the websites temporarily blocked access to their content. In addition, OGR issued a legislation action alert to ALA members asking them to contact their representatives to express opposition to the bills shortly after they were introduced.

In July 2012 the Library Copyright Alliance (LCA)—comprised of ALA, the Association of College and Research Libraries, and the Association of Research Libraries—filed a friends-of-the-court brief with the U.S. Supreme Court in support of petitioner Supap Kirtsaeng in the case *Kirtsaeng* v. *Wiley & Sons*. Wiley, a publisher of textbooks and other materials, claims Kirtsaeng infringed its copyrights by reselling cheaper foreign-produced editions of Wiley textbooks in the United States, copies that his family had lawfully purchased abroad. LCA believes an adverse decision in this "first sale" case could affect libraries' right to lend books and other materials manufactured abroad.

In October a court ruled that HathiTrust Digital Library's use of digitized works is a fair use permitted under the Copyright Act. The ruling allows HathiTrust to continue serving scholars and the print-disabled, and also provides helpful guidance on how future library services can comply with copyright law.

In the same month, the Association of American Publishers announced that it had reached a settlement in its lawsuit filed in 2005 against Google, Inc. The lawsuit was brought by authors who alleged that Google violated copyright by scanning books to create Google Book Search, a search tool similar to Google's Internet search engine. The settlement applies only to the publishers, and questions remain regarding "orphan works." ("Orphan works" are copyrighted works for which the copyright owner cannot be located.)

Emerging Advocacy Techniques

Using the Capwiz system, the ALA Washington Office continues to post advocacy action alerts online at the Legislative Action Center and through its e-mail-based messaging system. As of early 2013 the e-mail lists consisted of more than 70,000 supporters.

In 2011 ALA launched Mobile Commons, a new advocacy tool that allows library supporters to receive federal legislation text message alerts from OGR. Advocates can sign up for the text alerts from the Washington Office to receive the most up-to-date information on advocacy alerts and events by texting "library" to 877877. The opt-in service will allow ALA to communicate advocacy messages quickly and effectively using an innovative texting and calling feature. Advocacy subscribers have the option to call legislators to discuss particular issues toll-free through Mobile Commons. The text messages will provide subscribers with talking points on issues before automatically transferring the advocates to the offices of their legislators. Additionally, ALA uses social media channels such as Facebook and Twitter to connect with library supporters.

Open Access Legislation

In early February 2012 identical bills were introduced with bipartisan support aimed at improving access to federally funded research. In the House, the Federal Research Public Access Act (FRPAA) (H.R. 4004), was introduced by Rep. Mike Doyle (D-Pa.) and referred to the House Committee on Oversight and Government Reform. In the Senate, a bill by the same name (S. 2096) was introduced by Sen. John Cornyn (R-Texas) and then referred to the Senate Committee on Homeland Security and Government Affairs. ALA has a history of strong support for this legislation, as it builds on the success of the National Institutes of Health (NIH) Public Access Policy implemented in 2008.

In addition, FRPAA legislation is the antidote to the anti-open access Research Works Act (H.R. 3699) introduced in December 2011 by Rep. Darrell Issa (R-Calif.). In a somewhat unusual development in February 2012, the publishing house Elsevier announced it was retracting support for the Research Works Act, essentially rendering the bill dead. ALA will continue to voice strong opposition to anti-open access legislation while continuing to enthusiastically support FRPAA legislation.

E-books: Promising New Conversations

America's libraries began positioning themselves for a busy and creative 2013, expanding the publisher conversation beyond the largest publishers, collaborating with author groups and individual authors, working with publishers that focus on the school library market, and developing new paradigms to bring digital content to readers.

The ALA Digital Content and Libraries Working Group (DCWG) has been active in the e-book arena. In addition to co-releasing a report on the pricing of e-books, the group released "E-books and Libraries: An Economic Perspective," a report that was commissioned by ALA. The report explores and explains some of the economic underpinnings for the pricing of e-books. In August 2012 ALA Office for Information Technology Policy (OITP) Program Director Carrie Russell was a panelist on National Public Radio's Diane Rehm Show. DCWG member

Vailey Oehlke also participated in the session, which focused on e-books and library lending.

In the past year OITP released two digital supplements to *American Libraries* magazine: "E-Content: The Digital Dialogue" and "E-books: Making New Connections." In August ALA released "E-Book Business Models for Public Libraries," a report created by DCWG that describes general features and attributes of the current e-book environment and outlines constraints and restrictions on current business models. Additionally, the report suggests opportunities for publishers to showcase content through public libraries. In September ALA took an aggressive messaging approach by releasing an open letter from ALA 2012–2013 President Maureen Sullivan to U.S. publishers denouncing the refusal of several large trade publishers to sell e-books to libraries. Sullivan led an ALA delegation to New York to meet with publishers to discuss the many concerns of the library community about e-book publishing. Uppermost in their minds were the e-book complaints expressed by association members across the country—especially about pricing and availability and the slow pace of progress in finding solutions.

Surveillance Act Reauthorization

In December 2012 the Senate reauthorized the Foreign Intelligence Surveillance Act Amendments Act (FAA), a bill that gives the National Security Agency power to monitor the international phone calls and e-mails of Americans. ALA asked library supporters to contact their legislators to advocate for amendments that would increase privacy protections to the law and add transparency requirements. FAA is the 2008 law that, among other things, legalized the Bush administration's warrantless wiretapping program. As it did in 2008, ALA opposed the warrantless wiretap program because the public is at risk of being needlessly spied upon with little or no legal recourse, as the law reads now. On December 13 ALA sent out an FAA action alert. The alert asked supporters to write their senators to ask for more time for debate on the act instead of allowing it to be hastily reauthorized. Although the bill was eventually passed without debate, ALA was able to generate more than 675 messages to the Senate.

Whistleblower Protection Enhancement Act

Sen. Daniel Akaka (D-Hawaii) introduced the Whistleblower Protection Enhancement Act of 2012 (S. 743) on April 6, 2011, and on May 8, 2012, the bill passed the Senate by unanimous consent. This is a landmark bill that will expand the scope of whistleblower protections in the federal government, including providing whistleblower rights to employees of the Transportation Security Administration. The companion bill in the House was introduced by Rep. Darrell Issa (R-Calif.) on November 1, 2011, and passed the House on September 28, 2012, with an amendment. The Senate unanimously voted on November 13 to accept the bill with the House amendment and on November 16 it was sent to the president, who signed it the next day.

White House Responds to School Library Petition

In April 2012 the White House responded to a petition that was sent to President Barack Obama earlier in the year via the "We the People" section of the White House's website. The petition, which gained nearly 30,000 signatures, noted the importance that an effective school library program plays in a child's education and how it is necessary for school libraries to be included in an Elementary and Secondary Education Act (ESEA) reauthorization bill.

Pai, Rosenworcel Named to FCC

On May 7, 2012, the Senate unanimously confirmed the Federal Communications Commission's newest commissioners, Ajit Pai and Jessica Rosenworcel. ALA continues to have much interaction with FCC on numerous issues, including digital literacy and the E-rate, which provides lower "electronic" telecommunications rates for schools and libraries.

Funding Programs and Grant-Making Agencies

National Endowment for the Humanities

1100 Pennsylvania Ave. N.W., Washington, DC 20506
202-606-8400, 800-634-1121
TDD (hearing impaired) 202-606-8282 or 866-372-2930 (toll free)
E-mail info@neh.gov, World Wide Web http://neh.gov

The National Endowment for the Humanities (NEH) is an independent federal agency created in 1965. It is one of the largest funders of humanities programs in the United States.

Because democracy demands wisdom, NEH promotes excellence in the humanities and conveys the lessons of history to all Americans, seeking to develop educated and thoughtful citizens. It accomplishes this mission by providing grants for high-quality humanities projects in six funding areas: education, preservation and access, public programs, research, challenge grants, and digital humanities.

Grants from NEH enrich classroom learning, create and preserve knowledge, and bring ideas to life through public television, radio, new technologies, museum exhibitions, and programs in libraries and other community places. Recipients typically are cultural institutions, such as museums, archives, libraries, colleges and universities, and public television and radio stations, as well as individual scholars. The grants

- Strengthen teaching and learning in the humanities in schools and colleges
- Preserve and provide access to cultural and educational resources
- Provide opportunities for lifelong learning
- Facilitate research and original scholarship
- Strengthen the institutional base of the humanities

Over nearly half a century, NEH has reached millions of Americans with projects and programs that preserve and study the nation's culture and history while providing a foundation for the future.

The endowment's mission is to enrich cultural life by promoting the study of the humanities. According to the National Foundation on the Arts and the Humanities Act, "The term 'humanities' includes, but is not limited to, the study of the following: language, both modern and classical; linguistics; literature; history; jurisprudence; philosophy; archaeology; comparative religion; ethics; the history, criticism, and theory of the arts; those aspects of social sciences which have humanistic content and employ humanistic methods; and the study and application of the humanities to the human environment with particular attention to reflecting our diverse heritage, traditions, and history and to the relevance of the humanities to the current conditions of national life."

The act, adopted by Congress in 1965, provided for the establishment of the National Foundation on the Arts and the Humanities in order to promote progress and scholarship in the humanities and the arts in the United States. The act included the following findings:

- The arts and the humanities belong to all the people of the United States.
- The encouragement and support of national progress and scholarship in the humanities and the arts, while primarily matters for private and local initiative, are also appropriate matters of concern to the federal government.
- An advanced civilization must not limit its efforts to science and technology alone, but must give full value and support to the other great branches of scholarly and cultural activity in order to achieve a better understanding of the past, a better analysis of the present, and a better view of the future.
- Democracy demands wisdom and vision in its citizens. It must therefore foster and support a form of education, and access to the arts and the humanities, designed to make people of all backgrounds and locations masters of technology and not its unthinking servants.
- It is necessary and appropriate for the federal government to complement, assist, and add to programs for the advancement of the humanities and the arts by local, state, regional, and private agencies and their organizations. In doing so, the government must be sensitive to the nature of public sponsorship. Public funding of the arts and humanities is subject to the conditions that traditionally govern the use of public money. Such funding should contribute to public support and confidence in the use of taxpayer funds. Public funds provided by the federal government ultimately must serve public purposes the Congress defines.
- The arts and the humanities reflect the high place accorded by the American people to the nation's rich culture and history and to the fostering of mutual respect for the diverse beliefs and values of all persons and groups.

What NEH Grants Accomplish

Since its founding, NEH has awarded more than 68,000 competitive grants.

Interpretive Exhibitions

Interpretive exhibitions provide opportunities for lifelong learning in the humanities for millions of Americans. Since 1967 NEH has awarded nearly $300 million in grants for interpretive exhibitions, catalogs, and public programs, which are among the most highly visible activities supported by the endowment. During 2012 NEH support financed exhibitions; reading, viewing, and discussion programs; Web-based programs; and other public education programs at venues across the country.

Renewing Teaching

Over NEH's history, close to 100,000 high school and college teachers have deepened their knowledge of the humanities through intensive summer study supported by the endowment; tens of thousands of students benefit from these better-educated teachers every year.

Reading and Discussion Programs

Since 1982 NEH has supported reading and discussion programs in the nation's libraries, bringing people together to discuss works of literature and history. Scholars in the humanities provide thematic direction for the discussion programs. Using selected texts and themes such as "Work," "Family," "Diversity," and "Not for Children Only," these programs have attracted more than 2 million Americans to read and talk about what they've read.

Chronicling America

NEH's National Digital Newspaper Program is supporting projects to convert microfilm of historically important U.S. newspapers into fully searchable digital files. Developed in partnership with the Library of Congress, this long-term project ultimately will make more than 30 million pages of newspapers accessible online. For more on this project, visit http://chroniclingamerica.loc.gov.

Stimulating Private Support

Close to $2 billion in humanities support has been generated by NEH's Challenge Grants program, which requires most grant recipients to raise $3 in nonfederal funds for every dollar they receive.

Presidential Papers

Ten presidential papers projects, from Washington to Eisenhower, have received support from NEH. Matching grants for the ten projects have leveraged millions of dollars in nonfederal contributions.

New Scholarship

NEH grants enable scholars to do in-depth study. Jack Rakove explored the making of the Constitution in his *Original Meanings* and James McPherson chronicled the Civil War in his *Battle Cry of Freedom.* Projects supported by NEH grants have earned nearly 20 Pulitzer Prizes.

History on Screen

Since 1967 NEH has awarded nearly $300 million to support the production of films for broad public distribution, including the Emmy Award-winning series *The Civil War,* the Oscar-nominated films *Brooklyn Bridge, The Restless Conscience,* and *Freedom on My Mind,* and film biographies of John and Abigail Adams, Eugene O'Neill, and Ernest Hemingway. More than 20 million people have watched Ken Burns' critically acclaimed *The War* (2007), which chronicles the United States in World War II. More than 8 million saw the April 2010 debut of *The Bud-*

dha, a documentary made for PBS by filmmaker David Grubin, and it has been streamed into hundreds of classrooms across the country.

American Voices

NEH support for scholarly editions makes the writings of prominent and influential Americans accessible. Ten presidents are included, along with such key figures as Martin Luther King, Jr., George C. Marshall, and Eleanor Roosevelt. Papers of prominent writers—among them Emily Dickinson, Walt Whitman, Mark Twain, and Robert Frost—are also available.

Library of America

Millions of books have been sold as part of the Library of America series, a collection of the riches of the nation's literature. Begun with NEH seed money, the nearly 200 published volumes include the works of such figures as Henry Adams, Edith Wharton, William James, Eudora Welty, and W. E. B. Du Bois.

The Library of America also received a $150,000 grant for the publication of *American Poetry: The Seventeenth and Eighteenth Centuries* (two volumes) and an expanded volume of selected works by Captain John Smith—a key figure in the establishment of the first permanent English settlement in North America, at Jamestown, Virginia—and other early exploration narratives.

Technical Innovation

NEH support for the digital humanities is fueling innovation and new tools for research in the humanities. Modern 3D technology allows students to visit things ranging from ancient Egypt to the 1964–1965 New York World's Fair. Spectral imaging was used to create an online critical edition of explorer David Livingstone's previously unreadable field diary of 1871.

Science and the Humanities

The scientific past is being preserved with NEH-supported editions of the letters of Charles Darwin, the works of Albert Einstein, and the 14-volume papers of Thomas Edison. Additionally, NEH and the National Science Foundation have joined forces in Documenting Endangered Languages (DEL), a multiyear effort to preserve records of key languages that are in danger of becoming extinct.

EDSITEment

EDSITEment (http://edsitement.neh.gov) assembles the best humanities resources on the Web, drawing more than 400,000 visitors each month. Incorporating these Internet resources, particularly primary documents, from more than 350 peer-reviewed websites, EDSITEment features more than 500 online lesson plans in all areas of the humanities. Teachers use EDSITEment's resources to enhance lessons and to engage students through interactive technology tools that hone critical-thinking skills.

Federal-State Partnership

The Office of Federal-State Partnership links NEH with the nationwide network of 56 humanities councils, which are located in each state, the District of Columbia, Puerto Rico, the U.S. Virgin Islands, the Northern Mariana Islands, American Samoa. and Guam. Each council funds humanities programs in its own jurisdiction.

Directory of State Humanities Councils

Alabama

Alabama Humanities Foundation
1100 Ireland Way, Suite 101
Birmingham, AL 35205-7001
205-558-3980, fax 205-558-3981
http://www.ahf.net

Alaska

Alaska Humanities Forum
161 E. First Ave., Door 15
Anchorage, AK 99501
907-272-5341, fax 907-272-3979
http://www.akhf.org

Arizona

Arizona Humanities Council
Ellis-Shackelford House
1242 N. Central Ave.
Phoenix, AZ 85004-1887
602-257-0335, fax 602-257-0392
http://www.azhumanities.org

Arkansas

Arkansas Humanities Council
407 President Clinton Ave., Suite 201
Little Rock, AR 72201
501-320-5761, fax 501-537-4550
http://www.arkhums.org

California

Cal Humanities
312 Sutter St., Suite 601
San Francisco, CA 94108
415-391-1474, fax 415-391-1312
http://www.calhum.org

Colorado

Colorado Humanities
1490 Lafayette St., Suite 101
Denver, CO 80218
303-894-7951, fax 303-864-9361
http://www.coloradohumanities.org

Connecticut

Connecticut Humanities Council
37 Broad St.
Middletown, CT 06457
860-685-2260, fax 860-685-7597
http://www.ctculture.org

Delaware

Delaware Humanities Forum
100 W. Tenth St., Suite 1009
Wilmington, DE 19801
302-657-0650, fax 302-657-0655
http://www.dhf.org

District of Columbia

Humanities Council of Washington, D.C.
925 U St. N.W.
Washington, DC 20001
202-387-8393, fax 202-387-8149
http://wdchumanities.org

Florida

Florida Humanities Council
599 Second St. S.
St. Petersburg, FL 33701-5005
727-873-2000, fax 727-873-2014
http://www.flahum.org

Georgia

Georgia Humanities Council
50 Hurt Plaza S.E., Suite 595

Atlanta, GA 30303-2915
404-523-6220, fax 404-523-5702
http://www.georgiahumanities.org

Hawaii

Hawai'i Council for the Humanities
First Hawaiian Bank Bldg.
3599 Waialae Ave., Room 25
Honolulu, HI 96816
808-732-5402, fax 808-732-5432
http://www.hihumanities.org

Idaho

Idaho Humanities Council
217 W. State St.
Boise, ID 83702
208-345-5346, fax 208-345-5347
http://www.idahohumanities.org

Illinois

Illinois Humanities Council
17 N. State St., No. 1400
Chicago, IL 60602-3296
312-422-5580, fax 312-422-5588
http://www.prairie.org

Indiana

Indiana Humanities
1500 N. Delaware St.
Indianapolis, IN 46202
317-638-1500, fax 317-634-9503
http://www.indianahumanities.org

Iowa

Humanities Iowa
100 Library Room 4039
Iowa City, IA 52242-4038
319-335-4153, fax 319-335-4154
http://www.humanitiesiowa.org

Kansas

Kansas Humanities Council
112 S.W. Sixth Ave., Suite 210
Topeka, KS 66603
785-357-0359, fax 785-357-1723
http://www.kansashumanities.org

Kentucky

Kentucky Humanities Council
206 E. Maxwell St.
Lexington, KY 40508
859-257-5932, fax 859-257-5933
http://www.kyhumanities.org

Louisiana

Louisiana Endowment for the Humanities
938 Lafayette St., Suite 300
New Orleans, LA 70113-1782
504-523-4352, fax 504-529-2358
http://www.leh.org

Maine

Maine Humanities Council
674 Brighton Ave.
Portland, ME 04102-1012
207-773-5051, fax 207-773-2416
http://www.mainehumanities.org

Maryland

Maryland Humanities Council
108 W. Centre St.
Baltimore, MD 21201-4565
410-685-0095, fax 410-685-0795
http://www.mdhc.org

Massachusetts

Mass Humanities
66 Bridge St.
Northampton, MA 01060
413-584-8440, fax 413-584-8454
http://www.masshumanities.org

Michigan

Michigan Humanities Council
119 Pere Marquette Drive, Suite 3B
Lansing, MI 48912-1270
517-372-7770, fax 517-372-0027
http://michiganhumanities.org

Minnesota

Minnesota Humanities Center
987 E. Ivy Ave.
St. Paul, MN 55106-2046
651-774-0105, fax 651-774-0205
http://www.minnesotahumanities.org

Mississippi

Mississippi Humanities Council
3825 Ridgewood Rd., Room 311
Jackson, MS 39211
601-432-6752, fax 601-432-6750
http://www.mshumanities.org

Missouri

Missouri Humanities Council
543 Hanley Industrial Court, Suite 201
St. Louis, MO 63144-1905
314-781-9660, fax 314-781-9681
http://www.mohumanities.org

Montana

Humanities Montana
311 Brantly
Missoula, MT 59812-7848
406-243-6022, fax 406-243-4836
http://www.humanitiesmontana.org

Nebraska

Nebraska Humanities Council
215 Centennial Mall South, Suite 330
Lincoln, NE 68508
402-474-2131, fax 402-474-4852
http://www.nebraskahumanities.org/

Nevada

Nevada Humanities
1034 N. Sierra St.
Reno, NV 89507
775-784-6587, fax 775-784-6527
http://www.nevadahumanities.org

New Hampshire

New Hampshire Humanities Council
117 Pleasant St.
Concord, NH 03301-3852
603-224-4071, fax 603-224-4072
http://www.nhhc.org

New Jersey

New Jersey Council for the Humanities
28 W. State St., 6th floor
Trenton, NJ 08608
609-695-4838, fax 609-695-4929
http://www.njch.org

New Mexico

New Mexico Humanities Council
MSC06 3570
1 University of New Mexico
Albuquerque, NM 87131-0001
505-277-3705, fax 505-277-6056
http://www.nmhum.org

New York

New York Council for the Humanities
150 Broadway, Suite 1700
New York, NY 10038
212-233-1131, fax 212-233-4607
http://www.nyhumanities.org

North Carolina

North Carolina Humanities Council
122 North Elm St.
Greensboro, NC 27401
336-334-5325, fax 336-334-5052
http://www.nchumanities.org

North Dakota

North Dakota Humanities Council
418 E. Broadway, Suite 8
P.O. Box 2191
Bismarck, ND 58502
701-255-3360, fax 701-223-8724
http://www.nd-humanities.org

Ohio

Ohio Humanities Council
471 E. Broad St., Suite 1620
Columbus, OH 43215-3857
614-461-7802, fax 614-461-4651
http://www.ohiohumanities.org

Oklahoma

Oklahoma Humanities Council
Festival Plaza
428 W. California, Suite 270
Oklahoma City, OK 73102
405-235-0280, fax 405-235-0289
http://www.okhumanitiescouncil.org

Oregon

Oregon Council for the Humanities
813 S.W. Alder St., Suite 702

Portland, OR 97205
503-241-0543, fax 503-241-0024
http://www.oregonhum.org

Pennsylvania

Pennsylvania Humanities Council
325 Chestnut St., Suite 715
Philadelphia, PA 19106-2607
215-925-1005, fax 215-925-3054
http://www.pahumanities.org

Rhode Island

Rhode Island Council for the Humanities
131 Washington St., Suite 210
Providence, RI 02903
401-273-2250, fax 401-454-4872
http://www.rihumanities.org

South Carolina

Humanities Council of South Carolina
P.O. Box 5287
Columbia, SC 29250
803-771-2477, fax 803-771-2487
http://www.schumanities.org

South Dakota

South Dakota Humanities Council
1215 Trail Ridge Rd., Suite A
Brookings, SD 57006
605-688-6113, fax 605-688-4531
http://sdhumanities.org

Tennessee

Humanities Tennessee
306 Gay St., Suite 306
Nashville, TN 37201
615-770-0006, fax 615-770-0007
http://www.humanitiestennessee.org

Texas

Humanities Texas
1410 Rio Grande St.
Austin, TX 78701
512-440-1991, fax 512-440-0115
http://www.humanitiestexas.org

Utah

Utah Humanities Council
202 W. 300 North
Salt Lake City, UT 84103
801-359-9670, fax 801-531-7869
http://www.utahhumanities.org

Vermont

Vermont Humanities Council
11 Loomis St.
Montpelier, VT 05602
802-262-2626, fax 802-262-2620
http://www.vermonthumanities.org

Virginia

Virginia Foundation for the Humanities and
   Public Policy
145 Ednam Drive
Charlottesville, VA 22903-4629
434-924-3296, fax 434-296-4714
http://www.virginiafoundation.org

Washington

Humanities Washington
1204 Minor Ave.
Seattle, WA 98101-2825
206-682-1770, fax 206-682-4158
http://www.humanities.org

West Virginia

West Virginia Humanities Council
1310 Kanawha Blvd. East
Charleston, WV 25301
304-346-8500, fax 304-346-8504
http://www.wvhumanities.org

Wisconsin

Wisconsin Humanities Council
222 S. Bedford St., Suite F
Madison, WI 53703-3688
608-262-0706, fax 608-263-7970
http://www.wisconsinhumanities.org

Wyoming

Wyoming Humanities Council
1315 E. Lewis St.

Laramie, WY 82072-3459
307-721-9243, fax 307-742-4914
http://www.uwyo.edu/humanities

American Samoa

Amerika Samoa Humanities Council
P.O. Box 5800
Pago Pago, AS 96799
684-633-4870, fax 684-633-4873
http://amerikasamoahumanitiescouncil.org

Guam

Guam Humanities Council
222 Chalan Santo Papa
Reflection Center, Suite 106
Hagatna, Guam 96910
671-472-4460, fax 671-472-4465
http://www.guamhumanitiescouncil.org

Northern Marianas Islands

Northern Marianas Humanities Council
P.O. Box 506437
Saipan, MP 96950
670-235-4785, fax 670-235-4786
http://www.nmihumanities.org

Puerto Rico

Fundación Puertorriqueña de las Humanidades
Box 9023920
San Juan, PR 00902-3920
787-721-2087, fax 787-721-2684
http://www.fphpr.org

Virgin Islands

Virgin Islands Humanities Council
1826 Kongens Gade
St. Thomas, VI 00802-6746
340-776-4044, fax 340-774-3972
http://www.vihumanities.org

NEH Overview

Bridging Cultures

Bridging Cultures is a special endowment-wide initiative that highlights the role of the humanities in enhancing understanding and respect for diverse cultures and subcultures within America's borders and around the globe.

The initiative encourages projects that explore the ways in which cultures have influenced society. With the aim of revitalizing intellectual and civic life through the humanities, NEH welcomes projects that expand both scholarly and public discussion of diverse countries, peoples, and cultural and intellectual traditions worldwide.

Contact: 202-606-8337, e-mail bridgingcultures@neh.gov.

Division of Education Programs

Through grants to educational institutions and professional development programs for scholars and teachers, this division is designed to support study of the humanities at all levels of education.

Grants support the development of curriculum and materials, faculty study programs among educational institutions, and conferences and networks of institutions.

Contact: 202-606-8500, e-mail education@neh.gov.

Seminars and Institutes

Grants support summer seminars and institutes in the humanities for college and school teachers. These faculty development activities are conducted at colleges and universities in the United States and abroad. Those wishing to participate in seminars should submit their seminar applications to the seminar director.

Contact: 202-606-8471, e-mail sem-inst@neh.gov.

Landmarks of American History and Culture

Grants for Landmarks workshops provide support to school teachers and community college faculty. These professional development workshops are conducted at or near sites important to American history and culture (such as presidential residences or libraries, colonial era settlements, major battlefields, historic districts, and sites associated with major writers or artists) to address central themes and issues in American history, government, literature, art history, and related subjects in the humanities.

Contact: 202-606-8463, e-mail landmarks@neh.gov.

Division of Preservation and Access

Grants are made for projects that will create, preserve, and increase the availability of resources important for research, education, and public programming in the humanities.

Support may be sought to preserve the intellectual content and aid bibliographic control of collections; to compile bibliographies, descriptive catalogs, and guides to cultural holdings; and to create dictionaries, encyclopedias, databases, and electronic archives. Applications also may be submitted for education and training projects dealing with issues of preservation or access; for research and development leading to improved preservation and access standards, practices, and tools; and for projects to digitize historic U.S. newspapers and to document endangered languages. Grants are also made to help smaller cultural repositories preserve and care for their humanities collections. Proposals may combine preservation and access activities within a single project.

Contact: 202-606-8570, e-mail preservation@neh.gov.

Division of Public Programs

Public humanities programs promote lifelong learning in American and world history, literature, comparative religion, philosophy, and other fields of the humanities. They offer new insights into familiar subjects and invite conversation about important humanities ideas and questions.

The Division of Public Programs supports a wide range of public humanities programs that reach large and diverse public audiences through a variety of program formats, including interpretive exhibitions, radio and television broadcasts, lectures, symposia, interpretive multimedia projects, printed materials, and reading and discussion programs.

Grants support the development and production of television, radio, and digital media programs; the planning and implementation of museum exhibitions, the interpretation of historic sites, the production of related publications, multimedia components, and educational programs; and the planning and implementation of reading and discussion programs, lectures, symposia, and interpretive exhibitions of books, manuscripts, and other library resources.

Contact: 202-606-8269, e-mail publicpgms@neh.gov.

Division of Research Programs

Through fellowships to individual scholars and grants to support complex, frequently collaborative research, the Division of Research Programs contributes to the creation of knowledge in the humanities.

Fellowships and Stipends

Grants provide support for scholars to undertake full-time independent research and writing in the humanities. Grants are available for a maximum of one year and a minimum of two months of summer study.

Contact: 202-606-8200, e-mail (fellowships) fellowships@neh.gov, (summer stipends) stipends@neh.gov.

Research

Grants provide up to three years of support for collaborative research in the preparation of publication of editions, translations, and other important works in the humanities, and in the conduct of large or complex interpretive studies, including archaeology projects and humanities studies of science and technology. Grants also support research opportunities offered through independent research centers and international research organizations.

Contact: 202-606-8200, e-mail research@neh.gov.

Office of Challenge Grants

Nonprofit institutions interested in developing new sources of long-term support for educational, scholarly, preservation, and public programs in the humanities may be assisted in these efforts by an NEH Challenge Grant. Grantees are required to raise $3 in nonfederal donations for every federal dollar offered. Both federal and nonfederal funds may be used to establish or increase institutional endowments and therefore guarantee long-term support for a variety of humanities needs. Funds also may be used for limited direct capital expenditures where such needs are compelling and clearly related to improvements in the humanities.

Contact: 202-606-8309, e-mail challenge@neh.gov.

Office of Digital Humanities

The Office of Digital Humanities encourages and supports projects that utilize or study the impact of digital technology on research, education, preservation, and public programming in the humanities. Launched as an initiative in 2006, Digital Humanities was made permanent as an office within NEH in 2008.

NEH is interested in fostering the growth of digital humanities and lending support to a wide variety of projects, including those that deploy digital technologies and methods to enhance understanding of a topic or issue; those that study the impact of digital technology on the humanities; and those that digitize important materials, thereby increasing the public's ability to search and access humanities information.

The office coordinates the endowment's efforts in the area of digital scholarship. Currently, NEH has numerous programs throughout the agency that are actively funding digital scholarship, including Humanities Collections and Resources, Institutes for Advanced Topics in the Digital Humanities, Digital Humanities

Challenge Grants, Digital Humanities Start-Up Grants, and many others. NEH is also actively working with other funding partners in the United States and abroad in order to better coordinate spending on digital infrastructure for the humanities. *Contact:* 202-606-8401, e-mail odh@neh.gov.

A full list of NEH grants programs and deadlines is available on the endowment's website at http://www.neh.gov/grants.

Institute of Museum and Library Services
Office of Library Services

1800 M St. N.W., Ninth Floor, Washington, DC 20036-5802
202-653-4657, fax 202-653-4600
World Wide Web http://www.imls.gov

Susan H. Hildreth
Director

Vision and Mission

The vision of the Institute of Museum and Library Services (IMLS) is a democratic society where communities and individuals thrive with broad public access to knowledge, cultural heritage, and lifelong learning.

Its mission is to inspire libraries and museums to advance innovation, lifelong learning, and cultural and civic engagement. It provides leadership through research, policy development, and grantmaking.

Strategic Goals

- IMLS places the learner at the center and supports engaging experiences in libraries and museums that prepare people to be full participants in their local communities and our global society.
- IMLS promotes museums and libraries as strong community anchors that enhance civic engagement, cultural opportunities, and economic vitality.
- IMLS supports exemplary stewardship of museum and library collections and promotes the use of technology to facilitate discovery of knowledge and cultural heritage.
- IMLS advises the president and Congress on plans, policies, and activities to sustain and increase public access to information and ideas.
- IMLS achieves excellence in public management and performs as a model organization through strategic alignment of resources and prioritization of programmatic activities, maximizing value for the public.

There are 123,000 libraries and 17,500 museums in the United States. IMLS supports the full range of libraries, including public, academic, research, special, and tribal, and the full range of museums including art, history, science and technology, children's museums, historical societies, tribal museums, planetariums, botanic gardens, and zoos. Nearly 170 million people in the United States over the age of 14 (69 percent of the population) are library users, and every year 148 million over the age of 18 visit a museum.

Overview

U.S. museums and libraries are at the forefront of the movement to create a nation of learners. As stewards of cultural heritage, they provide learning experiences for everyone. With built infrastructure in nearly every community in the nation; robust online networks; and dedicated, knowledgeable staff, they connect people to one another and to the full spectrum of human experience.

The role of IMLS is to provide leadership and funding for museums and libraries—resources these institutions need to fulfill their mission of becoming centers of learning for life, crucial to achieving personal fulfillment, a productive work force, and an engaged citizenry.

The Museum and Library Services Act, which includes the Library Services and Technology Act (LSTA) and the Museum Services Act (MSA), authorizes IMLS to support the following activities:

LSTA

- Enhance coordination among federal programs that relate to library and information services
- Promote continuous improvement in library services in all types of libraries in order to better serve the public
- Facilitate access to resources in all types of libraries for the purpose of cultivating an educated and informed citizenry
- Encourage resource sharing among all types of libraries for the purpose of achieving economical and efficient delivery of library services
- Promote literacy, education, and lifelong learning and enhance and expand the services and resources provided by libraries, including those services and resources relating to work force development, 21st century skills, and digital literacy skills
- Enhance the skills of the current library work force and recruit future professionals to the field of library and information services
- Ensure the preservation of knowledge and library collections in all formats and enable libraries to serve their communities during disasters
- Enhance the role of libraries within the information infrastructure in order to support research, education, and innovation
- Promote library services that provide users with access to information through national, state, local, regional, and international collaborations and networks

MSA

- Encourage and support museums in carrying out their public service role of connecting the whole of society to the cultural, artistic, historical, natural, and scientific understandings that constitute the nation's heritage
- Encourage and support museums in carrying out their educational role as core providers of learning and in conjunction with schools, families, and communities
- Encourage leadership, innovation, and applications of the most current technologies and practices to enhance museum services through international, national, regional, state, and local networks and partnerships

- Assist, encourage, and support museums in carrying out their stewardship responsibilities to achieve the highest standards in conservation and care of the cultural, historic, natural, and scientific heritage to benefit future generations
- Assist, encourage, and support museums in achieving the highest standards of management and service, and ease the financial burden borne by museums as a result of their increasing use by the public
- Support resource sharing and partnerships among museums, libraries, schools, and other community organizations
- Encourage and support museums as a part of community economic development and revitalization
- Ensure that museums of various types and sizes in diverse geographic regions are afforded attention and support
- Support efforts at the state level to leverage museum resources and maximize museum services

A general provision of the Museum and Library Services Act calls for IMLS to develop and implement policy to ensure the availability of museum, library, and information services throughout the United States. Specific duties include the following: advising the president, Congress, and other federal agencies and offices on museum, library, and information services in order to ensure the creation, preservation, organization, and dissemination of knowledge; engaging federal, state, and local governmental agencies and private entities in assessing the museum, library, and information services needs of the people, and coordinating the development of plans, policies, and activities to meet such needs effectively; carrying out programs of research and development, data collection, and financial assistance to extend and improve the nation's museum, library, and information services; ensuring that museum, library, and information services are fully integrated into national information and education infrastructures.

Funding

In fiscal year (FY) 2012, Congress appropriated $184,704,000 for the programs authorized by LSTA. The Office of Library Services within IMLS, under the policy direction of the IMLS director and deputy director, administers LSTA programs. The office includes the Division of State Programs, which administers the Grants to States program, and the Division of Discretionary Programs, which administers the National Leadership Grants for Libraries program, the Laura Bush 21st Century Librarian Program, the Native American Library Services program, and the Native Hawaiian Library Services program. IMLS presents annual awards to libraries through the National Medal for Museum and Library Service program. Additionally, IMLS supports two award programs administered by the President's Committee on the Arts and the Humanities: the National Arts and Humanities Youth Program Awards and the National Student Poets Program.

Library Statistics

The president's budget request for FY 2012 included funds for IMLS to continue administering the Public Libraries Survey (PLS) and the State Library Agencies Survey. FY 2009 was the first year IMLS administered the two surveys over a full collection cycle, from planning to collection and dissemination. Responding to concerns from the professional community, IMLS has reduced the time it takes to release survey results by six months. In addition to producing annual reports of the survey data, IMLS introduced new, shorter research products to highlight report findings. These new reports leverage the survey data to address a wide range of public policy priorities, including education, employment, community and economic development, and telecommunications policy.

In the Library Statistics section of the IMLS website (http://www.imls.gov/research), visitors can link to data search tools, the latest available data for each survey, other publications, data files, and survey definitions.

Public Libraries Survey

Descriptive statistics for more than 9,000 public libraries are collected and disseminated annually through a voluntary census, the Public Libraries Survey. The survey is conducted through the Public Library Statistics Cooperative (PLSC, formerly the Federal-State Cooperative System [FSCS]). In FY 2013 IMLS will complete the 25th collection of this data.

The survey collects identifying information about public libraries and each of their service outlets, including street address, city, county, zip code, and telephone number. Additional identifying information is collected on public libraries including library Web address and mailing address. The survey collects data on staffing; type of legal basis; type of geographic boundary; type of administrative structure; type of interlibrary relationship; type and number of public service outlets; operating revenue and expenditures; capital revenue and expenditures; size of collection (including number of electronic books and databases); current serial subscriptions (including electronic); and service measures, such as number of reference transactions, interlibrary loans, circulation, public service hours, library visits, circulation of children's materials, number of children's programs, children's program attendance, total number of library programs, total attendance at library programs, number of Internet terminals used by the general public, and number of users of electronic resources a year.

This survey also collects several data items about outlets, including the location of an outlet relative to a metropolitan area, number of books-by-mail-only outlets, number of bookmobiles by bookmobile outlet, and square footage of the outlet.

The 50 states and the District of Columbia have participated in data collection from the survey's inception in 1989. In 1993 Guam, the Commonwealth of the Northern Mariana Islands, Puerto Rico, and the U.S. Virgin Islands joined in the survey. The first release of Public Libraries Survey data occurred with the launch of the updated Compare Public Libraries Tool on the Library Statistics section of the IMLS website (http://www.imls.gov/research). The data used in this Web tool are final but do not include imputations for missing data. (Imputation is a statistical means for providing an estimate for each missing data item.)

An important new feature of the public library data tools is the availability of locale codes for all administrative entities and outlets. These locale codes allow users to quickly identify which library outlets and administrative entities are located in cities, suburbs, towns, or rural areas. The new locale codes are based on an address's proximity to an urbanized area (a densely settled core with densely settled surrounding areas). The locale code system classifies territory into four major types: city, suburb, town, and rural. Each type has three subcategories. For city and suburb, these gradations are based on population size—large, midsize, and small. Towns and rural areas are further distinguished by their distance from an urbanized area. They can be characterized as fringe, distant, or remote. The coding methodology was developed by the U.S. Census Bureau as a way to identify the location of public schools in the National Center for Education Statistics' (NCES's) Common Core of Data. As of FY 2008 each library outlet and administrative entity survey has one of the 12 locale codes assigned to it.

Locale codes provide a new way to analyze U.S. library services. By incorporating objective measures of rurality and urbanicity into the data files, researchers and practitioners can benchmark services in a fundamentally different way by basing comparisons on community attributes as well as the attributes of the libraries themselves. In other words, library services in rural remote areas can now be compared with library services in other rural remote areas of the state or nation using a standardized urbanicity/rurality metric that is applied consistently to each library. Once communities of interest have been selected, comparisons can be made with any data that is available in the survey whether financial, operational, or service output related.

State Library Agencies Survey

The State Library Agencies Survey collects and disseminates information about the state library agencies in the 50 states and the District of Columbia. A State Library Administrative Agency (SLAA) is the official unit of state government charged with statewide library development and the administration of federal funds under the IMLS Grants to States program. SLAAs' administrative and developmental responsibilities affect the operation of thousands of public, academic, school, and special libraries. SLAAs provide important reference and information services to state government and sometimes also provide service to the general public. SLAAs often administer state library and special operations such as state archives and libraries for the blind and physically handicapped and the state Center for the Book.

The State Library Agencies Survey began in 1994 and was administered by NCES until 2007. Beginning with FY 1999 data, the survey used a Web-based data collection system and included imputations for missing data. IMLS has shifted to a biannual data collection of the SLAA Survey and began collecting the FY 2012 data at the end of calendar year 2012.

National Medal for Museum and Library Service

The National Medal for Museum and Library Service honors outstanding institutions that make significant and exceptional contributions to their communities. Selected institutions demonstrate extraordinary and innovative approaches to public service, exceeding the expected levels of community outreach and core programs generally associated with its services. The medal includes a prize of $5,000 to each recipient and an awards ceremony held in Washington, D.C. The 2012 ceremony was held in the White House on November 14.

The winners of the 2012 National Medal for Museum and Library Service were: (libraries) Contra Costa County Library, Pleasant Hill, California; Cumberland County Public Library, Fayetteville, North Carolina; Naturita (Colorado) Community Library; Park View High School Library Media Center, Sterling, Virginia; Shaler North Hills Library, Glenshaw, Pennsylvania; (museums) Bootheel Youth Museum, Malden, Missouri; Garfield Park Conservatory, Chicago; Long Island Children's Museum, Garden City, New York; Museum of Contemporary Art, North Miami, Florida; Pacific Science Center, Seattle.

State-Administered Programs

In FY 2012 approximately 85 percent ($156,365,300) of the annual federal appropriation under LSTA was distributed to SLAAs through the Grants to States program according to a formula set by the law. The formula consists of a base amount for each SLAA—the 50 states, Puerto Rico, and the District of Columbia receive $680,000 each; other U.S. territories receive $60,000 each—plus a supplemental amount based on population (Table 1).

Table 1 / Library Services and Technology Act, State Allotments, FY 2012
(P.L. 112-74)
Total Distributed to States: $156,365,300[1]

State	Federal Funds from IMLS (66%)[2]	State Matching Funds (34%)	Total Federal and State Funds
Alabama	$2,501,154	$1,288,473	$3,789,627
Alaska	952,947	490,912	1,443,859
Arizona	3,250,835	1,674,673	4,925,508
Arkansas	1,800,586	927,575	2,728,161
California	15,029,503	7,742,471	22,771,974
Colorado	2,641,949	1,361,004	4,002,953
Connecticut	2,038,047	1,049,903	3,087,950
Delaware	1,023,258	527,133	1,550,391
Florida	7,871,982	4,055,263	11,927,245
Georgia	4,495,213	2,315,716	6,810,929
Hawaii	1,159,084	597,104	1,756,188
Idaho	1,280,599	659,703	1,940,302
Illinois	5,664,245	2,917,944	8,582,189
Indiana	3,161,761	1,628,786	4,790,547
Iowa	1,844,037	949,958	2,793,995
Kansas	1,773,974	913,865	2,687,839
Kentucky	2,350,899	1,211,069	3,561,968
Louisiana	2,424,055	1,248,756	3,672,811
Maine	1,185,547	610,736	1,796,283
Maryland	2,889,137	1,488,343	4,377,480
Massachusetts	3,233,374	1,665,678	4,899,052

Michigan	4,504,022	2,320,254	6,824,276
Minnesota	2,717,086	1,399,711	4,116,797
Mississippi	1,819,928	937,539	2,757,467
Missouri	2,994,821	1,542,787	4,537,608
Montana	1,057,408	544,725	1,602,133
Nebraska	1,377,353	709,545	2,086,898
Nevada	1,702,212	876,897	2,579,109
New Hampshire	1,189,626	612,838	1,802,464
New Jersey	4,042,569	2,082,536	6,125,105
New Mexico	1,463,144	753,741	2,216,885
New York	8,146,018	4,196,434	12,342,452
North Carolina	4,322,143	2,226,559	6,548,702
North Dakota	931,737	479,986	1,411,723
Ohio	5,120,439	2,637,802	7,758,241
Oklahoma	2,114,098	1,089,081	3,203,179
Oregon	2,164,574	1,115,084	3,279,658
Pennsylvania	5,544,252	2,856,130	8,400,382
Rhode Island	1,086,948	559,943	1,646,891
South Carolina	2,450,059	1,262,152	3,712,211
South Dakota	995,771	512,973	1,508,744
Tennessee	3,120,490	1,607,525	4,728,015
Texas	10,388,436	5,351,619	15,740,055
Utah	1,769,981	911,808	2,681,789
Vermont	919,668	473,768	1,393,436
Virginia	3,741,963	1,927,678	5,669,641
Washington	3,277,624	1,688,473	4,966,097
West Virginia	1,382,914	712,410	2,095,324
Wisconsin	2,862,663	1,474,705	4,337,368
Wyoming	890,868	458,932	1,349,800
District of Columbia	915,107	471,419	1,386,526
Puerto Rico	2,140,076	1,102,463	3,242,539
American Samoa	81,378	41,922	123,300
Northern Marianas	80,748	41,597	122,345
Guam	121,361	62,519	183,880
Virgin Islands	100,971	52,015	152,986
Pacific Territories[3]	254,658	131,187	385,845
Total[4]	$156,365,300	$80,551,821	$236,917,121

1 Maintenance of effort (MOE) reductions that resulted from MOE shortfalls reported on the FY 2009 Financial Status Report (reported and reviewed in FY 2011) have been applied to the FY 2012 allotment distribution. Those funds deducted from the states that did not meet their MOE requirement have been distributed proportionately across the states that did meet their FY 2009 MOE requirements.

2 IMLS federal funds are calculated using the current minimum base set into law (20 USC 9131[b]) and population figures from the U.S. Census Bureau.
Data used in the state allotment table are the most current published population estimates available on the first day of the fiscal year. Therefore, the population data used in the FY 2012 table are what was available on the Census Bureau website (http://www.census.gov/popest/states/index.html) on October 1, 2011.
Population data for American Samoa, the Commonwealth of Northern Mariana Islands, Guam, the U.S. Virgin Islands, the Republic of the Marshall Islands, the Federated States of Micronesia, and the Republic of Palau reflect what was available on the Census Bureau website (http://www.census.gov/cgi-bin/ipc/idbrank.pl) on October 1, 2011.

3 Aggregate allotments (including administrative costs) for the Republic of Palau, the Republic of the Marshall Islands, and the Federated States of Micronesia are awarded on a competitive basis to eligible applicants, and are administered by Pacific Resources for Education and Learning (PREL).

4 Because of rounding to whole dollar amounts in the state allotments, some totals may be slightly adjusted to reflect actual total amounts.

SLAAs may use the appropriation for statewide initiatives and services. They may also distribute the funds through competitive subgrants or cooperative agreements to public, academic, research, school, or special libraries. For-profit and federal libraries are not eligible applicants. Grants to States funds have been used to meet the special needs of children, parents, teenagers, the unemployed, senior citizens, and the business community, as well as adult learners. Many libraries have partnered with community organizations to provide a variety of services and programs, including access to electronic databases, computer instruction, homework centers, summer reading programs, digitization of special collections, access to e-books and adaptive technology, bookmobile service, and development of outreach programs to the underserved. States are required by law to match the IMLS grant with non-federal funds at a 1-to-2 (non-federal to federal) ratio. No more than 4 percent of a state's program funds may be used for administrative costs.

A Special Rule, 20 USCA 9131(b)(3)(C), authorizes a small competitive grants program for four U.S. territories (Guam, American Samoa, the Commonwealth of the Northern Mariana Islands, and the U.S. Virgin Islands) and three Freely Associated States (the Federated States of Micronesia, the Republic of the Marshall Islands, and the Republic of Palau). The funds for this grant program are taken from the total allotment for the Freely Associated States. In FY 2012 a total of $254,658 was available for the seven entities. This amount included a set-aside of 5 percent for Pacific Resources for Education and Learning (PREL), based in Hawaii, to facilitate the grants review process. Therefore, the total amount awarded in FY 2012 was $241,925.

The IMLS-funded programs and services delivered by each SLAA support the purposes and priorities set forth in LSTA. The SLAAs determine goals and objectives for the Grants to States funds through a planning process that includes statewide needs assessments. These goals and objectives are included in each state's statutorily required five-year plan on file with IMLS.

On a rotating basis, IMLS Grants to States program staff conduct site visits to SLAAs to provide technical support and to monitor the states' success in administering the program. In 2012 program officers visited 12 SLAAs in Alaska, Arizona, Indiana, Louisiana, Maryland, Michigan, Nebraska, New Mexico, Oklahoma, Tennessee, Texas, and Virginia. Each site visit includes critical review of the administration of the LSTA program at the SLAA as well as trips into the field to visit libraries that are recipients of subgrants or beneficiaries of statewide IMLS-funded projects.

Discretionary Grants Programs

In FY 2012 IMLS's four library discretionary programs awarded the following total amounts: National Leadership Grants, $11,945,386; Laura Bush 21st Century Librarian Program, $10,406,038; Native American Library Services, $3,310,268; and Native Hawaiian Library Services, $552,000.

National Leadership Grants for Libraries

The National Leadership Grants for Libraries (NLG–Libraries) program provides funding for research and innovative model programs to enhance the quality of library services nationwide. The grants are competitive and intended to produce results useful for the broader library community.

Congress and the President appropriated $11,945,386 for NLG–Libraries for FY 2012. There were four categories:

Advancing Digital Resources (maximum award: $500,000)

This category supports the creation, use, preservation, and presentation of significant digital resources as well as the development of tools to manage digital assets, incorporating new technologies or new technology practice. This category included projects that develop and disseminate new tools to facilitate management, preservation, sharing, and use of digital resources; increase community access to institutional resources through innovative use of existing technology-based tools; develop or advance participation in library communities using social technologies in new ways; develop new approaches or tools for digital curation.

Demonstration (maximum award: $500,000)

Demonstration projects use available knowledge to address key needs and challenges facing libraries and archives, and transform that knowledge into formal practice. This category includes projects that demonstrate and/or test new practices in library and/or archives operations; demonstrate how libraries and/or archives serve their communities by fostering public value and implementing systemic changes in the field; establish and/or test standards and tools for innovative learning; or demonstrate and/or test an expansion of preservation or conservation practices.

Research (maximum award: $500,000)

Research grants support projects that have the potential to improve library and archives practice, resource use, programs, and services. Both basic and applied research projects are encouraged. This category includes projects that evaluate the impact of library or archival services; investigate how learning takes place in libraries and archives, and how use of library and/or archival resources enhances learning; investigate how to improve the quality, effectiveness, or efficiency of library or archives management programs or services; investigate ways to enhance the archiving, preservation, management, discovery, and use of digital assets and resources; or investigate or conduct research to add new knowledge or make improvements in the conservation and preservation of collections.

Library-Museum Collaboration (maximum award: $500,000)

This category helps to create new opportunities for libraries and museums to engage with each other, and with other organizations as appropriate, to support the educational, economic, and social needs of their communities. Both research and implementation projects are eligible. FY 2012 grant funds supported the agency's early learning priority through innovative collaborative projects, whether they were new partnerships or were building on an existing collaboration.

This category includes projects that address community civic and educational needs; increase the organizations' capacity to serve as effective venues and resources for learning; or use technology in innovative ways to serve audiences more effectively.

Collaborative Planning Grants

In addition to full project proposals, applicants had the opportunity to apply for Collaborative Planning Grants in any of the categories. These grants were offered at two levels: Level 1 planning grants of up to $50,000 enable project teams from libraries, museums, or other partner organizations to work together on the planning of a single collaborative project in any of the NLG categories; Level 2 planning grants of up to $100,000 support workshops, symposia, or other convenings of experts to discuss issues of national importance to libraries or archives (and museums when applicable), with the goal of producing a white paper that encourages multiple NLG proposals addressing issues raised in the report.

The program received 125 complete and eligible proposals in FY 2012, consisting of 86 full project proposals and 39 planning grant proposals. Collectively, these proposals requested nearly $35 million. In September 2012 the program announced 45 awards to libraries and archives, totaling $9,388,219 (Table 2). Among these funded NLG awards were 12 library-based early learning partnership projects, funded as part of the IMLS FY 2012–2013 initiative to support the national Campaign for Grade-Level Reading.

In addition to these 45 awards to libraries and archives, remaining program funds were used to sponsor special initiatives, out-of-cycle special opportunities, and other projects, including seven Sparks! Ignition Grants, three awards to U.S. research teams funded under the international Digging Into Data Challenge, eight grants to libraries as part of the Learning Labs for Libraries and Museums initiative, and multiple other small awards in support of such efforts as the National Medals and the Connecting to Collections implementation grants.

Table 2 / National Leadership Grants for Libraries, FY 2012

Advancing Digital Resources

Harvard College $249,714

The Digital Public Library of America, based at the Berkman Center for Internet and Society at Harvard, will partner with the Mountain West Digital Library and other collaborators to launch a digital hubs pilot program. The program will help fund a network of service hubs run by selected statewide digital library programs and "content hubs" consisting of large content repositories.

Hill Museum and Manuscript Library, St. John's University $350,930

The Hill Museum and Manuscript Library (HMML), a sponsored program of Saint John's, will lead a team of collaborators drawn from St. Louis University, the University of Kentucky, and other organizations to build vHMML, an integrated online environment for the discovery and use of digitized manuscripts.

Regents of the University of California, Riverside $250,000

The university's Center for Bibliographical Studies and Research will expand and enhance its growing database, A Union Catalog and Bibliography of Latin American Imprints to 1851. This database currently contains approximately 51,000 titles, and the project team will collect approximately 30,000 new title records from distributed online catalogs, printed bibliographies, and other sources to help the database to become a transformative tool in Latin American studies research.

Table 2 / National Leadership Grants for Libraries, FY 2012 *(cont.)*

University of California, Santa Cruz $400,000

The university library will partner with the Rosenzweig Center for History and New Media at George Mason University to develop and test a new "curator dashboard" plug-in for the Omeka Web-publishing system for digital collections. The partners will produce a suite of workflows and tools that help educators, scholars, and library and museum staff build, describe, manage, and prepare digital collections for deposit in digital preservation storage repositories.

University of Illinois $76,894

The University of Illinois Libraries will lead a project to update the IMLS Framework of Guidance for Building Good Digital Collections, a Web-based document created in 2001 that has served as a resource for libraries, museums, and archives creating digital collections. The document was last updated in 2007.

Research

American Library Association $486,587

The association (ALA) and the University of Maryland, in partnership with the International City/County Management Association, will conduct a three-year study of public libraries as providers of digitally inclusive services and resources. The study will generate new understanding of the roles public libraries are playing, and gaps or needs that must be addressed to help them fulfill their vision of equitable access for all.

Carnegie Mellon University Libraries $497,756

A team of Carnegie Mellon computer scientists and library staff currently are building Olive, an archiving system for executable content. The team will work with other collaborators at the University of Illinois and with publisher Reed Elsevier to identify the significant properties of executable content that must be preserved over time in a digital archive, and to explore possible refinements to existing models for building and evaluating digital archive systems.

South Carolina Research Foundation $498,812

Building on previous work, a team of scientists from the University of South Carolina and the Library of Congress will conduct a study to validate methods for measuring the degree of degradation in samples from magnetic tape collections. The team also will design a prototype device and software that could be shared between cultural heritage organizations to help them assess their tape collections' preservation needs.

University of Illinois $499,919

Researchers at the university's Graduate School of Library and Information Science and at the Johns Hopkins University Libraries will use this grant to study the motivations, needs, priorities, and workflows of small scientific research environments.

The Information School, University of Washington $460,337

The Information School will investigate the roles immigrant minority youths perform as technical intermediaries between their families and resources found in their local libraries. It will also explore the value of providing targeted information literacy and digital literacy training for these youths.

Demonstration

American Library Association $249,867

Building upon earlier planning work supported by IMLS, ALA and its partner StoryCorps will develop and implement "StoryCorps @ your library," a replicable program to be piloted at ten public libraries. The libraries will receive equipment, training, promotional materials, and other resources to help them implement community documentation projects using the StoryCorps interview model.

Table 2 / National Leadership Grants for Libraries, FY 2012 *(cont.)*

Association of College and Research Libraries $249,330

The Association for College and Research Libraries, a division of ALA, will partner with the Association for Institutional Research and the Association of Public and Land-grant Universities to design, implement, and evaluate a program that helps academic libraries develop new assessment plans that better reflect library contributions.

City of Omaha $407,175

The Omaha Public Library and the University of Nebraska at Omaha's Center for Public Affairs Research will produce a toolkit of useful resources and a replicable model to guide public libraries toward leadership roles in civic engagement efforts in their local communities.

Erie County of New York $319,809

The Buffalo and Erie County Public Library System will partner with the Buffalo Broadcasters Association, the University at Buffalo Center for Urban Studies, Cleveland State University's Center for Public History and Digital History, and Randforce Associates to demonstrate the concept of a "digitized commons" that emphasizes selection and digitization of collections that are tied directly to virtual and physical activities and events that encourage local civic engagement.

Middle Country Public Library, Centereach, New York $450,000

The library will work with 28 libraries across seven states to implement and evaluate Family Place Libraries, a library-based early childhood and family support service model. This program will focus on parents/caregivers as first teachers, will be organized around the developmental needs of the child, and will link library services with other regional and local family support agencies.

Orange County (Florida) Library System $212,070

Obituaries in local newspapers traditionally have provided rich genealogical and historical information. In recent years, the number of local newspapers has decreased, and the cost of publishing obituaries in them has increased significantly. As a consequence, a key source of historical information for many communities is in danger of disappearing. Building upon previous planning work funded by IMLS, the Orange County Library System will implement and evaluate a new service offering a free library-based community digital obituaries repository. Family and friends of deceased community members will be able to upload detailed obituaries, photographs, and related materials, and in doing so help document their local heritage.

Peninsula Library System, San Mateo, California $333,391

The library system will lead the California Audio-Visual Preservation Project (CAVPP), a two-year statewide collaborative effort by at least 36 libraries, museums, and archives to preserve and provide online access to the state's endangered historically significant audiovisual recordings. The project will bring to light hidden media collections via the Internet Archive and the Online Archive of California.

Syracuse University $150,000

The university's School of Information Studies will partner with the Massachusetts Institute of Technology's Education Arcade and ALA to plan, develop, and test an Alternate Reality Game Toolkit that could be used by libraries to create engaging game-based learning exercises. The toolkit's framework will permit libraries to insert their own local content and resources and customize the game experience and learning objectives to meet their own local needs without having to build the entire educational game from the ground up.

California Digital Library, University of California $149,070

California Digital Library will leverage the early success of its new Data Management Planning Tool (DMPTool) to continue developing a cohesive set of resources that help

Table 2 / National Leadership Grants for Libraries, FY 2012 *(cont.)*

academic libraries promote and provide better data management planning services for their campuses.

University of Illinois $213,932

The university libraries will partner with the William R. and Clarice V. Spurlock Museum; the McLean County Museum of History; Heritage Preservation, Inc.; the Chicago History Museum; the Illinois Heritage Association; and the Illinois State Library to develop the Preservation Self-Assessment Program, a free computer-based tool that will help library, museum, and archives staff to conduct physical assessment and prioritization of preservation needs for paper-based and photographic materials.

Library-Museum Collaboration

City of Houston, Houston Public Library $250,000

To encourage early learning, the Houston (Texas) Public Library will partner with the Children's Museum of Houston to establish the "Pop-up Library" program. Designed to reduce summer reading loss in children in grades K–3 and to involve families in summer reading programs, the Pop-up Library will be a transportable unit that brings library materials, resources, and programming into a variety of public spaces.

Eastern Iowa Community College District $449,714

Eastern Iowa Community College District Library will partner with seven entities including city museums, libraries, and cultural and educational organizations to develop programs to advance the science and information literacy skills of Davenport residents, attract new audiences to current programs, and engage residents in activities promoting environmental sustainability and energy efficiency.

Idaho Commission for Libraries $250,000

To encourage early learning, the commission will partner with the J. A. and Kathryn Albertson Foundation and Idaho Kids Count on a program titled "Routes to Reading: Idaho Paves the Way with Access to Print." The project will be designed to significantly increase the number of books shared with young children.

Public Library of Charlotte and Mecklenburg County, North Carolina $244,452

To encourage early learning, the library will partner with the Children's Museum of Wilmington and other municipal agencies and programs to create the "Read to Me, Charlotte" program. Part of a larger initiative, the program will be tested and evaluated for its ability to increase the number of children reading at a grade-appropriate level.

Springfield-Greene County (Missouri) Library District $97,091

To encourage early learning, the district will partner with the county health department's Women, Infants, and Children (WIC) program to train WIC staff and provide new early literacy programs for low-income families. The project will lay the foundation for expanding early literacy programs to additional community social service agencies in the future.

George A. Smathers Libraries, University of Florida $477,312

Financial pressures caused by the economic downturn caused the Panama Canal Museum to close in 2012. The libraries agreed not only to assume custody of and responsibility for the museum's collections, but also to explore ways to support and increase the community of donors, members, volunteers, and other supporters.

Planning

Young Adult Library Services Association $99,937

ALA's Young Adult Library Services Association will conduct a yearlong series of national forum activities to bring together key stakeholders from libraries, education, technology, adolescent development, and the for-profit and nonprofit sectors. Participants will produce a white paper that will provide direction on how these services need to adapt to better meet the needs of 21st century teens.

Table 2 / National Leadership Grants for Libraries, FY 2012 *(cont.)*

Arlington (Texas) Public Library $49,572

To encourage early learning, the library will partner in a planning project with the Arlington Independent School District, the Mansfield Independent School District, United Way of Tarrant County, and Child Care Associates. The team will establish a coordinating body for all partners to inventory current resources, programs, and families currently being served, and will identify gaps and needs not being met and formulate an action plan.

Colorado State Library $41,146

To encourage early learning, the state library will partner with the Fort Morgan Public Library and Museum, the Aurora Public Library, the Pikes Peak Library District, and the Lake County Public Library to plan for Project SPELL: Supporting Parents in Early Literacy Through Libraries. The planning team will review existing and new research to create a blueprint of promising practices for libraries working with other agencies to deliver early literacy information and resources to low-income families with young children.

Florida State University $98,789

In order to better measure the value and extent of services being delivered to diverse populations with diverse needs, public libraries need more specific data about their communities and about other libraries that serve similar populations. The university's School of Library and Information Studies will partner with ALA and the Chief Officers of State Library Agencies to develop a prototype Web-based mapping system that pulls data together from different sources.

Kansas City Public Library $41,935

To encourage early learning, the library will partner with the Family Conservancy in a planning project to identify and evaluate existing community programs that support school readiness. The planning team will produce a blueprint for collaboration among early educators, parent support groups, literacy organizations, social services, and others that share a common goal of promoting early language development.

Montana State University $47,952

Researchers at the university and ALA will explore the feasibility of an economic study of the Internet's impacts on public libraries. The project team will design and test a research questionnaire to see if it can elicit information that would be used to effectively model and quantify these economic impacts and provide insights into appropriate changes in public library operations.

Graduate School of Arts and Science, New York University $50,000

The Center for Creative Research and the Fales Library at NYU will partner with the Bebe Miller Dance Company, the Pick-Up Performance Company, and participants at Florida State University and Ohio State University in a planning project to explore the feasibility of a new model of archival engagement with artists and scholars.

Onondaga County (New York) Public Library $100,000

The library will partner with ProLiteracy and ALA to host a forum and related activities to develop a National Library Literacy Action Agenda that will address the need for adult literacy services, identify key stakeholders, and articulate a series of action steps to help public libraries and policymakers develop and advocate for accessible, effective, and innovative adult literacy programs, services, and resources.

Fleet Library, Rhode Island School of Design $50,000

The library will host a forum of stakeholders including artists, architects and designers, educators, researchers, and librarians to provide advice on the resources and documentation required to prepare art and design students for knowledgeable and responsible use of materials in their professional work.

Table 2 / National Leadership Grants for Libraries, FY 2012 *(cont.)*

Richland County (South Carolina) Public Library $50,000

The library will partner in a planning project with the University of South Carolina's Office of Program Evaluation and the Midlands Reading Consortium of the United Way of the Midlands. The planning team will pilot and evaluate Project Summer Stride, which will focus on reducing summer reading loss through effective tutoring, reading programs, and other interventions.

Richmond (California) Public Library $50,000

To increase digital literacy and access to computers among children and families in Richmond's Iron Triangle neighborhood, the library and the Building Blocks for Kids Collaborative will lead a planning group to assess currently available services and resources, identify best practices for achieving higher digital literacy rates in communities create a plan to identify local needs, and develop an action plan that includes consideration of issues that cannot be resolved with current resources.

Richmond (Virginia) Public Library $39,960

To encourage early learning, the library will partner with the Boys and Girls Club of Richmond, the YMCA of Richmond, and Woodville Day Nursery to develop a plan for working with a variety of community summer programs to combat summer reading loss among third-grade students in the city's Promise neighborhood.

Santa Barbara (California) Public Library $50,000

The library and the Santa Barbara Museum of Art will plan, pilot, and evaluate the potential for full implementation of the Siblings Project, an initiative to promote grade-level reading skills in children age 8 and younger by recruiting, training, and encouraging older siblings to read with younger ones.

South Carolina Research Foundation $98,491

The University of South Carolina's South Caroliniana Archival Library and College of Education will work with numerous campus partners, and with external organizations including the Southern Poverty Law Center, the Rosenzweig Center for History and New Media at George Mason University, the South Carolina State Library, and South Carolina State University to create a strategy for coordinating and improving access to and use of civil rights oral histories for study, presentation, and teaching.

Texas Tech Archive of Modern American Warfare $50,000

The archive will plan a strategy for collecting and documenting the stories of U.S. soldiers in the digital age. The project team will develop a strategy to identify and build partnerships with other organizations and collaborators, develop an outreach plan to involve service personnel, select appropriate technologies and policies for a digital archive, and involve key stakeholder communities such as veterans groups and military historians.

Trustees of Tufts College $49,488

Tufts University's Digital Collections and Archives will explore and pilot new approaches to the online creation and sharing of collection information and inventories, particularly digital resources.

University of Kansas Libraries $48,480

The libraries and the campus research office will partner with the Greater Western Library Alliance and the Great Plains Network to explore the potential for a shared regional approach to managing research data.

University of Massachusetts, Amherst Libraries $48,368

The university will partner with the Inter-University Consortium for Political and Social Research and the Centers for Nanotechnology and Society at Arizona State University and at the University of California, Santa Barbara in a planning project to explore

Table 2 / National Leadership Grants for Libraries, FY 2012 *(cont.)*

future integration of digital services for researchers studying ethical, legal, and social implications associated with the development of nanotechnology and other emerging technologies.

University of Tennessee $49,938

Librarians and digital humanities faculty at the University of Tennessee and the University of Illinois will partner in a planning grant to explore the feasibility of an online index, and possibly a full-text repository of individual poetry works published only in electronic format.

Laura Bush 21st Century Librarian Program (maximum award: $500,000)

The Laura Bush 21st Century Librarian Program provides competitive grants to support projects to recruit and educate the next generation of librarians and library leaders, build institutional capacity in graduate schools of library and information science and develop faculty who will help in this endeavor and support programs of continuing education and training in library and information science for librarians and library staff. In FY 2012 the program included the following categories:

Doctoral Programs

- To develop faculty to educate the next generation of library professionals; in particular, to increase the number of students enrolled in doctoral programs that will prepare faculty to teach master's students who will work in school, public, and academic libraries
- To develop the next generation of library leaders; in particular, to increase the number of students enrolled in doctoral programs that will prepare them to assume positions as library managers and administrators

Master's Programs

- To educate the next generation of librarians; in particular, to increase the number of students enrolled in nationally accredited graduate library programs preparing for careers of service in libraries

Early Career Development Program

- To support the early career development of new faculty members who are likely to become leaders in library and information science by supporting innovative research by untenured, tenure-track faculty

Programs to Build Institutional Capacity

- To develop or enhance curricula within graduate schools of library and information science; in particular, to develop or enhance courses or programs of study for library and archives professionals in the creation, management, preservation, presentation, and use of digital assets; to broaden curricula by incorporating perspectives from other disciplines and fields of scholarship; to develop or enhance programs of study that address knowledge, skills, abilities, and issues of common interest to libraries, museums, archives, and data repositories; and to develop projects or programs in data curation as training programs for graduate students in library and information science

Continuing Education

- To increase professional development and library and archive staff knowledge, skills, and abilities through programs of continuing formal education, informal education, and training

IMLS received a total of 106 applications in the 21st Century Librarian Program in FY 2012. Requests totaled $37,815,498 and $10,406,038 was awarded to 32 grants (Table 3). Matching funds equaled $6,650,021.

Table 3 / Laura Bush 21st Century Librarian Program, FY 2012

Doctoral Programs

University of Tennessee $339,593

The La SCALA program, a partnership between the University of Tennessee's College of Communication and Information and the University of Arizona's School of Information Resources and Library Science, will use its grant to recruit and educate four Hispanic/Latino doctoral students with the ultimate goal of placing them in faculty positions throughout the country.

University of Texas at Austin $498,359

The university will educate six doctoral students who will study the emerging roles of information professionals and translate findings into teaching materials and scholarly publications.

Scholarship Continuation

New York University $447,591

This grant will support NYU's Moving Image Archiving and Preservation program, which will educate library professionals in caring for collections on film. The project will provide paid internships for 30 students working in major film collections around the country.

Pacific Northwest Library Association, Ada Community Library, Boise, Idaho $70,225

The association will use its grant to support its PNLA Leads program, offering intensive weeklong training to degreed and non-degreed library staff in these largely rural states. PNLA Leads is designed to develop and enhance skills and aptitudes in areas such as visioning, conflict resolution, commitment to community, personal introspection and growth, mentoring, team building, and risk taking.

School of Information and Library Science, Pratt Institute $261,967

M-LEAD-TWO (Museum Library Education and Digitization Technology-Web-Online) is a partnership among Pratt's School of Information and Library Science, the Brooklyn Museum, the Frick Collection, and the New York Art Resource Consortium. It will provide scholarship support for 15 diverse MSLIS students (five a year) and a two-semester paid internship program at the Brooklyn Museum and the Frick.

School of Information Studies, Syracuse University $237,973

Syracuse will use its grant for Project ENABLE, which will extend a comprehensive continuing education program for school librarians to help them better serve the library and information needs of preschool students with disabilities. Thirty teams of general educators, special educators, and school librarians will collaboratively study types of disabilities, disability law, assistive technology, the Individualized Education Program process, accessibility, and Universal Design for Learning.

Table 3 / Laura Bush 21st Century Librarian Program, FY 2012 *(cont.)*

Morgridge College of Education, University of Denver $499,006

This grant will fund the Early Childhood Librarianship program, which is designed to increase the number of MLIS-degreed librarians who are prepared to serve the early literacy needs of very young children (0–5 years), caregivers, educators, and community coalitions.

University of Maryland $499,977

The University of Maryland at College Park, partnering with the ALA Office of Government Relations, will fund 15 scholarships for MLS students with a concentration in e-government.

University of Tennessee $478,258

The University of Tennessee's School of Information Sciences—partnering with Clinch Powell Regional Library, Fort Loudoun Regional Library, Sevier County Public Library, and Watauga Regional Library—will build on the existing information technology master's degree scholarship program to train 13 new rural paraprofessionals in information technology and management skills while they complete their online master's degrees.

Allen Memorial Library, Valley City (North Dakota) State University $290,014

To address the continuing need for professional librarians in rural areas, Valley City State University will offer scholarships for 15 master's degree candidates in its online Library and Information Technologies Master of Education concentration.

Master's Programs

Association of Research Libraries $481,751

The association's Career Enhancement Program will create a fellowship experience for 32 graduate students from traditionally underrepresented ethnic and racial minority groups. Over the course of three years, participants, selected through a competitive application process, will engage in an in-depth fellowship experience that includes a paid internship in an ARL member library, the potential for academic credit, mentoring, leadership development offered through ARL's annual leadership symposium, and career placement assistance.

McDaniel College $239,649

Addressing the critical shortage of school librarians in underserved Maryland regions, the college's school library program, partnering with the Maryland State Department of Education, will use its grant to recruit 12 teachers (or other currently employed school professionals) to receive full scholarships for master's degrees in school library media.

Texas Woman's University $469,999

Texas Woman's University School of Library and Information Studies, and its partners, the Texas Library Association and the Dallas Public Library, will recruit and educate 18 librarians specializing in early literacy with cultural sensitivity and competencies to provide library services for communities with underrepresented populations.

Catholic University of America $498,741

The university will educate and support 17 students in the Cultural Heritage Information Management concentration in its library science master's degree program. This three-year project will educate students in the organization, management, and preservation of materials in 21st century cultural heritage institutions.

University of Houston–Clear Lake $463,857

The university's LIS program will use its grant to recruit 15 teachers and educate them in a master's program focused on emerging readers (pre-kindergarten and kindergarten). As one of its goals, the project will increase the number of certified school librarians in Texas, particularly those who work with Hispanic populations.

Table 3 / Laura Bush 21st Century Librarian Program, FY 2012 *(cont.)*

Collaborative Planning Grant

Public Library Association $45,145

The Public Library Association, a division of ALA, in partnership with the International City/County Management Association (ICMA), will undertake a one-year collaborative planning project to design and develop a leadership training model for key staff in public libraries. This project will design, pilot test, and develop an outcomes-based evaluation plan to provide leadership training to public library administrators, senior managers, and staff who want to increase their capacity to lead within the library and the community.

Fundación Sila M. Calderón $38,200

Fundación Sila M. Calderón in San Juan will lead the effort to develop a continuing education plan for librarians and archivists working in Puerto Rico. The plan will be based on a needs assessment funded by the National Historical Publications and Records Commission of the National Archives and Records Administration.

University of Southern California Libraries $20,713

The USC Libraries, the Autry National Center, and California State University, Northridge will lead a project to develop a residency program that will provide continuing education opportunities for recent MLIS graduates and existing staff at neighborhood- and community-based archives throughout Southern California.

School of Information, University of Texas at Austin $44,790

The school will use its grant to partner with the American Indian Library Association on a curriculum planning project. The partners will assess the degree of awareness of indigenous ways among educators and recent graduates of programs that prepare entry-level professionals for library/archives/museum work settings.

Early Career Development

Rutgers University $272,996

This grant will fund an Early Career Development research project, in which Rutgers Assistant Professor Chirag Shah will investigate the need to introduce and support collaborative information-seeking for people working in such information-intensive domains as libraries. The intended audience includes, but is not limited to, students, educators, researchers, developers, and practitioners.

Library and Information Department, Rutgers University $399,995

Rutgers Assistant Professor Rebecca Reynolds will use a guided, discovery-based program to investigate the impact of gaming on learning among disadvantaged middle and high school students in three states.

University of North Carolina at Chapel Hill $218,063

Ryan Shaw, an assistant professor at the university's School of Information and Library Science, will use this grant to invent new tools for understanding large collections of histories through computational text-processing techniques. The specific histories to be used for this project are 80 scholarly monographs and 350 oral histories relating to the civil rights movement.

Institutional Capacity

Board of Trustees of the University of Illinois $498,777

The Graduate School of Library and Information Science at the University of Illinois at Urbana-Champaign will create a graduate specialization in Sociotechnical Data Analytics (SODA) as a way to help ensure that information will remain accessible over the long term. Particularly when large research data sets are involved, information stewards must apply a greater level of analysis to the materials they hold if they are to successfully preserve them and make them useable.

Table 3 / Laura Bush 21st Century Librarian Program, FY 2012 *(cont.)*

College of Information Science and Technology, Drexel University $345,270

Librarians are increasingly called upon to manage and preserve the resources created by an array of geo-location tools. The Geographic Information Librarianship (GIL) project is a two-year curricular research collaboration between Drexel and the University of Kentucky the goal of which is to formally integrate geographic information systems into LIS curricula at the two schools.

Continuing Education

Association of Tribal Archives, Libraries, and Museums $500,000

The association will provide 24 Web-based learning experiences and two international convenings focused on the continuing education needs of tribal archivists, librarians, and museum staff. These professional development programs, now in their tenth year, have proven highly effective in developing the knowledge, skills, and abilities of more than 750 caretakers of tribal materials and culture.

Council of State Historical Records Coordinators $489,880

The council will use its funding to support the State Electronic Records Initiative Education Program, which will improve electronic records management in state and territorial governments through a multifaceted continuing education program for state archives staff. Scholarships to each state archives will enable staff to attend existing electronic records management and digital preservation (ERM/DP) educational programs.

Linscheid Library, East Central University $65,147

East Central University and its partners will carry out the Oklahoma Library Skills Initiative, which seeks to create information literacy teaching resources through a collaborative effort. The project provides participating librarians with training in the technology and pedagogy required to address college students' information literacy deficiencies.

Illinois State Library $470,000

The state library's ILEAD USA project seeks to help librarians develop new technology skills by meeting a specific community need, all the while being supported by peer learners in a network of collaborating teams. The 18-month continuing education immersion initiative is designed to expand librarians' leadership abilities while also helping them build their participatory technology skills.

Mississippi Library Commission $212,938

The commission will create the Mississippi Library Leadership Institute to develop the state's next generation of library leaders. Designed for MLS-degreed librarians with less than 15 years of professional library experience, the institute will focus on developing participants' 21st century skills in the areas of critical thinking and problem solving, communication, and leadership and responsibility.

Regents of the University of California, Los Angeles $310,000

UCLA's School of Information Studies will use its grant to provide tuition and some travel and housing support for 36 mid-career special collections librarians to attend the California Rare Books School (CRBS). A continuing education program sponsored by UCLA, CRBS is one of the few institutions in the United States providing extended, high-level training in the knowledge and skills required by professionals working in all aspects of the rare book, special collections, and archives communities.

School of Library and Information Studies, University of Alabama $317,450

The Sustainable Training for Alabama Public Library Employees (STAPLE) initiative is a joint project between the school and the Alabama Public Library Service. It will provide management training to 60 of the state's public library administrators in two cohorts.

Table 3 / Laura Bush 21st Century Librarian Program, FY 2012 *(cont.)*

School of Religion, University of Southern California $399,714

The university's West Semitic Research Project's InscriptiFact Digital Image Library and the Archaeology Research Center will establish a training program to empower researchers, scholars, students, archivists, librarians, and museum professionals to carry out field projects involving sophisticated and innovative image documentation of ancient texts, artifacts, paintings, and other cultural heritage objects using such technologies as reflectance transformation imaging (RTI).

Native American/Native Hawaiian Library Services Grants

The Native American and Native Hawaiian Library Services program provides opportunities for improved library services to an important part of the nation's community of library users. The program offers three types of support:

- Basic library services grants in the amount of $6,000, which support core library operations on a noncompetitive basis for all eligible Indian tribes and Alaska Native villages and corporations that apply for such support
- Basic library services grants with a supplemental education/assessment option of $1,000, totaling $7,000; the purpose of the education/assessment option is to provide funding for library staff to attend continuing education courses and/or training workshops on- or off-site, for library staff to attend or give presentations at conferences related to library services, and/or to hire a consultant for an onsite professional library assessment
- Enhancement grants, which support new levels of library service for activities specifically identified under LSTA

Collectively, these programs received 287 applications in FY 2012. IMLS funded 253 of these proposals, totaling $3,862,268. This included basic grants to 28 tribes, basic grants with the education/assessment option to 208 tribes, and 14 enhancement grants (Table 4).

The Native Hawaiian Library Services program provides opportunities for improved library services through grants to nonprofit organizations that primarily serve and represent Native Hawaiians, as the term "Native Hawaiian" is defined in section 7207 of the Native Hawaiian Education Act (20 U.S.C. 7517). In FY 2012 IMLS awarded three grants in this program: $100,000 to Papahana Kuaola; $159,893 to Kanu o ka 'Aina Learning 'Ohana; and $292,107 to Alu Like, Inc. (Table 5).

Partnerships

Connecting to Collections

IMLS, along with the American Association for State and Local History (AASLH) and Heritage Preservation, launched the Connecting to Collections Online Community in early summer 2011. All collecting institutions are eligible to belong without cost, and the community as of early 2013 had 1,752 members. This interactive resource connects staff at small museums, archives, and libraries with each

(text continues on page 277)

Table 4 / Native American Library Services Enhancement Grants, FY 2012

Assiniboine and Sioux Tribes of the Fort Peck Indian Reservation $148,410

The Fort Peck Tribal Library at Fort Peck Community College will administer this grant on behalf of the Assiniboine and Sioux Tribes of the reservation. After extensive weeding, the library's collection will be refreshed with current materials, especially in science and health. A new community computer lab will provide computer skills classes and wireless Internet access as well as digital media services to all patrons. Workshops on making moccasins, flute playing, powwow dancing, and storytelling will allow participants to learn traditional skills.

Bear River Band of the Rohnerville Rancheria $149,982

Grant funds will go toward furnishing the new library in the recently completed Tish-Non Community Center and toward providing comprehensive training for a new library assistant. Collection development will double the children's collection and add materials of general community interest.

Chickasaw Nation $18,438

The Holisso Research Center will create the Chickasaw Nation Cultural Connection, an online repository of significant archival documents, records, maps, and photographs from the Chickasaw Nation Cultural Center and other tribal archive collections.

Chippewa Cree Indians of Rocky Boy's Reservation $149,193

On behalf of the Chippewa Cree Tribe, the Rocky Boy Community Library at Stone Child College will provide enhanced technology for library users by adding new computers and providing e-readers for community use. They will develop a collection of audiovisual media and materials that will be available for instructional use in the college, area schools, and other tribal institutions.

Confederated Salish and Kootenai Tribes $117,283

Salish Kootenai College, on behalf of the Confederated Salish and Kootenai Tribes, will update computer technology and furnishings in their library computer lab and implement new services. The library will also offer a downloadable library catalog mobile phone app and a weekly blog highlighting materials in the tribal archive collection.

Fort Belknap Indian Community $142,070

The Aaniiih Nakoda College Library will administer this grant on behalf of the community with the goal of supporting native language learning among young children on the Fort Belknap Indian Reservation.

Karuk Tribe of California $145,841

The tribe will enhance the professional skills of its library staff in order to increase their capacity to offer comprehensive library services to its two communities, in Happy Camp and Orleans. They will receive on-site training and participate in job shadowing at libraries in the region. Library staff will also particularly focus on community outreach and engagement by working closely with local schools to provide culturally appropriate materials and programs on Karuk history and culture.

Keweenaw Bay Indian Community $135,657

This cooperative effort between Keweenaw Bay Indian Community (KBIC), the Ojibwa Community Library, the Office of Violence Against Women (OVW), and the Department of Health and Human Services' "Positively You" teen program will increase library services and materials for at-risk families, teens, and the community as a whole.

Native Village of Port Graham $25,382

The Native Village of Port Graham, Alaska, will begin to identify and inventory material relating to the village's history held in a variety of Alaskan repositories and early visitors' personal collections. The librarian will receive hands-on training in research and basic archival management at several Anchorage archives that hold materials of interest.

Table 4 / Native American Library Services Enhancement Grants, FY 2012 *(cont.)*

Organized Village of Kasaan $150,000

The Organized Village of Kasaan in Alaska will expand the resources of the Kasaan Cu tural Learning Center and Library to create the most extensive collection of Kaigani Ha da print, photographic, and video materials in the United States, serving as the centerpiece for Haida research and cultural programming.

Pokagon Band of Potawatomi Indians $52,586

The Pokagon Band will enhance library services to its members by implementing job training services for those who want to improve their computer skills and work on career preparation. College planning, career development, and job search techniques will be provided through a comprehensive online program, while computer classes will be held on site for adults, complemented by childcare services with literacy activities.

Pueblo of Jemez $143,008

The community library in New Mexico's Pueblo of Jemez will continue to serve as a focal point for preserving the Towa language and Jemez Pueblo culture, traditions, and knowledge as well as to act as a strong community partner in meeting the educational needs of Jemez children, teens, adults, and elders.

Saint Paul Island $149,984

The Aleut Community of Saint Paul Island, Alaska, will develop a comprehensive website to support the need for both local and off-island Unangan (Aleut) community members, as well as all others interested in their history, to access information on Unangan traditional practices, language, family histories, art, and culture via the Internet.

Ysleta del Sur Pueblo of Texas $116,434

The pueblo empowerment department's library and education center will create "literacy circles" for children enrolled in the center's after-school program to instill the love of reading and to improve overall academic performance. The literacy circles will use a combination of library staff and trained tutors to facilitate guided reading for children grouped by reading level, age, and grade.

---

other and with solid information about collections care. The site offers a meeting room, featured resources, a discussion forum, a calendar, and an archive of past discussions. Recent online chats have engaged 80 to 100 people, most of them from smaller institutions.

Campaign for Grade-Level Reading

IMLS continues as a partner in the Campaign for Grade-Level Reading, a long-term effort by several national entities and more than 160 local funders, nonprofit partners, and states. Led by the Annie E. Casey Foundation, the campaign promotes third-grade reading proficiency and addresses the developmental and academic targets that children need to reach to be successful. In partnership with the National League of Cities, the National Civic League, and United Way Worldwide, the campaign is now working with more than 120 communities across the nation to invest in "what works" and achieve greater impact from strategically aligned grantmaking. For more information, see gradelevelreading.net.

In September 2012 IMLS announced $2,557,772 in grants to libraries and museums for 19 collaborative projects that address community early learning challenges. The agency is continuing to promote this as a priority in FY 2013. In addition, plans are proceeding for a publication geared toward policymakers that

Table 5 / Native Hawaiian Library Services Grants, FY 2012

Alu Like, Inc. $292,107

Alu Like's Native Hawaiian Library will use its funding to continue to provide library and information services to Native Hawaiians in both urban and rural communities through its central library in Kakaako (Oahu) and its three satellite libraries in Papakolea (Oahu), Milolii (Hawaii Island), and Hoolehua (Molokai). These sites have a combined collection of 25,000 Hawaiian resource materials. In addition, the Native Hawaiian Library branches will continue to provide computer access, genealogy, and language workshops, Hawaiian cultural demonstrations, homework assistance, storytelling, tutoring, summer reading programs, Native Hawaiian book launches, and family nights. Library staff will also conduct information literacy workshops and Motheread parent literacy workshops to develop skills for success in work and family life.

Kanu o ka 'Aina Learning 'Ohana $159,893

Kanu o ka 'Aina Learning 'Ohana (KALO), a nonprofit organization in Waimea on Hawaii Island, will provide college readiness and career development services to five target communities located in the South Kohala District, four of which are federally designated Hawaiian Homelands. They will use the resources of their newly built Halau Puke Native Hawaiian Library and will work in close partnership with six community-based and statewide organizations that specialize in college readiness and career/work force development. Together, they will provide a variety of services to local Native Hawaiian college-ready high school seniors and adults interested in attending college. They will also offer activities to develop career-related skills for Native Hawaiians seeking employment, a career change, or increased wages and to entrepreneurs wanting to start a small business.

Papahana Kuaola $100,000

Papahana Kuaola, a cultural learning center in Heeia, a rural community on Oahu, will develop a culture-based literacy program that emphasizes traditional Hawaiian mo'olelo (myths and legends) and incorporates Hawaiian cultural practices, traditional arts, language, and knowledge. Educational materials and activities focusing on three mo'olelo will be created for school groups from Oahu in grades 3, 4, and 5.

---

focuses on the role of libraries and museums in promoting effective early learning programs. It was scheduled for release in late April.

National Arts and Humanities Youth Program Awards

The National Arts and Humanities Youth Program (NAHYP) awards are an initiative of the President's Committee on the Arts and Humanities, implemented in partnership with the National Endowment for the Arts, the National Endowment for the Humanities, and IMLS. The awards are the nation's highest honor for out-of-school, after school, and summer arts and humanities programs that celebrate the creativity of youth, particularly the achievements of young people from underserved communities. Libraries and museums are encouraged to apply. Each year, the NAHYP Awards recognize and support excellence in programs that open new pathways to learning, self-discovery, and achievement, in addition to presenting high-quality arts and humanities learning opportunities. The awards are presented at a White House ceremony. Award recipients receive $10,000 each, a plaque, and an opportunity to attend the annual Awardees Conference in Washington, D.C., where they receive capacity-building and communications support designed to strengthen their organizations. The most recent award announcement occurred in November 2012 with a deadline of January 31, 2013. For more information, see http://www.nahyp.org.

Twenty First Century Skills, Competitive Work Force, Engaged Citizens

President Barack Obama has called for the development of 21st century skills, including problem solving, critical thinking, entrepreneurship, and creativity. Libraries and museums, with their strengths in creating powerful learning experiences, are well equipped to build the skills needed to succeed in the 21st century. The IMLS 2009 publication *Museums, Libraries, and 21st Century Skills* (http://www.imls.gov/assets/1/workflow_staging/AssetManager/293.pdf) continues to be enthusiastically received and provides a framework for museums and libraries to align their programs and services to deliver 21st century skills and outline possibilities for broader community partnerships and engagement. IMLS is continuing a dissemination, training, and communications effort to raise awareness and encourage action around 21st century skills. This involves grantmaking with a 21st century skills focus as well as outreach to federal, state, and local policymakers. New materials relating to libraries, museums, and 21st century skills, including additional case studies, practitioner videos, a bibliography, and a community workshop planning toolkit, are available on the IMLS website at http://www.imls.gov/about/21st_century_skills_home.aspx. For more information, see http://www.p21.org/tools-and-resources/p21blog.

Learning Labs at Libraries and Museums

In a speech to the National Academies of Science, President Obama challenged Americans to join in a national campaign to engage young people in STEM (science, technology, engineering, and mathematics) education. He announced a series called Educate to Innovate to highlight public-private partnerships to advance this goal. IMLS has collaborated with the White House Office of Science and Technology Policy to highlight ongoing IMLS support for library and museum STEM programming and to leverage private support.

In partnership with the John D. and Catherine T. MacArthur Foundation, along with the Urban Libraries Council and the Association for Science and Technology Centers, IMLS has supported a national grant competition to create up to 25 learning labs in libraries and museums across the country. Inspired by an innovative new teen space at the Chicago Public Library called YOUmedia and innovations in science and technology centers, these labs will help young people become creators of content rather than just consumers of it. In addition to the planning and development of the labs, grantees participate in a community of practice that encourages shared research, successful learning outcomes, and sustainable spaces that fulfill community needs and leverage community partnerships.

The first cohort of grantees, which includes eight libraries and four museums, is partnering with a wide range of such community institutions as libraries, museums, parks and recreation departments, media outlets, universities, and nonprofit community organizations. The initial group of 12 grantees convened twice in 2012, in Chicago and San Francisco. IMLS announced the second cohort of grantees, consisting of seven libraries and five museums, in November. A grantee convening, including the first and second cohorts, was scheduled to take place in Washington, D.C., in early 2013.

National Student Poets Program

The President's Committee on the Arts and the Humanities and IMLS have partnered with the Alliance for Young Artists and Writers to launch the National Student Poets Program (NSPP) for young poets presenting original work. Five outstanding high school poets, each from a different region of the country, whose work exhibits exceptional creativity, dedication to craft, and promise will be selected annually for a year of service as "national poetry ambassadors."

National Student Poets are chosen from among the national medalists in the Scholastic Art and Writing Awards by a jury of accomplished authors and leaders in education and the arts. They receive college scholarships and opportunities to present their work at writing and poetry events throughout their term, as well as a stipend to complete a service-learning project. The first student poets were appointed during a ceremony at the National Book Festival in Washington, D.C., in September 2012. Each had an opportunity to perform a selection of his or her poetry. During the book festival, the poets also visited its Pavilion of States, stopping by each state in his or her respective region. The poets are encouraged to team with libraries or museums in their region for events throughout their year of service. Another round of Scholastic Art and Writing Awards launched in fall 2012. For more information, see http://www.artandwriting.org/the-awards/national-student-poets-program.

Arts Education Partnership

IMLS and the Arts Education Partnership (AEP) have entered into a cooperative agreement to support research and provide technical support for an evolving community of practice on the role of libraries and museums as arts education hubs. AEP, a division of the Council of Chief State School Officers, serves as a hub for individuals and organizations committed to making high-quality arts education accessible to all students, improving arts education practice, and researching how art influences and strengthens American education. In collaboration with key partners, AEP gathers, analyzes, and disseminates evidence on how the arts contribute to student success; communicates and promotes reliable arts-based best practices that improve teaching and learning in and out of school; and makes the case for arts education as a critical component of a complete education. A recent AEP project, ArtsEdSearch (http://www.artsedsearch.org), is documenting peer-reviewed research as well as state-based arts education practice. In this partnership, AEP will work with IMLS and its Office of Research, Policy, and Evaluation to document and identify ways libraries and museums contribute to the arts education infrastructure and to identify a set of promising practices that can be used to expand the role of libraries and museums as premier community learning institutions.

Federal Interagency Collaboration

Department of Education

IMLS has worked on many programs with the Department of Education, most recently the Let's Read! Let's Move! series.

Department of Health and Human Services

IMLS has developed a partnership with the Department of Health and Human Services (HHS) Administration for Children and Families' (ACF)/Office of Head Start and ACF/Office of Child Care to encourage partnerships between care programs and public libraries. This agreement became official in May 2012 with the distribution of an information memorandum to all agencies funded by ACF.

Department of Labor

IMLS has an ongoing partnership with the Department of Labor to address work force development challenges. In September 2012 IMLS, together with the Employment and Training Administration (ETA), hosted two congressional staff briefings—one for the House and one for the Senate—on how libraries support work force development. In summer 2012 IMLS worked with ETA and the Federal Communications Commission (FCC) to highlight the roles that the nation's job centers and public libraries play in digital literacy and work force development.

Federal Communications Commission

IMLS shares FCC's goal of nationwide broadband connectivity and is working closely with FCC and the new nonprofit Connect to Compete (C2C) to support digital literacy efforts throughout the country. A national advertising campaign is being launched in 2013. IMLS is supporting digital literacy efforts at both the state and local library level.

Postal Service

In August 2012 IMLS began working with the U.S. Postal Service (USPS) and the State Library Administrative Agencies to encourage public libraries to consider becoming "village post offices." The initiative makes it possible for third parties to complement USPS's own network by offering the public retail access to postal products and services at non-post office locations.

Office of the First Lady

In a partnership designed to broaden the impact of First Lady Michelle Obama's Let's Move! initiative, 584 museums and gardens representing all 50 states are participating in "Let's Move Museums and Gardens." IMLS launched a newsletter for the program in July 2012.

International Collaboration

Salzburg Global Seminar

In October 2011 IMLS hosted a seminar on the topic "Libraries and Museums in an Era of Participatory Culture" in partnership with the Salzburg Global Seminar in Austria. The seminar convened 58 international library and museum leaders to explore and debate the changing roles and responsibilities of libraries and museums in society. IMLS published a follow-up report in April 2012 (http://www.

imls.gov/assets/1/AssetManager/SGS_Report_2012.pdf). An article on the seminar was published in the journal *Museums Australia* in July 2012, and another appeared in November in *History News,* published by the American Association for State and Local History.

In addition, an outgrowth of the seminar, Developing the Salzburg Curriculum, helped extend the reach of the seminar by developing a high-level curricular framework for library and museum professionals to help train them to work more effectively in this participatory society. An advisory committee has been established, the project website created, and the curriculum sent to the advisory group for final adjustments. In addition, the team has identified library and museum curricula to be mapped to the Salzburg Curriculum Framework and is pursuing partnerships with other major organizations in order to expand input into the curriculum and to encourage its adoption on a wider scale.

Film Forward

Now at the end of its second year, Film Forward is an international film/filmmaker exchange program designed to foster intercultural dialogue both in the United States and abroad. It is an initiative of the President's Committee on the Arts and Humanities and the Sundance Institute, in partnership with IMLS, the National Endowment for the Humanities, and the National Endowment for the Arts. The 2012 program included ten documentary and narrative films, six of them produced in the United States. The screening venues were Tucson, Arizona; the Imperial Valley in California; Sulphur, Oklahoma; San Juan and Caguas, Puerto Rico; and sites in China, India, Colombia, and Morocco. After viewing the films, audiences engaged in discussions with two of the filmmakers on the themes and craft involved in their productions. At most of the venues, events took place at libraries and museums. For more information, see http://www.sundance.org/filmforward.

Evaluation of IMLS Programs

In addition to outcome-based evaluation support for grantees, IMLS has instituted a new series of in-depth evaluations of its own programs. A retrospective evaluation of the Laura Bush 21st Century Librarian Program is currently under way. This evaluation will employ mixed-method techniques for measuring the impact of federal grants on individual program participants and the institutions that receive support. Data used for these studies include application data, financial and narrative reports, post-award follow-up surveys, and qualitative case studies.

Research Sponsored and Conducted by IMLS

The Office of Planning, Research, and Evaluation (OPRE), which advises the Department of Health and Human Services assistant secretary for children and families on increasing the effectiveness and efficiency of Administration for Children and Families (ACF) programs, released two major reports in FY 2012.

In July final imputed data files for the FY 2010 Public Libraries Survey (PLS) were made available in the data sets section of the IMLS website. PLS is designed as a universe survey whose FY 2010 frame consisted of 9,299 public libraries as identified by state library agencies (9,241 public libraries in the 50 states and the District of Columbia and 58 public libraries in Guam, the Northern Mariana Islands, Puerto Rico, and the U.S. Virgin Islands). A total of 9,100 of the public libraries in the survey frame responded to the survey for a unit response rate of 97.9 percent. The Compare Public Libraries Tool and the Find Public Libraries Tool on the IMLS website were updated with FY 2010 data, and a new resource called "Public Library Data Reports" was produced using the Data Ferret tool developed by U.S. Census Bureau. IMLS anticipates the release of a summary report based on the final data file ("Public Libraries in the United States: Fiscal Year 2010").

In January 2012 the FY 2010 State Library Administrative Agency (SLAA) Survey report was released. This report marks the fourth release of state library statistics data from IMLS and the 16th survey in the SLAA series. It contains data on state library agencies in the 50 states and the District of Columbia for FY 2010. The SLAA Survey is the product of a cooperative effort between Chief Officers of State Library Agencies (COSLA), IMLS, and the U.S. Census Bureau.

Future research from OPRE will examine library services in a variety of contexts from small towns and remote rural areas to central cities and suburbs. OPRE also will look at the intersection of library service with other public policy priorities, including education, employment, immigration, and public health.

Conferences and Activities

Grants to States Conference

The 12th Grants to States Conference was held in Philadelphia in March 2012. Fifty-three participants representing the SLAAs in the 50 states, the District of Columbia, Puerto Rico, and the U.S. Virgin Islands attended. The conference included a two-day grants management course on uniform administrative requirements, a primary area of federal grants administration. Other sessions included panels on statewide projects and subgrant programs; updates on the IMLS 2012–2016 Strategic Plan and the Measuring Success evaluation project; a review of basic financial management and cost principles; and perspectives from outside speakers on the Digital Public Library of America, civic engagement, and federal disability law.

WebWise

The 2012 WebWise conference was held in Baltimore. It addressed the theme "Tradition and Innovation," investigating how libraries and museums have used digital technologies to help scholars, students, educators, and the general public understand history and the humanities. Taking special note of the unique contributions that historical societies, public libraries, and other small and local organizations make to humanities scholarship and education, the conference addressed the challenges these organizations have faced in the course of their digital work, highlighted the often underappreciated contributions they have made in this area, and brought them into more fruitful conversation with colleagues in larger organizations and in the arts and sciences. Two sessions, "Sharing Public History Work: Crowdsourcing Data" and "Oral History in the Digital Age," were filmed and repurposed as webinars.

IMLS Website and Publications

The Grants to States program provides SLAA LSTA program administrators with access to a website that facilitates communication about program requirements and guidance.

The IMLS website (http://www.imls.gov) provides information on the various grant programs, the National Medal for Museum and Library Service, funded projects, application forms, and staff contacts. The website also highlights model projects developed by U.S. libraries and museums and provides information about IMLS-sponsored conferences, publications, and studies. Through an electronic newsletter, *Primary Source,* and "UpNext" blog, IMLS provides information on grant deadlines, success stories, and opportunities. Information on subscribing to the IMLS newsletter is located on the website. IMLS can be followed on Twitter @US_IMLS.

The following recent publications are available via the IMLS website: *Creating a Nation of Learners: Strategic Plan 2012–2016*; *Proposed Framework for Digitally Inclusive Communities: Final Report*; *Opportunity for All: How Library Policies and Practices Impact Public Internet Access*; the *National Medal for Museum and Library Service* brochure; and guidelines for each of the grant programs.

Part 3
Library/Information Science Education, Placement, and Salaries

Library Employment Sources on the Internet

Catherine Barr

Contributing Editor

The year 2012 "offered ongoing unemployment and stiff competition for jobs, especially for school library media specialists and reference librarians," according to *Library Journal*'s article "Placements and Salaries 2012: Emerging Jobs, New Titles." [See the following article for the full report.—*Ed.*] However, there were positive signs in both traditional and developing fields for librarians and information specialists, and salaries were slowly recovering.

The following is not a comprehensive list of the hundreds of job-related sites on the Internet of interest to librarians and information professionals. These are, however, the best starting places for a general job search in this area. Many offer additional information that will be helpful to those considering a career in librarianship, including advice on conducting a successful search, writing résumés, preparing for interviews, and negotiating salaries.

Before spending a lot of time on any website, users should check that the site has been updated recently and that out-of-date job listings no longer appear.

The Directory of Organizations in Part 6 of this volume may also prove useful.

Background Information

The Bureau of Labor Statistics of the Department of Labor provides a thorough overview of the work of a librarian, necessary qualifications, and the job and salary outlook at http://www.bls.gov/oco/ocos068.htm. Similar pages are available for archivists (http://www.bls.gov/ooh/education-training-and-library/archivists.htm), curators, museum technicians, and conservators (http://www.bls.gov/ooh/Education-Training-and-Library/Curators-and-museum-technicians.htm), and for library technicians and assistants http://www.bls.gov/oco/ocos316.htm). A useful page http://www.bls.gov/ooh/Education-Training-and-Library/Librarians.htm) lists similar occupations with their duties, education requirements, and average salaries.

The American Library Association (ALA) provides a user-friendly overview of librarianship at all levels—from pages and library assistants to managers and directors—at LibraryCareers.org (http://www.ala.org/educationcareers/careers/librarycareerssite/home), and Info*Nation: Choose a Career in Libraries (http://www.cla.ca/infonation/welcome.htm) is an excellent Canadian site that describes the work of librarians, combining brief information on a variety of career options with statements by individual librarians about why they love their jobs. These two sites will be particularly useful for young people considering a possible career in librarianship.

San José State University's School of Library and Information Science has created a "Career Development" page (http://slisweb.sjsu.edu/resources/career_development/index.htm) that aims to "help our students, alumni, and prospective students navigate a myriad of career opportunities, learn about emerging trends in the field, and develop an effective job search strategy." Various emerging job titles are described, such as "cloud/metadata support specialist" and "virtual services librarian," and there are tips on using social media effectively during job searches. "Library and Information Careers: Emerging Trends and Titles," a pdf updated in 2012, provides facts and figures on the profession and clearly lays out the responsibilities of librarians in various fields and the skills required.

The October 2010 issue of *Knowledge Quest* has a feature story titled "Public Librarian" in which three public librarians describe their jobs and the aspects that they particularly enjoy. And the April 2010 issue of *College & Research Library News* includes an article—"Making the Best of the Worst of Times: Global Turmoil and Landing Your First Library Job"—that looks at job listings and how to prepare for an interview.

Also of interest to aspiring librarians is Rachel Singer Gordon's article in the September 15, 2009, *Library Journal* (http://www.libraryjournal.com/article/CA605244.html), "How to Become a Librarian—Updated." In this, she covers all the basics and recommends paths to the profession.

Finally, How to Apply for a Library Job (http://www.liswiki.com/wiki/HOWTO:Apply_for_a_library_job) offers thoughtful advice and practical interview tips.

General Sites/Portals

American Library Association: Library Employment Resources
http://www.ala.org/educationcareers/employment/resources

Maintained by ALA, this site includes some useful information on applying for a library job and a link to ALA's "Guide to Employment Sources in the Library and Information Profession" (updated in 2011).

ALA JobList: Career Development Resources
http://joblist.ala.org/modules/jobseeker/controller.cfm

This ALA site lists job placement opportunities at forthcoming conferences, along with details of workshops and tips on various aspects of the job search. At the top of the page, you can do a quick search for job openings by state.

The main JobList site (http://joblist.ala.org) is a service of *American Libraries* magazine and *C&RL News*. Registration is free for jobseekers, who can post their résumés and search jobs by library type, date, state, institution name, salary range, and other parameters. Employers can choose from a menu of print and electronic posting combinations.

Canadian Library Association: Library Careers   http://www.cla.ca/AM/Template.cfm?Section=Library_Careers

The Canadian Library Association lists Canadian job openings here (select Job Search) and provides information on career development, plus guidance on recognition of foreign credentials.

San José State University Job Listing Sites and Resources http://slisweb.sjsu.edu/career-development/job-search/job-listing-sites-and-resources

This page provides an extensive list of library employment sites as well as tips on conducting an effective job search. A related page, Professional Associations in the Information Sciences (http://slisweb.sjsu.edu/resources/orgs.htm), is a comprehensive listing of associations in the United States and abroad.

Library Job Postings on the Internet   http://www.libraryjobpostings.org

Compiled by Sarah L. Johnson of Booth Library, Eastern Illinois University, author of "Career Development and Planning," in Ruddock, Bethan, ed., *The New Professional's Toolkit* (Facet Publishing, 2012), and coauthor of *The Information Professional's Guide to Career Development Online* (Information Today, Inc., 2002) (http://www.lisjobs.com/careerdev). This site provides links to library employment sites in the United States and abroad, with easy access by location and by category of job.

LIScareer.com: Career Strategies for Librarians   http://www.liscareer.com

Relaunched in 2009, this helpful site is maintained by Priscilla Shontz and offers "practical career development advice for new librarians and information professionals, MLS students, and those considering a library-related career." There are no job listings, but the site offers interesting articles in the areas of career exploration, education, job searching, experience, networking, mentoring, interpersonal skills, leadership, publishing and presenting, and work/life balance. This is an excellent place to begin research on library jobs. Shontz is also coauthor, with Richard A. Murray, of *What Do Employers Want? A Guide for Library Science Students* (Libraries Unlimited, 2012.)

I Need a Library Job   http://inalj.com

Maintained by Naomi House, this attractive and frequently updated site offers daily e-mails/digest of job openings, links to international jobs pages, and interviews with recent successful job hunters.

The Riley Guide   http://www.rileyguide.com

In addition to job listings, the Riley Guide allows users to explore all aspects of job hunting, from proper preparation to résumés and cover letters, researching and targeting employers, and networking, interviewing, and negotiating salaries and job conditions.

Sites by Sector

Public Libraries

Public library openings can be found at all the general sites/portals listed above.

Careers in Public Librarianship http://www.ala.org/pla/tools/careers

The Public Library Association offers information on public librarianship, with a webcast on finding and keeping public library jobs.

Competencies for Librarians Serving Children in Public Libraries
http://www.ala.org/ala/mgrps/divs/alsc/edcareeers/alsccorecomps

A detailed listing of skills and knowledge required to be a children's librarian in a public library.

School Libraries

School library openings can be found at many of the sites listed above. Sites with interesting material for aspiring school librarians include those listed below.

AASL: Recruitment to School Librarianship http://www.ala.org/ala/mgrps/
divs/aasl/aasleducation/recruitmentlib/aaslrecruitment.cfm

The American Association of School Librarians hosts this site, which describes the role of school librarians, salary and job outlooks, and mentoring programs; provides testimonials from working library media specialists; and offers state-by-state information on licensure, scholarships, library education, job hunting, mentoring, and recruitment efforts.

General education sites and comprehensive employment sites such as Monster. com often include school library openings.

Special and Academic Libraries

AALL Career Center http://www.aallnet.org/main-menu/
Careers/career-center

Maintained by the American Association of Law Librarians, this site has an online job board, an extensive FAQ section (under the heading "Support"), and useful tips for job seekers.

Careers in Law Librarianship http://www.lawlibrarycareers.org

This excellent site answers the question "Is a career as a law librarian right for you?" and provides broad information on the profession, educational require-ments, and available financial assistance.

Association of College and Research Libraries
See ALA JobLIST above.

ALISE: Job Placement http://www.alise.org/job-placement

ALISE, the Association for Library and Information Science Education, posts jobs for deans, directors, and faculty, organized by position and alphabetically by school/organization.

ASIS&T: Careers   http://www.asist.org/careers.html

The Careers page maintained by the American Society for Information Science and Technology offers access to a Jobline, profiles of selected members, and continuing education information.

Association of Research Libraries: Career Resources   http://www.arl.org/resources/careers/index.shtml

In addition to listings of openings at ARL member institutions and at other organizations, there is information on ARL's diversity programs plus a database of research library residency and internship programs. A video, *Faces of a Profession,* highlights the roles played by academic librarians and includes interviews with current staff.

Chronicle of Higher Education   http://chronicle.com/jobs

Listings can be browsed, with geographical options, under the category "Library/information sciences" (found under "Professional fields") or searched by simple keywords such as "library." Articles and advice on job searching are also available.

EDUCAUSE Job Posting Service   http://www.educause.edu/Jobs

EDUCAUSE member organizations post positions "in the broad field of information technology in higher education."

HigherEdJobs.com   http://www.higheredjobs.com

The category "Libraries" is found under Administrative Positions.

Major Orchestra Librarians' Association   http://www.mola-inc.org

A nice site for a field that might be overlooked. The Resources section includes an introduction to the work of an orchestra librarian.

Medical Library Association: Career Development   http://www.mlanet.org/career/index.html

The Medical Library Association offers much more than job listings here, with brochures on medical librarianship, a video, career tips, and a mentor program.

Music Library Association Job Openings   http://www.musiclibraryassoc.org/employment.aspx?id=95

Along with job postings and a résumé review service, this site features an article titled "Music Librarianship—Is It for You?" and a listing of resources for both beginning and mid-career music librarians.

SLA: Career Center   http://www.sla.org/content/jobs/index.cfm

In addition to salary information and searchable job listings that are available to all users, the Special Libraries Association provides many services for association members.

Government

Library of Congress   http://www.loc.gov/hr/employment

An extensive survey of what it's like to work at the library, the kinds of employees the library is seeking, the organizational structure, benefits, current job openings, internships, fellowships, and volunteering.

National Archives and Records Administration   http://www.archives.gov/careers

In addition to information on employment opportunities, internships, and volunteering, NARA provides profiles of employees and interns, describing the kinds of work they do.

Serials

NASIG Jobs   http://nasigjobs.wordpress.com

Managed by the North American Serials Interest Group. Accepts serials-related job postings.

Library Periodicals

American Libraries
See ALA JobList above.

Library Journal   http://www.libraryjournal.com

Job listings are found under the Job Zone tab. The Careers tab leads to archived articles relating to employment.

School Library Journal   http://www.schoollibraryjournal.com

Click on the Job Zone tab for access to a general list of job openings (jointly maintained with *Library Journal*; you must filter by Children's/Young Adult to access school positions.

Employment Agencies/Commercial Services

A number of employment agencies and commercial services in the United States and abroad specialize in library-related jobs. Among those that keep up-to-date listings on their websites are:

Advanced Information Management   http://www.aimusa.com

Specializes in librarians and support staff in a variety of types of libraries across the country.

LAC Group   http://careers.lac-group.com

An easy-to-use list of openings that can be sorted by function, location, and keyword.

Listservs and Networking Sites

Many listservs allow members to post job openings on a casual basis.

jESSE   http://web.utk.edu/~gwhitney/jesse.html

This worldwide discussion group focuses on library and information science education; LIS faculty position announcements frequently appear here.

LibGig   http://www.libgig.com

Along with news, blogs, career profiles, "who's hiring" job alerts, and résumé consultation, this professional networking site offers easily accessed job postings.

LIBJOBS   http://www.ifla.org/en/mailing-lists

LIBJOBS is a mailing list for librarians and information professionals seeking employment. It is managed by the International Federation of Library Associations and Institutions (IFLA). Subscribers to this list receive posted job opportunities by e-mail.

LIS New Professionals Network   http://lisnpn.spruz.com

A forum with news, blogs, and postings of general and specific (job openings, grants, and so on) interest.

PUBLIB   http://www.webjunction.org/documents/webjunction/
                                        PubLib_Overview.html

Public library job openings often appear on this list.

Blogs

Career Q&A with the Library Career People   http://www.lisjobs.com/
                                                     careerqa_blog

This attractive and user-friendly blog is maintained by librarians Tiffany Allen and Susanne Markgren and is intended to "create an enlightening discussion forum of professional guidance and advice for librarians, library staff, and those thinking of entering the profession." Categories include job satisfaction, job seeking, and professional development.

Placements and Salaries 2012:
Emerging Jobs, New Titles

Stephanie L. Maatta

"Challenges have been plentiful!" was the common refrain across the 2011 LIS graduating class. As the general economy continued its slow climb out of recession, there was ongoing unemployment and stiff competition for jobs, especially for school library media specialists and reference librarians.

However, despite erroneous reports that library and information science is a dying field, there were numerous bright spots and unprecedented gains, ranging from positive salary growth to increased numbers of placements in agencies outside library environments, and an exciting array of descriptors available to students seeking work inside the LIS field and elsewhere. More than 2,100 LIS graduates responded to *Library Journal*'s annual Placements and Salaries survey, representing 34.7 percent of the 2011 graduating class from the 41 participating programs.

Overall, the good news is supported by a healthy average starting salary increase of 5 percent, to $44,565, uplifted by several reports of annual salaries of more than $100,000. This is good news for a profession that has been battered in recent years by abysmal salary growth and an economy in recession. Graduates reporting minority status experienced the greatest impact in wage growth, increasing by 8.7 percent over the previous year's averages, although graduates landing in the West lost 2 percent during the same period.

Other signs of progress: a decrease in the number of temporary placements and a slight decrease in the number of part-time jobs reported. This good news was augmented by improved numbers of placements in public libraries—which have suffered significantly in salary and placement over the last several years—and by growth in academic library placements. Jobs in academic libraries in particular offered unique opportunities to work with emerging technologies, digital repositories, and instructional design. The average length of time to land a job also decreased slightly, dropping to just under five months, with the most frequently cited length being three months after graduation. However, some graduates were still searching more than a year later.

Nevertheless, finding and landing a job entails challenges and frustrations. Participants once again reported there were too few entry-level jobs, with many available jobs requiring three to five years of professional experience. For graduates, this presents an age-old bind: "It's hard to get a job without experience; it's hard to get professional experience when potential employers don't recognize volunteer activities or internships as professional enough." Once again, graduates spoke of competing with other information professionals in the job market owing to choice or circumstance, with their newly minted degrees often trumped by the availability of greater experience among the applicant pool. On the plus side, the unemployment rate among LIS graduates held steady at 6.8 percent, suggesting that jobs were largely available even if they required full-time effort to find.

Stephanie L. Maatta is an assistant professor at Wayne State University School of Library and Information Science, Detroit.

Adapted from *Library Journal,* October 15, 2012.

Emerging Jobs, New Titles

While the numbers tell the full story, the shifts in job nomenclature and description give their own high-level view of trends in employment for new library and information professionals. LIS programs and graduates alike reported an increase in the number of emerging job titles, including "emerging technologies librarian," "data assets manager," "digital initiatives librarian," and "digital curator." Still others included "market insights analyst," "repository librarian/manager," and "impact evaluation specialist."

Among the new responsibilities, graduates cited an emphasis on developing the agency's online presence through mobile and social media and Web accessibility, managing digitization initiatives and workflow, and gathering data and analytics. They were engaged in the development of digital research projects and services in academic institutions as well as in other types of research libraries and information agencies. The new titles appeared in a variety of places, particularly in academic institutions (inside the university library as well as in other academic units) and in corporate entities; the difference between the two came down largely to semantics—e.g., digital initiatives librarian or digital assets manager.

Graduates also emphasized the dual nature of many of their jobs—reference and digital services, adult services and community outreach librarian, for example—and they frequently used the term *blended* to describe this duality. They also focused on the highly collaborative nature of their positions, working across departments, such as with information technology (IT) staff and management, and as members of highly complex teams. Graduates added the ability to serve as a liaison among the multiple units of an institution to the list of job responsibilities. Even those few who described themselves as solo librarians indicated the necessity of working with other people outside the library.

While not a new or emerging responsibility, an emphasis on instruction and information literacy continued to appear throughout the job titles, although there was change in how the responsibilities were fulfilled. Today's LIS graduates are using emerging technologies to develop and design instructional resources, including interactive tutorials and virtual knowledge centers that can be accessed through mobile devices. They are coordinating and managing learning resource centers for K–12 schools and in higher education. And they are working with a variety of learning-management systems to integrate digital resources and services into the learning environment.

Some Disappointments

Full-time placements for the graduates of 2011 remained stable, holding at 75.4 percent of the reported jobs (nearly equivalent to the previous year's level of 75.8 percent and improved over earlier years' lows of 72.9 percent and 69.8 percent). Overall, 88.8 percent of the participants reported a job of any sort, either within or outside the LIS professions, a slight improvement from the previous survey when the figure was 86.5 percent. Positive reports of dream-job finds were equaled by reports of others who had joined the ranks of substitute teachers or retail clerks to fill the gap until a professional job materialized.

Full-time employment was also colored by another year of decline in permanent professional positions within LIS, with a slim 56.8 percent of all surveyed describing their jobs that way, a drop from 59.2 percent for the class of 2010 and 61 percent for 2009. However, this was also counterbalanced by an increase in the number of jobs described as "permanent and professional" outside LIS, such as software engineering and user interface design, and these often carried higher starting salaries. Jobs falling outside LIS rose from 10.1 percent for the graduates of 2010 to 18.3 percent of the placements for 2011's grads.

Another measure of stabilization comes in the form of temporary positions and part-time positions. Reverting to levels closer to those experienced by the 2009 graduates, just over 12 percent of the class of 2011 described their jobs as being temporary. This was a significant drop from the previous year, when 22.8 percent held temporary jobs. Part-time jobs saw a similar decline, though less dramatic, decreasing from 25 percent to 23.6 percent. Graduates finding jobs in the Northeast reported the highest levels of part-time placements at 34.4 percent, which was also an increase from 31.1 percent in the same region a year earlier. Graduates broadly shared the strategy of accepting temporary placements and part-time jobs as a possible route to full-time employment. For some the strategy paid off well as they moved from student assistant positions during graduate studies to part-time professional employment just before or upon graduation and ultimately to a permanent professional job.

For a second year, reports of nonprofessional full-time and part-time positions declined, dropping from 17.5 percent in 2010 to 15.4 percent in 2011. Jobs designated as "nonprofessional" fell into two distinct categories: an estimated 80 percent were within LIS and 20 percent outside. On one hand, the graduates accepted nonprofessional jobs in LIS agencies, in such positions as circulation clerk or media aide, and this created similar challenges to those experienced in temporary positions; among these challenges were receiving few fringe benefits and fearing that they would be the first let go if there were additional budget cuts. Meanwhile, other nonprofessional jobs fall outside the realm of library and information science into such areas as banking, retail, and food service; graduates in these positions expressed frustration that a master's degree seemed to be only a piece of high-quality paper that came with a high tuition price tag.

Nonprofessional full-time positions tended toward lower salaries, averaging $32,072 compared with $44,565 for all placements, with fewer employment benefits like paid time off and healthcare options. Some graduates in nonprofessional positions said they felt their coworkers, especially fellow librarians, did not recognize them as professionals even though they had the same credentials. Not surprisingly, public libraries held the highest proportion of nonprofessional placements at 21.9 percent of the new hires.

Approximately 37 percent of the survey participants remained with an employer while completing their studies for a master's degree. This is somewhat below the high of 47 percent for 2010. For some, a master's was required for career advancement or continuation of an existing job; in fact their jobs were dependent upon earning the advanced degree, and this was particularly evident among those entering school libraries. Approximately 12.6 percent of the graduates who remained with the same employer did not realize any benefits from their acquisition

(text continues on page 302)

Table 1 / Status of 2011 Graduates*

Region	Number of Schools Reporting	Number of Graduates Responding	Permanent Professional	Temporary Professional	Non-professional	Total	Graduates Outside of Profession	Unemployed or Status Unreported
Northeast	13	705	332	68	99	499	106	94
Southeast	9	205	126	12	34	172	47	26
Midwest	10	708	427	73	76	576	109	66
Southwest	5	221	82	3	28	113	38	26
West	4	298	112	34	54	200	38	59
Total	41	2,162	1,090	190	295	1,575	345	271

* Table based on survey responses from schools and individual graduates. Figures will not necessarily be fully consistent with some of the other data reported. Tables do not always add up, individually or collectively, since both schools and individuals omitted data in some cases.

Table 2 / Placements and Full-Time Salaries of 2011 Graduates by Region*

Region	Number of Placements	Salaries			Low Salary		High Salary		Average Salary			Median Salary		
		Women	Men	Total	Women	Men	Women	Men	Women	Men	All	Women	Men	All
Northeast	364	243	60	306	$15,000	$22,000	$82,500	150,000	$43,491	$54,163	$45,624	$42,700	$47,500	$43,844
Southeast	247	157	35	194	17,000	18,700	110,000	100,000	42,035	48,572	43,317	40,000	46,000	40,358
Midwest	390	251	74	326	10,000	13,000	100,000	125,000	41,149	46,715	42,376	40,000	45,050	40,624
Southwest	161	74	22	96	20,000	23,000	55,000	100,000	39,785	47,457	42,543	40,000	46,250	40,331
West	182	107	29	443	12,000	32,000	97,000	129,000	48,331	55,866	49,819	47,500	46,608	47,294
Canada/Intl.	18	10	3	13	22,500	43,000	57,628	65,000	41,701	51,667	44,001	43,000	47,000	47,000
Combined	1,447	860	227	1,095	$10,000	$13,000	$180,000	$150,000	$42,990	$50,500	$44,565	$41,000	$46,400	$42,000

* This table represents only salaries and placements reported as full-time. Some data were reported as aggregate without breakdown by gender or region. Comparison with other tables will show different numbers of placements.

Table 3 / 2011 Total Graduates and Placements by School

Schools	Graduates			Employed		
	Women	Men	Total	Women	Men	Total
Alabama	97	34	131	38	9	47
Albany	76	20	96	32	6	38
Buffalo	147	70	217	15	4	19
Catholic	12	—	12	11	—	—
Clarion	42	9	51	6	—	6
Denver	66	14	80	16	5	21
Dominican	197	58	255	56	12	69
Drexel	214	45	259	80	24	105
Florida State	170	59	229	20	6	26
Hawaii	1	1	3	1	1	2
Illinois	81	19	102	76	17	96
Indiana	180	59	239	64	17	81
Iowa	11	3	14	10	3	13
Kent State University	200	51	251	66	15	81
Kentucky	65	18	83	22	4	26
Long Island	123	33	156	5	—	5
Louisiana State	53	9	62	15	3	18
Michigan	—	—	179	97	51	146
Missouri–Columbia	74	21	95	20	2	22
N.C. Chapel Hill	95	37	132	38	13	51
N.C. Greensboro	1	—	1	1	—	1

North Texas	368	93	461	52	22	75
Oklahoma	40	7	47	12	2	14
Pittsburgh	206	54	260	9	—	9
Pratt	197	50	247	37	9	47
Queens College	130	70	200	26	11	38
Rhode Island	46	7	53	12	3	15
Rutgers	123	34	157	57	7	64
San Jose	412	142	554	154	25	180
Simmons	243	74	317	180	40	220
Southern Mississsippi	40	8	48	17	1	18
South Florida	117	24	141	23	3	26
St. John's University	22	9	31	—	—	—
Syracuse	74	17	91	30	5	36
Texas (Austin)	85	21	106	49	12	64
Texas Woman's	156	10	166	24	3	27
UCLA	56	13	69	20	1	22
Washington	—	—	161	21	6	30
Wayne State	157	51	208	38	4	42
Wisconsin (Madison)	65	14	79	—	—	—
Wisconsin (Milwaukee)	151	36	187	35	11	46
Total	4,593	1,294	6,230	1,485	357	1,846

Tables do not always add up, individually or collectively, since both schools and individuals omitted data in some cases.

For schools that did not fill out the institutional survey, data were taken from graduate surveys, thus there is not full representation of their graduating classes.

Some schools completed the institutional survey, but responses were not received from graduates, or schools conducted their own survey and provided reports. This table represents placements of any kind. Comparison with other tables will show different numbers of placements.

Table 4 / Placements by Average Full-Time Salary of Reporting 2011 Graduates

	Average Salary			Median Salary		Low Salary		High Salary		Salaries		Total Placements
	Women	Men	All	Women	Men	Women	Men	Women	Men	Women	Men	
Alabama	$37,696	$37,969	$37,770	$37,450	$36,250	$21,230	$21,408	$50,000	$58,500	16	6	47
Albany	42,913	40,500	42,511	42,300	28,000	24,000	22,000	70,000	84,000	20	4	38
Buffalo	38,899	42,480	39,695	42,000	42,480	15,000	24,960	50,000	60,000	7	2	19
Catholic University	45,800	—	45,800	45,000	—	28,000	—	72,000	—	10	—	11
Clarion	33,300	—	33,300	32,250	—	27,500	—	41,200	—	4	—	6
Denver	49,750	46,660	48,562	48,500	45,500	28,000	31,000	80,000	59,800	8	5	21
Dominican	39,342	43,102	40,078	38,500	43,000	12,000	30,070	80,000	65,000	37	9	69
Drexel	43,530	74,508	53,499	41,500	67,000	19,000	40,000	97,000	150,000	42	19	105
Florida State	39,462	57,519	44,879	41,750	44,500	17,000	34,116	63,000	100,000	14	6	26
Hawaii	80,000	43,000	61,000	80,000	43,000	80,000	43,000	80,000	43,000	1	1	2
Illinois	43,394	57,931	45,962	41,250	52,400	20,800	29,000	100,000	125,000	54	13	96
Indiana	42,731	44,976	43,083	40,500	46,750	20,000	25,500	70,000	62,000	43	8	81
Iowa	48,458	34,000	44,515	49,081	42,000	26,000	13,000	71,000	47,000	8	3	13
Kent State University	34,937	38,840	35,669	35,000	40,000	10,000	26,000	61,322	50,000	39	9	81
Kentucky	36,778	36,250	36,637	34,000	37,500	19,136	30,000	55,000	40,000	11	4	26
Long Island	45,200	—	45,200	45,400	—	40,000	—	50,000	—	4	—	5
Louisiana State	38,016	30,350	37,058	37,664	30,350	27,000	18,700	50,000	42,000	14	2	18
Michigan	55,000	64,000	58,000	—	—	—	—	—	—	51	32	144

School											
Missouri-Columbia	38,779	36,563	38,518	38,000	36,563	28,000	31,625	60,000	41,500	15	2	22
NC Chapel Hill	44,243	48,989	45,430	41,600	46,000	28,000	33,000	70,000	85,000	27	9	51
North Texas	39,592	36,955	38,902	38,800	36,000	25,000	23,000	60,000	48,000	31	11	75
Oklahoma	36,074	65,000	38,704	37,500	65,000	24,500	65,000	47,700	65,000	10	1	14
Pittsburgh	35,667	—	35,667	38,000	—	31,000	—	38,000	—	3	—	9
Pratt	43,140	64,578	36,960	40,000	75,000	24,000	39,000	72,500	80,000	27	5	47
Queens College	44,557	41,725	43,991	43,600	40,450	29,120	36,000	60,000	50,000	16	4	38
Rhode Island	36,100	40,050	36,758	36,000	40,050	20,000	38,500	47,000	41,000	10	2	15
Rutgers	48,474	54,800	49,378	50,300	55,000	28,000	22,000	75,000	84,000	30	5	64
San Jose	46,188	46,313	46,109	45,500	47,578	21,000	35,000	92,000	57,000	70	15	180
Simmons	42,424	44,129	42,752	40,000	43,000	19,000	28,000	110,000	60,000	105	25	220
Southern Mississippi	32,039	48,550	34,241	33,000	48,550	20,000	48,000	46,700	49,100	13	2	18
South Florida	35,326	41,333	36,386	35,750	42,000	24,648	35,000	45,000	47,000	14	3	26
Syracuse	44,342	45,988	44,644	43,000	46,000	31,200	39,000	65,000	52,950	19	4	36
Texas Woman's	43,708	46,300	44,013	46,000	46,300	28,000	40,600	57,000	52,000	15	2	27
UCLA	45,955	—	46,208	49,000	—	25,000	—	65,000	—	15	—	22
Washington	39,682	45,203	41,388	38,971	46,608	14,500	37,000	60,000	52,000	16	3	30
Wayne State	39,189	46,093	41,072	39,361	48,500	25,000	24,960	54,000	61,000	16	6	42
Wisconsin (Madison)	46,562	36,961	44,834	43,000	40,000	18,000	15,000	180,000	50,000	33	7	56
Wisconsin (Milwaukee)	40,886	41,400	40,985	39,000	38,000	29,000	30,000	72,000	54,000	21	5	46

This table represents only placements and salaries reported as full-time. Some individuals or schools omitted some information, rendering information unusable. University of Texas at Austin reports salary ranges, with $35,000–$39,999 the most frequently reported salary range. Comparisons with other tables will show different numbers of placement and salary.

(continued from page 296)

of a master's degree, staying in the same job classification with no salary or benefits increases. Others did not see immediate changes in status, though the degree granted them eligibility for higher positions if and when these became available and made it possible to move to other departments within the agency. The fortunate ones (13.7 percent) received a promotion or salary increase commensurate with the new position and advanced degree. Similarly to the previous year's participants, academic libraries were hardest hit by an inability to provide either a promotion or salary increase to newly degreed librarians, while public libraries were more successful in this regard despite widespread cutbacks and layoffs.

Regional Differences

Salaries for new LIS graduates exhibited healthy growth that was dependent upon multiple factors, including regional differences such as relative cost of living and population density, while longitudinal data indicates that region plays a role in salary levels. Nationally, average starting salaries rose by 5 percent from $42,556 to $44,565, with the highest regional average in the West ($49,819). However, the West also saw average starting salaries fall by 2 percent compared with the previ-

Table 5 / Average Salary Index Starting Library Positions 1990–2011

Year	Library Schools	Average Starting Salary	Dollar Increase in Average Salary	Salary Index	BLS-CPI*
1990	38	$25,306	$725	143	131
1991	46	25,583	277	145	136
1992	41	26,666	1,083	151	141
1993	50	27,116	450	153	144
1994	43	28,086	970	159	148
1995	41	28,997	911	164	153
1996	44	29,480	483	167	159
1997	43	30,270	790	171	162
1998	47	31,915	1,645	180	164
1999	37	33,976	2,061	192	169
2000	37	34,871	895	197	175
2001	40	36,818	1947	208	177
2002	30	37,456	638	212	180
2003	43	37,975	519	215	184
2004	46	39,079	1,104	221	189
2005	37	40,115	1,036	227	195
2006	45	41,014	899	232	202
2007	43	42,361	1347	239	207
2008	40	41,579	-782	235	215
2009	42	42,215	636	239	215
2010	38	42,556	341	241	218
2011	41	44,565	2,009	252	225

* U.S. Department of Labor, Bureau of Labor Statistics, Consumer Price index, All Urban Consumers (CPI-U), U.S. city average, all items, 1982–1984=100. The average beginning professional salary for that period was $17,693.

ous year ($50,792), with nonlibrary agencies—including jobs with an information science focus—losing approximately 20 percent ($52,778, down from $63,524). The Southeast held the winning hand in salary gains for the class of 2011, increasing $2,934 (from $40,383 to $43,317). Contributing to the improvement was the slight rise in salaries at the low end of the scale and the significantly higher top-rank salaries ($110,000–$180,000).

Regionally, academic libraries in the Southeast had the best salary growth among all types of library and information agencies, with reported salaries $7,685 above levels achieved a year earlier, for an average starting salary of $47,182. A major contributing factor was better-than-average starting salaries for academic

Table 6 / Salaries of Reporting Professionals* by Area of Job Assignment

Assignment	Number	Percent of Total	Low Salary	High Salary	Average Salary	Median Salary
Access Services	19	1	$34,000	$53,500	$41,901	$39,751
Acquisitions	15	1	18,700	46,000	32,172	32,000
Administration	77	4	26,000	150,000	48,979	41,124
Adult Services	38	2	12,000	50,000	37,765	38,800
Archives	107	6	21,000	57,000	38,926	38,000
Automation/Systems	12	1	28,000	90,000	55,090	51,250
Cataloging & Classification	74	4	19,000	70,000	39,303	39,500
Children's Services	74	4	18,000	53,124	37,229	37,500
Circulation	86	5	17,000	60,000	35,488	35,500
Collection Development	17	1	18,000	80,000	43,961	40,000
Database Management	22	1	28,000	84,000	49,385	41,000
Electronic or Digital Services	65	4	13,000	88,000	44,366	45,000
Government Documents	4	0	23,000	54,500	41,871	44,992
Information Architecture	11	1	41,000	84,000	62,643	65,000
Info Technology	66	4	20,800	110,000	56,388	52,475
Instruction	63	4	25,000	80,000	45,154	43,500
Interlibrary Loans/Document Delivery	20	1	22,000	48,000	35,597	39,250
Knowledge Management	13	1	30,000	68,000	49,496	48,250
Metadata	7	0	37,500	58,500	49,323	51,500
Other	299	17	12,000	180,000	46,130	42,000
Public Services	35	2	20,800	61,000	40,523	41,500
Records Management	17	1	34,000	70,000	45,773	43,000
Reference/Info Services	265	15	15,000	129,000	45,690	44,000
Research	13	1	30,000	75,000	46,813	43,250
School Library Media Specialist	178	10	12,000	71,000	45,221	44,350
Solo Librarian	57	3	14,500	70,000	40,408	40,000
Technical Services	36	2	15,600	60,000	40,313	41,000
Usability/User Experiences	46	3	30,000	100,000	56,971	57,750
Web Design/Development	6	0	37,750	95,000	68,550	70,000
Youth Services	55	3	10,000	72,500	38,277	38,906
Total	1,797		10,000	180,000	44,507	42,000

* This table represents placements of any type reported by job assignment, but only salaries reported as full-time. Some individuals omitted placement information, rendering some information unusable. Comparison with other tables will show different numbers of placements.

reference librarians ($52,560, or 10.2 percent higher than salaries reported by all new academic librarians in the Southeast).

The Midwest experienced the best overall wage growth and strongest placement rate for the graduates of 2010; for 2011 these gains took a roller-coaster ride. Despite lingering economic hardship, the unemployment rate among LIS grads in the Midwest was the lowest at 3.3 percent. And though this region showed the strongest placement again with 27 percent of the total reported jobs, this was below the previous year's level of 36.1 percent. While overall average salaries in the Midwest dipped by a slight 1.1 percent to $42,376, graduates claiming minority status experienced a nearly 13 percent rise in starting salaries, with an average of $45,489 compared with $39,609. Another bright spot for Midwesterners was the climb in starting salaries for academic librarians, with an increase of approximately $2,554 a year, bringing the average to $40,744—more than recovering the loss between 2009 ($39,072) and 2010 ($38,190).

In all regions, including the Midwest, men reported good gains in starting salaries, averaging 15.1 percent increases, ranging from 2.9 percent gains in the Midwest to 20.2 percent in the West. High salaries, topping $100,000, contributed to the much higher levels of achievement in 2011, as did an across-the-board increase in the lowest of the starting salaries among the men.

Specifics relating to type of agency and job responsibility likewise offer other images and measures of professional achievement. Public libraries, for example, while hard-hit by economic pressures, experienced modest growth in the percentage of overall placements. In 2010 public libraries lost jobs due to hiring freezes, early retirements, and attrition, dropping to 22.8 percent of the overall placements (compared with 24.2 percent in 2009); placements a year later in these same types of libraries recovered and comprised 25.5 percent of the overall placements. Surprisingly, however, in areas where strong placements might be anticipated, such as in children's services, there were declines. In the 2010 survey, children's librarians made up 7.3 percent of the jobs with an average starting salary of $35,211; these same children's librarians made up 4.1 percent of the overall placements a year later, reversing the gains made between 2009 and 2010. On the slightly brighter side, children's librarian salaries were 5.4 percent higher than the previous year, averaging $37,229, though this remains somewhat lower than the overall average of $44,565.

School library media specialist positions were another area of serious concern. Graduates of 2011 reported the reduction or outright elimination of library media positions in public school districts across the United States, and said that in many areas "specialty" educators such as school librarians, music teachers, and art teachers were hired at the last minute after other budget decisions were made and occasionally after the new school year officially began. School librarians comprised 13.5 percent of the overall placements, down from 15.4 percent the previous year. The decline was readily apparent in the Southwest, where placements fell from 17.1 percent to 9.7 percent. Salaries among new school librarians contracted by approximately 2 percent, averaging $44,515 and losing $900 from the previous year. A mild note was a 9.6 percent increase in salaries for school library media specialists in the Midwest ($44,404 compared with $40,150 a year earlier). New school librarians emphasized the need to know the hiring cycle for school systems as well as ensuring that teaching credentials were current.

Some Gains for Special Libraries

Special libraries recovered a slim margin of the losses of the previous year, with placements improving from 5.1 percent to 6.1 percent, helped along by an increase in filled positions in the Midwest and the West. Salaries for special librarians also saw recovery, with new graduates earning $45,659, regaining the decline noted in the previous survey ($41,791) and exceeding the levels of the year before that ($43,090) by 5.6 percent.

Graduates seeking jobs in special libraries looked toward archives and special collections as having comparable job functions and also considered positions in academic special libraries, such as academic law libraries, as viable options. The job functions in special libraries ranged from traditional roles relating to reference and archival functions to emerging roles in digital curation and digital content management. As in public libraries, these new information professionals—not all of them describe themselves as librarians—enjoy the challenge of having multiple responsibilities and exposure to numerous units within their places of employment.

Likewise, public librarians suggested that multitasking is the new norm, while assignment to one specific department or function is becoming less common and making it more difficult to describe their job with a single title or job focus.

Graduates of 2011 reported slightly more jobs in administration (directors, managers, coordinators, and so on), comprising 4.3 percent of reported placements (compared with 3 percent a year earlier). More important than the numbers of placements, administrative salaries expanded by 20.2 percent, from $39,072 to an average of $48,979, well above the overall average for salaries among the 2011 grads (9 percent higher). It is noteworthy, however, that not all of the administrative jobs were in libraries, but spread among nonprofit organizations and private industry as well as libraries. Administrative jobs were reported in academic units outside the university library as well as administration in government agencies; while they were not traditional library-related jobs, they required that graduates use the leadership and management skills developed through their degree programs.

Reference/information services jobs exhibited major changes in numbers, job function, and salary. Reports of reference as a primary job function declined from 23.8 percent of the placements to 14.7 percent. This drop, however, can be deceiving; reference is one of the jobs that graduates describe with multiple functions, including combinations with instruction, collection development/maintenance, or administration. Graduates indicated that they needed to exhibit skills relating to teaching as well as respond to reference queries during job interviews; they also had to be prepared to work within a learning or information commons environment where the focus is on the students' individualized needs. Not surprisingly, nearly half (47.1 percent) of the new reference librarians were hired by academic libraries, followed by public libraries (32.6 percent). Reference service is also one of the functions that solo librarians frequently point to as integral to their day-to-day responsibilities. A small number (approximately 1 percent) described conducting targeted searches and research analysis for clients and performing the same types of services as reference librarians. Reference skills and duties are also encompassed in jobs relating to electronic and digital services, including data management and development of scholarly repositories. However, while numbers may have drifted off the highs of previous years, the reported average salary for reference librarians increased by 10.8 percent, to $45,690 (slightly higher than the national average for all new graduates).

Eye on the 'Other'

Jobs in other sectors outside LIS, including private industry, were up once again, increasing to 18.3 percent of reported placements. The grads found themselves spread among nonprofit agencies (17.3 percent), private industry (30 percent), and other types of agencies, such as law, retail, or finance (52.7 percent). This offers good news about making ends meet, but can prolong the frustration of finding a job that matches the degree.

The graduates employed in nonprofit agencies were among the winners in salary increases, with an average annual rate of $43,093. This is a 27.5 percent salary differential in just a year. Among the various roles that the grads played in nonprofit organizations were impact analyst, prospect research analyst, and community relations coordinator at agencies such as the American Red Cross and AmeriCorps, as well as in museums, archives, and not-for-profit healthcare agencies.

The largest proportion of the nonprofit placements were located in the Northeast (36.7 percent), featuring slightly better-than-average salaries ($45,071). By comparison, placements declined in private industry, dropping from 9.4 percent of reported jobs to 5.4 percent. Annual salaries in private industry followed suit, coming in at an average of $51,897 compared with $56,526 in 2010 and a high of $58,194 in 2008. However, the private sector also held some of the highest-paying jobs, ranging from $100,000 to $180,000 a year. User interface design, analytics, software engineering, and digital asset management were among the most frequently identified roles in private sector jobs, with graduates landing in biotech firms, hospitals, high-tech companies, advertising and marketing, and publishing. Like the nonprofits, graduates in the Northeast claimed the largest proportion of private sector jobs (37.5 percent), echoing the trend of the previous year (32.6 percent); however, the highest salaries in private industry were obtained in the Midwest ($53,217 compared with the average salary for all private industry placements of $51,897 and $50,148 in the Northeast).

Finding employment outside the LIS professions became a delicate balancing act for many. Besides jobs in nonprofits and private industry, the graduating class also found employment in an array of "other" agencies but often using the skills learned during their master's degree programs. These included working with medical records; public radio and television; fund raising and grant writing; and local, state, and federal government agencies as well as in other academic units within institutions of higher education. On the down side, some also felt obligated to accept positions as clerical and secretarial employees, food service workers, and retail clerks in order to meet the monthly bills, and they expressed serious frustration in not finding employment reflecting their academic achievements. However, salaries did not completely mirror the disparity among the status of the positions, with an average starting salary of $47,604. While some graduates reported annual salaries well below the national average, salaries in the other agencies were boosted by the types of positions the grads obtained, including jobs relating to information and communication technology, e-commerce, and publishing.

Microcosms and Gaps

In a year that brought highs and lows for many graduates, the salary gap widened again with a 14.9 percent chasm between women and men. While women's salaries experienced a small upward spurt of 1.9 percent between 2010 ($42,205) and 2011 ($42,990), average annual salaries for men surged by 15.1 percent to $50,500 (up from $43,845). Regionally, the Southeast ($43,317) achieved the best rate of growth (6.8 percent) and outpaced both the Midwest ($42,376) and the Southwest ($42,543); women in the Southeast were recipients of some of the positive growth, with salaries that improved by 4.7 percent over the previous year ($42,035 in 2010 compared with $40,058 in 2009). However, women experienced declining salaries in the Midwest, Southwest, and West.

In attempting to pinpoint where the gaps occurred between men and women, jobs in administration ($72,108 and $41,791, respectively), private industry ($68,461 and $47,118, respectively), and information technology ($59,555 compared with $57,800) showed the greatest disparities between the sexes. Proportionally, a higher percentage of men (52.3 percent) earned salaries above the national average of $44,565, and achieved some of the top salaries among the graduates, receiving as much as $125,000 to $150,000.

Women dominated the public library job market (83.5 percent of the jobs), where the lowest average starting salaries were offered ($37,399 for new public librarians). This is further compounded by the percentage of women who accepted nonprofessional jobs (80.9 percent of the nonprofessional placements), which historically are lower paying and which were prominent in public libraries. This downward spiral was exacerbated by the low public library salaries in the Southeast, where women earned an average of $32,910, although this was 3.3 percent higher than men's salaries for the same positions ($31,822).

Women, for a second year in a row, did exceptionally well in negotiating higher salary levels in knowledge management ($50,833) relative to the national average, though not to the same level as in 2010 ($66,875). They also achieved better-than-average salaries in the area of information technology ($57,800), but again not reaching the high of $60,380 recorded for the previous year. These types of jobs contributed to the modest growth in women's salaries and helped to counterbalance the effects of lower paying public library jobs and nonprofessional positions.

Another way to examine the profession is through the experiences of the graduates claiming minority status. For the last several years minority graduates ranged from 10 percent to 13 percent of the survey participant pool; 2011 was no exception at 13 percent. Repeating past years' trends, minority grads achieved salaries that were above the national average by 8.8 percent ($48,841) and saw better growth in those salaries from 2010 to 2011 (up by 8.7 percent, or $4,239 higher), far outpacing the 5 percent rate in overall salaries. The gold winner is the 26.7 percent jump in salaries for other agencies, which climbed from $47,129 to $64,291.

Table 7 / Comparison of Salaries by Type of Organization

	Total Placements	Salaries		Low Salary		High Salary		Average Salary			Median Salary		
		Women	Men	Women	Men	Women	Men	Women	Men	All	Women	Men	All
Public Libraries													
All Public	430	183	36	$10,000	$15,000	$92,000	$55,000	$37,168	$38,847	$37,399	$38,000	$38,750	$38,000
Northeast	108	35	6	20,800	41,000	60,000	55,000	41,016	49,325	42,083	42,000	51,475	42,500
Southeast	58	34	6	17,000	21,408	46,794	46,000	32,910	31,822	32,747	33,650	33,558	33,650
Midwest	137	68	11	10,000	15,000	50,000	45,000	35,929	35,205	35,743	36,000	37,750	36,000
Southwest	45	19	7	20,000	31,000	47,700	40,600	36,185	36,790	36,290	40,000	37,780	40,000
West	74	24	9	14,500	19,000	92,000	53,124	43,229	43,650	43,334	40,660	43,039	40,660
College/University Libraries													
All Academic	471	233	86	15,000	13,000	110,000	121,647	42,936	45,787	43,554	41,000	45,750	42,000
Northeast	145	63	22	15,000	22,000	75,000	121,647	41,723	48,370	43,443	40,352	45,500	42,000
Southeast	75	44	13	24,000	18,700	110,000	88,000	45,739	51,323	47,182	42,000	49,100	42,500
Midwest	126	66	28	20,000	13,000	100,000	61,000	40,527	41,255	40,744	39,500	42,000	40,000
Southwest	34	16	12	25,000	23,000	53,364	67,000	39,918	48,939	43,388	40,000	49,194	45,250
West	73	35	12	24,000	32,000	66,000	55,000	47,481	42,901	46,207	49,000	44,000	47,000
Special Libraries													
All Special	104	64	9	20,800	25,000	80,000	150,000	45,079	49,786	45,659	45,000	39,000	43,275
Northeast	38	20	4	30,100	25,000	70,000	150,000	46,161	60,500	48,551	43,000	33,500	40,500
Southeast	10	8	—	33,000	—	67,000	—	46,613	—	46,613	45,000	—	45,000
Midwest	31	17	3	20,800	30,070	80,000	53,000	43,649	43,690	43,665	43,275	48,000	45,138
Southwest	8	5	2	32,000	36,000	52,000	39,000	39,792	37,500	39,137	37,960	37,500	37,960
West	15	12	—	31,500	—	72,000	—	46,579	—	46,579	46,500	—	46,500
Canada/International	2	2	—	39,000	—	50,000	—	44,500	—	44,500	44,500	—	44,500

Government Libraries													
All Government	34	23	4	26,000	42,000	72,000	62,000	38,833	54,875	47,159	44,000	57,750	44,000
Northeast	11	7	1	26,000	53,500	64,690	53,500	40,155	53,500	41,823	38,000	53,500	38,197
Southeast	13	9	3	35,000	42,000	72,000	62,000	45,812	55,333	48,193	44,000	62,000	45,750
Midwest	3	2	—	37,000	—	37,000	—	37,000	—	37,000	37,000	—	37,000
Southwest	2	1	—	55,000	—	55,000	—	55,000	—	55,000	55,000	—	55,000
West	3	2	—	54,000	—	56,400	—	55,200	—	55,200	55,200	—	55,200
Canada/International	1	1	—	51,000	—	51,000	—	51,000	—	51,000	51,000	—	51,000
Archives													
All Archives	49	32	4	21,000	34,900	57,000	53,000	38,133	42,825	38,654	37,500	41,700	37,750
Northeast	12	10	1	24,000	39,900	50,000	39,900	39,410	39,900	39,455	39,900	39,900	39,900
Southeast	10	6	1	25,000	34,900	57,000	34,900	38,333	34,900	37,843	37,000	34,900	36,000
Midwest	16	9	2	21,000	43,500	55,000	53,000	35,573	48,250	37,878	35,000	48,250	35,560
Southwest	4	4	—	25,000	—	48,000	—	37,250	—	37,250	38,000	—	38,000
West	7	3	—	38,000	—	47,000	—	42,333	—	42,333	42,000	—	42,000
Vendors													
All Vendors	18	11	2	20,000	40,000	70,000	50,000	40,545	45,000	41,500	38,000	45,000	39,000
Northeast	10	6	1	20,000	40,000	70,000	40,000	42,167	40,000	42,450	39,000	40,000	40,000
Southeast	3	1	—	33,000	—	33,000	—	33,000	—	33,000	33,000	—	33,000
Midwest	3	3	—	30,000	—	55,000	—	40,667	—	40,667	37,000	—	37,000
West	2	1	1	38,000	50,000	38,000	50,000	38,000	50,000	44,000	38,000	50,000	44,000

These tables represents only full-time salaries and placements reported by type. Some individuals omitted placement information, rendering some information unusable. Comparison with other tables will show different numbers of total placements due to completeness of the data reported by individuals and schools. Totals within the table represent all reported placement data but will not necessarily correspond to regional or gender breakdown.

Minority graduates also had the highest placement rates in other agencies (32.4 percent), landing in positions relating to information technology, user experience, and emerging technologies. As in the previous year, academic libraries offered lucrative opportunities to this group of graduates with strong employment rates (26 percent) and above-average salaries ($44,659 compared with $43,554 nationally).

Two aspects marred the picture for minority grads. One was a small decline in salary levels in the Northeast, where they fell by 3.3 percent to $48,478 (from $50,088 a year earlier), though these remained above the average for all grads in the same region ($45,624). The second was an increase in the number of graduates accepting part-time jobs (35.8 percent), which was somewhat higher than the national level of 23.6 percent; it is important to keep in mind, however, that in some cases part-time employment is a deliberate choice.

Women claiming minority status fared much worse in the gender gap, with average starting salaries showing a 25.5 percent disparity compared with their minority male counterparts ($45,775 compared with $61,482). However, they stayed ahead of the national average for all women ($42,990). Additionally, salaries achieved in 2011 by the minority women were 6.4 percent higher than the previous year.

Experience and Advice

The real stories of the graduates can be conveyed only in their words; numbers can show only trends. For the graduating class of 2011, there were exceptional highs and discouraging lows.

The job search was lengthy, and for many was a full-time job itself. For a lucky few, jobs were waiting when they graduated. But for the majority there were several months of nerve-wracking periods waiting to secure a permanent position. The most frustrating part was a lack of response from potential employers and discovering that "entry level" positions could still require years of experience.

On the positive side, graduates spoke of being fortunate in finding a job to love. Some were able to parlay an internship or practicum into a permanent position, capitalizing upon being in the right place when a position opened and letting the people in the position to hire know that they were interested in staying. They also took time to get to know staffers at the institutions where they were interning.

As a group, the graduating class of 2011 advised their upcoming colleagues to seek out experience wherever possible. Internships, practicums, and volunteering are critical in developing on-the-job skills; they also advised that the internship site supervisors are in the position to provide job references relating to practical experience. Numerous graduates said they sought part-time jobs while in school not only to supplement their income but to help build the requisite experience.

Networking with fellow students, professional colleagues, and faculty was another key to increasing the odds of finding employment. One graduate suggested that students need to "work your connections because it may lead to something upon graduation." Others said that personal connections and networks could reap big rewards and "you might find a job where you expected not to." Attending conferences and participating in professional activities were additional strategies that new grads strongly recommended in order to connect with the people and agencies that have the jobs. They also commented that not all of the jobs are publicly advertised, and students need to be insiders to hear about some of those opportunities.

The class of 2011 recommended that their future colleagues need to be strategic in the job search. Tailor cover letters and résumés to the specific job and make them "meaningful." Learn about the possible retirements in the area and arrange to complete an internship at the site in order to be in the right place when the agency is ready to hire; become a known entity. And the best piece of advice the grads offered: "The best thing to keep in mind during the job search process is that library and information/knowledge skills can transfer to so many different fields."

Survey Methods

For the 2012 Placements and Salaries Survey, *Library Journal* received responses either through the institutional survey or individuals representing 41 of the 48 LIS schools surveyed in the United States and from 2,162 of the reported LIS graduates. The University of Michigan and the University of Texas at Austin prepared their own surveys.

Schools were given the choice of responding by paper or electronic survey, with most choosing the latter. Some graduates and schools reported incomplete information, rendering some data unusable. For schools that did not complete the institutional survey, data were taken from graduate surveys, and thus are not a full representation of the entire graduating class.

The following schools declined to participate, did not respond to calls for participation, or had no graduate participation: University of Arizona, Emporia State University, University of Maryland, North Carolina Central, North Carolina Greensboro, University of Puerto Rico, University of South Carolina, Southern Connecticut State University, St. John's University, St. Katherine's University, University of Tennessee, and Valdosta State University. The Canadian programs—Alberta, British Columbia, Dalhousie, McGill, Montreal, Toronto, and Western Ontario—conduct their own annual salary and placements surveys, and do not participate in the *Library Journal* survey.

Accredited Master's Programs in Library and Information Studies

This list of graduate programs accredited by the American Library Association is issued by the ALA Office for Accreditation. Regular updates and additional details appear on the Office for Accreditation's Web site at http://www.ala.org/Template.cfm?Section=lisdirb&Template=/cfapps/lisdir/index.cfm. More than 150 institutions offering both accredited and nonaccredited programs in librarianship are included in the 66th edition (2013–2014) of *American Library Directory* (Information Today, Inc.)

Northeast: Conn., D.C., Md., Mass., N.J., N.Y., Pa., R.I.

Catholic University of America, School of Lib. and Info. Science, 620 Michigan Ave. N.E., Washington, DC 20064. L. R. Poos, interim dean. Tel. 202-319-5085, fax 202-219-5574, e-mail cua-slis@cua.edu, World Wide Web http://slis.cua.edu. Admissions contact: Louise Gray. Tel. 202-319-5085, fax 202-319-5574, e-mail grayl@cua.edu.

Clarion University of Pennsylvania, College of Educ. and Human Services, Dept. of Lib. Science, 210 Carlson Lib. Bldg., 840 Wood St., Clarion, PA 16214. Janice M. Krueger, chair. Tel. 866-272-5612, fax 814-393-2150, World Wide Web http://www.clarion.edu/libsci. Admissions contact: Lois Dulavitch. Tel. 866-272-5612, e-mail ldulavitch@clarion.edu.

Drexel University, College of Info. Science and Technology, 3141 Chestnut St., Philadelphia, PA 19104-2875. David E. Fenske, dean. Tel. 215-895-2474, fax 215-895-2494, e-mail istinfo@drexel.edu, World Wide Web http://www.ischool.drexel.edu. Admissions contact: Matthew Lechtenburg. Tel. 215-895-1951, e-mail ml333@ischool.drexel.edu.

Long Island University, Palmer School of Lib. and Info. Science, C. W. Post Campus, 720 Northern Blvd., Brookville, NY 11548-1300. Jody K. Howard, dir. and assoc. dean. Tel. 516-299-4109, fax 516-299-4168, e-mail palmer@cwpost.liu.edu, World Wide Web http://www.liu.edu/palmer. Admissions contact: Geraldine Kopczynski. Tel. 516-299-2857, e-mail gkopski@liu.edu.

Pratt Institute, School of Info. and Lib. Science, 144 W. 14 St., New York, NY 10011. Tula Giannini, dean. Tel. 212-647-7682, fax 202-367-2492, e-mail infosils@pratt.edu, World Wide Web http://www.pratt.edu/academics/information_and_library_sciences. Admissions contact: Quinn Lai. E-mail infosils@pratt.edu.

Queens College, City Univ. of New York, Grad. School of Lib. and Info. Studies, Rm. 254, Rosenthal Lib., 65-30 Kissena Blvd., Flushing, NY 11367-1597. James Marcum, chair/dir. Tel. 718-997-3790, fax 718-997-3797, e-mail gc_gslis@qc.cuny.edu, World Wide Web http://www.qc.cuny.edu/academics/degrees/dss/gslis/Pages/default.aspx. Admissions contact: Roberta Brody. E-mail roberta_brody@qc.edu.

Rutgers University, School of Communication and Info., Dept. of Lib. and Info. Science, New Brunswick, NJ 08901-1071. Marie L. Radford, chair. Tel. 732-932-7500 ext. 8218, fax 732-932-6916, e-mail scilsmls@comminfo.rutgers.edu, World Wide Web http://comminfo.rutgers.edu. Admissions contact: Kay Cassell. Tel. 732-932-7500 ext. 8264.

Saint John's University, College of Liberal Arts and Sciences, Div. of Lib. and Info. Science, 8000 Utopia Pkwy., Queens, NY 11439. Jeffery E. Olson, dir. Tel. 718-990-6200, fax 718-990-2071, e-mail dlis@stjohns.edu, World Wide Web http://www.stjohns.edu/dlis. Admissions contact: Deborah Martinez. Tel. 718-990-6200.

Simmons College, Grad. School of Lib. and Info. Science, 300 The Fenway, Boston, MA 02115. Michele Cloonan, dean. Tel. 617-521-2800, fax 617-521-3192, e-mail gslis@simmons.edu, World Wide Web http://www.

simmons.edu/gslis. Admissions contact: Sarah Petrakos.

Southern Connecticut State University, School of Educ., Communication, Dept. of Info., and Lib. Science, 501 Crescent St., New Haven, CT 06515. Chang Suk Kim, chair. Tel. 203-392-5781, fax 203-392-5780, e-mail ils@southernct.edu, World Wide Web http://www.southernct.edu/ils. Admissions contact: Kathy Muldowney.

Syracuse University, School of Info. Studies, 343 Hinds Hall, Syracuse, NY 13244. Elizabeth D. Liddy, dean. Tel. 315-443-2911, fax 315-443-6886, e-mail ischool@syr.edu, World Wide Web http://www.ischool.syr.edu. Admissions contact: Jill Hurst-Wahl, dir. Tel. 315-443-2911, e-mail mslis@syr.edu.

University at Albany, State Univ. of New York, College of Computing and Info., Dept. of Info. Studies, Draper 113, 135 Western Ave., Albany, NY 12222. Philip B. Eppard, chair. Tel 518-442-5110, fax 518-442-5367, e-mail infostudies@albany.edu, World Wide Web http://www.albany.edu/informationstudies/index.php. Admissions contact: Daphne Jorgensen. E-mail djorgensen@albany.edu.

University at Buffalo, State Univ. of New York, Graduate School of Educ., Lib. and Info. Studies, 534 Baldy Hall, Buffalo, NY 14260-1020. Jianqiang Wang, interim chair. Tel. 716-645-2412, fax 716-645-3775, e-mail ub-lis@buffalo.edu, World Wide Web http://gse.buffalo.edu/lis. Admissions contact: Radhika Suresh. Tel. 716-645-2110, e-mail gse-info@buffalo.edu.

University of Maryland, College of Info. Studies, 4105 Hornbake Bldg., College Park, MD 20742. Jennifer Preece, dean. Tel. 301-405-2033, fax 301-314-9145, e-mail ischooladmission@umd.edu, World Wide Web http://ischool.umd.edu. Admissions contact: Joanne Briscoe. Tel. 301-405-2038, e-mail ischooladmission@umd.edu.

University of Pittsburgh, School of Info. Sciences, 135 N. Bellefield Ave., Pittsburgh, PA 15260. Martin B. Weiss, acting chair and assoc. dean. Tel. 412-624-9420, fax 412-648-7001, e-mail lisinq@mail.sis.pitt.edu. World Wide Web http://www.ischool.pitt.edu. Admissions contact: Debbie Day. E-mail dday@sis.pitt.edu.

University of Rhode Island, Grad. School of Lib. and Info. Studies, Rodman Hall, 94 W. Alumni Ave., Kingston, RI 02881. Renee Hobbs, interim dir. Tel. 401-874-2878, fax 401-874-4964, e-mail gslis@etal.uri.edu, World Wide Web http://www.uri.edu/artsci/lsc.

Southeast: Ala., Fla., Ga., Ky., La., Miss., N.C., S.C., Tenn., P.R.

Florida State University, College of Communication and Info., School of Lib. and Info. Studies, 142 Collegiate Loop, P.O. Box 3062100, Tallahassee, FL 32306-2100. Kathleen Burnett, interim dir. Tel. 850-644-5775, fax 850-644-9763, World Wide Web http://slis.fsu.edu. Admissions e-mail slisgrad admissions@admin.fsu.edu, tel. 850-644-8121.

Louisiana State University, School of Lib. and Info. Science, 267 Coates Hall, Baton Rouge, LA 70803. Beth Paskoff, dean. Tel. 225-578-3158, fax 225-578-4581, e-mail slis@lsu.edu, World Wide Web http://slis.lsu.edu. Admissions contact: LaToya Coleman Joseph. E-mail lcjoseph@lsu.edu.

North Carolina Central University, School of Lib. and Info. Sciences, P.O. Box 19586, Durham, NC 27707. Irene Owens, dean. Tel. 919-530-6485, fax 919-530-6402, World Wide Web http://www.nccuslis.org.

University of Alabama, College of Communication and Info. Sciences, School of Lib. and Info. Studies, Box 870252, Tuscaloosa, AL 35487-0252. Heidi Julien, dir. Tel. 205-348-4610, fax 205-348-3746, e-mail info@slis.ua.edu, World Wide Web http://www.slis.ua.edu. Admissions contact: Beth Riggs. Tel. 205-348-1527, e-mail briggs@slis.ua.edu.

University of Kentucky, School of Lib. and Info. Science, 320 Little Lib., Lexington, KY 40506-0224. Jeffrey T. Huber, dir. Tel. 859-257-8876, fax 859-257-4205, e-mail ukslis@uky.edu, World Wide Web http://www.uky.edu/cis/slis. Admissions contact: Will Buntin. Tel. 859-257-3317, e-mail wjbunt0@uky.edu.

University of North Carolina at Chapel Hill, School of Info. and Lib. Science, CB 3360,

100 Manning Hall, Chapel Hill, NC 27599-3360. Gary Marchionini, dean. Tel. 919-962-8366, fax 919-962-8071, e-mail info@ils.unc.edu, World Wide Web http://www.sils.unc.edu. Admissions contact: Lara Bailey.

University of North Carolina at Greensboro, School of Educ., Dept. of Lib. and Info. Studies, 446 School of Educ. Bldg., Greensboro, NC 27402-6170. Clara M. Chu, chair. Tel. 336-334-3477, fax 336-334-4120, World Wide Web http://lis.uncg.edu. Admissions contact: Touger Vang. E-mail t_vang@uncg.edu.

University of Puerto Rico, Info. Sciences and Technologies, P.O. Box 21906, San Juan, PR 00931-1906. Mariano A. Maura, acting dir. Tel. 787-763-6199, fax 787-764-2311, e-mail egcti@uprrp.edu, World Wide Web http://egcti.upr.edu. Admissions contact: Migdalia Dávila-Perez. Tel. 787-764-0000 ext. 3530, e-mail migdalia.davila@upr.edu.

University of South Carolina, College of Mass Communications and Info. Studies, School of Lib. and Info. Science, 1501 Greene St., Columbia, SC 29208. Samantha K. Hastings, dir. Tel. 803-777-3858, fax 803-777-7938, e-mail hastings@sc.edu, World Wide Web http://www.libsci.sc.edu. Admissions contact: Tilda Reeder. Tel. 800-304-3153, e-mail tildareeder@sc.edu.

University of South Florida, College of Arts and Sciences, School of Lib. and Info. Science, 4202 E. Fowler Ave., CIS 1040, Tampa, FL 33620. James Andrews, dir. Tel. 813-974-3520, fax 813-974-6840, e-mail lisinfo@usf.edu, World Wide Web http://si.usf.edu. Admissions contact: Daniel Kahl. Tel. 813-974-8022, e-mail djkahl@usf.edu.

University of Southern Mississippi, College of Educ. and Psychology, School of Lib. and Info. Science, 118 College Drive, No. 5146, Hattiesburg, MS 39406-0001. M. J. Norton, dir. Tel. 601-266-4228, fax 601-266-5774, e-mail slis@usm.edu, World Wide Web http://www.usm.edu/slis. Admissions tel. 601-266-5137, e-mail graduatestudies@usm.edu.

University of Tennessee, College of Communication and Info., School of Info. Sciences, 451 Communication Bldg., Knoxville, TN 37996. Edwin M. Cortez, dir. Tel. 865-974-2148, fax 865-974-4967, World Wide Web http://www.sis.utk.edu. Admissions contact: Tanya Arnold. Tel. 865-974-2858, e-mail tnarnold@utk.edu.

Valdosta State Univ., Dept. of Info. Studies, 1500 N. Patterson St., Valdosta, GA 31698-0133. Wallace Koehler, dir. Tel. 229-333-5966, fax 229-259-5055, e-mail mlis@valdosta.edu, World Wide Web http://www.valdosta.edu/mlis. Admissions contact: Sheila Peacock.

Midwest: Ill., Ind., Iowa, Kan., Mich., Mo., Ohio, Wis.

Dominican Univ., Grad. School of Lib. and Info. Science, 7900 W. Division St., River Forest, IL 60305. Susan Roman, dean. Tel. 708-524-6845, fax 708-524-6657, e-mail gslis@dom.edu, World Wide Web http://www.dom.edu/gslis. Admissions contact: Teresa Espinoza. Tel. 708-524-6983, e-mail tespinoza@dom.edu.

Emporia State University, School of Lib. and Info. Management, 1200 Commercial, Campus Box 4025, Emporia, KS 66801. Gwen Alexander, dean. Tel. 620-341-5203, fax 620-341-5233, e-mail sliminfo@emporia.edu, World Wide Web http://slim.emporia.edu. Admissions contact: Matthew Upson. Tel. 620-341-6159, e-mail sliminfo@emporia.edu.

Indiana University, School of Lib. and Info. Science, 1320 E. 10 St., LI 011, Bloomington, IN 47405-3907. Debora Shaw, dean. Tel. 812-855-2018, fax 812-855-6166, e-mail slis@indiana.edu, World Wide Web http://www.slis.indiana.edu. Admissions contact: Rhonda Spencer.

Kent State University, School of Lib. and Info. Science, P.O. Box 5190, Kent, OH 44242-0001. Tomas A. Lipinski, dir. Tel. 330-672-2782, fax 330-672-7965, e-mail slisinform@kent.ed, World Wide Web http://www.kent.edu/slis. Admissions contact: Cheryl Tennant.

University of Illinois at Urbana-Champaign, Grad. School of Lib. and Info. Science, 501 E. Daniel St., Champaign, IL 61820-6211. Allen Renear, interim dean. Tel. 217-333-

3280, fax 217-244-3302, e-mail gslis@Illinois.edu, World Wide Web http://www.lis.illinois.edu. Admissions contact: Penny Ames. Tel. 217-333-7197, e-mail pames@illinois.edu.

University of Iowa, Graduate College, School of Lib. and Info. Science, 3087 Main Lib., Iowa City, IA 52242-1420. Daniel Berkowitz, interim dir. Tel. 319-335-5707, fax 319-335-5374, e-mail slis@uiowa.edu, World Wide Web http://slis.grad.uiowa.edu. Admissions contact: Kit Austin. Tel. 319-335-5709, e-mail caroline-austin@uiowa.edu.

University of Michigan, School of Info., 4322 North Quad, 105 S. State St., Ann Arbor, MI 48109-1285. Jeffrey Makie-Mason, dean. Tel. 734-763-2285, fax 734-764-2475, e-mail umsi.admissions@umich.edu, World Wide Web http://www.umsi.umich.edu. Admissions contact: Laura Elgas.

University of Missouri, College of Educ., School of Info. Science and Learning Technologies, 303 Townsend Hall, Columbia, MO 65211. John Wedman, dir. Tel. 877-747-5868, fax 573-884-0122, e-mail sislt@missouri.edu, World Wide Web http://sislt.missouri.edu. Admissions tel. 573-882-4546.

University of Wisconsin–Madison, College of Letters and Sciences, School of Lib. and Info. Studies, 600 N. Park St., Madison, WI 53706. Kristin Eschenfelder, dir. Tel. 608-263-2900, fax 608-263-4849, e-mail uw-slis@slis.wisc.edu, World Wide Web http://www.slis.wisc.edu. Admissions contact: Tanya Cobb. Tel. 608-263-2909, e-mail student-services@slis.wisc.edu.

University of Wisconsin–Milwaukee, School of Info. Studies, P.O. Box 413, Milwaukee, WI 53211. Thomas Walker, dir. Tel. 414-229-4707, fax 414-229-6699, e-mail soisinfo@uwm.edu, World Wide Web http://www4.uwm.edu/sois.

Wayne State University, School of Lib. and Info. Science, 106 Kresge Lib., Detroit, MI 48202. Stephen T. Bajjaly, assoc. dean. Tel. 313-577-1825, fax 313-577-7563, e-mail askcis@wayne.edu, World Wide Web http://www.slis.wayne.edu. Admissions contact: Matthew Fredericks. Tel. 313-577-2446, e-mail mfredericks@wayne.edu.

Southwest: Ariz., Okla., Texas

Texas Woman's University, School of Lib. and Info. Studies, P.O. Box 425438, Denton, TX 76204-5438. Ling Hwey Jeng, dir. Tel. 940-898-2602, fax 940-898-2611, e-mail slis@twu.edu, World Wide Web http://www.twu.edu/slis. Admissions contact: Brenda Mallory. E-mail bmallory@mail.twu.edu.

University of Arizona, College of Social and Behavioral Sciences, School of Info. Resources and Lib. Science, 1515 E. 1 St., Tucson, AZ 85719. P. Bryan Heidorn, dir. Tel. 520-621-3565, fax 520-621-3279, e-mail sirls@email.arizona.edu, World Wide Web http://www.sirls.arizona.edu. Admissions contact: Geraldine Fragoso. Tel. 520-621-5230, e-mail gfragoso@u.arizona.edu.

University of North Texas, College of Info., Dept. of Lib. and Info. Sciences, 1155 Union Circle, No. 311068, Denton, TX 76203-5017. Suliman Hawamdeh, chair. Tel. 940-565-3690, fax 940-369-7600, e-mail ci-dean@unt.edu, World Wide Web http://www.ci.unt.edu/main. Admissions contact: Toby Faber. Tel. 940-565-7873, e-mail john.pipes@unt.edu.

University of Oklahoma, School of Lib. and Info. Studies, College of Arts and Sciences, 401 W. Brooks, Norman, OK 73019-6032. Cecelia Brown, dir. Tel. 405-325-3921, fax 405-325-7648, e-mail slisinfo@ou.edu, World Wide Web http://www.ou.edu/cas/slis. Admissions contact: Maggie Ryan.

University of Texas at Austin, School of Info., Suite 5.202, 1616 Guadalupe St., Austin, TX 78701-1213. Andrew Dillon, dean. Tel. 512-471-3821, fax 512-471-3971, e-mail info@ischool.utexas.edu, World Wide Web http://www.ischool.utexas.edu. Admissions contact: Carla Criner. Tel. 512-471-5654, e-mail criner@ischool.utexas.edu.

West: Calif., Colo., Hawaii, Wash.

San José State University, School of Lib. and Info. Science, 1 Washington Sq., San José, CA 95192-0029. Sandy Hirsh, dir. Tel. 408-924-2490, fax 408-924-2476, e-mail sanjose slis@gmail.com, World Wide Web http://

slisweb.sjsu.edu. Admissions contact: Linda Main. Tel. 408-924-2494, e-mail linda. main@sjsu.edu.

University of California, Los Angeles, Graduate School of Educ. and Info. Studies, Dept. of Info. Studies, Box 951520, Los Angeles, CA 90095-1520. Gregory Leazer, chair. Tel. 310-825-8799, fax 310-206-3076, e-mail info@gseis.ucla.edu, World Wide Web http://is.gseis.ucla.edu. Admissions contact: Susan Abler. Tel. 310-825-5269, e-mail abler@gseis.ucla.edu.

University of Denver, Morgridge College of Educ., Lib. and Info. Science Program, 1999 E. Evans Ave., Denver, CO 80208-1700. Mary Stansbury, chair. Tel. 303-871-2747, fax 303-871-2709, e-mail mary.stansbury@ du.edu, World Wide Web http://www. du.edu/lis. Admissions contact: Nick Heckart. E-mail nheckart@du.edu.

University of Hawaii, College of Natural Sciences, Lib. and Info. Science Program, 2550 McCarthy Mall, Honolulu, HI 96822. Andrew Wertheimer, chair. Tel. 808-956-7321, fax 808-956-5835, e-mail slis@hawaii.edu, World Wide Web http://www.hawaii.edu/lis.

University of Washington, The Info. School, 370 Mary Gates Hall, Seattle, WA 98195-2840. Harry Bruce, dean. Tel. 206-685-9937, fax 206-616-3152, e-mail ischool@ uw.edu, World Wide Web http://ischool. uw.edu. Admissions contact: Tel. 206-543-1794, e-mail mlis@ischool.uw.edu.

Canada

Dalhousie University, School of Info. Management, Kenneth C. Rowe Management Bldg., Halifax, NS B3H 3J5. Louise Spiteri, dir. Tel. 902-494-3656, fax 902-494-2451, e-mail sim@dal.ca, World Wide Web http:// www.sim.management.dal.ca. Admissions contact: JoAnn Watson. Tel. 902-494-2471, e-mail joann.watson@dal.ca.

McGill University, School of Info. Studies, 3661 Peel St., Montreal, QC H3A 1X1. France Bouthillier, dir. Tel. 514-398-4204, fax 514-398-7193, e-mail sis@mcgill.ca, World Wide Web http://www.mcgill.ca/sis. Admissions contact: Kathryn Hubbard. Tel. 514-398-4204 ext. 0742, e-mail sis@mcgill. ca.

Université de Montréal, École de Bibliothéconomie et des Sciences de l'Information, C.P. 6128, Succursale Centre-Ville, Montreal, QC H3C 3J7. Clément Arsenault, dir. Tel. 514-343-6044, fax 514-343-5753, e-mail ebsiinfo@ebsi.umontreal.ca, World Wide Web http://www.ebsi.umontreal.ca. Admissions contact: Alain Tremblay. Tel. 514-343-6044, e-mail alain.tremblay.1@umontreal. ca.

University of Alberta, School of Lib. and Info. Studies, 3-20 Rutherford S., Edmonton, AB T6G 2J4. Ernie Ingles, dir. Tel. 780-492-4578, fax 780-492-2430, e-mail slis@ ualberta.ca, World Wide Web http://www. slis.ualberta.ca. Admissions contact: Lauren Romaniuk. Tel. 780-492-4140, e-mail slis admissions@ualberta.ca,

University of British Columbia, School of Lib., Archival, and Info. Studies, Irving K. Barber Learning Centre, Suite 470, 1961 East Mall, Vancouver, BC V6T 1Z1. Caroline Haythornthwaite, dir. Tel. 604-822-2404, fax 604-822-6006, e-mail slais@interchange. ubc.ca, World Wide Web http://www.slais. ubc.ca. Admissions contact: Michelle Mallette. E-mail slaisad@interchange.ubc.ca.

University of Toronto, Faculty of Info., 140 George St., Toronto, ON M5S 3G6. Seamus Ross, dean. Tel. 416-978-3202, fax 416-978-5762, e-mail inquire.ischool@utoronto. ca, World Wide Web http://www.ischool. utoronto.ca. Admissions contact: Adriana Rossini. Tel. 416-978-8589, e-mail adriana. rossini@utoronto.ca.

University of Western Ontario, Grad. Programs in Lib. and Info. Science, Faculty of Info. and Media Studies, Room 240, North Campus Bldg., London, ON N6A 5B7. Thomas Carmichael, dean. Tel. 519-661-4017, fax 519-661-3506, e-mail mlisinfo@uwo.ca, World Wide Web http://fims.uwo.ca. Admissions contact: Shelley Long.

Library Scholarship Sources

For a more complete list of scholarships, fellowships, and assistantships offered for library study, see *Financial Assistance for Library and Information Studies,* published annually by the American Library Association (ALA). The document is also available on the ALA website at http://www.ala.org/ala/educationcareers/education/financialassistance/index.cfm.

American Association of Law Libraries. (1) A varying number of scholarships of varying amounts for graduates of an accredited law school who are degree candidates in an ALA-accredited library school; (2) a varying number of scholarships of varying amounts for library school graduates working on a law degree and non-law graduates enrolled in an ALA-accredited library school; (3) the George A. Strait Minority Stipend for varying numbers of minority librarians working toward a library or law degree; and (4) a varying number of $200 scholarships for law librarians taking courses relating to law librarianship. For information, write to: AALL Scholarship Committee, 105 W. Adams, Suite 3300, Chicago, IL 60603.

American Library Association. (1) The Marshall Cavendish Scholarship and (2) the David H. Clift Scholarship, both of $3,000, for two students who have been admitted to ALA-accredited library schools; (3) the Tom and Roberta Drewes Scholarship of $3,000 for library support staff; (4) the Mary V. Gaver Scholarship of $3,000 for an individual specializing in youth services; (5) the Miriam L. Hornback Scholarship of $3,000 for an ALA or library support staff member; (6) the Christopher J. Hoy/ERT Scholarship of $5,000 for a student who has been admitted to an ALA-accredited library school; (7) the Tony B. Leisner Scholarship of $3,000 for a library support staff member; (8) the Peter Lyman Memorial/Sage Scholarship in New Media of $2,500 for a student admitted to an ALA-accredited library school who will specialize in new media; (9) the Cicely Phippen Marks Scholarship of $1,500 for a student admitted to an ALA-accredited program who will specialize in federal librarianship; (10) Spectrum Initiative Scholarships of $6,500 for a varying number of minority students admitted to a master's de-

gree program at an ALA-accredited library school. For information, write to: ALA Scholarship Clearinghouse, 50 E. Huron St., Chicago, IL 60611, or see http://www.ala.org/scholarships.

ALA/Association for Library Service to Children. (1) The Bound to Stay Bound Books Scholarship of $7,000 each for four U.S. or Canadian citizens who have been admitted to an ALA-accredited master's or doctoral program, and who will work with children in a library for one year after graduation; (2) the Frederic G. Melcher Scholarship of $6,000 each for two U.S. or Canadian citizens admitted to an ALA-accredited library school who will work with children in school or public libraries for one year after graduation. For information, write to: ALA Scholarship Clearinghouse, 50 E. Huron St., Chicago, IL 60611, or see http://www.ala.org/scholarships.

ALA/Association of College and Research Libraries and Thomson Reuters. (1) The ACRL Doctoral Dissertation Fellowship of $1,500 for a student who has completed all coursework, and submitted a dissertation proposal that has been accepted, in the area of academic librarianship; (2) the Samuel Lazerow Fellowship of $1,000 for a research, travel, or writing project in acquisitions or technical services in an academic or research library; (3) the ACRL and Coutts Nijhoff International West European Specialist Study Grant of $3,000 to pay travel expenses, room, and board for a ten-day trip to Europe for an ALA member (selection is based on a proposal outlining the purpose of the trip). Application is electronic only at http://www.ala.org/acrl/awards/researchawards.

ALA/Association of Specialized and Cooperative Library Agencies. Century Scholarship of up to $2,500 for a varying number of disabled U.S. or Canadian citizens admitted to an ALA-accredited library school. For information, write to: ALA Scholarship Clearinghouse, 50 E. Huron St., Chicago, IL 60611, or see http://www.ala.org/scholarships.

ALA/International Relations Committee. The Bogle Pratt International Library Travel Fund grant of $1,000 for a varying number of ALA members to attend a first international conference. For information, write to: Michael Dowling, ALA/IRC, 50 E. Huron St., Chicago, IL 60611.

ALA/Library and Information Technology Association. (1) The LITA/Christian Larew Memorial Scholarship of $3,000 for a disabled U.S. or Canadian citizen admitted to an ALA-accredited library school; (2) the LITA/OCLC Minority Scholarship in Library and Information Technology of $3,000 and (3) the LITA/LSSI Minority Scholarship of $2,500, each for a minority student admitted to an ALA-accredited program. For information, write to: ALA Scholarship Clearinghouse, 50 E. Huron St., Chicago, IL 60611, or see http://www.ala.org/scholarships.

ALA/Public Library Association. The Demco New Leaders Travel Grant Study Award of up to $1,500 for a varying number of PLA members with MLS degrees and five years or less experience. For information, write to: PLA Awards Program, ALA/PLA, 50 E. Huron St., Chicago, IL 60611.

American-Scandinavian Foundation. Fellowships and grants for 25 to 30 students, in amounts from $5,000 to $23,000, for advanced study in Denmark, Finland, Iceland, Norway, or Sweden. For information, write to: Fellowships and Grants, American-Scandinavian Foundation, 58 Park Ave., New York, NY 10026, or see http://www.amscan.org/fellowships_grants.html.

Association for Library and Information Science Education (ALISE). A varying number of research grants of up to $2,500 each for members of ALISE. For information, write to: Association for Library and Information Science Education, 65 E. Wacker Place, Suite 1900, Chicago, IL 60601.

Association of Bookmobile and Outreach Services (ABOS). (1) The Bernard Vavrek Scholarship of $1,000 for a student with a grade-point average of 3.0 or better admitted to an ALA-accredited program and interested in becoming an outreach/bookmobile librarian; (2) the John Philip Award of $300 to recognize outstanding contributions and leadership by an individual in bookmobile and outreach services; (3) the Carol Hole Conference Attendance Travel Grant of $500 for a public librarian working in outreach or bookmobile services. For information, write to: President, ABOS, c/o MLNC, 3610 Barrett Office Drive, Suite 206, Ballwin, MO 63021; e-mail abospresident@gmail.com; or visit http://www.abos-outreach.org.

Association of Jewish Libraries. The AJL Scholarship Fund offers up to two scholarships of $1,000 for MLS students who plan to work as Judaica librarians. For information, write to: Shulamith Berger, AJL Scholarship Committee, Yeshiva University Library, 500 W. 185 St., New York, NY 10033.

Association of Seventh-Day Adventist Librarians. The D. Glenn Hilts Scholarship of $1,200 for a member of the Seventh-Day Adventist Church in a graduate library program. For information, write to: Lee Wisel, Association of Seventh-Day Adventist Librarians, Columbia Union College, 7600 Flower Ave., Takoma Park, MD 20912.

Beta Phi Mu. (1) The Sarah Rebecca Reed Scholarship of $2,000 for a person accepted in an ALA-accredited library program; (2) the Frank B. Sessa Scholarship of $1,500 for a Beta Phi Mu member for continuing education; (3) the Harold Lancour Scholarship of $1,750 for study in a foreign country relating to the applicant's work or schooling; (4) the Blanche E. Woolls Scholarship for School Library Media Service of $2,250 for a person accepted in an ALA-accredited library program; (5) the Eugene Garfield Doctoral Dissertation Scholarship of $3,000 for a person who has approval of a dissertation topic. For information, write to Alison M. Lewis, Executive Director, Beta Phi Mu, c/o The iSchool, College of Information Science and Technology, Drexel University, Philadelphia, PA 19104. E-mail e-mail alewis@drexel.edu, World Wide Web http://www.beta-phi-mu.org

Canadian Association of Law Libraries. The Diana M. Priestly Scholarship of $2,500 for a student enrolled in an approved Canadian law school or accredited Canadian library school. For information, write to: Ann Marie Melvin, Librarian, Saskatchewan Court of Appeal, 2425 Victoria Ave., Regina, SK S4P 4W6.

Canadian Federation of University Women. (1) The Alice E. Wilson Award of $6,000 for five mature students returning to graduate studies in any field, with special consideration given to those returning to study after at least three years; (2) the Margaret McWilliams Pre-Doctoral Fellowship of $13,000 for a female student who has completed at least one full year as a full-time student in doctoral-level studies; (3) the Marion Elder Grant Fellowship of $11,000 for a full-time student at any level of a doctoral program; (4) the CFUW Memorial Fellowship of $10,000 for a student who is currently enrolled in a master's program in science, mathematics, or engineering in Canada or abroad; (5) the Beverly Jackson Fellowship of $2,000 for a student over the age of 35 at the time of application who is enrolled in graduate studies at an Ontario university; (6) the 1989 Ecole Polytechnique Commemorative Award of $7,000 for graduate studies in any field; (7) the Bourse Georgette LeMoyne award of $7,000 for graduate study in any field at a Canadian university (the candidate must be studying in French); (8) the Margaret Dale Philp Biennial Award of $3,000 for studies in the humanities or social sciences; (9) the Canadian Home Economics Association Fellowship of $6,000 for a student enrolled in a postgraduate program in Canada. For information, write to: Fellowships Program Manager, Canadian Federation of University Women, 251 Bank St., Suite 305, Ottawa, ON K2P 1X3, Canada, or visit http://www.cfuw.org/en-ca/fellowships/fellowshipsandawards.aspx.

Canadian Library Association. (1) The CLA Dafoe Scholarship of $5,000 and (2) the H. W. Wilson Scholarship of $2,000, each given to a Canadian citizen or landed immigrant to attend an accredited Canadian library school; (3) the Library Research and Development Grant of $1,000 for a member of the Canadian Library Association, in support of theoretical and applied research in library and information science. For information, write to: CLA Membership Services Department, Scholarship Committee, 1150 Morrison Drive, Suite 400, Ottawa, ON K2H 8S9, Canada.

Catholic Library Association. (1) The World Book, Inc., Grant of $1,500 divided among no more than three association members for continuing education in children's or school librarianship; (2) the Rev. Andrew L. Bouwhuis Memorial Scholarship of $1,500 for a student accepted into a graduate program in library science. For information, write to: Scholarship Committee, Catholic Library Association, 205 W. Monroe St., Suite 314, Chicago, IL 60606-5061.

Chinese American Librarians Association. (1) The Sheila Suen Lai Scholarship and (2) the C. C. Seetoo/CALA Conference Travel Scholarship, each $500, to a Chinese descendant who has been accepted in an ALA-accredited program. For information, write to: MengXiong Liu, Clark Library, San José State University, 1 Washington Sq., San Jose, CA 95192-0028.

Church and Synagogue Library Association. The Muriel Fuller Memorial Scholarship of $200 (including texts) for a correspondence course offered by the association. For information, write to: CSLA, 2920 S.W. Dolph Court, Suite 3A, Portland, OR 97280-0357.

Council on Library and Information Resources. (1) The Rovelstad Scholarship in International Librarianship, to enable a student enrolled in an accredited LIS program to attend the IFLA Annual Conference; (2) the A. R. Zipf Fellowship in Information Management of $10,000, to a U.S. citizen enrolled in graduate school who shows exceptional promise for leadership and technical achievement. For more information, write to: A. R. Zipf Fellowship, Council on Library and Information Resources, 1707 L St. N.W., Suite 650, Washington, DC 20036.

Massachusetts Black Librarians' Network. Two scholarships of at least $500 and $1,000 for minority students entering an ALA-accredited master's program in library science with no more than 12 semester hours completed toward a degree. For information, write to: Pearl Mosley, Chair, Massachusetts Black Librarians' Network, 17 Beech Glen St., Roxbury, MA 02119.

Medical Library Association. (1) The Cunningham Memorial International Fellowship of $3,500 for each of two health sciences librarians from countries other than the United States and Canada; (2) a scholarship of $5,000 for a person entering an ALA-accredited library program, with no more than one-half of the program yet to be completed; (3) a scholarship of $5,000 for a minority student for graduate study; (4) a varying number of Research, Development, and Demonstration Project Grants of $100 to $1,000 for U.S. or Canadian citizens, preferably MLA members; (5) the MLA Doctoral Fellowship of $2,000 for doctoral work in medical librarianship or information science; (6) the Rittenhouse Award of $500 for a student enrolled in an ALA-accredited library program or a recent graduate working as a trainee in a library internship program. For information, write to: Professional Development Department, Medical Library Association, 65 E. Wacker Place, Suite 1900, Chicago, IL 60601-7298.

Mountain Plains Library Association. A varying number of grants of up to $600 for applicants who are members of the association and have been for the preceding two years. For information, write to: Judy Zelenski, Executive Secretary, MPLA, 14293 W. Center Drive, Lakewood, SD 80228.

Society of American Archivists. (1) The F. Gerald Ham Scholarship of $7,500 for up to two graduate students in archival education at a U.S. university that meets the society's criteria for graduate education; (2) the Mosaic Scholarship of $5,000 for up to two U.S. or Canadian minority students enrolled in a graduate program in archival administration; (3) the Josephine Foreman Scholarship of $10,000 for a U.S. citizen or permanent resident who is a minority graduate student enrolled in a program in archival administration; (4) the Oliver Wendell Holmes Travel Award to enable foreign students involved in archival training in the United States or Canada to attend the SAA Annual Meeting; (5) the Donald Peterson Student Travel Award of up to $1,000 to enable graduate students or recent graduates to attend the meeting; and (6) the Harold T. Pinkett Minority Student Awards to enable minority students or graduate students to attend the meeting. For details, write to: Debra Noland, Society of American Archivists, 17 N. State St., Suite 1425, Chicago, IL 60607, or visit http://www2. archivists.org/governance/handbook/ section12.

Southern Regional Education Board. A varying number of grants of varying amounts to cover in-state tuition for graduate or postgraduate study in an ALA-accredited library school for residents of various southern U.S. states (qualifying states vary year by year). For information, write to: Academic Common Market, c/o Southern Regional Education Board, 592 Tenth St. N.W., Atlanta, GA 30318-5790.

Special Libraries Association. (1) Three $6,000 scholarships for students interested in special-library work; (2) the Plenum Scholarship of $1,000 and (3) the ISI Scholarship of $1,000, each also for students interested in special-library work; (4) the Affirmative Action Scholarship of $6,000 for a minority student interested in special-library work; and (5) the Pharmaceutical Division Stipend Award of $1,200 for a student with an undergraduate degree in chemistry, life sciences, or pharmacy entering or enrolled in an ALA-accredited program. For information on the first four scholarships, write to: Scholarship Committee, Special Libraries Association, 331 S. Patrick St., Alexandria, VA 22314-3501. For information on the Pharmaceutical Division Stipend, write to: Susan E. Katz, Awards Chair, Knoll Pharmaceuticals Science Information Center, 30 N. Jefferson St., Whippany, NJ 07981.

Library Scholarship and Award Recipients, 2012

Compiled by the staff of the *Library and Book Trade Almanac*

Scholarships and awards are listed by organization.

American Association of Law Libraries (AALL)

AALL and Thomson West/George A. Strait Minority Scholarship. *Winners:* Cattleya Concepcion, Donyele Darrough, Claire Hand.

AALL Distinguished Lectureship. *Winner:* Anne Klinefelter, director of the Law Library and associate professor of law, University of North Carolina School of Law. *Topic:* "Should Librarians Retire the Privacy Ethic?"

AALL Public Access to Government Information Award. *Winner:* Michele Timmons.

AALL Scholarships. *Winners:* (library degree for law school graduates) Katharine Hales; (law degree for library school graduates) Lucie Olejnikova; (dual library degree and law degree) Amy Lipford.

AALL Spectrum Article of the Year Award ($500). *Sponsor:* Wolters Kluwer. *Winner:* Steven A. Lastres for "Collection Development in the Age of the Virtual Law Firm Library."

AALL/Wolters Kluwer Law and Business Research Grant. *Winners:* Julie L. Kimbrough and Leslie A. Street for "Assessing Collection and Holding Patterns for Print Primary Legal Materials: A Fifty-State Database"; Melanie Knapp and Robert Willey for "Comparison of Research Speed and Accuracy Using Westlaw and WestlawNext."

Joseph L. Andrews Bibliographic Award. *Winners:* Richard A. Danner, Michael J. Hannon, Jules Winterton.

Marian Gould Gallagher Distinguished Service Award. To recognize extended and sustained service to law librarianship. *Winners:* Nancy P. Johnson, Harry S. Martin III.

Law Library Advocate Award. To a law library supporter in recognition of his or her substantial contribution toward the advancement and improvement of a state, court, or county law library's service or visibility. *Winner:* William J. Lavery.

Law Library Journal Article of the Year. *Sponsor:* Wolters Kluwer. *Winner:* Sarah Yates for "Black's Law Dictionary: The Making of an American Standard."

Law Library Publications Award. *Winners:* (nonprint division) Library of the U.S. Court of Appeals for the Sixth Circuit for *They Were Soldiers Once. . .* ; (print division) Library of the U.S. Court of Appeals for the Sixth Circuit for *Portraits of Justice: Judges of the United States Court of Appeals for the Sixth Circuit.*

LexisNexis/John R. Johnson Memorial Scholarships. *Winners:* (library degree for law school graduates) Catherine Biondo, Michelle Hook Dewey, Cassie DuBay, Jason Murray; (library degree for non-law school graduates) Rachel Decker, Claire Hand, Jessica Randall; (law degree for library school graduates) Lucie Olejnikova.

Minority Leadership Development Award. *Winner:* Eugenia J. Charles-Newton.

Robert L. Oakley Advocacy Award. To recognize an AALL member who has been an outstanding advocate and has contributed significantly to the AALL policy agenda at the federal, state, local, or international level. *Winner:* Barbara A. Bintliff.

American Library Association (ALA)

ALA Honorary Membership. To recognize outstanding contributions of lasting importance to libraries and librarianship. *Honorees:* Betty J. Turock, U.S. Sen. Jack Reed (D-R.I.).

ALA/Information Today Library of the Future Award ($1,500). For a library, consortium, group of librarians, or support organization for innovative planning for, applications of, or development of patron training programs about information technology in a library setting. *Donor:* Information Today, Inc. *Winner:* Artemis project, a training program developed by Katie Daugert and Lauren Sin for NPR.

ALA Presidential Citations for Innovative International Library Projects. To libraries outside the United States for significant contributions to the people they serve. *Winners:* "The World Is Just a Book Away" projects in Indonesia; Chinese Medicine Digital Projects at Hong Kong Baptist University; Riecken Foundation Community Libraries projects in Guatemala and Honduras; Helsinki (Finland) City Library's "The Urban Office."

Hugh C. Atkinson Memorial Award. For outstanding achievement (including risk taking) by academic librarians that has contributed significantly to improvements in library automation, management, and/or development or research. *Offered by:* ACRL, ALCTS, LLAMA, and LITA divisions. *Winner:* John F. Helmer, executive director, Orbis Cascade Alliance.

Carroll Preston Baber Research Grant (up to $3,000). For innovative research that could lead to an improvement in library services to any specified group(s) of people. *Donor:* Eric R. Baber. *Winners:* Libby Pollard and Melissa Fry for "Assessment of Non-Library Use at the Jeffersonville Township [Indiana] Public Library."

Beta Phi Mu Award ($1,000). For distinguished service in library education. *Donor:* Beta Phi Mu International Library Science Honorary Society. *Winner:* Mary M. Wagner.

Bogle-Pratt International Library Travel Fund Award ($1,000). To ALA member(s) to attend their first international conference. *Donors:* Bogle Memorial Fund and Pratt Institute School of Information and Library Science. *Winner:* Rebecca Kate Miller.

W. Y. Boyd Literary Novel Award. *Winner:* See "Literary Prizes, 2012" in Part 5.

David H. Clift Scholarship ($3,000). To worthy U.S. or Canadian citizens enrolled in an ALA-accredited program toward an MLS degree. *Winner:* Jenna Marie Goodall.

Melvil Dewey Medal ($2,000). To an individual or group for recent creative professional achievement in library management, training, cataloging and classification, and

the tools and techniques of librarianship. *Donor:* OCLC. *Winner:* Beverly P. Lynch.

Tom and Roberta Drewes Scholarship ($3,000). To a library support staff member pursuing a master's degree in an ALA-accredited program. *Donor:* Quality Books. *Winner:* Angela Kroeger.

EBSCO/ALA Conference Sponsorship Award ($1,000). To enable librarians to attend the ALA Annual Conference. *Donor:* EBSCO. *Winners:* Aimee Babcock-Ellis, Yu-Hui Chen, Susan K. S. Grigsby, Danielle Whren Johnson, Ann B. Perham, Susan Ridgeway, Anna Shelton.

Equality Award ($1,000). To an individual or group for an outstanding contribution that promotes equality in the library profession. *Donor:* Scarecrow Press. *Winner:* Patricia M. Y. Wong.

Elizabeth Futas Catalyst for Change Award ($1,000). A biennial award to recognize a librarian who invests time and talent to make positive change in the profession of librarianship. *Donor:* Elizabeth Futas Memorial Fund. *Winner:* Lyn Hopper.

Loleta D. Fyan Public Library Research Grant (up to $10,000). For projects in public library development. *Donor:* Fyan Estate. *Winner:* Carmen Patlan, Waukegan (Illinois) Public Library, for the proposed "Promotoras Ambassador Program," which will establish outreach to underserved Latino residents.

Gale Cengage Learning Financial Development Award ($2,500). To a library organization for a financial development project to secure new funding resources for a public or academic library. *Donor:* Gale Cengage Learning. *Winner:* Cedar Rapids (Iowa) Public Library Foundation.

Mary V. Gaver Scholarship ($3,000). To a student pursuing an MLS degree and specializing in youth services. *Winner:* Mary Hannah Farmer.

Greenwood Publishing Group Award for Best Book in Library Literature ($5,000). To recognize authors of U.S. or Canadian works whose books improve library management principles and practice. *Donor:* ABC-CLIO. *Winner:* R. David Lankes for *The Atlas of New Librarianship* (Association of College and Research Libraries and MIT Press).

Ken Haycock Award for Promoting Librarianship ($1,000). For significant contribution to public recognition and appreciation of librarianship through professional performance, teaching, or writing. *Winner:* Jeanne Drewes, Library of Congress.

Miriam L. Hornback Scholarship ($3,000). To an ALA or library support staff person pursuing a master's degree in library science. *Winner:* Mary Caitlin McMahon.

Paul Howard Award for Courage ($1,000). Awarded biennially to a librarian, library board, library group, or an individual for exhibiting unusual courage for the benefit of library programs or services. *Donor:* Paul Howard Memorial Fund. *Winner:* To be awarded next in 2013.

John Ames Humphry/OCLC/Forest Press Award ($1,000). To one or more individuals for significant contributions to international librarianship. *Donor:* OCLC/Forest Press. *Winner:* Jane Kinney Meyers.

Tony B. Leisner Scholarship ($3,000). To a library support staff member pursuing a master's degree. *Donor:* Tony B. Leisner. *Winner.* Oksana G. Prokhvacheva.

Joseph W. Lippincott Award ($1,000). For distinguished service to the library profession. *Donor:* Joseph W. Lippincott III. *Winner:* Carla J. Stoffle.

Peter Lyman Memorial/Sage Scholarship in New Media ($2,500). To support a student seeking an MLS degree in an ALA-accredited program and pursing a specialty in new media. *Donor:* Sage Publications. *Winner:* Samantha Jane Thomason.

James Madison Award. To recognize efforts to promote government openness. *Winner:* U.S. Rep. Zoe Lofgren (D-Calif.).

Marshall Cavendish Excellence in Library Programming Award ($2,000). To recognize either a school library or public library that demonstrates excellence in library programming by providing programs that have community impact and respond to community need. *Donor:* Marshall Cavendish. *Winner:* Waukegan (Illinois) Public Library for its Early Learning Center.

Marshall Cavendish Scholarship ($3,000). To a worthy U.S. or Canadian citizen to begin an MLS degree in an ALA-accredited program. *Winner:* Corinne Elizabeth Edgerton.

Schneider Family Book Awards. *Winners:* See "Literary Prizes, 2012" in Part 5.

Scholastic Library Publishing National Library Week Grant. ($3,000). For the best public awareness campaign in support of National Library Week. *Donor:* Scholastic Library Publishing. *Winner:* Sacramento (California) Public Library.

Spectrum Doctoral Fellowships. To provide full tuition support and stipends to minority U.S. and Canadian LIS doctoral students. *Donor:* Institute of Museum and Library Services. *Winners:* Not awarded in 2012.

Spectrum Initiative Scholarships ($5,000). To minority students admitted to ALA-accredited library schools. *Donors:* ALA and Institute of Museum and Library Services. *Winners:* Andrea Barkley, Anthony Bishop, Liza Booker, Moddie Breland, Brandon Cal, Brenda Carrillo, Rosa Cesaretti, Leonor Mabel Cortina, Jonathan DaSo, Amanda Davis, Alicia Diego, Orolando Duffus, Monica Figueroa, Melissa Floch, Sarah Gross, Ticha Gwaradzimba, Lori E. Harris, April Hathcock, Heath Horton, Eugene Hsue, Meena Jain, Basheer Kareem, Charlotte King, Monica Lagares, Vivienne Layne, Laura Liang, Kirk MacLeod, Ivelisse Maldonado, Marcia McIntosh, Marisa Mendez-Brady, Justin Mitchell, Sebastian Jose Moya, Christina Nhek, Maria Ornes, Thomas Padilla, Lauren Peters, Levertes Ragland, Saira Raza, Tamara Rhodes, Eva M. L. Rios-Alvarado, Charlotte Roh, Diana Rojas, Jose Miguel Ruiz, Elizabeth Sandoval-Marchand, Angelibel Soto, Christina Stone, June Thammasnong, Connie Thompson, Raina Tuakoi, Alicia Zuniga.

Sullivan Award for Public Library Administrators Supporting Services to Children. To a library supervisor/administrator who has shown exceptional understanding and support of public library services to children. *Donor:* Peggy Sullivan. *Winner:* Lynda Welborn Freas, director of family services, Anythink Libraries, Thornton, Colorado.

H. W. Wilson Library Staff Development Grant ($3,500). To a library organization for a program to further its staff development goals and objectives. *Donor:* H. W. Wilson Company. *Winner:* Virginia Beach Public Library for its staff training program "Petting Zoo."

Women's National Book Association/Ann Heidbreder Eastman Grant ($500). To support library association professional development in a state in which WNBA has a chapter. *Winner:* Not awarded in 2012.

World Book/ALA Information Literacy Goal Awards ($5,000). To promote exemplary information literacy programs in public and school libraries. *Donor:* World Book. *Winners:* Award suspended.

American Association of School Librarians (AASL)

AASL/ABC-CLIO Leadership Grant (up to $1,750). To AASL affiliates for planning and implementing leadership programs at state, regional, or local levels. *Donor:* ABC-CLIO. *Winner:* Iowa Association of School Librarians for "Growing the Next Generation of Leaders: A Leadership Academy."

AASL/Baker & Taylor Distinguished Service Award ($3,000). For outstanding contributions to librarianship and school library development. *Donor:* Baker & Taylor. *Winner:* Sharon Coatney.

AASL Collaborative School Library Award ($2,500). For expanding the role of the library in elementary and/or secondary school education. *Donor:* Highsmith, Inc. *Winners:* Sara Oremland, Darren McNally, Corinne Berletti, and Jessica Park, Albany (California) High School, for their "EDSET" research poster session and podcast project.

AASL Crystal Apple Award. To an individual, individuals, or group for a significant impact on school libraries and students. *Winner:* U.S. Sen. Jack Reed (D-R.I.).

AASL Distinguished School Administrators Award ($2,000). For expanding the role of the library in elementary and/or secondary school education. *Donor:* ProQuest. *Winner:* Mat McRae, Swan Valley High School, Sagninaw, Michigan.

AASL/Frances Henne Award ($1,250). To a school library media specialist with five or fewer years in the profession to attend an AASL regional conference or ALA Annual Conference for the first time. *Donor:* ABC-CLIO. *Winner:* Alisa Auchmoedy-Finck, Marbletown Elementary School, Stone Ridge, New York.

AASL Innovative Reading Grant ($2,500). To support the planning and implementation of an innovative program for children that motivates and encourages reading, especially with struggling readers. *Sponsor:* Capstone Publishers. *Winner:* Kristine Klopp, Lindbergh Elementary School, Madison, Wisconsin.

AASL Research Grants (up to $2,500). *Sponsor:* Capstone. *Winners:* Ann Dutton Ewbank for "The Role of Teacher Unions in School Library Advocacy: Case Study of the British Columbia Teacher-Librarians' Association and the British Columbia Teacher's Federation"; Daniella Smith for "An Examination of the Impact of Resiliency and School Organizational Structures on the Self-Perceived Leadership Behaviors of School Librarians."

Information Technology Pathfinder Award. To library media specialists for innovative approaches to microcomputer applications in the school library media center ($1,000 to the specialist, $500 to the library). *Donor:* Follett Software Company. *Winners:* (elementary) Sally Mays; (secondary) Elizabeth Kahn.

Intellectual Freedom Award ($2,000 plus $1,000 to the media center of the recipient's choice). To a school library media specialist and AASL member who has upheld the principles of intellectual freedom. *Donor:* ProQuest. *Winner:* Not awarded in 2012.

National School Library Media Program of the Year Award ($10,000). For excellence and innovation in outstanding library media programs. *Donor:* Follett Library Resources. *Winners:* Hinsdale Township (Illinois) High School District 86; South Texas Independent School District.

Association for Library Collections and Technical Services (ALCTS)

ALCTS/LBI George Cunha and Susan Swartzburg Preservation Award ($1,250). To recognize cooperative preservation projects and/or individuals or groups that foster collaboration for preservation goals. *Sponsor:* Hollinger Metal Edge. *Winner:* Gregor Trinkaus-Randall.

ALCTS Presidential Citations for Outstanding Service. *Winners:* Louise Ratliff, Deborah Ryszka.

Hugh C. Atkinson Memorial Award. *See under* American Library Association.

Ross Atkinson Lifetime Achievement Award ($3,000). To recognize the contribution of an ALCTS member and library leader who has demonstrated exceptional service to ALCTS and its areas of interest. *Donor:* EBSCO. *Winner:* Pamela Bluh.

Paul Banks and Carolyn Harris Preservation Award ($1,500). To recognize the contribution of a professional preservation specialist who has been active in the field of preservation and/or conservation for library and/or archival materials. *Donor:* Preservation Technologies. *Winner:* Julie Allen Page.

Blackwell's Scholarship Award. See Outstanding Publication Award.

Coutts Award for Innovation in Electronic Resources Management ($2,000). To recognize significant and innovative contributions to electronic collections management and development practice. *Donor:* Coutts Information Services. *Winner:* Lenore England.

First Step Award (Wiley Professional Development Grant). To enable librarians new to the serials field to attend the ALA Annual Conference. *Donor:* John Wiley & Sons. *Winner:* Beth Kumar.

Harrassowitz Award for Leadership in Library Acquisitions ($1,500). For significant contributions by an outstanding leader in the field of library acquisitions. *Donor:* Harrassowitz. *Winner:* Lisa German.

Margaret Mann Citation (includes $2,000 scholarship award to the U.S. or Canadian library school of the winner's choice). To a cataloger or classifier for achievement in the areas of cataloging or classification. *Donor:* Online Computer Library Center (OCLC). *Winner:* Jane Greenberg.

Outstanding Collaboration Citation. For outstanding collaborative problem-solving efforts in the areas of acquisition, access, management, preservation, or archiving of library materials. *Winners:* Queens (New York) Library and the Queens College Libraries Department of Special Collections and Archives, for the Queens Memory Project.

Outstanding Publication Award (formerly the Blackwell's Scholarship Award) ($250). To honor the year's outstanding monograph, article, or original paper in the field of acquisitions, collection development, and related areas of resource development in libraries. *Winner:* "Academic Library Databases and the Problem of Word-Sense Ambiguity," published in the *Journal of Academic Librarianship,* January 2011.

Esther J. Piercy Award ($1,500). To a librarian with no more than ten years' experience for contributions and leadership in the field of library collections and technical services. *Donor:* YBP Library Services. *Winner:* Timothy Strawn.

Edward Swanson Memorial Best of *LRTS* Award ($250). To the author(s) of the year's best paper published in the division's official journal. *Winners:* Erin Stalberg and Christopher Cronin for "Assessing the Cost and Value of Bibliographic Control."

Ulrich's Serials Librarianship Award ($1,500). For distinguished contributions to serials librarianship. *Sponsor:* ProQuest. *Winner:* Valerie Bross.

Association for Library Service to Children (ALSC)

ALSC/Book Wholesalers, Inc. BWI Summer Reading Program Grant ($3,000). To an ALSC member for implementation of an outstanding public library summer reading program for children. *Donor:* Book Wholesalers, Inc. *Winner:* Wichita Falls (Texas) Public Library.

ALSC/Booklist/YALSA Odyssey Award. To the producer of the best audiobook for children and/or young adults available in English in the United States. *Winner:* See "Literary Prizes, 2012" in Part 5.

ALSC/Candlewick Press "Light the Way: Library Outreach to the Underserved" Grant ($3,000). To a library conducting exemplary outreach to underserved populations. *Donor:* Candlewick Press. *Winner:* Memphis (Tennessee) Public Library and Information Center for its "Read With Me, Sign With Me" project.

May Hill Arbuthnot Honor Lectureship. To an author, critic, librarian, historian, or teacher of children's literature who prepares a paper considered to be a significant contribution to the field of children's literature. *Winner:* author Michael Morpurgo.

Mildred L. Batchelder Award. *Winner:* See "Literary Prizes, 2012" in Part 5.

Louise Seaman Bechtel Fellowship ($4,000). For librarians with 12 or more years of professional-level work in children's library collections, to read and study at Baldwin Library, University of Florida, Gainesville. *Donor:* Bechtel Fund. *Winner:* Allison Angell.

Pura Belpré Award. *Winners:* See "Literary Prizes, 2012" in Part 5.

Bookapalooza Program Awards. To provide three libraries with a collection of materials that will help transform their collection. *Winners:* First Regional Library, Hernando, Mississippi; Conley Elementary School Library, Whitman, Massachusetts; Saginaw Chippewa Indian Tribe, Saginaw Chippewa Academy, Mount Pleasant, Michigan.

Bound to Stay Bound Books Scholarships ($7,000). For men and women who intend to pursue an MLS or other advanced degree and who plan to work in the area of library service to children. *Donor:* Bound to Stay Bound Books. *Winners:* Michelle Ahern, Rebecca Baker, Lisa Jordan, Micaela Sanchez.

Randolph Caldecott Medal. *Winner:* See "Literary Prizes, 2012" in Part 5.

Andrew Carnegie Medal. To the U.S. producers of the most distinguished video for children in the previous year. *Sponsor:* Carnegie Corporation of New York. *Winners:* Paul R. Gagne and Melissa Reilly Ellard of Weston Woods Studios for *Children Make Terrible Pets.*

Carnegie-Whitney Awards (up to $5,000). For the preparation of print or electronic reading lists, indexes, or other guides to library resources that promote reading or the use of library resources at any type of library. *Donors:* James Lyman Whitney and Andrew Carnegie Funds. *Winners:* Wesley Boomgaarden for "Logan Elm Press Online Catalogue Raisonné"; Janne Boone for "Horses 101: Resources for Rescue Groups and Horse Advocates"; Wendi Bost for "Celebrate Florida! 500 Years of Hispanic Heritage"; Heather Doran and Helen Tanner for "American Indian History Collection";

Paul Kauppila for "Reggae and Ska Bibliography"; Janalyn Moss and Lisa Martinicik for "Graphic History: A Database for Graphic Novels about History"; Jere Odell for "Conscientious Objection in the Healing Professions: A Reader's Guide to the Ethical and Social Issues"; Frances Yates for "Seeing the World Through a Different Lens: Diversity in International Youth Films."

Century Scholarship (up to $2,500). For a library school student or students with disabilities admitted to an ALA-accredited library school. *Winner:* Anthony Trocchia.

Distinguished Service Award ($1,000). To recognize significant contributions to, and an impact on, library services to children and/ or ALSC. *Winner:* Linda A. Perkins.

Theodor Seuss Geisel Award. *Winner:* See "Literary Prizes, 2012" in Part 5.

Maureen Hayes Author/Illustrator Visit Award (up to $4,000). For an honorarium and travel expenses to make possible a library talk to children by a nationally known author/illustrator. *Sponsor:* Simon & Schuster Children's Publishing. *Winner:* Hartford (Connecticut) Public Library,

Frederic G. Melcher Scholarships ($6,000). To two students entering the field of library service to children for graduate work in an ALA-accredited program. *Winners:* Katie Clausen, Eileen Gilbert.

John Newbery Medal. *Winner:* See "Literary Prizes, 2012" in Part 5.

Penguin Young Readers Group Awards ($600). To children's librarians in school or public libraries with ten or fewer years of experience to attend the ALA Annual Conference. *Donor:* Penguin Young Readers Group. *Winners:* Heather Schubert, Eric Barbus, Linda Klein, Donna Alvis.

Robert F. Sibert Medal. *Winner:* See "Literary Prizes, 2012" in Part 5.

Laura Ingalls Wilder Medal. *Winner:* See "Literary Prizes, 2012" in Part 5.

Association of College and Research Libraries (ACRL)

ACRL Academic or Research Librarian of the Year Award ($5,000). For outstanding contribution to academic and research librarianship and library development. *Donor:* YBP Library Services. *Winner:* Paula Kaufman.

ACRL/CLS ProQuest Innovation in College Librarianship Award ($3,000). To academic librarians who show a capacity for innovation in the areas of programs, services, and operations; or creating innovations for library colleagues that facilitate their ability to better serve the library's community. *Winners:* Anne Burke, Adrienne Lai, and Adam Rogers, North Carolina State University Libraries.

ACRL/DLS Routledge Distance Learning Librarian Conference Sponsorship Award ($1,200). To an ACRL member working in distance-learning librarianship in higher education. *Winner:* Johanna Ruth Tuñón.

ACRL/EBSCO Community College Learning Resources Leadership/Library Program Achievement Awards ($500). To recognize outstanding achievement in library programs or leadership. *Sponsor:* EBSCO. *Winners:* Sheila Afnan-Manns, Kandice Mickelsen, Reyes Medrano.

ACRL/EBSS Distinguished Education and Behavioral Sciences Librarian Award ($2,500). To an academic librarian who has made an outstanding contribution as an education and/or behavioral sciences librarian through accomplishments and service to the profession. *Donor:* John Wiley & Sons. *Winner:* Scott Walter.

ACRL Special Presidential Recognition Award. To recognize an individual's special career contributions to ACRL and the library profession. *Winner:* Not awarded in 2012.

ACRL/STS Innovation in Science and Technology Librarianship Award ($3,000). To recognize creative, innovative approaches to solving problems or improving products and services in science and technology librarianship. *Sponsor* IEEE. *Winners:* Not awarded in 2012.

ACRL/WGSS Award for Career Achievement in Women and Gender Studies Librarianship. *Winner:* Ellen Greenblatt.

ACRL/WGSS Award for Significant Achievement in Women and Gender Studies Librarianship. *Winners:* Kayo Denda, Alicia Graham Rhonda Marker and Li Sun of Rutgers University Libraries, Kirsten Canfield and Lucy Vidal of Rutgers' Center for Women's Global Leadership.

Hugh C. Atkinson Memorial Award. *See under* American Library Association.

Miriam Dudley Instruction Librarian Award. For a contribution to the advancement of bibliographic instruction in a college or research institution. *Winner:* Barbara J. Mann.

Excellence in Academic Libraries Awards ($3,000).To recognize outstanding community college, college, and university libraries. *Donor:* YBP Library Services. *Winners:* (university) Grand Valley State University, Allendale, Michigan; (college) Champlain College, Burlington, Vermont; (community college) Seattle (Washington) Central Community College.

Instruction Section Innovation Award ($3,000). To librarians or project teams in recognition of a project that demonstrates creative, innovative, or unique approaches to information literacy instruction or programming. *Donor:* ProQuest. *Winners:* Joshua Vossler and John Watts for a series of information literacy videos, a collaborative professional development project created in cooperation with Coastal Carolina University's First Year Experience Program.

Marta Lange/CQ Press Award ($1,000). To recognize an academic or law librarian for contributions to bibliography and information service in law or political science. *Donor:* CQ Press. *Winner:* John Eaton.

Samuel Lazerow Fellowship for Research in Collections and Technical Services in Academic and Research Libraries. To foster advances in acquisitions or technical services by providing librarians a fellowship for travel or writing in those fields. *Winner:* Award discontinued.

Katharine Kyes Leab and Daniel J. Leab American Book Prices Current Exhibition Catalog Awards (citations). For the best catalogs published by American or Canadian institutions in conjunction with exhibitions of books and/or manuscripts. *Winners:* (expensive) Department of Prints and Drawings, Art Institute of Chicago, for "Altered and Adorned: Using Renaissance Prints in Daily Life"; (moderately expensive) University of Chicago Library for "Adventures in the Soviet Imaginary: Children's Books and Graphic Art"; (inexpensive) Chicago Public Library Special Collections and Preservation Division for "One Book, Many Interpretations: Second Edition"; (brochures) University of Pennsylvania Rare Book and

Manuscript Library for "Wharton Esherick and the Birth of the American Modern"; (electronic exhibitions) Folger Shakespeare Library for "Manifold Greatness: The Creation and Afterlife of the King James Bible" (http://www.manifoldgreatness.org).

Oberly Award for Bibliography in the Agricultural or Natural Sciences. Awarded biennially for the best English-language bibliography in the field of agriculture or a related science in the preceding two-year period. *Winner:* To be awarded next in 2013.

Ilene F. Rockman Instruction Publication of the Year Award ($3,000). To recognize an outstanding publication relating to instruction in a library environment. *Sponsor:* Emerald Group Publishing. *Winner:* Char Booth, Claremont Colleges Library, for *Reflective Teaching, Effective Learning: Instructional Literacy for Library Educators* (ALA Editions).

WESS De Gruyter European Librarianship Study Grant (formerly the Coutts Nijhoff International West European Specialist Study Grant) (€2,500). Supports research pertaining to European studies, librarianship, or the book trade. *Sponsor:* Walter de Gruyter Foundation for Scholarship and Research. *Winner:* Liladhar R. Pendse for his project to construct a bibliography and subject analysis of Indo-Portuguese periodicals held by the National Library of Portugal and other libraries in Lisbon.

Association of Library Trustees, Advocates, Friends and Foundations (ALTAFF). See United for Libraries.

Association of Specialized and Cooperative Library Agencies (ASCLA)

ASCLA Cathleen Bourdon Service Award. To recognize an ASCLA personal member for outstanding service and leadership to the division. *Winner:* Kathleen Moeller-Peiffe.

ASCLA Exceptional Service Award. To recognize exceptional service to patients, the homebound, inmates, and to medical, nursing, and other professional staff in hospitals. *Winner:* Kathleen Hegarty.

ASCLA Leadership and Professional Achievement Award. To recognize leadership and achievement in the areas of consulting, multitype library cooperation, statewide service and programs, and state library development. *Winner:* Laura Sherbo, branch library services program manager, Washington State Library.

Francis Joseph Campbell Award. For a contribution of recognized importance to library service for the blind and physically handicapped. *Winner:* Carole Rose, Indiana Talking Book and Braille Library.

KLAS/National Organization on Disability Award for Library Service to People with Disabilities ($1,000). To a library organization to recognize an innovative project to benefit people with disabilities. *Donors:* Aetna Inc., Keystone Systems, JCPenney Co. *Winner:* Port Washington (New York) Public Library for its "Books for Dessert" program for adults with intellectual and developmental disabilities.

Black Caucus of the American Library Association (BCALA)

BCALA Trailblazer's Award. Presented once every five years in recognition of outstanding and unique contributions to librarianship. *Winner:* To be awarded next in 2015.

DEMCO/BCALA Excellence in Librarianship Award. To a librarian who has made significant contributions to promoting the status of African Americans in the library profession. *Winner:* Andrew P. Jackson (Sekou Molefi Baako).

Ethnic and Multicultural Information and Exchange Round Table (EMIERT)

David Cohen Multicultural Award ($300). To recognize articles of significant research and publication that increase understanding and promote multiculturalism in North American libraries. *Donor:* Routledge. *Winner:* To be awarded next in 2014.

EMIERT Distinguished Librarian Award. To recognize significant accomplishments in library services that are national or international in scope and that include improving, spreading, and promoting multicultural librarianship. *Winner:* To be awarded next in 2013.

Gale Multicultural Award ($1,000). For outstanding achievement and leadership in serving the multicultural/multiethnic community. *Donor:* Gale Research. *Winner:* Not awarded in 2012.

Exhibits Round Table (ERT)

Christopher J. Hoy/ERT Scholarship ($5,000). To an individual or individuals who will work toward an MLS degree in an ALA-accredited program. *Donor:* Family of Christopher Hoy. *Winner:* Lora Lyn Worden.

Federal and Armed Forces Librarians Round Table (FAFLRT)

FAFLRT Achievement Award. For achievement in the promotion of library and information service and the information profession in the federal government community. *Winner:* Not awarded n in 2012.

FAFLRT Adelaide del Frate Conference Sponsorship Award ($1,000). To encourage library school students to become familiar with federal librarianship and ultimately seek work in federal libraries; for attendance at ALA Annual Conference and activities of FAFLRT. *Winner:* Lee C. Lipscomb.

Distinguished Service Award (citation). To honor a FAFLRT member for outstanding and sustained contributions to the association and to federal librarianship. *Winner:* Helen Q. Sherman, Defense Technical Information Center.

Cicely Phippen Marks Scholarship ($1,500). To a library school student with an interest in working in a federal library. *Winner:* Katie Rapp.

Rising Star Award. To a FAFLRT member new to the profession in a federal or armed forces library or government information management setting. *Winner:* Caralyn Champa, U.S. Army Knowledge Leaders Program.

Gay, Lesbian, Bisexual, and Transgendered Round Table (GLBTRT)

Stonewall Book Awards. *Winners:* See "Literary Prizes, 2012" in Part 5.

Government Documents Round Table (GODORT)

James Bennett Childs Award. To a librarian or other individual for distinguished lifetime contributions to documents librarianship. *Winner:* John B. Phillips, Oklahoma State University.

Bernadine Abbott Hoduski Founders Award. To recognize documents librarians who may not be known at the national level but who have made significant contributions to the field of local, state, federal, or international documents. *Winner:* Not awarded in 2012.

Margaret T. Lane/Virginia F. Saunders Memorial Research Award. *Winner:* Harold C. Relyea for "The Federal Register: Origins, Formulation, Realization, and Heritage" in *Government Information Quarterly,* July 2011.

NewsBank/Readex Catharine J. Reynolds Award. To documents librarians for travel and/or study in the field of documents librarianship or an area of study benefiting their performance. *Donor:* NewsBank and Readex Corporation. *Winners:* Helen Sheehy, Social Sciences Library, Pennsylvania State University; Kristene Unsworth, iSchool, Drexel University.

ProQuest/GODORT/ALA Documents to the People Award. To an individual, library, organization, or noncommercial group that most effectively encourages or enhances the use of government documents in library services. *Winner:* Association of Southeastern Research Libraries (ASERL) Collaborative Federal Depository Program (CFDP).

W. David Rozkuszka Scholarship ($3,000). To provide financial assistance to an individual who is currently working with government documents in a library while completing a master's program in library science. *Winner:* Not awarded in 2012.

Intellectual Freedom Round Table (IFRT)

John Phillip Immroth Memorial Award for Intellectual Freedom ($500). For notable contribution to intellectual freedom fueled by personal courage. *Winners:* Not awarded in 2012.

Eli M. Oboler Memorial Award. *Winner:* See "Literary Prizes, 2012" in Part 5.

ProQuest/SIRS State and Regional Achievement Award ($1,000). To an innovative and effective intellectual freedom project covering a state or region during the calendar year. *Donor:* ProQuest Social Issues Resource Series (SIRS). *Winner:* Award discontinued in 2011.

Library and Information Technology Association (LITA)

Hugh C. Atkinson Memorial Award. *See under* American Library Association.

Ex Libris Student Writing Award ($1,000 and publication in *Information Technology and Libraries*). For the best unpublished manuscript on a topic in the area of libraries and information technology written by a student or students enrolled in an ALA-accredited library and information studies graduate program. *Donor:* Ex Libris. *Winner:* Cynthia Cohen for "Extending LOCKSS: The Preservation Risks of Private LOCKSS Networks."

LITA/Christian Larew Memorial Scholarship ($3,000). To encourage the entry of qualified persons into the library and information technology field. *Sponsor:* Informata.com. *Winner:* William Edward Jones III.

LITA/Library Hi Tech Award ($1,000). To an individual or institution for a work that shows outstanding communication for continuing education in library and information technology. *Donor:* Emerald Group Publishing. *Winner:* Clifford Lynch, executive director, Coalition for Networked Information (CNI).

LITA/LSSI Minority Scholarship in Library and Information Technology ($2,500). To encourage a qualified member of a principal minority group to work toward an MLS degree in an ALA-accredited program with emphasis on library automation. *Donor:* Library Systems and Services. *Winner:* Brenda Bridgett Carrillo.

LITA/OCLC Frederick G. Kilgour Award for Research in Library and Information Technology ($2,000 and expense-paid attendance at the ALA Annual Conference). To bring attention to research relevant to the development of information technologies.

Donor: OCLC. *Winner:* G. Sayeed Choudhury, Sheridan Libraries, Johns Hopkins University.

LITA/OCLC Minority Scholarship in Library and Information Technology ($3,000). To encourage a qualified member of a principal minority group to work toward an MLS degree in an ALA-accredited program with an emphasis on library automation. *Donor:* OCLC. *Winner:* Eugene D. Hsue.

LITA/OITP Award for Cutting-Edge Technology in Library Services. To honor libraries that are serving their communities with novel and innovative methods. *Winners:* Boston College High School's Corcoran Library, Boston; Goethe-Institut New York Library and Pratt Institute School of Information and Library Science, New York; University of Arizona Libraries, Tucson; Orange County (Florida) Library System, Orlando; Genesee Valley Educational Partnership School Library System, Le Roy, New York.

Library History Round Table (LHRT)

Phyllis Dain Library History Dissertation Award ($500). Awarded biennially to the author of a dissertation treating the history of books, libraries, librarianship, or information science. *Winner:* Not awarded in 2012.

Donald G. Davis Article Award (certificate). Awarded biennially for the best article written in English in the field of U.S. and Canadian library history. *Winner:* Bernadette Lear for "Yankee Librarian in the Diamond City: Hannah Packard James, the Osterhout Free Library of Wilkes-Barre, and the Public Library Movement in Pennsylvania," in *Pennsylvania History: A Journal of Mid-Atlantic Studies* 78, 124–162.

Eliza Atkins Gleason Book Award. Presented every third year to the author of the best book in English in the field of library history. *Winner:* To be awarded next in 2013.

Justin Winsor Prize Essay ($100). Awarded biennially to the author of an outstanding essay embodying original historical research on a significant subject of library history. *Winner:* Ashley Maynor for "All the World's Memory: Implications for the Internet as Archive and Portal for Our Cultural Heritage."

Library Leadership and Management Association (LLAMA)

Hugh C. Atkinson Memorial Award. *See under* American Library Association.

John Cotton Dana Library Public Relations Awards. To libraries or library organizations of all types for public relations programs or special projects ended during the preceding year. *Donors:* H. W. Wilson Foundation and EBSCO. *Winners:* Arlington (Texas) Public Library; Cedar Rapids (Iowa) Public Library; Cleve J. Fredricksen Library, Camp Hill, Pennsylvania; Contra Costa County Library, Pleasant Hill, California; Emily Jones Pointer Library, Hernando, Mississippi; King County Library System, Issaquah, Washington; Minnesota Department of Transportation, Saint Paul; Utah Valley University, Orem.

Library Research Round Table (LRRT)

Jesse H. Shera Award for Distinguished Published Research. For a research article on library and information studies published in English during the calendar year. *Winners:* Shana Pribesh, Karen Gavigan, and Gail Dickinson for "The Access Gap: Poverty and Characteristics of School Library Media Centers" in *Library Quarterly,* April 2011.

Jesse H. Shera Award for Support of Dissertation Research. To recognize and support dissertation research employing exemplary research design and methods. *Winner:* Victor J. Sensenig for "Public Libraries and Literacy in Ecological Perspective."

Map and Geospatial Information Round Table (MAGIRT)

MAGIRT Honors Award. *Winners:* David Allen, Mary McInroy.

New Members Round Table (NMRT)

NMRT/Marshall Cavendish Award (tickets to the Newbery/Caldecott/Wilder Banquet at the ALA Annual Conference). *Winners:* April Grey, Kristin Maria Hylton.

Shirley Olofson Memorial Award ($1,000). To an individual to help defray costs of attending the ALA Annual Conference. *Winner:* Kirby McCurtis.

Student Chapter of the Year Award. To an ALA student chapter for outstanding contributions to the association. *Winner:* Student Chapter at San José State University.

3M/NMRT Professional Development Grant. To new NMRT members to encourage professional development and participation in national ALA and NMRT activities. *Donor:* 3M. *Winner:* Amy Honisett.

Office for Diversity

Achievement in Library Diversity Research Honor. To an ALA member who has made significant contributions to diversity research in the profession. *Winner:* Richard Chabrán, adjunct professor, School of Information Resources and Library Science, University of Arizona.

Diversity Research Grants ($2,500). To the authors of research proposals that address critical gaps in the knowledge of diversity issues within library and information science. *Winners:* Jamie C. Naidoo and Lance Simpson for "Beyond Broken Borders: Examining Library Services to Latino and Spanish-Speaking Populations in New Latino South States with Anti-Immigration Laws"; Danny P. Wallace for "LIS Diversity: A Longitudinal Study of the ALISE Statistics"; Wayne A. Wiegand for "This Hallowed Place: The Desegregation of Public Libraries in the American South, 1954–1968."

Office for Information Technology Policy

L. Ray Patterson Copyright Award. To recognize an individual who supports the constitutional purpose of U.S. copyright law, fair use, and the public domain. *Sponsor:* Freedom to Read Foundation. *Winner:* Winston Tabb.

Office for Intellectual Freedom

Freedom to Read Foundation Gordon M. Conable Conference Scholarship. To enable a library school student or new professional to attend the ALA Annual Conference. *Winner:* Steven Booth.

Freedom to Read Foundation Roll of Honor (citation): To recognize individuals who have contributed substantially to the foundation. *Winner:* Michael A. Bamberger, general counsel, the Media Coalition.

Office for Literacy and Outreach Services (OLOS)

Jean E. Coleman Library Outreach Lecture. *Sponsor:* OLOS Advisory Committee. *Winner:* Carol Brey-Casiano.

Diversity and Outreach Fair Awards. To outreach librarians for their institutions' diversity-in-action initiatives. *Winners:* (first place) California State Library for "Libraries Help CA Get Back to Work"; (second place) University of Illinois GSLIS for "Mix IT Up"; (third place) University of Wisconsin–Madison School of Library and Information Studies for "Convening Culture Keepers: Building Connections Between Library Students and American Indian Communities."

Estela and Raúl Mora Award ($1,000 and plaque). For exemplary programs celebrating Día de Los Niños/Día de Los Libros. *Winner:* Lynden Public Library, Whatcom County (Washington) Library System.

Public Awareness Committee

Scholastic Library Publishing National Library Week Grant ($3,000). To libraries or library associations of all types for a public awareness campaign in connection with National Library Week in the year the grant is awarded. *Sponsor:* Scholastic Library Publishing. *Winner:* Sacramento (California) Public Library for "You belong @ your library," a series of programs aimed at the gay, lesbian, bisexual, transgender, questioning, intersex, and ally (GLBTQIA) community.

Public Library Association (PLA)

Advancement of Literacy Award (plaque). To a publisher, bookseller, hardware and/or software dealer, foundation, or similar group that has made a significant contribution to the advancement of adult literacy. *Winner:* Award discontinued.

Baker & Taylor Entertainment Audio Music/Video Product Grant ($2,500 worth of audio music or video products). To help a public library to build or expand a collection of either or both formats. *Donor:* Baker & Tay-

lor. *Winner:* Tuscaloosa (Alabama) Public Library.

Gordon M. Conable Award ($1,500). To a public library staff member, library trustee, or public library for demonstrating a commitment to intellectual freedom and the Library Bill of Rights. *Sponsor:* LSSI. *Winner:* Not awarded in 2012.

Demco New Leaders Travel Grants (up to $1,500). To PLA members who have not attended a major PLA continuing education event in the past five years. *Winners:* Lisa Brock, Richard Lyda, Kirby McCurtis, April Wallace.

EBSCO Excellence in Small and/or Rural Public Service Award ($1,000). Honors a library serving a population of 10,000 or less that demonstrates excellence of service to its community as exemplified by an overall service program or a special program of significant accomplishment. *Donor:* EBSCO. *Winner:* Kinsley (Kansas) Public Library.

Highsmith Library Innovation Award ($2,000). To recognize a public library's innovative achievement in planning and implementing a creative community service program. *Donor:* Highsmith. *Winner:* San Diego County (California) Public Library for its efforts with partner Housing Opportunities Collaborative to provide foreclosure prevention clinics.

Allie Beth Martin Award ($3,000). To honor a public librarian who has demonstrated extraordinary range and depth of knowledge about books or other library materials and has distinguished ability to share that knowledge. *Donor:* Baker & Taylor. *Winner:* Kaite Mediatore Stover, Kansas City (Missouri) Public Library.

Polaris Innovation in Technology John Iliff Award. To a library worker, librarian, or library for the use of technology and innovative thinking as a tool to improve services to public library users. *Sponsor:* Polaris. *Winner:* Kinsley (Kansas) Public Library.

Charlie Robinson Award. To honor a public library director who, over a period of seven years, has been a risk taker, an innovator, and/or a change agent in a public library. *Donor:* Baker & Taylor. *Winner:* Pam Sandlian Smith, Anythink Libraries, Adams County, Colorado.

Romance Writers of America Library Grant ($4,500). To a library to build or expand a fiction collection and/or host romance fiction programming. *Donor:* Romance Writers of America. *Winner:* Tuscaloosa (Alabama) Public Library.

Public Programs Office

Sara Jaffarian School Library Program Award for Exemplary Humanities Programming ($4,000). To honor a K–8 school library that has conducted an outstanding humanities program or series. *Donors:* Sara Jaffarian and ALA Cultural Communities Fund. *Winner:* Inter-American Magnet School, Chicago.

Reference and User Services Association (RUSA)

ABC-CLIO Online History Award ($3,000). A biennial award to recognize professional achievement in historical reference and librarianship. *Donor:* ABC-CLIO. *Winners:* To be awarded next in 2013.

ALA/RUSA Zora Neale Hurston Award. To recognize the efforts of RUSA members in promoting African American literature. *Sponsored by:* Harper Perennial Publishing. *Winner:* Vanessa Irvin Morris, assistant professor, Drexel University.

Virginia Boucher-OCLC Distinguished ILL Librarian Award ($2,000). To a librarian for outstanding professional achievement, leadership, and contributions to interlibrary loan and document delivery. *Winner:* Cyril Oberlander, Milne Library, State University of New York, Geneseo.

BRASS Award for Outstanding Service to Minority Business Communities ($2,000). To a librarian or library to recognize creation of an innovative service to a minority business community or achievement of recognition from that community for providing outstanding service. *Winner:* Award suspended in 2011.

BRASS Business Expert Press Award for Academic Business Librarians ($1,250). To recognize a librarian new to the field of academic business librarianship and support his or her attendance at the ALA Annual Conference. *Sponsor:* Business Expert Press. *Winner:* Joel Glogowski.

BRASS Emerald Research Grant Awards ($5,000). To ALA members seeking support to conduct research in business librarianship. *Donor:* Emerald Group Publishing. *Winners:* Kerry Wu and Heidi E. K. Senior; Louise Mort Feldmann.

BRASS Gale Cengage Learning Student Travel Award ($1,000). To enable a student enrolled in an ALA-accredited master's program to attend the ALA Annual Conference. *Donor:* Gale Cengage Learning. *Winner:* Ilana Barnes.

Sophie Brody Medal. *Winner:* See "Literary Prizes, 2012" in Part 5.

Gale Cengage Award for Excellence in Business Librarianship ($3,000). For distinguished activities in the field of business librarianship *Donor:* Gale Cengage Learning. *Winner:* Rita W. Moss.

Gale Cengage Award for Excellence in Reference and Adult Library Services ($3,000). To recognize a library or library system for developing an imaginative and unique library resource to meet patrons' reference needs. *Donor:* Gale Cengage Learning. *Winner:* Richland County (South Carolina) Public Library Job Center.

Genealogical Publishing Company/History Section Award ($1,500). To encourage and commend professional achievement in historical reference and research librarianship. *Donor:* Genealogical Publishing Company. *Winner:* Jay L. Verkler.

MARS Achievement Recognition Certificate ("My Favorite Martian Award"). To recognize excellence in service to the RUSA section MARS—Emerging Technologies in Reference. *Winner:* Carolyn S. Larson.

Margaret E. Monroe Library Adult Services Award (citation). To a librarian for his or her impact on library service to adults. *Winner:* Neal Wyatt.

Morningstar Public Librarian Support Award ($1,000). To support attendance at the ALA Annual Conference of a public librarian who has performed outstanding business reference service. *Donor:* Morningstar. *Winner:* Anne MacDonald.

Isadore Gilbert Mudge–Gale Cengage Award ($5,000). For distinguished contributions to reference librarianship. *Donor:* Gale Cengage Learning. *Winner:* Robert Kieft.

Reference Service Press Award ($2,500). To the author or authors of the most outstanding article published in *RUSQ* during the preceding two volume years. *Donor:* Reference Service Press. *Winners:* Nancy D. Zionts, Janice H. Apter, Julianna Kuchta, and Pamela K. Greenhouse for "Promoting Consumer Health Literacy: Creation of a Health Information Librarian Fellowship" (*RUSQ* 49:4 Summer 2009); and Marie L. Radford, Lynn Silipigni Connaway, Patrick A. Confer, Susanna Sabolcsi-Boros, and Hannah Kwon for "Are We Getting Warmer?: Query Clarification in Live Chat Virtual Reference" (*RUSQ* 50:3 Spring 2010).

John Sessions Memorial Award (plaque). To a library or library system in recognition of work with the labor community. *Donor:* Department for Professional Employees, AFL/CIO. *Winner:* Labor Archives and Research Center, San Francisco State University.

Louis Shores–Greenwood Publishing Group Award ($3,000). To an individual, team, or organization to recognize excellence in reviewing of books and other materials for libraries. *Donor:* Greenwood Publishing Group. *Winner:* Sarah L. Johnson, professor of library services at Eastern Illinois University and author of the blog "Reading the Past."

STARS–Atlas Systems Mentoring Award ($1,250). To a library practitioner new to the field of interlibrary loan, resource sharing, or electronic reserves, to attend the ALA Annual Conference. *Donor:* Atlas Systems. *Winner:* Natalie D. Beam.

Social Responsibilities Round Table (SRRT)

Jackie Eubanks Memorial Award ($500). To honor outstanding achievement in promoting the acquisition and use of alternative media in libraries. *Donor:* SRRT Alternatives in Publication Task Force. *Winner:* Not awarded in 2012.

Coretta Scott King Awards. *Winners:* See "Literary Prizes, 2012" in Part 5.

United for Libraries (formerly ALTAFF, Association of Library Trustees, Advocates, Friends, and Foundations)

Trustee Citations. To recognize public library trustees for individual service to library development on the local, state, regional, or national level. *Winners:* Richard J. Ryan, Gwendolyn B. Guster Welch.

United for Libraries/Baker & Taylor Awards. To recognize library friends groups for outstanding efforts to support their libraries. *Donor:* Baker & Taylor. *Winners:* Batavia (Illinois) Public Library Foundation; Friends of Hackley Public Library, Muskegon, Michigan; Friends of the Troy (Michigan) Public Library.

United for Libraries/Gale Outstanding Trustee Conference Grant Award ($850). *Donor:* Gale Cengage Learning. *Winner:* Karen Parrilli.

United for Libraries Major Benefactors Citation. To individuals, families, or corporate bodies that have made major benefactions to public libraries. *Winner:* Not awarded in 2012.

United for Libraries Public Service Award. To a legislator who has been especially supportive of libraries. *Winner:* U.S. Rep. Rush Holt (D-N.J.).

Young Adult Library Services Association (YALSA)

Alex Awards. *Winners:* See "Literary Prizes, 2012" in Part 5.

Baker & Taylor/YALSA Scholarship Grants ($1,000). To young adult librarians in public or school libraries to attend the ALA Annual Conference for the first time. *Donor:* Baker & Taylor. *Winners:* Susan J. Smallsreed, Heather Schubert.

BWI/YALSA Collection Development Grants ($1,000). To YALSA members who represent a public library and work directly with young adults, for collection development materials for young adults. *Donor:* Book Wholesalers, Inc. *Winners:* Cynthia Shutts, Erik Carlson.

Margaret A. Edwards Award. *Winner:* See "Literary Prizes, 2012" in Part 5.

Great Books Giveaway (books, videos, CDs, and audiocassettes valued at a total of $25,000). *Winner:* Southeast Arkansas Regional Library System, Monticello.

Frances Henne/YALSA/VOYA Research Grant ($1,000). To provide seed money to an individual, institution, or group for a project to encourage research on library service to young adults. *Donor:* Greenwood Publishing Group. *Winner:* Sylvia Vardell.

Michael L. Printz Award. *Winner:* See "Literary Prizes, 2012" in Part 5.

YALSA/ABC-CLIO/Greenwood Publishing Group Service to Young Adults Achievement Award ($2,000). Awarded biennially to a YALSA member who has demonstrated unique and sustained devotion to young adult services. *Donor:* Greenwood Publishing Group. *Winner:* Not awarded in 2012.

YALSA/MAE Award ($500 for the recipient plus $500 for his or her library). For an exemplary young adult reading or literature program. *Sponsor:* Margaret A. Edwards Trust. *Winner:* Allison Cabaj.

YALSA William C. Morris YA Debut Award. *Winner:* See "Literary Prizes, 2012" in Part 5.

YALSA/Sagebrush Award. See YALSA/MAE Award.

American Society for Information Science and Technology (ASIS&T)

ASIS&T Award of Merit. For an outstanding contribution to the field of information science. *Winner:* Michael Buckland, University of California at Berkeley.

ASIS&T Best Information Science Book. *Winner:* Ricardo Baeza-Yates and Berthier Ribeiro-Neto for *Modern Information Retrieval: The Concepts and Technology Behind Search* (ACM).

ASIS&T New Leaders Award. To recruit, engage, and retain new ASIS&T members and to identify potential for new leadership in the society. *Winners:* Jonathan Colman, Jonathan Dorey, Catherine Dumas, Tamara Heck, Fidelia Ibekwe-SanJuan, Dorothy Porter, Elizabeth Rolando, Yin-Leng Theng.

ASIS&T ProQuest Doctoral Dissertation Award ($1,000 plus expense-paid attendance at ASIS&T Annual Meeting). *Winner:* Jaime Snyder, Syracuse University, for "Image-Enabled Discourse: Investigating the Creation of Visual Information as Communicative Practice."

ASIS&T Research in Information Science Award. For a systematic program of research in a single area at a level beyond the single study, recognizing contributions in the field of information science. *Winner:* Kalervo Jarvelin, University of Tampere (Finland).

James M. Cretsos Leadership Award. *Winner:* Naresh Agarwal, Simmons College.

Watson Davis Award. For outstanding continuous contributions and dedicated service to the society. *Winner:* K. T. Vaughan, University of North Carolina at Chapel Hill.

Pratt Severn Best Student Research Paper Award. To encourage student research and writing in the field of information science. *Winner:* April Lynne Earle, St. John's University, for "Design of an Application Profile for the St. John's University Oral History Collection."

Thomson Reuters Doctoral Dissertation Proposal Scholarship ($2,000). *Winner:* Lori McCay-Peet, Dalhousie University, for "At the Intersection: Investigating the Qualities of the Serendipitous Digital Environment and the Serendipity-Prone Person."

Thomson Reuters Outstanding Teacher Award ($1,500). To recognize the unique teaching contribution of an individual as a teacher of information science. *Winner:* Dietmar Wolfram, University of Wisconsin–Milwaukee.

John Wiley Best *JASIST* Paper Award. *Winners:* Sukomal Pal, Mandar Mitra, and Jaap Kamps for "Evaluation Effort, Reliability, and Reusability in XML Retrieval" in *JASIST* 62:2.

Art Libraries Society of North America (ARLIS/NA)

ARLIS/NA Distinguished Service Award. To honor an individual whose exemplary service in art librarianship, visual resources curatorship, or a related field, has made an outstanding national or international contribution to art information. *Winner:* Rosemary Furtak.

ARLIS/NA Internship Award. To provide financial support for students preparing for a career in art librarianship or visual resource librarianship. *Winner:* Lindsey Reynolds.

ARLIS/NA Student Conference Attendance Award. *Winner:* Stephanie Grimm.

ARLIS/NA Worldwide Books Award for Electronic Resources. *Winner:* Not awarded in 2012.

ARLIS/NA Worldwide Books Award for Publications. *Winner:* Eric Michael Wolf for *American Art Museum Architecture: Documents and Design* (Norton).

AskART Conference Attendance Award. *Winner:* Tony White.

Andrew Cahan Photography Award ($1,000). *Winner:* Adam Hess.

Melva J. Dwyer Award. To the creators of exceptional reference or research tools relating to Canadian art and architecture. *Winners:* François-Marc Gagnon, Nancy Senior, and Réal Ouellet for *The Codex Canadensis* (McGill-Queen's University Press).

Judith A. Hoffberg Award for Student Attendance. *Winner:* Effie Patelos.

Howard and Beverly Joy Karno Award. *Winner:* Joyce Weaver.

Gerd Muehsam Award. To one or more graduate students in library science programs to recognize excellence in a graduate paper or project. *Winner:* Katrina Windon for "The Right to Decay with Dignity: Documentation and the Negotiation between an Artist's Sanction and the Cultural Interest."

Merrill Wadsworth Smith Travel Award in Architecture Librarianship. *Winner:* Kathy Edwards.

Student Chapter of the Year award. *Winner:* San José State University.

H. W. Wilson Foundation Research Award. *Winner:* Heather Gendron for "Studio Archives: Voices of Living Artists, Their Assistants, and Archivists/Phase II: Artists Working in Digital and Video Media."

George Wittenborn Memorial Book Awards. *Winner:* See "Literary Prizes, 2012" in Part 5.

Asian/Pacific Americans Libraries Association (APALA)

APALA Emerging Leaders sponsorship (up to $1,000). *Winner:* Tina Chan.

APALA Scholarship ($1,000). For a student of Asian or Pacific background who is enrolled in, or has been accepted into, a master's or doctoral degree program in library and/or information science at an ALA-accredited school. *Winner:* Paul Lai.

APALA Travel Award ($500). To a library professional possessing a master's-level degree in library and/or information science to attend the ALA Annual Conference. *Winner:* Catherine Phan.

Association for Library and Information Science Education (ALISE)

ALISE Award for Teaching Excellence in the Field of Library and Information Science Education. *Winner:* Sandra Hughes-Hassell, University of North Carolina at Chapel Hill.

ALISE Best Conference Paper Award. *Winners:* Kafi Kumasi, Wayne State University, and Renee Franklin Hill, Syracuse University, for "Are We There Yet? Results of a Gap Analysis to Measure LIS Students' Prior Knowledge and Actual Learning of Cultural Competence Concepts"; Bharat Mehra, Kimberly Black, Vandana Singh, and Jenna Nolt, University of Tennessee, for "What Is the Value of LIS Education? A Qualitative Study of the Perspectives of Tennessee's Rural Librarians"; Susan E. Searing, University of Illinois Urbana-Champaign, and Alison M. Greenlee, University of Tulsa, for "Faculty Responses to Library Service Innovations: A Case Study"; Linda R. Most, Valdosta State University, for "Hands on from a Distance: The Community-Embedded Learning Model Contextualizes Online Student."

ALISE/Eugene Garfield Doctoral Dissertation Award ($500). *Winner:* Eric M. Meyers, University of Washington, for "The Nature and Impact of Information Problem Solving in the Middle School Classroom."

ALISE/Norman Horrocks Leadership Award ($500). To recognize a new ALISE member who has demonstrated outstanding leadership qualities in professional ALISE activities. *Winner:* Renate Chancellor, Catholic University.

ALISE/LMC Paper Award. *Sponsor:* Libraries Unlimited/Linworth. *Winner:* Eric M. Meyers, University of British Columbia, for "The Group6: Toward the Development of a Collaborative Information Problem Solving."

ALISE/Pratt-Severn Faculty Innovation Award ($1,000). To recognize innovation by full-time faculty members in incorporating evolving information technologies in the curricula of accredited master's degree programs in library and information studies. *Winner:* Leanne Bowler, University of Pittsburgh.

ALISE Professional Contribution to Library and Information Science Education Award. *Winner:* Eileen Abels, Drexel University.

ALISE/ProQuest Methodology Paper Competition. *Winners:* Mahria Lebow and Heather L. O'Brien, University of British Columbia, for "Is There a Role for Physiological Methods in the Evaluation of Human-Information Interaction?"

ALISE Research Grant Awards (one or more grants totaling $5,000). *Winners:* Carolyn Hank, McGill University; Cassidy Sugimoto, Indiana University, and Jeffrey Pomerantz, University of North Carolina at Chapel Hill, for "Teaching in the Age of Facebook and Other Social Media: LIS Faculty and Students 'Friending' and 'Poking' in the Social Sphere."

ALISE Service Award. *Winner:* Linda C. Smith.

ALISE/Jean Tague Sutcliffe Doctoral Student Research Poster Competition. *Winner:* Lysanne Lessard, University of Toronto.

ALISE/University of Washington Information School Youth Services Graduate Student Travel Award ($750). To support the costs associated with travel to and participation in the ALISE Annual Conference. *Winner:*

Robin Fogle Kurz, University of South Carolina.

ALISE/Bohdan S. Wynar Research Paper Competition. *Winner:* Jessica F. Lingel, Rutgers University, for "Improvisation, Tactics, and Wandering: Urban Information Practices of Migrational Individuals."

Doctoral Students to ALISE Grant ($500). To support the attendance of one or more promising LIS doctoral students at the ALISE Annual Conference. *Sponsor:* Libraries Unlimited/Linworth. *Winner:* Jackie Brodsky, University of Alabama.

OCLC/ALISE Library and Information Science Research Grant Competition. To promote independent research that helps librarians integrate new technologies into areas of traditional competence and contributes to a better understanding of the library environment. *Winners:* Abdulhussain Mahdi and Arash Joorabchi, University of Limerick, Ireland, for "A New Unsupervised Approach to Automatic Topical Indexing of Scientific Documents According to Library Controlled Vocabularies"; Laura Saunders and Mary Wilkins Jordan, Simmons College, for "Reference Competencies from the Practitioner's Perspective: An International Comparison"; Carolyn Hank, McGill University, and Cassidy Sugimoto, Indiana University–Bloomington, for "The Biblioblogosphere: A Comparison of Communication and Preservation Perceptions and Practices Between Blogging LIS Scholar-Practitioners and LIS Scholar-Researchers."

Association of Jewish Libraries (AJL)

AJL Scholarships ($1,000). For students enrolled in accredited library schools who plan to work as Judaica librarians. *Winners:* Rina Krautwirth, Joyce Wortsman.

Fanny Goldstein Merit Award. To honor loyal and ongoing contributions to the association and to the profession of Jewish librarianship. *Winner:* Sylvia Firschein.

Life Membership Award. To recognize outstanding leadership and professional contributions to the association and to the profession of Jewish librarianship. *Winner:* Elhanan Adler.

Association of Research Libraries

ARL Diversity Scholarships (stipend of up to $10,000). To a varying number of MLS students from under-represented groups who are interested in careers in research libraries. *Sponsors:* ARL member libraries and the Institute of Museum and Library Services. *Winners (2012–2014):* Christina Chan-Park, Sabrina D. Dyck, Lisa Hardman, Mario Macias, Ebony Magnus, Christian Minter, Na Qin, Peace Ossom, Thomas Padilla, Eva Rios-Alvarado, Bredny Rodriguez, Camille Salas, Amber Saundry, Curtis Small.

Association of Seventh-Day Adventist Librarians

D. Glenn Hilts Scholarship ($1,500) for a member of the Seventh-Day Adventist Church in a graduate library program. *Winner:* Daniel Alvsbert.

Beta Phi Mu

Beta Phi Mu Award. *See under* American Library Association.

Eugene Garfield Doctoral Dissertation Fellowships ($3,000). *Winners:* C. Sean Burns, Laura Christopherson, Marianne Martens, Xi Niu, Sarah Roberts, Ji Teon Yang.

Harold Lancour Scholarship for Foreign Study ($1,750). For graduate study in a country related to the applicant's work or schooling. *Winner:* Nic Weber.

Sarah Rebecca Reed Scholarship ($2,250). For study at an ALA-accredited library school. *Winner:* Daniela Rovida.

Frank B. Sessa Scholarship for Continuing Professional Education ($1,500). For continuing education for a Beta Phi Mu member. *Winner:* Margaret Swanson.

Blanche E. Woolls Scholarship ($2,250). For a beginning student in school library media services. *Winner:* Laura Browning.

Bibliographical Society of America (BSA)

BSA Fellowships ($1,500–$6,000). For scholars involved in bibliographical inquiry and research in the history of the book trades and in publishing history. *Winners:* (Fredson Bowers Award, $1,500) Not awarded in 2012; (BSA-ASECS Fellowship for Bibliographical Studies in the 18th Century, $3,000) Anne Weinshenker; (BSA-Mercantile Library Fellowship in North American Bibliography, $2,000) Not awarded in 2012; (Folter Fellowship in the History of Bibliography, $2,000) Not awarded in 2012; (McCorison Fellowship for the History and Bibliography of Printing in Canada and the United States, $2,000) Trish Travis; (one-month fellowships, $2,000) Linde Brocato, Godfried Croenen, Kyle Dugdale; (Katharine F. Pantzer Senior Fellowship in Bibliography and the British Book Trades, $6,000) James Carley; (Katharine Pantzer Fellowship in the British Book Trades, $2,000) Joseph Rezek; (Reese Fellowship for American Bibliography and the History of the Book in the Americas, $2,000) Martha Scotford.

William L. Mitchell Prize for Research on Early British Serials ($1,000). Awarded triennially for the best single work published in the previous three years. *Winner:* Not awarded in 2012.

New Scholars Program. To promote the work of scholars who are new to the field of bibliography. *Winners:* Steven Carl Smith, Barbara Heritage, Juliette Atkinson.

St. Louis Mercantile Library Prize in American Bibliography ($2,000). Awarded triennially to encourage scholarship in the bibliography of American history and literature. *Sponsor:* St. Louis Mercantile Library, University of Missouri, St. Louis. *Winner:* To be awarded next in 2014.

Justin G. Schiller Prize for Bibliographical Work on Pre-20th Century Children's Books ($2,000). A triennial award to encourage scholarship in the bibliography of historical children's books. *Winner:* Kyle B. Roberts.

Canadian Library Association (CLA)

Olga B. Bishop Award (C$200). To a library school student for the best paper on government information or publications. *Winner:* Award discontinued in 2012.

Chancellor Group Conference Grant (C$500). To support attendance of newly qualified teacher-librarians at the next conference of the Canadian Association for School Libraries (CASL). *Winners:* Carole Fleetham.

CLA Award for the Advancement of Intellectual Freedom in Canada. *Winner:* Calgary Freedom to Read Committee.

CLA Elizabeth Dafoe Scholarship (C$5,000). *Winner:* Grant Hurley.

CLA/Ken Haycock Award for Promoting Librarianship (C$1,000). For significant contributions to the public recognition and appreciation of librarianship. *Winner:* Pilar Martinez.

CLA Library Research and Development Grant (C$1,000). *Winner:* Not awarded in 2012.

CLA/OCLC Award for Innovative Technology. *Donor:* OCLC Canada. *Winner:* Windsor (Ontario) Public Library.

CLA Outstanding Service to Librarianship Award. *Donor:* Bowker. *Winner:* Ken Roberts.

CLA Student Article Award. *Winner:* Nicole Dalmer for "Women in Archives: Present Contexts and Future Implications."

CLA/3M Canada Award for Achievement in Technical Services (C$1,000). *Winner:* Award discontinued in 2012.

CLA/H. W. Wilson Scholarship ($2,000). *Winner:* Leila Meshgini.

CLA/YBP Award for Outstanding Contribution to Collection Development and Management (C$1,000). To recognize a CLA member who has made an outstanding local, national, or international contribution in the field of library collection development or management. *Sponsor:* YBP Library Services. *Winner:* Award discontinued in 2012.

W. Kaye Lamb Award for Service to Seniors. Awarded biennially to recognize a library that has developed an ongoing service, program, or procedure of benefit to seniors and/or a design and organization of buildings or facilities that improve access and encourage use by seniors. *Sponsors:* Ex Libris Association and CLA. *Winner:* Coquitlam (British Columbia) Public Library.

Canadian Association for School Libraries (CASL)

CASL Follett International Teacher Librarian of the Year Award. *Winner:* Award discontinued in 2012.

CASL Margaret B. Scott Award of Merit. For the development of school libraries in Canada. *Winner:* Award discontinued in 2012.

CASL Angela Thacker Memorial Award. To honor teacher-librarians who have made contributions to the profession through publications, productions, or professional development activities. *Winner:* Not awarded in 2012.

Canadian Association of College and University Libraries (CACUL)

CACUL/Robert H. Blackburn Distinguished Paper Award ($200). To acknowledge notable research published by CACUL members. *Winners:* Lorie Kloda, Denise Koufogiannakis, and Katrine Mallan, for "Transferring Evidence Into Practice: What Evidence Summaries of Library and Information Studies Research Tell Practitioners" (*Information Research,* March 2011).

CACUL/Miles Blackwell Award for Outstanding Academic Librarian. *Sponsor:* Baker & Taylor/YBP Library Services. *Winner:* Award discontinued in 2012.

CACUL Innovation Achievement Award ($1,000). *Sponsor:* OCLC. *Winner:* Award discontinued in 2012.

CTCL Award for Outstanding College Librarian. *Winner:* Awarded discontinued in 2012.

CTCL Innovation Achievement Award. *Sponsor:* OCLC. *Winners:* Award discontinued in 2012.

Canadian Association of Public Libraries (CAPL)

CAPL/Brodart Outstanding Public Library Service Award. *Winner:* Award discontinued in 2012.

Canadian Association of Special Libraries and Information Services (CASLIS)

CASLIS Award for Special Librarianship in Canada. *Winner:* Award discontinued in 2012.

Canadian Library Trustees Association (CLTA)

CLTA/Stan Heath Achievement in Literacy Award. For an innovative literacy program by a public library board. *Donor:* ABC Canada. *Winners:* Award discontinued in 2012.

CLTA Merit Award for Distinguished Service as a Public Library Trustee. *Winner:* Award discontinued in 2012.

Catholic Library Association

Regina Medal. For continued, distinguished contribution to the field of children's literature. *Winner:* author and illustrator Kevin Henkes.

Chinese American Librarians Association (CALA)

CALA Distinguished Service Award. To a librarian who has been a mentor, role model, and leader in the fields of library and information science. *Winner:* Barbara Ford, University of Illinois, Urbana-Champaign.

CALA President's Recognition Award. *Winners:* Clara Chu, Mengxiong Liu, Sha Li Zhang.

CALA Scholarship of Library and Information Science ($500). *Winner:* Wai Yi Ma.

Sheila Suen Lai Scholarship ($500). *Winner:* Yuting Wu.

C. C. Seetoo/CALA Conference Travel Scholarship ($500). For a student to attend the ALA Annual Conference and CALA program. *Winner:* Not awarded in 2012.

Sally C. Tseng Professional Development Grant ($1,000). *Winner:* Not awarded in 2012.

Huang Tso-ping and Wu Yao-yu Scholarship Memorial Research Grant ($200): *Winner:* Not awarded in 2012.

Church and Synagogue Library Association (CSLA)

CSLA Award for Outstanding Congregational Librarian. For distinguished service to the congregation and/or community through devotion to the congregational library. *Winner:* Paula Altschul, Temple Emanuel of South Hills Library, Pittsburgh.

CSLA Award for Outstanding Congregational Library. For responding in creative and innovative ways to the library's mission of reaching and serving the congregation and/or the wider community. *Winner:* William Smith Culbertson Memorial Library, Satellite Library and Archives, the National Presbyterian Church, Washington, D.C.

CSLA Award for Outstanding Contribution to Congregational Libraries. For providing inspiration, guidance, leadership, or resources to enrich the field of church or synagogue librarianship. *Winner:* Maryann Dotts Barth, New Port Richey, Florida.

Helen Keating Ott Award for Outstanding Contribution to Children's Literature. *Winner:* Not awarded in 2012.

Rodda Book Award. *Winner:* See "Literary Prizes, 2012" in Part 5.

Coalition for Networked Information

Paul Evan Peters Award. Awarded biennially to recognize notable and lasting international achievements relating to high-performance networks and the creation and use of information resources and services that advance scholarship and intellectual productivity. *Sponsors:* Association of Research Libraries, Coalition for Networked Information, EDUCAUSE. *Winner:* Not awarded in 2012.

Paul Evan Peters Fellowship ($5,000 a year for two years). Awarded biennially to a student pursuing a graduate degree in librarianship or the information sciences. *Sponsors:* Association of Research Libraries, Coalition for Networked Information, EDUCAUSE. *Winner:* Courtney Loder.

Council on Library and Information Resources (CLIR)

CLIR Postdoctoral Fellowships in Scholarly Information Resources. *Current fellows:* Katherine Akers, Benjamin Dewayne Branch, Jason Brodeur, Brock Dubbels, Vessela Ensberg, Inna Kouper, Matthew J. Lavin, Natsuko Hayashi Nicholls, Jennifer Parrott, Fe Consolacion Sferdean, Ting Wang, Wei Yang; *Continuing current fellows* Jessica Aberle, Peter Broadwell, Arthur "Mitch" Fraas, Jennifer Redmond, Christopher Teeter, Yi Shen.

Mellon Fellowship Program for Dissertation Research in the Humanities in Original Sources (stipends of up to $20,000 to support dissertation research). *Current fellows:* Elise Bonner, Adam Boss, William Brown, Rebecca Herman, Thomas Hooker, Jang Wook Huh, Neelima Jeychandran, Seth LeJacq, Kara Moskowitz, Sylvia Mullins, Elizabeth Nelson, Kimberly Powers, Matthew Rarey, Frederick Schenker, Rafal Stepien, Stephanie Stillo, Mirela Tanta, Zita Worley.

Rick Peterson Fellowship. To an early-career information technology professional or librarian who has reached beyond traditional boundaries to resolve a significant challenge facing digital libraries. *Cosponsors:* CLIR and the National Institute for Technology in Liberal Education (NITLE). *Winner:* Joshua Honn.

Rovelstad Scholarship in International Librarianship. To enable a student enrolled in an accredited LIS program to attend the IFLA World Library and Information Congress. *Winner:* Molly Schwartz, University of Maryland at College Park.

A. R. Zipf Fellowship in Information Management ($10,000). To a student enrolled in graduate school who shows exceptional promise for leadership and technical achievement. *Winner:* Jodi Schneider, Ph.D. candidate at the Digital Enterprise Research Institute, National University of Ireland, Galway.

EDUCAUSE

EDUCAUSE Leadership Award. To acknowledge leadership in higher education information technology. *Winners:* Earving L. Blythe, David G. Schwartz.

EDUCAUSE Rising Star Award. To recognize an early-career information technology professional who demonstrates exceptional achievement in the area of information technology in higher education. *Winner:* Melissa Woo.

Friends of the National Library of Medicine

Michael E. DeBakey Library Services Outreach Award. To recognize outstanding service and contributions to rural and underserved communities by a practicing health sciences librarian. *Winner:* Anna Ercoli Schnitzer, disability issues librarian at the Taubman Health Sciences Library, University of Michigan.

Bill and Melinda Gates Foundation

Access to Learning Award ($1 million). To public libraries or similar organizations outside the United States for innovative programs that provide the public free access to information technology. *Administered by:* Gates Foundation Global Libraries initiative. *Winner:* The Dominican Republic's network of nearly 100 Community Technology Centers (CTCs), which provide public access to technological equipment and services.

Institute of Museum and Library Services

National Medal for Museum and Library Service. For extraordinary civic, educational, economic, environmental, and social contributions ($5,000). *Winners:* (libraries) Contra Costa County Library, Pleasant Hill, California; Cumberland County Public Library, Fayetteville, North Carolina; Naturita (Colorado) Community Library; Park View

High School Library Media Center, Sterling, Virginia; Shaler North Hills Library, Glenshaw, Pennsylvania.

International Association of School Librarians (IASL)

Ken Haycock and Jean Lowrie Leadership Development Grants ($1,000). To enable applicants in developing nations to attend their first IASL Annual Conference. *Winners:* (Haycock award) Kenneth M. Kozel, Jordan; (Lowrie award) Daniel N. Mangale, Kenya.

IASL School Librarianship Award. To IASL members for their contribution to the national development of school libraries and services within their own country or internationally. *Winner:* Nancy Everhart, Florida State University.

IASL/Softlink International Excellence Award ($1,000). To recognize significant contributions to school librarianship by school library specialists, educators, and/or researchers. *Winner:* S. L. Faizal, Kerala, India.

Takeshi Murofushi Research Award ($500 toward funding of a research project). *Winner:* Lyn Hay, Charles Sturt University, Canberra, Australia.

International Federation of Library Associations and Institutions (IFLA)

De Gruyter Saur/IFLA Research Paper Award (€1,000). For the best unpublished research paper on a topic of importance to publishing and access to information by an author or authors with no more than eight years of professional experience in library and information services. *Sponsors:* IFLA and De Gruyter Saur. *Winner:* Adam Girard for "E-books Are Not Books: The Challenges and Chances in the New Media Context."

Honorary Fellowship. For long and distinguished service to IFLA. *Winners:* Winston Tabb, Ellen Tise.

IFLA Medal. To a person or organization for a distinguished contribution either to IFLA or to international librarianship. *Winners:*

Helena Asamoah-Hassan, Jay Jordan, Eeva Kristiina Murtomaa.

Jay Jordan IFLA/OCLC Early Career Development Fellowships. To library and information science professionals from countries with developing economies who are in the early stages of their careers. *Sponsors:* IFLA, OCLC, American Theological Library Association. *Fellows:* Dwaymian Brissette, Jamaica; Caroline Nyaga, Kenya; David Ofili, Nigeria; Rozita Petrinska-Labudovikj, Macedonia; Chona San Pedro, Philippines.

Dr. Shawky Salem Conference Grant (up to $1,900). To enable an expert in library and information science who is a national of an Arab country to attend the IFLA Conference for the first time. *Winner:* Heba Mohamed Ismail, Integrated Care Society (ICS), Cairo.

Frederick Thorpe Organizational Award (up to £15,000). To a library organization for development of service delivery to the visually impaired. *Winners:* To be announced in mid-2013.

Ulverscroft Foundation/IFLA Libraries Serving Persons with Print Disabilities Section Best Practice Awards. To assist the development of library services for print-disabled people and foster cooperation between library services serving these persons. *Winners:* To be announced in mid-2013.

Library Journal

DEMCO/LJ Paralibrarian of the Year Award. *Winner:* Linda Dahlquist, New Smyrna Beach (Florida) Regional Library.

Gale/LJ Library of the Year. *Sponsor:* Gale Cengage Learning. *Winner:* San Diego County (California) Library.

LJ Best Small Library in America ($15,000). To honor a public library that profoundly demonstrates outstanding service to populations of 25,000 or less. *Co-sponsors:* *Library Journal* and the Bill and Melinda Gates Foundation. *Winner:* Independence (Kansas) Public Library.

LJ Librarian of the Year. *Winner:* Luis Herrera, San Francisco City Librarian.

LJ Teaching Award ($5,000). To recognize excellence in LIS education. *Offered by:* *Library Journal.* *Sponsored by:* ProQuest.

Winner: Lilia Pavlovsky, School of Communication and Information, Rutgers University.

Medical Library Association (MLA)

Virginia L. and William K. Beatty MLA Volunteer Service Award. To recognize a medical librarian who has demonstrated outstanding, sustained service to the Medical Library Association and the health sciences library profession. *Winner:* Janet L. Cowen.

Estelle Brodman Award for the Academic Medical Librarian of the Year. To honor significant achievement, potential for leadership, and continuing excellence at midcareer in the area of academic health sciences librarianship. *Winner:* Bart Ragon.

Lois Ann Colaianni Award for Excellence and Achievement in Hospital Librarianship. To a member of MLA who has made significant contributions to the profession in the area of overall distinction or leadership in hospital librarianship. *Winner:* Mary Virginia Taylor.

Cunningham Memorial International Fellowships. Provides grants and travel expenses in the United States and Canada for one or more librarians from other countries. Includes attendance at the MLA Annual Meeting and observation and supervised work in one or more medical libraries. *Winners:* Michael Chimalizeni, South Africa; Silvia Ciubrei, Republic of Moldova; Valerie Clarke, Barbados; Elaine Garrett, United Kingdom; Gussun Gunes, Turkey; Nguyen Hai Ha, Vietnam; Shona Kirtley, United Kingdom; Carol Lefebvre, United Kingdom; Richard Ssenono, Uganda; Mary Louise Thompson, St. Vincent and the Grenadines.

Louise Darling Medal. For distinguished achievement in collection development in the health sciences. *Winner:* Laurie L. Thompson.

Janet Doe Lectureship. *Winner:* Mark E. Funk. Topic: "Our World, Our Story: A Textual Analysis of Articles Published in the Bulletin of the Medical Library Association/ Journal of the Medical Library Association from 1961 to 2010."

EBSCO/MLA Annual Meeting Grants (up to $1,000). To enable four health sciences librarians to attend the MLA Annual Meeting. *Winners:* Aleta Embrey, Aleshia Heckel, Alisha Miles, Jennifer Walker.

Ida and George Eliot Prize. To recognize a work published in the preceding calendar year that has been judged most effective in furthering medical librarianship. *Winners:* Margaret M. Bandy and Rosalind F. Dudden for "The Medical Library Association Guide to Managing Health Care Libraries."

Carla J. Funk Governmental Relations Award ($500). To recognize a medical librarian who has demonstrated outstanding leadership in the area of governmental relations at the federal, state, or local level, and who has furthered the goal of providing quality information for improved health. *Sponsor:* Kent A. Smith. *Winner:* Lynne K. Siemers.

Murray Gottlieb Prize. For the best unpublished essay on the history of medicine and allied sciences written by a health sciences librarian. *Donors:* Ralph and Jo Grimes. *Winner:* Not awarded in 2012.

T. Mark Hodges International Service Award. To honor outstanding achievement in promoting, enabling, or delivering improved health information internationally. *Winner:* Alice E. Hadley.

David A. Kronick Traveling Fellowship ($2,000). *Sponsor:* Bowden-Massey Foundation. *Winner:* Not awarded in 2012.

Joseph Leiter NLM/MLA Lectureship. *Winner:* Frederick "Skip" Burkle, Jr., M.D. Topic: "Future Humanitarian Crises: Challenges to Practice, Policy, and Public Health."

Donald A. B. Lindberg Research Fellowship ($10,000). To fund research aimed at expanding the research knowledge base, linking the information services provided by librarians to improved health care and advances in biomedical research. *Winner:* Mary J. Moore. Topic: "The Investment in Health Sciences Libraries in Relation to U.S. National Rankings for Medical Education and Research."

Lucretia W. McClure Excellence in Education Award. To an outstanding educator in the field of health sciences librarianship and informatics. *Winner:* Janet G. Schnall.

John P. McGovern Award Lectureship. *Winner:* Steven Johnson.

Majors/MLA Chapter Project of the Year Award. *Sponsor:* J. A. Majors Co. *Winner:* South Central Chapter.

Medical Informatics Section Career Development Grant ($1,500). To support a career development activity that will contribute to advancement in the field of medical informatics. *Winner:* Not awarded in 2012.

MLA Continuing Education Awards ($100–$500). *Winner:* Alisha Miles.

MLA Scholarship (up to $5,000). For graduate study at an ALA-accredited library school. *Winner:* Kevin Pardon.

MLA Scholarship for Minority Students (up to $5,000). For graduate study at an ALA-accredited library school. *Winner:* Ligia Patricia Groff.

Marcia C. Noyes Award. For an outstanding contribution to medical librarianship. *Winner:* Jacqueline D. Doyle.

President's Award. To an MLA member for a notable or important contribution made during the past association year. *Winner:* Connie Schardt.

Rittenhouse Award. For the best unpublished paper on medical librarianship submitted by a student enrolled in, or having been enrolled in, a course for credit in an ALA-accredited library school or a trainee in an internship program in medical librarianship. *Donor:* Rittenhouse Book Distributors. *Winner:* Eva Jurczyk for "Developing a Custom Health Search Tool to Meet Diverse Health Literacy Needs."

Thomson Reuters/Frank Bradway Rogers Information Advancement Award. To recognize outstanding contributions for the application of technology to the delivery of health science information, to the science of information, or to the facilitation of the delivery of health science information. *Sponsor:* Thomson Reuters. *Winner:* Not awarded in 2012.

Music Library Association

Carol June Bradley Award. To support studies that involve the history of music libraries or special collections. *Winner:* Jim Carrier.

Vincent H. Duckles Award. For the best book-length bibliography or other research tool in music. *Winner:* Christophe Grabowski and John Rink for *Annotated Catalogue of Chopin's First Editions* (Cambridge University Press).

Dena Epstein Award for Archival and Library Research in American Music. To support research in archives or libraries internationally on any aspect of American music. *Winner:* Mark Burford.

Kevin Freeman Travel Grants. To colleagues who are new to the profession to enable them to attend the MLA Annual Meeting. *Winners:* Sonia Archer-Capuzzo, Sofia Becerra-Licha, Victoria Chu, Stephanie Lewin-Lane, Pamela Pagels.

Walter Gerboth Award. To members of the association who are in the first five years of their professional library careers, to assist research-in-progress in music or music librarianship. *Winner:* Bonnie "Beth" Fleming.

Richard S. Hill Award. For the best article on music librarianship or article of a music-bibliographic nature. *Winners:* Kate van Orden and Alfredo Vitolo for "Padre Martini, Gaetano Gaspari, and the 'Pagliarini Collection': A Renaissance Music Library Rediscovered" in *Early Music History* 29 (2010).

MLA Citation. Awarded in recognition of contributions to the profession over a career. *Winner:* Not awarded in 2012.

Eva Judd O'Meara Award. For the best review published in *Notes*. *Winner:* Pieter Mannaerts, for a review of Charles M. Atkinson's *The Critical Nexus: Tone-system, Mode, and Notation in Early Medieval Music* in *Notes* 66:3 (March 2010).

National Library Service for the Blind and Physically Handicapped, Library of Congress

Library of the Year Awards ($1,000). *Winners:* (network library of the year) Texas Talking Book Program, a division of the Texas State Library and Archives Commission; (network subregional library of the year) Chicago Public Library Talking Book Center, part of the Illinois Network of Talking Book and Braille Libraries.

REFORMA (National Association to Promote Library and Information Services to Latinos and the Spanish-Speaking)

REFORMA scholarships (up to $1,500). To students who qualify for graduate study in library science and who are citizens or permanent residents of the United States. *Winners:* Claire Bartlett, Brenda Carrillo, Alexandra Doval, Karen Orellana, Jade B. Torres-Morrison.

Arnulfo D. Trejo Librarian of the Year Award. To recognize a librarian who has promoted and advocated services to the Spanish-speaking and Latino communities and made outstanding contributions to REFORMA. *Winner:* Silvia Cisneros, senior librarian, Santa Ana (California) Public Library.

Society of American Archivists (SAA)

C. F. W. Coker Award for Description. To recognize creators of tools that enable archivists to produce more effective finding aids. *Winner:* Not awarded in 2012.

Council Exemplary Service Award. *Winners:* Native American Protocols Forum Working Group, Michael J. Fox, Nancy P. Beaumont.

Distinguished Service Award. To recognize an archival institution, education program, nonprofit organization, or governmental organization that has given outstanding service to its public and has made an exemplary contribution to the archives profession. *Winner:* Archival Education Collaborative.

Diversity Award. To an individual, group, or institution for outstanding contributions to advancing diversity within the archives profession, SAA, or the archival record. *Winner:* Chicano Studies Research Center (CSRC), University of California, Los Angeles.

Emerging Leader Award. To recognize early-career archivists who have completed archival work of broad merit, demonstrated significant promise of leadership, performed commendable service to the archives profession, or have accomplished a combina-

tion of these requirements. *Winner:* Mark A. Matienzo, Yale University Library.

Fellows' Ernst Posner Award. For an outstanding essay dealing with a facet of archival administration, history, theory, or methodology, published in American Archivist. *Winner:* Douglas Cox for "National Archives and International Conflicts," *American Archivist* 74:2.

Josephine Forman Scholarship ($10,000). *Sponsor:* General Commission on Archives and History of the United Methodist Church. *Winner:* Nathasha Alvarez.

F. Gerald Ham Scholarship ($7,500). To recognize an individual's past performance in a graduate archival studies program and his or her potential in the field. *Winners:* Nathan Sowry, Jarrett M. Drake.

Philip M. Hamer and Elizabeth Hamer Kegan Award. For individuals and/or institutions that have increased public awareness of a specific body of documents. *Winner:* Immigration History Research Center at the University of Minnesota.

Oliver Wendell Holmes Travel Award. To enable overseas archivists already in the United States or Canada for training to attend the SAA annual meeting. *Winners:* Lara Mancuso, Georgia Barlaoura.

J. Franklin Jameson Award. For individuals and/or organizations that promote greater public awareness of archival activities and programs. *Winners:* Eve Kahn, Bebe Miller, Philip W. Stewart.

Sister M. Claude Lane, O.P., Memorial Award. For a significant contribution to the field of religious archives. *Winner:* Mark J. Duffy.

Waldo Gifford Leland Prize. For writing of superior excellence and usefulness in the field of archival history, theory, or practice. *Winners:* Francis X. Blouin, Jr. and William G. Rosenberg for *Processing the Past: Contesting Authority in History and the Archives* (Oxford University Press).

Theodore Calvin Pease Award. For the best student paper. *Winner:* Pam Mayer for "Like a Box of Chocolates: A Case Study of User-Contributed Content at Footnote."

Donald Peterson Student Scholarship Award (up to $1,000). To enable a student or recent graduate to attend the SAA Annual Meeting. *Winner:* Amanda Strauss.

Harold T. Pinkett Minority Student Award. To encourage minority students to consider careers in the archival profession, and to promote minority participation in SAA. *Winner:* Kapena Shim.

Preservation Publication Award. To recognize an outstanding work published in North America that advances the theory or the practice of preservation in archival institutions. *Winner:* the GeoMAPP project for Geospatial Multistate Archive and Preservation Partnership (GeoMAPP) Best Practices for Archival Processing for Geospatial Datasets.

SAA Fellows. To a limited number of members for their outstanding contribution to the archival profession. *Honored:* Scott Cline, Peter Gottlieb, Nancy Lenoil, Ben Primer, Timothy D. Pyatt.

SAA Mosaic Scholarship ($5,000). To minority students pursuing graduate education in archival science. *Winner:* Aditi Sharma Worcester.

SAA Spotlight Award. To recognize the contributions of individuals who work for the good of the profession and of archival collections, and whose work would not typically receive public recognition. *Winners:* Cindy Ditzler and Joan Metzger, Northern Illinois University.

Special Libraries Association (SLA)

Diversity Leadership Development Program Award ($1,000 stipend). *Sponsor:* EBSCO. *Winner:* Sophia Guevara, chair, Consortium of Foundation Libraries.

Dow Jones Leadership Award ($2,000). For excellence in special librarianship. *Winner:* NPR librarian Christine "Kee" Malesky.

SLA John Cotton Dana Award. For exceptional support and encouragement of special librarianship. *Winner:* Jesus Lau.

ProQuest and Dialog Member Achievement Award ($1,000). To an SLA member for raising visibility, awareness, and appreciation of the profession, SLA unit, or the association. *Winner:* Daniel Lee.

SLA Fellows. *Honored:* Scott Brown, Ann Cullen, Ruth Kneale, Chris Olson, Roberto Sarmiento.

SLA Hall of Fame Award. For outstanding performance and distinguished service to SLA. *Winners:* Sharon Lenius, Susan Fifer Canby.

SLA Rising Stars Award. To SLA members in the first five years of membership who demonstrate exceptional promise of leadership. *Winners:* Davis Erin Anderson, Janel Kinlaw, Moy McIntosh, Chris Zammarelli.

SLA Research Grant (incorporating the Steven I. Goldspiel Memorial Research Grant Fund) (up to $25,000). To support outstanding research. *Winner:* Not awarded in 2012.

Rose L. Vormelker Award. To SLA members for exceptional service through the education and mentoring of students and working professionals. *Winners:* Denise Callihan, Bruce Rosenstein.

Theatre Library Association

Distinguished Service in Performing Arts Librarianship Award. For extraordinary contributions to performing arts librarianship. *Winner:* Nena Couch, curator, Lawrence and Lee Theatre Research Institute, Ohio State University.

Brooks McNamara Performing Arts Librarian Scholarship. *Winner:* Lisbeth Wells-Pratt.

Other Awards of Distinction

Robert B. Downs Intellectual Freedom Award. To recognize individuals or groups who have furthered the cause of intellectual freedom, particularly as it impacts libraries and information centers and the dissemination of ideas. *Offered by:* Graduate School of Library and Information Science, University of Illinois at Urbana-Champaign. *Sponsor:* ABC-CLIO. *Winner:* Librotraficante, a movement led by Tony Diaz, for its efforts to oppose the censorship of ethnic and cultural studies materials in Arizona.

I Love My Librarian Awards ($5,000, a plaque, and a $500 travel stipend to attend the awards ceremony). To recognize librarians for service to their communities, schools, and campuses. Winners are nominated by library patrons. *Sponsors:* Carnegie Corporation of New York and the New York Times. *Winners:* Dorothy J. Davison, Horrmann

Library, Wagner College; Roberto Carlos Delgadillo, Peter J. Shields Library, University of California, Davis; Beatriz Adriana Guevara, Charlotte Mecklenburg Library, Charlotte, North Carolina; Rachel Hyland, Tunxis Community College Library, Farmington, Connecticut; Susan Kowalski, Pine Grove Middle School Library, East Syracuse, New York; Rae Anne Locke, Saugatuck Elementary "Secret Garden" Library, Westport, Connecticut; Greta E. Marlatt, Dudley Knox Library, Naval Postgraduate School, Monterey, California; Mary Ellen Pellington, Octavia Fellin Public Library, Gallup, New Mexico; Madlyn S. Schneider, Queens Library, Queens Village, New York;

Julie Hatsell Wales, McNair Magnet School, Rockledge, Florida.

RWA Librarian of the Year. To a librarian who demonstrates outstanding support of romance authors and the romance genre. *Offered by:* Romance Writers of America. *Winner:* Mary Moore, Huntsville-Madison County (Alabama) Public Library.

Women's National Book Association Award. Awarded biennially to a living American woman who derives part or all of her income from books and allied arts and who has done meritorious work in the world of books. *Offered by:* Women's National Book Association (WNBA). *Winner:* Ann Patchett.

Part 4
Research and Statistics

Library Research and Statistics

Research and Statistics on Libraries and Librarianship in 2012

Kathy Rosa

Director, Office for Research and Statistics, American Library Association

During 2012 libraries continued to struggle with the effects of the continuing recession while trying to keep pace with a growing demand for technology resources and services. Libraries face a challenge to return to pre-recession levels of staff, open hours, collections, and services. The year ended, however, with cautious optimism based on trend data from the 2012–2013 Chief Officers of State Library Agencies Survey (COSLA)[1] and the 2012 *Library Journal* survey.[2] Fewer funding decreases occurred in 2012 and, in some instances, there were slight increases.

Funding continues to be a challenge, however, as does the demand for technology resources and services. The "Libraries Connect Communities" Public Library Funding and Technology Access Study[3] and the Pew study "Library Services in the Digital Age"[4] show that while Americans still look to libraries for books, they see library computers and Internet access as crucial resources for homework, e-government, and social networking. The demand for more e-books than are available continues to be problematic. Publishers struggle with an uncertain future and have yet to develop business models relating to price, copyright, and lending that are acceptable to libraries.

This article highlights research and statistics about public, school, and academic libraries and librarianship. Sources include the Institute of Museum and Library Services, the National Center for Education Statistics, the American Library Association (ALA), the Pew Research Center, the American Association of School Librarians, the Association of College and Research Libraries, the Association of Research Libraries, and *Library Journal*.

Winners of research awards and grants conferred by ALA and its divisions and by Beta Phi Mu, the American Society for Information Science and Technology, the Association for Library and Information Science Education, and the Medical Library Association are also included.

Notable Research

Library Journal's Patron Profiles[5] are studies that provide quantitative data from the user's perspective about issues relevant to public and academic libraries. Study titles released in 2012 included "Mobile Devices, Mobile Content and Library

Apps," "Media Consumption and the Library User," "Library Websites and Virtual Services," "Library Patrons and the Changing Ebook Landscape," and "Patron Profiles: Academic Library Edition: 2012 Report."

Public Libraries

The 2012–2013 Chief Officers of Library State Agencies (COSLA)[6] survey results include responses from 46 of the 50 states about funding, library closures, and public library hours. Cuts in state funding for public libraries fell for the first time in three years, with decreases reported by 21.7 percent in fiscal year (FY) 2012–2013, compared with 46 percent in FY 2011–2012 and 41.5 percent in FY 2010–2011. Direct state aid for public libraries increased in 6 states, decreased in 10 states, and remained flat in 16 states. No state aid to public libraries was reported in 11 states.

Previously, the COSLA survey collected data about public libraries but not about the state library; a new question on the FY 2011–2012 survey asked about funding to state libraries. The findings include that funding for state libraries increased in 9 states, decreased in 17 states, and remained flat in another 17 states. In another study, *Library Journal*[7] surveyed 2,060 U.S. public libraries and reported findings for the 388 respondents. Funding improved in 60 percent of the responding libraries, decreased in 36 percent, and remained flat for 4 percent.

Library closures held steady, with 11 states reporting closures for the past two years, a welcome change from closures in 17 states during FY 2010–2011. All participating states reported closures of five library outlets or fewer. An article in the *Wall Street Journal*[8] reported that a cutback in open hours has public library patrons scrambling to find access to computers and the Internet for homework and study. The COSLA study[9] bears this out, finding 65.2 percent of states reporting that libraries had to cut hours during 2012–2013 in addition to the 82 percent that reported hours cut during 2011–2012.

The Institute of Museum and Library Services conducts the annual Public Libraries Survey,[10] which includes data on the 50 states plus the District of Columbia, Guam, and Puerto Rico. The most recent results, released in January 2013, include data collected for 2010 from 9,100 of the 9,299 eligible public libraries. The survey shows that of the 3.75 million programs offered in public libraries, 61.5 percent were for children. Knitters and quilters continued to meet at the library, while "makerspaces" increased and provided opportunities for such activities as creating Lego robots and experimenting with 3D printing.[11] During 2010 a total of 2.46 billion books, audio and video materials, and e-books circulated in public libraries, sustaining a ten-year increase. Children's materials accounted for more than one-third of all circulation and increased by 28.3 percent over the past decade. Books were still the dominant material type in public libraries, making up 87.1 percent of the total collection. Audio, video, and digital materials had increased, with 18.5 million e-books available for circulation, triple the number available in 2003. The demand for public-access computers increased and libraries responded by doubling the number of public computers available ten years earlier. Physical visits to libraries showed a decrease of 1.1 percent in 2010, but data were not collected for online visits or transactions. There remained a longer-term increase in the number of physical visits to the library—up 32.7 percent from FY 2001 to FY 2010.

The Pew "Library Services in the Digital Age" report discusses Americans' views of their libraries. Telephone interviews were conducted with a nationally representative sample of 2,252 individuals ages 16 and older. The majority of Americans surveyed said they consider "very important" library services to be borrowing books (80 percent), service of reference librarians (80 percent), and free access to computers and the Internet (77 percent). Patrons would like to have access to several other customer service benefits adapted from retail shopping, such as apps-based access to library materials and programs, the ability to try out new technology devices, and GPS navigation apps to help patrons locate material inside library buildings.

Academic Libraries

The Association of College and Research Libraries (ACRL), a division of ALA, published *ACRL 2011 Academic Library Trends and Statistics* during the year.[12] The study gathered data about the expenditures, collections, staffing, and services of academic libraries by Carnegie classification. Notably, all types of academic libraries greatly increased spending for e-books during 2011. Baccalaureate schools increased their spending on e-books by an average of 109.5 percent, comprehensive degree-granting schools by 102.7 percent, associate degree-granting schools by 109.2 percent, and doctorate-granting institutions by 78.9 percent. All types of institutions except baccalaureate schools spent less on serials. Serials accounted for 52.56 percent of materials budgets at baccalaureate schools, 57.62 percent at comprehensive schools, 33.87 percent at associate degree-granting institutions, and 66.12 percent at doctorate-granting institutions. Salaries and wages increased slightly in doctoral and comprehensive institutions (by 0.94 percent and 0.98 percent, respectively). Salaries and wages decreased at associate degree-granting institutions by 1.85 percent and at baccalaureate schools by 0.64 percent.

The ACRL Research Planning and Review Committee conducted an environmental scan to identify trends and issues in academic librarianship.[13] The following were identified:

* Academic libraries must prove the value they provide to the academic enterprise.
* Data curation challenges are increasing as standards for all types of data continue to evolve; more repositories, many of them cloud-based, will emerge; librarians and other information workers will collaborate with their research communities to facilitate this process.
* As digital collections mature, concerns grow about the general lack of long-term planning for their preservation. No strategic leadership for establishing architecture, policy, or standards for creating, accessing, and preserving digital content is likely to emerge in the near term.
* Higher education institutions are entering a period of flux, and potentially even turmoil. Trends to watch for are the rise of online instruction and degree programs, globalization, and an increased skepticism about the "return on investment" in a college degree.
* Technology continues to drive much of the futuristic thinking within academic libraries. The key trends driving educational technology identified

in the 2012 Horizon Report are equally applicable to academic libraries: people's desire for information and access. (The Horizon Report series is part of the New Media Consortium [NMC] Horizon Project, a comprehensive research venture established in 2002 that identifies and describes emerging technologies likely to have a large impact over the coming five years in education.)

- Mobile devices are changing the way information is delivered and accessed.

- Patron-driven acquisition (PDA) of e-books is poised to become the norm. For this to occur, licensing options and models for library lending of e-books must become more sustainable.

- New scholarly communication and publishing models are developing at an ever-faster pace, requiring libraries to be actively involved or be left behind.

- Academic libraries must develop the staff needed to meet new challenges through creative approaches to hiring new personnel and deploying/re-training existing staff.

- User convenience affects all aspects of information seeking.

The Association of Research Libraries surveyed member institutions on current library practice and policies. SPEC Kits[14] were created to guide research libraries in decision making and planning. Among the SPEC Kits released in 2012 were *SPEC Kit 333: Art and Artifact Management, SPEC Kit 332: Organization of Scholarly Communication Services,* and *SPEC Kit 329: Managing Born-Digital Special Collections and Archival Materials.*

School Libraries

The 2012 edition of *School Libraries Count!*[15]—published by the American Association of School Librarians (AASL)—is based on a longitudinal study that had 4,385 respondents. The report provides trend data for U.S. public and private K–12 school libraries. School libraries continue to rely on books as a significant learning resource. More books were purchased on average during 2012 (13,517 titles) than in 2011 (12,989 titles). The number of periodicals across subscriptions and video materials remained consistent with 2011, although the number of video materials was directionally lower than 2009. The trend toward digital access continues, with more than 8 in 10 schools reporting that students could access their library resources remotely. The average number of computers outside of the library with networked access to library services, including licensed databases, increased by 7.6 percent with an average of 193.4 in 2011 and 208.2 in 2012. Notably, the increase is attributed to all school categories: elementary schools, public schools, schools with enrollment of less than 300 and between 300 and 999, schools in the Midwest and South, in non-metro areas, and in areas of low poverty. The average number of computers in libraries increased by 5 percent from 2011 (27.9) to 2012 (29.29).

The 2012 *School Libraries Count!* includes a supplemental report on Internet filtering. Most schools or school libraries filter content for social media, entertainment, and news and education consumption. Most likely to be filtered are social networking sites (88 percent), IM/online chatting (74 percent), gaming sites (69 percent), and video services such as YouTube (66 percent). Fewer schools report filtering newsgroups (17 percent) and professional development tools for education (9 percent). Filtering of portable electronic devices, required by half of the schools that allow such devices, is managed most often with an acceptable-use policy (48 percent) and by making students log on through school networks (47 percent).

Awards and Grants that Support Excellent Research

The professional library associations offer many awards and grants to recognize and encourage research. The 2012 awards and grants here are listed under the name of the sponsoring association, and in the case of ALA by the awarding division, in alphabetical order. More-detailed information about the prizes and prize-winners can be found at the association websites. [For additional library awards, see "Library Scholarship and Award Recipients, 2012" in Part 3—*Ed.*]

American Library Association

Carroll Preston Baber Research Grant
Winners: Libby Pollard and Melissa Fry for "Assessment of Non-Library Use at the Jeffersonville Township [Indiana] Public Library."

Jesse H. Shera Award for Excellence in Published Research
Winners: Shana Pribesh, Karen Gavigan, and Gail Dickinson for "The Access Gap: Poverty and Characteristics of School Library Media Centers" in *Library Quarterly* 81(2): 143–160, April 2011.

Jesse H. Shera Award for Support of Dissertation Research
Winner: Victor J. Sensenig for "Public Libraries and Literacy in Ecological Perspective."

American Association of School Libraries

AASL Research Grant
Winners: Ann Dutton Ewbank for "The Role of Teacher Unions in School Library Advocacy: Case Study of the British Columbia Teacher-Librarians' Association and the British Columbia Teacher's Federation"; Daniella Smith for "An Examination of the Impact of Resiliency and School Organizational Structures on the Self-Perceived Leadership Behaviors of School Librarians."

Association of College and Research Libraries

WESS De Gruyter European Librarianship Study Grant
Winner: Liladhar R. Pendse, Princeton University, for his project to construct a bibliography and subject analysis of Indo-Portuguese periodicals held by the National Library of Portugal and other libraries in Lisbon.

Academic/Research Librarian of the Year Award
Winner: Paula T. Kaufman.

Ilene F. Rockman Instruction Publication of the Year Award
Winner: Char Booth, Claremont Colleges Library, for *Reflective Teaching, Effective Learning: Instructional Literacy for Library Educators* (ALA Editions).

Library and Information Technology Association/OCLC

Frederick G. Kilgour Award for Research in Library and Information Technology
Winner: G. Sayeed Choudhury, Johns Hopkins University.

American Society for Information Science and Technology

ASIS&T Best Information Science Book Award
Winners: Ricardo Baeza-Yates and Berthier Ribeiro-Neto for *Modern Information Retrieval: The Concepts and Technology Behind Search* (ACM).

John Wiley Best *JASIST* Paper
Winners: Sukomal Pal, Mandar Mitra, and Jaap Kamps for "Evaluation Effort, Reliability, and Reusability in XML Retrieval" in *JASIST* 62(2).

Pratt Severn Best Student Research Paper
Winner: April Lynne Earle, St. John's University, for "Design of an Application Profile for the St. John's University Oral History Collection." *JASIST* 62(2).

ProQuest Doctoral Dissertation
Winner: Jaime Snyder, Syracuse University, for "Image-Enabled Discourse: Investigating the Creation of Visual Information as Communicative Practice."

Research in Information Science Award
Winner: Kalervo Jarvelin, University of Tampere (Finland).

James Cretsos Leadership Award
Winner: Naresh Agarwal, Simmons College.

Thomson Reuters Doctoral Dissertation Proposal Scholarship
Winner: Lori McCay-Peet, Dalhousie University, for "At the Intersection: Investigating the Qualities of the Serendipitous Digital Environment and the Serendipity-Prone Person."

Watson Davis Award
Winner: K. T. Vaughan, University of North Carolina at Chapel Hill.

Association for Library and Information Science Education

ALISE/Eugene Garfield Doctoral Dissertation Competition
Winner: Eric M. Meyers, University of Washington, for "The Nature and Impact of Information Problem Solving in the Middle School Classroom."

ALISE Research Grant Competition
Winner: Carolyn Hank, McGill University; Cassidy Sugimoto, Indiana University; and Jeffrey Pomerantz, University of North Carolina at Chapel Hill, for "Teaching in the Age of Facebook and other Social Media: LIS Faculty and Students 'Friending' and 'Poking' in the Social Sphere."

ALISE/Bohdan S. Wynar Research Paper Competition

Winner: Jessica F. Lingel, Rutgers University, for "Improvisation, Tactics, and Wandering: Urban Information Practices of Migrational Individuals."

ALISE/ProQuest Methodology Paper Competition

Winners: Mahria Lebow and Heather L. O'Brien, University of British Columbia, for "Is There a Role for Physiological Methods in the Evaluation of Human-Information Interaction?"

Medical Library Association

Donald A. B. Lindberg Research Fellowship

Winner: Mary J. Moore for "The Investment in Health Sciences Libraries in Relation to U.S. National Rankings for Medical Education and Research."

Ida and George Eliot Prize

Winners: Margaret M. Bandy and Rosalind F. Dudden for "The Medical Library Association Guide to Managing Health Care Libraries."

Janet Doe Lectureship

Winner: Mark E. Funk for "Our World, Our Story: A Textual Analysis of Articles Published in the *Bulletin of the Medical Library Association/Journal of the Medical Library Association* from 1961 to 2010."

Notes

1. 2012–2013 Chief Officers of State Library Agencies Survey (COSLA). Available from the American Library Association Office for Research and Statistics.

2. Schwartz, M. "The Budget Balancing Act: LJ's Budget Survey Shows Modest Improvement, and Signs of More to Come." *Library Journal.* Retrieved January 20, 2013, from http://lj. libraryjournal.com/2013/01/funding/the-budget-balancing-act-library-budgets-show-modest-improvement-and-signs-of-more-to-come.

3. Hoffman, J., J. C. Bertot, and D. M. Davis. "Libraries Connect Communities: Public Library Funding and Technology Access Study 2011–2012." Digital supplement to *American Libraries*, June 2012. Retrieved January 20, 2013, from http://viewer.zmags.com/ publication/4673a369.

4. Zickuhr, K., L. Rainie, and K. Purcell. "Library Services in the Digital Age." Pew Internet and American Life Project. Retrieved January 20, 2013, from http://libraries.pewinternet. org/2013/01/22/library-services.

5. Patron Profiles are published by *Library Journal* and Bowker PubTrack Consumer. Available at http://www.thedigitalshift.com/research/patron-profiles/public/subscribe-2.

6. 2012-2013 Chief Officers of State Library Agencies Survey (COSLA), op. cit.

7. Schwartz, op. cit.

8. Troianovski, A. "The Web-Deprived Study at McDonald's." *Wall Street Journal.* Retrieved January 28, 2013, from http://online.wsj.com/article/SB10001424127887324731304578189 794161056954.html.

9. 2012–2013 Chief Officers of State Library Agencies Survey (COSLA), op. cit.

10. Institute of Museum and Library Services. "IMLS 2010 Public Library Survey Results Announced." Retrieved January 22, 2013, from http://www.imls.gov/imls_2010_public_ library_survey_results_announced.aspx.

11. *American Libraries.* "Manufacturing Makerspaces." Retrieved February 6, 2013, from http://americanlibrariesmagazine.org/features/02062013/manufacturing-makerspaces.

12. *2011 Academic Library Trends and Statistics* (2012). American Library Association. http://www.alastore.ala.org/detail.aspx?ID=4209.

13. ACRL Research Planning and Review Committee. "2012 Top Ten Trends in Academic Libraries: A Review of the Trends and Issues Affecting Academic Libraries in Higher Education." *College & Research Libraries News* 73(6): 311–320. Retrieved January 20, 2013, from http://crln.acrl.org/content/73/6/311.full.

14. The SPEC Kits are available from the Association of Research Libraries at http://publications.arl.org/SPEC_Kits.

15. American Library Association. American Association of School Librarians. *School Libraries Count! 2012* Retrieved January 20, 2013, from http://www.ala.org/aasl/sites/ala.org.aasl/files/content/researchandstatistics/slcsurvey/2012/AASL-SLC-2012-WEB.pdf.

Number of Libraries in the United States and Canada

Statistics are from *American Library Directory (ALD) 2012–2013* (Information Today, Inc., 2012). Data are exclusive of elementary and secondary school libraries.

Libraries in the United States

Public Libraries	16,912*
Public libraries, excluding branches	9,709†
Main public libraries that have branches	1,414
Public library branches	7,203
Academic Libraries	3,730*
Community college	1,151
Departmental	195
Law	1
Medical	9
Religious	11
University and college	2,579
Departmental	1,327
Law	184
Medical	236
Religious	238
Armed Forces Libraries	275*
Air Force	81
Medical	6
Army	128
Medical	27
Marine Corps	12
Navy	54
Law	1
Medical	11
Government Libraries	1,060*
Law	389
Medical	145
Special Libraries (excluding public, academic, armed forces, and government)	6,756*
Law	818
Medical	1,346
Religious	498
Total Special Libraries (including public, academic, armed forces, and government)	8,014
Total law	1,393
Total medical	1,780
Total religious	990
Total Libraries Counted(*)	28,733

Libraries in Regions Administered by the United States

Public Libraries	28*
Public libraries, excluding branches	11†
Main public libraries that have branches	3
Public library branches	17
Academic Libraries	37*
Community college	4
Departmental	3
Medical	0
University and college	33
Departmental	21
Law	3
Medical	2
Religious	1
Armed Forces Libraries	2*
Air Force	1
Army	1
Navy	0
Government Libraries	4*
Law	1
Medical	1
Special Libraries (excluding public, academic, armed forces, and government)	6*
Law	3
Medical	1
Religious	1
Total Special Libraries (including public, academic, armed forces, and government)	14
Total law	7
Total medical	4
Total religious	2
Total Libraries Counted(*)	77

Libraries in Canada

Public Libraries	2,046*
Public libraries, excluding branches	812†
Main public libraries that have branches	136
Public library branches	1,234
Academic Libraries	346*
Community college	84
Departmental	14
Medical	0
Religious	4
University and college	262
Departmental	177

Law	16
Medical	20
Religious	33
Government Libraries	275*
Law	38
Medical	7
Special Libraries (excluding public, academic, armed forces, and government)	854*
Law	101
Medical	170
Religious	25
Total Special Libraries (including public, academic, armed forces, and government)	972
Total law	155
Total medical	197
Total religious	87
Total Libraries Counted(*)	3,521

Summary

Total U.S. Libraries	28,733
Total Libraries Administered by the United States	77
Total Canadian Libraries	3,521
Grand Total of Libraries Listed	32,331

Note: Numbers followed by an asterisk are added to find "Total libraries counted" for each of the three geographic areas (United States, U.S.-administered regions, and Canada). The sum of the three totals is the "Grand total of libraries listed" in *ALD*. For details on the count of libraries, see the preface to the 65th edition of *ALD—Ed.*

†Federal, state, and other statistical sources use this figure (libraries *excluding* branches) as the total for public libraries.

Highlights of IMLS and NCES Surveys

The Institute of Museum and Library Services (IMLS) and the National Center for Education Statistics (NCES) collect and disseminate statistical information about libraries in the United States and its outlying areas. Two major surveys are conducted by NCES, the Academic Libraries Survey and the School Library Media Centers Survey; two others, the Public Libraries Survey and the State Library Agencies Survey, were formerly conducted by NCES, but are now handled by IMLS. Both NCES and IMLS also conduct surveys on related topics.

This article presents highlights from two of the most recently conducted surveys. For more information on the surveys, see "National Center for Education Statistics Library Statistics Program" in Part 1 and "Institute of Museum and Library Services Library Programs" in Part 2 of this volume.

Public Libraries

The following are highlights from the publication *Public Libraries in the United States Survey: Fiscal Year 2010,* released in January 2013 by IMLS.

Services and Operations

- In fiscal year (FY) 2010 public libraries served 297.6 million people throughout the United States, a number that is equivalent to 96.4 percent of the total U.S. population. There were 8,951 public libraries in the 50 states and the District of Columbia, with 17,078 public library branches and bookmobiles.
- While physical visits to library buildings decreased from the prior year for the first time in ten years, visitation remained strong with an overall ten-year increase of 32.7 percent. On average, Americans visited a public library 5.3 times per year, a ten-year increase of 21.7 percent. Although the national visitation rate was down slightly in FY 2010 from the previous year, the story at the state level was mixed, with most states showing a decrease but some having increases.
- The total of programs offered to the public by public libraries in FY 2010 was 3.75 million, which amounts to an average of at least one program a day for every library system in the nation. The majority of these programs (61.5 percent) were designed for children.
- Attendance at programs has continued to rise, indicating an increased demand for these services; it reached 86.64 million in FY 2010, a six-year increase of 28.8 percent.
- Program offerings differed across locales. Public libraries in rural areas offered significantly more programs per capita, with 16.7 per 1,000 people, which was a one-year increase of 2.3 percent from FY 2009. Suburban and town libraries offered 12.9 and 13.3 programs per 1,000 people, respectively, similar to the national rate of 12.6. Libraries in cities had the lowest rate, 10.5 per 1,000 people.

Collections

- The composition of public library collections has changed dramatically in recent years. While printed books continue to dominate the physical portion of collections, making up 87.1 percent of the total in FY 2010, the share of nonprint materials—including audio and video materials and electronic books—has increased.

- The number of e-books has tripled since FY 2003. In FY 2010 there were 18.50 million e-books available for circulation, a one-year increase of 22.5 percent. E-book volume increased by 323.5 percent between 2003 (the first time this metric was collected in the survey) and 2010.

- In addition to e-books, the number of nonprint materials in public library collections, including audio and video materials in both physical and downloadable formats, has increased greatly since FY 2001. In FY 2010 there were 55.05 million total audio materials, both physical and downloadable, which include music and audiobooks. This was a one-year increase of 4.3 percent and a ten-year increase of 61.2 percent. There were 53.21 million total video materials, both physical and downloadable. This was a one-year increase of 5.0 percent and a ten-year increase of 112.4 percent.

- Public-access computer use continued to be one of the fastest-growing services in public libraries. In FY 2010 public libraries reported a computer use rate of more than one use for every five visits to the library. Public libraries have responded to demand by increasing access, doubling the number of public computers in the past decade.

- Physical visits to libraries decreased 1.1 percent in FY 2010, but there was an overall ten-year increase of 32.7 percent FY 2001–FY 2010. On average, Americans visited a public library 5.3 times per year, a ten-year increase of 21.7 percent.

Revenue

- Public libraries had $11.3 billion in revenue in FY 2010, a decrease of 3.5 percent from FY 2009 after adjusting for inflation. Although local governments have generally been the largest source of revenue for public libraries, they have had to take on an even larger role as state support has declined.

- Total operating revenue for public libraries was $11.30 billion in FY 2010, falling for the first time in ten years, most likely a result of budget cuts attributable to the recession. From FY 2009 to 2010 total revenue decreased by $407.79 million. Revenue per capita was $37.97, which reflected a 1-year decrease of 3.9 percent, but a ten-year increase of 3.1 percent from FY 2001.

- In FY 2010 revenue from local governments accounted for 84.8 percent of total revenue, an increase of 9.7 percent since FY 2001. In contrast, revenue from state government was 7.1 percent of total revenue, a ten-year decrease of 44.6 percent.

Expenditures

- Operating expenditures of $10.77 billion were reported by public libraries in FY 2010, the first decrease since FY 2001.
- Although expenditures across all U.S. public libraries were $36.18 per capita, expenditures per capita varied greatly by state, with spending as low as $15.99 and as high as $67.78. Highest per capita expenditures among public libraries were found in the District of Columbia ($67.78), and the states of Illinois ($59.46) and New York ($58.01). States with the lowest per capita expenditures were Mississippi ($15.99), Tennessee ($16.17), and West Virginia ($18.04).
- Thirty-six states had decreases in their per capita operating expenditures from FY 2009. The largest decreases were in the District of Columbia (14.6 percent) and Georgia (12.3 percent); the largest increases were in New Hampshire (30.6 percent) and Louisiana (6.8 percent).

Circulation

- Public libraries circulated 2.46 billion materials in FY 2010, a one-year increase of 2.1 percent and a ten-year increase of 38.0 percent. Circulation per capita was 8.3, an increase of 26.4 percent over ten years. Circulation per 1,000 visits was 1,567.2, an increase of 4.0 percent over ten years.
- Circulation of children's materials comprised 34.0 percent of total circulation, at 837.12 million materials. This reflects an increase of 2.7 percent since FY 2009 and a ten-year increase of 28.3 percent. There was a strong positive relationship between circulation per capita and expenditures on collections.
- Public libraries in suburban areas had the highest circulation per capita, both in total circulation and for children's materials. Circulation per capita for all materials in suburban libraries was 9.8, an increase of 2.2 percent from FY 2009. Circulation per capita for children's materials was 3.5, an increase of 2.6 percent.

Work Force

- The recession has had an impact on the public library work force, which decreased by 6,385 full-time equivalent (FTE) staff between FY 2008 and 2010, a drop of 3.9 percent. Staff-related expenditures were $7.21 billion, or 67 percent of public library expenses in FY 2010.
- Librarians made up one-third of all library staff. Although the majority of these librarians held a master's degree in library science from a program accredited by the American Library Association (ALA-MLS), only half of all libraries reported having a librarian with an ALA-MLS on staff.

The full report is available at http://www.imls.gov/assets/1/AssetManager/PLS2010.pdf.

Academic Libraries

The following are highlights from the First Look publication *Academic Libraries, 2010*, released in December 2011 by NCES.

Services

- Academic libraries lent some 11.2 million documents to other libraries in fiscal year 2010 and borrowed approximately 10.2 million documents from other libraries and commercial services. Documents from commercial services accounted for about 176,000 of those documents borrowed.
- The majority of academic libraries, 2,362, were open between 60 and 99 hours during a typical week in fall 2010. Another 564 were open 100 or more hours per typical week.
- In FY 2010 academic libraries conducted approximately 34.6 million information services to individuals, including computer searches.

Collections

- At the end of FY 2010 there were 227 academic libraries that held at least 1 million or more books, serial backfiles, and other paper materials including government documents.
- Academic libraries held approximately 158.7 million e-books and about 1.8 million electronic reference sources and aggregation services at the end of FY 2010. During the fiscal year academic libraries added about 12.9 million audiovisual material units, making their total audiovisual material holdings more than 1.12 billion units.

Staff

- Academic libraries reported 88,943 FTE staff working in academic libraries during fall 2010, and 26,706 FTE librarians working during the same period. Librarians accounted for about 30 percent of the total number of FTE staff in academic libraries.

Expenditures

- Just under half of academic libraries, 1,739, had total expenditures of $500,000 or more in FY 2010. Another 581 academic libraries had total expenditures under $100,000.
- During the fiscal year academic libraries spent about $3.4 billion on salaries and wages, representing approximately 50 percent of total library expenditures.
- Academic libraries spent approximately $152.4 million for electronic books, serial backfiles, and other materials in FY 2010. Expenditures for electronic current serial subscriptions totaled about $1.2 billion. During the fiscal year academic libraries spent approximately $142.7 million for computer hardware and software.

Electronic Services

- In fall 2010 about 41 percent of academic libraries reported providing documents digitized by staff.
- More than half (54 percent) reported providing technology to assist patrons with disabilities.

Virtual Reference

- During FY 2010 about 72 percent of academic libraries reported that they supported virtual reference services.
- About 32 percent reported that they used instant messaging applications.

Public Library State Rankings, 2010

State	Library Visits per Capita	Reference Transactions per Capita	Circulation Transactions per Capita	Interlibrary Loans per 1,000 Population	Average Public-use Computers per Outlet
Alabama	46	22	46	33	17
Alaska	32	46	38	31	47
Arizona	37	39	27	24	4
Arkansas	43	30	42	43	39
California	35	23	37	21	13
Colorado	11	12	5	18	10
Connecticut	3	11	17	16	19
Delaware	25	41	9	6	14
District of Columbia	38	4	3	50	2
Florida	33	2	34	46	1
Georgia	45	14	45	25	5
Hawaii	4	44	4	51	51
Idaho	16	20	12	27	36
Illinois	7	8	15	7	23
Indiana	5	13	3	38	8
Iowa	12	45	19	19	44
Kansas	14	21	8	13	40
Kentucky	36	29	35	41	6
Louisiana	47	3	48	36	28
Maine	21	49	25	9	48
Maryland	23	6	13	32	3
Massachusetts	13	27	20	4	32
Michigan	22	15	22	10	20
Minnesota	28	35	11	15	26
Mississippi	51	47	51	48	37
Missouri	19	18	14	26	31
Montana	31	50	30	14	41
Nebraska	15	32	16	34	42
Nevada	39	42	29	30	24
New Hampshire	1	28	7	17	49
New Jersey	20	16	28	12	18
New Mexico	29	37	36	45	30
New York	18	5	24	8	22
North Carolina	34	7	40	49	11
North Dakota	40	36	33	20	46
Ohio	2	1	1	5	21
Oklahoma	30	38	32	44	34
Oregon	9	34	2	2	29
Pennsylvania	44	31	41	11	33
Rhode Island	24	33	31	3	15
South Carolina	41	10	39	39	9
South Dakota	27	43	26	29	45
Tennessee	50	48	50	42	25
Texas	48	40	44	40	7
Utah	8	9	4	47	27

State	Library Visits per Capita	Reference Transactions per Capita	Circulation Transactions per Capita	Interlibrary Loans per 1,000 Population	Average Public-use Computers per Outlet
Vermont	6	25	23	23	50
Virginia	26	17	18	35	12
Washington	10	26	6	37	16
West Virginia	49	51	49	28	43
Wisconsin	17	24	10	1	35
Wyoming	4	19	21	22	38

State	Public-use Internet Computers per 5,000 Population	Print Materials per Capita	Audio Materials per 1,000 Population	Video Materials per 1,000 Population	Current Print Serial Subscriptions per 1,000 Population
Alabama	16	41	42	44	48
Alaska	28	21	25	5	12
Arizona	45	51	40	41	46
Arkansas	33	31	47	45	38
California	49	43	43	42	45
Colorado	23	36	20	16	29
Connecticut	11	7	6	8	15
Delaware	44	37	35	27	25
District of Columbia	12	22	24	23	30
Florida	30	46	36	32	40
Georgia	39	50	51	50	51
Hawaii	51	29	48	46	47
Idaho	14	23	27	26	31
Illinois	18	16	5	14	8
Indiana	4	6	2	3	4
Iowa	6	12	9	12	3
Kansas	2	10	16	4	18
Kentucky	24	42	34	36	36
Louisiana	17	30	46	34	27
Maine	8	3	19	11	11
Maryland	40	32	23	28	32
Massachusetts	31	4	14	13	16
Michigan	15	18	18	22	20
Minnesota	21	25	26	33	23
Mississippi	34	45	50	48	44
Missouri	26	20	21	31	9
Montana	13	24	38	29	26
Nebraska	5	9	22	18	6
Nevada	50	49	30	24	42
New Hampshire	7	1	3	2	2
New Jersey	29	17	17	21	22
New Mexico	27	27	32	37	17
New York	25	15	10	20	10
North Carolina	42	48	49	51	43
North Dakota	19	11	29	25	13
Ohio	20	14	1	1	1

State	Public-use Internet Computers per 5,000 Population	Print Materials per Capita	Audio Materials per 1,000 Population	Video Materials per 1,000 Population	Current Print Serial Subscriptions per 1,000 Population
Oklahoma	36	35	37	43	41
Oregon	38	28	13	19	28
Pennsylvania	48	38	11	38	35
Rhode Island	10	8	33	17	24
South Carolina	35	40	41	40	33
South Dakota	9	13	28	15	19
Tennessee	46	44	44	49	50
Texas	43	47	45	47	49
Utah	47	33	12	10	34
Vermont	1	2	7	7	5
Virginia	37	34	31	39	39
Washington	32	39	15	30	21
West Virginia	41	26	39	35	37
Wisconsin	22	19	8	6	14
Wyoming	3	5	4	9	7

State	Paid FTE Staff per 25,000 Population	Paid FTE Librarians per 25,000 Population	ALA-MLS Librarians per 25,000 Population	Other Paid FTE Staff per 25,000 Population	Total Operating Revenue per Capita
Alabama	41	31	44	44	46
Alaska	29	30	28	28	15
Arizona	45	45	36	39	37
Arkansas	37	50	49	21	43
California	49	47	32	46	33
Colorado	16	29	14	10	8
Connecticut	7	6	1	12	9
Delaware	32	33	37	30	30
District of Columbia	8	27	5	4	1
Florida	43	43	23	33	35
Georgia	50	51	40	42	47
Hawaii	33	37	12	27	44
Idaho	20	32	46	13	32
Illinois	6	9	8	5	2
Indiana	3	11	10	1	6
Iowa	17	4	27	34	27
Kansas	4	7	20	7	14
Kentucky	27	12	35	43	24
Louisiana	23	17	29	24	13
Maine	11	5	11	26	29
Maryland	15	15	16	15	16
Massachusetts	19	10	7	29	20
Michigan	24	24	13	22	18
Minnesota	35	34	22	31	22
Mississippi	38	23	51	45	51
Missouri	13	35	34	6	19
Montana	39	19	42	49	41

State	Paid FTE Staff per 25,000 Population	Paid FTE Librarians per 25,000 Population	ALA-MLS Librarians per 25,000 Population	Other Paid FTE Staff per 25,000 Population	Total Operating Revenue per Capita
Nebraska	14	8	30	20	23
Nevada	47	48	43	40	25
New Hampshire	2	1	2	16	11
New Jersey	10	26	4	8	4
New Mexico	36	28	33	36	38
New York	9	18	6	9	5
North Carolina	46	49	38	37	45
North Dakota	42	21	45	50	42
Ohio	5	13	9	2	3
Oklahoma	31	20	31	41	31
Oregon	26	36	18	17	12
Pennsylvania	40	42	25	32	40
Rhode Island	18	16	3	18	17
South Carolina	30	38	21	23	39
South Dakota	28	14	47	38	36
Tennessee	51	46	50	48	50
Texas	48	44	39	47	49
Utah	34	41	41	25	34
Vermont	12	2	24	35	26
Virginia	25	39	17	14	28
Washington	22	40	15	11	10
West Virginia	44	22	48	51	48
Wisconsin	21	25	19	19	21
Wyoming	1	3	26	3	7

State	State Operating Revenue per Capita	Local Operating Revenue per Capita	Other Operating Revenue per Capita	Total Operating Expenditures per Capita	Collection Expenditures per Capita
Alabama	31	45	32	46	46
Alaska	28	13	27	14	27
Arizona	43	34	47	38	33
Arkansas	12	42	46	44	38
California	33	26	30	28	43
Colorado	48	6	14	11	6
Connecticut	37	11	7	5	10
Delaware	5	35	36	29	18
District of Columbia	50	1	49	1	19
Florida	23	31	45	30	36
Georgia	9	47	43	48	50
Hawaii	2	51	21	43	48
Idaho	34	29	22	31	37
Illinois	11	2	12	2	1
Indiana	8	7	19	10	3
Iowa	29	23	16	25	21
Kansas	18	14	10	15	14
Kentucky	21	20	24	35	29
Louisiana	22	12	40	23	24

State	State Operating Revenue per Capita	Local Operating Revenue per Capita	Other Operating Revenue per Capita	Total Operating Expenditures per Capita	Collection Expenditures per Capita
Maine	39	36	1	24	40
Maryland	4	21	6	13	12
Massachusetts	24	19	15	17	11
Michigan	26	15	28	18	20
Minnesota	15	22	13	22	23
Mississippi	10	50	41	51	51
Missouri	27	16	20	19	5
Montana	36	39	23	42	42
Nebraska	38	18	25	26	15
Nevada	25	33	3	33	31
New Hampshire	45	8	11	8	8
New Jersey	35	3	29	4	9
New Mexico	19	37	50	37	39
New York	13	9	4	3	7
North Carolina	16	43	39	45	47
North Dakota	17	41	26	41	30
Ohio	1	40	5	7	2
Oklahoma	30	24	34	34	22
Oregon	42	10	18	12	16
Pennsylvania	6	46	9	40	41
Rhode Island	3	27	8	16	25
South Carolina	20	38	42	39	32
South Dakota	51	32	44	36	35
Tennessee	44	48	48	50	49
Texas	40	44	51	47	45
Utah	41	28	33	32	13
Vermont	49	30	2	20	28
Virginia	14	25	37	27	34
Washington	47	5	35	9	4
West Virginia	7	49	38	49	44
Wisconsin	32	17	31	21	26
Wyoming	46	4	17	6	17

State	Staff Expenditures per Capita	Salaries and Wages Expenditures per Capita	Registered Borrowers per Capita
Alabama	46	45	37
Alaska	13	19	21
Arizona	40	42	10
Arkansas	45	46	20
California	28	32	29
Colorado	15	13	24
Connecticut	4	2	40
Delaware	32	34	32
District of Columbia	1	1	44
Florida	35	36	17
Georgia	47	47	51

State	Staff Expenditures per Capita	Salaries and Wages Expenditures per Capita	Registered Borrowers per Capita
Hawaii	42	29	16
Idaho	31	31	25
Illinois	7	5	49
Indiana	11	11	8
Iowa	25	24	9
Kansas	17	15	2
Kentucky	38	39	23
Louisiana	29	28	27
Maine	22	18	11
Maryland	10	12	26
Massachusetts	16	10	35
Michigan	20	22	39
Minnesota	19	23	1
Mississippi	51	51	48
Missouri	23	21	15
Montana	41	41	43
Nebraska	26	26	4
Nevada	27	27	46
New Hampshire	6	4	5
New Jersey	5	7	33
New Mexico	36	37	6
New York	2	3	31
North Carolina	43	44	28
North Dakota	44	43	45
Ohio	8	8	3
Oklahoma	34	33	19
Oregon	12	16	38
Pennsylvania	39	40	47
Rhode Island	14	14	34
South Carolina	37	38	30
South Dakota	33	30	36
Tennessee	50	50	41
Texas	48	48	42
Utah	30	35	14
Vermont	21	17	12
Virginia	24	25	22
Washington	9	9	18
West Virginia	49	49	50
Wisconsin	18	20	13
Wyoming	3	6	7

FTE=full-time equivalent.

"Per capita" is based on the total unduplicated population of legal service areas.

"Total" includes the 50 states and the District of Columbia but excludes outlying areas and libraries that do not meet the FSCS Public Library Definition.

The District of Columbia, although not a state, is included in the state rankings. Special care should be used in comparing its data to state data.

Caution should be used in making comparisons with the state of Hawaii, as Hawaii reports only one public library for the entire state.

Source: Compiled by Carol Collier from Survey of Public Libraries in the United States, Fiscal Year 2010, Institute of Museum and Library Services, 2013.

Library Acquisition Expenditures, 2011–2012: U.S. Public, Academic, Special, and Government Libraries

The information in these tables is taken from current edition of *American Library Directory* (*ALD*) (Information Today, Inc.). The tables report acquisition expenditures by public, academic, special, and government libraries.

The total number of libraries in the United States and in regions administered by the United States listed in this 65th edition of *ALD* is 28,810, including 16,940 public libraries, 3,767 academic libraries, 6,762 special libraries, and 1,064 government libraries.

Understanding the Tables

Number of libraries includes only those U.S. libraries in *ALD* that reported annual acquisition expenditures (1,864 public libraries, 784 academic libraries, 129 special libraries, and 42 government libraries). Libraries that reported annual income but not expenditures are not included in the count. Academic libraries include university, college, and junior college libraries. Special academic libraries, such as law and medical libraries, that reported acquisition expenditures separately from the institution's main library are counted as independent libraries.

The amount in the *total acquisition expenditures* column for a given state is generally greater than the sum of the categories of expenditures. This is because the total acquisition expenditures amount also includes the expenditures of libraries that did not itemize by category.

Figures in *categories of expenditure* columns represent only those libraries that itemized expenditures. Libraries that reported a total acquisition expenditure amount but did not itemize are only represented in the total acquisition expenditures column.

Table 1 / Public Library Acquisition Expenditures

Categories of Expenditures (in U.S. dollars)

State	Number of Libraries	Total Acquisition Expenditures	Books	Other Print Materials	Periodicals/ Serials	Manuscripts & Archives	AV Equipment	AV Materials	Microforms	Electronic Reference	Preservation
Alabama	26	18,208,992	1,309,576	9,400	43,038	2,000	297	208,249	2,013	3,826	400
Alaska	14	917,622	179,339	1,100	27,894	0	0	33,540	500	23,160	6,871
Arizona	21	12,693,304	2,872,076	4,815,715	189,756	575	0	2,181,700	48,786	1,982,708	8,876
Arkansas	18	4,364,551	2,696,585	22,064	181,835	0	23,105	484,518	1,640	346,435	8,270
California	72	82,885,645	33,708,844	2,590,921	3,618,897	6,500	13,430	8,959,512	134,245	7,958,380	85,395
Colorado	36	17,617,905	6,405,953	15,300	494,590	0	17,200	3,506,034	1,000	1,470,326	450
Connecticut	65	13,525,393	4,496,153	666,213	861,449	600	10,600	1,012,106	118,040	1,131,861	25,444
Delaware	7	710,064	166,285	0	4,679	0	0	34,540	0	3,480	0
District of Columbia	0	0	0	0	0	0	0	0	0	0	0
Florida	36	30,834,083	9,608,252	60,247	880,393	1,500	129,966	4,890,964	9,131	2,269,320	2,000
Georgia	16	8,361,804	2,153,058	326	84,035	0	3,081	384,620	800	227,327	945
Hawaii	1	11,054,314	111,215	0	159,338	0	0	0	51,293	2,891,021	0
Idaho	10	412,305	111,215	500	0	0	0	14,199	0	14,064	0
Illinois	96	40,178,421	8,822,665	84,388	703,173	10,000	88,253	2,954,089	45,346	3,218,666	16,869
Indiana	66	26,032,706	10,902,162	12,000	1,120,915	0	111,460	4,036,628	199,288	1,715,524	75,647
Iowa	62	7,069,268	1,924,548	90,141	211,522	15	13,768	596,503	3,555	228,941	0
Kansas	38	12,924,555	2,557,930	179,124	854,413	0	23,600	926,782	3,879	682,409	400
Kentucky	20	6,826,072	1,964,248	2,486	91,811	0	15,329	839,989	15,085	412,000	0
Louisiana	7	6,346,603	2,399,628	5,000	299,786	3,000	111,897	811,895	54,882	571,199	0
Maine	47	1,536,311	849,400	1,350	120,075	2,000	5,350	135,072	800	201,461	1,000
Maryland	3	10,353,632	1,823,665	0	85,337	0	0	974,786	0	175,455	0
Massachusetts	88	20,188,969	3,816,547	94,854	433,980	0	3,815	1,120,037	34,959	432,793	3,200
Michigan	84	34,187,354	8,857,556	187,280	634,020	0	144,831	2,019,670	10,768	1,488,468	12,475
Minnesota	37	15,214,424	2,712,699	7,447	127,486	0	4,500	619,824	10,678	369,451	668
Mississippi	10	1,105,620	470,815	0	21,467	0	0	99,375	26,000	93,028	2,162

Missouri	33	18,760,564	2,089,804	0	198,303	0	25,796	758,146	3,909	912,554	0
Montana	19	865,557	531,777	1,000	90,166	200	10,316	134,977	2,873	71,748	2,500
Nebraska	30	2,129,362	1,186,327	399,871	44,957	0	47	63,549	540	242,267	2,346
Nevada	5	1,172,070	128,500	1,193	10,558	0	0	34,634	0	20,000	0
New Hampshire	65	2,513,267	1,125,205	500	136,702	0	7,428	267,288	13,791	91,776	7,050
New Jersey	76	28,969,447	13,924,948	77,587	1,363,873	500	21,500	3,348,806	105,249	1,833,855	5,850
New Mexico	13	4,153,739	2,141,167	207,615	59,199	0	6,000	446,382	11,539	435,758	0
New York	136	40,994,353	22,286,985	357,920	2,029,340	5,000	147,577	4,192,455	99,167	2,406,171	22,783
North Carolina	27	13,144,635	7,483,265	1,344,458	250,136	0	31,840	936,685	14,040	510,209	0
North Dakota	16	1,725,586	739,755	4,085	88,029	0	35,000	135,161	3,500	121,887	1,000
Ohio	69	52,739,536	23,843,610	498,861	3,637,637	6,921	39,329	11,436,292	379,637	6,758,178	338,159
Oklahoma	10	12,259,235	5,556,143	11,831	851,876	0	0	1,563,188	3,305	1,444,448	0
Oregon	40	7,667,614	3,010,968	22,827	343,014	0	1,500	801,911	23,699	175,563	1,872,003
Pennsylvania	77	19,580,012	6,486,760	895,879	1,725,380	156,260	14,208	2,854,102	397,884	1,587,029	106,789
Rhode Island	9	9,925,724	532,374	71,214	63,807	0	0	96,962	70	770,614	1,000
South Carolina	17	10,980,560	6,204,533	22,222	407,116	5,000	90,907	1,930,806	23,809	1,439,876	12,235
South Dakota	18	1,911,963	973,589	1,000	97,149	0	395	308,448	50	92,165	0
Tennessee	24	5,645,932	1,405,868	0	149,357	0	16,600	342,193	1,200	424,960	1,724
Texas	96	56,792,147	10,553,210	334,782	940,652	200	287,296	1,648,710	64,872	1,642,953	9,450
Utah	11	3,827,367	2,023,678	1,203	65,063	245,000	0	851,771	30,367	419,209	70,000
Vermont	47	1,380,613	591,172	571	26,905	0	0	118,272	276	21,771	500
Virginia	30	11,642,409	3,815,257	3,148	432,029	38,278	0	963,360	77,322	909,491	1,503,000
Washington	24	19,351,424	2,859,325	536,079	138,160	0	54,230	731,045	3,211	546,963	400
West Virginia	16	4,065,232	1,498,143	4,086	113,400	9,000	24,000	245,236	13,810	862,874	2,900
Wisconsin	63	7,649,970	3,873,367	82,021	241,274	0	6,475	1,157,488	11,892	576,116	2,700
Wyoming	13	1,509,073	425,477	4,694	40,577	0	6,000	91,433	55	43,039	0
Puerto Rico	0	0	0	0	0	0	0	0	0	0	0
Total	1,864	724,907,308	236,100,406	13,730,503	24,794,548	492,549	1,546,926	72,303,932	2,058,755	52,272,777	4,213,461
Estimated % of Acquisition Expenditures		33	2	3	0	0	10	0	7	1	

Table 2 / Academic Library Acquisition Expenditures

State	Number of Libraries	Total Acquisition Expenditures	Categories of Expenditures (in U.S. dollars)								
			Books	Other Print Materials	Periodicals/ Serials	Manuscripts & Archives	AV Equipment	AV Materials	Microforms	Electronic Reference	Preservation
Alabama	14	17,401,673	1,414,083	4,017	4,205,807	0	10,000	124,360	108,162	2,205,977	86,002
Alaska	5	6,777,613	560,433	20,000	2,446,408	0	300	77,387	16,807	938,392	18,827
Arizona	9	2,948,097	527,441	2,500	224,043	4,997	1,495	130,529	28,227	1,705,813	12,030
Arkansas	8	10,898,543	1,701,276	354,042	6,257,749	34,264	1,000	100,483	208,023	1,692,679	41,604
California	59	89,900,774	8,684,443	790,679	15,000,843	5,203	659,715	460,833	306,964	13,494,798	557,981
Colorado	11	8,782,818	1,133,026	31,239	2,634,333	0	0	188,583	0	1,389,529	49,384
Connecticut	12	9,243,517	1,539,347	250	3,923,175	0	63,924	154,063	87,307	1,635,990	95,665
Delaware	3	8,346,310	40,000	0	8,419	0	0	0	0	0	0
District of Columbia	3	11,890,787	1,973,224	110,000	6,131,228	0	0	8,531	99,300	1,263,882	94,154
Florida	31	33,170,942	5,910,011	941,932	14,397,063	0	26,000	522,339	199,112	8,885,790	211,499
Georgia	21	14,737,972	1,072,219	2,000	1,450,501	0	4,075	148,069	51,714	1,937,872	56,037
Hawaii	2	659,932	128,000	0	176,200	0	3,000	16,047	14,000	77,438	18,700
Idaho	4	9,324,254	368,331	54,040	1,886,840	0	0	11,776	0	597,018	24,910
Illinois	30	64,865,678	9,136,531	1,010	16,854,244	0	34,435	328,017	43,809	13,457,839	162,000
Indiana	18	22,887,113	3,908,469	24,211	13,238,742	0	44,452	187,987	25,275	1,722,280	104,453
Iowa	18	24,834,200	3,002,497	564,763	13,409,174	0	31,139	104,827	34,325	2,293,161	115,081
Kansas	17	8,899,385	1,347,721	24,000	6,486,431	0	8,718	38,478	35,018	816,644	62,840
Kentucky	13	19,264,497	2,022,167	11,387	6,377,828	76,230	4,212	156,163	148,925	8,050,607	133,281
Louisiana	8	5,546,605	547,193	36,361	3,236,304	3,427	3,720	9,134	68,382	1,393,211	36,718
Maine	3	7,905,379	1,509,525	0	5,842,437	0	0	44,812	62,500	251,231	74,374
Maryland	11	8,667,134	1,201,304	6,209	5,174,482	14,926	0	64,522	11,535	1,171,303	68,381
Massachusetts	27	182,954,950	4,066,278	36,256	13,239,722	0	57,000	248,170	41,575	6,685,563	113,329
Michigan	28	21,307,985	3,286,079	157,690	7,504,010	26,000	40,000	156,320	201,810	6,721,232	99,924
Minnesota	17	12,882,202	2,226,552	31,664	4,914,301	300	53,455	259,512	67,722	1,357,034	110,537
Mississippi	6	3,714,166	335,367	0	1,365,001	0	1,000	36,353	116,000	1,397,997	44,200

Missouri	16	11,573,315	558,330	19,916	1,297,471	2,326	6,928	108,459	115,395	788,347	38,315
Montana	5	3/4,3/5	164,269	0	154,718	0	10,000	9,028	3,000	20,000	0
Nebraska	9	11,083,072	711,188	123,250	2,178,472	15,000	0	146,270	48,324	831,478	17,948
Nevada	2	415,295	136,754	0	11,877	0	0	15,908	217	49,926	613
New Hampshire	6	9,351,484	1,195,724	0	4,180,222	0	0	700	21,116	1,351,794	76,271
New Jersey	12	8,800,932	1,113,668	69,154	2,139,374	0	0	81,736	25,708	1,212,233	8,585
New Mexico	4	624,302	44,000	0	8,800	0	0	11,000	4,300	24,400	2,200
New York	53	72,442,305	10,601,212	395,716	21,615,938	29,242	164,973	584,230	204,089	14,900,038	346,561
North Carolina	31	95,478,694	9,360,216	43,297	24,390,859	2,000	31,332	554,693	563,804	3,733,767	136,446
North Dakota	3	5,139,898	396,179	10,000	2,380,610	0	1,080	23,797	684	515,813	19,579
Ohio	33	29,439,084	5,654,820	78,695	9,177,935	2,461	22,254	278,110	135,370	6,649,533	279,867
Oklahoma	9	6,462,424	688,701	0	2,518,421	2,000	0	130,646	18,127	2,156,045	12,899
Oregon	17	27,244,514	1,322,626	4,052	3,244,326	0	46,350	116,011	0	2,236,027	79,679
Pennsylvania	32	24,356,816	4,129,140	80,632	9,173,728	36,489	71,203	350,604	219,698	3,687,638	201,493
Rhode Island	4	2,314,060	467,521	2,100	1,016,191	9,500	36,338	40,537	21,021	609,916	16,930
South Carolina	17	10,352,605	2,192,778	53,414	2,830,946	20,000	10,000	111,678	79,717	2,434,228	101,623
South Dakota	4	3,219,219	279,889	0	743,406	0	764	16,145	12,451	555,088	18,666
Tennessee	15	19,068,645	902,473	0	1,551,936	0	0	48,596	68,400	2,805,231	7,538
Texas	37	47,668,295	8,605,724	41,909	20,489,053	6,050	92,562	261,214	253,354	5,350,151	238,729
Utah	5	7,009,607	1,254,090	0	3,101,740	0	6,000	66,500	3,500	907,180	5,383
Vermont	6	1,661,816	437,277	0	795,983	3,500	5,000	31,695	1,770	348,091	9,000
Virginia	28	34,060,071	6,549,160	625,166	13,040,952	2,000	27,747	264,716	102,695	6,372,039	94,901
Washington	15	13,196,898	2,350,016	0	6,348,220	14,564	50,000	267,322	7,900	1,683,749	26,673
West Virginia	14	3,518,263	349,337	11,985	501,290	10,000	19,000	44,485	70,550	813,797	12,283
Wisconsin	19	22,401,187	2,867,270	7,093	6,284,323	2,000	23,569	176,886	111,475	1,257,697	65,597
Wyoming	3	7,480,309	3,458,937	0	2,201,321	0	0	13,200	0	863,481	0
Puerto Rico	7	6,231,740	784,208	1,000	4,648,724	5,000	34,490	44,940	0	696,183	9,800
Total	784	1,088,781,751	124,217,024	4,771,629	302,411,821	327,479	1,707,230	7,376,401	4,069,157	143,997,150	4,219,490
Estimated % of Acquisition Expenditures			11	0	28	0	0	1	0	13	0

Table 3 / Special Library Acquisition Expenditures

State	Number of Libraries	Total Acquisition Expenditures	Books	Other Print Materials	Periodicals/ Serials	Manuscripts & Archives	AV Equipment	AV Materials	Microforms	Electronic Reference	Preservation
Alabama	1	1,375	250	0	525	0	0	0	0	500	100
Alaska	0	0	0	0	0	0	0	0	0	0	0
Arizona	4	20,324	3,500	0	324	0	0	0	0	0	1,000
Arkansas	0	0	0	0	0	0	0	0	0	0	0
California	14	416,748	51,698	2,000	171,059	0	0	1,100	0	65,891	7,500
Colorado	2	66,575	27,000	0	27,379	0	0	2,000	0	3,621	6,575
Connecticut	0	0	0	0	0	0	0	0	0	0	0
Delaware	0	0	0	0	0	0	0	0	0	0	0
District of Columbia	2	869,577	121,000	0	52,000	0	0	261	25,000	13,000	504,877
Florida	5	97,760	46,650	1,000	31,230	0	0	0	0	6,630	11,400
Georgia	0	0	0	0	0	0	0	0	0	0	0
Hawaii	0	0	0	0	0	0	0	0	0	0	0
Idaho	0	0	0	0	0	0	0	0	0	0	0
Illinois	9	2,966,800	93,300	30,500	147,700	200	1,900	4,000	1,500	72,000	4,700
Indiana	1	3,075	275	0	120	500	0	0	680	0	1,500
Iowa	2	203,058	35,362	0	12,408	0	0	0	155,288	0	0
Kansas	2	12,581	4,400	4,000	4,081	0	0	0	0	0	100
Kentucky	0	0	0	0	0	0	0	0	0	0	0
Louisiana	0	0	0	0	0	0	0	0	0	0	0
Maine	1	200	0	0	0	0	0	0	0	0	0
Maryland	3	166,950	23,150	0	130,450	50	0	0	0	12,000	100
Massachusetts	3	81,891	0	0	0	0	0	0	0	0	0
Michigan	1	12,000	3,000	500	3,600	0	0	400	0	0	0
Minnesota	2	54,850	21,350	5,000	11,500	0	0	1,000	0	16,000	0
Mississippi	0	0	0	0	0	0	0	0	0	0	0

State										
Missouri	2	68,745	24,000	0	30,145	0	0	0	600	14,000	0
Montana	1	17,348	15,848	0	0	0	0	0	0	1,500	0
Nebraska	2	2,600	950	0	1,500	0	0	0	0	0	0
Nevada	1	1,000	0	0	0	0	0	0	0	0	0
New Hampshire	2	92,000	16,000	10,000	5,000	20,000	0	0	0	32,000	9,000
New Jersey	4	21,700	9,000	0	5,500	0	6,000	0	0	0	1,200
New Mexico	2	12,500	0	0	0	0	0	0	0	0	0
New York	22	467,133	118,574	50	53,450	20,000	3,800	11,662	1,000	8,475	8,320
North Carolina	0	0	0	0	0	0	0	0	0	0	0
North Dakota	2	11,598	2,660	0	5,475	2,000	0	0	0	0	1,463
Ohio	11	1,587,756	112,763	550	674,382	0	150	1,798	3,249	777,524	12,160
Oklahoma	3	101,050	15,000	1,250	36,800	12,000	20,000	1,000	3,000	12,000	0
Oregon	1	600	200	0	0	20,000	0	0	0	400	0
Pennsylvania	4	633,057	51,108	78,312	112,259	18,351	0	9,671	10,000	328,322	25,034
Rhode Island	1	75,313	44,726	0	5,000	15,387	0	0	0	0	10,200
South Carolina	1	29,600	14,000	0	5,000	0	0	6,000	3,000	0	0
South Dakota	0	0	0	0	0	0	0	0	0	0	0
Tennessee	2	26,000	12,500	0	6,000	0	500	3,000	0	4,000	0
Texas	7	1,319,360	37,556	43,992	2,393	500	670	765	0	29,000	2,056
Utah	1	75,000	5,000	5,000	10,000	0	5,000	0	0	50,000	0
Vermont	0	0	0	0	0	0	0	0	0	0	0
Virginia	5	382,323	101,968	12,600	51,030	39,903	48,265	5,224	4,200	27,975	91,158
Washington	1	1,500	0	0	0	0	0	0	0	0	0
West Virginia	0	0	0	0	0	0	0	0	0	0	0
Wisconsin	2	128,500	11,300	0	74,000	0	0	0	0	43,000	0
Wyoming	0	0	0	0	0	0	0	0	0	0	0
Puerto Rico	0	0	0	0	0	0	0	0	0	0	0
Total	129	10,028,447	1,024,088	194,754	1,670,310	128,891	82,785	53,881	207,517	1,517,838	698,443
Estimated % of Acquisition Expenditures		10	10	2	17	1	1	1	2	15	7

Table 4 / Government Library Acquisition Expenditures

State	Number of Libraries	Total Acquisition Expenditures	Books	Other Print Materials	Periodicals/ Serials	Manuscripts & Archives	AV Equipment	AV Materials	Microforms	Electronic Reference	Preservation
							Categories of Expenditures (in U.S. dollars)				
Alabama	2	626,295	243,777	0	575	0	0	0	0	381,472	471
Alaska	0	0	0	0	0	0	0	0	0	0	0
Arizona	0	0	0	0	0	0	0	0	0	0	0
Arkansas	0	0	0	0	0	0	0	0	0	0	0
California	9	2,068,871	591,325	10,000	526,313	0	3,740	6,207	8,000	296,951	1,950
Colorado	0	0	0	0	0	0	0	0	0	0	0
Connecticut	0	0	0	0	0	0	0	0	0	0	0
Delaware	1	50,000	7,000	1,000	9,000	0	0	0	0	33,000	0
District of Columbia	0	0	0	0	0	0	0	0	0	0	0
Florida	1	19,545	3,750	0	14,170	0	0	1,625	0	0	0
Georgia	0	0	0	0	0	0	0	0	0	0	0
Hawaii	0			0	0	0	0	0	0	0	0
Idaho	0			0	0	0	0	0	0	0	0
Illinois	0	0	0	0	0	0	0	0	0	0	0
Indiana	0	0	0	0	0	0	0	0	0	0	0
Iowa	0	0	0	0	0	0	0	0	0	0	0
Kansas	2	789,260	296,852	0	400,491	0	0	0	0	85,690	6,227
Kentucky	0	0	0	0	0	0	0	0	0	0	0
Louisiana	2	1,042,318	28,500	0	123,000	0	500	1,000	0	15,000	0
Maine	1	257,079	0	0	0	0	0	0	0	0	0
Maryland	3	589,000	358,000	11,800	196,000	0	0	7,700	0	0	3,500
Massachusetts	3	348,868	195,036	0	0	0	0	0	0	68,332	7,500
Michigan	1	35,000	0	0	0	0	0	0	0	0	0
Minnesota	2	134,500	18,000	0	61,500	0	0	0	0	55,000	0
Mississippi	0	0	0	0	0	0	0	0	0	0	0

Missouri	0	0	0	0	0	0	0	0	0	0
Montana	1	425,961	328,391	0	0	0	0	0	97,570	0
Nebraska	0	0	0	0	0	0	0	0	0	0
Nevada	1	768,769	562,656	0	10,803	0	0	3,151	186,357	5,802
New Hampshire	1	70,000	0	0	0	0	0	0	0	0
New Jersey	0	0	0	0	0	0	0	0	0	0
New Mexico	0	0	0	0	0	0	0	0	0	0
New York	3	1,367,180	0	0	0	0	0	0	0	5,300
North Carolina	0	0	0	0	0	0	0	0	0	0
North Dakota	1	40,000	5,000	0	30,000	0	0	0	5,000	0
Ohio	0	0	0	0	0	0	0	0	0	0
Oklahoma	0	0	0	0	0	0	0	0	0	0
Oregon	0	0	0	0	0	0	0	0	0	0
Pennsylvania	4	575,000	71,500	0	500	0	0	0	10,000	0
Rhode Island	1	43,425	9,961	0	31,764	0	814	0	886	0
South Carolina	0	0	0	0	0	0	0	0	0	0
South Dakota	0	0	0	0	0	0	0	0	0	0
Tennessee	0	0	0	0	0	0	0	0	0	0
Texas	0	0	0	0	0	0	0	0	0	0
Utah	0	0	0	0	0	0	0	0	0	0
Vermont	0	0	0	0	0	0	0	0	0	0
Virginia	1	63,090	13,355	0	42,453	0	6,271	0	1,011	0
Washington	0	0	0	0	0	0	0	0	0	0
West Virginia	1	650,000	50,000	0	400,000	0	0	0	200,000	0
Wisconsin	1	81,000	45,000	0	0	0	0	0	36,000	0
Wyoming	0	0	0	0	0	0	0	0	0	0
Puerto Rico	0	0	0	0	0	0	0	0	0	0
Total	42	10,045,161	2,828,103	22,800	1,846,569	4,240	23,617	11,151	1,472,269	30,750
Estimated % of Acquisition Expenditures			28	0	18	0	0	0	15	0

Library Buildings 2012: Waves of the Future

Bette-Lee Fox

Managing Editor, *Library Journal*

The year's library architectural landscape encompasses combination spaces, meticulous renovations and restorations, and innovative thinking in the reuse of existing structures. The 107 public library capital projects and 19 academic buildings completed between July 1, 2011, and June 30, 2012, present fascinating and functioning responses to library service needs that are shaking up the design front.

A number of libraries have gone "open concept," featuring an atrium around which service areas revolve. The new Visitacion Valley Branch Library in San Francisco has a central atrium and arched entryways, while the Spencer Road Branch of St. Charles City-County Library District in Missouri has a two-story atrium, a gas fireplace, and a water feature in what it calls its "community commons." The new Lyman Beecher Brooks Library at Norfolk State University in Virginia introduced a three-story atrium along with a circular staircase, glass curtain walls, mobile service desks, and tables that are curved, waved, or elliptical. Malibu (California) Library has retractable glass walls that open the inside space to the outside reading garden.

Perfect Partnerships

Combination spaces in partnership with civic institutions keep the library at the center of the community. The Ocotillo Library and Workforce Literacy Center in Phoenix, Arizona, provides one access point for the Phoenix Workforce Connection, while the Fairview Park Branch in Ohio incorporated a Job and Career Center.

The new Millcreek Community Center Library in Salt Lake City joins with a senior center and a café in a building that is state-of-the-art. Several public libraries invoke academic terminology and a unified vibe in referring to their locations as a "civic campus." Utah's new West Jordan Library and Viridian Event Center, home to an outdoor amphitheater, overlaps municipal and recreational spaces. Bifold doors connect interior library areas with the outdoor event zones. The Fountaindale Public Library in Bolingbrook, Illinois, was conceived as a dream environment within its "civic reality." The South County Library in Roanoke, Virginia, is on a 26-acre parcel of land situated across from an elementary school, adjacent to athletic fields, and accessible by miles of pedestrian and bike trails. Even the new Chicago Theological Seminary Learning Commons is integrated with chapels and academic and administrative centers.

The renovated Ortega Branch in San Francisco is at the center of a civic plaza near a playground and three schools. The Loveland (Colorado) Public Library has achieved Leadership in Energy and Environmental Design (LEED) Gold certification in its civic center locale. The Ramsey County Library in New Brighton, Minnesota, also calls a community center collaboration home, inviting patrons to enjoy its fireplace and comfortable reading room.

Adapted from *Library Journal,* November 15, 2012

Talk about partnerships, the Kent Branch of Toledo-Lucas County Public Library was transformed into a Library/Technology Access Center through a collaboration with 56 community-focused partners, including Mayor Michael Bell, Congresswoman Marcy Kaptur, and a dozen local businesses and foundations. It also revved up a cybermobile tech classroom on wheels.

Kid Stuff

Focusing on younger users, a creative children's space took center stage at the renovated Farmingdale (New York) Public Library with the installation of a 500-gallon saltwater aquarium. The children's wing at Los Gatos Library in California includes a pop-out teen room that is cantilevered over a plaza, providing great views. The innovation sphere rocked with Oakland California's Rockridge Library Teen Zone, the 9,800-square-foot teen space at Central Arkansas Library System in Little Rock, the Dansville (New York) Public Library's Teen Mezzanine, and Sachem Public Library in Holbrook, New York, with its "desTEENation."

Student Unions

Academic libraries are doing their bit to offer amenities and flexibility for their clientele. Renner Academic Library at Elgin Community College in Illinois focused on making connections through social spaces and lounge seating and connecting with nature through courtyard views that make the most of natural light. The Pattee and Paterno Library at Penn State has a demountable wall system that is easily scalable and reconfigurable.

The Richard J. Daley Library at University of Illinois at Chicago offers an IDEA (Information, Data, Expertise, Access) Commons for high-tech collaborations. The Levi Watkins Learning Center at Alabama State University in Montgomery incorporates open flexible learning spaces with a wide range of exhibit options. A sunken outdoor courtyard with media walls at the Yale University Center for Science and Social Science Information combines three formerly separate spaces.

Innovate While Renovating

Many of the year's projects targeted LEED certification for sustainability or had already achieved it—Topanga Library in California earned Gold certification, as did West Hollywood (California) Library, Manoa Public Library in Hawaii, and Patrick Heath Public Library in Boerne, Texas; Franklin Avenue Library in Des Moines reached a LEED Platinum rating. The Old Town Library in Fort Collins, Colorado, carried through on its dream of net-zero energy usage.

The "greenest" library, however, is often the one created from an existing structure and making adaptive reuse of that building. The Lincoln Branch in Peoria, Illinois, is a restored 1911 Carnegie building, with a 12,000-square-foot addition that features a hot-air balloon theme in the story-time room.

Major building projects have brought New Orleans back in part with four new libraries that replaced facilities destroyed by Hurricane Katrina in 2005. The

Rosa F. Keller Library and Community Center project managed to restore a historic bungalow and add a library space. The Stone County Library in Crane, Missouri, is the result of the remodel of a 100-year-old historic district structure, and the Washington Public Library, also in Missouri, reconnected two floors of what was formerly the library and the police department. A new central staircase with glass railings, clerestory windows, a new entryway, and a children's garden/plaza update the facility. The Sherburne (New York) Public Library project restored a 1911 Carnegie building that was originally designed by Edward Lippincott Tilton.

Problem-Solving While Preserving

After converting a 10,000-square-foot chain restaurant, the Union Township Branch in Cincinnati established laptop "touchdown areas" to enable patrons to make use of the building's wifi service. The Allendale County (South Carolina) Library was an auto parts store, and the Otay Ranch Branch Library in Chula Vista, California, has a three-year "rent-free" lease on its former pizza restaurant shopping center site. The Mesa County Palisade Branch in Grand Junction, Colorado, started out as a lumber yard. But the most impressive conversion project has to be the McAllen (Texas) Public Library, which transformed a former Walmart store into a 124,000-square-foot library, the biggest single-level library in the country. With movable furnishings, transportable stacks, and flexible configurations, the year's library buildings were designed for long-term service and room to grow. Creativity, innovation, and a big wave to the future.

Table 1 / New Academic Library Buildings, 2012

Institution	Project Cost	Gross Area (Sq. Ft.)	Sq. Ft. Cost	Construction Cost	Furniture/ Equip. Cost	Book Capacity	Architect
Lyman Beecher Brooks Library, Norfolk (Va.) State University	$43,000,000	134,000	$261.19	$35,000,000	$2,546,000	631,000	Moseley Architects; John Portman & Associates; Tappe Associates
Russell Special Collections Libraries Building, University of Georgia, Athens	41,500,000	115,000	290.63	33,423,000	8,077,000	4,000,000*	Collins Cooper Carusi
Learning Commons, Chicago Theological Seminary	n.a.	80,000	375.00	30,000,000	n.a.	100,000	Nagle Hartray
Botanical Research Institute of Texas, Fort Worth	25,000,000	70,000	300.00	21,000,000	n.a.	175,000**	H3 Hardy Collaboration
American Bureau of Shipping Information Commons, Massachusetts Maritime Academy, Buzzards Bay	24,000,000	43,000	418.60	18,000,000	228,000	44,300	Perry Dean Rogers
Renner Academic Library and Learning Resources, Elgin (Ill.) Community College	n.a.	73,000	202.49	14,782,000	1,148,400	107,900	Dewberry
Wilson S. Rivers Library and Media Center, Florida Gateway College, Lake City	7,366,000	37,955	169.04	6,416,000	950,000	50,000	Harvard Jolly
Roland Library, Hannibal-LaGrange University, Hannibal, MO	3,000,000	19,980	n.a.	n.a.	n.a.	200,000	Bleigh Construction, Architechnics; Klingner Associates

* Mainly used for archives at 220,000 linear feet
** Along with the books are one million botanical specimens
n.a.=not available

Table 2 / Academic Library Buildings, Renovations Only, 2012

Institution	Project Cost	Gross Area (Sq. Ft.)	Sq. Ft. Cost	Construction Cost	Furniture/ Equip. Cost	Book Capacity	Architect
Pattee and Paterno Library, Penn State University, University Park	$7,500,000	35,300	$158.64	$5,600,000	$800,000	1,700	WTW Architects
Business, Engineering, Science and Technology Library, Miami University, Oxford, Ohio	5,740,000	23,000	157.17	3,615,000	570,000	150,000	BHDP Architecture
Roland G. Parrish Library of Management and Economics, Purdue University, West Lafayette, In.	3,628,150	16,100	184.73	2,974,100	654,050	1,630	Mark R. Beebe; Moody Nolan; RQAW Corp.; McGee Designhouse
Richard J. Daley Library, University of Illinois at Chicago	3,584,000	15,475	225.14	3,484,000	100,000	0	David Woodhouse
Harmony Library, Front Range Community College, Fort Collins, CO	824,628	30,000	19.36	580,800	243,828	n.a.	Architectural Resource
Cowles Library, Drake University, Des Moines	530,000	4,280	98.04	419,599	106,000	n.a.	Daniel Sloan
Center for Science and Social Science Information (CSSSI), Yale University	n.a.	28,900	n.a.	n.a.	n.a.	180,000	Apicella & Bunton

n.a.=not available

Table 3 / Academic Library Buildings, Additions and Renovations, 2012

Institution	Status	Project Cost	Gross Area (Sq. Ft.)	Sq. Ft. Cost	Construction Cost	Furniture/ Equip. Cost	Book Capacity	Architect
J. Paul Leonard Library/Sutro Library, San Francisco State University	Total	$125,810,305	361,542	$287.16	$103,820,760	$5,799,000	1,500,000	
	New	47,807,916	79,042	493.81	39,031,574	579,900	1,250,000	HMC
	Renovated	78,002,389	282,500	229.34	64,789,186	5,219,100	250,000	
William E. Morgan Library, Colorado State University, Fort Collins	Total	19,900,000	146,000	95.41	13,930,000	1,750,000	1,400,000	Studiotrope Design Collective
	New	2,500,000	7,000	250.00	1,750,000	250,000	0	
	Renovated	17,400,000	139,000	87.63	12,180,000	1,500,000	1,400,000	
Levi Watkins Learning Center, Alabama State University, Montgomery	Total	16,742,711	147,813	113.27	16,742,711	n.a.	432,715	
	New	7,820,000	60,475	129.31	7,820,000	n.a.	n.a.	NHB Group
	Renovated	8,922,711	87,338	102.16	8,922,711	n.a.	n.a.	
Patricia W. and J. Douglas Perry Library, Old Dominion University, Norfolk, Va.	Total	12,916,125	28,000	n.a.	n.a.	751,630	n.a.	
	New	n.a.	8,000	n.a.	n.a.	n.a.	n.a.	Clark Nexsen
	Renovated	n.a.	20,000	n.a.	n.a.	n.a.	3,400	

n.a. = not available

Table 4 / New Public Library Buildings, 2012

	Pop ('000)	Code	Project Cost	Const. Cost	Gross Area (Sq. Ft.)	Sq. Ft. Cost	Equip. Cost	Site Cost	Other Costs	Volumes	Architect
California											
Los Gatos	29	MS	$17,999,921	$12,733,321	29,240	$435.48	$2,100,000	Owned	$3,166,600	142,228	Noll & Tam
San Francisco	18	B	13,462,489	7,870,450	9,945	791.38	500,000	$2,241,989	2,850,050	3,382	Dept. of Public Works
Topanga	9	B	n.a.	n.a.	11,293	n.a.	n.a.	Owned	n.a.	42,000	Gkk Works
West Hollywood	36	M	60,000,000	42,200,000	45,000	937.78	3,100,000	4,000,000	10,700,000	150,000	Johnson/Favaro
District of Columbia											
Washington	25	B	18,085,281	13,760,358	22,500	611.57	1,105,656	Owned	3,219,267	80,000	Wiencek Associates; Adjaye Associates
Washington	25	B	16,238,553	12,565,260	22,500	558.46	968,556	Leased	2,704,737	80,000	Wiencek Associates; Adjaye Associates
Florida											
Loxahatchee	43	B	13,760,049	10,915,733	30,000	363.86	1,004,054	Owned	1,840,262	159,055	Slattery & Associates
Georgia											
Senoia	10	B	1,725,000	950,000	7,000	135.71	160,000	77,000	538,000	25,000	KA Oldham Design
Hawaii											
Honolulu	21	B	12,090,553	9,500,000	32,437	292.88	240,617	1,633,200	716,736	94,740	Architecture Plus
Illinois											
Bolingbrook	68	M	39,500,000	24,209,289	110,900	218.30	4,707,039	Owned	10,583,672	19,000	Nagle Hartray Architecture
Chicago	61	B	9,871,401	8,461,361	16,300	519.10	172,510	1,217,567	19,963	45,000	Harley Ellis Devereaux
Kentucky											
Louisville	8	B	2,188,493	1,964,719	7,840	250.60	61,274	Owned	162,500	486	MS&R Ltd.
Louisiana											
New Orleans	70	B	9,085,040	7,690,500	28,158	273.12	1,205,870	Owned	188,670	6,162	Gould Evans
New Orleans	70	B	8,839,088	7,182,500	27,235	263.72	1,061,500	Owned	595,088	7,210	Gould Evans
New Orleans	70	B	6,723,302	5,399,200	18,081	298.61	937,354	Owned	386,748	5,808	Lee Ledbetter & Associates
New Orleans	70	B	5,522,094	4,125,600	12,746	323.68	1,145,548	Owned	250,946	4,626	Lee Ledbetter & Associates
Massachusetts											
Osterville	n.a.	M	5,500,000	4,480,000	20,100	222.89	250,000	Owned	770,000		Ford3 Architects
Walpole	24	M	9,553,689	7,431,667	31,506	235.88	606,382	Owned	1,515,640	10,500	Lerner Ladds Bartels

Symbol Code: B=Branch Library; BS=Branch and System Headquarters; M=Main Library; MS=Main and System Headquarters; S=System Headquarters; O=combined use space; n.a.=not available

Missouri									
Saint Peters	217	B	7,623,646	6,334,294	56,232	112.65	855,997	Owned	433,355	Cornerstone Architecture
Nebraska									
North Bend	2	M	1,200,000	900,000	7,150	125.87	150,000	n.a.	150,000	Carlson, West, Povandra
Pawnee City	3	M	870,500	686,150	7,200	95.30	83,000	28,000	73,350	Larry Chilese
Ohio									
Cortland	7	B	2,242,000	1,700,000	10,636	159.83	396,000	Owned	146,000	Baker, Bednar, Snyder
Warrensville Hgts.	16	B	9,503,098	7,958,883	27,500	289.41	84,985	Owned	1,459,230	HBM Architects
Oklahoma									
Oklahoma City	54	B	11,808,270	8,396,180	35,000	239.89	1,386,476	992,230	1,033,384	richŠárd+bauer; LWPB Architecture
Oklahoma City	392	B	5,800,000	3,710,150	19,348	191.75	585,000	292,995	1,211,855	Cratton Tull
South Carolina									
New Ellenton	2	B	421,548	283,500	2,400	118.13	103,900	Owned	34,148	Craig Gaulden Davis
Texas									
Alpine	9	M	2,158,733	1,208,127	9,216	131.09	297,424	400,000	253,182	hatch ulland + owen
Boerne	33	M	6,742,960	5,642,474	30,000	188.08	628,026	Owned	472,460	OCO Architects
Utah									
Salt Lake City	40	B	6,520,900	4,383,300	19,981	219.37	1,104,500	Owned	1,033,100	Architectural Nexus
Springville	30	M	9,859,582	8,054,484	49,756	161.88	1,125,673	Owned	679,425	JRCA Architects.
West Jordan	105	BS	19,750,800	16,133,300	71,665	225.12	1,720,500	Owned	1,897,000	MHTN Architects
Virginia									
Roanoke	93	MS	15,150,000	11,000,000	54,000	203.70	1,636,000	Owned	2,514,000	HBM Architects
Washington									
Fife	9	B	4,123,682	1,301,288	6,000	216.88	480,244	1,677,766	664,384	SHKS Architects
Kenmore	21	B	7,255,000	4,181,000	10,000	418.10	569,000	1,655,000	850,000	Weinstein AU Architects

Symbol Code: B=Branch Library; BS=Branch and System Headquarters; M=Main Library; MS=Main and System Headquarters; S=System Headquarters; O=combined use space; n.a.=not available

Table 5 / Public Library Buildings, Additions and Renovations, 2012

Community	Pop ('000)	Code	Project Cost	Const. Cost	Gross Area (Sq. Ft.)	Sq. Ft. Cost	Equip. Cost	Site Cost	Other Costs	Volumes	Architect
Arizona											
Phoenix	89	B	$1,755,562	$1,234,119	7,200	$171.41	$141,897	Owned	$379,546	24,638	durkin + durkin Architects
Arkansas											
Little Rock	346	MS	6,435,307	5,142,080	64,345	79.91	913,721	Owned	379,506	75,000	Stocks Mann Architects
California											
Berkeley	113	B	4,814,240	2,994,393	8,110	369.22	420,000	Owned	1,399,847	3,208	Gould Evans
Berkeley	113	B	5,955,989	4,498,765	9,555	470.83	410,000	Owned	1,047,224	2,649	Architectural Resources Group
Chula Vista	n.a.	B	530,000	260,000	3,412	76.20	170,000	Leased	100,000	8,000	Group 4 Architecture
Keyes	5	O	11,350	11,350	1,000	11.35	0	Leased	0	n.a.	Carpet One
Malibu	n.a.	BS	7,100,000	5,100,000	16,530	308.53	550,000	Owned	1,450,000	n.a.	LPA Architecture
Menlo Park	32	M	249,384	81,814	2,077	39.39	126,570	Owned	41,000	176,217	Noll & Tam
Oakland	10	B	483,227	263,418	650	405.26	106,400	Owned	113,409	4,500	Noll & Tam
Salida	14	B	2,542,000	1,786,000	65,165	27.40	560,000	Owned	196,000	n.a.	Pacific Design Associates
San Francisco	19	B	7,779,809	4,513,450	7,432	607.30	500,000	Owned	2,766,359	2,286	Paulett Taggart; Tom Eliot Fisch
San Francisco	30	B	10,520,492	7,066,454	9,300	759.83	500,000	Owned	2,954,038	3,372	Dept. of Pubic Works
Colorado											
Elizabeth	24	BS	176,000	91,314	5,000	18.26	21,000	Leased	63,686	17,000	Humphries Poli
Fort Collins	170	B	4,746,408	2,972,113	40,387	73.59	1,120,866	Owned	653,429	165,000	OZ Architecture
Loveland	85	M	8,200,000	5,300,000	57,300	92.50	750,000	Owned	2,150,000	170,000	Belford Watkins Group
New Castle	5	B	2,979,000	2,160,000	11,000	196.36	456,000	Owned	363,000	33,000	A4 Architecture
Palisade	3	B	503,136	472,884	5,000	94.58	12,081	Owned	18,171	13,000	none reported
Florida											
Boynton Beach	98	B	2,722,065	1,885,999	17,538	107.54	337,083	Owned	498,983	144,051	Colome & Associates
West Palm Beach	27	M	4,650,717	3,342,365	46,480	71.91	370,688	Owned	937,664	15,768	Colome & Associates

Symbol Code: B=Branch Library; BS=Branch and System Headquarters; M=Main Library; MS=Main and System Headquarters; S=System Headquarters; O=combined use space; n.a.=not available.

Georgia											
Rockmart	30	B	1,899,000	1,437,750	17,000	84.57	300,000	Leased	161,250	60,000	CAS Architecture
Thomasville	43	MS	2,617,575	2,003,068	31,200	67.11	347,260	Owned	170,330	10,490	Ellis, Ricket & Associates
Illinois											
Peoria	115	B	850,608	722,858	12,500	57.82	35,000	Owned	92,750	77,562	Farnsworth Group
Peoria	115	B	6,098,554	5,140,453	16,300	315.37	380,260	Owned	577,841	39,483	Farnsworth Group; Dewberry; BCA
Peoria	115	B	667,407	482,394	4,270	112.97	80,250	Owned	104,763	26,388	Farnsworth Group; Dewberry; BCA
Quincy	52	M	5,750,000	5,033,000	52,096	96.61	410,000	Owned	307,000	171,340	Poepping Stone Bach
Romeoville	35	M	12,000,000	6,000,000	46,000	130.43	850,000	$2,500,000	2,650,000	100,000	Dewberry
Iowa											
Des Moines	50	B	7,662,011	5,455,504	28,590	190.82	895,300	Owned	1,311,207	110,000	Benjamin Design Collaborative
Sioux City	83	M	1,845,949	1,273,285	35,620	35.75	214,137	Owned	358,527	170,000	FEH Associates
Kentucky											
Warsaw	9	M	929,229	729,481	9,984	73.07	112,302	Owned	82,446	29,136	Robert Ehmet Hayes
Louisiana											
New Orleans	70	B	6,372,553	4,821,200	9,707	496.67	882,205	Owned	669,148	930	Eskew+Dumez+Ripple
Maryland											
District Heights	52	B	997,000	867,000	23,600	36.74	36,000	Owned	94,000	70,000	Gant Brunnett Architects
Massachusetts											
Boston	625	MS	1,800,000	1,500,000	5,760	286.46	150,000	Owned	150,000	*	Gensler
Michigan											
Traverse City	77	MS	208,500	83,500	1,368	61.03	113,500	Owned	11,500	n.a.	Riemenschneider/Quinn Evans
Minnesota											
New Brighton**	31	O	989,510	751,510	6,600	113.87	142,000	Leased	96,000	40,000	HGA Architects
Missouri											
Crane	6	B	522,537	383,471	3,295	116.38	47,316	65,000	26,750	12,000	Paragon Architecture
Trenton	10	MS	16,390	15,653	870	17.99	0	Owned	737	n.a.	Joe DeVorss Construction
Washington	14	M	3,405,396	2,638,776	22,460	117.49	422,232	Owned	344,388	5,805	Horn Architects

* 200,000 original historic maps, 5,000 atlases; 195 linear feet for regular-sized books; 180 folio shelves for 600 folio atlases and reference books; 36 extra-large shelves for 75 extra-large atlases; 240 five-drawer flat files, with capacity for 12,000–15,000 single sheet maps; two cabinets with five shelves each for 3-D artifacts, e.g., globes and geographic games.

** Co-located with an existing community center

Symbol Code: B=Branch Library; BS=Branch and System Headquarters; M=Main Library; MS=Main and System Headquarters; S=System Headquarters; O=combined use space; n.a.=not available.

Table 5 / Public Library Buildings, Additions and Renovations, 2012 (cont.)

Community	Pop ('000)	Code	Project Cost	Const. Cost	Gross Area (Sq. Ft.)	Sq. Ft. Cost	Equip. Cost	Site Cost	Other Costs	Volumes	Architect
Nebraska											
Kearney	31	M	$5,628,376	$4,754,274	49,052	$96.92	$343,458	Owned	$530,644	180,000	Wilkins Hinrichs Stober
Minden	3	M	230,340	127,510	4,350	29.31	102,830	Owned	0	22,175	Knispel Construction; Tri-County Glass
Omaha***	53	O	1,650,876	1,340,000	20,450	65.53	208,316	Owned	99,900	108,883	Alley Poyner Macchietto
Valley	4	O	522,184	326,402	3,600	90.67	13,970	125,000	56,812	1,088	Clavin L. Hinz Architects
New Jersey											
Cliffside Park	24	M	1,682,000	1,400,000	8,800	159.09	200,000	Owned	82,000	5,200	Arcari & Iovino
Franklin Lakes	11	M	31,000	21,000	40	525.00	0	Owned	10,000	n.a.	Janice Davis Design
Franklin Park	13	B	309,000	240,000	3,650	65.75	50,000	Leased	19,000	1,452	Arcari & Iovino
Upper Saddle River	8	M	42,000	31,000	1,200	25.83	0	Owned	11,000	n.a.	Janice Davis Design
Wyckoff	17	M	4,404,615	3,400,000	28,000	121.43	669,134	Owned	335,481	79,314	Beatty, Harvey Coco
New York											
Albertson	27	M	6,969,736	5,156,827	23,787	216.79	595,000	Owned	1,217,909	127,693	Beatty, Harvey Coco
Cortland	28	M	884,000	750,000	12,000	62.50	0	Owned	134,000	80,000	Crawford & Stearns
Dansville	10	M	2,900,000	2,400,000	8,100	296.30	200,000	150,000	150,000	20,000	LaBella Associates
Farmingdale	8	M	3,008,178	2,061,527	41,722	49.41	309,034	Owned	637,617	154,563	Beatty, Harvey Coco
Holbrook	83	M	315,845	231,023	4,328	53.38	58,822	Owned	26,000	12,086	Beatty, Harvey Coco
Islip	20	M	1,231,925	838,318	8,278	101.27	197,790	Owned	195,817	119,296	Beatty, Harvey Coco
Sherburne	4	O	296,807	236,147	5,900	40.02	0	Owned	60,660	n.a.	Klepper, Hahn & Hyatt
Ohio											
Beachwood	12	B	1,187,034	993,848	18,626	53.36	4,233	Owned	188,953	53,842	CBLH Design
Cincinnati	42	B	5,300,000	2,672,165	20,709	129.03	1,030,609	875,000	722,226	66,085	KBA

*** Joint facility with Omaha Parks and Recreation Department

Symbol Code: B=Branch Library; BS=Branch and System Headquarters; M=Main Library; MS=Main and System Headquarters; S=System Headquarters; O=combined use space; n.a.=not available.

City		Symbol									Architect
Cleveland	401	M	1,267,967	551,213	7,403	74.46	277,994	Owned	438,760	n.a.	Bostwick Design Partnership
Fairview Park	17	B	935,569	785,111	44,225	17.75	3,201	Owned	147,257	68,132	Van Dyke Architects
Solon	24	B	1,100,244	883,926	22,000	40.18	6,157	Owned	210,161	76,597	CBLH Design
Toledo	17	B	2,280,398	1,732,015	17,766	97.49	371,000	Owned	177,383	34,178	Buehrer Group Architecture
Oregon											
Clackamas	5	M	2,903,281	2,121,626	18,300	115.94	315,670	Owned	465,985	78,875	Scott Edwards Architecture
Rhode Island											
North Scituate	11	M	1,641,000	1,177,000	7,925	148.52	180,000	30,000	254,000	38,043	Lerner Ladds Bartels
South Carolina											
Allendale	10	BS	3,142,288	2,738,618	12,000	228.22	200,000	50,000	153,670	35,566	jsms
Wagener	2	B	421,598	304,750	2,700	112.87	82,700	Owned	34,148	15,000	Craig Gaulden Davis
Texas											
Honey Grove	2	M	77,405	25,413	1,886	13.47	41,000	Owned	10,992	22,000	Vance Hunt
Houston	2,099	M	28,083,000	25,909,000	90,300	286.92	1,760,000	Owned	414,000	15,000	Gensler
Huntsville	25	M	4,005,403	3,168,914	22,000	144.04	366,789	Owned	469,700	58,901	Aguirre Roden
McAllen	212	M	23,807,890	14,105,491	124,500	113.30	2,781,420	5,000,000	1,920,979	21,378	MS&R Ltd.
Magnolia	138	B	37,277	13,250	1,624	8.16	24,027	Owned	0	1,497	none reported
Virginia											
Henrico	n.a.	B	4,765,990	2,344,038	12,672	184.98	1,307,377	Owned	1,114,575	50,000	BCWH
Honaker	7	B	176,704	126,125	1,950	64.68	38,359	Owned	12,220	16,500	Colley Architects
Waynesboro	20	M	1,867,319	1,333,605	11,600	114.97	230,000	Owned	303,714	3,000,000	BCWH
Washington											
Lake Forest Park	13	B	1,446,000	806,000	5,841	137.99	431,000	Leased	209,000	41,858	Hutteball & Oremus
Tukwila	19	B	303,000	240,000	3,322	72.25	63,000	Leased	0	21,564	SHKS Architects

Symbol Code: B=Branch Library; BS=Branch and System Headquarters; M=Main Library; MS=Main and System Headquarters; S=System Headquarters; O=combined use space; n.a.=not available.

Book Trade Research and Statistics

2012: Digital Delivery Has Ever-Greater Role in Publishing

Jim Milliot

Co-Editorial Director, *Publishers Weekly*

The increased importance of the digital delivery of content touched all parts of the publishing business in 2012.

For much of the year the industry watched as the U.S. Department of Justice sued Apple and publishing houses Hachette, Simon & Schuster, HarperCollins, Penguin, and Macmillan over what the government charged was a conspiracy by Apple and the five houses to fix e-book prices when the publishers moved to the so-called agency pricing model for e-books. The April announcement of the charges was accompanied by the news that three of the publishers—S&S, Hachette, and HarperCollins—had reached a settlement agreement with the Justice Department, while Macmillan, Penguin, and Apple would continue to fight the case.

Under the agreement, the publishers terminated their contracts with all e-book retailers and agreed to new terms allowing online retailers to discount individual titles so long as the discount for all titles does not exceed 30 percent off the retail price for the full year. The limit was put in place to ease fears by publishers, booksellers, and online retailers that Amazon would use e-books as loss leaders to draw customers to its website and in the process drive other online e-book retailers as well as physical bookstores out of business. During the comment period between the initial agreement and final September hearing before Judge Denise Cote, publishers, booksellers, distributors, authors, and agents all filed statements with the court claiming that the agreement would give Amazon—which already controlled at least 60 percent of the e-book market—too much power and would eventually lead to higher, not lower, prices for e-books, the goal of the lawsuit. Despite the groundswell of industry opposition, Judge Cote approved the agreement with no public hearings and no changes to the deal. She argued that the case was a straightforward price-fixing case, and that even if Amazon was engaged in predatory pricing, it would not excuse unlawful price-fixing.

Along with the federal government, 49 states also sued Apple and the five publishers over e-book pricing, reaching agreements with S&S, Hachette, and HarperCollins. Terms were similar to those reached with the Justice Department and also included provisions for the publishers to issue rebates to consumers who bought e-books during a specified period. On the civil side, the numerous class-action lawsuits filed against the publishers and Apple in late 2011 continued with no agreements reached with any publisher or Apple by the end of 2012.

While Penguin had been an initial hold-out to a deal with the Justice Department, in December it came to terms with the government in order to clear the path for what was the other big story of 2012—the merger of Penguin and Random House, the nation's two largest trade publishers. At the end of 2012 the merger was still undergoing regulatory review by government agencies in several different countries, although approval was expected sometime in 2013. When united, the two companies will control about 25 percent of the U.S. trade book market with Penguin Group Chairman John Makinson serving as chairman and Random House Chairman Markus Dohle running day-to-day operations as CEO.

The nation's largest bookstore chain was also involved with a major transaction in 2012 that reflected the changing bookselling environment. Barnes & Noble and Microsoft completed a deal in October that gave the software giant a 17.6 percent stake in a new unit, Nook Media, that is made up of B&N's Nook digital business and its college stores. For a total five-year investment of more than $600 million, Microsoft gained another chance to participate in the booming consumer digital hardware and content market, while B&N received a much needed cash infusion to help fund not only the development of Nook reading devices but its international expansion as well. The company's first overseas venture was to the United Kingdom where it opened an e-bookstore and signed deals with various retailers to sell the device. B&N is considering a move to spin off Nook Media into its own company, leaving the trade bookstores as a separate entity. Very late in 2012 Nook Media picked up another investor when Pearson announced it was investing $89 million in the venture.

Independent booksellers reacted to the increase in sales of e-books by replacing a failed agreement with Google with a three-year partnership with Kobo. Under the agreement, which was in place by the 2012 holiday season, American Booksellers Association (ABA) members not only can sell e-books through the Kobo e-bookstore but can sell Kobo reading devices as well.

The relationship between publishers—especially the major trade houses—and librarians over the issue of lending e-books remained contentious throughout 2012. Publishers have been reluctant to allow libraries to lend all of their e-books for fear that the ease of use would discourage book sales. At the end of 2012 Macmillan and Simon & Schuster had no e-book library plan in place (although Macmillan announced a test in January 2013). Penguin and Hachette had tests in place while Harper allowed libraries to lend e-books 26 times before buying a new "copy" while Random House was selling libraries e-books for about three times the retail price.

Greater access to digital content helped to add more fuel to the growth of self-publishing. The publishing phenomenon of the year was EL James's "Fifty Shades of Grey" trilogy. Begun as fan fiction and posted on various websites, the erotica-tinged trilogy was first picked up by a small Australian publisher before being acquired by Random House's Vintage Press imprint. The three titles plus a boxed set ended up selling more than 35 million copies in print and digital formats in 2012 and James was named on many "most interesting people of the year" lists as well as chosen as *Publishers Weekly*'s Publishing Person of the Year. James's success led other publishers to sign other authors—many self-published—who had written erotic novels.

Distribution deals are usually run-of-the mill news in publishing, but that was not the case when Amazon announced that its publishing subsidiary had signed a licensing agreement with Houghton Mifflin Harcourt for HMH to publish print editions of its digital titles. HMH formed the New Harvest imprint to publish and sell the books, but a number of bricks-and-mortar stores, including Barnes & Noble, Books-A-Million, and many independents, declined to carry the books. Despite lukewarm sales of its print titles, Amazon said it would expand its publishing operation into Europe in 2013. Vicky Griffith, publisher of Amazon's West Coast group, is leading the expansion, while in the United States Larry Kirshbaum, publisher of the Amazon East Coast group, assumed editorial leadership for the Seattle and New York adult imprints, as well as Amazon Children's Publishing. The expansion will focus on expanding the English-language audience through its English-language bookstores in Britain, Germany, France, Italy, and Spain.

A year wouldn't be complete without a controversy involving Amazon, and the dispute came early in 2012. In a push to get more co-op money from publishers, the online retailer was seeking a hefty increase in promotional books as well as for e-books. When distributor IPG declined to renew its agreement with Amazon, the company removed the "buy" buttons from all of IPG's e-books, and the dispute dragged on for several weeks before a deal was struck. Shortly after it was resolved, Educational Development Corp., which sells children's books, took something of a preemptive strike, announcing that it would stop selling all of its titles through Amazon.

Mergers and Acquisitions

The largest acquisition of 2012 was the preliminary agreement signed by Apollo Management Group to buy McGraw-Hill Education for $2.5 billion. The deal was expected to be completed early in 2013. Parent company McGraw-Hill Cos. began exploring ways to divest itself of the education and publishing group in September 2011 to focus on its financial businesses. The original plan had involved spinning off MHE into its own company, but MHC also talked to a number of potential suitors before signing the deal with Apollo. The education group will continue to be known as McGraw-Hill Education under the direction of Buzz Waterhouse, who was named president and CEO in June 2012. Its corporate offices will remain in New York.

John Wiley was one of the more active deal makers in 2012, selling and buying a number of properties. It sold its travel assets, including Frommer's, to Google for $22 million. As it did with Zagat, which Google bought in 2011, Google added the content from Frommer's into its search engine to help boost local search results Later in the year, Wiley sold its cookbooks, CliffsNotes, and reference assets to Houghton Mifflin Harcourt for $11 million. The divestitures were part of Wiley's strategy to get out of consumer publishing in favor of professional and career development areas. To do that, Wiley paid $85 million for Inscape, which has annual revenue of about $20 million, and $24 million for Electronic Learning Systems, which has annual sales of approximately $7 million. Books are not the main product of Inscape or ELS; rather, they provide digital tools and services to professionals in a variety of businesses. Wiley made a third major acquisition in 2012, buying Deltak.edu in October for $220 million. With annual sales of about $54 million, Deltak is now part of Wiley's global education group.

In a purchase that showed the acceptance of self-publishing by mainstream publishers, Pearson/Penguin bought Author Solutions Inc., one of the world's largest self-publishing ventures, for $116 million from Bertram Capital. ASI, owner of some of the best-known self-publishing brands, had sales of $100 million in 2011.

Following an auction that concluded August 28, Amazon Publishing acquired the publication contracts of more than 1,000 books from Dorchester Publishing after that mass market publisher ended its publishing program and auctioned off its assets. Earlier in the year, Amazon Publishing acquired publication rights to more than 3,000 backlist titles from Avalon Books. Founded in 1950, Avalon Books specialized in such major genres as mystery, romance, and westerns. Like the Dorchester books, the Avalon titles will be published by Amazon in e-book and print editions under its Amazon Publishing, Montlake Romance, and Thomas & Mercer imprints. The company also brought on editor and publisher James Atlas to publish a series of short biographies.

In one of the larger deals made by an independent publisher, F+W Media acquired Aspire Media, the parent company of Interweave, a move that united two of the country's largest publishers of niche content. Best known for its craft books and magazines, Interweave has a backlist of 350 craft books and publishes 15 magazines and more than 30 special newsstand publications. In addition, the company operates 33 websites and ten online communities. New York private equity firm Wicks Group purchased a majority share in Bendon Publishing, a leading purveyor of coloring, activity, and other mass market book formats. Worthy Publishing purchased the Ellie Claire Gift and Paper Expressions imprint from Guideposts, including the Ellie Claire brand and product lines. The deal also included the acquisition of all nonfiction gift and inspirational books from Guideposts' Summerside Press. Harlequin acquired the book club assets of Heartsong Presents Book Club, the inspiration book club owned by the Christian publisher Barbour Publishing.

Bloomsbury Publishing acquired Fairchild Books, the New York publisher of educational materials for fashion students. Leon Black, CEO of the private equity firm Apollo Group, bought art publisher Phaidon Press. ZelnickMedia sold its book-packaging division, Alloy Entertainment, to Warner Bros. Television Group.

Among smaller acquisitions, Cherry Lake Publishing, a Mankato, Minnesota-based educational publisher, acquired Sleeping Bear Press from Gale, a Cengage Learning company. Sleeping Bear, which is based in Ann Arbor, is known for its illustrated state alphabet series of 50 books. Sleeping Bear's ten employees will remain in their Ann Arbor offices.

The only significant deal in retail involved Family Christian Stores, the largest Christian retail chain, which was acquired by a group of Atlanta-based investors. The digital services provider Aptara was acquired by iEnergizer, an international business process outsourcing company that has offices around the world. The purchase price was $144 million. Acquisitions also extended into the literary agency field; in a deal that brought a number of bold-faced names to its client list, Lippincott Massie McQuilkin acquired Russell & Volkening, Inc.

In a deal north of the border, Random House of Canada took over 100 percent ownership of McClelland & Stewart, one of Canada's oldest publishers. In a deal that didn't happen, Barnes & Noble pulled its Sterling Publishing subsidiary off the block after offers came in far below what B&N would accept.

People

Skip Prichard, who helped to integrate the various Ingram divisions into the Ingram Content Group, left the company as CEO and president and was succeeded by company Chairman John Ingram. Madeline McIntosh was promoted to chief operating officer of Random House. As part of a worldwide reorganization, John Sargent was appointed head of Holtzbrinck's global trade division, while Annette Thomas, CEO of Macmillan UK, was named head of the global science and education group. David Young announced in the fall that he would resign in April 2013 as CEO of Hachette Book Group to return to Britain where he would serve in a variety of roles for Hachette, including as chairman of HBG. Michael Pietsch, publisher of Little, Brown, was named to succeed Young as CEO, while Ken Michaels was named president. Also at Hachette, Evan Schnittman was appointed to the new post of executive vice president, chief marketing and sales officer.

Laurence Orbach, cofounder and CEO of Quarto Publishers, was replaced by Tim Chadwick after a special meeting in which shareholders voted for Orbach's removal. Mary Lee Schneider, former president of Digital Solutions and chief technology officer at Donnelley, was named president and CEO of Follett Corp., the first person outside the Follett family to run the college bookstores and distribution company.

Basic Books publisher John Sherer left to become director of University of North Carolina Press; David Perry, its longtime editor-in-chief, announced plans to retire in March 2013. To succeed Sherer, Lara Heimert was named publisher, and Clive Priddle was named publisher of PublicAffairs. Susan Weinberg was promoted to group publisher of Basic Books. Jeff Pinkser was named president of Scholastic's Klutz imprint. Steve Smith was appointed publisher of Oasis Audio after Tammy Faxel resigned to join Brilliance Audio.

Amanda Cook joined Crown Publishing from Houghton Mifflin Harcourt as vice president and executive editor. Open Road added a number of new people in 2012, including a new publisher, Tina Pohlman, who had been vice president and publisher of trade paperbacks at Crown. Betsy Mitchell, longtime Del Rey editor, joined the company early in 2012 to acquire science fiction and fantasy properties for the e-book publisher. Ileene Smith moved from Yale University Press to Farrar, Straus and Giroux as vice president and executive editor. After 17 years at Gibbs Smith, Publishers, CEO Christopher Robbins resigned to start a family media company. Michael Taeckens, Algonquin Books online and paperback director, left to become marketing director of Graywolf Press.

Frances Coady, longtime head of Macmillan's Picador imprint, stepped down in March as part of a restructuring of Macmillan's trade paperback operations. Following Coady's departure, Penguin Books' Stephen Morrison was named Picador publisher. To replace Morrison, Patrick Nolan was named editor-in-chief and associate publisher of Penguin Books. Kate Lyall Grant was named publisher of Severn House.

Sara Nelson, book editor of *O, the Oprah Magazine,* was appointed editorial director of Amazon.com Books. Alistair Burtenshaw stepped down as director of the London Book Fair and was replaced by Jacks Thomas. Kelly Gallagher, head of Bowker's publishing solutions team, was appointed vice president of content acquisition for Ingram. Peter Berkery, Jr. was named executive director of the Association of American University Presses, effective March 1. Berkery replaced longtime director Peter Givler.

In bookselling, Todd Noden was appointed chief financial officer of Books-A-Million. After 13 years as director of the Southern California Independent Booksellers Association, Jennifer Bigelow resigned at the end of 2012.

There were a fair number of major personnel shifts in children's publishing in 2012. At Amazon Publishing, Tim Ditlow was named associate publisher of its Marshall Cavendish Children's Books division. Joy Peskin joined Macmillan Children's Publishing Group as division vice president and editorial director of Farrar, Straus & Giroux Books for Young Readers. Brian Buerkle moved to Kingfisher as associate publisher and director of marketing. Children's book publishing veteran Lisa Holton left Fourth Story Media to head Classroom Inc.

Restructurings and Start-Ups

HarperCollins parent company News Corp. said it would split into two separate companies with Harper joining a group that will include News Corp.'s newspaper assets. Robert Thomson was named CEO of the new company. The spinoff is expected to be completed by the summer of 2013 and will keep the News Corp. name. Also at Harper, the company formed a new Christian publishing group after its purchase of Thomas Nelson was finally approved. The new group consists of Nelson and Zondervan and is being led by Mark Schoenwald. Zondervan President Scott MacDonald resigned.

Random House announced plans late in the year to start three digital-only imprints: Alibi, a mystery/thriller line; Flirt, a YA/new adult list; and Hydra, a science fiction line. Grand Central Publishing launched a digital-only imprint, Forever Yours, that will publish new works in digital format as well as backlist romance titles. The company also announced its intention to start Redhook, an imprint of its Orbit unit, in 2013 to publish commercial fiction. NBC News entered the publishing business with NBC Publishing, a unit whose goal is to use its video and audio assets to create digital books. Two print industry veterans, Peter Costanzo and Brian Perrin, were appointed creative director and director of digital development, respectively.

After nearly two years of development, Scholastic launched Storia, its proprietary platform for selling children's e-books. Bookish, the online bookstore backed by Penguin, Hachette, and Simon & Schuster, lost its second CEO in September when Caroline Marks resigned and the launch of the site was delayed once again. Ardy Khazaei was named to replace Marks and Bookish launched on February 5, 2013. Conservative publisher Regnery Publishing launched a children's book imprint, Little Patriot Press. Italian publishing giant DeAgostini began a staggered entry into the U.S. market, releasing its first official line of adult and children's books with an emphasis on book-plus packages. Seven Stories launched Triangle Square Editions, its first children's imprint. Penguin's Berkley/NAL division started a graphic novel line called InkLit, overseen by Richard Johnson. Le French Book, which publishes e-book editions of popular French titles, released its first titles early in 2012 under the direction of Anne Trager. Harlequin announced plans to start Kiss, a contemporary romance imprint that will publish in both e-book and mass market paperback formats. Tantor Audio started a book imprint to complement its audiobook and e-book operations. Abrams reorganized its adult management team, naming Steve Tager senior vice president and chief marketing and development officer.

IAC chairman Barry Diller and producer Scott Rudin announced the creation of Brightline, a multiplatform publishing house that will do more than e-books. Frances Coady, former Picador publisher, was named president and publisher. Medallion Media Group bought Triple Threat Mobile Development with plans to use the company to launch a new e-book platform in 2013. Independent book publisher Chelsea Green made the transition to an employee-owned company.

Home Depot stopped selling all but a small line of its own-branded books at its stores in late spring.

Tor/Forge Books dropped DRM (digital rights management) protection for all of its e-books starting in July. DRM is used by most traditional publishers to guard against piracy of books.

Disney Publishing Worldwide closed down its White Plains, New York, office and moved employees to Disney Consumer Products headquarters in Glendale, California. Callaway Digital Arts shut its New York studio and moved all of its operations to its San Francisco office.

Houghton Mifflin Harcourt filed for prepackaged bankruptcy in the spring as part of a plan to eliminate $3.1 billion in debt and reduce its annual interest payment by $250 million. HMH emerged from Chapter 11 in the summer. One of Canada's largest independent book publishers, D&M Publishers, filed for bankruptcy in October. On the Canadian bookselling side, the Canadian Booksellers Association, faced with declining membership and financial resources, voted to become part of the Retail Council of Canada. Books-A-Million formed a special committee to explore the possible buyout of the bookseller by the Anderson family, which is the majority shareholder in the company. The Anderson offer of $3.05 per share was eventually withdrawn when outside shareholders deemed the bid too low. Barnes & Noble closed its Tikatok unit, which it bought in 2009 to allow parents and children to create their own books.

HarperCollins restructured its sales and marketing department, adding more analytics and cutting eight spots. Perseus Books began phasing out its Vanguard Books imprint, which had been established in 2007 to offer low advances but higher royalties and more marketing. Vanguard publisher Roger Cooper left the company at the end of the year. Vantage Press, one of the original "vanity presses," closed in December after a restructuring by new owner David Lamb failed to turn the company around.

Simon & Schuster reorganized its adult publishing operations, creating four groups—Atria Publishing Group, Scribner Publishing Group, Simon & Schuster Publishing Group, and Gallery Publishing Group. One consequence of the realignment was moving the Free Press into the S&S group with Martha Levin and Dominick Anfuso, publisher and editorial director, respectively, of Free Press leaving the company. The restructuring also led to the promotion of Nan Graham to publisher of Scribner. In a separate high-level departure, Anthony Ziccardi stepped down as deputy publisher of Gallery Books, Threshold Editions, and Pocket Books. Toward the end of 2012 S&S signed with the self-publishing giant Author Solutions to create Archway Publishing, a division that will offer self-publishing services in fiction, nonfiction, business, and children's. Finally, Simon & Schuster relaunched its dormant mass market paperback line, Pocket Star, as an e-book only line, releasing new and backlist titles in a variety of genres.

Bestsellers

With a huge boost from EL James's Fifty Shades trilogy, Random House increased its share of *Publishers Weekly*'s paperback bestsellers lists in 2012, taking 35.1 percent of slots in trade and mass market paperback, up by just over two percentage points from 2011. (Bestsellers are based on print sales only.) *Fifty Shades of Grey, Fifty Shades Darker,* and *Fifty Shades Freed* took the top three trade paperback spots in 2012 and accounted for just under 15 percent of trade paperback "book weeks" in the year. On the mass market paperback side, Random House's position was helped by the strong performances of John Grisham (*The Litigators*) and George R. R. Martin (*A Game of Thrones*).

Penguin once again had the second-greatest presence on the paperback lists, with 70 titles hitting the lists for a combined 281 weeks and giving Penguin a 17.7 percent share of paperback bestsellers, down from 19.3 percent in 2011. Hachette Book Group had a strong year in paperback with its share of bestsellers rising by almost three percentage points to 16.7 percent. Simon & Schuster's slice of paperback bestsellers slipped to 8.4 percent from 9.7 percent and it was challenged by Harlequin for the fourth spot in the paperback rankings. Harlequin's share of paperback bestsellers rose to 8.2 percent from 6.1 percent in 2011.

Random House actually lost market share on the hardcover bestseller lists but still controlled 27 percent of slots in 2012, easily outdistancing Penguin, which had a 15.5 percent share of hardcover bestsellers. Random House titles that spent the most time on the hardcover lists were *Gone Girl* (30 weeks), *A Dance with Dragons* (27), and *Wild* (22). *No Easy Day* was Penguin's steadiest hardcover seller, staying on the list for 17 weeks.

While Random House and Penguin lost share on the hardcover list, Simon & Schuster picked up just over three percentage points and took 14.4 percent of hardcover bestseller slots in the year, led by the Steve Jobs biography, which spent 27 weeks on the hardcover list. Hachette's share of hardcover bestsellers fell from 16.2 percent to 13.9 percent, dropping it from third to fourth in the hardcover ranking. HarperCollins also saw its share of hardcover bestsellers rise in the year and it accounted for 10.5 percent of top hardcovers in 2012, up from 8.2 percent.

Prices of U.S. and Foreign Published Materials

Narda Tafuri

Editor, ALA ALCTS Library Materials Price Index Editorial Board

The Library Materials Price Index (LMPI) Editorial Board of the American Library Association's Association for Library Collections and Technical Services' Publications Committee continues to monitor prices for a range of library materials from sources within North America and from other key publishing centers around the world.

The U.S. Consumer Price Index (CPI) increased by 1.6 percent in 2012. This was similar to the increase seen in 2010 (1.5), but a substantial decrease from 2011. Indexes for gasoline, natural gas, and fuel oil exhibited declines. All indexes showed a smaller increase than in 2011 except for U.S. hardcover books and U.S. e-books. During 2012 all of the price indexes outperformed the CPI with the exception of audiobooks, which posted another steep decline. U.S. e-books demonstrated the greatest gain with an increase of 15.03 percent. CPI data are obtained from the Bureau of Labor Statistics website at http://www.bls.gov.

The U.S. Periodical Price Index (USPPI) (Table 1) continues to be reproduced as it appeared in the 2010 article. The LMPI Editorial Board is working on re-establishing this index and hopes to make it available in the future. Percent changes in average prices from previous years are noted in the chart below under the category "Periodicals."

Table 8, Average Price of Serials, continues in this year's article and provides the average price trends of serials from 2009 through 2013. The table is based on titles indexed in ISI Arts and Humanities Citation Index, ISI Science Citation Index, ISI Social Sciences Citation Index, EBSCO Academic Search Premier, and EBSCO Masterfile Premier. It differs from the data that appear in the U.S. Periodicals Price Index (USPPI) by its inclusion of foreign serials prices as well as by using approximately three times the number of serials in its compilation. Because the same data set of titles is not treated every year, price changes may differ from year to year. This table measures the changes in price for more than 10,000 academic titles over a period of five years.

U.S. E-Books (Table 7B), established last year by compiler Catherine Barr, has been continued in this year's article. Data for this index continue to be provided by Baker & Taylor. Changes in average price for this index are noted in the chart below under the category "U.S. E-Books." Table 4A, "North American Academic E-Books" covers only those titles treated for academic library approval plan customers by Ingram Content Group (formerly Coutts Information Services) and YBP Library Services. Changes in average prices for Table 4A are noted in the chart below under the category "Academic E-Books." The British Academic Book Index (Table 9) continues this year with a new compiler, George Aulisio.

Readers should note that the data source for the North American Academic Books Index (Table 4) changed in 2009 and that this table is being indexed using combined data from Ingram Content Group and YBP Library Services. Prior years' data may not be applicable if compared with those presented in this year's table.

Table 1 / U.S Periodicals: Average Prices and Price Indexes, 2008–2010

Index Base: 1984 = 100

Subject Area	1984 Average Price	2008 Average Price	2008 Index	2009 Average Price	2009 Index	2010 Average Price	2010 Index
U.S. periodicals excluding Russian translations	$54.97	$436.90	794.8	$467.82	851.1	$497.63	905.3
U.S. periodicals including Russian translations	72.47	559.96	772.7	603.85	833.3	642.62	886.8
Agriculture	24.06	169.99	706.5	181.40	754.0	201.60	837.9
Business and economics	38.87	245.27	631.0	263.64	678.3	287.64	740.0
Chemistry and physics	228.90	2,333.37	1,019.4	2,482.16	1,084.4	2,622.14	1,145.5
Children's periodicals	12.21	29.98	245.5	33.43	273.8	35.87	293.8
Education	34.01	240.80	708.0	258.73	760.8	276.33	812.5
Engineering	78.70	688.98	875.5	734.14	932.8	786.72	999.6
Fine and applied arts	26.90	84.94	315.8	89.40	332.4	94.10	349.8
General interest periodicals	27.90	60.11	215.5	63.91	229.1	66.70	239.1
History	23.68	106.55	450.0	113.94	481.2	123.57	521.8
Home economics	37.15	225.51	549.5	246.26	600.1	260.64	635.1
Industrial arts	30.40	170.51	560.9	172.22	566.5	188.27	619.3
Journalism and communications	39.25	182.41	464.8	192.89	491.4	210.49	536.3
Labor and industrial relations	29.87	201.12	673.3	220.96	739.8	234.50	785.1
Law	31.31	141.02	450.4	149.04	476.0	157.88	504.2
Library and information sciences	38.85	161.15	414.8	172.63	444.4	179.80	462.8
Literature and language	23.02	96.35	418.5	102.92	447.1	109.32	474.9
Mathematics, botany, geology, general science	106.56	925.61	868.6	991.88	930.8	1,024.13	961.1
Medicine	125.57	1,224.41	975.1	1,317.81	1,049.5	1,427.56	1,136.9
Philosophy and religion	21.94	99.33	452.8	107.44	489.7	117.24	534.3
Physical education and recreation	20.54	81.79	398.2	87.73	427.1	91.48	445.4
Political science	32.43	241.37	744.3	261.05	805.0	273.80	844.3
Psychology	69.74	631.79	905.9	686.52	984.4	726.87	1,042.3
Russian translations	381.86	3,080.51	806.7	3,390.04	887.8	3,580.13	937.6
Sociology and anthropology	43.87	367.59	837.9	400.08	912.0	432.76	986.5
Zoology	78.35	911.89	1,163.9	980.66	1,251.6	1,047.35	1,336.8
Total number of periodicals							
Excluding Russian translations	3,731	3,728		3,728		3,728	
Including Russian translations	3,942	3,910		3,910		3,912	

Compiled by Brenda Dingley, University of Missouri, Kansas City, based on subscription information supplied by Swets Information Services.

Index	Percent Change				
	2008	2009	2010	2011	2012
CPI	0.1	2.7	1.5	3.0	1.6
Periodicals	8.0	6.4	n.a.	n.a.	n.a.
Legal serials services	n.a.	n.a.	3.5	11.0	10.5
*Hardcover books	2.81	0.34	5.54	0.87	4.17
+Academic books	3.9	-1.2	12.4	4.6	n.a.
+Academic E-Books	13.1	-18.4	13.7	-0.3	n.a.
+Textbooks	2.8	1.7	0.7	3.5	n.a.
College books	3.3	4.1	-2.3	4.6	2.15
*Mass market paperbacks	1.56	3.08	1.94	2.34	0.72
*Trade paperbacks	-9.75	-0.41	7.30	-9.99	9.59
*Audiobooks	11.39	9.88	-1.19	-4.39	-10.61
*U.S. E-Books	n.a.	-22.80	-6.07	-41.17	15.03
++Serials	n.a.	n.a.	4.1	5.8	5.8
British academic books	n.a.	n.a.	-1.8	14.7	9.7

n.a. = not available
* = figures revised based on BISAC categories
+ Beginning with 2009, new data source
++Data set changes each year.

U.S. Published Materials

Tables 1 through 7B indicate average prices and price indexes for library materials published primarily in the United States. These indexes are U.S. Periodicals (Table 1), Legal Serials Services (Table 2), U.S. Hardcover Books (Table 3), North American Academic Books (Table 4), North American Academic E-Books (Table 4A), North American Academic Textbooks (Table 4B), U.S. College Books (Table 5), U.S. Mass Market Paperback Books (Table 6), U.S. Paperbacks (Excluding Mass Market) (Table 7), U.S. Audiobooks (Table 7A), and U.S. E-Books (Table 7B).

Periodical and Serials Prices

The LMPI Committee and Swets Information Services jointly produced the U.S. Periodicals Price Index (Table 1). The subscription prices shown are publishers' list prices, excluding publisher discount or vendor service charges. This report includes 2008, 2009, and 2010 data indexed to the base year of 1984. Table 1 was compiled by Brenda Dingley using data provided by Swets Information Services. This index is being repeated from previous years. It is hoped that an updated table will appear in next year's *Library and Book Trade Almanac*.

More extensive reports from the periodicals price index were published annually in the April 15 issue of *Library Journal* through 1992, in the May issue of *American Libraries* from 1993 to 2002, and in the October 2003 issue of *Library Resources and Technical Services*.

The Legal Serials Services Index (Table 2) was compiled by Ajaye Bloomstone using data collected from a number of different legal serials vendors. The base year for this index is 2009. This index presents price data covering the years 2009 through 2013. Vendors were asked again to provide cost data on particular titles with the assumption that the title/set has been held by a large academic research law library, and the cost recorded in the index is that for the upkeep of the title in question, *not* the cost incurred with purchasing a new set. It should be noted that although legal serials in print format continue to be produced, titles are migrating, albeit slowly, to an electronic-only format.

Table 2 / Legal Serials Services: Average Prices and Price Indexes, 2009–2013
Index Base: 2009=100

Year	Number of Titles	Average Price	Percent Change	Index
2009	217	$1,658.20	n.a.	100.0
2010	217	1,716.30	3.5%	103.5
2011	217	1,905.20	11.0	114.9
2012	217	2,020.83	6.1	124.1
2013	217	2,233.00	10.5	134.7

Book Prices

Tables 3 (hardcover books), 6 (mass market paperbacks), 7 (other—trade—paperbacks), 7A (audiobooks), and table 7B (e-books), prepared by Catherine Barr, are derived from data provided by book wholesaler Baker & Taylor. Figures for 2011 are revised to reflect late updates to the Baker & Taylor database (publishers were still adding 2011 titles in early 2012); the 2012 figures given here may be similarly revised in next year's tables and should be considered preliminary. These five tables use the Book Industry Study Group's BISAC categories; for more information on the BISAC categories, visit http://www.bisg.org.

Average book prices were mixed in 2011 and 2012. List prices for hardcovers overall (Table 3) rose only 0.87 percent but were up 4.17 percent in preliminary data for 2012. Mass market paperback prices (Table 6) remained in positive territory but gained a mere 2.34 percent in 2011 and 0.72 percent in 2012. In contrast, trade paperbacks (Table 7)—whose numbers swelled in 2011—saw prices fall 9.99 percent that year but recover nearly that total in 2012. Audiobook prices (Table 7A) have been falling since 2009, with declines of 4.39 percent in 2011 and 10.61 percent in 2012. E-books (Table 7B) showed a wide range of prices and price changes across categories, with an overall drop of 41.17 percent in 2011 followed by an increase of 15 percent in 2012.

The North American Academic Books Price Indexes (Tables 4, 4A, and 4B) are prepared by Stephen Bosch. The current version of North American Academic Books: Average Prices and Price Indexes 2009–2011 (Table 4) should not be compared with the versions published in 2009 or prior years. The North American Academic Books Price Index (NAABPI) now contains many more titles in the source data, which has impacted the index considerably. This is mainly due to the fact that Coutts has treated far more titles in their approval programs than Blackwell Book Services. Blackwell was purchased in 2011 by YBP and the vendor data used to create the index changed at that time. The year-to-year comparisons from 2007 on are now based on this new data model and the changes in price and number of titles are not as dramatic as when looking at comparable data in the indexes that were published prior to 2009.

The overall average price for books in the North American Academic Books Price Index (NAABPI) for 2011 increased moderately when compared with 2010. The average price increased to $93.26 (2011) from $89.15 (2010), a 4.6 percent increase. The overall number of titles in the 2011 index (120,482) increased by approximately 12 percent. Price increases and increased availability of titles will pressure library budgets. This year's price increase was not the result of increases in the costs for e-books as the e-book-only index showed relatively little change in price. This index looks at all titles treated by approval book vendors and includes e-books.

Since 2008, two additional indexes have been available, one for academic e-books only (Table 4A) and another for textbooks (Table 4B). Both of these indexes are of high interest to users and, based on that input, the indexes will continue to be published with the base index year set to 2007. In the academic market, it has always been assumed that e-books are more expensive than their print counterparts. Users might be surprised to find that the $9.95 versions of e-books, available to consumers through channels such as Amazon and the Apple Store, are not available to libraries at similar prices. The new index clearly points out the difference in price: the average price of an e-book in 2011 was $115.86 while the average price for all books was $93.26. The average price of a print book was $76.52. The price for e-books is not that surprising as most pricing models for academic e-books generally charge a large percentage of list print price for multiuser access to e-books. In some cases even single-user academic e-book titles are more expensive than their print counterparts. Responding to customer demands, vendors offer e-books on multiple platforms with multiple pricing models; consequently there can be multiple prices for the same title. Only the first instance of a unique ISBN is included in the data, so if the same book was treated by a vendor from one e-book aggregator and then treated again from another aggregator, only the first instance of the e-book is in the index. Because electronic access is where the market is going it is appropriate to have e-books as a separate index. It is also important to note that the e-book market is changing rapidly. This is reflected in the large swing in numbers of titles supplied between 2007, 2009, 2010, and 2011. Vendors continue to report large jumps in numbers of titles treated due to adding "catch up" titles to their database or adding titles from new publishers.

The cost of textbooks has been a hot topic on many college campuses. The index for textbooks documents price changes in this area. Indications are that textbooks tend to be much more expensive than other types of books, with an average price of $111.69 in 2011. There was not a big increase in the average price (3.5 percent) of textbooks in 2011 but the increase was above the Consumer Price Index (1.6 percent) so the increase is not inconsequential. Textbooks are expensive and the prices seem to be on the rise. Since "e" versions are in the textbook index, a migration to "e" format does not seem to be lowering costs. This is not much consolation for cash-strapped students.

The average price of North American Academic Books in 2011 (Table 4) increased by 4.6 percent as compared with the 2010 average price. This is mainly

(text continues on page 412)

Table 3 / Hardcover Books: Average Prices and Price Indexes, 2009–2012

Index Base: 2005 = 100

BISAC Category	2005 Average Prices	2009 Final Volumes	2009 Final Average Prices	2009 Final Index	2010 Final Volumes	2010 Final Average Prices	2010 Final Index	2011 Final Volumes	2011 Final Average Prices	2011 Final Index	2012 Preliminary Volumes	2012 Preliminary Average Prices	2012 Preliminary Index
Antiques and collectibles	$71.07	159	$46.98	66.1	179	$51.44	72.4	150	$53.07	74.7	118	$72.68	102.3
Architecture	66.99	842	84.46	126.1	742	85.52	127.7	743	77.19	115.2	752	81.97	122.4
Art	62.33	1,688	75.13	120.5	1,687	71.53	114.8	1,686	71.06	114.0	1,744	70.73	113.5
Bibles	48.05	165	46.32	96.4	185	37.50	78.0	221	46.28	96.3	199	37.14	77.3
Biography and autobiography	46.20	1,652	50.08	108.4	1,658	53.41	115.6	1,711	49.00	106.1	1,654	50.19	108.6
Body, mind and spirit	26.76	194	27.60	103.1	177	36.91	137.9	155	30.18	112.8	124	36.92	138.0
Business and economics	120.56	3,913	123.46	102.4	3,977	134.61	111.7	4,105	136.53	113.2	4,060	135.91	112.7
Children	23.14	12,396	25.01	108.1	11,675	24.63	106.4	11,704	26.80	115.8	11,607	22.76	98.4
Comics and graphic novels	32.75	732	32.07	97.9	679	31.51	96.2	801	34.64	105.8	739	37.93	115.8
Computers	113.07	786	155.86	137.8	834	138.53	122.5	884	138.05	122.1	1,004	164.11	145.1
Cooking	28.68	814	29.54	103.0	1,016	30.91	107.8	972	30.82	107.5	1,107	28.37	98.9
Crafts and hobbies	28.82	237	29.94	103.9	217	33.28	115.5	218	30.44	105.6	214	32.05	111.2
Design	59.41	331	66.52	112.0	435	76.59	128.9	441	68.63	115.5	516	63.56	107.0
Drama	60.81	81	83.00	136.5	133	42.91	70.6	138	40.77	67.0	61	74.80	123.0
Education	95.10	1,392	105.56	111.0	1,345	117.59	123.6	1,569	130.14	136.8	1,470	141.77	149.1
Family and relationships	25.37	296	33.57	132.3	277	32.24	127.1	229	33.72	132.9	215	44.25	174.4
Fiction	28.37	4,556	28.78	101.4	4,464	32.20	113.5	4,491	29.51	104.0	4,217	30.06	106.0
Foreign language study	116.89	120	132.01	112.9	123	132.47	113.3	158	136.08	116.4	147	124.18	106.2
Games	32.07	167	37.48	116.9	163	52.07	162.4	112	34.75	108.4	109	36.74	114.6
Gardening	38.20	140	36.98	96.8	118	36.42	95.3	118	40.00	104.7	133	40.09	104.9
Health and fitness	54.05	356	50.78	94.0	309	48.51	89.8	321	60.01	111.0	318	67.62	125.1
History	88.17	4,687	84.41	95.7	4,927	82.65	93.7	4,543	82.80	93.9	4,879	83.01	94.1
House and home	31.51	113	40.44	128.3	90	44.61	141.6	90	38.30	121.5	93	43.63	138.5

Humor	19.00	229	20.24	106.5	221	21.94	115.5	199	19.33	101.7	240	20.05	105.5
Language arts and disciplines	120.71	1,485	131.36	108.8	1,613	117.67	97.5	1,587	115.71	95.9	1,127	129.68	107.4
Law	155.28	1,515	166.60	107.3	1,714	174.48	112.4	1,756	179.16	115.4	1,745	177.69	114.4
Literary collections	74.92	373	90.08	120.2	325	83.49	111.4	357	88.34	117.9	269	91.03	121.5
Literary criticism	123.84	1,903	108.05	87.2	1,955	117.63	95.0	1,964	120.90	97.6	1,930	118.96	96.1
Mathematics	144.88	895	117.08	80.8	1,028	133.23	92.0	1,030	135.56	93.6	979	140.18	96.8
Medical	156.54	2,924	165.92	106.0	3,153	171.13	109.3	2,976	165.38	105.6	3,565	174.54	111.5
Music	77.63	520	77.34	99.6	502	87.84	113.2	488	91.25	117.5	520	84.16	108.4
Nature	67.75	411	65.83	97.2	377	74.89	110.5	400	73.56	108.6	376	86.42	127.6
Performing arts	71.74	540	80.97	112.9	531	76.27	106.3	534	82.49	115.0	580	88.25	123.0
Pets	25.45	176	25.04	98.4	138	24.66	96.9	122	21.16	83.1	86	22.66	89.0
Philosophy	127.22	990	93.78	73.7	1,044	108.93	85.6	1,004	96.68	76.0	1,179	101.55	79.8
Photography	56.77	805	81.82	144.1	800	107.99	190.2	822	60.45	106.5	842	85.67	150.9
Poetry	36.58	293	45.48	124.3	294	40.76	111.4	318	35.16	96.1	221	46.14	126.1
Political science	103.39	2,698	108.10	104.6	2,671	110.32	106.7	2,578	110.27	106.7	2,693	107.46	103.9
Psychology	93.85	1,031	104.29	111.1	1,138	109.85	117.0	1,082	119.76	127.6	1,130	135.57	144.5
Reference	202.23	558	274.83	135.9	541	302.69	149.7	599	351.48	173.8	512	422.35	208.8
Religion	62.29	2,353	72.64	116.6	2,590	80.88	129.8	2,370	73.53	118.0	2,527	82.56	132.5
Science	203.44	3,161	190.41	93.6	3,557	192.20	94.5	3,459	194.96	95.8	3,504	191.35	94.1
Self-help	22.43	311	21.51	95.9	257	27.11	120.9	219	23.92	106.6	219	23.75	105.9
Social science	96.17	3,019	102.73	106.8	3,027	100.47	104.5	3,069	105.66	109.9	3,141	111.20	115.6
Sports and recreation	38.77	619	38.66	99.7	652	41.23	106.3	645	44.69	115.3	651	51.14	131.9
Study aids	105.28	24	114.64	108.9	17	101.54	96.4	20	96.26	91.4	15	106.95	101.6
Technology and engineering	187.80	2,439	160.83	85.6	2,455	164.66	87.7	2,633	167.64	89.3	2,803	172.40	91.8
Transportation	68.68	245	75.98	110.6	292	84.28	122.7	326	61.92	90.2	218	67.49	98.3
Travel	37.11	384	41.22	111.1	367	41.32	111.3	340	42.35	114.1	206	45.65	123.0
True crime	29.28	93	29.36	100.3	67	34.83	119.0	73	31.48	107.5	75	31.06	106.1
Young adult	50.17	2,466	37.38	74.5	2,653	35.99	71.7	2,602	37.47	74.7	2,185	34.43	68.6
Totals	$80.36	68,277	$84.84	105.6	69,389	$89.54	111.4	69,132	$90.32	112.4	69,018	$94.09	117.1

Compiled by Catherine Barr from data supplied by Baker & Taylor.

Table 4 / North American Academic Books: Average Prices and Price Indexes 2009–2011
Index Base: 1989 = 100

Subject Area	LC Class	1989		2009		2010		2010			
		No. of Titles	Average Price	No. of Titles	Average Price	No. of Titles	Average Price	No. of Titles	Average Price	% Change 2010–2011	Index
Agriculture	S	897	$45.13	1,253	$98.24	1,139	$107.44	1,321	$100.51	-6.5%	222.7
Anthropology	GN	406	32.81	488	73.55	609	91.96	558	101.56	10.4	309.5
Botany	QK	251	69.02	286	118.52	260	125.84	283	139.62	10.9	202.3
Business and economics	H	5,979	41.67	10,070	89.33	10,916	97.31	11,237	103.11	6.0	247.4
Chemistry	QD	577	110.61	562	225.48	667	223.03	686	214.45	-3.8	193.9
Education	L	1,685	29.61	4,295	75.75	4,688	86.47	4,728	88.90	2.8	300.3
Engineering and technology	T	4,569	64.94	7,137	124.72	6,913	133.45	8,089	135.40	1.5	208.5
Fine and applied arts	M-N	3,040	40.72	6,647	54.07	5,535	57.17	7,866	63.68	11.4	156.4
General works	A	333	134.65	116	57.09	80	75.60	115	76.52	1.2	56.8
Geography	G	396	47.34	1,124	102.13	1,144	104.98	1,219	108.35	3.2	228.9
Geology	QE	303	63.49	278	125.35	276	114.34	298	115.36	0.9	181.7
History	C-D-E-F	5,549	31.34	10,415	55.98	10,079	65.29	10,729	74.99	14.9	239.3
Home economics	TX	535	27.10	961	42.85	812	44.35	878	48.94	10.3	180.6
Industrial arts	TT	175	23.89	281	38.05	265	52.60	322	44.03	-16.3	184.3
Law	K	1,252	51.10	4,522	113.24	4,596	125.35	6,277	126.55	1.0	247.7
Library and information science	Z	857	44.51	738	86.67	636	90.18	867	88.75	-1.6	199.4
Literature and language	P	10,812	24.99	19,707	48.32	19,364	57.31	21,247	60.21	5.1	240.9
Mathematics and computer science	QA	2,707	44.68	3,902	103.90	3,965	103.85	4,295	106.72	2.8	238.9
Medicine	R	5,028	58.38	8,603	101.97	8,679	112.66	9,613	114.54	1.7	196.2
Military and naval science	U-V	715	33.57	849	62.51	773	79.99	812	71.69	-10.4	213.6
Philosophy and religion	B	3,518	29.06	7,574	67.91	7,386	81.75	8,706	88.74	8.5	305.4
Physical education and recreation	GV	814	20.38	1,807	49.75	1,788	56.03	1,914	67.58	20.6	331.6
Physics and astronomy	QB	1,219	64.59	1,551	128.92	1,627	128.36	1,669	134.88	5.1	208.8
Political science	J	1,650	36.76	3,196	85.12	3,549	99.70	3,863	105.19	5.5	286.2
Psychology	BF	890	31.97	1,626	63.97	1,730	76.65	1,889	85.09	11.0	266.1
Science (general)	Q	433	56.10	552	122.02	631	108.40	611	115.87	6.9	206.5
Sociology	HM	2,742	29.36	6,240	73.58	6,666	88.75	7,273	89.96	1.4	306.4
Zoology	QH,L,P,R	1,967	71.28	2,973	126.24	3,029	140.26	3,117	147.90	5.4	207.5
Average for all subjects		59,299	$41.69	107,753	$79.32	107,802	$89.15	120,482	$93.26	4.6	223.7

Compiled by Stephen Bosch, University of Arizona from electronic data provided by Ingrams Content Group (Coutts Information Services), and YBP Library Services. The data represents all titles (includes hardcover, trade & paperback books, as well as annuals) treated for all approval plan customers serviced by the vendors. This table covers titles published or distributed in the United States and Canada during the calendar years listed.

This index does include paperback editions. The inclusion of these items does impact pricing in the index.

Table 4A / North American Academic E-Books: Average Prices and Price Indexes 2009–2011

Index Base: 2007 = 100

Subject Area	LC Class	2007		2009		2010		2011			
		No. of Titles	Average Price	No. of Titles	Average Price	No. of Titles	Average Price	No. of Titles	Average Price	% Change 2010–2011	Index
Agriculture	S	894	$128.59	1,416	$141.69	697	$168.73	793	$125.68	-25.5%	97.7
Anthropology	GN	382	105.28	521	87.65	385	109.96	357	109.99	0.0	104.5
Botany	QK	287	168.18	347	167.31	190	175.23	169	169.98	-3.0	101.1
Business and economics	H	9,807	97.25	12,542	87.02	8,481	102.87	8,796	106.45	3.5	109.5
Chemistry	QD	934	213.76	1,559	244.65	521	232.57	675	258.38	11.1	120.9
Education	L	2,565	107.62	3,650	84.24	2,852	99.96	2,707	108.27	8.3	100.6
Engineering and technology	T	7,176	133.60	9,128	142.86	4,976	152.33	5,662	144.34	-5.2	108.0
Fine and applied arts	M-N	1,141	84.30	2,174	70.91	1,493	83.35	1,802	84.88	1.8	100.7
General works	A	60	107.85	83	81.79	53	89.13	43	115.99	30.1	107.5
Geography	G	888	132.67	1,308	109.83	829	117.83	833	119.81	1.7	90.3
Geology	QE	201	136.49	358	135.90	178	146.85	196	129.39	-11.9	94.8
History	C-D-E-F	4,452	93.55	8,519	73.99	5,189	89.42	6,288	91.40	2.2	97.7
Home economics	TX	255	104.31	468	80.49	211	78.08	245	72.80	-6.8	69.8
Industrial arts	TT	20	52.73	72	36.91	23	46.11	157	150.98	227.5	286.3
Law	K	1,743	99.61	3,711	113.49	2,433	147.66	2,591	153.51	4.0	154.1
Library and information science	Z	308	74.70	561	84.44	387	89.43	525	91.94	2.8	123.1
Literature and language	P	5,517	90.59	11,470	84.08	7,664	103.12	8,582	100.63	-2.4	111.1
Mathematics and computer science	QA	4,285	102.93	4,387	109.20	3,000	112.65	3,357	121.44	7.8	118.0
Medicine	R	7,420	123.59	10,680	118.45	6,404	134.60	7,184	127.12	-5.6	102.9
Military and naval science	U-V	684	82.89	736	86.28	487	105.07	645	71.69	-31.8	86.5
Philosophy and religion	B	3,612	93.77	6,843	87.18	4,262	110.31	5,648	115.85	5.0	123.5
Physical education and recreation	GV	610	96.00	1,255	61.11	791	76.57	1,114	79.19	3.4	82.5
Physics and astronomy	QB	1,965	142.11	2,197	143.77	1,288	147.50	1,350	136.13	-7.7	95.8
Political science	J	2,447	102.72	4,053	88.44	2,638	110.10	2,695	114.27	3.8	111.2
Psychology	BF	1,113	83.51	1,729	77.42	1,062	91.35	1,290	92.65	1.4	110.9
Science (general)	Q	468	117.19	640	107.75	462	122.51	528	119.86	-2.2	102.3
Sociology	HM	4,139	98.02	7,141	82.60	4,520	103.73	4,883	100.82	-2.8	102.9
Zoology	QH,L,P,R	3,394	154.01	4,066	145.77	2,336	164.82	2,442	170.60	3.5	110.8
Average for all subjects		66,767	$110.82	101,614	$102.21	63,812	$116.25	71,557	$115.86	-0.3	104.6

Compiled by Stephen Bosch, University of Arizona, from electronic data provided by Ingrams Content Group (formerly Coutts Information Services), and YBP Library Services. The data represents all e-book titles treated for all approval plan customers serviced by the vendors. This table covers titles published or distributed in the United States and Canada during the calendar years listed. It is important to note that e-books that were released in a given year may have been published in print much earlier.

(continued from page 407)

due to a large increase in the number of titles treated in the higher part of the price bands ($120 and up) as well as a large increase in the prices in the top price band. Nearly all price bands showed only modest growth in the number of titles between 2007 and 2011 except for the price band above $120, which showed very large increases. This led to a large increase in the average price for all books. The increase in the upper price bands was primarily due to the increased cost of e-books. Remove e-books from this sample, and the upper price bands shrink considerably. See Figure 1.

Figure 1 / Comparison of Titles in Sample Grouped by Price

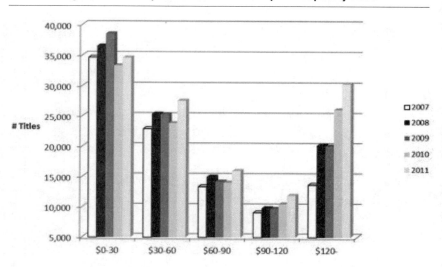

One thing that really stands out when looking at the data by price band is that the highest end of the price bands ($120 and up) has seen huge growth in the past four years, more than doubling in overall costs from $2.6 million (2007) to $6.7 million (2011). The impact on pricing from the titles in the $120 and up price band is confirmed if you look at the actual dollar values in groups (sum of all prices for titles in the group). It is clear that the increase in the top end of the index was the main component in the overall increase in the index for 2011. Although the $0–$30 price area has the largest number of titles, dollar-wise it remains the smallest portion as far as total cost (sum of all prices) goes in the index. The increase in the prices in the upper end of the index was what added to the overall level of increase. Over the last four years, the costs (titles x prices) for books pricing above $120 has increased 153 percent, while the overall costs for all books increased 76 percent. The increases in the costs of books in the upper price band represents 85 percent of the entire increase over the past four years. E-books are the significant driver in that increase. Within the price bands, the average price remains fairly constant except for the area with prices above $120, which displayed a 21 percent increase over the past four years. See Figures 2 and 3.

Figure 2 / Comparison of Total Costs in Sample Grouped by Price

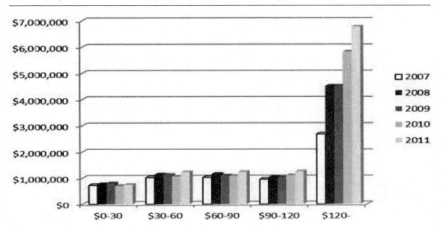

Figure 3 / Comparison of Average Price Grouped by Price Band

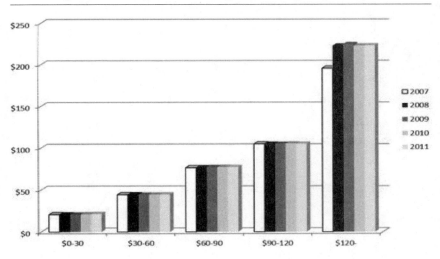

The data used for this index are derived from all titles treated by the Ingram Content Group (formerly Coutts Information Services) and YBP Library Services in their approval plans during the calendar years listed. The index includes e-books as well as paperback editions as supplied by these vendors, and this inclusion of paperbacks and e-books as distributed as part of the approval plans has clearly influenced the prices reflected in the index figures. The index is inclusive of the broadest categories of materials as that is the marketplace in which academic libraries operate, and the index attempts to chart price changes that impact that market.

(text continues on page 421)

Table 4B / North American Academic Text Books: Average Prices and Price Indexes 2009–2011

Index Base: 2007 = 100

Subject Area	LC Class	2007 No. of Titles	2007 Average Price	2009 No. of Titles	2009 Average Price	2010 No. of Titles	2010 Average Price	2011 No. of Titles	2011 Average Price	% Change 2010–2011	Index
Agriculture	S	68	$134.75	50	$102.37	49	$115.80	120	$118.80	2.6%	88.2
Anthropology	GN	40	89.15	27	82.21	35	90.65	59	88.71	-2.1	99.5
Botany	QK	4	98.00	21	126.81	11	109.52	17	114.79	4.8	117.1
Business and economics	H	666	110.18	674	115.47	694	121.36	1,556	113.53	-6.4	103.0
Chemistry	QD	80	138.70	76	131.24	94	134.59	169	154.21	14.6	111.2
Education	L	235	79.58	220	84.49	271	87.75	667	82.90	-5.5	104.2
Engineering and technology	T	668	106.13	790	113.64	744	116.38	1,736	120.21	3.3	113.3
Fine and applied arts	M-N	82	73.69	72	86.44	73	93.33	173	86.78	-7.0	117.8
General works	A	1	48.00	1	90.00	0	0.00	4	80.88	0.0	89.9
Geography	G	59	100.42	82	104.79	78	105.21	190	110.18	4.7	109.7
Geology	QE	26	118.28	20	124.78	36	117.97	56	117.57	-0.3	99.4
History	C-D-E-F	72	78.41	72	87.34	81	81.49	205	78.84	-3.2	100.5
Home economics	TX	54	68.23	32	92.59	39	89.52	46	87.78	-1.9	128.7
Industrial arts	TT	13	73.90	13	91.87	14	84.72	23	821.82	870.0	1112.1
Law	K	163	87.67	241	100.38	242	102.09	513	105.89	3.7	120.8
Library and information science	Z	24	65.54	21	71.61	19	70.30	49	76.14	8.3	116.2
Literature and language	P	269	71.35	284	73.56	309	77.71	864	78.90	1.5	110.6
Mathematics and Computer science	QA	732	91.42	679	89.50	683	96.11	1,544	112.26	16.8	122.8
Medicine	R	1,210	126.37	1,375	131.12	1,512	126.75	3,357	130.46	2.9	103.2
Military and naval science	U-V	10	104.58	8	138.90	3	122.65	24	98.38	-19.8	94.1
Philosophy and religion	B	85	55.51	98	57.11	101	72.13	216	65.42	-9.3	117.8
Physical education and recreation	GV	47	72.14	45	84.99	51	79.39	118	87.56	10.3	121.4
Physics and astronomy	QB	237	107.05	200	109.28	243	107.38	537	116.51	8.5	108.8
Political science	J	104	74.21	100	86.36	110	80.09	277	84.69	5.7	114.1
Psychology	BF	120	100.17	102	101.51	138	95.95	327	95.86	-0.1	95.7
Science (general)	Q	24	111.30	24	86.36	33	97.14	64	87.63	-9.8	78.7
Sociology	HM	330	84.88	261	84.05	353	86.97	844	88.31	1.5	104.0
Zoology	QH,L,P,R	250	116.73	231	114.93	227	109.82	511	120.33	9.6	103.1
Average for all subjects		5,673	$102.52	5,819	$107.17	6,243	$107.94	14,266	$111.69	3.5	108.9

Compiled by Stephen Bosch, University of Arizona, from electronic data provided by YBP Library Services and Ingrams Content Group. The data represents all textbook titles treated for all approval plan customers serviced by the vendors. This table covers titles published or distributed in the United States and Canada during the calendar years listed. This index does include paperback editions. The inclusion of these items does impact pricing in the index.

Table 5 / U.S. College Books: Average Prices and Price Indexes 1989, 2010–2012
Index Base for all years: 1989=100

Subject	1989 No. of Titles	1989 Avg. Price per Title	2010 No. of Titles	2010 Avg. Price per Title	2010 Indexed to 1989	2010 Indexed to 2009	2011 No. of Titles	2011 Avg. Price per Title	2011 Indexed to 1989	2011 Indexed to 2010	2012 No. of Titles	2012 Avg. Price per Title	2012 Indexed to 1989	2012 Indexed to 2011	Percent Change 2011–2012
General*	19	$40.19	n.a.	n.a.	n.a.	n.a.	n.a.	n.a.	n.a.	n.a.	n.a.	n.a.	n.a.	n.a.	n.a.
Humanities	21	32.33	91	$58.99	182.5	106.5	87	$60.90	188.4	103.2	99	$69.36	214.5	113.9	13.9%
Art & Architecture	276	55.56	149	61.69	111.0	105.8	170	64.61	116.3	104.7	176	68.40	123.1	105.9	5.9
Fine Arts**	n.a.	n.a.	92	67.13	n.a.	103.6	93	65.46	n.a.	97.5	117	67.49	n.a.	103.1	3.1
Architecture**	n.a.	n.a.	48	61.53	n.a.	98.6	51	67.72	n.a.	110.1	58	75.15	n.a.	111.0	11.0
Photography	24	44.11	28	53.02	120.2	97.4	25	51.87	117.6	97.8	31	63.50	144.0	122.4	22.4
Communication	42	32.70	112	59.97	183.4	98.3	111	73.51	224.8	122.6	85	68.36	209.1	93.0	-7.0
Language and Literature	110	35.17	94	68.66	195.2	113.0	124	70.09	199.3	102.1	122	73.30	208.4	104.6	4.6
Africa and Middle East**	n.a.	n.a.	24	62.28	n.a.	127.9	30	63.93	n.a.	102.6	21	66.77	n.a.	104.4	4.4
Asia and Oceania**	n.a.	n.a.	24	71.99	n.a.	128.7	18	78.89	n.a.	109.6	20	61.66	n.a.	78.2	-21.8
Classical	75	43.07	24	78.76	182.9	105.7	34	92.32	214.3	117.2	27	94.71	219.9	102.6	2.6
English and American	547	30.27	394	61.96	204.7	98.8	376	68.92	227.7	111.2	412	70.77	233.8	102.7	2.7
Germanic	38	32.18	22	70.36	218.7	106.9	26	67.99	211.3	96.6	29	71.17	221.2	104.7	4.7
Romance	97	30.30	70	59.00	194.7	92.5	70	68.69	226.7	116.4	67	69.54	229.5	101.2	1.2
Slavic	41	27.92	32	35.95	128.8	65.2	21	55.46	198.6	154.3	13	50.78	181.9	91.6	-8.4
Other*	63	25.09	n.a.	n.a.	n.a.	n.a.	n.a.	n.a.	n.a.	n.a.	n.a.	n.a.	n.a.	n.a.	n.a.
Performing Arts	20	29.41	30	61.97	210.7	111.1	26	46.03	156.5	74.3	27	62.56	212.7	135.9	35.9
Film	82	33.00	130	64.13	194.3	95.9	138	64.97	196.9	101.3	148	66.69	202.1	102.6	2.6
Music	156	35.34	123	61.01	172.6	111.7	146	65.12	184.3	106.7	137	66.48	188.1	102.1	2.1
Theater and Dance	58	34.18	45	62.38	182.5	99.9	49	70.28	205.6	112.7	37	68.87	201.5	98.0	-2.0
Philosophy	185	37.25	198	63.45	170.3	90.6	206	70.28	188.7	110.8	236	71.79	192.7	102.1	2.1
Religion	174	33.49	272	57.18	170.7	113.8	243	60.99	182.1	106.7	259	83.71	250.0	137.3	37.3
Total Humanities	2,009	$36.09	2,002	$61.60	170.7	101.2	2,044	$66.89	185.3	108.6	2,121	$68.96	191.1	103.1	3.1

Table 5 / U.S. College Books: Average Prices and Price Indexes 1989, 2010–2012 *(cont.)*
Index Base for all years: 1989=100

Subject	1989		2010				2011				2012				
	No. of Titles	Avg. Price per Title	No. of Titles	Avg. Price per Title	Indexed to 1989	Indexed to 2009	No. of Titles	Avg. Price per Title	Indexed to 1989	Indexed to 2010	No. of Titles	Avg. Price per Title	Indexed to 1989	Indexed to 2011	Percent Change 2011–2012
Science and Technology	99	$46.90	110	$58.09	123.9	90.1	93	$57.99	123.6	99.8	104	$57.10	121.7	98.5	-1.5%
History of Science and Technology	74	40.56	78	54.10	133.4	88.0	79	50.72	125.0	93.8	77	59.84	147.5	118.0	18.0
Astronautics and Astronomy	22	50.56	63	55.58	109.9	102.2	69	55.96	110.7	100.7	50	52.82	104.5	94.4	-5.6
Biology	97	51.01	151	72.74	142.6	100.9	153	73.42	143.9	100.9	136	81.29	159.4	110.7	10.7
Botany	29	63.91	85	85.09	133.1	98.8	75	70.92	111.0	83.3	75	90.52	141.6	127.6	27.6
Zoology	53	49.21	121	64.33	130.7	100.1	114	61.00	124.0	94.8	95	68.49	139.2	112.3	12.3
Chemistry	21	70.76	42	115.42	163.1	111.7	48	96.06	135.8	83.2	46	90.74	128.2	94.5	-5.5
Earth Science	34	79.44	102	63.33	79.7	82.0	113	64.02	80.6	101.1	100	82.49	103.8	128.9	28.9
Engineering	87	66.74	103	88.38	132.4	86.1	89	102.12	153.0	115.5	60	98.52	147.6	96.5	-3.5
Health Sciences	94	34.91	146	56.14	160.8	106.1	154	57.98	166.1	103.3	155	60.78	174.1	104.8	4.8
Information and Computer Science	70	40.35	83	73.50	182.2	78.6	96	70.03	173.6	95.3	73	69.63	172.6	99.4	-0.6
Mathematics	60	48.53	108	61.97	127.7	91.5	104	69.89	144.0	112.8	92	64.44	132.8	92.2	-7.8
Physics	22	43.94	50	54.74	124.6	85.1	64	65.59	149.3	119.8	53	52.85	120.3	80.6	-19.4
Sports and Physical Education	18	27.46	67	54.06	196.9	104.3	52	63.91	232.7	118.2	47	80.83	294.4	126.5	26.5
Total Science	780	49.54	1,309	67.13	135.5	94.6	1,303	$67.65	136.6	100.8	1,163	71.29	143.9	105.4	5.4

Social and Behavioral Sciences	92	$37.09	129	$66.32	178.8	102.2	143	$68.64	185.1	103.5	158	$70.11	189.0	102.1	2.1
Anthropology	96	39.94	139	63.60	159.2	93.3	134	68.46	171.4	107.6	126	68.60	171.8	100.2	0.2
Business Management and Labor	145	35.72	150	58.00	162.4	105.7	161	54.37	152.2	93.7	169	56.52	158.2	104.0	4.0
Economics	332	40.75	270	61.16	150.1	96.2	281	59.01	144.8	96.5	264	63.84	156.7	108.2	8.2
Education	71	34.50	158	62.56	181.3	107.3	153	69.54	201.6	111.2	162	70.85	205.4	101.9	1.9
History, Geography, and Area Studies	59	42.10	154	58.16	138.2	108.5	109	71.73	170.4	123.3	125	66.85	158.8	93.2	-6.8
Africa	44	34.85	38	69.05	198.1	108.6	46	65.28	187.3	94.5	44	67.96	195.0	104.1	4.1
Ancient History**	n.a.	n.a.	49	57.90	n.a.	91.8	62	74.41	n.a.	128.5	66	80.73	n.a.	108.5	8.5
Asia and Oceania	76	34.75	72	60.88	175.2	84.8	61	61.86	178.0	101.6	84	66.78	192.2	108.0	8.0
Central and Eastern Europe**	n.a.	n.a.	56	66.53	n.a.	96.6	61	64.22	n.a.	96.5	74	54.03	n.a.	84.1	-15.9
Latin America and Caribbean	42	37.23	54	59.31	159.3	107.6	59	60.28	161.9	101.6	66	63.00	169.2	104.5	4.5
Middle East and North Africa	30	36.32	43	65.57	180.5	95.8	51	60.69	167.1	92.6	38	72.37	199.3	119.2	19.2
North America	349	30.56	444	45.50	148.9	92.3	445	47.43	155.2	104.2	416	49.91	163.3	105.2	5.2
United Kingdom**	n.a.	n.a.	80	69.56	n.a.	107.8	68	80.32	n.a.	115.5	88	78.10	n.a.	97.2	-2.8
Western Europe	287	42.08	138	59.14	140.5	85.0	141	69.66	165.5	117.8	134	68.45	162.7	98.3	-1.7
Political Science	28	33.56	4	84.36	251.4	81.9	4	132.50	394.8	157.1	2	105.00	312.9	79.2	-20.8
Comparative Politics	236	37.82	183	66.34	175.4	93.5	211	72.76	192.4	109.7	195	70.51	186.4	96.9	-3.1
International Relations	207	35.74	213	65.64	183.7	99.2	167	72.47	202.8	110.4	170	67.30	188.3	92.9	-7.1
Political Theory	59	37.76	73	56.74	150.3	92.8	91	59.06	156.4	104.1	86	58.54	155.0	99.1	-0.9
U.S. Politics	212	29.37	253	53.03	180.6	105.4	213	55.86	190.2	105.3	246	56.52	192.4	101.2	1.2
Psychology	179	36.36	126	60.55	166.5	92.5	115	64.12	176.3	105.9	114	73.84	203.1	115.2	15.2
Sociology	178	36.36	226	60.71	167.0	101.4	241	64.48	177.3	106.2	230	69.04	189.9	107.1	7.1

Table 5 / U.S. College Books: Average Prices and Price Indexes 1989, 2010–2012 *(cont.)*

Index Base for all years: 1989=100

Subject	1989		2010				2011				2012				
	No. of Titles	Avg. Price per Title	No. of Titles	Avg. Price per Title	Indexed to 1989	Indexed to 2009	No. of Titles	Avg. Price per Title	Indexed to 1989	Indexed to 2010	No. of Titles	Avg. Price per Title	Indexed to 1989	Indexed to 2011	Percent Change 2011–2012
Total Social and Behavioral Sciences	2,722	$36.43	3,052	$59.09	162.2	97.4	3,017	$62.75	172.2	106.2	3,057	$64.19	176.2	102.3	2.3
Total General, Humanities, Science and Social Sciences	5,511	$38.16	6,363	$61.53	161.2	97.7	6,364	$65.08	170.5	105.8	6,341	$67.09	175.8	103.1	3.1
Reference	636	$61.02	29	$61.17	65.5	65.5	31	$91.40	149.8	149.4	37	$93.04	152.5	101.8	1.8
Humanities**	n.a.	n.a.	128	117.12	n.a.	103.9	109	126.39	n.a.	107.9	138	110.23	n.a.	87.2	-12.8
Science and Technology**	n.a.	n.a.	76	133.19	n.a.	113.8	58	136.46	n.a.	102.5	43	151.19	n.a.	110.8	10.8
Social and Behavioral Sciences**	n.a.	n.a.	216	152.91	n.a.	101.5	216	144.23	n.a.	94.3	210	136.53	n.a.	94.7	-5.3
Total Reference	636	$61.02	449	$133.44	218.7	103.8	414	$134.49	220.4	100.8	428	$125.76	206.1	93.5	-6.5
Grand Total	6,147	40.52	6,812	$66.27	163.6	98.7	6,778	$69.32	171.1	104.6	6,769	$70.80	174.7	102.1	2.1

Compiled by Frederick Lynden, Brown University.

* General category no longer appears.

**Began appearing as separate sections after 1989. n.a. = not available.

Table 6 / U.S. Mass Market Paperback Books: Average Prices and Price Indexes, 2009–2012

Index Base: 2005 = 100

BISAC Category	2005 Average Prices	2009 Final			2010 Final			2011 Final			2012 Preliminary		
		Volumes	Average Prices	Index	Volumes	Average Prices	Index	Volumes	Average Prices	Index	Volumes	Average Prices	Index
Antiques and collectibles	$7.69	9	$8.66	112.6	9	$8.77	114.0	5	$8.79	114.3	5	$8.99	116.9
Architecture	n.a.	n.a.	n.a.	n.a.	n.a.	n.a.	n.a.	n.a.	n.a.	n.a.	n.a.	n.a.	n.a.
Art	n.a.	n.a.	n.a.	n.a.	n.a.	n.a.	n.a.	n.a.	n.a.	n.a.	n.a.	n.a.	n.a.
Bibles	n.a.	n.a.	n.a.	n.a.	n.a.	n.a.	n.a.	n.a.	n.a.	n.a.	n.a.	n.a.	n.a.
Biography and autobiography	7.83	13	7.48	95.5	13	7.51	95.9	8	8.62	110.1	4	6.73	86.0
Body, mind and spirit	7.11	13	7.99	112.4	17	7.99	112.4	17	7.93	111.5	14	8.13	114.3
Business and economics	12.47	1	9.99	80.1	3	9.32	74.7	2	7.99	64.1	1	7.99	64.1
Children	5.29	238	6.12	115.7	257	6.22	117.6	253	6.56	124	246	6.46	122.1
Comics and graphic novels	8.47	n.a.	n.a.	n.a.	n.a.	n.a.	n.a.	n.a.	n.a.	n.a.	n.a.	n.a.	n.a.
Computers	n.a.	n.a.	n.a.	n.a.	n.a.	n.a.	n.a.	n.a.	n.a.	n.a.	n.a.	n.a.	n.a.
Cooking	7.50	n.a.	n.a.	n.a.	n.a.	n.a.	n.a.	1	7.99	106.5	n.a.	n.a.	n.a.
Crafts and hobbies	n.a.	n.a.	n.a.	n.a.	n.a.	n.a.	n.a.	n.a.	n.a.	n.a.	n.a.	n.a.	n.a.
Design	n.a.	n.a.	n.a.	n.a.	n.a.	n.a.	n.a.	n.a.	n.a.	n.a.	n.a.	n.a.	n.a.
Drama	6.32	3	5.98	94.6	3	6.30	99.7	1	8.95	141.6	2	4.95	78.3
Education	n.a.	n.a.	n.a.	n.a.	n.a.	n.a.	n.a.	n.a.	n.a.	n.a.	n.a.	n.a.	n.a.
Family and relationships	6.98	1	4.99	71.5	1	7.99	114.5	1	8.99	128.8	1	4.99	71.5
Fiction	6.34	4,013	6.68	105.4	3,952	6.80	107.3	3,997	6.97	109.9	3,883	7.03	110.9
Foreign language study	n.a.	4	6.99	n.a.	6	7.08	n.a.	n.a.	n.a.	n.a.	n.a.	n.a.	n.a.
Games	7.14	5	4.99	69.9	n.a.	n.a.	n.a.	n.a.	n.a.	n.a.	n.a.	n.a.	n.a.
Gardening	n.a.	n.a.	n.a.	n.a.	n.a.	n.a.	n.a.	n.a.	n.a.	n.a.	n.a.	n.a.	n.a.
Health and fitness	7.43	15	7.79	104.8	14	7.92	106.6	11	8.17	110	16	8.24	110.9
History	7.90	5	7.89	99.9	1	9.95	125.9	7	8.56	108.4	3	8.66	109.6
House and home	5.99	n.a.	n.a.	n.a.	n.a.	n.a.	n.a.	n.a.	n.a.	n.a.	n.a.	n.a.	n.a.
Humor	6.99	n.a.	n.a.	n.a.	2	13.25	189.6	1	3.50	50.1	n.a.	n.a.	n.a.
Language arts and disciplines	6.99	n.a.	n.a.	n.a.	n.a.	n.a.	n.a.	n.a.	n.a.	n.a.	n.a.	n.a.	n.a.
Law	n.a.	n.a.	n.a.	n.a.	n.a.	n.a.	n.a.	n.a.	n.a.	n.a.	n.a.	n.a.	n.a.
Literary collections	n.a.	1	7.95	n.a.	1	5.95	n.a.	1	7.95	n.a.	2	5.95	n.a.

Table 6 / U.S. Mass Market Paperback Books: Average Prices and Price Indexes, 2009–2012 (cont.)

Index Base: 2005 = 100

BISAC Category	2005 Average Prices	2009 Final Volumes	2009 Final Average Prices	2009 Final Index	2010 Final Volumes	2010 Final Average Prices	2010 Final Index	2011 Final Volumes	2011 Final Average Prices	2011 Final Index	2012 Preliminary Volumes	2012 Preliminary Average Prices	2012 Preliminary Index
Literary criticism	7.95	1	7.99	100.5	1	7.99	100.5	1	9.99	125.7	n.a.	n.a.	n.a.
Mathematics	n.a.	n.a.	n.a.	n.a.	n.a.	n.a.	n.a.	n.a.	n.a.	n.a.	n.a.	n.a.	n.a.
Medical	7.83	n.a.	n.a.	n.a.	1	8.99	114.8	n.a.	n.a.	n.a.	1	8.99	114.8
Music	7.95	n.a.	n.a.	n.a.	1	n.a.	n.a.	1	7.95	n.a.	n.a.	n.a.	n.a.
Nature	n.a.	n.a.	n.a.	n.a.	n.a.	n.a.	n.a.	1	n.a.	n.a.	1	7.99	n.a.
Performing arts	8.23	1	9.99	121.4	1	9.99	121.4	2	8.99	109.2	1	9.99	121.4
Pets	n.a.	n.a.	n.a.	n.a.	1	7.99	n.a.	1	7.99	n.a.	n.a.	n.a.	n.a.
Philosophy	7.49	n.a.	n.a.	n.a.	2	6.47	86.4	n.a.	n.a.	n.a.	n.a.	n.a.	n.a.
Photography	n.a.	n.a.	n.a.	n.a.	n.a.	n.a.	n.a.	n.a.	n.a.	n.a.	n.a.	n.a.	n.a.
Poetry	5.75	5	6.95	120.9	1	7.95	138.3	1	7.95	138.3	2	7.45	129.6
Political science	n.a.	1	5.95	n.a.	2	7.97	n.a.	1	5.95	n.a.	n.a.	n.a.	n.a.
Psychology	7.97	n.a.	n.a.	n.a.	n.a.	n.a.	n.a.	1	7.99	100.3	n.a.	n.a.	n.a.
Reference	6.85	3	7.66	111.8	1	7.99	116.6	2	7.99	116.6	3	8.31	121.3
Religion	9.96	3	6.98	70.1	2	7.99	80.2	3	7.99	80.2	2	7.49	75.2
Science	n.a.	n.a.	n.a.	n.a.	n.a.	n.a.	n.a.	n.a.	n.a.	n.a.	n.a.	n.a.	n.a.
Self-help	12.45	2	7.99	64.2	1	7.99	64.2	1	7.99	64.2	1	7.99	64.2
Social science	7.08	n.a.	n.a.	n.a.	n.a.	n.a.	n.a.	1	n.a.	n.a.	1	9.99	141.1
Sports and recreation	7.62	3	6.99	91.7	1	7.99	104.9	1	7.99	104.9	1	7.99	104.9
Study aids	n.a.	n.a.	n.a.	n.a.	n.a.	n.a.	n.a.	n.a.	n.a.	n.a.	n.a.	n.a.	n.a.
Technology and engineering	n.a.	n.a.	n.a.	n.a.	n.a.	n.a.	n.a.	n.a.	n.a.	n.a.	n.a.	n.a.	n.a.
Transportation	12.95	1	14.00	108.1	n.a.	n.a.	n.a.	n.a.	n.a.	n.a.	n.a.	n.a.	n.a.
Travel	n.a.	1	4.95	n.a.	n.a.	n.a.	n.a.	n.a.	n.a.	n.a.	n.a.	n.a.	n.a.
True crime	7.19	52	7.47	103.9	54	7.64	106.3	44	7.83	108.9	38	8.31	115.6
Young adult	6.46	96	7.63	118.1	83	8.13	125.9	47	8.48	131.3	55	9.04	139.9
Totals	$6.34	4,490	$6.70	105.7	4,430	$6.83	107.7	4,411	$6.99	110.3	4,283	$7.04	111.0

Compiled by Catherine Barr from data supplied by Baker & Taylor.

n.a. = not available

(continued from page 413)

E-books are also now being treated in a separate index (Table 4A), so the differences in the indexes will be interesting to observe. Currently the vast majority of titles are not published in both print and "e" version, so the number of titles in the e-book index should remain much smaller than the broader index. It is safe to say that in the future the number of titles in the broader index could decline and at the same time the number of e-books should rise, especially as we see more publishers move to publishing electronic versions of their books. Many e-book pricing models add extra charges of as much as 50 percent to 100 percent to the retail price for a multi-user license. This pricing model is reflected in the higher prices for e-books. The overall price for e-books did show a decline from 2007 to 2009 but in 2010 the prices shot up again. The year 2011 saw the price remain relatively unchanged (-0.3 percent). As the number of titles treated has had a huge variation, it is not really possible to draw absolute conclusions about pricing trends in e-books at this time. The overall trend seems to indicate that prices are going up. The index does clearly show that for the library market, e-books are much more expensive than print. Many publishers and e-book aggregators are still adding "e" versions of print books from backlists, and these are showing up in the index; this is also the basis of the wide swings in numbers of titles in the index from year to year.

The price index for textbooks (Table 4B) shows a 3.5 percent increase for overall prices between 2010 and 2011. This increase is smaller than the increase seen for the broader print index, but the overall prices are higher. These are indicators that the angst experienced by students as they purchase their texts may well be justified; prices appear to be much higher than those for regular academic books.

Price changes vary, as always, among subject areas. This year there were many double-digit increases in subject areas and a few areas showed price decreases. The subjects with the highest price increases, as indicated by the 2011 data, were the social sciences and humanities. This may be due to increases in e-book publishing in these subject areas. STM publishers have tended to be early adopters and have been publishing e-books for a while. The large price increases in the social sciences and humanities reflect the availability of a lot more e-books in these areas.

It is good to remember that price indexes become less accurate at describing price changes the smaller the sample becomes. Industrial arts and military science are small samples and showed very large price changes, but to conclude all books in those areas increased or decreased at like amounts is not correct. These areas have a small sample size (fewer than 1,000 titles) and the inclusion/exclusion of just a few large expensive items can have a major impact on prices for the category. The huge increases in industrial arts, for example, were due to two very expensive titles that showed up in the textbook and e-book price data. Since the sample is very small, these titles caused the overall price to jump dramatically.

The U.S. College Books Price Index (Table 5), prepared by Frederick C. Lynden, contains price and indexing information for the years 2010 through 2012 (index base year of 1989), and also the percentage change between 2011 and 2012. Data for the index were compiled from 6,769 reviews of books published in *Choice*

(text continues on page 428)

Table 7 / U.S. Paperback Books (Excluding Mass Market): Average Prices and Price Indexes, 2009–2012
Index Base: 2005 = 100

BISAC Category	2005 Average Prices	2009 Final Volumes	2009 Final Average Prices	2009 Final Index	2010 Final Volumes	2010 Final Average Prices	2010 Final Index	2011 Final Volumes	2011 Final Average Prices	2011 Final Index	2012 Preliminary Volumes	2012 Preliminary Average Prices	2012 Preliminary Index
Antiques and collectibles	$24.80	191	$27.25	109.9	178	$25.53	102.9	158	$25.85	104.2	178	$28.88	116.5
Architecture	38.90	692	44.89	115.4	752	45.31	116.5	739	42.71	109.8	633	40.68	104.6
Art	31.28	1,491	37.63	120.3	1,506	38.25	122.3	1,706	37.64	120.3	1,688	35.87	114.7
Bibles	36.87	307	40.67	110.3	430	38.66	104.9	755	41.08	111.4	632	45.07	122.2
Biography and autobiography	19.19	2,347	20.54	107.0	2,434	20.35	106.0	4,946	18.93	98.6	4,551	19.12	99.6
Body, mind and spirit	17.48	1,009	18.16	103.9	995	18.03	103.1	1,717	17.88	102.3	1,700	17.29	98.9
Business and economics	71.12	5,930	62.07	87.3	5,791	69.30	97.4	5,789	68.02	95.6	8,189	80.04	112.5
Children	11.11	9,716	10.91	98.2	8,612	10.42	93.8	9,474	11.05	99.5	9,364	12.37	111.3
Comics and graphic novels	12.75	2,173	15.42	120.9	1,863	16.11	126.4	3,415	16.24	127.4	2,180	16.31	127.9
Computers	57.01	3,795	97.47	171.0	3,460	70.42	123.5	3,495	71.41	125.3	3,629	78.09	137.0
Cooking	18.30	1,006	19.59	107.0	1,101	19.95	109.0	1,242	19.80	108.2	1,251	20.64	112.8
Crafts and hobbies	18.49	1,002	19.29	104.3	1,052	19.34	104.6	1,091	19.41	105.0	1,049	19.75	106.8
Design	32.87	397	37.00	112.6	440	63.98	194.6	414	42.72	130.0	384	40.67	123.7
Drama	16.40	581	21.70	132.3	739	18.95	115.5	559	18.80	114.6	565	18.50	112.8
Education	35.10	3,262	41.43	118.0	3,545	42.98	122.5	3,565	41.21	117.4	3,633	44.23	126.0
Family and relationships	17.10	884	19.63	114.8	782	18.72	109.5	1,288	17.87	104.5	1,185	18.05	105.6
Fiction	15.74	9,694	17.32	110.0	9,546	17.99	114.3	18,402	18.22	115.8	15,958	17.62	111.9
Foreign language study	41.90	977	32.31	77.1	1,280	31.33	74.8	1,247	36.30	86.6	1,090	39.27	93.7
Games	16.53	787	17.59	106.4	792	16.57	100.2	705	16.61	100.5	653	16.14	97.6
Gardening	20.59	256	20.96	101.8	241	23.45	113.9	249	23.33	113.3	231	23.03	111.9
Health and fitness	22.81	1,333	23.67	103.8	1,271	26.95	118.1	1,477	26.98	118.3	1,276	25.10	110.0
History	33.53	6,436	31.80	94.8	6,952	35.79	106.7	7,456	36.45	108.7	7,096	38.18	113.9
House and home	19.33	226	21.96	113.6	200	21.19	109.6	153	20.43	105.7	150	21.76	112.6

Humor	12.96	486	13.79	106.4	430	14.37	110.9	581	14.97	115.5	510	14.90	115.0
Language arts and disciplines	49.14	2,088	65.85	134.0	2,317	64.46	131.2	1,835	72.19	146.9	2,157	71.00	144.5
Law	60.92	2,711	75.41	123.8	3,179	72.07	118.3	3,220	70.43	115.6	3,045	71.30	117.0
Literary collections	28.07	581	35.01	124.7	672	36.42	129.7	541	29.36	104.6	473	32.49	115.7
Literary criticism	31.99	1,770	38.66	120.9	1,612	36.57	114.3	1,750	38.50	120.4	1,522	39.79	124.4
Mathematics	75.77	885	68.93	91.0	1,312	86.13	113.7	1,611	81.10	107.0	1,706	90.65	119.6
Medical	64.27	3,937	76.34	118.8	5,378	90.22	140.4	6,107	83.04	129.2	5,531	96.03	149.4
Music	22.66	2,975	23.22	102.5	3,020	22.83	100.8	2,837	24.53	108.3	2,586	24.62	108.6
Nature	26.90	613	27.02	100.4	565	37.28	138.6	586	35.86	133.3	604	33.11	123.1
Performing arts	27.85	934	33.65	120.8	1,030	33.53	120.4	938	32.40	116.3	952	36.19	129.9
Pets	18.86	299	19.01	100.8	249	17.34	91.9	235	18.70	99.2	211	18.85	99.9
Philosophy	31.40	1,465	34.33	109.3	1,391	52.66	167.7	1,587	42.41	135.1	1,503	45.15	143.8
Photography	27.74	539	31.13	112.2	546	31.30	112.8	541	32.14	115.9	522	31.09	112.1
Poetry	16.09	1,720	16.88	104.9	1,720	16.73	104.0	3,811	16.26	101.1	3,433	16.13	100.2
Political science	45.65	3,220	37.91	83.0	3,908	41.00	89.8	3,472	41.07	90.0	3,501	42.36	92.8
Psychology	45.74	1,256	43.08	94.2	1,578	47.98	104.9	1,685	53.84	117.7	1,807	60.12	131.4
Reference	52.54	1,307	90.69	172.6	1,057	84.85	161.5	1,217	89.01	169.4	1,214	99.58	189.5
Religion	20.54	6,052	21.31	103.7	6,955	22.08	107.5	8,639	20.58	100.2	8,728	21.07	102.6
Science	71.05	2,462	78.19	110.0	4,004	116.37	163.8	4,685	99.37	139.9	3,886	98.74	139.0
Self-help	16.36	1,047	17.84	109.0	1,121	17.84	109.0	2,043	17.31	105.8	2,371	16.64	101.7
Social science	36.83	3,998	42.51	115.4	4,270	45.05	122.3	4,013	43.93	119.3	4,551	47.78	129.7
Sports and recreation	21.82	1,259	23.39	107.2	1,315	22.30	102.2	1,310	24.79	113.6	1,178	23.24	106.5
Study aids	30.90	669	30.82	99.7	1,499	49.24	159.4	985	33.84	109.5	591	41.30	133.7
Technology and engineering	85.80	2,681	153.11	178.4	2,427	111.20	129.6	2,426	105.98	123.5	3,037	115.26	134.3
Transportation	40.19	459	36.61	91.1	507	36.26	90.2	458	36.76	91.5	411	34.73	86.4
Travel	19.18	2,852	20.51	106.9	2,585	20.93	109.1	2,513	19.82	103.3	2,171	19.96	104.1
True crime	17.71	156	19.00	107.3	195	20.94	118.2	227	19.00	107.3	197	19.18	108.3
Young adult	14.06	2,462	16.79	119.4	2,173	14.86	105.7	2,555	18.59	132.2	3,241	16.92	120.3
Totals	$33.90	105,375	$39.20	115.6	110,977	$42.06	124.1	132,450	$37.86	111.7	128,904	$41.49	122.4

Compiled by Catherine Barr from data supplied by Baker & Taylor.

Table 7A / U.S. Audiobooks: Average Prices and Price Indexes, 2009–2012

Index Base: 2005 = 100

BISAC Category	2005 Average Prices	2009 Final Volumes	2009 Final Average Prices	2009 Final Index	2010 Final Volumes	2010 Final Average Prices	2010 Final Index	2011 Final Volumes	2011 Final Average Prices	2011 Final Index	2012 Preliminary Volumes	2012 Preliminary Average Prices	2012 Preliminary Index
Antiques and collectibles	n.a.	1	$74.95	n.a.	3	$36.66	n.a.	n.a.	n.a.	n.a.	n.a.	n.a.	n.a.
Architecture	$68.95	n.a.	n.a.	n.a.	4	41.24	59.8	3	$39.97	58.0	2	$32.45	47.1
Art	57.51	7	59.41	103.3	9	58.21	101.2	9	40.36	70.2	12	37.40	65.0
Bibles	47.08	9	75.53	160.4	7	43.28	91.9	10	44.49	94.5	23	48.76	103.6
Biography and autobiography	37.68	685	50.75	134.7	751	50.79	134.8	749	51.25	136.0	991	47.43	125.9
Body, mind and spirit	26.74	87	37.95	141.9	69	32.98	123.3	103	37.62	140.7	133	37.74	141.1
Business and economics	42.11	436	46.15	109.6	346	49.70	118.0	401	45.20	107.3	465	38.26	90.9
Children	26.57	832	36.22	136.3	899	37.80	142.3	978	34.74	130.7	1,215	32.89	123.8
Comics and graphic novels	n.a.	n.a.	n.a.	n.a.	n.a.	n.a.	n.a.	29	19.99	n.a.	4	37.48	n.a.
Computers	41.39	5	46.99	113.5	2	45.00	108.7	12	53.99	130.4	4	42.73	103.2
Cooking	14.45	14	44.70	309.3	2	44.97	311.2	14	42.77	296.0	13	42.83	296.4
Crafts and hobbies	n.a.	4	38.72	n.a.	1	24.98	n.a.	n.a.	n.a.	n.a.	1	24.95	n.a.
Design	n.a.	n.a.	n.a.	n.a.	n.a.	n.a.	n.a.	n.a.	n.a.	n.a.	3	57.30	n.a.
Drama	23.45	151	34.54	147.3	95	33.21	141.6	104	28.03	119.5	110	23.99	102.3
Education	27.46	22	45.34	165.1	20	45.71	166.5	34	44.04	160.4	35	36.00	131.1
Family and relationships	24.58	54	39.41	160.3	69	41.17	167.5	110	41.20	167.6	151	42.75	173.9
Fiction	41.47	6,278	52.62	126.9	7,649	50.38	121.5	7,174	48.19	116.2	11,167	42.10	101.5
Foreign language study	70.04	260	40.74	58.2	186	45.11	64.4	223	50.61	72.3	164	60.46	86.3
Games	32.68	6	14.12	43.2	n.a.	n.a.	n.a.	5	46.98	143.8	5	44.98	137.6
Gardening	n.a.	n.a.	n.a.	n.a.	6	47.82	n.a.	n.a.	n.a.	n.a.	5	31.99	n.a.
Health and fitness	26.61	82	46.09	173.2	85	43.09	161.9	110	47.00	176.6	89	44.10	165.7
History	41.61	450	57.69	138.6	563	58.07	139.6	446	59.36	142.7	598	50.56	121.5
House and home	25.00	n.a.	n.a.	n.a.	n.a.	n.a.	n.a.	1	34.95	139.8	3	55.32	221.3
Humor	29.60	79	42.37	143.1	95	36.62	123.7	103	40.46	136.7	81	33.36	112.7

Category													
Language arts and disciplines	60.84	18	46.65	76.7	13	38.34	63.0	38	44.87	73.8	25	46.05	75.7
Law	55.32	9	49.75	89.9	10	64.49	116.6	7	70.42	127.3	18	50.82	91.9
Literary collections	24.71	20	32.34	130.9	11	52.07	210.7	33	51.64	209.0	35	39.72	160.7
Literary criticism	26.41	20	42.43	160.7	18	42.53	161.0	188	30.59	115.8	95	33.38	126.4
Mathematics	n.a.	n.a.	n.a.	n.a.	n.a.	n.a.	n.a.	1	24.95	n.a.	3	51.32	n.a.
Medical	153.72	13	60.66	39.5	28	40.13	26.1	24	45.74	29.8	24	48.56	31.6
Music	29.83	108	38.41	128.8	74	35.67	119.6	57	48.44	162.4	44	39.00	130.7
Nature	28.92	37	47.09	162.8	57	41.20	142.5	44	46.71	161.5	13	51.60	178.4
Performing arts	25.78	21	46.23	179.3	16	40.60	157.5	9	65.08	252.4	16	34.42	133.5
Pets	33.05	23	43.51	131.6	52	38.33	116.0	25	43.14	130.5	20	42.93	129.9
Philosophy	35.30	36	51.39	145.6	38	53.05	150.3	73	46.86	132.7	39	40.13	113.7
Photography	n.a.	n.a.	n.a.	n.a.	n.a.	n.a.	n.a.	n.a.	n.a.	n.a.	n.a.	n.a.	n.a.
Poetry	22.87	50	35.88	156.9	28	33.59	146.9	16	23.03	100.7	14	29.62	129.5
Political science	42.66	177	49.69	116.5	230	48.04	112.6	220	48.22	113.0	234	46.77	109.6
Psychology	35.70	54	52.13	146.0	46	45.42	127.2	91	48.58	136.1	79	40.23	112.7
Reference	21.20	7	40.55	191.3	2	59.99	283.0	19	42.62	201.0	11	35.44	167.2
Religion	26.52	418	33.50	126.3	425	33.94	128.0	465	31.81	119.9	569	32.81	123.7
Science	39.86	64	47.75	119.8	66	51.89	130.2	90	54.30	136.2	113	41.56	104.3
Self-help	23.58	289	38.30	162.4	192	39.43	167.2	197	41.65	176.6	369	36.42	154.5
Social science	35.73	79	50.36	140.9	90	48.07	134.5	102	48.64	136.1	118	43.27	121.1
Sports and recreation	28.46	41	45.78	160.9	58	48.48	170.3	38	45.51	159.9	40	43.38	152.4
Study aids	41.85	21	33.92	81.1	7	19.41	46.4	2	27.66	66.1	6	213.56	510.3
Technology and engineering	61.47	7	48.56	79.0	23	53.33	86.8	26	46.41	75.5	10	40.58	66.0
Transportation	28.00	3	36.66	130.9	7	46.28	165.3	1	24.95	89.1	7	46.27	165.3
Travel	41.91	15	51.57	123.0	47	50.96	121.6	20	61.17	146.0	49	35.65	85.1
True crime	35.97	45	50.69	140.9	37	52.58	146.2	36	50.04	139.1	79	44.69	124.2
Young adult	35.68	527	44.85	125.7	888	44.81	125.6	960	41.71	116.9	1,434	34.20	95.9
Totals	$40.49	11,564	$48.58	120.0	13,324	$48.00	118.5	13,400	$45.89	113.3	18,738	$41.02	101.3

Compiled by Catherine Barr from data supplied by Baker & Taylor.
n.a. = not available

Table 7B / U.S. E-Books: Average Prices and Price Indexes, 2009–2012

Index Base: 2008 = 100

BISAC Category	2008 Average Prices	2010 Final Volumes	2010 Final Average Prices	2010 Final Index	2011 Final Volumes	2011 Final Average Prices	2011 Final Index	2012 Preliminary Volumes	2012 Preliminary Average Prices	2012 Preliminary Index
Antiques and collectibles	$55.97	62	$30.24	54.0	229	$21.46	38.3	166	$34.71	62.0
Architecture	70.50	268	66.57	94.4	312	60.38	85.6	865	63.03	89.4
Art	45.41	199	41.56	91.5	729	16.89	37.2	1,231	23.92	52.7
Bibles	25.79	119	6.11	23.7	113	11.34	44.0	154	12.61	48.9
Biography and autobiography	14.58	1,828	15.47	106.1	3,824	10.23	70.2	6,309	20.20	138.5
Body, mind and spirit	12.41	628	13.95	112.4	1,378	11.54	93.0	2,200	14.39	116.0
Business and economics	57.52	5,603	44.82	77.9	7,198	40.64	70.7	11,296	45.39	78.9
Children	12.01	4,239	13.82	115.1	14,867	16.42	136.7	18,197	12.61	105.0
Comics and graphic novels	25.04	26	11.39	45.5	269	6.02	24.0	504	7.34	29.3
Computers	66.87	3,057	62.09	92.9	4,383	61.72	92.3	3,941	77.96	116.6
Cooking	20.20	715	16.79	83.1	1,561	12.42	61.5	1,892	12.78	63.3
Crafts and hobbies	14.35	340	17.63	122.9	785	15.26	106.3	804	12.09	84.3
Design	36.04	125	37.03	102.7	104	38.69	107.4	275	23.04	63.9
Drama	29.49	443	4.86	16.5	2,758	3.19	10.8	1,472	7.50	25.4
Education	51.98	1,537	45.95	88.4	1,787	50.25	96.7	3,368	51.45	99.0
Family and relationships	19.88	717	14.79	74.4	1,210	10.13	51.0	1,714	15.43	77.6
Fiction	8.71	18,043	7.06	81.1	56,776	4.83	55.5	73,848	12.07	138.6
Foreign language study	43.01	97	46.68	108.5	304	19.69	45.8	710	28.46	66.2
Games	17.73	120	12.85	72.5	324	10.79	60.9	377	9.53	53.8
Gardening	20.40	68	17.41	85.3	169	13.34	65.4	249	17.39	85.2
Health and fitness	18.54	920	18.78	101.3	1,988	13.20	71.2	2,286	15.45	83.3
History	57.53	2,641	48.20	83.8	4,163	33.22	57.7	8,467	35.52	61.7
House and home	22.89	121	21.57	94.2	187	14.90	65.1	209	13.27	58.0
Humor	11.27	322	11.15	98.9	619	7.53	66.8	1,052	13.04	115.7

Category										
Language arts and disciplines	03.27	582	75.61	81.1	1,075	59.54	63.8	1,747	53.41	57.3
Law	81.23	609	112.19	138.1	872	76.17	93.8	1,781	79.31	97.6
Literary collections	24.50	226	20.27	82.7	1,757	4.41	18.0	1,397	10.74	43.8
Literary criticism	86.62	608	87.17	100.6	936	50.59	58.4	2,214	39.76	45.9
Mathematics	106.16	801	112.32	105.8	1,332	95.28	89.8	1,623	77.92	73.4
Medical	135.21	1,575	135.71	100.4	4,299	100.28	74.2	4,815	103.25	76.4
Music	33.83	331	32.65	96.5	4,390	14.12	41.7	9,723	7.10	21.0
Nature	59.76	370	59.48	99.5	527	32.10	53.7	757	40.52	67.8
Performing arts	38.06	474	32.17	84.5	863	26.70	70.2	1,134	34.73	91.3
Pets	15.91	176	14.50	91.1	581	11.17	70.2	624	16.04	100.8
Philosophy	79.19	598	71.43	90.2	948	44.17	55.8	2,016	42.23	53.3
Photography	30.30	202	27.23	89.9	387	18.19	60.0	463	23.84	78.7
Poetry	13.66	332	9.54	69.8	1,807	5.73	41.9	1,548	8.33	61.0
Political science	59.03	1,427	59.74	101.2	2,208	43.34	73.4	4,483	46.75	79.2
Psychology	65.30	914	56.42	86.4	2,139	49.01	75.1	2,578	50.07	76.7
Reference	48.33	646	22.92	47.4	788	19.77	40.9	811	46.43	96.1
Religion	27.29	2,874	27.81	101.9	5,669	17.29	63.4	8,004	18.93	69.4
Science	210.57	2,915	155.80	74.0	3,634	131.61	62.5	5,357	108.63	51.6
Self-help	14.15	746	14.06	99.4	2,497	8.10	57.2	3,943	14.01	99.0
Social science	69.42	1,513	56.83	81.9	2,240	53.61	77.2	4,029	60.29	86.8
Sports and recreation	22.44	643	19.22	85.7	1,223	17.09	76.2	1,858	19.81	88.3
Study aids	21.95	305	13.94	63.5	859	9.20	41.9	398	44.59	203.1
Technology and engineering	153.73	2,618	158.44	103.1	2,831	123.20	80.1	3,829	112.50	73.2
Transportation	35.47	97	33.12	93.4	193	19.12	53.9	286	26.90	75.8
Travel	15.61	1,223	15.84	101.5	2,745	9.10	58.3	3,148	9.49	60.8
True crime	11.60	210	10.37	89.4	321	8.81	75.9	496	17.21	148.4
Young adult	8.83	1,892	11.96	135.4	2,821	21.47	243.1	4,465	15.85	179.5
Totals	$57.38	67,145	$41.61	72.5	155,979	$24.48	42.7	215,113	$28.16	49.1

Compiled by Catherine Barr from data supplied by Baker & Taylor.

(continued from page 421)
during 2012; expensive titles ($500 or more) were omitted from the analysis, thus the total number of titles reported is smaller than the number reviewed. As with the North American Academic Books: Average Prices and Price Indexes data (Table 4), this index includes some paperback prices; as a result, the average price of books is less than if only hardcover books were included. Table 5 reports the number of titles, dollar amounts, percentages, and average prices for books for the years 2010 through 2012 in each *Choice* subject category.

The average price for humanities titles in 2012 increased by 3.09 percent over the previous year. The average price for science and technology titles increased at the faster rate of 5.38 percent, and the average price for social and behavioral sciences titles increased by 2.29 percent. Calculated separately, reference books for 2012 showed a 6.49 percent decrease over the previous year. For all titles, there was a 2.14 percent average price increase for 2012, and a 75 percent average price increase since 1989.

For 2012 the overall average price for books in the humanities, sciences, and social and behavioral sciences (including reference books) was $70.80, an increase of 2.14 percent over the average 2011 book price of $69.32. Reference books calculated separately had an average price decrease of 6.49 percent over the previous year, with a 2012 average price of $125.76 compared with last year's average price of $134.49. Excluding reference books, the 2012 average price was $67.09, a 3.09 percent increase compared with the average 2011 price of $65.08.

Questions regarding this index should be addressed to the author: Frederick Lynden, Retired Director, Scholarly Communication and Library Research, Brown University Library, Providence, RI 02912 (e-mail flynden@stanfordalumni.org).

Foreign Prices

During 2012 the dollar continued its decline against the Canadian dollar, British pound sterling, and the euro. The dollar regained some strength against the Japanese yen. The dollar's overall decline may be reflected in book and serials pricing.

Dates	12/31/08*	12/31/09*	12/31/10*	12/31/11*	12/31/12*
Canada	1.1910	1.0510	1.0200	1.0180	0.9950
Euro	0.7310	0.6950	0.7700	0.7650	0.7590
U.K.	0.6570	0.6160	0.6400	0.6370	0.6180
Japan	92.6500	92.3900	83.8300	78.0000	6.1600

* Data from Financial Management Services. U.S. Treasury Department (http://fms.treas.gov/intn. html).

Serials Prices

Average Price of Serials (Table 8), compiled by Stephen Bosch, provides the average prices and percent increases for serials based on titles in select serials indexes. The serials included here are published in the United States as well as overseas and are indexed in ISI Arts and Humanities Citation Index, ISI Science

Citation Index, ISI Social Sciences Citation Index, EBSCO Academic Search Premier, and EBSCO Masterfile Premier.

Table 8 covers prices for periodicals and serials for a five-year period, 2009 through 2013. The 2013 pricing is the actual renewal pricing for 2013 for serials that were indexed in the selected products. This table is derived from pricing data supplied by EBSCO Subscription Services and reflects broad pricing changes aggregated from titles that are indexed in the five major products mentioned above. The USPPI (Table 1) is based on price changes seen in a static set of approximately 3,700 serials titles, while Table 8 is based on a much broader set of more than 10,000 titles. Due to the fact that every year titles fall off and new titles are added to the indexes on which Table 8 is based, there may be differences in the figures presented in this table when compared with those published in previous years. The titles are not static, so this pricing study does not rise to the level of a price index. This study is still useful in showing price changes for periodicals. The indexes selected for this price survey were deemed to be fairly representative of serials that are frequently purchased in academic and public libraries. There are some foreign titles in the indexes, so the scope is broader and this may give a better picture of the overall price pressures experienced in libraries.

The most important trend seen in this data is that after the modest increase of 4.1 percent between 2009 and 2010, increases in prices have remained fairly constant since the economic recovery began. Price increases hovered around 5.8 percent annually since 2010. The respite in price increases seen in 2010 appears over. Libraries were very vocal about not being able to sustain high rates of inflation, and in 2010 price increases moderated significantly, but since then rates have continued to climb to just under 6 percent.

Another interesting trend is that science areas do not dominate the list of subjects with the largest price increases. The subject areas that displayed large increases were quite varied. Education, health sciences, and library science saw higher increases than most areas. Average prices of journals in the science and technology areas are by far higher than in other areas and that trend continues with the average cost of chemistry and physics journals being $4,296 and $3,834, respectively. Although these STM titles are not inflating at high rates, the impact of a 5.0 percent increase on a $4,000 title is much higher than a 9 percent increase on a $300 title.

In this price study, as in similar price surveys, the data become less accurate at describing price changes as the sample becomes smaller. For that reason, drawing conclusions about price changes in subject areas with a limited number of titles will be less accurate than for large areas or the broader price survey. Price changes are far more volatile where smaller data sets are used. For example, military and naval science (about 43 titles) showed price changes of 11.0 percent, 11.1 percent, 5.4 percent, and 1.6 percent between 2009 and 2013. Librarians are encouraged to look at an average price change over the period (military and naval science averaged 7.3 percent) or the overall number for the price study (5.9 percent) to calculate inflation rates. Year-to-year price changes are too unstable to be used for this purpose.

(text continues on page 433)

Table 8 / Average Price of Serials, Based on Titles in Select Serial Indices: 2009–2013

Subject	LC Class	2009 No. of Titles	2009 Avg. Price	2010 No. of Titles	2010 Avg. Price	2010 % of Price Increase	2011 No. of Titles	2011 Avg. Price	2011 % of Price Increase	2012 No. of Titles	2012 Avg. Price	2012 % of Price Increase	2013 No. of Titles	2013 Avg. Price	2013 % of Price Increase
Agriculture	S	270	$966	272	$1,019	5.5%	276	$1,072	5.2%	276	$1,128	5.2%	276	$1,212	7.4%
Anthropology	GN	83	407	85	420	3.3	88	445	6.0	88	469	5.3	88	500	6.8
Arts and architecture	N	161	236	168	254	7.5	170	271	6.6	170	285	5.1	171	303	6.4
Astronomy	QB	46	1,883	46	2,001	6.3	47	2,084	4.2	47	2,213	6.2	47	2,294	3.7
Biology	QH	794	2,037	798	2,140	5.1	798	2,269	6.0	799	2,395	5.6	801	2,517	5.1
Botany	QK	88	1,518	88	1,612	6.2	90	1,705	5.8	91	1,780	4.4	91	1,890	6.2
Business and economics	HA-HJ	782	691	796	725	4.8	798	777	7.2	801	821	5.6	806	871	6.0
Chemistry	QD	287	3,511	289	3,660	4.3	295	3,901	6.6	296	4,091	4.9	296	4,296	5.0
Education	L	417	452	416	479	5.9	419	513	7.1	418	542	5.7	419	590	8.7
Engineering	T	688	1,728	689	1,820	5.3	690	1,935	6.3	692	2,045	5.7	693	2,171	6.2
Food science	TX	61	777	62	823	5.9	62	881	7.1	62	934	6.0	63	988	5.8
General science	Q	137	966	141	1,007	4.2	144	1,080	7.2	146	1,151	6.6	148	1,193	3.7
General works	A	212	123	215	130	5.4	214	138	5.8	214	143	3.6	214	150	5.2
Geography	G-GF	168	909	170	958	5.4	168	1,020	6.5	171	1,068	4.7	173	1,139	6.6
Geology	QE	122	1,459	123	1,528	4.7	117	1,640	7.3	117	1,739	6.0	121	1,825	4.9
Health sciences	R	1,892	1,058	1,891	1,112	5.1	1,908	1,188	6.8	1,915	1,268	6.7	1,919	1,369	8.0
History	C,D,E,F	594	262	621	280	6.9	627	298	6.5	629	316	6.1	629	336	6.3
Language and literature	P	605	236	640	260	10.3	675	276	6.2	673	291	5.5	675	312	7.2

Subject	LC class													
Law	K	196	304	212	334	9.9	219	350	4.9	220	372	6.4	220	392	5.3
Library science	Z	130	334	130	353	5.8	134	365	3.4	133	383	4.9	128	417	8.9
Math and computer science	QA	347	1,360	347	1,416	4.1	359	1,488	5.1	359	1,570	5.5	359	1,594	1.5
Military and naval science	U,V	45	287	42	319	11.0	42	354	11.1	42	373	5.4	43	379	1.6
Music	M	96	182	98	190	4.4	99	199	4.9	99	210	5.3	101	223	6.3
Philosophy and religion	B-BD; BH-BX	333	270	380	292	8.1	386	311	6.8	387	330	6.0	394	345	4.5
Physics	QC	309	3,184	313	3,296	3.5	316	3,410	3.5	311	3,653	7.1	316	3,834	5.0
Political science	J	176	484	181	506	4.6	185	542	7.3	185	574	5.9	186	608	5.9
Psychology	BF	272	627	278	665	6.1	279	712	7.1	278	746	4.8	281	789	5.7
Recreation	QV	74	242	73	261	7.8	73	284	8.9	75	304	7.0	75	326	7.4
Social sciences	H	107	496	110	511	2.9	111	534	4.6	111	560	4.9	113	586	4.7
Sociology	HM-HX	573	550	583	582	6.0	587	626	7.5	587	662	5.7	590	705	6.5
Technology	TA-TT	124	1,091	123	1,169	7.2	126	1,235	5.7	126	1,303	5.4	126	1,383	6.2
Zoology	QL	170	1,348	176	1,400	3.8	179	1,456	4.0	179	1,539	5.7	179	1,615	5.0
Totals		10,359	$1,025	10,556	$1,067	4.1	10,681	$1,129	5.8	10,697	$1,195	5.8%	10,741	$1,265	5.9

Compiled by Stephen Bosch, University of Arizona, from data on serial pricing supplied by EBSCO based on titles indexed in ISI Arts and Humanities Citation Index, ISI Science Citation Index, ISI Social Sciences Citation Index, EBSCO Academic Search Premier and EBSCO Masterfile Premier

Table 9 / British Academic Books: Average Prices and Price Indexes 2009–2012

Index Base: 2009 = 100

Subject	LC Class	2009		2010		2011		2012			
		No. of Titles	Average Price (£)	No. of Titles	Average Price (£)	No. of Titles	Average Price (£)	No. of Titles	Average Price (£)	% Change 2011–2012	Index
Agriculture	S	140	53.96	154	63.97	177	58.83	183	69.29	17.8%	128.4
Anthropology	GN	109	53.60	154	50.85	111	59.74	145	45.73	-23.5	85.3
Botany	QK	22	145.94	45	66.08	39	85.29	45	97.50	14.3	66.8
Business and economics	H-HJ	2,439	59.12	2,874	61.09	1,690	63.89	2,022	76.41	19.6	129.2
Chemistry	QD	88	101.14	96	105.68	87	116.07	144	155.82	34.2	154.1
Education	L	386	49.70	558	52.21	456	52.98	547	64.36	21.5	129.5
Engineering and technology	T	716	65.60	655	65.73	639	81.66	830	72.68	-11.0	110.8
Fine and applied arts	M, N	762	39.71	1,037	37.00	949	44.63	1,092	45.84	2.7	115.4
General works	A	15	76.73	30	60.03	24	69.50	26	78.67	13.2	102.5
Geography	G-GF, GR-GT	233	50.98	660	64.95	294	52.61	276	63.48	20.7	124.5
Geology	QE	41	53.80	33	52.28	35	57.97	51	79.33	36.8	147.5
History	C,D,E,F	1,572	41.01	1,822	48.13	1,586	48.51	1,794	49.65	2.4	121.1
Home economics	TX	59	39.02	46	30.48	34	48.40	47	61.06	26.2	156.5
Industrial arts	TT	21	24.32	41	28.47	42	36.62	42	25.47	-30.4	104.7
Law	K	1,117	76.13	1,153	83.10	1,159	78.79	1,312	87.74	11.4	115.3
Library and information science	Z	98	60.32	100	53.58	104	61.51	105	65.96	7.2	109.4
Literature and language	P	2,928	34.77	3,987	31.58	3,526	32.71	3,966	37.34	14.2	107.4
Mathematics and computer science	QA	216	49.30	207	48.29	245	55.79	266	54.93	-1.5	111.4
Medicine	R	1,110	48.50	1,182	55.12	1,177	55.02	1,280	55.88	1.6	115.2
Military and naval sciences	U, V	112	83.99	184	38.00	133	45.16	126	51.55	14.1	61.4
Philosophy and religion	B	1,091	46.45	1,336	45.24	1,151	48.30	1,590	53.98	11.8	116.2
Physics and astronomy	QB, QC	196	54.54	214	59.69	215	62.78	240	64.83	3.3	118.9
Political Science	J	621	59.74	737	71.88	671	62.95	797	69.98	11.2	117.1
Psychology	BF	195	44.46	265	39.69	264	46.77	297	50.93	8.9	114.6
Science (general)	Q	55	42.12	69	36.32	60	51.05	72	72.50	42.0	172.1
Sociology	HM-HX	153	74.17	208	70.13	1,069	62.67	1,195	53.58	-14.5	72.2
Sports & Recreation	GV	181	30.90	192	36.76	145	46.83	202	56.70	21.1	183.5
Zoology	QH, QL-QR	326	66.20	373	72.30	370	81.77	434	69.83	-14.6	105.5
Total, All Books		15,432	52.91	18,490	51.97	16,452	59.60	19,126	65.39	9.7	123.6

Compiled by George Aulisio, University of Scranton, based on information provided by YBK U.K./Baker & Taylor.

(continued from page 429)
Book Prices

British Academic Books (Table 9), now compiled by George Aulisio, indicates the average prices and price indexes from 2009 through 2012 with the percent of change from 2011 to 2012. This index is compiled using data from YBP U.K. and utilizes prices from cloth editions except when not available. YBP U.K. also profiles select titles from continental Europe and Africa. The index does not separate out more expensive reference titles. Small numbers of titles that include higher-priced reference sets may not be reliable indicators of price changes. This index does not include e-book prices.

British academic book production has considerably increased from the previous year's steep drop. In 2011 there were 16,452 new British academic books, an 11.02 percent decrease from the 18,490 British academic books profiled in 2010. In 2012 there were 19,126 British academic books profiled, which is the largest output recorded by this list and a 16.25 percent increase from 2011. This large increase may be attributable to YBP U.K. now profiling titles published by The Stationery Office (http://www.ybp.com/book_price_update.html).

The average price in pounds of a British academic book went from £59.60 in 2011 to £65.39 in 2012, an increase of 9.7 percent. Though a relatively steep increase, this is slightly lower than the increase seen from 2009 to 2010, which was 14.7 percent. The 2012 increase of 9.7 percent outpaces the United Kingdom's Consumer Price Index which, according to the Office of National Statistics, was at 2.7 percent inflation in December 2012 http://www.ons.gov.uk). The lower 9.7 percent increase is not attributable to the low average cost of titles published by The Stationery Office as these books were not included in the price calculation.

Using the Price Indexes

Librarians are encouraged to monitor trends in the publishing industry and changes in economic conditions when preparing budget forecasts and projections. The ALA ALCTS Library Materials Price Index Editorial Board endeavors to make information on publishing trends readily available by sponsoring the annual compilation and publication of price data contained in Tables 1 to 9. The indexes cover newly published library materials and document prices and rates of percent changes at the national and international level. They are useful benchmarks against which local costs can be compared, but because they reflect retail prices in the aggregate, they are not a substitute for cost data that reflect the collecting patterns of individual libraries, and they are not a substitute for specific cost studies.

Differences between local prices and those found in national indexes arise partially because these indexes exclude discounts, service charges, shipping and handling fees, and other costs that the library might incur. Discrepancies may also relate to a library's subject coverage; mix of titles purchased, including both current and backfiles; and the proportion of the library's budget expended on domestic or foreign materials. These variables can affect the average price paid by an individual library, although the individual library's rate of increase may not differ greatly from the national indexes.

LMPI is interested in pursuing studies that would correlate a particular library's costs with the national prices. The group welcomes interested parties to its meetings at ALA Annual and Midwinter conferences.

The Library Materials Price Index Editorial Board consists of compilers George Aulisio, Catherine Barr, Ajaye Bloomstone, Stephen Bosch, Frederick C. Lynden, and editor Narda Tafuri.

Book Title Output and Average Prices: 2008–2012

Catherine Barr
Contributing Editor

Constance Harbison
Baker & Taylor

Overall American book title output registered a high of 190,502 titles in 2007 before declining with the economic downturn. However, there are signs of recovery, with a revised total of 190,533 titles for 2011 and an encouraging preliminary figure of 185,933 for 2012 (this number is likely to be revised upward as late-arriving materials are added to the database; publishers were still submitting late 2012 titles in early 2013). The number of titles published dropped by 5.5 percent in 2008 and 0.66 percent in 2009, but rose by 4.2 percent in 2010 and a further 2.25 percent in 2011.

The figures for this edition of the *Library and Book Trade Almanac* were provided by book wholesaler Baker & Taylor and are based on the Book Industry Study Group's BISAC categories. The BISAC juvenile category (fiction and nonfiction) has been divided into children's and young adult. Figures for 2011 have been restated, reflecting late updates to the Baker & Taylor database. Figures for 2012 are preliminary.

For more information on the BISAC categories, visit http://www.bisg.org.

Output by Format and by Category

Revised results were mixed in 2011, with the following formats showing varying degrees of decline: hardcover (down 0.37 percent following growth of 1.63 percent the previous year), hardcovers less than $81 (down 2.02 percent after a drop of 3.46 percent), and mass market paperbacks (down 0.43 percent, less than the previous decline of 1.34 percent). Trade paperbacks, however, registered a surprising 19.35 percent increase following a rise of 5.32 percent in 2010, while audiobook output rose only slightly in 2011 (up 0.57 percent) after a gain of 15.22 percent in 2010. Output of e-books continued to soar, registering a revised gain of 132.30 percent in 2011 and a promising increase of 37.91 percent in 2012. Preliminary results for 2012 in categories other than audiobooks and e-books did not appear to predict large gains.

Fiction, a key category, rose 18.03 percent in 2011 after a disappointing performance in 2010 and registered a revised overall output of 21,211; preliminary results for 2012 did not suggest a similar increase. Output of hardcover fiction (less than $81) has held fairly steady for the last few years, falling 2.43 percent in 2010 and rising just 0.95 percent in 2011; 2012 promised similar results. In the paperback sector, mass market fiction dropped 1.52 percent in 2010 but recovered slightly with a posting of 1.14 percent in 2011 while trade fiction fell 1.53 percent in 2010 but recovered by a striking 92.77 percent in 2011 and appeared to be sustaining that recovery in 2012. Audiobook fiction, which fell 6.21 percent in 2011, registered a preliminary increase of 55.66 percent for 2012. E-book output may

Table 1 / American Book Production, 2008–2012

BISAC Category	2008	2009	2010	2011	2012
Antiques and collectibles	445	359	366	294	280
Architecture	1,548	1,534	1,495	1,468	1,368
Art	3,261	3,181	3,213	3,325	3,379
Bibles	554	474	614	976	831
Biography and autobiography	3,935	4,012	4,105	4,496	4,069
Body, mind and spirit	1,319	1,216	1,189	1,324	1,123
Business and economics	9,593	10,006	10,024	9,813	12,066
Children	22,603	22,395	20,562	21,300	21,103
Comics and graphic novels	2,869	2,906	2,542	4,212	2,915
Computers	4,014	4,589	4,312	4,391	4,667
Cooking	2,294	1,835	2,131	2,142	2,307
Crafts and hobbies	1,212	1,240	1,271	1,301	1,260
Design	739	728	878	856	903
Drama	714	665	875	606	540
Education	5,277	4,673	4,955	4,923	4,908
Family and relationships	1,256	1,185	1,064	981	954
Fiction	18,638	18,272	17,971	21,211	18,129
Foreign language study	1,550	1,114	1,464	1,463	1,258
Games	958	959	955	792	737
Gardening	517	397	359	368	362
Health and fitness	1,847	1,710	1,601	1,654	1,439
History	10,658	11,157	11,975	11,634	11,625
House and home	412	340	290	230	233
Humor	708	715	651	626	609
Language arts and disciplines	2,967	3,590	3,985	3,530	3,327
Law	5,363	4,266	4,925	4,979	4,795
Literary collections	922	955	998	870	706
Literary criticism	3,158	3,679	3,580	3,673	3,426
Mathematics	1,888	1,829	2,549	2,781	2,828
Medical	7,092	6,891	8,574	9,021	9,047
Music	3,408	3,497	3,541	3,313	3,064
Nature	1,039	1,025	944	948	948
Performing arts	1,610	1,481	1,569	1,449	1,497
Pets	474	475	388	330	277
Philosophy	2,246	2,456	2,447	2,465	2,536
Photography	1,417	1,344	1,345	1,359	1,360
Poetry	2,126	2,018	2,015	2,321	1,928
Political science	5,655	5,927	6,703	5,925	6,065
Psychology	2,456	2,339	2,882	2,817	3,006
Reference	1,975	1,872	1,601	1,687	1,592
Religion	8,276	8,415	9,550	9,117	9,032
Science	5,324	5,740	7,782	8,266	7,532
Self-help	1,474	1,360	1,379	1,336	1,440
Social science	6,998	7,037	7,353	7,056	7,628
Sports and recreation	2,081	1,882	1,968	1,836	1,737
Study aids	898	694	1,519	999	619
Technology and engineering	4,739	5,134	4,907	5,060	5,834
Transportation	742	706	800	769	617
Travel	3,542	3,238	2,953	2,778	2,315
True crime	291	301	316	299	277
Young adult	4,950	5,028	4,909	5,163	5,435
Totals	180,032	178,841	186,344	190,533	185,933

explain a lot of the declines in other fiction formats, with totals rising from 7,414 in 2008 to a whopping 56,776 in 2011 and 73,848 in 2012 (increases of 214.67 percent and 30.07 percent, respectively).

The important juveniles category is broken down into children's (PreK–6) and young adult (YA; grades 7–12) titles. Overall children's books output has moved up and down in a fairly tight range, with a revised increase of 3.59 percent in 2011. Hardcover books priced at less than $81 fell 0.61 percent in 2011, while mass market lost 1.56 percent and trade paperbacks rose 10.01 percent in the same period. Children's audiobooks and e-books showed consistent growth, with audiobooks up more than 8 percent in 2010 and 2011, followed by a 24.23 increase in preliminary 2012 results; e-books meanwhile surged 250.72 percent in 2011 and were up a further 22.4 percent in 2012.

Output of YA titles rose to 5,163 in 2011 (up 5.17 percent) and had already surpassed this in preliminary data for 2012. Hardcover titles priced at less than $81 lost ground, falling 2.68 percent in 2011; mass market paperbacks fell 43.37 percent in 2011 but showed new strength in 2012; and trade paperbacks registered hike of 17.6 percent in 2011 and 26.85 percent in early 2012 data. YA audiobook production continued to climb (up 8.11 percent in 2011 and 49.38 percent in 2012).

A review of overall output in nonfiction categories (Table 1) shows the usual variations. Of the 51 categories, 27 lost ground in 2011 and 33 in 2012. The only categories that registered significant increases in 2011 were Bibles (up 58.96 percent), comics and graphic novels (up 65.70 percent), and fiction (up 18.03 percent); none of these seemed likely to provide similar results in 2012. Double-digit losses were common and covered the gamut from antiques and collectibles to study aids (down 34.23 percent).

Average Book Prices

Average book prices were mixed in 2011. List prices for hardcovers overall (Table 2) rose only 0.87 percent but were up 4.17 percent in preliminary data for 2012; hardcovers under $81 (Table 3) fell 32 cents (0.94 percent) in 2011 and 4 cents (0.12 percent) in 2012. Mass market paperback (Table 4) prices remained in positive territory, gaining 2.34 percent in 2011 and 0.72 percent in 2012. In contrast, trade paperbacks (Table 5)—whose numbers swelled in 2011—saw prices fall 9.99 percent that year but recover nearly that total in 2012. Audiobook prices (Table 6) have been falling since 2009, with declines of 4.40 percent in 2011 and 10.61 percent in 2012. After declining for several years (down 41.17 percent in 2011), e-book prices rose a preliminary 15.03 percent in 2012.

Average book prices for fiction were also mixed. Hardcover fiction titles priced at less than $81 edged up a mere 2 cents (0.07 percent) in 2011 but seemed set to fare slightly better in 2012. Mass market fiction rose 2.50 percent and trade paperback fiction was up 1.28 percent. Audiobook fiction prices continued a decline that started in 2010, and e-book pricing fell in 2011 but recovered dramatically in 2012.

(text continues on page 450)

Table 2 / Hardcover Average Per-Volume Prices, 2009–2012

BISAC Category	2009			2010			2011			2012		
	Vols.	$ Total	Prices	Vols.	$ Total	Prices	Vols.	$ Total	Prices	Vols.	$ Total	Prices
Antiques and collectibles	159	$7,469.68	$46.98	179	$9,208.36	$51.44	150	$7,960.50	$53.07	118	$8,576.32	$72.68
Architecture	842	71,115.56	84.46	742	63,455.32	85.52	743	57,353.10	77.19	752	61,643.09	81.97
Art	1,688	126,824.23	75.13	1,687	120,672.85	71.53	1,686	119,808.64	71.06	1,744	123,355.70	70.73
Bibles	165	7,643.10	46.32	185	6,937.14	37.50	221	10,228.39	46.28	199	7,390.81	37.14
Biography and autobiography	1,652	82,734.86	50.08	1,658	88,546.37	53.41	1,711	83,835.30	49.00	1,654	83,019.55	50.19
Body, mind and spirit	194	5,355.04	27.60	177	6,532.28	36.91	155	4,678.47	30.18	124	4,578.35	36.92
Business and economics	3,913	483,112.81	123.46	3,977	535,329.39	134.61	4,105	560,439.24	136.53	4,060	551,775.14	135.91
Children	12,396	310,031.58	25.01	11,675	287,595.70	24.63	11,704	313,717.81	26.80	11,607	264,131.61	22.76
Comics and graphic novels	732	23,474.46	32.07	679	21,394.39	31.51	801	27,745.57	34.64	739	28,031.57	37.93
Computers	786	122,508.69	155.86	834	115,535.07	138.53	884	122,038.70	138.05	1,004	164,770.83	164.11
Cooking	814	24,041.89	29.54	1,016	31,405.09	30.91	972	29,952.24	30.82	1,107	31,404.07	28.37
Crafts and hobbies	237	7,094.80	29.94	217	7,222.08	33.28	218	6,636.46	30.44	214	6,857.80	32.05
Design	331	22,019.63	66.52	435	33,317.52	76.59	441	30,266.36	68.63	516	32,796.89	63.56
Drama	81	6,723.29	83.00	133	5,706.38	42.91	138	5,625.83	40.77	61	4,562.88	74.80
Education	1,392	146,944.34	105.56	1,345	158,158.85	117.59	1,569	204,182.22	130.14	1,470	208,407.84	141.77
Family and relationships	296	9,936.85	33.57	277	8,931.75	32.24	229	7,722.37	33.72	215	9,514.38	44.25
Fiction	4,556	131,127.58	28.78	4,464	143,724.29	32.20	4,491	132,527.00	29.51	4,217	126,779.87	30.06
Foreign language study	120	15,840.79	132.01	123	16,293.93	132.47	158	21,500.20	136.08	147	18,254.61	124.18
Games	167	6,258.91	37.48	163	8,486.77	52.07	112	3,891.77	34.75	109	4,005.09	36.74
Gardening	140	5,177.87	36.98	118	4,297.09	36.42	118	4,720.14	40.00	133	5,332.42	40.09
Health and fitness	356	18,078.72	50.78	309	14,990.57	48.51	321	19,262.41	60.01	318	21,502.63	67.62
History	4,687	395,609.19	84.41	4,927	407,233.60	82.65	4,543	376,140.58	82.80	4,879	404,982.00	83.01
House and home	113	4,569.88	40.44	90	4,014.78	44.61	90	3,447.30	38.30	93	4,057.93	43.63

Humor	229	4,635.89	20.24	221	4,849.44	21.94	199	3,847.01	19.33	240	4,812.37	20.05
Language arts and disciplines	1,485	195,087.50	131.36	1,613	189,802.42	117.67	1,587	183,632.32	115.71	1,127	146,151.46	129.68
Law	1,515	252,397.29	166.60	1,714	299,062.75	174.48	1,756	314,608.71	179.16	1,745	310,077.44	177.69
Literary collections	373	33,600.00	90.00	325	27,134.42	83.49	357	31,536.51	88.34	269	24,487.11	91.03
Literary criticism	1,903	205,616.68	108.05	1,955	229,962.69	117.63	1,964	237,447.45	120.90	1,930	229,589.96	118.96
Mathematics	895	104,786.72	117.08	1,028	136,962.32	133.23	1,030	139,631.75	135.56	979	137,233.93	140.18
Medical	2,924	485,153.60	165.92	3,153	539,557.59	171.13	2,976	492,181.51	165.38	3,565	622,252.86	174.54
Music	520	40,214.72	77.34	502	44,097.69	87.84	488	44,531.57	91.25	520	43,764.64	84.16
Nature	411	27,055.02	65.83	377	28,234.52	74.89	400	29,422.57	73.56	376	32,493.44	86.42
Performing arts	540	43,721.93	80.97	531	40,500.99	76.27	534	44,052.03	82.49	580	51,182.73	88.25
Pets	176	4,407.15	25.04	138	3,402.88	24.66	122	2,580.92	21.16	86	1,948.57	22.66
Philosophy	990	92,845.84	93.78	1,044	113,724.14	108.93	1,004	97,070.12	96.68	1,179	119,724.81	101.55
Photography	805	65,864.70	81.82	800	86,393.32	107.99	822	49,691.09	60.45	842	72,137.11	85.67
Poetry	293	13,324.37	45.48	294	11,982.30	40.76	318	11,181.99	35.16	221	10,196.91	46.14
Political science	2,698	291,658.10	108.10	2,671	294,673.30	110.32	2,578	284,265.43	110.27	2,693	289,391.57	107.46
Psychology	1,031	107,518.67	104.29	1,138	125,012.56	109.85	1,082	129,576.30	119.76	1,130	153,196.20	135.57
Reference	558	153,354.85	274.83	541	163,753.31	302.69	599	210,538.27	351.48	512	216,241.72	422.35
Religion	2,353	170,926.23	72.64	2,590	209,468.75	80.88	2,370	174,269.39	73.53	2,527	208,622.82	82.56
Science	3,161	601,882.90	190.41	3,557	683,655.73	192.20	3,459	674,361.10	194.96	3,504	670,494.68	191.35
Self-help	311	6,690.61	21.51	257	6,967.70	27.11	219	5,239.28	23.92	219	5,201.95	23.75
Social science	3,019	310,154.24	102.73	3,027	304,118.83	100.47	3,069	324,271.08	105.66	3,141	349,291.18	111.20
Sports and recreation	619	23,927.64	38.66	652	26,883.77	41.23	645	28,825.82	44.69	651	33,294.27	51.14
Study aids	24	2,751.35	114.64	17	1,726.24	101.54	20	1,925.29	96.26	15	1,604.30	106.95
Technology and engineering	2,439	392,271.18	160.83	2,455	404,250.43	164.66	2,633	441,397.42	167.64	2,803	483,238.33	172.40
Transportation	245	18,614.53	75.98	292	24,609.98	84.28	326	20,185.88	61.92	218	14,712.33	67.49
Travel	384	15,827.41	41.22	367	15,164.44	41.32	340	14,400.62	42.35	206	9,403.64	45.65
True crime	93	2,730.42	29.36	67	2,333.57	34.83	73	2,298.15	31.48	75	2,329.66	31.06
Young adult	2,466	92,170.46	37.38	2,653	95,478.35	35.99	2,602	97,498.64	37.47	2,185	75,235.27	34.43
Totals	68,277	$5,792,863.75	$84.84	69,389	$6,212,754.00	$89.54	69,132	$6,244,148.82	$90.32	69,018	$6,494,042.63	$94.09

Table 3 / Hardcover Average Per-Volume Prices, Less Than $81, 2009–2012

BISAC Category	2009			2010			2011			2012		
	Vols.	$ Total	Prices	Vols.	$ Total	Prices	Vols.	$ Total	Prices	Vols.	$ Total	Prices
Antiques and collectibles	140	$5,250.25	$37.50	147	$4,501.00	$30.62	124	$4,832.07	$38.97	90	$3,431.94	$38.13
Architecture	564	29,288.70	51.93	493	25,651.77	52.03	531	26,758.87	50.39	496	25,169.25	50.74
Art	1,364	63,705.85	46.71	1,335	62,565.70	46.87	1,339	62,333.12	46.55	1,377	64,325.49	46.71
Bibles	158	6,370.23	40.32	177	5,953.20	33.63	207	7,484.93	36.16	192	6,610.90	34.43
Biography and autobiography	1,482	45,428.56	30.65	1,466	46,136.67	31.47	1,529	47,544.96	31.10	1,475	46,299.44	31.39
Body, mind and spirit	183	4,031.74	22.03	166	4,356.88	26.25	146	3,789.58	25.96	115	2,732.35	23.76
Business and economics	1,814	72,002.39	39.69	1,617	64,601.18	39.95	1,618	66,319.32	40.99	1,555	66,464.66	42.74
Children	12,073	236,547.64	19.59	11,295	220,108.19	19.49	11,226	217,931.06	19.41	11,341	217,404.80	19.17
Comics and graphic novels	710	20,811.69	29.31	659	18,799.44	28.53	766	23,644.60	30.87	701	22,656.73	32.32
Computers	181	10,900.85	60.23	185	11,010.71	59.52	228	13,644.29	59.84	209	12,923.01	61.83
Cooking	805	23,192.54	28.81	977	25,089.56	25.68	949	25,459.16	26.83	1,091	29,383.93	26.93
Crafts and hobbies	232	6,590.35	28.41	209	6,158.08	29.46	211	5,976.56	28.32	211	5,662.80	26.84
Design	277	13,520.48	48.81	339	15,713.02	46.35	352	17,121.41	48.64	426	19,884.17	46.68
Drama	37	1,680.29	45.41	106	2,642.48	24.93	112	2,624.48	23.43	38	1,687.13	44.40
Education	649	36,057.56	55.56	471	24,227.11	51.44	497	26,169.88	52.66	402	21,378.28	53.18
Family and relationships	271	6,413.10	23.66	254	6,098.65	24.01	208	4,844.78	23.29	184	4,316.81	23.46
Fiction	4,530	127,152.18	28.07	4,420	124,701.19	28.21	4,462	125,949.05	28.23	4,168	119,034.16	28.56
Foreign language study	46	2,152.49	46.79	37	1,732.59	46.83	47	2,280.52	48.52	47	2,404.47	51.16
Games	161	5,377.91	33.40	157	4,176.77	26.60	106	3,103.78	29.28	106	3,395.09	32.03
Gardening	134	4,558.07	34.02	115	3,933.09	34.20	114	4,245.14	37.24	126	4,212.47	33.43
Health and fitness	303	10,085.59	33.29	260	8,412.02	32.35	262	7,824.20	29.86	229	7,073.53	30.89
History	3,066	136,103.66	44.39	3,076	140,793.51	45.77	2,749	119,506.01	43.47	2,893	127,062.65	43.92
House and home	107	3,928.93	36.72	85	3,060.93	36.01	86	2,809.40	32.67	89	3,634.13	40.83

Humor	226	4,301.94	19.04	218	4,491.49	20.60	198	3,722.01	18.80	236	4,442.42	18.82
Language arts and disciplines	551	32,192.66	58.43	669	38,841.54	58.06	600	35,250.83	58.75	301	16,825.96	55.90
Law	278	15,704.82	56.49	332	17,978.77	54.15	263	14,269.14	54.26	266	14,600.41	54.89
Literary collections	237	10,737.27	45.30	211	9,636.37	45.67	210	9,172.96	43.68	154	6,764.71	43.93
Literary criticism	872	47,594.62	54.58	783	44,251.02	56.51	779	44,425.92	57.03	725	42,487.90	58.60
Mathematics	264	16,163.72	61.23	227	14,162.41	62.39	188	11,725.87	62.37	206	12,774.91	62.01
Medical	450	25,644.77	56.99	448	24,869.75	55.51	397	22,552.35	56.81	412	23,311.14	56.58
Music	352	15,543.74	44.16	320	14,115.74	44.11	309	13,585.82	43.97	314	14,116.72	44.96
Nature	294	10,642.04	36.20	255	9,633.42	37.78	270	9,520.87	35.26	235	8,657.89	36.84
Performing arts	314	14,787.15	47.09	326	15,627.22	47.94	274	13,364.73	48.78	318	15,801.49	49.69
Pets	173	4,112.20	23.77	137	3,257.88	23.78	122	2,580.92	21.16	86	1,948.57	22.66
Philosophy	441	23,240.50	52.70	441	24,659.66	55.92	481	25,282.98	52.56	500	28,139.64	56.28
Photography	706	31,564.61	44.71	705	33,865.63	48.04	719	34,351.66	47.78	732	35,162.56	48.04
Poetry	255	7,652.03	30.01	263	7,886.00	29.98	301	8,760.54	29.10	193	5,753.46	29.81
Political science	1,175	57,443.46	48.89	1,030	49,757.20	48.31	910	43,026.72	47.28	944	43,887.84	46.49
Psychology	477	24,580.38	51.53	456	23,807.86	52.21	446	22,949.08	51.46	389	20,031.22	51.49
Reference	238	8,588.83	36.09	219	7,565.84	34.55	202	6,492.48	32.14	172	5,717.07	33.24
Religion	1,614	53,692.99	33.27	1,645	54,558.92	33.17	1,593	54,819.43	34.41	1,530	51,983.48	33.98
Science	683	33,617.88	49.22	655	33,131.00	50.58	579	27,707.21	47.85	558	27,034.43	48.45
Self-help	309	6,458.71	20.90	249	5,867.50	23.56	217	5,024.33	23.15	217	4,995.96	23.02
Social science	1,622	85,039.38	52.43	1,464	76,354.23	52.15	1,320	69,515.12	52.66	1,143	62,754.70	54.90
Sports and recreation	579	18,414.49	31.80	592	18,796.17	31.75	572	17,643.62	30.85	567	17,653.98	31.14
Study aids	15	661.50	44.10	12	514.59	42.88	15	649.59	43.31	9	439.65	48.85
Technology and engineering	269	15,258.54	56.72	248	13,114.69	52.88	280	15,773.29	56.33	264	15,876.12	60.14
Transportation	196	8,252.63	42.11	237	9,164.23	38.67	270	9,767.73	36.18	172	6,648.88	38.66
Travel	365	11,560.17	31.67	330	9,563.71	28.98	325	9,925.47	30.54	183	5,451.89	29.79
True crime	91	2,550.42	28.03	64	1,880.58	29.38	71	2,068.15	29.13	73	2,043.71	28.00
Young adult	2,333	67,217.00	28.81	2,540	71,701.20	28.23	2,472	70,155.32	28.38	2,090	54,785.96	26.21
Totals	44,666	$1,524,369.50	$34.13	43,122	$1,469,478.36	$34.08	42,252	$1,426,281.31	$33.76	40,550	$1,367,240.86	$33.72

Table 4 / Mass Market Paperbacks Average Per-Volume Prices, 2009–2012

BISAC Category	2009			2010			2011			2012		
	Vols.	$ Total	Prices	Vols.	$ Total	Prices	Vols.	$ Total	Prices	Vols.	$ Total	Prices
Antiques and collectibles	9	$77.91	$8.66	9	$78.91	$8.77	5	$43.95	$8.79	5	$44.95	$8.99
Architecture	n.a.	n.a.	n.a.	n.a.	n.a.	n.a.	n.a.	n.a.	n.a.	n.a.	n.a.	n.a.
Art	n.a.	n.a.	n.a.	n.a.	n.a.	n.a.	n.a.	n.a.	n.a.	n.a.	n.a.	n.a.
Bibles	n.a.	n.a.	n.a.	n.a.	n.a.	n.a.	n.a.	n.a.	n.a.	n.a.	n.a.	n.a.
Biography and autobiography	13	97.30	7.48	13	97.67	7.51	8	68.92	8.62	4	26.92	6.73
Body, mind and spirit	13	103.87	7.99	17	135.83	7.99	17	134.83	7.93	14	113.86	8.13
Business and economics	1	9.99	9.99	3	27.97	9.32	2	15.98	7.99	1	7.99	7.99
Children	238	1,456.16	6.12	257	1,597.94	6.22	253	1,658.44	6.56	246	1,588.54	6.46
Comics and graphic novels	n.a.	n.a.	n.a.	n.a.	n.a.	n.a.	n.a.	n.a.	n.a.	n.a.	n.a.	n.a.
Computers	n.a.	n.a.	n.a.	n.a.	n.a.	n.a.	n.a.	n.a.	n.a.	n.a.	n.a.	n.a.
Cooking	n.a.	n.a.	n.a.	n.a.	n.a.	n.a.	1	7.99	7.99	n.a.	n.a.	n.a.
Crafts and hobbies	n.a.	n.a.	n.a.	n.a.	n.a.	n.a.	n.a.	n.a.	n.a.	n.a.	n.a.	n.a.
Design	n.a.	n.a.	n.a.	n.a.	n.a.	n.a.	n.a.	n.a.	n.a.	n.a.	n.a.	n.a.
Drama	3	17.93	5.98	3	18.89	6.30	1	8.95	8.95	2	9.90	4.95
Education	n.a.	n.a.	n.a.	n.a.	n.a.	n.a.	n.a.	n.a.	n.a.	n.a.	n.a.	n.a.
Family and relationships	1	4.99	4.99	1	7.99	7.99	1	8.99	8.99	1	4.99	4.99
Fiction	4,013	26,824.43	6.68	3,952	26,882.67	6.80	3,997	27,865.23	6.97	3,883	27,281.13	7.03
Foreign language study	4	27.96	6.99	6	42.45	7.08	n.a.	n.a.	n.a.	n.a.	n.a.	n.a.
Games	5	24.95	4.99	n.a.	n.a.	n.a.	n.a.	n.a.	n.a.	n.a.	n.a.	n.a.
Gardening	n.a.	n.a.	n.a.	n.a.	n.a.	n.a.	n.a.	n.a.	n.a.	n.a.	n.a.	n.a.
Health and fitness	15	116.85	7.79	14	110.86	7.92	11	89.89	8.17	16	131.84	8.24
History	5	39.46	7.89	1	9.95	9.95	7	59.89	8.56	3	25.97	8.66
House and home	n.a.	n.a.	n.a.	n.a.	n.a.	n.a.	n.a.	n.a.	n.a.	n.a.	n.a.	n.a.

Humor	n.a.	n.a.	n.a.	n.a.	n.a.	n.a.	1	3.50	3.50	n.a.	n.a.	n.a.
Language arts and disciplines	n.a.	n.a.	n.a.	2	26.49	13.25	n.a.	n.a.	n.a.	n.a.	n.a.	n.a.
Law	n.a.	n.a.	n.a.	n.a.	n.a.	n.a.	n.a.	n.a.	n.a.	n.a.	n.a.	n.a.
Literary collections	1	7.95	7.95	1	5.95	5.95	1	7.95	7.95	2	11.90	5.95
Literary criticism	1	7.99	7.99	1	7.99	7.99	1	9.99	9.99	n.a.	n.a.	n.a.
Mathematics	n.a.	n.a.	n.a.	n.a.	n.a.	n.a.	n.a.	n.a.	n.a.	n.a.	n.a.	n.a.
Medical	n.a.	n.a.	n.a.	1	8.99	8.99	n.a.	n.a.	n.a.	1	8.99	8.99
Music	n.a.	n.a.	n.a.	n.a.	n.a.	n.a.	1	7.95	7.95	n.a.	n.a.	n.a.
Nature	n.a.	n.a.	n.a.	n.a.	n.a.	n.a.	n.a.	n.a.	n.a.	1	7.99	7.99
Performing arts	1	9.99	9.99	1	9.99	9.99	2	17.98	8.99	1	9.99	9.99
Pets	n.a.	n.a.	n.a.	1	7.99	7.99	1	7.99	7.99	n.a.	n.a.	n.a.
Philosophy	n.a.	n.a.	n.a.	2	12.94	6.47	n.a.	n.a.	n.a.	n.a.	n.a.	n.a.
Photography	n.a.	n.a.	n.a.	n.a.	n.a.	n.a.	n.a.	n.a.	n.a.	n.a.	n.a.	n.a.
Poetry	5	34.75	6.95	1	7.95	7.95	1	7.95	7.95	2	14.90	7.45
Political science	1	5.95	5.95	2	15.94	7.97	1	5.95	5.95	n.a.	n.a.	n.a.
Psychology	n.a.	n.a.	n.a.	n.a.	n.a.	n.a.	1	7.99	7.99	n.a.	n.a.	n.a.
Reference	3	22.97	7.66	1	7.99	7.99	2	15.98	7.99	3	24.93	8.31
Religion	3	20.93	6.98	2	15.98	7.99	3	23.97	7.99	2	14.98	7.49
Science	n.a.	n.a.	n.a.	n.a.	n.a.	n.a.	n.a.	n.a.	n.a.	n.a.	n.a.	n.a.
Self-help	2	15.98	7.99	1	7.99	7.99	1	7.99	7.99	1	7.99	7.99
Social science	0	0.00	n.a.	n.a.	n.a.	n.a.	n.a.	n.a.	n.a.	1	9.99	9.99
Sports and recreation	3	20.97	6.99	1	7.99	7.99	1	7.99	7.99	1	7.99	7.99
Study aids	n.a.	n.a.	n.a.	n.a.	n.a.	n.a.	n.a.	n.a.	n.a.	n.a.	n.a.	n.a.
Technology and engineering	n.a.	n.a.	n.a.	n.a.	n.a.	n.a.	n.a.	n.a.	n.a.	n.a.	n.a.	n.a.
Transportation	1	14.00	14.00	n.a.	n.a.	n.a.	n.a.	n.a.	n.a.	n.a.	n.a.	n.a.
Travel	1	4.95	4.95	n.a.	n.a.	n.a.	n.a.	n.a.	n.a.	n.a.	n.a.	n.a.
True crime	52	388.48	7.47	54	412.46	7.64	44	344.56	7.83	38	315.62	8.31
Young adult	96	732.61	7.63	83	674.68	8.13	47	398.53	8.48	55	497.43	9.04
Totals	4,490	$30,089.32	$6.70	4,430	$30,242.45	$6.83	4,411	$30,839.33	$6.99	4,283	$30,168.79	$7.04

n.a.=not available

Table 5 / Trade Paperbacks Average Per-Volume Prices, 2009–2012

BISAC Category	2009			2010			2011			2012		
	Vols.	$ Total	Prices	Vols.	$ Total	Prices	Vols.	$ Total	Prices	Vols.	$ Total	Prices
Antiques and collectibles	191	$5,204.12	$27.25	178	$4,544.12	$25.53	158	$4,084.94	$25.85	178	$5,140.48	$28.88
Architecture	692	31,060.73	44.89	752	34,075.86	45.31	739	31,559.04	42.71	633	25,753.06	40.68
Art	1,491	56,100.80	37.63	1,506	57,609.66	38.25	1,706	64,211.49	37.64	1,688	60,547.71	35.87
Bibles	307	12,484.70	40.67	430	16,622.32	38.66	755	31,013.64	41.08	632	28,487.06	45.07
Biography and autobiography	2,347	48,201.37	20.54	2,434	49,532.67	20.35	4,946	93,609.40	18.93	4,551	87,007.56	19.12
Body, mind and spirit	1,009	18,319.98	18.16	995	17,940.04	18.03	1,717	30,695.43	17.88	1,700	29,397.82	17.29
Business and economics	5,930	368,094.31	62.07	5,791	401,291.31	69.30	5,789	393,764.09	68.02	8,189	655,422.80	80.04
Children	9,716	105,976.59	10.91	8,612	89,751.55	10.42	9,474	104,689.10	11.05	9,364	115,835.78	12.37
Comics and graphic novels	2,173	33,503.48	15.42	1,863	30,016.52	16.11	3,415	55,465.86	16.24	2,180	35,557.07	16.31
Computers	3,795	369,895.63	97.47	3,460	243,654.22	70.42	3,495	249,579.85	71.41	3,629	283,397.35	78.09
Cooking	1,006	19,711.24	19.59	1,101	21,962.25	19.95	1,242	24,597.47	19.80	1,251	25,822.40	20.64
Crafts and hobbies	1,002	19,331.96	19.29	1,052	20,343.06	19.34	1,091	21,175.04	19.41	1,049	20,714.50	19.75
Design	397	14,690.39	37.00	440	28,152.04	63.98	414	17,684.75	42.72	384	15,618.96	40.67
Drama	581	12,607.20	21.70	739	14,006.42	18.95	559	10,506.88	18.80	565	10,451.29	18.50
Education	3,262	135,148.69	41.43	3,545	152,347.38	42.98	3,565	146,902.07	41.21	3,633	160,679.21	44.23
Family and relationships	884	17,351.78	19.63	782	14,642.51	18.72	1,288	23,020.33	17.87	1,185	21,391.06	18.05
Fiction	9,694	167,906.96	17.32	9,546	171,735.66	17.99	18,402	335,323.99	18.22	15,958	281,104.50	17.62
Foreign language study	977	31,564.73	32.31	1,280	40,097.96	31.33	1,247	45,261.94	36.30	1,090	42,802.43	39.27
Games	787	13,844.60	17.59	792	13,127.18	16.57	705	11,712.67	16.61	653	10,539.35	16.14
Gardening	256	5,364.93	20.96	241	5,651.33	23.45	249	5,810.32	23.33	231	5,319.26	23.03
Health and fitness	1,333	31,558.58	23.67	1,271	34,253.18	26.95	1,477	39,849.21	26.98	1,276	32,031.94	25.10
History	6,436	204,677.72	31.80	6,952	248,808.28	35.79	7,456	271,738.66	36.45	7,096	270,954.05	38.18
House and home	226	4,963.14	21.96	200	4,238.03	21.19	153	3,125.76	20.43	150	3,264.61	21.76

Category											
Humor	486	6,700.28	13.79	430	6,176.99	14.37	581	8,694.93	14.97	510	7,598.07	14.90
Language arts and disciplines	2,088	137,490.40	65.85	2,317	149,344.28	64.46	1,835	132,469.86	72.19	2,157	153,147.88	71.00
Law	2,711	204,427.95	75.41	3,179	229,116.93	72.07	3,220	226,786.54	70.43	3,045	217,114.66	71.30
Literary collections	581	20,338.04	35.01	672	24,471.28	36.42	541	15,881.19	29.36	473	15,367.12	32.49
Literary criticism	1,770	68,422.50	38.66	1,612	58,945.92	36.57	1,750	67,367.67	38.50	1,522	60,557.85	39.79
Mathematics	885	61,007.20	68.93	1,312	113,002.65	86.13	1,611	130,653.27	81.10	1,706	154,650.45	90.65
Medical	3,937	300,540.69	76.34	5,378	485,210.97	90.22	6,107	507,144.40	83.04	5,531	531,155.80	96.03
Music	2,975	69,079.36	23.22	3,020	68,935.86	22.83	2,837	69,596.60	24.53	2,586	63,657.57	24.62
Nature	613	16,565.41	27.02	565	21,064.03	37.28	586	21,015.68	35.86	604	19,996.16	33.11
Performing arts	934	31,428.80	33.65	1,030	34,531.78	33.53	938	30,390.41	32.40	952	34,451.71	36.19
Pets	299	5,683.91	19.01	249	4,317.85	17.34	235	4,395.04	18.70	211	3,977.32	18.85
Philosophy	1,465	50,292.43	34.33	1,391	73,256.72	52.66	1,587	67,304.33	42.41	1,503	67,863.98	45.15
Photography	539	16,778.30	31.13	546	17,087.12	31.30	541	17,387.11	32.14	522	16,230.92	31.09
Poetry	1,720	29,025.11	16.88	1,720	28,775.89	16.73	3,811	61,979.20	16.26	3,433	55,377.52	16.13
Political science	3,220	122,070.40	37.91	3,908	160,217.61	41.00	3,472	142,581.41	41.07	3,501	148,300.99	42.36
Psychology	1,256	54,111.63	43.08	1,578	75,710.56	47.98	1,685	90,713.21	53.84	1,807	108,645.23	60.12
Reference	1,307	118,538.30	90.69	1,057	89,691.16	84.85	1,217	108,322.32	89.01	1,214	120,891.44	99.58
Religion	6,052	128,974.55	21.31	6,955	153,538.88	22.08	8,639	177,831.51	20.58	8,728	183,923.29	21.07
Science	2,462	192,498.92	78.19	4,004	465,938.99	116.37	4,685	465,535.92	99.37	3,886	383,702.50	98.74
Self-help	1,047	18,675.96	17.84	1,121	20,002.38	17.84	2,043	35,371.73	17.31	2,371	39,460.95	16.64
Social science	3,998	169,968.27	42.51	4,270	192,361.40	45.05	4,013	176,295.60	43.93	4,551	217,436.14	47.78
Sports and recreation	1,259	29,445.35	23.39	1,315	29,326.75	22.30	1,310	32,479.61	24.79	1,178	27,381.06	23.24
Study aids	669	20,617.83	30.82	1,499	73,805.65	49.24	985	33,330.29	33.84	591	24,410.48	41.30
Technology and engineering	2,681	410,478.85	153.11	2,427	269,875.47	111.20	2,426	257,108.54	105.98	3,037	350,058.68	115.26
Transportation	459	16,804.27	36.61	507	18,385.24	36.26	458	16,835.71	36.76	411	14,275.25	34.73
Travel	2,852	58,486.95	20.51	2,585	54,099.71	20.93	2,513	49,806.57	19.82	2,171	43,323.32	19.96
True crime	156	2,964.75	19.00	195	4,083.57	20.94	227	4,313.89	19.00	197	3,779.00	19.18
Young adult	2,462	41,325.07	16.79	2,173	32,281.38	14.86	2,555	47,506.66	18.59	3,241	54,843.92	16.92
Totals	105,375	$4,130,305.11	$39.20	110,977	$4,667,960.57	$42.06	132,450	$5,014,481.13	$37.86	128,904	$5,348,819.51	$41.49

Table 6 / Audiobook Average Per-Volume Prices, 2009–2012

BISAC Category	2009 Vols.	2009 $ Total	2009 Prices	2010 Vols.	2010 $ Total	2010 Prices	2011 Vols.	2011 $ Total	2011 Prices	2012 Vols.	2012 $ Total	2012 Prices
Antiques and collectibles	1	$74.95	$74.95	3	$109.97	$36.66	n.a.	n.a.	n.a.	n.a.	n.a.	n.a.
Architecture	n.a.	n.a.	n.a.	4	164.97	41.24	3	$119.90	$39.97	2	$64.90	$32.45
Art	7	415.86	59.41	9	523.90	58.21	9	363.27	40.36	12	448.82	37.40
Bibles	9	679.75	75.53	7	302.93	43.28	10	444.86	44.49	23	1,121.54	48.76
Biography and autobiography	685	34,762.98	50.75	751	38,142.55	50.79	749	38,389.55	51.25	991	47,005.91	47.43
Body, mind and spirit	87	3,302.01	37.95	69	2,275.35	32.98	103	3,874.54	37.62	133	5,019.86	37.74
Business and economics	436	20,121.06	46.15	346	17,195.20	49.70	401	18,126.12	45.20	465	17,789.62	38.26
Children	832	30,132.89	36.22	899	33,981.63	37.80	978	33,971.16	34.74	1,215	39,967.35	32.89
Comics and graphic novels	n.a.	n.a.	n.a.	n.a.	n.a.	n.a.	29	579.71	19.99	4	149.92	37.48
Computers	5	234.95	46.99	2	89.99	45.00	12	647.86	53.99	4	170.92	42.73
Cooking	14	625.78	44.70	2	89.94	44.97	14	598.74	42.77	13	556.79	42.83
Crafts and hobbies	4	154.88	38.72	1	24.98	24.98	n.a.	n.a.	n.a.	1	24.95	24.95
Design	n.a.	n.a.	n.a.	n.a.	n.a.	n.a.	n.a.	n.a.	n.a.	3	171.90	57.30
Drama	151	5,214.79	34.54	95	3,154.48	33.21	104	2,915.63	28.03	110	2,638.75	23.99
Education	22	997.47	45.34	20	914.22	45.71	34	1,497.28	44.04	35	1,260.14	36.00
Family and relationships	54	2,128.07	39.41	69	2,840.86	41.17	110	4,531.51	41.20	151	6,454.70	42.75
Fiction	6,278	330,348.73	52.62	7,649	385,381.14	50.38	7,174	345,701.76	48.19	11,167	470,185.04	42.10
Foreign language study	260	10,592.04	40.74	186	8,390.07	45.11	223	11,285.56	50.61	164	9,915.99	60.46
Games	6	84.74	14.12	n.a.	n.a.	n.a.	5	234.91	46.98	5	224.88	44.98
Gardening	n.a.	n.a.	n.a.	6	286.89	47.82	n.a.	n.a.	n.a.	5	159.93	31.99
Health and fitness	82	3,779.22	46.09	85	3,662.56	43.09	110	5,170.40	47.00	89	3,925.23	44.10
History	450	25,959.35	57.69	563	32,691.39	58.07	446	26,475.56	59.36	598	30,233.27	50.56
House and home	0	0.00	n.a.	n.a.	n.a.	n.a.	1	34.95	34.95	3	165.97	55.32

Category											
Humor	79	3,347.29	42.37	95	3,479.34	36.62	103	4,167.81	40.46	81	2,701.87	33.36
Language arts and disciplines	18	839.65	46.65	13	498.43	38.34	38	1,705.23	44.87	25	1,151.25	46.05
Law	9	447.79	49.75	10	644.94	64.49	7	492.96	70.42	18	914.69	50.82
Literary collections	20	646.71	32.34	11	572.74	52.07	33	1,704.26	51.64	35	1,390.31	39.72
Literary criticism	20	848.60	42.43	18	765.61	42.53	188	5,750.62	30.59	95	3,170.80	33.38
Mathematics	0	0.00	n.a.	n.a.	n.a.	n.a.	1	24.95	24.95	3	153.97	51.32
Medical	13	788.59	60.66	28	1,123.66	40.13	24	1,097.85	45.74	24	1,165.52	48.56
Music	108	4,148.22	38.41	74	2,639.78	35.67	57	2,761.16	48.44	44	1,715.90	39.00
Nature	37	1,742.43	47.09	57	2,348.20	41.20	44	2,055.28	46.71	13	670.79	51.60
Performing arts	21	970.78	46.23	16	649.63	40.60	9	585.74	65.08	16	550.68	34.42
Pets	23	1,000.67	43.51	52	1,993.21	38.33	25	1,078.57	43.14	20	858.69	42.93
Philosophy	36	1,850.21	51.39	38	2,015.98	53.05	73	3,420.46	46.86	39	1,565.05	40.13
Photography	n.a.	n.a.	n.a.	n.a.	n.a.	n.a.	n.a.	n.a.	n.a.	n.a.	n.a.	n.a.
Poetry	50	1,794.08	35.88	28	940.46	33.59	16	368.54	23.03	14	414.65	29.62
Political science	177	8,795.18	49.69	230	11,050.07	48.04	220	10,608.99	48.22	234	10,944.88	46.77
Psychology	54	2,815.00	52.13	46	2,089.19	45.42	91	4,420.40	48.58	79	3,178.56	40.23
Reference	7	283.85	40.55	2	119.98	59.99	19	809.77	42.62	11	389.81	35.44
Religion	418	14,002.55	33.50	425	14,426.23	33.94	465	14,790.98	31.81	569	18,669.94	32.81
Science	64	3,055.70	47.75	66	3,425.01	51.89	90	4,887.33	54.30	113	4,696.83	41.56
Self-help	289	11,067.31	38.30	192	7,571.23	39.43	197	8,205.68	41.65	369	13,439.63	36.42
Social science	79	3,978.46	50.36	90	4,326.20	48.07	102	4,961.38	48.64	118	5,105.79	43.27
Sports and recreation	41	1,877.15	45.78	58	2,811.69	48.48	38	1,729.47	45.51	40	1,735.29	43.38
Study aids	21	712.23	33.92	7	135.88	19.41	2	55.32	27.66	6	1,281.33	213.56
Technology and engineering	7	339.94	48.56	23	1,226.54	53.33	26	1,206.57	46.41	10	405.78	40.58
Transportation	3	109.97	36.66	7	323.93	46.28	1	24.95	24.95	7	323.86	46.27
Travel	15	773.58	51.57	47	2,395.08	50.96	20	1,223.46	61.17	49	1,747.00	35.65
True crime	45	2,281.13	50.69	37	1,945.35	52.58	36	1,801.29	50.04	79	3,530.45	44.69
Young adult	527	23,638.46	44.85	888	39,789.54	44.81	960	40,041.92	41.71	1,434	49,044.57	34.20
Totals	11,564	$561,765.05	$48.58	13,324	$639,530.92	$48.00	13,400	$614,944.21	$45.89	18,738	$768,574.27	$41.02

n.a.=not available

Table 7 / E-Book Average Per-Volume Prices, 2009–2012

BISAC Category	2009			2010			2011			2012		
	Vols.	$ Total	Prices	Vols.	$ Total	Prices	Vols.	$ Total	Prices	Vols.	$ Total	Prices
Antiques and collectibles	11	$989.68	$89.97	62	$1,875.04	$30.24	229	$4,913.87	$21.46	166	$5,762.06	$34.71
Architecture	205	14,190.05	69.22	268	17,839.50	66.57	312	18,837.60	60.38	865	54,518.77	63.03
Art	166	4,635.21	27.92	199	8,270.92	41.56	729	12,309.78	16.89	1,231	29,451.27	23.92
Bibles	22	342.78	15.58	119	727.27	6.11	113	1,281.94	11.34	154	1,941.36	12.61
Biography and autobiography	1,464	20,866.88	14.25	1,828	28,271.22	15.47	3,824	39,105.73	10.23	6,309	127,458.82	20.20
Body, mind and spirit	362	4,238.07	11.71	628	8,759.51	13.95	1,378	15,899.16	11.54	2,200	31,666.87	14.39
Business and economics	4,707	228,107.43	48.46	5,603	251,141.29	44.82	7,198	292,515.94	40.64	11,296	512,761.45	45.39
Children	3,554	41,682.27	11.73	4,239	58,588.74	13.82	14,867	244,048.77	16.42	18,197	229,380.12	12.61
Comics and graphic novels	16	193.82	12.11	26	296.18	11.39	269	1,619.40	6.02	504	3,697.32	7.34
Computers	2,574	158,668.53	61.64	3,057	189,819.37	62.09	4,383	270,498.10	61.72	3,941	307,255.52	77.96
Cooking	508	8,147.74	16.04	715	12,007.93	16.79	1,561	19,388.60	12.42	1,892	24,182.04	12.78
Crafts and hobbies	211	2,724.58	12.91	340	5,995.40	17.63	785	11,979.56	15.26	804	9,724.33	12.09
Design	59	2,061.86	34.95	125	4,629.14	37.03	104	4,023.47	38.69	275	6,335.72	23.04
Drama	137	1,720.28	12.56	443	2,152.39	4.86	2,758	8,809.25	3.19	1,472	11,045.27	7.50
Education	1,397	77,081.31	55.18	1,537	70,625.15	45.95	1,787	89,804.00	50.25	3,368	173,292.07	51.45
Family and relationships	650	9,252.18	14.23	717	10,600.99	14.79	1,210	12,252.48	10.13	1,714	26,441.32	15.43
Fiction	13,364	109,681.11	8.21	18,043	127,403.62	7.06	56,776	274,064.81	4.83	73,848	891,690.24	12.07
Foreign language study	116	4,745.40	40.91	97	4,528.10	46.68	304	5,986.97	19.69	710	20,208.84	28.46
Games	84	1,394.05	16.60	120	1,542.19	12.85	324	3,495.71	10.79	377	3,594.48	9.53
Gardening	51	1,197.94	23.49	68	1,184.03	17.41	169	2,254.01	13.34	249	4,330.81	17.39
Health and fitness	755	13,762.20	18.23	920	17,276.85	18.78	1,988	26,236.83	13.20	2,286	35,314.57	15.45
History	1,929	90,563.42	46.95	2,641	127,292.83	48.20	4,163	138,309.34	33.22	8,467	300,742.38	35.52
House and home	103	2,441.51	23.70	121	2,610.21	21.57	187	2,787.16	14.90	209	2,773.75	13.27
Humor	232	2,875.31	12.39	322	3,589.47	11.15	619	4,660.76	7.53	1,052	13,721.33	13.04
Language arts and disciplines	566	49,885.85	88.14	582	44,003.09	75.61	1,075	64,004.71	59.54	1,747	93,313.13	53.41

Category											
Law	487	44,616.45	91.61	609	68,324.51	112.19	872	66,422.78	76.17	1,781	141,259.17	79.31
Literary collections	94	2,912.93	30.99	226	4,580.60	20.27	1,757	7,757.14	4.41	1,397	15,004.09	10.74
Literary criticism	447	36,454.50	81.55	608	53,002.07	87.17	936	47,348.25	50.59	2,214	88,023.04	39.76
Mathematics	530	54,040.15	101.96	801	89,965.18	112.32	1,332	126,913.95	95.28	1,623	126,465.10	77.92
Medical	1,676	207,275.36	123.67	1,575	213,740.04	135.71	4,299	431,112.16	100.28	4,815	497,140.15	103.25
Music	262	9,151.49	34.93	331	10,808.03	32.65	4,390	62,006.71	14.12	9,723	69,065.52	7.10
Nature	209	6,777.67	32.43	370	22,006.25	59.48	527	16,917.81	32.10	757	30,674.10	40.52
Performing arts	335	11,911.61	35.56	474	15,246.76	32.17	863	23,042.10	26.70	1,134	39,381.85	34.73
Pets	113	1,701.62	15.06	176	2,552.35	14.50	581	6,492.44	11.17	624	10,010.17	16.04
Philosophy	664	40,289.40	60.68	598	42,712.85	71.43	948	41,871.46	44.17	2,016	85,136.26	42.23
Photography	158	4,507.88	28.53	202	5,501.27	27.23	387	7,038.13	18.19	463	11,037.58	23.84
Poetry	257	3,521.91	13.70	332	3,167.52	9.54	1,807	10,345.56	5.73	1,548	12,891.93	8.33
Political science	1,451	90,231.19	62.19	1,427	85,245.96	59.74	2,208	95,687.88	43.34	4,483	209,578.04	46.75
Psychology	845	45,122.14	53.40	914	51,568.40	56.42	2,139	104,824.79	49.01	2,578	129,077.30	50.07
Reference	284	8,854.79	31.18	646	14,809.54	22.92	788	15,578.45	19.77	811	37,658.65	46.43
Religion	2,676	56,810.95	21.23	2,874	79,918.02	27.81	5,669	98,002.50	17.29	8,004	151,549.35	18.93
Science	2,770	538,120.20	194.27	2,915	454,162.54	155.80	3,634	478,281.26	131.61	5,357	581,938.40	108.63
Self-help	743	8,865.50	11.93	746	10,489.68	14.06	2,497	20,217.11	8.10	3,943	55,243.12	14.01
Social science	1,357	77,863.22	57.38	1,513	85,986.29	56.83	2,240	120,078.07	53.61	4,029	242,927.97	60.29
Sports and recreation	546	11,240.95	20.59	643	12,360.63	19.22	1,223	20,906.04	17.09	1,858	36,816.10	19.81
Study aids	147	2,346.28	15.96	305	4,250.35	13.94	859	7,903.67	9.20	398	17,746.33	44.59
Technology and engineering	1,633	234,354.76	143.51	2,618	414,799.35	158.44	2,831	348,789.41	123.20	3,829	430,747.52	112.50
Transportation	64	2,536.78	39.64	97	3,212.56	33.12	193	3,689.30	19.12	286	7,692.28	26.90
Travel	710	9,596.24	13.52	1,223	19,367.97	15.84	2,745	24,973.53	9.10	3,148	29,878.37	9.49
True crime	169	1,930.69	11.42	210	2,177.10	10.37	321	2,826.65	8.81	496	8,535.62	17.21
Young adult	1,861	17,889.85	9.61	1,892	22,635.77	11.96	2,821	60,577.82	21.47	4,465	70,772.96	15.85
Totals	53,731	$2,380,373.97	$44.30	67,145	$2,793,622.02	$41.61	155,979	$3,818,692.92	$24.48	215,113	$6,056,854.81	$28.16

(continued from page 437)

Average prices for hardcovers under $81 in the important children's category have been fairly stable over the last few years, falling 0.51 percent in 2010 and 0.41 percent in revised data for 2011. Children's mass market paperback prices, on the other hand, rose steadily, posting gains of 1.63 percent in 2010 and 5.47 percent in 2011; the more important sector of trade paperbacks saw price hikes of 6.05 percent in 2011 and 11.95 percent in preliminary 2012 data. Children's audiobook prices fell 8.10 percent in 2011 after climbing 4.36 percent in 2010, and the decline appeared to be continuing in 2012. Children's e-book prices rose 18.81 percent in 2011 but preliminary results for 2012 suggest that they may be dropping back to earlier levels.

Prices for young adult materials held fairly steady in the hardcover sector, while trade paperback prices jumped 25.10 percent in 2011 before falling 8.98 percent in preliminary 2012 data. YA audiobooks declined 6.92 percent in 2011 and were down 18.00 percent for 2012; e-book prices showed a puzzling surge in 2011 and appeared to be retreating in 2012.

Price declines and increases were evenly distributed throughout the hardcover sector in 2011 (Table 2). Preliminary results for 2012, however, showed many of the declines being reversed.

The Competitive Advantage of U.S. Book Publishers in the International Market for Books

Albert N. Greco

Emily Osman

Gabelli School of Business, Fordham University
E-mail agreco@fordham.edu

Introduction

Impact of Digital Books on the U.S. Book Industry

The economics of publishing are harsh and unforgiving unless you understand the way supply and demand operate in the eclectic U.S. book publishing industry (Greco, Milliot, and Wharton 2013). For decades the U.S. book publishing industry—including publishers, retailers, and distributors—relied on the international trade in printed books for competitive advantages (Porter 1980; Porter 1996; Porter 1999; Hall 2012) because of the following:

- A steady increasing revenue stream for U.S. book exports (Greco 2011; Greco 2012a; Greco 2012b; Nissan and Nicoomand 2009; Kaplan, Sensoy, and Stromberg 2009)

- A constant supply of books printed and published abroad (for example, in Canada, the United Kingdom, Italy) to be sold into the diverse and growing U.S. channels of distribution (especially the traditional academic market as well as nontraditional retail markets including price clubs, mass merchants, supermarkets, convenience stores, toy stores, and so forth) (Anderson 2004; Chacholiades 1970; Greco 2011; Greco 2012a; Greco 2012b; Keh 1998; Krause 1962)

- Inexpensive books printed abroad (i.e., books printed—not printed and published—abroad, perhaps in China, Singapore, or Hong Kong) with a lower unit manufacturing cost and a higher profit margin than titles printed in the United States, effectively saving U.S. publishers money in typesetting, printing, paper, and binding costs (Lane 2004; Leichenko 2000; O'Loughlin and Anselin 1996; Rai and Jagannathan 2012; Sirgy, Dong-Jin, Miller, Littlefield, and Atay 2007; Vignarajah 2009)

The bottom line was significant. U.S. publishers, retailers, and distributors had a supply of popular trade books (adult hardcovers and paperbacks, juvenile and young adult hardcovers and paperbacks, mass market paperbacks, and religious hardcover and paperback titles); high-impact scholarly and professional hardcovers and paperbacks (Caves 2000; Coser, Kadushin, and Powell 1985; Gre-

Detailed statistical data from the United States Department of Commerce, International Trade Administration (ITA) was used in the preparation of this article. The authors are grateful for the considerable assistance of Jim Rice at ITA, who provided detailed statistical datasets that made it possible to update previous articles with the latest figures for 2011 and 2012.

Table 1 / U.S. Book Export Totals 2002–2012

($'000)

Year	Religion	Textbooks	Professional	Art and Pictorial	Hardbound Books	Mass Market Paperbacks	Encyclopedias	Dictionaries	Total	% Change
2002	73,893	380,637	376,576	20,701	110,390	165,273	14,759	2,493	1,144,722	n.a.
2003	72,127	355,071	371,129	20,962	114,055	208,822	10,518	3,188	1,155,872	1.0
2004	86,352	402,057	391,532	11,113	146,608	228,901	8,292	2,953	1,277,808	10.5
2005	88,303	413,408	475,407	10,582	164,373	216,541	9,204	2,236	1,380,054	8.0
2006	94,863	425,951	478,336	15,766	162,749	216,712	6,852	3,115	1,404,344	1.8
2007	114,065	430,058	560,938	26,328	160,123	239,495	6,436	3,792	1,541,235	9.7
2008	106,001	513,022	504,002	32,477	193,006	271,768	7,017	3,338	1,630,631	5.8
2009	96,319	476,625	434,888	17,109	203,062	307,358	3,497	1,984	1,540,842	-5.5
2010	90,971	453,482	453,384	18,388	221,637	313,937	4,190	1,964	1,557,953	1.1
2011	103,646	463,284	338,007	25,639	250,336	385,627	1,873	1,445	1,569,857	0.8
2012	96,868	455,584	310,604	25,375	277,316	468,714	2,979	571	1,638,011	4.3

Source: U.S. Department of Commerce, International Trade Administration.
All numbers are rounded off to one decimal place and may not always equal 100%.
n.a. = not available or not applicable

Table 2 / Total U.S. Book Imports 2002–2012
($'000)

Year	Religion	Textbooks	Professional	Art and Pictorial >$5	Art and Pictorial <$5	Hardbound Books	Mass Market Paperbacks	Encyclopedias	Dictionaries	Total	% Change
2002	79,083	162,733	189,124	23,239	30,251	584,255	70,012	7,703	11,557	1,157,957	n.a.
2003	83,631	197,175	225,889	21,699	24,341	555,460	83,700	12,816	11,572	1,216,283	5.0
2004	99,478	217,413	265,561	28,265	23,686	577,274	128,727	6,458	15,407	1,362,269	12.0
2005	108,631	232,518	291,244	29,005	21,465	596,036	112,633	6,057	18,133	1,415,722	3.9
2006	114,254	243,489	249,248	33,324	22,695	657,237	108,883	5,912	11,775	1,446,817	2.2
2007	132,687	310,491	275,844	29,927	24,791	725,052	108,883	3,110	9,907	1,620,692	12.0
2008	131,858	291,914	262,352	31,803	18,829	718,631	112,537	5,662	7,534	1,581,120	-2.4
2009	122,195	246,473	177,169	26,394	13,848	528,402	84,415	1,980	5,517	1,206,393	-23.7
2010	132,100	259,537	198,006	43,816	23,245	532,863	89,209	1,261	5,930	1,285,967	6.6
2011	132,621	219,562	185,266	43,535	21,257	466,362	71,571	2,244	5,338	1,147,756	-10.8
2012	138,218	196,699	175,108	47,780	20,284	470,094	89,990	2,094	4,010	1,144,277	-0.3

Source: U.S. Department of Commerce, International Trade Administration.

co 2005; Greco, Estelami, Wharton, and Jones 2007; Throsby 2001); and hardcover and paperback K–12 and higher education textbooks.

These developments generated, overall, an impressive positive balance of trade for printed books. Total exports reached $1,638,011,000 in 2012, up 4.3 percent from 2011. Imports stood at $1,144,277,000 in 2012, a decline of 0.3 percent from 2011. Table 1 and Table 2 list export and import revenues for the years 2002 to 2012.

The emergence of e-readers such as the Nook and the Kindle and tablets such as the iPAD and the Surface Pro sparked the release of an abundance of e-books. It took a few years for e-books to begin to affect the sale of printed trade books, with small e-book revenues in both 2008 and 2009, but the situation changed in 2010 when digital book revenues topped $825 million, as shown in Table 3. The results for 2011 and 2012 were impressive, reaching $3.55 billion in 2012, and the outlook for the years 2013 to 2015 is striking.

The success of e-books triggered reductions in the revenues for all printed trade books, with noticeable declines posted for adult and mass market books for 2011 and 2012 and forecast through 2015.

Adult trade books account for about 90 percent of all e-books, with juvenile/young adult books holding an 8 percent share. The religion category accounts for about 2 percent of the total. In a digital world, there are no paperback reprints. Our models predicted that digital trade e-books will capture almost half of all revenues by 2015.

Table 3 / Printed and Digital Trade Books: Net Publishers' Revenues 2008–2015
($ million)

	2008	2009	2010	2011	2012	2013	2014	2015
Adult/Print	5,380	5,163	4,904	4,574	4,117	3,581	3,116	2,711
Juvenile/YA/Print	3,164	3,325	3,192	3,286	3,295	3,000	2,730	2,429
Mass Market/Print	1,662	1,596	1,517	1,075	806	645	516	413
Religion/Print	2,044	1,882	1,750	1,698	1,630	1,549	1,394	1,258
Print Totals	12,250	11,966	11,363	10,633	9,848	8,775	7,756	6,811
Consumer/Trade Digital	78	166	825	1,700	3,550	4,438	5,447	6,650
Trade Totals	12,328	12,132	12,188	12,233	13,398	13,213	13,303	13,745
% Digital of Total Trade	0.6	1.4	6.8	13.8	26.5	33.6	41.3	49.4

Source: Greco and Wharton. Estimates for 2013–2015. Net publishers' revenues refers specifically to domestic and export net revenues. Gross sales minus returns equals net revenues.

However, not all book categories will move quickly to digital formats. Professional and scholarly titles, which are "must have, need-to-know" books, will also approach the 50 percent mark by 2015. K–12 textbooks rely on state funding, and this may lead to a trend toward e-textbooks. Nationally, about 47 percent of the typical K–12 budget comes from the state, about 44 percent from local taxes (principally property taxes), and the remaining 9 percent from the federal government (although the level of federal funding varies from place to place). With a decline in state and local taxes, the K–12 sector will move toward digital e-textbooks. Table 4 outlines these trends. Projections indicate that e-textbooks will approach 18 percent of total K–12 purchases by 2015.

**Table 4 / Professional and Scholarly Books and K–12 Textbooks:
Net Publishers' Revenues 2008–2015**

($ million)

	2008	2009	2010	2011	2012	2013	2014	2015
Professional and Scholarly								
Print	5,292	5,516	5,773	6,033	5,810	5,653	5,100	4,575
Digita	1,142	1,337	1,552	1,827	2,206	2,596	3,142	3,770
Total	6,434	6,853	7,325	7,860	8,016	8,249	8,242	8,345
% Digital of Total	17.8	19.5	21.2	23.2	27.5	31.5	38.1	45.3
K–12 Textbooks								
Print	2,760	2,420	2,730	2,377	2,196	2,698	2,812	2,775
Digita	151	143	136	145	154	165	300	600
Total	2,911	2,563	2,866	2,522	2,350	2,863	3,112	3,375
% Digital of Total	5.2	5.6	4.8	5.8	6.6	5.8	9.6	17.8

Source: Greco and Wharton. Estimates for 2013–2015.

Higher education is likely to adopt digital books at an exceptionally fast pace because of the adverse financial impact that used and rental print textbooks have on publishers' balance sheets. More than 92 percent of college students have a computer or tablet, and this publishing sector is positioned to go considerably more digital by 2014–2015.

University presses want to move toward digital publishing in order to capitalize on the fact that two of their principal markets—the pivotal academic community and general readers—have largely accepted digital journals and e-books. Yet far too many university presses lack the financial resources to release both print and digital versions of major titles. Table 5 illustrates these two book categories.

**Table 5 / College/Higher Education Textbooks and University Press Books:
Net Publishers' Revenues 2008–2015**

($ million)

	2008	2009	2010	2011	2012	2013	2014	2015
College/Higher Education Textbooks								
Print	4,280	4,350	4,546	4,650	4,185	3,767	3,389	1,694
Digital	200	400	750	1,140	1,730	2,840	4,120	6,530
Total	4,480	4,750	5,296	5,790	5,915	6,606	7,509	8,224
% Digital of Total	4.5	8.4	14.2	19.7	29.3	43.0	54.9	79.4
University Press Books								
Print	451	425	407	383	360	338	317	298
Digital	8	10	12	30	51	75	109	141
Total	459	435	419	413	411	413	426	439
% Digital of Total	1.7	2.3	2.9	7.3	12.4	18.2	25.6	32.1

Source: Greco and Wharton. Estimates for 2013–2015.

Christensen (2000) analyzed the impact of what he called "disruptive technologies" and Porter (2008), in his "Five Competitive Forces that Shape Strategy," discussed the threat of new entrants into the marketplace and the impact of substitute products.

Clearly, e-readers and e-books are prime examples of disruptive technologies and the threat of substitute products affects the entire book-publishing industry. Margins are unquestionably higher on a digital book than a print book (Greco, Milliot, and Wharton 2013), but there is a "dark side of the moon" when you analyze e-books. Every e-book purchased is a print book that is not purchased. While some analysts might argue that e-books do not greatly affect printed book sales, our research indicated the opposite. We studied actual print unit sales for 2008 to 2012 and modeled out to 2015 (Greco, Milliot, and Wharton 2013). Our projections show that all eight print categories are likely to see declines—in some instances steep declines—between 2008 and 2015. For example, we project that adult trade books will see a 51.5 percent sales decline between 2008 and 2015, that mass market paperbacks will drop 78.7 percent during those years, and that higher education textbooks will decline by 69.7 percent. Book export revenues are likely to remain relatively "stable" for the next few years, at least to 2016–2017. Table 6 shows the results of our research on unit declines.

Table 6 / Trade Books Units: Adult, Juvenile/YA, Mass Market Paperbacks, Religion, Professional and Scholarly, K–12 Textbooks, Higher Education Textbooks, and University Press Books: Net Publishers' Units

(million units)

	2008	2009	2010	2011	2012	2013	2014	2015
Adult	474.6	453.9	424.0	394.0	354.0	308.0	266.0	230.0
Juvenile/YA	464.6	486.6	482.0	484.3	488.7	444.7	399.0	352.0
Mass market	470.0	450.0	435.0	315.0	238.0	190.0	136.0	100.0
Religion	276.8	252.9	231.4	224.5	208.0	185.0	166.5	149.9
Professional and scholarly	85.7	86.7	88.2	89.7	86.1	80.1	72.1	64.2
K–12 textbooks	95.5	82.3	75.7	38.8	63.3	57.6	60.4	64.2
Higher education textbooks	58.7	56.7	56.8	55.4	47.6	41.9	36.4	17.8
University press books	25.5	23.1	22.0	20.9	19.6	18.2	17.0	15.9

Source: Greco and Wharton. Estimates for 2013–2015.

U.S. Book Exports 2009–2012

The impact of economic uncertainty and recessions in various nations affected total U.S. book exports between 2009 and 2012, with declines posted in 2011 and 2012 for five of the eight major book categories.

The dictionary market suffered through years of stark declines (the value of exports dropped 60.5 percent between 2011 and 2012) because of the impact of digital dictionaries, and this sector is unlikely to rebound. What were rather odd were the 2012 results for traditionally "strong" U.S. book categories: textbooks (down 1.7 percent) and technical, scientific, and professional books (down 8.1 percent). While the 2012 results were, perhaps, single-year anomalies, publishers might be wise to look into these reversals and try to ascertain why they happened. Table 7 lists the results for all book categories during those years.

Table 7 / U.S. Exports of Books: 2009–2012
($'000)

Category	2009	2010	2011	2012	Percent Change 2011–2012
Dictionaries and thesauruses	$1,984	1,964	1,445	571	-60.5
Encyclopedias	3,497	4,190	1,873	2,979	59.1
Art	17,109	18,388	25,639	25,375	-1.0
Textbooks	476,625	453,482	463,284	455,584	-1.7
Relig on	96,319	90,971	103,646	96,868	-6.5
Technical, scientific, and professional	434,888	453,384	338,007	310,604	-8.1
Hardcover books, n.e.s.	203,062	221,637	250,336	277,316	10.8
Mass market paperbacks	307,358	313,937	385,627	468,714	21.5

Source: U.S. Department of Commerce, International Trade Administration.
n.e.s. = not elsewhere specified

Overall, the mass market paperback category posted positive results in 2012. However, Canada—a traditional market for these titles—purchased fewer books, recording a 7.2 percent decline from 2011. This may have been the result of relative currency values, but this unusual situation also warrants additional research by the large U.S. trade book houses. Fortunately, impressive increases in exports to the United Kingdom (up 108.2 percent), the Philippines (up 57.7 percent), and Brazil (up 63.9 percent) compensated for the slippage in the Canadian market. Table 8 illustrates these developments.

Table 8 / U.S. Exports of Mass Market Paperbacks (Rack Sized):
Top Ten Markets 2009–2012
($'000)

Country	2009	2010	2011	2012	Percent Change 2011–2012
Canada	$158,689	$178,581	$178,790	$165,864	-7.2
United Kingdom	43,064	38,602	75,816	157,859	108.2
Australia	20,574	15,811	14,661	15,671	6.9
Japar	11,680	10,357	14,869	13,185	-11.3
Philippines	11,007	8,148	9,894	15,605	57.7
Singapore	10,875	13,513	14,074	18,897	34.3
South Africa	10,826	13,708	12,376	8,770	-29.1
China	5,731	5,284	9,855	10,490	6.5
Brazil	4,100	2,357	8,460	13,864	63.9
Thailand	3,728	2,329	5,184	4,654	-10.2

Source: U.S. Department of Commerce, International Trade Administration.

Technical, scientific, and professional books are critically important to academics and researchers throughout the world even with their high suggested retail prices. It therefore was inevitable that as publishers in this sector moved away from printed titles toward digital books, the export of printed books would see declines. This was the pattern in both 2011 and 2012, and our models indicate that the trend will continue well beyond 2015. Consequently, the statistical data-sets for this category revealed declines in eight of the ten major destinations for these printed books. Table 9 outlines the results for Canada (down 7.7 percent), the United Kingdom (down 2.5 percent), and Australia (down 34.4 percent). The tallies for Singapore (down 38.7 percent) and Brazil (down 44.8 percent) exacer-bated the situation.

Table 9 / U.S. Exports of Technical, Scientific, and Professional Books: Top Ten Markets 2009–2012
(\$'000)

Country	2009	2010	2011	2012	Percent Change 2011–2012
Canada	\$129,830	\$124,587	\$115,665	\$106,742	-7.7
United Kingdom	92,344	83,546	31,538	30,738	-2.5
Japan	26,497	41,090	30,952	32,997	6.6
Mexico	23,134	35,840	28,335	27,654	-2.4
Australia	21,753	26,718	21,994	14,431	-34.4
Germany	16,385	17,448	8,284	7,600	-8.3
Hong Kong	15,676	12,142	10,609	8,846	-16.6
Singapore	14,755	9,651	8,057	4,941	-38.7
India	10,159	12,199	8,403	12,034	43.2
Brazil	9,931	15,131	6,695	3,699	-44.8

Source: U.S. Department of Commerce, International Trade Administration.

Textbooks, long a bellwether printed book export category, had patterns that mirrored the results for technical, scientific, and professional books. Again, the movement toward digital textbooks will continue to impact this once-vibrant ex-port category, with anticipated deep declines in the years after 2016–2017. Table 10 lists negative results for Australia (down 11.8 percent), Singapore (down 32.4 percent), Germany (down 15.7 percent), and other nations.

Table 10 / U.S. Exports of Textbooks 2009–2012: Top Ten Markets
(\$'000)

Country	2009	2010	2011	2012	Percent Change 2011–2012
Canada	\$108,956	\$101,748	\$83,120	\$87,016	4.7
United Kingdom	89,816	95,592	109,868	126,671	15.3
Australia	34,666	32,032	25,896	22,829	-11.8
Korea	26,518	26,445	23,561	25,736	9.2
Singapore	25,368	24,574	37,892	25,634	-32.4
Japan	23,682	15,610	17,458	15,142	-13.3
Germany	18,665	10,925	13,548	11,422	-15.7
Mexico	14,850	15,298	10,824	13,405	23.8
United Arab Emirates	12,968	13,828	17,773	15,557	-12.5
Taiwan	9,983	6,179	6,334	6,005	-5.2

Source: U.S. Department of Commerce, International Trade Administration.

The first book printed in what is now the United States was *The Whole Booke of Psalmes Faithfully Translated into English Metre,* generally known as the "Bay Psalm Book," in 1640. So there is a long national tradition of book publishing in this area, and most religious organizations have book-publishing operations. However, this once-dynamic book category shared the fate of numerous other categories in 2012, with a number of deep declines: exports to Canada were down 20.1 percent, and to the United Kingdom down a staggering 50.9 percent. Religion books are likely to move quite slowly toward e-book formats, primarily because many of them are used in religious ceremonies; these declines are unsettling and worthy of close examination by publishers. Table 11 reveals the state of this sector.

Table 11 / U.S. Exports of Religion Books 2009–2012: Top Ten Markets
($'000)

Country	2009	2010	2011	2012	Percent Change 2011–2012
Canada	$20,078	$19,060	$22,871	$18,283	-20.1
United Kingdom	14,064	13,670	15,395	7,566	-50.9
Mexico	8,894	7,918	6,725	6,657	-1.0
Nigeria	8,030	8,807	9,485	8,370	-11.8
Australia	7,157	3,178	2,784	3,765	35.2
Argentina	2,336	4,160	3,319	3,418	3.0
Venezuela	2,320	1,989	4,554	4,973	9.2
Philippines	2,055	2,033	2,204	1,975	-10.4
Guatemala	1,968	1,310	1,790	1,365	-23.8
Colombia	1,670	1,796	2,416	3,924	62.4

Source: U.S. Department of Commerce, International Trade Administration.

In many ways, hardbound books have been, and are likely to remain, the "star" book category in the United States. Many of the authors of these titles have become celebrities with international reach, among them John Grisham, Mary Higgins Clark, James Patterson, and Janet Evanovich. So if any book category had the strength to withstand global economic uncertainties, currency issues, and high unemployment rates, it would be the hardcover book sector.

As it turned out, hardcover books exhibited great market strength in 2012, with almost unbelievable tallies: exports to the United Kingdom were up 101.4 percent, and to the Philippines up 75.2 percent. Six other nations posted higher results in 2012. Yet as more publishers trim print runs as a result of increased e-book sales, this category is likely to show a decline, and probably a stark drop, in exports around 2017. Table 12 lists the success of hardbound books between 2009 and 2012.

Two categories adversely affected by digitization are encyclopedias and serial installments (Table 13) and dictionaries (Table 14). Their results in recent years have been marginal, and sooner or later these two groups will be dropped from this analysis.

Table 12 / U.S. Exports of Hardbound Books 2009–2012: Top Ten Markets
($'000)

Country	2009	2010	2011	2012	Percent Change 2011–2012
Canada	$160,246	$176,225	$184,833	$187,960	1.7
United Kingdom	12,552	9,720	18,107	36,464	101.4
India	4,498	7,364	1,758	1,975	12.3
Australia	3,938	5,486	9,894	8,004	-19.1
Singapore	1,941	998	1,926	2,259	17.3
Japan	1,909	2,530	6,078	7,034	15.7
Mexico	1,840	1,816	2,009	592	-70.5
Philippines	1,089	1,590	870	1,524	75.2
South Korea	1,071	791	1,492	1,598	7.1
New Zealand	817	440	561	603	7.5

Source: U.S. Department of Commerce, International Trade Administration.

Table 13 / U.S. Exports of Encyclopedias and Serial Installments 2009–2012: Top Ten Markets
($'000)

Country	2009	2010	2011	2012	Percent Change 2011–2012
Canada	$1,297	$1,216	$863	$1,279	48.3
South Africa	274	163	108	149	39.0
Philippines	273	312	34	106	215.6
United Kingdom	253	59	165	161	-2.5
Australia	252	198	131	239	82.7
Taiwan	226	418	583	52	-91.1
Mexico	168	1,140	206	83	-59.7
Indonesia	123	n.a.	n.a.	n.a.	n.a.
Saudi Arabia	115	728	2,155	2,904	34.8
Korea	104	791	1,492	1,598	7.1

Source: U.S. Department of Commerce, International Trade Administration.
n.a. = not applicable

Art and pictorial books are also challenged by a growing number of innovative digital options. While exports are significant to a cluster of markets (mainly the United Kingdom, Canada, Singapore, and Mexico), it remains to be seen how much longer art titles generate enough export revenues to be part of this analysis. Table 15 outlines trends in this category.

U.S. Book Imports: 2009–2012

While U.S. book exports were under severe pressure in 2012, the import category will sustain the deepest declines in coming years because of the effect of e-book sales on print book sales. Of the eight book import categories, four posted de-

Table 14 / U.S. Exports of Dictionaries (including Thesauruses) 2009–2012:
Top Ten Markets
($'000)

Country	2009	2010	2011	2012	Percent Change 2011–2012
Canada	$589	n.a.	n.a.	n.a.	n.a.
Mexico	130	179	116	90	-22.2
Chile	114	n.a.	n.a.	n.a.	n.a.
Colombia	112	n.a.	n.a.	n.a.	n.a.
Brazil	64	0	24	10	-57.1
Costa Rica	50	12	0	61	n.a.
Peru	27	n.a.	n.a.	n.a.	n.a.
Guatemala	26	0	11	5	-51.0
United Kingdom	26	21	16	48	191.6
Singapore	21	11	11	10	-4.3

Source: U.S. Department of Commerce, International Trade Administration.
n.a. = not applicable

Table 15 / U.S. Exports of Art and Pictorial Books 2009–2012: Top Ten Markets
($'000)

Country	2009	2010	2011	2012	Percent Change 2011–2012
United Kingdom	$7,295	$6,617	$9,335	$9,679	3.5
Canada	2,731	3,534	4,179	5,072	21.4
Mexico	1,106	721	777	1,027	32.1
Netherlands	797	539	1,965	1,487	24.3
Singapore	610	733	165	241	45.8
Chile	525	n.a.	n.a.	n.a.	n.a.
Australia	391	658	2,182	2,046	-6.2
United Arab Emirates	390	211	151	165	8.8
South Korea	349	1,324	1,448	248	-82.9
Germany	236	593	688	391	-43.3

Source: U.S. Department of Commerce, International Trade Administration.
n.a. = not applicable

clines, three exhibited modest single-digit increases, and just one (mass market paperbacks) showed strong growth (up 25.7 percent). While domestic unit totals were not available when this report was being prepared, it is possible (probably likely) that much of these gains resulted from the phenomenal success of a small cluster of mass market paperback titles. Table 16 lists the categories and their results.

The textbook category saw import declines from seven trading partners, notably Hong Kong (down 56.3 percent), Mexico (down 25.5 percent), India (down 26.4 percent), Germany (down 22.3 percent), and Colombia (down 23.4 percent). China as a whole remained a major source of printed textbooks, its figures up 19.9 percent. Yet it is only a matter of time before U.S. textbook publishers move more aggressively—for economic reasons—to a mainly digital format.

Table 16 / U.S. Imports of Books: 2009–2012
($'000)

Category	2009	2010	2011	2012	Percent Change 2011–2012
Encyclopedias	$1,980	$1,261	$2,244	$2,094	-6.7
Textbooks	246,473	259,537	219,562	196,699	-10.4
Religion books	122,195	132,100	135,621	138,218	1.9
Technical, scientific, and professional	177,169	198,006	185,266	175,108	-5.5
Hardcover books	528,402	532,863	466,362	470,094	0.8
Mass market paperbacks	84,415	89,209	71,571	89,990	25.7
Art and pictorial books (valued more than $5.00)	26,394	43,816	43,535	47,780	9.8
Dictionaries and thesauruses	5,517	5,930	5,338	4,010	-24.9

Source: U.S. Department of Commerce, International Trade Administration.

According to the National Association of College Stores, which represents 4,000 U.S. college bookstores, about 35 percent of all textbooks sold in the United States are used print copies, and another 12 percent are rental printed books. Because of this, publishers are losing about 45 percent of the potential market for their titles each year, and are moving rather rapidly away from print into e-textbooks in an effort to regain those losses. In a digital textbook world, there is no printed used book or printed rental book.

For example, Philip Kotler and Kevin Keller's highly popular *Marketing Management* 14th edition (Prentice-Hall) has a suggested retail price of $241.73 for a new print copy. Coursesmart offers pdf versions of textbooks, and Coursesmart is owned by the "Big 5" textbooks companies (Prentice-Hall, Cengage, McGraw-Hill, John Wiley, and Macmillan). They are also a third-party distributor of textbooks; and all of their pdf books are under license agreements with publishers. Their pdf version of Kotler-Keller is $96.99 for a six-month rental. However, this title is also available as a used textbook from a variety of "shopbots" (online robot shopping services that offer price comparisons). Used copies are available from various Internet vendors; prices listed include shipping and handling: Abebooks.com ($28.98), Biblio.com ($29.17), and eCampus.com ($43.73). Rental copies are available from Chegg.com at $46.48 (again, including shipping and handling). An international version of the book is also available ("international" refers to a new paperback version imported into the United States). Biblio.com offers it at $29.17, Abebooks.com at $41.09. The International version is subject of a major 2013 U.S. Supreme Court case.

All of the prices listed above for used print, rental print, and the international versions are examples of dynamic pricing, which means these prices can change every second.

In the last few years, "enriched" textbooks (that is, digital books with audio and video) entered the marketplace with competitive sale prices for entire books and individual chapters. Inkling has a license agreement with textbook publishers, and Pearson PLC (the parent company of Prentice-Hall) and McGraw-Hill have invested in Inkling. Kotler-Keller's *Marketing Management* has a suggested

Inkling retail price of $159.99, but Inkling offers individual chapters for sale for $7.99.

Business administration/accounting/economics is the largest textbook category, accounting for between 18 percent and 21 percent of all textbooks sold. Inkling offers a number of enriched textbooks in this diverse category: 4 titles in accounting, 5 in business statistics, 25 in finance, 4 in financial accounting, 2 in information systems, 4 in international business, 6 in microeconomics, 16 in management, 14 in marketing, 3 in negotiation, 16 in operations management, 8 in organization behavior, 2 in strategy, and 7 in other categories.

The textbook sector's move toward digital texts will transform this book category, generating significantly better margins (about 52 percent) than those for print books (about 23 percent). The impact on companies involved in printing, paper, and binding printed texts will be severe.

Table 17 outlines the countries providing textbooks for the U.S. market.

Table 17 / U.S. Imports of Textbooks 2009–2012: Top Ten Markets
($'000)

Country	2009	2010	2011	2012	Percent Change 2011–2012
Canada	$68,651	$53,666	$46,109	$45,291	-1.8
United Kingdom	57,547	55,071	61,809	48,089	-22.2
China	54,253	71,984	38,153	45,751	19.9
Hong Kong	16,823	27,657	23,155	10,127	-56.3
Singapore	10,309	10,377	7,365	10,138	37.7
United Arab Emirates	3,940	3,178	3,844	4,016	4.5
Mexico	3,678	2,854	4,589	3,420	-25.5
India	2,920	3,808	4,455	3,278	-26.4
Colombia	2,696	4,161	4,385	3,361	-23.4
Germany	2,689	2,285	2,342	1,821	-22.3

Source: U.S. Department of Commerce, International Trade Administration.

Table 18 / U.S. Imports of Bibles, Testaments, Prayer Books, and Other Religion Books 2009–2012: Top Ten Markets
($'000)

Country	2009	2010	2011	2012	Percent Change 2011–2012
China	$37,174	$47,967	$59,939	$63,820	6.5
Colombia	19,896	20,232	15,199	12,280	-19.2
South Korea	19,343	19,427	19,199	21,062	9.7
Israel	9,402	9,913	8,515	7,991	-6.5
Canada	4,910	3,607	2,846	1,456	-48.0
United Kingdom	3,994	2,578	3,428	4,057	18.3
Spain	3,644	2,604	4,089	2,716	-33.0
Mexico	2,797	2,901	1,601	2,590	61.8
Italy	2,647	1,355	4,939	4,423	-10.4
Hong Kong	2,440	3,157	1,234	1,955	58.4

Source: U.S. Department of Commerce, International Trade Administration.

While religion books also posted uneven results (Table 18), with imports from five nations reporting declines between 2011 and 2012 (Canada down 48 percent, Colombia 19.2 percent, Spain 33 percent, Italy 10.4 percent, and Israel 6.5 percent), technical, scientific, and professional books, hardcover books, and mass market paperback books again mirrored the steep declines in the textbook category.

The technical, scientific, and professional category saw imports from seven nations decrease in 2012; for example, Hong Kong was down 13.0 percent, India 48.8 percent, Singapore 25.6 percent, and Mexico 47.4 percent. Because a number of global publishers are active in this sector (among them Elsevier, Kluwer, Sage, Wiley, Informa, Springer, Pearson, and McGraw-Hill), and because many of these firms moved into digital journals a number of years ago, books in this category will move as aggressively as textbooks away from print into digital.

Table 19 / U.S. Imports of Technical, Scientific, and Professional Books 2009–2012: Top Ten Markets
($'000)

Country	2009	2010	2011	2012	Percent Change 2011–2012
China	$33,721	$34,393	$36,824	$49,489	34.4
Japan	28,403	39,002	16,862	18,034	6.9
Germany	26,291	17,630	17,820	11,474	-35.6
Canada	24,144	27,399	25,097	23,713	-5.5
United Kingdom	22,653	30,414	25,314	21,749	-14.1
Hong Kong	7,805	2,495	3,441	2,993	-13.0
India	5,898	7,935	15,047	7,708	-48.8
Singapore	5,710	6,109	7,451	5,537	-25.6
Mexico	4,357	9,918	11,738	6,173	-47.4
France	3,566	3,353	3,451	3,959	14.7

Source: U.S. Department of Commerce, International Trade Administration.

In hardcover books, five nations saw declines in shipments to the United States, paced by Singapore (down 23.22 percent) and Hong Kong (down 27.7 percent). China reported a small increase of 3.4 percent, and South Korea was up 4.6 percent. Some generated robust results: the United Kingdom was up 58 percent, Germany 30.5 percent, and France 15.4 percent. See Table 20.

Although China achieved an impressive 63.5 percent surge in the value of mass market paperback books sent to the United States, this book category showed increasing vulnerability in 2012. Seven nations' U.S. exports figures were down, with small declines for Hong Kong (4.4 percent) and Japan (1.6 percent). Singapore's decline hovered near the 12.4 percent mark, slightly better than the results for the United Kingdom, which was down 19.2 percent. Spain's slippage was huge: 85.5 percent. Table 21 illustrates these developments.

Encyclopedias and serial installments (Table 22) and dictionaries and thesauruses (Table 23) were marginal book categories at best during the past few years, and lackluster performances are likely in the next few years. Art and pictorial books, while under pressure because of competing digital products, are likely to continue to exhibit some market resiliency. Italy dominates all revenues with $13.6 million, eclipsing the United Kingdom's $11.2 million. Germany's $7.4 mil-

Table 20 / U.S. Imports of Hardbound Books 2009–2012: Top Ten Markets
($'000)

Country	2009	2010	2011	2012	Percent Change 2011–2012
China	$312,453	$346,284	$293,195	$303,043	3.4
Singapore	42,250	33,108	26,004	19,964	-23.2
United Kingdom	36,712	38,462	28,977	45,777	58.0
Hong Kong	23,405	14,824	18,034	13,031	-27.7
Canada	21,647	19,004	19,374	14,433	-25.5
Italy	19,971	20,769	26,713	23,842	-10.7
Spain	10,628	9,352	7,810	5,418	-30.6
Germany	9,131	7,713	7,291	9,516	30.5
France	7,294	4,524	5,651	6,524	15.4
South Korea	6,329	2,841	2,324	2,433	4.6

Source: U.S. Department of Commerce, International Trade Administration.

Table 21 / U.S. Imports of Mass Market Paperbacks (Rack Size) 2009–2012: Top Ten Markets
($'000)

Country	2009	2010	2011	2012	Percent Change 2011–2012
China	$24,503	$46,139	$32,832	$53,686	63.5
Canada	21,021	15,879	12,761	11,723	-8.1
United Kingdom	18,716	7,854	8,311	6,716	-19.2
Hong Kong	4,418	2,571	2,689	2,568	-4.4
Italy	3,528	4,000	942	1,429	51.6
Singapore	3,498	4,218	3,433	3,006	-12.4
Spain	2,178	2,195	2,922	1,575	-85.5
Japan	1,146	548	672	661	-1.6
Malaysia	684	783	1,973	3,276	66.0
Germany	636	477	333	1,455	333.9

Source: U.S. Department of Commerce, International Trade Administration

Table 22 / U.S. Imports of Encyclopedias and Serial Installments 2009–2012: Top Ten Markets
($'000)

Country	2009	2010	2011	2012	Percent Change 2011–2012
Mexico	$460	$296	$214	$253	18.2
Singapore	280	263	0	570	n.a.
China	279	301	1,436	754	-47.5
Taiwan	264	0	0	0	0.0
United Arab Emirates	233	154	266	185	-30.5
Germany	105	n.a.	n.a.	n.a.	n.a.
Hong Kong	84	0	4	29	625.0
United Kingdom	83	41	79	69	-14.5
Canada	76	0	4	29	625.0
Netherlands	32	n.a.	n.a.	n.a.	n.a.

Source: U.S. Department of Commerce, International Trade Administration.
n.a. = not applicable

lion and China's $6.6 million rounded out the top four in 2012. The declines of Hong Kong (down 36 percent) and Spain (down 57.4 percent) were noteworthy. See Table 24.

Table 23 / U.S. Imports of Dictionaries and Thesauruses 2009–2012:
Top Ten Markets
($'000)

Country	2009	2010	2011	2012	Percent Change 2011–2012
China	$1,377	$1,464	$943	$737	-21.8
United Kingdom	1,362	1,363	1,144	837	-26.8
Italy	516	n.a.	n.a.	n.a.	n.a.
France	445	176	821	45	-94.5
Spain	378	104	189	208	10.1
Canada	220	103	97	37	-61.9
India	142	89	192	166	-13.5
Colombia	140	121	164	151	-7.9
United Arab Emirates	87	202	172	117	-31.9

Source: U.S. Department of Commerce, International Trade Administration.
n.a. = not applicable

Table 24 / U.S. Imports of Art and Pictorial Books 2009–2012
Valued $5 or More Each: Top Ten Markets
($'000)

Country	2009	2010	2011	2012	Percent Change 2011–2012
Germany	$5,927	$8,875	$10,557	$7,424	-29.7
China	4,766	5,640	4,996	6,624	24.6
United Kingdom	4,567	6,217	7,752	11,151	43.8
Italy	3,768	12,980	11,624	13,589	16.9
Hong Kong	2,063	1,680	1,029	659	-36.0
Singapore	925	1,801	729	1,056	44.9
Netherlands	552	896	1,007	947	-6.0
France	535	1,475	1,795	2,653	47.8
Spain	496	621	1,576	671	-57.4
Canada	479	384	123	287	128.5

Source: U.S. Department of Commerce, International Trade Administration.

Conclusion

The acceptance of e-readers and e-books in the United States has been well publicized. Printed books will not disappear in the coming years and decades—there just will be fewer of them published and sold. But a review of the available data indicates conclusively that this change from print to digital will produce winners and losers in the marketplace.

The winners will include

- Publishers able to produce high-profit e-books while reducing, if not eliminating, the impact of the used and rental printed book market
- Authors who can share in the anticipated financial rewards because their books will be available only as digital books
- Agents, whose share of an author's royalties will increase to perhaps 20 percent or more
- Retailers selling e-books
- Owners and stockholders of publishing firms, because content will remain "king" and content will be monetized by publishers able to supply a steady supply of popular or high-impact titles

On the losing side, export revenues ultimately will sag. Companies dependent on exports will suffer some financial reversals, although these should be relatively modest for the foreseeable future. The real losers will be:

- Companies in developing nations involved in the printing, paper, and binding operations of books sent to the United States
- Shipping companies in developing nations transporting those books
- U.S.-based transportation companies moving shipments of books from dockside to a distribution warehouse
- People shipping books to retailers and distributors and handling returns
- Surety bond companies writing policies for books imported into the United States

How severe will the loss of books sent to the United States be for printers, binders, etc., in developing nations? (The term "developing nations" is based on definitions used by the World Bank, UNESCO, and the International Monetary Fund; see Greco 2012a; pages 2–3.)

Using the statistics found in the import tables above, the authors prepared a list of book categories (textbooks, professional, hardbound, mass market paperbacks, and art books) likely to go digital in the next few years, with data on the dollar revenues in 2012 for certain developing nations. For example, China's total exposure in these categories is $458.59 million, Hong Kong's $29.38 million, Singapore's $39.7 million, India's $10.99 million, and Mexico's $9.59 million. While print will not disappear in the short term, some erosion in the export revenues of certain companies in the developing nations is inevitable, especially in the textbook and hardcover book categories.

In addition to Porter and Christensen, three other scholars wrote extensively about the problems certain nations will face as the U.S. market for their printed books begins to decline. Levitt (2004) remarked that many companies declined as technology advanced because they defined themselves too narrowly. He insisted that to continue growing, companies must: (a) determine and act on their customers' wants and needs and desires; and (b) not assume on the longevity of their product(s). He wrote that U.S. railroads ended up in trouble not because the need for passengers and freight transportation declined; they suffered through decades of economic problems because they were not filling this need. Railroads thought they were in the railroad business when they were really in the transportation business, and they allowed other forms of transportation to take their customers away. They were, unfortunately, product-oriented and not market-oriented.

Hayes and Abernathy (1980) wrote that success in most industries today requires an organizational commitment to compete in the marketplace on technological grounds—that is, to compete over the long run by offering superior products. The key to long-term success—even survival—in business is what it has always been: to invest, to innovate, to lead, and to create value where none existed before.

Levitt and Hayes and Abernathy were correct. Certain printing and binding production firms in developing nations must re-evaluate their "product"-oriented strategies and adopt market-based strategies able to succeed in the changing marketplace. While the future does look very attractive for firms able to harness digital-book technologies (for example, digital typesetting companies in India) and thus effectively becoming technology companies, some printing and binding firms will languish.

Creative managers must craft intelligent plans in a constantly changing business environment in order to manage in what are, clearly, turbulent times. But the inevitable question is whether companies in developing nations have the time and the financial and human resources needed to develop effective strategies and plans. As boxing champion Mike Tyson once said, "Everyone has a plan until they get hit."

References

Anderson, Patricia. "Imports, Exports, and Jobs: What Does Trade Mean for Employment and Job Loss?" (review of Kletzer 2002), *Relations Industrielles* 59:2 (Spring 2004), 423–424.

Caves, Richard E. *Creative Industries: Contracts Between Art and Commerce.* (Harvard University Press, 2000).

Chacholiades, Miltiades. "Balance of Trade Equilibrium with Imports as a Factor of Production," *Oxford Economic Papers* 22:2 (July 1970), 173.

Christensen, Clayton M. *The Innovator's Dilemma* (HarperCollins, 2000).

Coser, Lewis A., Charles Kadushin, and Walter W. Powell. *Books: The Culture and Commerce of Publishing.* (University of Chicago Press, 1985).

Greco, Albert N. "A Bibliography of Books and Journal Articles on Scholarly Publishing;" *Journal of Scholarly Publishing* 37:1(October 2005), 48–54.

Greco, Albert N., ed. *Essential JSP: Critical Insights into the World of Scholarly Publishing: Vol. 3 Scholarly Journals: Print, Digital, Open Access, and Search Engines* (University of Toronto Press; 2012a).

———. *Essential JSP: Critical Insights into the World of Scholarly Publishing: Vol. 2 Scholarly Publishing in Emerging Nations* (University of Toronto Press; 2012b).

————. *Essential JSP: Critical Insights into the World of Scholarly Publishing: Vol. 1 University Presses* (University of Toronto Press 2011).

Greco, Albert N., Hooman Estelami, Robert Wharton, and Robert Jones. "The Changing College and University Library Market for Non-Profit University Press Books and Journals: 1997–2005," *Journal of Scholarly Publishing* 39:1 (October 2007), 1–32.

Greco, Albert N., Jim Milliot, and Robert M. Wharton. *The Book Publishing Industry,* 3rd ed. (Routledge, 2013; in press).

Hall, James W. *Hit Lit: Cracking the Code of the Twentieth Century's Biggest Bestsellers* (Random, 2012).

Hayes, Robert H., and William J. Abernathy. "Managing Our Way to Economic Decline." *Harvard Business Review* 58 (July–August 1980), 67–77.

Kaplan, Steven N., Berk A. Sensoy, and Peter Stromberg. "Should Investors Bet on the Jockey or the Horse? Evidence from the Evolution of Firms from Early Business Plans to Public Companies," *Journal of Finance* LXIV:1 (February 2009), 75–115.

Keh, Hean Tat. "Evolution of the Book Publishing Industry: Structural Changes and Strategic Implications," *Journal of Management History* 4:2 (1998), 104.

Kletzer, Lori G. *Imports, Exports, and Jobs: What Does Trade Mean for Employment and Job Loss?* (W. E. Upjohn Institute for Employment Research, 2002).

Krause, Lawrence B. "United States Imports, 1947–1958," *Econometrica* 30:2 (April 1962), 221.

Lane, Julia. "Imports, Exports and Jobs: What Does Trade Mean for Employment and Job Loss?" (review of Kletzer 2002), *Journal of Regional Science* 44:2 (May 2004), 372–373.

Leichenko, Robin M. "Exports, Employment, and Production: A Casual Assessment of U.S. States and Regions," *Economic Geography* 76:4 (October 2000), 303–325.

Levitt, Ted. "Marketing Myopia," *Harvard Business Review* 82:7/8 (July 2004), 138–149.

Nissan, Edward, and Farhand Nicoomand. "Geographic and Income Anatomy of International Exports," *Journal of Economic Studies* 36:1 (2009), 5–16.

O'Loughlin, John, and Luc Anselin. "Geo-Economic Competition and Trade Bloc Formation: United States, Germany, and Japanese Exports, 1968–1992," *Economic Geography* 72:2 (April 1996), 131.

Porter, Michael E. *Competitive Advantage: Creating and Sustaining Superior Performance* (Free Press, 1999).

————. *Competitive Strategy: Techniques for Analyzing Industries and Competitors.* (Free Press, 1980).

————. *On Competition* (Harvard Business Review Book Series, 1996).

————. "The Five Competitive Forces that Shape Strategy," *Harvard Business Review* 86:1 (January 2008), 78–93.

Rai, Rajnish Kumar, and Srinath Jagannathan. "Parallel Imports and Unparallel Laws: Does the WTO Need to Harmonize the Parallel Import Law?" *Journal of World Trade* 46:3 (June 2012), 657–694.

Sirgy, M. Joseph, Lee Dong-Jin, Chad Miller, James E. Littlefield, and Eda Gurel Atay. "The Impact of Imports and Exports on a Country's Quality of Life," *Social Indicators Research* 83:2 (September 2007), 245.

Throsby, David. *Economics and Culture* (Cambridge University Press, 2001).

Vignarajah, Krishanti. "Reconciling Free Trade and Safe Trade: New Paradigms for Regulating Imports in the Twenty-First Century," *Journal of World Trade* 43:4 (August 2009), 771–795.

Notes

For this article, the authors excluded all data for "printed matter" (a) less than 4 pages long; (b) 5 to 48 pages long; and (c) more than 49 pages long. This was done because they were unable to ascertain the type of book categories for these printed matter exports and imports. New calculations were undertaken for the years 2002 to 2009 to reflect this change, and this affected the export and import totals listed in this 58th edition of the *Library and Book Trade Almanac,* which differ from previous totals in earlier editions of the book. Note that: (1) the terms "professional," "technical, scientific, and professional," and "professional and scholarly professional" were used interchangeably in this article; (2) ITA aggregated university press books into the "technical, scientific, and professional" category; and (3) revenues for the exportation or importation of digital e-books were not available at the time the article was prepared, and it is difficult to say when, or even if, e-book revenue totals will be available from ITA in coming years. However, for this article, the authors developed statistical models for e-book U.S. publisher revenues in various book categories, and it is likely that some of these revenues were the result of the exportation of certain e-books. Again, it is impossible to ascertain with any precision the percentage of revenues from exported e-books because publishers have yet to release these totals.

Number of Book Outlets
in the United States and Canada

The *American Book Trade Directory* (Information Today, Inc.) has been published since 1915. Revised annually, it features lists of booksellers, wholesalers, periodicals, reference tools, and other information about the U.S. and Canadian book markets. The data shown in Table 1, the most current available, are from the 2013–2014 edition of the directory.

The 16,520 stores of various types shown are located throughout the United States, Canada, and regions administered by the United States. "General" bookstores stock trade books and children's books in a general variety of subjects. "College" stores carry college-level textbooks. "Educational" outlets handle school textbooks up to and including the high school level. "Mail order" outlets sell general trade books by mail and are not book clubs; all others operating by mail are classified according to the kinds of books carried. "Antiquarian" dealers sell old and rare books. Stores handling secondhand books are classified as "used." "Paperback" stores have more than 80 percent of their stock in paperbound books. Stores with paperback departments are listed under the appropriate major classification ("general," "department store," "stationer," and so forth). Bookstores with at least 50 percent of their stock on a particular subject are classified by subject.

Table 1 / Bookstores in the United States and Canada, 2012

Category	United States	Canada
Antiquarian General	632	57
Antiquarian Mail Order	246	7
Antiquarian Specialized	118	4
Art Supply Store	60	2
College General	2,968	139
College Specialized	109	5
Comics	201	27
Computer Software	2	0
Cooking	267	10
Department Store	1,520	9
Educational*	176	33
Federal Sites†	231	1
Foreign Language*	16	2
General	2,601	521
Gift Shop	121	6
Juvenile*	82	16
Mail Order General	68	6
Mail Order Specialized	298	13
Metaphysics, New Age, and Occult	128	18
Museum Store and Art Gallery	472	30
Nature and Natural History	37	4
Newsdealer	22	2
Office Supply	10	1
Other‡	2,375	424
Paperback§	59	3

Table 1 / Bookstores in the United States and Canada, 2012 *(cont.)*

Category	United States	Canada
Religious*	1,558	135
Self Help/Development	18	5
Stationer	3	3
Toy Store	40	20
Used*	501	78
Totals	14,939	1,581

* Includes Mail Order Shops for this topic, which are not counted elsewhere in this survey.

† National Historic Sites, National Monuments, and National Parks.

‡ Stores specializing in subjects or services other than those covered in this survey.

§ Includes Mail Order. Excludes used paperback bookstores, stationers, drugstores, or wholesalers handling paperbacks.

Review Media Statistics

Compiled by the staff of the *Library and Book Trade Almanac*

Number of Books and Other Media Reviewed by Major Reviewing Publications 2011–2012

	Adult		Juvenile		Young Adult		Total	
	2011	2012	2011	2012	2011	2012	2011	2012
Booklist[1]	4,479	n.a.	3,499	n.a.	—	—	7,978	n.a.
Bookmarks	711	709	—	—	16	22	727	731
BookPage[2]	653	576	116	74	59	32	828	682
Bulletin of the Center for Children's Books[3]	—	—	n.a.	n.a.	—	—	n.a.	n.a.
Chicago Sun Times	n.a.	n.a.	n.a.	n.a.	—	—	n.a.	n.a.
Chicago Tribune Sunday Book Section[4]	260	1,460	240	320	—	—	500	1,780
Choice[5]	6,833	6,817	—	—	—	—	6,833	6,817
Horn Book Guide	—	—	3,155	3,257	1,111	949	4,266	4,206
Horn Book Magazine[6]	5	—	351	357	126	183	482	540
Kirkus Reviews[4]	3,231	3,846	2,966	3,082	—	—	6,197	7,178
Library Journal[7]	6,590	5,447	—	—	—	—	6,590	5,447
Los Angeles Times	n.a.	n.a.	—	—	—	—	n.a.	n.a.
Multicultural Review[8]	n.a.	n.a.	n.a.	n.a.	n.a.	n.a.	n.a.	n.a.
New York Journal of Books[9]	1,192	1,257	120	100	60	80	1,372	1,437
New York Review of Books[10]	n.a.	n.a.	—	—	—	—	n.a.	n.a.
New York Times Sunday Book Review	n.a.	n.a.	n.a.	n.a.	—	—	n.a.	n.a.
Publishers Weekly[11]	6,131	7,319	1,704	1,819	—	—	7,835	9,138
School Library Journal[4]	220	200	5,999	5,600	—	—	6,219	5,800
Washington Post Book World	1,100	1,100	36	36	—	—	1,136	1,136

n.a. = not available

1 All figures are for a 12-month period from September 1, 2010, to August 31, 2011 (vol. 107). YA books are included in the juvenile total.

2 *BookPage* also published 37 audio reviews. In addition, it published 183 online-only reviews, of which 91 were of adult, 51 juvenile, and 41 young adult works. The grand total of reviews for the year was 888.

3 All figures are for a 12-month period beginning September and ending July/August. YA books are included in the juvenile total.

4 YA books are included in the juvenile total.

5 All materials reviewed in *Choice* are scholarly publications intended for undergraduate libraries. *Choice* also reviewed 413 Internet sites and 1 DVD.

6 *Horn Book Magazine* also reviewed 15 audiobooks.

7 In addition, *Library Journal* reviewed 362 audiobooks; 70 databases; 363 DVDs/videos; 197 books and 63 DVDs in Collection Development; 96 online databases; and previewed 1,385 books in "Prepub Alert."

8 *MultiCultural Review* suspended publication late in 2010, and publication had not resumed in 2012.

9 *New York Journal of Books*, which began publication in 2010, is online only.

10 *New York Review of Books* in 2010 published 280 articles dealing directly with books or other media. These articles treated a cumulative 435 individual items, of which 10 were films, 2 operas, 2 television series, 3 plays, and 24 art exhibitions. The remainder (394) were adult books. Figures for 2011 and 2012 were unavailable.

11 Of the total of 9,138 reviews, 1,351 were online only. A total of 350 audiobooks are included in *Publishers Weekly*'s total count.

Part 5
Reference Information

Bibliographies

The Librarian's Bookshelf

Karen Muller
Librarian, American Library Association

Most of the books on this selective bibliography have been published since 2009; a few earlier titles are retained because of their continuing importance. Many are also available as e-books.

General

American Library Directory, 2012–2013. Information Today, Inc., 2012. Print and online.

Annual Review of Information Science and Technology (ARIST). Ed. by Blaise Cronin. Information Today, Inc., 2011.

The Atlas of New Librarianship. By R. David Lankes. MIT Press, 2011.

Books: A Living History. By Martyn Lyons. J. Paul Getty Museum, 2011.

Encyclopedia of Library and Information Science, 3rd ed. Ed. by Miriam A. Drake. CRC, 2009. Print and online.

The Library: An Illustrated History. By Stuart A. P. Murray. Skyhorse, 2009.

Library and Book Trade Almanac, 58th ed. Ed. by Dave Bogart. Information Today, Inc., 2013.

Library and Information Science Source. EBSCO Publishing. Online database.

Library Literature and Information Science Full Text, 1984–. EBSCO Publishing (formerly H. W. Wilson). Online database.

Library Literature and Information Science Retrospective: 1905–1983. EBSCO Publishing (formerly H. W. Wilson). Online database.

Library World Records, 2nd ed. By Godfrey Oswald. McFarland, 2009.

Library, Information Science & Technology Abstracts (LISTA). EBSCO Publishing. Online database.

Library, Information Science & Technology Abstracts with Full Text. EBSCO Publishing. Online database.

The Oxford Guide to Library Research, 3rd ed. By Thomas Mann. Oxford University Press, 2005.

The Whole Library Handbook 5: Current Data, Professional Advice, and Curiosa. Ed. by George Eberhart. American Library Association, 2013.

Academic Libraries

A Field Guide to the Information Commons. By Charles Forrest and Martin Halbert. Scarecrow, 2009.

Academic Librarianship. By Camila A. Alire and G. Edward Evans. Neal-Schuman, 2010.

Building Bridges: Connecting Faculty, Students, and the College Library. By Monty L. McAdoo. American Library Association, 2010.

The Changing Academic Library: Operations, Culture, Environments, 2nd ed. By John M. Budd. Association of College and Research Libraries, 2012.

Embedded Librarians: Moving Beyond One-shot Instruction. Ed. by Cassandra Kvenild and Kaijsa Calkins. Association of College and Research Libraries, 2011.

The Expert Library: Staffing, Sustaining, and Advancing the Academic Library in the 21st Century. Ed. by Scott Walter and Karen Williams. Association of College and Research Libraries, 2010.

Managing the Small College Library. By Rachel Applegate. Libraries Unlimited, 2010.

Administration

Balancing the Books: Accounting for Librarians. By Rachel A. Kirk. Libraries Unlimited, 2013.

The Complete Library Trustee Handbook. By Sally Gardner Reed and Jillian Kolonick. Neal-Schuman, 2010.

Convergence of Project Management and Knowledge Management. Ed. by T. Kanti Srikantaiah, Michael E. D. Koenig, and Suliman Hawamdeh. Scarecrow, 2010.

The Digital Librarian's Legal Handbook. By John N. Gathegi. Neal-Schuman, 2012.

Greening Libraries. Ed. by Monika Antonelli and Mark McCullough. Library Juice, 2012.

How to Thrive as a Solo Librarian. Ed. by Carol Smallwood and Melissa J. Clapp. Scarecrow, 2012.

Implementing for Results: Your Strategic Plan in Action. By Sandra Nelson. American Library Association, 2009.

Joint Libraries: Models that Work. By Claire B. Gunnels, Susan E. Green, and Patricia M. Butler. American Library Association, 2012.

Library and Information Center Management, 8th ed. By Barbara B. Moran, Robert D. Stueart, and Claudia J. Morner. Libraries Unlimited, 2013.

Managing in the Middle: The Librarian's Handbook Ed. by Robert Farrell and Kenneth Schlesinger. ALA Editions, 2013.

Moving Materials: Physical Delivery in Libraries. Ed. by Valerie Horton and Bruce Smith. American Library Association, 2010.

New Planning for Results: A Streamlined Approach. By Sandra Nelson. Public Library Association, 2001.

Strategic Planning for Results. By Sandra Nelson. American Library Association, 2008.

Advocacy and Funding

Advocacy, Outreach and the Nation's Academic Libraries: A Call for Action. Ed. by William C. Welburn, Janice Welburn, and Beth McNeil. Association of College and Research Libraries, 2010.

Activism and the School Librarian: Tools for Advocacy and Survival. Ed. by Deborah D. Levitov. Libraries Unlimited, 2012.

ALA Book of Library Grant Money, 8th ed. American Library Association, 2012.

A Book Sale How-to Guide: More Money, Less Stress. By Pat Ditzler and JoAnn Dumas. American Library Association. 2012.

From Awareness to Funding: A Study of Library Support in America. OCLC, 2008.

Grassroots Library Advocacy: A Special Report. By Lauren Comito, Aliqae Geraci, and Christian Zabriskie. American Library Association, 2012.

Inside, Outside, and Online: Building Your Library Community. By Chrystie Hill. American Library Association, 2009.

Librarian's Handbook for Seeking, Writing, and Managing Grants. By Sylvia D. Hall-Ellis, Stacey L. Bowers, Christopher Hudson, Claire Williamson, and Joanne Patrick. Libraries Unlimited, 2011.

Archives and Special Collections

Academic Archives: Managing the Next Generation of College and University Archives, Records, and Special Collections. By Aaron D. Purcell. Neal-Schuman, 2012.

Archives: Principles and Practices. By Laura A. Millar. Neal-Schuman, 2010.

Rare Book Librarianship: An Introduction and Guide. By Steven K Galbraith and Geoffrey D. Smith. Libraries Unlimited, 2012.

Special Collections 2.0: New Technologies for Rare Books, Manuscripts, and Archival Collections. By Beth M. Whittaker and Lynne M. Thomas. Libraries Unlimited, 2009.

Starting, Strengthening, and Managing Institutional Repositories: A How-to-Do-It Manual. By Jonathan A. Nabe. Neal-Schuman, 2010.

Buildings and Space Planning

The Academic Library Building in the Digital Age: A Study of Construction, Planning, and Design of New Library Space. By Christopher Stewart. Association of College and Research Libraries, 2010.

Building Blocks for Planning Functional Library Space, 3rd ed. By the Library Leadership and Management Association. Scarecrow, 2011.

Building Science 101: A Primer for Librarians. By Lynn M. Piotrowicz and Scott Osgood. American Library Association, 2010.

Countdown to a New Library: Managing the Building Project, 2nd ed. By Jeannette Woodward. American Library Association, 2010.

Moving Your Library: Getting the Collection from Here to There. By Steven Carl Fortriede. American Library Association, 2010.

Planning Academic and Research Library Buildings, 3rd ed. By Philip D. Leighton and David C. Weber. American Library Association, 1999.

Teen Spaces: The Step-by-Step Library Makeover, 2nd ed. By Kimberly Bolan. American Library Association, 2009.

Cataloging and Bibliographic Control

Cataloging Correctly for Kids: An Introduction to the Tools, 5th ed. By Sheila S. Intner and Joanna F. Fountain. American Library Association, 2011.

Describing Electronic, Digital, and Other Media Using AACR2 and RDA. By Mary Beth Weber and Fay Austin. Neal-Schuman, 2010.

FRBR: A Guide for the Perplexed. By Robert L. Maxwell. American Library Association, 2008.

Information Resource Description: Creating and Managing Metadata. By Philip Hider. ALA Editions, 2013.

The Library Catalogue as Social Space. By Laurel Tarulli. Libraries Unlimited, 2012.

The Organization of Information, 3rd ed. By Arlene G. Taylor and Daniel N. Joudrey. Libraries Unlimited, 2009.

RDA and Serials Cataloging. By Ed Jones. ALA Editions, 2013.

RDA Toolkit. Joint Steering Committee for Development of RDA (JSC). American Library Association, 2011–.

RDA: Resource Description and Access Print Joint Steering Committee for Development of RDA (JSC). American Library Association, 2011–.

RDA: Strategies for Implementation. By Magda El-Sherbini. ALA Editions, 2013.

Structures for Organizing Knowledge: Exploring Taxonomies, Ontologies, and Other Schemas. By June Abbas. Neal-Schuman, 2010.

Children's and Young Adult Services and Materials

Children's Services: Partnerships for Success. Ed. by Betsy Diamant-Cohen. American Library Association, 2010.

The Coretta Scott King Awards, 1970–2009, 4th ed. Ed. by Henrietta M. Smith, the Ethnic and Multicultural Information Exchange Round Table, and the Coretta Scott King Book Awards Committee. American Library Association, 2009.

Crash Course in Library Services to Preschool Children. By Betsy Diamant-Cohen. Libraries Unlimited, 2010.

In the Words of the Winners: The Newbery and Caldecott Medals, 2001–2010. By the Association for Library Service to Children and the *Horn Book.* American Library Association, 2011.

Integrating Young Adult Literature through the Common Core Standards. By Rachel L. Wadham and Jonathan W. Ostenson. Libraries Unlimited, 2013.

Managing Children's Services in Libraries, 4th ed. By Adele M. Fasick and Leslie Edmonds Holt. Libraries Unlimited, 2013.

More Than MySpace: Teens, Librarians, and Social Networking. Ed. by Robyn M. Lupa. Libraries Unlimited, 2009.

The Newbery and Caldecott Awards 2013: A Guide to the Medal and Honor Books. Association for Library Service to Children/ American Library Association, 2013.

Risky Business: Taking and Managing Risks in Library Services for Teens. By Linda W.

Braun, Hillias J. Martin, and Connie Urquhart. American Library Association, 2010.

Serving Urban Teens. By Paula Brehm-Heeger. Libraries Unlimited, 2008.

Young Adults Deserve the Best: YALSA's Competencies in Action. By Sarah Flowers. American Library Association, 2010.

Collection Development

Choice's Outstanding Academic Titles, 2007–2011. Ed. by Rebecca Ann Bartlett. Association of College and Research Libraries, 2012.

Collection Management Basics, 6th ed. By G. Edward Evans and Margaret Zarnosky Saponaro. Libraries Unlimited, 2013.

The Collection Program in Schools: Concepts and Practices, 5th ed. By Kay Bishop. Libraries Unlimited, 2012.

Developing an Outstanding Core Collection. By Carol Alabaster. American Library Association, 2010.

Fundamentals of Collection Development and Management, 2nd ed. By Peggy Johnson. American Library Association, 2009.

Guide to Implementing and Managing Patron-Driven Acquisitions. By Suzanne M. Ward. Association for Library Collections and Technical Services, 2012.

The Kovacs Guide to Electronic Library Collection Development, 2nd ed. By Diane K. Kovacs. Neal-Schuman, 2009.

Copyright

Complete Copyright for K–12 Librarians and Educators. By Carrie Russell. American Library Association, 2012.

Copyright Law for Librarians and Educators: Creative Strategies and Practical Solutions, 3rd ed. By Kenneth D. Crews. American Library Association, 2012.

Copyright Questions and Answers for Information Professionals: From the Columns of Against the Grain. By Laura N. Gasaway. Purdue University Press, 2013.

Licensing Digital Content: A Practical Guide for Librarians, 2nd ed. By Lesley Ellen Harris. American Library Association, 2009.

Digital Libraries

Digital Library Futures: User Perspectives and Institutional Strategies. Ed. by Ingeborg Verheul, Anna Maria Tammaro, and Steve Witt. De Gruyter Saur, 2009.

Digitization in the Real World: Lessons Learned from Small and Medium-Sized Digitization Projects. Ed. by Kwong Bor Ng and Jason Kucsma. Metropolitan New York Library Council, 2010.

No Shelf Required: E-Books in Libraries. By Sue Polanka. American Library Association, 2011.

No Shelf Required 2: Use and Management of Electronic Books. By Sue Polanka. American Library Association, 2012.

History

Books, Bluster, and Bounty: Local Politics and Carnegie Library Building Grants in the Intermountain West, 1890–1920. By Susan H. Swetnam. Utah State University Press, 2012.

The Great Depression: Its Impact on Forty-six Large American Public Libraries: an Inquiry Based on a Content Analysis of Published Writings of their Directors. By Robert Scott Kramp. Library Juice, 2010.

Main Street Public Library. By Wayne Wiegand. University of Iowa Press, 2011.

The MLS Project: An Assessment After Sixty Years. By Boyd Keith Swigger. Scarecrow, 2010.

Reading Places: Literacy, Democracy, and the Public Library in the Cold War. By Christine Pawley. University of Massachusetts Press, 2010.

Right Here I See My Own Books: The Woman's Building Library at the World's Columbian Exposition. By Wayne A. Wiegand and Sarah Wadsworth. University of Massachusetts Press, 2012.

Human Resources and Leadership

Being Indispensable: A School Librarian's Guide to Becoming an Invaluable Leader.

By Ruth Toor and Hilda K. Weisburg. American Library Association, 2011.

Coaching in the Library: a Management Strategy for Achieving Excellence, 2nd ed. By Ruth F. Metz. American Library Association, 2011.

Fundamentals of Library Supervision. By Joan Giesecke and Beth McNeil. American Library Association, 2010.

Hiring, Training, and Supervising Library Shelvers. By Patricia Tunstall. American Library Association, 2010.

Interpersonal Skills, Theory, and Practice: The Librarian's Guide to Becoming a Leader. By Brooke E. Sheldon. Libraries Unlimited, 2010.

'Leading from the Middle' and Other Contrarian Essays on Library Leadership. By John Lubans, Jr. Libraries Unlimited, 2010.

Managing Library Volunteers. By Preston Driggers and Eileen Dumas. American Library Association, 2011.

Personal Learning Networks: Professional Development for the Isolated School Librarian. By Mary Ann Harlan. Libraries Unlimited, 2009.

Shaping the Future: Advancing the Understanding of Leadership. Ed. by Peter Hernon. Libraries Unlimited, 2010.

Staff Development: A Practical Guide, 4th ed. Ed. by Andrea Wigbels Stewart, Carlette Washington-Hoagland, and Carol T. Zsulya. ALA Editions, 2013.

Succession Planning in the Library: Developing Leaders, Managing Change. By Paula M. Singer with Gail Griffith. American Library Association, 2010.

Instructional Design for Librarians and Information Professionals. By Lesley S. J. Farmer. Neal-Schuman, 2011.

Reflective Teaching, Effective Learning: Instructional Literacy for Library Educators. By Char Booth. American Library Association, 2011.

Teaching Generation M: A Handbook for Librarians and Educators. By Robert J. Lackie and Vibiana Bowman Cvetkovic. Neal-Schuman, 2009.

Transforming Information Literacy Programs: Intersecting Frontiers of Self, Library Culture, and Campus Community. Ed. by Carroll Wilkinson and Courtney Bruch. Association of College and Research Libraries, 2011.

Web of Deceit: Misinformation and Manipulation in the Age of Social Media. Ed. by Anne P. Mintz. CyberAge, 2012.

Information Science

Foundations of Library and Information Science, 3rd. ed. By Richard E. Rubin. Neal-Schuman, 2010.

Information Technology in Librarianship: New Critical Approaches. Ed. by Gloria J. Leckie and John E. Buschman. Libraries Unlimited, 2009.

Introduction to Information Science and Technology. By Charles H. Davis and Debora Shaw. Information Today, Inc. 2011.

Knowledge Management: An Introduction. By Kevin C. Desouza and Scott Paquette. Neal-Schuman, 2011.

Information Literacy

Going Beyond Google: The Invisible Web in Learning and Teaching. By Jane Devine and Francine Egger-Sider. Neal-Schuman, 2009.

Information Literacy and Information Skills Instruction: Applying Research to Practice in the 21st Century School Library, 3rd ed. By Nancy Pickering Thomas, Sherry R. Crow, and Lori L. Franklin. Libraries Unlimited, 2011.

Information Literacy Instruction: Theory and Practice, 2nd ed. By Esther S. Grassian and Joan R. Kaplowitz. Neal-Schuman, 2009.

Intellectual Freedom

Banned Books Resource Guide. American Library Association/Office of Intellectual Freedom, 2010.

Intellectual Freedom Manual, 8th ed. American Library Association/Office of Intellectual Freedom, 2010.

Library Ethics. By Jean L. Preer. Libraries Unlimited, 2008.

Privacy and Confidentiality Issues: A Guide for Libraries and their Lawyers. By Theresa Chmara. American Library Association, 2009.

Protecting Intellectual Freedom in Your Academic Library. By Barbara M. Jones. American Library Association, 2009.

Protecting Intellectual Freedom in Your Public Library. By June Pinnell-Stephens. American Library Association, 2012.

Protecting Intellectual Freedom in Your School Library. By Pat R. Scales. American Library Association, 2009.

VOYA's Guide to Intellectual Freedom for Teens. By Margaret Auguste. VOYA Press, 2012.

Librarians and Librarianship

A Librarian's Guide to an Uncertain Job Market. By Jeannette Woodward. American Library Association, 2011.

Libraries in the Information Age: An Introduction and Career Exploration, 2nd ed. By Denise K. Fourie and David R. Dowell. Libraries Unlimited, 2009.

Mob Rule Learning: Camps, Unconferences, and Trashing the Talking Head. By Michelle Boule. CyberAge, 2011.

A Strong Future for Public Library Use and Employment. By Jose-Marie Griffiths and Donald W. King. American Library Association, 2011.

Outreach and Services

50+ Services: Innovation in Action. By Diantha Dow Schull. ALA Editions, 2013.

Academic Library Outreach: Beyond the Campus Walls. By Nancy Courtney. Libraries Unlimited, 2008.

Assistive Technologies in the Library. By Barbara T. Mates, with contributions by William R. Reed IV. American Library Association, 2011.

Easy Information Sources for ESL, Adult Learners, and New Readers. By Rosemarie Riechel. Neal-Schuman, 2008.

The Embedded Librarian: Innovative Strategies for Taking Knowledge Where It's Needed. By David Shumaker. Information Today, Inc. 2012.

¡Hola, Amigos! A Plan for Latino Outreach. By Susana G. Baumann. Libraries Unlimited, 2010.

The Librarian's Guide to Micropublishing: Helping Patrons and Communities Use Free and Low-cost Publishing Tools to Tell their Stories. By Walt Crawford. Information Today, Inc., 2012.

Librarians Serving Diverse Populations: Challenges and Opportunities. By Lori Mestre. Association of College and Research Libraries, 2010.

Lifelong Learning in Public Libraries: Principles, Programs, and People. By Donna L. Gilton. Scarecrow, 2012.

Literacy: A Way Out for At-Risk Youth. By Jennifer Sweeney. Libraries Unlimited, 2012.

Open Conversations: Public Learning in Libraries and Museums. By David Carr. Libraries Unlimited, 2011.

The Prison Library Primer: A Program for the 21st Century. By Brenda Vogel. Scarecrow, 2009.

Public Library Services to the Poor: Doing All We Can. By Leslie Edmonds Holt and Glen E. Holt. American Library Association, 2010.

Small Business and the Public Library: Strategies for a Successful Partnership. By Luise Weiss, Sophia Serlis-McPhillips, and Elizabeth Malafi. American Library Association, 2011.

Successful Community Outreach: A How-to-do-it Manual for Librarians. By Barbara Blake, Robert S. Martin, and Yunfei Du. Neal-Schuman, 2011.

Technology Training in Libraries. By Sarah Houghton-Jan. Neal-Schuman, 2010.

UContent: The Information Professional's Guide to User-Generated Content. By Nicholas G. Tomaiuolo. Information Today, Inc., 2012.

Without a Net: Librarians Bridging the Digital Divide. By Jessamyn C. West. Libraries Unlimited, 2011.

Preservation, Disaster Response, and Security: Comprehensive Guide to Emergency Preparedness and Disaster Recovery. By Frances C. Wilkinson, Linda K. Lewis, and Nancy K. Dennis. Association of College and Research Libraries, 2010.

Disaster Response and Planning for Libraries. By Miriam B. Kahn. American Library Association, 2012.

Guide to Security Considerations and Practices for Rare Book, Manuscript, and Spe-

cial Collection Libraries. Ed. by Everett C. Wilkie, Jr. Association of College and Research Libraries, 2011.

The Library Security and Safety Guide to Prevention, Planning, and Response. By Miriam B. Kahn. American Library Association, 2008.

Programming

El Día de los Niños/El Día de los Libros: Building a Culture of Literacy in Your Community Through Día. By Jeanette Larson. American Library Association, 2011.

Everyone Plays at the Library: Creating Great Gaming Experiences for All Ages. By Scott Nicholson. Information Today, Inc., 2010.

Game On! Gaming at the Library. By Beth Gallaway. Neal-Schuman, 2009.

Gaming in Libraries. By Kelly N. Czarnecki. Neal-Schuman, 2010.

Library Programs Online: Possibilities and Practicalities of Web Conferencing. By Thomas A. Peters. Libraries Unlimited, 2009.

Library Videos and Webcasts. By Sean Robinson. Neal-Schuman, 2010.

Multicultural Programs for 'Tweens and Teens. By Linda B. Alexander and Nahyun Kwon. American Library Association, 2010.

Start-to-finish YA Programs: Hip-hop Symposiums, Summer Reading Programs, Virtual Tours, Poetry Slams, Teen Advisory Boards, Term Paper Clinics, and More! By Ella W. Jones. Neal-Schuman, 2009.

Technology and Literacy: 21st Century Library Programming for Children and Teens. By Jennifer Nelson and Keith Braafladt. American Library Association, 2012.

Public Libraries

The American Public Library Handbook. By Guy A. Marco. Libraries Unlimited, 2012.

IFLA Public Library Service Guidelines. Ed. by Christie Koontz and Barbara Gubbin. De Gruyter Saur, 2010.

Opportunity for All: How Library Policies and Practices Impact Public Internet Access: the U.S. IMPACT Study: A Research Initiative Examining the Impact of Free Access

to Computers and the Internet in Public Libraries. By Samantha Becker et al. IMLS, 2011.

Public Libraries and Internet Service Roles: Measuring and Maximizing Internet Services. By Charles R. McClure and Paul T. Jaeger. American Library Association, 2008.

Public Libraries and the Internet: Roles, Perspectives, and Implications. By John Carlo Bertot and Paul T. Jaeger. Libraries Unlimited, 2010.

Public Libraries in the 21st Century. By Ann E. Prentice. Libraries Unlimited, 2011.

The Public Library Policy Writer: A Guidebook with Model Policies on CD-ROM. By Jeanette C. Larson and Herman L. Totten. Neal-Schuman, 2008.

Small Public Library Management. By Jane Pearlmutter and Paul Nelson. American Library Association, 2012.

Public Relations/Marketing

Bite-Sized Marketing: Realistic Solutions for the Overworked Librarian. By Nancy Dowd, Mary Evangelista, and Jonathan Silberman. American Library Association, 2010.

Building a Buzz: Libraries and Word-of-Mouth Marketing. By Peggy Barber and Linda Wallace. American Library Association, 2010.

The Customer-Focused Library: Reinventing the Library From the Outside In. By Joseph R. Matthews. Libraries Unlimited, 2009.

DIY Programming and Book Displays: How to Stretch Your Programming Without Stretching Your Budget and Staff. By Amanda Moss Struckmeyer and Svetha Hetzler. Libraries Unlimited, 2010.

Listening to the Customer. By Peter Hernon and Joseph R. Matthews. Libraries Unlimited, 2011.

Marketing Your Library: Tips and Tools That Work. Ed. By Carol Smallwood, Vera Gubnitskaia, and Kerol Harrod. McFarland, 2012.

The Mobile Marketing Handbook: A Step-by-Step Guide to Creating Dynamic Mobile Marketing Campaigns, 2nd ed. By Kim Dushinski. Information Today, Inc., 2012.

A Social Networking Primer for Librarians. By Cliff Landis. Neal-Schuman, 2010.

Wikis for Libraries. By Lauren Pressley. Neal-Schuman, 2010.

Readers' Advisory

Integrated Advisory Service: Breaking Through the Book Boundary to Better Serve Library Users. Ed. by Jessica E. Moyer. Libraries Unlimited, 2010.

Outstanding Books for the College Bound: Titles and Programs for a New Generation. Ed. by Angela Carstensen. American Library Association, 2011.

Readers' Advisory Service for Children and 'Tweens. By Penny Peck. Libraries Unlimited, 2010.

Research-Based Readers' Advisory. By Jessica E. Moyer. American Library Association, 2008.

The Readers' Advisory Guide to Genre Fiction, 2nd ed. By Joyce G. Saricks. American Library Association, 2009.

The Readers' Advisory Guide to Street Literature. By Vanessa Irvin Morris. American Library Association, 2012.

The Reader's Advisory Handbook. Ed. by Jessica E. Moyer and Kaite Mediatore Stover. American Library Association, 2010.

Serving Boys Through Readers' Advisory. By Michael Sullivan. American Library Association, 2010.

Reference Services

Conducting the Reference Interview: a How-to-do-it Manual for Librarians, 2nd ed. By Catherine Sheldrick Ross, Kristi Nilsen, and Marie L. Radford. Neal-Schuman, 2009.

Essential Reference Services for Today's School Media Specialists, 2nd ed. By Scott Lanning and John Bryner. Libraries Unlimited, 2010.

Fundamentals of Managing Reference Collections By Carol A. Singer. ALA Editions, 2012.

Guide to Reference. American Library Association. Online database at http://www.guidetoreference.org.

Interlibrary Loan Practices Handbook, 3rd ed. Ed. by Cherié L. Weible and Karen L. Janke. American Library Association, 2011.

The Librarian as Information Consultant: Transforming Reference for the Information Age. By Sarah Anne Murphy. American Library Association, 2011.

Reference and Information Services: An Introduction, 4th ed. Ed. by Richard E. Bopp and Linda C. Smith. Libraries Unlimited, 2011.

Reference Renaissance: Current and Future Trends. Ed. by Marie L. Radford and R. David Lankes. Neal-Schuman, 2010.

Reference Sources and Services for Youth. By Meghan Harper. Neal-Shuman, 2011.

Training Paraprofessionals for Reference Service. By Pamela J. Morgan. Neal-Schuman, 2008.

Research and Statistics

Academic Library Trends and Statistics. Association of College and Research Libraries/American Library Association. Annual, print and online.

The ALA-APA Salary Survey 2012: Librarian—Public and Academic. ALA-Allied Professional Association. Print and online.

ARL Annual Salary Survey. Association of Research Libraries. Annual, print and online.

ARL Statistics. Association of Research Libraries. Annual, print and online.

Assessing Information Needs: Managing Transformative Library Services. By Robert J. Grover, Roger C. Greer, and John Agada. Libraries Unlimited, 2010.

Assessing Service Quality: Satisfying the Expectations of Library Customers, 2nd ed. By Peter Hernon and Ellen Altman. American Library Association, 2010.

Basic Research Methods for Librarians, 5th ed. By Lynn Silipigni Connaway and Ronald R. Powell. Libraries Unlimited, 2010.

Engaging in Evaluation and Assessment Research. By Peter Hernon, Robert E. Dugan, and Danuta A. Nitecki. Libraries Unlimited, 2011.

Knowledge Into Action: Research and Evaluation in Library and Information Science. By Danny P. Wallace and Connie Van Fleet. Libraries Unlimited, 2012.

Public Libraries in the United States Survey: Fiscal Year 2010. Institute of Museum and

Library Services. Online at http://www.imls.gov/assets/1/AssetManager/PLS2010.pdf.
Public Library Data Service Statistical Report (PLDS). Public Library Association/American Library Association. Online database.

School Libraries

21st Century Learning in School Libraries: Putting the AASL Standards to Work. Ed. by Kristin Fontichiaro. Libraries Unlimited, 2009.

Administering the School Library Media Center, 5th ed. By Betty J. Morris. Libraries Unlimited, 2010.

Empowering Learners: Guidelines for School Library Programs. American Association of School Librarians, 2009.

Essential Documents for School Libraries, 2nd ed. By Colleen MacDonell. Linworth, 2010.

Fundamentals of School Library Media Management. By Barbara Stein Martin and Marco Zannier. Neal-Schuman, 2009.

Guide for Developing and Evaluating School Library Programs, 7th ed. By Nebraska Educational Media Association. Libraries Unlimited, 2010.

Independent School Libraries: Perspectives on Excellence. Ed. by Dorcas Hand. Libraries Unlimited, 2010.

Simply Indispensable: An Action Guide for School Librarians. By Janice Gilmore-See. Libraries Unlimited, 2010.

The School Library Media Manager, 4th ed. By Blanche Woolls. Libraries Unlimited, 2008.

The School Library Media Specialist's Policy and Procedure Writer. By Elizabeth Downs. Neal-Schuman, 2010.

Standards for the 21st Century Learner. American Association of School Librarians, 2007.

Standards for the 21st Century Learner in Action. American Association of School Librarians, 2009.

Technology and the School Library: A Comprehensive Guide for Media Specialists and Other Educators. By Odin Jurkowski. Scarecrow, 2010.

Using Web 2.0 and Social Networking Tools in the K–12 Classroom. By Beverley E. Crane. Neal-Schuman, 2012.

Technical Services

Acquisitions in the New Information Universe: Core Competencies and Ethical Practices. By Jesse Holden. Neal-Schuman, 2010.

Electronics Resources Management in the Academic Library: A Professional Guide. By Karin Wikoff. Libraries Unlimited, 2012.

Fundamentals of Technical Services Management. By Sheila S. Intner, with Peggy Johnson. American Library Association, 2008.

Integrated Library Systems: Planning, Selecting, and Implementing. By Desiree Webber and Andrew Peters. Libraries Unlimited, 2010.

Introduction to Technical Services, 8th ed. By C. Edward Evans, Sheila S. Intner, and Jean Weihs. Libraries Unlimited, 2011.

Technology

Mobile Technology and Libraries. By Jason Griffey. Neal-Schuman, 2010.

Neal-Schuman Library Technology Companion: A Basic Guide for Library Staff, 3rd ed. By John J. Burke. Neal-Schuman, 2009.

The Neal-Schuman Technology Management Handbook for School Library Media Centers. By Lesley S. J. Farmer and Marc E. McPhee. Neal-Schuman, 2010.

Web Service APIs and Libraries. By Jason Paul Michel. ALA Editions, 2013.

Periodicals

This listing of key library publications includes ISSNs for print and online formats. All titles have been verified against the EBSCO database as active periodicals.

Against the Grain (1043-2094)

American Archivist (0360-9081)

American Libraries (0002-9769)

American Libraries Direct (online, 1559-369X)

Ariadne: A Web and Print Magazine of Internet Issues for Librarians and Information Specialists (1361-3197)

Art Documentation (print, 0730-7187; online, 2161-9417)

Behavioral and Social Sciences Librarian (print, 0163-9269; online, 1544-4546)

Booklist (0006-7385)

Bottom Line: Managing Library Finances (0888-045X)

Cataloging and Classification Quarterly (print, 0163-9374; online, 1544-4554)

Catholic Library World (0008-820X)

Children and Libraries: The Journal of the Association for Library Service to Children (1542-9806)

Children's Programming Monthly (online, 2156-8685)

CHOICE: Current Reviews for Academic Libraries (print, 0009-4978; online, 1523-8253)

Code4Lib Journal (1940-5758)

Collection Building (0160-4953)

Collection Management (print, 0146-2679; online, 1545-2549)

College & Research Libraries (print, 0099-0086; online, 2150-6701)

Computers in Libraries (1041-7915)

D-Lib (1082-9873)

DttP: A Quarterly Journal of Government Information Practice and Perspective (0091-2085)

Electronic Library (print, 0264-0473; online, 1758-616X)

Electronic Journal of Knowledge Management (1479-4411)

First Monday (1396-0466)

Government Information Quarterly (0740-624X)

Horn Book Magazine (0018-5078)

IFLA Journal (print, 0340-0352; online, 1745-2651)

In the Library with the Lead Pipe (1944-6195)

Indexer (print, 0019-4131; 1756-0632)

Information & Culture (2164-8034)

Information Outlook (online, 1938-3819)

Information Research—An International Electronic Journal (1368-1613)

Information Standards Quarterly (1041-0031)

Information Technology and Libraries (online, 2163-5226)

Interlending & Document Supply (print, 0264-1615; online 1995-2006)

Internet @ Schools (2156-843X)

Internet Reference Services Quarterly (print, 1087-5301; online, 1540-4749)

Issues in Science and Technology Librarianship (online, 1092-1206)

Journal of Academic Librarianship (0099-1333)

Journal of Documentation (print, 0022-0418; online, 1758-7379)

Journal of Education for Library and Information Science (0748-5786)

Journal of Electronic Resources Librarianship (print, 1542-4065; online, 1532-3269)

Journal of Information Ethics (1061-9321)

Journal of Information Science (print, 0165-5515; online, 1061-9321)

Journal of Interlibrary Loan, Document Delivery and Information Supply (print, 1072-303X; online, 1540-3572)

Journal of Librarianship & Information Science (print, 0961-0006; online 1741-6477)

Journal of Library Administration (print, 0193-0826; online, 1540-3564)

Journal of Library Metadata (print, 1938-6389; online, 1937-5034)

Journal of Research on Libraries and Young Adults (2157-3980)

Journal of the American Society for Information Science and Technology (1532-2882)

Journal of the Medical Library Association (1536-5050)

Journal of Web Librarianship (print, 1932-2909; online, 1932-2917)

Knowledge Quest (1094-9046)

Law Library Journal (0023-9283)

Legal Reference Services Quarterly (print, 0270-319X; online, 1540-949X)

Library & Archival Security (print, 0196-0075; online 1540-9511)

Library & Information Science Research (LIBRES) (0740-8188)

Library Collections Acquisitions & Technical Services (1464-9055)

Library Hi-Tech Journal (0737-8831)

Library Journal (0363-0277)

Library Leadership & Management (Online, 1945-8851)

Library Management (0143-5124)

Library Media Connection (1542-4715)

The Library Quarterly (print, 0024-2519; online, 1549-652X)

Library Resources & Technical Services (print, 0024-2527; online, 2159-9610)

Library Technology Reports (print, 0024-2586; online, 1945-4538)

Library Trends (print, 0024-2594; online, 1559-0682)

Library Worklife: HR E-news for Today's Leaders (1550-3534)

Librarysparks (1544-9092)

New Review of Children's Literature and Librarianship (print, 1361-4541; online, 1740-7885)

Newsletter on Intellectual Freedom (online, 0028-9485)

Notes (Music Library Association) (print, 0027-4380; online, 1534-150X)

Online Searcher (2324-9684)

portal: Libraries and the Academy (print, 1531-2542; online, 1530-7131)

Public Libraries (0163-5506)

Public Library Quarterly (print, 0161-6846; online, 1541-1540)

Publishing Research Quarterly (print, 1053-8801; online, 1936-4792)

RBM: A Journal of Rare Books, Manuscripts, and Cultural Heritage (1529-6407)

Reference & User Services Quarterly (online, 1094-9054)

Reference Librarian (print, 0276-3877; online, 1541-1117)

Research Libraries Issues (1947-4911)

RSR: Reference Services Review (0090-7324)

School Library Journal (0362-8930)

School Library Research (2165-1019)

Serials Librarian (print, 0361-526X; online, 1541-1095)

Serials Review (0098-7913)

State of America's Libraries Report (annual, online only)

Technical Services Quarterly (print, 0731-7131; online, 1555-3337)

Technicalities (0272-0884)

Voice of Youth Advocates (*VOYA*) (0160-4201)

Blogs

025.431: The Dewey Blog. Jonathan Furner, editor (http://ddc.typepad.com)

AASL Blog (http://www.aasl.ala.org/aaslblog)

ACRL Insider (http://www.acrl.ala.org/acrl insider)

ACRLog (http://acrlog.org)

AL Inside Scoop (http://americanlibraries magazine.org/insidescoop)

ALA Editions Blog (http://www.alaeditions.org/blog)

ALA Membership Blog (http://americanlibraries magazine.org/ala-members-blog)

ALA Student Member Blog (http://american librariesmagazine.org/student-member-blog)

ALSC Blog (http://www.alsc.ala.org/blog)

Annoyed Librarian (http://www.libraryjournal.com/annoyedlibrarian)

AOTUS: Collector in Chief. By David Ferriero (http://blogs.archives.gov/aotus)

Ask the ALA Library (http://www.ala.org/tools/ask-ala-library)

Attempting Elegance. By Jennica Rogers. (http://www.attemptingelegance.com)

Audiobooker. By Mary Burkey (http://audio booker.booklistonline.com)

Awful Library Books. By Holly Hibner and Mary Kelly (http://awfullibrarybooks.net)

Blue Skunk. By Doug Johnson (http://doug-johnson.squarespace.com)

Book Group Buzz (http://bookgroupbuzz.booklistonline.com)

Bookends. By Cindy Dobrez and Lynn Rutan (http://bookends.booklistonline.com)

Catalogablog. By David Bigwood (http://catalogablog.blogspot.com)

Celeripedean. By Jennifer Eustis (http://celeripedean.wordpress.com)

A Chair, a Fireplace, and a Tea Cozy. By Liz Burns (http://blog.schoollibraryjournal.com/teacozy)

Copyfight: The Politics of IP. By Donna Wentworth, Ernest Miller, Elizabeth Rader, Jason Schultz, Wendy Seltzer, Aaron Schwartz, and Adam Wexelblat (http://copyfight.corante.com)

Copyright Matters: Digitization and Public Access (http://blogs.loc.gov/copyright digitization)

Copyrightlaws.com. By Lesley Ellen Harris (http://www.copyrightlaws.com)

Coyle's InFormation. By Karen Coyle (http://kcoyle.blogspot.com)

David Lee King. By David Lee King (http://www.davidleeking.com)

Designing Better Libraries: Exploring the Application of Design, Innovation, and New Media to Create Better Libraries and User Experiences (http://dbl.lishost.org/blog)

The Digital Shift (http://www.thedigitalshift.com)

Digitization 101. By Jill Hurst-Wahl (http://hurstassociates.blogspot.com)

District Dispatch. By the ALA Washington Office (http://www.districtdispatch.org)

Early Word. By Nora Rawlinson (http://www.earlyword.com)

E-Content. (http://americanlibrariesmagazine.org/e-content)

Free Range Librarian. By Karen G. Schneider (http://freerangelibrarian.com)

A Fuse #8 Production. By Elizabeth Bird. (http://blog.schoollibraryjournal.com/afuse8production)

GLBT-RT Reviews. By the ALA Gay, Lesbian, Bisexual, and Transgender Round Table (http://www.glbtrt.ala.org/reviews)

Go to Hellman. By Eric Hellman (http://go-to-hellman.blogspot.com)

Hack Library School (http://hacklibschool.wordpress.com)

Hangingtogether.org (http://hangingtogether.org)

Hey Jude. By Judy O'Connell (http://heyjude.wordpress.com)

The Hub: Your Connection to Teen Reads. By the Young Adult Library Services Association (http://www.yalsa.ala.org/thehub)

INFOdocket. By Gary Price and Shirl Kennedy (http://infodocket.com)

Information Wants to Be Free. By Meredith Farkas (http://meredith.wolfwater.com/wordpress)

John Battelle's Searchblog (http://battelle media.com)

Leads from LLAMA (http://www.llama.ala.org/llamaleads)

Librarian.net. By Jessamyn West (http://www.librarian.net)

LibrarianInBlack. By Sarah Houghton-Jan (http://librarianinblack.net/librarianinblack)

Library as Incubator Project. By Laura Damon-Moore, Erinn Batykefer, and Christina Endres (http://www.libraryasincubatorproject.org)

Library History Buff Blog. By Larry T. Nix (http://libraryhistorybuff.blogspot.com)

Library Juice. By Rory Litwin (http://library juicepress.com/blog)

Library of Congress Blog (http://blogs.loc.gov/loc)

Library Renewal (http://libraryrenewal.org/blog)

A Library Writer's Blog. By Corey Seeman (http://librarywriting.blogspot.com)

LibraryLaw Blog. By Mary Minow (http://blog.librarylaw.com)

Likely Stories. By Keir Graff (http://blog.booklistonline.com)

LIS News. By Blake Carver (http://lisnews.org)

LITA Blog (http://litablog.org)

Lorcan Dempsey's Weblog (http://orweblog.oclc.org)

The 'M' Word—Marketing in Libraries. By Kathy Dempsey (http://themwordblog.blogspot.com)

NeverEndingSearch. By Joyce Valenza (http://blog.schoollibraryjournal.com/neverendingsearch)

NMRT Notes (http://www.nmrt.ala.org/notes)

No Shelf Required. By Sue Polanka (http://www.libraries.wright.edu/noshelfrequired)

Office for Intellectual Freedom Blog (http://www.oif.ala.org/oif)

Pattern Recognition. By Jason Griffey (http://www.jasongriffey.net/wp)

Peer to Peer Review. By Barbara Fister (http://lj.libraryjournal.com/author/bfister)

Phil Bradley's Weblog. By Phil Bradley (http://www.philbradley.typepad.com)

PLA Blog (http://plablog.org)

Planet Cataloging (http://planetcataloging.org)

Programming Librarian Blog (http://www.programminglibrarian.org/blog.html)

RDA Toolkit Blog (http://www.rdatoolkit.org/blog)

RUSA Blog (http://rusa.ala.org/blog)

ShelfRenewal. By Karen Kleckner Keefe and Rebecca Vnuk (http://shelfrenewal.booklist online.com).

The Signal: Digital Preservation (http://blogs.loc.gov/digitalpreservation)

SLA Blog (http://slablogger.typepad.com/sla_blog)

Solutions and Services (http://americanlibraries magazine.org/solutions-and-services)

Stephen's Lighthouse. By Stephen Abram (http://stephenslighthouse.com)

Swiss Army Librarian. By Brian Herzog (http://www.swissarmylibrarian.net)

Tame the Web: Libraries and Technology. By Michael Stephens (http://tametheweb.com)

Teen Librarian Toolbox. By Karen Jensen, Stephanie Wilkes, Christie Ross Gibrich, and Heather Booth. (http://www.teenlibrarian toolbox.com)

TechSource Blog. By Jason Griffey, Tom Peters, Kate Sheehan, Michael Stephens, Cindi Trainor, Michelle Boule, and Richard Wallis (http://www.alatechsource.org/blog)

TeleRead: News and views on e-books, libraries, publishing and related topics (http://www.teleread.com)

The Travelin' Librarian. By Michael Sauers (http://www.travelinlibrarian.info)

Walking Paper. By Aaron Schmidt (http://www.walkingpaper.org)

Walt at Random. By Walt Crawford (http://walt.lishost.org)

YALSA Blog (http://yalsa.ala.org/blog)

Ready Reference

How to Obtain an ISBN

Beat Barblan

United States ISBN/SAN Agency

The International Standard Book Numbering (ISBN) system was introduced into the United Kingdom by J. Whitaker & Sons Ltd. in 1967 and into the United States in 1968 by R. R. Bowker. The Technical Committee on Documentation of the International Organization for Standardization (ISO TC 46) is responsible for the international standard.

The purpose of this standard is to "establish the specifications for the International Standard Book Number (ISBN) as a unique international identification system for each product form or edition of a monographic publication published or produced by a specific publisher." The standard specifies the construction of an ISBN, the rules for assignment and use of an ISBN, and all metadata associated with the allocation of an ISBN.

Types of monographic publications to which an ISBN may be assigned include printed books and pamphlets (in various product formats); electronic publications (either on the Internet or on physical carriers such as CD-ROMs or diskettes); educational/instructional films, videos, and transparencies; educational/instructional software; audiobooks on cassette or CD or DVD; braille publications; and microform publications.

Serial publications, printed music, and musical sound recordings are excluded from the ISBN standard as they are covered by other identification systems.

The ISBN is used by publishers, distributors, wholesalers, bookstores, and libraries, among others, in 217 countries and territories as an ordering and inventory system. It expedites the collection of data on new and forthcoming editions of monographic publications for print and electronic directories used by the book trade. Its use also facilitates rights management and the monitoring of sales data for the publishing industry.

The "new" ISBN consists of 13 digits. As of January 1, 2007, a revision to the ISBN standard was implemented in an effort to substantially increase the numbering capacity. The 10-digit ISBN identifier (ISBN-10) is now replaced by the ISBN 13-digit identifier (ISBN-13). All facets of book publishing are now expected to use the ISBN-13, and the ISBN agencies throughout the world are now issuing only ISBN-13s to publishers. Publishers with existing ISBN-10s need to convert their ISBNs to ISBN-13s by the addition of the EAN prefix 978 and recalculation of the new check digit:

ISBN-10: 0-8352-8235-X
ISBN-13: 978-0-8352-8235-2

When the inventory of the ISBN-10s has been exhausted, the ISBN agencies will start assigning ISBN-13s with the "979" prefix instead of the "978." There is no 10-digit equivalent for 979 ISBNs.

Construction of an ISBN

An ISBN currently consists of 13 digits separated into the following parts:

1 A prefix of "978" for an ISBN-10 converted to an ISBN-13
2 Group or country identifier, which identifies a national or geographic grouping of publishers
3 Publisher identifier, which identifies a particular publisher within a group
4 Title identifier, which identifies a particular title or edition of a title
5 Check digit, the single digit at the end of the ISBN that validates the ISBN-13

For more information regarding ISBN-13 conversion services provided by the U.S. ISBN Agency at R. R. Bowker, LLC, visit the ISBN Agency website at http://www.isbn.org, or contact the U.S. ISBN Agency at isbn-san@bowker.com.

Publishers requiring their ISBNs to be converted from the ISBN-10 to ISBN-13 format can use the U.S. ISBN Agency's free ISBN-13 online converter at http://isbn.org/converterpub.asp. Publishers can also view their ISBNs online by accessing their personal account at http://www.myidentifiers.com.

Displaying the ISBN on a Product or Publication

When an ISBN is written or printed, it should be preceded by the letters ISBN, and each part should be separated by a space or hyphen. In the United States, the hyphen is used for separation, as in the following example: ISBN 978-0-8352-8235-2. In this example, 978 is the prefix that precedes the ISBN-13, 0 is the group identifier, 8352 is the publisher identifier, 8235 is the title identifier, and 2 is the check digit. The group of English-speaking countries, which includes the United States, Australia, Canada, New Zealand, and the United Kingdom, uses the group identifiers 0 and 1.

The ISBN Organization

The administration of the ISBN system is carried out at three levels—through the International ISBN Agency in the United Kingdom, through the national agencies, and through the publishing houses themselves. The International ISBN Agency, which is responsible for assigning country prefixes and for coordinating the worldwide implementation of the system, has an advisory panel that represents the International Organization for Standardization (ISO), publishers, and libraries. The International ISBN Agency publishes the *Publishers International ISBN Directory,* which is a listing of all national agencies' publishers with their assigned ISBN publisher prefixes. R. R. Bowker, as the publisher of *Books In Print* with its extensive and varied database of publishers' addresses, was the obvious place to initiate the ISBN system and to provide the service to the U.S. publishing industry. To date, the U.S. ISBN Agency has entered more than 180,000 publishers into the system.

ISBN Assignment Procedure

Assignment of ISBNs is a shared endeavor between the U.S. ISBN Agency and the publisher. Publishers can apply online through the ISBN Agency's website http://www.myidentifiers.com. Once the order is processed, an e-mail confirmation will be sent with instructions for managing the account. The publisher then has the responsibility to assign an ISBN to each title, keep an accurate record of each number assigned, and register each title in the *Books In Print* database at http://www.myidentifiers.com. It is the responsibility of the ISBN Agency to validate assigned ISBNs and keep a record of all ISBN publisher prefixes in circulation.

ISBN implementation is very much market-driven. Major distributors, wholesalers, retailers, and so forth recognize the necessity of the ISBN system and request that publishers register with the ISBN Agency. Also, the ISBN is a mandatory bibliographic element in the International Standard Bibliographical Description (ISBD). The Library of Congress Cataloging in Publication (CIP) Division directs publishers to the agency to obtain their ISBN prefixes.

Location and Display of the ISBN

On books, pamphlets, and other printed material, the ISBN shall be printed on the verso of the title leaf or, if this is not possible, at the foot of the title leaf itself. It should also appear on the outside back cover or on the back of the jacket if the book has one (the lower right-hand corner is recommended). It should also appear on any accompanying promotional materials following the provisions for location according to the format of the material.

On other monographic publications, the ISBN shall appear on the title or credit frames and any labels permanently affixed to the publication. If the publication is issued in a container that is an integral part of the publication, the ISBN shall be displayed on the label. If it is not possible to place the ISBN on the item or its label, then the number should be displayed on the bottom or the back of the container, box, sleeve, or frame. It should also appear on any accompanying material, including each component of a multi-type publication.

Printing of ISBN in Machine-Readable Coding

All books should carry ISBNs in the EAN-13 bar code machine-readable format. All ISBN EAN-13 bar codes start with the EAN prefix 978 for books. As of January 1, 2007, all EAN bar codes should have the ISBN-13 appearing immediately above the bar code in eye-readable format, preceded by the acronym "ISBN." The recommended location of the EAN-13 bar code for books is in the lower right-hand corner of the back cover (see Figure 1).

Figure 1 / Printing the ISBN in Bookland/EAN Symbology

Five-Digit Add-On Code

In the United States, a five-digit add-on code is used for additional information. In the publishing industry, this code is used for price information. The lead digit of the five-digit add-on has been designated a currency identifier, when the add-on is used for price. Number 5 is the code for the U.S. dollar, 6 denotes the Canadian dollar, 1 the British pound, 3 the Australian dollar, and 4 the New Zealand dollar. Publishers that do not want to indicate price in the add-on should print the code 90000 (see Figure 2).

**Figure 2 / Printing the ISBN Bookland/EAN Number in Bar Code
with the Five-Digit Add-On Code**

978 = ISBN Bookland/EAN prefix   90000 means no information
5 = Code for U.S. $ in the add-on code
0995 = $9.95

Reporting the Title and the ISBN

After the publisher reports a title to the ISBN Agency, the number is validated and the title is listed in the many R. R. Bowker hard-copy and electronic publications, including *Books in Print; Forthcoming Books; Paperbound Books in Print; Books in Print Supplement; Books Out of Print; Books in Print Online; Books in Print Plus-CD ROM; Children's Books in Print; Subject Guide to Children's Books in Print: Books Out Loud: Bowker's Guide to AudioBooks; Bowker's Complete Video Directory; Software Encyclopedia; Software for Schools;* and other specialized publications.

For an ISBN application and information, visit the ISBN Agency website at http://www.myidentifiers.com, call the toll-free number 877-310-7333, fax 908-219-0188, or write to the United States ISBN Agency, 630 Central Ave., New Providence, NJ 07974.

The ISSN, and How to Obtain One

U.S. ISSN Center
Library of Congress

In the early 1970s the rapid increase in the production and dissemination of information and an intensified desire to exchange information about serials in computerized form among different systems and organizations made it increasingly clear that a means to identify serial publications at an international level was needed. The International Standard Serial Number (ISSN) was developed and became the internationally accepted code for identifying serial publications.

The ISSN is an international standard, ISO 3297: 2007, as well as a U.S. standard, ANSI/NISO Z39.9. The 2007 edition of ISO 3297 expands the scope of the ISSN to cover continuing resources (serials, as well as updating databases, looseleafs, and some websites).

The number itself has no significance other than as a brief, unique, and unambiguous identifier. The ISSN consists of eight digits in Arabic numerals 0 to 9, except for the last ("check") digit, which can be an X. The numbers appear as two groups of four digits separated by a hyphen and preceded by the letters ISSN—for example, ISSN 1234-5679.

The ISSN is not self-assigned by publishers. Administration of the ISSN is coordinated through the ISSN Network, an intergovernmental organization within the UNESCO/UNISIST program. The ISSN Network consists of national ISSN centers, coordinated by the ISSN International Centre, located in Paris. National ISSN Centers are responsible for registering serials published in their respective countries. Responsibility for the assignment of ISSN to titles from multinational publishers is allocated among the ISSN Centers in which the publisher has offices. A list of these publishers and the corresponding ISSN centers is located on the ISSN International Centre's website, http://www.issn.org.

The ISSN International Centre handles ISSN assignments for international organizations and for countries that do not have a national center. It also maintains and distributes the ISSN Register and makes it available in a variety of products, most commonly via the ISSN Portal, an online subscription database. The ISSN Register is also available via Z39.50 access, and as a data file. Selected ISSN data can also be obtained in customized files or database extracts that can be used, for example, to check the accuracy or completeness of a requestor's list of titles and ISSN. Another available ISSN service is OAI-PMH, a customizable "harvesting" protocol through which external applications can automatically and regularly gather new and updated metadata on a defined schedule. The ISSN Register contains bibliographic records corresponding to each ISSN assignment as reported by national ISSN centers. The database contains records for around 1.7 million ISSNs.

The ISSN is used all over the world by serials publishers to identify their serials and to distinguish their titles from others that are the same or similar. It is used by subscription services and libraries to manage files for orders, claims, and back issues. It is used in automated check-in systems by libraries that wish to process receipts more quickly. Copyright centers use the ISSN as a means to collect and disseminate royalties. It is also used as an identification code by postal services and legal deposit services. The ISSN is included as a verification element in interlibrary lending activities and for union catalogs as a collocating device. In recent years, the ISSN has been incorporated into bar codes for optical recognition of serial publications and into the standards for the identification of issues and articles in serial publications. Other growing uses for the ISSN are in online systems where it can serve to connect catalog records or citations in abstracting and indexing databases with full-text journal content via OpenURL resolvers or reference linking services, and as an identifier and link in archives of electronic and print serials.

Because serials are generally known and cited by title, assignment of the ISSN is inseparably linked to the key title, a standardized form of the title derived from information in the serial issue. Only one ISSN can be assigned to a title in a particular medium. For titles issued in multiple media—e.g., print, online, CD-ROM—a separate ISSN is assigned to each medium version. If a major title change occurs or the medium changes, a new ISSN must be assigned. Centers responsible for assigning ISSNs also construct the key title and create an associated bibliographic record.

A significant new feature of the 2007 ISSN standard is the Linking ISSN (ISSN-L), a mechanism that enables collocation or linking among different media versions of a continuing resource. The Linking ISSN allows a unique designation (one of the existing ISSNs) to be applied to all media versions of a continuing resource while retaining the separate ISSN that pertains to each version. When an ISSN is functioning as a Linking ISSN, the eight digits of the base ISSN are prefixed with the designation "ISSN-L." The Linking ISSN facilitates search, retrieval, and delivery across all medium versions of a serial or other continuing resource for improved ISSN functionality in OpenURL linking, search engines, library catalogs, and knowledge bases. The 2007 standard also supports interoperability by specifying the use of ISSN and ISSN-L with other systems such as DOI, OpenURL, URN, and EAN bar codes. ISSN-L was implemented in the ISSN Register in 2008. To help ISSN users implement the ISSN-L in their databases, two free tables are available from the ISSN International Centre's home page: one lists each ISSN and its corresponding ISSN-L; the other lists each ISSN-L and its corresponding ISSNs.

In the United States, the U.S. ISSN Center at the Library of Congress is responsible for assigning and maintaining the ISSNs for all U.S. serial titles. Publishers wishing to have an ISSN assigned should download an application from the Center's website, and mail, e-mail, or fax the form to the U.S. ISSN Center. Assignment of the ISSN is free, and there is no charge for use of the ISSN.

To obtain an ISSN for a U.S. publication, or for more information about ISSN in the United States, libraries, publishers, and other ISSN users should visit the U.S. ISSN Center's website, http://www.loc.gov/issn, or contact the U.S. ISSN Center, U.S. and Publisher Liaison Division, Library of Congress, 101 Independence Ave. S.E., Washington, DC 20540-4284 (telephone 202-707-6452, fax 202-707-6333, e-mail issn@loc.gov).

For information about ISSN products and services, and for application procedures that non-U.S. parties should use to apply for an ISSN, visit the ISSN International Centre's website, http://www.issn.org, or contact the International Centre at 45 rue de Turbigo, 75003 Paris, France (telephone 33-1-44-88-22-20, fax 33-1-40-26-32-43, e-mail issnic@issn.org).

How to Obtain an SAN

Beat Barblan

United States ISBN/SAN Agency

SAN stands for Standard Address Number. The SAN system, an American National Standards Institute (ANSI) standard, assigns a unique identification number that is used to positively identify specific addresses of organizations in order to facilitate buying and selling transactions within the industry. It is recognized as the identification code for electronic communication within the industry.

For purposes of this standard, the book industry includes book publishers, book wholesalers, book distributors, book retailers, college bookstores, libraries, library binders, and serial vendors. Schools, school systems, technical institutes, and colleges and universities are not members of this industry, but are served by it and therefore included in the SAN system.

The purpose of the SAN is to ease communications among these organizations, of which there are several hundreds of thousands that engage in a large volume of separate transactions with one another. These transactions include purchases of books by book dealers, wholesalers, schools, colleges, and libraries from publishers and wholesalers; payments for all such purchases; and other communications between participants. The objective of this standard is to establish an identification code system by assigning each address within the industry a unique code to be used for positive identification for all book and serial buying and selling transactions.

Many organizations have similar names and multiple addresses, making identification of the correct contact point difficult and subject to error. In many cases, the physical movement of materials takes place between addresses that differ from the addresses to be used for the financial transactions. In such instances, there is ample opportunity for confusion and errors. Without identification by SAN, a complex record-keeping system would have to be instituted to avoid introducing errors. In addition, problems with the current numbering system—such as errors in billing, shipping, payments, and returns—are significantly reduced by using the SAN system. The SAN also eliminates one step in the order fulfillment process: the "look-up procedure" used to assign account numbers. Previously a store or library dealing with 50 different publishers was assigned a different account number by each of the suppliers. The SAN solved this problem. If a publisher prints its SAN on its stationery and ordering documents, vendors to whom it sends transactions do not have to look up the account number, but can proceed immediately to process orders by SAN.

Libraries are involved in many of the same transactions as book dealers, such as ordering and paying for books and charging and paying for various services to other libraries. Keeping records of transactions—whether these involve buying, selling, lending, or donations—entails operations suited to SAN use. SAN stationery speeds up order fulfillment and eliminate errors in shipping, billing, and crediting; this, in turn, means savings in both time and money.

History

Development of the Standard Address Number began in 1968 when Russell Reynolds, general manager of the National Association of College Stores (NACS), approached R. R. Bowker and suggested that a "Standard Account Number" system be implemented in the book industry. The first draft of a standard was prepared by an American National Standards Institute (ANSI) Committee Z39 subcommittee, which was co-chaired by Reynolds and Emery Koltay of Bowker. After Z39 members proposed changes, the current version of the standard was approved by NACS on December 17, 1979.

Format

The SAN consists of six digits plus a seventh *Modulus 11* check digit; a hyphen follows the third digit (XXX-XXXX) to facilitate transcription. The hyphen is to be used in print form, but need not be entered or retained in computer systems. Printed on documents, the Standard Address Number should be preceded by the identifier "SAN" to avoid confusion with other numerical codes (SAN XXXXXXX).

Check Digit Calculation

The check digit is based on *Modulus 11,* and can be derived as follows:

1. Write the digits of the basic number.   2 3 4 5 6 7
2. Write the constant weighting factors associated with each position by the basic number.   7 6 5 4 3 2
3. Multiply each digit by its associated weighting factor.   14 18 20 20 18 14
4. Add the products of the multiplications. $14 + 18 + 20 + 20 + 18 + 14 = 104$
5. Divide the sum by Modulus 11 to find the remainder.   104 -: 11 = 9 plus a remainder of 5
6. Subtract the remainder from the Modulus 11 to generate the required check digit. If there is no remainder, generate a check digit of zero. If the check digit is 10, generate a check digit of X to represent 10, since the use of 10 would require an extra digit. $11 - 5 = 6$
7. Append the check digit to create the standard seven-digit Standard Address Number.   SAN 234-5676

SAN Assignment

R. R. Bowker accepted responsibility for being the central administrative agency for SAN, and in that capacity assigns SANs to identify uniquely the addresses of organizations. No SANs can be reassigned; in the event that an organization should cease to exist, for example, its SAN would cease to be in circulation entirely. If an organization using an SAN should move or change its name with no change in ownership, its SAN would remain the same, and only the name or address would be updated to reflect the change.

The SAN should be used in all transactions; it is recommended that the SAN be imprinted on stationery, letterheads, order and invoice forms, checks, and all other documents used in executing various book transactions. The SAN should always be printed on a separate line above the name and address of the organization, preferably in the upper left-hand corner of the stationery to avoid confusion with other numerical codes pertaining to the organization, such as telephone number, zip code, and the like.

SAN Functions

The SAN is strictly a Standard Address Number, becoming functional only in applications determined by the user; these may include activities such as purchasing, billing, shipping, receiving, paying, crediting, and refunding. It is the method used by Pubnet and PubEasy systems and is required in all electronic data interchange communications using the Book Industry Systems Advisory Committee (BISAC) EDI formats. Every department that has an independent function within an organization could have a SAN for its own identification.

For additional information or to make suggestions, write to ISBN/SAN Agency, R. R. Bowker, LLC, 630 Central Ave., New Providence, NJ 07974, call 877-310-7333, or fax 908-219-0188. The e-mail address is san@bowker.com. The SAN website for online applications is at http://www.isbn.org.

Distinguished Books

Notable Books of 2012

The Notable Books Council of the Reference and User Services Association, a division of the American Library Association, selected these titles for their significant contribution to the expansion of knowledge or for the pleasure they can provide to adult readers.

Fiction

Díaz, Junot. *This is How You Lose Her* (Riverhead).

Edugyan, Esi. *Half-Blood Blues* (Picador).

Eggers, Dave. *A Hologram for the King* (McSweeney's).

Erdrich, Louise. *The Round House* (Harper).

Ford, Richard. *Canada.* (Ecco).

Fountain, Ben. *Billy Lynn's Long Halftime Walk* (Ecco).

Heller, Peter. *The Dog Stars* (Knopf).

Johnson, Adam. *The Orphan Master's Son* (Random).

Joyce, Rachel. *The Unlikely Pilgrimage of Harold Fry* (Random).

Lam, Vincent. *The Headmaster's Wager* (Hogarth).

Tropper, Jonathan. *One Last Thing Before I Go* (Dutton).

Watkins, Claire Vaye. *Battleborn* (Riverhead).

Nonfiction

Boo, Katherine. *Behind the Beautiful Forevers: Life, Death, and Hope in a Mumbai Undercity* (Random).

Cain, Susan. *Quiet: The Power of Introverts in a World That Can't Stop Talking* (Crown).

Colby, Tanner. *Some of My Best Friends are Black: The Strange Story of Integration in America* (Viking).

Dyson, George. *Turing's Cathedral: The Origins of the Digital Universe* (Knopf).

Egan, Timothy. *Short Nights of the Shadow Catcher: The Epic Life and Immortal Photographs of Edward Curtis* (Houghton Mifflin Harcourt).

Holt, Jim. *Why Does the World Exist? An Existential Detective Story* (Norton).

Ingrassia, Paul. *Engines of Change: A History of the American Dream in Fifteen Cars.* (Simon & Schuster).

Iverson, Kristen. *Full Body Burden: Growing Up in the Nuclear Shadow of Rocky Flats* (Crown).

King, Ross. *Leonardo and the Last Supper* (Walker).

Murphy, Paul Thomas. *Shooting Victoria: Madness, Mayhem, and the Rebirth of the British Monarchy* (Pegasus).

Roberts, Callum. *The Ocean of Life: The Fate of Man and the Sea* (Viking).

Winterson, Jeanette. *Why Be Happy When You Could be Normal?* (Grove).

Poetry

Alighieri, Dante (translator Mary Jo Bang, illustrator Henrik Drescher). *Inferno* (Graywolf).

Olds, Sharon. *Stag's Leap* (Knopf).

Best Fiction for Young Adults

Each year a committee of the Young Adult Library Services Association (YALSA), a division of the American Library Association, compiles a list of the best fiction appropriate for young adults ages 12 to 18. Selected on the basis of each book's proven or potential appeal and value to young adults, the titles span a variety of subjects as well as a broad range of reading levels.

Anderson, Jodi Lynn. *Tiger Lily* (HarperCollins).

Andrews, Jesse. *Me and Earl and the Dying Girl* (Abrams/Amulet).

Bacigalupi, Paolo. *The Drowned Cities* (Little, Brown).

Bardugo, Leigh. *Shadow and Bone* (Holt).

Barnaby, Hannah. *Wonder Show* (Houghton Mifflin Harcourt).

Barnes, Jennifer Lynn. *Every Other Day* (Egmont).

Barraclough, Lindsey. *Long Lankin* (Candlewick).

Bray, Libba. *The Diviners* (Little, Brown),

Brennan, Sarah Rees. *Unspoken: The Lynburn Legacy* (Random).

Calame, Don. *Call the Shots* (Candlewick).

Cameron, Sharon. *The Dark Unwinding* (Scholastic).

Carey, Janet Lee. *Dragonswood* (Penguin/Dial).

Carlton, Susan. *Love and Haight* (Holt).

Cashore, Kristin. *Bitterblue* (Penguin/Dial).

Coats, Jillian Anderson. *The Wicked and the Just* (Houghton Mifflin Harcourt).

Cronn-Mills, Kirstin. *Beautiful Music for Ugly Children* (Flux).

Cross, Sarah. *Kill Me Softly* (Egmont).

Crowley, Cath. *Graffiti Moon* (Random).

Damico, Gina. *Croak* (Houghton Mifflin Harcourt).

Danforth, Emily M. *The Miseducation of Cameron Post* (HarperCollins).

Derting, Kimberly *The Pledge* (McElderry).

Doller, Trish. *Something Like Normal* (Bloomsbury).

Jordan, Dream. *Bad Boy* (St. Martin's).

Ellison, Kate. *Butterfly Clues* (Egmont).

Fama, Elizabeth. *Monstrous Beauty* (Farrar, Straus & Giroux).

Farish, Terry. *The Good Braider* (Amazon).

Fforde, Jasper. *The Last Dragonslayer* (Houghton Mifflin Harcourt).

Fitzpatrick, Huntley. *My Life Next Door* (Penguin/Dial).

Gagnon, Michelle. *Don't Turn Around* (HarperCollins).

Gaughen, A. C. *Scarlet* (Walker).

Grant, Michael. *BZRK* (Egmont).

Grant, Michael, and Katherine Applegate. *Eve and Adam* (Macmillan).

Green, John. *The Fault in Our Stars* (Penguin/Dutton).

Halpern, Julie. *Have a Nice Day* (Macmillan).

Hand, Elizabeth. *Radiant Days* (Penguin/Viking).

Harrington, Hannah. *Speechless* (Harlequin).

Hartman, Rachel. *Seraphina* (Random).

Hiaasen, Carl. *Chomp* (Knopf).

Johnson, Angela. *A Certain October* (Simon & Schuster).

Kagawa, Julie. *The Immortal Rules* (Harlequin).

Kincaid, S. J. *Insignia* (HarperCollins).

Kindl, Patrice. *Keeping the Castle* (Penguin/Viking).

King, A. S. *Ask the Passengers* (Little, Brown).

Knowles, Jo. *See You At Harry's* (Candlewick).

Kokie, E. M. *Personal Effects* (Candlewick).

Kontis, Alethea. *Enchanted* (Houghton Mifflin Harcourt).

Lacey, Josh. *Island of Thieves* (Houghton Mifflin Harcourt).

LaCour, Nina. *The Disenchantments* (Penguin/Dutton).

LaFevers, Robin. *Grave Mercy* (Houghton Mifflin Harcourt).

Lake, Nick. *In Darkness* (Bloomsbury).

Lanagan, Margo. *The Brides of Rollrock Island* (Knopf).

Larbalestier, Justine, and Sarah Rees Brennan. *Team Human* (HarperCollins).

Leavitt, Martine. *My Book of Life by Angel* (Farrar, Straus & Giroux).

Lee, Y. S. *The Traitor and the Tunnel* (Candlewick).

Lerangis, Peter, and Harry Mazer. *Somebody Please Tell Me Who I Am* (Simon & Schuster).

Leveen, Tom. *Zero* (Random).

Levine, Kristin. *Lions of Little Rock* (Penguin/Putnam).

Levithan, David. *Every Day* (Random).

Lyga, Barry. *I Hunt Killers* (Little, Brown).

Maas, Sarah. *Throne of Glass* (Bloomsbury).

MacColl, Michaela. *Promise the Night* (Chronicle).

Mackall, Dandi. *The Silence of Murder* (Knopf).

Magoon, Kekla. *Fire in the Streets* (Aladdin).

Marchetta, Melina. *Froi of the Exiles: The Lumatere Chronicles* (Candlewick).

Mariller, Juliet. *Shadowfell* (Knopf).

Matson, Morgan. *Second Chance Summer* (Simon & Schuster).

McCormick, Patricia. *Never Fall Down* (HarperCollins).

McDonald, Ian. *Planesrunner* (Prometheus).

McQuerry, Maureen Doyle. *The Peculiars* (Abrams/Amulet).

Meyer, Marissa. *Cinder* (Macmillian).

Michaelis, Antonia. *The Storyteller* (Abrams/Amulet).

Mieville, China. *Railsea* (Random).

Myers, Kate Kae. *The Vanishing Game* (Bloomsbury).

Nelson, Vaunda Micheaux. *No Crystal Stair: A Documentary Novel of the Life and Work of Lewis Micheaux, Harlem Bookseller* (Carolrhoda).

Newman, Leslea. *October Mourning: A Song for Matthew Shepard* (Candlewick).

Nielsen, Jennifer. *The False Prince* (Scholastic).

Nix, Garth. *A Confusion of Princes* (HarperCollins).

Oppel, Kenneth. *Such Wicked Intent: The Apprenticeship of Victor Frankenstein, Book Two* (Simon & Schuster).

Pearce, Jackson. *Purity* (Little, Brown).

Poblocki, Dan. *The Ghost of Graylock* (Scholastic).

Pratchett, Terry. *Dodger* (HarperCollins).

Quick, Matthew. *Boy 21* (Little, Brown).

Rivers, Karen. *The Encyclopedia of Me* (Scholastic).

Rossi, Veronica. *Under the Never Sky* (HarperCollins).

Rubens, Michael. *Sons of the 613* (Houghton Mifflin Harcourt).

Saenz, Benjamin Alire. *Aristotle and Dante Discover the Secrets of the Universe* (Simon & Schuster).

Schrefer, Eliot. *Endangered* (Scholastic).

Schumacher, Julie. *The Unbearable Book Club for Unsinkable Girls* (Delacorte).

Selfors, Suzanne. *The Sweetest Spell* (Walker).

Sherman, Delia. *The Freedom Maze* (Big Mouth House).

Schreiber, Joe. *Au Revoir Crazy European Chick* (Houghton Mifflin Harcourt).

Sonnenblick, Jordan. *Curveball: The Year I Lost My Grip* (Scholastic).

Stiefvater, Maggie. *The Raven Boys* (Scholastic).

Summers, Courtney. *This is Not a Test* (St. Martin's).

Tregay, Sarah. *Love and Leftovers* (HarperCollins).

Vivian, Siobhan. *The List* (Scholastic).

Volponi, Paul. *The Final Four* (Penguin/Viking).

Wasserman, Robin. *The Book of Blood and Shadow* (Knopf).

Wein, Elizabeth. *Code Name Verity* (Disney/Hyperion).

Woodson, Jacqueline. *Beneath a Meth Moon* (Penguin).

Woolston, Blythe. *Catch and Release* (Carolrhoda).

Zettel, Sarah. *Dust Girl* (Random).

Quick Picks for Reluctant Young Adult Readers

The Young Adult Library Services Association, a division of the American Library Association, annually chooses a list of outstanding titles that will stimulate the interest of reluctant teen readers. This list is intended to attract teens who, for whatever reason, choose not to read.

The list includes fiction and nonfiction titles published from late 2011 through 2012.

Fiction

Andrews, Jesse. *Me and Earl and the Dying Girl* (Abrams/Amulet).

Atwood, Megan. The Paranormalists series: *Case 1: The Haunting in Apt. 101; Case 2: The Terror of Black Eagle Tavern; Case 3: The Mayhem on Mohawk Avenue; Case 4: The Bridge of Death* (Lerner).

Bick, Ilsa J. *Ashes* (Egmont).

Blake, Kendare. *Girl of Nightmares* (Tor Teen).

Bodeen, S. A. *The Raft* (Farrar, Straus & Giroux).

Brooks, Kevin. *Johnny Delgado: Private Detective* (Stoke).

Brown, Jeffrey. *Darth Vader and Son* (Chronicle).

Crawford, Brent. *Carter's Unfocused, One-Track Mind* (Hyperion).

Damico, Gina. *Croak* (Houghton Mifflin Harcourt).

Devine, Eric. *Tap Out* (Running Press).

Doller, Trish. *Something Like Normal* (Bloomsbury).

Fukuda, Andrew. *The Hunt* (Macmillan).

Halliday, Gemma. *Deadly Cool* (HarperCollins).

Halliday, Gemma. *Social Suicide* (Deadly Cool series). (HarperCollins).

Henry, April. *The Night She Disappeared* (Holt).

Hopkins, Ellen. *Tilt* (McElderry).

Jordan, Dream. *Bad Boy* (Macmillan).

Keplinger, Kody. *A Midsummer's Nightmare* (Little, Brown).

Kinney, Jeff. *Diary of a Wimpy Kid: The Third Wheel* (Amulet).

Lacey, Josh. *Island of Thieves* (Houghton Mifflin Harcourt).

Laybourne, Emmy. *Monument 14* (Feiwel and Friends).

Lorentz, Dayna. *No Safety in Numbers* (Penguin/Dial).

Lyga, Barry. *I Hunt Killers* (Little, Brown).

Lynch, Chris. Vietnam series: *Vietnam No. 1: I Pledge Allegiance; Vietnam No. 2: Sharpshooter; Vietnam No. 3: Free-Fire Zone* (Scholastic).

McClintock, Norah. *Guilty* (Orca).

McDaniel, Lurlene. *Red Heart Tattoo* (Delacorte).

McDowell, Beck. *This is Not a Drill* (Nancy Paulsen Books).

McGarry, Katie. *Pushing the Limits* (Harlequin).

McMann, Lisa. *Dead To You* (Simon & Schuster).

McNeil, Gretchen. *Ten* (Balzer + Bray).

Monsen, Avery, and Jory John. *All My Friends Are Still Dead* (Chronicle).

Morel, Alex. *Survive* (Razorbill).

O'Connor, George. *Hades: Lord of the Dead* (Olympians series) (Roaring Brook).

Patrick, Cat. *Revived* (Little, Brown).

Price, Lissa. *Starters* (Delacorte).

Ross, Jeff. *Dawn Patrol* (Orca).

Ryan, Amy Kathleen. *Glow* (Macmillan).

Ryan, Tom. *Way to Go* (Orca).

Shan, Darren. *Zom-B* (Little, Brown).

Springer, Nancy. *My Sister's Stalker* (Holiday House).

Stones, Greg. *Zombies Hate Stuff* (Chronicle).

Summers, Courtney. *This is Not a Test* (Macmillan).

TenNapel, Doug. *Cardboard* (Scholastic/Graphix).

Tillit, L. B. *Unchained* (Saddleback Educational).

Travel Team series: Fehler, Gene. *Forced Out*; Glaser, Jason. *The Prospect*; Higgins, M. G. *Power Hitter*; Jasper, Rick. *The Catch* and

Out of Control; Karre, Andrew. *High Heat* (Lerner).

Van Tol, Alex. *Shallow Grave* (Orca).

Volponi, Paul. *The Final Four* (Penguin).

Williams, Carol Lynch. *Waiting* (Simon & Schuster).

Woodson, Jacqueline. *Beneath a Meth Moon: An Elegy* (Penguin).

Nonfiction

Backderf, Derf. *My Friend Dahmer* (Abrams ComicArts).

Bender, Mike, and Doug Chernack. *Awkward Family Pet Photos* (Random).

Briggs, Amy. *Angry Birds Space: A Furious Flight into the Final Frontier* (National Geographic).

Brooks, Stacey Leigh. *Diary of Creepy-Ass Dolls* (Krause).

Failblog.org community. *Fail Harder: Ridiculous Illustrations of Epic Fails* (Andrews McMeel).

Halls, Kelly Milner. *Alien Investigation: Searching for the Truth About UFOs and Aliens* (Lerner).

Jenkins, Beverly. *Photobombed! Making Bad Pictures Great and Good Pictures Awesomely Bad* (Sourcebooks).

John, Jory and Avery Monsen. *K is for Knifeball: An Alphabet of Terrible Advice* (Chronicle).

Johnson, Rich. *The Ultimate Survival Manual: 333 Skills That Will Get You Out Alive* (Weldon Owen).

Kyi, Tanya Lloyd, and Steve Rolston (illustrator). *Seeing Red: The True Story of Blood* (PBK Annick).

Marciuliano, Francesco. *I Could Pee on This: And Other Poems by Cats* (Chronicle).

National Geographic. *Weird But True! Stupid Criminals: 100 Brainless Baddies Busted, plus Wacky Facts* (National Geographic).

Nemtin, Ben, Dave Lingwood, Duncan Penn, and Jonnie Penn. *What Do You Want to Do Before You Die?* (Workman).

Patenaude, Jeremy. *Halo: The Essential Visual Guide* (DK).

Raatma, Lucia. *The Science of Soldiers* (Capstone).

Rodriguez, Gaby, and Jenna Glatzer. *The Pregnancy Project: A Memoir* (Simon & Schuster).

Ross, Richard. *Juvenile in Justice* (Richard Ross).

Shoket, Ann. *Seventeen Ultimate Guide to Beauty: The Best Hair, Skin, Nails and Makeup Ideas for You* (Running Press).

Wasdin, Howard E., and Stephen Templin. *I Am a SEAL Team Six Warrior: Memoirs of an American Soldier* (Macmillan).

Amazing Audiobooks for Young Adults

Each year a committee of the Young Adult Library Services Association, a division of the American Library Association, compiles a list of the best audiobooks for young adults ages 12 to 18. The titles are selected for their teen appeal and recording quality, and because they enhance the audience's appreciation of any written work on which the recordings may be based. While the list as a whole addresses the interests and needs of young adults, individual titles need not appeal to this entire age range but rather to parts of it.

Nonfiction

Warriors Don't Cry by Melba Pattillo Beals, read by Lisa Renee Pitts. Tantor, 13 hours, 10 discs or 2 MP3 CDs.

Witches! by Rosalyn Schanzer, read by Jessica Almasy. Recorded Books, 2 hours and 25 minutes, 2 discs.

Fiction

Almost Perfect by Brian Katcher, read by Kirby Heyborne. Listening Library, 10 hours and 40 minutes, 9 discs.

Artemis Fowl: The Last Guardian by Eoin Colfer, read by Nathaniel Parker. Listening Library, 7 hours and 40 minutes, 6 discs.

Au Revoir, Crazy European Chick by Joe Schreiber, read by Steven Boyer. Recorded Books, 5 hours, 5 discs.

The Catastrophic History of You and Me by Jess Rothenberg, read by Suzy Jackson. Recorded Books, 9 hours and 30 minutes, 8 discs.

Code Name Verity by Elizabeth Wein, read by Morven Christie and Lucy Gaskell. Bolinda, 10 hours, 9 discs.

Crusher by Niall Leonard, read by Daniel Weyman. Listening Library, 6 hours and 42 minutes, 6 discs.

Curveball: the Year I Lost My Grip by Jordan Sonnenblick, read by Luke Daniels. Brilliance, 5 hours and 8 minutes, 5 discs.

Dancing Carl by Gary Paulsen, read by Nick Podehl. Brilliance, 2 hours and 21 minutes, 2 discs.

Diary of a Wimpy Kid: Cabin Fever by Jeff Kinney, read by Ramón De Ocampo. Recorded Books, 2 hours and 15 minutes, 2 discs.

The Diviners by Libba Bray, read by January LaVoy. Listening Library, 18 hours and 15 minutes, 15 discs.

Enchanted by Alethea Kontis, read by Katherine Kellgren. Brilliance, 7 hours and 49 minutes, 7 discs.

The Fault in Our Stars by John Green, read by Kate Rudd. Candlewick on Brilliance, 7 hours and 19 minutes, 6 discs.

The Fire Chronicle by John Stephens, read by Jim Dale. Listening Library, 12 hours and 22 minutes, 10 discs.

The Freak Observer by Blythe Woolston, read by Jessica Almasy. Brilliance, 5 hours and 36 minutes, 5 discs.

Graffiti Moon by Cath Crowley, read by Ben MacLaine, Hamish R. Johnson, and Chelsea Bruland. Listening Library, 6 hours and 5 minutes, 5 discs.

I Hunt Killers by Barry Lyga, read by Charlie Thurston. AudioGo, 9 hours and 30 minutes, 8 discs.

Inheritance by Christopher Paolini, read by Gerard Doyle. Listening Library, 31 hours and 5 minutes, 24 discs.

The Isle of Blood by Rick Yancey, read by Steven Boyer. Recorded Books, 14 hours and 30 minutes, 12 discs.

A Monster Calls by Patrick Ness, read by Jason Isaacs. Candlewick on Brilliance, 4 hours and 1 minute, 5 discs.

Monstrous Beauty by Elizabeth Fama, read by Katherine Kellgren. Macmillan Audio, 8 hours, 7 discs.

October Mourning by Leslea Newman, read by Emily Beresford, Luke Daniels, Tom Parks, Nick Podehl, Kate Rudd, and Christina Traister. Candlewick on Brilliance, 1 hour and 20 minutes, 2 discs.

Personal Effects by E. M. Kokie, read by Nick Podehl. Candlewick on Brilliance, 9 hours and 8 minutes, 8 discs.

See You At Harry's by Jo Knowles, read by Kate Rudd. Candlewick on Brilliance, 5 hours and 49 minutes, 5 discs.

Son by Lois Lowry, read by Bernadette Dunne. Books on Tape, 8 hours and 11 minutes, 7 discs.

Three Times Lucky by Sheila Turnage, read by Michal Friedman. Penguin Audio, 8 hours, 7 discs.

The Watch That Ends the Night by Allan Wolf, read by Michael Page, Phil Gigante, Christopher Lane, Laural Merlington, and Angela Dawe. Candlewick on Brilliance, 10 hours and 16 minutes, 9 discs.

Wonder by R. J. Palacio, read by Diana Steele, Nick Podehl, and Kate Rudd. Brilliance, 8 hours and 12 minutes, 7 discs.

Words in the Dust by Trent Reedy, read by Ariana Delawari. Scholastic Audiobooks, 8 hours and 28 minutes, 7 discs.

The Reading List

Established in 2007 by the Reference and User Services Association (RUSA), a division of the American Library Association, this list highlights outstanding genre fiction that merits special attention by general adult readers and the librarians who work with them.

RUSA's Reading List Council, which consists of 12 librarians who are experts in readers' advisory and collection development, selects books in eight categories: Adrenaline (suspense, thrillers, and action adventure), Fantasy, Historical Fiction, Horror, Mystery, Romance, Science Fiction, and Women's Fiction.

Adrenaline

Gone Girl by Gillian Flynn (Crown).

Fantasy

The Rook by Daniel O'Malley (Little, Brown).

Historical Fiction

Bring Up the Bodies by Hilary Mantel (Holt).

Horror

The Ritual by Adam Nevill (St. Martin's).

Mystery

The Gods of Gotham by Lyndsay Faye (Putnam).

Romance

Firelight by Kristen Callihan (Grand Central).

Science Fiction

Caliban's War by James S. A. Corey (Orbit).

Women's Fiction

The Care and Handling of Roses with Thorns by Margaret Dilloway (Putnam).

The Listen List

Established in 2010 by the Reference and User Services Association (RUSA), the Listen List highlights outstanding audiobooks that merit special attention by general adult listeners and the librarians who work with them.

They are chosen by RUSA's Listen List Council, which annually selects a list of 12 titles including fiction, nonfiction, poetry, and plays. To be eligible, titles must be available for purchase and circulation by libraries. An annotated version of the list on the RUSA website includes more information on each choice.

Angelmaker by Nick Harkaway, narrated by Daniel Weyman (AudioGO).

Bring Up the Bodies by Hilary Mantel, narrated by Simon Vance (Macmillan Audio).

The Chalk Girl by Carol O'Connell, narrated by Barbara Rosenblat (Recorded Books).

The Death of Sweet Mister by Daniel Woodrell, narrated by Nicholas Tecosky (AudioGo).

The Garden Intrigue by Lauren Willig, narrated by Kate Reading (Books on Tape).

Heft by Liz Moore, narrated by Kirby Heyborne and Keith Szarabajka (Blackstone Audiobooks).

The House of Silk: A Sherlock Holmes Novel by Anthony Horowitz, narrated by Derek Jacobi (Hachette Audio and AudioGO).

The Inquisitor by Mark Allen Smith, narrated by Ari Fliakos (Macmillan Audio).

Macbeth by William Shakespeare, narrated by Alan Cumming (Simon & Schuster Audio).

Miles: The Autobiography by Miles Davis and Quincy Troupe, narrated by Dion Graham (AudioGO).

Mr. Penumbra's 24-Hour Bookstore by Robin Sloan, narrated by Ari Fliakos (Macmillan Audio).

The Pickwick Papers by Charles Dickens, narrated by David Timson (Naxos Audiobooks).

The Remains of the Day by Kazuo Ishiguro, narrated by Simon Prebble (Tantor Media).

Notable Recordings for Children

This list of notable CD recordings for children was selected by the Association for Library Service to Children, a division of the American Library Association. Recommended titles are chosen by children's librarians and educators on the basis of their originality, creativity, and suitability. Running times are rounded to nearest hour or half hour.

Artemis Fowl: The Last Guardian Listening Library, 7 hours and 30 minutes. Grades 5–9. Nathaniel Parker narrates this tale involving Artemis Fowl's archenemy, Opal Koboi.

Ballet for Martha: Making Appalachian Spring. Brilliance Audio, 45 minutes. Grades 2–6. The creation of Martha Graham's and Aaron Copland's "Appalachian Spring" is documented in this collaboration between Sarah Jessica Parker and the Seattle Symphony.

Can You Canoe? Okee Dokee Brothers, 39 minutes. All Ages. Music, storytelling, and video feature in this adventure on the Mississippi.

The Cheshire Cheese Cat: A Dickens of a Tale. Listening Library, 4 hours. Grades 4–7. Katherine Kellgren narrates a cat-and-mouse tale set in the England of Charles Dickens's time.

A Dog's Way Home. Listening Library, 7 hours. Grades 4–7. A dog and his owner seek to find each other after a long separation. The story is told by Chuck Carrington and Emily Eiden.

Edwina, the Dinosaur Who Didn't Know She Was Extinct. Weston Woods, 7 minutes. Grades K–2. Mo and Cher Willems recite the tale of a dinosaur and a boy.

The False Prince. Scholastic Audio, 8 hours. Grades 5–8. Charlie McWade narrates the story of an orphan who tries to impersonate a prince.

The Fire Chronicle. Listening Library, 12 hours and 30 minutes. Grades 4–8. Jim Dale tells of Michael's and Emma's hunt for a legendary book while their sister Kate is stranded a hundred years in the past in this sequel to *The Emerald Atlas.*

Ghost Knight. Listening Library, 5 hours. Grades 4–6. Young Jon and his new friend Ella seek to solve a century-old mystery, as danger constantly threatens. Elliot Hill is the narrator.

Goodnight, Goodnight, Construction Site. Weston Woods, 8 minutes. Pre-K–Grade 2. Big trucks on a construction site settle in for the night in this tale read by Dion Graham.

The Great Cake Mystery: Precious Ramotswe's Very First Case. Listening Library, 1 hour. Grades 2–4. Precious Ramotswe shows she has what it takes to be a detective. Adjoa Andoh narrates this Alexander McCall Smith story for young readers.

Knuffle Bunny Free: An Unexpected Diversion. Weston Woods, 10 minutes. Pre-K–Grade 2. Knuffle Bunny takes a surprise detour on a long-distance family outing. Voiced by Trixie, Cher, and Mo Willems.

The Library Dragon. Peachtree, 21 minutes. Grades K–3. Carmen Agra Deedy tells her tale of a library dragon who loses her scales.

Little Seed: Songs for Children by Woody Guthrie. Smithsonian Folkways, 30 minutes. All Ages. Elizabeth Mitchell performs Guthrie's songs for young listeners, including "Bling Blang" and "Riding in My Car."

Merry Christmas, Splat. Weston Woods, 6 minutes. Pre-K–Grade 2. John Keating's narration and Scotty Huff's music highlight Splat the Cat's attempts to behave well enough that Santa will visit.

The Mighty Miss Malone. Listening Library, 8 hours. Grades 4–7. Deza Malone and her family bravely struggle through the Great Depression in this story read by Bahni Turpin.

The Mighty Sky. BNC Records, 31 minutes. Grades 2–5. Art and science blend in this musical celebration of astronomy.

The Notorious Benedict Arnold. Listening Library, 7 hours. Grades 6–8. The story of traitorous Revolutionary War officer Benedict Arnold is told by Mark Bramhall.

One Year in Coal Harbor. Listening Library, 5 hours and 30 minutes. Grades 4–7. Kathleen McInerney narrates the continuing story of Primrose Squarp.

Ozomatli Presents OzoKidz. Hornblow Recordings/Megaforce Records, 37 minutes. All Ages. A lively blend of various musical genres is designed to inspire singing and dancing.

The Red Hen. Weston Woods, 5 minutes. Pre-K–Grade 2. A creative rendering of the traditional story is told by Walter Mayes with music by Caleb Miles. Lively illustrations accompany the storytelling.

Same Sun Here. Brilliance Audio, six hours. Grades 5–8. River and Meena live many miles apart but become friends through correspondence. The narrators are the story's authors, Silas House and Neela Vaswani.

A Sick Day for Amos McGee. Weston Woods, 8 minutes. Pre-K–Grade 2. David de Vries voices the story of zoo animals' affection for their keeper.

Temple Grandin: How the Girl Who Loved Cows Embraced Autism and Changed the World. AudioGO, 3 hours. Grades 5–8. Meredith Mitchell convincingly portrays the scientist and her efforts to develop humane ways to treat animals.

Titanic: Voices from the Disaster. Listening Library, 5 hours. Grades 4–8. Several narrators tell the story of this famous disaster from the viewpoints of a number of survivors.

Wonder. Brilliance Audio, 8 hours. Grades 4–7. Diana Steele, Nick Podehl, and Kate Rudd recount the story of Auggie, who was born with severe facial abnormalities, and the challenges and triumphs of his first year at school.

Words in the Dust. Scholastic Audio, 8 hours and 30 minutes. Grades 5–8. The story of Zulaikha and the challenges she faces as a young woman in modern Afghan society is narrated by Ariana Delawari.

Notable Children's Books

A list of notable children's books is selected each year by the Notable Children's Books Committee of the Association for Library Service to Children, a division of the American Library Association. Recommended titles are selected by children's librarians and educators based on originality, creativity, and suitability for children. [See "Literary Prizes, 2012" later in Part 5 for Caldecott, Newbery, and other award winners—Ed.]

Books for Younger Readers

And Then It's Spring by Julie Fogliano, illustrated by Erin E. Stead (Roaring Brook/Neal Porter).

Bear Has a Story to Tell by Philip C. Stead, illustrated by Erin E. Stead (Roaring Brook/Neal Porter).

Black Dog by Levi Pinfold, illustrated by the author (Candlewick/Templar).

Charley's First Night by Amy Hest, illustrated by Helen Oxenbury (Candlewick).

Creepy Carrots! by Aaron Reynolds, illustrated by Peter Brown (Simon & Schuster).

Demolition by Sally Sutton, illustrated by Brian Lovelock (Candlewick).

Dogs on Duty by Dorothy Hinshaw Patent. Illustrated. (Walker).

Dreaming Up: A Celebration of Building by Christy Hale, illustrated by the author (Lee & Low).

Extra Yarn by Mac Barnett, illustrated by Jon Klassen (HarperCollins).

Golden Domes and Silver Lanterns: A Muslim Book of Colors by Hena Khan, illustrated by Mehrdokht Amini (Chronicle).

Goldilocks and the Three Dinosaurs by Mo Willems, illustrated by the author. (HarperCollins).

Green by Laura Vaccaro Seeger, illustrated by the author (Roaring Brook/Neal Porter).

Hippopposites by Janik Coat (Appleseed).

Infinity and Me by Kate Hosford, illustrated by Gabi Swiatkowska. (Lerner/Carolrhoda).

Just Ducks by Nicola Davies, illustrated by Salvatore Rubbino (Candlewick).

Let's Go for a Drive! by Mo Willems, illustrated by the author (Hyperion).

Machines Go to Work in the City by William Low, illustrated by the author (Holt).

Magritte's Marvelous Hat : A Picture Book by D. B. (Donald B.) Johnson, illustrated by the author (Houghton Mifflin Harcourt).

Martin de Porres: The Rose in the Desert by Gary D. Schmidt, illustrated by David Diaz (Houghton Mifflin Harcourt).

More by I. C. Springman, illustrated by Brian Lies (Houghton Mifflin Harcourt).

Nighttime Ninja by Barbara DaCosta, illustrated by Ed Young (Little, Brown).

Oh, No! by Candace Fleming, illustrated by Eric Rohmann (Random/Schwartz & Wade).

One Cool Friend by Toni Buzzeo, illustrated by David Small (Dial/Penguin).

One Special Day: A Story for Big Brothers and Sisters by Lola M. Schaefer, illustrated by Jessica Meserve (Disney/Hyperion).

Penny and Her Doll by Kevin Henkes, illustrated by the author (Greenwillow).

Pete the Cat and His Four Groovy Buttons by Eric Litwin, illustrated by James Dean (HarperCollins).

Rabbit and Robot: The Sleepover by Cece Bell, illustrated by the author (Candlewick).

Sleep Like a Tiger by Mary Logue, illustrated by Pamela Zagarenski (Houghton Mifflin Harcourt).

This Is Not My Hat by Jon Klassen, illustrated by the author (Candlewick).

This Moose Belongs to Me by Oliver Jeffers, illustrated by the author (Philomel/Penguin).

Up, Tall, and High! by Ethan Long, illustrated by the author (Putnam/Penguin).

Z Is for Moose by Kelly Bingham, illustrated by Paul O. Zelinsky (Greenwillow).

Middle Readers

Abraham Lincoln and Frederick Douglass: The Story behind an American Friendship by Russell Freedman. Illustrated. (Houghton Mifflin Harcourt).

The Beetle Book by Steve Jenkins, illustrated by the author (Houghton Mifflin Harcourt).

A Black Hole Is Not a Hole by Carolyn Cinami DeCristofano, illustrated by Michael Carroll (Charlesbridge).

Bomb: The Race to Build—and Steal—the World's Most Dangerous Weapon by Steve Sheinkin. Illustrated. (Roaring Brook).

Brothers at Bat: The True Story of an Amazing All-Brother Baseball Team by Audrey Vernick, illustrated by Steven Salerno (Houghton Mifflin Harcourt).

Chuck Close: Face Book by Chuck Close. Illustrated. (Abrams).

Each Kindness by Jacqueline Woodson, illustrated by E. B. Lewis (Penguin/Nancy Paulsen).

Electric Ben: The Amazing Life and Times of Benjamin Franklin by Robert Byrd, illustrated by the author (Dial/Penguin).

George Bellows: Painter with a Punch! by Robert Burleigh, illustrated by George Bellows (Abrams).

Helen's Big World: The Life of Helen Keller by Doreen Rappaport, illustrated by Matt Tavares (Disney/Hyperion).

Iceberg, Right Ahead! The Tragedy of the Titanic by Stephanie Sammartino McPherson. Illustrated. (Lerner/Twenty-First Century).

In a Glass Grimmly by Adam Gidwitz. Illustrated. (Dutton/Penguin).

Island: A Story of the Galápagos by Jason Chin, illustrated by the author (Roaring Brook/Neal Porter).

Liar and Spy by Rebecca Stead (Random/Wendy Lamb).

Lulu and the Duck in the Park by Hilary McKay, illustrated by Priscilla Lamont (Albert Whitman).

May B. by Caroline Starr Rose (Random/Schwartz & Wade).

The Mighty Mars Rovers: The Incredible Adventures of Spirit and Opportunity by Elizabeth Rusch. Illustrated. (Houghton Mifflin Harcourt).

Moonbird : A Year on the Wind with the Great Survivor B95 by Phillip M. Hoose. Illustrated. (Farrar, Straus & Giroux).

The One and Only Ivan by Katherine Applegate, illustrated by Patricia Castelao. (HarperCollins).

See You at Harry's by Jo Knowles (Candlewick).

Splendors and Glooms by Laura Amy Schlitz (Candlewick).

Starry River of the Sky by Grace Lin, illustrated by the author (Little, Brown).

Three Times Lucky by Sheila Turnage (Dial/Penguin).

Titanic: Voices from the Disaster by Deborah Hopkinson. Illustrated. (Scholastic).

Twelve Kinds of Ice by Ellen Bryan Obed, illustrated by Barbara McClintock (Houghton Mifflin Harcourt).

Unspoken: A Story from the Underground Railroad by Henry Cole, illustrated by the author (Scholastic).

Wonder by R. J. Palacio (Knopf).

Zombie Makers: True Stories of Nature's Undead by Rebecca L. Johnson. Illustrated. (Lerner/Millbrook).

Older Readers

Aristotle and Dante Discover the Secrets of the Universe by Benjamin Alire Sáenz (Simon & Schuster).

Beyond Courage: The Untold Story of Jewish Resistance during the Holocaust by Doreen Rappaport. Illustrated. (Candlewick).

Drama by Raina Telgemeier, illustrated by the author (Graphix/Scholastic).

A Game for Swallows: To Die, to Leave, to Return by Zeina Abirached, illustrated by the author (Lerner/Graphic Universe).

Invincible Microbe: Tuberculosis and the Never-Ending Search for a Cure by Jim Murphy and Alison Blank. Illustrated. (Houghton Mifflin Harcourt).

My Family for the War by Anne C. Voorhoeve, translated by Tammi Reichel (Dial/Penguin).

My Sister Lives on the Mantelpiece by Annabel Pitcher (Little, Brown).

The Revolution of Evelyn Serrano by Sonia Manzano (Scholastic).

Seraphina by Rachel Hartman (Random).

Son by Lois Lowry (Houghton Mifflin Harcourt).

Son of a Gun by Anne de Graaf (Eerdmans).

Steve Jobs: The Man Who Thought Different by Karen Blumenthal. Illustrated. (Macmillan).

Temple Grandin: How the Girl who Loved Cows Embraced Autism and Changed the World by Sy Montgomery. Illustrated. (Houghton Mifflin Harcourt).

We've Got a Job: The 1963 Birmingham Children's March by Cynthia Y. Levinson. Illustrated. (Peachtree).

All Ages

Little Bird by Germano Zullo, illustrated by Albertine (Enchanted Lion).

National Geographic Book of Animal Poetry: 200 Poems with Photographs that Squeak, Soar, and Roar! edited by J. Patrick Lewis. Illustrated. (National Geographic).

Step Gently Out by Helen Frost, illustrated by Rick Lieder (Candlewick).

The Year Comes Round : Haiku through the Seasons by Sid Farrar, illustrated by Ilse Plume (Albert Whitman).

Water Sings Blue: Ocean Poems by Kate Coombs, illustrated by Meilo So (Chronicle).

Notable Children's Videos

These DVD titles are selected by a committee of the Association for Library Service to Children, a division of the American Library Association. Recommendations are based on originality, creativity, and suitability for children.

55 Socks. National Film Board of Canada, 8 minutes. Ages 8–14.

Anna, Emma and the Condors. Green Planet Films, 20 minutes. Ages 7 and up.

Are You a Bully? Test. Human Relations Media, 23 minutes. Ages 10 and up.

Big Drive. National Film Board of Canada, 9 minutes. Ages 8 and up.

Bink and Gollie. Weston Woods, 14 minutes. Ages 4–8.

Edwina, the Dinosaur Who Didn't Know She Was Extinct. Weston Woods, 10 minutes. Ages 4–8.

Hi! Fly Guy. Weston Woods, 7 minutes. Ages 4–8

Kali the Little Vampire. National Film Board of Canada, 9 minutes. Ages 12 and up.

Knuffle Bunny Free: An Unexpected Diversion. Weston Woods, 13 minutes. Ages 4–8.

The Other Side. Weston Woods, 8 minutes. Ages 5–9.

Scaredy Squirrel Makes a Friend. Weston Woods, 12 minutes. Ages 4–8.

A Sick Day for Amos McGee. Weston Woods, 10 minutes. Ages 3–8.

Show Way. Weston Woods, 12 minutes. Ages 5 and up.

Sky Color. Weston Woods, 7 minutes. Ages 4–8.

Wind Flyers. Nutmeg Media, 7 minutes. Ages 5–9.

Bestsellers of 2012

Trend to Digital Books Heats Up

Daisy Maryles

Contributing Editor, *Publishers Weekly*

All the publishers that shared digital book information with *Publishers Weekly* (*PW*) were houses that rack up enough print sales to compete in the bestsellers race. And while we estimate that we have more than 1,000 e-books with sales of 25,000+, we know this does not reflect all e-book sales in the book industry. Still, a look at this quantity underscores that the book business is quickly moving to digital.

It would be safe to say that the lackluster performance in mass market has a lot to do with the fact that readers are enjoying the convenience of electronic devices instead of the more traditional convenience of the paperback.

Also, it is clear where backlist sales have gone. Peruse the list and you will see double-digit numbers of titles for most of the bestselling veterans. Nora Roberts may be the most prolific author in this area; she has 40 titles on the e-book list, adding up to about 3.2 million in total e-sales; James Patterson has 29 books on the list, with a total of more than 2.6 million; Janet Evanovich scores close to 1.8 million with 19 books.

We've also compiled a list of the top-selling children's and young adult e-books of 2012, which is led by the powerhouse Hunger Games trilogy, which sold a combined 12.7 million e-books. [See the Children's Books section later in this article—*Ed.*].

In *PW*'s call for information we mistakenly asked for e-books that had sold more than 25,000 copies in 2012 without explaining that we were only collecting titles published in 2011 and 2012 or those titles that are still on the magazine's weekly print charts. All the better! Most publishers complied with the written instructions, and we were inundated with long lists of e-book topsellers, and what a picture it paints of a changed sales landscape! Looking at these lists provided some fascinating insights into the world of e-books, so we changed the rules this time and honored our miscommunication.

Note: Titles submitted in confidence, for use only in ranking the titles on the list, have asterisks. Penguin USA and Random House Publishing Group were among those that shared sales numbers for ranking purposes only.

Adapted from *Publishers Weekly*, March 18, 2013.

E-Book Sales, 2012

15 Million+ for All Three

*Fifty Shades of Grey Book One. EL James. Vintage.

*Fifty Shades Darker Book Two. EL James. Vintage.

*Fifty Shades Freed Book Three. EL James. Vintage.

1,000,000+

*Gone Girl. Gillian Flynn. Crown.

850,000+

*Fifty Shades Trilogy bundle. EL James. Vintage.

*Bared to You. Sylvia Day. Berkley.

500,000+

*The Racketeer. John Grisham. Doubleday.

*Reflected in You. Sylvia Day. Berkley.

The Lucky One. Nicholas Sparks. Grand Central (569,544).

400,000+

*No Easy Day. Mark Owen. Dutton.

*Defending Jacob. William Landay. Delacorte.

*The Girl with the Dragon Tattoo: Book 1 of the Millennium Trilogy. Steig Larsson. Vintage.

*A Game of Thrones. George R. R. Martin. Bantam.

11/22/53. Stephen King. Scribner (441,152).

The Innocent. David Baldacci. Grand Central (432,098).

*The Girl Who Kicked the Hornet's Nest: Book 3 of the Millennium Trilogy. Steig Larsson. Vintage.

*The Last Boyfriend. Nora Roberts. Berkley.

*The Help. Kathryn Stockett. Berkley.

*A Dance with the Dragons. George R. R. Martin. Bantam.

300,000+

*Unbroken. Laura Hillenbrand. Random House.

*The Girl Who Played with Fire: Book 2 of the Millennium Trilogy. Steig Larsson. Vintage.

11th Hour. James Patterson and Maxine Paetro. Little, Brown (372,071).

*The Witness. Nora Roberts. Berkley.

Extremely Loud and Incredibly Close. Jonathan Safran Foer. Houghton Mifflin Harcourt (365,488).

Water for Elephants. Sara Gruen. Algonquin (355,466).

*The Perfect Hope. Nora Roberts. Berkley.

*Killing Lincoln: The Shocking Assassination that Changed America Forever. Bill O'Reilly and Martin Dugard. Henry Holt.

Kill Shot: An American Assassin. Vince Flynn. Emily Bestler (335,422).

Guilty Wives. James Patterson and David Ellis. Little, Brown (330,924).

Kill Alex Cross. James Patterson. Little, Brown (322,982).

Steve Jobs. Walter Isaacson. Simon & Schuster (311,727).

The Perks of Being a Wallflower. Stephen Chbosky. Gallery (305,634).

The Drop. Michael Connelly. Little, Brown (302,681).

200,000+

*A Wanted Man. Lee Child. Delacorte.

*A Clash of Kings. George R. R. Martin. Bantam.

*Wild. Cheryl Strayed. Knopf.

The Best of Me. Nicholas Sparks. Grand Central (282,847).

*Deadlocked. Charlaine Harris. Ace.

*Explosive Eighteen. Janet Evanovich. Bantam.

*A Storm of Swords. George R. R. Martin. Bantam.

*Game of Thrones, 4-Copy. George R. R. Martin. Bantam.

Unfinished Business. Nora Roberts. Silhouette (275,279).

Where We Belong. Emily Giffin. St. Martin's (269,907).

*The Next Always. Nora Roberts. Berkley.

The Last Man. Vince Flynn. Atria (260,776).

Private: No. 1 Suspect. James Patterson and Maxine Paetro. Little, Brown (262,379).

*Calico Joe. John Grisham. Doubleday.

*Deep Down: A Jack Reacher Story. Lee Child. Delacorte.

The Casual Vacancy. J. K. Rowling. Little, Brown (246,301).

Abraham Lincoln: Vampire Hunter. Seth Grahame-Smith. Grand Central (244,975).

*A Feast for Crows. George R. R. Martin. Bantam.

*Notorious Nineteen. Janet Evanovich. Bantam.

*Shadow of Night. Deborah Harkness. Viking.

*Winter of the World. Ken Follett. Dutton.

Lone Wolf. Jodi Picoult. Emily Bestler (232,026).

The Light Between Oceans. M. L. Stedman. Scribner (228,133).

*Killing Kennedy: The End of Camelot. Bill O'Reilly and Martin Dugard. Henry Holt.

Private Games. James Patterson and Mark T. Sullivan. Little, Brown (218,396).

Zero Day. David Baldacci. Grand Central (218,344).

American Sniper. Chris Kyle. Morrow (211,897).

NYPD Red. James Patterson and Marshall Karp. Little, Brown (208,092).

*Stolen Prey. John Sandford. Penguin.

7 Habits of Highly Effective People. Stephen R. Covey. Free Press (203,352).

*The Litigators. John Grisham. Doubleday.

I, Michael Bennett. James Patterson. Little, Brown (202,270).

170,000+

*Snatched (novella, e-original). Karin Slaughter. Dell.

*A Discovery of Witches. Deborah Harkness. Penguin.

Bossypants. Tina Fey. Little, Brown/Reagan Arthur (190,699).

*The Bone Bed. Patricia Cornwell. Putnam.

*Fall of Giants. Ken Follett. Signet.

One for the Money: A Stephanie Plum Novel. Janet Evanovich. Scribner (179,449).

*The Power of Habit. Charles Duhigg. Random House.

Act Like a Lady, Think Like a Man. Steve Harvey. Harper/Amistad (178,000).

The Amateur: Barack Obama in the White House. Edward Klein. Regnery (175,750).

*In the Garden of Beasts: Love, Terror, and an American Family in Hitler's Berlin. Erik Larson. Crown.

*The Paris Wife. Paula McLain. Ballantine.

Lone Wolf. Jodi Picoult. Atria (172,448).

The Art of Racing in the Rain. Garth Stein. Harper (172,000).

The Fallen Angel. Daniel Silva. Harper (170,000).

160,000+

Black List. Brad Thor. Atria (168,624).

Zoo. James Patterson and Michael Ledwidge. Little, Brown (168,244).

*Celebrity in Death. J. D. Robb. Berkley.

I've Got Your Number. Sophie Kinsella. Random House (165,753).

Proof of Heaven. Eben Alexander. Simon & Schuster (164,883).

Stay Close. Harlan Coben. Signet.

The Night Circus. Erin Morgenstern. Anchor.

150,000+

*Victims. Jonathan Kellerman. Ballantine.

*The Immortal Life of Henrietta Lacks. Rebecca Skloot. Crown.

The Pact. Jodi Picoult. Avon (157,408).

*Catch Me. Lisa Gardner. Signet.

The Shoemaker's Wife. Adriana Trigiani. Harper (153,000).

Merry Christmas, Alex Cross. James Patterson. Little, Brown (151,005).

*Killing Floor. Lee Child. Jove.

140,000+

Beautiful Disaster. Jamie McGuire. Atria (149,051).

Life of Pi. Yann Martel. Houghton Mifflin Harcourt (148,272).

*Mad River. John Sandford. Putnam.

*Dark Paces. Gillian Flynn. Crown.

*Let's Pretend This Never Happened. Jenny Lawson. Putnam/Amy Einhorn.

Mile 81. Stephen King. Scribner (144,492).

*Backfire. Catherine Coulter. Putnam.

*The 7th Month. Lisa Gardner. Dutton.

*Friends Forever. Danielle Steel. Delacorte.

*Lover Reborn. J. R. Ward. Signet.

The Panther. Nelson DeMille. Grand Central (142,100).

*The Inn at Rose Harbor. Debbie Macomber. Ballantine.

*Delusion in Death. J. D. Robb. Putnam.

125,000+

*Wicked Business. Janet Evanovich. Bantam.

Home Front. Kristin Hannah. St. Martin's (137,912).

*Cloud Business. David Mitchell. Random House.

*The Moonlit Mind (e-original). Dean Koontz. Bantam.

*Odd Interlude (e-original). Dean Koontz. Bantam.

Black List. Brad Thor. Atria (168,624).

*Betrayal. Danielle Steel. Delacorte.

*Death Comes to Pemberley. P. D. James. Vintage.

*Catherine the Great. Robert K. Massie. Random House.

*Quiet: The Power of Introverts in a World that Can't Stop Talking. Susan Cain. Crown.

10th Anniversary. James Patterson and Maxine Paetro. Little, Brown (126,929).

The Forgotten. David Baldacci. Grand Central (126,513).

Safe Haven. Nicholas Sparks. Grand Central (125,474).

*Cutting for Stone. Abraham Verghese. Vintage.

100,000+

*The Affair. Lee Child. Dell.

I Used to Know That. Caroline Taggart. Reader's Digest (123,594).

Redwood Bend. Robyn Carr. Mira (123,731).

*Sharp Objects. Gillian Flynn. Crown.

*The Storm. Clive Cussler. Putnam.

*Red Mist. Patricia Cornwell. Berkley.

Angel of Investigation (e-original). Michael Connelly. Little, Brown (120,265).

My Kind of Christmas. Robyn Carr. Mira (119,206).

Island of the Lost Girls. Jennifer McMahon. Morrow (118,703).

The Lost Years. Mary Higgins Clark. Simon & Schuster (118,397).

*Gabriel's Inferno. Sylvain Reynard. Berkley.

*Threat Vector. Tom Clancy. Putnam.

*Criminal. Karin Slaughter. Dell.

*Locked On. Tom Clancy. Berkley.

Low Pressure. Sandra Brown. Grand Central (112,839).

Stolen Life. Jaycee Dugard. Simon & Schuster (112,706).

The Kitchen House. Kathleen Grissom. Touchstone (112,173).

The State of Wonder. Ann Patchett. Harper (112,000).

Two for the Dough: A Stephanie Plum Novel. Janet Evanovich. Scribner (111,999).

*The Litigators. John Grisham. Bantam.

The Great Gatsby. F. Scott Fitzgerald. Scribner (111,117).

*Second Son (e-original). Lee Child. Dell.

The Time Keeper. Mitch Albom. Hyperion (110,479).

The Art of Fielding. Chad Harbach. Little, Brown (110,312).

The Wind Through the Keyhole: A Dark Tower Novel. Stephen King. Scribner (109,783).

*Odd Apocalypse. Dean Koontz. Bantam.

All Summer Long. Susan Mallery. HQN (109,521).

*Odd Interlude No. 2 (e-original). Dean Koontz. Bantam.

*Last to Die. Tess Gerritsen. Ballantine.

*Smokin' Seventeen. Janet Evanovich. Bantam.

*The Language of Flowers. Vanessa Diffenbaugh. Ballantine.

*Odd Interlude No. 3 (e-original). Dean Koontz. Bantam.

Rainshadow Road. Lisa Kleypas. St. Martin's (106,123).

*The Sense of an Ending. Julian Barnes. Vintage.

Love in a Nutshell. Janet Evanovich and Dorien Kelly. St. Martin's (104,758).

*Rules of Civility. Amor Towles. Penguin.

Sunrise Point. Robyn Carr. Mira (103,205).

*The Tiger's Wife. Téa Obreht. Random House.

The Round House. Louise Erdrich. Harper (102,000).

The Black Box. Michael Connelly. Little, Brown (101,940).

Only Time Will Tell. Jeffrey Archer. St. Martin's (101,670).

The Speed of Trust: The One Thing that Changes Everything. Stephen M. R. Covey. Free Press (101,171).

Bloodlines. James Rollins. Morrow (100,502).

90,000+

No Time Left (e-original). David Baldacci. Grand Central (99,947).

The Glass Castle: A Memoir. Jeannette Walls. Scribner (99,685).

*Gabriel's Rapture. Sylvain Reynard. Berkley.

Matter of Honor. Jeffrey Archer. St. Martin's (98,919).

The Next Best Thing. Jennifer Weiner. Atria (98,602).

*Atlas Shrugged. Ayn Rand. Plume.

The Secret Keeper. Kate Morton. Atria (98,262).

One Good Dog. Susan Wilson. St. Martin's (97,408).

Sarah's Key. Tatiana De Rosnay. St. Martin's (96,826).

*Poseidon's Arrow. Clive Cussler. Putnam.

To Heaven and Back: A Doctor's Extraordinary Account of Her Death, Heaven, Angels, and Life Again: A True Story. Mary C. Neal, M.D. WaterBrook (96,804).

*The Devil in the White City. Erik Larson. Vintage.

Eat to Live, Revised. Joel Fuhrman. Little, Brown (95,892).

*77 Shadow Street. Dean Koontz. Bantam.

*The Twelve. Justin Cronin. Ballantine.

*World War Z: An Oral History of the Zombie War. Max Brooks. Crown.

Summerland. Elin Hilderbrand. Little, Brown/ Reagan Arthur (93,548).

*Taken. Robert Crais. Putnam.

Keeping Faith. Jodi Picoult. Avon (93,320).

17 Day Diet: A Doctor's Plan Designed for Rapid Results. Dr. Mike Moreno. Free Press (92,787).

The Shack. William P. Young. Windblown Media (91,993).

Sins of the Father. Jeffrey Archer. St. Martin's (91,627).

Because You Are Mine, Part 1. Beth Kery. Interlude (91,310).

*The Girl with the Dragon Tattoo trilogy bundle. Steig Larsson. Vintage.

Rescue Me. Rachel Gibson. Avon (91,158).

A Will and a Way. Nora Roberts. Silhouette (90,915).

*Die Trying. Lee Child. Jove.

What Doesn't Kill You. Iris Johansen. St. Martin's (90,702).

*The Claim of Sleeping Beauty. A. Roquelaure. Plume.

Beautiful Ruins. Jess Walter. Harper (90,000).

80,000+

*The Passage. Justin Cronin. Ballantine.

Heart of the Matter. Emily Giffin. St. Martin's (87,879).

Mrs. Kennedy and Me: An Intimate Memoir. Clint Hill. Gallery (87,681).

Simply Irresistible. Jill Shalvis. Grand Central/ Forever (87,476).

Team of Rivals. Doris Kearns Goodwin. Simon & Schuster (87,212).

Lethal. Sandra Brown. Grand Central (86,904).

Rainshadow Road. Lisa Kleypas. St. Martin's Griffin (86,862).

*The Big Miss: My Years Coaching Tiger Woods. Hank Haney. Crown Archetype.

Summer Days. Susan Mallery. HQN (85,541).

Lone Survivor. Marcus Luttrell. Little, Brown (85,410).

*Outlander. Diane Gabaldon. Bantam/Dell.

*Unnatural Acts. Stuart Woods. Signet.

Three to Get Ready: A Stephanie Plum Novel. Janet Evanovich. Scribner (83,342).

The Chaperone. Laura Moriarty. Riverhead (83,092).

The Dovekeepers. Alice Hoffman. Scribner (82,909).

Cold Days. Jim Butcher. Roc (82,872).

Outliers. Malcolm Gladwell. Little, Brown (82,197).

*When First They Met (e- original). Debbie Macomber. Ballantine.

*Is Everyone Hanging Out Without Me? (And Other Concerns). Mindy Kaling. Crown Archetype.

The Last Coyote. Michael Connelly. Little, Brown (80,554).

*On the Island. Tracey Garvis Graves. Plume.

A Perfect Blood. Kim Harrison. Harper Voyager (80,526).

*The Columbus Affair. Steve Berry. Ballantine.

Room. Emma Donoghue. Little, Brown (80,508).

70,000+

*Bring Up the Bodies. Hilary Mantel. Henry Holt.

*Sweet Talk. Julie Garwood. Dutton.

*Tripwire. Lee Child. Jove.

The Marriage Trap. Jennifer Probst. Gallery (77,928).

Throttle. Joe Hill. Morrow (77,818).

Suicide Run (e-original). Michael Connelly. Little, Brown (77,619).

*Behind Beautiful Forevers. Katherine Boo. Random House.

*The Sins of the Mother. Danielle Steel. Delacorte.

*The Tombs. Clive Cussler. Putnam.

*The Thief. Clive Cussler. Putnam.

Hidden Summit. Robyn Carr. Mira (76,954).

Unorthodox. Deborah Feldman. Simon & Schuster (76,829).

*Believing the Lie. Elizabeth George. NAL.

*The Wolf Gift. Anne Rice. Anchor.

With Open Eyes. Iris Johansen. St. Martin's (75,616).

The Christmas Wedding. James Patterson. Little, Brown (75,588).

*Severe Clear. Stuart Wood. Putnam.

What to Expect When You Are Expecting, 4th edition. Heidi Murkoff and Sharon Mazel. Workman (74,872).

Simply Irresistible. Rachel Gibson. Avon (74,687).

Almost Summer. Susan Mallery. HQN (73,702).

The Summer Garden. Sherryl Woods. Mira (73,296).

Once Burned. Jeaniene Frost. Avon (73,265).

The Marriage Bargain. Jennifer Probst. Gallery (72,686).

The Fall of Shane Mackade. Nora Roberts. Silhouette (72,085).

*V Is for Vengeance. Sue Grafton. Berkley.

The Third Gate. Lincoln Child. Doubleday.

Presidents Club. Nancy Gibbs and Michael Duffy. Simon & Schuster (71,967).

A Brewing Storm (e-original). Richard Castle. Hyperion (71,602).

In One Person. John Irving. Simon & Schuster (71,421).

Crazy on You. Rachel Gibson. Avon Impulse (71,199).

Before I Go to Sleep. S. J. Watson. Harper (71,000).

Summer Nights. Susan Mallery. HQN (70,883).

*Born to Run. Christopher McDougall. Vintage.

*Running Blind. Lee Child. Jove.

60,000+

The Return of Rafe Mackade. Nora Roberts. Silhouette (69,742).

Under the Dome. Stephen King. Scribner (69,626).

Four to Score. Janet Evanovich. St. Martin's (69,593).

*The Wolf Gift. Anne Rice. Knopf.

Lothaire. Kresley Cole. Gallery (69,211).

The Host. Stephenie Meyer. Little, Brown (69,072).

The Concrete Blonde. Michael Connelly. Little, Brown (68,927).

*The Skinny Rules. Bob Harper. Ballantine.

*The Pillars of the Earth. Ken Follett. Signet.

*Hotel on the Corner of Bitter and Sweet. Jamie Ford. Ballantine.

*Sweet Tooth. Ian McEwan. Doubleday/Nan A. Talese.

The Happiness Project. Gretchen Rubin. Harper (68,000).

*Dead Reckoning. Charlaine Harris. Ace.

The Marriage Mistake. Jennifer Probst. Gallery (67,858).

Because You Are Mine, Part II. Beth Kery. Intermix (67,773).

Outlaw Platoon. Sean Parnell. Morrow (67,457).

How to Win Friends and Influence People. Dale Carnegie. Simon & Schuster (67,351).

What the Dead Know. Laura Lippman. Morrow (67,228).

To Have and to Kill. Mary Jane Clark. Morrow (67,099).

*The Expats. Chris Pavone. Crown.

Cross Fire. James Patterson. Little, Brown (66,690).

A Night Like This. Julia Quinn. Avon (66,192).

*Dark Lover. J. R. Ward. Signet.

Flight Behavior. Barbara Kingsolver. Harper (66,000).

Sleep No More. Iris Johansen. St. Martin's (65,927).

Heat Wave. Richard Castle. Hyperion (65,831).

Pride and Prejudice and Zombies. Seth Grahame Smith. Quirk (65,801).

Silenced. Allison Brennan. Minotaur (65,621).

Seriously . . . I'm Kidding. Ellen DeGeneres. Grand Central (65,374).

*The Descendants. Kaui Hart Hemmings. Random House.

The Darkest Seduction. Gena Showalter. HQN (64,830).

*Drift: The Unmooring of American Military Power. Rachel Maddow. Crown.

The Heart of Devin Mackade. Nora Roberts. Silhouette (64,685).

Silenced. Allison Brennan. Minotaur (64,610).

Seven Up. Janet Evanovich. St. Martin's (64,418).

Growing Up Amish: A Memoir. Ira Wagler. Tyndale (64,130).

Bones Are Forever. Kathy Reichs. Scribner (64,048).

Barefoot Season. Susan Mallery. Mira (64,004).

*Broken Harbor. Tana French. Viking.

*Spellbound. Nora Roberts. Jove.

*High Five. Janet Evanovich. St. Martin's (62,964).

*Escape from Camp 14. Blaine Harden. Viking.

The Cowboy Takes a Bride. Lori Wilde. Avon (62,657).

*The Age of Miracles. Karen Walker Thomson. Random House.

Hard Eight. Janet Evanovich. St. Martin's (62,155).

*Once Upon a Secret. Mimi Alford. Random House.

Something Blue. Emily Giffin. St. Martin's (61,808).

Because You Are Mine, Part III. Beth Kery. Intermix (61,626)

*Ready Player One. Ernest Cline. Crown

*Untraceable. Laura Griffin. Pocket

Now You See Her. James Patterson. Little, Brown (61,500)

Hot Six. Janet Evanovich. St. Martin's (61,431)

Pleasures of the Night. Sylvia Day. Avon Red (61,429)

The Pride of Jared Mackade. Nora Roberts. Silhouette (61,415)

American Assassin. Vince Flynn. Atria (61,322)

Plum Island. Nelson DeMille. Grand Central (61,151)

The Power of Now: A Guide to Spiritual Enlightenment. Eckhart Tolle. New World Library (61,000)

The Safe Man (e-original). Michael Connelly. Little, Brown (60,998)

Love Unrehearsed. Tina Reber. Atria (60,808)

Porch Light. Dorothea Benton Frank. Morrow (60,745)

The Princess Bride. William Goldman. Houghton Mifflin Harcourt (60,515)

Ameritopia: The Unmaking of America. Mark R. Levin. Threshold Editions (60,485)

11/22/63 (enhanced e-book). Stephen King. Scribner (60,139)

Life of Pi, Illustrated Edition. Yann Martel. Houghton Mifflin Harcourt (60,073)

50,000+

*Kiss the Dead. Laurell Hamilton. Berkley.

*Dead Until Dark. Charlaine Harris. Ace.

The Ugly Duchess. Eloisa James. Avon (59,333).

*The Signal and the Noise. Nate Silver. Penguin.

Sizzling Seventeen. Janet Evanovich. St. Martin's (59,156).

*The Lost Wife. Alyson Richman. Berkley.

I'll Walk Alone. Mary Higgins Clark. Simon & Schuster (58,995).

Partners. Nora Roberts. Intermix (58,966).

*Without Fail. Lee Child. Jove.

1225 Christmas Tree Lane. Debbie Macomber. Mira (58,644).

Head Over Heels. Jill Shalvis. Grand Central/Forever (58,564).

Private. James Patterson. Little, Brown (58,432).

*Echo Burning. Lee Child. Jove.

To the Nines. Janet Evanovich. St. Martin's (58,344).

*Down the Darkest Road. Tami Hoag. Signet.

Under a Vampire Moon. Lynsay Sands. Avon (58,242).

The Sixth Man. David Baldacci. Grand Central (58,090).

Risky Business. Nora Roberts. Silhouette (58,075).

Because You Are Mine, Part IV. Beth Kery. Intermix (58,011).

Micro. Michael Crichton. Harper (58,000).

Sh*t My Dad Says. Justin Halpern. It Books (58,000).

I Suck at Girls. Justin Halpern. It Books (58,000).

The Snow Child. Eowyn Ivey. Little, Brown (57,926).

Fahrenheit 451. Ray Bradbury. Simon & Schuster (57,894)

Night Road. Kristin Hannah. St. Martin's (57,480).

Frozen Heart. Richard Castle. Hyperion (57,460).

The Fifth Witness. Michael Connelly. Little, Brown (57,051).

The 9th Judgment. James Patterson. Little, Brown (56,954).

*Bringing Up Bebe: One American Mother Discovers the Wisdom of French Parenting. Pamela Druckerman. Penguin.

*Fair Game. Pamela Briggs. Ace.

Wicked Appetite. Janet Evanovich. St. Martin's (56,717).

Ten Big Ones. Janet Evanovich. St. Martin's (56,657).

The Warlord Wants Forever. Kresley Cole. Pocket (56,494).

*New York to Dallas. J. D. Robb. Berkley.

Bonnie. Iris Johansen. St. Martin's (56,060).

Big Sky Mountain. Linda Lael Miller. HQN (55,636).

1984. George Orwell. Houghton Mifflin Harcourt (55,601).

*Witchful Thinking. H. P. Mallory. Bantam.

Something Borrowed. Emily Giffin. St. Martin's (55,506).

Mudbound. Hillary Jordan. Algonquin (55,476).

*Tinker, Tailor, Soldier, Spy. John le Carré. Penguin.

Big Sky Country. Linda Lael Miller. HQN (55,370).

*Invisible Thread: The True Story of an 11-Year-Old Panhandler, a Busy Sales Executive, and an Unlikely Meeting and Destiny. Laura Schroff and Alex Tresnowski. Howard (55,360).

Along Came a Spider. James Patterson. Little, Brown (55,332).

*Lots of Candles, Plenty of Cake. Anna Quindlen. Random House.

The Capture of the Earl of Glencrae. Stephanie Laurens. Avon (55,093).

Portrait of a Spy. Daniel Silva. Harper (55,000).

Judgment Call. J. A. Jance. Morrow (54,881).

The Notebook. Nicholas Sparks. Grand Central (54,831).

Secret Daughter. Shilpi Somaya Gowda. Morrow (54,797).

Eleven on Top. Janet Evanovich. St. Martin's (54,713).

First to Die. James Patterson. Little, Brown (54,576).

The Transfer of Power. Vince Flynn. Atria (54,472).

*Jack Reacher: One Shot. Lee Child. Dell.

Creole Belle. James Lee Burke. Simon & Schuster (54,435).

*The Confession. John Grisham. Bantam.

*Darker After Midnight. Lara Adrian. Dell.

Come Home. Lisa Scottoline. St. Martin's (53,976).

*Mission to Paris. Alan Furst. Random House.

*Because You Are Mine, Part V. Beth Kery. Intermix.

The Five People You Meet in Heaven. Mitch Albom. Hyperion (53,691).

Wicked. Gregory Maguire. Morrow (53,574).

*A Taste of Midnight (e-original). Lara Adrian. Dell.

The Beautiful Mystery. Louise Penny. SMP/Minotaur Books (53,247).

*Sweet Addiction. Maya Banks, Berkley.

*The Leopard. Jo Nesbø. Vintage.

The Lord of the Rings. J. R. R. Tolkien. Houghton Mifflin Harcourt (53,128).

*1Q84. Haruki Murakami. Vintage.

The Name of the Wind. Patrick Rothfuss. DAW (53,097).

Virgin River. Robyn Carr. Mira (53,013).

John Doe: Short Story (e-original). Tess Gerritsen. Ballantine.

Twelve Sharp. Janet Evanovich. St. Martin's (52,814).

House at Riverton. Kate Morton. Atria (52,836).

*Love You More. Lisa Gardner. Bantam.

This Is How You Lose Her. Junot Diaz. Riverhead (52,487).

Wicked Nights. Gena Showalter. HQN (52,446).

*The Last Honest Woman. Nora Roberts. Intermix.

*Hotel Vendome. Danielle Steel. Delacorte.

*Most Talkative: Stories from the Frontline of Pop Culture. Andy Cohen. Henry Holt.

A Face in the Crowd. Stephen King and Stewart O'Nan. Scribner (52,183).

*World Without End. Ken Follett. Signet.

Finger Lickin' Fifteen. Janet Evanovich. St. Martin's (52,061).

Trunk Music. Michael Connelly. Little, Brown (51,973).

*Lover Eternal. J. R. Ward. Signet.

*The Stand. Stephen King. Anchor.

Close Your Eyes. Iris Johansen and Roy Johansen. St. Martin's (51,488).

Kingmaker's Daughter. Philippa Gregory. Touchstone. (51,451).

*Persuader. Lee Child. Dell.

*Dragonfly in Amber. Diana Gabaldon. Delta.

Crooked Letter, Crooked Letter. Tom Franklin. Morrow (51,206).

*The Gunslinger. Stephen King. Signet.

*The Passage of Power. Robert A. Caro. Knopf.

Lean Mean Thirteen. Janet Evanovich. St. Martin's (50,792).

The Rescue. Nicholas Sparks. Grand Central (50,777).

The Choice. Nicholas Sparks. Grand Central. (50,747).

Heat Rises. Richard Castle. Hyperion. (50,700)

*Belong to Me. Shayla Black. Berkley.

*Because You Are Mine, Part VI. Beth Kery. Intermix.

Fearless Fourteen. Janet Evanovich. St. Martin's (50,293).

What the Most Important People Do Before Breakfast. Laura Vanderkam. Portfolio (50,273).

From Ashes. Molly McAdams. Morrow Paperbacks (50,243).

Somebody to Love. Kristan Higgins. HQN (50,223).

*Lovers Awakened. J. R. Ward. Signet.

40,000+

Forgotten Garden. Kate Morton. Atria (49,884).

A Fool's Gold Christmas. Susan Mallery. HQN (49,853).

*Echoes at Dawn. Maya Banks. Berkley.

The Wise Man's Fear. Patrick Rothfuss. DAW (49,731).

Pray for Silence. Linda Castillo. SMP/Minotaur (49,684).

*The 4-Hour Body: An Uncommon Guide to Rapid Fat-Loss, Incredible Sex, and Becoming Superhuman. Timothy Ferriss. Harmony.

*Whispers in the Dark. Maya Banks. Berkley.

The Bridge. Karen Kingsbury. Howard (49,218).

The Last Lecture. Randy Pausch with Jeffrey Zaslow. Hyperion (49,199).

*The Buddha in the Attic. Julie Otsuka. Vintage.

*The Sandcastle Girls. Chris Bohjalian. Doubleday.

Where'd You Go, Bernadette. Maria Semple. Little, Brown (48,940).

Spring Fever. Mary Kay Andrews. St. Martin's (48,650).

Becoming Sister Wives: The Story of an Unconventional Marriage. Kody Brown. Gallery (48,503).

Price of Politics. Bob Woodward. Simon & Schuster (48,401).

Full Black. Brad Thor. Atria (48,297).

Third Option. Vince Flynn. Atria (48,251).

Fatal Justice. Marie Force. Carina (48,219).

*Darkness Under the Sun (e-original). Dean Koontz. Bantam.

*Because You Are Mine, Part VII. Beth Kery. Intermix.Whispering Rock. Robyn Carr. Mira (48,082).

The Guardian. Nicholas Sparks. Grand Central (48,055).

Fearless: The Undaunted Courage and Ultimate Sacrifice of Navy SEAL Team SIX Operator Adam Brown. Eric Blehm. WaterBrook (47,993).

The Duke Is Mine. Eloisa James. Avon (47,983).

Taking Chances. Molly McAdams. Morrow Paperbacks (47,981).

The End of Illness. David B. Agus. Free Press (47,946).

Shelter Mountain. Robyn Carr. Mira (47,729).

A Raging Storm: A Derrick Storm Short (e-original). Richard Castle. Hyperion (47,130).

Wishin' and Hopin'. Wally Lamb. Harper (47,000).

*Because You Are Mine, Part VIII. Beth Kery. Intermix.

The Lifeboat. Charlotte Rogan. Little, Brown/ Reagan Arthur (46,897).

Spontaneous. Brenda Jackson. Harlequin Blaze (46,883).

Forever and a Day. Jill Shalvis. Grand Central/ Forever (46,735).

Dream Lake. Lisa Kleypas. St. Martin's (46,645).

*Samurai Game. Christine Feehan. Jove.

Bring Me Home for Christmas. Robyn Carr. Mira (46,581).

Sins of a Wicked Duke. Sophie Jordan. Avon (46,487).

The Perfect Christmas. Debbie Macomber. Mira (46,440).

*Angels at the Table. Debbie Macomber. Ballantine.

The Great Escape. Susan Elizabeth Phillips. Morrow (46,194).

*The Witch Is Back. H. P. Mallory. Bantam.

*Lover Revealed. J. R. Ward. Signet.

The Blood Sugar Solution. Mark Hyman. Little, Brown (46,117).

*Robert Parker's Lullaby. Ace Atkins. Putnam.

The Master of Disguise. Antonio J. Mendez. Morrow Paperbacks (45,816).

Raylen. Elmore Leonard. Morrow (45,693).

A Virgin River Christmas. Robyn Carr. Mira (45,616)

*Lover Unleashed. J. R. Ward. Signet.

*Caleb's Crossing. Geraldine Brooks. Penguin.

The Handmaid's Tale. Margaret Atwood. Houghton Mifflin Harcourt (45,035).

*The Dressmaker. Kate Alcott. Doubleday.

Cross. James Patterson. Little, Brown (44,953).

A Week to Be Wicked. Tessa Dare. Avon (44,792).

*Beauty. Laurell Hamilton. Berkley.

*The Enemy. Lee Child. Dell.

The Reversal. Michael Connelly. Little, Brown (44,524).

Power Down. Ben Coes. St. Martin's (44,474).

A Rogue. Any Other Name. Sarah MacLean. Avon (44,380).

Lucky in Love. Jill Shalvis. Grand Central/Forever (44,338).

*Why We Get Fat: And What to Do About It. Gary Taubes. Anchor.

You Are Next. Katia Lief. Avon (44,270).

*D.C. Dead. Stuart Woods. Signet.

*44 Charles. Danielle Steel. Delacorte.

*The Unlikely Pilgrimage of Harold Fry. Rachel Joyce. Random House.

Live. Night. Dennis Lehane. Morrow (44,068).

Wishes Fulfilled. Wayne W. Dyer. Hay House (44,020).

*Buried Prey. John Sandford. Berkley.

Fatal Flaw. Marie Force. Carina (43,892).

*Crystal Gardens. Amanda Quick. Putnam.

*The Weird Sisters. Eleanor Brown. Berkley.

*The Dog Stars. Peter Heller. Knopf.

*Lover Unbound. J. R. Ward. Signet.

*Dead in the Family. Charlaine Harris. Ace.

*Lord of the Flies. William Goldman. Penguin.

The Breach. Patrick Lee. Avon (43,342).

Mystic River. Dennis Lehane. Morrow (43,113).

How to Be a Woman. Caitlin Moran. Harper (43,000).

A Tree Grows in Brooklyn. Betty Smith. Harper (43,000).

The Black Echo. Michael Connelly. Little, Brown (42,914).

Dead Witch Walking. Kim Harrison. Harper Voyager (42,852).

A Prayer for Owen Meany. John Irving. Morrow (42,842).

Dog on It. Spencer Quinn. Atria (42,735).

A Kiss at Midnight. Eloisa James. Avon (42,624).

*The Dukan Diet: 2 Steps to Lose the Weight, 2 Steps to Keep It Off Forever. Pierre Dukan. Harmony.

Then Came You. Jennifer Weiner. Atria (42,580).

Dream Lake. Lisa Kleypas. St. Martin's Griffin (42,549).

Anything He Wants, Serial No. 5. Sara Fawkes. St. Martin's Griffin (42,450).

*Seating Arrangements. Maggie Shipstead. Knopf.

*Wicked Ties. Shayla Black. Berkley.

Redeeming Love. Francine Rivers. Multnomah (42,142).

*Living Dead in Dallas. Charlaine Harris. Ace.

*Still Alice. Lisa Genova. Pocket.

The Sweetest Thing Jill Shalvis. Grand Central/Forever (42,080).

What It Was. George Pelecanos. Little, Brown/Reagan Arthur (42,079).

A Perfect Storm. Lori Foster. HQN (42,075).

The Devil Colony. James Rollin. Morrow (41,967).

Thoughtless. S. C. Stephens. Gallery (41,934).

The Closers. Michael Connelly. Little, Brown (41,743).

*Shock Wave. John Sandford. Berkley.

They're Watching. Gregg Hurwitz. St. Martin's (41,555).

*Voyager. Diana Gabaldon. Delta.

Consent to Kill. Vince Flynn. Atria (41,404).

*Wreck This. Ken Smith. Perigee.

*A Visit from the Goon Squad. Jennifer Egan. Anchor.

*Copper Beach. Jayne Krentz. Putnam.

*Mine to Hold. Shayla Black. Berkley.

Empire of the Summer Moon. Quanah Parker and the Rise and Fall of the Comanches, the Most Powerful Indian Tribe. S. C. Gwynne. Scribner (41,292).

*Lover Enshrined. J. R. Ward. Signet.

At Last. Jill Shalvis. Grand Central/Forever (41,178).

*The Lean Startup: How Today's Entrepreneurs Use Continuous Innovation to Create Radically Successful Businesses. Eric Ries. Crown Business.

No One Heard Her Scream. Jordan Dane. Avon (41,116).

*Lover Mine. J. R. Ward. Signet.

The Last Kingdom. Bernard Cornwell. Harper (41,000).

Death of Kings. Bernard Cornwell. Harper (41,000).

Slammed. Colleen Hoover. Atria (41,000).

*Happy Birthday. Danielle Steel. Delacorte.

Winning the Wallflower. Eloisa James. Avon Impulse (40,954).

Child 44. Tom Rob Smith. Grand Central (40,947).

One Thousand Gifts: A Dare to Live Fully Right Where You Are. Ann Voskamp. Zondervan (40,875).

*Bad Luck and Trouble. Lee Child. Dell.

Those Who Save Us. Jenna Blum. Houghton Mifflin Harcourt (40,844).

*All Necessary Force. Brad Taylor. Signet.

2nd Chance. James Patterson. Little, Brown (40,738).

Sacre Bleu. Christopher Moore. Morrow (40,714).

Every Day a Friday. Joel Osteen. FaithWords (40,644).

Tracker: A Short Story Exclusive. James Rollin. Morrow (40,555).

*The Ultimate Hitchhiker's Guide to the Galaxy. Douglas Adams. Del Rey.

*Wicked Burn. Beth Kery. Berkley.

Gideon's Corpse. Douglas Preston. Grand Central (40,280).

Gun Games. Faye Kellerman. Morrow (40,258).

*The Orphan Master's Son. Adam Johnson. Random House.

A Heartbeat Away. Michael Palmer. St. Martin's (40,220).

American Gods. Neil Gaiman. Morrow (40,181).

Point of Retreat. Colleen Hoover. Atria (40,171).

Fatal Consequences. Marie Force. Carina (40,042).

The Secret. Rhonda. rne. Atria (40,023).

*Dark Storm. Christine Feehan. Berkley.

Telegraph Avenue. Michael Chabon. Harper (40,000).

30,000+

*Lover Avenged. J. R. Ward. Signet.

*The Twelve Tribes of Hattie. Ayana Mathis. Knopf.

*Maine. J. Courtney Sullivan. Vintage.

*Major Pettigrew's Last Stand. Helen Simonson. Random House.

The Last Song. Nicholas Sparks. Grand Central (39,667).

Separation of Power. Vince Flynn. Atria (39,504).

*The Keeper of Lost Causes. Jussi Adler-Olsen. Plume.

The Lady Is a Vamp. Lynsay Sands. Avon (39,293).

The Wedding. Nicholas Sparks. Grand Central (39,250).

Kill Me if You Can. James Patterson. Little, Brown (39,194).

*Moonlight in the Morning. Jude Deveraux. Pocket.

A Bloody Storm: A Derrick Storm Short (e-original). Richard Castle. Hyperion (39,168).

*Haven. Kay Hooper. Berkley.

I Declare. Joel Osteen. FaithWords (39,079).

A Walk to Remember. Nicholas Sparks. Grand Central (38,994).

Half Broke Horses: A True-Life Novel. Jeannette Walls. Scribner (38,772).

Left for Dead. J. A. Jance. Touchstone (38,770).

*Blackberry Winter. Sarah Jio. Plume.

*The Partner. John Grisham. Bantam.

What I Did for a Duke. Julie Anne Long. Avon (38,666).

*Never Seduce a Scot. Maya Banks. Ballantine.

*The Hard Way. Lee Child. Dell.

*Happy Ever After. Nora Roberts. Jove.

Choose to Lose: The 7-Day Carb Cycle Solution. Chris Powell. Hyperion (38,505).

White Girl Problems. Babe Walker. Hyperion (38,315).

Plain Truth. Jodi Picoult. Atria (38,392).

Dark Craving. Donna Grant. St. Martin's (38,266).

Naked Heat. Richard Castle. Hyperion (38,254).

Of Mice and Men. John Steinbeck. Penguin (38,243).

Smooth Talking Stranger. Lisa Kleypas. St. Martin's (38,205).

Still Life. Louise Penny. SMP/Minotaur (38,205).

City of Screams. James Rollins. Morrow (38,129).

Unglued: Making Wise Choices in the Midst of Raw Emotions. Lysa TerKeurst .Zondervan (38,125).

*Dead and Gone. Charlaine Harris. Ace.

The Tipping Point. Malcolm Gladwell. Little, Brown (38,054).

*Phantom. Jo Nesbø. Knopf.

*The Dressmaker. Kate Alcott. Anchor.

What Remains: A Memoir of Fate, Friendship, and Love. Carole Radziwill. Scribner (37,868).

Fairy Tale Interrupted: A Memoir of Life, Love, and Loss. Rosemarie Terenzio. Gallery (37,850).

Secret Daughter. Shilpi Somaya Gowda. St. Martin's (37,720).

Time Untime. Sherrilyn Kenyon. St. Martin's (37,720).

*Sweet Surrender. Maya Banks. Berkley.

*Dreams of Joy. Lisa See. Random House.

Robert Ludlum's The Bourne Imperative. Eric Van Lustbader. Grand Central (37,693).

*Beauty's Punishment. A. Roquelaure. Plume.

*Devil's Gate. Clive Cussler. Berkley.

Where Azaleas Bloom. Sherryl Woods. Mira (37,337).

Still Missing. Chevy Stevens. St. Martin's (37,318).

Extraction (e-original). Douglas Preston. Grand Central (37,309).

*This Is Where I Leave You. Jonathan Tropper. Plume.

*The Welcoming. Nora Roberts. Intermix.

*The Silent Girl. Tess Gerritsen. Ballantine.

*Drums of Autumn. Diana Gabaldon. Delta.

*Darkfever. Karen Marie Moning. Dell.

Three Brides, No Groom. Debbie Macomber. Mira (37,078).

The Magic. Rhonda. rne. Atria (37,024).

How Will You Measure Your Life?. Clayton M. Christensen. Harper (37,000).The 8th Confession. James Patterson. Little, Brown (36,997).

*Doublecross: The True Story of the D-Day Spies. Ben Macintyre. Crown.

Effortless. S. C. Stephens. Gallery (36,970).

The God Delusion. Richard Dawkins. Houghton Mifflin Harcourt (36,846).

True Colors. Kristin Hannah. St. Martin's (36,826).

*Public Secrets. Nora Roberts. Bantam.

*Club Dead. Charlaine Harris. Ace.

Anything He Wants, Serial No. 1. Sara Fawkes. St. Martin's Griffin (36,690).

*Dead to the World. Charlaine Harris. Ace.

*What Alice Forgot. Liane Moriarty. Berkley.

Boundary Lines. Nora Roberts. Intermix (36,521).

3rd Degree. James Patterson. Little, Brown (36,310).

Woman Of Grace. Kathleen Morgan. Revell (36,274).

*Naked in Death. J. D. Robb. Berkley.

*Tricked. Kevin Hearne. Del Rey.

Love the One You're With. Emily Giffin. St. Martin's (36,154).

Dying to Be Me. Anita Moorjani. Hay House (36,067).

Cowards: What Politicians, Radicals, and the Media Refuse to Say. Glenn Beck. Threshold Editions (36,064).

*The Cold Dish. Craig Johnson. Penguin.

The Redbreast. Jo Nesbø. Harper (36,000).

Good to Great. Jim Collins. HarperBusiness (36,000).

Forbidden. Ted Dekker. Center Street (35,963).

*Iced. Karen Marie Moning. Dell.

Memorial Day. Vince Flynn. Atria (35,874).

No Mark Upon Her. Deborah Crombie. Morrow (35,770).

Catching Fireflies. Sherryl Woods. Mira (35,744).

Spellman Files. Lisa Lutz. Simon & Schuster (35,706).

Wanted: Undead or Alive. Kerrelyn Sparks. Avon (35,687)

*From Dead to Worse. Charlaine Harris. Ace.

Blindsighted. Karin Slaughter. Morrow (35,537).

*The Surgeon. Tess Gerritsen. Ballantine.

*Dead as a Doornail. Charlaine Harris. Ace.

Temptation Ridge. Robyn Carr. Mira (35,408).

The Brass Verdict. Michael Connelly. Little, Brown (35,382).

Stygian's Honor. Lora Leigh. Berkley (35,244).

*The Snowman. Jo Nesbø. Vintage.

*A Dangerous Fortune. Ken Follett. Random House.

Assholes Finish First. Max Tucker. Gallery (35,174).

*On Dublin Street. Samantha Young. NAL.

Freakonomics, Rev. Ed. Steven D. Levitt. Morrow (35,152).

John Dies at the End. David Wong. St. Martin's (35,130).

*I Hate Everyone . . . Starting with Me. Joan Rivers. Berkley.

Amazing Gracie: A Dog's Tale. Dan Dye and Mark Beckloff. Workman. (35,101).

*Heads in Beds. Jacob Tomsky. Doubleday.

Paradise Valley. Robyn Carr. Mira (34,995).

7th Heaven. James Patterson. Little, Brown (34,985).

*Worth Dying For. Lee Child. Dell.

The Darkest Night. Gena Showalter. HQN (34,932).

The Winner. David Baldacci. Grand Central (34,961).

*Gone Tomorrow. Lee Child. Dell.

The Limpopo Academy of Private Detection. Alexander McCall Smith. Pantheon.

1105 Yakima Street. Debbie Macomber. Mira (34,862).

4th of July. James Patterson. Little, Brown (34,820).

Phantom. Ted Bell. Morrow (34,782).

Midnight Promises. Sherryl Woods. HQN (34,680).

I, Alex Cross. James Patterson. Little, Brown (34,679).

*Definitely Dead. Charlaine Harris. Ace.

*All Together Dead. Charlaine Harris. Ace.

Zen and the Art of Motorcycle Maintenance. Robert M. Pirsig. Avon (34,518).

Seduced. a Pirate. Eloisa James. Avon Impulse (34,516).

Harvest Moon. Robyn Carr. Mira (34,439).

Let It Go: Forgive So You Can Be Forgiven. T. D. Jakes. Atria (34,364).

*Taking a Shot. Jaci Burton. Berkley.

*61 Hours. Lee Child. Dell.

*The Ideal Man. Julie Garwood. Signet.

A Lady Never Surrenders. Sabrina Jeffries. Pocket (34,290).

XO. Jeffery Deaver. Simon & Schuster (34,287).

Beginning: An eShort Prequel to The Bridge. Karen Kingsbury. Howard (34,283).

Only Us: A Fool's Gold Holiday. Susan Mallery. HQN (34,271).

*Captivated. Nora Roberts. Intermix.

*The Beginner's Goodbye. Anne Tyler. Ballantine.

*Savor the Moment. Nora Roberts. Jove.

*The Fiery Cross. Diana Gabaldon. Dell.

One Thousand White Women. Jim Fergus. St. Martin's (34,018).

A Darkness More than Night. Michael Connelly. Little, Brown (33,971).

A Bend in the Road. Nicholas Sparks. Grand Central (33,957).

Nineteen Minutes. Jodi Picoult. Atria (33,941).

Losing It. Cora Carmack. Morrow (33,903).

Second Chance Pass. Robyn Carr. Mira (33,885).

*The Lost Symbol. Dan Brown. Anchor.

American Heiress. Daisy Goodwin. St. Martin's (33,860).

Protect and Defend. Vince Flynn. Atria (33,845).

Term Limits. Vince Flynn. Atria (33,798).

Road to Grace. Richard Paul Evans. Simon & Schuster (33,712).

An Outlaw's Christmas. Linda Lael Miller. HQN (33,693).

*Split Second. Catherine Coulter. Jove.

Firefly Lane. Kristin Hannah. St. Martin's (33,628).

Haunted. Heather Graham. Mira (33,595).

The Things They Carried. Tim O'Brien. Houghton Mifflin Harcourt (33,544).

Baby Proof. Emily Giffin. St. Martin's (33,502).

16 Lighthouse Road. Debbie Macomber. Mira (33,393).

The House I Loved. Tatiana De Rosnay. St. Martin's (33,362).

*Tom Clancy Presents: Act of Valor. Dick Couch. Berkley.

*The Scottish Prisoner. Diana Gabaldon. Dell.

Not a Fan: Becoming a Completely Committed Follower of Jesus. Kyle Idleman. Zondervan (33,250).

Flowers for Algernon. Daniel Keys. Houghton Mifflin Harcourt (33,154).

*Swamplandia!. Karen Russell. Vintage.

*Something Witchy This Way Comes. H. P. Mallory. Bantam.

Real Marriage: The Truth about Sex, Friendship, and Life Together. Mary Driscoll. Thomas Nelson (31,952).

In Plain Sight. Lorena McCourtney. Revell (32,923).

The 100-Year-Old Man Who Climbed Out the Window and Disappeared. Jonas Jonasson. Hyperion (32,859).

*Echo In the Bone. Diana Gabaldon. Dell.

Nine Dragons. Michael Connelly. Little, Brown (32,793).

The 6th Target. James Patterson. Little, Brown (32,764).

She Woke Up Married. Suzanne Macpherson. Avon (32,742).

*The Zombie Survival Guide: Complete Protection from the Living Dead. Max Brooks. Broadway.

Lady of the Rivers. Philippa Gregory. Touchstone (32,731).

Imperfect Justice. Jeff Ashton. Morrow (32,724).

*Then Again. Diane Keaton. Random House.

*Getting Things Done. David Allen. Penguin.

*The Admirals Mark (e-original). Steve Berry. Ballantine.

*Colters' Promise. Maya Banks. Berkley.

Moonlight Road. Robyn Carr. Mira (32,557).

*Fallen. Karin Slaughter. Delacorte.

*Storm Front. Jim Butcher. Roc.

*The Lost Night. Jayne Castle. Jove.

Jack & Jill. James Patterson. Little, Brown (32,328).

Against the Night. Kat Martin. Mira (32,305).

*Rapture. J. R. Ward. NAL.

*The House at Tyneford. Natasha Solomons. Plume.

*Sweet Persuasion. Maya Banks. Berkley.

Executive Power. Vince Flynn. Atria (32,152).

Are You There, Vodka? It's Me, Chelsea. Chelsea Handler. Gallery (32,143).

Capitol Murder. Phillip Margolin. Harper (32,000).

Final Appeal. Lisa Scottoline. Harper (32,000).

Moloka'I. Alan Brennert. St. Martin's (31,989).

Real Marriage: The Truth about Sex, Friendship, and Life Together. Mary Driscoll. Thomas Nelson (31,952).

Blink. Malcolm Gladwell. Little, Brown (31,852).

*Aleph. Paul Coelho. Vintage.

Eve. Iris Johansen. St. Martin's (31,824).

In the Tall Grass. Stephen King. Scribner (31,782).

Full-Time Father. Susan Mallery. Silhouette (31,688).

*Shadowfever. Karen Marie Moning. Dell.

Lions of Lucerne. Brad Thor. Atria (31,618).

*In the Woods. Tana French. Penguin.

Neverwhere. Neil Gaiman. Morrow (31,581).

Pictures of You. Caroline Leavitt. Algonquin (31,565).

Silver Girl. Elin Hilderbrand. Little, Brown (31,552).

Back to Blood. Tom Wolfe. Little, Brown (31,506).

Shantaram. Gregory David Roberts. St. Martin's (31,504).

*First Impressions. Nora Roberts. Intermix.

*Gabriel's Angel. Nora Roberts. Intermix.

Istanbul Passage. Joseph Kanon. Atria (31,433).

*The Kite Runner. Khaled Hosseini. Riverhead.

*Covert Warriors. W. E. B. Griffin. Jove.

*The Secret Race. Tyler Hamilton. Bantam.

The Worst Hard Time. Timothy Egan. Houghton Mifflin Harcourt (31,366).

Wild Man Creek. Robyn Carr. Mira (31,348).

*Moonwalking with Einstein. Joshua Foer. Penguin.

A Quick Bite. Lynsay Sands. Avon (31,285).

*Holiday Wishes. Nora Roberts. Intermix.

*Bed of Roses. Nora Roberts. Jove.

Kiss the Girls. James Patterson. Little, Brown (31,223).

Savages. Don Winslow. Simon & Schuster (31,205).

The 4-Hour Workweek: Expanded and Updated. Timothy Ferriss. Harmony (31,066).

*Elizabeth the Queen. Sally Bedell Smith. Random House.

Death Benefits (e-original). Nelson DeMille. Grand Central (31,044).

The Seduction of Sebastian Trantor. Stephanie Laurens. Avon Impulse (31,027).

The Lacuna. Barbara Kingsolver. Harper (31,000).

*Force of Nature. C. J. Box. Putnam.

How We Decide. Jonah Lehrer. Houghton Mifflin Harcourt (30,987).

Lost Light. Michael Connelly. Little, Brown (30,922).

Look Away. Lisa Scottoline. St. Martin's (30,947).

*Can You Keep a Secret?. Sophie Kinsella. Random House.

*A Breath of Snow and Ashes. Diana Gabaldon. Dell.

*The Jungle. Clive Cussler. Berkley.

Only His. Susan Mallery. HQN (30,877).

*The $100 Startup: Reinvent the Way You Make a Living, Do What You Love, and Create a New Future. Chris Guillebeau. Crown Business

*The Hunter. John Lescroart. Signet.

Another Piece of My Heart. Jane Green. St. Martin's (30,802).

Angel's Peak. Robyn Carr. Mira (30,789).

Recalculating. Jennifer Weiner. Atria (30,789).

*City of Women. David R. Gillham. Putnam/ Amy Einhorn.

Tick Tock. James Patterson. Little, Brown (30,729).

Obama's America: Unmaking the American Dream. Dinesh D'Souza. Regnery (30,700).

Witch's Daughter. Paula Brackston. St. Martin's (30,656).

*Chasing Fire. Nora Roberts. Jove.

*Shanghai Girls. Lisa See. Random House.

*The Shadow Patrol. Alex Berenson. Jove.

Quinn. Iris Johansen. St. Martin's (30,560).

*A Devil Is Waiting. Jack Higgins. Berkley.

Switch. Megan Hart. Spice (30,532).

*Vision in White. Nora Roberts. Jove.

*Beauty's Release. A. Roquelaure. Plume.

Pursuit of Honor. Vince Flynn. Atria (30,460).

This Matter of Marriage. Debbie Macomber. Mira (30,434).

Fall from Grace. Richard North Patterson. Scribner (30,388).

Hell's Corner. David Baldacci. Grand Central (30,337).

A Faint Cold Fear. Karin Slaughter. Morrow (30,335).

*Never Love a Highlander. Maya Banks. Ballantine.

*Mystery. Jonathan Kellerman. Ballantine.

*The Invisible Bridge. Julie Orringer. Vintage.

The Black Ice. Michael Connelly. Little, Brown (30,163).

The Prague Cemetery. Umberto Eco. Houghton Mifflin Harcourt (30,121)

*Coming Apart: The State of White America, 1960–2010. Charles Murray. Crown Forum.

*Land of Painted Caves. Jean M. Auel. Bantam.

Lost in Shangri-La. Mitchell Zuckoff. Harper (30,000).

Game Change. John Heilemann. Harper (30,000).

Bel Canto. Ann Patchett. Harper (30,000).

25,000+

Soulless. Gail Carriger. Orbit (29,969).

*Star Wars: Darth Plagueis. James Luceno. Lucas. Flash and Bones. Kathy Reichs. Scribner (29,827).

Chelsea Chelsea Bang Bang. Chelsea Handler. Grand Central (29,797).

Monday Mornings. Sanjay Gupta. Grand Central (29,797).

*The Spymasters. W. E. B. Griffin. Putnam.

*The Jefferson Key. Steve Berry. Ballantine.

Heat of the Night. Sylvia Day. Avon Red (29,636).

Drop Dead Healthy. A. J. Jacobs. Simon & Schuster (29,627).

*Decadent. Shayla Black. Berkley.

Echo Park. Michael Connelly. Little, Brown (29,599).

*The Guernsey Literary and Potato Peel Pie Society. Mary Ann Shaffer and Annie Barrows. Random House.

*The End of Your Life Book Club. Will Schwalbe. Knopf.

Winter Garden. Kristin Hannah. St. Martin's (29,504).

She Tempts the Duke. Lorraine Heath. Avon (29,382).

The Bite Before Christmas. Lynsay Sands. Morrow (29,373).

*Gunmetal Magic. Ilona Andrews. Ace.

The Narrows. Michael Connelly. Little, Brown (29,360).

*Without a Trace. Nora Roberts. Intermix.

*The Warmth of Other Suns. Isabel Wilkerson. Vintage.

Swinging On a Star. Janice Thompson. Revell (29,172).

A Secret Kept. Tatiana De Rosnay. St. Martin's (29,156).

*Forks Over Knives: The Plant-Based Way to Health, Gene Stone, editor. Experiment (29,111).

The Lady Risks All. Stephanie Laurens. Avon (29,100).

*Life as I Blow It. Sara Colonna. Ballantine.

Stranger in the Moonlight. Jude Deveraux. Pocket.

One Foot in the Grave. Jeaniene Frost. Avon (28,970).

Halfway to the Grave. Jeaniene Frost. Avon (28,951).

Promise Canyon. Robyn Carr. Mira (28,938).

*Mission Flats. William Landay. Bantam/Dell.

Where Are You Now? Mary Higgins Clark. Simon & Schuster (28,889).

The Emperor of All Maladies: A Biography of Cancer. Siddhartha Mukherjee. Scribner (28,856).

Sidney Sheldon's Angel of the Dark. Sidney Sheldon. Morrow (28,851).

*Dead or Alive. Tom Clancy. Berkley.

Summer Desserts. Nora Roberts. Silhouette (28,741).

Fatal Deception. Marie Force. Carina (28,735).

A Turn in the Road. Debbie Macomber. Mira (28,595).

*In Bed with a Highlander. Maya Banks. Ballantine.

Soft Target. Stephen Hunter. Simon & Schuster (28,527).

*One Rough Man. Brad Taylor. Signet Select.

Oath Of Office. Michael Palmer. St. Martin's (28,508).

The Rope. Nevada Barr. SMP/Minotaur (28,492).

Winter's Tale. Mark Helprin. Houghton Mifflin Harcourt (28,472).

*Seduction of a Highland Lass. Maya Banks. Ballantine.

And Then There Were None. Agatha Christie. Morrow Paperbacks (28,334).

*The Meaning of Marriage. Timothy Keller. Dutton.

The Unseen. Heather Graham. Mira (28,267).

Night's Awakening. Donna Grant. St. Martin's (28,202).

Gone With the Wind. Margaret Mitchell. Scribner (28,183).

One Summer. Nora Roberts. Silhouette (28,178).

Cold Vengeance. Douglas Preston. Grand Central (28,178).

The Overlook. Michael Connelly. Little, Brown (28,178).

*Night Watch. Linda Fairstein. Dutton.

Act of Treason. Vince Flynn. Atria (28,111).

Mulholland Dive (e-original). Michael Connelly. Little, Brown (28,088).

Wings of Morning. Kathleen Morgan. Revell (28,042).

It Had to Be You. Susan Elizabeth Phillips. Avon (28,014).

Men Are from Mars, Women Are from Venus. John Gray. Harper (28,000).

Their Eyes Were Watching God. Zora Neale Hurston. Harper (28,000).

*Tell the Wolves I'm Home. Carol Rifka Brunt. Random House.

Chasing Perfect. Susan Mallery. HQN (27,962).

*Midnight in Death. J. D. Robb. Berkley.

Being George Washington: The Indispensable Man, as You've Never Seen Him. Glenn Beck. Threshold (27,937).

*The Road. Cormac McCarthy. Vintage.

*Be Witched. H. P. Mallory. Bantam.

Free Will. Sam Harris. Free Press (27,858).

Lucky Man: A Memoir. Michael J. Fox. Hyperion (27,845).

*Home. Toni Morrison. Vintage.

Waiting for Nick. Nora Roberts. Silhouette (27,821).

Forbidden Falls. Robyn Carr. Mira (27,810).

Sing You Home. Jodi Picoult. Atria (27,801).

Lady of Light. Kathleen Morgan. Revell (27,793).

*About that Night. Julie James. Berkley.

*Rules of Prey. John Sandford. Berkley.

*Wild Cat. Jennifer Ashley. Berkley.

Mob Daughter. Karen Gravano. St. Martin's (27,602).

Love Unscripted. Tina Weber. Atria (27,568).

*The Kill Artist. Daniel Silva. Signet.

*The Innocent Man. John Grisham. Bantam.

Run the Risk. Lori Foster. HQN (27,467).

Good Christian Bitches. Kim Gatlin. Hyperion (27,452).

*Glory in Death. J. D. Robb. Berkley.

*Deal Breaker. Harlan Coben. Bantam/Dell.

*The Cat's Table. Michael Ondaatje. Vintage.

*Bloodfever. Karen Marie Moning. Bantam/Dell.

Choosing to See. Mary Beth Chapman with Ellen Vaughn. Revell (27,340).

Kisses from Katie: A Story of Relentless Love and Redemption. Katie J. Davis. Howard (27,337).

*Dreamfever. Karen Marie Moning. Dell.

*Sister. Rosamund Lupton. Crown.

Undone. Her Tender Touch. Susan Mallery. Harlequin Desire (27,314).

*Beyond Outrage. Robert B. Reich. Vintage.

In the Bleak Midwinter. Julia Spencer Fleming. SMP/Minotaur (27,268).

The Sun Also Rises. Ernest Hemingway. Scribner (27,266).

City of Bones. Michael Connelly. Little, Brown (27,242).

Born of Silence. Sherrilyn Kenyon. Grand Central (27,139).

Greater Journey. David McCullough. Simon & Schuster (27,096).

Skinnydipping. Bethenny Frankel. Touchstone (27,069).

*The Neighbor. Lisa Gardner. Bantam.

Nemesis. Jo Nesbø. Harper (27,000).

The Devil's Star. Jo Nesbø. Harper (27,000).

Elegy for Eddie. Jacqueline Winspear. Harper (27,000).

When It Happens to You. Molly Ringwald. It Books (27,000).

Extreme Measures. Vince Flynn. Atria (26,935).

*Tuesdays with Morrie: An Old Man, a Young Man, and Life's Greatest Lesson. Mitch Albom. Broadway.

*Snow Flower and the Secret Fan. Lisa See. Random House.

*Robert B. Parker's Fool Me Twice. Michael Brandman. Putnam.

*Nothing to Lose. Lee Child. Dell.

Dear John. Nicholas Sparks. Grand Central (26,897).

Robert Ludlum's the Janson Command. Paul Garrison. Grand Central (26,842).

*Live to Tell. Lisa Gardner. Bantam.

At Grave's End. Jeaniene Frost. Avon (26,772).

*Dance to the Piper. Nora Roberts. Intermix.

Against the Sun. Kat Martin. Mira (26,761).

*Skin Deep. Nora Roberts. Intermix.

What a Westmoreland Wants. Brenda Jackson. Harlequin Desire (26,667).

Sleepwalker. Karen Robards. Gallery (26,607).

*One Day. David Nicholls. Vintage.

*Hounded. Kevin Hearne. Del Rey.

*The Baker's Daughter. Sarah McCoy. Crown.

*The Secret. Julie Garwood. Dutton.

1022 Evergreen Place. Debbie Macomber. Mira (26,501).

Split Second. David Baldacci. Grand Central (26,476).

*Home Again. Kristin Hannah. Ballantine.

The Fall of Rogue Gerrard. Stephanie Laurens. Avon Impulse (26,466).

Jack Kennedy. Chris Matthews. Simon & Schuster (26,458)

*The Righteous Mind. Jonathan Haidt. Vintage.

Return to Willow Lake. Susan Wiggs. Mira (26,353).

American Sniper (enhanced e-book). Chris Kyle. Morrow (26,337).

*The Search. Nora Roberts. Jove.

*The Woman in Black. Susan Hill. Vintage.

Faefever. Karen Marie Moning. Dell (26,295).

Angels Flight. Michael Connelly. Little, Brown (26,281).

Tiger's Claw. Dale Brown. Morrow (26,196).

Kris Jenner . . . and All Things Kardashian. Kris Jenner. Gallery (26,189).

Nearing Home: Life, Faith, and Finishing Well. Billy Graham. Thomas Nelson (26,178).

Seal Team Six. Howard E. Wasdin. St. Martin's (26,176).

Playing the Odds. Nora Roberts. Intermix.

*Custom of the Army. Diana Gabaldon. Dell.

Infinite Jest. David Foster Wallace. Back Bay (26,113).

One Grave at a Time. Jeaniene Frost. Avon (26,039).

*Charmed. Nora Roberts. Intermix.

Stolen Innocence. Elissa Wall. Morrow (26,007).

*In Cold Blood. Truman Capote. Vintage.

How the Marquess Was Won. Julie Anne Long. Avon (25,980).

15 Seconds. Andrew Gross. Morrow (25,980).

Anything He Wants, Serial 1–5. Sara Fawkes. St. Martin's Griffin (25,945).

Only Yours. Susan Mallery. HQN (25,941).

*Easy. Tammara Webber. Berkley.

*Eat, Pray, Love. Elizabeth Gilbert. Penguin.

*The Righteous Mind. Jonathan Haidt. Pantheon.

Reckoning. Jeaniene Frost. Avon (25,770).

The Great Destroyer: Barack's Obama's War on the Republic. David Limbaugh. Regnery (25,650).

*The Last Victim. Karen Robards. Ballantine.

The Duke and I. Julia Quinn. Avon (25,640).

*Into the Fire. Dakota Meyer. Random House.

*Magic Hour. Kristin Hannah. Ballantine.

American Gods: 10th Anniversary Edition. Neil Gaiman. Morrow (25,577).

The Postcard Killers. James Patterson. Little, Brown (25,534).

Anything He Wants, Serial No. 4. Sara Fawkes. St. Martin's Griffin (25,519).

Sister of the Bride. Susan Mallery. Mira (25,515).

*A Blaze of Glory. Jeff Shaara. Ballantine.

*The Darkest Hour. Maya Banks. Berkley.

The Hiding Place: 35th Anniversary Edition. Corrie Ten Boom with John and Elizabeth Sherrill. Revell (25,421).

The Red Book. Deborah Copaken Kogan. Hyperion/Voice (25,354).

Eyes Wide Open. Andrew Gross. Morrow (25,314).

Twenty Wishes. Debbie Macomber. Mira (25,285).

An O'Brien Family Christmas. Sherryl Woods. Mira (25,263).

*No Place to Run. Maya Banks. Berkley.

Devil's Bride. Stephanie Laurens. Avon (25,229).

*Ghost Story. Jim Butcher. Roc.

Happily Never After. Jeaniene Frost. Avon (25,221).

Anything He Wants, Serial No. 2. Sara Fawkes. St. Martin's Griffin (25,202).

*Surrender to Me. Shayla Black. Berkley.

Dirty. Megan Hart. Spice (25,160).

The Lovely Bones. Alice Sebold. Little, Brown (25,138).

*The Joy of Hate: How to Triumph over Whiners in the Age of Phony Outrage. Greg Gutfeld. Crown Forum.

SuperFreakonomics. Steven D. Leavitt. Morrow (25,123).

*Entranced. Nora Roberts. Intermix.

*Into the Wild. John Krakauer. Anchor.

*Hot in Handcuffs. Shayla Black. Berkley.

Carry the One. Carol Anshaw. Simon & Schuster (25,083).

Take Me. Bella Andre. Pocket (25,071).

Diary of a Young Girl. Anne Frank. Anchor (25,064).

Anything He Wants, Serial No. 3. Sara Fawkes. St. Martin's Griffin (25,031).

*Immortal in Death. J. D. Robb. Berkley.

Brain on Fire: My Month of Madness. Susannah Cahalan. Free Press (25,008).

Ali in Wonderland. Ali Wentworth. Harper (25,000).

Eyes Wide Open. Andrew Gross. Harper (25,000).

Prague Winter. Madeleine Albright. Harper (25,000).

Faith. Jennifer Haigh. Harper (25,000).

It Worked for Me. Colin Powell. Harper (25,000).

The Orchardist. Amanda Coplin. Harper (25,000).

Great. Choice. Jim Collins. Harper Business (25,000).

Hardcover: The Big Didn't Get Bigger

Daisy Maryles

Familiar Names Dominate, Units Continue to Erode

Last year at the end of this annual article we made the obvious prediction that unit sales for hardcover bestsellers would be even lower for 2012 books, and that the "e-book explosion could be the culprit." There were no naysayers to that comment and the lists below prove that we were all right on the money.

The count for 2012 topsellers with 100,000+ in sales is 91 for hardcover fiction and 74 for hardcover nonfiction—and both figures are record lows. In 2011 it was 113 for fiction and 83 for nonfiction; in 2010 it was 126 for fiction and 108 for nonfiction. And while these figures dwindled, the opposite was the case for e-books, as can be observed in our extensive listing in the previous section of this article.

What does not change from year to year is the content/authors of these end-of-the-year lists. The fiction top 15 include the usual veterans—Patterson, Evanovich, Grisham, Clancy, Baldacci, Harris, Beck, Connelly, Child, and Vince Flynn. All have graced these lists many times and some for decades. Kudos to John Grisham, who has not missed a year in the top 15 since his first appearance with *The Firm* in 1991. There are two newcomers on the fiction list. In the No. 1

slot is J. K. Rowling for her novel *The Casual Vacancy*—her first foray into the adult market. Of course, Rowling has been a habitual lead player on the children's charts with her Harry Potter books. Another Flynn, Gillian, is No. 3 with sales of more than 900,000 copies of *Gone Girl*. It is her third book. There are two debut fiction titles on this list of 113 bestsellers—*Rules of Civility* by Amor Towles and *The Light Between Oceans* by M. L. Stedman; both enjoyed glowing reviews as well as impressive sales.

On the nonfiction side, familiar subjects—politics, cooking, and religion—reigned. Past presidents—Kennedy, Lincoln, and Jefferson—were the focus of three books in the top ten, as was a book critical of the current president. Peruse the nonfiction list and there are at least six more books focusing on past and current presidents, making the presidency the subject of almost 15 percent of the topsellers. Cookbooks, both healthful and decadent, had 13 spots on the nonfiction list; the religion category has 12 bestselling titles, three in the top ten. Another popular subject was Navy Seals, with two winners in the top ten and one more in the top 73.

Our prediction for 2013 books: more of the same winners in hardcover fiction and nonfiction, but with fewer titles and lower units. In e-books, the sky is the limit.

The Usual Disclaimer

As in previous years, all the calculations on the following pages are based on shipped-and-billed figures for new books with sales of 100,000 units or more in hardcover or paper. While many publishers did calculate early returns, sales figures should not be considered final, especially for books published in the last quarter of the year. That's not a problem for e-books, where returns are not part of the scenario, as all books are direct to consumer and not returnable.

Totals for titles preceded by an asterisk were submitted in confidence, for use only in ranking the titles on the list.

Fiction

900,000+

The Casual Vacancy. J. K. Rowling. Little, Brown (1,318,605).
*The Racketeer. John Grisham. Doubleday.
*Gone Girl. Gillian Flynn. Crown.

400,000+

*Notorious Nineteen. Janet Evanovich. Bantam.
Merry Christmas, Alex Cross. James Patterson. Little, Brown (447,418).
*Calico Joe. John Grisham. Doubleday.
*Winter of the World. Ken Follett. Dutton.

The Last Man. Vince Flynn. Atria/Emily Bestler (435,715).
*Threat Vector. Tom Clancy with Mark Greaney. Putnam.

300,000+

The Forgotten. David Baldacci. Grand Central (384,128).
Deadlocked. Charlaine Harris. Ace (350,000).
Agenda 21. Glenn Beck. Threshold Editions (348,227).
11th Hour. James Patterson and Maxine Paetro. Little, Brown (330,914).
The Black Box. Michael Connelly. Little, Brown (321,561).

*A Wanted Man. Lee Child. Delacorte.
The Time Keeper. Mitch Albom. Hyperion (306,581).

200,000+

Love in a Nutshell. Janet Evanovich and Dorien Kelly. St. Martin's (299,869).
NYPD Red. James Patterson and Marshall Karp. Little, Brown (296,498).
The Wind Through the Keyhole: A Dark Tower Novel. Stephen King. Scribner (293,165).
*The Sins of the Mother. Danielle Steel. Delacorte.
Where We Belong. Emily Giffin. St. Martin's (288,966).
Kill Shot: An American Assassin Thriller. Vince Flynn. Atria/Emily Bestler (288,355).
*A Dance with Dragons. George R. R. Marin. Bantam.
*The Bone Bed. Patricia Cornwell. Putnam.
The Innocent. David Baldacci. Grand Central (281,152).
*Of Mice and Men. John Steinbeck. Penguin.
The Fanther. Nelson DeMille. Grand Central (265,264).
Guilty Wives. James Patterson and David Ellis. Little, Brown (252,667).
I, Michael Bennett. James Patterson and Michael Ledwidge. Little, Brown (249,916).
Private: #1 Suspect. James Patterson and Maxine Paetro. Little, Brown (247,287).
Zoo. James Patterson and Michael Ledwidge. Little, Brown (246,178).
*Poseidon's Arrow: A Dirk Pitt Novel. Clive Cussler and Dirk Cussler. Putnam.
*The Witness. Nora Roberts. Putnam.
*Friends Forever. Danielle Steel. Delacorte.
Private Games. James Patterson and Mark T. Sullivan. Little, Brown (223,852).
The Bridge. Karen Kingsbury. Howard (219,706).
Flight Behavior. Barbara Kingsolver. Harper (211,000).

170,000+

*Wicked Business. Janet Evanovich. Bantam.
*Betrayal. Danielle Steel. Delacorte.
*Shadow of Night: A Novel. Deborah Harkness. Viking.
Winter Dream. Richard Paul Evans. Simon & Schuster (183,333).

Home Front. Kristin Hannah. St. Martin's (175,668).
Lost Years. Mary Higgins Clark. Simon & Schuster (173,986).
*Angels at the Table. Debbie Macomber. Ballantine.
*Stolen Prey. John Sandford. Putnam.

150,000+

*Odd Apocalypse. Dean Koontz. Bantam.
Cold Days. Jim Butcher. Roc (165,000).
Low Pressure. Sandra Brown. Grand Central (159,022).
Back to Blood. Tom Wolfe. Little, Brown (156,953).
*Mad River. John Sandford. Putnam.
Bring Up the Bodies. Hilary Mantel. Henry Holt. (155,673)
Live by Night. Dennis Lehane. Morrow (154,738).
*Defending Jacob. William Landay. Delacorte.
*The Inn at Rose Harbor. Debbie Macomber. Ballantine.

125,000+

*Stay Close. Harlan Coben. Dutton.
*Rules of Civility. Amor Towles. Penguin.
*Delusion in Death. J. D. Robb. Putnam.
*Celebrity in Death. J. D. Robb. Putnam.
*The Twelve. Justin Cronin. Ballantine.
*The Twelve Tribes of Hattie. Ayana Mathis. Knopf.
The Fallen Angel. Daniel Silva. Harper (141,000).
The Round House. Louise Erdrich. Harper (139,000).
*The Tombs: A Fargo Adventure. Clive Cussler and Thomas Perry. Putnam.
*The Storm: A Novel from the NUMA Files. Clive Cussler and Graham Brown. Putnam,
15 Seconds. Andrew Gross. Morrow (130,509).
Come Home. Lisa Scottoline. St. Martin's (128,010).
*Backfire. Catherine Coulter. Putnam.

100,000+

The Hobbit, Deluxe Pocket Edition. J. R. R. Tolkien. Houghton Mifflin Harcourt (123,821).
What Doesn't Kill You. Iris Johansen. St. Martin's (122,077).

Bloodline. James Rollin. Morrow (121,516).
*I've Got Your Number. Sophie Kinsella. Dial.
The Light Between Oceans. M. L. Stedman. Scribner (118,457).
*The Thief: An Isaac Bell Adventure. Clive Cussler and Justin Scott. Putnam.
*Believing the Lie. Elizabeth George. Dutton.
Two Graves. Douglas Preston and Lincoln Child. Grand Central (116,924).
Sleep No More. Iris Johansen. St. Martin's (115,463).
*Sweet Tooth. Ian McEwan. Doubleday/Nan A. Talese.
Porch Light. Dorothea Benton Frank. Morrow (113,132).
*Catch Me. Lisa Gardner. Dutton.
*Sweet Talk. Julie Garwood. Dutton.
*Lover Reborn. J. R. Ward. NAL.
The Wolf Gift. Anne Rice. Knopf (102,577).
A Perfect Blood. Kim Harrison. Harper Voyager (102,156).
Telegraph Avenue. Michael Chabon. Harper (102,000).
Sins of the Father. Jeffrey Archer. St. Martin's (101,002).
*Kiss the Dead. Laurell K. Hamilton. Berkley.
Spring Fever. Mary Kay Andrews. St. Martin's (100,543).
Sacre Bleu. Christopher Moore. Morrow (100,057).

Nonfiction

1,000,000+

Killing Kennedy: The End of Camelot. Bill O'Reilly and Martin Dugard. Holt (1,516,778).
*No Easy Day: The Firsthand Accounts of the Mission that Killed Osama Bin Laden. Mark Owen with Kevin Maurer. Dutton.

700,000+

Killing Lincoln: The Shocking Assassination that Changed America. Bill O'Reilly and Martin Dugard (928,377).
Barefoot Contessa Foolproof: Recipes You Can Trust. Ina Garten. Clarkson Potter (763,483).
Cross Roads. William Paul Young. Faith Words (748,543).

500,000+

The Pioneer Woman Cooks: Food from My Frontier. Ree Drummond. Morrow (551,721).
American Sniper. Chris Kyle. Morrow (547,781).

400,000+

I Declare: 31 Promises to Speak Over Your Life. Joel Osteen. Faith Words (495,453).
The Amateur: Barack Obama in the White House. Edward Klein. Regnery (449,940).
*Thomas Jefferson: The Art of Power. Jon Meacham. Random House.

300,000+

*Wild: From Lost to Found on the Pacific Crest Trail. Cheryl Strayed. Knopf.
America Again: Re-becoming the Greatness We Never Weren't. Stephen Colbert. Grand Central (361,143).
*Unbroken. Laura Hillenbrand. Random House.
Jesus Calling: Enjoying Peace in His Presence. Sarah Young. Thomas Nelson (317,952).

200,000+

*In the Kitchen with David. David Venable. Random House.
Jesus Today: Experience Hope Through His Presence. Sarah Young. Thomas Nelson (285,682).
Thinking Fast and Slow. Daniel Kahneman. Farrar, Straus & Giroux (280,514).
*Quiet: The Power of Introverts in a World that Can't Stop Talking. Susan Cain. Crown.
Shred: The Revolutionary Diet: 6 Weeks 4 Inches 2 Sizes. Ian K. Smith. St. Martin's (273,890).
One Thousand Gifts: A Dare to Live Fully Right Where You Are. Ann Voskamp. Zondervan (266,000).
Heaven Changes Everything: Living Every Day with Eternity in Mind. Todd and Sonja Burpo. Thomas Nelson (264,453).
My Year in Meals. Rachael Ray. Atria (264,111).
Steve Jobs. Walter Isaacson. Simon & Schuster (259,592).

The Blood Sugar Solution: The Ultrahealthy Program for Losing Weight, Preventing Disease, and Feeling Great Now! Mark Hyman. Little, Brown (253,152).

*The Power of Habit. Charles Duhigg. Random House.

Go the F**k to Sleep. Adam Mansbach. Akashic (200,000).

175,000+

Total Recall. Arnold Schwarzenegger. Simon & Schuster (192,432).

*Weeknights with Giada: Quick and Simple Recipes to Revamp Dinner. Giada De Laurentiis. Clarkson Potter.

*The Big Mess: My Years Coaching Tiger Woods. Hank Haney. Crown Archetype.

*Behind the Beautiful Forevers: Life, Death, and Hope in a Mumbai Undercity. Katherine Boo. Random House.

It Worked for Me. Colin Powell. Harper (180,000).

*Fifty Shades of Chicken: A Parody in a Cookbook. F. L. Fowler. Clarkson Potter.

170,000+

Heaven Is for Real. Todd Burpo with Lynn Vincent. Thomas Nelson (177,251).

The Great Destroyer: Barack Obama's War on the Republic. David Limbaugh. Regnery (175,320).

The Pioneer Woman Cooks. Ree Drummond. Morrow (174,868).

The Price of Politics. Bob Woodward. Simon & Schuster (174,509).

Obama's America: Unmaking the American Dream. Dinesh D'Souza. Regnery (174,480).

*The Signal and the Noise: Why So Many Predictions Fail but Some Don't. Nate Silver. Penguin.

Let It Go: Forgive So You Can Be Forgiven. T. D. Jakes. Atria (168,829).

*Rod. Rod Stewart. Crown Archetype.

*Drift: The Unmooring of American Military Power. Rachel Maddow. Crown.

*The Skinny Rules. Bob Harper. Random House.

*The Smitten Kitchen Cookbook. Deb Perelman. Knopf.

Cowards: What Politicians, Radicals, and the Media Won't Tell You. Glenn Beck. Threshold (165,054).

*The Passage of Power: The Years of Lyndon Johnson. Robert A. Caro. Knopf.

150,000+

Trickle Down Tyranny: Crushing Obama's Dream of the Socialist States of America. Michael Savage. Morrow (153,957).

The 4-Hour Chef: The Simple Path to Cooking Like a Pro, Learning Anything, and Living the Good Life. Timothy Ferriss. Houghton Mifflin Harcourt (151,146).

Change Your Words, Change Your Life: Understanding the Power of Every Word You Speak. Joyce Meyer. Faith Words (150,748).

Good to Great. Jim Collins. HarperBusiness (150,000).

130,000+

Bruce. Peter Ames Carlin. Touchstone (143,480).

Grace. Max Lucado. Thomas Nelson (141,417).

Who I Am. Pete Townshend. Harper (140,000).

Presidents Club: Inside the World's Most Exclusive Fraternity. Nancy Gibbs and Michael Duffy. Simon & Schuster (138,729).

Roll Me Up and Smoke Me When I Die. Willie Nelson. Morrow (136,690).

Do Yourself a Favor . . . Forgive: Learn How to Take Control of Your Life Through Forgiveness. Joyce Meyer. Faith Words (134,300).

The Last Lion: Winston Spencer Churchill: Defender of the Realm, 1940–1965. William Manchester with Paul Reid. Little, Brown (133,983).

*Waging Heavy Peace. Neil Young. Blue Rider.

My Cross to Bear. Gregg Allman. Morrow (131,235).

Good to Great. Jim Collins. HarperBusiness (130,000).

125,000+

Chronicles of Downton Abbey. Jessica Fellowes. St. Martin's (126,283).

*The World Until Yesterday: What Can We Learn from Traditional Societies? Jared Diamond. Viking.

17 Day Diet: A Doctor's Plan Designed for Rapid Results. Dr. Mike Moreno. Free Press (125,542).

100,000+

The Circle Maker: Praying Circles Around Your Biggest Dreams and Greatest Fears. Mark Batterson. Zondervan (118,350).

How Children Succeed: Grit, Curiosity, and the Hidden Power of Character. Paul Tough. Houghton Mifflin Harcourt (116,661).

Great by Choice. Jim Collins. HarperBusiness (114,000).

Change: Activating the 10 Human Drives that Make You Feel Alive. Brendon Burchard. Free Press (109,633).

The End of Illness. David B. Agus. Free Press (109,044).

The Cake Boss: Family Favorites as Only Buddy Can Serve Them Up. Buddy Valastro. Atria (106,273).

Tap Dancing to Work: Warren Buffett on Practically Everything, 1966–2012. Carol Loomis. Portfolio (106,076).

*Let's Pretend This Never Happened (A Mostly True Memoir). Jenny Lawson. Putnam/Amy Einhorn.

*Lots of Candles, Plenty of Cake. Anna Quindlen. Random House.

Fearless: The Undaunted Courage and Ultimate Sacrifice of Navy SEAL Team SIX Operator Adam Brown. Eric Blehm. WaterBrook (105,085).

The Hobbit: An Unexpected Journey Chronicles: Art & Design. Weta. HarperDesign (101,000).

One Last Strike. Tony La Russa. Morrow (100,057).

Paperbacks: Highs and Lows in a Dramatic Year

Daisy Maryles

Looking at 2012's huge drop in the number of mass market bestsellers with sales of more than 500,000 copies is alarming. In 2012 only 26 titles hit that figure and only three in the group reached the million mark. Not that long ago—back in 2006—116 enjoyed sales of 500,000+ and that group had 26 one million+ players. In 2005 40 books went over the million mark. The fall-off is dramatic even when we go back only one year; in 2011 we lamented that only 48 books had hit the 500,000+ copy level and six of those made it to 1 million and more.

The number of books that hit the weekly *Publishers Weekly* mass market charts also went down in 2012, to a record low of 196 titles. The record high was set in 2007 with 212 books making it to the weekly list.

There were certainly no surprises in who the winning authors were—George R. R. Martin leads the list with *A Game of Thrones,* and two more from the Fire and Ice series are among the 26 mass market bestsellers. The award-winning HBO fantasy series returns later this month for a third season, so sales should continue to climb for all of Martin's titles. Nicholas Sparks has two in the top five, and movie tie-ins have also buoyed his sales. In fact, movies had a positive effect on a number of other books, including Tolkien's *The Hobbit* and Lee Child's *One Shot.* Familiar mass market icons are the only authors making it to the half-million mark. And while actual numbers are lower for most of their 2012 titles than in previous years, check out the very lengthy e-book list of 2012 sales earlier in this article and you will find these regulars and their colleagues with numerous titles.

There was no dearth of trade paperback bestsellers in 2012, and in fact a record 121 books landed on the weekly charts, jumping the previous record of 84 books set in 2011. Trade paperbacks with sales of more than 100,000 sold numbered at 156 books; the 2011 figure was 119 books.

That's all good news, but not the big news. EL James took over the weekly charts with her Fifty Shades books and by the end of the year had more than 29 million copies sold for the three books and the trilogy. The books' on-sale date was April 1, and the speed of sales broke all records ever set for a bestseller; it is highly unlikely that these numbers will ever again be matched. James's books also whetted the appetite for other erotic titles, especially the books by Sylvia Day. She has two titles in the top eight, *Bared to You* and *Reflected in You,* giving eroticism more than 50 percent of the top-ten trade paper bestsellers.

Nonetheless, the list continues to be eclectic, with commercial and literary titles throughout. Food for the soul and stomach are still strong performers on this chart.

Note: All the figures that follow on the two paperback lists were provided by publishers. An asterisk denotes a title for which sales figures were provided in confidence, to be used for ranking purposes only. Penguin USA and the Random House Book Group supplied numbers for ranking purposes only. Kensington declined to participate.

Mass Market

1,000,000+

*A Game of Thrones (movie tie-in). George R. R. Martin. Bantam.

The Lucky One. Nicholas Sparks. Grand Central (1,039,167).

*Chasing Fire. Nora Roberts. Jove.

900,000+

*A Clash of Kings (movie tie-in). George R. R. Martin. Bantam.

Safe Haven. Nicholas Sparks. Grand Central (949,713).

800,000+

*A Storm of Swords. George R. R. Martin. Bantam.

*The Hobbit (movie tie-in). J. R. R. Tolkien. Ballantine.

*The Litigators. John Grisham. Dell.

*A Feast for Crows. George R. R. Martin. Bantam.

600,000+

To Kill a Mockingbird. Harper Lee. Grand Central (745,975).

*Live Wire. Harlan Coben. Signet.

*Red Mist. Patricia Cornwell. Berkley.

*Buried Prey. John Sandford. Berkley.

525,000+

Kill Alex Cross. James Patterson. Grand Central (565,363).

*Split Second. Catherine Coulter. Jove.

Micro. Michael Crichton. Harper (533,740).

*The Jungle. Clive Cussler. Berkley.

500,000+

*Shock Wave. John Sandford. Berkley.

*One Shot: A Jack Reacher Novel (movie tie-in). Lee Child. Dell.

What Doesn't Kill You. Iris Johansen. St. Martin's (511,400).

*Hotel Vendome. Danielle Steel. Dell.

*V Is for Vengeance. Sue Grafton. Berkley.

*The Devil Colony. James Rollin. Harper (503,648).

*Down the Darkest Road. Tami Hoag. Berkley.

*Locked On. Tom Clancy. Berkley.

*Catch Me. Lisa Gardner. Signet.

Trade Paperback

29 Million+

*Fifty Shades of Grey: Book One. EL James. Vintage.

*Fifty Shades Darker: Book Two. EL James. Vintage.

*Fifty Shades Freed: Book Three. EL James. Vintage.

700,000+

*Fifty Shades Trilogy bundle: 3-volume boxed set. EL James. Vintage.

*Bared to You. Sylvia Day. Berkley.

*Proof of Heaven: A Neurosurgeon's Journey into the Afterlife. Eben Alexander. Simon & Schuster (755,861).

600,000+

The Perks of Being a Wallflower. Stephen Chbosky. Gallery (648,413).

*Reflected in You. Sylvia Day. Berkley.

To Heaven and Back: A Doctor's Extraordinary Account of Her Death, Heaven, Angels, and Life Again: A True Story. Mary C. Neal, M.D. WaterBrook (617,648).

The Lucky One. Nicholas Sparks. Grand Central (602,785).

500,000+

*The Perfect Hope. Nora Roberts. Berkley.

The Great Gatsby. F. Scott Fitzgerald. Scribner (552,139).

The Hobbit (movie tie-in). J. R. R. Tolkien. Houghton Mifflin Harcourt (509,179).

*The Last Boyfriend. Nora Roberts. Berkley.

400,000+

Safe Haven. Nicholas Sparks. Grand Central (451,308).

Bossypants. Tina Fey. Little, Brown/Reagan Arthur (449,935).

Wheat Belly. Dr. William Davis. Rodale (428,681).

What to Expect When You're Expecting, Fourth Edition. Heidi Murkoff and Sharon Mazel. Workman (428,323).

The Best of Me. Nicholas Sparks. Grand Central (413,842).

*The Girl Who Kicked the Hornet's Nest: Book 3 of the Millennium Trilogy. Steig Larsson. Vintage.

300,000+

*The Immortal Life of Henrietta Lacks. Rebecca Skloot. Broadway.

*In the Garden of Beasts: Love, Terror, and an American Family in Hitler's Berlin. Erik Larson. Broadway.

*Cloud Atlas (movie tie-in). David Mitchell. Random House.

Not a Fan: Becoming a Completely Committed Follower of Jesus. Kyle Idleman. Zondervan (358,000).

The Happiness Project. Gretchen Rubin. Harper Paperbacks (340,000).

Fahrenheit 451. Ray Bradbury. Simon & Schuster (326,193).

The Magic. Rhonda Byrne. Atria (315,373).

Life of Pi (movie tie-in). Yann Martell. Houghton Mifflin Harcourt (308,356).

*Wreck This Journal: Expanded Edition. Keri Smith. Perigee.

Private London. James Patterson and Mark Pearson. Grand Central (307,805).

Abraham Lincoln: Vampire Hunter. Seth Grahame-Smith. Grand Central (306,338).

200,000+

*Of Mice and Men. John Steinbeck. Penguin.

The Hobbit. J. R. R. Tolkien. Houghton Mifflin Harcourt (254,529).

Lone Wolf. Jodi Picoult. Emily Bestler (244,159).

Team of Rivals (*Lincoln* film tie-in edition). Doris Kearns Goodwin. Simon & Schuster (238,267).

Beautiful Disaster. Jamie McGuire. Atria (233,854).

Eat to Live (Revised). Dr. Jack Fuhrman. Little, Brown (231,834).

*The Night Circus. Erin Morgenstern. Vintage.

Hungry Girl to the Max! The Ultimate Guilt-Free Cookbook. Lisa Lillien. St. Martin's (224,444).

*The Paris Wife. Paula McLain. Ballantine.

State of Wonder. Ann Patchett. Harper (221,000).

Nearing Home: Life, Faith, and Finishing Well. Billy Graham. Thomas Nelson (220,788).

*The Tiger's Wife. Téa Obreht. Random House.

*World War Z: An Oral History of the Zombie War. Max Brooks. Broadway.

Unlikely Friendships: 47 Remarkable Stories from the Animal Kingdom. Jennifer Holland. Workman (214,453).

Kill Alex Cross. James Patterson. Grand Central (212,976).

The Things They Carried. Tim O'Brien. Houghton Mifflin Harcourt (210,437).

*The Language of Flowers. Vanessa Diffenbaugh. Random House.

7 Habits of Highly Effective People: Powerful Lessons in Personal Change. Stephen R. Covey. Free Press (203,352).

The Innocent. David Baldacci. Grand Central (202,574).

*The Weird Sisters. Eleanor Brown. Berkley.

The Art of Racing Rain. Garth Stein. Harper (200,000).

170,000+

10th Anniversary. James Patterson and Maxine Paetro. Grand Central (199,606).

Outliers: The Story of Success. Malcolm Gladwell. Back Bay (193,077).

Battlefield of the Mind: Winning the Battle in Your Mind. Joyce Meyer. Faith Words (192,969).

American Heiress. Daisy Goodwin. St. Martin s (191,697).

11/22/63. Stephen King. Gallery (189,560).

*Things Fall Apart. Chinua Achebe. Vintage.

The Fiddler. Beverly Lewis. Bethany House (187,771).

A Stolen Life. Jaycee Dugard. Simon & Schuster (185,452).

Save Me. Lisa Scottoline. St. Martin's (185,137).

*The Zombie Survival Guide: Complete Protection from the Living Dead. Max Brooks. Broadway.

What to Expect the First Year (2nd edition). Sandee Hathaway, Arlene Eisenberg, Heidi Murkoff. Workman (182,514).

Now You See Her. James Patterson and Michael Ledwidge. Grand Central (175,480).

Guilty Wives. James Patterson and David Ellis. Grand Central (175,277).

*The House on Mango Street. Sandra Cisneros. Vintage.

160,000+

The Bridesmaid. Beverly Lewis. Bethany House (169,870).

*The Girl Who Played with Fire. Steig Larsson. Vintage.

*A Game of Thrones (movie tie-in). George R. R. Martin. Bantam.

Brave New World. Aldous Huxley. Harper (165,000).

Then Came You. Jennifer Weiner. Washington Square (162,482).

Every Day a Friday: How to be Happy 7 Days a Week. Joel Osteen. Faith Words (162,474).

*The Devil in the White City. Erik Larson. Vintage.

150,000+

*Maine. J. Courtney Sullivan. Vintage.

Kitchen House. Kathleen Grissom. Touchstone (156,375).

Zero Day. David Baldacci. Grand Central (155,557).

The Host (movie tie-in). Stephenie Meyer. Little, Brown (152,164).

Kill Me if You Can. James Patterson and Marshall Karp. Grand Central (151,439).

The Wind Through the Keyhole: A Dark Tower Novel. Stephen King. Gallery (151,422).

140,000+

The Other Wes Moore: One Name, Two Lives. Wes Moore. Spiegel and Grau (143,311).

The Lord of the Rings (one-volume movie tie-in edition). J. R. R. Tolkien. Houghton Mifflin Harcourt (148,796).

*The Sense of an Ending. Julian Barnes. Vintage.

The Dovekeepers. Alice Hoffman. Scribner (148,715).

The Glass Castle. Jeannette Walls. Scribner (147,105).

Crucial Conversations Tools for Talking When Stakes Are High, Second Edition. Kerry Patterson, Joseph Grenny, Ron McMillan, and Al Switzler. McGraw-Hill (146,252).

*Rules of Civility. Amor Towles. Penguin.

*Lady Almina and the Real Downton Abbey: The Lost Legacy of Highclere Castle. The Countess of Carnarvon. Broadway.

The Art of Fielding. Chad Harbach. Little, Brown (142,284).

130,000+

*Into the Wild. John Krakauer. Vintage.

7 Habits of Highly Effective Teens. Sean Covey. Touchstone (138,385).

Sarah's Key. Tatiana De Rosnay. St. Martin's Paperbacks (138,064).

Lethal. Sandra Brown. Grand Central (137,992).

Rainshadow Road. Lisa Kleypas. St. Martin's (137,114).

*The Litigators. John Grisham. Bantam.

*Sharp Objects. Gillian Flynn. Broadway.

What's New Cupcake? Ingeniously Simple Designs for Every Occasion. Karen Tack and Alan Richardson. Houghton Mifflin Harcourt (134,158).

*Dark Places. Gillian Flynn. Broadway.

The Shack: Where Tragedy Confronts Eternity. William Paul Young. Windblown Media (130,790).

The Kite Runner. Khaled Hosseini. Riverhead (130,749).

*Born to Run. Christopher McDougall. Vintage.

120,000+

Radical: Taking Back Your Faith from the American Dream. David Platt. Multnomah Books (129,419).

The Boy Who Came Back from Heaven. Kevin and Alex Malarkey. Tyndale (128,605).

Hunger Pains: A Parody. Harvard Lampoon. Touchstone (128,285).

The Drop. Michael Connelly. Grand Central (127,962).

Alex Cross (movie tie-in). James Patterson. Grand Central (127,423).

Wolf Hall. Hilary Mantel. Picador (127,281).

To Kill a Mockingbird. Harper Lee. Harper (127,000).

The Chew: Food, Life, Fun. The Chew Team. Hyperion (125,517).

Empire of the Summer Moon: Quanah Parker and the Rise and Fall of the Comanches, the Most Powerful Indian Tribe. S. C. Gwynne. Scribner (124,485).

Seal Team Six: Memoirs of an Elite Navy Seal Sniper. Howard E. Wasdin. St. Martin's (124,289).

How to Read Literature Like a Professor. Thomas C. Foster. Harper (124,000).

Forks Over Knives—The Cookbook. Del Sroufe. Experiment (123,419).

Their Eyes Were Watching God. Zora Neale Hurston. Harper (123,000).

Team of Rivals: The Political Genius of Abraham Lincoln. Doris Kearns Goodwin. Simon & Schuster (122,560).

100,000+

Seriously . . . I'm Kidding. Ellen DeGeneres. Grand Central (119,776).

Chicken Soup for the Soul: Messages from Heaven. Jack Canfield, Mark Victor Hansen, and Amy Newmark. Chicken Soup for the Soul Publishing (119,433).

The Fellowship of the Ring. J. R. R. Tolkien. Houghton Mifflin Harcourt (119,314).

Unglued: Making Wise Choices in the Midst of Raw Emotions. Lysa TerKeurst. Zondervan (118,600).

*Mindset: The New Psychology of Success. Carol Dweck. Ballantine.

The Two Towers. J. R. R. Tolkien. Houghton Mifflin Harcourt (115,011).

Anything He Wants. Sara Fawkes. St. Martin's (114,778).

The Return of the King. J. R. R. Tolkien. Houghton Mifflin Harcourt (114,359).

*Tuesdays with Morrie: An Old Man, a Young Man, and Life's Greatest Lesson. Mitch Albom. Broadway.

*The Eighty-Dollar Champion: The Horse that Inspired a Nation. Elizabeth Letts. Ballantine.

How to Win Friends and Influence People. Dale Carnegie. Gallery (113,797).

Private Games. James Patterson and Mark Sullivan. Grand Central (113,594).

*Home Again. Kristin Hannah. Ballantine.

Is Everyone Hanging Out Without Me? (And Other Concerns). Mindy Kaling. Three Rivers (112,333).

*A Clash of Kings (movie tie-in). George R. R. Martin. Bantam.

The Shoemaker's Wife. Adriana Trigiani. Harper Paperbacks (111,000).

*Cutting for Stone. Abraham Verghese. Vintage.

*Half the Sky: Turning Oppression into Opportunity for Women Worldwide. Nicholas D. Kristoff and Sheryl WuDunn. Vintage.

Lady of the Rivers. Philippa Gregory. Touchstone (109,052).

*The Road. Cormac McCarthy. Vintage.

Switch. Megan Hart. Harlequin Mira (107,396).

Blink: The Power of Thinking Without Thinking. Malcolm Gladwell. Back Bay (106,563).

The House I Loved. Tatiana De Rosnay. St. Martin's (105,479).

The Old Man and the Sea. Ernest Hemingway. Scribner (104,411).

One Summer. David Baldacci. Grand Central (104,307).

Summer Rental. Mary Kay Andrews. St. Martin s (103,162).

The Power of Now: A Guide to Spiritual Enlightenment. Eckhart Tolle. New World Library (103,000).

Love Does: Discover A Secretly Incredible Life in an Ordinary World. Bob Goff. Thomas Nelson (102,958).

Dream Lake. Lisa Kleypas. St. Martin's (102,443)

The Marriage Plot. Jeffrey Eugenides. Picador (102,271).

Forks Over Knives: The Plant-Based Way to Health. Gene Stone. Experiment (101,726).

Pleasures of the Night. Sylvia Day. Morrow (101,569).

The Book of Burger. Rachael Ray. Atria (100,397).

Speed of Trust: The One Thing that Changes Everything. Stephen M. R. Covey. Free Press (101,171).

Inside of a Dog: What Dogs See, Smell, and Know. Alexandra Horowitz. Scribner (100,662).

*Sisterhood Everlasting. Ann Brashares. Random House.

Freakonomics. Steven D. Leavitt. Morrow (100,353).

The Heaven Answer Book. Billy Graham. Thomas Nelson (100,224).

Picture This. Jacqueline Sheehan. William Morrow (100,001).

Children's Books: Hunger Games Leads the Way

Diane Roback
Senior Editor, Children's Books, *Publishers Weekly*

For children's books, without a doubt, Hunger Games was the story of the year. Its performance far exceeded all other books for children and teens. In 2012 Suzanne Collins's dystopian trilogy sold an astounding 27.7 million copies: 15 million print books and 12.7 million e-books. Of that print number, 8.8 million was for hardcovers, since only the first of the three books is available in paperback.

The original Hunger Games title sold 11.7 million copies on its own (903,000 in hardcover, 6.2 million in paperback, and 4.6 million digitally). The only series with higher digital sales, for either adults or children, was the Fifty Shades of Grey trilogy at 15+ million—soft-core porn edging out kids battling to the death.

Although the Hunger Games was already a huge phenomenon before the March 2012 release of the Lionsgate film, the movie launched book sales into the stratosphere. Back in 2010 Hunger Games books sold 4.3 million copies, which jumped to 9.2 million in 2011; that number tripled in 2012, making for a 201 percent increase over previous year sales. Clearly—as previously demonstrated by the Twilight and Harry Potter series—while a hot movie franchise is ongoing, demand for the books is unrelenting.

Rick Riordan's books show a different sales pattern, because a movie is not currently driving sales (the first film from his Percy Jackson and the Olympians series, *The Lightning Thief,* was released in 2010; Sea of Monsters is due in theaters in August). Riordan's various myth-based series sold a combined 5.6 million copies in 2012 (2.52 million in hardcover, 1.79 million in paper, and 1.27 million e-books). Those numbers are up slightly from 2011, when 5 million books were sold, though still down from 2010's high-water mark of 10 million.

Other bestselling franchises of note: a combined 2.7 million copies sold of James Patterson's assorted series; 2.1 million copies sold of Rachel Renée Russell's Dork Diaries; 2 million copies of the first two books in Veronica Roth's Divergent trilogy (No. 3 is due out this October); and 1.4 million Big Nate books by Lincoln Peirce. Stephenie Meyer's Twilight series may have declined from its glory days, but it still sold 1.1 million in 2012, with almost half of that coming from e-books. Harry Potter, however, is virtually gone from the lists, with just one title (the first in the series) appearing on our paperback backlist chart.

Figures were supplied by Random House in confidence for ranking purposes only; Penguin supplied e-book figures in confidence for ranking purposes only.

Hardcover Frontlist

500,000+

The Mark of Athena (Heroes of Olympus No. 3). Rick Riordan. Disney-Hyperion (1,425,754).

The Third Wheel (Diary of a Wimpy Kid). Jeff Kinney. Abrams/Amulet (1,401,799).

The Serpent's Shadow (Kane Chronicles No. 3). Rick Riordan. Disney-Hyperion (783,180).

Tales From a Not-So-Graceful Ice Princess (Dork Diaries No. 4). Rachel Renée Russell. Simon & Schuster/Aladdin (727,660).

Insurgent. Veronica Roth. HarperCollins/Tegen (615,411).

Tales From a Not So Smart Miss Know-It-All (Dork Diaries No. 5). Rachel Renée Russell. Simon & Schuster/Aladdin (607,929).

300,000+

Middle School: Get Me Out of Here! James Patterson and Chris Tebbetts. Little, Brown (498,894).

Junie B., First Grader: Turkeys We Have Loved and Eaten (and Other Thankful Stuff.) (Junie B., First Grader No. 28). Barbara Park, illustrated by Denise Brunkus. Random House.

Hidden. P. C. Cast and Kristin Cast. St. Martin's Griffin (428,469).

"Who Could That Be at This Hour?" (All the Wrong Questions No. 1). Lemony Snicket, illustrated by Seth. Little, Brown (383,274).

Big Nate Goes for Broke. Lincoln Peirce. HarperCollins (382,984).

Justin Bieber: Just Getting Started. Justin Bieber. HarperCollins (340,088).

I Funny: A Middle School Story. James Patterson and Chris Grabenstein. Little, Brown (327,315).

A Perfect Time for Pandas (Magic Tree House No. 48). Mary Pope Osborne, illustrated by Sal Murdocca. Random House.

Lincoln's Last Days. Bill O'Reilly and Dwight Jon Zimmerman. Holt (316,696).

Disney Bedtime Favorites. Disney (310,838).

Nancy Clancy, Super Sleuth. Jane O'Connor, illustrated by Robin Preiss Glasser. HarperCollins (308,566).

Pete the Cat and His Four Groovy Buttons. Eric Litwin, illustrated by James Dean. HarperCollins (308,065).

200,000+

Olivia and the Fairy Princesses. Ian Falconer. Simon & Schuster/Atheneum (299,393).

The Fault in Our Stars. John Green. Dutton (292,747).

Confessions of a Murder Suspect. James Patterson and Maxine Paetro. Little, Brown (284,887).

Nevermore: The Final Maximum Ride Adventure. James Patterson. Little, Brown/Patterson Young Readers (275,340).

Dr. Seuss's ABC. Dr. Seuss. Random House.

Captain Underpants and the Terrifying Return of Tippy Tinkletrousers. Dav Pilkey. Scholastic (266,181).

Fancy Nancy and the Mermaid Ballet. Jane O'Connor, illustrated by Robin Preiss Glasser. HarperCollins (253,572).

Horton Hears a Who. Dr. Seuss. Random House.

Rapture (Fallen No. 4). Lauren Kate. Delacorte (248,184).

The Rise of Nine. Pittacus Lore. HarperCollins (245,440).

Wonder. R. J. Palacio. Knopf.

Reached. Ally Condie. Dutton (242,537).

Caught. Margaret Peterson Haddix. Simon & Schuster (226,699).

Pete the Cat Saves Christmas. Eric Litwin, illustrated by James Dean. HarperCollins (223,158).

5-Minute Disney Pixar Stories. Disney (221,401).

Between the Lines. Jodi Picoult. Atria/Bestler (205,357).

The Demigod Diaries (Heroes of Olympus). Rick Riordan. Disney-Hyperion (203,484).

Chomp. Carl Hiaasen. Knopf.

100,000+

The Accused (Theodore Boone No. 3). John Grisham. Dutton (181,600).

The World of the Hunger Games. Kate Egan. Scholastic (179,814).

The Kill Order (Maze Runner Prequel). James Dashner. Delacorte (177,534).

The Mighty Avengers. Billy Wrecks, illustrated by Patrick Spaziante. Random House.

The LEGO Ninjago Character Encyclopedia. DK (165,740).

Brave Little Golden Book. Random House.

Big Nate Fun Blaster. Lincoln Peirce. HarperCollins (161,910).

A Mutiny in Time (Infinity Ring No. 1). James Dashner. Scholastic (161,348).

Nancy Clancy, Secret Admirer. Jane O'Connor, illustrated by Robin Preiss Glasser. HarperCollins (161,270).

Llama Llama Time to Share. Anna Dewdney. Viking (157,221).

Finale (Hush, Hush). Becca Fitzpatrick. Simon & Schuster (154, 332).

Lenobia's Vow. P. C. Cast and Kristin Cast. St. Martin's Griffin (153,296).

Goldilocks and the Three Dinosaurs. Mo Willems. HarperCollins/Balzer + Bray (151,599).

Star Wars Origami. Chris Alexander. Workman (151,233).

The Enchantress (Secrets of the Immortal Nicholas Flamel No. 6). Michael Scott. Delacorte.

The Duckling Gets a Cookie!? Mo Willems. Hyperion (144,916).

Infamous. Sherrilyn Kenyon. St. Martin's Griffin (144,090).

The Last Guardian. Eoin Colfer. Disney Hyperion (142,323).

Llama Llama Nighty-Night. Anna Dewdney. Viking (141,515).

Michael Vey 2: Rise of the Elgen. Richard Paul Evans. Simon Pulse/Mercury Ink (136,725).

Brave Big Golden Book. Random House.

I Am a Princess (Disney Princess). Andrea Posner-Sanchez, illustrated by Francesco Legramandi and Gabriella Matta. Random House.

My Brave Year of Firsts. Jamie Lee Curtis, illustrated by Laura Cornell. HarperCollins (130,095).

Good Night, I Love You. Caroline Jayne Church. Scholastic/Cartwheel (129,553).

Son. Lois Lowry. Houghton Mifflin (128,097).

Wake (Watersong No. 1). Amanda Hocking. St. Martin's Griffin (126,964).

Stunning (Pretty Little Liars No. 11). Sara Shepard. HarperTeen (126,292).

The Amazing Spider-Man Storybook Collection. Marvel (125,517).

The Secret of the Fortune Wookiee (Origami Yoda). Tom Angleberger. Abrams/Amulet (123,912).

The Amazing Spider-Man. Frank Berrios, illustrated by Francesco Legramandi and Andrea Cagol. Random House.

Shatterproof (The 39 Clues: Cahills vs. Vespers No. 4). Roland Smith. Scholastic (122,435).

The Dead of Night (The 39 Clues: Cahills vs. Vespers No. 3). Peter Lerangis. Scholastic (121,934).

The Land of Stories: The Wishing Spell. Chris Colfer. Little, Brown (121,766).

Fated (Soul Seekers No. 1). Alyson Noël. St. Martin's Griffin (121,156).

The Fame Game. Lauren Conrad. HarperCollins (119,776).

City of Lost Souls (The Mortal Instruments). Cassandra Clare. Simon & Schuster/
McElderry (118,821).

The Kane Chronicles Survival Guide. Rick Riordan. Disney-Hyperion (118,190).

Fallen in Love. Lauren Kate. Delacorte.

The Extraordinary Education of Nicholas Benedict. Trenton Lee Stewart. Little,
Brown (117,360).

Monster High: Ghoulfriends Forever. Gitty Daneshvari. Little, Brown (117,283).

The Empty City (Survivors No. 1). Erin Hunter. HarperCollins (116,874).

Pretty Little Secrets. Sara Shepard. HarperTeen (114,493).

Rocket Writes a Story. Tad Hills. Random House/Schwartz & Wade.

Safari: A Photicular Book. Carol Kaufman. Workman (113,588).

The Invincible Iron Man. Billy Wrecks, illustrated by Patrick Spaziante. Random
House.

Pandemonium. Lauren Oliver. HarperCollins (108,145).

Star Wars: A Galactic Pop-Up Adventure. Matthew Reinhart. Scholastic/Orchard
(107,924).

The Big Purple Book of Beginner Books. Random House.

The Golden Lily (Bloodlines). Richelle Mead. Razorbill (107,234).

The Fantastic Flying Books of Mr. Morris Lessmore. William Joyce. Simon &
Schuster/Atheneum (106,645).

The Wimpy Kid Movie Diary. Jeff Kinney. Abrams/Amulet (106,043).

It's Time for Bubble Puppy! Random House/Golden.

This Is Not My Hat. Jon Klassen. Candlewick (105,250).

Fox in Socks (board book). Dr. Seuss. Random House.

A Series of Unfortunate Events No. 1: The Bad Beginning: The Short-Lived Edition. Lemony Snicket, illustrated by Brent Helquist. HarperCollins (104,665).

Burned (Pretty Little Liars No. 12). Sara Shepard. HarperTeen (104,443).

Liar & Spy. Rebecca Stead. Random House/Lamb.

Divide and Conquer (Infinity Ring No. 2). Carrie Ryan. Scholastic (101,274).

Princess and the Popstar. Mary Tillworth. Random House/Golden.

Trust No One (The 39 Clues: Cahills vs. Vespers No. 2). Linda Sue Park. Scholastic (100,922).

Lullaby (Watersong No. 2). Amanda Hocking. St. Martin's Griffin (100,863).

Lauren Conrad Beauty. Lauren Conrad. HarperCollins (100,751).

The Last Hope (Warriors: Omen of the Stars No. 6). Erin Hunter. HarperCollins
(100,409).

Hardcover Backlist

500,000+

Catching Fire. Suzanne Collins. Scholastic, 2009 (4,431,869).

Mockingjay. Suzanne Collins. Scholastic, 2010 (3,427,354).

The Hunger Games. Suzanne Collins. Scholastic, 2008 (903,457).

Green Eggs and Ham. Dr. Seuss. Random House, 1960.

One Fish Two Fish Red Fish Blue Fish. Dr. Seuss. Random House, 1960.

Goodnight Moon (board book). Margaret Wise Brown, illustrated by Clement Hurd. HarperFestival, 1991 (605,779).

Cabin Fever (Diary of a Wimpy Kid). Jeff Kinney. Abrams/Amulet, 2011 (584,234).

The Lorax. Dr. Seuss. Random House, 1971.

The Cat in the Hat. Dr. Seuss. Random House, 1957.

300,000+

Oh, the Places You'll Go! Dr. Seuss. Random House, 1990.

The Wimpy Kid Do-It-Yourself Book. Jeff Kinney. Abrams/Amulet, 2011 (446,123).

Dr. Seuss's ABC (board book). Dr. Seuss. Random House, 1996.

Guess How Much I Love You (board book). Sam McBratney, illustrated by Anita Jeram. Candlewick, 1995 (414,455).

Brown Bear, Brown Bear, What Do You See? (board book). Bill Martin, Jr., illustrated by Eric Carle. Holt, 1996 (385,126).

Little Blue Truck (board book). Alice Schertle, illustrated by Jill McElmurry. Houghton Mifflin Harcourt, 2008 (381,808).

The Very Hungry Caterpillar (board book). Eric Carle. Philomel, 1994 (369,560).

5-Minute Princess Stories. Disney, 2011 (354,797).

Mr. Brown Can Moo! Can You? (board book). Dr. Seuss. Random House, 1996.

Princess Bedtime Stories. Disney, 2010 (314,104).

200,000+

Fox in Socks. Dr. Seuss. Random House, 1965.

I Love You Through and Through. Bernadette Rossetti Shustak, illustrated by Caroline Jayne Church. Scholastic/Cartwheel, 2005 (289,896).

Goodnight, Goodnight, Construction Site. Sherri Duskey Rinker, illustrated by Tom Lichtenheld. Chronicle, 2011 (283,859).

Giraffes Can't Dance. Giles Andreae, illustrated by Guy Parker-Rees. Scholastic/ Orchard, 2001 (277,741).

Hop on Pop. Dr. Seuss. Random House, 1963.

Go, Dog. Go! P. D. Eastman. Random House, 1961.

Dog Days (Diary of a Wimpy Kid). Jeff Kinney. Abrams/Amulet, 2009 (261,106).

The Ugly Truth (Diary of a Wimpy Kid). Jeff Kinney. Abrams/Amulet, 2010 (243,312).

Are You My Mother? (board book). P. D. Eastman. Random House, 1998.

Are You My Mother? P. D. Eastman. Random House, 1960.

The Last Straw (Diary of a Wimpy Kid). Jeff Kinney. Abrams/Amulet, 2009 (237,663).

Diary of a Wimpy Kid. Jeff Kinney. Abrams/Amulet, 2007 (236,515).

Dr. Seuss's ABC. Dr. Seuss. Random House, 1960.

Rodrick Rules (Diary of a Wimpy Kid). Jeff Kinney. Abrams/Amulet, 2008 (231,526).

Miss Peregrine's Home for Peculiar Children. Ransom Riggs. Quirk, 2011 (223,979).

On the Night You Were Born (board book). Nancy Tillman. Feiwel and Friends, 2010 (210,971).

The Giving Tree. Shel Silverstein. HarperCollins, 1964 (207,473).

Tales From a Not-So-Fabulous Life (Dork Diaries No. 1). Rachel Renée Russell. Simon & Schuster/Aladdin, 2009 (203,646).

Press Here. Hervé Tullet. Chronicle, 2011 (202,779).

150,000+

Where the Sidewalk Ends (30th anniversary edition). Shel Silverstein. HarperCollins, 2003 (198,361).

Baby Einstein: First Words. Disney, 2008 (192,246).

Heaven Is for Real for Kids. Todd Burpo. Thomas Nelson, 2011 (187,893).

Hand, Hand, Fingers, Thumb. Al Perkins. Random House, 1998.

How to Dork Your Diary (Dork Diaries No. 3½). Rachel Renée Russell. Simon & Schuster/Aladdin, 2011 (186,679).

Down by the Cool of the Pool. Tony Mitton, illustrated by Guy Parker-Rees. Scholastic/Orchard, 2002 (185,288).

Big Nate: In a Class by Himself. HarperCollins, 2010 (185,108).

How the Grinch Stole Christmas. Dr. Seuss. Random House, 1957.

The Foot Book (board book). Dr. Seuss. Random House, 1996.

The Polar Express. Chris Van Allsburg. Houghton Mifflin, 1985 (177,328).

If You Give a Mouse a Cookie. Laura Joffe Numeroff, illustrated by Felicia Bond. HarperCollins, 1985 (172,627).

A Ball for Daisy. Chris Raschka. Random House/Schwartz & Wade, 2011.

My First Read and Learn Bible. American Bible Society. Scholastic/Little Shepherd, 2006 (165,799).

I Love You Stinky Face (board book). Lisa McCourt. Scholastic/Cartwheel, 2004 (164,420).

The Poky Little Puppy. Janette Sebring Lowrey, illustrated by Gustaf Tenggren. Random House, 2001.

Disney Princess Collection. Disney, 2009 (162,112).

Tales From a Not-So-Talented Pop Star (Dork Diaries No. 3). Rachel Renée Russell. Simon & Schuster/Aladdin, 2011 (154,988).

Hop on Board (board book). Dr. Seuss. Random House, 2004.

Brown Bear, Brown Bear, What Do You See? (Slide and Find). Bill Martin, Jr., illustrated by Eric Carle. Priddy, 2010 (154,163).

Little Blue Truck Leads the Way (board book). Alice Schertle, illustrated by Jill McElmurry. Houghton Mifflin Harcourt, 2009 (152,871).

Big Blue Book of Beginner Books. Random House, 2008.

I Can Read with My Eyes Shut! Dr. Seuss. Random House, 1978.

Pat the Bunny. Dorothy Kunhardt. Random House, 2001.

100,000+

Every Thing on It. Shel Silverstein. HarperCollins, 2011 (149,442).

Happy Birthday to You! Dr. Seuss. Random House, 1959.

Walt Disney's Classic Storybook. Disney, 2009 (148,537).

Disney Pixar Storybook Collection. Disney, 2011 (148,222).

Peek-a-Who? Nina Laden. Chronicle, 2000 (147,341).

The Invention of Hugo Cabret. Brian Selznick. Scholastic, 2007 (147,209).

First 100 Words (board book). Roger Priddy. Priddy, 2005 (139,958).

Where the Wild Things Are. Maurice Sendak. HarperCollins, 1963 (139,362).

Oh, the Thinks You Can Think! Dr. Seuss. Random House, 1975.

Oh Say, Can You Say Di-no-saur? Bonnie Worth, illustrated by Steve Haefele. Random House, 1999.

You Are My Sunshine. Jimmie Davis, illustrated by Caroline Jayne Church. Scholastic/Cartwheel, 2011 (138,243).

Oh, the Thinks You Can Think! (board book). Dr. Seuss. Random House, 2009.

The Runaway Bunny (board book). Margaret Wise Brown, illustrated by Clement Hurd. HarperFestival, 1991 (136,095).

Tales From a Not-So-Popular Party Girl: (Dork Diaries No. 2). Rachel Renée Russell. Simon & Schuster/Aladdin, 2010 (133,016).

Divergent. Veronica Roth. HarperCollins/Tegen, 2011 (130,680).

Cars Storybook Collection. Disney, 2011 (129,953).

Pete the Cat: I Love My White Shoes. Eric Litwin, illustrated by James Dean. HarperCollins, 2010 (129,646).

I Want My Hat Back. Jon Klassen. Candlewick, 2011 (129,316).

There's No Place Like Space. Tish Rabe, illustrated by Aristedes Ruiz. Random House, 1999.

Disney Christmas Storybook Collection. Disney, 2009 (126,607).

Big Nate on a Roll. Lincoln Peirce. HarperCollins, 2011 (125,505).

Wacky Wednesday. Dr. Seuss. Random House, 1974.

Wipe Clean Letters. Roger Priddy. Priddy, 2004 (118,955).

The Big Green Book of Beginner Books. Dr. Seuss. Random House, 2009.

There's a Wocket in My Pocket (board book). Dr. Seuss. Random House, 1996.

On the Night You Were Born. Nancy Tillman. Feiwel and Friends, 2006 (115,517).

The Night Before Christmas. Clement C. Moore, illustrated by Corinne Malvern. Random House, 2011.

Ten Apples Up on Top! Dr. Seuss. Random House, 1961.

My Big Book of Beginner Books About Me. Random House, 2011.

Disney Nursery Rhymes and Fairy Tales. Disney, 2008 (111,028).

Dead End in Norvelt. Jack Gantos. Farrar, Straus & Giroux, 2011 (109,700).

Richard Scarry's Book of Cars and Trucks and Things That Go. Richard Scarry. Random House, 1998.

Disney Storybook Collection. Disney, 2006 (108,853).

Big Nate Strikes Again. Lincoln Peirce. HarperCollins, 2011 (108,163).

Five Little Monkeys Jumping on the Bed (board book). Eileen Christelow. Houghton Mifflin Harcourt, 1989 (107,657).

If You Give a Dog a Donut. Laura Numeroff, illus by Felicia Bond. HarperCollins/ Balzer + Bray, 2011 (106,814).

The Strange Case of Origami Yoda. Tom Angleberger. Abrams/Amulet, 2010 (105,256).

Wherever You Are, My Love Will Find You. Nancy Tillman. Feiwel and Friends, 2010 (103,793).

Middle School, the Worst Years of My Life. James Patterson and Chris Tebbetts. Little Brown, 2011 (103,494).

Where's Spot? Eric Hill. Putnam, 2003 (103,353).

I'm a Big Sister. Joanna Cole, illustrated by Rosalinda Kightly. HarperFestival (102,764).

Simple First Words: Let's Talk. Roger Priddy. Priddy, 2011 (102,344).

Pete the Cat: Rocking in My School Shoes. Eric Litwin, illustrated by James Dean. HarperCollins, 2011 (102,229).

A Bad Kitty Christmas. Nick Bruel. Roaring Brook, 2011 (101,899).

Go, Dog. Go! (board book). P. D. Eastman. Random House, 1997.

Pinkalicious. Victoria Kann. HarperCollins, 2006 (101,447).

Slide and Find: Trucks. Roger Priddy. Priddy, 2007 (100,312).

The Christmas Story. Jane Werner Watson. Random House, 2000.

The Nose Book. Al Perkins, illustrated by Joe Mathieu. Random House, 2003.

Dr. Seuss's Sleep Book. Dr. Seuss. Random House, 1962.

My Book About Me. Dr Seuss. Random House, 1969.

Paperback Frontlist

300,000+

Divergent. Veronica Roth. HarperCollins/Tegen (690,314).

Look for the Lorax (Dr. Seuss). Tish Rabe, illustrated by Christopher Moroney and Jan Gerardi. Random House.

One Direction: Dare to Dream. One Direction. HarperCollins (514,734).

A Fairy-Tale Adventure (Barbie). Tish Rabe, illustrated by Christopher Moroney and Jan Gerardi. Random House.

Pinkalicious: The Princess of Pink Slumber Party. Victoria Kann. HarperCollins (450,121).

Happy Birthday, Princess! (Disney). Jennifer Weinberg, illustrated by Elisa Marrucchi. Random House.

Game On! (Disney's Wreck-It Ralph). Susan Amerikaner. Random House.

The Hunger Games Tribute Guide. Emily Seife. Scholastic (349,333).

Breaking Dawn (Twilight No. 4). Stephenie Meyer. Little, Brown (342,948).

The Lost Hero (Heroes of Olympus No. 1). Rick Riordan. Disney-Hyperion (342,405).

The Gift (Witch and Wizard No. 2) (mass market). James Patterson and Ned Rust. Little, Brown (333,544).

200,000+

The Hunger Games Official Illustrated Movie Companion. Kate Egan. Scholastic (297,368).

Big Nate: What Could Possibly Go Wrong? Lincoln Peirce. HarperCollins (268,170).

Big Bear, Little Bear (Disney/Pixar Brave). Random House/Disney.

The Archer's Quest (Disney/Pixar Brave). Random House/Disney.

Out of My Mind. Sharon M. Draper. Simon & Schuster/Atheneum (229,141).

Color Our World (Disney Princess). Random House/Golden.

Mater's Birthday Surprise (Disney/Pixar Cars). Melissa Lagonegro. Random House.

Fairy Magic (Dora the Explorer). Illustrated by Jason Fruchter. Random House/ Golden.

National Geographic Kids Almanac 2013. National Geographic (218,048).

Brave Junior Novelization (Disney/Pixar Brave). Irene Trimble. Random House.

Torn. Amanda Hocking. St. Martin's Griffin (212,490).

Pinkalicious and the Pinkatastic Zoo Day. Victoria Kann. HarperCollins (210,473).

One Direction: Behind the Scenes. One Direction. HarperCollins (208,746).

A Fin-tastic Journey (Barbie). Mary Man-Kong. Random House.

Splat the Cat Takes the Cake. Rob Scotton. HarperCollins (204,124).

Merida's Challenge (Disney/Pixar Brave). Random House.

Ascend. Amanda Hocking. St. Martin's Griffin (201,137).

100,000+

The Great Crayon Race (Bubble Guppies). Random House.

Middle School, the Worst Years of My Life. James Patterson and Chris Tebbetts. Little, Brown (194,732).

These Are the Avengers. Marvel (190,419).

Inheritance (Inheritance Cycle No. 4). Christopher Paolini. Knopf.

A Friend for Merida (Disney/Pixar Brave). Random House.

Masters of Spinjitzu (Lego Ninjago Reader No. 2). Tracey West. Scholastic (186,481).

Star Power. Mary Man-Kong. Random House.

A Mother's Love (Disney/Pixar Brave). Random House.

Big Nate: Here Goes Nothing. Lincoln Peirce. HarperCollins (178,672).

The Throne of Fire (Kane Chronicles No. 2). Rick Riordan. Disney-Hyperion (174,750).

Pinkalicious: Fairy House. Victoria Kann. HarperCollins (173,653).

How to Help the Earth—By the Lorax (Dr. Seuss). Tish Rabe, illustrated by Christopher Moroney and Jan Gerardi. Random House.

The Abduction (Theodore Boone No. 2). John Grisham. Puffin (166,944).

Pinkalicious: Soccer Star. Victoria Kann. HarperCollins (165,730).

An Egg-cellent Easter (Barbie). Rebecca Frazer, illustrated by Kellee Riley. Random House.

Beautiful Creatures (mass market tie-in). Kami Garcia and Margaret Stohl. Little, Brown (163,450).

Fancy Nancy: Fancy Day in Room 1-A. Jane O'Connor, illustrated by Robin Preiss Glasser. HarperCollins (162,719).

Friends, Fashion, and Fun! (Barbie). Mary Man-Kong, illustrated by Das Grup. Random House.

Way of the Ninja (Lego Ninjago Reader No. 1). Greg Farshtey. Scholastic (153,934).

Royal Coloring Fun (Disney Princess). Random House.

Snow White & the Huntsman. Lily Blake et al. Little, Brown (150,891).

Finish-Line Friends (Disney/Pixar Cars). Random House.

Secret of the Wings Junior Novelization (Disney Fairies). Random House.

A Tree for Me! (Dr. Seuss). Illustrated by Jan Gerardi. Random House/Golden.

Splat the Cat: The Name of the Game. Rob Scotton. HarperCollins (143,873).

Oh, Brother! (Disney/Pixar Brave). Apple Jordan. Random House.

Rise of the Snakes (Lego Ninjago Reader No. 4). Tracey West. Scholastic (139,837).

Surf Princess (Barbie). Chelsea Eberly. Random House.

Cute and Cuddly (Disney Princess). Random House.

Delirium. Lauren Oliver. HarperCollins (134,784).

Alvin and the Chipmunks: Alvin Gets an A. Kristen Mayer. HarperCollins (134,310).

Leprechaun in Late Winter (Magic Tree House No. 43). Mary Pope Osborne, illustrated by Sal Murdocca. Random House.

The Fire (Witch and Wizard No. 3). James Patterson and Jill Dembowski. Little, Brown (130,519).

Jewels for a Princess (Disney Princess). Ruth Homberg. Random House.

Pandas and Other Endangered Species (Magic Tree House Fact Tracker No. 26). Mary Pope Osborne and Natalie Pope Boyce, illustrated by Sal Murdocca. Random House.

Glam It Up (Barbie). Random House.

City of Fallen Angels (The Mortal Intruments). Cassandra Clare. Simon & Schuster/McElderry (125,568).

The Golden Weapons (Lego Ninjago Reader No. 3). Tracey West. Scholastic (123,995).

Angel (Maximum Ride No. 7). James Patterson. Little, Brown/Patterson Young Readers (123,634).

Kite Riders! (Team Umizumi). Illustrated by Jason Fruchter. Random House.

Wreck-It Ralph Junior Novelization. Irene Trimble. Random House.

I Am a Seal Team Six Warrior. Howard E. Wasdin. St. Martin's Griffin (121,889).

Walkin' in a Sticker Wonderland! (Dr. Seuss/Cat in the Hat). Illustrated by Christopher Moroney. Random House.

New Friends (Disney Fairies). Random House.

A Ghost Tale for Christmas Time (Magic Tree House No. 44). Mary Pope Osborne, illustrated by Sal Murdocca. Random House.

High Score! (Disney Wreck-It Ralph). Cynthia Hands. Random House.

I Can Be President (Barbie). Christy Webster, illustrated by Kellee Riley. Random House.

Awakened. P. C. Cast and Kristin Cast. St. Martin's Griffin (115,859).

This Is Spider-Man. Marvel (113,584).

Green Team! (Teenage Mutant Ninja Turtles). Christy Webster, illustrated by Patrick Spaziante. Random House.

Sparkle and Shine (Disney Princess). Random House.

Switched. Amanda Hocking. St. Martin's Griffin (112,663).

Cinderella (Diamond) Step into Reading (Disney Princess). Melissa Lagonegro. Random House.

A Night to Sparkle (Disney Princess). Random House.

The Power of Six. Pittacus Lore. HarperCollins (109,358).

Between Shades of Gray. Ruta Sepetys. Penguin (108,251).

The Avengers Assemble. Marvel (107,626).

McKenna. Mary Casanova. American Girl (106,424).

Passion (Fallen No. 3). Lauren Kate. Delacorte.

Bad Kitty for President. Nick Bruel. Macmillan/Square Fish (102,412).

Arcade Brigade (Disney Wreck-It Ralph). Cynthia Hands. Random House.

Saved by the Shell! (Teenage Mutant Ninja Turtles). Random House.

Moon over Manifest. Clare Vanderpool. Delacorte.

A Perfect Match (Disney Fairies). Random House.

Princess Hearts (Disney Princess). Jennifer Liberts Weinberg, illustrated by Francesco Legramandi. Random House.

Good Night, Princess! (Disney Princess). Andrea Posner-Sanchez, illustrated by Francesco Legramandi and Gabriella Matta. Random House.

The Lorax Doodle Book. Illustrated by Jan Gerardi. Random House.

Rock and Rule (Barbie). Mary Tillworth. Random House.

The Cup of Ankh (House of Anubis). Peter McGrath. Random House.

Invincible. Sherrilyn Kenyon. St. Martin's Griffin (100,346).

Paperback Backlist

300,000+

The Hunger Games. Suzanne Collins. Scholastic, 2010 (6,203,307).

The Giver. Lois Lowry. Random House, 2002.

Love You Forever. Robert Munsch. Firefly, 1986 (395,223).

The Lightning Thief (Percy Jackson and the Olympians No. 1). Rick Riordan. Disney-Hyperion, 2006 (378,061).

Dinosaurs Before Dark (Magic Tree House No. 1). Mary Pope Osborne, illustrated by Sal Murdocca. Random House, 1992.

The Book Thief. Markus Zusak. Knopf, 2007.

The Outsiders. S. E. Hinton. Penguin/Speak, 1997 (301,119).

200,000+

Where the Wild Things Are. Maurice Sendak. HarperCollins, 1988 (286,059).

The Maze Runner (Maze Runner No. 1). James Dashner. Random House/Ember, 2010.

The Knight at Dawn (Magic Tree House No. 2). Mary Pope Osborne, illustrated by Sal Murdocca. Random House, 1993.

Charlotte's Web. E. B. White, illustrated by Garth Williams. HarperCollins, 1974 (235,457).

Fairytale Collection (Barbie) Random House, 2011.

Pirates Past Noon (Magic Tree House No. 4). Mary Pope Osborne, illustrated by Sal Murdocca. Random House, 1994.

Fancy Nancy: Hair Dos and Hair Don'ts. Jane O'Connor, illustrated by Robin Preiss Glasser. HarperCollins, 2011 (223,746).

The Sea of Monsters (Percy Jackson and the Olympians No. 2). Rick Riordan. Disney-Hyperion, 2007 (215,288).

Holes. Louis Sachar. Random House/Yearling, 2000.

Frindle. Andrew Clements. Atheneum, 1998 (203,910).

The Care and Keeping of You: The Body Book for Girls. Valorie Schaefer. American Girl, 1998 (203,337).

A Wrinkle in Time. Madeleine L'Engle. Macmillan/Square Fish, 2007 (200,465).

100,000+

The Titan's Curse (Percy Jackson and the Olympians No. 3). Rick Riordan. Disney-Hyperion, 2008 (193,671).

Fancy Nancy and the Delectable Cupcakes. Jane O'Connor, illustrated by Robin Preiss Glasser. HarperCollins, 2010 (193,573).

Pinkalicious: School Rules! Victoria Kann. HarperCollins, 2010 (193,299).

Number the Stars. Lois Lowry. Houghton Mifflin Harcourt/Sandpiper, 1989 (192,540).

The Last Olympian (Percy Jackson and the Olympians No. 5). Rick Riordan. Disney-Hyperion, 2011 (188,998).

Fancy Nancy and the Too-Loose Tooth. Jane O'Connor, illustrated by Robin Preiss Glasser. HarperCollins, 2011 (188,645).

Night of the Ninjas (Magic Tree House No. 5). Mary Pope Osborne, illustrated by Sal Murdocca. Random House, 1995.

The Absolutely True Diary of a Part-Time Indian. Sherman Alexie. Little, Brown, 2009 (185,747).

Hatchet. Gary Paulsen. Simon & Schuster, 2006 (178,421).

The Battle of the Labyrinth (Percy Jackson and the Olympians No. 4). Rick Riordan. Disney-Hyperion, 2009 (176,636).

Goodnight Moon. Margaret Wise Brown, illustrated by Clement Hurd. HarperCollins, 1977 (175,602).

Ramona Quimby, Age 8. Beverly Cleary, illustrated by Jacqueline Rogers. HarperCollins, 1992 (170,714).

Biscuit Goes to School. Alyssa Satin Capucilli, illustrated by Pat Schories. HarperCollins, 2003 (168,691).

Super Friends Flying High. Random House, 2008.

Because of Winn-Dixie. Kate DiCamillo. Candlewick, 2000 (167,581).

Danny and the Dinosaur. Syd Hoff. HarperCollins, 1978 (167,215).

Frog and Toad Are Friends. Arnold Lobel. HarperCollins, 1979 (164,461).

Freckle Juice. Judy Blume. Random/Yearling, 1978.

Junie B. Jones and the Stupid Smelly Bus (Junie B. Jones No. 1). Barbara Park, illustrated by Denise Brunkus. Random House, 1993.

The Boy in the Striped Pajamas. John Boyne. Random/Ember, 2007.

Midnight on the Moon (Magic Tree House No. 8). Mary Pope Osborne, illustrated by Sal Murdocca. Random House, 1996.

Matched. Ally Condie. Penguin, 2011 (159,174).

Afternoon on the Amazon (Magic Tree House No. 6). Mary Pope Osborne, illustrated by Sal Murdocca. Random House, 1995.

The Mouse and the Motorcycle. Beverly Cleary, illustrated by Tracy Dockray. HarperCollins, 2000 (152,668).

The Lion, the Witch and the Wardrobe. C. S. Lewis, illustrated by Pauline Baynes. HarperCollins, 1994 (148,777).

Beezus and Ramona. Beverly Cleary, illustrated by Jacqueline Rogers. HarperCollins, 1990 (148,543).

City of Bones (The Mortal Instruments series). Cassandra Clare. Simon & Schuster/McElderry, 2008 (147,557).

What Is a Princess? (Disney Princess). Random House/Disney, 2004.

War Horse (movie tie-in). Michael Morpurgo. Scholastic, 2011 (145,011).

Pinkalicious: Pink Around the Rink. Victoria Kann. HarperCollins, 2010 (143,226).

Biscuit. Alyssa Satin Capucilli, illustrated by Pat Schories. HarperCollins, 1997 (143,054).

The Scorch Trials (Maze Runner No. 2). James Dashner. Random/Ember, 2011.

Harry Potter and the Sorcerer's Stone. J. K. Rowling. Scholastic, 2009 (142,016).

Ivy and Bean. Annie Barrows, illustrated by Sophie Blackall. Chronicle, 2007 (141,998).

The Mysterious Benedict Society. Trenton Lee Stewart. Little, Brown/Tingley, 2008 (141,635).

Pinkalicious: The Pinkerrific Playdate. Victoria Kann. HarperCollins, 2011 (140,366).

Ramona the Pest. Beverly Cleary, illustrated by Jacqueline Rogers. HarperCollins, 1992 (139,812).

Pinkalicious: Pinkie Promise. Victoria Kann. HarperCollins, 2011 (139,671).

Bad Kitty Gets a Bath. Nick Bruel. Macmillan/Square Fish, 2009 (139,134).

Dolphins at Daybreak (Magic Tree House No. 9). Mary Pope Osborne, illustrated by Sal Murdocca. Random House, 1997.

Judy Moody. Megan McDonald. Candlewick, 2000 (137,953).

The Phantom Tollbooth. Norton Juster, illustrated by Jules Feiffer. Random/Yearling, 1988.

Fancy Nancy See Stars. Jane O'Connor, illustrated by Robin Preiss Glasser. HarperCollins, 2008 (136,309).

Amelia Bedelia. Peggy Parish, illustrated by Fritz Siebel. Greenwillow, 1992 (134,561).

Island of the Blue Dolphins. Scott O'Dell. Houghton Mifflin Harcourt/Sandpiper, 1960 (132,767).

Breaking Dawn (Twilight No. 4). Stephenie Meyer. Little, Brown/Tingley, 2010 (131,751).

Thirteen Reasons Why. Jay Asher. Razorbill, 2011 (131,665).

Junie B. Jones and a Little Monkey Business (Junie B. Jones No. 2). Barbara Park, illustrated by Denise Brunkus. Random House, 1993.

Sunset of the Sabertooth (Magic Tree House No. 7). Mary Pope Osborne, illustrated by Sal Murdocca. Random House, 1996.

The Red Pyramid (Kane Chronicles No. 1). Rick Riordan, Disney-Hyperion, 2011 (129,210).

Flat Stanley: His Original Adventure! Jeff Brown, illustrated by Mackey Pamintuan. HarperCollins, 2003 (126,090).

Esperanza Rising. Pam Muñoz Ryan. Scholastic, 2002 (125,432).

Hoot. Carl Hiaasen. Random/Yearling, 2005.

Pretty Little Liars. Sara Shepard. HarperTeen, 2007 (124,563).

Mr. Popper's Penguins. Richard and Florence Atwater. Little, Brown, 1992 (123,453).

Kid Lawyer (Theodore Boone No. 1). John Grisham. Puffin, 2011 (122,516).

Fancy Nancy and the Boy from Paris. Jane O'Connor, illustrated by Robin Preiss Glasser. HarperCollins, 2008 (121,336).

Looking for Alaska. John Green. Penguin/Speak, 2006 (121,172).

I Can Be a Teacher (Barbie). Mary Man-Kong, illustrated by Kellee Riley. Random House, 2011.

Smile. Raina Teigemeier. Scholastic/Graphix, 2010 (120,608).

Twilight. Stephenie Meyer. Little, Brown/Tingley, 2006 (119,340).

Junie B. Jones and Her Big Fat Mouth (Junie B. Jones No. 3). Barbara Park, illustrated by Denise Brunkus. Random House, 1993.

Fancy Nancy and the Mean Girl. Jane O'Connor, illustrated by Robin Preiss Glasser. Harper-Collins, 2011 (118,881).

The Night Before Kindergarten. Natasha Wing, illustrated by Julie Durrell. Grosset & Dunlap, 2001 (117,568).

Tales of a Fourth Grade Nothing. Judy Blume. Puffin, 2007 (117,383).

Fallen. Lauren Kate. Delacorte, 2010.

Junie B. Jones and Some Sneaky Peeky Spying (Junie B. Jones No. 4). Barbara Park, illustrated by Denise Brunkus. Random House, 1994.

Tonight on the Titanic (Magic Tree House No. 17). Mary Pope Osborne, illustrated by Sal Murdocca. Random House, 1999.

Biscuit and the Little Pup. Alyssa Satin Capucilli, illustrated by Pat Schories. HarperCollins, 2007 (116,317).

The Graveyard Book. Neil Gaiman, illustrated by Dave McKean. HarperCollins, 2010 (116,146).

Happy Birthday, Bad Kitty. Nick Bruel. Macmillan/Square Fish, 2010 (115,453).

Ramona and Her Father. Beverly Cleary, illustrated by Jacqueline Rogers. HarperCollins, 1990 (114,751).

Fancy Nancy at the Museum. Jane O'Connor, illustrated by Robin Preiss Glasser. HarperCollins, 2008 (113,691).

Fancy Nancy: Every Day Is Earth Day. Jane O'Connor, illustrated by Robin Preiss Glasser. Harper-Collins, 2010 (112,955).

Max's Easter Surprise. Rosemary Wells. Grosset & Dunlap, 2008 (111,716).

Maniac Magee. Jerry Spinelli. Little, Brown, 1999 (110,664).

Tuck Everlasting. Natalie Babbitt. Macmillan/Square Fish, 2007 (110,309).

Tangerine. Edward Bloor. Houghton Mifflin Harcourt/Sandpiper, 1997 (110,072).

A Cricket in Times Square. George Selden, illustrated by Garth Williams. Macmillan/Square Fish, 2008 (110,011).

Junie B., First Grader: Toothless Wonder (Junie B. Jones No. 20). Barbara Park, illustrated by Denise Brunkus. Random House, 2003.

Fancy Nancy: Spectacular Spectacles. Jane O'Connor, illustrated by Robin Preiss Glasser. Harper-Collins, 2010 (109,455).

Harold and the Purple Crayon. Crockett Johnson. HarperCollins, 1981 (108,479).

Frog and Toad Together. Arnold Lobel. HarperCollins, 1979 (107,568).

I Can Be a Pet Vet (Barbie). Mary Man-Kong, illustrated by Jiyoung An. Random House, 2010.

The Name of This Book Is Secret. Pseudonymous Bosch. Little, Brown, 2008 (106,616).

Fancy Nancy: Poison Ivy Expert. Jane O'Connor, illustrated by Robin Preiss Glasser. HarperCollins, 2008 (106,602).

Polar Bears Past Bedtime (Magic Tree House No. 12). Mary Pope Osborne, illustrated by Sal Murdocca. Random House, 1998.

Turtle in Paradise. Jennifer L. Holm. Random/Yearling, 2011.

Ghost Town at Sundown (Magic Tree House No. 10). Mary Pope Osborne, illustrated by Sal Murdocca. Random House, 1997.

The Adventures of Captain Underpants. Dav Pilkey. Scholastic, 1997 (103,708).

Fancy Nancy: The Dazzling Book Report. Jane O'Connor, illustrated by Robin Preiss Glasser. HarperCollins, 2009 (103,661).

Freak the Mighty. Rodman Philbrick. Scholastic, 1993 (103,575).

Hour of the Olympics (Magic Tree House No. 16). Mary Pope Osborne, illustrated by Sal Murdocca. Random House, 1998.

Kingdom of Color (Disney Tangled). Melissa Lagonegro, illustrated by Jean-Paul Orpinas et al. Random House, 2010.

Ramona and Her Mother. Beverly Cleary, illustrated by Jacqueline Rogers. HarperCollins, 1990 (101,826).

I Was So Mad (Little Critter). Mercer Mayer. Random House, 2000.

Judy Moody Gets Famous! Megan McDonald. Candlewick, 2001 (101,782).

Splat the Cat: Good Night, Sleep Tight. Rob Scotton. HarperCollins, 2011 (101,536).

Speak. Laurie Halse Anderson. Macmillan/Square Fish, 2011 (101,244).

There Was an Old Lady Who Swallowed a Bat! Lucille Colandro, illustrated by Jared Lee. Scholastic, 1995 (101,082).

The Boxcar Children Mysteries No. 1. Gertrude Chandler Warner. Albert Whitman, 1942 (101,023).

Bad Kitty Meets the Baby. Nick Bruel. Macmillan/Square Fish, 2011 (100,973).

High-Speed Adventures (Disney/Pixar Cars). Frank Berrios. Random House, 2010.

Hungry, Hungry Sharks. Joanna Cole. Random House, 1986.

Be a Ballerina (Dora the Explorer). Illustrated by Warner McGee. Random House, 2010.

When You Reach Me. Rebecca Stead. Random/Yearling, 2010.

Room on the Broom. Julia Donaldson, illustrated by Axel Scheffler. Puffin, 2003 (100,313).

E-books

200,000+

The Hunger Games. Suzanne Collins. Scholastic (4,595,739).

Catching Fire. Suzanne Collins. Scholastic (4,218,680).

Mockingjay. Suzanne Collins. Scholastic (3,941,753).

The Mark of Athena (Heroes of Olympus No. 3). Rick Riordan. Disney-Hyperion (305,734).

Divergent. Veronica Roth. HarperCollins/Tegen (291,005).

Insurgent. Veronica Roth. HarperCollins/Tegen (281,470).

Artemis Fowl. Eoin Colfer. Disney-Hyperion (224,723).

100,000+

War Horse. Michael Morpurgo. Scholastic (195,942).

The Serpent's Shadow (Kane Chronicles No. 3). Rick Riordan. Disney-Hyperion (190,081).

The Fault in Our Stars. John Green. Dutton.

Breaking Dawn. Stephenie Meyer. Little, Brown (160,975).

Twilight. Stephenie Meyer. Little, Brown (157,708).

The Giver. Lois Lowry. Houghton Mifflin (152,678).

Inheritance (Inheritance Cycle No. 4). Christopher Paolini. Knopf.

The Son of Neptune (Heroes of Olympus No. 2). Rick Riordan. Disney-Hyperion (130,568).

Miss Peregrine's Home for Peculiar Children. Ransom Riggs. Quirk (124,211).

City of Lost Souls (The Mortal Instruments). Cassandra Clare. Simon & Schuster/ McElderry (123,666).

Witch and Wizard. James Patterson. Little, Brown (122,369).

Matched. Ally Condie. Penguin/Speak.

The Third Wheel (Diary of a Wimpy Kid). Jeff Kinney. Abrams/Amulet (114,995).

Gregor the Overlander. Suzanne Collins. Scholastic (113,975).

The Lightning Thief (Percy Jackson and the Olympians No. 1). Rick Riordan. Disney-Hyperion (105,563).

The Lost Hero (Heroes of Olympus No. 1). Rick Riordan. Disney-Hyperion (101,361).

City of Bones (The Mortal Instruments). Cassandra Clare. Simon & Schuster/ McElderry (100,908).

The Book Thief. Markus Zusak. Knopf.

Crossed. Ally Condie. Dutton.

75,000+

The Fire. James Patterson, Little, Brown (93,546).

The Maze Runner. James Dashner. Delacorte.

New Moon. Stephenie Meyer. Little, Brown (87,503).

The Sea of Monsters (Percy Jackson and the Olympians No. 5). Rick Riordan. Disney-Hyperion, (85,976).

Eclipse. Stephenie Meyer. Little, Brown (84,218).

The Rise of Nine. Pittacus Lore. HarperCollins (83,369).

Clockwork Prince (The Infernal Devices). Cassandra Clare. Simon & Schuster/ McElderry (82,827).

The Titan's Curse (Percy Jackson and the Olympians No. 3). Rick Riordan. Disney-Hyperion (76,705).

The Last Olympian (Percy Jackson and the Olympians No. 5). Rick Riordan. Disney-Hyperion (75,145).

50,000+

Nevermore. James Patterson, Little, Brown (72,985).

Delirium. Lauren Oliver. HarperCollins (71,853).

The Battle of the Labyrinth (Percy Jackson and the Olympians No. 4). Rick Riordan. Disney-Hyperion (71,460).

The Death Cure (Maze Runner No. 3). James Dashner. Delacorte.

Reached. Ally Condie. Dutton.

The Throne of Fire (Kane Chronicles No. 2). Rick Riordan. Disney-Hyperion (68,151).

The Scorch Trails (Maze Runner No. 2). James Dashner. Delacorte.

The Red Pyramid (Kane Chronicles No. 1). Rick Riordan. Disney-Hyperion (63,869).

Destined (House of Night). P. C. Cast and Kristin Cast. St. Martin's Griffin (63,410).

Thirteen Reasons Why. Jay Asher. Razorbill.

Rapture (Fallen No. 4). Lauren Kate. Delacorte.

The Power of Six. Pittacus Lore. HarperCollins (59,365).

Pandemonium. Lauren Oliver. HarperCollins (58,645).

Ruthless (Pretty Little Liars No. 10). Sara Shepard. HarperTeen (58,535).

Pretty Little Liars. Sara Shepard. HarperTeen (57,805).

The Borrowers. Mary Norton. Houghton Mifflin (56,364).

City of Fallen Angels (The Mortal Instruments). Cassandra Clare. Simon & Schuster/McElderry (53,084).

The Accused (Theodore Boone No. 3). John Grisham. Dutton.

The Vampire Diaries: The Awakening. L. J. Smith. HarperTeen (50,871).

Gregor and the Prophecy of Bane. Suzanne Collins. Scholastic (50,482).

25,000+

Looking for Alaska. John Green. Penguin/Speak.

The Gift. James Patterson. Little, Brown (49,627).

Graceling. Kristin Cashore. Harcourt (48,439).

Born at Midnight (Shadow Falls). C. C. Hunter. St. Martin's Griffin (47,931).

I Am Number Four. Pittacus Lore. HarperCollins (47,682).

Free Four. Veronica Roth. HarperCollins/Tegen (45,422).

Kid Lawyer (Theodore Boone No. 1). John Grisham. Puffin.

The Enchantress (Secrets of the Immortal Nicholas Flamel No. 6). Michael Scott. Delacorte.

City of Ashes (The Mortal Instruments). Cassandra Clare. Simon & Schuster/McElderry (45,344).

The Twilight Saga Collection. Stephenie Meyer. Little, Brown (45,311).

The Golden Lily. Richelle Mead. Razorbill.

City of Glass (The Mortal Instruments). Cassandra Clare. Simon & Schuster/McElderry (41,764).

Uglies. Scott Westerfeld. Simon Pulse (41,729).

Hatchet. Gary Paulsen. Simon & Schuster (41,347).

The Abduction (Theodore Boone No. 2). John Grisham. Puffin.

Stunning (Pretty Little Liars No. 11). Sara Shepard. HarperTeen (40,325).

Flawless (Pretty Little Liars No. 2). Sara Shepard. HarperTeen (40,202).

Tales From a Not-So-Graceful Ice Princess (Dork Diaries No. 4). Rachel Renée Russell. Simon & Schuster/Aladdin (39,633).

Marked (House of Night). P. C. Cast and Kristin Cast. St. Martin's Griffin (38,888).

A Wrinkle in Time. Madeleine L'Engle. Macmillan (38,466).

Beautiful Creatures. Kami Garcia and Margaret Stohl. Little, Brown (37,731).

Clockwork Angel (The Infernal Devices). Cassandra Clare. Simon & Schuster/McElderry (36,825).

Silence (Hush, Hush). Becca Fitzpatrick. Simon & Schuster/Aladdin (36,715).

Into the Wild (Warriors No. 1). Erin Hunter. HarperCollins (36,619).

Because of Winn-Dixie. Kate Camillo. Candlewick (35,589).

The Bad Beginning (A Series of Unfortunate Events No. 1). Lemony Snicket, illustrated by Brett Helquist. HarperCollins (34,823).

I Am Number Four (The Lost Files: Six's Legacy). Pittacus Lore. HarperCollins (34,785).

Catching Jordan. Miranda Kenneally. Sourcebooks Fire (34,749).

Entwined. Heather Dixon. Greenwillow (34,361).

The Lost Files: Nine's Legacy (I Am Number Four). Pittacus Lore. HarperCollins (33,654).

Wonder. R. J. Palacio. Knopf.

Seconds Away. Harlan Coben. Putnam.

Bitterblue. Kristin Cashore. Dial.

Infamous (Chronicles of Nick). Sherrilyn Kenyon. St. Martin's Griffin (32,955).

The Selection. Kiera Cass. HarperTeen (32,917).

Holes. Louis Sachar. Random/Yearling.

Confessions of a Murder Suspect. James Patterson. Little, Brown/Patterson Young Readers (32,658).

Switched (A Trylle Novel). Amanda Hocking. St. Martin's Griffin (32,323).

Out of Sight, Out of Mind (Gallagher Girls No. 5) Ally Carter. Disney-Hyperion (32,266).

Perfect (Pretty Little Liars No. 3). Sara Shepard. HarperTeen (32,195).

Legend. Marie Lu. Putnam.

Warriors: Hollyleaf's Story. Erin Hunter. HarperCollins (31,758).

Ten Things We Did (and Probably Shouldn't Have). Sarah Mlynowski. Harper-Teen (31,481).

Fallen. Lauren Kate. Delacorte.

Passion (Fallen No. 3). Lauren Kate. Delacorte.

The Outsiders. S. E. Hinton. Penguin/Speak.

The Lion, the Witch, and the Wardrobe. C. S. Lewis. HarperCollins (30,987).

Where the Red Fern Grows. Wilson Rawls. Delacorte.

Tales From a Not-So-Talented Pop Star (Dork Diaries No. 3). Rachel Renée Russell. Simon & Schuster/Aladdin (30,837).

Pretties. Scott Westerfeld. Simon Pulse (30,809).

Number the Stars. Lois Lowry. Houghton Mifflin Harcourt (30,670).

Taken at Dusk (Shadow Falls). C. C. Hunter. St. Martin's Griffin (30,605).

Torn (Trylle trilogy, Book 2). Amanda Hocking. St. Martin's Griffin (30,302).

Tales From a Not-So-Fabulous Life (Dork Diaries No. 1). Rachel Renée Russell. Simon & Schuster/Aladdin (30,129).

The Kill Order (Maze Runner Prequel). James Dashner. Delacorte.

The Mysterious Benedict Society. Trenton Lee Stewart. Little, Brown (29,916).

Gone. Michael Grant. HarperCollins/Tegen (29,885).

Inheritance Cycle E-Omni. Christopher Paolini. Knopf.

The Boy in the Striped Pajamas. John Boyne. Random/Fickling.

Finale (Hush, Hush). Becca Fitzpatrick. Simon & Schuster (29,100).

Eragon (Inheritance Cycle No. 1). Christopher Paolini. Knopf.

Fear (A Gone Novel). Michael Grant. HarperCollins/Tegen (28,908).

Evermore (The Immortals No. 1). Alyson Noël. St. Martin's Griffin (28,858).

Between the Lines. Jodi Picoult. Atria/Bestler (28,856).

Awake at Dawn (Shadow Falls). C. C. Hunter. St. Martin's Griffin (28,843).

Ascend (A Trylle Novel). Amanda Hocking. St. Martin's Griffin (28,714).

Ivy and Bean. Annie Barrows, illustrated by Sophie Blackall. Chronicle (28,618).

Unbelievable (Pretty Little Liars No. 4). Sara Shepard. HarperTeen (28,607).

Enclave. Ann Aguirre. Macmillan (28,533).

Twisted (Pretty Little Liars No. 9). Sara Shepard. HarperTeen (28,533).

Diary of a Wimpy Kid. Jeff Kinney. Abrams/Amulet (28,234).

Dinosaurs Before Dark Magic (Magic Tree House No. 1). Mary Pope Osborne, illustrated by Sal Murdocca. Random House.

Crescendo (Hush, Hush). Becca Fitzpatrick. Simon & Schuster (28,004).

No News Is Good News (Ivy and Bean No. 8). Annie Barrows, illustrated by Sophie Blackall. Chronicle (27,869).

The Angel Experiment. James Patterson. Little, Brown/Patterson Young Readers (27,823).

Shelter. Harlan Coben. Penguin/Speak.

Two Truths and a Lie (The Lying Game No. 3). Sara Shepard. HarperTeen (27,651).

Warriors: Omen of the Stars No. 6: The Last Hope. Erin Hunter. HarperCollins (27,635).

Torment (Fallen No. 2). Lauren Kate. Delacorte.

Perfect Chemistry. Simon Elkeles. Walker (27,370).

Awakened (House of Night). P. C. Cast and Kristin Cast. St. Martin's Griffin (27,332).

Daughter of Smoke and Bone. Laini Taylor. Little, Brown (27,167).

Hush, Hush. Becca Fitzpatrick. Simon & Schuster (27,009).

Gathering Blue. Lois Lowry. Houghton Mifflin (26,999).

Cabin Fever (Diary of a Wimpy Kid). Jeff Kinney. Abrams/Amulet (26,951).

Before I Fall. Lauren Oliver. HarperCollins (26,882).

Middle School, The Worst Years of My Life. James Patterson. Little, Brown (26,680).

The City of Ember. Jeanne DuPrau. Random House.

The Phantom Tollbooth. Norton Juster, illustrated by Jules Feiffer. Knopf.

Brisingr (Inheritance Cycle No. 3). Christopher Paolini. Knopf.

Wicked (Pretty Little Liars No. 5). Sara Shepard. HarperTeen (25,979).

Betrayed (House of Night). P. C. Cast and Kristin Cast. St. Martin's Griffin (25,689).

The Vampire Diaries: The Struggle. L. J. Smith. HarperTeen (25,429).

Warriors No. 2: Fire and Ice. Erin Hunter. HarperCollins (25,268).

The Lemonade War. Jackie Davies. Houghton Mifflin (25,229).

The Invaders. John Flanagan. Philomel.

Burned (House of Night). P. C. Cast and Kristin Cast. St. Martin's Griffin (25,071).

Goodnight, Goodnight, Construction Site. Sherri Duskey Rinker, illustrated by Tom Lichtenheld. Chronicle (25,000).

Literary Prizes, 2012

Compiled by the staff of the *Library and Book Trade Almanac*

Jane Addams Children's Book Awards. For children's books that effectively promote the cause of peace, social justice, world community, and equality. *Offered by:* Women's International League for Peace and Freedom and the Jane Addams Peace Association. *Winners:* (younger children) Susan L. Roth and Cindy Trumbore for *The Mangrove Tree: Planting Trees to Feed Families* (Lee & Low); (older children) Winifred Conkling for *Sylvia and Aki* (Random).

Aesop Prize. For outstanding work in children's folklore, both fiction and nonfiction. *Offered by:* American Folklore Society. *Winners:* George Ella Lyon and Christopher Cardinale, illustrator, for *Which Side Are You On?* (Cinco Puntos).

Agatha Awards. For mystery novels written in the method exemplified by author Agatha Christie. *Offered by:* Malice Domestic Ltd. *Winners:* (novel) Margaret Maron for *Three-Day Town* (Grand Central); (best first novel) Sara J. Henry for *Learning to Swim* (Crown); (nonfiction) Leslie Budewitz for *Books, Crooks, and Counselors: How to Write Accurately About Criminal Law and Courtroom Procedure* (Linden); (short story) Dana Cameron for "Disarming" in *Ellery Queen Mystery Magazine,* June 2011; (children's/young adult) Chris Grabenstein for *The Black Heart Crypt* (Random); (historical novel) Rhys Bowen for *Naughty in Nice* (Berkley).

Ambassador Book Awards. To honor an exceptional contribution to the interpretation of life and culture in the United States. *Offered by:* English-Speaking Union of the United States. *Winners:* To be awarded next in 2013.

American Academy of Arts and Letters Award of Merit ($10,000). Given annually, in rotation, for the short story, sculpture, novel, poetry, drama, and painting. *Offered by:* American Academy of Arts and Letters. *Winner:* painter Joyce Pensato.

American Academy of Arts and Letters Awards in Literature ($7,500). To honor writers of fiction and nonfiction, poets, dramatists, and translators of exceptional accomplishment. *Offered by:* American Academy of Arts and Letters. *Winners:* Andre Dubus III, Adam Hochschild, David Lindsay-Abaire, Christopher Middleton, Julie Otsuka, Michael Palmer, Frederick Seidel, Timothy Snyder.

American Academy of Arts and Letters Gold Medals for distinguished achievement in belles lettres and criticism, biography, fiction, history, poetry, and drama. *Offered by:* American Academy of Arts and Letters. *Winner:* (biography) David McCullough.

American Academy of Arts and Letters Rome Fellowships. For a one-year residency at the American Academy in Rome for young writers of promise. *Offered by:* American Academy of Arts and Letters. *Winners:* Lucy Corin, Jessica Fisher.

American Book Awards. For literary achievement by people of various ethnic backgrounds. *Offered by:* Before Columbus Foundation. *Winners:* Annia Ciezadlo for *Day of Honey: A Memoir of Food, Love, and War* (Free Press); Arlene Kim for *What Have You Done to Our Ears to Make Us Hear Echoes?* (Milkweed); Ed Bok Lee for *Whorled* (Coffee House); Adilifu Nama for *Super Black: American Pop Culture and Black Superheroes* (University of Texas Press); Rob Nixon for *Slow Violence and the Environmentalism of the Poor* (Harvard University Press); Shann Ray for *American Masculine* (Graywolf); Alice Rearden, translator, and Ann Fienup-Riordan, editor, for *Qaluyaarmiuni Nunamtenek Qanemciput (Our Nelson Island Stories)* (University of Washington Press); Touré for *Who's Afraid of Post-Blackness? What It Means to Be Black Now* (Free Press); Amy Waldman for *The Submission* (Farrar, Straus & Giroux); Mary Winegarden for *The Translator's Sister* (Mayapple); Kevin Young for *Ardency: A Chronicle of the Amistad Rebels* (Knopf); (lifetime achievement) Eugene B. Redmond.

American Indian Youth Literature Awards. Offered biennially to recognize excellence in books by and about American Indians. *Of-*

fered by: American Indian Library Association. *Winners:* Virginia Driving Hawk Sneve and Ellen Beier, illustrator, for *The Christmas Coat: Memories of My Sioux Childhood* (Holiday House); Jacqueline Guest for *Free Throw* and *Triple Threat* (Lorimer); and Adam Fortunate Eagle for *Pipestone: My Life in an Indian Boarding School* (University of Oklahoma Press).

American Poetry Review/Honickman First Book Prize in Poetry ($3,000). To encourage excellence in poetry and to provide a wide readership for a deserving first book of poems. *Winner:* Tomás Q. Morín for *A Larger Country* (American Poetry Review).

Américas Book Award for Children's and Young Adult Literature. To recognize U.S. works of fiction, poetry, folklore, or selected nonfiction that authentically and engagingly portray Latin America, the Caribbean, or Latinos in the United States. *Sponsored by:* Consortium of Latin American Studies Programs (CLASP). *Winners:* Margarita Engle for *Hurricane Dancers: The First Caribbean Pirate Shipwreck* (Henry Holt); Monica Brown and Julie Paschkis, illustrator, for *Pablo Neruda: Poet of the People* (Henry Holt).

Rudolfo and Patricia Anaya Premio Aztlán Literary Prize ($1,000 and a lectureship). To honor a Chicano or Chicana fiction writer who has published no more than two books. *Offered by:* National Hispanic Cultural Center. *Winner:* Lucrecia Guerrero for *Tree of Sighs* (Bilingual Review).

Hans Christian Andersen Awards. Awarded biennially to an author and an illustrator whose body of work has made an important and lasting contribution to children's literature. *Offered by:* International Board on Books for Young People (IBBY). *Sponsor:* Nami Island, Inc. *Winners:* (writer) María Teresa Andruetto (Argentina); (illustrator) Peter Sís (Czech Republic).

Hans Christian Andersen Literature Award (500,000 Danish kroner, about $87,000). To a writer whose work can be compared with that of Andersen. *Offered by:* Hans Christian Andersen Literary Committee. *Winner:* Isabel Allende.

Anthony Awards. For superior mystery writing. *Offered by:* Bouchercon World Mystery Convention. *Winners:* (novel) Louise Penny

for *A Trick of the Light* (Minotaur); (first novel) Sara J. Henry for *Learning to Swim* (Crown); (paperback original) Julie Hyzy for *Buffalo West Wing* (Berkley); (short story) Dana Cameron for "Disarming" in *Ellery Queen Mystery Magazine*; (critical nonfiction) Charlaine Harris, editor, for *The Sookie Stackhouse Companion* (Ace).

Asia Society Bernard Schwartz Book Award ($20,000). *Winner:* Brahma Chellaney for *Water: Asia's New Battleground* (Georgetown University Press).

Asian/Pacific American Awards for Literature. For books that promote Asian/Pacific American culture and heritage. *Sponsor:* Asian/Pacific American Librarians Association (APALA). *Winners:* (2011–2012) (picture book) Ed Young for *The House Baba Built: An Artist's Childhood in China* (Little, Brown); (children's literature) Wendy Wan-Long Shang for *The Great Wall of Lucy Wu* (Scholastic); (young adult) Holly Thompson for *Orchards* (Delacorte); (adult fiction) Amy Waldman for *The Submission* (Farrar, Straus & Giroux); (adult nonfiction) Ying-Ying Chang for *The Woman Who Could Not Forget: Iris Chang Before and Beyond the Rape of Nanking—A Memoir* (Pegasus).

Audio Publishers Association awards (Audies). To recognize excellence in audiobooks. *Winners:* (audiobook of the year) *Bossypants* by Tina Fey, read by the author (Hachette Audio); (distinguished achievement in production) *The Watch That Ends the Night: Voices from the Titanic* by Allan Wolf, read by Michael Page, Phil Gigante, Christopher Lane, Laural Merlington, and Angela Dawe (Brilliance Audio); (solo narration, female) *The Winter Sea* by Susanna Kearsley, read by Rosalyn Landor (Audible); (solo narration, male) *The King's Speech: How One Man Saved the British Monarchy* by Mark Logue and Peter Conradi, read by Simon Vance (Tantor); (narration by the author or authors) *Beauty Queens* by Libba Bray (Scholastic Audio); (audio drama) *I, Claudius* by Robert Graves, read by Derek Jacobi, Tim McInnerny, Harriet Walter, and others (AudioGo); (biography/memoir) *Bossypants* by Tina Fey (Hachette Audio); (business/educational) *The Barefoot Executive: The Ultimate Guide for Being Your Own Boss and Achieving Financial Freedom* by Carrie

W_lkerson, read by the author (Oasis); (children's, ages 0–8) *Django: World's Greatest Jazz Guitarist* by Bonnie Christensen, read by George Guidall (Live Oak Media); (children's, ages 8–12) *Heart and Soul* by Kadir Nelson, read by Debbie Allen (HarperAudio); (classic) *The Life and Adventures of Nicholas Nickelby* by Charles Dickens, read by Simon Vance (Tantor); (fantasy) *Daughter of Smoke and Bone* by Laini Taylor, read by Khristine Hvam (Hachette Audio); (fiction) *Alas, Babylon* by Pat Frank, read by Will Patton (Audible); (history) *1861: The Civil War Awakening* by Adam Goodheart, read by Jonathan Davis (Audible); (humor) *Shatner Rules: Your Guide to Understanding the Shatnerverse and the World at Large* by William Shatner with Chris Regan, read by William Shatner (Penguin Audio); (inspirational/faith-based fiction) *Courageous* by Randy Alcorn, read by Roger Mueller (Oasis); (inspirational/faith-based nonfiction) *The Story: The Bible as One Continuing Story of God and His People,* read by Michael Blain-Rozgay, Allison Moffett, and others (Zondervan); (literary fiction) *State of Wonder* by Ann Patchett, read by Hope Davis (HarperAudio); (multi-voiced performance) *A Raisin in the Sun* by Lorraine Hansberry, read by Judyann Elder, Rutina Wesley, Mirron Willis, and others (L.A. Theatre Works); (mystery) *Feast Day of Fools* by James Lee Burke, read by Will Patton (Simon & Schuster Audio); (nonfiction) *The Murder of the Century: The Gilded Age Crime That Scandalized a City and Sparked the Tabloid Wars* by Paul Collins, read by William Dufris (AudioGo); (original work) *METAtropolis: Cascadia* by Jay Lake, Mary Robinette Kowal, Elizabeth Bear, Ken Scholes, Karl Schroeder, and Tobias Buckell, read by René Auberjonois, Kate Mulgrew, Wil Wheaton, Gates McFadden, Jonathan Frakes, and LeVar Burton (Audible); (paranormal) *Hard Magic* by Larry Correia, read by Bronson Pinchot (Audible); (personal development) *Prime Time: Love, Health, Sex, Fitness, Friendship, Spirit, and Making the Most of All of Your Life* by Jane Fonda, read by the author (Random House Audio); (romance) *New York to Dallas* by J. D. Robb, read by Susan Ericksen (Brilliance Audio); (science fiction) *Fuzzy Nation* by John

Scalzi, read by Wil Wheaton (Audible); (short stories/collections) *Selected Shorts: New American Stories* by Aleksandar Hemon, Jhumpa Lahiri, Chimamanda Ngozi Adichie, and Sherman Alexie, read by Boyd Gaines, Rita Wolf, Condola Rashad, and BD Wong (Symphony Space); (teen) *The Wake of the Lorelei Lee* by L. A. Meyer, read by Katherine Kellgren (Listen & Live); (thriller/suspense) *The Nightmare Thief* by Meg Gardiner, read by Susan Ericksen (Brilliance Audio); (package design) *Jane Austen: Classic BBC Radio Productions,* read by Angharad Rees, Hannah Gorden, Juliet Stevenson, Annette Crosbie, and full casts, package designed by Tri-Plex (AudioGo).

Bad Sex in Fiction Award (United Kingdom). *Sponsor: Literary Review. Winner:* Nancy Huston for *Infrared* (Grove).

Bakeless Literary Prizes (publication by Graywolf and fellowships to attend the 2012 Bread Loaf Writers' Conference). For promising new writers. *Offered by:* Bread Loaf Writers' Conference of Middlebury College. *Winners:* (fiction) Ben Stroud for *Byzantium: Stories*; (poetry) Brian Russell for *The Year of What Now*; (creative nonfiction) Not awarded in 2012.

Bancroft Prizes ($10,000). For books of exceptional merit and distinction in American history, American diplomacy, and the international relations of the United States. *Offered by:* Columbia University. *Winners:* Anne F. Hyde for *Empires, Nations, and Families: A History of the North American West, 1800–1860* (University of Nebraska Press); Daniel T. Rodgers for *Age of Fracture* (Belknap Press of Harvard University Press); Tomiko Brown-Nagin for *Courage to Dissent: Atlanta and the Long History of the Civil Rights Movement* (Oxford University Press).

Barnes & Noble Discover Great New Writers Awards. To honor a first novel and a first work of nonfiction by American authors. *Offered by:* Barnes & Noble. *Winners:* (fiction) Scott O'Connor for *Untouchable* (Tyrus); (nonfiction) Michael Levy for *Kosher Chinese: Living, Teaching, and Eating with China's Other Billion* (Henry Holt).

Mildred L. Batchelder Award. For an American publisher of a children's book originally published in a language other than English and subsequently published in English in the United States. *Offered by:* American Library Association, Association for Library Service to Children. *Winner:* Eerdmans Books for Young Readers for *Soldier Bear* by Bibi Dumon Tak, illustrated by Philip Hopman and translated by Laura Watkinson.

BBC National Short Story Award (£15,000). *Winner:* Miroslav Penkov for "East of the West."

Beacon of Freedom Award. For the best title introducing American history, from colonial times through the Civil War, to young readers. *Offered by:* Williamsburg (Virginia) Regional Library and the Colonial Williamsburg Foundation. *Winner:* Afua Cooper for *My Name is Phillis Wheatley: A Story of Slavery and Freedom* (KCP Fiction).

Pura Belpré Awards. To a Latino/Latina writer and illustrator whose work portrays, affirms, and celebrates the Latino cultural experience in an outstanding work of literature for children and youth. *Offered by:* American Library Association, Association for Library Service to Children. *Winners:* (writer) Guadalupe Garcia McCall for *Under the Mesquite* (Lee and Low); (illustrator) Duncan Tonatiuh, writer and illustrator, for *Diego Rivera: His World and Ours* (Abrams).

Helen B. Bernstein Award for Excellence in Journalism ($15,000). To a journalist who has written at book length about an issue of contemporary concern. *Offered by:* New York Public Library. *Winner:* Ellen E. Schultz for *Retirement Heist: How Companies Plunder and Profit from the Nest Eggs of American Workers* (Portfolio Hardcover).

Black Caucus of the American Library Association (BCALA) Literary Awards. *Winners:* (fiction) Not awarded in 2012; (fiction honor books) Tayari Jones for *Silver Sparrow* (Algonquin) and Martha Southgate for *The Taste of Salt* (Algonquin); (nonfiction) Lawrence P. Jackson for *The Indignant Generation: A Narrative History of African American Writers and Critics, 1934–1960* (Princeton University Press); (poetry) Rachel Eliza Griffiths for *Mule and Pear* (Western Michigan University Press); (outstanding contribution to publishing citation) Cheryl Finley, Laurence Glasco, and Joe W. Trotter for *Teenie Harris, Photographer: Image, Memory, History* (University of

Pittsburgh Press); (first novelist award) Not awarded in 2012.

Irma Simonton Black and James H. Black Award for Excellence in Children's Literature. To a book for young children in which the text and illustrations work together to create an outstanding whole. *Offered by:* Bank Street College of Education. *Winner:* Fiona Robinson, writer and illustrator, for *What Animals Really Like* (Abrams).

James Tait Black Memorial Prize (United Kingdom) (£10,000). To recognize literary excellence in biography and fiction. *Offered by:* University of Edinburgh. *Winners:* (fiction) Padgett Powell for *You and I* (Serpent's Tail); (biography) Fiona MacCarthy for *The Last Pre-Raphaelite: Edward Burne-Jones and the Victorian Imagination* (Harvard University Press).

Blue Peter Book of the Year (United Kingdom). To recognize excellence in children's books. Winners are chosen by a jury of viewers, ages 8–12, of the children's BBC television program "Blue Peter." *Winner:* Gareth P. Jones for *The Considine Curse* (Bloomsbury); (Blue Peter Best Children's Book of the Last Ten Years) *Winner:* Jeff Kinney for *Diary of a Wimpy Kid* (Puffin).

Rebekah Johnson Bobbitt National Prize for Poetry ($10,000). *Offered biennially by:* Library of Congress. *Winner:* Gerald Stern for *Early Collected Poems: 1965–1992* (Norton).

Bookseller/Diagram Prize for Oddest Title of the Year. *Sponsor: The Bookseller* magazine. *Winner: Cooking with Poo* by Saiyuud "Poo" Diwong (Urban Neighbors of Hope).

BookSense Book of the Year Awards. See Indies Choice Book Awards.

Booktrust Teenage Prize (United Kingdom) (£2,500). *Offered by:* Booktrust. *Winner:* Award discontinued.

Boston Globe/Horn Book Awards. For excellence in children's literature. *Winners:* (fiction) Vaunda Micheaux Nelson and R. Gregory Christie, illustrator, for *No Crystal Stair: A Documentary Novel of the Life and Work of Lewis Michaux, Harlem Bookseller* (Carolrhoda Lab); (nonfiction) Chuck Close for *Chuck Close: Face Book* (Abrams); (picture book) Mac Barnette and Jon Klassen, illustrator, for *Extra Yarn* (Balzer + Bray).

Boyd Literary Award ($5,000). For a military novel that honors the service of American veterans during a time of war. *Offered by:* American Library Association. *Donor:* W. Y. Boyd II. *Winner:* P. T. Deutermann for *Pacific Glory* (St. Martin's Griffin).

Branford Boase Award (United Kingdom). To the author and editor of an outstanding novel for young readers by a first-time writer. *Winners:* Annabel Pitcher and Fiona Kennedy, editor, for *My Sister Lives on the Mantelpiece* (Orion).

Michael Braude Award for Light Verse ($5,000). *Offered biennially by:* American Academy of Arts and Letters. *Winner:* Roger Angell.

Bridport International Creative Writing Prizes (United Kingdom). For poetry and short stories. *Offered by:* Bridport Arts Centre. *Winners:* (short story, £5,000) Helen Barton for "Being David"; (poetry, £5,000) Claudia Daventry for "Alakazam"; (flash fiction, 250-word maximum, £1,000) Gregory Jackson for "Nearly New."

British Council Award for ELT writing (£1,000). To celebrate the best writing for English language teaching. *Winners:* Michael Swan and Catherine Walter for *Oxford English Grammar Course—Advanced* (Oxford University Press).

British Fantasy Awards (United Kingdom). *Offered by:* British Fantasy Society. *Winners:* (fantasy novel) Jo Walton for *Among Others* (Tor); (horror novel) Adam Neville for *The Ritual* (St. Martin's Griffin); (novella) Lavie Tidhar for *Gorel and the Pot Bellied God* (PS); (short fiction) Angela Slatter for "The Coffin-Maker's Daughter" in *A Book of Horrors* (St. Martin's Griffin); (anthology) Jeff and Ann Vandermeer, editors, for *The Weird* (Corvus); (collection) Robert Shearman for *Everyone's Just So So Special* (Big Finish); (screenplay) Woody Allen for "Midnight in Paris"; (magazine/periodical) "Black Static," edited by Andy Cox (TTA Press); (comic/graphic novel) Joe Hill and Gabriel Rodriguez for "Locke and Key" (IDW); (nonfiction) Grant Morrison for *Supergods: Our World in the Age of the Super Hero* (Jonathan Cape).

Sophie Brody Medal. For the U.S. author of the most distinguished contribution to Jewish literature for adults, published in the preceding year. *Donors:* Arthur Brody and the Brodart Foundation. *Offered by:* American Library Association, Reference and User Services Association. *Winners:* Adina Hoffman and Peter Cole for *Sacred Trash: The Lost and Found World of the Cairo Geniza* (Schocken).

Witter Bynner Poetry Fellowships ($10,000). To encourage poets and poetry. *Sponsor:* Witter Bynner Foundation for Poetry. *Winners:* L. S. Asekoff, Sheila Black.

Caine Prize for African Writing (£10,000). For a short story by an African writer, published in English. *Winner:* Rotimi Babatunde for "Bombay's Republic" in the online magazine *Mirabilia Review,* Vol. 3, No. 9.

Randolph Caldecott Medal. For the artist of the most distinguished picture book. *Offered by:* American Library Association, Association for Library Service to Children. *Winner:* Chris Raschka for *A Ball for Daisy* (Random).

California Book Awards. To California residents to honor books of fiction, nonfiction, and poetry published in the previous year. *Offered by:* Commonwealth Club of California. *Winners:* (poetry) Giovanni Singleton for *Ascension* (Counterpath); (nonfiction) Jason Felch and Ralph Frammolino for *Chasing Aphrodite: The Hunt for Looted Antiquities at the World's Richest Museum* (Houghton Mifflin Harcourt); (first fiction) Alice LaPlante for *Turn of Mind* (Atlantic Monthly); Héctor Tobar for *The Barbarian Nurseries* (Farrar, Straus & Giroux); (juvenile) Joanne Rocklin for *One Day and One Amazing Morning on Orange Street* (Amulet); (young adult) Maile Meloy for *The Apothecary* (Penguin); (contribution to publishing) City Lights Publishers for *Ten Years that Shook the City: San Francisco 1968–1978,* edited by Chris Carlsson; (Californiana) David Rains Wallace for *Chuckwalla Land: The Riddle of California's Desert* (University of California Press).

John W. Campbell Award. For the best new science fiction or fantasy writer whose first work of science fiction or fantasy was published in a professional publication in the previous two years. *Offered by:* Dell Magazines. *Winner:* E. Lily Yu for "The Cartographer Wasps and the Anarchist Bees" in *Clarkesworld* magazine.

John W. Campbell Memorial Award. For science fiction writing. *Offered by:* Center for the Study of Science Fiction. *Winners:* Christopher Priest for *The Islanders* (Gollancz); Joan Slonczewski for *The Highest Frontier* (Tor).

Canadian Library Association Book of the Year for Children. *Sponsor:* Library Services Centre. *Winner:* Kit Pearson for *The Whole Truth* (HarperCollins).

Canadian Library Association Amelia Frances Howard-Gibbon Illustrator's Award. *Sponsor:* Library Services Centre. *Winner:* Matthew Forsythe for *My Name Is Elizabeth,* written by Annika Dunklee (Kids Can).

Canadian Library Association Young Adult Book Award. *Winner:* Catherine Austen for *All Good Children* (Orca).

Andrew Carnegie Medal for Excellence in Fiction and Nonfiction. For adult books published during the previous year in the United States. *Sponsors:* Carnegie Corporation of New York, ALA/RUSA, and *Booklist. Winners:* Anne Enright for *The Forgotten Waltz* (Norton); (nonfiction) Robert K. Massie for *Catherine the Great: Portrait of a Woman* (Random).

Carnegie Medal (United Kingdom). See CILIP Carnegie Medal.

Center for Fiction Flaherty-Dunnan First Novel Prize ($10,000). *Offered by:* Center for Fiction, Mercantile Library of New York. *Winner:* Ben Fountain for *Billy Lynn's Long Halftime Walk* (Ecco).

Chicago Tribune Nelson Algren Short Story Award ($5,000). For unpublished short fiction. *Offered by: Chicago Tribune. Winner:* Jeremy T. Wilson for "Everything Is Going to Be Okay."

Chicago Tribune Heartland Prize for Fiction ($7,500). *Offered by: Chicago Tribune. Winner:* Richard Ford for *Canada* (Ecco).

Chicago Tribune Heartland Prize for Nonfiction ($7,500). *Offered by: Chicago Tribune. Winner:* Paul Hendrickson for *Hemingway's Boat: Everything He Loved in Life, and Lost* (Bodley Head).

Chicago Tribune Literary Prize. For a lifetime of literary achievement by an author whose body of work has had great impact on American society. *Offered by: Chicago Tribune. Winner:* Elie Wiesel.

Chicago Tribune Young Adult Literary Prize. To recognize a distinguished literary career. *Winner:* John Green.

Children's Africana Book Awards. To recognize and encourage excellent children's books about Africa. *Offered by:* Outreach Council of the African Studies Association. *Winner:* Trilby Kent for *Stones for My Father* (Tundra).

Children's Book Council of Australia Children's Book of the Year Awards. *Winners:* (older readers) Scott Gardner for *The Dead I Know* (Allen & Unwin); (younger readers) Kate Constable for *Crow Country* (Allen & Unwin); (early childhood) Nick Bland and Freya Blackwood, illustrator, for *The Runaway Hug* (Scholastic); (picture book) Bob Graham for *A Bus Called Heaven* (Walker); (Eve Pownall Book of the Year) Alison Lester and Coral Tulloch for *One Small Island: The Story of Macquarie Island* (Penguin).

Children's Poet Laureate ($25,000). For lifetime achievement in poetry for children. Honoree holds the title for two years. *Offered by:* The Poetry Foundation. *Winner:* J. Patrick Lewis.

Cholmondeley Awards for Poets (United Kingdom) (£2,000). For a poet's body of work and contribution to poetry. *Winners:* Christine Evans, Don Paterson, Peter Riley, Robin Robertson.

CILIP Carnegie Medal (United Kingdom). For the outstanding children's book of the year. *Offered by:* CILIP: The Chartered Institute of Library and Information Professionals (formerly the Library Association). *Winner:* Patrick Ness for *Monsters of Men* (Walker).

CILIP Kate Greenaway Medal and Colin Mears Award (United Kingdom) (£5,000 plus £500 worth of books donated to a library of the winner's choice). For children's book illustration. *Offered by:* CILIP: The Chartered Institute of Library and Information Professionals. *Winner:* Jim Kay for *A Monster Calls* (Walker).

Arthur C. Clarke Award (United Kingdom). For the best science fiction novel published in the United Kingdom. *Offered by:* British Science Fiction Association. *Winner:* Jane Rogers for *The Testament of Jessie Lamb* (Harper).

David Cohen Prize for Literature (United Kingdom) (£40,000). Awarded biennially to a living British writer, novelist, poet, essayist, or dramatist in recognition of an entire body of work written in the English language. *Offered by:* David Cohen Family Charitable Trust. *Winner:* To be awarded next in 2013.

Matt Cohen Award: In Celebration of a Writing Life (Canada) (C$20,000). To a Canadian author whose life has been dedicated to writing as a primary pursuit, for a body of work. *Offered by:* Writers' Trust of Canada. *Sponsors:* Marla and David Lehberg. *Winner:* Jean Little.

Commonwealth Writers' Prize (United Kingdom). To reward and encourage new Commonwealth fiction and ensure that works of merit reach a wider audience outside their country of origin. *Offered by:* Commonwealth Institute. *Winners:* (book) Shehan Karunatilaka, Sri Lanka, for *Chinaman: The Legend of Pradeep Mathew* (Random); (short story) Emma Martin, New Zealand, for "Two Girls in a Boat."

Olive Cook Prize (United Kingdom) (£1,000). For a short story. *Offered by:* Society of Authors. *Winner:* Award discontinued in 2011.

Cork City–Frank O'Connor Short Story Award (€35,000). An international award for a collection of short stories. *Offered by:* Munster Literature Centre, Cork, Ireland. *Sponsor:* Cork City Council. *Winner:* Nathan Englander for *What We Talk About When We Talk About Anne Frank* (Knopf).

Costa Book Awards (United Kingdom) (formerly Whitbread Book Awards). For literature of merit that is readable on a wide scale. *Offered by:* Booksellers Association of Great Britain and Costa Coffee (£5,000 plus an additional £25,000 for Book of the Year). *Winners:* (novel and Book of the Year) Hilary Mantel for *Bring Up the Bodies* (Henry Holt); (first novel) Francesca Segal for *The Innocents* (Voice); (biography) Mary M. Talbot and Bryan Talbot, illustrator, for *Dotter of Her Father's Eyes* (Dark Horse); (poetry) Kathleen Jamie for *The Overhaul* (Picador); (children's) Sally Gardner for *Maggot Moon* (Candlewick).

Crab Orchard Review Literary Prizes ($2,000). *Winners:* (Jack Dyer Fiction Prize) Amy Merrick for "Laura, Lost"; (John Guyon Literary Nonfiction Prize) Jim Fairhall for "Núi Khê Revisited"; (Richard Peterson Poetry Prize) Teresa Leo for "Memory Is a Kind of Broken Promise," "Suicide Is a Mind Stripping Petals Off Flowers," and "I Have Drinks with My Dead Friend's Ex-Boyfriend."

Crime Writers' Association (CWA) Dagger Awards (United Kingdom). *Winners:* (Gold Dagger, for outstanding achievement in the field of crime writing) Gene Kerrigan for *The Rage* (Harvill Secker); (Ian Fleming Steel Dagger) Charles Cumming for *A Foreign Country* (HarperCollins); (John Creasey New Blood Dagger, for a first book by a previously unpublished writer) Wiley Cash for *Land More Kind than Home* (Bantam); (International Dagger) Andrea Camilleri for *The Potter's Field*, translated by Stephen Sartarelli (Mantle); (Ellis Peters Historical Dagger) Aly Monroe for *Icelight* (John Murray); (Nonfiction Dagger) Anthony Summers and Robbyn Swan for *The Eleventh Day* (Doubleday); (Short Story Dagger—tie) Margaret Murphy for "The Message," Cath Staincliffe for "Laptop," both in *Best Eaten Cold and Other Stories* (History Press); (Debut Dagger, for an author who has not yet had a novel published commercially) Sandy Gingras for "Beached"; (Dagger in the Library, to the author of crime fiction whose work is currently giving the greatest enjoyment to library users) Steve Mosby.

Roald Dahl Funny Prize (United Kingdom) (£2,500). *Offered by:* Booktrust. *Winners:* (ages 0–6) Rebecca Patterson for *My Big Shouting Day* (Jonathan Cape); (ages 7–14) Jamie Thomson for *Dark Lord: Teenage Years,* illustrated by Freya Hartas (Orchard).

Benjamin H. Danks Award ($20,000). To a promising young writer, playwright, or composer, in alternate years. *Offered by:* American Academy of Arts and Letters. *Winner:* composer Adam Roberts.

Dartmouth Medal. For creating current reference works of outstanding quality and significance. *Donor:* Dartmouth College. *Offered by:* American Library Association, Reference and User Services Division. *Winner:* Jonathon Green for *Green's Dictionary of Slang* (Oxford University Press).

Derringer Awards. To recognize excellence in short crime and mystery fiction. *Sponsor:* Short Mystery Fiction Society. *Winners:* (flash story, up to 1,000 words) Allan

Leverone for "Lessons Learned" in *Shotgun Honey*; (short story, 1,001–4,000 words) B. V. Lawson for "Touch of Death" in *Absent Willow Review*; (long story, 4,001–8,000 words—tie) Art Taylor for "A Drowning at Snow's Cut" in *Ellery Queen's Mystery Magazine*; Karen Pullen for "Brea's Tale" in *Ellery Queen's Mystery Magazine*; (novelette, 8,001–17,500 words) Earl Staggs for "Where Billy Died" (Untreed Reads); (Edward D. Hoch Memorial Golden Derringer for Lifetime Achievement) Bill Pronzini.

Philip K. Dick Award. For a distinguished science fiction paperback published in the United States. *Sponsor:* Philadelphia Science Fiction Society and the Philip K. Dick Trust. *Winner:* Simon Moden for the Samuil Petrovitch trilogy, *Equations of Life, Degrees of Freedom,* and *Theory of Flight* (Orbit).

Dundee International Book Prize (Scotland) (£10,000 and publication by Cargo). For an unpublished novel on any theme, in any genre. *Winner:* Jacob M. Appel for *The Man Who Wouldn't Stand Up.*

Dundee Picture Book Award (Scotland) (£1,000). To recognize excellence in storytelling for children. The winner is chosen by the schoolchildren of Dundee. *Winner:* (0–7 years) Ross Collins for *Dear Vampa*; (8–11 years) Ross MacKenzie for *Zac and the Dream Pirates.*

Educational Writers' Award (United Kingdom) (£2,000). For noteworthy educational nonfiction for children. *Offered by:* Authors' Licensing and Collecting Society and Society of Authors. *Winner:* Ruth Thomson for *Terezín: A Story of the Holocaust* (Franklin Watts).

Margaret A. Edwards Award ($2,000). To an author whose book or books have provided young adults with a window through which they can view their world and which will help them to grow and to understand themselves and their role in society. *Donor: School Library Journal. Winner:* Susan Cooper, whose books include the Dark Is Rising sequence.

Encore Award (United Kingdom) (£10,000). Awarded biennially for the best second novel of the previous two years. *Offered by*: Society of Authors. *Sponsor:* Lucy Astor.

Winner: Joe Dunthorne for *Wild Abandon* (Random House).

European Union Prize for Literature (€5,000). To recognize outstanding European writing. *Sponsors:* European Commission, European Booksellers Federation, European Writers' Council, Federation of European Publishers. The 2012 round of the competition involved writers from Austria, Croatia, France, Hungary, Ireland, Italy, Lithuania, Norway, Poland, Portugal, Slovakia, and Sweden. *Winners:* (Austria) Anna Kim for *Die Gefrorene Zeit* (*Frozen Time*); (Croatia) Lada Žigo for *Rulet* (*Roulette*); (France) Laurence Plazenet for *L'Amour Seul* (*Love Alone*); (Hungary) Viktor Horváth for *Török Tükör* (*Turkish Mirror*); (Ireland) Kevin Barry for *City of Bohane*; (Italy) Emanuele Trevi for *Qualcosa di Scritto* (*Something Written*); (Lithuania) Giedra Radvilavičiūtė for *Šįnakt Aš Miegosiu Prie Sienos* (*Tonight I Shall Sleep By the Wall*); (Norway) Gunstein Bakke for *Maud og Aud—Ein Roman om Trafikk* (*Maud and Aud—A Novel on Traffic*); (Poland) Piotr Paziński for *Pensjonat* (*Boarding House*); (Portugal) Alfonso Cruz for *A Boneca de Kokoschka* (*The Kokoschka's Doll*); (Slovakia) Jana Beňová for *Café Hyena* (*Plán Odprevádzania*) (*Café Hyena [Seeing People Off]*); (Sweden); Sara Mannheimer for *Handlingen* (*The Action*).

Fairfax Prize ($10,000). For a body of work that has "made significant contributions to American and international culture." *Sponsors:* Fairfax County (Virginia) Public Library Foundation and George Mason University. *Winner:* Michael Chabon.

FIELD Poetry Prize ($1,000). For a book-length poetry collection. *Offered by: FIELD: Contemporary Poetry and Poetics. Winner:* Mary Ann Samyn for "My Life in Heaven" (to be published by Oberlin College Press).

FIL Literary Award in Romance Languages (formerly the Juan Rulfo International Latin American and Caribbean Prize) (Mexico) ($150,000). For lifetime achievement in any literary genre. *Offered by:* Juan Rulfo International Latin American and Caribbean Prize Committee. *Winner:* Alfredo Bryce Echenique.

Financial Times/Goldman Sachs Business Book of the Year Award (£30,000). To recognize books that provide compelling and enjoyable insight into modern business issues. *Winner:* Steve Coll for *Private Empire: ExxonMobil and American Power* (Penguin).

Sid Fleischman Award for Humor. See Golden Kite Awards.

ForeWord Magazine Book of the Year Awards ($1,500). For independently published books. *Offered by: ForeWord* magazine. *Winners:* Leonard Rosen for *All Cry Chaos* (Permanent); (nonfiction) Erzsébet Gilbert and Sherise Talbott, illustrator, for *Logodaedaly, or, Sleight of Words* (Wolverine Farm).

E. M. Forster Award ($20,000). To a young writer from England, Ireland, Scotland, or Wales, for a stay in the United States. *Offered by:* American Academy of Arts and Letters. *Winner:* David Mitchell.

Forward Prizes (United Kingdom). For poetry. *Offered by: The Forward. Winners:* (best collection, £10,000) Jorie Graham for *Place* (Ecco); (Felix Dennis Prize for best first collection, £5,000) Sam Riviere for *81 Austerities* (Faber); (best single poem, £1,000) Denise Riley for "A Part Song."

H. E. Francis Short Story Competition ($1,000). For an unpublished short story no more than 5,000 words in length. *Sponsors:* Ruth Hindman Foundation and English Department, University of Alabama, Huntsville. *Winner:* Allison Slavick for " Balsam of Gilead."

Josette Frank Award (formerly the Children's Book Award). For a work of fiction in which children or young people deal in a positive and realistic way with difficulties in their world and grow emotionally and morally. *Offered by:* Bank Street College of Education and the Florence M. Miller Memorial Fund. *Winner:* Pat Schmatz for *Bluefish* (Candlewick).

George Freedley Memorial Award. For the best English-language work about live theater published in the United States. *Offered by:* Theatre Library Association. *Winner:* Jonathan Kalb for *Great Lengths: Seven Works of Marathon Theatre* (University of Michigan Press); (special jury prize) Steven Serafin. editor of *BAM: The Complete Works* (Brooklyn Academy of Music and Quantuck Lane).

French-American Foundation Translation Prizes. For a translation or translations from French into English of works of fiction and nonfiction. *Offered by:* French-American Foundation. *Winners:* Marina Harss for *The Mirador: Dreamed Memories of Irène Némirovsky by Her Daughter* by Elisabeth Gille (New York Review of Books); Arthur Goldhammer for *The Ancien Régime and the French Revolution* by Alexis de Tocqueville (Cambridge University Press); Richard Howard for *When the World Spoke French* by Marc Fumaroli (New York Review of Books).

Frost Medal. To recognize achievement in poetry over a lifetime. *Offered by:* Poetry Society of America. *Winner:* Marilyn Nelson.

Lewis Galantière Award. Awarded biennially for a literary translation into English from any language other than German. *Offered by:* American Translators Association. *Winner:* Arthur Goldhammer for his translation from French of Alexis-Charles-Henri Clérel de Tocqueville's *The Ancien Régime and the French Revolution* (Cambridge University Press).

Galaxy National Book Awards. See Specsavers National Book Awards.

Theodor Seuss Geisel Medal. For the best book for beginning readers. *Offered by:* American Library Association, Association for Library Service to Children. *Winner:* Josh Schneider, writer and illustrator, for *Tales for Very Picky Eaters* (Clarion).

David Gemmell Legend Awards for Fantasy. For novels published for the first time in English during the year of nomination. *Winners:* (Legend Award for best fantasy novel) Patrick Rothfuss for *The Wise Man's Fear* (DAW); (Morningstar Award for best debut novel) Helen Lowe for *Heir of Night* (EOS); (Ravenheart Award for best cover art) Raymond Swanland for *Blood of Aenarion* by William King (Black Library).

Giller Prize (Canada). See Scotiabank Giller Prize.

Gival Press Novel Award ($3,000 and publication by Gival Press). *Winner:* Mark Brazaitis for *Julia and Rodrigo.*

Giverny Award. For an outstanding children's science picture book. *Offered by:* 15 Degree Laboratory. *Winners:* Andrea Zimmerman and Ju Hong Chen, illustrator, for *Eliza's Cherry Trees: Japan's Gift to America* (Pelican).

Alexander Gode Medal. To an individual or institution for outstanding service to the translation and interpreting professions. *Offered by:* American Translators Association. *Winner:* Not awarded in 2012.

Goldberg Prize for Jewish Fiction by Emerging Writers ($2,500). To highlight new works by contemporary writers exploring Jewish themes. *Offered by:* Foundation for Jewish Culture. *Donor:* Samuel Goldberg and Sons Foundation. *Winner:* Ned Beauman for *Boxer, Beetle* (Bloomsbury).

Golden Duck Awards for Excellence in Children's Science Fiction Literature. *Sponsored by:* Super-Con-Duck-Tivity. *Winners:* (picture book) Pam Smallcomb and Joe Berger, illustrator, for *Earth to Clunk* (Dial); (Eleanor Cameron middle grades award) Hena Kahn and David Borgenicht for *Worst-Case Scenario Ultimate Adventure No. 2: Mars!* (Chronicle); (Hal Clement young adult award—tie) David Weber for *A Beautiful Friendship* (Baen) and Anna Sheehan for *A Long, Long Sleep* (Candlewick).

Golden Kite Awards. For children's books. *Offered by:* Society of Children's Book Writers and Illustrators. *Winners:* (fiction) Ruta Sepetys for *Between Shades of Gray* (Philomel); (nonfiction) Candace Fleming for *Amelia Lost: The Life and Disappearance of Amelia Earhart* (Schwartz & Wade); (picture book text) Kate Messner for *Over and Under the Snow* (Chronicle); (picture book illustration) Melissa Sweet for *Balloons Over Broadway* (Houghton Mifflin Harcourt); (Sid Fleischman Award for Humor) Chris Rylander for *The Fourth Stall* (HarperCollins).

Governor General's Literary Awards (Canada) (C$25,000, plus C$3,000 to the publisher). For works, in English and in French, of fiction, nonfiction, poetry, drama, and children's literature, and for translation. *Offered by:* Canada Council for the Arts. *Winners:* (fiction, English) Linda Spalding for *The Purchase* (Random House); (fiction, French) France Daigle for *Pour Sûr* (Éditions du Boréal); (poetry, English) Julie Bruck for *Monkey Ranch* (Brick); (poetry, French) Maude Smith Gagnon for *Un Drap. Une Place* (Éditions Triptyque); (drama, English) Catherine Banks for *It Is Solved by Walking* (Playwrights Canada); (drama,

French) Geneviève Billette for *Contre le Temps* (Leméac Éditeur); (nonfiction, English) Ross King for *Leonardo and the Last Supper* (Bond Street); (nonfiction, French) Normand Chaurette for *Comment Tuer Shakespeare* (Presses de l'Université de Montréal); (children's literature, text, English) Susin Nielsen for *The Reluctant Journal of Henry K. Larsen* (Tundra); (children's literature, text, French) Aline Apostolska for *Un Été d'Amour et de Cendres* (Leméac Éditeur); (children's literature, illustration, English) Isabelle Arsenault for *Virginia Wolf*, text by Kyo Maclear (Kids Can); (children's literature, illustration, French) Élise Gravel for *La Clé à Molette* (Éditions de la Courte Échelle); (translation, French-English) Nigel Spencer for *Mai at the Predators' Ball* by Marie-Claire Blais (House of Anansi); (translation, English-French) Alain Roy for *Glenn Gould* by Mark Kingwell (Éditions du Boréal).

Dolly Gray Children's Literature Awards. Presented biennially for fiction or biographical children's books with positive portrayals of individuals with developmental disabilities. *Offered by:* Council for Exceptional Children, Division on Autism and Developmental Disabilities. *Winners:* To be awarded next in 2014.

Kate Greenaway Medal and Colin Mears Award. See CILIP Kate Greenaway Medal.

Eric Gregory Awards (United Kingdom) (£3,000). For a published or unpublished collection by poets under the age of 30. *Winners:* Sophie Baker, Joey Connolly, Holly Corfield Carr, Caleb Klaces, Rachael Nicholas, Phoebe Power, Jon Stone.

Griffin Poetry Prizes (Canada) (C$65,000). To a living Canadian poet or translator and a living poet or translator from any country, which may include Canada. *Offered by:* Griffin Trust. *Winners:* (international) David Harsent for *Night* (Faber); (Canadian) Ken Babstock for *Methodist Hatchet* (House of Anansi).

Gryphon Award ($1,000). To recognize a noteworthy work of fiction or nonfiction for younger children. *Offered by:* The Center for Children's Books. *Winner:* Julie Sternberg and Matthew Cordell, illustrator, for *Like Pickle Juice on a Cookie* (Amulet/Adams).

Guardian Children's Fiction Prize (United Kingdom) (£1,500). For an outstanding children's or young adult novel. *Offered by:* The *Guardian. Winner:* Frank Cottrell Boyce for *The Unforgotten Coat* (Candlewick).

Guardian First Book Award (United Kingdom) (£10,000). To recognize a first book. *Offered by:* The *Guardian. Winner:* Kevin Powers for *The Yellow Birds* (Little, Brown).

Dashiell Hammett Prize. For a work of literary excellence in the field of crime writing. *Offered by:* North American Branch, International Association of Crime Writers. *Winner:* James Sallis for *The Killer Is Dying* (Walker).

Harvey Awards. To recognize outstanding work in comics and sequential art. *Winners:* (syndicated strip or panel) Richard Thompson for "Cul De Sac" (Universal Press Syndicate); (online comics) Kate Beaton for "Hark! A Vagrant"; (writer) Mark Waid for "Daredevil" (Marvel); (cover artist) J. H. Williams for "Batwoman" (DC).

Hatchet Job of the Year (United Kingdom). To reward book critics who have the courage to overturn received opinion, and who do so with style. *Sponsor:* The Fish Society. *Winner:* Adam Mars-Jones for his *Observer* review of *By Nightfall* by Michael Cunningham (Farrar, Straus & Giroux).

R. R. Hawkins Award. For the outstanding professional/scholarly work of the year. *Offered by:* Association of American Publishers. *Winner:* Peter Brown for *Through the Eye of a Needle: Wealth, the Fall of Rome, and the Making of Christianity in the West, 350–550 AD* (Princeton University Press).

Anthony Hecht Poetry Prize ($3,000 and publication by Waywiser Press). For an unpublished first or second book-length poetry collection. *Winner:* Chris Andrews for *Green Lime Chair.*

Drue Heinz Literature Prize ($15,000 and publication by University of Pittsburgh Press). For short fiction. *Winner:* Beth Bosworth for *The Source of Life and Other Stories.*

O. Henry Awards. See PEN/O. Henry Prize.

William Dean Howells Medal. In recognition of the most distinguished novel published in the preceding five years. *Offered by:* American Academy of Arts and Letters. *Winner:* To be awarded next in 2015.

Hugo Awards. For outstanding science fiction writing. *Offered by:* World Science Fiction Convention. *Winners:* (novel) Jo Walton for *Among Others* (Tor); (novella) Kij Johnson for *The Man Who Bridged the Mist* in *Asimov's*; (novelette) Charlie Jane Anders for "Six Months, Three Days" (Tor.com); (short story) Ken Liu for "The Paper Menagerie" in the *Magazine of Fantasy and Science Fiction*; (related work) John Clute, David Langford, Peter Nicholls, and Graham Sleight, editors, for *The Encyclopedia of Science Fiction, Third Edition* (Gollancz); (graphic story) Ursula Vernon for *Digger* (Sofawolf); (John W. Campbell Award for best new writer) E. Lily Yu.

Hurston/Wright Legacy Awards. To writers of African American descent for a book of fiction, a book of nonfiction, and a book of poetry. *Offered by:* Hurston/Wright Foundation. *Sponsor:* Busboys and Poets. *Winners:* (fiction) Helen Oyeyemi for *Mr. Fox* (Riverhead); (nonfiction) Tomiko Brown-Nagin for *Courage to Dissent: Atlanta and the Long History of the Civil Rights Movement* (Oxford University Press); (poetry) Evie Shockley for *The New Black* (Wesleyan).

IMPAC Dublin Literary Award (Ireland) (€100,000). For a book of high literary merit, written in English or translated into English. *Offered by:* IMPAC Corp. and the City of Dublin. *Winner:* Jon McGregor for *Even the Dogs* (Bloomsbury).

Independent Foreign Fiction Prize (United Kingdom) (£5,000 each for author and translator). For a work of fiction by a living author that has been translated into English from any other language and published in the United Kingdom. *Winners:* Aharon Appelfeld and Jeffrey M Green, translator from Hebrew, for *Blooms of Darkness* (Alma).

Indies Choice Book Awards (formerly Book-Sense Book of the Year Awards). Chosen by owners and staff of American Booksellers Association member bookstores. *Winners:* (adult fiction) Jeffrey Eugenides for *The Marriage Plot* (Farrar, Straus & Giroux); (adult nonfiction) Gabrielle Hamilton for *Blood, Bones and Butter: The Inadvertent Education of a Reluctant Chef* (Random); (adult debut book) Téa Obreht for *The Tiger's Wife* (Random); (young adult) Ruta Sepetys for *Between Shades of Gray*

(Philomel); (most engaging author) Ann Patchett.

International Prize for Arabic Fiction ($50,000). To reward excellence in contemporary Arabic creative writing. *Sponsors:* Booker Prize Foundation, Emirates Foundation for Philanthropy. *Winner:* Rabee Jaber for *The Druze of Belgrade* (Al-Markez al-Thaqafi al-Arabi).

Iowa Poetry Prize. For book-length poetry collections by new or established poets. *Sponsor:* University of Iowa Press. *Winner:* Stephanie Pippin for *The Messenger* (University of Iowa Press).

IPPY Peacemaker Award. To honor the best books promoting world peace and human tolerance. *Offered by:* Jenkins Group and *Independent Publisher. Winners:* Parker W. Borg, Maureen J. Carroll, Patricia MacDermot Kasdan, and Stephen W. Wells for *Answering Kennedy's Call: Pioneering the Peace Corps in the Philippines* (Peace Corps Writers); Jay Chen, editor, for *A Small Key Opens Big Doors: 50 Years of Amazing Peace Corps Stories—Vol. 3, The Heart of Eurasia)* (Travelers' Tales).

IRA Children's and Young Adult Book Awards. For first or second books in any language published for children or young adults. *Offered by:* International Reading Association. *Winners:* (primary fiction) Stephen Savage for *Where's Walrus?* (Scholastic); (intermediate fiction) Sheila O'Connor for *Sparrow Road* (Putnam), Lucy Christopher for *Flyaway* (Scholastic); (young adult fiction) Ruta Sepetys for *Between Shades of Gray* (Philomel); (primary nonfiction) Jeanne Walker Harvey for *My Hands Sing the Blues: Romare Bearden's Childhood Journey* (Marshall Cavendish); (young adult nonfiction) Georgia Bragg for *How They Croaked: The Awful Ends of the Awfully Famous* (Walker).

Rona Jaffe Foundation Writers' Awards ($30,000). To identify and support women writers of exceptional talent in the early stages of their careers. *Offered by:* Rona Jaffe Foundation. *Winners:* Julia Elliott, Christina Nichol, Lauren Goodwin Slaughter, Rachel Swearingen, Kim Tingley, Inara Verzemnieks.

Jerusalem Prize (Israel). Awarded biennially to a writer whose works best express the theme of freedom of the individual in society. *Offered by:* Jerusalem International Book Fair. *Winner:* To be awarded next in 2013.

Jewish Book Council American Jewish Studies Award (Celebrate 350 Award). *Winner:* Laura Arnold Leibman for *Messianism, Secrecy, and Mysticism: A New Interpretation of Early American Jewish Life* (Vallentine Mitchell).

Jewish Book Council Lifetime Achievement Award. *Winner:* Eric R. Kandel.

Jewish Book of the Year (Everett Family Foundation Award). For outstanding writing. *Offered by:* Jewish Book Council. *Winners:* Howard B. Rock, Annie Polland and Daniel Soyer, Jeffrey S. Gurock, and Deborah Dash Moore, editor, for *City of Promises: A History of the Jews of New York* (New York University Press).

Samuel Johnson Prize for Nonfiction (United Kingdom) (£20,000). For an outstanding work of nonfiction. *Offered by:* British Broadcasting Corporation. *Winner:* Wade Davis for *Into the Silence: The Great War, Mallory and the Conquest of Everest* (Bodley Head).

Sue Kaufman Prize for First Fiction ($5,000). For a first novel or collection of short stories. *Offered by:* American Academy of Arts and Letters. *Winner:* Ismet Prcic for *Shards* (Grove).

Ezra Jack Keats Awards. For children's picture books. *Offered by:* New York Public Library and the Ezra Jack Keats Foundation. *Winners:* (new writer award) Meg Medina for *Tía Isa Wants a Car* (Candlewick); (new illustrator award) Jenny Sue Kostecki-Shaw for *Same, Same but Different* (Henry Holt).

Kerlan Award. To recognize singular attainments in the creation of children's literature and in appreciation for generous donation of unique resources to the Kerlan Collection for the study of children's literature. *Offered by:* Kerlan Children's Literature Research Collections, University of Minnesota. *Winner:* Karen Nelson Hoyle, retired curator of the University of Minnesota Children's Literature Research Collections.

Coretta Scott King Book Awards ($1,000). To an African American author and illustrator of outstanding books for children and young adults. *Offered by:* American Library Association, Social Responsibilities Round

Table. *Winners:* (author) Kadir Nelson for *Heart and Soul: The Story of America and African Americans* (HarperCollins); (illustrator) Shane W. Evans for *Underground: Finding the Light to Freedom* (Roaring Brook).

Coretta Scott King/John Steptoe Award for New Talent. To offer visibility to a writer or illustrator at the beginning of a career. *Sponsor:* Coretta Scott King Book Award Committee. *Winner:* Not awarded in 2012.

Coretta Scott King/Virginia Hamilton Award for Lifetime Achievement. Given in even-numbered years to an African American author, illustrator, or author/illustrator for a body of books for children or young adults. In odd-numbered years, the award honors substantial contributions through active engagement with youth, using award-winning African American literature for children or young adults. *Winner:* Ashley Bryan.

Kiriyama Pacific Rim Book Prize ($30,000). For a book of fiction or a book of nonfiction that best contributes to a fuller understanding among the nations and peoples of the Pacific Rim. *Offered by:* Pacific Rim Voices. *Winner:* Award discontinued.

Lambda Literary Awards. To honor outstanding lesbian, gay, bisexual, and transgender (LGBT) literature. *Offered by:* Lambda Literary Foundation. *Winners:* (lesbian debut fiction) Laurie Weeks for *Zipper Mouth* (Feminist Press at CUNY); (lesbian general fiction) Farzana Doctor for *Six Metres of Pavement* (Dundurn); (lesbian memoir/biography) Jeanne Córdova for *When We Were Outlaws: A Memoir of Love and Revolution* (Spinsters Ink); (lesbian mystery) Kim Baldwin and Xenia Alexiou for *Dying to Live* (Bold Strokes); (lesbian poetry) Leah Lakshmi Piepzna-Samarasinha for *Love Cake* (TSAR); (lesbian romance) Kenna White for *Taken by Surprise* (Bella); (lesbian erotica) Debra Hyde for *Story of L* (Ravenous Romance); (gay debut fiction) Rahul Mehta for *Quarantine: Stories* (Harper Perennial); (gay general fiction) Colm Tóibín for *The Empty Family* (Scribner); (gay memoir/biography) Glen Retief for *The Jack Bank: A Memoir of a South African Childhood* (St. Martin's); (gay mystery) Richard Stevenson for *Red White Black and Blue* (MLR); (gay poetry) David Trinidad,

editor, for *A Fast Life: The Collected Poems of Tim Dlugos* (Nightboat); (gay romance) Jim Provenzano for *Every Time I Think of You* (CreateSpace/Myrmidude); (gay erotica) Dirk Vanden for *All Together* (loveyoudivine Alerotica); (transgender fiction) Tristan Taormino, editor, for *Take Me There: Trans and Genderqueer Erotica* (Cleis); (transgender nonfiction) Justin Vivian Bond for *Tango: My Childhood, Backwards and in High Heels* (Feminist Press at CUNY); (bisexual fiction) Barbara Browning for *The Correspondence Artist* (Two Dollar Radio); (bisexual nonfiction) Jan Steckel for *The Horizontal Poet* (Zeitgeist); (LGBT Anthology) Michael Hames-García and Ernesto Javier Martínez, editors, for *Gay Latino Studies: A Critical Reader* (Duke University Press); (LGBT children's/young adult) Bil Wright for *Putting Makeup on the Fat Boy* (Simon & Schuster); (LGBT drama) Peggy Shaw for *A Menopausal Gentleman: The Solo Performances of Peggy Shaw* (University of Michigan Press); (LGBT nonfiction) Michael Bronski for *A Queer History of the United States* (Beacon); (LGBT SF/fantasy/horror) Lee Thomas for *The German* (Lethe); (LGBT studies) Lisa L. Moore for *Sister Arts: The Erotics of Lesbian Landscapes* (University of Minnesota Press).

Harold Morton Landon Translation Award ($1,000). For a book of verse translated into English by a single translator. *Offered by:* Academy of American Poets. *Winner:* Jen Hofer for her translation from Spanish of *Ivory Black,* a bilingual edition of *Negro Marfil* by Myriam Moscona (Les Figues).

David J. Langum, Sr. Prize in American Historical Fiction ($1,000). To honor a book of historical fiction published in the previous year. *Winner:* Julie Otsuka for *The Buddha in the Attic* (Knopf).

David J. Langum, Sr. Prize in American Legal History or Biography ($1,000). For a university press book that is accessible to the educated general public, rooted in sound scholarship, with themes that touch upon matters of general concern. *Winners:* Stuart Banner for *American Property: A History of How, Why, and What We Own* (Harvard University Press); Joanna L. Grossman and Lawrence M. Friedman for *Inside the Castle: Law and the Family in 20th Century America* (Princeton University Press).

Lannan Foundation Literary Awards and Fellowships. To recognize young and mid-career writers of distinctive literary merit who demonstrate potential for continued outstanding work. *Offered by:* Lannan Foundation. *Winners:* Natalie Diaz, Dennis O'Driscoll.

James Laughlin Award ($5,000). To commend and support a second book of poetry. *Offered by:* Academy of American Poets. *Winner:* Catherine Barnett for *The Game of Boxes* (Graywolf).

Claudia Lewis Awards. For the year's best poetry book or books for young readers. *Offered by:* Bank Street College of Education and the Florence M. Miller Memorial Fund. *Winners:* (younger readers) Kristine O'Connell George and Nancy Carpenter, illustrator, for *Emma Dilemma: Big Sister Poems* (Houghton Mifflin Harcourt); (older readers) Allan Wolf for *The Watch That Ends the Night* (Candlewick).

Library of Congress Lifetime Achievement Award for the Writing of Fiction. For a distinguished body of work. *Offered by:* Library of Congress. *Winner:* Not awarded in 2012.

Ruth Lilly Fellowships ($15,000). To emerging poets to support their continued study and writing of poetry. *Offered by:* the Poetry Foundation. *Winners:* Reginald Dwayne Betts, Nicholas Friedman, Richie Hofmann, Rickey Laurentiis, Jacob Saenz.

Ruth Lilly Poetry Prize ($100,000). To a U.S. poet in recognition of lifetime achievement. *Offered by:* the Poetry Foundation. *Winner:* W. S. Di Piero.

Astrid Lindgren Memorial Award (Sweden) (5 million kroner, approximately $868,500). In memory of children's author Astrid Lindgren, to honor outstanding children's literature and efforts to promote it. *Offered by:* Government of Sweden and the Swedish Arts Council. *Winner:* Dutch author Guus Kuijer.

Locus Awards. For science fiction writing. *Offered by:* Locus Publications. *Winners:* (novel) China Miéville for *Embassytown* (Macmillan); (fantasy) George R. R. Martin for *A Dance with Dragons* (Bantam); (first novel) Erin Morgenstern for *The Night Cir-*

cus (Doubleday); (young adult) Catherynne M. Valente for *The Girl Who Circumnavigated Fairyland in a Ship of Her Own Making* (Feiwel and Friends); (novella) Catherynne M. Valente for *Silently and Very Fast* in *Clarkesworld*; (novelette) Catherynne M. Valente for "White Lines on a Green Field" in *Subterranean*; (short story) Neil Gaiman for "The Case of Death and Honey" in *A Study in Sherlock* (Poisoned Pen); (anthology) Gardner Dozois, editor, for *The Year's Best Science Fiction: Twenty-eighth Annual Collection* (St. Martin's Griffin); (collection) Tim Powers for *The Bible Repairman and Other Stories* (Tachyon); (nonfiction) Gary K. Wolfe for *Evaporating Genres: Essays on Fantastic Literature* (Wesleyan); (art books) Cathy Fenner and Arnie Fenner for *Spectrum 18: The Best in Contemporary Fantastic Art* (Underwood).

London Book Festival Awards. To honor books worthy of further attention from the international publishing community. *Winner:* (grand prize) Simeon Courtie for *The Long and Whining Road* (Simantics Ltd.).

Elizabeth Longford Prize for Historical Biography (United Kingdom) (£5,000). *Sponsors:* Flora Fraser and Peter Soros. *Winner:* Frances Wilson for *How to Survive the Titanic, or The Sinking of J. Bruce Ismay* (Bloomsbury).

Los Angeles Times Book Prizes. To honor literary excellence. *Offered by:* Los Angeles Times. *Winners:* (biography) John A. Farrell for *Clarence Darrow: Attorney for the Damned* (Doubleday); (current interest) Daniel Kahneman for *Thinking Fast and Slow* (Farrar, Straus & Giroux); (fiction) Alex Shakar for *Luminarium* (Soho); (Art Seidenbaum Award for First Fiction) Ismet Prcic for *Shards* (Grove); (graphic novel) Carla Speed McNeil for *Finder: Voice* (Dark Horse); (history) Richard White for *Railroads: The Transcontinentals and the Making of Modern America* (Norton); (mystery/thriller) Stephen King for *11/22/1963* (Scribner); (poetry) Carl Phillips for *Double Shadow: Poems* (Farrar, Straus & Giroux); (science and technology) Sylvia Naser for *Grand Pursuit: The Story of Economic Genius* (Simon & Schuster); (young adult) Pete Hautman for *The Big Crunch* (Scholastic); (Robert Kirsch Award for Lifetime Achievement) Rudolfo Anaya; (Innovator's Award) Dana Goodyear and Jacob Lewis, co-founders of Figment, a digital writing community.

Amy Lowell Poetry Traveling Scholarship. For one or two U.S. poets to spend one year outside North America in a country the recipients feel will most advance their work. *Offered by:* Amy Lowell Poetry Traveling Scholarship. *Winners:* Joshua Weiner, Penelope Pelizzon.

J. Anthony Lukas Awards. For nonfiction writing that demonstrates literary grace, serious research, and concern for an important aspect of American social or political life. *Offered by:* Columbia University Graduate School of Journalism and the Nieman Foundation for Journalism at Harvard. *Winners:* (Lukas Book Prize) ($10,000) Daniel J. Sharfstein for *The Invisible Line: Three American Families and the Secret Journey from Black to White* (Penguin); (Mark Lynton History Prize) ($10,000) Sophia Rosenfeld for *Common Sense: A Political History* (Harvard University Press); (Lukas Work-in-Progress Award) ($30,000) Jonathan M. Katz for *The Big Truck That Went By: How the World Came to Save Haiti and Left Behind a Disaster* (Palgrave Macmillan).

Macavity Awards. For excellence in mystery writing. *Offered by:* Mystery Readers International. *Winners:* (novel) Sara Gran for *Claire DeWitt and the City of the Dead* (Houghton Mifflin Harcourt); (first novel) Leonard Rosen for *All Cry Chaos* (Permanent); (mystery-related nonfiction) Charlaine Harris for *The Sookie Stackhouse Companion* (Ace); (short story) Dana Cameron for "Disarming" in *Ellery Queen Mystery Magazine*; (Sue Feder Historical Mystery Award) Catriona McPherson for *Dandy Gilver and the Proper Treatment of Bloodstains* (Minotaur).

McKitterick Prize (United Kingdom) (£4,000). To an author over the age of 40 for a first novel, published or unpublished. *Winner:* Ginny Baily for *Africa Junction* (Harvill Secker).

Man Asian Literary Prize ($30,000). For a novel by an Asian writer, either written in English or translated into English, and published in the previous calendar year. *Winner:* Kyung-sook Shin for *Please Look After Mom* (Weidenfeld & Nicolson).

Man Booker International Prize (United Kingdom) (£60,000). Awarded biennially to a living author for a significant contribution to world literature. *Offered by:* Man Group. *Winner:* To be awarded next in 2013.

Man Booker Prize for Fiction (United Kingdom) (£50,000). For the best novel written in English by a Commonwealth author. *Offered by:* Booktrust and the Man Group. *Winner:* Hilary Mantel for *Bring Up the Bodies* (Henry Holt).

Lenore Marshall Poetry Prize ($25,000). For an outstanding book of poems published in the United States. *Offered by:* Academy of American Poets. *Winner:* David Wojahn for *World Tree* (University of Pittsburgh Press).

Mason Award ($10,000). To honor an author whose body of work has made extraordinary contributions to bringing literature to a wide reading public. *Sponsors:* George Mason University and Fall for the Book. *Winner:* Neil Gaiman.

Somerset Maugham Awards (£3,500) (United Kingdom). For works in any genre except drama by a writer under the age of 35, to enable young writers to enrich their work by gaining experience of foreign countries. *Winners:* Not awarded in 2012.

Addison M. Metcalf Award in Literature ($10,000). Awarded biennially to a young writer of great promise. *Offered by:* American Academy of Arts and Letters. *Winner:* To be awarded next in 2013.

Vicky Metcalf Award for Children's Literature (Canada) (C$20,000). To a Canadian writer of children's literature for a body of work. *Offered by:* Metcalf Foundation. *Winner:* Paul Yee.

Midwest Booksellers Choice Awards. *Offered by:* Midwest Booksellers Association. *Winners:* (adult fiction) Chad Harbach for *The Art of Fielding* (Little, Brown); (adult nonfiction) Cheryl Strayed for *Wild: From Lost to Found on the Pacific Crest Trail* (Knopf); (poetry) Todd Boss for *Pitch* (Norton); (children's literature) Brian Selznick for *Wonderstruck* (Scholastic); (children's picture books) Loren Long for *Otis and the Tornado* (Philomel).

William C. Morris YA Debut Award. To honor a debut book published by a first-time author writing for teens and celebrating impressive new voices in young adult literature. *Offered by:* American Library Association, Young Adult Library Services Association. *Donor:* William C. Morris Endowment. *Winner:* John Corey Whaley for *Where Things Come Back* (Simon & Schuster).

Gustavus Myers Awards. For outstanding books that extend understanding of the root causes of bigotry. *Offered by:* Gustavus Myers Center for the Study of Bigotry and Human Rights in North America. *Winners:* Awarded suspended in 2009.

Mythopoeic Fantasy Awards. To recognize fantasy or mythic literature for children and adults that best exemplifies the spirit of the Inklings, a group of fantasy writers that includes J. R. R. Tolkien, C. S. Lewis, and Charles Williams. *Offered by:* Mythopoeic Society. *Winners:* (adult literature) Lisa Goldstein for *The Uncertain Places* (Tachyon); (children's literature) Delia Sherman for *The Freedom Maze* (Big Mouth House); (Mythopoeic Scholarship Award in Inklings Studies) Carl Phelpstead for *Tolkien and Wales: Language, Literature and Identity* (University of Wales Press); (Mythopoeic Scholarship Award in Myth and Fantasy Studies) Jack Zipes for *The Enchanted Screen: The Unknown History of Fairy-Tale Films* (Routledge).

National Book Awards. To celebrate the best in American literature. *Offered by:* National Book Foundation. *Winners:* (fiction) Lois Erdrich for *The Round House* (Harper); (nonfiction) Katherine Boo for *Behind the Beautiful Forevers: Life, Death, and Hope in a Mumbai Undercity* (Random); (poetry) David Ferry for *Bewilderment: New Poems and Translations* (University of Chicago Press); (young people's literature) William Alexander for *Goblin Secrets* (McElderry).

National Book Awards (United Kingdom). See Specsavers National Book Awards.

National Book Critics Circle Awards. For literary excellence. *Offered by:* National Book Critics Circle. *Winners:* (fiction) Edith Pearlman for *Binocular Vision: New and Selected Stories* (Lookout); (general nonfiction) Maya Jasanoff for *Liberty's Exiles: American Loyalists in the Revolutionary World* (Knopf); (biography) John Lewis Gaddis for *George F. Kennan: An American Life* (Penguin); (poetry) Laura Kasischke for *Space, in Chains* (Copper Canyon); (au-

tobiography) Mira Bartók for *The Memory Palace* (Free Press); (Nona Balakian Citation for Excellence in Reviewing) Kathryn Schulz; (Ivan Sandrof Lifetime Achievement Award) Robert B. Silvers.

National Book Festival Award for Creative Achievement. *Offered by:* Center for the Book, Library of Congress. *Winner:* Philip Roth.

National Book Foundation Literarian Award for Outstanding Service to the American Literary Community. *Offered by:* National Book Foundation. *Winner:* Arthur O. Sulzberger, Jr., chairman and publisher, the *New York Times.*

National Book Foundation Medal for Distinguished Contribution to American Letters ($10,000). To a person who has enriched the nation's literary heritage over a life of service or corpus of work. *Offered by:* National Book Foundation. *Winner:* Elmore Leonard.

National Endowment for the Arts Literature Fellowships for Creative Writing (poetry) ($25,000). *Winners:* Jose Perez Beduya, Miriam Bird Greenberg, Sarah Blake, Traci Brimhall, Jenny Browne, Suzanne Buffam, Ken Chen, Maxine Chernoff, Eduardo Corral, Lisa Fay Coutley, Meg Day, Ansel Elkins, Jill Alexander Essbaum, Reginald L. Flood, Sarah Gorham, Pamela Hart, Sy Hoahwah, Elizabeth Hughey, Joshua Kryah, Rickey Laurentiis, Sarah Mangold, Kerrin McCadden, Shane McCrae, Philip Metres, Simone Muench, John Murillo, Jacob Rakovan, Srikanth Reddy, Roger W. Reeves, James Richardson, Rachel Richardson, David Rigsbee, Atsuro Riley, Allison Seay, Solmaz Sharif, B. T. Shaw, Ryan Teitman, Sarah Vap, Jake Adam York, Rachel Zucker.

National Translation Awards ($5,000). To honor translators whose work has made a valuable contribution to literary translation into English. *Offered by:* American Literary Translators Association. *Winners:* Sinan Antoon for his translation from Arabic of *In the Presence of Absence* by Mahmoud Darwish (Archipelago); (Lucien Stryk Asian Translation Prize) Don Mee Choi for *All the Garbage of the World, Unite!* by Kim Hyesoon (Action).

Nebula Awards. For science fiction writing. *Offered by:* Science Fiction and Fantasy Writers of America (SFWA). *Winners:* (novel) Jo

Walton for *Among Others* (Tor); (novella) K.j Johnson for *The Man Who Bridged the Mist* in *Asimov's Science Fiction*; (novelette) Geoff Ryman for "What We Found" in the *Magazine of Fantasy and Science Fiction*; (short story) Ken Liu for "The Paper Menagerie" in the *Magazine of Fantasy and Science Fiction*; (Ray Bradbury Award) Neil Gaiman, writer, and Richard Clark, director, for "Doctor Who: The Doctor's Wife" (BBC Wales); (Andre Norton Award) Delia Sherman for *The Freedom Maze* (Big Mouth House); (Damon Knight Grand Master Award) Connie Willis.

John Newbery Medal. For the most distinguished contribution to literature for children. *Offered by:* American Library Association, Association for Library Service to Children. *Winner:* Jack Gantos for *Dead End in Norvelt* (Farrar, Straus & Giroux).

Nimrod Literary Awards ($2,000 plus publication). *Offered by: Nimrod International Journal of Prose and Poetry. Winners:* (Pablo Neruda Prize in Poetry) Chelsea Wagenaar for "Penance IV" and other poems; (Katherine Anne Porter Prize in Fiction) Judith E. Johnson for "The Tarot of Lost Names."

Nobel Prize in Literature (Sweden). For the total literary output of a distinguished career. *Offered by:* Swedish Academy. *Winner:* Mo Yan.

Eli M. Oboler Memorial Award. Given biennially to an author of a published work in English or in English translation dealing with issues, events, questions, or controversies in the area of intellectual freedom. *Offered by:* Intellectual Freedom Round Table, American Library Association. *Winner:* Evgeny Morozov for *The Net Delusion: The Dark Side of Internet Freedom* (PublicAffairs).

Flannery O'Connor Awards for Short Fiction. For collections of short fiction. *Offered by:* University of Georgia Press. *Winners:* Jacquelin Gorman for "The Viewing Room"; Tom Kealey for "Thieves I've Known."

Frank O'Connor Short Story Award. See Cork City–Frank O'Connor Short Story Award.

Oddest Book Title of the Year Award. See Bookseller/Diagram Prize for Oddest Title of the Year.

Scott O'Dell Award for Historical Fiction ($5,000). *Offered by: Bulletin of the Center for Children's Books,* University of Chicago. *Winner:* Jack Gantos for *Dead End in Norvelt* (Farrar, Straus & Giroux).

Odyssey Award. To the producer of the best audiobook for children and/or young adults available in English in the United States. *Sponsors:* American Library Association, ALSC/Booklist/YALSA. *Winner:* Listening Library for *Rotters* by Daniel Kraus, read by Kirby Heyborne.

Sean O'Faoláin Short Story Competition (€1,500 and publication in the literary journal *Southword. Offered by:* Munster Literature Centre, Cork, Ireland. *Winner:* Sophie Hampton for "White Socks and Weirdos."

Dayne Ogilvie Prize (C$4,000). To an emerging Canadian writer from the LGBT community who demonstrates promise through a body of quality work. *Offered by:* Writers' Trust of Canada. *Sponsor:* Robin Pacific. *Winner:* Amber Dawn.

Orange Award for New Writers (United Kingdom) (£10,000). For a first novel or short story collection written by a woman and published in the United Kingdom. *Offered by:* Orange plc and Arts Council London. *Winner:* Award discontinued in 2011.

Orange Prize for Fiction (United Kingdom) (£30,000). For the best novel written by a woman and published in the United Kingdom. *Offered by:* Orange plc. *Winner:* Madeline Miller *The Song of Achilles* (Bloomsbury). (Starting in 2013, the prize will be privately funded and known as the Women's Prize for Fiction.)

Orbis Pictus Award. For outstanding nonfiction for children. *Offered by:* National Council of Teachers of English. *Winner:* Melissa Sweet for *Balloons over Broadway: The True Story of the Puppeteer of Macy's Parade* (Houghton Mifflin Harcourt).

Orion Book Award ($3,000). To recognize books that deepen connection to the natural world, present new ideas about mankind's relationship with nature, and achieve excellence in writing. *Sponsors: Orion Magazine* and the Geraldine R. Dodge Foundation. *Winner:* Carl Safina for *The View from Lazy Point* (Henry Holt).

PEN Award for Poetry in Translation ($3,000). For a book-length translation of poetry from any language into English and published in the United States. *Offered by:* PEN

American Center. *Winner:* Jen Hofer for her translation from Spanish of *Ivory Black,* a bilingual edition of *Negro Marfil* by Myriam Moscona (Les Figues).

PEN/Saul Bellow Award for Achievement in American Fiction ($25,000). Awarded biennially to a distinguished living American author of fiction. *Offered by:* PEN American Center. *Winner:* E. L. Doctorow.

PEN/Bellwether Prize for Socially Engaged Fiction ($25,000). To the author of a previously unpublished novel that addresses issues of social justice and the impact of culture and politics on human relationships. *Founder:* Barbara Kingsolver. *Winner:* Susan Nussbaum for *Good Kings Bad Kings* (Algonquin).

PEN Beyond Margins Awards. See PEN Open Book Awards.

PEN/Robert Bingham Fellowship ($25,000). To a writer whose first novel or short story collection represents distinguished literary achievement and suggests great promise. *Offered by:* PEN American Center. *Winner:* Vanessa Veselka for *Zazen* (Red Lemonade).

PEN/Diamonstein-Spielvogel Award for the Art of the Essay ($5,000). For a book of essays by a single author that best exemplifies the dignity and esteem of the essay form. *Winner:* Christopher Hitchins for *Arguably* (Twelve).

PEN/ESPN Award for Literary Sports Writing ($5,000). To a living writer for exceptional contributions to the field of literary sports writing. *Winner:* Dan Barry for *Bottom of the 33rd: Hope, Redemption, and Baseball's Longest Game* (Harper).

PEN/ESPN Lifetime Achievement Award for Literary Sports Writing ($5,000). For a writer whose body of work represents an exceptional contribution to the field. *Winner:* Dan Jenkins.

PEN/Faulkner Award for Fiction ($15,000). To honor the best work of fiction published by an American. *Winner:* Julie Otsuka for *The Buddha in the Attic* (Knopf).

PEN/John Kenneth Galbraith Award ($10,000). Given biennially for a distinguished book of general nonfiction. *Offered by:* PEN American Center. *Winner:* To be awarded next in 2013.

PEN/Ernest Hemingway Foundation Award. For a distinguished work of first fiction by

an American. *Offered by:* PEN New England. *Winner:* Teju Cole for *Open City* (Random).

PEN/Steven Kroll Award ($5,000). To an author of exceptional writing in an illustrated children's book. *Winner:* Patricia C. McKissack for *Never Forgotten* (Schwartz & Wade).

PEN/Nora Magid Award ($5,000). Awarded biennially to honor a magazine editor who has contributed significantly to the excellence of the publication he or she edits. *Winner:* To be awarded next in 2013.

PEN/Ralph Manheim Medal for Translation. Given triennially to a translator whose career has demonstrated a commitment to excellence. *Winner:* Margaret Sayers Peden.

PEN/Phyllis Naylor Working Writer Fellowship ($5,000). To a published author of children's or young adults' fiction to aid in completing a book-length work in progress. *Offered by:* PEN American Center. *Winner:* Sarah Dooley for *Free Verse* (to be published by Putnam).

PEN New England Awards. For works of fiction, nonfiction, and poetry by New England writers or with New England topics or settings. *Winners:* (fiction) Yannick Murphy for *The Call* (Harper); (nonfiction) Mitchell Zuckoff for *Lost in Shangri-La* (HarperCollins); (poetry) Elizabeth Willis for *Address* (Wesleyan University Press).

PEN New England Susan P. Bloom Children's Book Discovery Award. For noteworthy unpublished children's or young adult literature. *Winners:* Amitha Knight for *Landwalker*; Heather Demetrios for *Streaming*.

PEN New England Henry David Thoreau Prize for Literary Excellence in Nature Writing. *Winner:* Gary Snyder.

PEN/O. Henry Prize. For short stories of exceptional merit, in English, published in U.S. and Canadian magazines. *Winners:* John Berger for "A Brush" in *Harper's*; Wendell Berry for "Nothing Living Lives Alone" in the *Threepenny Review*; Anthony Doerr for "The Deep" in *Zoetrope*; Dagoberto Gilb for "Uncle Rock" in the *New Yorker*; Karl Taro Greenfeld for "Mickey Mouse" in *Santa Monica Review*; Lauren Groff for "Eyewall" in *Subtropics*; Yiyun Li for "Kindness" in *A Public Space*; Hisham Matar for "Naima" in the *New Yorker*; Alice Mattison for "The

Vandercook" in *Ecotone*; Steven Millhauser for "Phantoms" in *McSweeney's Quarterly Concern*; Alice Munro for "Corrie" in the *New Yorker*; Ann Packer for "Things Said or Done" in *Zoetrope*; Miroslav Penkov for "East of the West" in *Orion*; Keith Ridgway for "Rothko Eggs" in *Zoetrope*; Sam Ruddick for "Leak" in the *Threepenny Review*; Salvatore Scibona for "The Woman Who Lived in the House" in *A Public Space;* Jim Shepard for "Boys Town" in the *New Yorker*; Mark Slouka for "The Hare's Mask" in *Harper's*; Christine Sneed for "The First Wife" in *New England Review*; Kevin Wilson for "A Birth in the Woods" in *Ecotone.*

PEN Open Book Award (formerly PEN Beyond Margins Award) ($1,000). For book-length writings by authors of color, published in the United States during the current calendar year. *Offered by:* PEN American Center. *Winner:* Siddhartha Deb for *The Beautiful and the Damned: A Portrait of the New India* (Faber).

PEN/Joyce Osterweil Award for Poetry ($5,000). A biennial award to recognize a new and emerging American poet. *Offered by:* PEN American Center. *Winner:* To be awarded next in 2013.

PEN/Laura Pels Foundation Awards for Drama. To recognize a master American dramatist and an American playwright in mid-career. *Offered by:* PEN American Center. *Winners:* (master dramatist) Christopher Durang; (mid-career) Will Eno, Adam Rapp.

PEN Prison Writing Awards. To provide support and encouragement to prison inmates whose writing shows merit or promise. *Offered by:* PEN American Center. *Winners:* (poetry) Charles Norman for "How Should I Look?"; (fiction) Scott Gutches for "Siddhartha's Loop"; (memoir) Ezekiel Caligiuri for "The Last Visit from the Girl in the Willow Tree"; (essay) Atif Rafay for "Bleak Housing and Black Americans"; (drama) Robert Weaver for "Somewhere Between."

PEN Translation Fund Grants ($1,000–$3,000). To support the translation of book-length works of fiction, creative nonfiction, poetry, or drama that have not previously appeared in English or have appeared only in an egregiously flawed translation. *Winners:* Bernard Adams, Alexander Booth, Brent Edwards, Joshua Daniel Edwin, Musharraf Ali

Farooqi, Deborah Garfinkle, Hillary Gulley, Bonnie Huie, Jacquelyn Pope, Matt Reeck and Aftab Ahmad, Carrie Reed, Nathanaël.

PEN Translation Prize ($3,000). To promote the publication and reception of translated world literature in English. *Winner:* Bill Johnston for *Stone Upon Stone* by Wiesław Myśliwski (Archipelago).

PEN/Edward and Lily Tuck Award for Paraguayan Literature ($3,000). To the author of a major work of Paraguayan literature not yet translated into English. *Winner:* Delfina Acosta for *Versos de Amor y de Locura* (ServLibro).

PEN/Voelcker Award for Poetry. Given in even-numbered years to an American poet at the height of his or her powers. *Offered by:* PEN American Center. *Winner:* Toi Derricotte for *The Undertaker's Daughter* (University of Pittsburgh Press).

PEN/Jacqueline Bograd Weld Award for Biography ($5,000). To the author of a distinguished biography published in the United States during the previous calendar year. *Offered by:* PEN American Center. *Winner:* Robert K. Massie for *Catherine the Great: Portrait of a Woman* (Random).

PEN/E. O. Wilson Literary Science Writing Award ($10,000). For a book of literary nonfiction on the subject of the physical and biological sciences. *Winner:* James Gleick for *The Information: A History, a Theory, a Flood* (Parthenon).

Maxwell E. Perkins Award. To honor an editor, publisher, or agent who has discovered, nurtured, and championed writers of fiction in the United States. *Offered by:* Center for Fiction, Mercantile Library of New York. *Winner:* Deborah Treisman, fiction editor, the *New Yorker.*

Phoenix Award. To the author of an English-language children's book that failed to win a major award at the time of its publication 20 years earlier. *Winner:* Karen Hesse for *Letters from Rifka* (Henry Holt, 1992).

Edgar Allan Poe Awards. For outstanding mystery, suspense, and crime writing. *Offered by:* Mystery Writers of America. *Winners:* (novel) Mo Hayder for *Gone* (Atlantic Monthly); (first novel) Lori Roy for *Bent Road* (Penguin); (paperback original) Robert Jackson Bennett for *The Company Man* (Hachette); (fact crime) Candice Millard for *Destiny of the Republic: A Tale of Madness, Medicine and the Murder of a President* (Random); (critical biographical) Michael Dirda for *On Conan Doyle: Or, the Whole Art of Storytelling* (Princeton University Press); (short story) Peter Turnbull for "The Man Who Took His Hat Off to the Driver of the Train" in *Ellery Queen Mystery Magazine*; (juvenile) Matthew J. Kirby for *Icefall* (Scholastic); (young adult) Dandi Daley Mackall for *The Silence of Murder* (Random); (play) Ken Ludwig for "The Game's Afoot" (Cleveland Playhouse); (television episode teleplay) Alex Gansa, Howard Gordon, and Gideon Raff for the pilot to "Homeland" (Showtime); (Robert L. Fish Memorial Award) David Ingram for "A Good Man of Business" in *Ellery Queen Mystery Magazine*; (Mary Higgins Clark Award) Sara J. Henry for *Learning to Swim* (Crown); (grand master) Martha Grimes.

Poets Out Loud Prize ($1,000 and publication by Fordham University Press). For a book-length poetry collection. *Sponsor:* Fordham University at Lincoln Center. *Winners:* Amy Sara Carroll for "Fannie + Freddie/The Sentimentality of Post-9/11 Pornography"; (editor's prize) Nicolas Hundley for "The Revolver in the Hive."

Katherine Anne Porter Award ($20,000). Awarded biennially to a prose writer of demonstrated achievement. *Offered by:* American Academy of Arts and Letters. *Winner:* Maureen Howard.

Michael L. Printz Award. For excellence in literature for young adults. *Offered by:* American Library Association, Young Adult Library Services Association. *Winner:* John Corey Whaley for *Where Things Come Back* (Simon & Schuster).

V. S. Pritchett Memorial Prize (United Kingdom) (£1,000). For a previously unpublished short story. *Offered by:* Royal Society of Literature. *Winner:* Martina Devlin for "Singing Dumb."

Pritzker Military Library Literature Award ($100,000). To recognize a living author for a body of work that has profoundly enriched the public understanding of American military history. *Sponsor:* Tawani Foundation. *Winner:* Max Hastings.

Prix Aurora Awards (Canada). For science fiction writing. *Winners:* (novel) Robert J. Sawyer for *Wonder* (Penguin); (short fiction) Suzanne Church for "The Needle's Eye" in *Chilling Tales: Evil Did I Dwell; Lewd I Did Live* (Edge); (poem/song) Helen Marshall for "Skeleton Leaves" (Kelp Queen); (graphic novel) Tarol Hunt for the webcomic *Goblins*; (related work) *On Spec* magazine (Copper Pig Writers' Society); (artist) Dan O'Driscoll; (fan publication) Eileen Bell, Ryan McFadden, Billie Milholland, and Randy McCharles for *Bourbon and Eggnog* (10th Circle Project).

Prix Goncourt (France). For "the best imaginary prose work of the year." *Offered by:* Société des Gens des Lettres. *Winner:* Jérôme Ferrari for *Sermon sur la Chute de Rome* (*Sermon on the Fall of Rome*) (Actes Sud).

Pulitzer Prizes in Letters ($10,000). To honor distinguished work dealing preferably with American themes. *Offered by:* Columbia University Graduate School of Journalism. *Winners:* (biography/autobiography) John Lewis Gaddis for *George F. Kennan: An American Life* (Penguin); (fiction) Not awarded in 2012; (general nonfiction) Stephen Greenblatt for *The Swerve: How the World Became Modern* (Norton); (poetry) Tracy K. Smith for *Life on Mars* (Graywolf); (drama) Quiara Alegría Hudes for "Water by the Spoonful" (Theatre Communications Group); (music) Kevin Puts for "Silent Night: Opera in Two Acts" (Aperto).

Raiziss/De Palchi Translation Award ($5,000 prize and a $25,000 fellowship, awarded in alternate years). For a translation into English of a significant work of modern Italian poetry by a living translator. *Offered by:* Academy of American Poets. *Winner:* (prize, $5,000) Jennifer Scappettone for her translation from Italian of *Locomotrix: Selected Poetry and Prose* by Amelia Rosselli.

RBC Bronwen Wallace Award for Emerging Writers (Canada) ($5,000). For a writer under the age of 35 who has not yet been published in book form. *Sponsor:* RBC Foundation. *Winner:* Jen Neale for "Elk-Headed Man."

Arthur Rense Poetry Prize ($20,000). Awarded triennially to an exceptional poet. *Offered by:* American Academy of Arts and Letters. *Winner:* To be awarded next in 2014.

John Llewellyn Rhys Prize (United Kingdom) (£5,000). For a work of literature by a British or Commonwealth author 35 or younger and published in the United Kingdom. *Offered by: Booktrust. Winner:* Not awarded in 2012.

Harold U. Ribalow Prize. For Jewish fiction published in English. *Sponsor: Hadassah* magazine. *Winner:* Edith Pearlman for *Binocular Vision: New and Selected Stories* (Lookout).

Rita Awards. *Offered by:* Romance Writers of America. *Winners:* (paranormal romance) Thea Harrison for *Dragon Bound* (Berkley); (romance novella) Caroline Linden for *I Love the Earl* (Avon Impulse); (novel with strong romantic elements) Barbara O'Neal for *How to Bake a Perfect Life* (Ballantine Bantam Dell); (first book) Darynda Jones for *First Grave on the Right* (St. Martin's); (historical romance) Joanna Bourne for *The Black Hawk* (Berkley); (inspirational romance) Serena Miller for *The Measure of Katie Calloway* (Revell); (contemporary series romance, suspense/adventure) Cindy Dees for *Soldier's Last Stand* (Harlequin); (contemporary single title romance) Fiona Lowe for *Boomerang Bride* (Carina); (regency historical romance) Tessa Dare for *A Night to Surrender* (Avon); (young adult romance) Ann Aguirre for *Enclave* (Macmillan); (contemporary series romance) Sarah Morgan for *Doukakis's Apprentice* (Harlequin); (romantic suspense) J. D. Robb for *New York to Dallas* (Penguin).

Rita Golden Heart Awards. For worthy unpublished romance manuscripts. *Offered by:* Romance Writers of America. *Winners:* (paranormal romance) Lorenda Christensen for "Never Deal with Dragons"; (novel with strong romantic elements) Lisa Lain for "Song without Words"; (historical romance) Elisa Beatty for "The Devil May Care"; (inspirational romance) Karen Fleming, writing as KD Flemming, for "Love's Advocate"; (contemporary single title romance) Tamar Bihari, writing as Talia Quinn Daniels, for "No Peeking"; (regency historical romance) Kimberly Ohara, writing as April Bennet, for "The Perfect Heiress"; (young adult romance) Romily Bernard for "Wired"; (contemporary series romance) Tamra Baumann for "Cyrano at Your Service"; (romantic suspense) Elizabeth Bemis for "Edge of Deception."

Rodda Book Award. To recognize a book that exhibits excellence in writing and has contributed significantly to congregational libraries through promotion of spiritual growth. The award is given to books for adults, young adults, and children on a three-year-rotational basis. *Offered by:* Church and Synagogue Library Association. *Winner:* (adult book) Barbara Brown Taylor for *An Altar in the World* (Harper One).

Rogers Writers' Trust Fiction Prize (Canada) (C$25,000). To a Canadian author of a novel or short story collection. *Offered by:* Rogers Communications. *Winner:* Tamas Dobozy for *Siege 13* (Thomas Allen).

Sami Rohr Prize for Jewish Literature ($100,000 first place, $25,000 first runner-up). For emerging writers of Jewish literature. *Offered by:* Family of Sami Rohr. *Winners:* (first place) Gal Beckerman for *When They Come for Us, We'll Be Gone: The Epic Struggle to Save Soviet Jewry* (Houghton Mifflin Harcourt); (first runner-up) Abigail Green for *Moses Montefiore: Jewish Liberator, Imperial Hero* (Belknap).

Rosenthal Foundation Award ($5,000). To a young novelist of considerable literary talent. *Offered by:* American Academy of Arts and Letters. *Winner:* Teju Cole for *Open City* (Random).

Royal Society of Literature Benson Medal (United Kingdom). To recognize meritorious works in poetry, fiction, history, and belles letters, honoring an entire career. The recipient may be someone who is not a writer but has done conspicuous service to literature. *Winners:* David Pease, Jenny Uglow.

Royal Society of Literature Jerwood Awards for Nonfiction (United Kingdom). For authors engaged on their first major commissioned works of nonfiction. *Offered by:* Royal Society of Literature. *Winners:* (£10,000) Ramita Navai for "City of Lies: The Undercover Truth About Tehran"; (£5,000) Edmund Gordon for "Angela Carter: The Biography," Gwen Adshead for "A Short Book About Evil."

Royal Society of Literature Ondaatje Prize (£10,000). For a distinguished work of fiction, nonfiction, or poetry evoking the spirit of a place. *Offered by:* Royal Society of Literature. *Winner:* Rahul Bhattacharya for *The Sly Company of People Who Care* (Picador).

Juan Rulfo International Latin American and Caribbean Prize (Mexico). See FIL Literary Award in Romance Languages.

Carl Sandburg Literary Awards. To honor a significant body of work that has enhanced public awareness of the written word. *Sponsor:* Chicago Public Library Foundation. *Winners:* (Sandburg Award) Don DeLillo, Walter Isaacson; (21st Century Award, recognizing a Chicago-area writer for recent noteworthy accomplishments) Nami Mun.

Schneider Family Book Awards ($5,000). To honor authors and illustrators for books that embody artistic expressions of the disability experience of children and adolescents. *Offered by:* American Library Association. *Donor:* Katherine Schneider. *Winners:* (middle school readers) Brian Selznick for *Wonderstruck: A Novel in Words and Pictures* (Scholastic), Joan Bauer for *Close to Famous* (Penguin); (teen readers) Wendelin Van Draanen for *The Running Dream* (Knopf).

Scotiabank Giller Prize (Canada) (C$50,000). For the best Canadian novel or short story collection written in English. *Offered by:* Giller Prize Foundation and Scotiabank. *Winner:* Will Ferguson for *419* (Viking).

Scottish Book of the Year Awards. *Sponsor:* Scottish Arts Council. *Donor:* Scottish Mortgage Investment Trust. *Winners:* (book of the year, £30,000) Janice Galloway for *All Made Up* (Granta); (category winners, £5,000) (fiction) Ali Smith for *There but for the* (Hamish Hamilton); (poetry) Angus Peter Campbell for *Aibisidh* (Polygon); (first book) Simon Stephenson for *Let Not the Waves of the Sea* (John Murray).

Shamus Awards. To honor mysteries featuring independent private investigators. *Offered by:* Private Eye Writers of America. *Winners:* (hardcover novel) Michael Wiley for *A Bad Night's Sleep* (Minotaur); (first novel) P. G. Sturges for *The Shortcut Man* (Scribner); (paperback original) Duane Swierczynski for *Fun and Games* (Mulholland); (short story) Michael Z. Lewin for "Who I Am" in *Ellery Queen Mystery Magazine.*

Roger Shattuck Prize for Criticism ($5,000). To support and encourage emerging critics. *Offered by:* Center for Fiction, Mercantile Library of New York. *Winners:* Ruth Franklin, David Yaffe.

Shelley Memorial Award ($6,000 to $9,000). To a poet or poets living in the United States, chosen on the basis of genius and need. *Offered by:* Poetry Society of America. *Winner:* Wanda Coleman.

Robert F. Sibert Medal. For the most distinguished informational book for children. *Offered by:* American Library Association, Association for Library Service to Children. *Winner:* Melissa Sweet for *Balloons over Broadway: The True Story of the Puppeteer of Macy's Parade* (Houghton Mifflin Harcourt).

Society of Authors Travelling Scholarships (£2,000) (United Kingdom). *Winners:* Stella Duffy, Matthew Hollis, Justin Marozzi.

Specsavers National Book Awards (United Kingdom) (formerly the Galaxy National Book Awards, earlier the British Book Awards). *Winners:* (book of the year and popular fiction) EL James for *Fifty Shades of Grey* (Arrow); (outstanding achievement award) Ian Rankin; (UK author of the year) Hilary Mantel for *Bring Up the Bodies* (Henry Holt); (international author of the year) Eowyn Ivey for *The Snow Child* (Headline Review); (children's book) David Edward Walliams for *Ratburger* (HarperCollins); (new writer) Rachel Joyce for *The Unlikely Pilgrimage of Harold Fry* (Doubleday); (biography/autobiography) Clare Balding for *My Animals and Other Family* (Viking); (popular nonfiction) Miranda Hart for *Is It Just Me?* (Hodder & Stoughton); (audiobook) Sue Townsend for *The Woman Who Went to Bed for a Year,* read by Caroline Quentin (Whole Story); (thriller and crime novel) Lee Child for *A Wanted Man* (Bantam); (food and drink) Si King and Dave Myers for *The Hairy Dieters* (Weidenfeld & Nicholson).

Spur Awards. *Offered by:* Western Writers of America. *Winners:* (short novel) Johnny D. Boggs for *Legacy of a Lawman* (Five Star); (long novel) Stephen Harrigan for *Remember Ben Clayton* (Knopf); (original paperback) Johnny D. Boggs for *West Texas Kill* (Pinnacle); (first novel) Meg Mims for *Double Crossing* (Astraea); (nonfiction biography) Paul Magid for *George Crook* (University of Oklahoma Press); (nonfiction historical) David L. Bigler and Will Bagley for *The Mormon Rebellion* (University of

Oklahoma Press); (nonfiction contemporary) Frederick H. Swanson for *The Bitteroot and Mr. Brandborg* (University of Utah Press); (short story) Rod Miller for "The Death of Delgado" (Western Fictioneers), Clay Reynolds for "The Deacon's Horse" (Ink Brush); (short nonfiction) Paul Andrew Hutton for "The Alamo, Well Remembered" in *Wild West Magazine*; (juvenile fiction) Candace Simar for *Birdie* (North Star); (juvenile nonfiction) Don Nardo for *Migrant Mother* (Capstone); (storyteller award) Bryan Langdo for *Tornado Slim and the Magic Cowboy Hat* (Marshall Cavendish); (fiction drama script) John Logan for "Rango" (Nickelodeon Movies); (documentary script) Cindy Meehl and Julie Goldman for "Buck" (Cedar Creek Productions); (poem) Rod Miller for "Tabula Rasa" (Port Yonder); (song) Jon Chandler for "Morning Star Moon" (Western Dog).

Wallace Stevens Award ($100,000). To recognize outstanding and proven mastery in the art of poetry. *Offered by:* Academy of American Poets. *Winner:* Gary Snyder.

Bram Stoker Awards. For superior horror writing. *Offered by:* Horror Writers Association. *Winners:* (novel) Joe McKinney for *Flesh Eaters* (Pinnacle); (first novel) Allyson Bird for *Isis Unbound* (Dark Regions); (young adult novel—tie) Nancy Holder for *The Screaming Season* (Razorbill), Jonathan Maberry for *Dust and Decay* (Simon & Schuster); (graphic novel) Alan Moore for *Neonomicon* (Avatar); (long fiction) Peter Straub for "The Ballad of Ballard and Sandrine" in *Conjunctions* online magazine; (short fiction) Stephen King for "Herman Wouk Is Still Alive" in the *Atlantic*; (screenplay) Jessica Sharzer for "American Horror Story," episode 12, "Afterbirth" (20th Century Fox); (fiction collection) Joyce Carol Oates for *The Corn Maiden and Other Nightmares* (Mysterious); (anthology) John Skipp, editor, for *Demons: Encounters with the Devil and His Minions, Fallen Angels and the Possessed* (Black Dog & Leventhal); (nonfiction) Rocky Wood for *Stephen King: A Literary Companion* (McFarland); (poetry collection) Linda Addison for *How to Recognize a Demon Has Become Your Friend* (Necon Ebooks); (vampire novel of the century) Richard Matheson for *I Am*

Legend (ORB); (lifetime achievement) Rick Hautala, Joe R. Lansdale.

Stonewall Book Awards. *Offered by:* Gay, Lesbian, Bisexual, and Transgender Round Table, American Library Association. *Winners:* (children's and young adult literature) Bil Wright for *Putting Makeup on the Fat Boy* (Simon & Schuster); (Barbara Gittings Literature Award) Wayne Hoffman for *Sweet Like Sugar* (Kensington); (Israel Fishman Nonfiction Award) Jonathan D. Katz and David C. Ward for *Hide/Seek: Difference and Desire in American Portraiture* (Smithsonian); Michael Bronski for *A Queer History of the United States* (Beacon).

Story Prize. For a collection of short fiction. *Offered by: Story* magazine. *Winner:* Steven Millhauser for *We Others: New and Selected Stories* (Knopf).

Flora Stieglitz Straus Award. For nonfiction books that serve as an inspiration to young readers. *Offered by:* Bank Street College of Education and the Florence M. Miller Memorial Fund. *Winners:* (younger readers) Melissa Sweet for *Balloons Over Broadway: The True Story of the Puppeteer of Macy's Parade* (Houghton Mifflin Harcourt); (older readers) Albert Marrin for *Flesh and Blood So Cheap: The Triangle Fire and Its Legacy* (Knopf).

Mildred and Harold Strauss Livings ($50,000 a year for five years). To two writers of English prose literature to enable them to devote their time exclusively to writing. *Winners:* To be awarded next in 2013.

Theodore Sturgeon Memorial Award. For the year's best short science fiction. *Offered by:* Center for the Study of Science Fiction. *Winner:* Paul McAuley for "The Choice" in *Mammoth Book of Best New SF 25* (Robinson).

Sunburst Awards for Canadian Literature of the Fantastic (C$1,000). *Winners:* (adult) Geoff Ryman for *Paradise Tales* (Small Beer); (young adult) Catherine Austen for *All Good Children* (Orca).

Sunday Times EFG Private Bank Short Story Award (United Kingdom) (£30,000). To an author from any country for an English-language story of 6,000 words or less *Winner:* Kevin Barry for "Beer Trip to Llandudno."

Tanizaki Prize (Japan) (1 million yen, approximately $10,500). For a full-length work of fiction or drama by a professional writer. *Offered by:* Chuokoron-Shinsha, Inc. *Winner:* Genichiro Takahashi for *Sayonara Christopher Robin* (Shinchosha).

Charles Taylor Prize for Literary Nonfiction (Canada) (C$25,000). To honor a book of creative nonfiction widely available in Canada and written by a Canadian citizen or landed immigrant. *Offered by:* Charles Taylor Foundation. *Winner:* Andrew Westoll for *The Chimps of Fauna Sanctuary: A Canadian Story of Resilience and Recovery* (HarperCollins).

Sydney Taylor Children's Book Awards. For a distinguished contribution to Jewish children's literature. *Offered by:* Association of Jewish Libraries. *Winners:* (younger readers) Michael J. Rosen and Robert Sabuda, illustrator, for *Chanukah Lights* (Candlewick); (older readers) Susan Goldman Rubin for *Music Was It: Young Leonard Bernstein* (Charlesbridge); (teen readers) Robert Sharenow for *The Berlin Boxing Club* (HarperTeen).

Sydney Taylor Manuscript Competition ($1,000). For the best fiction manuscript appropriate for readers ages 8–11, both Jewish and non-Jewish, revealing positive aspects of Jewish life, and written by an unpublished author. *Winner:* Not awarded in 2012.

Theatre Library Association Award. See Richard Wall Memorial Award.

Dylan Thomas Prize (£30,000). For a published or produced literary work in the English language, written by an author under 30. *Offered by:* University of Wales. *Winner:* Maggie Shipstead for *Seating Arrangements* (Knopf).

Thriller Awards. *Offered by:* International Thriller Writers. *Winners:* (hardcover novel) Stephen King for *11/23/63* (Scribner); (paperback original) Jeff Abbott for *The Last Minute* (Little, Brown); (first novel) Paul McEuen for *Spiral* (Dial); (short story) Tim L. Williams for "Half-Lives" in *Ellery Queen Mystery Magazine.*

Thurber Prize for American Humor ($5,000). For a humorous book of fiction or nonfiction. *Offered by:* Thurber House. *Winner:* Calvin Trillin for *Quite Enough of Calvin Trillin: Forty Years of Funny Stuff* (Random).

Tom-Gallon Trust Award (United Kingdom) (£1,000). For a short story. *Offered by:* Society of Authors. *Winner:* To be awarded next in 2014.

Betty Trask Prize and Award (United Kingdom). To Commonwealth writers under the age of 35 for "romantic or traditional" first novels. *Offered by:* Society of Authors. *Winners:* (Betty Trask Prize, £8,000) David Whitehouse for *Bed* (Canongate); (Betty Trask Awards, £3,000) Kalinda Ashton for *The Danger Game* (Tindal Street); Elizabeth Day for *Scissors, Paper, Stone* (Bloomsbury); Annabel Pitcher for *My Sister Lives on the Mantelpiece* (Orion); Emma Jane Unsworth for *Hungry the Stars and Everything* (Hidden Gem).

Kate Tufts Discovery Award ($10,000). For a first or very early book of poetry by an emerging poet. *Offered by:* Claremont Graduate School. *Winner:* Katherine Larson for *Radial Symmetry* (Yale University Press).

Kingsley Tufts Poetry Award ($100,000). For a book of poetry by a mid-career poet. *Offered by:* Claremont Graduate School. *Winner:* Timothy Donnelly for *The Cloud Corporation* (Wave).

21st Century Award. To honor recent achievement in writing by an author with ties to Chicago. See Carl Sandburg Literary Awards.

UKLA Children's Book Awards (United Kingdom). *Sponsor:* United Kingdom Literacy Association. *Winners:* (ages 3–6) Catherine Rayner for *Iris and Isaac* (Little Tiger); (ages 7–11) Gill Lewis for *Sky Hawk* (Oxford University Press); (ages 12–16) Patrick Ness and Jim Kay, illustrator, for *A Monster Calls* (Walker).

Ungar German Translation Award. Awarded biennially for a distinguished literary translation from German into English that has been published in the United States. *Offered by:* American Translators Association. *Winner:* To be awarded next in 2013.

John Updike Award ($20,000). Given biennially to a writer in mid-career who has demonstrated consistent excellence. *Offered by:* American Academy of Arts and Letters. *Winner:* To be awarded next in 2013.

VCU/Cabell First Novelist Award ($5,000). For a first novel published in the previous year. *Offered by:* Virginia Commonwealth

University. *Winner:* Justin Torres for *We the Animals!* (Houghton Mifflin Harcourt).

Harold D. Vursell Memorial Award ($10,000). To a writer whose work merits recognition for the quality of its prose style. *Offered by:* American Academy of Arts and Letters. *Winner:* Peter Carey.

Amelia Elizabeth Walden Award ($5,000). To honor a book relevant to adolescents that has enjoyed a wide teenage audience. *Sponsor:* Assembly on Literature for Adolescents, National Council of Teachers of English. *Winner:* Lauren Myracle for *Shine* (Amulet).

Richard Wall Memorial Award (formerly the Theatre Library Association Award). To honor an English-language book of exceptional scholarship in the field of recorded performance, including motion pictures, television, and radio. *Offered by:* Theatre Library Association. *Winners:* Christopher Sieving for *Soul Searching: Black-Themed Cinema from the March on Washington to the Rise of Blaxploitation* (Wesleyan University Press); (special jury prize) Susan Orlean for *Rin Tin Tin: The Life and the Legend* (Simon & Schuster).

Kim Scott Walwyn Prize (United Kingdom) (£1,000). To recognize the professional achievements of women in publishing. *Offered by:* Booktrust. *Winner:* Rukhsana Yasmin.

George Washington Book Prize ($50,000). To recognize an important new book about America's founding era. *Offered by:* Washington College and the Gilder Lehrman Institute of American History. *Winner:* Maya Jasanoff for *Liberty's Exiles: America Loyalists in a Revolutionary World* (Knopf).

Carole Weinstein Poetry Prize ($10,000). To poets with strong connections to the Commonwealth of Virginia who have made a "significant recent contribution to the art of poetry." *Winner:* Kelly Cherry.

Hilary Weston Writers' Trust of Canada Prize for Nonfiction (C$60,000). *Winner:* Candace Savage for *A Geography of Blood: Unearthing Memory from a Prairie Landscape* (Greystone).

Whitbread Book Awards. See Costa Book Awards.

E. B. White Read-Aloud Awards. For children's books with particular appeal as read-aloud books. *Offered by:* American Booksellers Association/Association of Booksellers for Children. *Winners:* (picture book) John Klassen for *I Want My Hat Back* (Candlewick); (middle readers) Maile Meloy and Ian Schoenherr, illustrator, for *The Apothecary* (Putnam), and Colin Meloy and Carson Ellis, illustrator, for *Wildwood* (Balzer + Bray).

Whiting Writers' Awards ($50,000). For emerging writers of exceptional talent and promise. *Offered by:* Mrs. Giles Whiting Foundation. *Winners:* (fiction) Alan Heathcock, Anthony Marra, Hanna Pylväinen; (nonfiction) Sharifa Rhodes-Pitts; (poetry) Ciaran Berry, Atsuro Riley; (plays) Danai Gurira, Samuel D. Hunter, Mona Mansour, Meg Miroshnik.

Walt Whitman Award ($5,000). To a U.S. poet who has not published a book of poems in a standard edition. *Offered by:* Academy of American Poets. *Winner:* Matt Rasmussen for *Black Aperture* (LSU Press).

Richard Wilbur Award ($1,000 and publication by University of Evansville Press). For a book-length poetry collection. *Winner:* William F. Bell for *The Picnic in the Rain.*

Laura Ingalls Wilder Award. Awarded biennially to an author or illustrator whose books have made a substantial and lasting contribution to children's literature. *Offered by:* American Library Association, Association for Library Service to Children. *Winner:* To be awarded next in 2013.

Thornton Wilder Prize for Translation ($20,000). To a practitioner, scholar, or patron who has made a significant contribution to the art of literary translation. *Offered by:* American Academy of Arts and Letters. *Winner:* Michael Hofmann.

Robert H. Winner Memorial Award ($2,500). To a mid-career poet over 40 who has published no more than one book of poetry. *Offered by:* Poetry Society of America. *Winner:* Lise Goett.

George Wittenborn Memorial Book Awards. To North American art publications that represent the highest standards of content, documentation, layout, and format. *Offered by:* Art Libraries Society of North America

(ARLIS/NA). *Winners:* Peter Kort Zegers and Douglas W. Druick, editors, for *Windows on the War: Soviet TASS Posters at Home and Abroad, 1941–1945* (Art Institute of Chicago and Yale University Press).

Thomas Wolfe Award and Lecture. To honor writers with distinguished bodies of work. *Offered by:* Thomas Wolfe Society and University of North Carolina at Chapel Hill. *Winner:* Josephine Humphreys.

Thomas Wolfe Fiction Prize ($1,000). For a short story that honors Thomas Wolfe. *Offered by:* North Carolina Writers Network. *Winner:* Laurel Ferejohn for "That Other Story."

Helen and Kurt Wolff Translator's Prize ($10,000). For an outstanding translation from German into English, published in the United States. *Offered by:* Goethe Institut Inter Nationes, Chicago. *Winner:* Burton Pike for his translation of Gerhard Meier's *Isle of the Dead,* originally published as *Toteninsel* (Dalkey Archive).

Women's Prize for Fiction (United Kingdom). See Orange Prize for Fiction.

World Fantasy Convention Awards. For outstanding fantasy writing. *Offered by:* World Fantasy Convention. *Winners:* (novel) Lavie Tidhar for *Osama* (PS); (novella) K. J. Parker for *A Small Price to Pay for Birdsong* in *Subterranean,* winter 2011; (short story) Ken Liu for "The Paper Menagerie" in *Fantasy & Science Fiction,* March–April 2011; (anthology) Ann and Jeff VanderMeer, editors, for *The Weird* (Tor); (collection) Tim Powers for *The Bible Repairman and Other Stories* (Tachyon and Subterranean); (artist) John Coulthart; (lifetime achievement) Alan Garner, George R. R. Martin.

Writers' Trust Distinguished Contribution Award (Canada). To an individual or an organization in recognition of their long-standing involvement with the Writers' Trust of Canada. *Winner:* Metcalf Foundation.

Writers' Trust Engel/Findley Award (C$25,000). To a Canadian writer predominantly of fiction, for a body of work. *Winner:* Nino Ricci.

Writers' Trust Shaughnessy Cohen Prize for Political Writing (Canada) (C$25,000). For a nonfiction book that captures a subject of political interest. *Sponsor:* CTV. *Winner:* Richard Gwyn for *Nation Maker: Sir John A. Macdonald: His Life, Our Times; Volume Two: 1867–1891* (Random Canada).

Writers' Trust/McClelland & Stewart Journey Prize (Canada) (C$10,000). To a new, developing Canadian author for a short story or an excerpt from a novel in progress. *Offered by:* McClelland & Stewart. *Winner:* Alex Pugsley for "Crisis on Earth-X" in the *Dalhousie Review.*

Writers' Trust Hilary Weston Prize for Nonfiction (Canada). See Hilary Weston Writers' Trust of Canada Prize for Nonfiction.

YALSA Award for Excellence in Nonfiction. For a work of nonfiction published for young adults (ages 12–18). *Offered by:* American Library Association, Young Adult Library Services Association. *Winner:* Steve Sheinkin for *The Notorious Benedict Arnold: A True Story of Adventure, Heroism, and Treachery* (Flash Point/Roaring Brook).

Young Lions Fiction Award ($10,000). For a novel or collection of short stories by an American under the age of 35. *Offered by:* Young Lions of the New York Public Library. *Winner:* Karen Russell for *Swamplandia!* (Knopf).

Morton Dauwen Zabel Award ($10,000). Awarded biennially to a progressive and experimental writer. *Offered by:* American Academy of Arts and Letters. *Winner:* Andrew Sarris.

Zoetrope Short Fiction Prizes. *Offered by:* Zoetrope: All-Story. *Winners:* (first, $1,000) Cody Klippenstein for "Case Studies in Ascension"; (second, $500) Sara C. Thomason for "Liberation Day"; (third, $250) Gillian Colson French for "Ain't You Scared?"

Charlotte Zolotow Award. For outstanding writing in a picture book published in the United States in the previous year. *Offered by:* Cooperative Children's Book Center, University of Wisconsin–Madison. *Winner:* Patrick McDonnell for *Me . . . Jane* (Little, Brown).

Part 6
Directory of Organizations

Directory of Library and Related Organizations

Networks, Consortia, and Other Cooperative Library Organizations

This list is taken from the current edition of *American Library Directory* (Information Today, Inc.), which includes additional information on member libraries and primary functions of each organization.

United States

Alabama

Alabama Health Libraries Assn., Inc. (AL-HeLa), Lister Hill Lib., Univ. of Alabama, Birmingham 35294-0013. SAN 372-8218. Tel. 205-975-8313, fax 205-934-2230. *Pres.* Lee Vacovich.

Library Management Network, Inc. (LMN), 2132 6th Ave S.E., Suite 106, Decatur 35601. SAN 322-3906. Tel. 256-308-2529, fax 256-308-2533. *Systems Coord.* Charlotte Moncrief.

Marine Environmental Sciences Consortium, Dauphin Island Sea Laboratory, Dauphin Island 36528. SAN 322-0001. Tel. 251-861-2141, fax 251-861-4646, e-mail disl@disl.org *Coord.* John Dindo.

Network of Alabama Academic Libraries, c/o Alabama Commission on Higher Education, Montgomery 36104. SAN 322-4570. Tel. 334-242-2211, fax 334-242-0270. *Dir.* Ron P. Leonard.

Alaska

Alaska Library Network (ALN), P.O. Box 100585, Anchorage 99501-0585. SAN 371-0688. Tel. 907-269-6567. *Exec. Dir.* Nina Malyshev.

Arizona

Maricopa County Community College District/Library Technology Services, 2411 W. 14 St., Tempe 85281-6942. SAN 322-0060. Tel. 480-731-8774, fax 480-731-8787. *Dir. of Technical Services* Thomas Saudargas.

Arkansas

Arkansas Area Health Education Center Consortium (AHEC), Sparks Regional Medical Center, Fort Smith 72917-7006. SAN 329-3734. Tel. 479-441-5337, fax 479-441-5339. *Dir.* Grace Anderson.

Arkansas Independent Colleges and Universities, Firstar Bldg., 1 Riverfront Place, Suite 610, North Little Rock 72114. SAN 322-0079. Tel. 501-378-0843, fax 501-374-1523. *Pres.* Kearney E. Dietz.

Mid-America Law Library Consortium (MALLCO), UALR Bowen School of Law Lib., 1203 McMath Ave., Little Rock 72202. Tel. 501-324-9980, fax 501-324-9447, e-mail sdgoldner@ualr.edu. *Exec. Dir.* Susan Goldner.

Northeast Arkansas Hospital Library Consortium, 223 E. Jackson, Jonesboro 72401. SAN 329-529X. Tel. 870-972-1290, fax 870-931-0839. *Dir.* Karen Crosser.

South Arkansas Film Coop., c/o Malvern-Hot Spring County Lib., Malvern 72104. SAN 321-5938. Tel. 501-332-5441, fax 501-332-6679, e-mail hotspringcountylibrary@yahoo.com. *Dir.* Tammy Carter.

California

49-99 Cooperative Library System, c/o Southern California Lib. Cooperative, Monrovia 91016. SAN 301-6218. Tel. 626-359-6111, fax 626-359-0001. *Dir.* Rosario Garza.

Bay Area Library and Information Network (BayNet), c/o San Francisco Public Lib., San Francisco 94702. SAN 371-0610. Tel. 415-355-2826, e-mail infobay@baynetlibs.org. *Pres.* Nicole Greenland.

Berkeley Information Network (BIN), Berkeley Public Lib., Berkeley 94704. Tel. 510-981-6166; 510-981-6150, fax 510-981-6246. *Mgr.* Jane Scantlebury.

Califa, 32 W. 25 Ave., Suite 201, San Mateo 94403. Tel. 650-572-2746, fax 650-349-5089, e-mail califa@califa.org. *Exec. Dir.* Linda Crowe.

Claremont University Consortium (CUC), 150 E. 8 St., Claremont 91711. Tel. 909-621-8026; 909-621-8150, fax 909-621-8681. *CEO* Robert Walton.

Consumer Health Information Program and Services (CHIPS), 12350 Imperial Hwy., Norwalk 90650. SAN 372-8110. Tel. 562-868-4003, fax 562-868-4065, e-mail reference services@gw.colapl.org. *Libn.* Amy Beteilho.

Gold Coast Library Network, 3437 Empresa Drive, Suite C, San Luis Obispo 93401-7355. Tel. 805-543-6082, fax 805-543-9487. *Admin. Dir.* Maureen Theobald.

Monterey Bay Area Cooperative Library System (MOBAC), 2471 Flores St., San Mateo 94403. SAN 301-2921. Tel. 650-349-5538, fax 650-349-5089. *Exec. Dir.* Linda Crowe.

Mountain Valley Library System (MVLS), 2471 Flores St., San Mateo 94403. Tel. 650-349-5538. *Exec. Dir.* Linda Crowe.

National Network of Libraries of Medicine–Pacific Southwest Region (NN/LM-PSR), Louise M. Darling Biomedical Lib., Los Angeles 90095-1798. SAN 372-8234. Tel. 310-825-1200, fax 310-825-5389, e-mail psr-nnlm@library.ucla.edu. *Dir.* Judy Consales.

Nevada Medical Library Group (NMLG), Barton Memorial Hospital Lib., South Lake Tahoe 96150. SAN 370-0445. Tel. 530-543-5844, fax 530-541-4697. *Senior Exec. Coord.* Laurie Anton.

Northern California Assn. of Law Libraries (NOCALL), 268 Bush St., No. 4006, San Francisco 94104. SAN 323-5777. E-mail admin@nocall.org. *Pres.* Coral Henning.

Northern California Consortium of Psychology Libraries (NCCPL), Argosy Univ., San Francisco Bay Area Campus, Alameda 94133. SAN 371-9006. Tel. 510-837-3715. *Pres.* Julie Griffith.

Peninsula Libraries Automated Network (PLAN), 2471 Flores St., San Mateo 94403-4000. SAN 371-5035. Tel. 650-349-5538, fax 650-349-5089. *Dir., Information Technology.* Monica Schultz.

San Bernardino, Inyo, Riverside Counties United Library Services (SIRCULS), 555 W. 6th St., San Bernadino 92410. Tel. 909-381-8257, fax 909-888-3171, e-mail ils@inlandlib.org. *Exec. Dir.* Vera Skop.

San Francisco Biomedical Library Network (SFBLN), San Francisco General Hospital UCSF/Barnett-Briggs Medical Lib., San Francisco 94110. SAN 371-2125. Tel. 415-206-6639, e-mail fishbon@ucsfmedctr.org.

Santa Clarita Interlibrary Network (SCILNET), Powell Lib., Santa Clarita 91321. SAN 371-8964. Tel. 661-259-3540 ext. 3420, fax 661-222-9159. *Libn.* John Stone.

Southern California Library Cooperative (SCLC), 248 E. Foothill Blvd., Suite 101, Monrovia 91016-5522. SAN 371-3865. Tel. 626-359-6111, fax 626-359-0001, e-mail sclchq@socallibraries.org. *Dir.* Rosario Garza.

Substance Abuse Librarians and Information Specialists (SALIS), P.O. Box 9513, Berkeley 94709-0513. SAN 372-4042. Tel. 510-769-1831, fax 510-865-2467, e-mail salis@salis.org. *Exec. Dir.* Andrea L. Mitchell.

Colorado

Automation System Colorado Consortium (ASCC), c/o Delta Public Lib., Delta 81416.

Tel. 970-872-4317. *Technology Consultant* Connie Wolfrom.

Colorado Alliance of Research Libraries, 3801 E. Florida Ave., Suite 515, Denver 80210. SAN 322-3760. Tel. 303-759-3399, fax 303-759-3363. *Exec. Dir.* Alan Charnes.

Colorado Assn. of Law Libraries, P.O. Box 13363, Denver 80201. SAN 322-4325. Tel. 303-492-7535, fax 303-492-2707. *Pres.* Tracy Leming.

Colorado Council of Medical Librarians (CCML), P.O. Box 101058, Denver 80210-1058. SAN 370-0755. Tel. 303-724-2124, fax 303-724-2154. *Pres.* Gene Gardner.

Colorado Library Consortium (CLiC), 7400 E. Arapahoe Rd., Suite 75, Centennial 80112. SAN 371-3970. Tel. 303-422-1150, fax 303-431-9752. *Exec. Dir.* Jim Duncan.

Connecticut

Bibliomation, 32 Crest Rd., Middlebury 06762. Tel. 203-577-4070, fax 203-577-4077. *CEO* Mike Simonds.

Capital Area Health Consortium, 270 Farmington Ave., Suite 352, Farmington 06032-1994. SAN 322-0370. Tel. 860-676-1110, fax 860-676-1303. *Pres.* Karen Goodman.

Connecticut Library Consortium, 234 Court St., Middletown 06457-3304. SAN 322-0389. Tel. 860-344-8777, fax 860-344-9199, e-mail clc@ctlibrarians.org. *Exec. Dir.* Jennifer Keohane.

Council of State Library Agencies in the Northeast (COSLINE), Connecticut State Lib., Hartford 06106. SAN 322-0451. Tel. 860-757-6510, fax 860-757-6503.

CTW Library Consortium, Olin Memorial Lib., Middletown 06459-6065. SAN 329-4587. Tel. 860-685-3887, fax 860-685-2661. *Man. Dir.* Patricia Tully.

Hartford Consortium for Higher Education, 950 Main St., Suite 314, Hartford 06103. SAN 322-0443. Tel. 860-906-5016, fax 860-906-5118. *Exec. Dir.* Rosanne Druckman.

Libraries Online, Inc. (LION), 100 Riverview Center, Suite 252, Middletown 06457. SAN 322-3922. Tel. 860-347-1704, fax 860-346-3707. *Exec. Dir.* Alan Hagyard.

Library Connection, Inc., 599 Matianuck Ave., Windsor 06095-3567. Tel. 860-298-5322, fax 860-298-5328. *Exec. Dir.* George Christian.

Delaware

Central Delaware Library Consortium, Dover Public Lib., Dover 19901. SAN 329-3696. Tel. 302-736-7030, fax 302-736-5087. *Dir.* Margery Kirby Cyr.

Delaware Library Consortium (DLC), Delaware Academy of Medicine, Newark 19713. SAN 329-3718. Tel. 302-733-1122, fax 302-733-3885, e-mail library@delamed.org. *Dir.* P. J. Grier.

District of Columbia

Computer Sciences Corporation/ERIC Project, 655 15th St. N.W., Suite 500, Washington 20005. SAN 322-161X. Tel. 202-741-4200, fax 202-628-3205. *Dir.* Lawrence Henry.

Council for Christian Colleges and Universities, 321 8th St. N.E., Washington 20002. SAN 322-0524. Tel. 202-546-8713, fax 202-546-8913, e-mail council@cccu.org. *Pres.* Paul R. Corts.

District of Columbia Area Health Science Libraries (DCAHSL), PO Box 96920, Washington 20090. SAN 323-9918. Tel. 202-863-2518, fax 202-484-1595, e-mail resources@acog.org. *Pres.* Debra Scarborough.

FEDLINK/Federal Library and Information Network, c/o Federal Lib. and Info. Center Committee, Washington 20540-4935. SAN 322-0761. Tel. 202-707-4800, fax 202-707-4818, e-mail flicc@loc.gov. *Exec. Dir.* Roberta I. Shaffer.

Interlibrary Users Assn. (IUA), c/o Urban Institute Lib., Washington 20037. SAN 322-1628. Tel. 202-261-5534, fax 202-223-3043. *Pres.* Nancy L. Minter.

Transportation Research Board, 500 5th St. N.W., Washington 20001. SAN 370-582X. Tel. 202-334-2990, fax 202-334-2527. *Mgr., Info. Services* Barbara Post.

Washington Theological Consortium, 487 Michigan Ave. N.E., Washington 20017-1585. SAN 322-0842. Tel. 202-832-2675, fax 202-526-0818, e-mail wtc@washtheocon.org. *Exec. Dir.* Larry Golemon.

Florida

Central Florida Library Cooperative (CFLC), 431 E. Horatio Ave., Suite 230, Maitland 32751. SAN 371-9014. Tel. 407-644-9050, fax 407-644-7023, e-mail contactus@cflc. net. *Exec. Dir.* Marta Westall.

College Center for Library Automation (CCLA), 1753 W. Paul Dirac Drive, Tallahassee 32310. Tel. 850-922-6044, fax 850-922-4869, e-mail servicedesk@cclaflorida. org. *Exec. Dir.* Richard Madaus.

Florida Center for Library Automation (FCLA), 5830 N.W. 39 Ave., Gainesville 32606. Tel. 352-392-9020, fax 352-392-9185, e-mail fclmin@ufl.edu. *Dir.* James Corey.

Florida Library Information Network, R. A. Gray Bldg., Tallahassee 32399-0250. SAN 322-0869. Tel. 850-245-6600, fax 850-245-6744, e-mail library@dos.myflorida.com. *Bureau Chief* Cathy Moloney.

Northeast Florida Library Information Network (NEFLIN), 2233 Park Ave., Suite 402, Orange Park 32073. Tel. 904-278-5620, fax 904-278-5625, e-mail office@neflin.org. *Exec. Dir.* Brad Ward.

Panhandle Library Access Network (PLAN), Five Miracle Strip Loop, Suite 8, Panama City Beach 32407-3850. SAN 370-047X. Tel. 850-233-9051, fax 850-235-2286. *Exec. Dir.* William P. Conniff.

SEFLIN/Southeast Florida Library Information Network, Inc, Wimberly Lib., Office 452, Boca Raton 33431. SAN 370-0666. Tel. 561-208-0984, fax 561-208-0995. *Exec. Dir.* Jeannette Smithee.

Southwest Florida Library Network (SWFLN), Bldg. III, Unit 7, Fort Myers 33913. Tel. 239-225-4225, fax 239-225-4229, e-mail swfln@fgcu.edu. *Exec. Dir.* Sondra Taylor-Furbee.

Tampa Bay Library Consortium, Inc., 1202 Tech Blvd., Suite 202, Tampa 33619. SAN 322-371X. Tel. 813-740-3963; 813-622-8252, fax 813-628-4425. *Exec. Dir.* Charlie Parker.

Tampa Bay Medical Library Network (TA-BAMLN), Florida Hospital College of Health Sciences, Orlando 32803-1226. SAN 322-0885. Tel. 407-303-9798, fax 407-303-9408. *Pres.* Deanna Stevens.

Georgia

Assn. of Southeastern Research Libraries (ASERL), c/o LYRASIS, Atlanta 30309-2955. SAN 322-1555. Tel. 404-892-0943, fax 404-892-7879. *Exec. Dir.* John Burger.

Atlanta Health Science Libraries Consortium, Fran Golding Medical Lib. at Scottish Rite, Atlanta 30342-1600. Tel. 404-785-2157, fax 404-785-2155. *Pres.* Kate Daniels.

Atlanta Regional Council for Higher Education (ARCHE), 50 Hurt Plaza, Suite 735, Atlanta 30303-2923. SAN 322-0990. Tel. 404-651-2668, fax 404-880-9816, e-mail arche@ atlantahighered.org. *Admin. Coord.* Jackie Smith.

Georgia Online Database (GOLD), c/o Public Lib. Services, Atlanta 30345-4304. SAN 322-094X. Tel. 404-235-7200, fax 404-235-7201. *Asst. State Libn. for Lib. Development* Alan Harkness.

LYRASIS, 1438 W. Peachtree St. N.W., Suite 200, Atlanta 30309-2955. SAN 322-0974. Tel. 404-892-0943, fax 404-892-7879. *Exec. Dir.* Kate Nevins.

Metro Atlanta Library Assn. (MALA), P.O. Box 14948, Atlanta 30324. SAN 378-2549. Tel. 678-915-7207, fax 678-915-7471, e-mail mala-a@comcast.net. *Pres.* Steven Vincent.

Hawaii

Hawaii Library Consortium (HLC), c/o Hawaii Business Research Lib., Kihei 96753. Tel. 808-875-2408. *Pres.* Sonia I. King.

Hawaii-Pacific Chapter, Medical Library Assn. (HPC-MLA), Health Sciences Lib., Honolulu 96813. SAN 371-3946. Tel. 808-692-0810, fax 808-692-1244. *Chair* A. Lee Adams.

Idaho

Canyon Owyhee Library Group, Ltd. (COLG), 203 E. Owyhee Ave., Homedale 83628. Tel. 208-337-4613, fax 208-337-4933. *Pres.* Sara Murphy.

Cooperative Information Network (CIN), 8385 N. Government Way, Hayden 83835-9280. SAN 323-7656. Tel. 208-772-5612, fax 208-772-2498, e-mail hay@cin.kcl.org. *Fiscal Agent* John W. Hartung.

Idaho Health Information Assn. (IHIA), c/o Eastern Idaho Regional Medical Center, Idaho Falls 83403. SAN 371-5078. Tel. 208-529-6077, fax 208-529-7014. *Dir.* Kathy Fatkin.

Library Consortium of Eastern Idaho (LCEI), 149 South Main, Soda Springs 83276. SAN 323-7699. Tel. 208-547-2606. *Pres.* Cindy Erickson.

LYNX Consortium, c/o Boise Public Lib., Boise 83702-7195. SAN 375-0086. Tel. 208-384-4238, fax 208-384-4025.

Illinois

American Theological Library Assn. (ATLA), 300 S. Wacker Drive, Suite 2100, Chicago 60606-5889. SAN 371-9022. Tel. 312-454-5100, fax 312-454-5505, e-mail atla@atla.com. *Exec. Dir.* Brenda Bailey-Hainer.

Areawide Hospital Library Consortium of Southwestern Illinois (AHLC), c/o St. Elizabeth Hospital Health Sciences Lib., Belleville 62222. SAN 322-1016. Tel. 618-234-2120 ext. 2011, fax 618-222-4614.

Assn. of Chicago Theological Schools (ACTS), Univ. of St. Mary of the Lake, Mundelein 60060-1174. SAN 370-0658. Tel. 847-566-6401. *Chair* Thomas Baima.

Center for Research Libraries, 6050 S. Kenwood, Chicago 60637-2804. SAN 322-1032. Tel. 773-955-4545, fax 773-955-4339. *Pres.* Bernard F. Reilly.

Chicago and South Consortium, Jackson Park Hospital and Medical Center, Chicago 60649-3993. SAN 322-1067. Tel. 773-947-7653. *Coord.* Andrew Paradise.

Chicago Area Museum Libraries (CAML), c/o Lib., Field Museum, Chicago 60605-2496. SAN 371-392X. Tel. 312-665-7970, fax 312-665-7893. *Museum Libn.* Christine Giannoni.

Committee on Institutional Cooperation, 1819 S. Neil St., Suite D, Champaign 61820-7271. Tel. 217-333-8475, fax 217-244-7127, e-mail cic@staff.cic.net. *Dir.* Barbara Mcfadden Allen.

Consortium of Academic and Research Libraries in Illinois (CARLI), 100 Trade Center Drive, Suite 303, Champaign 61820. SAN 322-3736. Tel. 217-244-7593, fax 217-244-7596, e-mail support@carli.illinois.edu. *Exec. Dir.* Susan Singleton.

Council of Directors of State University Libraries in Illinois (CODSULI), Southern Illinois Univ. School of Medicine Lib., Springfield 62702-4910. SAN 322-1083. Tel. 217-545-0994, fax 217-545-0988.

East Central Illinois Consortium, Booth Lib., Eastern Illinois Univ., Charleston 61920. SAN 322-1040. Tel. 217-581-7549, fax 217-581-7534. *Mgr.* Stacey Knight-Davis.

Fox Valley Health Science Library Consortium, c/o Delnor-Community Hospital, Geneva 60134. SAN 329-3831. Tel. 630-208-4299.

Heart of Illinois Library Consortium, 511 N.E. Greenleaf, Peoria 61603. SAN 322-1113. *Chair* Leslie Menz.

Illinois Library and Information Network (IL-LINET), c/o Illinois State Lib., Springfield 62701-1796. SAN 322-1148. Tel. 217-782-2994, fax 217-785-4326. *Dir.* Anne Craig.

Illinois Office of Educational Services, 2450 Foundation Drive, Suite 100, Springfield 62703-5464. SAN 371-5108. Tel. 217-786-3010, fax 217-786-3020, e-mail info@ioes.org. *Dir.* Rebecca Woodhull.

LIBRAS, Inc., North Park Univ., Chicago 60625-4895. SAN 322-1172. Tel. 773-244-5584, fax 773-244-4891. *Pres.* Mark Vargas.

Metropolitan Consortium of Chicago, Chicago School of Professional Psychology, Chicago 60610. SAN 322-1180. Tel. 312-329-6633, fax 312-644-6075. *Coord.* Margaret White.

National Network of Libraries of Medicine– Greater Midwest Region (NN/LM-GMR), c/o Lib. of Health Sciences, Univ. of Illinois at Chicago, Chicago 60612-4330. SAN 322-1202. Tel. 312-996-2464, fax 312-996-2226. *Dir.* Kathryn Carpenter.

Network of Illinois Learning Resources in Community Colleges (NILRC), PO Box 120, Blanchardville 53516-0120. Tel. 608-523-4094, fax 608-523-4072. *Business Mgr.* Lisa Sikora.

System Wide Automated Network (SWAN), c/o Metropolitan Lib. System, Burr Ridge 60527-5783. Tel. 630-734-5000, fax 630-734-5050. *Dir.* Aaron Skog.

Indiana

Central Indiana Health Science Libraries Consortium, Indiana Univ. School of Medicine Lib., Indianapolis 46202. SAN 322-1245.

Tel. 317-274-8358, fax 317-274-4056. *Officer* Elaine Skopelja.

Consortium of College and University Media Centers (CCUMC), Indiana Univ., Bloomington 47405-1223. SAN 322-1091. Tel. 812-855-6049, fax 812-855-2103, e-mail ccumc @ccumc.org. *Exec. Dir.* Aileen Scales.

Evansville Area Library Consortium, 3700 Washington Ave., Evansville 47750. SAN 322-1261. Tel. 812-485-4151, fax 812-485-7564. *Coord.* Jane Saltzman.

Evergreen Indiana Consortium, Indiana State Lib., Indianapolis 46202. Tel. 317-605-4518, fax 317-232-0002. *Coord.* Shauna Borger.

Indiana State Data Center, Indiana State Lib., Indianapolis 46202. SAN 322-1318. Tel. 317-232-3733, fax 317-232-3728. *Coord.* Katie Springer.

Northeast Indiana Health Science Libraries Consortium (NEIHSL), Univ. of Saint Francis Vann Lib., Fort Wayne 46808. SAN 373-1383. Tel. 260-399-7700 ext. 6065, fax 260-399-8166. *Coord.* Lauralee Aven.

Iowa

Consortium of User Libraries (CUL), Lib. for the Blind and Physically Handicapped, Des Moines 50309-2364. Tel. 515-281-1333, fax 515-281-1378; 515-281-1263.

Dubuque (Iowa) Area Library Information Consortium, c/o Burton Payne Lib., N.E. Iowa Community College, Peosta 52068. Tel. 563-556-5110 ext. 269, fax 563-557-0340. *Coord.* Deb Seiffert.

Iowa Private Academic Library Consortium (IPAL), c/o Buena Vista Univ. Lib., Storm Lake 50588. SAN 329-5311. Tel. 712-749-2127, 712-749-2203, fax 712-749-2059, e-mail library@bvu.edu. *Pres.* Rodney N. Henshaw.

Linn County Library Consortium, Russell D. Cole Lib., Mount Vernon 52314-1012. SAN 322-4597. Tel. 319-895-4259. *Pres.* Jason Bengtson.

Polk County Biomedical Consortium, c/o Broadlawns Medical Center Lib., Des Moines 50314. SAN 322-1431. Tel. 515-282-2394, fax 515-282-5634. *Treas.* Elaine Hughes.

Quad City Area Biomedical Consortium, Great River Medical Center Lib., West Burlington 52655. SAN 322-435X. Tel. 319-768-4075, fax 319-768-4080. *Coord.* Sarah Goff.

Sioux City Library Cooperative (SCLC), c/o Sioux City Public Lib., Sioux City 51101-1203. SAN 329-4722. Tel. 712-255-2933 ext. 255, fax 712-279-6432. *Chair* Betsy Thompson.

State of Iowa Libraries Online (SILO), State Lib. of Iowa, Des Moines 50319. SAN 322-1415. Tel. 515-281-4105, fax 515-281-6191. *State Libn.* Mary Wegner.

Kansas

Associated Colleges of Central Kansas (ACCK), 210 S. Main St., McPherson 67460. SAN 322-1474. Tel. 620-241-5150, fax 620-241-5153.

Dodge City Library Consortium, c/o Comanche Intermediate Center, Dodge City 67801. SAN 322-4368. Tel. 620-227-1609, fax 620-227-4862.

Kansas Regents Library Database Consortium (RLDC), c/o Emporia State Univ., Emporia 66801. Tel. 620-341-5480, e-mail rldc@ ku.edu. *Chair* Cynthia Akers.

State Library of Kansas/Statewide Resource Sharing Div., 300 S.W. 10 Ave., Room 343 N., Topeka 66612-1593. SAN 329-5621. Tel. 785-296-3875, fax 785-368-7291. *Dir.* Patti Butcher.

Kentucky

Assn. of Independent Kentucky Colleges and Universities (AIKCU), 484 Chenault Rd., Frankfort 40601. SAN 322-1490. Tel. 502-695-5007, fax 502-695-5057. *Pres.* Gary S. Cox.

Eastern Kentucky Health Science Information Network (EKHSIN), c/o Camden-Carroll Lib., Morehead 40351. SAN 370-0631. Tel. 606-783-6860, fax 606-784-2178. *Lib. Dir.* Tammy Jenkins.

Kentuckiana Metroversity, Inc., 109 E. Broadway, Louisville 40202. SAN 322-1504. Tel. 502-897-3374, fax 502-895-1647.

Kentucky Medical Library Assn., VA Medical Center, Lib. Serices 142D, Louisville 40206-1499. SAN 370-0623. Tel. 502-287-6240, fax 502-287-6134. *Head Libn.* Gene M. Haynes.

Southeastern Chapter of the American Assn. of Law Libraries (SEAALL), c/o Univ. of Kentucky Law Lib., Lexington 40506-0048. Tel. 859-257-8347, fax 859-323-4906. *Pres.* Amy Osborne.

Theological Education Assn. of Mid America (TEAM-A), Southern Baptist Theological Seminary, Louisville 40280. SAN 377-5038. Tel. 502-897-4807, fax 502-897-4600. *Dir., Info. Resources* Ken Boyd.

Louisiana

Central Louisiana Medical Center Library Consortium (CLMLC), 2495 Shreveport Hwy., 142D, Alexandria 71306. Tel. 318-619-9102, fax 318-619-9144, e-mail clmlc 8784@yahoo.com. *Coord.* Miriam J. Brown.

Health Sciences Library Assn. of Louisiana (HSLAL), LSUHSC Lib., Shreveport 71103. SAN 375-0035. *Pres.* Marlene Bishop.

Loan SHARK, State Lib. of Louisiana, Baton Rouge 70802. SAN 371-6880. Tel. 225-342-4920, 342-4918, fax 225-219-4725. *Head, Access Services* Kytara A. Gaudin.

LOUIS/Louisiana Library Network, Info. Technology Services, Baton Rouge 70803. *Exec. Dir.* Sara Zimmerman.

New Orleans Educational Telecommunications Consortium, 6400 Press Dr., New Orleans 70126. SAN 329-5214. Tel. 504-524-0350, e-mail noetc@noetc.org.

Maine

Health Science Library Information Consortium (HSLIC), 211 Marginal Way, No 245, Portland 04101. SAN 322-1601. Tel. 207-795-2561, fax 207-795-2569. *Chair* Kathy Brunjes.

Maryland

Maryland Assn. of Health Science Librarians (MAHSL), VA Medical HealthCare System Medical Lib., Baltimore 21201. SAN 377-5070. Tel. 401-605-7093. *Co-Pres.* Brittany Rice.

Maryland Interlibrary Loan Organization (MILO), c/o Enoch Pratt Free Lib., Baltimore 21201-4484. SAN 343-8600. Tel. 410-396-5498, fax 410-396-5837, e-mail milo@ prattlibrary.org. *Mgr.* Emma E. Beaven.

National Network of Libraries of Medicine (NN/LM), National Lib. of Medicine, Bethesda 20894. SAN 373-0905. Tel. 301-496-4777, fax 301-480-1467. *Dir.* Angela Ruffin.

National Network of Libraries of Medicine–Southeastern Atlantic Region (NN/LM-SEA), Univ. of Maryland Health Sciences and Human Services Lib., Baltimore 21201-1512. SAN 322-1644. Tel. 410-706-2855, fax 410-706-0099, e-mail hshsl-nlmsea@ hshsl.umaryland.edu. *Dir.* Mary J. Tooey.

U.S. National Library of Medicine (NLM), 8600 Rockville Pike, Bethesda 20894. SAN 322-1652. Tel. 301-594-5983, fax 301-402-1384, e-mail custserv@nlm.nih.gov. *Coord.* Martha Fishel.

Washington Research Library Consortium (WRLC), 901 Commerce Drive, Upper Marlboro 20774. SAN 373-0883. Tel. 301-390-2000, fax 301-390-2020. *Exec. Dir.* Mark Jacobs.

Massachusetts

Boston Biomedical Library Consortium (BBLC), c/o Dana Farber Cancer Trust, Boston 02115. SAN 322-1725. *Interim Exec. Dir.* Margret Branschofsky.

Boston Library Consortium, Inc., McKim Bldg., Boston 02117. SAN 322-1733. Tel. 617-262-6244, fax 617-262-0163, e-mail admin@blc.org. *Exec. Dir.* Melissa Trevvett.

Cape Libraries Automated Materials Sharing Network (CLAMS), 270 Communication Way, Unit 4E, Hyannis 02601. SAN 370-579X. Tel. 508-790-4399, fax 508-771-4533. *Exec. Dir.* Gayle Simundza.

Central and Western Massachusetts Automated Resource Sharing (C/W MARS), 67 Millbrook St., Suite 201, Worcester 01606. SAN 322-3973. Tel. 508-755-3323 ext. 30, fax 508-755-3721. *Exec. Dir.* Joan Kuklinski.

Cooperating Libraries of Greater Springfield (CLGS), Springfield Technical Community College, Springfield 01102. SAN 322-1768. Tel. 413-755-4565, fax 413-755-6315, e-mail lcoakley@stcc.edu. *Coord.* Lynn Coakley.

Fenway Libraries Online, Inc. (FLO), c/o Wentworth Institute of Technology, Boston 02115. SAN 373-9112. Tel. 617-442-2384, fax 617-442-1519. *Exec. Dir.* Walter Stine.

Massachusetts Health Sciences Libraries Network (MAHSLIN), Lamar Soutter Lib., Univ. of Massachusetts Medical School, Worcester 01655. SAN 372-8293. http://nahsl.libguides.com/mahslin/home. *Chair* Jane Ichord.

Merrimack Valley Library Consortium, 1600 Osgood St., North Andover 01845. SAN 322-4384. Tel. 978-557-1050, fax 978-557-8101, e-mail netmail@mvlc.org. *Exec. Dir.* Lawrence Rungren.

Minuteman Library Network, 10 Strathmore Rd., Natick 01760-2419. SAN 322-4252. Tel. 508-655-8008, fax 508-655-1507. *Exec. Dir.* Susan McAlister.

National Network of Libraries of Medicine–New England Region (NN/LM-NER), Univ. of Massachusetts Medical School, Shrewsbury 01545-2732. SAN 372-5448. Tel. 508-856-5979, fax 508-856-5977. *Dir.* Elaine Martin.

North of Boston Library Exchange, Inc. (NOBLE), 26 Cherry Hill Drive, Danvers 01923. SAN 322-4023. Tel. 978-777-8844, fax 978-750-8472. *Exec. Dir.* Ronald A. Gagnon.

Northeast Consortium of Colleges and Universities in Massachusetts (NECCUM), Merrimack College, North Andover 01845. SAN 371-0602. Tel. 978-556-3400, fax 978-556-3738. *Pres.* Richard Santagati.

Northeastern Consortium for Health Information (NECHI), Lowell General Hospital Health Science Lib., Lowell 01854. SAN 322-1857. Tel. 978-937-6247, fax 978-937-6855. *Libn.* Donna Beales.

SAILS, Inc., 547 W. Groves St., Suite 4, Middleboro 02346. SAN 378-0058. Tel. 508-946-8600, fax 508-946-8605. *Pres.* Robin Glasser.

Southeastern Massachusetts Consortium of Health Science Libraries (SEMCO), Charlton Medical Lib., Fall River 02720. SAN 322-1873. Tel. 508-679-7196, fax 508-679-7458. *Chair* Nicola Pallotti.

Western Massachusetts Health Information Consortium, Baystate Medical Center Health Sciences Lib., Springfield 01199. SAN 329-4579. Tel. 413-794-1865, fax 413-794-1974. *Pres.* Susan La Forter.

Michigan

Detroit Area Consortium of Catholic Colleges, c/o Sacred Heart Seminary, Detroit 48206.

SAN 329-482X. Tel. 313-883-8500, fax 313-883-8594. *Dir.* Chris Spilker.

Detroit Area Library Network (DALNET), 6th Floor SEL, 5048 Gullen Mall, Detroit 48202. Tel. 313-577-6789, fax 313-577-1231, info@dalnet.org. *Exec. Dir.* Steven K. Bowers.

Lakeland Library Cooperative, 4138 Three Mile Rd. N.W., Grand Rapids 49534-1134. SAN 308-132X. Tel. 616-559-5253, fax 616-559-4329. *Dir.* Sandra Wilson.

The Library Network (TLN), 41365 Vincenti Ct., Novi 48375. SAN 370-596X. Tel. 248-536-3100, fax 248-536-3099. *Dir.* James Pletz.

Michigan Health Sciences Libraries Assn. (MHSLA), 1407 Rensen St., Suite 4, Lansing 48910. SAN 323-987X. Tel. 517-394-2774, fax 517-394-2675. *Pres.* Sheila Bryant.

Mideastern Michigan Library Cooperative, 503 S. Saginaw St., Suite 839, Flint 48502. SAN 346-5187. Tel. 810-232-7119, fax 810-232-6639. *Dir.* Denise Hooks.

Mid-Michigan Library League, 210 1/2 N Mitchell, Cadillac 49601-1835. SAN 307-9325. Tel. 231-775-3037, fax 231-775-1749. *Dir.* James Lawrence.

PALnet, 1040 W Bristol Rd., Flint 48507. Tel. 810-766-4070. *Dir.* Vince Molosky.

Southeastern Michigan League of Libraries (SEMLOL), Lawrence Technological Univ., Southfield 48075. SAN 322-4481. Tel. 248-204-3000, fax 248-204-3005. *Treas.* Gary Cocozzoli.

Southwest Michigan Library Cooperative, Willard Public Library, Battle Creek, 49017. SAN 308-2156. Tel. 269-968-8166, e-mail rhulsey@willard.lib.mi.us. *Dir.* Rick Hulsey.

Suburban Library Cooperative (SLC), 44750 Delco Blvd., Sterling Heights 48313. SAN 373-9082. Tel. 586-685-5750, fax 586-685-3010. *Interim Dir.* Arthur M. Woodford.

Upper Peninsula of Michigan Health Science Library Consortium, c/o Marquette Health System Hospital, Marquette 49855. SAN 329-4803. Tel. 906-225-3429, fax 906-225-3524. *Lib. Mgr.* Janis Lubenow.

Upper Peninsula Region of Library Cooperation, Inc., 1615 Presque Isle Ave., Marquette 49855. SAN 329-5540. Tel. 906-228-7697, fax 906-228-5627. *Treas.* Suzanne Dees.

Valley Library Consortium, 3210 Davenport Ave., Saginaw 48602-3495. Tel. 989-497-0925, fax 989-497-0918. *Exec. Dir.* Randall Martin.

Minnesota

Capital Area Library Consortium (CALCO), c/o Minnesota Dept. of Transportation, Lib. MS155, Saint Paul 55155. SAN 374-6127. Tel. 651-296-5272, fax 651-297-2354. *Libn.* Shirley Sherkow.

Central Minnesota Libraries Exchange (CMLE), Miller Center, Room 130-D, Saint Cloud 56301-4498. SAN 322-3779. Tel. 320-308-2950, fax 320-654-5131, e-mail cmle@stcloudstate.edu. *Dir.* Patricia A. Post.

Cooperating Libraries in Consortium (CLIC), 1619 Dayton Ave., Suite 204, Saint Paul 55104. SAN 322-1970. Tel. 651-644-3878, fax 651-644-6258. *Exec. Dir.* Ruth Duke-low.

Metronet, 1619 Dayton Ave., Suite 314, Saint Paul 55104. SAN 322-1989. Tel. 651-646-0475, fax 651-649-3169, e-mail information @metrolibraries.net. *Exec. Dir.* Ann Walker Smalley.

Metropolitan Library Service Agency (MEL-SA), 1619 Dayton Ave., No. 314, Saint Paul 55104-6206. SAN 371-5124. Tel. 651-645-5731, fax 651-649-3169, e-mail melsa@ melsa.org. *Exec. Dir.* Chris D. Olson.

MINITEX Library Information Network, 15 Andersen Lib., Univ. of Minnesota–Twin Cities, Minneapolis 55455-0439. SAN 322-1997. Tel. 612-624-4002, fax 612-624-4508. *Assoc. Dir.* Mary Parker.

Minnesota Library Information Network (MnLINK), Univ. of Minnesota–Twin Cities, Minneapolis 55455-0439. Tel. 612-624-8096, fax 612-624-4508. *Info. Specialist* Nick Banitt.

Minnesota Theological Library Assn. (MTLA), Luther Seminary Lib., Saint Paul 55108. SAN 322-1962. Tel. 651-641-3447. *Chair* David Stewart.

North Country Library Cooperative, 5528 Emerald Ave., Mountain Iron 55768-2069. SAN 322-3795. Tel. 218-741-1907, fax 218-741-1908. *Dir.* Linda J. Wadman.

Northern Lights Library Network, 103 Graystone Plaza, Detroit Lakes 56501-3041. SAN 322-2004. Tel. 218-847-2825, fax 218-

847-1461, e-mail nloffice@nlln.org. *Exec. Dir.* Kathy B. Enger.

SMILE (Southcentral Minnesota Inter-Library Exchange), 1400 Madison Ave., No. 622, Mankato 56001. SAN 321-3358. Tel. 507-625-7555, fax 507-625-4049, e-mail smile@tds.lib.mn.us. *Dir.* Nancy Katharine Steele.

Southeastern Libraries Cooperating (SELCO), 2600 19th St. N.W., Rochester 55901-0767. SAN 308-7417. Tel. 507-288-5513, fax 507-288-8697. *Exec. Dir.* Ann Hutton.

Southwest Area Multicounty Multitype Interlibrary Exchange (SAMMIE), 109 S. 5 St., Suite 30, Marshall 56258-1240. SAN 322-2039. Tel. 507-532-9013, fax 507-532-2039, e-mail info@sammie.org. *Dir.* Robin Chaney.

Twin Cities Biomedical Consortium (TCBC), c/o Fairview Univ. Medical Center, Minneapolis 55455. SAN 322-2055. Tel. 612-273-6595, fax 612-273-2675. *Mgr.* Colleen Olsen.

Mississippi

Central Mississippi Library Council (CMLC), c/o Millsaps College Lib., Jackson 39210. SAN 372-8250. Tel. 601-974-1070, fax 601-974-1082. *Admin./Treas.* Tom Henderson.

Mississippi Electronic Libraries Online (MELO), Mississippi State Board for Community and Junior Colleges, Jackson 39211. Tel. 601-432-6518, fax 601-432-6363, e-mail melo@colin.edu. *Dir.* Audra Kimball.

Missouri

Greater Western Library Alliance (GWLA), 5109 Cherry St., Kansas City 64110. Tel. 816-926-8765, fax 816-926-8790. *Exec. Dir.* Joni Blake.

Health Sciences Library Network of Kansas City (HSLNKC), Univ. of Missouri–Kansas City Health Sciences Lib., Kansas City 64108-2792. SAN 322-2098. Tel. 816-235-1880, fax 816-235-6570. *Dir.* Peggy Mullaly-Quijas.

Kansas City Library Service Program (KC-LSP), 14 W. 10 St., Kansas City 64105. Tel. 816-701-3520, fax 816-701-3401, e-mail kclcsupport@kclibrary.org. *Dir. of Business and Library Systems* Steven Knapp.

Mid-America Library Alliance/Kansas City Metropolitan Library and Information Network, 15624 E. 24 Hwy., Independence 64050. SAN 322-2101. Tel. 816-521-7257, fax 816-461-0966. *Exec. Dir.* Susan Burton.

Saint Louis Regional Library Network, 341 Sappington Rd., Saint Louis 63122. SAN 322-2209. Tel. 314-395-1305.

Western Council of State Libraries, Inc., c/o Missouri State Lib., P.O. Box, 387, Jefferson City 65102-0387. Tel. 573-751-2751, e-mail margaret.conroy@sos.mo.gov. *Pres.* Margaret M. Conroy.

Nebraska

ICON Library Consortium, McGoogan Lib. of Medicine, Univ. of Nebraska, Omaha 68198-6705. Tel. 402-559-7099, fax 402-559-5498.

Southeast Nebraska Library System, 5730 R St., Suite C-1, Lincoln 68505. SAN 322-4732. Tel. 402-467-6188, fax 402-467-6196. *Pres.* Glenda Willnerd.

Nevada

Desert States Law Library Consortium, Wiener-Rogers Law Lib., William S. Boyd School of Law, Las Vegas 89154-1080. Tel. 702-895-2400, fax 702-895-2416. *Collection Development Libn.* Matthew Wright.

Information Nevada, Interlibrary Loan Dept., Nevada State Lib. and Archives, Carson City 89701-4285. SAN 322-2276. Tel. 775-684-3328, fax 775-684-3330. *Asst. Admin., Lib. and Development Services* Karen Starr.

New Hampshire

GMILCS, Inc., 1701B Hooksett Rd., Hooksett 03106. Tel. 603-485-4286, fax 603-485-4246, e-mail helpdesk@gmilcs.org. *Chair* Dianne Hathaway.

Health Sciences Libraries of New Hampshire and Vermont, Breene Memorial Lib., New Hampshire Hospital, Concord 03246. SAN 371-6864. Tel. 603-527-2837, fax 603-527-7197. *Admin. Coord.* Marion Allen.

Librarians of the Upper Valley Coop. (LUV Coop), c/o Hanover Town Lib., Etna 03750. SAN 371-6856. Tel. 603-643-3116. *Coord.* Barbara Prince.

Merri-Hill-Rock Library Cooperative, c/o Kimball Lib., Atkinson 03811-2299. SAN 329-5338. Tel. 603-362-5234, fax 603-362-4791. *Interim Dir.* Caroline Birr.

New England Law Library Consortium, Inc. (NELLCO), 9 Drummer Rd., Keene 03431. SAN 322-4244. Tel. 603-357-3385, fax 603-357-2075. *Exec. Dir.* Tracy L. Thompson-Przylucki.

New Hampshire College and University Council, 3 Barrell Court, Suite 100, Concord 03301-8543. SAN 322-2322. Tel. 603-225-4199, fax 603-225-8108. *Pres.* Thomas R. Horgan.

Nubanusit Library Cooperative, c/o Peterborough Town Lib., Peterborough 03458. SAN 322-4600. Tel. 603-924-8040, fax 603-924-8041.

New Jersey

Basic Health Sciences Library Network (BHSL), Overlook Hospital Health Science Lib., Summit 07902. SAN 371-4888. Tel. 908-522-2886, fax 908-522-2274. *Coord.* Pat Regenberg.

Bergen Passaic Health Sciences Library Consortium, c/o Health Sciences Lib., Englewood Hospital and Medical Center, Englewood 07631. SAN 371-0904. Tel. 201-894-3069, fax 201-894-9049. *Coord.* Lia Sabbagh.

Burlington Libraries Information Consortium (BLINC), 5 Pioneer Blvd., Westampton 08060. Tel. 609-267-9660, fax 609-267-4091, e-mail hq@bcls.lib.nj.us. *Coord.* Gale Sweet.

Integrated Information Solutions, 600 Mountain Ave., Room 1B 202, Murray Hill 07974. SAN 329-5400. Tel. 908-582-4840, fax 908-582-3146. *Mgr.* M. E. Brennan.

Libraries of Middlesex Automation Consortium (LMxAC), 1030 Saint Georges Ave., Suite 203, Avenel 07001. SAN 329-448X. Tel. 732-750-2525, fax 732-750-9392. *Exec. Dir.* Eileen Palmer.

LibraryLinkNJ, New Jersey Library Cooperative, 44 Stelton Rd., Suite 330, Piscataway 08854. SAN 371-5116. Tel. 732-752-7720, fax 732-752-7785. *Exec. Dir.* Cheryl O'Connor.

Monmouth-Ocean Biomedical Information Consortium (MOBIC), Community Medical

Center, Toms River 08755. SAN 329-5389. Tel. 732-557-8117, fax 732-557-8354. *Libn.* Reina Reisler.

Morris Automated Information Network (MAIN), c/o Morris County Lib., 30 East Hanover Ave., Whippany 07981. SAN 322-4058. Tel. 973-631-5353, fax 973-631-5356. *Dir.* Jeremy Jenynak.

Morris-Union Federation, 214 Main St., Chatham 07928. SAN 310-2629. Tel. 973-635-0603, fax 973-635-7827.

New Jersey Health Sciences Library Network (NJHSN), Overlook Hospital Lib., Summit 07902. SAN 371-4829. Tel. 908-522-2886, fax 908-522-2274. *Lib. Mgr.* Patricia Regenberg.

New Jersey Library Network, Lib. Development Bureau, Trenton 08608. SAN 372-8161. Tel. 609-278-2640 ext. 152, fax 609-278-2650. *Assoc. State Libn. for Lib. Development* Kathleen Moeller-Peiffer.

Virtual Academic Library Environment (VALE), William Paterson Univ. Lib., Wayne 07470-2103. Tel. 973-720-3179, fax 973-720-3171. *Coord.* Judy Avrin.

New Mexico

Alliance for Innovation in Science and Technology Information (AISTI), 369 Montezuma Ave., No. 237, Santa Fe 87501. *Exec. Dir.* Corinne Lebrunn.

Estacado Library Information Network (ELIN), 509 N. Shipp, Hobby 88240. Tel. 505-397-9328, fax 505-397-1508.

New Mexico Consortium of Academic Libraries. Dean's Office, Albuquerque 87131-0001. SAN 371-6872. *Pres.* Ruben Aragon.

New Mexico Consortium of Biomedical and Hospital Libraries, c/o St. Vincent Hospital, Santa Fe 87505. SAN 322-449X. Tel. 505-820-5218, fax 505-989-6478. *Chair* Albert Robinson.

New York

Academic Libraries of Brooklyn, Long Island Univ. Lib. LLC 517, Brooklyn 11201. SAN 322-2411. Tel. 718-488-1081, fax 718-780-4057.

Associated Colleges of the Saint Lawrence Valley, SUNY Potsdam, Potsdam 13676-2299. SAN 322-242X. Tel. 315-267-3331, fax

315-267-2389. *Exec. Dir.* Anneke J. Larrance.

Brooklyn-Queens-Staten Island-Manhattan-Bronx Health Sciences Librarians (BQSIMB), 150 55th St., Brooklyn 11220. Tel. 718-630-7200, fax 718-630-8918. *Pres.* Irina Meyman.

Capital District Library Council (CDLC), 28 Essex St., Albany 12206. SAN 322-2446. Tel. 518-438-2500, fax 518-438-2872. *Exec. Dir.* Jean K. Sheviak.

Central New York Library Resources Council (CLRC), 6493 Ridings Rd., Syracuse 13206-1195. SAN 322-2454. Tel. 315-446-5446, fax 315-446-5590. *Exec. Dir.* Penelope J. Klein.

ConnectNY, Rochester Institute of Technology, Rochester 14623. Tel. 585-475-2050. *Exec. Dir.* Bart Harloe.

Council of Archives and Research Libraries in Jewish Studies (CARLJS), 330 7th Ave., 21st flr., New York 10001. SAN 371-053X. Tel. 212-629-0500, fax 212-629-0508, e-mail fjc@jewishculture.org. *Operations Dir.* Michelle Moskowitz Brown.

Library Assn. of Rockland County (LARC), P.O. Box 917, New City 10956-0917. Tel. 845-359-3877. *Pres.* Sara Nugent.

Library Consortium of Health Institutions in Buffalo (LCHIB), Abbott Hall, SUNY at Buffalo, Buffalo 14214. SAN 329-367X. Tel. 716-829-3900 ext. 143, fax 716-829-2211, e-mail hubnet@buffalo.edu; ulb-lchib@buffalo.edu. *Exec. Dir.* Martin E. Mutka.

Long Island Library Resources Council (LILRC), 627 N. Sunrise Service Rd., Bellport 11713. SAN 322-2489. Tel. 631-675-1570. *Dir.* Herbert Biblo.

Medical and Scientific Libraries of Long Island (MEDLI), c/o Palmer School of Lib. and Info. Science, Brookville 11548. SAN 322-4309. Tel. 516-299-2866, fax 516-299-4168. *Chair* Mary Westermann-Cicio.

Metropolitan New York Library Council (METRO), 57 E. 11 St., 4th flr., New York 10003-4605. SAN 322-2500. Tel. 212-228-2320, fax 212-228-2598. *Exec. Dir.* Dottie Hiebing.

New York State Higher Education Initiative (NYSHEI), 22 Corporate Woods Blvd., Albany 12211-2350. Fax 518-432-4346, e-mail nyshei@nyshei.org. *Exec. Dir.* Jason Kramer.

Northeast Foreign Law Libraries Cooperative Group, Columbia Univ. Lib., New York 10027. SAN 375-0000. Tel. 212-854-1411, fax 212-854-3295. *Coord.* Silke Sahl.

Northern New York Library Network, 6721 U.S. Hwy. 11, Potsdam 13676. SAN 322-2527. Tel. 315-265-1119, fax 315-265-1881, e-mail info@nnyln.org. *Exec. Dir.* John J. Hammond.

Nylink, 22 Corporate Woods, 3rd flr., Albany 12211. SAN 322-256X. Tel. 518-443-5444, fax 518-432-4346, e-mail nylink@nylink. org. *Exec. Dir.* David Penniman.

Research Library Assn. of South Manhattan, Bobst Lib., New York Univ., New York 10012. SAN 372-8080. Tel. 212-998-2477, fax 212-995-4366. *Dean of Lib.* Carol Mandel.

Rochester Regional Library Council, 390 Packetts Landing, Fairport 14450. SAN 322-2535. Tel. 585-223-7570, fax 585-223-7712, e-mail rrlc@rrlc.org. *Exec. Dir.* Kathleen M. Miller.

South Central Regional Library Council, Clinton Hall, Ithaca 14850. SAN 322-2543. Tel. 607-273-9106, fax 607-272-0740, e-mail scrlc@scrlc.org. *Exec. Dir.* Mary-Carol Lindbloom.

Southeastern New York Library Resources Council (SENYLRC), 21 S. Elting Corners Rd., Highland 12528-2805. SAN 322-2551. Tel. 845-883-9065, fax 845-883-9483. *Exec. Dir.* John L. Shaloiko.

SUNYConnect, Office of Lib. and Info. Services, Albany 12246. Tel. 518-443-5577, fax 518-443-5358. *Asst. Provost for Lib. and Info. Services* Carey Hatch.

United Nations System Electronic Information Acquisitions Consortium (UNSEIAC), c/o United Nations Lib., New York 10017. SAN 377-855X. Tel. 212-963-2026, fax 212-963-2608, e-mail unseiac@un.org. *Coord.* Kikuko Maeyama.

Western New York Library Resources Council, 4455 Genesee St., Buffalo 14225. SAN 322-2578. Tel. 716-633-0705, fax 716-633-1736. *Exec. Dir.* Sheryl Knab.

North Carolina

Cape Fear Health Sciences Information Consortium, 1601 Owen Drive, Fayetteville 28301. SAN 322-3930. Tel. 910-671-5046, fax 910-671-5337. *Dir.* Katherine Mcginniss.

North Carolina Area Health Education Centers, Univ. of North Carolina Health Sciences Lib., CB 7585, Chapel Hill 27599-7585. SAN 323-9950. Tel. 919-962-0700. *Dir.* Diana McDuffee.

North Carolina Community College System, 200 W. Jones St., Raleigh 27603-1379. SAN 322-2594. Tel. 919-807-7100, fax 919-807-7175; 919-807-7164. *Assoc. V.P. for Learning Technology Systems* Bill Randall.

Northwest AHEC Library at Hickory, Catawba Medical Center, Hickory 28602. SAN 322-4708. Tel. 828-326-3662, fax 828-326-3484. *Dir.* Karen Lee Martinez.

Northwest AHEC Library at Salisbury, c/o Rowan Regional Medical Center, Salisbury 28144. SAN 322-4589. Tel. 704-210-5069, fax 704-636-5050.

Northwest AHEC Library Information Network, Wake Forest Univ. School of Medicine, Winston-Salem 27157-1060. SAN 322-4716. Tel. 336-713-7700, fax 336-713-7701. *Dir.* Mike Lischke.

Triangle Research Libraries Network, Wilson Lib., Chapel Hill 27514-8890. SAN 329-5362. Tel. 919-962-8022, fax 919-962-4452. *Dir.* Mona C. Couts.

Western North Carolina Library Network (WNCLN), c/o Appalachian State Univ., Boone 28608. SAN 376-7205. Tel. 828-262-2774, fax 828-262-3001. *Libn.* Catherine Wilkinson.

North Dakota

Central Dakota Library Network, Morton Mandan Public Lib., Mandan 58554-3149. SAN 373-1391. Tel. 701-667-5365, e-mail mortonmandanlibrary@cdln.info. *Dir.* Kelly Steckler.

Mid-America Law Library Consortium (MALLCO), Univ. of North Dakota School of Law, Grand Forks 58202. SAN 371-6813. Tel. 701-777-2204, fax 701-777-4956. *Interim Dir.* Rhonda Schwartz.

Tri-College University Libraries Consortium, NDSU Downtown Campus, Fargo 58102. SAN 322-2047. Tel. 701-231-8170, fax 701-231-7205. *In Charge* Sonia Hohnadel.

Ohio

Assn. of Christian Librarians (ACL), P.O. Box 4, Cedarville 45314. Tel. 937-766-2255, fax 937-766-5499, e-mail info@acl.org. *Pres.* Frank Quinn.

Central Ohio Hospital Library Consortium, 127 S. Davis Ave., Columbus 43222. SAN 371-084X. Tel. 614-234-5214, fax 614-234-1257, e-mail library@mchs.com. *Dir.* Stevo Roksandic.

Christian Library Consortium (CLC), c/o ACL, Cedarville 45314. Tel. 937-766-2255, fax 937-766-5499, e-mail info@acl.org. *Coord.* Beth Purtee.

Columbus Area Library and Information Council of Ohio (CALICO), c/o Westerville Public Lib., Westerville 43081. SAN 371-683X. Tel. 614-882-7277, fax 614-882-5369.

Consortium of Popular Culture Collections in the Midwest (CPCCM), c/o Popular Culture Lib., Bowling Green 43403-0600. SAN 370-5811. Tel. 419-372-2450, fax 419-372-7996. *Head Libn.* Nancy Down.

Five Colleges of Ohio, 102 Allen House, Gambier 43022. Tel. 740-427-5377, fax 740-427-5390, e-mail ohiofive@gmail.com. *Exec. Dir.* Susan Palmer.

Northeast Ohio Regional Library System (NEO-RLS), 4445 Mahoning Ave. N.W., Warren 44483. SAN 322-2713. Tel. 330-847-7744, fax 330-847-7704. *Exec. Dir.* William Martino.

Northwest Regional Library System (NOR-WELD), 181½ S. Main St., Bowling Green 43402. SAN 322-273X. Tel. 419-352-2903, fax 419-353-8310. *Dir.* Allan Gray.

OCLC Online Computer Library Center, Inc., 6565 Kilgour Place, Dublin 43017-3395. SAN 322-2748. Tel. 614-764-6000, fax 614-718-1017, e-mail oclc@oclc.org. *Pres./CEO* Jay Jordan.

Ohio Health Sciences Library Assn. (OHSLA), Medical Lib., South Pointe Hospital, Warrensville Heights 44122. Tel. 216-491-7454, fax 216-491-7650. *Pres.* Michelle Kraft.

Ohio Library and Information Network (Ohio-LINK), 2455 N. Star Rd., Suite 300, Columbus 43221. SAN 374-8014. Tel. 614-728-3600, fax 614-728-3610, e-mail info@ohiolink.edu. *Exec. Dir.* Gwen Evans.

Ohio Network of American History Research Centers, Ohio Historical Society Archives-Lib., Columbus 43211-2497. SAN 323-9624. Tel. 614-297-2510, fax 614-297-2546, e-mail reference@ohiohistory.org.

Ohio Public Library Information Network (OPLIN), 2323 W. 5 Ave., Suite 130, Columbus 43204. Tel. 614-728-5252, fax 614-728-5256, e-mail support@oplin.org. *Exec. Dir.* Stephen Hedges.

OHIONET, 1500 W. Lane Ave., Columbus 43221-3975. SAN 322-2764. Tel. 614-486-2966, fax 614-486-1527. *Exec. Officer* Michael P. Butler.

Rural Ohio Valley Health Sciences Library Network (ROVHSLN), Southern State Community College–South, Sardinia 45171. Tel. 937-695-0307 ext. 3681, fax 937-695-1440. *Mgr.* Mary Ayres.

Southeast Regional Library System (SERLS), 252 W. 13 St., Wellston 45692. SAN 322-2756. Tel. 740-384-2103, fax 740-384-2106, e-mail dirserls@oplin.org. *Exec. Dir.* Mary Leffler.

SouthWest Ohio and Neighboring Libraries (SWON), 10250 Alliance Rd., Suite 225, Blue Ash 45242. SAN 322-2675. Tel. 513-751-4422, fax 513-751-0463, e-mail info@swonlibraries.org. *Exec. Dir.* Melanie A. Blau-McDonald.

Southwestern Ohio Council for Higher Education (SOCHE), Miami Valley Research Park, Dayton 45420-4015. SAN 322-2659. Tel. 937-258-8890, fax 937-258-8899, e-mail soche@soche.org.

State Assisted Academic Library Council of Kentucky (SAALCK), c/o SWON Libs., Cincinnati 45241. SAN 371-2222. Tel. 513-751-4422, fax 513-751-0463, e-mail saalck @saalck.org. *Exec. Dir.* Anne Abate.

Theological Consortium of Greater Columbus (TCGC), Trinity Lutheran Seminary, Columbus 43209-2334. Tel. 614-384-4646, fax 614-238-0263. *Lib. Systems Mgr.* Ray Olson.

Oklahoma

Greater Oklahoma Area Health Sciences Library Consortium (GOAL), Resource Center, Mercy Memorial Health Center, Ardmore 73401. SAN 329-3858. Tel. 580-220-6625, fax 580-220-6599. *Pres.* Catherine Ice.

Oklahoma Health Sciences Library Assn. (OHSLA), HSC Bird Health Science Lib., Univ. of Oklahoma, Oklahoma City 73190. SAN 375-0051. Tel. 405-271-2285 ext. 48755, fax 405-271-3297. *Dir.* Clinton M. Thompson.

Oregon

Chemeketa Cooperative Regional Library Service, c/o Chemeketa Community College, Salem 97305-1453. SAN 322-2837. Tel. 503-399-5105, fax 503-399-7316, e-mail cocl@chemeketa.edu. *Coord.* Linda Cochrane.

Coastal Resource Sharing Network (CRSN), c/o Tillamook County Lib., Tillamook 97141. Tel. 503-842-4792, fax 503-815-8194. *Pres.* Jill Tierce.

Coos County Library Service District, Tioga Hall, 3rd flr., 1988 Newmark, Coos Bay 97420. SAN 322-4279. Tel. 541-888-1529, fax 541-888-1529. *Dir.* Mary Jane Fisher.

Gorge LINK Library Consortium, c/o Hood River County Lib., Hood River 97031. Tel. 541-386-2535, fax 541-386-3835, e-mail gorgelinklibrary@gorge.net. *System Admin.* Jayne Guidinger.

Library Information Network of Clackamas County (LINCC), 16239 S.E. McLoughlin Blvd., Suite 208, Oak Grove 97267-4654. SAN 322-2845. Tel. 503-723-4888, fax 503-794-8238. *Lib. System Analyst* George Yobst.

Orbis Cascade Alliance, 2288 Oakmont Way, Eugene 97401. SAN 377-8096. Tel. 541-246-2470. *Exec. Dir.* John F. Helmer.

Oregon Health Sciences Libraries Assn. (OHSLA), Oregon Health and Science Univ. Lib., Portland 97239-3098. SAN 371-2176. Tel. 503-494-3462, fax 503-494-3322, e-mail library@ohsu.edu.

Portland Area Library System (PORTALS), Port Community College, SYLIB202, Portland 97219. Tel. 503-977-4571, fax 503-977-4977. *Coord.* Roberta Richards.

Southern Oregon Library Federation, c/o Klamath County Lib., Klamath Falls 97601. SAN 322-2861. Tel. 541-882-8894, fax 541-882-6166. *Dir.* Andy Swanson.

Southern Oregon Library Information System (SOLIS), 724 S. Central Ave., Suite 112, Medford 97501. Tel. 541-772-2141, fax 541-772-2144, e-mail solis_97501@yahoo.com. *System Admin.* Marian Stoner.

Washington County Cooperative Library Services, 111 N.E. Lincoln St., MS No. 58, Hillsboro 97124-3036. SAN 322-287X. Tel. 503-846-3222, fax 503-846-3220. *Mgr.* Eva Calcagno.

Pennsylvania

Associated College Libraries of Central Pennsylvania, c/o 648 State St., Lancaster 17603. E-mail webmaster@aclcp.org. *Pres.* Sharon Neal.

Berks County Library Assn. (BCLA), Reading Public Lib., Reading 19602. SAN 371-0866. Tel. 610-478-9035; 610-655-6350. *Pres.* Jennifer Balas.

Central Pennsylvania Consortium (CPC), Dickinson College, Carlisle 17013. SAN 322-2896. Tel. 717-245-1984, fax 717-245-1807, e-mail cpc@dickinson.edu. *Pres.* Katherine Haley Will.

Central Pennsylvania Health Sciences Library Assn. (CPHSLA), Office for Research Protections, Pennsylvania State Univ., University Park 16802. SAN 375-5290. Fax 814-865-1775. *Pres.* Tracie Kahler.

Cooperating Hospital Libraries of the Lehigh Valley Area, Estes Lib., Saint Luke's Hospital, Bethlehem 18015. SAN 371-0858. Tel. 610-954-3407, fax 610-954-4651. *Chair* Sharon Hrabina.

Delaware Valley Information Consortium (DEVIC), St. Mary Medical Center Medical Lib., Langhorne 19047. Tel. 215-710-2012, fax 215-710-4638. *Dir.* Jacqueline Luizzi.

Eastern Mennonite Associated Libraries and Archives (EMALA), 2215 Millstream Rd., Lancaster 17602. SAN 372-8226. Tel. 717-393-9745, fax 717-393-8751. *Chair* Edsel Burdge.

Erie Area Health Information Library Cooperative (EAHILC), Nash Lib., Gannon Univ., Erie 16541. SAN 371-0564. Tel. 814-871-7667, fax 814-871-5566. *Chair* Deborah West.

Greater Philadelphia Law Library Assn. (GPLLA), Wolf, Block, Schorr and Solis-Cohen LLP Lib., 25th flr., Philadelphia 19103. SAN 373-1375. *Pres.* Monica Almendarez.

HSLC/Access PA (Health Science Libraries Consortium), 3600 Market St., Suite 550, Philadelphia 19104-2646. SAN 323-9780. Tel. 215-222-1532, fax 215-222-0416, e-mail support@hslc.org. *Exec. Dir.* Joseph C. Scorza.

Interlibrary Delivery Service of Pennsylvania (IDS), c/o Bucks County IU, No. 22, Doylestown 18901. SAN 322-2942. Tel. 215-348-2940 ext. 1620, fax 215-348-8315, e-mail ids@bucksiu.org. *Admin. Dir.* Pamela Newman Dinan.

Keystone Library Network, Dixon Univ. Center, Harrisburg 17110-1201. Tel. 717-720-4088, fax 717-720-4453. *Coord.* Mary Lou Sowden.

Laurel Highlands Health Science Library Consortium, 361 Sunrise Rd., Dayton 16222. SAN 322-2950. Tel. 814-341-0242, fax 814-266-8230. *Dir.* Rhonda Yeager.

Lehigh Valley Assn. of Independent Colleges, 130 W. Greenwich St., Bethlehem 18018. SAN 322-2969. Tel. 610-625-7888, fax 610-625-7891. *Exec. Dir.* Bonnie Lynch.

Montgomery County Library and Information Network Consortium (MCLINC), 301 Lafayette St., 2nd flr., Conshohocken 19428. Tel. 610-238-0580, fax 610-238-0581, e-mail webmaster@mclinc.org. *Pres.* Anne Frank.

National Network of Libraries of Medicine–Middle Atlantic Region (NN/LM-MAR), Univ. of Pittsburgh, Pittsburgh 15261. E-mail nnlmmar@pitt.edu. *Exec. Dir.* Renae Barger.

Northeastern Pennsylvania Library Network, c/o Marywood Univ. Lib., Scranton 18509-1598. SAN 322-2993. Tel. 570-348-6260, fax 570-961-4769. *Exec. Dir.* Catherine H. Schappert.

Northwest Interlibrary Cooperative of Pennsylvania (NICOP), Mercyhurst College Lib., Erie 16546. SAN 370-5862. Tel. 814-824-2190, fax 814-824-2219. *Archivist* Earleen Glaser.

Pennsylvania Library Assn., 220 Cumberland Pkwy, Suite 10, Mechanicsburg 17055. Tel. 717-766-7663, fax 717-766-5440. *Exec. Dir.* Glenn R. Miller.

Philadelphia Area Consortium of Special Collections Libraries (PACSCL), P.O. Box 22642, Philadelphia 19110-2642. Tel. 215-985-1445, fax 215-985-1446, email lblanchard@pacscl.org. *Exec. Dir.* Laura Blanchard.

Southeastern Pennsylvania Theological Library Assn. (SEPTLA), c/o Biblical Seminary, Hatfield 19440. SAN 371-0793. Tel. 215-368-5000 ext. 234. *Chair* Daniel LaValla.

State System of Higher Education Library Cooperative (SSHELCO), c/o Bailey Lib., Slippery Rock 16057. Tel. 724-738-2630, fax 724-738-2661. *Dir.* Philip Tramdack.

Susquehanna Library Cooperative (SLC), Stevenson Lib., Lock Haven Univ., Lock Haven 17745. SAN 322-3051. Tel. 570-484-2310, fax 570-484-2506. *Interim Dir. of Lib. and Info. Services* Joby Topper.

Tri-State College Library Cooperative (TCLC), c/o Rosemont College Lib., Rosemont 19010-1699. SAN 322-3078. Tel. 610-525-0796, fax 610-525-1939, e-mail office@tclclibs.org. *Coord.* Ellen Gasiewski.

Rhode Island

Library of Rhode Island Network (LORI), c/o Office of Lib. and Info. Services, Providence 02908-5870. SAN 371-6821. Tel. 401-574-9300, fax 401-574-9320. *Lib. Services Dir.* Howard Boksenbaum.

Ocean State Libraries (OSL), 300 Centerville Rd., Suite 103S, Warwick 02886-0226. SAN 329-4560. Tel. 401-738-2200, fax 401-736-8949, e-mail support@oslri.net. *Exec. Dir.* Joan Gillespie.

South Carolina

Charleston Academic Libraries Consortium (CALC), P.O. Box 118067, Charleston 29423-8067. SAN 371-0769. Tel. 843-574-6088, fax 843-574-6484. *Chair* Drucie Gullion.

Columbia Area Medical Librarians' Assn. (CAMLA), School of Medicine Lib., Univ. of South Carolina, Columbia 29209. SAN 372-9400. Tel. 803-733-3361, fax 803-733-1509. *Pres.* Roz Anderson.

Partnership Among South Carolina Academic Libraries (PASCAL), 1333 Main St., Suite 305, Columbia 29201. Tel. 803-734-0900, fax 803-734-0901. *Exec. Dir.* Rick Moul.

South Carolina AHEC, c/o Medical Univ. of South Carolina, Charleston 29425. SAN

329-3998. Tel. 843-792-4431, fax 843-792-4430. *Exec. Dir.* David Garr.

South Carolina Library Network, 1430 and 1500 Senate St., Columbia 29201. SAN 322-4198. Tel. 803-734-8666, fax 803-734-8676. *Dir., Lib. Development* Denise Lyons.

South Dakota

South Dakota Library Network (SDLN), 1200 University, Unit 9672, Spearfish 57799-9672. SAN 371-2117. Tel. 605-642-6835, fax 605-642-6472. *Dir.* Warren Wilson.

Tennessee

Consortium of Southern Biomedical Libraries (CONBLS), Meharry Medical College, Nashville 37208. SAN 370-7717. Tel. 615-327-6728, fax 615-327-6448. *Chair* Barbara Shearer.

Knoxville Area Health Sciences Library Consortium (KAHSLC), Univ. of Tennessee Preston Medical Lib., Knoxville 37920. SAN 371-0556. Tel. 865-305-9525, fax 865-305-9527. *Pres.* Cynthia Vaughn.

Tennessee Health Science Library Assn. (THeSLA), Holston Valley Medical Center Health Sciences Lib., Kingsport 37660. SAN 371-0726. Tel. 423-224-6870, fax 423-224-6014. *Coord., Lib. Services* Sharon M. Brown.

Tri-Cities Area Health Sciences Libraries Consortium (TCAHSLC), James H. Quillen College of Medicine, East Tennessee State Univ., Johnson City 37614. SAN 329-4099. Tel. 423-439-6252, fax 423-439-7025. *Dir.* Biddanda Ponnappa.

Wolf River Library Consortium, c/o Germantown Community Lib., Germantown 38138-2815. Tel. 901-757-7323, fax 901-756-9940. *Dir.* Melody Pittman.

Texas

Abilene Library Consortium, 3305 N. 3 St., Suite 301, Abilene 79603. SAN 322-4694. Tel. 325-672-7081, fax 325-672-7082. *Coord.* Edward J. Smith.

Amigos Library Services, Inc., 14400 Midway Rd., Dallas 75244-3509. SAN 322-3191. Tel. 972-851-8000, fax 972-991-6061, e-mail amigos@amigos.org. *Exec. Dir.* Bonnie Juergens.

Council of Research and Academic Libraries (CORAL), P.O. Box 290236, San Antonio 78280-1636. SAN 322-3213. Tel. 210-458-4885. *Coord.* Rosemary Vasquez.

Del Norte Biosciences Library Consortium, El Paso Community College, El Paso 79998. SAN 322-3302. Tel. 915-831-4149, fax 915-831-4639. *Coord.* Kristin Sanchez.

Harrington Library Consortium, 413 E. 4 Ave., Amarillo 79101. SAN 329-546X. Tel. 806-378-6037, fax 806-378-6038. *Dir.* Donna Littlejohn.

Health Libraries Information Network (Health LINE), Univ. of Texas Southwestern Medical Center Lib., Dallas 75390-9049. SAN 322-3299. Tel. 214-648-2626, fax 214-648-2826.

Houston Area Library Automation Network (HALAN), Houston Public Lib., Houston 77002. Tel. 832-393-1411, fax 832-393-1427, e-mail website@hpl.lib.tx.us. *Chief* Judith Hiott.

Houston Area Research Library Consortium (HARLiC), c/o Univ. of Houston Libs., Houston 77204-2000. SAN 322-3329. Tel. 713-743-9807, fax 713-743-9811. *Pres.* Dana Rooks.

National Network of Libraries of Medicine–South Central Region (NN/LM-SCR), c/o HAM-TMC Library, Houston 77030-2809. SAN 322-3353. Tel. 713-799-7880, fax 713-790-7030, e-mail nnlm-scr@exch.library.tmc.edu. *Dir.* L. Maximillian Buja.

South Central Academic Medical Libraries Consortium (SCAMeL), c/o Lewis Lib.-UNTHSC, Fort Worth 76107. SAN 372-8269. Tel. 817-735-2380, fax 817-735-5158. *Dir.* Daniel Burgard.

Texas Council of Academic Libraries (TCAL), VC/UHV Lib., Victoria 77901. SAN 322-337X. Tel. 361-570-4150, fax 361-570-4155. *Chair* Joe Dahlstrom.

Texas State Library and Archives Commission (TexSHARE), P.O. Box 12927, Austin 78711. Tel. 512-463-5465, fax 512-936-2306, e-mail texshare@tsl.state.tx.us. *Consortia Services* Beverley Shirley.

Texas Navigator Group, P.O. Box 12927, Austin 78711. SAN 322-3396. Tel. 512-463-5406, fax 512-936-2306. *Coord.* Sue Bennett.

Utah

National Network of Libraries of Medicine–MidContinental Region (NN/LM-MCR), Spencer S. Eccles Health Sciences Lib., Univ. of Utah, Salt Lake City 84112-5890. SAN 322-225X. Tel. 801-587-3412, fax 801-581-3632. *Dir.* Wayne J. Peay.

Utah Academic Library Consortium (UALC), Univ. of Utah, Salt Lake City 84112-0860. SAN 322-3418. Tel. 801-581-7701, 801-581-3852, fax 801-585-7185, e-mail UALC mail@library.utah.edu. *Fiscal Agent* Carol Jost.

Utah Health Sciences Library Consortium, c/o Spencer S. Eccles Health Sciences Lib., Univ. of Utah, Salt Lake City 84112-5890. SAN 376-2246. Tel. 801-585-5743, fax 801-581-3632. *Chair* Emily Eresuma.

Vermont

North Atlantic Health Sciences Libraries, Inc. (NAHSL), Dana Medical Lib., Univ. of Vermont Medical School, Burlington 05405. SAN 371-0599. Tel. 508-656-3483, fax 508-656-0762. *Chair* Sally Gore.

Vermont Resource Sharing Network, c/o Vermont Dept. of Libs., Montpelier 05609-0601. SAN 322-3426. Tel. 802-828-3261, fax 802-828-1481. *Ref. Libn.* Gerrie Denison.

Virgin Islands

Virgin Islands Library and Information Network (VILINET), c/o Div. of Libs., Archives, and Museums, Saint Thomas 00802. SAN 322-3639. Tel. 340-773-5715, fax 340-773-3257, e-mail info@vilinet.net. *Territorial Dir. of Libs., Archives, and Museums* Ingrid Bough.

Virginia

American Indian Higher Education Consortium (AIHEC), 121 Oronoco St., Alexandria 22314. SAN 329-4056. Tel. 703-838-0400, fax 703-838-0388, e-mail info@aihec.org.

Lynchburg Area Library Cooperative, c/o Sweet Briar College Lib., Sweet Briar 24595. SAN 322-3450. Tel. 434-381-6315, fax 434-381-6173.

Lynchburg Information Online Network (LION), 2315 Memorial Ave., Lynchburg 24503. SAN 374-6097. Tel. 434-381-6311, fax 434-381-6173. *Dir.* John G. Jaffee.

NASA Libraries Information System–NASA Galaxie, NASA Langley Research Center, MS 185-Technical Lib., Hampton 23681-2199. SAN 322-0788. Tel. 757-864-2356, fax 757-864-2375, e-mail tech-library@larc.nasa.gov.

Richmond Academic Library Consortium (RALC), James Branch Cabell Lib., Virginia Commonwealth Univ., Richmond 23284. SAN 322-3469. Tel. 804-828-1110, fax 804-828-1105. *Univ. Libn.* John E. Ulmschneider.

Southside Virginia Library Network (SVLN), Longwood Univ., Farmville 23909-1897. SAN 372-8242. Tel. 434-395-2431; 434-395-2433, fax 434-395-2453. *Dir.* Suzy Szasz.

Southwestern Virginia Health Information Librarians (SWVAHILI), Carilion Health Sciences Lib., Roanoke 24033. SAN 323-9527. Tel. 540-433-4166, fax 540-433-3106. *Chair* George Curran.

United States Army Training and Doctrine Command (TRADOC)/Lib. Program Office, U.S. Army Hq TRADOC, Fort Monroe 23651. SAN 322-418X. Tel. 757-788-2155, fax 757-788-5544. *Dir.* Amy Loughran.

Virginia Independent College and University Library Assn., c/o Mary Helen Cochran Lib., Sweet Briar 24595. SAN 374-6089. Tel. 434-381-6139, fax 434-381-6173. *Dir.* John Jaffee.

Virginia Tidewater Consortium for Higher Education (VTC), 4900 Powhatan Ave., Norfolk 23529. SAN 329-5486. Tel. 757-683-3183, fax 757-683-4515, e-mail lgdotolo@aol.com. *Pres.* Lawrence G. Dotolo.

Virtual Library of Virginia (VIVA), George Mason Univ., Fairfax 22030. Tel. 703-993-4652, fax 703-993-4662. *Dir.* Katherine Perry.

Washington

Cooperating Libraries in Olympia (CLIO), Evergreen State College Library, L2300, Olympia 98505. SAN 329-4528. Tel. 360-867-6260, fax 360-867-6790. *Dean, Lib. Services* Lee Lyttle.

Inland NorthWest Health Sciences Libraries (INWHSL), P.O. Box 10283, Spokane 99209-0283. SAN 370-5099. Tel. 509-368-6973, fax 509-358-7928. *Treas.* Robert Pringle.

National Network of Libraries of Medicine–Pacific Northwest Region (NN/LM-PNR), T-344 Health Sciences Bldg., Univ. of Washington, Seattle 98195. SAN 322-3485. Tel. 206-543-8262, fax 206-543-2469, e-mail nnlm@u.washington.edu. *Assoc. Dir.* Catherine Burroughs.

Palouse Area Library Information Services (PALIS), c/o Neill Public Lib., Pullman 99163. SAN 375-0132. Tel. 509-334-3595, fax 509-334-6051. *Dir.* Andriette Pieron.

Washington Idaho Network (WIN), Foley Center Lib., Gonzaga Univ., Spokane 99258. Tel. 509-323-6545, fax 509-324-5904, e-mail winsupport@gonzaga.edu. *Pres.* Eileen Bell-Garrison.

Wisconsin

Arrowhead Health Sciences Library Network, Wisconsin Indianhead Technical College, Shell Lake 54817. SAN 322-1954. Tel. 715-468-2815 ext. 2298, fax 715-468-2819. *Coord.* Judy Lyons.

Fox River Valley Area Library Consortium (FRVALC), c/o Polk Lib., Univ. of Wisconsin–Oshkosh, Oshkosh 54901. SAN 322-3531. Tel. 920-424-3348, 920-424-4333, fax 920-424-2175.

Fox Valley Library Council, c/o OWLS, Appleton 54911. SAN 323-9640. Tel. 920-832-6190, fax 920-832-6422. *Pres.* Joy Schwarz.

North East Wisconsin Intertype Libraries, Inc. (NEWIL), 515 Pine St., Green Bay 54301. SAN 322-3574. Tel. 920-448-4413, fax 920-448-4420. *Coord.* Jamie Matczak.

Northwestern Wisconsin Health Science Library Consortium, c/o Gundersen Lutheran Medical Center, Lacrosse 54601. Tel. 608-775-5410, fax 608-775-6343. *Treas.* Eileen Severson.

South Central Wisconsin Health Science Library Consortium, c/o Fort Healthcare Medical Lib., Fort Atkinson 53538. SAN 322-4686. Tel. 920-568-5194, fax 920-568-5195. *Coord.* Carrie Garity.

Southeastern Wisconsin Health Science Library Consortium, Veterans Admin. Center Medical Lib., Milwaukee 53295. SAN 322-3582. Tel. 414-384-2000 ext. 42342, fax 414-382-5334. *Coord.* Janice Curnes.

Southeastern Wisconsin Information Technology Exchange, Inc. (SWITCH), 6801 N. Yates Rd., Milwaukee 53217-3985. SAN 371-3962. Tel. 414-351-2423, fax 414-228-4146. *Coord.* William A. Topritzhofer.

University of Wisconsin System School Library Education Consortium (UWSSLEC), Graduate and Continuing Educ., Univ. of Wisconsin–Whitewater, Whitewater 53190. Tel. 262-472-1463, fax 262-472-5210, e-mail lenchoc@uww.edu. *Co-Dir.* E. Anne Zarinnia.

Wisconsin Library Services (WILS), 728 State St., Room 464, Madison 53706-1494. SAN 322-3612. Tel. 608-265-0580, 608-263-4981, 608-265-4167, fax 608-262-6067, 608-263-3684. *Dir.* Kathryn Schneider Michaelis.

Wisconsin Public Library Consortium (WPLC), c/o South Central Lib. System, Madison 53718. *Dir.* Phyllis Davis.

Wisconsin Valley Library Service (WVLS), 300 N. 1 St., Wausau 54403. SAN 371-3911. Tel. 715-261-7250, fax 715-261-7259. *Dir.* Marla Rae Sepnafski.

WISPALS Library Consortium, c/o Gateway Technical College, Kenosha 53144-1690. Tel. 262-564-2602, fax 262-564-2787. *Coord.* Jennifer Brosek.

Wyoming

WYLD Network, c/o Wyoming State Lib., Cheyenne 82002-0060. SAN 371-0661. Tel. 307-777-6339, fax 307-777-6289, e-mail wyldstaff@will.state.wy.us. *State Libn.* Lesley Boughton.

Canada

Alberta

The Alberta Library (TAL), 6-14, 7 Sir Winston Churchill Sq., Edmonton T5J 2V5. Tel. 780-414-0805, fax 780-414-0806, e-mail admin@thealbertalibrary.ab.ca. *CEO* Maureen Woods.

NEOS Library Consortium, Cameron Lib., 5th flr., Edmonton T6G 2J8. Tel. 780-492-0075, fax 780-492-8302. *Mgr.* Anne Carr-Wiggin.

British Columbia

British Columbia Academic Health Council (BCAHC), 402-1770 W. 7 Ave., Vancouver V6J 4Y6. Tel. 604-739-3910 ext. 228, fax 604-739-3931, e-mail info@bcahc.ca. *CEO* Laureen Styles.

British Columbia College and Institute Library Services, Langara College Lib., Vancouver V5Y 2Z6. SAN 329-6970. Tel. 604-323-5639, fax 604-323-5544, e-mail cils@langara.bc.ca. *Dir.* Mary Anne Epp.

British Columbia Electronic Library Network (BCELN), WAC Bennett Lib., 7th flr., Simon Fraser Univ., Burnaby V5A 1S6. Tel. 778-782-7003, fax 778-782-3023, e-mail office@eln.bc.ca. *Exec. Dir.* Anita Cocchia.

Council of Prairie and Pacific University Libraries (COPPUL), 2005 Sooke Rd., Victoria V9B 5Y2. Tel. 250-391-2554, fax 250-391-2556, e-mail coppul@royalroads.ca. *Exec. Dir.* Alexander Slade.

Electronic Health Library of British Columbia (e-HLbc), c/o Bennett Lib., Burnaby V5A 1S6. Tel. 778-782-5440, fax 778-782-3023, e-mail info@ehlbc.ca. *Coord.* JoAnne Newyear-Ramirez.

Public Library InterLINK, c/o Burnaby Public Lib.–Kingsway Branch, Burnaby V5E 1G3. SAN 318-8272. Tel. 604-517-8441, fax 604-517-8410, e-mail info@interlinklibraries. ca. *Operations Mgr.* Rita Avigdor.

Manitoba

Manitoba Government Libraries Council (MGLC), c/o Instructional Resources Unit, Winnipeg R3G 0T3. SAN 371-6848. Tel. 204-945-7833, fax 204-945-8756. *Chair* John Tooth.

Manitoba Library Consortium, Inc. (MLCI), c/o Lib. Admin., Univ. of Winnipeg, Winnipeg R3B 2E9. SAN 372-820X. Tel. 204-786-9801, fax 204-783-8910. *Chair* Patricia Burt.

Nova Scotia

Maritimes Health Libraries Assn. (MHLA-ABSM), W. K. Kellogg Health Sciences Lib., Halifax B3H 1X5. SAN 370-0836. Tel. 902-494-2483, fax 902-494-3750. *Libn.* Shelley McKibbon.

NOVANET, 84 Chain Lake Drive, Suite 402, Halifax B3S 1A2. SAN 372-4050. Tel. 902-453-2461, fax 902-453-2369, e-mail office@novanet.ns.ca. *Mgr.* Bill Slauenwhite.

Ontario

Canadian Assn. of Research Libraries (Association des Bibliothèques de Recherche du Canada), 350 Albert St., Suite 600, Ottawa K1R 1B1. SAN 323-9721. Tel. 613-562-5385, fax 613-562-5297, e-mail carladm@uottawa.ca. *Exec. Dir.* Brent Roe.

Canadian Health Libraries Assn. (CHLA-ABSC), 39 River St., Toronto M5A 3P1. SAN 370-0720. Tel. 416-646-1600, fax 416-646-9460, e-mail info@chla-absc.ca. *Pres.* Miriam Ticoll.

Canadian Research Knowledge Network (CRKN), Preston Sq., Tower 2, Ottawa K1S 1N4. Tel. 613-907-7040, fax 866-903-9094. *Exec. Dir.* Deb deBruijn.

Consortium of Ontario Libraries (COOL), 111 Peter St., Suite 902, Toronto M5V 2H1. Tel. 416-961-1669, fax 416-961-5122. *Dir.* Barbara Franchetto.

Hamilton and District Health Library Network, c/o St Josephs Healthcare Hamilton, Sherman Lib., Room T2305, Hamilton L8N 4A6. SAN 370-5846. Tel. 905-522-1155 ext. 3410, fax 905-540-6504. *Coord.* Jean Maragno.

Health Science Information Consortium of Toronto, c/o Gerstein Science Info. Center, Univ. of Toronto, Toronto M5S 1A5. SAN 370-5080. Tel. 416-978-6359, fax 416-971-2637. *Exec. Dir.* Miriam Ticoll.

Ontario Council of University Libraries (OCUL), 130 Saint George St., Toronto M5S 1A5. Tel. 416-946-0578, fax 416-978-6755. *Exec. Dir.* Kathy Scardellato.

Ontario Health Libraries Assn. (OHLA), c/o Salt Area Hospital Lib., Sault Ste. Marie P6A 2C4. SAN 370-0739. Tel. 705-759-3434, fax 705-759-3640, e-mail askohla@accessola.com. *Pres.* Toni Janik.

Ontario Library Consortium (OLC), Owen Sound and North Grey Union Public Lib., Owen Sound N4K 4K4. *Pres.* Judy Armstrong.

Parry Sound and Area Access Network, c/o Parry Sound Public Lib., Parry Sound P2A 1E3. Tel. 705-746-9601, fax 705-746-9601, e-mail pspl@vianet.ca. *Chair* Laurine Tremaine.

Perth County Information Network (PCIN), c/o Stratford Public Lib., Stratford N5A 1A2. Tel. 519-271-0220, fax 519-271-3843, e-mail webmaster@pcin.on.ca. *CEO* Sam Coglin.

Shared Library Services (SLS), South Huron Hospital, Exeter N0M 1S2. SAN 323-9500. Tel. 519-235-5168, fax 519-235-4476, e-mail shha.sls@shha.on.ca. *Libn.* Linda Wilcox.

Southwestern Ontario Health Libraries and Information Network (SOHLIN), St. Joseph's Health Care London–Regional Mental Health Staff Libs., St. Thomas N5P 3V9. Tel. 519-631-8510 ext. 49685. *Pres.* Elizabeth Russell.

Toronto Health Libraries Assn. (THLA), 3409 Yonge St., Toronto M4N 2L0. SAN 323-9853. Tel. 416-485-0377, fax 416-485-6877, e-mail medinfoserv@rogers.com. *Pres.* Graziela Alexandria.

Quebec

Assn. des Bibliothèques de la Santé Affiliées a l'Université de Montréal (ABSAUM), c/o Health Lib., Univ. of Montreal, Montreal H3C 3J7. SAN 370-5838. Tel. 514-343-6826, fax 514-343-2350. *Dir.* Monique St-Jean.

Canadian Heritage Information Network (CHIN), 15 Eddy St., 4th flr., Gatineau K1A 0M5. SAN 329-3076. Tel. 819-994-1200, fax 819-994-9555, e-mail service@chin.gc.ca. *Acting Exec. Dir.* Claudette Levesque.

Réseau BIBLIO de l'Ouatouais, 2295 Saint-Louis St., Gatineau, Quebec J8T 5L8. SAN 319-6526. Tel. 819-561-6008. *Exec. Gen.* Sylvie Thibault.

National Library and Information-Industry Associations, United States and Canada

American Association of Law Libraries

Executive Director, Kate Hagan
105 W. Adams St., Suite 3300, Chicago, IL 60603
312-939-4764, fax 312-431-1097, e-mail khagan@aall.org
World Wide Web http://www.aallnet.org

Object

The American Association of Law Libraries (AALL) is established for educational and scientific purposes. It shall be conducted as a nonprofit corporation to promote and enhance the value of law libraries to the public, the legal community, and the world; to foster the profession of law librarianship; to provide leadership in the field of legal information; and to foster a spirit of cooperation among the members of the profession. Established 1906.

Membership

Memb. 5,000+. Persons officially connected with a law library or with a law section of a state or general library, separately maintained. Associate membership available for others.

Dues (Indiv.) $222; (Associate) $222; (Retired) $56; (Student) $56. Year. July 1–June 30.

Officers (2013–2014)

Pres. Steven P. Anderson. E-mail steve.anderson@courts.state.md.us; *V.P.* Holly M. Riccio. E-mail hriccio@omm.com; *Secy.* Deborah L. Rusin. E-mail deborah.rusin@kattenlaw.com; *Treas.* Gail Warren. E-mail gail.warren.56@comcast.net; *Past Pres.* Jean M. Wenger. E-mail jean.wenger@cookcountyil.gov.

Executive Board

Kathleen Brown, Femi Cadmus, Amy J. Eaton, Kenneth J. Hirsh, Gregory R. Lambert, Suzanne Thorpe.

American Library Association

Executive Director, Keith Michael Fiels
50 E. Huron St., Chicago, IL 60611
800-545-2433, 312-280-1392, fax 312-440-9374
World Wide Web http://www.ala.org

Object

The mission of the American Library Association (ALA) is to provide leadership for the development, promotion, and improvement of library and information services and the profession of librarianship in order to enhance learning and ensure access to information for all. Founded 1876.

Membership

Memb. (Indiv.) 55,013; (Inst.) 2,633; (Corporate) 205; (Total) 57,851 (as of November 2012). Any person, library, or other organization interested in library service and librarians. Dues (Indiv.) 1st year, $65; 2nd year, $98; 3rd year and later, $130; (Trustee and Assoc. Memb.) $59; (Lib. Support Staff) $46; (Student) $33; (Foreign Indiv.) $78; (Other) $46; (Inst.) $110 and up, depending on operating expenses of institution.

Officers (2012–2013)

Pres. Maureen Sullivan, Organization Development Consultant. E-mail msull317@aol.com; *Pres.-Elect* Barbara Stripling, Syracuse Univ. E-mail bstripli@syr.edu; *Past Pres.* Molly Raphael, Multnomah County (Oregon) Lib. E-mail mraphael@rapgroup.com; *Treas.* James Neal, Columbia Univ. E-mail jneal@columbia.edu.

Executive Board

Robert E. Banks (2015), Dora Ho (2014), Alexia Hudson-Ward (2015), John Moorman (2015), Sylvia Norton (2014), Michael Porter (2014), Kevin Reynolds (2013), J. Linda Williams (2013).

Endowment Trustees

John Vitali (chair), Rodney M. Hersberger, Kate Nevins, Robert A. Walton; *Exec. Board Liaison* James Neal; *Staff Liaison* Gregory L. Calloway.

Divisions

See the separate entries that follow: American Assn. of School Libns.; Assn. for Lib. Collections and Technical Services; Assn. for Lib. Service to Children; Assn. of College and Research Libs.; Assn. of Specialized and Cooperative Lib. Agencies; Lib. Leadership and Management Assn.; Lib. and Info. Technology Assn.; Public Lib. Assn.; Reference and User Services Assn.; United for Libraries; Young Adult Lib. Services Assn.

Publications

ALA Handbook of Organization (online).
American Libraries (6 a year with four quarterly digital supplements; memb.; organizations $45; foreign $60; single copy $7.50).
Booklist (22 a year with 4 *Book Links* print issues; U.S. and Canada $147.50; foreign $170; single copy $9).

Round Table Chairs

(ALA staff liaison in parentheses)
Ethnic and Multicultural Information Exchange. Tess Tobin (John Amundsen).
Exhibits. Gene Shimshock (Amy McGuigan).
Federal and Armed Forces Libraries. Anne Harrison (Rosalind Reynolds).
Games and Gaming. JP Porcaro (Jenny Levine).
Gay, Lesbian, Bisexual, Transgendered. David S. Vess (John Amundsen).

Government Documents. Barbara Miller (Rosalind Reynolds).

Intellectual Freedom. Julia M. G. Warga (Shumeca Pickett).

International Relations. Loriene Roy (Delin Guerra).

Learning. Louise G. Whitaker (Kimberly Redd).

Library History. Mark McCallon (Norman Rose).

Library Instruction. Mardi Mahaffy (Beatrice Calvin).

Library Research. Lynn Silipigni Connaway (Norman Rose).

Library Support Staff Interests. Jason Pendleton (Darlena Davis).

Map and Geospatial Information. Tracey Hughes (Danielle M. Alderson).

New Members. Janel Kinlaw (Kimberly Sanders).

Retired Members. Therese G. Bigelow (Danielle M. Alderson).

Social Responsibilities. Laura Koltutsky (John Amundsen).

Staff Organizations. Leon S. Bey (Kimberly Redd).

Video. Scott Spicer (Danielle M. Alderson).

Committee Chairs

(ALA staff liaison in parentheses)

Accreditation (Standing). Brian L. Andrew (Laura Dare).

American Libraries Advisory (Standing). Paul Joseph Signorelli (Laurie Borman).

Appointments (Standing). Barbara Stripling (Kerri Price).

Awards (Standing). Camila Alire (Cheryl Malden).

Budget Analysis and Review (Standing). Clara Nalli Bohrer (Gregory L. Calloway).

Chapter Relations (Standing). Joseph M. Eagan (Michael Dowling).

Committee on Committees (Elected Council Committee). Barbara Stripling (Lois Ann Gregory-Wood).

Conference Committee (Standing). Rose T. Dawson (Alicia Babcock).

Conference Program Coordinating Team. (Amy McGuigan).

Constitution and Bylaws (Standing). Carlen Ruschoff (JoAnne M. Kempf).

Council Orientation (Standing). Pamela J. Hickson-Stevenson (Lois Ann Gregory-Wood).

Diversity (Standing). Alexandra Rivera (Gwendolyn Prellwitz).

Education (Standing). Karen E. Downing (Lorelle R. Swader).

Election (Standing). Karen Danczak-Lyons (Lois Ann Gregory-Wood).

Human Resource Development and Recruitment (Standing). Kathleen M. DeLong (Lorelle R. Swader).

Information Technology Policy Advisory (Standing). Bonnie Tijerina (Alan Inouye).

Intellectual Freedom (Standing). Theresa Liedtka (Nanette Perez).

International Relations (Standing). Nancy M. Bolt (Michael P. Dowling).

Legislation (Standing). Vivian R. Wynn (Lynne E. Bradley).

Literacy (Standing). Sandra Dobbins Andrews (Dale Lipschultz).

Literacy and Outreach Services Advisory (Standing). Fantasia A. Thorne (Dale Lipschultz).

Membership (Standing). Kay Cassell (Cathleen Bourdon).

Membership Meetings. Loida Garci-Febo (Lois Ann Gregory-Wood).

Nominating. Stephen L. Matthews (Joanne Kempf).

Organization (Standing). James R. Rettig (Kerri Price).

Policy Monitoring (Standing). Erlene Bishop Killeen (Lois Ann Gregory-Wood).

Professional Ethics (Standing). Martin L. Garnar (Angela Maycock).

Public and Cultural Programs Advisory (Standing). Carolyn A. Anthony (Deborah Anne Robertson).

Public Awareness (Standing). Sonia Alcantara-Antoine (Megan McFarlane).

Publishing (Standing). Ernest A. DiMattia, Jr. (Donald E. Chatham).

Research and Statistics (Standing). Wanda V. Dole (Norman Rose).

Resolutions. Irene L. Briggs (Lois Ann Gregory-Wood).

Rural, Native, and Tribal Libraries of All Kinds. Liana Juliano (John Amundsen).

Scholarships and Study Grants. Lynne O. King (Lorelle R. Swader).

Status of Women in Librarianship (Standing). Deborah G. Tenofsky (Lorelle R. Swader). Training, Orientation, and Leadership Devel-opment. Cal Shepard (Lorelle Swader). Web Site Advisory. Christopher T. Jones (Sherri L. Vanyek).

American Library Association
American Association of School Librarians

Executive Director, Julie A. Walker
50 E. Huron St., Chicago, IL 60611
312-280-4382, 800-545-2433 ext. 4382, fax 312-280-5276, e-mail aasl@ala.org
World Wide Web http://www.aasl.org.

Object

The mission of the American Association of School Librarians (AASL) is to advocate excellence, facilitate change, and develop leaders in the school library field. AASL works to ensure that all members of the field collaborate to provide leadership in the total education program; participate as active partners in the teaching/learning process; connect learners with ideas and information; and prepare students for lifelong learning, informed decision making, a love of reading, and the use of information technologies.

Established in 1951 as a separate division of the American Library Association.

Membership

Memb. 7,000+. Open to all libraries, school librarians, interested individuals, and business firms, with requisite membership in ALA.

Officers (2012–2013)

Pres. Susan D. Ballard; *Pres.-Elect* Gail K. Dickinson; *Treas.* Karen R. Lemmons; *Past Pres.* Carl A. Harvey II.

Board of Directors

Deborah Jean Christensen, Audrey P. Church, Valerie Diggs, Valerie A. Edwards, Karen L. Egger, Catherine G. Evans, Louis Matthew Greco, Jr., Susi Parks Grissom, Sara Kelly Johns, Bonnie S. Kelley, Catherine E. Marriott, Robbie L. Nickel, Cindy Pfeiffer, Cecelia L. Solomon, David A. Sonnen.

Publications

AASL Hotlinks (mo.; electronic, memb.).
Knowledge Quest (5 a year; $50, $60 outside USA). *Ed.* Markisan Naso. E-mail mnaso@ala.org.
School Library Media Research (electronic, free, at http://www.ala.org/aasl.slmr). *Eds.* Jean Donham. E-mail jean.donham@uni.edu; Carol L. Tilley. E-mail ctilley@uiuc.edu.

Section Leadership

AASL/ESLS Executive Committee. Judy T. Bivens, Audrey P. Church, Jody K. Howard, Ramona N. Kerby, Michelle Kowalsky.
AASL/ISS Executive Committee. Cheri Ann Dobbs, Catherine G. Evans, Judith L. Hill, Barbara L. Spivey, Alicia S. Q. Yao.
AASL/SPVS Executive Committee. John P. Brock, Bonnie S. Kelley, Kathryn Roots Lewis, Catherine E. Marriott.

Committee Chairs

AASL/ACRL Joint Information Literacy Committee. Lesley S. J. Farmer, Scott B. Mandernack.
AASL/ALSC/YALSA Interdivisional Committee on School/Public Library Cooperation. Julie Bartel.
Advocacy. Judi Repman.

Affiliate Assembly. Pamela Renfrow.

Alliance for Association Excellence. Karen R. Lemmons.

American University Press Book Selection. Merlyn K. Miller.

Annual Conference. Margaret L. Sullivan.

Awards. Richard L. Hasenyager, Jr.

Best Web Sites for Teaching and Learning. Donna G. Baratta.

Beyond Words Grant Jury. Donald C. Adcock.

Blog Group. Frances Reeve, Carolyn J. Starkey.

Bylaws and Organization. Rebecca J. Pasco.

Essential Links Editorial Board. Vicki C. Bullta.

Intellectual Freedom. Annalisa R. Keuler.

Knowledge Quest Editorial Board. Judi Moreillon.

Leadership Development Committee. Sharon Coatney.

Legislation. Connie Hamner Williams.

National Conference 2013. Terri G. Kirk, Ken W. Stewart.

National Institute 2012. Barbara A. Jansen.

NCATE Coordinating Committee. Mary A. Berry.

Nominating. Carol A. Gordon.

Research/Statistics. Jody K. Howard.

School Library Month Committee. Cassandra G. Barnett.

SLR Editorial Board. Jean Donham, Carol L. Tilley.

Task Force Chairs

Best Apps for Curriculum. Melissa Jacobs-Israel.

Educator Pre-Service. David Schuster.

Planned Giving Initiative. Frances R. Roscello.

Senior Project/Capstone Project. Sarah Justice.

Standards and Guidelines Implementation. Karen W. Gavigan.

Awards Committees and Chairs

AASL Research Grant. Nancy Everhart.

ABC-CLIO Leadership Grant. Charles Edwin Hockersmith.

Collaborative School Library Award. Harriet Lapointe.

Distinguished School Administrator Award. Paul K. Whitsitt.

Distinguished Service Award. Violet H. Harada.

Frances Henne Award. Mary Fran Daley.

Information Technology Pathfinder Award. Christopher G. Harris.

Innovative Reading Grant. Sabrina Carnesi.

Intellectual Freedom Award. Helen Ruth Adams.

National School Library Program of the Year Award. Katherine E. Lowe.

Advisory Group Staff Liaisons

Professional Development. Melissa Jacobsen.

Publications. Stephanie Book.

American Library Association
Association for Library Collections and Technical Services

Executive Director, Charles Wilt
50 E. Huron St., Chicago, IL 60611
800-545-2433 ext. 5030, fax 312-280-5033, e-mail cwilt@ala.org
World Wide Web http://www.ala.org/alcts

Object

The Association for Library Collections and Technical Services (ALCTS) envisions an environment in which traditional library roles are evolving. New technologies are making information more fluid and raising expectations. The public needs quality information anytime, anyplace. ALCTS provides frameworks to meet these information needs.

ALCTS provides leadership to the library and information communities in developing principles, standards, and best practices for creating, collecting, organizing, delivering, and preserving information resources in all forms. It provides this leadership through its members by fostering educational, research, and professional service opportunities. ALCTS is committed to quality information, universal access, collaboration, and lifelong learning.

Standards—Develop, evaluate, revise, and promote standards for creating, collecting, organizing, delivering, and preserving information resources in all forms.

Best practices—Research, develop, evaluate, and implement best practices for creating, collecting, organizing, delivering, and preserving information resources in all forms.

Education—Assess the need for, sponsor, develop, administer, and promote educational programs and resources for lifelong learning.

Professional development—Provide opportunities for professional development through research, scholarship, publication, and professional service.

Interaction and information exchange—Create opportunities to interact and exchange information with others in the library and information communities.

Association operations—Ensure efficient use of association resources and effective delivery of member services.

Established 1957; renamed 1988.

Membership

Memb. 4,200. Any member of the American Library Association may elect membership in this division according to the provisions of the bylaws.

Officers (2012–2013)

Pres. Carolynne Myall, Kennedy Lib., Eastern Washington Univ., 816 F St., Cheney, WA 99004. Tel. 509-359-6967, fax 509-359-2476, e-mail cmyall@ewu.edu; *Pres.-Elect* Genevieve Owens, Williamsburg Regional Libraries, 7700 Croaker Rd. Williamsburg, VA 23188. Tel. 757-259-7740, fax 757-259-4079, e-mail gowens@wrl.org; *Past Pres.* Betsy Simpson, Smathers Lib., Univ. of Florida, P.O. Box

117004, Gainesville, FL 32611. Tel. 352-273-2730, fax 352-392-7365, e-mail betsys@uflib.ufl.edu; *Councilor* Brian E. C. Schottlaender, Lib., Univ. of California, San Diego, 9500 Gilman Dr., No. 0175G, La Jolla, CA 92093. Tel. 858-534-3060, fax 858-534-6193, e-mail becs@ucsd.edu.

Address correspondence to the executive director.

Board of Directors

Susan A. Davis, James Dooley, Erica Findley, Elaine Franco, Andrew Hart, Emily McElroy, Norm Medeiros, Carolynne Myall, Jacob Nadal, Genevieve Owens, Alice Platt, Jacquie Samples, Brian E. C. Schottlaender, Betsy Simpson, Erin Stalberg, Timothy Strawn, Cory Tucker, Marie Waltz, Charles Wilt.

Publications

ALCTS Newsletter Online (q.; free; posted at http://www.ala.org/alcts). *Ed.* Alice Platt, Boston Athenaeum, 10Ω Beacon St., Boston, MA 02108. Tel. 617-720-7609 ext. 241, e-mail platt@bostonathenaeum.org.

Library Resources and Technical Services (q.; nonmemb. $110; international $120). *Ed.* Mary Beth Weber, Technical and Automated Services Dept., Rutgers Univ. Libs., 47 Davidson Rd., Piscataway, NJ 08854. Tel. 732-445-0500, fax 732-445-5888, e-mail mbfecko@rci.rutgers.edu.

Section Chairpersons

Acquisitions. James Dooley.
Cataloging and Metadata Management. Erin Stalberg.
Collection Management. Cory Tucker.
Continuing Resources. Jacquie Samples.
Preservation and Reformatting. Jacob Nadal.

Committee Chairpersons

ALCTS Outstanding Publications Award Jury. Janet Lute.

Hugh C. Atkinson Memorial Award (ALCTS/ACRL/LLAMA/LITA). Lisa Thomas.
Ross Atkinson Lifetime Achievement Award Jury. John Duke.
Budget and Finance. Emily McElroy.
Continuing Education. Keri Cascio.
Fund Raising. Lenore England.
International Relations. David Miller.
Leadership Development. Miranda Bennett.
LRTS Editorial Board. Mary Beth Weber.
Membership. Deborah Ryszka.
Nominating. Cynthia Whitacre.
Organization and Bylaws. Marie Waltz.
Outstanding Collaboration Citation Jury. Arthur Miller.
Esther J. Piercy Award Jury. Karen Darling.
Planning. Andrew Hart.
Program. Mary Page, Catherine Gardiner.
Publications. Dina Giambi.
Edward Swanson Memorial Best of *LRTS* Award Jury. Margaret Mering.

Interest Groups

Authority Control (ALCTS/LITA). Caroline Miller.
Automated Acquisitions/In-Process Control Systems. To be announced.
Creative Ideas in Technical Services. Wyoma VanDuinkerken.
Electronic Resources. Clara Ruttenberg.
FRBR. Debra Shapiro.
Linked Library Data (ALCTS/LITA). Theodore Gerontakos, Debra Shapiro.
MARC Formats (ALCTS/LITA). Stacie Traill, Sarah Beth Weeks.
New Members. Elizabeth Siler.
Newspapers. Brian Geiger.
Public Libraries Technical Services. Megan Dazey.
Role of the Professional in Academic Research Technical Service Departments. Charles McElroy, Allison Yanos.
Scholarly Communications. Melanie Feltner-Reichert.
Technical Services Directors of Large Research Libraries. James Mouw.
Technical Services Managers in Academic Libraries. Judy Garrison.
Technical Services Workflow Efficiency. Eric Brownell, Nancy Gonzales.

American Library Association
Association for Library Service to Children

Executive Director, Aimee Strittmatter
50 E. Huron St., Chicago, IL 60611
312-280-2163, 800-545-2433 ext. 2163, fax 312-280-5271, e-mail alsc@ala.org
World Wide Web http://www.ala.org/alsc

Object

The core purpose of the Association for Library Service to Children (ALSC) is to create a better future for children through libraries. Its primary goal is to lead the way in forging excellent library services for all children. ALSC offers creative programming, information about best practices, continuing education, an awards and media evaluation program, and professional connections. Founded 1901.

Membership

Memb. 4,000. Open to anyone interested in library services to children. For information on dues, see ALA entry.

Address correspondence to the executive director.

Officers

Pres. Carolyn S. Brodie; *V.P./Pres.-Elect* Marina "Starr" LaTronica; *Past Pres.* Mary Fellows; *Fiscal Officer* Tali Balas; *Div. Councilor* Andrew Medlar.

Directors

Rita Auerbach, Ernie Cox, Nina Lindsay, Jamie Campbell Naidoo, Michael Santangelo, Megan Schliesman, Lisa Von Drasek, Jan Watkins.

Publications

ALSConnect (q., electronic; memb. Not available by subscription.)
Children and Libraries: The Journal of the Association for Library Service to Children (q.; memb; nonmemb. $40; foreign $50).

Committee Chairs

AASL/ALSC/YALSA Interdivisional Committee on School/Public Library Cooperation. Julie Thomas-Bartel.
Advocacy and Legislation. Penny Markey.
ALSC/Booklist/YALSA Odyssey Award Selection 2013. Teri Lesesne.
ALSC/Booklist/YALSA Odyssey Award Selection 2014. Ellen Spring.
Arbuthnot Honor Lecture 2013. Susan Pine.
Arbuthnot Honor Lecture 2014. Susan Moore.
Arbuthnot Honor Lecture 2015. Sue McCleaf Nespeca.
Mildred L. Batchelder Award 2013. Jean Hatfield.
Mildred L. Batchelder Award 2014. Maureen White.
Pura Belpré Award 2013. Charmette Kuhn-Kendrick.
Pura Belpré Award 2014. Ruth Tobar.
Budget. Alison Ernst.
Randolph Caldecott Award 2013. Sandra Imdieke.
Randolph Caldecott Award 2014. Marion Hanes Rutsch.
Andrew Carnegie Medal/Notable Children's Videos. Joan Atkinson.
Children and Libraries Advisory Committee. Africa Hands.
Children and Technology. Gretchen Caserotti.
Distinguished Service Award 2013. Carol Doll.

Distinguished Service Award 2014. Maria Salvadore.
Early Childhood Programs and Services. Jennifer Nemec.
Education. Katharine Todd.
Every Child Ready to Read Oversight. Judy Nelson
Theodor Seuss Geisel Award 2013. Carla Morris.
Theodor Seuss Geisel Award 2014. Penny Peck.
Grant Administration Committee. Nancy Baumann.
Great Web Sites. Kimberly Grad, John Peters.
Intellectual Freedom. Heather Acerro.
Liaison with National Organizations. Stephanie Bange, Betsy Diamant-Cohen.
Library Service to Special Population Children and Their Caregivers. Paula Holmes.
Local Arrangements (Chicago). Maria Xochitl Peterson.
Managing Children's Services. Ann Schwab.
Membership. C. Gaye Hinchliff.
John Newbery Award 2013. Steven Engelfried.
John Newbery Award 2014. Elizabeth Orsburn.
Nominating 2013. Thom Barthelmess.
Nominating 2014. Julie Corsaro.
Notable Children's Books. Wendy Woodfill.
Notable Children's Recordings. Lynda Salem-Poling.
Oral History. Jean Gaffney.
Organization and Bylaws. Susan Polos, Alene Sterlief.
Program Coordinating. Karen Kessel.
Public Awareness. Robin Howe.
Quicklists Consulting. Rachel Godwin Payne, Frances Veit.
Charlemae Rollins President's Program 2013. Wendy Lukehart.
Scholarships. Marianne Martens.
School Age Programs and Service. Sarah Stippich.
Robert F. Sibert Award 2013. Kathie Meizner.
Robert F. Sibert Award 2014. Cecilia McGowan.
Special Collections and Bechtel Fellowship. Angela Leeper.
Laura Ingalls Wilder Award 2013. Martha Parravano.
Laura Ingalls Wilder Award 2014. Karen Nelson Hoyle.

American Library Association
Association of College and Research Libraries

Executive Director, Mary Ellen K. Davis
50 E. Huron St., Chicago, IL 60611-2795
312-280-2523, 800-545-2433 ext. 2523, fax 312-280-2520, e-mail acrl@ala.org
World Wide Web http://www.ala.org/acrl

Object

The Association of College and Research Libraries (ACRL) leads academic and research librarians and libraries in advancing learning and scholarship. Founded 1940.

Membership

Memb. 11,857. For information on dues, see ALA entry.

Officers

Pres. Steven J. Bell, Paley Lib., Temple Univ., Philadelphia, PA 19122-6086. Tel. 215-204-5023, fax 215-204-5201, e-mail bells@temple.edu; *Pres.-Elect* Trevor A. Dawes, Circulation Services Dir., Princeton Univ. Lib., Princeton, NJ 08544-2002. Tel. 609-258-3231, fax 609-258-0441, e-mail tdawes@princeton.edu; *Past Pres.* Joyce L. Ogburn, 327 J. Willard Marriott Lib., Univ. of Utah, Salt Lake City, UT 84103-3322. Tel. 801-585-9775, fax 801-585-7185, e-mail joyce.ogburn@utah.edu; *Budget and Finance Chair* Cynthia K. Steinhoff, Anne Arundel Community College, 101 College Pkwy., Arnold, MD 21012-1895. Tel. 410-777-2483, fax 410-777-4483, e-mail cksteinhoff@aacc.edu; *ACRL Councilor* Maggie Ferrell, Univ. of Wyoming, 1000 E. University Ave., Laramie, WY 82071-2000. Tel. 307-766-3279, fax 307-766-2510, e-mail farrell@uwyo.edu.

Board of Directors

Officers; Lisabeth A. Chabot, Mark Emmons, Julie Ann Garrison, Irene M. H. Herold, Marilyn Naiba Ochoa, Loretta R. Parham, Ann Campion Riley, Mary Ann Sheble.

Publications

Choice (12 a year; $390; Canada and Mexico $440; other international $510). *Ed.* Irving Rockwood.

Choice Reviews-on-Cards (available only to subscribers of *Choice* and/or *Choice Reviews Online*) $480; Canada and Mexico $530; other international $610).

Choice Reviews Online 2.0 (academic libraries FTE 10,000+ $560; academic libraries FTE 2,500–9,999 $540; academic libraries FTE fewer than 2,500 $515; school library K–12 $375; foreign academic libraries [includes Mexico and Canada] $560; public library $515; government library $600; other libraries $600; publishers/dealers $600).

College & Research Libraries (*C&RL*) (6 a year; memb.; nonmemb. $75; Canada and other PUAS countries $80; other international $85). *Ed.* Joseph J. Branin.

College & Research Libraries News (*C&RL News*) (11 a year; memb.; nonmemb. $50; Canada and other PUAS countries $55; other international $60). *Ed.* David Free.

Publications in Librarianship (formerly ACRL Monograph Series) (occasional). *Ed.* Craig Gibson.

RBM: A Journal of Rare Books, Manuscripts, and Cultural Heritage (s. ann.; $45; Canada and other PUAS countries $55; other international $60). *Ed.* Beth M. Whittaker.

Committee and Task Force Chairs

AASL/ACRL Information Literacy (interdivisional). Lesley S. J. Farmer, Scott B. Mandernack.

Academic/Research Librarian of the Year Award. David D. Oberhelman.

ACRL Academic Library Trends and Statistics Survey. Charles C. Stuart.
ACRL 2013 Contributed Papers. Scott Vine, Janice D. Welburn.
ACRL 2013 Coordinating Committee (Indianapolis). Erika C. Linke.
ACRL 2013 Cyber Zed Shed. Arlene V. Salazar, Lynn Sutton.
ACRL 2013 Innovations. John P. Culshaw, Courtney Greene.
ACRL 2013 Invited Papers. Trevor A. Dawes, Alyssa Koclanes.
ACRL 2013 Keynote Speakers. Georgie Lynn Donovan, Kenley E. Neufeld.
ACRL 2013 Local Arrangements. James L. Mullins, William H. Weare, Jr.
ACRL 2013 Panel Sessions. Carrie Donovan, Rebecca Kate Miller.
ACRL 2013 Poster Sessions. Theresa S. Byrd, Joan Plungis.
ACRL 2013 Preconference. Kathryn R. Bartelt, Sarah E. Sheehan.
ACRL 2013 Roundtable Discussions. Tim Gritten, Douglas K. Lehman.
ACRL 2013 Scholarships. Toni Anaya, Deanne M. Peterson.
ACRL 2013 Virtual Conference. Kaijsa J. Calkins, Barbara G. Preece.
ACRL 2013 Volunteers. June L. DeWeese, Beth McNeil.
ACRL 2013 Workshop Programs. Rhonda Kay Huisman, Jennifer E. Nutefall.
ACRL/LLAMA Interdivisional Committee on Building Resources. Ann H. Hamilton, Felice E. Maciejewski.
Appointments. Kenley E. Neufeld.
Hugh C. Atkinson Memorial Award. Larry P. Alford.
Budget and Finance. Cynthia K. Steinhoff.
Choice Editorial Board. Keith R. Stetson.
Colleagues. Marianne I. Gaunt, Lorraine J. Haricombe.
College & Research Libraries Editorial Board. Joseph Branin.
College & Research Libraries News Editorial Board. Joan F. Cheverie.
Diversity. Rayette Sterling.
Ethics. Jean S. Caspers.
Excellence in Academic Libraries Award. Lisa Janicke Hinchliffe.
Friends Fund. Carolyn H. Allen.
Friends Fund Disbursement. Louise S. Sherby.
Government Relations. Rachel Bridgewater.

Immersion Program. Carrie Donovan.
Information Literacy Professional Development. Sheila Stoeckel.
Information Literacy Standards. Diane M. Fulkerson.
Information Literacy Web Site. Lisa A. Ancelet.
Intellectual Freedom. Theresa Liedtka.
Dr. E. J. Josey Spectrum Scholar Mentor Program. Jade Alburo.
Leadership Recruitment and Nomination. Sarah Barbara Watstein.
Liaison Assembly. Kim L. Eccles.
Liaison Coordinating. Bruce Henson.
Liaison Grants. Andrea M. Falcone.
Liaisons Training and Development. Kim L. Eccles.
Membership. Meghan Elizabeth Sitar.
New Publications Advisory. Joan K. Lippincott.
President's Program Planning Committee, 2013. Valeda Dent.
President's Program Planning Committee, 2014. Debbie L. Malone, Adi Redzic.
Professional Development. Jim Elmborg.
Publications Coordinating. Kim Leeder.
Publications in Librarianship Editorial Board. Craig Gibson.
RBM Editorial Board. Beth M. Whittaker.
Research Planning and Review. Bradford L. Eden.
Resources for College Libraries Editorial Board. Nancy P. O'Brien.
Section Membership. Jaena Alabi.
Standards. H. Frank Cervone.
Value of Academic Libraries. Lisa Janicke Hinchliffe, Megan Jane Oakleaf.

Discussion Group Chairs

Assessment. Sarah M. Passonneau, Joan Ellen Stein.
Balancing Baby and Book. Laura Bonella, Cynthia M. Dudenhoffer.
Continuing Education/Professional Development. Elizabeth A. Avery.
Copyright. Tomas A. Lipinski.
Digital Humanities. Angela Courtney, Craig Martin Harkema.
First Year Experience. Carissa Ann Tomlinson.
Heads of Public Services. Jan H. Kemp.
Information Commons. Michael Whitchurch.

Leadership. Rudy Leon.

Libraries and Information Science Collections. Rebecca Vargha.

Marketing. Katy Kelly, Heidi M. Steiner.

Media Resources. Monique L. Threatt, Chimene Elise Tucker.

MLA International Bibliography. Sarah G. Wenzel.

New Members. John Morris Jackson II, Elizabeth Psyck.

Personnel Administrators and Staff Development Officers. Emily Backe, Brian William Keith.

Philosophical, Religious, and Theological Studies. Wayne Bivens-Tatum.

Popular Cultures. Kimberley Bugg.

Regional Campus Libraries. John J. Burke.

Scholarly Communications. Scott Paul Lapinski.

Sponsored Research Administrators and Grants Managers. To be appointed.

Student Retention. Nicole Pagowsky.

Undergraduate Libraries. Pamela Joan MacKintosh.

Interest Group Conveners

Academic Library Services to International Students. Hui-Fen Chang.

Digital Curation. Patricia M. Hswe.

Health Sciences. Sue Phelps.

Image Resources. Robin Leech.

Librarianship in For-Profit Educational Institutions. Kit M. Keller.

Library and Information Science (LIS) Education. To be appointed.

Numeric and Geospatial Data Services in Academic Libraries. Lynda M. Kellam.

Residency Programs. Latisha Marrita Reynolds.

Universal Accessibility. Debra Riley-Huff.

Virtual Worlds. Valerie J. Hill.

Section Chairs

African American Studies Librarians. Gennice W. King.

Anthropology and Sociology. Jennifer Darragh.

Arts. Alessia Zanin-Yost.

Asian, African, and Middle Eastern. Deepa Banerjee.

College Libraries. Gillian S. Gremmels.

Community and Junior College Libraries. Ann Coder.

Distance Learning. Sandra Lee Hawes.

Education and Behavioral Sciences. Vanessa Earp.

Instruction. Susan G. Miller.

Law and Political Science. LeRoy Jason LaFleur.

Literatures in English. Melissa S. Van Vuuren.

Rare Books and Manuscripts. Erika Dowell.

Science and Technology. Lori J. Ostapowicz-Critz.

Slavic and East European. Patricia K. Thurston.

University Libraries. Stephanie S. Atkins.

Western European Studies. Heidi Madden.

Women and Gender Studies. Jennifer Mayer.

American Library Association
Association of Specialized and Cooperative Library Agencies

Executive Director, Susan Hornung
50 E. Huron St., Chicago, IL 60611-2795
312-280-4395, 800-545-2433 ext. 4395, fax 312-280-5273, e-mail shornung@ala.org
World Wide Web http://www.ala.org/ascla

Object

The Association of Specialized and Cooperative Library Agencies (ASCLA) represents specialized library agencies, state library agencies, library cooperatives, and independent librarians.

Library agencies provide library materials and service to populations with special needs, such as those with sensory, physical, health, or behavioral conditions or those who are incarcerated or detained. The ASCLA LSSP (Library Services to Special Populations) Interest Group represents members with interests in this area.

State library agencies are those organizations created or authorized by the state government to promote library services in the state through the organization and coordination of a variety of library services. The ASCLA SLA (State Library Agencies) Interest Group represents members with interests in this area.

Library cooperatives are combinations, mergers, or contractual associations of one or more types of libraries (academic, public, special, or school) crossing jurisdictional, institutional, or political boundaries, working together to achieve maximum effective use of funds to provide library and information services to all citizens above and beyond those that can be provided through one institution. Such cooperative organizations or agencies may be designated to serve a community, a metropolitan area, a region within a region, or may serve a statewide or multi-state area. The ASCLA ICAN (InterLibrary Cooperation and Networking) Interest Group represents members with interests in this area.

The ASCLA ILEX (Independent Librarians' Exchange) Interest Group represents independent librarians who work outside traditional library settings.

Within the interests of these types of library organizations, ASCLA has specific responsibility for:

1. Development and evaluation of goals and plans for state library agencies and library cooperatives to facilitate the implementation, improvement, and extension of library activities designed to foster improved user services, coordinating such activities with other appropriate ALA units

2. Representation and interpretation of the role, function, and services of state library agencies, specialized library agencies, and library cooperatives within and outside the profession, including contact with national organizations and government agencies

3. Development of policies, studies, and activities in matters affecting state library agencies and library cooperatives relating to: (a) state and local library legislation, (b) state grants-in-aid and appropriations, and (c) relationships among state, federal, regional, and local governments, coordinating such activities with other appropriate ALA units

4. Establishment, evaluation, and promotion of standards and services guidelines relating to the concerns of the association

5. Identifying the library interests and needs of all persons, encouraging the creation of services to meet these needs within the areas of concern of the association, and promoting the use of these services provided by state library agencies, specialized library agencies, and library cooperatives

6. Stimulating the professional growth and promoting the specialized training and continuing education of library personnel

at all levels in the areas of concern of this association and encouraging membership participation in appropriate type-of-activity divisions within ALA

7. Assisting in the coordination of activities of other units within ALA that have a bearing on the concerns of this association

8. Granting recognition for outstanding library service within the areas of concern of this association

9. Acting as a clearinghouse for the exchange of information and encouraging the development of materials, publications, and research within the areas of concern of this association

Membership

Memb. 800+. For information on dues, see ALA entry.

Officers (2012–2013)

Pres. Stacy Aldrich; *Pres.-Elect* Sara G. Laughlin; *Past Pres.* Carol Ann Desch; *Div. Councilor* Lizbeth Bishoff.

Directors

Officers; Anne Abate, Hulen E. Bivins, Tracy Byerly, Marti Goddard, Lori Allen Guenther, Susan Hornung, Shannon O'Grady, Kathleen Moeller-Peiffer, Lisa Priebe, Stephen Prine, Jeannette Smithee.

Interest Groups

ASCLA ICAN (InterLibrary Cooperation and Networking) Consortium Management Discussion Interest Group; ASCLA ICAN Collaborative Digitization Interest Group; ASCLA ICAN Interlibrary Cooperation Interest Group; ASCLA ICAN Physical Delivery Interest Group; ASCLA Library Consultants Interest Group; ASCLA Library Services for Incarcerated Youth (LSSP); ASCLA LSSP Bridging Deaf Cultures @your library Interest Group; ASCLA LSSP (Libraries Serving Special Populations) Library Services to People with Visual or Physical Disabilities that Prevent Them from Reading Standard Print Interest Group; ASCLA LSSP Library Services to the Incarcerated and Detained; ASCLA LSSP Universal Access Interest Group; ASCLA SLA State Library Agencies/Library Development Interest Group; ASCLA SLA/LSTA Coordinators Interest Group; ASCLA SLA Youth Services Consultants Interest Group.

Publication

Interface (q.; online). *Ed.* Anne Abate. E-mail anne@librarydiscountnetwork.com.

Committees

Accessibility Assembly; Awards; Finance and Planning; Guidelines for Library and Information Services for the American Deaf Community; Legislation; Membership; Nominating; Online Continuing Education; Publications; Standards Review; Web Presence.

American Library Association
Library Leadership and Management Association

Executive Director, Kerry Ward
50 E. Huron St., Chicago, IL 60611
312-280-5032, 800-545-2433 ext. 5032, fax 312-280-5033
e-mail kward@ala.org
World Wide Web http://www.ala.org/llama

Object

The Library Leadership and Management Association (LLAMA) Strategic Plan sets out the following:

Mission: The Library Leadership and Management Association advances outstanding leadership and management practices in library and information services by encouraging and nurturing individual excellence in current and aspiring library leaders.

Vision: As the foremost organization developing present and future leaders in library and information services, LLAMA provides a welcoming community where aspiring and experienced library leaders and library supporters from all types of libraries can seek and share knowledge and skills in leadership, administration, and management in a manner that creates meaningful transformation in libraries around the world.

Core Values: LLAMA believes advancing leadership and management excellence is achieved by fostering the following values: exemplary and innovative service to and for our members; and leadership development and continuous learning opportunities for our members.

Established 1957.

Membership

Memb. 4,100. For information on dues, see ALA entry.

Officers (July 2012–June 2013)

Pres. Pat Hawthorne; *V.P.* Catherine Friedman; *Past Pres.* Janine Golden.

Address correspondence to the executive director.

Publication

Library Leadership and Management (LL&M) (open access: http://journals.tdl.org/llm/index.php/llm). *Ed.* Elizabeth Blakesley.

Committee Chairs

Competencies. Keith Swigger.
Continuing Education. Miriam Matteson.
Financial Advancement. Alison Ames Galstad.
Leadership Development. Janet Bishop, Estella Maria Richardson.
LL&M Editorial Board. Elizabeth Blakesley.
Marketing Communications. Eric C. Shoaf.
Membership. Eileen Marie Theodore-Shusta.
Mentoring. Holly Okuhara.
Nominating. Gail Kennedy.
President's Program. Lila Daum Fredenburg.
Program. Lee Anne Hooley.

American Library Association
Library and Information Technology Association

Executive Director, Mary C. Taylor
50 E. Huron St., Chicago, IL 60611
312-280-4267, 800-545-2433, e-mail mtaylor@ala.org
World Wide Web http://www.lita.org

Object

As a center of expertise about information technology, the Library and Information Technology Association (LITA) leads in exploring and enabling new technologies to empower libraries. LITA members use the promise of technology to deliver dynamic library collections and services.

LITA educates, serves, and reaches out to its members, other ALA members and divisions, and the entire library and information community through its publications, programs, and other activities designed to promote, develop, and aid in the implementation of library and information technology.

Membership

Memb. 3,269. For information on dues, see ALA entry.

Officers (2012–2013)

Pres. Elizabeth A. Stewart-Marshall; *V.P./ Pres.-Elect* Cindi Trainor; *Past Pres.* Colleen Cuddy.

Directors

John F. Blyberg, Jason Griffey, Cody Hanson, David Lee King, Lauren Pressley, Rachel Vacek; *Exec. Dir.* Mary C. Taylor.

Publication

Information Technology and Libraries (*ITAL*) (open source at http://ejournals.bc.edu/ojs/index.php/ital/issue/current). *Ed.* Robert Gerrity. For information or to send manuscripts, contact the editor.

American Library Association
Public Library Association

Executive Director, Barbara A. Macikas
50 E. Huron St., Chicago, IL 60611
312-280-5752, 800-545-2433 ext. 5752, fax 312-280-5029, e-mail pla@ala.org
World Wide Web http://www.pla.org

The Public Library Association (PLA) has specific responsibility for

1. Conducting and sponsoring research about how the public library can respond to changing social needs and technical developments

2. Developing and disseminating materials useful to public libraries in interpreting public library services and needs

3. Conducting continuing education for public librarians by programming at national and regional conferences, by publications such as the newsletter, and by other delivery means

4. Establishing, evaluating, and promoting goals, guidelines, and standards for public libraries

5. Maintaining liaison with relevant national agencies and organizations engaged in public administration and human ser-

vices, such as the National Association of Counties, the Municipal League, and the Commission on Postsecondary Education

6. Maintaining liaison with other divisions and units of ALA and other library organizations, such as the Association for Library and Information Science Education and the Urban Libraries Council

7. Defining the role of the public library in service to a wide range of user and potential user groups

8. Promoting and interpreting the public library to a changing society through legislative programs and other appropriate means

9. Identifying legislation to improve and to equalize support of public libraries

PLA enhances the development and effectiveness of public librarians and public library services. This mission positions PLA to

• Focus its efforts on serving the needs of its members

• Address issues that affect public libraries

• Commit to quality public library services that benefit the general public

The goals of PLA are

• Advocacy and Awareness: PLA is an essential partner in public library advocacy.

• Leadership and Transformation: PLA is the leading source for learning opportunities to advance transformation of public libraries.

• Literate Nation: PLA will be a leader and valued partner of public libraries' initiatives to create a literate nation.

• Organizational Excellence: PLA is positioned to sustain and grow its resources to advance the work of the association.

Membership

Memb. 9,000+. Open to all ALA members interested in the improvement and expansion of public library services to all ages in various types of communities.

Officers (2012–2013)

Pres. Eva Poole, District of Columbia Public Lib. E-mail eva.poole@dc.gov; *Pres.-Elect* Carolyn Anthony, Skokie (Illinois) Public Library. E-mail canthony@skokielibrary.info; *Past Pres.* Marcia Warner. E-mail mwarner@grpl.org.

Publication

Public Libraries (bi-mo.; memb.; nonmemb. $65; foreign $75; single copy $10). *Ed.* Kathleen Hughes, PLA, 50 E. Huron St., Chicago, IL 60611. E-mail khughes@ala.org.

Committee Chairs

Annual Conference Program Subcommittee. Mary Lee Hastler.

Baker & Taylor Entertainment Audio Music/Video Product Award. Todd Krueger.

Budget and Finance. Jo Ann Pinder.

Gordon M. Conable Award Jury. Terese G. Bigelow.

Continuing Education Advisory Group. Sara Dallas.

DEMCO New Leaders Travel Grant Jury. Dale McNeill.

EBSCO Excellence in Small and/or Rural Public Library Service Award. Cathy Duty Ziegler.

Highsmith Library Innovation Award Jury. Sydney Leigh McCoy.

Intellectual Freedom. Robert Hubsher.

Leadership Development Task Force. Jay Lamar Turner.

Legislation and Advocacy. Victoria L. Yarbrough.

Allie Beth Martin Award Jury. Lorraine M. Lessey.

Membership Advisory Group. Kristin Kirk.

Nominating 2013. Audra L. Caplan.

Nominating 2014. Marcia Warner.

PLA/ALSC Every Child Ready to Read Oversight Committee. Judy T. Nelson.

PLA National Conference 2014. Larry Neal.

PLA National Conference 2014 Program Subcommittee. Georgia Lomax.

PLA 2014 Local Arrangements. Jackie Nytes.

PLDS Statistical Report Advisory. Sian Dorian Brannon.

Polaris Innovation in Technology John Iliff Award. Cynthia DeLanty.

Public Libraries Advisory. Latasha Baker.

Charlie Robinson Award Jury. Cheryl Napsha.

Romance Writers of America Library Grant Jury. Christine Caputo.

Technology Committee. Amy Frances Terlaga.

American Library Association
Reference and User Services Association

Executive Director, Susan Hornung
50 E. Huron St., Chicago, IL 60611
800-545-2433 ext. 4395, 312-280-4395, fax 312-280-5273
e-mail shornung@ala.org
World Wide Web http://www.ala.org/rusa

Object

The Reference and User Services Association (RUSA) is responsible for stimulating and supporting excellence in the delivery of general library services and materials, and the provision of reference and information services, collection development, readers' advisory, and resource sharing for all ages, in every type of library.

The specific responsibilities of RUSA are:

1. Conduct of activities and projects within the association's areas of responsibility
2. Encouragement of the development of librarians engaged in these activities, and stimulation of participation by members of appropriate type-of-library divisions
3. Synthesis of the activities of all units within the American Library Association that have a bearing on the type of activities represented by the association
4. Representation and interpretation of the association's activities in contacts outside the profession
5. Planning and development of programs of study and research in these areas for the total profession
6. Continuous study and review of the association's activities

Membership

Memb. 3,800+

Officers (2012–2013)

Pres. Mary Pagliero Popp; *Pres.-Elect* M. Kathleen Kern; *Secy.* Carolyn Larson; *Past Pres.* Gary White; *Div. Councilor* Jennifer C. Boettcher.

Publication

Reference and User Services Quarterly, online only, http://rusa.metapress.com. (memb.). *Ed.* Barry Trott, Williamsburg Regional Lib., 7770 Croaker Rd., Williamsburg, VA 23188-7064. E-mail btrott@wrl.org.

Sections

Business Reference and Services (BRASS); Collection Development and Evaluation (CODES); History (HS); Emerging Technologies in Reference (MARS); Reference Services (RSS); Sharing and Transforming Access to Resources (STARS).

Committees

Access to Information; AFL/CIO Joint Committee on Library Services to Labor Groups; Awards; Budget and Finance; Conference Program; Membership; Nominating; Organization and Planning; Professional Development; Publications and Communications; Standards and Guidelines.

American Library Association
United for Libraries: Association of Library Trustees, Advocates, Friends, and Foundations

Executive Director, Sally Gardner Reed
109 S. 13 St., Suite 117B, Philadelphia, PA 19107
312-280-2161, fax 215-545-3821, e-mail sreed@ala.org
World Wide Web http://www.ala.org/united

Object

United for Libraries was founded in 1890 as the American Library Trustee Association (ALTA). It was the only division of the American Library Association dedicated to promoting and ensuring outstanding library service through educational programs that develop excellence in trusteeship and promote citizen involvement in the support of libraries. ALTA became an ALA division in 1961. In 2008 the members of ALTA voted to expand the division to more aggressively address the needs of friends of libraries and library foundations, and through a merger with Friends of Libraries USA (FOLUSA) became Association of Library Trustees, Advocates, Friends and Foundations (ALTAFF). In 2012 members voted to add "United for Libraries" to its title.

Memb. 5,200. Open to all interested persons and organizations. For dues and membership year, see ALA entry.

Officers (2012–2013)

Pres. Gail Guidry Griffin; *Pres.-Elect* Rod Wagner; *Councilor* Susan Schmidt; *Past Pres.* Donna McDonald.

Publications

The Complete Trustee Handbook.
101+ Great Ideas for Libraries and Friends.
Even More Great Ideas for Libraries and Friends.
The Voice for America's Libraries (q.; memb.).

Committee Chairs

Annual Conference Program. Shirley Bruursema, Dora Sims.
Library Issues. Ronald Friedman, Ruth Newell.
Newsletter and Web Site Advisory. Martha Grahame, Joan Ress Reeves.
Nominating. Gwendolyn Amamoo, Rose Mosley.
PLA Conference Program. Tanya Butler, Ron Heezen.
United for Libraries Leaders Orientation. Peggy Danhof.

American Library Association
Young Adult Library Services Association

Executive Director, Beth Yoke
50 E. Huron St., Chicago, IL 60611
312-280-4390, 800-545-2433 ext. 4390, fax 312-280-5276, e-mail yalsa@ala.org
World Wide Web http://www.ala.org/yalsa
YALSA blog http://yalsa.ala.org/blog, The Hub (http://yalsa.ala.org/thehub),
Wiki (http://wikis.ala.org/yalsa), Twitter (http://twitter.com/yalsa),
Facebook (http://www.facebook.com/YALSA)

Object

In every library in the nation, high-quality library service to young adults is provided by a staff that understands and respects the unique informational, educational, and recreational needs of teenagers. Equal access to information, services, and materials is recognized as a right, not a privilege. Young adults are actively involved in the library decision making process. The library staff collaborates and cooperates with other youth-serving agencies to provide a holistic, community-wide network of activities and services that support healthy youth development. To ensure that this vision becomes a reality, the Young Adult Library Services Association (YALSA)

1. Advocates extensive and developmentally appropriate library and information services for young adults ages 12 to 18

2. Promotes reading and supports the literacy movement

3. Advocates the use of information and communications technologies to provide effective library service

4. Supports equality of access to the full range of library materials and services, including existing and emerging information and communications technologies, for young adults

5. Provides education and professional development to enable its members to serve as effective advocates for young people

6. Fosters collaboration and partnerships among its individual members with the library community and other groups involved in providing library and information services to young adults

7. Influences public policy by demonstrating the importance of providing library and information services that meet the unique needs and interests of young adults

8. Encourages research and is in the vanguard of new thinking concerning the provision of library and information services for youth

Membership

Memb. 5,200. Open to anyone interested in library services, literature, and technology for young adults. For information on dues, see ALA entry.

Officers

Pres. Jack Martin. E-mail hillias@gmail.com; *Pres.-Elect* Shannon Peterson. E-mail shannonpeterson@gmail.com; *Division Councilor* Vicki Emery. E-mail vemery@fcps.edu; *Fiscal Officer* Penny Johnson. E-mail pjlibrarylady@gmail.com; *Secy.* Sarajo Wentling. E-mail sjwentling@gmail.com; *Past Pres.* Sarah Flowers. E-mail sarahflowers@charter.net.

Directors

Linda W. Braun, Priscille Dando, Sandra Hughes-Hassell, Carrie Kausch, Renee McGrath, Candice Mack, Chris Shoemaker, Sarah Sogigian, Gail Tobin, Christian Zabriskie.

Publications

Journal of Research on Libraries and Young Adults (q.) (online, open source, peer-reviewed). *Ed.* Sandra Hughes-Hassell.

Young Adult Library Services (q.) (memb.; nonmemb. $70; foreign $80). *Ed.* Linda W. Braun.

YALSA E-News (memb.) *Ed.* Jaclyn Finneke.

AIIM—The Enterprise Content Management Association

President, John F. Mancini
1100 Wayne Ave., Suite 1100, Silver Spring, MD 20910
800-477-2446, 301-587-8202, fax 301-587-2711, e-mail aiim@aiim.org
World Wide Web http://www.aiim.org
European Office: 8 Canalside, Lowesmoor Wharf, Worcester WR1 2RR, England.
Tel. 44-1905-727613, fax 44-1905-727609, e-mail info@aiim.org.uk

Object

AIIM is an international authority on enterprise content management, the tools and technologies that capture, manage, store, preserve, and deliver content in support of business processes. Founded in 1943 as the Association for Information and Image Management.

Officers

Chair John Newton, Alfresco Software; *V. Chair* Timothy Elmore, Bank-Fund Staff Federal Credit Union; *Treas.* Paul Engel, VeBridge; *Past Chair* John Chickering, Fidelity Investments.

Publication

Connect (weekly, memb., online).

American Indian Library Association

President, Janice Kowemy
World Wide Web http://www.ailanet.org

Object

To improve library and information services for American Indians. Founded in 1979; affiliated with American Library Association 1985.

Membership

Any person, library, or other organization interested in working to improve library and information services for American Indians may become a member. Dues (Inst.) $40; (Indiv.) $20; (Student) $10.

Officers (July 2012–June 2013)

Pres. Janice Kowemy. E-mail jkowemy@lagunatribe.org; *V.P./Pres.-Elect* Heather Devine. E-mail hhdevine@gmail.com; *Secy.* Naomi Bishop. E-mail naopoleon@gmail.com; *Treas.* Carlene Engstrom. E-mail carleneengstrom@yahoo.com; *Exec. Dir.* Kelly Webster. E-mail kellypster@gmail.com.

Publication

AILA Newsletter (irregular).

American Merchant Marine Library Association

Executive Director, Roger T. Korner
635 Fourth Ave., Brooklyn, NY 11232
718-369-3818, fax 718-369-3024, e-mail ussammla@ix.netcom.com
World Wide Web http://unitedseamensservice.org

Object

Known as "the public library of the high seas," the association provides ship and shore library service for American-flag merchant vessels, and for the Military Sealift Command, the U.S. Coast Guard, and other waterborne operations of the U.S. government. Established 1921.

Executive Committee

John M. Bowers; Joseph J. Cox, John L. De-Gurse, Jr.; Fred Finger; Florence R. Fleming, Philip M. Grill, Robert E. Hart; David Heindel; James Henry; Edward Honor; Donald E. Kadlac; Edward J. Kelly; Roger T. Korner; Richard M. Larrabee; Edward R. Morgan; George E. Murphy; F. Anthony Naccarato; C. James Patti; William D. Potts; Philip Shapiro; Richard A. Simpson; Augustin Tellez; Gloria Cataneo; Edward Tregurtha; Kenneth R. Wykle.

American Theological Library Association

Executive Director, Brenda Bailey-Hainer
300 S. Wacker Drive, Suite 2100, Chicago, IL 60606-6701
888-665-2852, 312-454-5100, fax 312-454-5505, e-mail atla@atla.com
World Wide Web http://www.atla.com

Mission

The mission of the American Theological Library Association (ATLA) is to foster the study of theology and religion by enhancing the development of theological and religious libraries and librarianship.

Membership

(Inst.) 249; (International Inst.) 19; (Indiv.) 401; (Student) 99; (Lifetime) 92; (Affiliates) 69.

Officers

Pres. Andrew Keck, Luther Seminary, 2481 Como Ave., St. Paul, MN 55108. Tel. 651-641-3592, fax 651-641-3280, e-mail akeck001@luthersem.edu; *V.P.* Beth Bidlack, 6025 Baker-Berry Lib., Dartmouth College, Hanover, NH 03755. Tel. 603-646-3342, e-mail beth.bidlack@dartmouth.edu; *Secy.* Eileen K. Saner, Associated Mennonite Biblical Seminary Lib., 3003 Benham Ave., Elkhart, IN 46517-1999. Tel. 574-296-6233, fax 574-295-0092, e-mail esaner@ambs.edu.

Directors

H. D. "Sandy" Ayer, Kelly Campbell, Douglas L. Gragg, Carrie M. Hackney, Tammy L. Johnson, Timothy D. Lincoln, Saundra Lipton, Melody Layton McMahon, John B. Weaver.

Publications

ATLA Indexes in MARC Format (q.).
ATLA Religion Database, 1949– (q., on EBSCO, Ovid).
ATLASerials, 1949– (q., full-text, on EBSCO, Ovid).

ATLA Catholic Periodical and Literature Index (q., on EBSCO).

Old Testament Abstracts (ann., on EBSCO).

New Testament Abstracts (ann., on EBSCO).

Proceedings (ann.; memb.; nonmemb. $60). *Ed.* Tawny Burgess.

Research in Ministry: An Index to Doctor of Ministry Project Reports (ann.) online. *Ed.* Justin Travis.

Archivists and Librarians in the History of the Health Sciences

President, Chris Lyons
E-mail christopher.lyons@mcgill.ca
World Wide Web http://www.alhhs.org

Object

The association was established exclusively for educational purposes, to serve the professional interests of librarians, archivists, and other specialists actively engaged in the librarianship of the history of the health sciences by promoting the exchange of information and by improving the standards of service.

Officers

Pres. Christopher Lyons. E-mail christopher.lyons@mcgill.ca; *Past Pres.* Stephen J. Greenberg. E-mail patzere4@gmail.com; *Secy.* Phoebe Evans Letocha. E-mail pletocha@jhmi.edu; *Treas.* Arlene Shaner. E-mail ashaner@nyam.org; *Membs.-at-Large* Megan Curran, Melissa Grafe, John Hellebrand, Rachel Ingold.

Membership

Memb. 149. Dues $15.

Publication

Watermark (q.; memb.). *Ed.* Stephen E. Novak, Archives and Special Collections, Columbia Univ. Medical Center. E-mail sen13@columbia.edu.

ARMA International

Executive Director, Marilyn Bier
11880 College Blvd., Suite 450, Overland Park, KS 66210
800-422-2762, 913-341-3808, fax 913-341-3742
World Wide Web http://www.arma.org

Object

To advance the practice of records and information management as a discipline and a profession; to organize and promote programs of research, education, training, and networking within that profession; to support the enhancement of professionalism of the membership; and to promote cooperative endeavors with related professional groups.

Membership

Memb. 11,000. Annual dues $175 for international affiliation (student/retired $25). Chapter dues vary.

Officers

Pres. Komal Gulich, FirstEnergy Corp., 76 S. Main St., Akron, OH 44308; *Pres.-Elect* Julie J. Colgan, Merrill Corp., 105 Winding Way, Columbia, SC 29212; *Treas.* Brenda Prowse, Prima Info. Solutions, 11 Austin St., St. John's, NL A1B-4C1, Canada; *Past Pres.* Galina Datskovsky, Autonomy, 21-00 Rte. 208 S., Fair Lawn, NJ 07410.

Directors

Jason R. Baron, Patricia Burns, Melissa G. Dederer, Ilona Koti, Peter Kurilecz, William LeFevre, Brian A. Moriki, Alison North, Denise Pickett, Steven Roberts, Paula Sutton, Alice B. Young.

Publication

Information Management (*IM*) (bi-mo.).

Art Libraries Society of North America

President, Deborah Kempe
Executive Management, Scott Sherer
414-768-8000 ext. 104, fax 414-768-8001, e-mail sherer@techenterprises.net

Object

The object of the Art Libraries Society of North America (ARLIS/NA) is to foster excellence in art librarianship and visual resources curatorship for the advancement of the visual arts. Established 1972.

Membership

Memb. 1,000+. Dues (Inst./Business Affiliate) $145; (Introductory) $90 (one-year limit); (Indiv.) $120; (Student) $50 (three-year limit); (Retired/Unemployed) $60. Year. Jan. 1–Dec. 31. Membership is open to all those interested in visual librarianship, whether they be professional librarians, students, library assistants, art book publishers, art book dealers, art historians, archivists, architects, slide and photograph curators, or retired associates in these fields.

Officers

Pres. Deborah Kempe, Frick Art Reference Lib., 10 E. 71 St., New York, NY 10021. Tel. 212-547-0658, e-mail kempe@frick.org; *V.P./ Pres.-Elect* Gregory P. J. Most, National Gallery of Art, Washington, DC 20565. Tel. 202-842-6100, e-mail g-most@nga.gov; *Secy.* Alan Michelson, Built Environments Lib., Univ. of

Washington Libs., Gould Hall, Box 355730, Seattle, WA 98195. Tel. 206-543-7091, e-mail alanmich@u.washington.edu; *Treas.* Deborah Barlow Smedstad, William Morris Hunt Memorial Lib., Museum of Fine Arts, Boston, 465 Huntington Ave., Boston, MA 02115. Tel. 617-369-3107, e-mail dbarlowsmedstad@mfa.org; *Past Pres.* Jon Evans, Hirsch Lib., Museum of Fine Arts–Houston, P.O. Box 6826, Houston, TX 77265-6826. Tel. 713-639-7393, e-mail jevans@mfah.org.

Address correspondence to Scott Sherer, Technical Enterprises, Inc., 7044 S. 13 St., Oak Creek, WI 53154.

Publications

ARLIS/NA Update (bi-mo.; memb.).
Art Documentation (2 a year; memb., subscription).
Handbook and List of Members (ann.; memb.).
Occasional papers (price varies).
Miscellaneous others (request current list from headquarters).

Committee Chairs

Awards. Rebecca Cooper.
Cataloging Advisory. Maria Oldal.

Communications and Publications. Amy Lucker.
Development. Kathryn Wayne.
Diversity. Patrick Tomlin.
Document Advisory. V. Heidi Hass, Tony White.
Finance. Tom Riedel.
International Relations. Holly Hatheway.

Membership. Jamie Lausch Vander Broek.
Nominating. Alba Fernandez-Keys.
Professional Development. Stacy Brinkman.
Public Policy. Carmen Orth-Alfie, Patrick Tomlin.
Strategic Planning. Hannah Bennett.

Asian/Pacific American Librarians Association

Executive Director, Buenaventura "Ven" Basco
P.O. Box 1669, Goleta, CA 93116-1669
E-mail buenaventura.basco@ucf.edu
World Wide Web http://www.apalaweb.org

Object

To provide a forum for discussing problems and concerns of Asian/Pacific American librarians; to provide a forum for the exchange of ideas by Asian/Pacific American librarians and other librarians; to support and encourage library services to Asian/Pacific American communities; to recruit and support Asian/Pacific American librarians in the library/information science professions; to seek funding for scholarships in library/information science programs for Asian/Pacific Americans; and to provide a vehicle whereby Asian/Pacific American librarians can cooperate with other associations and organizations having similar or allied interests. Founded in 1980; incorporated 1981; affiliated with American Library Association 1982.

Membership

Open to all librarians and information specialists of Asian/Pacific descent working in U.S. libraries and information centers and other related organizations, and to others who support the goals and purposes of the association. Asian/Pacific Americans are defined as people residing in North America who self-identify as Asian/Pacific American.

Officers (July 2012–June 2013)

Pres. A. Jade Alburo, UCLA. E-mail jalburo@ library.ucla.edu; *V.P./Pres.-Elect* Eugenia Beh, Texas A&M. E-mail eugenia_beh@yahoo.com; *Secy.* Lessa K. Pelayo-Lozada, Glendale Public Lib. E-mail lpelayo-lozada@ci.glendale.ca.us; *Treas.* Shoko Tokoro, Univ. of North Carolina at Charlotte. E-mail stokoro@uncc.edu; *Past Pres.* Sandy Wee, San Mateo County Lib., 1 Library Ave., Millbrae, CA 94030. Tel. 650-697-7607, e-mail wee@smcl.org.

Publication

APALA Newsletter (q.).

Committee Chairs

Constitution and Bylaws. Florante Peter Ibanez.
Finance and Fund Raising. Eileen Bosch.
Literature Awards. Ven Basco, Dora Ho.
Membership and Mentoring. Maria Pontillas.
Newsletter and Publications. Gary A. Colmenar, Melissa Cardenas-Dow.
Nominating. Sandy Wee.
Program Planning, 2013. Cynthia Mari Orozco.
Program Planning, 2014. Linda Absher, Safi Saffiulah.
Publicity. Heawon Paick.
Scholarships and Awards. Tassanee Chitcharoen, Gayatri Singh.
Web. Young Lee.

Association for Information Science and Technology

Executive Director, Richard B. Hill
1320 Fenwick Lane, Suite 510, Silver Spring, MD 20910
301-495-0900, fax 301-495-0810, e-mail asis@asis.org
World Wide Web http://www.asis.org

Object

The Association for Information Science and Technology (formerly the American Society for Information Science and Technology, or ASIS&T) provides a forum for the discussion, publication, and critical analysis of work dealing with the design, management, and use of information, information systems, and information technology.

Membership

Memb. (Indiv.) 3,000; (Student) 800; (Inst.) 250. Dues (Indiv.) $140; (Student) $40; (Inst.) $650 and $800.

Officers

Pres. Andrew Dillon, Univ. of Texas at Austin; *Pres.-Elect* Harry Bruce, Univ. of Washington; *Treas.* Vicki Gregory, Univ. of South Florida; *Past Pres.* Diane Sonnenwald, Univ. College Dublin (Ireland).

Address correspondence to the executive director.

Board of Directors

Dirs.-at-Large Katriina Byström, Prudence Dalrymple, Jens-Erik Mai, Diane Neal, Cassidy Sugimoto, Elaine Toms, Shelly Warwick, Marcia Lei Zeng.

Publications

ASIS&T Thesaurus of Information Science, Technology, and Librarianship, 3rd edition, ed. by Alice Redmond-Neal and Marjorie M. K. Hlava.

Computerization Movements and Technology Diffusion: From Mainframes to Ubiquitous Computing, ed. by Margaret S. Elliott and Kenneth L. Kraemer.

Covert and Overt: Recollecting and Connecting Intelligence Service and Information Science, ed. by Robert V. Williams and Ben-Ami Lipetz.

Editorial Peer Review: Its Strengths and Weaknesses, by Ann C. Weller.

Electronic Publishing: Applications and Implications, ed. by Elisabeth Logan and Myke Gluck.

Evaluating Networked Information Services: Techniques, Policy and Issues, by Charles R. McClure and John Carlo Bertot.

From Print to Electronic: The Transformation of Scientific Communication, by Susan Y. Crawford, Julie M. Hurd, and Ann C. Weller.

Historical Information Science: An Emerging Unidiscipline, by Lawrence J. McCrank.

Historical Studies in Information Science, ed. by Trudi Bellardo Hahn and Michael Buckland.

The History and Heritage of Scientific and Technological Information Systems, ed. by W. Boyd Rayward and Mary Ellen Bowden.

Information and Emotion: The Emergent Affective Paradigm in Information Behavior Research and Theory, ed. by Dania Bilal and Diane Nahl.

Information Management for the Intelligent Organization: The Art of Environmental Scanning, 3rd edition, by Chun Wei Choo.

Information Representation and Retrieval in the Digital Age, by Heting Chu.

Intelligent Technologies in Library and Information Service Applications, by F. W. Lancaster and Amy Warner.

Introduction to Information Science and Technology, ed. by Charles H. Davis and Debora Shaw.

Introductory Concepts in Information Science, by Melanie J. Norton.

Knowledge Management for the Information Professional, ed. by T. Kanti Srikantaiah and Michael E. D. Koenig.

Knowledge Management in Practice: Connections and Context, ed. by T. Kanti Srikantaiah and Michael E. D. Koenig.

Knowledge Management Lessons Learned: What Works and What Doesn't, ed. by T. Kanti Srikantaiah and Michael E. D. Koenig.

Knowledge Management: The Bibliography, compiled by Paul Burden.

Proceedings of ASIS&T Annual Meetings.

Statistical Methods for the Information Professional, by Liwen Vaughan.

Theories of Information Behavior, ed. by Karen E. Fisher, Sanda Erdelez, and Lynne E. F. McKechnie.

The Web of Knowledge: A Festschrift in Honor of Eugene Garfield, ed. by Blaise Cronin and Helen Barsky Atkins.

The above publications are available from Information Today, Inc., 143 Old Marlton Pike, Medford, NJ 08055.

Association for Library and Information Science Education

Executive Director, Kathleen Combs
ALISE Headquarters, 65 E. Wacker Place, Suite 1900, Chicago, IL 60601-7246
312-795-0996, fax 312-419-8950, e-mail contact@alise.org
World Wide Web http://www.alise.org

The Association for Library and Information Science Education (ALISE) is an independent nonprofit professional association whose mission is to promote excellence in research, teaching, and service for library and information science education through leadership, collaboration, advocacy, and dissemination of research. Its enduring purpose is to promote research that informs the scholarship of teaching and learning for library and information science, enabling members to integrate research into teaching and learning. The association provides a forum in which to share ideas, discuss issues, address challenges, and shape the future of education for library and information science. Founded in 1915 as the Association of American Library Schools, it has had its present name since 1983.

Membership

700+ in four categories: Personal, Institutional, International Affiliate Institutional, and Associ-

ate Institutional. Personal membership is open to anyone with an interest in the association's objectives.

Officers (2013–2014)

Pres. Eileen Abels, Drexel Univ. E-mail ega26@drexel.edu; *V.P./Pres.-Elect* Clara Chu, Univ. of North Carolina–Greensboro; *Past Pres.* Melissa Gross, Florida State Univ.; *Secy.-Treas.* Steven MacCall, Univ. of Alabama; *Dirs.* Louise Spiteri, Dalhousie Univ.; Don Latham, Florida State Univ.; Laurie Bonnici, Univ. of Alabama.

Publications

Journal of Education for Library and Information Science (JELIS) (q.). *Co-Eds.* Michelle Kazmer, Kathleen Burnett. E-mail jeliseditors@gmail.com.

ALISE News (q.)

Association for Rural and Small Libraries

201 E. Main St., Suite 1405, Lexington, KY 40507.
859-514-9178, e-mail szach@amrms.com
World Wide Web http://www.arsl.info.

Object

The Association for Rural and Small Libraries (ARSL) was established in 1978 as the Center for Study of Rural Librarianship in the Department of Library Science at Clarion University of Pennsylvania.

ARSL is a network of persons throughout the United States dedicated to the positive growth and development of libraries. ARSL believes in the value of rural and small libraries, and strives to create resources and services that address national, state, and local priorities for libraries situated in rural communities.

Its objectives are

- To organize a network of members concerned about the growth and development of useful library services in rural and small libraries
- To provide opportunities for the continuing education of members
- To provide mechanisms for members to exchange ideas and to meet on a regular basis
- To cultivate the practice of librarianship and to foster a spirit of coopera-

tion among members of the profession, enabling them to act together for mutual goals

- To serve as a source of current information about trends, issues, and strategies
- To partner with other library and non-library groups and organizations serving rural and small library communities
- To collect and disseminate information and resources that are critical to this network
- To advocate for rural and small libraries at the local, state, and national levels

Officers

Pres. Andrea Berstler, Wicomico Public Lib., 122 S. Division St., Salisbury, MD 21801. Tel. 410-749-3612, e-mail andrea.berstler@gmail.com; *V.P./Pres.-Elect* Tena Hanson, Estherville Public Lib., 613 Central Ave., Estherville, IA 51334. Tel. 712-362-7731, e-mail thansonlibrarian@gmail.com; *Past Pres.* Becky Heil, Iowa Lib. Services/State Lib., 1112 E. Grand Ave., Des Moines, IA 50319. Tel. 563-542-0519, e-mail becky.heil@lib.state.ia.us.

Association of Academic Health Sciences Libraries

Executive Director, Louise S. Miller
2150 N. 107 St., Suite 205, Seattle, WA 98133
206-367-8704, fax 206-367-8777, e-mail aahsl@sbims.com
World Wide Web http://www.aahsl.org

Object

The Association of Academic Health Sciences Libraries (AAHSL) comprises the libraries serving the accredited U.S. and Canadian medical schools belonging to or affiliated with the Association of American Medical Colleges. Its goals are to promote excellence in academic health science libraries and to ensure that the next generation of health practitioners is trained in information-seeking skills that enhance the quality of health care delivery, education, and research. Founded in 1977.

Membership

Memb. 150+. Full membership is available to nonprofit educational institutions operating a school of health sciences that has full or provisional accreditation by the Association of American Medical Colleges. Full members are represented by the chief administrative officer of the member institution's health sciences library. Associate membership (and nonvoting representation) is available to organizations having an interest in the purposes and activities of the association.

Officers (2012–2013)

Pres. M. J. Tooey, Health Sciences and Human Services Lib., Univ. of Maryland, Baltimore; *Pres.-Elect* A. James Bothmer, Health Science Lib./Learning Resource Center, Creighton Univ.; *Secy./Treas.* Jett McCann, Dahlgren Memorial Lib., Georgetown Univ. Medical Center; *Past Pres.* Gary Freiburger, Arizona Health Sciences Lib., Univ. of Arizona.

Directors

Karen Butter, Lib. and Center for Knowledge Management, Univ. of California, San Francisco; Barbara Epstein, Health Sciences Lib. System, Univ. of Pittsburgh; Neil Rambo, NYU Health Sciences Lib., NYU Langone Medical Center.

Association of Independent Information Professionals

8550 United Plaza Blvd., Suite 1001, Baton Rouge, LA 70809
225-408-4400, fax 225-408-4422, e-mail office@aiip.org
World Wide Web http://www.aiip.org

Object

Members of the Association of Independent Information Professionals (AIIP) are owners of firms providing such information-related services as online and manual research, document delivery, database design, library support, consulting, writing, and publishing. The objectives of the association are

- To advance the knowledge and understanding of the information profession
- To promote and maintain high professional and ethical standards among its members
- To encourage independent information professionals to assemble to discuss common issues
- To promote the interchange of information among independent information professionals and various organizations
- To keep the public informed of the profession and of the responsibilities of the information professional

Membership

Memb. 50+.

Officers (2012–2013)

Pres. Scott Brown, Social Information Group. E-mail president@aiip.org; *Pres.-Elect* Jocelyn Sheppard, Red House Consulting; *Secy.* Joann M. Wleklinski, Wleklinski Information Services; *Treas.* Marilyn Harmacek, MHConsulting; *Past Pres.* Cynthia Hetherington, Hetherington Group.

Publications

AIIP Connections (q.).
Membership Directory (ann.).
Professional papers series.

Association of Jewish Libraries

P.O. Box 1118, Teaneck, NJ 07666
201-371-3255
World Wide Web http://www.jewishlibraries.org

Object

The Association of Jewish Libraries (AJL) promotes Jewish literacy through enhancement of libraries and library resources and through leadership for the profession and practitioners of Judaica librarianship. The association fosters access to information, learning, teaching, and research relating to Jews, Judaism, the Jewish experience, and Israel.

AJL membership is open to individuals and libraries, library workers, and library supporters. There are two divisions within AJL: RAS (Research Libraries, Archives, and Special Collections) and SSC (Schools, Synagogues, and Centers). The diverse membership includes libraries in synagogues, JCCs, day schools, yeshivot, universities, Holocaust museums, and the Library of Congress. Membership is drawn from North America and beyond, including from China, the Czech Republic, the Netherlands, Israel, Italy, South Africa, Switzerland, and the United Kingdom.

Goals

- Maintain high professional standards for Judaica librarians and recruit qualified individuals into the profession
- Facilitate communication and exchange of information on a global scale
- Encourage quality publication in the field in all formats and media
- Stimulate publication of high-quality children's literature
- Facilitate and encourage establishment of Judaica library collections
- Enhance information access for all through application of advanced technologies
- Publicize the organization and its activities in all relevant venues
- Stimulate awareness of Judaica library services among the public at large
- Promote recognition of Judaica librarianship within the wider library profession
- Encourage recognition of Judaica library services by other organizations and related professions
- Ensure continuity of the association through sound management, financial security, effective governance, and a dedicated and active membership

AJL conducts an annual convention in the United States or Canada in late June.

Membership

Memb. 1,000+. For dues information, contact the association. Year. July 1–June 30.

Officers (July 2012–June 2014)

Pres. Heidi Estrin. E-mail president@jewish libraries.org; *V.P./Pres.-Elect* Yaffa Weisman; *V.P. Memb.* Sheryl Stahl; *V.P. Publications* Joyce Levine; *Recording Secy.* Shoshanah Seidman; *Corresponding Secy.* Elana Gensler; *Treas.* Deborah Stern; *Past Pres.* James P. Rosenbloom; *RAS Pres.* Daniel Scheide; *SSC Pres.* Lisa Silverman.

Address correspondence to the association.

Publications

AJL Conference Proceedings.
AJL News (q., digital).
AJL Reviews (q., digital).
Judaica Librarianship (annual).

Association of Research Libraries

Executive Director, Elliott Shore
21 Dupont Circle N.W., Suite 800, Washington, DC 20036
202-296-2296, fax 202-872-0884, e-mail arlhq@arl.org
World Wide Web http://www.arl.org

Object

The Association of Research Libraries (ARL) is a nonprofit organization of 125 research libraries in the United States and Canada. Its mission is to influence the changing environment of scholarly communication and the public policies that affect research libraries and the diverse communities they serve. ARL pursues this mission by advancing the goals of its member research libraries, providing leadership in public and information policy to the scholarly and higher education communities, fostering the exchange of ideas and expertise, facilitating the emergence of new roles for research libraries, and shaping a future environment that leverages its interests with those of allied organizations.

Membership

Memb. 125. Membership is institutional. Dues: $25,579 for 2013.

Officers

Pres. Wendy Pradt Lougee, Univ. of Minnesota; *V.P./Pres.-Elect* Carol Pitts Diedrichs, Ohio State Univ.; *Past Pres.* Winston Tabb, Johns Hopkns Univ.

Board of Directors

Larry Alford, Univ. of Toronto; Deborah Carver, Univ. of Oregon; Carol Pitts Diedrichs, Ohio State Univ.; Connie Vinita Dowell, Vanderbilt Univ.; Thomas Hickerson, Univ. of Calgary; Ernie Ingels, Univ. of Alberta; Anne R. Kenney, Cornell Univ.; Wendy Pradt Lougee, Univ. of Minnesota; Charles B. Lowry (ex oficio), ARL; Olivia M. A. Madison, Iowa State Univ.; Carton Rogers (ex officio), Univ. of Pennsylvania; Judith C. Russell, Univ. of Florida; Jay Schafer, Univ. of Massachusetts Amherst; Brian E. C. Schottlaender (ex officio), Univ. of California, San Diego; Winston Tabb, Johns Hopkins Univ.; James F. Williams II (ex officio), Univ. of Colorado at Boulder.

Publications

Research Library Issues: A Quarterly Report from ARL, CNI, and SPARC (q.).
ARL Academic Health Sciences Library Statistics (ann.).
ARL Academic Law Library Statistics (ann.).
ARL Annual Salary Survey (ann.).
ARL Statistics (ann.).
SPEC Kit series (6 a year).

Committee and Working Group Chairs

Advancing Scholarly Communication. Brian E. C. Schottlaender, Univ. of California, San Diego.
ARL Licensing Working Group. Jay Starratt, Washington State Univ.
Diversity and Leadership. Marianne Gaunt, Rutgers Univ.
E-Research Working Group. Harriette Hemmas., Brown Univ.
Fair Use and Related Exemptions Working Group. Betsy Wilson, Univ. of Washington.

Influencing Public Policies. James F. Williams II, Univ. of Colorado at Boulder.
Membership. Fred Heath, Univ. of Texas at Austin.
Regional Federal Depository Libraries Working Group. Judith C. Russell, Univ. of Florida.
Statistics and Assessment. Robert E. Fox, Jr., Univ. of Louisville.
Transforming Research Libraries. Carton Rogers, Univ. of Pennsylvania.
Transforming Special Collections in the Digital Age Working Group, Thomas Hickerson, Univ. of Calgary.

ARL Membership

Non-university Libraries

Boston Public Lib., Center for Research Libs., Knowledge Management, Lib. of Congress, National Agricultural Lib., National Archives, National Lib. of Medicine, National Research Council, New York Public Lib., New York State Lib., Smithsonian Institution Libs.

University Libraries

Alabama; Albany (SUNY); Alberta; Arizona; Arizona State; Auburn; Boston College; Boston Univ.; Brigham Young; British Columbia; Brown; Buffalo (SUNY); Calgary; California, Berkeley; California, Davis; California, Irvine; California, Los Angeles; California, Riverside; California, San Diego; California, Santa Barbara; Case Western Reserve; Chicago; Cincinnati; Colorado; Colorado State; Columbia; Connecticut; Cornell; Dartmouth; Delaware; Duke; Emory; Florida; Florida State; George Washington; Georgetown; Georgia; Georgia Inst. of Technology; Guelph; Harvard; Hawaii; Houston; Howard; Illinois, Chicago; Illinois, Urbana-Champaign; Indiana; Iowa; Iowa State; Johns Hopkins; Kansas; Kent State; Kentucky; Laval; Louisiana State; Louisville; McGill; McMaster; Manitoba; Maryland; Massachusetts; Massachusetts Inst. of Technology; Miami (Florida); Michigan; Michigan State; Minnesota; Missouri; Montreal; Nebraska, Lincoln; New Mexico; New York; North Carolina; North Carolina State; Northwestern; Notre Dame; Ohio; Ohio State; Oklahoma; Oklahoma State; Oregon; Ottawa; Pennsylvania; Pennsylvania State; Pittsburgh; Princeton; Purdue; Queen's (Kingston, Ontario); Rice; Rochester; Rutgers; Saskatchewan; South Carolina; Southern California; Southern Illinois; Stony Brook (SUNY); Syracuse; Temple; Tennessee; Texas; Texas A&M; Texas Tech; Toronto; Tulane; Utah; Vanderbilt; Virginia; Virginia Tech; Washington; Washington (Saint Louis); Washington State; Waterloo; Wayne State; Western Ontario; Wisconsin; Yale; York.

Association of Vision Science Librarians

Chair, 2012–2014 D. J. Matthews
World Wide Web http://www.avsl.org

Object

To foster collective and individual acquisition and dissemination of vision science information, to improve services for all persons seeking such information, and to develop standards for libraries to which members are attached. Founded in 1968.

Officers

Chair D. J. Matthews, M. B. Ketchum Memorial Lib., Southern California College of Optometry, Fullerton; *Secy./Chair-Elect* Nancy Henderson, Pacific Univ. Lib., Forest Grove, Oregon; *Treas.* Elaine Wells, Harold Kohn Vision Science Lib., SUNY College of Optometry, New York, N.Y.

Publications

Core List of Audio-Visual Related Serials.
Guidelines for Vision Science Libraries.
Opening Day Book, Journal and AV Collection–Visual Science.
Publication Considerations in the Age of Electronic Opportunities.
Standards for Vision Science Libraries.
Union List of Vision-Related Serials (irreg.).

Meetings

Annual meeting held in the fall, mid-year mini-meeting with the Medical Library Association.

Beta Phi Mu
(International Library and Information Studies Honor Society)

Executive Director, Alison M. Lewis
The iSchool, College of Information Science and Technology
Drexel University, Philadelphia, PA 19104
215-895-5959, fax 215-895-2494, e-mail alewis@drexel.edu
World Wide Web http://www.beta-phi-mu.org

Object

To recognize distinguished achievement in and scholarly contributions to librarianship, information studies, or library education, and to sponsor and support appropriate professional and scholarly projects relating to these fields. Founded at the University of Illinois in 1948.

Membership

Memb. 36,000. Open to graduates of library school programs accredited by the American Library Association who fulfill the following requirements: complete the course requirements leading to a fifth year or other advanced degree in librarianship with a scholastic average of 3.75 where A equals 4 points (this provision shall also apply to planned programs of advanced study beyond the master's degree that require full-time study for one or more academic years). Each chapter is allowed to invite no more than 25 percent of the annual graduating class, and the faculty of participating library schools must attest to their initiates' professional promise.

Officers

Pres. Beth Paskoff, Louisiana State Univ., Baton Rouge, LA 70803; *V.P./Pres.-Elect* Amanda Ros, Tulane Libs. Recovery Center, New Orleans, LA 70123; *Treas.* Kate Inman, Drexel Univ., College of Info. Science and Technology, Philadelphia, PA 19104; *Exec. Dir.* Alison M. Lewis, Drexel Univ., College of Info. Science and Technology, Philadelphia, PA 19104. Tel. 215-895-5959, fax 215-895-2494, e-mail alewis@drexel.edu or betaphimu@drexel.edu.

Directors

Eileen G. Abels, Susan W. Alman, John M. Budd, Elizabeth Figa, Carrie Hurst, Charles McElroy, Shannon Tennant. *Dirs.-At-Large* Elaine Yontz, Melissa A. Hofmann.

Publications

Beta Phi Mu Monograph Series. Book-length scholarly works based on original research in subjects of interest to library and information professionals. Available from ABC-CLIO, 130 Cremona Drive, Santa Barbara, CA 93117. *Ed.* Lorraine J. Haricombe; *Assoc. Ed.* Keith Russell.
The Pipeline (electronic only). *Ed.* Erin Gabriele.

Chapters

Alpha. Univ. of Illinois at Urbana-Champaign, Grad. School of Lib. and Info. Science; *Gamma.* Florida State Univ., College of Communication and Info.; *Epsilon.* Univ. of North Carolina at Chapel Hill, School of Info. and Lib. Science; *Theta.* Pratt Inst., Grad. School of Lib. and Info. Science; *Iota.* Catholic Univ. of America, School of Lib. and Info. Science; Univ. of Maryland, College of Info. Studies; *Lambda.* Univ. of Oklahoma, School of Lib. and Info. Studies; *Xi.* Univ. of Hawaii at Manoa, School of Lib. and Info. Studies; *Omicron.* Rutgers Univ., Grad. School of Communication, Info. and Lib. Studies; *Pi.* Univ. of Pittsburgh, School of Info. Sciences; *Rho.* Kent State Univ., School of Lib. and Info. Science; *Sigma.* Drexel Univ., College of Info. Science and Technology; *Upsilon.* Univ. of Kentucky,

School of Lib. and Info. Science; *Phi.* Univ. of Denver, Grad. School of Lib. and Info. Science; *Chi.* Indiana Univ., School of Lib. and Info. Science; *Psi.* Univ. of Missouri at Columbia, School of Lib. and Info. Science; *Omega.* San Jose State Univ., School of Lib. and Info. Science; *Beta Alpha.* Queens College, City College of New York, Grad. School of Lib. and Info. Studies; *Beta Beta.* Simmons College, Grad. School of Lib. and Info. Science; *Beta Delta.* State Univ. of New York at Buffalo, Dept. of Lib. and Info. Studies; *Beta Epsilon.* Emporia State Univ., School of Lib. and Info. Management; *Beta Zeta.* Louisiana State Univ., School of Lib. and Info. Science; *Beta Eta.* Univ. of Texas at Austin, Grad. School of Lib. and Info. Science; *Beta Iota.* Univ. of Rhode Island, Grad. School of Lib. and Info. Studies; *Beta Kappa.* Univ. of Alabama, School of Lib. and Info. Studies; *Beta Lambda.* Texas Woman's Univ., School of Lib. and Info. Sciences; *Beta Mu.* Long Island Univ., Palmer School of Lib. and Info. Science; *Beta Nu.* Saint John's Univ., Div. of Lib. and Info. Science; *Beta Xi.* North Carolina Central Univ., School of Lib. and Info. Sciences; *Beta Omicron.* Univ. of Tennessee at Knoxville, School of Info. Sciences;

Beta Pi. Univ. of Arizona, School of Info. Resources and Lib. Science; *Beta Rho.* Univ. of Wisconsin at Milwaukee, School of Info.; *Beta Sigma.* Clarion Univ. of Pennsylvania, Dept. of Lib. Science; *Beta Tau.* Wayne State Univ., Lib. and Info. Science Program; *Beta Phi.* Univ. of South Florida, School of Lib. and Info. Science; *Beta Psi.* Univ. of Southern Mississippi, School of Lib. and Info. Science; *Beta Omega.* Univ. of South Carolina, College of Lib. and Info. Science; *Beta Beta Gamma.* Dominican Univ., Grad. School of Lib. and Info. Science; *Beta Beta Epsilon.* Univ. of Wisconsin at Madison, School of Lib. and Info. Studies; *Beta Beta Zeta.* Univ. of North Carolina at Greensboro, Dept. of Lib. and Info. Studies; *Beta Beta Theta.* Univ. of Iowa, School of Lib. and Info. Science; *Beta Beta Iota.* State Univ. of New York, Univ. at Albany, School of Info. Science and Policy; *Beta Beta Kappa.* Univ. of Puerto Rico, Grad. School of Info. Sciences and Technologies; *Pi Lambda Sigma.* Syracuse Univ., School of Info. Studies; *Beta Beta Mu.* Valdosta State Univ., School of Lib. and Info. Science; *Beta Beta Nu.* Univ. of North Texas, College of Info.; *Beta Beta Xi.* St. Catherine Univ., Master of Library and Information Science program.

Bibliographical Society of America

Executive Secretary, Michèle E. Randall
P.O. Box 1537, Lenox Hill Sta., New York, NY 10021
212-452-2710 (tel./fax), e-mail bsa@bibsocamer.org
World Wide Web http://www.bibsocamer.org

Object

To promote bibliographical research and to issue bibliographical publications. Organized 1904.

Membership

Memb. Dues (Indiv.) $65; (Sustaining) $250; (Contributing) $100; (Student) $20; (Inst.) $100; (Lifetime) $1,250. Year. Jan.–Dec.

Officers

Pres. Claudia Funke. E-mail claudiafunke@mac.com; *V.P.* John Crichton. E-mail jcrichton@brickrow.com; *Secy.* Caroline Duroselle-Melish. E-mail cmelish@fas.harvard.edu; *Treas.* G. Scott Clemons. E-mail scott.clemons@bbh.com; *Past Pres.* John Neal Hoover. E-mail jhoover@umsl.edu.

Council

(2013) Gerald Cloud, Eugene S. Flamm, David Alan Richards, Carolyn L. Smith; (2014) Douglas F. Bauer, Joan Friedman, Nina Musinsky, Gregory A. Pass; (2015) Christina Geiger, Michael Suarez, David J. Supino, Michael Thompson.

Publication

Papers of the Bibliographical Society of America (q.; memb.). *Ed.* Gregory A. Pass;

Managing Ed. Travis Gordon. E-mail travis gordon@mindspring.com.

Committee Chairs

Audit. R. Dyke Benjamin.
Fellowship. Gerald Cloud.
Finance. David J. Supino.
Program. Marcia Reed.
Publications. Gregory A. Pass.

Bibliographical Society of Canada
(La Société Bibliographique du Canada)

President, Janet Friskney
P.O. Box 575, Postal Station P, Toronto, ON M5S 2T1
World Wide Web http://www.bsc-sbc.ca/index.html

Object

The Bibliographical Society of Canada is a bilingual (English/French) organization that has as its goal the scholarly study of the history, description, and transmission of texts in all media and formats, with a primary emphasis on Canada, and the fulfillment of this goal through the following objectives:

- To promote the study and practice of bibliography: enumerative, historical, descriptive, analytical, and textual
- To further the study, research, and publication of book history and print culture
- To publish bibliographies and studies of book history and print culture
- To encourage the publication of bibliographies, critical editions, and studies of book history and print culture
- To promote the appropriate preservation and conservation of manuscript, archival, and published materials in various formats
- To encourage the utilization and analysis of relevant manuscript and archival sources as a foundation of bibliographical scholarship and book history
- To promote the interdisciplinary nature of bibliography, and to foster relationships

with other relevant organizations nationally and internationally
- To conduct the society without purpose of financial gain for its members, and to ensure that any profits or other accretions to the society shall be used in promoting its goal and objectives

Membership

The society welcomes as members all those who share its aims and wish to support and participate in bibliographical research and publication.

Officers

Pres. Janet Friskney. E-mail president@bsc-sbc.ca; *Senior V.P.* Linda Quirk; *2nd V.P.* Don McLeod; *Secy.* Greta Golick. E-mail secretary@bsc-sbc.ca; *Treas.* Tom Vincent.

Publications

Papers of the Bibliographical Society of Canada/Cahiers de la Société Bibliographique du Canada (s. ann).
The Bulletin/Le Bulletin (s. ann).

For a full list of the society's publications, see http://www.library.utoronto.ca/bsc/publicationseng.html.

Committee Chairs

Awards. Jillian Tomm.
Fellowships. Scott Schofield.
Publications. Geoffrey Little.

Black Caucus of the American Library Association

President, Jerome Offord, Jr.
World Wide Web http://www.bcala.org

Mission

The Black Caucus of the American Library Association (BCALA) serves as an advocate for the development, promotion, and improvement of library services and resources for the nation's African American community and provides leadership for the recruitment and professional development of African American librarians. Founded in 1970.

Membership

Membership is open to any person, institution, or business interested in promoting the development of library and information services for African Americans and other people of African descent and willing to maintain good financial standing with the organization. The membership is currently composed of librarians and other information professionals, library support staff, libraries, publishers, authors, vendors, and other library-related organizations in the United States and abroad. Dues (Corporate) $200; (Institutional) $60; (Regular) $45; (Student) $10.

Officers

Pres. Jerome Offord, Jr. E-mail jeromeoffordjr@gmail.com; *V.P./Pres.-Elect* Kelvin A. Watson. E-mail kantoniow@yahoo.com; *Secy.* Diane Covington. E-mail dianec@andrew.cmu.edu; *Treas.* Annie M. Ford. E-mail annieford@gmail.com; *Past Pres.* Jos N. Holman. E-mail jholman@tcpl.lib.in.us.

Executive Board

Jason K. Alston, Stanton Biddle, Bettye Black, Elizabeth Brumfield, Eboni Curry, D. L. Grant, Kymberley Keeton, Em Claire Knowles, Derek Mosley, Carol Nurse, Akilah Nosakhere, Lambert Shell, Gladys Smiley Bell, Eboni Stokes.

Publication

BCALA Newsletter (bi-mo; memb.). *Contact* Jason K. Alston. E-mail jasonalston@gmail.com.

Committee Chairs

Affiliate Chapters. Lambert Shell.
Affirmative Action. Howard F. McGinn.
ALA Relations. Allene Hayes.
Awards. Richard Bradberry, ayo dayo.
Budget/Audit. Wanda Brown, Kelvin Watson.
Constitution and Bylaws. D. L. Grant.
History. Sibyl E. Moses.
International Relations. Vivian Bordeaux, Eboni M. Stokes.
E. J. Josey Scholarship. Sylvia Sprinkle Hamlin.
Literary Awards. Jennifer Baxmeyer, Gladys Smiley Bell.
Membership. Rudolph Clay.
National Conference of African American Librarians 2013. Fannie Cox, Dennyvetta Davis.
Newsletter. Jason K. Alston.
Nominations/Elections. Karolyn Thompson.
Program. Jerome Offord, Jr.

Recruitment and Professional Development. Andrew P. Jackson (Sekou Molefi Baako), Charlene Maxey-Harris.

Services to Children of Families of African Descent. Karen Lemmons.

Smiley Fund. Gladys Smiley Bell.

Gladys Smiley Travel Grant. Gladys Smiley Bell.

Technology Advisory. Chanitra Bishop.

Dr. John C. Tyson Award. Esmeralda M. Kale.

Canadian Association for Information Science (L'Association Canadienne des Sciences de l'Information)

President, Anabel Quan-Haase
World Wide Web http://www.cais-acsi.ca

Object

To promote the advancement of information science in Canada and encourage and facilitate the exchange of information relating to the use, access, retrieval, organization, management, and dissemination of information.

Membership

Institutions and individuals interested in information science and involved in the gathering, organization, and dissemination of information (such as information scientists, archivists, librarians, computer scientists, documentalists, economists, educators, journalists, and psychologists) and who support CAIS's objectives can become association members.

Officers

Pres. Anabel Quan-Haase, Univ. of Western Ontario, London. E-mail anabel.quanhaase@gmail.com; *V.P.* Diane Rasmussen, Univ. of Western Ontario, London. E-mail dneal2@uwo.ca; *Secy.* Jen Pecoskie, Wayne State Univ. E-mail jpecoskie@wayne.edu; *Treas.* Anatoliy Gruzd, Dalhousie Univ. E-mail gruzd@dal.ca; *Past Pres.* Siobhan Stevenson, Univ. of Toronto. E-mail siobhan.stevenson@utoronto.ca.

Publication

Canadian Journal of Information and Library Science. Ed. Clément Arsenault, Univ. de Montréal. E-mail clement.arsenault@u montreal.ca.

Canadian Association of Research Libraries
(Association des Bibliothèques de Recherche du Canada)

Executive Director, Brent Roe
600-350 Albert St., Ottawa, ON K1R 1B1
613-482-9344, e-mail brent.roe@carl-abrc.ca
World Wide Web http://www.carl-abrc.ca

Membership

The Canadian Association of Research Libraries (CARL), established in 1976, is the leadership organization for the Canadian research library community. The association's members are the 29 major academic research libraries across Canada together with Library and Archives Canada and the Canada Institute for Scientific and Technical Information (CISTI). Membership is institutional, open primarily to libraries of Canadian universities that have doctoral graduates in both the arts and the sciences. CARL is an associate member of the Association of Universities and Colleges of Canada (AUCC) and is incorporated as a not-for-profit organization under the Canada Corporations Act.

Mission

The association provides leadership on behalf of Canada's research libraries and enhances their capacity to advance research and higher education. It promotes effective and sustainable scholarly communication, and public policy that enables broad access to scholarly information.

Officers

Pres. Thomas Hickerson, Univ. of Calgary. E-mail tom.hickerson@ucalgary.ca; *V.P./Pres.-Elect* Gerald Beasley, Concordia Univ. E-mail gerald.beasley@concordia.ca; *Secy.* Richard Dumont, Univ. de Montréal. E-mail richard.dumont@umontreal.ca; *Treas.* John Teskey, Univ. of New Brunswick. E-mail jteskey@unb.ca; *Past Pres.* Ernie Ingles, Univ. of Alberta. E-mail ernie.ingles@ualberta.ca; *Dirs.* Charles Eckman, Simon Fraser Univ. E-mail ceckman@sfu.ca; Martha Whitehead, Queen's Univ. E-mail martha.whitehead@queensu.ca.

Member Institutions

Univ. of Alberta, Univ. of British Columbia, Brock Univ., Univ. of Calgary, Carleton Univ., CISTI (Canada Institute for Scientific and Technical Information), Concordia Univ., Dalhousie Univ., Univ. of Guelph, Université Laval, Lib. and Archives Canada, McGill Univ., McMaster Univ., Univ. of Manitoba, Memorial Univ. of Newfoundland, Université de Montréal, Univ. of New Brunswick, Univ. of Ottawa, Université du Québec à Montréal, Queen's Univ., Univ. of Regina, Ryerson Univ., Univ. of Saskatchewan, Université de Sherbrooke, Simon Fraser Univ., Univ. of Toronto, Univ. of Victoria, Univ. of Waterloo, Univ. of Western Ontario, Univ. of Windsor, York Univ.

Canadian Library Association
(Association Canadienne des Bibliothèques)

Executive Director, Kelly Moore
1150 Morrison Drive, Suite 400, Ottawa, ON K2H 8S9
613-232-9625 ext. 306, fax 613-563-9895, e-mail kmoore@cla.ca
World Wide Web http://www.cla.ca

Object

The Canadian Library Association (CLA) is the national voice for Canada's library communities. CLA champions library values and the value of libraries, influences public policy affecting libraries, inspires and supports learning, and collaborates to strengthen the library community. The association represents Canadian librarianship to the federal government and media, carries on international liaison with other library associations and cultural agencies, offers professional development programs, and supports such core library values as intellectual freedom and access to information, particularly for disadvantaged populations. Founded in 1946, CLA is a not-for-profit voluntary organization governed by an elected executive council.

Membership

Memb. (Indiv.) 3,475; (Inst.) 470. Open to individuals, institutions, library boards, and groups interested in librarianship and in library and information services.

Officers

Pres. Pilar Martinez, Edmonton Public Lib; *V.P./Pres.-Elect* Marie DeYoung, Saint Mary's Univ.; *Treas.* Mary-Jo Romaniuk, Univ. of Alberta; *Past Pres.* Karen Adams, Univ. of Manitoba.

Publications

Feliciter: Linking Canada's Information Professionals (6 a year; electronic journal).
CLA Digest (bi-weekly; electronic newsletter).

Catholic Library Association

Acting Executive Director, Malachy R. McCarthy
205 W. Monroe St., Suite 314, Chicago, IL 60606
312-739-1776, fax 312-739-1778, e-mail cla@cathla.org
World Wide Web http://www.cathla.org

Object

The promotion and encouragement of Catholic literature and library work through cooperation, publications, education, and information. Founded in 1921.

Membership

Memb. 1,000. Dues $55–$500. Year. July–June.

Officers (2011–2013)

Pres. Malachy R. McCarthy, Claretian Missionaries Archives, 205 W. Monroe St., Chicago, IL 60606; *V.P./Pres.-Elect* Sara B. Baron, Regent Univ. Lib., 1000 Regent University Drive, Virginia Beach, VA 23464; *Past Pres.* Nancy K. Schmidtmann, 174 Theodore Drive, Coram, NY 11727.

Address correspondence to the executive director.

Executive Board

Officers; Jean Elvekrog, 401 Doral Court, Waunakee, WI 53597; Susan B. Finney, St. Mary's Dominican H.S., 7701 Walmsley Ave., New Orleans, LA 70125; Cait C. Kokolus, St. Charles Borromeo Seminary, 100 E. Wynnewood Rd., Wynnewood, PA 19096; Frances O'Dell, OSF, Barry Univ. Lib., 11300 N.E. 2 Ave., Miami Shores, FL 33161.

Publication

Catholic Library World (q.; memb.; nonmemb. $125). *General Ed.* Sigrid Kelsey.

Chief Officers of State Library Agencies

Association Director, Laura Singler
201 E. Main St., Suite 1405, Lexington, KY 40507
859-514-9151, fax 859-514-9166, e-mail lsingler@amrms.com
World Wide Web http://www.cosla.org

Object

Chief Officers of State Library Agencies (CO-SLA) is an independent organization of the chief officers of state and territorial agencies designated as the state library administrative agency and responsible for statewide library development. Its purpose is to identify and address issues of common concern and national interest; to further state library agency relationships with federal government and national organizations; and to initiate cooperative action for the improvement of library services to the people of the United States.

COSLA's membership consists solely of these top library officers, variously designated as state librarian, director, commissioner, or executive secretary. The organization provides a continuing mechanism for dealing with the problems and challenges faced by these officers. Its work is carried on through its members, a board of directors, and committees.

Board of Directors (2012–2014)

Pres. Ann Joslin, State Libn., Idaho Commission for Libs., 325 W. State St., Boise, ID 83702. Tel. 208-334-2150, e-mail ann.joslin@libraries.idaho.gov; *V.P./Pres.-Elect* Kendall Wiggin, State Libn., Connecticut State Lib., 231 Capitol Ave., Hartford, CT 06106. Tel. 860-757-6510, e-mail kendall.wiggin@ct.gov; *Treas.* Sandra Treadway, Libn. of Virginia, Lib. of Virginia, 800 E. Broad St., Richmond, VA 23219. Tel. 804-692-3535, e-mail sandra.treadway@lva.virginia.gov; *Secy.* Wayne Onkst, State Libn. and Commissioner, Kentucky Dept. for Libs. and Archives, P.O. Box 537, Frankfort, KY 40602. Tel. 502-564-8300, e-mail wayne.onkst@ky.gov; *Past Pres.* Lamar Veatch, State Libn., Georgia Public Lib. Service, 1800 Century Place, Suite 150, Atlanta, GA 30345-4304. Tel. 404-235-7200, e-mail lveatch@georgialibraries.org; *Dirs.* Stacey Aldrich, Deputy Secy. for Libs., Office of Commonwealth Libs., Pennsylvania Dept. of Educ., 607 South Drive, Forum Bldg., Room 200, Harrisburg, PA 17120-0600. Tel. 717-787-2646, e-mail saldrich@pa.gov; Martha Reid, State Libn., Vermont Dept. of Libs., 109 State St., Montpelier, VT 05609. Tel. 802-828-3265, e-mail martha.reid@state.vt.us.

Chinese American Librarians Association

Executive Director, Haipeng Li
E-mail haipeng4cala@gmail.com
World Wide Web http://www.cala-web.org

Object

To enhance communications among Chinese American librarians as well as between Chinese American librarians and other librarians; to serve as a forum for discussion of mutual problems and professional concerns among Chinese American librarians; to promote Sino-American librarianship and library services; and to provide a vehicle whereby Chinese American librarians can cooperate with other associations and organizations having similar or allied interests.

Membership

Memb. 1,500+. Open to anyone who is interested in the association's goals and activities. Dues (Regular) $30; (International/Student/Nonsalaried) $15; (Inst.) $100; (Affiliated) $100; (Life) $300.

Officers

Pres. Esther Lee. E-mail eyw888lee@gmail.com; *V.P./Pres.-Elect* Lisa Zhao. E-mail zhls50@yahoo.com; *Incoming V.P./Pres.-Elect* Carol Gee. E-mail kachuen.gee@lehman.cuny.edu; *Treas.* Maria Fung. E-mail maria4cala@gmail.com; *Past Pres.* Min Chou. E-mail minchou.njcu@gmail.com.

Publications

CALA Newsletter (2 a year; memb.; online). *Eds.* Priscilla Yu. E-mail pcyu@illinois.edu; Sai Deng. E-mail saideng@gmail.com.

Journal of Library and Information Science (JLIS) (2 a year). *Editorial Board Chair* (2012–2015) Chengzhi Wang, Columbia Univ. Libs. E-mail cw2165@columbia.edu.

Membership Directory (memb.).

Occasional Paper Series (OPS) (online). *Ed.* (2012–2015) Yunshan Ye. E-mail yye@jhu.edu.

Committee Chairs

Annual Conference, Program Planning (2012–2013). Lisa Zhao.

Annual Conference, Program Planning (2013–2014). Carol Gee.

Awards. Frank Xu.

Best Book Award. Carol Gee, Jianye He.

Constitution and Bylaws. Kuei Chiu, Manuel Urrizola.

Elections. Haipeng Li.

Finance. Clement Lau.

International Relations. Michael Bailou Huang.

Membership. Weiling Liu, Lian Ruan.

Mentorship Program. Hong Miao, Ying Zhong.

Nominating. Min Chou.

Public Relations/Fund Raising. Jia Mi, Sally Tseng.

Publications. Jia Mi, Dajin Sun.

Scholarship Committee. Min Liu, Yongyi Song.

Sally C. Tseng's Professional Development Grant Committee. Songqian Lu, Ying Xu.

Web Committee. Vincci Kwong, Weiling Liu.

Church and Synagogue Library Association

10157 SW Barbur Blvd., No.102C, Portland, OR 97219
503-244-6919, 800-542-2752, fax 503-977-3734, e-mail CSLA@worldaccessnet.com
World Wide Web http://www.cslainfo.org

Object

The Church and Synagogue Library Association (CSLA) provides educational guidance in the establishment and maintenance of congregational libraries.

Its purpose is to act as a unifying core for congregational libraries; to provide the opportunity for a mutual sharing of practices and problems; to inspire and encourage a sense of purpose and mission among congregational librarians; to study and guide the development of congregational librarianship toward recognition as a formal branch of the library profession. Founded in 1967.

Membership

Memb. 1,000. Dues (Inst.) $200; (Affiliated) $100; (Church or Synagogue) $70 ($75 foreign); (Indiv.) $50 ($55 foreign).

Officers (July 2012–July 2013)

Pres. Evelyn Pockrass; *1st V.P./Pres.-Elect* Cheryl Cutchin; *2nd V.P.* David Reid; *Treas.* Alice Campbell; *Past Pres.* Marjorie Smink; *Ed., Congregational Libraries Today* Jeri Zulli; *Admin.* Judith Janzen.

Executive Board

Officers; committee chairs.

Publications

Bibliographies (4; price varies).
Congregational Libraries Today (q.; memb.; nonmemb. $50; Canada $60).
CSLA Guides (price varies).

Committee Chairs

Awards. Glenda Strombom.
Conference. Marjorie Smink, Naomi Kauffman.
Finance. Pat Shufeldt.
Publications. Dotty Lewis.

Coalition for Networked Information

Executive Director, Clifford A. Lynch
21 Dupont Circle, Suite 800, Washington, DC 20036
202-296-5098, fax 202-872-0884, e-mail http://www.cni.org/contact
World Wide Web http://www.cni.org

Mission

The Coalition for Networked Information (CNI) is an organization to advance the transformative promise of networked information technology for the advancement of scholarly communication and the enrichment of intellectual productivity.

Membership

Memb. 224. Membership is institutional. Dues $7,100. Year. July–June.

Steering Committee

Daniel Cohen, George Mason Univ.; Jeffrey Horrell, Dartmouth College; Thomas C. Leonard, Univ. of California; Clifford A. Lynch, CNI; Kathryn Joan Monday, Univ. of Richmond; Diana G. Oblinger, EDUCAUSE; Carrie E. Regenstein, Carnegie Mellon Univ.; Elliott Shore, Assn. of Research Libs.; Tyler O. Walters, Virginia Polytechnic Institute and State Univ.; Donald J. Waters, Andrew W. Mellon Foundation.

Publication

CNI-Announce (subscribe by e-mail to cni-announce-subscribe@cni.org).

Council on Library and Information Resources

1707 L St. N.W., Suite 650, Washington, DC 20036
202-939-4750, fax 202-939-4765
World Wide Web http://www.clir.org

Object

In 1997 the Council on Library Resources (CLR) and the Commission on Preservation and Access (CPA) merged and became the Council on Library and Information Resources (CLIR). CLIR is an independent, nonprofit organization that forges strategies to enhance research, teaching, and learning environments in collaboration with libraries, cultural institutions, and communities of higher learning.

CLIR promotes forward-looking collaborative solutions that transcend disciplinary, institutional, professional, and geographic boundaries in support of the public good. CLIR identifies and defines the key emerging issues relating to the welfare of libraries and the constituencies they serve, convenes the leaders who can influence change, and promotes collaboration among the institutions and organizations that can achieve change. The council's interests embrace the entire range of information resources and services from traditional library and archival materials to emerging digital formats. It assumes a particular interest in helping institutions cope with the accelerating pace of change associated with the transition into the digital environment.

While maintaining appropriate collaboration and liaison with other institutions and organizations, CLIR operates independently of any particular institutional or vested interests. Through the composition of its board, it brings the broadest possible perspective to bear upon defining and establishing the priority of the issues with which it is concerned.

Board

CLIR's Board of Directors currently has 19 members.

Officers

Chair Herman Pabbruwe; *Pres.* Charles Henry. E-mail chenry@clir.org; *V. Chair* David Rum-sey; *Secy.* Karin Wittenborg; *Treas.* David Gift. Address correspondence to headquarters.

Publications

Annual Report.

CLIR Issues (bi-mo.).

Technical reports.

Federal Library and Information Network

Executive Director, Blane K. Dessy
Library of Congress, Washington, DC 20540-4935
202-707-4800
World Wide Web http://www.loc.gov/flicc

Object

The Federal Library and Information Network (FEDLINK) is an organization of federal agencies working together to achieve optimum use of the resources and facilities of federal libraries and information centers by promoting common services, coordinating and sharing available resources, and providing continuing professional education for federal library and information staff. FEDLINK serves as a forum for discussion of the policies, programs, procedures, and technologies that affect federal libraries and the information services they provide to their agencies, to Congress, the federal courts, and the public.

Membership

The FEDLINK voting membership is composed of representatives of the following U.S. federal departments and agencies: Each of the national libraries (the Library of Congress, National Agricultural Library, National Library of Education, National Library of Medicine, and the National Transportation Library); each cabinet-level executive department, as defined in 5 U.S.C. § 101; additional departments and agencies (the Defense Technical Information Center; departments of the Air Force, Army, and Navy; Executive Office of the President, Government Accountability Office, General Services Administration, Government Printing Office, Institute of Museum and Library Services, National Aeronautics and Space Administration, National Archives and Records Administration, National Technical Information Service [Department of Commerce], Office of Management and Budget, Office of Personnel Management, Office of Scientific and Technical Information [Department of Energy], Office of the Director of National Intelligence, and the Smithsonian Institution); the U.S. Supreme Court and the Administrative Office of the U.S. Courts; the District of Columbia; and other federal independent agencies and government corporations.

Officers

Co-Chairs Roberta I. Shaffer and Kathryn Mendenhall, Library of Congress; *Exec. Dir.* Blane K. Dessy. Address correspondence to the executive director.

Medical Library Association

Executive Director, Carla Funk
65 E. Wacker Place, Suite 1900, Chicago, IL 60601-7298
312-419-9094, fax 312-419-8950, e-mail info@mlahq.org
World Wide Web http://www.mlanet.org

Object

The Medical Library Association (MLA) is a nonprofit professional education organization with more than 4,000 health sciences information professional members and partners worldwide. MLA provides lifelong educational opportunities, supports a knowledgebase of health information research, and works with a global network of partners to promote the importance of high-quality information for improved health to the health care community and the public.

Membership

Memb. (Inst.) 600+; (Indiv.) 3,400+, in more than 50 countries. Institutional members are medical and allied scientific libraries. Individual members are people who are (or were at the time membership was established) engaged in professional library or bibliographic work in medical and allied scientific libraries or people who are interested in medical or allied scientific libraries. Members can be affiliated with one or more of MLA's more than 20 special-interest sections and its regional chapters.

Officers

Pres. Jane Blumenthal. E-mail janeblum@umich.edu; *Pres.-Elect* Dixie Jones. E-mail djon17@lsuhsc.edu; *Past Pres.* Gerald Perry. E-mail jerry.perry@ucdenver.edu; *Secy.* Michelle Kraft; *Treas.* Marianne Comegys.

Directors

Marianne Comegys (2013), Julia Esparza (2015), Cynthia Henderson (2012), Michelle Kraft (2014), Rikke Ogawa (2013), Jodi L. Philbrick (2014); Gabriel Rios (2014), Chris Shaffer (2015), Julia Shaw-Kokot (2013), Joy Summers-Ables (2014).

Publications

Journal of the Medical Library Association (q.; $190).

MLA News (10 a year; $120).

Miscellaneous (request current list from association headquarters).

Music Library Association

8551 Research Way, Suite 180, Middleton, WI 53562
608-836-5825, e-mail mla@areditions.com
World Wide Web http://www.musiclibraryassoc.org

Object

The Music Library Association provides a professional forum for librarians, archivists, and others who support and preserve the world's musical heritage. To achieve this mission, it

- Provides leadership for the collection and preservation of music and information about music in libraries and archives
- Develops and delivers programs that promote continuing education and professional development in music librarianship
- Ensures and enhances intellectual access to music for all by contributing to the development and revision of national and international codes, formats, and other standards for the bibliographic control of music
- Ensures and enhances access to music for all by facilitating best practices for housing, preserving, and providing access to music
- Promotes legislation that strengthens music library services and universal access to music
- Fosters information literacy and lifelong learning by promoting music reference services, library instruction programs, and publications
- Collaborates with other groups in the music and technology industries, government, and librarianship, to promote its mission and values

Membership

Memb. 1,200+. Dues (Inst.) $135; (Indiv.) $100; (Retired or Assoc.) $70; (Paraprofessional) $55; (Student) $45. (Foreign, add $10.) Year. July 1–June 30.

Officers

Pres. Jerry L. McBride. E-mail jerry.mcbride@stanford.edu; *V.P./Pres.-elect* Michael Colby. E-mail mdcolby@ucdavis.edu; *Recording Secy.* Pamela Bristah. E-mail pbristah@wellesley.edu; *Admin. Officer* Linda W. Blair. E-mail lblair@esm.rochester.edu; *Past Pres.* Ruthann B. McTyre, 2000 Voxman Music Bldg., Univ. of Iowa, Iowa City, IA 52242-1795. Tel. 319-335-3088, fax 319-335-2637, e-mail ruthann-mctyre@uiowa.edu.

Members-at-Large

(2011–2013) Daniel Boomhower, Kirstin Dougan, Laurie J. Sampsel; (2012–2014) Paula Hickner, Stephen Landstreet, Mark Scharff.

Publications

MLA Index and Bibliography Series (irreg.; price varies).
MLA Newsletter (q.; memb.).
MLA Technical Reports (irreg.; price varies).
Music Cataloging Bulletin (mo.; online subscription only, $35).
Notes (q.; indiv. $85; inst. $100).

National Association of Government Archives and Records Administrators

1450 Western Ave., Suite 101, Albany, NY 12203
518-694-8472, e-mail nagara@caphill.com
World Wide Web http://www.nagara.org

Object

Founded in 1984, NAGARA is a growing nationwide association of local, state, and federal archivists and records administrators, and others interested in improved care and management of government records. NAGARA promotes public awareness of government records and archives management programs, encourages interchange of information among government archives and records management agencies, develops and implements professional standards of government records and archival administration, and encourages study and research into records management problems and issues.

Membership

Most NAGARA members are federal, state, and local archival and records management agencies.

Officers

Pres. Daphne DeLeon, Nevada State Lib. and Archives, 100 N. Stewart St., Carson City, NV 89701-4285. Tel. 775-684-3315, fax 775-684-3311, e-mail ddeleon@nevadaculture.org; *V.P.* Tanya Marshall, Vermont State Archivist, Vermont State Archives and Records Admin., 1078 U.S. Route 2, Middlesex, Montpelier, VT 05633-7701. Tel. 802-828-0405, fax 802-828-3710, e-mail tmarshall@sec.state.vt.us; *Secy.* Lisa C. Johnston, City of Artesia, P.O.

Box 1310, Artesia, NM 88211. Tel. 575-748-8290, fax 575-746-3886, e-mail ljohnston@artesianm.gov; *Treas.* Nancy Fortna, National Archives and Records Administration, Seventh and Pennsylvania Ave. N.W., Room G-13 NWCC, Washington, DC 20408-0001. Tel. 202-357-5288, e-mail nancy.fortna@nara.gov; *Past Pres.* Paul R. Bergeron, City of Nashua, 229 Main St., Nashua, NH 03060. Tel. 603-589-3010, fax 603-589-3029, e-mail bergeronp@nashuanh.gov; *Memb. Services and Publications Coord.* Steve Grandin.

Directors

Douglas K. King, Sedgwick County (Kansas) Government; Wayne Moore, Tennessee State Lib. and Archives; Arian Ravanbakhsh, National Archives and Records Admin.; Michael Sherman, Chatham County (Georgia) Admin. Services; Melanie Sturgeon, Polly Rosenbaum Archives and History Building, Phoenix, Arizona; Galen R. Wilson, National Archives and Records Admin.; Val Wood, San Diego County, California.

Publications

Clearinghouse (q.; memb.).
Crossroads (q.; memb.).
Government Records Issues (series).
Preservation Needs in State Archives.
Program Reporting Guidelines for Government Records Programs.

National Federation of Advanced Information Services

Executive Director, Bonnie Lawlor
1518 Walnut St., Suite 1004, Philadelphia, PA 19102
215-893-1561, fax 215-893-1564, e-mail nfais@nfais.org
World Wide Web http://www.nfais.org

Object

The National Federation of Advanced Information Services (NFAIS) is an international nonprofit membership organization composed of leading information providers. Its membership includes government agencies, nonprofit scholarly societies, private sector businesses, and libraries. NFAIS is committed to promoting the value of credible, high-quality content. It serves all groups that create, aggregate, organize, or facilitate access to such information. In order to improve members' capabilities and to contribute to their ongoing success, NFAIS provides opportunities for education, advocacy, and a forum in which to address common interests. Founded in 1958.

Membership

Memb. 60. Full members are organizations whose main focus is any of the following activities: information creation, organization, aggregation, dissemination, access, or retrieval. Organizations are eligible for associate member status if they do not meet the qualifications for full membership.

Officers (2012–2013)

Pres. Barbara Dobbs Mackenzie, RILM Abstracts of Music Literature; *Pres.-Elect* Suzanne BeDell, Elsevier; *Past Pres.* Keith MacGregor, Thomson Reuters IP and Science; *Treas.* Chris McCue, CAS; *Secy.* Mark Gauthier, H. W. Wilson.

Directors

David Brown, Ric Davis, Ellen Herbst, Judith Russell, Judy Salk, Mary Sauer-Games, Lynn Willis; ex officio, David Gillikin, Jeff Massa.

Staff

Exec. Dir. Bonnie Lawlor. E-mail blawlor@nfais.org; *Dir., Planning and Communications* Jill O'Neill. E-mail jilloneill@nfais.org; *Customer Service* Margaret Manson. E-mail mmanson@nfais.org.

Publications

For a detailed list of NFAIS publications, see the NFAIS website, http://www.nfais.org.

National Information Standards Organization (NISO)

Executive Director, Todd Carpenter
3600 Clipper Mill Rd., Suite 302, Baltimore, MD 21211
301-654-2512, fax 410-685-5278, e-mail nisohq@niso.org
World Wide Web http://www.niso.org

Object

The National Information Standards Organization (NISO) fosters the development and maintenance of standards that facilitate the creation, persistent management, and effective interchange of information so that it can be trusted for use in research and learning. To fulfill this mission, NISO engages libraries, publishers, information aggregators, and other organizations that support learning, research, and scholarship through the creation, organization, management, and curation of knowledge. NISO works with intersecting communities of interest and across the entire lifecycle of an information standard. NISO standards apply both traditional and new technologies to the full range of information-related needs, including discovery, retrieval, repurposing, storage, metadata, business information, and preservation.

NISO also develops and publishes recommended practices, technical reports, white papers, and information publications. NISO holds regular educational programs on standards, technologies, and related topics where standards-based solutions can help solve problems. These programs include webinars, online virtual conferences, in-person forums, and teleconferences.

Experts from the information industry, libraries, systems vendors, and publishing participate in the development of NISO standards and recommended practices. The standards are approved by the consensus body of NISO's voting membership, representing libraries, publishers, vendors, government, associations, and private businesses and organizations. NISO is supported by its membership and grants.

NISO is a not-for-profit association accredited by the American National Standards Institute (ANSI) and serves as the U.S. Technical Advisory Group Administrator to ISO/TC 46 Information and Documentation as well as the secretariat for ISO/TC 46/SC 9, Identification and Description.

Membership

Voting Members: 80+. Open to any organization, association, government agency, or company willing to participate in and having substantial concern for the development of NISO standards. Library Standards Alliance Members: 60+. Open to any academic, public, special, or government-supported library interested in supporting the mission of NISO.

Officers

Chair Barbara Preece, California State Univ., San Marcos; *V. Chair/Chair-Elect* Heather Reid, Copyright Clearance Center, Danvers, Massachusetts; *Treas.* Bruce Rosenblum, INERA, Inc., Belmont, Massachusetts; *Past Chair* Bruce Heterick, JSTOR and Portico, New York.

Directors

Janice Fleming, American Psychological Assn.; Gerry Grenier, IEEE; Chuck Koscher, CrossRef; Wendy Pradt Lougee, Univ. of Minnesota Libs.; Mairéad Martin, Pennsylvania State Univ.; Patricia A. Steele, Univ. of Maryland; Mike Teets, OCLC; Tyler Walters, Virginia Tech Univ. Libs.; Keith Webster, John Wiley and Sons.

Publications

Information Standards Quarterly (print: $130/year domestic, $165/year international, back issues $36; electronic version available in open access from the NISO website).

NISO Newsline (free e-newsletter released on the first Wednesday of each month; distributed through e-mail and posted on the NISO website).

Working Group Connection (free quarterly e-newsletter supplement to *Newsline* that provides updates on the activities of NISO's working groups; distributed through e-mail and posted on the NISO website).

For other NISO publications, see the article "National Information Standards Organization (NISO) Standards" later in Part 6.

NISO's published standards, recommended practices, and technical reports are available free of charge as downloadable PDF files from the NISO website (http://www.niso.org). Hardcopy documents are available for sale from the website.

Patent and Trademark Resource Center Association

World Wide Web http://www.ptrca.org

Object

The Patent and Trademark Resource Center Association (PTRCA) provides a support structure for the more than 80 patent and trademark resource centers (PTRCs) affiliated with the U.S. Patent and Trademark Office (USPTO). The association's mission is to discover the interests, needs, opinions, and goals of the PTRCs and to advise USPTO in these matters for the benefit of PTRCs and their users, and to assist USPTO in planning and implementing appropriate services. Founded in 1983 as the Patent Depository Library Advisory Council; name changed to Patent and Trademark Depository Library Association in 1988; became an American Library Association affiliate in 1996. In 2011 the association was renamed the Patent and Trademark Resource Center Association.

Membership

Open to any person employed in a patent and trademark depository library whose responsibilities include the patent collection. Affiliate membership is also available. Dues $50 in 2013, increasing to $65 in 2014.

Officers (2012–2013)

Pres. Walt Johnson. E-mail wjohnson@hclib. org; *V.P./Pres.-Elect* Ran Raider. E-mail ran. raider@wright.edu; *Secy.* Martin Wallace. E-mail martin.wallace@umit.maine.edu; *Treas.* Jim Miller. E-mail jmiller2@umd.edu; *Past Pres.* Marian Armour Gemmen. E-mail marmour@wvu.edu

Divisional Representatives

(Academic) Suzanne Reinman. E-mail suzanne.reinman@okstate.edu (2011–2013); Paulina Borrego. E-mail pborrego@library. umass.edu (2012–2014); (Public) Spruce Fraser. E-mail sfraser@slpl.org (2011–2013); Monique Mason. E-mail mmason@akronlibrary. org (2012–2014).

Publications

PTDLA Newsletter. Ed. Suzanne Reinman. E-mail suzanne.reinman@okstate.edu.
Intellectual Property (IP). Electronic at http://www.ptdla.org/ipjournal.html. *Ed.* Michael White.

REFORMA (National Association to Promote Library and Information Services to Latinos and the Spanish-Speaking)

President, Denice Adkins
P.O. Box 4386, Fresno, CA 93744
480-734-4460, e-mail officemgr@reforma.org
World Wide Web http://www.reforma.org

Object

Promoting library services to the Spanish-speaking for nearly 40 years, REFORMA, an affiliate of the American Library Association, works in a number of areas to promote the development of library collections to include Spanish-language and Latino-oriented materials; the recruitment of more bilingual and bicultural professionals and support staff; the development of library services and programs that meet the needs of the Latino community; the establishment of a national network among individuals who share its goals; the education of the U.S. Latino population in regard to the availability and types of library services; and lobbying efforts to preserve existing library resource centers serving the interest of Latinos.

Membership

Memb. 800+. Any person who is supportive of the goals and objectives of REFORMA.

Officers

Pres. Denice Adkins, School of Info. Science and Learning Technologies, Univ. of Missouri. Tel. 573-884-9804, e-mail president@reforma. org; *V.P./Pres.-Elect* Isabel Espinal, W. E. B. Du Bois Lib., Univ. of Massachusetts. Tel. 413-545-6817, e-mail vice-president@reforma.org; *Secy./Recorder* Louis Munoz, Brooklyn Public Lib. Tel. 718-230-2417, secretary@reforma. org; *Treas.* Sarah Dahlen, California State Univ., Monterey Bay. Tel. 831-582-4432, e-mail treasurer@reforma.org; *Memb.-at-Large* Cristina Ramirez, Richmond (Virginia) Pub-lic Lib. Tel. 804-646-8488, e-mail cristina. ramirez@richmondgov.com; *Past Pres.* Maria Kramer, Redwood City (California) Public Lib. Tel. 650-780-7043, e-mail past-president@reforma.org.

Committees

Pura Belpré Award. Jamie Campbell Naidoo.
Children's and Young Adult Services. Lucía González, Ana E. Pavon.
Education. Mario A. Ascencio.
Finance. Maria Kramer.
Fund Raising. Sylvia D. Hall-Ellis.
Information Technology. Juan Carlos Rodríguez.
International Relations. Miguel Garcia Colon.
Legislative. Loida Garcia-Febo.
Librarian of the Year Award. Susan Luevano.
Membership. Daniel Berdaner.
Nominations. Monica Chapa Domercq.
Organizational Development. Martha A. Parker.
Program. Isabel Espinal.
Public Relations. Yago Cura.
Recruitment and Mentoring. Minerva Alaniz.
Scholarship. Mary A. Donley.
Translations. Armando Trejo.

Publication

REFORMA Newsletter (s. ann; memb.).

Meetings

General membership and board meetings take place at the American Library Association Midwinter Meeting and Annual Conference.

Society for Scholarly Publishing

Executive Director, Ann Mehan Crosse
10200 W. 44 Ave., Suite 304, Wheat Ridge, CO 80033
303-422-3914, fax 303-422-8894, e-mail info@sspnet.org or amcrosse@resourcecenter.org
World Wide Web http://www.sspnet.org

Object

To draw together individuals involved in the process of scholarly publishing. This process requires successful interaction of the many functions performed within the scholarly community. The Society for Scholarly Publishing (SSP) provides the leadership for such interaction by creating opportunities for the exchange of information and opinions among scholars, editors, publishers, librarians, printers, booksellers, and all others engaged in scholarly publishing.

Membership

Memb. 1,100. Open to all with an interest in the scholarly publishing process and dissemination of information. Dues (New Member) $145; (Indiv. Renewal) $160; (Libn.) $80; (Student) $35; (Supporting) $1,430; (Sustaining) $3,475. Year. Jan. 1–Dec. 31.

Executive Committee

Pres. Carol Anne Meyer, CrossRef. E-mail cmeyer@crossref.org; *Pres.-Elect* Kent Anderson, *Journal of Bone and Joint Surgery.* E-mail kanderson@jbjs.org; *Secy./Treas.* Todd Carpenter, National Info. Standards Organization. E-mail tcarpenter@niso.org; *Past Pres.* Theresa Van Schaik, American Society of Clinical Oncology. E-mail: terry.vanschaik@asco.org.

Directors

Michael T. Clarke, Alice Meadows, Ann Michael, Eileen Kiley Novak, Anne Orens, Kristen Fisher Ratan, David Smith, Heather Staines, Adrian Stanley, William M. Wakeling.

Meetings

An annual meeting is held in late May/early June. SSP also conducts a Librarian Focus Group (February), the IN Conference (September), and the Fall Seminar Series (November).

Society of American Archivists

Executive Director, Nancy Perkin Beaumont
17 N. State St., Suite 1425, Chicago, IL 60602
866-722-7858, 312-606-0722, fax 312-606-0728, e-mail nbeaumont@archivists.org
World Wide Web http://www.archivists.org

Object

Founded in 1936, the Society of American Archivists (SAA) is North America's oldest and largest national archival professional association. SAA's mission is to serve the education and information needs of more than 6,100 individual and institutional members and to provide leadership to ensure the identification, preservation, and use of records of historical value.

Membership

Memb. 6,100+. Dues (Indiv.) $48 to $240, graduated according to salary; (Assoc.) $90, domestic; (Student or Bridge) $48; (Inst.) $285; (Sustaining Inst.) $525.

Officers (2012–2013)

Pres. Jackie Dooley, OCLC Research, San Clemente, CA 92673. Tel. 949-492-5060, e-mail dooleyj@oclc.org; *V.P.* Danna Bell-Russel, Library of Congress. Tel. 202-707-4159, e-mail dbellr@att.net.

Staff

Exec. Dir. Nancy Perkin Beaumont. E-mail nbeaumont@archivists.org; *Dir., Publishing* Teresa Brinati. E-mail tbrinati@archivists.org; *Dir., Educ.* Solveig De Sutter. E-mail sdesutter @archivists.org; *Dir., Finance and Admin.* Tom Jurczak. E-mail tjurczak@archivists.org; *Mgr., Service Center* Carlos Salgado. E-mail csalgado@archivists.org; *Program Coord.* René Mueller. E-mail rmueller@archivists.org; *Editorial and Production Coord.* Anne Hartman. E-mail ahartman@archivists.org; *Educ. Program Coord.* Amanda Look. E-mail alook@ archivists.org; *Service Center Reps.* Lee Gonzalez. E-mail lgonzalez@archivists.org; Jeanette Spears. E-mail jspears@archivists.org.

Publications

American Archivist (2 a year) individual print or online edition, $169; print and online, $199; institutional, $209 print or online, $259 print and online). *Ed.* Gregory Hunter; *Reviews Ed.* Amy Cooper Cary.
Archival Outlook (bi-mo.; memb.). *Eds.* Teresa Brinati, Anne Hartman.

Software and Information Industry Association

1090 Vermont Ave. N.W., Washington, DC 20005-4095
202-289-7442, fax 202-289-7097
World Wide Web http://www.siia.net

Membership

Mem⊃. 500+ companies. The Software and Information Industry Association (SIIA) was formed January 1, 1999, through the merger of the Software Publishers Association (SPA) and the Information Industry Association (IIA). Open to companies involved in the creation, distribution, and use of software, information products, services, and technologies. For details on membership and dues, see the SIIA website.

Staff

Pres. Kenneth Wasch. E-mail kwasch@siia. net; *General Counsel* Keith Kupferschmid; *Senior V.P.s* Tom Davin, Brian Rosenberg; *V.P.s*

Karen Billings, Rhianna Collier, Eric Fredell, Mike Hettinger, Mark MacCarthy, Tom Meldrum, Kathy Greenler Sexton; *Senior Dirs.* David LeDuc, Mark Schneiderman.

Board of Directors

Mark Bohannon, Red Hat; Cynthia Braddon, McGraw-Hill; Cindy Cook, Cengage Learning; Mary Cullinane, Houghton Mifflin Harcourt; Kate Friedrich, Thomson Reuters; Kenneth Glueck, Oracle; Randall Hopkins, NASDAQ OMX; Steven Kingsley, Pearson; Steve Manzo, Reed Elsevier; Randy Marcinko, Marcinko Enterprises; Bernard McKay, Intuit; Timothy Sheehy, IBM Corporation (chair); Johanna Shelton, Google; Daniel Smith, Dow Jones; Michael Ward, Cisco; Ken Wasch, SIIA.

SPARC

Executive Director, Heather Joseph
21 Dupont Circle, Suite 800, Washington, DC 20036
202-296-2296, fax 202-872-0884, e-mail sparc@arl.org
World Wide Web http://www.arl.org/sparc

SPARC, the Scholarly Publishing and Academic Resources Coalition, is a global organization that promotes expanded sharing of scholarship in the networked digital environment. Developed by the Association of Research Libraries, SPARC has become a catalyst for change. Its pragmatic focus is to stimulate the emergence of new scholarly communication models that expand the dissemination of scholarly research and reduce financial pressures on libraries. Action by SPARC in collaboration with stakeholders—including authors, publishers, and libraries—builds on the unprecedented opportunities created by the networked digital environment to advance the conduct of scholarship.

SPARC's role in stimulating change focuses on

- Educating stakeholders about the problems facing scholarly communication and the opportunities for them to play a role in achieving positive change

- Advocating policy changes that advance scholarly communication and explicitly recognize that dissemination of scholarship is an essential, inseparable component of the research process

- Incubating demonstrations of new publishing and sustainability models that benefit scholarship and academe

SPARC is a visible advocate for changes in scholarly communication that benefit more than the academic community alone. Founded in 1997, it has expanded to represent more than 800 academic and research libraries in North America, the United Kingdom, Europe, and Japan.

Membership

SPARC membership is open to international academic and research institutions, organizations, and consortia that share an interest in creating a more open and diverse marketplace for scholarly communication. Dues are scaled by membership type and budget. For more information, visit SPARC's website at http://www.arl.org/sparc, SPARC Europe at http://www.sparceurope.org, or SPARC Japan at http://www.nii.ac.jp/sparc.

Publications

Open Access Spectrum Guide (2012), by SPARC in collaboration with PLOS and OASPA (http://www.plos.org/about/open-access/howopenisit).

You've Signed the Boycott, Now What? A SPARC Guide for Campus Action (2012) (http://www.arl.org/sparc/bm~doc/sparc_boycott_next_steps.pdf).

Open-Access Journal Publishing Resource Index (2011) by Raym Crow.

Library Publishing Services: Strategies for Success (2011) by Raym Crow, October Ivins, Allyson Mower, Daureen Nesdill, Mark Newton, Julie Speer, and Charles Watkinson.

Library Publishing Services: Strategies for Success Report, Version 1.0 (2011) by Raym Crow, October Ivins, Allyson Mower, Daureen Nesdill, Mark Newton, Julie Speer, and Charles Watkinson.

Campus-Based Open-Access Publishing Funds: A Practical Guide to Design and Implementation (2010) by Greg Tananbaum.

Campus-Based Publishing Partnerships: A Guide to Critical Issues (2009) by Raym Crow.

Income Models for Open Access: An Overview of Current Practice (2009) by Raym Crow.

The Right to Research: The Student Guide to Opening Access to Scholarship (2008), part of a campaign to engage students on the issue of research access.

Greater Reach for Research: Expanding Readership Through Digital Repositories (2008), the initiative to educate faculty on the benefits of open repositories and emerging research access policies.

Author Rights (2006), an educational initiative and introduction to the SPARC Author Addendum, a legal form that enables authors of journal articles to modify publishers' copyright transfer agreements and allow authors to keep key rights to their articles.

"Open Access News Blog," daily updates on the worldwide movement for open access to science and scholarship, written by Peter Suber and cosponsored by SPARC.

SPARC Open Access Newsletter, a monthly roundup of developments relating to open access publishing written by Peter Suber.

SPARC e-news, SPARC's monthly newsletter featuring SPARC activities, an industry roundup, upcoming workshops and events, and articles relating to developments in scholarly communication.

Publishing Cooperatives: An Alternative for Society Publishers (2006) by Raym Crow.

Sponsorships for Nonprofit Scholarly and Scientific Journals: A Guide to Defining and Negotiating Successful Sponsorships (2005) by Raym Crow.

A more-complete list of SPARC publications, including brochures, articles, and guides, is available at http://www.arl.org/sparc.

Special Libraries Association (SLA)

Chief Executive Officer, Janice R. Lachance
331 S. Patrick St., Alexandria, VA 22314
703-647-4900, fax 703-647-4901, e-mail resources@sla.org
World Wide Web http://www.sla.org

Mission

The Special Libraries Association promotes and strengthens its members through learning, advocacy, and networking initiatives.

Strategic Vision

SLA is a global association of information and knowledge professionals who are employed in every sector of the economy. Its members thrive where data, information, and knowledge intersect, and its strategic partners support SLA because they believe in the association's mission and the future of its members. SLA's goal is to support information professionals as they contribute, in their varied and evolving roles, to the opportunities and achievements of organizations, communities, and society.

Membership

Memb 9,000. Dues (Organizational) $750; (Indiv.) $114–$200; (Student/Retired/Salary less than $18,000 a year) $40.

Officers

Pres. Deb Hunt, Information Edge. E-mail dhunt@information-edge.com; *Pres.-Elect* Kate Arnold. E-mail katearnold64@yahoo.co.uk; *Treas.* John DiGilio, E-mail jdigilio@reedsmith.com, Reed Smith LLP; *Chapter Cabinet Chair* Debbie Schachter, Douglas College. E-mail schachterd@douglas.bc.ca; *Chapter Cabinet Chair-Elect* Kama Siegel, Libs. of Stevens County (Washington). E-mail kamasue@gmail.com; *Div. Cabinet Chair* Ann Koopman, Thomas Jefferson Univ. E-mail ann.koopman@jefferson.edu; *Div. Cabinet Chair-Elect* Tara Murray, American Philatelic Research Lib. E-mail tmurray@stamps.org.

Directors

Officers; Marilyn Bromley, Jill Hurst-Wahl, Hal Kirkwood, Sara Tompson.

Publication

Information Outlook (memb., nonmemb. $125/yr.).

Theatre Library Association

c/o New York Public Library for the Performing Arts
40 Lincoln Center Plaza, New York, NY 10023
E-mail info@tla-online.org
World Wide Web http://www.tla-online.org

Object

To further the interests of collecting, preserving, and using theater, cinema, and performing arts materials in libraries, museums, and private collections. Founded in 1937.

Membership

Memb. 300. Dues (Indiv.) $20–$40, (Inst.) $40–$50. Year. Jan. 1–Dec. 31.

Officers

Pres. Nancy Friedland, Columbia Univ.; *V.P.* Angela Weaver, Univ. of Washington; *Exec. Secy.* Rebecca Lord, New York Univ.; *Treas.* Colleen Reilly, Slippery Rock Univ.

Executive Board

Diana Bertolini, Susan Brady, John Calhoun, Charlotte Cubbage, Leahkim Gannett, Beth Kattelman, Diana King, Francesca Marini, Karen Nickeson, Tiffany Nixon, Doug Reside, Morgen Stevens-Garmon; *Honorary* Louis A. Rachow, Marian Seldes; *Legal Counsel* Georgia Harper; *Past Pres.* Kenneth Schlesinger.

Publications

Broadside (3 a year; memb.). *Ed.* Angela Weaver.

Performing Arts Resources (occasional; memb.).

Membership Directory (annual; memb.). *Ed.* Rebecca Lord.

Committee Chairs

Book Awards. To be announced.
Conference Planning. Angela Weaver.
Membership. Beth Kerr.
Nominating. Kenneth Schlesinger.
Professional Awards. Francesca Marini.
Publications. Leahkim Gannett.
Strategic Planning. Angela Weaver.

Urban Libraries Council

125 S. Wacker Drive, Suite 1050, Chicago, IL 60606
312-676-0999, fax 312-676-0950, e-mail info@urbanlibraries.org
World Wide Web http://www.urbanlibraries.org

Object

Since 1971 the Urban Libraries Council (ULC) has worked to strengthen public libraries as an essential part of urban life. A member organization of North America's leading public library systems, ULC serves as a forum for research widely recognized and used by public and private sector leaders. Its members are thought leaders dedicated to leadership, innovation, and the continuous transformation of libraries to meet community needs.

ULC's work focuses on helping public libraries to identify and utilize skills and strategies that match the challenges of the 21st century.

Membership

Membership is open to public libraries and to corporate partners specializing in library-related materials and services. The organization also offers associate memberships.

Officers (2012–2013)

Chair Joan Prince; *V. Chair/Chair-Elect* Mela-nie Huggins; *Secy./Treas.* John F. Szabo; *Past Chair* Keith B. Simmons; *Member-at-Large* Karen "Kari" Glover.

Officers serve one-year terms, members of the executive board two-year terms. New officers are elected and take office at the summer annual meeting of the council.

Executive Board

Susan Adams, Ruth Anna, Melinda Cervantes, Jan Harder, Dennis B. Martinez, Vailey Oehlke, Matthew K. Poland, Gloria Rubio-Cortés, Michael Sherrod, Gary A. Wasdin, Rashad Young.

Key Staff

CEO and Pres. Susan Benton; *Project Mgr.* Mary Colleen Bragiel; *Senior Program Mgr.* Jake Cowan; *Program Leader for Educ.* Amy Eshleman; *Finance and Admin.* Angela Goodrich; *Communications and Member Services* Jodi Lazar; *Program Communications Mgr.* Sheila Murphy; *Senior Communications Mgr.* Alison Saffold; *Exec. Asst. to the Pres.* Erika Slaughter.

State, Provincial, and Regional Library Associations

The associations in this section are organized under three headings: United States, Canada, and Regional. Both the United States and Canada are represented under Regional associations.

United States

Alabama

Memb. 1,200. Term of Office. Apr. 2012–Apr. 2013. Publication. *The Alabama Librarian* (q.). *Pres.* Emily Tish, Trussville Public Lib., 201 Parkway Drive, Trussville 35173. Tel. 205-559-4639, e-mail etish@bham.lib.al.us; *Pres.-Elect* Jeff Simpson, Rosa Parks Lib., Troy Univ.–Montgomery, 252 Montgomery St., Montgomery 36104. Tel. 334-241-8604, e-mail simpson@troy.edu; *Secy.* Paula Sue Whittaker Laurita, Athens-Limestone Public Lib., 405 E. South St., Athens 35611. Tel 256-232-1233, e-mail drago.biblioteche@gmail.com; *Treas.* Tim Bailey, Auburn Univ. at Montgomery, P.O. Box 244023, Montgomery 36124-4023. Tel. 334-398-0825, e-mail tbailey1@aum.edu; *Past Pres.* Steven Yates, Mountain Brook H.S., 3650 Bethune Drive, Birmingham 35223. Tel. 205-826-3303, e-mail yatess@mtnbrook.k12.al.us.

Address correspondence to the association, 9154 Eastchase Pkwy., Suite 418, Montgomery 36117. Tel. 334-414-0113, e-mail admin@allanet.org.

World Wide Web http://allanet.org.

Alaska

Memb. 450+. Publication. *Newspoke* (q.). *Pres.* Linda Wynne. E-mail lindaleewynne@gmail.com; *Pres.-Elect* Stacey Glaser. E-mail sglaser@alaska.edu; *Secy.* Julie Niederhauser. E-mail julie.niederhauser@alaska.gov; *Treas.* Patricia Linville. E-mail plinville@cityofseward.net; *Conference Coord.* Mollie Good. E-mail mgood@ci.valdez.ak.us; *Past Pres.* Michael Robinson. E-mail afmcr@uaa.alaska.edu; *Exec. Officer* Mary Jennings. E-mail maryj@gci.net.

Address correspondence to the secretary, Alaska Lib. Assn., P.O. Box 81084, Fairbanks 99708. Fax 877-863-1401, e-mail akla@akla.org.

World Wide Web http://www.akla.org.

Arizona

Memb. 1,000. Term of Office. Nov. 2012–Nov. 2013. Publication. *AzLA Newsletter* (mo.). *Pres.* Tom Wilding, SIRLS, Univ. of Arizona, 1515 E. 1 St., Tucson 85719. E-mail president@azla.org or wilding@email.arizona.edu; *Pres.-Elect* Ann Boles, Wickenburg Public Lib. Tel. 928-533-2276, e-mail ann.boles@gmail.com; *Secy.* Erin MacFarlane, Northwest Regional Lib., 16089 N. Bullard Ave., Surprise 85374. Tel. 602-652-3406, e-mail erin macfarlane@mcldaz.org; *Treas.* Claudia Leon, Glendale Public Lib. Tel. 623-930-3570, e-mail cleon@glendaleaz.com; *Past Pres.* Nancy Deegan, South Mountain Community College, 7050 S. 24 St., Phoenix 85042-5806. Tel. 602-305-5877, e-mail president@azla.org or nancy.deegan@smcmail.maricopa.edu; *Exec. Secy.* Debbie J. Hanson, Arizona Lib. Assn., 1030 E. Baseline Rd., No. 105-1025, Tempe 85283. Tel. 480-609-3999, fax 480-609-3939, e-mail admin@azla.org.

Address correspondence to the executive secretary.

World Wide Web http://www.azla.org.

Arkansas

Memb. 600. Term of Office. Jan.–Dec. 2013. Publication. *Arkansas Libraries* (bi-mo.). *Pres.* Patricia Miller, Remington College, 19 Remington Rd., Little Rock 72204. Tel. 501-312-0007, e-mail trish.miller@remington college.edu; *V.P./Pres.-Elect* Holly Mercer, East Central Arkansas Regional Lib., 410 E. Merriman Ave., Wynn 72396. Tel. 870-238-3850, e-mail hmercer@crosscountrylibrary.org; *Secy./Treas.* Jamie Melson, Central Arkansas Lib. System, 100 Rock St., Little Rock 72201. Tel. 501-918-3074, e-mail jamiem@cals.lib.ar.us; *Past Pres.* Jim Robb, North Arkansas College, 1515 Pioneer Drive, Harrison 72601. Tel. 870-391-3359, e-mail jrobb@ northark.edu; *Exec. Admin.* Lynda Hampel, Arkansas Lib. Assn., P.O. Box 958, Benton 72018-0958. Tel. 501-860-7585, fax 501-778-4014, e-mail arlib2@sbcglobal.net.

Address correspondence to the executive administrator.

World Wide Web http://www.arlib.org.

California

Memb. 2,500. Publication. *CLA Insider* (online).

Pres. Derek Wolfgram, Santa Clara County Lib. E-mail derekclaprez@gmail.com; *V.P./ Pres.-Elect* Deborah Doyle, CALTAC. E-mail zorrah@gmail.com; *Treas.* Barbara Flynn, Contra Costa County Libs. E-mail bflynn@ ccclib.org; *Past Pres.* Wayne Disher, Disher Lib. Services. E-mail disherlibraryservices@ gmail.com; *Exec. Dir.* Rosario Garza. E-mail rgarza@socallibraries.org.

Address correspondence to the executive director, California Lib. Assn., 248 E. Foothill Blvd., Suite 101, Monrovia, CA 91016. Tel. 650-376-0886, fax 650-539-2341.

World Wide Web http://www.cla-net.org.

Colorado

Pres. Stephen Sweeney. E-mail stephen.sweeney @archden.org; *V.P./Pres.-Elect* Kari May. E-mail director@elbertcountylibrary.org; *Secy.* Dinah Kress. E-mail dinah.kress@asd20.org; *Treas.* Chris Brogan. E-mail cgbrogan@msn. com; *Past Pres.* Linda Conway. E-mail linda conway@rocketmail.com.

Address correspondence to the president, Colorado Assn. of Libs., 3030 W. 81 Ave., Westminster 80031. Tel. 303-463-6400, fax 303-458-0002.

World Wide Web http://www.cal-webs.org.

Connecticut

Memb. 1,000+. Term of Office. July 2012–June 2013. Publication. *CLA Today* (online). E-mail editor@ctlibrarians.org.

Pres. Carl R. DeMilia, New Milford Public Lib., 24 Main St., New Milford 6776. Tel. 860 355-1191 ext. 210, fax 860-350-9579, e-mail cdemilia@biblio.org; *V.P./Pres.-Elect* Richard Conroy, Essex Lib. Assn., 33 West Ave., Essex 06426. Tel. 860-767-1560, e-mail rconroy@ essexlib.org; *Recording Secy.* Beth Crowley, Scranton Lib., 801 Boston Post Rd., Madison 06443. Tel. 203-245-7365, e-mail crowleyb@ madisonct.org; *Treas.* Christina Baum, Southern Connecticut State Univ. Tel. 203 392-5760, e-mail baum1@southernct.edu; *Past Pres.* Elizabeth Anne Reiter, Groton Public Lib. Tel. 860-441-6750, fax 860-448-0363, e-mail breiter @town.groton.ct.us.

Address correspondence to Connecticut Lib. Assn., 234 Court St., Middletown 06457. Tel. 860-346-2444, fax 860-344-9199, e-mail cla@ ctlibrarians.org.

World Wide Web http://www.ctlibrary association.org.

Delaware

Memb. 200+. Term of Office. Apr. 2012–Apr. 2013. Publication. *DLA Bulletin* (online only).

Pres. Terri Jones, Hockessin Lib., 1023 Valley Rd., Hockessin 19707. Tel. 302-239-5160, e-mail terrijones18@gmail.com; *V.P.* Christine Payne, Appoquinimink H.S., 1080 Bunker Hill Rd., Middletown 19709. Tel. 302-449-3840, e-mail christine.payne@appo.k12. de.us; *Secy.* Maureen S. Miller, Lewes Public Lib., 111 Adams Ave., Lewes 19958. Tel. 302-645-4633, e-mail maureen.miller@lib.de.us; *Treas.* Ed Goyda, Lewes Public Lib., 111 Adams Ave., Lewes 19958. E-mail ed.goyda@lib. de.us; *Past Pres.* Patty Langley, Delaware Div. of Libs., 121 Duke of York St., Dover 19901. Tel. 302-257-3011, fax 302-739-6787, e-mail patty.langley@state.de.us; *Exec. Dir.* Cathay Crosby, Delaware Div. of Libs., 121 Duke of York St., Dover 19901. Tel. 302-983-1430, fax 302-739-6787.

Address correspondence to the association, Box 816, Dover 19903-0816. E-mail dla@dla. lib.de.us.

World Wide Web http://www2.lib.udel.edu/ dla.

District of Columbia

Memb. 300+. Term of Office. July 2012–June 2013. Publication. *Capital Librarian* (s. ann.).

Pres. Jacqueline Protka; *V.P./Pres.-Elect* Amanda Wilson; *Secy.* Jessica McGilvray; *Treas.* Roman Santillan; *Past Pres.* Megan

Sheils; *Membership Secy.* Rebecca Trinite; *Dirs.* Barbara Conaty, Vickie Crawley, Karen Quash.

Address correspondence to the association, Box 14177, Benjamin Franklin Sta., Washington 20044.

World Wide Web http://www.dcla.org.

Florida

Memb. (Indiv.) 1,000+. Publication. *Florida Libraries* (s. ann.). *Ed.* Maria Gebhardt. Tel. 954-357-7570, e-mail mariagfla@gmail.com. *Pres.* Barbara Stites, Florida Gulf Coast Univ. Lib., 10501 FGCU Blvd. S., Fort Myers 33965-6501. Tel. 239-590-7602, e-mail bstites@fgcu.edu; *V.P./Pres.-Elect* Gladys Roberts, Polk County Lib. Cooperative. Tel. 863-519-7958, e-mail gladys.roberts@mypclc. info; *Secy.* Ruth O'Donnell, Tallahassee. Tel. 850-668-6911, e-mail ruth.odonnell@comcast. net; *Treas.* Mary Anne Hodel, Orange County Lib. Dist. Tel. 407-835-7611, e-mail hodel. maryanne@ocls.info; *Past Pres.* Gloria Colvin, 2505 Blarney Drive, Tallahassee 32309. Tel. 850-645-1680, e-mail gpcolvin@yahoo.com; *Exec. Dir.* Faye Roberts, P.O. Box 1571, Lake City 32056-1571. Tel. 386-438-5795, fax 386-438-5796, e-mail faye.roberts@comcast.net.

Address correspondence to the executive director.

World Wide Web http://www.flalib.org.

Georgia

Memb. 800+. Publication. *Georgia Library Quarterly.* *Ed.* Jeff Heck, Reese Lib., Augusta State Univ., 2500 Walton Way, Augusta 30904-2200. E-mail jheck@aug.edu. *Pres.* Diana Very, Georgia Public Lib. Service. Tel. 404-235-7156, e-mail dvery@georgia libraries.org; *1st V.P./Pres.-Elect* Susan Morris, Univ. of Georgia. Tel. 706-542-0642, e-mail smorris@uga.edu; *2nd V.P./Membership Chair* Amelia Glawe, Georgia Perimeter College. Tel. 678-458-0006, e-mail amelia.glawe@gpc.edu; *Secy.* Jessica Everingham, Altamaha Technical College. Tel. 912-427-1928, e-mail jeveringham @altamahatech.edu; *Treas.* Ashley Dupuy, Kennesaw State Univ. Tel. 770-499-3590, e-mail adupuy@kennesaw.edu; *Past Pres.* Elizabeth Bagley, Agnes Scott College. Tel. 404-471-5277, e-mail ebagley@agnesscott.edu.

Address correspondence to the president, Georgia Lib. Assn., P.O. Box 793, Rex 30273-0793.

World Wide Web http://gla.georgialibraries. org.

Hawaii

Memb. 250. Publication. HLA Blog, "Hawaii Library Association" (http://hawaiilibraryasso-ciation.blogspot.com). *Pres.* Christina Abelardo, Sgt. Yano Lib. E-mail christinathelibrarian@gmail.com; *V.P./ Pres.-Elect* To be announced; *Secy.* Susan Hammer, Mid Pacific Institute; *Treas.* Jude Y. Yang, Univ. of Hawaii at Manoa; *Past Pres.* Christine Pawliuk, Hawaii Business Research Lib. E-mail christine.pawliuk@hisbdc.org.

Address correspondence to the association at hawaii.library.association@gmail.com.

World Wide Web http://hla.chaminade.edu.

Idaho

Memb. 420. Term of Office. Oct. 2012–Oct. 2013 *Pres.* Karen Yother, Community Lib. Network, 8385 N. Government Way, Hayden 83835. Tel. 208-772-5612 ext. 121, e-mail kareny@communitylibrary.net; *V.P./Pres.-Elect* Rami Attebury, Univ. of Idaho Lib., P.O. Box 442350, Moscow 88344-2350. Tel. 208-885-2503, e-mail rattebur@uidaho.edu; *Secy.* Megan Egbert, Meridian Lib. Dist., 1326 W. Cherry Lane, Meridian 83642. Tel. 208-888-4451, e-mail megan@mld.org; *Treas.* Cheri Rendler, Meridian Lib. Dist., 1326 W. Cherry Lane, Meridian 83642. Tel. 208-472-1751; e-mail cheri@mld.org; *Past Pres.* Gena Marker, Centennial H.S., 12400 W. McMillan Rd., Boise 83713. Tel. 208-855-4261, e-mail marker. gena@meridianschools.org.

Address correspondence to the association, P.O. Box 8533, Moscow 83844.

World Wide Web http://www.idaholibraries. org.

Illinois

Memb. 3,500. Term of Office. July–July. Publication. *ILA Reporter* (bi-mo.). *Pres.* Pamela Van Kirk, 708 N. I St., Monmouth 61462. Tel. 309-734-3922, e-mail pamela.

vankirk@gmail.com; *V.P./Pres.-Elect* Su Erickson, Robert Morris Univ., 905 Meridan Lake Drive, Aurora 60504. Tel. 630-375-8209, fax 630-375-8193, e-mail serickson@robertmorris.edu; *Treas.* Leslie Warren, American Bar Assn., 321 N. Clark St., Chicago 60654-7598. Tel. 312-988-5737, fax 312-988-5494, e-mail leslieann.warren@gmail.com; *Past Pres.* Lynn Elam, Algonquin Area Public Lib. Dist., 2600 Harnish Drive, Algonquin 60102. Tel. 847-458-6069, fax 847-458-9370, e-mail lelam@aapld.org; *Exec. Dir.* Robert P. Doyle, Illinois Lib. Assn., 33 W. Grand Ave., Suite 401, Chicago 60654-6799. Tel. 312-644-1896, fax 312-644-1899, e-maildoyle@ila.org.

Address correspondence to the executive director.

World Wide Web http://www.ila.org.

Indiana

Memb. 2,000+. Publications. *Indiana Libraries* (s. ann.). *Ed.* Kristi Palmer, IUPUI Univ. Lib., 755 W. Michigan, Indianapolis 46202. Tel. 317-274-8230, e-mail klpalmer@iupui.edu; *Focus on Indiana Libraries* (11 a year, memb.). *Ed.* Diane J. Bever, Kokomo Lib., Indiana Univ., 2300 S. Washington St., P.O. Box 9003, Kokomo 46904-9003. Tel. 765-455-9345, fax 765-455-9276, e-mail dbever@iuk.edu.

Pres. Robin Crumrin, IUPUI Univ. Lib., Indianapolis. E-mail rcrumrin@iupui.edu; *Pres.-Elect* Marcia Learned Au, Evansville Vanderburgh Public Lib. E-mail mau@evpl.org; *Secy.* Kelly Ehinger, Adams Public Lib. System, Decatur. E-mail ehinger@apls.lib.in.us; *Treas.* Amy Harshbarger, Logan Lib., Rose-Hulman Institute of Technology, Terre Haute. E-mail harshbarg@rose-hulman.edu; *Past Pres.* Dennis LeLoup, Avon Intermediate School East, Avon 46123. E-mail djleloup@avon-schools.org; *Exec. Dir.* Susan Akers. Tel. 317-257-2040 ext. 101, e-mail sakers@ilfonline.org.

Address correspondence to Indiana Lib. Federation, 941 E. 86 St., Suite 260, Indianapolis 46240. Tel. 317-257-2040, fax 317-257-1389.

World Wide Web http://www.ilfonline.org.

Iowa

Memb. 1,500. Publication. *The Catalyst* (bi-mo.).

Pres. Mary Heinzman, St. Ambrose Univ., 518 W. Locust St., Davenport 52803. Tel. 563-333-6241, e-mail heinzmanmaryb@sau.edu; *V.P./Pres.-Elect* Sarah Willeford; *Exec. Board* Mary Cameron, Maeve Clark, Katherine Howsare, Kathy Kaldenberg, John Lerdal, Marilyn Murphy, Kathy Parsons, Jill Sandres, Duncan Stewart; *Past Pres.* Lorraine Borowski. E-mail lborowski@decorah.lib.ia.us.

Address correspondence to the association, 525 S.W. 5 St., Suite A, Des Moines 50309. Tel. 515-273-5322, fax 515-309-4576.

World Wide Web http://www.iowalibrary association.org.

Kansas

Memb. 1,500. Term of Office. July 2012–June 2013. Publication. *KLA Connects* (q.).

Pres. Mickey Coalwell, Northeast Kansas Lib. System, 4317 W. 6 St., Lawrence 66049. Tel. 785-838-4090, e-mail mcoalwell@nekls.org; *V.P.* Cathy Reeves, Dodge City Public Lib., 1001 N. 2 Ave., Dodge City 67801. Tel. 620-225-0248, e-mail cathyr@dcpl.info; *2nd V.P.* Terri Summey, Emporia State Univ. Libs. and Archives, Campus Box 4051, Emporia 66801. Tel. 620-341-5058, e-mail tsummey@emporia.edu; *Secy.* Kim Gile, Johnson County Lib., 9875 W. 87 St., Overland Park 66212. Tel. 913-826-4600 ext. 64479, e-mail gilek@jocolibrary.org; *Treas.* Candi Hemel, Cimarron City Lib., 120 N. Main, P.O. Box 645, Cimarron 67835. Tel. 620-855-3808, e-mail director@cimarroncitylibrary.org; *Past Pres.* Royce Kitts, Tonganoxie Public Lib., 303 S. Bury, Tonganoxie 66086. Tel. 913-845-3281, fax 913-845-2962, e-mail director@tonganoxie library.org; *Exec. Secy.* Lisa Beebe.

Address correspondence to the president, Kansas Lib. Assn., 1020 S.W. Washburn, Topeka 66604. Tel. 785-580-4518, fax 785-580-4595, e-mail kansaslibraryassociation@yahoo.com.

World Wide Web http://www.kslibassoc.org.

Kentucky

Memb. 1,600. Term of Office. Oct. 2012–Oct. 2013. Publication. *Kentucky Libraries* (q.).

Pres. Lisa Rice, Warren County Public Lib., 1225 State St., Bowling Green 42101. Tel. 270-781-4882 ext. 202, e-mail lisar@warrenpl.org;

Pres.-Elect Brenda Metzger, Lone Oak H.S., 225 John E. Robinson Ave., Paducah 42003. Tel. 270-554-2920, e-mail brenda.metzger@ mccracken.kyschools.us; *Secy.* Abby Thorne, Bluegrass Community and Technical College, 460 Cooper Drive, Lexington 40506. E-mail abby.thorne@gmail.com; *Past Pres.* Terry Buckner, Learning Resource Center, Bluegrass Community and Technical College, 222B Oswald Bldg., 460 Cooper Drive, Lexington 40506. Tel. 859-246-6397, e-mail terry.buckner @kctcs.edu; *Exec. Dir.* Tom Underwood, 1501 Twilight Trail, Frankfort 40601. Tel. 502-223-5322, fax 502-223-4937, e-mail info@kylibasn. org.

Address correspondence to the executive director.

World Wide Web http://www.klaonline.org

Louisiana

Memb. 1,000+. Term of Office. July 2012–June 2013. Publication. *Louisiana Libraries* (q.). *Ed.* Vivian Solar. Tel. 225-647-8924, e-mail vsolar@state.lib.la.us.

Pres. Charlene Picheloup. Tel. 337-229-4701, e-mail crpeachy@yahoo.com; *1st V.P.* Vivian McCain. Tel. 318-251-5030, e-mail vmccain@mylpl.org; *2nd V.P.* Betsy Miguez. Tel. 337-482-1173, e-mail bbmiguez@gmail. com; *Secy.* Allison "Al" Barron. Tel. 985-515-7071, e-mail abarron@state.lib.la.us; *Past Pres.* Carla Clark. Tel. 801-223-5734, e-mail carla.clark@sirsidynix.com; *Exec. Dir.* Bland O'Connor. E-mail execdirector@llaonline.org.

Address correspondence to Louisiana Lib. Assn., 8550 United Plaza Blvd., Suite 1001, Baton Rouge 70809. Tel. 225-922-4642, 877-550-7890, fax 225-408-4422, e-mail office@ llaonline.org.

World Wide Web http://www.llaonline.org.

Maine

Memb. 950. Publication. *MLA-to-Z* (q., online).

Pres. Andi Jackson-Darling, Falmouth Memorial Lib., 5 Lunt Rd., Falmouth 04105. Tel. 207-781-2351, e-mail ajdarling@falmouth.lib. me.us; *V.P./Pres.-Elect* Nissa Flanagan, Merrill Memorial Lib., 215 Main St., Yarmouth 04096. Tel. 207-846-4763; *Secy.* Leigh Hallett, Newport Public Lib., 154 Main St., Newport 04953.

Tel. 207-368-2193; *Treas.* Donna Rasche, Brewer Public Lib., 100 S. Main St., Brewer 04412. E-mail drasche@brewermaine.gov; *Past Pres.* Sonja Plummer-Morgan, Mark and Emily Turner Memorial Lib., 39 Second St., Presque Isle 04769. Tel. 207-764-2571, e-mail sonjapmorgan@presqueislelibrary.org.

Address correspondence to the association, P.O. Box 634, Augusta 04332-0634. Tel. 207-441-1410.

World Wide Web http://mainelibraries.org.

Maryland

Memb. 1,000+. Term of Office. July 2012–July 2013. Publication. *The Crab* (q., online). *Ed.* Annette Haldeman. E-mail annette.haldeman @mlis.state.md.us.

Pres. Lynn Wheeler; *1st V.P./Pres.-Elect* Carrie Willson-Plymire; *Secy.* Eileen Kuhl; *Treas.* Daria Parry; *Past Pres.* Lucy Holman; *Exec. Dir.* Margaret Carty. E-mail mcarty@ carr.org.

Address correspondence to the association, 1401 Hollins St., Baltimore 21223. Tel. 410-947-5090, fax 410-947-5089, e-mail mla@ mdlib.org.

World Wide Web http://www.mdlib.org.

Massachusetts

Memb. (Indiv.) 1,000; (Inst.) 100. Publication. *Bay State Libraries* (q.).

Pres. Dinah O'Brien, Plymouth Public Lib., 132 South St., Plymouth 02360. Tel. 508-830-4250, e-mail do'brien@townhall.plymouth. ma.us; *V.P.* Elizabeth Marcus, Brockton Public Lib., 304 Main St., Brockton 02301. Tel. 508-580-7890 ext. 101, e-mail emarcus@cobma. us; *Secy.* Laura Bernheim, Waltham Public Lib., Waltham 02451. Tel. 781-314-3435, e-mail lbernheim@minlib.net; *Treas.* Bernadette D. Rivard, Bellingham Public Lib., 100 Blackstone St., Bellingham 02019. Tel. 508-966-1660, e-mail brivard@bellinghamma.org; *Past Pres.* Ruth Urell, Reading Public Lib., 64 Middlesex Ave., Reading 01867. Tel. 781-942-6725, e-mail urell@noblenet.org; *Exec. Mgr.* Elizabeth Hacala, Massachusetts Lib. Assn., P.O. Box 535, Bedford 01730. Tel. 781-275-7729, fax 781-998-0393, e-mail mlaoffice@ masslib.org.

Address correspondence to the executive manager.

World Wide Web http://www.masslib.org.

Michigan

Memb. (Indiv.) 2,000+. Publications. *Michigan Librarian* (6 a year), *Michigan Library Association Forum* (s. ann., online).

Pres. Lance Werner, Kent Lib. Dist.; *Pres.-Elect* Cathy Wolford, DALNET; *Secy.* Carolyn Nash, Genesee District Lib.; *Treas.* Richard Schneider, Muskegon District Lib.; *Past Pres.* Richard Cochran, Central Michigan Univ.

Address correspondence to Gail Madziar, Exec. Dir., Michigan Lib. Assn., 1407 Rensen St., Suite 2, Lansing 48910. Tel. 517-394-2774 ext. 224, e-mail madziarg@mlcnet.org.

World Wide Web http://www.mla.lib.mi.us.

Minnesota

Memb. 1,100. Term of Office. (*Pres., Pres.-Elect*) Jan.–Dec. 2013.

Pres. Kristen Mastel, Univ. of Minnesota Libs.–Twin Cities. E-mail meye0539@umn.edu; *Pres.-Elect* Michele McGraw, Hennepin County Lib. E-mail mmcgraw@hclib.org; *Secy.* Carla Powers, Duluth Public Lib. E-mail cpowers@duluth.lib.mn.us; *Treas.* Anna Hulseberg, Gustavus Adolphus College. E-mail ahulsebe@gac.edu; *Past Pres.* Carla Urban. E-mail dewey002@umn.edu.

Address correspondence to the association, 1821 University Ave. W., Suite S256, Saint Paul 55104. Tel. 651-999-5343, fax 651-917-1835.

World Wide Web http://www.mnlibraryassociation.org.

Mississippi

Memb. 625. Term of Office. Jan.–Dec. 2013. Publication. *Mississippi Libraries* (q.).

Pres. Lynn Shurden, Bolivar County Lib. System. Tel. 662-843-2774 ext. 102, e-mail lshurden@bolivar.lib.ms.us; *V.P./Pres.-Elect* Amanda Clay Powers, MSU-Mitchell Memorial Lib. Tel. 662-325-7677, e-mail apowers@library.msstate.edu; *Secy.* Mara Villa, Central Mississippi Regional Lib. System. Tel. 601-932-2562, e-mail pearl@cmrls.lib.ms.us; *Treas.* Kathy Buntin, Mississippi Lib. Commis-

sion. Tel. 601-432-4111, e-mail kbuntin@mlc.lib.ms.us; *Past Pres.* Stephen Cunetto, MSU-Mitchell Memorial Lib. Tel. 662-325-8542, e-mail scunetto@library.msstate.edu; *Exec. Secy.* Mary Julia Anderson, P.O. Box 13687, Jackson 39236-3687. Tel. 601-981-4586, e-mail info@misslib.org or marjulia@misslib.org.

Address correspondence to the executive secretary.

World Wide Web http://www.misslib.org.

Missouri

Memb. 800+. Term of Office. Jan.–Dec. 2013. Publication. *MO INFO* (bi-mo.).

Pres. Carol Smith, James C. Kirkpatrick Lib., JCKL 2464, Univ. of Central Missouri. Tel. 660-543-8639, e-mail csmith@libserv.ucmo.edu; *Secy.* Jane Theissen, Fontbonne Univ. Tel. 314-889-4570, e-mail jtheissen@fontbonne.edu; *Treas.* Brandy Sanchez, Daniel Boone Regional Lib., Columbia. E-mail brandysanchez@gmail.com; *Past Pres.* Glenda Hunt, Adair County Public Lib., Kirksville. Tel. 660-665-6038, e-mail ghunt@adairco.org.

Address correspondence to the president.

World Wide Web http://www.molib.org.

Montana

Memb. 600. Term of Office. July 2012–June 2013. Publication. *Focus* (bi-mo.).

Pres. Anne Kish, Carson Lib., Univ. of Montana–Western, Dillon 59725. Tel. 406-683-7495, fax 406-683-7493, e-mail a_kish@umwestern.edu; *V.P.* Beth Boyson, Bozeman Public Lib., 626 Main St., Bozeman 59715. Tel. 406-582-2402, fax 406-582-2424, e-mail bboyson@bozeman.net; *Secy./Treas.* Cherie Heser, Rosebud County Lib., P.O. Box 7, Forsyth 59327. Tel. 406-346-7561, fax 406-346-7685, e-mail cheser@rosebudcountymt.com; *Past Pres.* Kim Crowley, Flathead County Lib. System, 247 First Ave. E., Kalispell 59901. Tel. 406-758-5820, fax 406-758-5868, e-mail kcrowley@flathead.mt.gov; *Admin. Dir.* Debra Kramer, P.O. Box 1352, Three Forks 59752. Tel. 406-579-3121, fax 406-285-3091, e-mail debkmla@hotmail.com.

Address correspondence to the administrative director.

World Wide Web http://www.mtlib.org.

Nebraska

Term of Office. Jan.–Dec. 2013.
Pres. Gordon Wynant, Bellevue Public Lib. E-mail gordon.wyant@bellevue.net; *V.P./ Pres.-Elect* Robin Clark, Sump Memorial Lib. E-mail robin.r.clark@gmail.com; *Secy.* Rose Barcal, LaVista Public Lib. E-mail rbarcal@ cityoflavista.org; *Treas.* Barbara Hegr, Nebraska City Lib. E-mail barbarahegr@neb.rr.com; *Past Pres.* Jan Boyer, UNO. E-mail jboyer@ mail.unomaha.edu; *Exec. Dir.* Michael Straatmann.

Address correspondence to the executive director, P.O. Box 21756, Lincoln 68542-1756. Tel. 402-216-0727, e-mail nlaexecutivedirector @gmail.com.

World Wide Web http://www.nebraska libraries.org.

Nevada

Memb. 450. Term of Office. Jan.–Dec. 2013. Publication. *Nevada Libraries* (q.).
Pres. John Crockett, Washoe County Lib. System. E-mail jcrockett@washoecounty. us; *Pres.-Elect* Ann-Marie White, Las Vegas-Clark County Lib. System. E-mail whitea@ lvccld.org; *Treas.* Tammy Westergard, Carson City Lib. E-mail twestergard@carson.org; *Past Pres.* Robbie DeBuff, Las Vegas-Clark County Lib. System. E-mail rjdebuff@hotmail.com; *Exec. Secy.* Lauren Campbell, Las Vegas-Clark County Lib. Dist. E-mail ltcampbell10@gmail. com.

Address correspondence to the executive secretary.

World Wide Web http://www.nevadalibraries. org.

New Hampshire

Memb. 700. Publication. *NHLA News* (q.).
Pres. Diane Lynch, Laconia Public Lib., 695 Main St., Laconia 03246. Tel. 603-524-4775, e-mail dlynchlpl@metrocast.net; *V.P./Pres.- Elect* Linda Taggart, Nashua Public Lib., 2 Court St., Nashua 03060. Tel. 603-589-4600, e-mail linda.taggart@nashualibrary.org; *Secy.* Carl Heidenblad, Nesmith Lib., 8 Fellows Rd., Windham 03087. Tel. 603-432-7154, e-mail cheidenblad@nesmithlibrary.org; *Treas.* Tim Sheehan, Chester Public Lib., 3 Chester St.,

P.O. Box 277, Chester 03036. Tel. 603-887-3404, e-mail chesterpubliclibrary@gmail.com; *Past Pres.* Lori Fisher, Baker Free Lib., 509 South St., Bow 03304. Tel. 603-224-7113, e-mail bfldirector@comcast.net.

Address correspondence to the association, 53 Regional Drive, Suite 1, Concord 03301.

World Wide Web http://nhlibrarians.org.

New Jersey

Memb. 1,800. Term of Office. July 2012–June 2013. Publication. *New Jersey Libraries NEWSletter* (q.).
Pres. Karen Klapperstuck, Monroe Twp. Pubic Lib., 4 Municipal Plaza, Monroe Twp. 08831. Tel. 732-521-5000, fax 732-521-4766, e-mail librarykar@gmail.com; *V.P.* Eileen Palmer, Libs. of Middlesex Automation Consortium, 1030 St. Georges Ave., Suite 203, Avenel 00701. Tel. 732-750-2525, e-mail empalmer@lmxac.org; *2nd V.P.* Terrie McColl, New Milford Public Lib., 200 Dahlia Ave., New Milford 07646. Tel. 201-262-1221, e-mail mccoll@bccls.org; *Secy.* Chris Carbone, South Brunswick Public Lib., 110 Kingston Lane, Monmouth Junction 08852. Tel. 609-329-4000 ext. 7287, e-mail ccarbone@sbpl.info; *Treas.* James Keehbler, Piscataway Public Lib., 500 Hoes Lane, Piscataway 08854. Tel. 732-463-1633, e-mail jkeehbler@piscatawaylibrary.org; *Past Pres.* Susan O'Neal, Middletown Twp. Public Lib., 55 New Monmouth Rd., Middletown 07748. Tel. 732-671-3703, fax 732-671-5839, e-mail soneal@mtpl.org; *Exec. Dir.* Patricia Tumulty, NJLA, P.O. Box 1534, Trenton 08607. Tel. 609-394-8032, fax 609-394-8164, e-mail ptumulty@njla.org.

Address correspondence to the executive director.

World Wide Web http://www.njla.org.

New Mexico

Memb. 550. Term of Office. Apr. 2012–Apr. 2013. Publication. *New Mexico Library Association Newsletter* (6 a year).
Pres. Tina Glatz. E-mail tglatz66@gmail. com; *V.P.* Mary Ellen Pellington. E-mail library @ci.gallup.nm.us; *Secy.* Casandra Osterloh. E-mail costerloh@sandiaprep.org; *Treas.* Norice Lee. E-mail nlee@nmsu.edu; *Past Pres.* Mary Alice Tsosie. E-mail mtsosie@unm.edu.

Address correspondence to the association, Box 26074, Albuquerque 87125. Tel. 505-400-7309. fax 505-891-5171, e-mail admin@nmla.org.
World Wide Web http://nmla.org.

New York

Memb. 4,000. Term of Office. Nov. 2012–Nov. 2013. Publication. *NYLA e-Bulletin* (q.). *Pres.* Carol Anne Germain. Tel. 518-442-3590, e-mail cgermain@albany.edu; *Pres.-Elect* Sara Kelly Johns. Tel. 518-891-2339, e-mail skjohns@gmail.com; *Treas.* Christine McDonald. Tel. 518-587-9662, e-mail ckcine@nycap.rr.com; *Past Pres.* Matthew Bollerman. Tel. 631-979-1600, e-mail mbollerm@suffolk.lib.ny.us; *Exec. Dir.* Jeremy Johannesen.

Address correspondence to the executive director, New York Lib. Assn., 6021 State Farm Rd., Guilderland 12084. Tel. 518-432-6952, fax 518-427-1697, e-mail director@nyla.org.
World Wide Web http://www.nyla.org.

North Carolina

Memb. 1,100. Term of Office. Oct. 2011–Oct. 2013. Publications. *North Carolina Library Association E-news* (bi-mo.). *Ed.* Marilyn Schuster, Local Documents/Special Collections, Univ. of North Carolina–Charlotte. E-mail mbschust@email.uncc.edu; *North Carolina Libraries Online* (2 a year). *Ed.* Ralph Scott, Joyner Lib., East Carolina Univ., Greenville 27858. Tel. 252-328-0265, e-mail scottr@ecu.edu.

Pres. Wanda Brown, Z. Smith Reynolds Lib., Wake Forest Univ., Box 7777 Reynolda Sta., Winston-Salem 27109. Tel. 336-758-5094, e-mail brownw@wfu.edu; *V.P./Pres.-Elect* Dale Cousins, Wake County Public Libs., 1930 Clark Ave., Raleigh 27605. Tel. 919-856-6726, dale.cousins@wakegov.com; *Secy.* Eleanor Cook, Joyner Lib., East Carolina Univ., E. Fifth St., Greenville 27858. Tel. 252-328-2598, e-mail cooke@ecu.edu; *Treas.* Mary Sizemore, High Point Public Lib., 301 N. Main St., High Point 27262. Tel. 336-883-3694, e-mail marysizemore@highpointnc.org; *Past Pres.* Sherwin Rice, Bladen Community College, P.O. Box 266, Dublin 28332. Tel. 910-879-5641, e-mail srice@bladencc.edu; *Admin. Asst.* Kim Parrot, North Carolina Lib. Assn., 1841 Capi-

tal Blvd., Raleigh 27604. Tel. 919-839-6252, fax 919-839-6253, e-mail nclaonline@gmail.com.
Address correspondence to the administrative assistant.
World Wide Web http://www.nclaonline.org.

North Dakota

Memb. (Indiv.) 317; (Inst.) 9. Term of Office. Sept. 2012–Sept. 2013. Publication. *The Good Stuff* (q.). *Ed.* Marlene Anderson, Bismarck State College Lib., Box 5587, Bismarck 58506-5587. Tel. 701-224-5578.

Pres. Alfred L. Peterson, North Dakota State Lib. Tel. 701-328-3495, fax 701-328-2040, e-mail alpeterson@nd.gov; *Pres.-Elect* Victor Lieberman, Chester Fritz Lib., Univ. of North Dakota. Tel. 701-777-4639, fax 701-777-3319, e-mail victor.lieberman@library.und.edu; *Secy.* Beth Sorenson, Chester Fritz Lib., Univ. of North Dakota. Tel. 701-277-2919, e-mail beth.sorenson@library.und.edu; *Treas.* Michael Safratowich, Harley French Lib. of the Health Sciences, Univ. of North Dakota, Box 9002, Grand Forks 58202-9002. Tel. 701-777-2602, fax 701-777-4790, e-mail michael.safratowich@med.und.edu; *Past Pres.* Aubrey Madler, Univ. of North Dakota Center for Rural Health, School of Medicine and Health Sciences, Room 4520, 501 N. Columbia Rd., Stop 9037, Grand Forks 58202-9037. Tel. 701-777-6025, e-mail aubrey.madler@med.und.edu.
Address correspondence to the president.
World Wide Web http://www.ndla.info.

Ohio

Memb. 2,700+. Term of Office. Jan.–Dec. 2013. Publication. *Access* (memb., weekly, online).

Pres. Chris Taylor, Upper Arlington Public Lib., 2800 Tremont Rd., Columbus 43221. Tel. 614-486-0900, e-mail ctaylor@uslibrary.org; *V.P./Pres.-Elect* Margaret Delaney, Toledo-Lucas County Public Lib., 325 N. Michigan St., Toledo 43624. Tel. 419-259-5333; *Secy./Treas.* Audrey Cole, 3435 Hollister Rd., Cleveland Heights 44118. E-mail t_prevo@sbcglobal.net; *Past Pres.* Virginia Sharp March, Perry Public Lib., 3753 Main St., Perry 44081-8501. Tel. 440-259-3300, e-mail marchvi@oplin.org;

Exec. Dir. Douglas S. Evans. E-mail devans@olc.org.

Address correspondence to the executive director, OLC, 1105 Schrock Rd., Suite 440, Columbus 43229-1174. Tel. 614-410-8092, fax 614-410-8098, e-mail olc@olc.org.

World Wide Web http://www.olc.org.

Oklahoma

Memb. (Indiv.) 1,000; (Inst.) 60. Term of Office. July 2012–June 2013. Publication. *Oklahoma Librarian* (bi-mo.).

Pres. Sarah Robbins; *V.P./Pres.-Elect* Lynda Reynolds; *Secy.* Gloria Farmer; *Treas.* Tim Miller; *Past Pres.* Cheryl Suttles; *Exec. Dir.* Kay Boies, 300 Hardy Drive, Edmond 73013. Tel. 405-525-5100, fax 405-525-5103, e-mail kboies@sbcglobal.net.

Address correspondence to the executive director.

World Wide Web http://www.oklibs.org.

Oregon

Memb. (Indiv.) 1,000+. Publications. *OLA Hotline* (bi-w.), *OLA Quarterly.*

Pres. Michele Burke, Chemeketa Community College Lib. E-mail michele.burke@chemeketa.edu; *V.P./Pres.-Elect* Penny Hummel, Canby Public Lib. E-mail hummelp@ci.canby.or.us; *Secy.* Brian Greene, Columbia Gorge Community College. E-mail bgreene@cgcc.cc.or.us; *Treas.* Liisa Sjoblom, Deschutes Public Lib. E-mail liisas@deschuteslibrary.org; *Past Pres.* Abigail Elder, Tualatin Public Lib. E-mail aelder@ci.tualatin.or.us.

Address correspondence to Oregon Lib. Assn., P.O. Box 3067, La Grande 97850. Tel. 541-962-5824, e-mail olaweb@olaweb.org.

World Wide Web http://www.olaweb.org.

Pennsylvania

Memb. 1,900+. Term of Office. Jan.–Dec. 2013. Publication. *PaLA Bulletin* (10 a year).

Pres. Paula Gilbert, Martin Lib. Tel. 717-846-5300, e-mail pgilbert@yorklibraries.org; *1st V.P.* Janis Stubbs, Delaware County Lib. System. Tel. 610-891-8622, e-mail jstubbs@delcolibraries.org; *2nd V.P./Conference Chair* Barbara Zaborwoski, Pennsylvania Highlands Community College. Tel. 814-262-6425, e-mail bzabor@pennhighlands.edu; *Treas.* David

Schappert, Moravian College. Tel. 610-861-1540; *Past Pres.* Debbie Malone, DeSales Univ. Tel. 610-282-1100 ext. 253, e-mail debbie.malone@desales.edu; *Exec. Dir.* Glenn R. Miller, Pennsylvania Lib. Assn., 220 Cumberland Pkwy., Suite 10, Mechanicsburg 17055. Tel. 717-766-7663, fax 717-766-5440, e-mail glenn@palibraries.org.

Address correspondence to the executive director.

World Wide Web http://www.palibraries.org.

Rhode Island

Memb. (Indiv.) 350+; (Inst.) 50+. Term of Office. June 2011–June 2013. Publication. *RILA Bulletin.*

Pres. Eileen Dyer, Cranston Public Lib., 140 Sockanossett Cross Rd., Cranston 02920. Tel. 401-943-9080 ext. 119, e-mail president@rilibraryassoc.org; *V.P./Pres.-Elect* Jenifer Bond, Douglas and Judith Krupp Lib., Bryant Univ., Smithfield 02917. Tel. 401-232-6299, e-mail vicepresident@rilibraryassoc.org; *Secy.* Adrienne Gallo. Tel. 401-942-1787, e-mail secretary@rilibraryassoc.org; *Treas.* Patricia Schultz. Tel. 401-232-6296, e-mail treasurer@rilibraryassoc.org; *Past Pres.* Laura Marlane, Providence Community Lib., South Providence Lib., 441 Prairie Ave., Providence 02905. Tel. 401-467-2700 ext. 1610, e-mail pastpresident@rilibraries.org.

Address correspondence to Rhode Island Library Assn., P.O. Box 6765, Providence 02940.

World Wide Web http://www.rilibraries.org.

South Carolina

Memb. 350+. Term of Office. Jan.–Dec. 2013. Publication. *News and Views.*

Pres. Jonathan Newton, Greenville County Lib. System, 25 Heritage Green Place, Greenville 29601. Tel. 864-527-9296, e-mail jnewton@greenvillelibrary.org; *1st V.P.* Edward Rock, Clemson Univ. Libs., Box 343001, Clemson 29643. Tel. 864-656-1879, e-mail erock@clemson.edu; *2nd V.P.* Crystal Johnson, Richland Lib., 1431 Assembly St., Columbia 29201. Tel. 803-929-3400, e-mail cjohnson@myrcpl.com; *Secy.* Georgia Coleman, Richland Lib., Columbia 29201. Tel. 803-929-3479, e-mail gcoleman@richlandlibrary.com; *Treas.*

Kathy Snediker, Elliott White Springs Business Lib., Univ. of South Carolina, Columbia 29201. Tel. 803-777-2346, e-mail snediker@mailbox.sc.edu; *Past Pres.* Yvonne Davis, Rogers Lib., Francis Marion Univ., P.O. Box 100547, Florence 29502. Tel. 843-661-1303, e-mail ydavis@fmarion.edu; *Exec. Secy.* Donald Wood, SCLA, P.O. Box 1763, Columbia 29202. Tel. 803-252-1087, fax 803-252-0589. E-mail scla@capconsc.com.

Address correspondence to the executive secretary.

World Wide Web http://www.scla.org.

South Dakota

Memb. (Indiv.) 462; (Inst.) 67. Term of Office. Oct. 2012–Oct. 2013. Publication. *Book Marks* (q.).

Pres. Jan Brue Enright, Augustana College Lib., Sioux Falls. E-mail jenright@augie.edu; *V.P./Pres.-Elect* Scott Ahola, Black Hills State Univ. Lib., Spearfish. E-mail scott.ahola@bhsu.edu; *Recording Secy.* Cindy Messenger, Hot Springs Public Lib. E-mail hsplib@gwtc.net; *Past Pres.* Annie Brunskill, Haakon County Public Lib., Philip. E-mail library@gwtc.net; *Exec. Secy./Treas.* Laura G. Olson. E-mail sdlaest@gmail.com.

Address correspondence to the executive secretary, SDLA, 28363 472nd Ave., Worthing 57077-5722. Tel. 605-372-0235, e-mail sdlaest@gmail.com.

World Wide Web http://www.sdlibraryassociation.org.

Tennessee

Memb. 600+. Term of Office. July 2012–June 2013. Publications. *Tennessee Libraries* (q.), *TLA Newsletter* (bi-mo.). Both online at http://www.tnla.org.

Pres. Dinah Harris. E-mail dhtla1213@gmail.com; *V.P./Pres.-Elect* Ruth Kinnersley. E-mail rkinnersley@trevecca.edu; *Recording Secy.* Jodie Gambill. E-mail jodie.gamibll@gmail.com; *Past Pres.* Wendy Cornelisen. E-mail wendy.cornelisen@gmail.com; *Exec. Dir.* Annelle R. Huggins, Tennessee Lib. Assn., Box 241074, Memphis 38124. Tel. 901-485-6952, e-mail arhuggins1@comcast.net.

Address correspondence to the executive director.

World Wide Web http://tnla.org.

Texas

Memb. 6,500+. Term of Office. Apr. 2012–Apr. 2013 Publications. *Texas Library Journal* (q.), *TLACast* (9 a year).

Pres. Sherilyn Bird, Texas Woman's Univ.; *Pres.-Elect* Yvonne Chandler, Univ. of North Texas; *Treas.* Jesús Campos, South Texas College; *Past Pres.* Jerilynn A. Williams, Montgomery County Lib. System; *Exec. Dir.* Patricia H. Smith, TXLA, 3355 Bee Cave Rd., Suite 401, Austin 78746-6763. Tel. 512-328-1518, fax 512-328-8852, e-mail pats@txla.org or tla@txla.org.

Address correspondence to the executive director.

World Wide Web http://www.txla.org.

Utah

Memb. 650. Publication. *Utah Libraries News* (bi-mo.) (online at http://www.ula.org/newsletter).

Pres. Adriane Juarez, Salt Lake City Public Lib., Day-Riverside Branch Lib., 1575 West 1100 North, Salt Lake City 84116. Tel. 801-594-8630, e-mail ajuarez@slcpl.org; *V.P./Pres.-Elect* Patricia Hull, Magna Branch, Salt Lake County Lib. System, 8339 West 3500 South, Magna 84044. Tel. 801-944-7626, e-mail phull@slcolibrary.org; *Recording Secy.* Brooke Corbin. E-mail brooke.corbin@yahoo.com; *Treas.* Javaid Lal. E-mail jlal@slcolibrary.org; *Past Pres.* Linda Tillson, Park City Lib., P.O. Box 668, Park City 84060. Tel. 435-615-5605, e-mail ltillson@parkcity.org; *Exec. Dir.* Anna Neatrour, No. 101, 845 East 100 South, Salt Lake City 84102. Tel. 801-200-3129, e-mail anna.neatrour@gmail.com.

Address correspondence to the executive director.

World Wide Web http://www.ula.org.

Vermont

Memb. 400. Publication. *VLA News* (6 a year).

Pres. Deborah Gadwah-Lambert, Alice M. Ward Memorial Lib., P.O. Box 134, Canaan 05903. Tel. 802-266-7135, e-mail deborahlle@yahoo.com; *V.P./Pres.-Elect* Amber Billey, Bailey/Howe Lib., Univ. of Vermont, 538 Main St., Burlington 05405-0036. Tel. 802-656-

8568, e-mail amber.billey@uvm.edu; *Secy.* Heidi Steiner, Kreitzberg Lib., Norwich Univ., 158 Harmon Drive, Northfield 05663. Tel. 802-485-2171, e-mail hsteiner@norwich.edu; *Treas.* Wynne Browne, Downs Rachlin Martin, St. Johnsbury 05819-0099. Tel. 802-473-4216, e-mail wbrowne@drm.com; *Past Pres.* Joseph Farara, Willey Lib., Johnson State College, 337 College Hill, Johnson 05656. Tel. 802-635-1272, e-mail joseph.farara@jsc.edu.

Address correspondence to VLA, Box 803, Burlington 05402.

World Wide Web http://www.vermontlibraries.org.

Virginia

Memb. 950+. Term of Office. Oct. 2012–Oct. 2013. Publication. *Virginia Libraries* (q.).

Pres. Lisa Lee Broughman, Randolph College, 2500 Rivermont Ave., Lynchburg 24503. Tel. 434-947-8481, e-mail llee@randolphcollege.edu; *V.P./Pres.-Elect* Kevin Smith, York County Public Lib., 100 Long Green Blvd., Yorktown, VA 23693. E-mail smithk@yorkcounty.gov; *2nd V.P.* Mark Lenker, Longwood Univ., 201 High St., Farmville 23909. Tel. 434-395-257, e-mail lenkermn@longwood.edu; *Secy.* Marilyn J Scott, James Branch Cabell Lib., Virginia Commonwealth Univ. Tel. 804-828-9049, e-mail mjscott@vcu.edu; *Treas.* Maryke Barber, Hollins Univ. Lib., P.O. Box 9000, Roanoke 24020. Tel. 540-362-6328, e-mail mbarber@hollins.edu; *Past Pres.* Connie Gilman, Chinn Park Regional Lib., 13065 Chinn Park Drive, Prince William 22192. Tel. 703-792-6199, e-mail cgilman@pwcgov.org; *Exec. Dir.* Lisa Varga, P.O. Box 56312, Virginia Beach 23456. Tel. 757-689-0594, fax 757-447-3478, e-mail vla.lisav@cox.net.

Address correspondence to the executive director.

World Wide Web http://www.vla.org.

Washington

Memb. 750+. Term of Office. Apr. 2011–Apr. 2013. Publication. *Alki: The Washington Library Association Journal* (3 a year). *Ed.* Bo Kinney, Seattle Public Lib., 1000 Fourth Ave., Seattle 98104. E-mail alkieditor@wla.org.

Pres. Brian Soneda, Mount Vernon City Lib., 315 Snoqualmie St., Mount Vernon 98273.

Tel. 360-336-6209, e-mail brians@ci.mountvernon.wa.us; *V.P./Pres.-Elect* Jennifer Wiseman, King County Lib. System, P.O. Box 199, Snoqualmie 98068. Tel. 425-369-3221, e-mail jlwiseman@kcls.org; *Secy./Treas.*Phil Heikkinen, Orcas Island Public Lib., 500 Rose St., Eastsound 98245. Tel. 360-376-2308, e-mail pheikkinen@orcaslibrary.org; *Exec. Dir.* Dana Murphy-Love, WLA, 23607 Hwy. 99, Suite 2-C, Edmonds 98026. Tel. 425-967-0739, fax 425-771-9588, e-mail dana@wla.org.

Address correspondence to the executive director.

World Wide Web http://www.wla.org.

West Virginia

Memb. 650+. Publication. *West Virginia Libraries* (6 a year).

Pres. Myra Ziegler, Summers County Public Lib., 201 Temple St., Hinton 25951. Tel. 304-466-4490, e-mail zieglm@mail.mln.lib.wv.us; *1st V.P./Pres.-Elect* Beth Royall, Evansdale Lib., West Virginia Univ. Libs., P.O. Box 6105, Morgantown 26506-6105. Tel. 304-293-9755, fax 304-293-7330, e-mail beth.royall@mail.wvu.edu; *2nd V.P.* Amy Lilly, 221 N. Kanawha St., Beckley 25801. Tel. 304-255-0511, fax 304-255-9161, e-mail amy.lilly@raleigh.lib.wv.us; *Secy.* Angela Strait, Cabell County Public Lib., 455 Ninth St., Huntington 25701. Tel. 304-528-5700, fax 304-528-5701, e-mail angela.strait@cabell.lib.wv.us; *Treas.* Brian E. Raitz, Parkersburg and Wood County Public Lib., 3100 Emerson Ave., Parkersburg 26104-2414. Tel. 304-420-4587 ext. 11, fax 304-420-4589, e-mail raitzb@mail.mln.lib.wv.us; *Past Pres.* Crystal Hamrick, Bridgeport Public Lib., 1200 Johnson Ave., Bridgeport 26330. Tel. 304-842-8248, e-mail chamrick@bridgeportwv.com.

Address correspondence to the president.

World Wide Web http://www.wvla.org.

Wisconsin

Memb. 1,900. Term of Office. Jan.–Dec. Publication. *WLA Newsletter* (q.).

Pres. Paula Ganyard, Cofrin Lib., Univ. of Wisconsin–Green Bay. Tel. 920-465-2537, e-mail ganyardp@uwgb.edu; *Secy.* Tasha Saecker, Appleton Public Lib. Tel. 920-832-6168, e-mail tsaecker@apl.org; *Treas.* Jen Gerber,

Oscar Grady Public Lib., Saukville. Tel. 262-284-6022, e-mail jgerber@esls.lib.wi.us; *Past Pres.* Ron McCabe, McMillan Memorial Lib., Wisconsin Rapids 54494-4898. E-mail rmccabe @wctc.net; *Exec. Dir.* Lisa Strand, Wisconsin Lib. Assn., 4610 S. Biltmore Lane, Suite 100, Madison 53718-2153. Tel. 608-245-3640, fax 608-245-3646, e-mail wla@wisconsinlibraries. org.

Address correspondence to the association. World Wide Web http://wla.wisconsin libraries.org.

Wyoming

Memb. 450+. Term of Office. Oct. 2012–Oct. 2013.

Pres. Debbie McCarthy, Coe Lib., Univ. of Wyoming. Tel. 307-766-4228, e-mail mccarthy @uwyo.edu; *V.P.* Scott Kinney, Sweetwater County Lib. System. Tel. 307-872-3200 ext. 5200, e-mail skinney@sweetwaterlibraries. com; *Past Pres.* Sukey Hohl; *Exec. Secy.* Laura Grott Box 1387, Cheyenne 82003. Tel. 307-632-7622, fax 307-638-3469, e-mail grottski@ aol.com.

Address correspondence to the executive secretary.

World Wide Web http://www.wyla.org.

Canada

Alberta

Memb. 500. Term of Office. May 2012–Apr. 2013. Publication. *Letter of the LAA* (q.).

Pres. Diane Clark, 5-02A Cameron Lib., Univ. of Alberta Libs., Edmonton, AB T6G 2J8. Tel. 780-492-9364, e-mail president@laa. ca; *1st V.P.* Lisa Hardy, Calgary Public Lib., 390 Elgin Way S.E., Calgary, AB T2Z 4A7. Tel. 403-260-2797, e-mail 1stvicepresident@ laa.ca; *2nd V.P.* Lindsay Johnston, 1-51 Cameron Science and Technology Lib., Univ. of Alberta, Edmonton, AB T5R 5P8. Tel. 780-492-5946, e-mail 2ndvicepresident@laa.ca; *Treas.* Julia Reinhart, Alberta Lib. E-mail treasurer@ laa.ca; *Exec. Dir.* Christine Sheppard, 80 Baker Crescent N.W., Calgary T2L 1R4. Tel. 403-284-5818, fax 403-282-6646, e-mail info@laa. ca.

Address correspondence to the executive director.

World Wide Web http://www.laa.ca.

British Columbia

Memb. 750+. Term of Office. April 2012–April 2013. Publication. *BCLA Browser* (online at http://bclabrowser.ca). *Ed.* Leanna Jantzi.

Pres. June Stockdale, Nelson Municipal Lib. E-mail jstockdale@nelson.ca; *V.P./Pres.-Elect* Gwen Bird, Council of Prairie and Pacific Univ. Libs. E-mail execdir@coppul.ca; *2nd V.P.* Heather Morrison, Electronic Lib. Network. E-mail heatherm@eln.bc.ca; *Treas.* Heather Compeau, Univ. of the Fraser Valley. E-mail hcompeau@gmail.com; *Past Pres.* Christopher Kevlahan, Vancouver Public Lib., 7110 Kerr St., Vancouver, BC V5S 4W2. Tel. 604-665-3955, e-mail christopher.kevlahan@ vpl.ca; *Exec. Dir.* Annette DeFaveri. E-mail execdir@bcla.bc.ca.

Address correspondence to the association, 500-900 Howe St., Suite 150, Vancouver V6Z 2M4. Tel. 604-683-5354, e-mail exdir@bcla. bc.ca.

World Wide Web http://www.bcla.bc.ca.

Manitoba

Memb. 500+. Term of Office. May 2012–May 2013. Publication. *Newsline* (mo.).

Pres. Stephen Carney, Canadian Museum for Human Rights, 269 Main St., Winnipeg R3C 1B3. E-mail stephen_carney@outlook. com; *V.P.* Dawn Bassett, Canadian Grain Commission. E-mail dbassett69@gmail.com; *Secy.* Evelyn Bruneau, 128 Elizabeth Dafoe Lib., Univ. of Manitoba Libs., Winnipeg R3T 2N2. Tel. 204-474-6780, e-mail evelyn_bruneau@ umanitoba.ca; *Treas.* Kathy Rusnak, Univ. of Manitoba Libs., Winnipeg R3T 2N2. Tel. 204-474-8858, fax 204-474-7581, e-mail kathy_ rusnak@umanitoba.ca; *Past Pres.* Emma Hill Kepron, Elizabeth Dafoe Lib., Winnipeg. Tel. 204-474-6710, e-mail emma_kepron@u manitoba.ca.

Address correspondence to the association, 606-100 Arthur St., Winnipeg R3B 1H3. Tel. 204-943-4567, e-mail manitobalibrary@gmail. com.

World Wide Web http://www.mla.mb.ca.

Ontario

Memb. 5,000+. Publications. *Access* (q.); *Teaching Librarian* (3 a year).

Pres. Susanna Hubbard Krimmer, London Public Lib. E-mail susanna.krimmer@lpl. london.on.ca; *V.P./Pres.-Elect* Anita Brooks-Kirkland, Waterloo Region District School Board. E-mail anita_brooks-kirkland@wrdsb. on.ca; *Treas.* Lita Barrie, Hamilton Public Lib. E-mail lbarrie@hpl.ca; *Past Pres.* Karen Mc-Grath, Niagara College Libs. E-mail kmcgrath niagara@gmail.com; *Exec. Dir.* Shelagh Paterson. E-mail spaterson@accessola.com.

Address correspondence to the association, 50 Wellington St. E., Suite 201, Toronto M5E 1C8. Tel. 416-363-3388, fax 416-941-9581, e-mail info@accessola.com.

World Wide Web http://www.accessola. com.

Quebec

Memb. (Indiv.) 100+. Term of Office. May 2012–April 2013. Publication. *ABQLA Bulletin* (3 a year).

Pres. Luigina Vileno. E-mail luigina.vileno @concordia.ca; *V.P.* Robin Canuel. E-mail robin.canuel@mcgill.ca; *Treas.* Anne Wade; *Past Pres.* Julie-Anne Cardella; *Exec. Secy.* Margaret Goldik, P.O. Box 26717, CPS Beaconsfield, Beaconsfield QC H9W 6G7. Tel./fax 514-697-0146, e-mail abqla@abqla.qc.ca.

Address correspondence to the executive secretary.

World Wide Web http://www.abqla.qc.ca.

Saskatchewan

Memb. 200+. Publication. *Forum* (q.).

Pres. Robert G. Thomas, Dr. John Archer Lib., Univ. of Regina, 3737 Wascana Pkwy., Regina S4S 0A2. Tel. 306-585-4398, e-mail robert.thomas@uregina.ca; *V.P., Membership and Publications* Colleen Murphy; *V.P., Advocacy and Development* Deborah McConkey; *Treas.* Gwen Schmidt; *Membs.-at-Large* Blanche Bird, Gillian Nowlan, Michael Shires, Theresa Slind; *Past Pres.* Amber Christensen, Prince of Wales Branch, Regina Public Lib. E-mail msamberdawn@gmail.com; *Exec. Dir.* Loraine Thompson, Saskatchewan Lib. Assn., 2010 Seventh Ave., No. 15, Regina S4R 1C2.

Tel. 306-780-9413, fax 306-780-9447, e-mail slaexdir@sasktel.net.

Address correspondence to the executive director.

World Wide Web http://www.saskla.ca.

Regional

Atlantic Provinces: N.B., N.L., N.S., P.E.I.

Memb. (Indiv.) 300+; (Inst.) 26. Publication. *APLA Bulletin* (4 a year).

Pres. Lou Duggan, Patrick Power Lib., Saint Mary's Univ., 923 Robie St., Halifax, NS B3H 3C3. Tel. 902-420-5534, e-mail lou.duggan@ smu.ca; *V.P./Pres.-Elect* Louise White, Marine Institute, Memorial Univ. of Newfoundland, P.O. Box 4920, St. John's, NL A1C 5R3. Tel. 709-757-0719, e-mail louise.white@mi.mun. ca; *V.P., Membership* Suzanne van den Hoogen, Angus L. Macdonald Lib., St. Francis Xavier Univ., P.O. Box 5000, Antigonish, NS B2G 2W5. Tel. 902-867-4535, e-mail svandenh@ stfx.ca; *Secy.* Debbie Costelo, Nova Scotia Community College. Tel. 902-491-1031, fax 902-491-1292, e-mail debbie.costelo@nscc. ca; *Treas.* Bill Slauenwhite, Novanet. Tel. 902-453-2461, fax 902-453-2369, e-mail bill. slauenwhite@novanet.ns.ca; *Past Pres.* Jocelyne Thompson, Univ. of New Brunswick Libs. E-mail jlt@unb.ca.

Address correspondence to Atlantic Provinces Lib. Assn., c/o School of Info. Mgt., Faculty of Mgt., Kenneth C. Rowe Mgt. Bldg., Dalhousie Univ., 6100 University Ave., Halifax, NS B3H 3J5.

World Wide Web http://www.apla.ca.

Mountain Plains: Ariz., Colo., Kan., Mont., Neb., Nev., N.Dak., N.M., Okla., S.Dak., Utah, Wyo.

Memb. 700. Term of Office. Oct. 2012–Oct. 2013. Publications. *MPLA Newsletter* (bimo., online only). *Ed./Advertising Mgr.* Judy Zelenski, 14293 W. Center Drive, Lakewood, CO 80228. Tel. 303-985-7795, e-mail editor@ mpla.us.

Pres. JaNae Kinikin, Stewart Lib., Weber State Univ., 2901 University Circle, Ogden, UT 84408-2901. Tel. 801-626-6093, fax 801-626-8521, e-mail president@mpla.us; *V.P./Pres.-*

Elect Wendy Wendt, Grand Forks Public Lib. Tel. 701-772-8116, fax 701-771-1379, e-mail vicepresident@mpla.us; *Past Pres.* Dana Braccia, Scottsdale Public Lib. System; *Recording Secy.* Lea Briggs, Univ. of New Mexico. Tel. 505-277-9439, e-mail secretary@mpla.us; *Exec. Secy.* Judy Zelenski, 14293 W. Center Drive, Lakewood, CO 80228. Tel. 303-985-7795 e-mail execsecretary@mpla.us.

Address correspondence to the executive secretary.

World Wide Web http://www.mpla.us.

New England: Conn., Maine, Mass., N.H., R.I., Vt.

Memb. (Indiv.) 661. Term of Office. Nov. 2012–Oct. 2013. Publication. *NELA News* (online, mo.).

Pres. Deborah Kelsey, Medfield Public Lib., 468 Main St., Medfield, MA 02052. Tel. 508-359-4544, e-mail president@nela1.org; *V.P./ Pres.-Elect* Deb Hoadley, Massachusetts Lib. System, 225 Cedar Hill St., Suite 229, Marlborough, MA 01752. Tel. 508-357-2121, e-mail vicepresident@nela1.org; *Secy.* Kirsten Corbett, Lane Memorial Lib., 2 Academy Ave., Hampton, NH 03842. Tel. 603-926-4729, e-mail secretary@nela1.org; *Treas.* Karen Patterson, South Windsor, Connecticut. E-mail treasurer@nela1.org; *Senior Dir.* Theresa Maturevich, Bedford Public Lib., 7 Mudge Way, Bedford, MA 01730. Tel. 781-275-9440, e-mail director-sr@nela1.org; *Junior Dir.* Jennifer Hinderer, Nashua Public Lib., 2 Court St., Nashua, NH 03060. Tel. 603-589-4620, e-mail director-jr@nela1.org; *Past Pres.* Mary Ann List, Portsmouth Public Lib., 175 Parrott Ave., Portsmouth, NH 03801. Tel. 603-766-1710, e-mail pastpresident@nela1.org; *Admin.* Bob Scheier, New England Lib. Assn., 55 N. Main St., Unit 49, Belchertown, MA 01007. Tel. 413-813-5254, e-mail libraryassociation-administrator@nela1.org.

World Wide Web http://www.nelib.org.

Pacific Northwest: Alaska, Idaho, Mont., Ore., Wash., Alberta, B.C.

Memb. (Active) 170+. Term of Office. Aug.–Aug. Publication. *PNLA Quarterly. Ed.* Mary Bolin. 322B Love Lib., Univ. of Nebraska, P.O. Box 881140, Lincoln, NE 68588-4100. Tel. 402-472-4281, e-mail mbolin2@unlnotes.unl. edu.

Pres. Heidi Chittim, Eastern Washington Univ. Libs., 100 LIB, 816 F St., Cheney, WA 99004-2453. Tel. 509-359-2303, fax 509-359-2476, e-mail hchittim@ewu.edu; *1st V.P./Pres.-Elect* Kelsey Keyes, Albertsons Lib., Boise State Univ., Boise, ID. Tel. 208-426-1139, e-mail kelseykeyes@boisestate.edu; *2nd V.P.* Jason Openo, Alberta Public Lib. Electronic Network, Suite 6-14, 7 Sir Winston Churchill Sq. Edmonton, AB T5J 2V5. Tel. 780-414-0805 ext. 228, e-mail jopeno@thealbertalibrary. ab.ca; *Secy.* Darlene Hert, Montana State Univ.–Billings Lib., 1500 University Drive, Billings, MT 59101. Tel. 406-657-1661, fax 406-657-2037, e-mail dhert@msubillings.edu; *Treas.* Katie Cargill, Eastern Washington Univ. Libs., 816 F St., Cheney, WA 99004. Tel. 509-359-2385, fax 509-359-2476, e-mail kcargill@ mail.ewu.edu; *Past Pres.* Michael Burris, Public Lib. InterLINK, 7252 Kingsway, Burnaby, BC V5E 1G3. Tel. 604-517-8441, fax 604-517-8410, e-mail michael.burris@interlinklibraries. ca.

Address correspondence to the president, Pacific Northwest Lib. Assn.

World Wide Web http://www.pnla.org.

Southeastern: Ala., Ark., Fla., Ga., Ky., La., Miss., N.C., S.C., Tenn., Va., W.Va.

Memb. 500. Publication. *The Southeastern Librarian (SELn)* (q.). *Ed.* Perry Bratcher, 503A Steely Lib., Northern Kentucky Univ., Highland Heights, KY 41099. Tel. 859-572-6309, fax 859-572-6181, e-mail bratcher@nku.edu.

Pres. Gordon N. Baker, Clayton State Univ. Lib., 2000 Clayton State Blvd., Morrow, GA 30260. Tel. 678-466-4334, fax 679-466-4349, e-mail gordonbaker@clayton.edu; *V.P.* Camille McCutcheon. E-mail cmccutcheon@ uscupstate.edu; *Secy.* Lorene Flanders. E-mail lflanders@westga.edu; *Treas.* Beverly James. E-mail bjames@greenvillelibrary.org; *Past Pres.* Michael Seigler. E-mail mjseigler@msn. com.

Address correspondence to Southeastern Lib. Assn., Admin. Services, P.O. Box 950, Rex, GA 30273-0950. Tel. 770-961-3520, fax 770-961-3712.

World Wide Web http://selaonline.org.

State and Provincial Library Agencies

The state library administrative agency in each of the U.S. states will have the latest information on its state plan for the use of federal funds under the Library Services and Technology Act (LSTA). The directors and addresses of these state agencies are listed below.

Alabama

Rebecca Mitchell, Dir., Alabama Public Lib. Service, 6030 Monticello Drive, Montgomery 36130-6000. Tel. 334-213-3902, fax 334-213-3993, e-mail rmitchell@apls.state.al.us. World Wide Web http://statelibrary.alabama.gov/Content/Index.aspx.

Alaska

Linda S. Thibodeau, State Libn. and Dir., Alaska Dept. of Educ., Div. of Libs., Archives, and Museums, P.O. Box 110571, Juneau 99811. Tel. 907-465-2911, fax 907-465-2151, e-mail linda.thibodeau@alaska.gov. World Wide Web http://library.state.ak.us.

Arizona

Joan Clark, State Libn., Arizona State Lib., Archives, and Public Records, 1700 W. Washington, Phoenix 85007. Tel. 602-926-4035, fax 602-256-7983, e-mail lclark@lib.az.us. World Wide Web http://www.lib.az.us.

Arkansas

Carolyn Ashcraft, State Libn., Arkansas State Lib., 900 W. Capitol, Suite 100, Little Rock 72201-3108. Tel. 501-682-1526, fax 501-682-1899, e-mail carolyn@library.arkansas.gov. World Wide Web http://www.asl.lib.ar.us.

California

Gerry Maginnity, Acting State Libn., California State Lib., P.O. Box 942837, Sacramento 94237. Tel. 916-654-0188, fax 916-654-0064, e-mail gerald.maginnity@library.ca.gov. World Wide Web http://www.library.ca.gov.

Colorado

Eugene Hainer, Dir. and State Libn., Colorado State Lib., Rm. 309, 201 E. Colfax Ave., Denver 80203-1799. Tel. 303-866-6733, fax 303-866-6940, e-mail hainer_g@cde.state.co.us. World Wide Web http://www.cde.state.co.us/cdelib.

Connecticut

Kendall F. Wiggin, State Libn., Connecticut State Lib., 231 Capitol Ave., Hartford 06106. Tel. 860-757-6510, fax 860-757-6503, e-mail kendall.wiggin@ct.gov. World Wide Web http://www.cslib.org.

Delaware

Anne Norman, State Libn. and Dir., Delaware Div. of Libs., 121 Duke of York St., Dover 19901. Tel. 302-739-4748 ext. 5126, fax 302-739-8436, e-mail annie.norman@state.de.us. World Wide Web http://www.state.lib.de.us.

District of Columbia

Ginnie Cooper, Chief Libn., District of Columbia Public Lib., 901 G St. N.W., Suite 400, Washington 20001-4599. Tel. 202-727-1101, fax 202-727-1129, e-mail ginnie.cooper@dc.gov. World Wide Web http://www.dclibrary.org.

Florida

Judith A. Ring, State Libn., Div. of Lib. and Info. Services, R. A. Gray Bldg., 500 S. Bronough St., Tallahassee 32399-0250. Tel. 850-245-6604, fax 850-488-2746, e-mail jring@dos.state.fl.us. World Wide Web http://dlis.dos.state.fl.us/stlib.

Georgia

Lamar Veatch, State Libn., Georgia Public Lib. Services, 1800 Century Place N.E., Suite 150, Atlanta 30345-4304. Tel. 404-235-7120, fax 404-235-7201, e-mail lveatch@georgialibraries.

org. World Wide Web http://www.georgia libraries.org.

Hawaii

Richard Burns, State Libn., Hawaii State Public Lib. System, 44 Merchant St., Honolulu 96813. Tel. 808-586-3704, fax 808-586-3715, e-mail stlib@librarieshawaii.org. World Wide Web http://www.librarieshawaii.org.

Idaho

Ann Joslin, State Libn., Idaho Commission for Libs., 325 W. State St., Boise 83702-6072. Tel. 208-334-2150, fax 208-334-4016, e-mail ann.joslin@libraries.idaho.gov. World Wide Web http://libraries.idaho.gov.

Illinois

Anne Craig, Dir., Illinois State Lib., 300 S. 2 St., Springfield 62701-1703. Tel. 217-782-2994, fax 217-785-4326, e-mail acraig@ilsos.net. World Wide Web http://www.cyberdrive illinois.com/departments/library/home.html.

Indiana

Roberta L. Brooker, Dir. and State Libn., Indiana State Lib., 315 W. Ohio St., Indianapolis 46202. Tel. 317-232-3692, fax 317-232-3728, e-mail rbrooker@library.in.gov. World Wide Web http://www.in.gov/library.

Iowa

Mary Wegner, State Libn., State Lib. of Iowa, 1112 E. Grand Ave., Des Moines 50319. Tel. 515-281-4105, fax 515-281-6191, e-mail mary.wegner@lib.state.ia.us. World Wide Web http://www.statelibraryofiowa.org.

Kansas

Jo Budler, State Libn., State Lib. of Kansas, Rm.312-N, 300 S.W. 10 Ave., Topeka 66612-1593. Tel. 785-506-5466, fax 785-296-6650, e-mail jo.budler@library.ks.gov. World Wide Web http://skyways.lib.ks.us/KSL.

Kentucky

Wayne Onkst, State Libn. and Commissioner, Kentucky Dept. for Libs. and Archives, P.O. Box 537, Frankfort 40602-0537. Tel. 502-564-8300 ext. 312, fax 502-564-5773, e-mail wayne.onkst@ky.gov. World Wide Web http://www.kdla.ky.gov.

Louisiana

Rebecca Hamilton, State Libn., State Lib. of Louisiana, P.O. Box 131, 701 N. 4 St., Baton Rouge 70821-0131. Tel. 225-342-4923, fax 225-219-4804, e-mail rhamilton@crt.state.la.gov. World Wide Web http://www.state.lib.la.us.

Maine

Linda Lord, State Libn., Maine State Lib., 64 State House Sta., Augusta 04333-0064. Tel. 207-287-5620, fax 207-287-5624, e-mail linda.lord@maine.gov. World Wide Web http://www.maine.gov/msl.

Maryland

Irene Padilla, Asst. State Superintendent for Libs., State Dept. of Educ., Div. of Lib. Development and Services, 200 W. Baltimore St., Baltimore 21201. Tel. 410-767-0435, fax 410-333-2507, e-mail ipadilla@msde.state.md.us. World Wide Web http://www.marylandpublic schools.org/MSDE/divisions/library.

Massachusetts

Robert C. Maier, Dir., Massachusetts Board of Lib. Commissioners, 98 N. Washington St., Suite 401, Boston 02114-1933. Tel. 617-725-1860 ext. 249, fax 617-725-0140, e-mail robert.maier@state.ma.us. World Wide Web http://mblc.state.ma.us.

Michigan

Nancy R. Robertson, State Libn., Lib. of Michigan, 702 W. Kalamazoo St., P.O. Box 30007, Lansing 48909-7507. Tel. 517-373-9464, fax 517-373-5700, e-mail robertsonn@michigan.gov. World Wide Web http://www.michigan.gov/libraryofmichigan.

Minnesota

Nancy K. Walton, State Libn. and Dir., Minnesota State Lib. Agency, Div. of State Lib. Services, Dept. of Educ., 1500 Hwy. 36 W.,

Roseville 55113-4266. Tel. 651-582-8881, fax 651-582-8752, e-mail nancy.walton@state. mn.us. World Wide Web http://education.state. mn.us/MDE/stusuc/lib.statelibserv/index.html.

Mississippi

Sharman Bridges Smith, Exec. Dir., Mississippi Lib. Commission, 3881 Eastwood Drive, Jackson 39211. Tel. 601-432-4039, fax 601-432-4480, e-mail sharman@mlc.lib.ms.us. World Wide Web http://www.mlc.lib.ms.us.

Missouri

Margaret Conroy, State Libn., Missouri State Lib., P.O. Box 387, Jefferson City 65102-0387. Tel. 573-526-2751, fax 573-751-3612, e-mail margaret.conroy@sos.mo.gov. World Wide Web http://www.sos.mo.gov/library.

Montana

Jennie Stapp, State Libn., Montana State Lib., 1515 E. 6 Ave., P.O. Box 201800, Helena 59620-1800. Tel. 406-444-3116, fax 406-444-0266, e-mail jstapp2@mt.gov. World Wide Web http://msl.mt.gov.

Nebraska

Rodney G. Wagner, Dir., Nebraska Lib. Commission, Suite 120, The Atrium, 1200 N St., Lincoln 68508-2023. Tel. 402-471-4001, fax 402-471-2083, e-mail rod.wagner@nebraska. gov. World Wide Web http://www.nlc.nebraska. gov.

Nevada

Daphne DeLeon, State Lib. and Archives Admin., Nevada State Lib. and Archives, 100 N. Stewart St., Carson City 89710-4285. Tel. 775-684-3315, fax 775-684-3311, e-mail ddeleon@admin.nv.gov. World Wide Web http://nsla.nevadaculture.org.

New Hampshire

Michael York, State Libn., New Hampshire State Lib., 20 Park St., Concord 03301-6314. Tel. 603-271-2397, fax 603-271-6826, e-mail michael.york@dcr.nh.gov. World Wide Web http://www.nh.gov/nhsl.

New Jersey

Mary Chute, State Libn., New Jersey State Lib., P.O. Box 520, Trenton 08625-0520. Tel. 609-278-2640 ext. 101, fax 609-278-2652, e-mail mchute@njstatelib.org. World Wide Web http://www.njstatelib.org.

New Mexico

Devon Skeele, State Libn., New Mexico State Lib., 1209 Camino Carlos Rey, Santa Fe 87507. Tel. 505-476-9762, fax 505-476-9761, e-mail devon.skeele@state.nm.us. World Wide Web http://www.nmstatelibrary.org.

New York

Bernard A. Margolis, State Libn. and Assistant Commissioner for Libs., New York State Lib., Room 10C34, Cultural Educ. Center, Empire State Plaza, Albany 12230. Tel. 518-486-4865, fax 518-486-6880, e-mail bmargolis@mail. nysed.gov. World Wide Web http://www.nysl. nysed.gov.

North Carolina

Caroline "Cal" Shepard, State Libn., State Lib. of North Carolina, 4640 Mail Service Center, 109 E. Jones St., Raleigh 27699-4640. Tel. 919-807-7410, fax 919-733-8748, e-mail cal. shepard@ncdcr.gov. World Wide Web http:// statelibrary.ncdcr.gov.

North Dakota

Hulen Bivins, State Libn., North Dakota State Lib., 604 E. Boulevard Ave., Bismarck 58505-0800. Tel. 701-328-2492, fax 701-328-2040, e-mail hbivins@nd.gov. World Wide Web http:// ndsl.lib.state.nd.us.

Ohio

Beverly Cain, State Libn., State Lib. of Ohio, Suite 100, 274 E. 1 Ave., Columbus 43201. Tel. 614-644-6843, fax 614-466-3584, e-mail bcain@library.ohio.gov. World Wide Web http://www.library.ohio.gov.

Oklahoma

Susan C. McVey, Dir., Oklahoma Dept. of Libs., 200 N.E. 18 St., Oklahoma City 73105-

3298. Tel. 405-522-3173, fax 405-522-1077, e-mail smcvey@oltn.odl.state.ok.us. World Wide Web http://www.odl.state.ok.us.

Oregon

MaryKay Dahlgreen, State Libn., Oregon State Lib., 250 Winter St. N.E., Salem 97301. Tel. 503-378-5012, fax 503-585-8059, e-mail marykay.dahlgreen@state.or.us. World Wide Web http://oregon.gov/OSL.

Pennsylvania

Stacey Aldrich, Deputy Secy. of Educ. and Commissioner for Libs., 607 South Drive, Harrisburg 17120-0600. Tel. 717-783-2466, fax 717-772-3265, e-mail saldrich@pa.gov. World Wide Web http://www.statelibrary.state.pa.us/libraries/site/default.asp.

Rhode Island

Howard Boksenbaum, Chief Lib. Officer, Rhode Island Office of Lib. and Info. Services, 1 Capitol Hill, 2nd flr., Providence 02908-5803. Tel. 401-574-9301, fax 401-574-9320, e-mail howard.boksenbaum@olis.ri.gov. World Wide Web http://www.olis.ri.gov.

South Carolina

Leesa Benggio, Interim Agency Dir., South Carolina State Lib., 1430 Senate St., P.O. Box 11469, Columbia 29211. Tel. 803-734-8626, fax 803-734-8676, e-mail lbenggio@statelibrary.sc.gov. World Wide Web http://www.statelibrary.sc.gov.

South Dakota

Daria Bossman, State Libn., South Dakota State Lib., 800 Governors Drive, Pierre 57501-2294. Tel. 605-773-3167, fax 605-773-6962, e-mail daria.bossman@state.sd.us. World Wide Web http://library.sd.gov.

Tennessee

Chuck Sherrill, State Libn. and Archivist, Tennessee State Lib. and Archives, 403 Seventh Ave. N., Nashville 37243-0312. Tel. 615-741-7996, fax 615-532-9293, e-mail chuck.sherrill@tn.gov. World Wide Web http://www.tennessee.gov/tsla.

Texas

Edward Seidenberg, Interim Dir. and Libn., Texas State Lib. and Archives Commission, P.O. Box 12927, Austin 78711-2927. Tel. 512-463-5459, fax 512-463-5436, e-mail eseidenberg@tsl.state.tx.us. World Wide Web http://www.tsl.state.tx.us.

Utah

Donna Jones Morris, Dir. and State Libn., Utah State Lib. Div., Suite A, 250 N. 1950 W., Salt Lake City 84116. Tel. 801-715-6770, fax 801-715-6767, e-mail dmorris@utah.gov. World Wide Web http://library.utah.gov.

Vermont

Martha Reid, State Libn., Vermont Dept. of Libs., 109 State St., Montpelier 05609. Tel. 802-828-3265, fax 802-828-2199, e-mail martha.reid@mail.dol.state.vt.us. World Wide Web http://dol.state.vt.us.

Virginia

Sandra G. Treadway, Libn. of Virginia, Lib. of Virginia, 800 E. Broad St., Richmond 23219-8000. Tel. 804-692-3535, fax 804-692-3594, e-mail sandra.treadway@lva.virginia.gov. World Wide Web http://www.lva.virginia.gov.

Washington

Rand Simmons, State Libn., Washington State Lib., P.O. Box 42460, Olympia 98504. Tel. 360-570-5585, fax 360-586-7575, e-mail rand.simmons@sos.wa.gov. World Wide Web http://www.sos.wa.gov/library.

West Virginia

Karen Goff, Dir./State Libn., West Virginia Lib. Commission, Cultural Center, 1900 Kanawha Blvd. E., Charleston 25305. Tel. 304-558-2041, fax 304-558-2044, e-mail karen.e.goff@wv.gov. World Wide Web http://www.librarycommission.wv.gov.

Wisconsin

Kurt Kiefer, Asst. State Superintendent, Wisconsin Dept. of Public Instruction, Div. for Libs. and Technology, P.O. Box 7841, Madison

53707-7841. Tel. 608-266-2205, fax 608-266-9207, e-mail kurt.kiefer@dpi.wi.gov. World Wide Web http://dpi.wi.gov/dltcl/index.html.

Wyoming

Lesley Boughton, State Libn., Wyoming State Lib., 2800 Central Ave., Cheyenne 82002. Tel. 307-777-5911, fax 307-777-6289, e-mail lbough@wyo.gov. World Wide Web http://www-wsl.state.wy.us.

American Samoa

Cheryl Morales, Territorial Libn., Feleti Barstow Public Lib., P.O. Box 997687, Pago Pago, AS 96799. Tel. 684-633-5816, fax 684-633-5823, e-mail feletibarstow@yahoo.com. World Wide Web http://fbpl.org.

Federated States of Micronesia

Augustine Kohler, Acting Dir., National Archives, Culture, and Historic Preservation, P.O. Box PS 175, Palikir, Pohnpei, FM 96941. Tel. 691-320-2343, fax 691-320-5634, e-mail hpo@mail.fm. World Wide Web http://www.fsmgov.org.

Guam

Sandra Stanley, Admin. Officer, Guam Public Lib. System, 254 Martyr St., Hagatna 96910-5141. Tel. 671-475-4765, fax 671-477-0888, e-mail sandra.stanley@gpls.guam.gov. World Wide Web http://gpls.guam.gov.

Northern Mariana Islands

John Oliver Gonzales, Exec. Dir., CNMI Joeten-Kiyu Public Lib., P.O. Box 501092, Saipan, MP 96950-1092. Tel. 670-235-7322, fax 670-235-7550, e-mail joetenkiyupublic library@gmail.com. World Wide Web http://www.cnmilibrary.com.

Palau

Masa-Aki N. Emesiochl, Minister of Educ., Republic of Palau, P.O. Box 189, Koror, PW 96940. Tel. 680-488-2952, fax 680-488-8465, e-mail memesiochl@palaumoe.net. World Wide Web http://www.palaugov.net/palaugov/executive/ministries/MOE/MOE.htm.

Puerto Rico

Sandra Castro, Dir., Lib. and Info. Services Program, Puerto Rico Dept. of Educ., P.O. Box 190759, San Juan 00919-0759. Tel. 787-773-3564, fax 787-753-6945, e-mail castroas @de.gobierno.pr. World Wide Web http://de.gobierno.pr/deportal/escuelas/bibliotecas/bibliotecarios.aspx.

Republic of the Marshall Islands

Newton Lajuan, Dir., Alele Museum and Public Lib., P.O. Box 629, Majuro, MH 96960. Tel. 692-625-3372, fax 692-625-3226, e-mail alele_inc@ntamar.net. World Wide Web http://rmigovernment.org/index.jsp.

U.S. Virgin Islands

Ingrid A. Bough, Territorial Dir., Div. of Libs., Archives, and Museums, 23 Dronningens Gade, St. Thomas 00802. Tel. 340-773-5715, fax 340-773-5327, e-mail ingrid.bough@dpnr.gov.vi. World Wide Web http://www.virginislandspace.org/Division%20of%20Libraries/dlamhome.htm.

Canada

Alberta

Diana Davidson, Dir., Public Lib. Services Branch, Alberta Municipal Affairs, 803 Standard Life Centre, 10405 Jasper Ave., Edmonton T5J 4R7. Tel. 780-427-4871, fax 780-415-8594, e-mail diana.davidson@gov.ab.ca or libraries@gov.ab.cam. World Wide Web http://www.municipalaffairs.alberta.ca/mc_libraries.cfm.

British Columbia

Jacqueline van Dyk, Dir., Public Lib. Services Branch, Ministry of Educ., 605 Robson St., Suite 850, Vancouver V6B 5J3. Tel. 250-356-1791, fax 250-953-3225, e-mail jacqueline.vandyk@gov.bc.ca. World Wide Web http://www.bced.gov.bc.ca/pls.

Manitoba

Dir., Public Lib. Services, Manitoba Dept. of Culture, Heritage, and Tourism, 300-1011

Rosser Ave., Brandon R7A OL5. Tel. 204-726-6590, e-mail pls@gov.mb.ca. World Wide Web http://www.gov.mb.ca/chc/pls/index.html.

New Brunswick

Sylvie Nadeau, Exec. Dir., New Brunswick Public Lib. Service, Place 2000, 250 King St., P.O. Box 6000, Fredericton E3B 5H1. Tel. 506-453-2354, fax 506-444-4064, e-mail sylvie.nadeau@gnb.ca. World Wide Web http://www.gnb.ca/0003/index-e.asp.

Newfoundland and Labrador

Shawn Tetford, Exec. Dir., Provincial Info. and Lib. Resources Board, 48 St. George's Ave., Stephenville A2N 1K9. Tel. 709-643-0902, fax 709-643-0925, e-mail stetford@nlpl.ca. World Wide Web http://www.nlpl.ca.

Northwest Territories

Alison Hopkins, Territorial Libn., NWT Lib. Services, 75 Woodland Drive, Hay River X0E 1G1. Tel. 867-874-6531, fax 867-874-3321, e-mail alison_hopkins@gov.nt.ca. World Wide Web http://www.nwtpls.gov.nt.ca.

Nova Scotia

Jennifer Evans, Dir., Nova Scotia Provincial Lib., 2021 Brunswick St., P.O. Box 578, Halifax B3J 2S9. Tel. 902-424-2455, fax 902-424-0633, e-mail evansjl@gov.ns.ca. World Wide Web http://www.library.ns.ca.

Nunavut

Ron Knowling, Mgr., Nunavut Public Lib. Services, Box 270, Baker Lake X0C 0A0. Tel. 867-793-3353, fax 867-793-3360, e-mail rknowling@gov.nu.ca. World Wide Web http://www.publiclibraries.nu.ca.

Ontario

Rod Sawyer, Ontario Government Ministry of Tourism, Culture, and Sport, Hearst Block, 900 Bay St., Toronto M7A 2E1. Tel. 416-326-9326. World Wide Web http://www.mtc.gov.on.ca/en/libraries/contact.shtml.
Ontario Lib. Service–North, 334 Regent St., Sudbury P3C 4E2. Tel. 705-675-6467. World Wide Web http://www.olsn.ca. Joyce Cunningham, Chair.
Southern Ontario Lib. Service, 111 Peter St., Suite 902, Toronto M5V 2H1. Tel. 416-961-1669 ext. 5118. World Wide Web http://www.sols.org. Laurey Gillies, CEO. E-mail lgillies@sols.org.

Prince Edward Island

Public Lib. Service of Prince Edward Island, P.O. Box 7500, Morell C0A 1S0. Tel. 902-961-7320, fax 902-961-7322, e-mail plshq@gov.pe.ca. World Wide Web http://www.library.pe.ca.

Quebec

Guy Berthiaume, Chair and CEO, Bibliothèque et Archives Nationales du Québec (BAnQ), 2275 rue Holt, Montreal H2G 3H1. Tel. 800-363-9028 or 514-873-1100, fax 514-873-9312, info@banq.qc.ca. World Wide Web http://www.banq.qc.ca/portal/dt/accueil.jsp.

Saskatchewan

Brett Waytuck, Provincial Libn., Provincial Lib. and Literacy Office, Ministry of Educ., 409A Park St., Regina S4N 5B2. Tel. 306-787-2972, fax 306-787-2029, e-mail brett.waytuck@gov.sk.ca. World Wide Web http://www.education.gov.sk.ca/provincial-library/public-library-system.

Yukon Territory

Julie Ourom, Dir., Public Libs., Community Development Div., Dept. of Community Services, Government of Yukon, P.O. Box 2703, Whitehorse Y1A 2C6. Tel. 867-667-5447, fax 867-393-6333, e-mail julie.ourom@gov.yk.ca. World Wide Web http://www.ypl.gov.yk.ca.

State School Library Media Associations

Alabama

Children's and School Libns. Div., Alabama Lib. Assn. Memb. 650. Publication. *The Alabama Librarian* (q.).

Chair Carolyn Starkey, Buckhorn H.S., 25 Warren Rd., Albertville 35950. Tel. 256-302-1009, e-mail admin@jojo-starkey.com; *V. Chair/Chair-Elect* Susan Cordell, Sta. 33, Univ. of West Alabama, Livingston 35470. Tel. 205-652-5421, fax 205-652-3706, e-mail scordell@uwa.edu; *Secy.* Michelle Wilson, North Highland Elementary School, 2021 29th Ave. N., Hueytown 35023. Tel. 205-379-4950, e-mail mwilson518@gmail.com; *Past Chair* Jana Fine, Tuscaloosa Public Lib., 1801 Jack Warner Pkwy., Tuscaloosa 35401. Tel. 205-391-9025, e-mail jfine@tuscaloosa-library.org.

Address correspondence to the association administrator, Alabama Lib. Assn., 9154 Eastchase Pkwy., Suite 418, Montgomery 36117. Tel. 334-414-0113, e-mail admin@allanet.org. World Wide Web http://allanet.org.

Alaska

Alaska Assn. of School Libns. Memb. 130. Publication. *The Puffin* (3 a year), online at http://puffin.akasl.org. *Ed.* Alta Collins, Northern Lights ABC School, Anchorage. E-mail puffin@akasl.org.

Pres. Nicole Roohi, Goldenville Middle School, Anchorage. E-mail roohi_nicole@asdk12.org; *Pres.-Elect* Wendy Stout, Larson Elementary, Wasilla. E-mail wendy.stout@matsuk12.us; *Secy.* Janet Madson, West Valley H.S., Fairbanks. E-mail janet.madsen@k12northstar.org; *Treas.* Laura Guest, Turnagain Elementary, Anchorage. E-mail guest_laura@asdk12.us; *Past Pres.* Robin Turk, Palmer. E-mail rturk@matsuk12.us.

World Wide Web http://www.akasl.org.

Arizona

Teacher-Libn. Div., Arizona Lib. Assn. Memb. 1,000. Publication. *AZLA Newsletter.*

Chair Tanya Molina, Centerra Mirage Elementary School. E-mail tmolina@avondale.k12.az.us; *Past Co-Chairs* Jean Kilker, Maryvale H.S.; Kerrlita Westrick, Verrado Middle School.

Address correspondence to the chairperson. WorldWideWebhttp://www.azla.affiniscape.com.

Arkansas

Arkansas Assn. of School Libns., Div. of Arkansas Lib. Assn.

Chair Tracy McAllister, Bob Courtway Middle School, 1200 Bob Courtway Drive, Conway 72032. Tel. 501-450-4832, e-mail mcallistert@conwayschools.net; *Conference Chair* Erin Shaw, Greenbrier Middle School, 13 School Drive, Greenbrier 72058. Tel. 501-679-2113, e-mail shawe@greenbrierschools.org; *Past Chair* Cathy Toney, Sally Cone Elementary, 1629 South Blvd., Conway 72034. Tel. 501-450-4835, e-mail toneyc@conwayschools.net.

Address correspondence to the president. World Wide Web http://www.arlib.org/organization/aasl/index.php.

California

California School Lib. Assn. Memb. 1,200+. Publications. *CSLA Journal* (2 a year). *Ed.* Marilyn Robertson. E-mail mnroberts@earthlink.net; *CSLA Newsletter* (10 a year).

(Northern Region) *Pres.* Katie Williams, Gale Ranch Middle School, 6400 Main Branch Rd., San Ramon 94582. Tel. 925-479-1500, e-mail kjwbooks@comcast.net; *Pres.-Elect* Andrea Stephenson, El Camino H.S., 1310 Silver Spur Circle, Lincoln 95648. Tel. 916-645-8301, e-mail astephenson@ci.lincoln.ca.us; *Secy.* Christina Larrechea, Mission Oak H.S., Tulare Joint Union H.S. Dist., 3442 E. Bardsley, Tulare 93274. E-mail jcm_larrechea@hotmail.com; *Treas.* Renee Ousley-Swank, Daniel J. Savage Middle School, 1900 Maid Mariane Lane, Modesto 95355. Tel. 209-552-

3300, e-mail rousley-swank@sylvan.k12. ca.us; *Past Pres.* Teresa Lai, A. P. Giannini Middle School, 3151 Ortega St., San Francisco 94122. Tel. 415-759-2770, e-mail info spec@gmail.com; (Southern Region) *Pres.* Marie Slim, Fullerton Joint Union H.S. Dist., 2200 E. Dorothy Lane, Fullerton 92831. Tel. 714-458-5309, e-mail sraslim@sbcglobal. net; *Pres.-Elect* Yvonne Weinstein, Frank Augustus Miller Middle School, 5140 Monterey Rd., Riverside 92506. Tel. 951-789-8181, e-mail mrsweinstein@fastmail.fm; *Secy.* Claudia Durnerin, Temecula Valley USD, 32231 Corte Gabaiva, Temecula 92592. Tel. 619-987-190, e-mail cdurnerin@tvusd.k12.ca.us; *Treas.* Becky Johnston, Redlands East Valley H.S., 31000 E. Colton Ave., Redlands 92374. Tel. 909-389-2500, e-mail rkjohns@adelphia.net; *Past Pres.* Kathie Maier, Savanna H.S., 301 N. Gilbert St., Anaheim 92801. Tel. 714-220-4262, e-mail karmak1@cox.net.

Address correspondence to the association at 6444 E. Spring St., No. 237, Long Beach 90815-1553. Tel./fax 888-655-8480, e-mail info@csla.net.

World Wide Web http://www.csla.net.

Colorado

Colorado Assn. of School Libns. Memb. 260+.

Pres. Christine Schein, Academy Dist. 20. E-mail caslprez@gmail.com; *V.P./Pres.-Elect* Paula Busey, ThunderRidge H.S. E-mail paula. busey@dcsdk12.org; *Secy.* Yvonne Miller, Douglas County School Dist. E-mail yvonne. miller@dcsdk12.org; *Past Pres.* Becky Johnson, Mesa County Valley School Dist. 51. E-mail rebecca.johnson@d51schools.org; *Business Mgr.* Jesse Haynes, Colorado Assn. of School Libns., Westminster 80031. Tel. 303-463-6400, e-mail jesse@cal-webs.org.

World Wide Web http://www.cal-webs. org/?page=CASL.

Connecticut

Connecticut Assn. of School Libns. (formerly Connecticut Educ. Media Assn.). Memb. 500+. Term of Office. July 2012–June 2013.

Pres. Sara Kelley-Mudie. E-mail librarian. skm@gmail.com; *V.P.* Mary Ellen Minichiello.

E-mail meminichiello@milforded.org; *Recording Secy.* Christopher Barlow. E-mail christoph barlow@sbcglobal.net; *Treas.* Martha Djang. E-mail mdjang@hamdenhall.org; *Admin. Secy.* Anne Weimann, 25 Elmwood Ave., Trumbull 06611. Tel. 203-372-2260, e-mail anne weimann@gmail.com.

Address correspondence to the administrative secretary.

World Wide Web http://www.ctcasl.com.

Delaware

Delaware School Lib. Assn., div. of Delaware Lib. Assn. Memb. 100+. Publications. *DSLA Newsletter* (online; irreg.); column in *DLA Bulletin* (3 a year).

Pres. Janice Haney, Appoquinimink H.S., 1080 Bunker Hill Rd., Middletown 19709. E-mail janice.haney@appo.k12.de.us; *V.P./ Pres.-Elect* Jen Delgado. E-mail jennifer. delgado@redclay.k12.de.us; *Secy.* Tamra Pearson. E-mail tamra.pearson@appo.k12.de.us; *Past Pres.* Charles E. "Ed" Hockersmith, Delcastle Technical H.S., 1417 Newport Rd., Wilmington 19804. Tel. 302-995-8100, e-mail charles.hockersmith@nccvt.k12.de.us.

Address correspondence to the president.

World Wide Web http://www2.lib.udel. edu/dla/divisions/dsla13.htm and https://sites. google.com/site/delawaresla.

District of Columbia

District of Columbia Assn. of School Libns. Memb. 8. Publication. *Newsletter* (4 a year).

Pres. André Maria Taylor. E-mail diva librarian2@aol.com.

Address correspondence to André Maria Taylor, 330 10th St. N.E., Washington, DC 20002. Tel. 301-502-4203.

Florida

Florida Assn. for Media in Educ. Memb. 1,400+. Term of Office. Nov. 2012–Oct. 2013. Publication. *Florida Media Quarterly. Ed.* Rhoda Cribbs. E-mail rcribbs@pasco.k12. fl.us.

Pres. Cora P. Dunkley. E-mail cdunkley@ usf.edu; *Pres.-Elect* Henry Haake. E-mail henry.

haake@polk-fl.net; *Secy.* Deborah McNeil. E-mail Debora.mcneil@ocps.net; *Treas.* Lorri Cosgrove. E-mail cosgrol@stjohns.k12.fl.us; *Past Pres.* Lou Greco. E-mail grecol@stjohns.k12.fl.us; *Exec. Dir.* Larry E. Bodkin, Jr. Tel. 850-531-8351, fax 850-531-8344, e-mail lbodkin@floridamedia.org.

Address correspondence to FAME, 1876-B Eider Court, Tallahassee 32308. Tel. 850-531-8351, fax 850-531-8344, e-mail info@floridamedia.org.

World Wide Web http://www.floridamedia.org.

Georgia

School Lib. Media Div., Georgia Lib. Assn.

Chair Stephanie Jones, Georgia Southern Univ. College of Education, P.O. Box 8131, Statesboro 30460-8131. Tel. 912-478-5250, e-mail sjones@georgiasouthern.edu; *Chair-Elect* Lucy Green, Dept. of Leadership, Technology, and Human Development, Georgia Southern Univ. E-mail lgreen@georgiasouthern.edu; *Past Chair* Tim Wojcik, Our Lady of Mercy Catholic H.S. Tel. 770-461-2202, e-mail wojcikt@bellsouth.net.

Address correspondence to School Lib. Media Div., Georgia Lib. Assn., P.O. Box 793, Rex, GA 30273.

World Wide Web http://gla.georgialibraries.org/div_media.htm.

Georgia Lib. Media Assn. Memb. 700+.

Pres. Andy Spinks; *Pres.-Elect* Beth Miller; *Secy.* Karii Zimmerman; *Treas.* Lora Taft; *Past Pres.* Betsy Razza; *Exec. Dir.* Lasa Joiner.

Address correspondence to GLMA Executive Office, 2711 Irvin Way, Suite 111, Decatur 30030. Tel. 404-299-7700, fax 404-299-7029, e-mail glma@jlh-consulting.com.

World Wide Web http://www.glma-inc.org.

Hawaii

Hawaii Assn. of School Libns. Memb. 145. Term of Office. June 2012–May 2013. Publication. *HASL Newsletter* (3 a year).

Co-Pres. Patty Louis, Diane Mokuau; *V.P., Programming* Michelle Colte; *V.P., Membership* Denise Sumida; *Corresponding Secy.* Terry Heckman; *Recording Secy.* Sandra Takishita; *Treas.* Jarri Kagawa.

Address correspondence to the association, P.O. Box 235284, Honolulu 96823.

World Wide Web https://sites.google.com/site/haslsite.

Idaho

Educational Media Div., Idaho Lib. Assn. Memb. 40+.

Chair Dennis Hahs, Rocky Mountain H.S., 5450 N. Linder Rd., Meridian 83646. Tel. 208-350-4340 ext. 1530, e-mail hahs.dennis@meridianschools.org; *Past Chair* Glynda Pflieger, Melba School Dist., 6870 Stokes Lane, P.O. Box 185, Melba 83641. Tel. 208-495-2221, e-mail gpflieger@melbaschools.org.

Address correspondence to the chairperson.

World Wide Web http://www.idaholibraries.org/node/94.

Illinois

Illinois School Lib. Media Assn. Memb. 1,000. Term of Office. July 2012–June 2013. Publications. *ISLMA News* (4 a year); *Linking for Learning: The Illinois School Library Media Program Guidelines* (3rd ed., 2010); *Powerful Libraries Make Powerful Learners: The Illinois Study.*

Pres. Christine Graves, Jefferson Middle School, 1151 Plum St., Aurora 60506. Tel. 630-301-5320, fax 630-844-5711, e-mail cgraves@sevarg.net; *Pres.-Elect* Debra Turner, Metea Valley H.S., 1801 N. Eola Rd., Aurora, IL 60502. Tel. 630-375-8851; *Secy.* Jennifer Bromann-Bender, Lincoln-Way West H.S. E-mail bromannj@hotmail.com; *Past Pres.* Sarah Hill, Paris Cooperative H.S., 309 S. Main St., Paris 61944. Tel. 217-466-1175, fax 217-466-1903, e-mail gsarahthelibrarian@gmail.com; *Exec. Secy.* Kay Maynard, ISLMA, P.O. Box 598, Canton 61520. Tel. 390-649-0911, fax 309-649-0916, e-mail islma@islma.org.

World Wide Web http://www.islma.org.

Indiana

Assn. of Indiana School Library Educators (AISLE). Publications. *Focus on Indiana Libraries* (mo.); *Indiana Libraries* (q.).

Pres. Leslie Sutherlin, South Dearborn Community School Corp., 5850 Squire Place, Aurora 47001. Tel. 812-926-6298, e-mail leslie.sutherlin@sdcsc.k12.in.us; *Pres.-Elect* Susie

Highley, Creston Middle School, 10925 E. Prospect, Indianapolis 46239. Tel. 812-532-6806, fax 812-532-6891, e-mail shighley@warren.k12.in.us; *Treas.* To be announced; *Past Pres.* Denise Keogh, Tipton Middle School, 817 S Main St., Tipton 46072. Tel. 765-675-7521 ext. 225, e-mail dkeogh@tcsc.k12.in.us.

Address correspondence to the association, c/o Indiana Lib. Federation, 941 E. 86 St., Suite 260, Indianapolis 46240. Tel. 317-257-2040, fax 317-257-1389, e-mail ilf@indy.net.

World Wide Web http://www.ilfonline.org/units/aisle.

Iowa

Iowa Assn. of School Libns., Subdivision of the Iowa Lib. Assn. Memb. 180+. Term of Office. Jan.–Jan. Publication. *IASL Journal* (online, 4 a year).

Chair Susan Feuerbach. E-mail susan.feuerbach@camanche.k12.ia.us; *V.P./Pres.-Elect* Christine Sturgeon. E-mail csturgeon@mnwcougars.com; *Secy./Treas.* Sue Inhelder. E-mail sinhelder@marshalltown.k12.ia.us; *Past Chair* Becky Johnson, Jefferson H.S., Cedar Rapids. E-mail bcjohnson@cr.k12.ia.us.

Address correspondence to the chairperson. World Wide Web http://www.iasl-ia.org.

Kansas

Kansas Assn. of School Libns. Memb. 600. Publication. *KASL News* (online; q.).

Pres. Gwen Lehman. Tel. 620-285-8430, e-mail gwen.lehman@usd495.net; *Secy.* Susie Whitaker. Tel. 785-597-5124. e-mail swhitaker@usd.343.org; *Treas.* Diane Leupold. Tel. 785-295-3941, e-mail dleupold@topeka.k12.ks.us; *Past Pres.* Juanita Jameson. Tel. 620-805-8412, e-mail juanitajameson@cox.net; *Exec. Secy.* Barb Bahm. Tel. 913-845-2627, e-mail bbahm@tong464.org.

Address correspondence to the executive secretary.

World Wide Web http://kasl.typepad.com/kasl.

Kentucky

Kentucky Assn. of School Libns. (KASL), Section of the Kentucky Lib. Assn. Memb. 600+. Publication. *KASL Newsletter* (q.).

Pres. Adele Koch, St. Patrick School, 1000 N. Beckley Station Rd., Louisville 40245. E-mail akoch@stpatrick-lou.org; *Pres.-Elect* Janet Wells, Rockcastle County H.S., 1545 Lake Cumberland Rd., Mt. Vernon 40456. E-mail janet.wells@rockcastle.kyschools.us; *Secy.* Fred Tilsley. E-mail ftilsley@windstream.net; *Past Pres.* Tara Griffith, W. R. McNeill Elementary School, 1800 Creason Drive, Bowling Green 42101. E-mail tara.griffith@bgreen.kyschools.us.

Address correspondence to the president. World Wide Web http://www.kysma.org.

Louisiana

Louisiana Assn. of School Libns. Memb. 230. Term of Office. July 2012–June 2013.

Pres. Catherine Smith. Tel. 318-603-6374, e-mail catlib2000@yahoo.com; *1st V.P./Pres.-Elect* Amanda Graves. Tel. 225-383-0397 ext.118, e-mail agraves@catholichigh.org; *2nd V.P.* Kristy Sturm. Tel. 337-981-0917, e-mail kasturm@lpssonline.com; *Past Pres.* Paula Clemmons. E-mail pclemmons@episcopaldayschool.org.

Address correspondence to the association, c/o Louisiana Lib. Assn., 8550 United Plaza Blvd., Suite 1001, Baton Rouge 70809. Tel. 225-922-4642, fax 225-408-4422, e-mail office@llaonline.org.

World Wide Web http://llaonline.org/sig/lasl.

Maine

Maine School Lib. Assn. Memb. 200+.

Pres. Eileen Broderick. E-mail ebroderick@rus10.org; *Pres.-Elect* Joyce Lucas. E-mail jolukeme@gmail.com; *Secy.* Tina Taggart. E-mail tina.taggart@staff.foxcroftacademy.org; *Treas.* Dorothy Hall-Riddle. E-mail dorothyhallriddle@gmail.com; *Past Pres.* Peg Becksvoort. E-mail pegbecksvoort@gmail.com; *Business Mgr.* Edna Comstock. E-mail empoweredna@gwi.net.

Address correspondence to the president. World Wide Web http://www.maslibraries.org.

Maryland

Maryland Assn. of School Libns. (formerly Maryland Educ. Media Organization).

Pres. Mary Jo Richmond, Frederick County Public Schools. E-mail marylandmasl@gmail.com; *Secy.* To be announced; *Treas.* Lynda Baker, Frederick County Public Schools. E-mail superbooklady@gmail.com; *Past Pres.* Michele Forney, Prince Georges County Public Schools. E-mail michele.forney@gmail.com.

Address correspondence to the association, Box 21127, Baltimore 21228.

World Wide Web http://maslmd.org.

Massachusetts

Massachusetts School Lib. Assn. Memb. 800. Publication. *MSLA Forum* (3 a year).

Pres. Valerie Diggs, Chelmsford H.S. Tel. 978-251-5111; *Pres.-Elect* Judi Paradis, Plympton Elementary School, Waltham. Tel. 781-314-5767, e-mail judiparadis@gmail.com; *Secy.* Carrie Tucker. E-mail ctucker240@gmail.com; *Treas.* Linda Friel. E-mail lafriel@comcast.net; *Exec. Dir.* Kathy Lowe, Massachusetts School Lib. Assn., P.O. Box 658, Lunenburg 01462. Tel. 978-582-6967, e-mail klowe@maschoolibraries.org.

Address correspondence to the executive director.

World Wide Web http://www.maschoolibraries.org.

Michigan

Michigan Assn. for Media in Educ. Memb. 1,200. Publications. *Media Spectrum* (2 a year); *MAME Newsletter* (6 a year).

Pres. Tom Stream, 15681 High Ridge Drive, Grand Haven 49417. Tel. 616-842-3335, e-mail tom.stream@mimame.org; *Pres.-Elect* Kathy Lester, Parker Middle School Lib., Howell Public Schools, 400 Wright Rd., Howell 4884. E-mail klester1@comcast.net; *Secy.* Jeanna Walker, Portage Public Schools, 1000 Idaho St., Portage 49024. Tel. 269-323-5489, e-mail jwalker@portageps.org; *Past Pres.* Sue Lay, Derby Middle School, 1300 Derby Rd., Birmingham 48009. Tel. 248-203-5052, e-mail suel@mimame.org.

Address correspondence to MAME, 1407 Rensen, Suite 3, Lansing 48910. Tel. 517-394-2808, fax 517-394-2096, e-mail mame@mimame.org.

World Wide Web http://www.mimame.org.

Minnesota

Minnesota Educ. Media Organization. Memb. 832. Term of Office. July 2012–July 2013. Publication. *MEMOrandom.*

Pres. Dhaivyd Hilgendorf, Park Center Senior H.S., 7300 Brooklyn Blvd., Brooklyn Park 55443. Tel. 763-569-7629, e-mail memodhaivyd@gmail.com; *Co-Pres.-Elect* Karen Qualey, Hubert Olson Middle School, 4551 W. 102 St., Bloomington 55437. E-mail karenjoy113@gmail.com; Donna Ohlgren, Oak View Elementary, 6710 E. Fish Lake Rd., Maple Grove 55369. E-mail ohlgrend@gmail.com; *Secy.* Mary Mehsikomer, TIES, 1667 Snelling Ave. N., St. Paul 55108. Tel 651-999-6510, e-mail mary.mehsikomer@ties.k12.mn.us; *Treas.* Laura Gudmundson, Kingsland Public School, 705 North Section Ave., Spring Valley 55975. E-mail lauragud79@gmail.com; *Past Pres.* Sally Mays, Robbinsdale Spanish Immersion School, 8808 Medicine Lake Rd., New Hope 55427. Tel. 763-504-4408, e-mail sally_mays@rdale.org; *Admin. Asst.* Deanna Sylte, P.O. Box 130555, Roseville 55113. Tel. 651-771-8672, e-mail admin@memoweb.org.

World Wide Web http://memoweb.org.

Mississippi

School Section, Mississippi Lib. Assn. Memb. 1,300.

Co-Chairs Susan Sparkman, Rowan Middle School. Tel. 601-960-5349, e-mail ssparkman@jackson.k12.ms.us; Venetia Oglesby, New Hope Elementary. Tel. 662-244-4769, e-mail venetia.oglesby@lowndes.k12.ms.us; *Exec. Secy.* Mary Julia Anderson.

Address correspondence to School Section, Mississippi Lib. Assn., P.O. Box 13687, Jackson 39236-3687. Tel. 601-981-4586, fax 601-981-4501, e-mail info@misslib.org.

World Wide Web http://www.misslib.org.

Missouri

Missouri Assn. of School Libns. Memb. 1,000. Term of Office. July 2012–June 2013. Publication. *Connections* (q.).

Pres. Vickie Howard, retired. E-mail ms mediacenter@harrisonville.k12.mo.us; *1st V.P./Pres.-Elect* Ellen Wickham, Raytown South H.S. E-mail wickhame@raytownschools.org; *2nd V.P.* Lysha Thompson, Tuscumbia County

R-3 Schools. E-mail lthompson@tuscumbia lions.k12.mo.us; *Secy.* Amy Hertzberg, Nevada Middle School. E-mail ahertzberg@nevada. k12.mo.us; *Treas.* Jenny Robins, UCMO. E-mail robins@ucmo.edu; *Past Pres.* Curtis Clark, Harrisonville Middle school. E-mail msmediacenter@harrisonville.k12.mo.us.

Address correspondence to the association, P.O. Box 2107, Jefferson City 65102. Tel. 573-893-4155, fax 573-635-2858, e-mail info@ maslonline.org.

World Wide Web http://www.maslonline. org.

Montana

Montana School Lib. Media Div., Montana Lib. Assn. Memb. 200+. Publication. *FOCUS* (published by Montana Lib. Assn.) (q.).

Exec. Asst., Montana Lib. Assn. Debra Kramer, P.O. Box 1352, Three Forks 59752. Tel. 406-285-3090, fax 406-285-3091, e-mail debkmla@hotmail.com.

World Wide Web http://www.mtlib.org.

Nebraska

Nebraska School Libns. Assn. Memb. 300+. Term of Office. July 2012–June 2013. Publication. *NSLA News* (q.).

Pres. Stacy Lickteig. E-mail stacy.lickteig@ ops.org; *Pres.-Elect* Sherry Crow. E-mail S4crows@msn.com; *Secy.* Beth Kabes. E-mail neschoollibsecretary@gmail.com; *Treas.* Tammi Mans. E-mail tmans@fairburyjeffs. org; *Past Pres.* Karen Buckley. E-mail karen. buckley@piusx.net; *Exec. Secy.* Kim Gangwish. E-mail contactsla@gmail.com.

Address correspondence to the executive secretary, Bellevue West H.S., 1501 Thurston Ave., Bellevue 68123.

World Wide Web https://sites.google.com/ site/neschoollibrariansassociation.

Nevada

Nevada School and Children's Libs. Section, Nevada Lib. Assn. Memb. 120.

Chair Carla Land, Las Vegas-Clark County Lib. Dist. E-mail landc@lvccld.org; *Past Chair* Leona Vittum-Jones, Henderson Dist. Public Libs.; *Exec. Secy.* Lauren Campbell, Las Vegas-Clark County Lib. Dist. E-mail ltcampbell 10@gmail.com.

World Wide Web http://www.nevadalibraries. org/handbook/nscls.html.

Address correspondence to the executive secretary.

New Hampshire

New Hampshire School Lib. Media Assn. (NHSLMA), Box 418, Concord 03302-0418. Memb. 271. Term of Office. June 2012–June 2013. Publication. *Online News* (winter, spring; online and print).

Pres. Helen Burnham, Lincoln Street School, 25 Lincoln St., Exeter 03833. Tel. 603-775-8851, e-mail hburnham@sau16.org; *V.P.* Pam Harland, Sanborn Regional H.S., Kingston 03833. E-mail pharland@sau17.org; *Recording Secy.* Jill Canillas Daley, Plainfield Elementary School. E-mail jdaley@plainfield school.org; *Treas.* Jeff Kent, 43 E. Ridge Rd., Merrimack 03054. E-mail jkent@comcast.net; *Past Pres.* Kathy Lane, G. H. Hood Middle School, Derry 03038. E-mail klane@derry. k12.nh.us.

Address correspondence to the president. World Wide Web http://nhslma.org.

New Jersey

New Jersey Association of School Librarians (NJASL). Memb. 1,000+. Term of Office. Aug. 2012–July 2013.

Pres. Amy Rominiecki E-mail president@ njasl.org; *Pres.-Elect* Pam Gunter. E-mail presidentelect@njasl.org; *V.P.* Arlen Kimmelman. E-mail vicepresident@njasl.org; *Recording Secy.* Kay Baggs. E-mail recording secretary@njasl.org; *Corresponding Secy.* Lisa Bakanas. E-mail correspondingsecretary@ njasl.org; *Treas.* Michelle Marhefka. E-mail treasurer@njasl.org; *Past Pres.* Pat Massey. E-mail immediatepastpresident@njasl.org.

Address correspondence to Elizabeth McArthur, Assn. Mgr., NJASL, Box 610, Trenton 08607. E-mail associationmanager@njasl.org.

World Wide Web http://www.njasl.org.

New York

New York Lib. Assn./Section of School Libns, 252 Hudson St., Albany 12210. Tel. 518-432-6952. Memb. 820. Term of Office. Nov. 2012–Oct. 2013. Publications. *SLMSGram* (q.); participates in *NYLA Bulletin* (mo. except July and Aug.).

Pres. Sue Kowalski. E-mail kowalski423@yahoo.com; *Pres.-Elect* Karen Sperrazza. E-mail krnsprzz@gmail.com; *V.P. Conferences* Livia Sabourin. E-mail livtiv@yahoo.com; *V.P. Communications* Beth Stancil. E-mail bstancl @clar.wnyric.org; *Secy.* Michelle Miller. E-mail mmiller@mwcsd.org; *Treas.* Patty Martire. E-mail pmartire@mtmorriscsd.org; *Past Pres.* Pauline Herr. E-mail pherr@acsdny.org.

World Wide Web http://www.nyla.org/max/4DCGI/cms/review.html?Action=CMS_Document&DocID=136&MenuKey=ssl.

North Carolina

North Carolina School Lib. Media Assn. Memb. 1,000+. Term of Office. Nov. 2012–Oct. 2013.

Pres. April Dawkins, Porter Ridge H.S., 2839 Ridge Rd., Indian Trail 28079. Tel. 704-292-7662, fax 704-296-9733, e-mail april.dawkins@ucps.k12.nc.us; *Pres.-Elect* Joann Absi, New Hanover County Schools, 555 Halyburton Memorial Pkwy., Wilmington 28412. Tel. 910-790-2360, fax 910-790-2356, e-mail joann.absi@nhcs.net; *Treas.* Laura Bowers, Westwood Elementary School, 4083 U.S. Hwy. 221 S., West Jefferson 28694. Tel. 336-877-2921, e-mail laura.bowers@ashe.k12.nc.us; *Past Pres.* Sarah Justice, Transylvania County Schools, 749 Pickens Hwy., Rosman 28772. Tel. 828-862-4284, fax 828-885-5572, e-mail sjustice@tcsnc.org; *Secy.* Jennifer Umbarger, Durham Public Schools, 911 W. Cornwallis Rd., Durham 27707. Tel. 919-560-3970, fax 919-560-2439, e-mail jennifer.umbarger@dpsnc.net.

Address correspondence to the president. World Wide Web http://www.ncslma.org.

North Dakota

School Lib. and Youth Services Section, North Dakota Lib. Assn. Memb. 100. Publication. *The Good Stuff* (q.).

Chair Lesley Gunderson, Sunrise Elementary, Bismarck Public Schools. Tel. 701-323-4300, e-mail lesley_gunderson@bismarckschools.org.

World Wide Web http://ndlaonline.org.

Ohio

Ohio Educ. Lib. Media Assn. Memb. 1,000. Publications. *OELMA News* (3 a year); *Ohio Media Spectrum* (q.).

Pres. Susan Yutzey. E-mail oelmasdy@gmail.com; *V.P.* Jen Flaherty. E-mail oelma.jlf@gmail.com; *Secy.* Sheila Campbell. E-mail librarian@columbuszoo.com; *Treas.* Brenda Gehm. E-mail bgehm@monroelocalschools.com; *Past Pres.* Sue Subel. E-mail sue.subel@kenstonlocal.org; *Dir. of Services* Kate Brunswick, 17 S. High St., Suite 200, Columbus 43215. Tel. 614-221-1900, fax 614-221-1989, e-mail kate@assnoffices.com.

Address correspondence to the director of services.

World Wide Web http://www.oelma.org.

Oklahoma

Oklahoma School Libs. Div., Oklahoma Lib. Assn. Memb. 200+. Publication. *Oklahoma Librarian.*

Chair Earon Cunningham; *Chair-Elect* Calypso Gilstrap; *Secy.* Stacy Ford; *Treas.* Michelle Robertson; *Past Chair* John Allen.

Address correspondence to the chairperson, School Libs. Div., Oklahoma Lib. Assn., 300 Hardy Drive, Edmond 73013. Tel. 405-348-0506.

World Wide Web http://www.oklibs.org/displaycommon.cfm?an=1&subarticlenbr=174.

Oregon

Oregon Assn. of School Libs. Memb. 600. Publication. *Interchange* (3 a year).

Pres. Susan Stone. E-mail sstone@pps.net; *Pres.-Elect* Nancy Sullivan. E-mail nsullivan@gmail.com; *Secy.* Jenny Takeda. E-mail jenny_takeda@beavton.k12.or.us; *Treas.* Stuart Levy. E-mail oasltreasurer@gmail.com; *Past Pres.* Ruth Murray. E-mail murrayr@pdx.edu.

Address correspondence to the association, 860 S. Clematis Rd., West Linn 97068.

World Wide Web http://ola.memberclicks.net/oasl-home.

Pennsylvania

Pennsylvania School Libns. Assn. Memb. 800+. Publication. *Learning and Media* (q.).

Pres. Eileen Kern. E-mail ekern@psla. org; *V.P./Pres.-Elect* Michael Nailor. E-mail mnailor@psla.org; *Secy.* Lindsey Long. E-mail pslaboard@psla.org; *Treas.* Natalie Hawley. E-mail pslaboard@psla.org; *Past Pres.* Doug Francis. E-mail pslaboard@psla.org.

Address correspondence to the president. World Wide Web http://www.psla.org.

Rhode Island

School Libns. of Rhode Island (formerly Rhode Island Educ. Media Assn.). Memb. 350+.

Pres. Darshell Silva. E-mail ucaplibrarian@ verizon.net; *V.P.* To be announced; *Secy.* Jane Perry; *Treas.* Jen Simoneau. E-mail jsimoneau 4@cox.net; *Past Pres.* Jamie Greene. E-mail greenej@bw.k12.ri.us.

Address correspondence to the president. World Wide Web http://www.slri.info.

South Carolina

South Carolina Assn. of School Libns. Memb. 900. Term of Office. July 1, 2012–June 30, 2013.

Pres. Heather Loy. E-mail hloy@mac. com; *V.P./Pres.-Elect* Anne Lemieux. E-mail lemieux.anne@gmail.com; *Secy.* Charlene Zehner. E-mail zehnerc@bcsdschools.net; *Treas.* Steve Reed. E-mail screed3103 @aol.com; *Past Pres.* Kathy Sutusky. E-mail ksutusky@ sc.rr.com; *Exec. Secy.* Diane Ervin. E-mail ervinscasl@gmail.com.

Address correspondence to the association, P.O. Box 2442, Columbia 29202. Tel./fax 803-492-3025.

World Wide Web http://www.scasl.net.

South Dakota

South Dakota School Lib. Media Section, South Dakota Lib. Assn., 28363 472nd Ave., Worthing 57077. Tel. 605-372-0235. Memb. 140+. Term of Office. Oct. 2012–Oct. 2013.

Chair Jeanne Conner, Roosevelt H.S., Sioux Falls. E-mail jeanne.conner@k12.sd.us.

Tennessee

Tennessee Assn. of School Libns. Memb. 450. Term of Office. Jan.–Dec. 2013. Publication. *TASL Talks.*

Pres. Beth Frerking, Northwest H.S., 800 Lafayette Rd., Clarksville 37042. E-mail frerking.tasl@gmail.com; *V.P./Pres.-Elect* Mona Batchelor. E-mail mona.batchelor.tasl@gmail. com; Lora Ann Black. E-mail loraannblack. tasl@gmail.com; *Treas.* Nancy Dickinson. E-mail fsufan23@gmail.com; *Past Pres.* Hannah Little. E-mail hlittle@webbschool.com.

Address correspondence to the president. World Wide Web http://www.tasltn.org.

Texas

Texas Assn. of School Libns., Div. of Texas Lib. Assn. Memb. 4,000+. Term of Office. Apr. 2012–Apr. 2013.

Chair Mary Woodard, Mesquite Independent School Dist. Tel. 972-882-5548, e-mail mwoodard@mesquiteisd.org; *Chair-Elect* Karen Kessel. E-mail karen_kessel@yahoo.com; *Secy.* Nora Galvan. Tel. 956-354-2041, e-mail nora.galvan@psjaisd.us; *Past Chair* Naomi Bates, Northwest ISD. Tel. 214-491-9485, e-mail nbates@nisdtx.org.

Address correspondence to Texas Lib. Assn., 3355 Bee Cave Rd., Suite 401, Austin 78746. Tel. 512-328-1518, fax 512-328-8852, e-mail tla@txla.org.

World Wide Web http://www.txla.org/ groups/tasl.

Utah

Utah Educ. Lib. Media Assn. Memb. 500+. Publication. *UELMA Newsletter* (q.).

Pres. Shelly Ripplinger, Polk Elementary, 2615 Polk Ave., Ogden 84401. Tel. 801-737-8308, e-mail ripplingers@ogdensd.org; *Pres.-Elect* Angie Woodring, Odyssey Elementary, 375 Goddard Ave., Ogden 84401. Tel. 801-737-8426, e-mail woodringa@ogdensd.org; *Secy.* Amy Jamison, Bonneville Elementary School, 490 Gramercy, Ogden 84404. Tel. 801-737-8900, e-mail adjamison@yahoo.com; *Past Pres.* Andrea Woodring, Bonneville H.S., 251 E. Laker Way, Ogden 84405. Tel. 801-452-4050, e-mail anwoodring@weber.k12.ut.us; *Exec. Dir.* John L. Smith, High Ridge Media, 714 W. 1900 N., Clinton 84015. Tel. 801-776-6829, e-mail jlsutah@comcast.net.

Address correspondence to the executive director.

World Wide Web http://www.uelma.org.

Vermont

Vermont School Lib. Assn. (formerly Vermont Educ. Media Assn.). Memb. 220+. Term of Office. May 2012–May 2013. Publication. *VSLA Newsletter Online* (q.).

Pres. Anna Bolognani, Twin Valley H.S., 1 School St., Wilmington 05363. Tel. 802-464-5255 ext. 119, e-mail rebolibrary@hotmail.com; *Pres.-Elect* Denise Wentz, Allen Brook School, 497 Talcott Rd., Williston 05495. Tel. 802-879-5848, e-mail dwentz@cssu.org; *Secy.* Kate Davie, Blue Mountain Union School, 2420 Rte. 302, Wells River 05081. Tel. 802-757-2711 ext.1142, e-mail kate.davie@bmuschool.org; *Treas.* Donna Smyth, 4 Homer Ave., Queensbury, NY 12804. Tel. 802-459-2225 ext. 2005, e-mail smythd@rcsu.org; *Past Pres.* Claire Buckley, South Burlington H.S., 550 Dorset St., South Burlington 05403. Tel. 802-652-7085, e-mail cbuckley@sbschools.net.

Address correspondence to the president.

World Wide Web https://sites.google.com/site/vermontschoolibraries/home.

Virginia

Virginia Assn. of School Librarians (VAASL) (formerly Virginia Educ. Media Assn., or VEMA). Memb. 1,200. Term of Office. (Pres., Pres.-Elect) Nov. 2012–Nov. 2013 (other officers two years in alternating years). Publication. *VAASL VOICE* (q.).

Pres. Frances Reeve, Longwood Univ. E-mail president@vaasl.org; *Pres.-Elect* Lori Donovan, Chesterfield Public Schools. E-mail presidentelect@vaasl.org; *Secy.* Earlene Lester. E-mail secretary@vaasl.org; *Treas.* Beth Lee, Lee Hall Elementary School, Newport News. E-mail treasurer@vaasl.org; *Past Pres.* Julie Tate, Hanover Public Schools, E-mail pastpresident@vaasl.org; *Exec. Dir.* Margaret Baker. Tel. 540-416-6109, e-mail executive@vaasl.org.

Address correspondence to the association, P.O. Box 2015, Staunton 24402-2015.

World Wide Web http://vaasl.org.

Washington

Washington Lib. Media Assn. Memb. 849. Term of Office. Oct.–Oct. Publication. The *Medium* (3 a year).

Pres. Leigh Lohrasbi. E-mail leigh.lohrasbi@gmail.com; *Pres.-Elect* Anne Bingham. E-mail infoanne@gmail.com; *V.P.* Sharyn Merrigan. E-mail smerrigan28@gmail.com; *Secy.* Alyse Fritz. E-mail alyse_fritz@eatonville.wednet.edu; *Treas.* Merrilyn Tucker. E-mail wlmatreasurer@gmail.com; *Past Pres.* Craig Seasholes. E-mail seasholes@gmail.com.

Address correspondence to the association, 10924 Mukilteo Speedway, PMB 142, Mukilteo 98275. E-mail wlma@wlma.org.

World Wide Web http://www.wlma.org.

West Virginia

School Lib. Div., West Virginia Lib. Assn. Memb. 50. Term of Office. Nov.–Nov. Publication. *WVLA School Library News* (5 a year).

Chair Melissa Hinerman, Bridgeport Middle School, Bridgeport 26330. E-mail mhinerman@access.k12.av.us; *Past Chair* Cathy Davis, East Fairmont Junior H.S., 1 Orion Lane, Fairmont 26554. Tel. 304-367-2123, e-mail ctdavis@access.k12.wv.us.

Address correspondence to the chairperson.

World Wide Web http://www.wvla.org.

Wisconsin

Wisconsin Educ. Media and Technology Assn. Memb. 1,100+. Publication. *WEMTA Dispatch* (q.).

Pres. Annette Smith. E-mail arsmith14@gmail.com; *Pres.-Elect* Jo Ann Carr. E-mail carr@education.wisc.edu; *Secy.* Vicki Santacroce. E-mail vsantacroce@ashwaubenon.k12.wi.us; *Treas.* Sandy Heiden. E-mail sheiden@seymour.k12.wi.us; *Assn. Mgr.* Courtney Rounds. Tel. 608-375-6020, e-mail wemamanager@hughes.net.

Address correspondence to WEMA, P.O. Box 206, Boscobel 53805.

World Wide Web http://www.wemaonline.org.

Wyoming

Teacher-Librarian Interest Group, Wyoming Lib. Assn. Memb. 100+.

Co-Chairs Lori Clark-Erickson. E-mail lclark-erickson@tcsd.org; Mary Wegher. E-mail mwegher@ccsd.k12.wy.us.

Address correspondence to the co-chairpersons.

World Wide Web https://sites.google.com/site/wlateacherlibrarians.

International Library Associations

International Association of Agricultural Information Specialists

Federico Sancho Guevara, President
IAALD, P.O. Box 63, Lexington, KY 40588-0063
Fax 859-257-8379, e-mail info@iaald.org
World Wide Web http://www.iaald.org

Object

The International Association of Agricultural Information Specialists (IAALD) facilitates professional development of and communication among members of the agricultural information community worldwide. Its goal is to enhance access to and use of agriculture-related information resources. To further this mission, IAALD will promote the agricultural information profession, support professional development activities, foster collaboration, and provide a platform for information exchange. Founded 1955.

Membership

Memb. 400+ in 80 countries. Dues (Inst.) US$130; (Indiv.) US$60.

Officers

Pres. Federico Sancho Guevara (Costa Rica); *Secy.-Treas.* Toni Greider (USA), P.O. Box 63, Lexington, KY 40588-0063. Tel. 859-254-0752, fax 859-257-8379, e-mail toni.greider@iaald.org; *Past Pres.* Edith Hesse (Austria). E-mail hesseedith@gmail.com.

Publication

Agricultural Information Worldwide (q.) (memb.).

International Association of Law Libraries

Petal Kinder, President
High Court of Australia, Canberra, ACT 2600
61-2-6270-6922, fax 61-2-6273-2110, e-mail pkinder@hcourt.gov.au
World Wide Web http://www.iall.org

Object

The International Association of Law Libraries (IALL) is a worldwide organization of librarians, libraries, and other persons or institutions concerned with the acquisition and use of legal information emanating from sources other than their jurisdictions and from multinational and international organizations.

IALL's purpose is to facilitate the work of librarians who acquire, process, organize, and provide access to foreign legal materials. IALL has no local chapters but maintains liaison with national law library associations in many countries and regions of the world.

Membership

More than 800 members in more than 50 countries on five continents.

Officers

Pres. Petal Kinder, High Court of Australia, Parkes Place, Parkes, Canberra, ACT 2600. Tel. 61-2-6270-6922, fax 61-2-6273-2110, e-mail pkinder@hcourt.gov.au; *1st V.P.* Jeroen Vervliet, Peace Palace Lib., Carnegieplein 2, 2517 KJ The Hague, Netherlands. Tel. 31-70-302-4242, e-mail j.vervliet@ppl.nl; *2nd V.P.* Jennefer Aston, 47 St. Kevin's Park, Dublin 6, Ireland. Tel. 353-1-497-4385, e-mail jennefera@gmail.com; *Secy.* Barbara Garavaglia, Univ. of Michigan Law Lib., Ann Arbor, MI 48109-1210. Tel. 734-764-9338, fax 734-764-5863, e-mail bvaccaro@umich.edu; *Treas.* Xinh Luu, Univ. of Virginia Law Lib., 580 Massie Rd., Charlottesville, VA 22903. E-mail xtl5d@virginia.edu; *Past Pres.* Jules Winterton, Institute of Advanced Legal Studies, Univ. of London, 17 Russell Sq., London WCIB 5DR, England. Tel. 44-20-7862-5884, fax 44-20-7862-5850, e-mail julesw@sas.ac.uk.

Board Members

Ruth Bird, Bodleian Law Lib., Oxford Univ., England; Mark D. Engsberg (ex officio), MacMillan Law Lib., Emory Univ. School of Law, Atlanta; Ligita Gjortlere, Riga Graduate School of Law Lib., Riga, Latvia; Marci Hoffman (ex officio), Univ. of California, Berkeley, School of Law Lib.; Janice L. Johnston, Albert E. Jenner, Jr. Memorial Law Lib., Univ. of Illinois; Uma Narayan, Bombay High Court, Mumbai, India; Pedro Padilla-Rosa, Univ. of Puerto Rico Law Lib., San Juan; Anita Soboleva, JURIX (Jurists for Constitutional Rights and Freedoms), Moscow, Russia; Bård Tuseth, Dept. of Public and International Law Lib., Oslo, Norway; Ivo Vogel, Sondersammelgebiet und Virtuellen Fachbibliothek Recht, Berlin, Germany.

Publication

International Journal of Legal Information (3 a year; US$60 indiv.; US$95 institutions).

International Association of Music Libraries, Archives and Docusumentation Centres

Pia Shekhter, Secretary-General
Gothenburg University Library, P.O. Box 210, SE 405 30 Gothenburg, Sweden
46-31-786-4057, cell 46-703-22-62, fax 46-31-786-40-59, e-mail secretary@iaml.info
World Wide Web http://www.iaml.info

Object

The object of the International Association of Music Libraries, Archives, and Documentation Centres (IAML) is to promote the activities of music libraries, archives, and documentation centers and to strengthen the cooperation among them; to promote the availability of all publications and documents relating to music and further their bibliographical control; to encourage the development of standards in all areas that concern the association; and to support the protection and preservation of musical documents of the past and the present.

Membership

Memb. 2,000.

Board Members

Pres. Roger Flury, National Lib. of New Zealand, P.O. Box 1467, Wellington, NZ. Tel. 64-4-474-3039, fax 64-4-474-3035; *Secy.-Gen.* Pia Shekhter, Academy of Music and Drama, Univ. of Gothenburg Lib., Box 210, SE-405 30 Gothenburg, Sweden. Tel. 46-31-786-40-57, fax 46-31-786-40-59; *V.P.s* Stanislaw Hrabia, Biblioteka i Fonoteka, Instytut Muzykologii, Uniwersytet Jagiellonski, ul. Westerplatte 10,

31-033 Kraków, Poland. Tel. 48-12-663-1673, fax 48-12-663-1671; Antony Gordon, British Lib. Sound Archive, 96 Euston Rd., London NW1 2DB, England. Tel. 44-20-7412-7412, fax 44-20-7412-7441; Johan Eeckeloo, Koninklijk Conservatorium Brussel, Regentschapsstraat 30, B-1000 Brussels, Belgium. Tel. 32-2-213-41-30; Jutta Lambrecht, WDR D&A / Recherche, Leitung Musik und Notenarchiv, Appellhofplatz 1, D-50667 Köln, Germany. Tel. 49-221-220-3376, fax 49-221-220-9217; *Treas.* Kathryn Adamson, Royal Academy of Music, Marylebone Rd., London NW1 5HT, England. Tel. 44-20-7873-7321; *Past Pres.* Martie Severt, Netherlands Radio Music Lib., Postbus 125, NL-1200 AC Hilversum, Netherlands. Tel. 31-35-6714181, fax 31-35-6714189.

Publication

Fontes Artis Musicae (4 a year; memb.). *Ed.* Maureen Buja, Hong Kong Gold Coast Block 22, Flat 1-A, 1 Castle Peak Rd., Tuen Mun, NT, Hong Kong. Tel. 852-2146-8407, e-mail fontes@iaml.info.

Professional Branches

Archives and Documentation Centres. Marguerite Sablonnière, Bibliothèque Nationale de France, Département de la Musique, 58 rue de Richelieu, 75002 Paris.

Broadcasting and Orchestra Libraries. Angela Escott, Royal College of Music, Prince Consort Rd., London SW7 2BS, England.

Libraries in Music Teaching Institutions. Pia Shekhter, Gothenburg Univ. Lib., P.O. Box 210, SE 405 30 Gothenburg, Sweden.

Public Libraries. Hanneke Kuiper, Public Lib., Oosterdoksstraat 143, 1011 DK Amsterdam, Netherlands.

Research Libraries. Stanislaw Hrabia, Uniwersytet Jagiellonski Instytut Muzykologii Biblioteka, ul. Westerplatte 10 31-033 Kraków, Poland.

International Association of School Librarianship

Carla Funk, Executive Director
65 E. Wacker Place, Suite 1900, Chicago, IL 60601
e-mail iasl@mlahq.org
World Wide Web http://www.iasl-online.org

Mission and Objectives

The mission of the International Association of School Librarianship (IASL) is to provide an international forum for those people interested in promoting effective school library media programs as viable instruments in the educational process. IASL also provides guidance and advice for the development of school library programs and the school library profession. IASL works in cooperation with other professional associations and agencies.

Membership is worldwide, and includes school librarians, teachers, librarians, library advisers, consultants, educational administrators, and others who are responsible for library and information services in schools. The membership also includes professors and instructors in universities and colleges where there are programs for school librarians, and students who are undertaking such programs.

The objectives of IASL are to advocate the development of school libraries throughout all countries; to encourage the integration of school library programs into the instructional and curriculum development of the school; to promote the professional preparation and continuing education of school library personnel; to foster a sense of community among school librarians in all parts of the world; to foster and extend relationships between school librarians and other professionals connected with children and youth; to foster research in the field of school librarianship and the integration of its conclusions with pertinent knowledge from related fields; to promote the publication and dissemination of information about successful advocacy and program initiatives in school librarianship; to share information about programs and materials for children and youth throughout the international community; and to initiate and coordinate activities, conferences, and other projects in the field of school librarianship and information services. Founded 1971.

Australia; *Treas.* Katy Manck, USA; *Dirs.* Geraldine Howell, Oceania; Busi Dlamini, Africa-Sub Sahara; Lourdes T. David, East Asia; Luisa Marquardt, Europe; Dianne Oberg, Canada; Ingrid Skirrow, International Schools; Blanche Woolls, USA; Ayse Yuksel-Durukan, North Africa/Middle East; Madhu Bhargava, Asia; Paulette Stewart, Latin America/Caribbean.

Membership

Approximately 600.

Officers and Executive Board

Pres. Diljit Singh, Malaysia; *V.P.s* Lourense Das, Association Operations, Netherlands; Lesley Farmer, Association Relations, USA; Elizabeth Greef, Advocacy and Promotion,

Publications

Proceedings of annual conferences (see http://www.iasl-online.org/pubs/publications-proceedings.html).

School Libraries Worldwide (http://www.iasl-online.org/pubs/slw/index.htm) (2 a year), the association's refereed research and professional journal.

IASL Newsletter (http://www.iasl-online.org/pubs/newsletter/index.htm) (3 a year).

International Association of Scientific and Technological University Libraries (IATUL)

President, Reiner Kallenborn
World Wide Web http://www.iatul.org

Object

The main object of the International Association of Scientific and Technological University Libraries (IATUL) is to provide a forum where library directors and senior managers can meet to exchange views on matters of current significance and to provide an opportunity for them to develop a collaborative approach to solving problems. IATUL also welcomes into membership organizations that supply services to university libraries, if they wish to be identified with the association's activities.

Membership

239 (in 42 countries).

Officers

Pres. Reiner Kallenborn, Technische Universität München, Munich, Germany; *V.P.* Imogen Garner, Curtin Univ Lib., Perth, WA, Australia; *Secy.* Elisha R. T. Chiware, Cape Peninsula Univ. of Technology, South Africa; *Treas.* Irma Pasanen, Aalto Univ. Lib., Helsinki, Finland.

Publication

IATUL Conference Proceedings (on IATUL website, http://www.iatul.org). (ann.).

International Council on Archives

David A. Leitch, Secretary-General
60 rue des Francs-Bourgeois, 75003 Paris, France
33-1-40-27-63-06, fax 33-1-42-72-20-65, e-mail ica@ica.org
World Wide Web http://www.ica.org

Object

The mission of the International Council on Archives (ICA) is to establish, maintain, and strengthen relations among archivists of all lands. and among all professional and other agencies or institutions concerned with the custody, organization, or administration of archives, public or private, wherever located. Established 1948.

Membership

Memb. approximately 1,400 (representing nearly 200 countries and territories).

Officers

Pres. Martin Berendse, Netherlands; *V.P.s* Didier Bondue, France; Vu Thi Minh Huong, Vietnam; Andreas Kellerhals, Switzerland; Henri Zuber, France.

Executive Board

Daniel J. Caron, Canada; Abdelmajid Chikhi, Algeria; Margaret Crockett, United Kingdom; Jaime Antunes DaSilva, Brazil; Joel Das Neves Tembe, Mozambique; Hervé Lemoine, France; Christine Martinez, France; Angelika Menne-Haritz, Germany; Dominique Taffin, Martinique, France; Antoine Lumenganeso Kiobe, Congo; Amatuni Virabyan, Armenia; Bryan Corbett, Canada; Amela Silipa, Western Samoa; Vu Thi Minh Huong, Vietnam; Saroja Wettasinghe, Sri Lanka; Fatoumata Cissé Diarra, Senegal; Geir Magnus Walderhaug, Norway; Emilie Gagnet Leumas, United States; Paola Caroli, Italy; Esther Cruces Blanco, Spain; Bruce Smith, Australia; Milovan Misic, Switzerland; Gwigeun Song, Republic of Korea; David Sutton, United Kingdom; Deborah Jenkins, United Kingdom; Fred Van Kan, Netherlands; Kenth Sjöblom, Finland; Günther Schefbeck, Austria; William J. Maher, United States; Atakilty Assefa Asegedom, Ethiopia.

Publications

Comma (memb.) (2 a year, memb.)

Flash (2 a year; memb.).

Guide to the Sources of the History of Nations (Latin American Series, 11 vols. pub.; Africa South of the Sahara Series, 20 vols. pub.; North Africa, Asia, and Oceania Series, 15 vols. pub.).

Guide to the Sources of Asian History (English-language series [India, Indonesia, Korea, Nepal, Pakistan, Singapore], 14 vols. pub.; national language series [Indonesia, Korea, Malaysia, Nepal, Thailand], 6 vols. pub.; other guides, 3 vols. pub.).

International Federation of Film Archives
(Fédération Internationale des Archives du Film)

Secretariat, 1 rue Defacqz, B-1000 Brussels, Belgium
32-2-538-3065, fax 32-2-534-4774, e-mail info@fiafnet.org
World Wide Web http://www.fiafnet.org

Object

Founded in 1938, the International Federation of Film Archives (FIAF) brings together not-for-profit institutions dedicated to rescuing films and any other moving-image elements considered both as cultural heritage and as historical documents.

FIAF is a collaborative association of the world's leading film archives whose purpose has always been to ensure the proper preservation and showing of motion pictures.More than 150 archives in more than 75 countries collect, restore, and exhibit films and cinema documentation spanning the entire history of film.

FIAF seeks to promote film culture and facilitate historical research, to help create new archives around the world, to foster training and expertise in film preservation, to encourage the collection and preservation of documents and other cinema-related materials, to develop cooperation between archives, and to ensure the international availability of films and cinema documents.

Officers

Pres. Eric Le Roy; *Secy.-Gen.* Meg Labrum; *Treas.* Patrick Loughney; *Membs.* Francisco Gaytan Fernandez, Anne Fiaccarini, Sylvia Frank, Olga Futemma, Mimi Gjorgoska-Ilievska, Lise Gustavson, Dennis Maake, Hisashi Okajima, Vladimir Opela, Esteve Riambau.

Address correspondence to Christophe Dupin, Senior Administrator, c/o FIAF Secretariat. E-mail c.dupin@fiafnet.org.

Publications

Journal of Film Preservation.
International Index to Film Periodicals.
FIAF International Filmarchive database (OVID).
FIAF International Index to Film Periodicals (ProQuest).

For additional FIAF publications, see http://www.fiafnet.org.

International Federation of Library Associations and Institutions

Jennefer Nicholson, Secretary-General
P.O. Box 95312, 2509 CH The Hague, Netherlands
31-70-314-0884, fax 31-70-383-4827
E-mail ifla@ifla.org, World Wide Web http://www.ifla.org

Object

The object of the International Federation of Library Associations and Institutions (IFLA) is to promote international understanding, cooperation, discussion, research, and development in all fields of library activity, including bibliography, information services, and the education of library personnel, and to provide a body through which librarianship can be represented in matters of international interest. IFLA is the leading international body representing the interests of library and information services and their users. It is the global voice of the library and information profession. Founded 1927.

Officers and Governing Board

Pres. Ingrid Parent, Univ. of British Columbia; *Pres.-Elect* Sinikka Sipilä, Finnish Lib. Assn.; *Treas.* Donna Scheeder, Lib. of Congress.

Governing Board

Kent Skov Andreasen, Odense Central Public Lib.; Frédéric Blin, Bibliothèque Nationale et Universitaire de Strasbourg; Ingrid Bon, Biblioservice Gelderland; Genevieve Clavel-Merrin, Swiss National Lib.; Barbara Lison, Bremen Public Libs.; Inga Lundén, Stockholm Public Lib.; Christine Mackenzie, Yarra Plenty Regional Lib.; Buhle Mbambo-Thata, UNISA; Paul Whitney, Vancouver Public Lib.; Ann Okerson, Yale Univ.; Lynne M. Rudasill, Univ. of Illinois at Urbana-Champaign; Tone Eli Moseid, ABM-Utvikling; Anna Maria Tammaro, Univ. of Parma; Filiberto Felipe Martínez-Arellano, National Autonomous Univ. of Mexico; Gerald Leitner, Austrian Lib. Assn.; *Secy.-Gen.* Jennefer Nicholson.

Publications

IFLA Annual Report.
IFLA Journal (4 a year).

IFLA Professional Reports.
IFLA Publications Series.
IFLA Series on Bibliographic Control.
International Preservation News.

American Membership

Associations

American Lib. Assn., Assn. for Lib. and Info. Science Educ., Assn. of Research Libs., Chief Officers of State Lib. Agencies, Medical Lib. Assn., Special Libs. Assn., Urban Libs. Council, Chinese American Libns. Assn.

Institutional Members

There are 130 libraries and related institutions that are institutional members or consultative bodies and sponsors of IFLA in the United States (out of a total of 1,130 members globally), and 125 individual affiliates (out of a total of 357 members globally).

International Organization for Standardization

Robert Steele, Secretary-General
ISO Central Secretariat, 1 ch. de la Voie-Creuse, Case postale 56,
CH-1211 Geneva 20, Switzerland
41-22-749-01-11, fax 41-22-733-34-30, e-mail central@iso.org
World Wide Web http://www.iso.org

Object

The International Organization for Standardization (ISO) is a worldwide federation of national standards bodies, founded in 1947, at present comprising 162 members, one in each country. The object of ISO is to promote the development of standardization and related activities in the world with a view to facilitating international exchange of goods and services, and to developing cooperation in the spheres of intellectual, scientific, technological, and economic activity. The scope of ISO covers international standardization in all fields except electrical and electronic engineering standardization, which is the responsibility of the International Electrotechnical Commission

(IEC). The results of ISO technical work are published as international standards.

Officers

Pres. Terry Hill, United Kingdom; *V.P. (Policy)* Sadao Takeda, Japan; *V.P. (Technical Management)* Elisabeth Stampfl-Blaha, Austria; *V.P. (Finance)* Olivier Peyrat, France; *Treas.* Julien Pitton, Switzerland.

Technical Work

The technical work of ISO is carried out by more than 200 technical committees. These include:

ISO/TC 46-Information and documentation (Secretariat, Association Française de Normalization, 11 ave. Francis de Pressensé, 93571 Saint-Denis La Plaine, Cedex, France). Scope: Standardization of practices relating to libraries, documentation and information centers, indexing and abstracting services, archives, information science, and publishing.

ISO/TC 37-Terminology and language and content resources (Secretariat, INFOTERM, Aichholzgasse 6/12, 1120 Vienna, Austria, on behalf of Österreichisches Normungsinstitut). Scope: Standardization of principles, methods, and applications relating to terminology and other language and content resources in the contexts of multilingual communication and cultural diversity.

ISO/IEC JTC 1-Information technology (Secretariat, American National Standards Institute, 25 W. 43 St., 4th fl., New York, NY 10036). Scope: Standardization in the field of information technology.

Publications

ISO Annual Report.
ISO Catalogue on CD-ROM (combined catalog of published standards and technical work program) (ann.).
ISO Focus+ (10 a year).
ISO International Standards.
ISO Memento (ann.).
ISO Online information service on World Wide Web (http://www.iso.org).

Foreign Library Associations

The following is a list of regional and national library associations around the world. A more complete list can be found in *International Literary Market Place* (Information Today, Inc.).

Regional

Africa

Standing Conference of Eastern, Central, and Southern African Lib. and Info. Assns. (SCECSAL), c/o Constantine M. Nyamboga, Chair, Kenya Assn. of Lib. and Info. Professionals, P.O. Box 46031, Nairobi 00100, Kenya. E-mail constantinebu@yahoo.com or constantinenyamboga@gmail.com.

The Americas

Asociación de Bibliotecas Universitarias, de Investigación e Institucionales del Caribe (ACURIL) (Assn. of Caribbean Univ., Research, and Institutional Libs.), Box 23317, UPR Sta., San Juan, PR 00931-3317. Tel./fax 787-790-8054, e-mail acurilsec@yahoo.com or acuril@gmail.com, World Wide Web http://acuril.uprrp.edu. *Pres.* Françoise Beaulieu Thybulle; *Exec. Secy.* Luisa Vigo-Cepeda. E-mail executivesecretariat@acuril.org.

Seminar on the Acquisition of Latin American Lib. Materials (SALALM), c/o *Exec. Secy.* Hortensia Calvo, SALALM Secretariat, Latin American Lib., 422 Howard Tilton Memorial Lib., Tulane Univ., 7001 Freret St., New Orleans, LA 70118-5549. Tel. 504-247-1366, fax 504-247-1367, e-mail salalm@tulane.edu, World Wide Web http://www.salalm.org. *Pres.* Lynn Shirey. E-mail shirey@fas.harvard.edu.

Asia

Congress of Southeast Asian Libns. (CONSAL), c/o Jl Salemba Raya 28A, Jakarta 10430, Indonesia. Tel. 21-310-3554, World Wide Web http://www.consal.org. *Secy.-Gen.* Aristaianto Hakim.

The Commonwealth

Commonwealth Lib. Assn. (COMLA), P.O. Box 144, Mona, Kingston 7, Jamaica. Tel. 876-927-0083, fax 876-927-1926, e-mail nkpodo@uwimonal.edu.jm.

National and State Libs. Australasia, c/o State Lib. of Victoria, 328 Swanston St., Melbourne, Vic. 3000, Australia. Tel. 3-8664-7512, fax 3-9639-4737, e-mail nsla@slv.vic.gov.au, World Wide Web http://www.nsla.org.au. *Chair* Alan Smith.

Standing Conference on Lib. Materials on Africa (SCOLMA), Social Science Collections and Research, British Library St. Pancras, 96 Euston Rd., London NW1 2DB, England. Tel. 20-7412-7567, fax 20-7747-6168, e-mail scolma@hotmail.com, World Wide Web http://www2.lse.ac.uk/library/scolma.

Europe

Ligue des Bibliothèques Européennes de Recherche (LIBER) (Assn. of European Research Libs.), Postbus 90407, 2509 LK The Hague, Netherlands. Tel. 070-314-07-67, fax 070-314-01-97, e-mail liber@kb.nl, World Wide Web http://www.libereurope.eu. *Pres.* Hans Geleijnse. E-mail hans.geleijnse@uvt.nl; *Secy.-Gen.* Ann Matheson. E-mail a.matheson@tinyworld.co.uk.

National

Argentina

Asociación de Bibliotecarios Graduados de la República Argentina (ABGRA) (Assn. of Graduate Libns. of Argentina), Parana 918, 2do Piso, C1017AAT Buenos Aires. Tel. 11-4811-0043, fax 11-4816-3422, e-mail info@abgra.org.ar, World Wide Web http://www.abgra.org.ar. *Pres.* Gloria Priore.

Australia

Australian Lib. and Info. Assn., Box 6335, Kingston, ACT 2604. Tel. 2-6215-8222, fax 2-6282-2249, e-mail enquiry@alia.org.au, World Wide Web http://www.alia.org.au. *Pres.* Vanessa Little. E-mail vanessa.little@act.gov.au; *Exec. Dir.* Sue Hutley. E-mail sue.hutley@alia.org.au.

Australian Society of Archivists, Suite 2, Level 4, 360 Queen St., Brisbane, Qld 4000. Tel. 800-622-251, fax 7-3221-6885, e-mail office@archivists.org.au, World Wide Web http://www.archivists.org.au. *Pres.* Patricia Jackson.

Austria

Österreichische Gesellschaft für Dokumentation und Information (Austrian Society for Documentation and Info.), c/o OGDI, Wollzeile 1-3, P.O. Box 46, 1010 Vienna. E-mail office@oegdi.at, World Wide Web http://www.oegdi.at. *Chair* Gabriele Sauberer.

Vereinigung Österreichischer Bibliothekarinnen und Bibliothekare (Assn. of Austrian Libns.), Voralberg State Lib., Fluherstr. 4, 6900 Bregenz. E-mail voeb@ub.tuwein.ac.at, World Wide Web http://www.univie.ac.at/voeb/php. *Pres.* Harald Weigel.

Bangladesh

Lib. Assn. of Bangladesh, Nilkhet H.S. Bhaban, 2nd flr., Dhaka 1000. Tel. 171-3020-266, e-mail libraryassociation.bd@gmail.com, World Wide Web http://www.lab.org.bd. *Pres.* Nasir Uddin Munshi; *Secy.-Gen.* Mizanur Rahman.

Barbados

Lib. Assn. of Barbados, P.O. Box 827E, Bridgetown, Barbados. E-mail milton@uwichill.edu.bb. *Pres.* Junior Browne.

Belgium

Archief- en Bibliotheekwezen in België (Belgian Assn. of Archivists and Libns.), Keizerslaan 4, 1000 Brussels. Tel. 2-519-53-93, fax 2-519-56-10.

Association Belge de Documentation/Belgische Vereniging voor Documentatie (Belgian Assn. for Documentation), chaussée de Wavre 1683, B-1160 Brussels. Tel. 2-675-58-62, fax 2-672-74-46, e-mail abdbvd@abd-bvd.be, World Wide Web http://www.abd-bvd.be. *Pres.* Christopher Boon; *Secy.-Gen.* Dominique Vanpee.

Association Professionnelle des Bibliothécaires et Documentalistes (Assn. of Libns. and Documentation Specialists), Place de la Wallonie 15, 6140 Fontaine-l'Eveque. Tel. 71-52-31-93, fax 71-52-23-07, World Wide Web http://www.apbd.be. *Pres.* Laurence Boulanger; *Secy.* Fabienne Gerard.

Vlaamse Vereniging voor Bibliotheek-, Archief-, en Documentatiewezen (Flemish Assn. of Libns., Archivists, and Documentalists), Statiestraat 179, B-2600 Berchem, Antwerp. Tel. 3-281-44-57, e-mail vvbad@vvbad.be, World Wide Web http://www.vvbad.be.

Belize

Belize National Lib. Service and Info. System (BNLSIS), P.O. Box 287, Belize City. Tel. 223-4248, fax 223-4246, e-mail nls@btl.net, World Wide Web http://www.nlsbze.bz. *Chief Libn.* Joy Ysaguirre.

Bolivia

Centro Nacional de Documentación Cientifica y Tecnologica (National Scientific and Technological Documentation Center), Av. Mariscal Santa Cruz 1175, Esquina c Ayacucho, La Paz. Tel. 02-359-583, fax 02-359-586, e-mail iiicndct@huayna.umsa.edu.bo, World Wide Web http://www.bolivian.com/industrial/cndct.

Bosnia and Herzegovina

Drustvo Bibliotekara Bosne i Hercegovine (Libns. Society of Bosnia and Herzegovina), Zmaja od Bosne 8B, 71000 Sarajevo. Tel. 33-275-5325, fax 33-212-435, e-mail nubbih@nub.ba, World Wide Web http://www.nub.ba. *Pres.* Nevenka Hajdarovic. E-mail nevenka@nub.ba; *Secy.* Dijana Bilos. E-mail dijana@nub.ba.

Botswana

Botswana Lib. Assn., Box 1310, Gaborone. Tel. 371-750, fax 371-748, World Wide Web http://www.bla.org.bw. *Pres.* Kgomotso Radijeing.

Brazil

Associação dos Arquivistas Brasileiros (Assn. of Brazilian Archivists), Av. Presidente Vargas 1733, Sala 903, 20210-030 Rio de Janiero RJ. Tel. 21-2507-2239, fax 21-3852-2541, e-mail aab@aab.org.br, World Wide Web http://www.aab.org.br. *Pres.* Lucia Maria Velloso de Oliveira.

Brunei Darussalam

Persatuan Perpustakaan Negara Brunei Darussalam (National Lib. Assn. of Brunei), c/c Class 64 Lib., SOASC, Jl Tengah, Bandar Seri Begawan BS8411. Fax 2-222-330, World Wide Web http://bruneilibrary association.wordpress.com. *Hon. Secy.* Hjh Rosnani.

Cameroon

Association des Bibliothécaires, Archivistes, Documentalistes et Muséographes du Cameroun (Assn. of Libns., Archivists, Documentalists, and Museum Curators of Cameroon), BP 14077, Yaoundé. World Wide Web http://www.abadcam.sitew.com. *Pres.* Jerome Ndjock.

Chile

Colegio de Bibliotecarios de Chile (Chilean Lib. Assn.), Avda. Diagonal Paraguay 383, Torre 11, Of. 122, 6510017 Santiago. Tel. 2-222-5652, e-mail cbc@bibliotecarios.cl, World Wide Web http://www.bibliotecarios. cl. *Pres.* Gabriela Pradenas Bobadilla; *Secy.-Gen.* Victor Candia Arancibia.

China

Lib. Society of China, 33 Zhongguancun S, Beijing 100081. Tel. 10-8854-5283, fax 10-6841-7815, e-mail ztxhmsc@nlc.gov. cn, World Wide Web http://www.nlc.gov.cn. *Secy.-Gen.* Gensheng Tang.

Colombia

Asociación Colombiana de Bibliotecólogos y Documentalistas (Colombian Assn. of Libns. and Documentalists), Calle 21, No. 6-58, Of. 404, Bogotá. Tel. 1-282-3620, fax 1-282-5487, e-mail secretaria@ascolbi.org, World Wide Web http://www.ascolbi.org. *Pres.* Edgar Allan Degado.

Congo (Republic of)

Association des Bibliothécaires, Archivistes, Documentalistes et Muséologues du Congo (ABADOM) (Assn. of Librarians, Archivists, Documentalists, and Museologists of Congo), BP 3148, Kinshasa-Gombe. *Pres.* Desire Didier Tengeneza. E-mail didier teng@yahoo.fr.

Côte d'Ivoire

Direction des Archives Nationales et de la Documentation, BP V 126, Abidjan, Tel. 20-21-75-78. *Dir.* Venance Bahi Gouro.

Croatia

Hrvatsko Knjiznicarsko Drustvo (Croatian Lib. Assn.), c/o National and Univ. Lib., Hrvatske bratske zajednice 4, 10 000 Zagreb. Tel./fax 385-1-615-93-20, e-mail hkd@nsk.hr, World Wide Web http://www.hkdrustvo.hr. *Pres.* Marijana Misetic. E-mail mmisetic@ffzg.hr.

Cuba

Asociación Cubana de Bibliotecarios (ASCUBI) (Lib. Assn. of Cuba), Biblioteca Nacional Jose Marti, Ave. Independencia 20 de Mayo, Plaza de la Revolucion, Havana. Tel. 7-555-442, fax 7-816-224, e-mail ascubi@bnjm.cu, World Wide Web http://www.bnjm.cu/ascubi. *Pres.* Margarita Bellas Vilarino.

Cyprus

Kypriakos Synthesmos Vivliothicarion (Lib. Assn. of Cyprus), c/o Pedagogical Academy, P.O. Box 1039, Nicosia.

Czech Republic

Svaz Knihovniku a Informacnich Pracovniku Ceske Republiky (SKIP) (Assn. of Lib. and Info. Professionals of the Czech Republic), National Lib., Klementinum 190, 110 00

Prague 1. Tel. 221-663-379, fax 221-663-175, e-mail vit.richter@nkp.cz, World Wide Web http://skip.nkp.cz. *Pres.* Vit Richter.

Denmark

Arkivforeningen (Archives Society), c/o Rigsarkivet, Rigsdagsgarden 9, 1218 Copenhagen. Tel. 3392-3310, fax 3315-3239, World Wide Web http://www.arkivarforeningen. no. *Chair* Lars Schreiber Pedersen. E-mail lape02@frederiksberg.dk.

Danmarks Biblioteksforening (Danish Lib. Assn.), Vartov, Farvergade 27D, 1463 Copenhagen K. Tel. 3325-0935, fax 3325-7900, e-mail db@db.dk, World Wide Web http://www.db.dk. *Dir.* Vagn Ytte Larsen. E-mail vyl@odsherred.dk.

Danmarks Forskningsbiblioteksforening (Danish Research Lib. Assn.), c/o Statsbiblioteket, Tangen 2, 8200 Arhus N. Tel. 89-46-22-07, e-mail df@statsbiblioteket.dk, World Wide Web http://www.dfdf.dk. *Pres.* Michael Cotta-Schonberg. E-mail mcs@kb.dk; *Secy.* Hanne Dahl.

Dansk Musikbiblioteks Forening (Assn. of Danish Music Libs.), c/o Koge Lib., Kirkestr. 18, 4600 Koge. E-mail sekretariat@dmbf.nu, World Wide Web http://www.dmbf.nu. *Pres.* Emilie Wieth-Knudsen. E-mail emwk@ltk.dk.

Kommunernes Skolebiblioteksforening (Assn. of Danish School Libs.), Farvergade 27 D, 2 sal, 1463 Copenhagen K. Tel. 33-11-13-91, e-mail ksbf@ksbf.dk, World Wide Web http://www.ksbf.dk. *Dir.* Gitte Frausing. E-mail gf@ksbf.dk.

Dominican Republic

Asociación Dominicana de Bibliotecarios (Dominican Assn. of Libns.), c/o Biblioteca Nacional, Cesar Nicolás Penson 91, Plaza de la Cultura, Pichincha, Santo Domingo. Tel. 809-688-4086, fax 809-688-5841.

Ecuador

Asociación Ecuatoriana de Bibliotecarios (Ecuadoran Lib. Assn.), c/o Casa de la Cultura Ecuatoriana, Casilla 87, Quito. Tel. 9832-258-7666, fax 9832-258-8516, e-mail aso ebfp@hotmail.com. *Pres.* Amparo Nuñez.

El Salvador

Asociación de Bibliotecarios de El Salvador (ABES) (Assn. of Salvadorian Libns.), Jardines de la Hacienda Block D pje, 19 No. 158, Ciudad Merliot, Antiguo Cuscatlan, La Libertad. Tel. 503-2241-4464, fax 523-2228-2956, World Wide Web http://www. abes.org.sv. *Pres.* Yensi Vides.

Finland

Suomen Kirjastoseura (Finnish Lib. Assn.), Runeberginkatu 15 A 23, 00100 Helsinki. Tel. 44-522-2941, e-mail info@fla.fi, World Wide Web http://www.fla.fi. *Exec. Dir.* Sinikka Sipila.

France

Association des Archivistes Français (Assn. of French Archivists), 8 rue Jean-Marie Jego, 75013 Paris. Tel. 1-46-06-39-44, fax 1-46-06-39-52, e-mail secretariat@archivistes. org, World Wide Web http://www.archivistes. org. *Pres.* Xavier de la Selle; *Secy.* Jean-Philippe Legois.

Association des Bibliothécaires Français (Assn. of French Libns.), 31 rue de Chabrol, F-75010 Paris. Tel. 1-55-33-10-30, fax 1-55-30-10-31, e-mail info@abf.asso.fr, World Wide Web http://www.abf.asso.fr. *Pres.* Pascal Wagner; *Gen. Secy.* Maité Vanmarque.

Association des Professionnels de l'Information et de la Documentation (Assn. of Info. and Documentation Professionals), 25 rue Claude Tillier, F-75012 Paris. Tel. 1-43-72-25-25, fax 1-43-72-30-41, e-mail adbs@adbs.fr, World Wide Web http://www.adbs. fr. *Commissioner Gen.* Flora Lagneau.

Germany

Arbeitsgemeinschaft der Spezialbibliotheken (Assn. of Special Libs.), c/o Herder-Institute eV, Bibliothek, Gisonenweg 5-7, 35037 Marburg. Tel. 6421-184-151, fax 6421-184-139, e-mail geschaeftsstelle@aspb.de, World Wide Web http://www.aspb.de. *Chair* Henning Frankenberger. E-mail frankenberger@mpisoc.mpg.de; *Contact* Jadwiga Warmbrunn.

Berufsverband Information Bibliothek (Assn. of Info. and Lib. Professionals), Gartenstr. 18, 72764 Reutlingen. Tel. 7121-3491-0, fax 7121-3004-33, e-mail mail@bib-info. de, World Wide Web http://www.bib-info. de. *Pres.* Kirsten Marschall. E-mail kirsten. marschall@buecherhallen.de.

Deutsche Gesellschaft für Informationswissenschaft und Informationspraxis eV (German Society for Info. Science and Practice), W.ndmühlstr. 3, 603294 Frankfurt-am-Main 1. Tel. 69-43-03-13, fax 69-490-90-96, e-mail mail@dgi-info.de, World Wide Web http://www.dgd.de. *Pres.* Stefan Gradmann.

Deutscher Bibliotheksverband eV (German Lib. Assn.), Fritschestr. 27–28, 10585 Berlin. Tel. 30-644-98-99-10, fax 30-644-98-99-29, e-mail dbv@bibliotheksverband.de, World Wide Web http://www.bibliotheks verband.de. *Chair* Monika Ziller. E-mail monika.ziller@stadt-heilbronn.de; *Managing Dir.* Barbara Schleihagen. E-mail schleihagen@bibliotheksverband.de.

VdA—Verband Deutscher Archivarinnen und Archivare (Assn. of German Archivists), Woerthstr. 3, 36037 Fulda. Tel. 661-29-109-72, fax 661-29-109-74, e-mail info@ vda.archiv.net, World Wide Web http://www.vda.archiv.net. *Chair* Michael Diefenbacher. E-mail michael.diefenbacher@stadt. nuernberg.de.

Verein Deutscher Bibliothekare eV (Society of German Libns.), Universitaetsbibliothek Munchen, Geschwister-scholl-Platz 1, 80539 Munich. Tel. 89-2180-2420, e-mail vdb@ub.uni-muenchen.de, World Wide Web http://www.vdb-online.org. *Chair* Klaus-Rainer Brintzinger.

Ghana

Ghana Lib. Assn., c/o INSTI, P.O. Box GP 4105, Accra. Tel. 244-17-4930, e-mail info@gla-net.org, World Wide Web http:// gla-net.org. *Pres.* Valentina J. A. Bannerman. E-mail valnin@yahoo.com.

Greece

Enosis Hellinon Bibliothekarion (Assn. of Greek Libns.), Skoufa 52, P.O. Box 10672, Athens. Tel./fax 210-330-2128, e-mail info@eebep.gr, World Wide Web http://

www.eebep.gr. *Pres.* George Glossa. E-mail glossiotis@gmail.com.

Guyana

Guyana Lib. Assn., c/o National Lib., P.O. Box 10240, Georgetown. Tel. 222-486, fax 223-596, e-mail londonh@uog.ed.gy, World Wide Web http://www.natlib.gov.gy. *Pres.* Wenda R. Stephenson, *Secy.* Althea John.

Honduras

Asociación de Bibliotecarios y Archiveros de Honduras (Assn. of Libns. and Archivists of Honduras), 11a Calle, 1a y 2a Avdas., No. 105, Comayagüela DC, Tegucigalpa. *Secy. Gen.* Juan Angel R. Ayes.

Hong Kong

Hong Kong Lib. Assn., GPO Box 10095, Hong Kong. E-mail hkla@hkla.org, World Wide Web http://www.hkla.org. *Pres.* Peter Sidroko. E-mail peters@hkucc.hku.hk.

Hungary

Magyar Könyvtárosok Egyesülete (Assn. of Hungarian Libns.), Hold u 6, H-1054 Budapest. Tel./fax 1-311-8634, e-mail mke@ oszk.hu, World Wide Web http://www.mke. oszk.hu. *Pres.* Klara Bakos; *Secy. Gen.* Miklos Feher.

Iceland

Upplysing—Felag bokasafns-og upplysingafraeoa (Information—The Icelandic Lib. and Info. Science Assn.), Lyngas 18, 210 Gardabaer. Tel. 864-6220, e-mail upplysing@upplysing.is, World Wide Web http:// www.upplysing.is.

India

Indian Assn. of Special Libs. and Info. Centres, P-291, CIT Scheme 6M, Kankurgachi, Kolkata 700054. Tel. 33-2362-9651, e-mail iaslic@vsnl.net, World Wide Web http:// www.iaslic1955.org.in. *Pres.* Jatindranath Satpathi. E-mail satpathijn@rediffmail.com; *Gen. Secy.* Pijushkanti Panigrahi. E-mail panigrahipk@yahoo.com.

Indian Lib. Assn., A/40-41, Flat 201, Ansal Bldg., Mukerjee Nagar, New Delhi 110009. Tel./fax 11-2765-1743, e-mail dvs-srcc@ rediffmail.com, World Wide Web http:// www.ilaindia.net. *Pres.* Dharm Veer Singh. E-mail dvs_srcc@rediffmail.com; *Gen. Secy.* Anuradha Gupta. E-mail anugupta160@ yahoo.com.

Indonesia

Ikatan Pustakawan Indonesia (Indonesian Lib. Assn.), Jl Merdeka Selatan No. 11, 10110 Jakarta, Pusat. Tel./fax 21-385-5729, World Wide Web http://ipi.pnri.go.id.

Ireland

Cumann Leabharlann na hEireann (Lib. Assn. of Ireland), c/o 138–144 Pearce St., Dublin 2. E-mail president@libraryassociation.ie, World Wide Web http://www.libraryassociation. ie. *Pres.* Fionnuala Hanrahan.

Israel

Israeli Center for Libs., 22 Baruch Hirsch St., 51108 Bnei Brak. Tel. 03-618-0151, fax 3-579-8048, e-mail icl@icl.org.il, World Wide Web http://www.icl.org.il.

Israeli Society for Libs. and Info. Centers (ASMI), Blum 8, 253 44 Kfar Saba. Tel. 77-215-1800, fax 77-434-0509, e-mail agudat asmi@gmail.com, World Wide Web http:// www.asmi.org.il. *Chair* Shachaf Hagafni.

Italy

Associazione Italiana Biblioteche (Italian Lib. Assn.), Biblioteca Nazionale Centrale, Viale Castro Pretorio 105, 00185 Rome RM. Tel. 6-446-3532, fax 6-444-1139, e-mail aib@ legalmail.it, World Wide Web http://www. aib.it. *CEO* Palmira Maria Barbini. E-mail barbini@aib.it.

Jamaica

Lib. and Info. Assn. of Jamaica., P.O. Box 125, Kingston 5. Tel./fax 876-927-1614, e-mail liajapresident@yahoo.com, World Wide Web http://www.liaja.org.jm. *Pres.* Pauline Nicholas.

Japan

Joho Kagaku Gijutsu Kyokai (Info. Science and Technology Assn.), Sasaki Bldg., 2-5-7 Koisikawa, Bunkyo-ku, Tokyo 112-0002. Tel. 3-3813-3791, fax 3-3813-3793, e-mail infosta@infosta.or.jp, World Wide Web http://www.infosta.or.jp. *Pres.* Onodera Natsuo.

Nihon Toshokan Kyokai (Japan Lib. Assn.), 1-11-14 Shinkawa, Chuo-ku, Tokyo 104 0033. Tel. 3-3523-0811, fax 3-3523-0841, e-mail info@jla.or.jp, World Wide Web http://www.jla.or.jp. *Pres.* Shiomi Noboru.

Senmon Toshokan Kyogikai (Japan Special Libs. Assn.), c/o Japan Lib. Assn., Bldg. F6, 1-11-14 Shinkawa Chuo-ku, Tokyo 104-0033. Tel. 3-3537-8335, fax 3-3537-8336, e-mail jsla@jsla.or.jp, World Wide Web http://www.jsla.or.jp.

Jordan

Arab Archives Institute, P.O. Box 815454, Amman. Tel. 6-465-6694, fax 6-465-6693, e-mail aainstitute@gmail.com, World Wide Web http://www.alarcheef.com. *Dir.* Sa'eda Kilani.

Jordan Lib. and Info. Assn., P.O. Box 6289, Amman 11118. Tel./fax 6-462-9412, e-mail jorla_1963@yahoo.com, World Wide Web http://www.jorla.org. *Pres.* Omar Mohammad Jaradat.

Kenya

Kenya Assn. of Lib. and Info. Professionals (formerly Kenya Lib. Assn.), P.O. Box 46031, 00100 Nairobi. Tel. 20-733-732-799, fax 20-811-455, e-mail talktochairman@ gmail.com, World Wide Web http://www. klas.or.ke. *Chair* Rosemary Gitachu. E-mail gitachur@yahoo.com.

Korea (Democratic People's Republic of)

Lib. Assn. of the Democratic People's Republic of Korea, c/o Grand People's Study House, P.O. Box 200, Pyongyang. E-mail nsj@ co.chesin.com.

Korea (Republic of)

Korean Lib. Assn., San 60-1, Banpo-dong, Seocho-gu, Seoul 137-702. Tel. 2-535-4868, fax 2-535-5616, e-mail license@kla.kr, World Wide Web http://www.kla.kr.

Laos

Association des Bibliothécaires Laotiens (Lao Lib. Assn.), c/o Direction de la Bibliothèque Nationale, Ministry of Educ., BP 704, Vientiane. Tel. 21-21-2452, fax 21-21-2408, e-mail bailane@laotel.com.

Latvia

Latvian Libns. Assn., Terbatas iela 75, Riga LV-1001. Tel./fax 6731-2791, e-mail lbb@lbi lnb.lv, World Wide Web http://www.lnb.lv.

Lebanon

Lebanese Lib. Assn., P.O. Box 13-5053, Beirut 1102 2801. Tel. 1-786-456, e-mail kjaroudy@lau.edu.lb; World Wide Web http://www.llaweb.org. *Pres.* Fawz Abdalleh. E-mail fatdalla@lau.edu.lb.

Lesotho

Lesotho Lib. Assn., Private Bag A26, Maseru 100. Tel. 213-420, fax 340-000, e-mail s.mohai@nul.ls. *Contact* Makemang Ntsasa.

Lithuania

Lietuvos Bibliotekininku Draugija (Lithuanian Libns. Assn.), S Dariaus ir S Gireno g 12, LT-59212 Birstonas. Tel./fax 5-262-5570, e-mail lbd_sekretore@gmail.com, World Wide Web http://www.lbd.lt. *Pres.* Irma Kleiziene. E-mail bmb@is.lt.

Luxembourg

Association Luxembourgeoise des Bibliothécaires, Archivistes, et Documentalistes (ALBAD) (Luxembourg Assn. of Libns., Archivists, and Documentalists), c/o National Lib. of Luxembourg, BP 295, L-2012 Luxembourg. Tel. 352-22-97-55-1, fax 352-47-56-72, World Wide Web http://www.albad.lu. *Pres.* Jean-Marie Reding. E-mail jean-marie.reding@bnl.etat.lu; *Secy. Gen.* Michel Donven. E-mail michel.donven@bnl.etat.lu.

Malawi

Malawi Lib. Assn., c/o Univ. Libn., P.O. Box 429, Zomba. Tel. 524-265, fax 525-255. *Chair* Geoffrey F Salanja; *Secy. Gen.* Francis F. C. Kachala.

Malaysia

Persatuan Pustakawan Malaysia (Libns. Assn. of Malaysia), P.O. Box 12545, 50782 Kuala Lumpur. Tel./fax 3-2694-7390, e-mail ppm55@po.jaring.my, World Wide Web http://ppm55.org. *Pres.* Mohd Sharif Mohd Saad. E-mail mohd.sharif@gmail.com.

Mali

Association Malienne des Bibliothécaires, Archivistes et Documentalistes (Mali Assn. of Libns., Archivists, and Documentalists) (AMBAD), BP E4473, Bamako. Tel. 20-29-94-23, fax 20-29-93-76, e-mail dnbd@afribone.net.ml.

Malta

Malta Lib. and Info. Assn. (MaLIA), c/o Univ. of Malta Lib., Msida MSD 2080. E-mail info@malia-malta.org, World Wide Web http://www.malia-malta.org. *Chair* Laurence Zerafa.

Mauritania

Association Mauritanienne des Bibliothécaires, Archivistes, et Documentalistes (Mauritanian Assn. of Libns., Archivists, and Documentalists), c/o Bibliothèque Nationale, BP 20, Nouakchott. Tel. 525-18-62, fax 525-18-68, e-mail bibliothequenationale@yahoo.fr.

Mauritius

Mauritius Lib. Assn., Ministry of Educ. Public Lib., Moka Rd., Rose Hill. Tel. 403-0200, fax 454-9553. *Pres.* Abdool Fareed Soogali.

Mexico

Asociación Mexicana de Bibliotecarios (Mexican Assn. of Libns.), Apdo. 12-800, Admon Postal Obrero Mundial, 03001 México DF. Tel. 155-55-75-33-96, fax 155-5575-1136, e-mail correo@ambac.org.mx, World Wide Web http://www.ambac.org.mx. *Pres.* Oscar Saavedra; *Secy. Gen.* Guadalupe Vega.

Myanmar

Myanmar Lib. Assn., c/o National Lib., 85 Thirimingalar Yeiktha Lane, Kabar Aye Pagoda Rd., Yankin Township, Yangon. Tel. 1-28-3332.

Nepal

Nepal Lib. Assn., GPO 2773, Kathmandu. Tel. 977-1-441-1318, e-mail info@nla.org. np, World Wide Web http://www.nla.org. np. *Pres.* Prakash Kumar Thapa. E-mail kyammuntar@yahoo.com.

The Netherlands

Nederlandse Vereniging voor Beroepsbeoefenaren in de Bibliotheek-Informatie-en Kennissector (Netherlands Assn. of Libns., Documentalists, and Info. Specialists), Mariaplaats 3, 3511 LH Utrecht. Tel. 30-233-00-50, fax 30-238-00-30, e-mail info@ nvbonline.nl, World Wide Web http://www. nvbonline.nl. *Chair* Michel G. Wesseling. E-mail m.g.wesseling@gmail.com.

New Zealand

New Zealand Lib. Assn. (LIANZA), P.O. Box 12212, Thorndon, Wellington 6144. Tel. 4-801-5542, fax 4-801-5543, e-mail admin @lianza.org.nz, World Wide Web http:// www.lianza.org.nz. *Exec. Dir.* Alli Smith. E-mail alli@lianza.org.nz.

Nicaragua

Asociación Nicaraguense de Bibliotecarios y Profesionales Afines (ANIBIPA) (Nicaraguan Assn. of Libns.), Bello Horizonte, Tope Sur de la Rotonda 1/2 cuadra abajo, J-11-57, Managua. Tel. 277-4159, e-mail anibipa@hotmail.com. *Pres.* Yadira Roque. E-mail r-yardira@hotmail.com.

Nigeria

Nigerian Lib. Assn., c/o National Lib. of Nigeria, Sanusi Dantata House, Central Business District, PMB 1, Abuja GPO 900001. Tel. 805-536-5245, fax 9-234-6773, e-mail info@nla-ng.org, World Wide Web http://www.nla-ng.org. *Pres.* Lenrie Aina.

Norway

Arkivarforeningen (Assn. of Archivists), Fredrik Glads gate 1, 0482 Oslo. Tel. 913-16-895, e-mail imb@steria.no, World Wide Web http://www.arkivarforeningen.no. *Chair* Inge Manfred Bjorlin. E-mail inge.bjorlin@ gmail.com.

Norsk Bibliotekforening (Norwegian Lib. Assn.), Postboks 6540, 0606 Etterstad, Oslo. Tel. 23-24-34-30, fax 22-67-23-68, e-mail nbf@norskbibliotekforening.no, World Wide Web http://www.norskbibliotekforening.no. *Gen. Secy.* Hege Newth Nouri. E-mail hege. newth.nouri@norskbibliotekforening.no.

Pakistan

Library Promotion Bureau, Karachi Univ. Campus, P.O. Box 8421, Karachi 75270. Tel./fax 21-857-6301. *Vice Chancellor* Pirzada Qasim Raza Siddiqui. E-mail vc@ uok.edu.pk.

Panama

Asociación Panameña de Bibliotecarios (Panama Lib. Assn.), c/o Biblioteca Interamericana Simón Bolivar, Estafeta Universitaria, Panama City. E-mail biblis2@arcon.up.ac. pa.

Paraguay

Asociación de Bibliotecarios Graduados del Paraguay (Assn. of Paraguayan Graduate Libns.), Facultad Politecnica, Universidad Nacional de Asunción, 2160 San Lorenzo. Tel. 21-585-588, e-mail abigrap@pol.una. py, World Wide Web http://www.pol.una.py/ abigrap.

Peru

Asociación de Archiveros del Perú (Peruvian Assn. of Archivists), Av. Manco Capac No. 1180, Dpto 201, La Victoria, Lima. Tel. 1-472-8729, fax 1-472-7408, e-mail contactos@adapperu.com. *Pres.* Juan Manuel Serrano Valencia.
Asociación Peruana de Bibliotecarios (Peruvian Assn. of Libns.), Bellavista 561 Miraflores, Apdo. 995, Lima 18. Tel. 1-474-869.

Philippines

Assn. of Special Libs. of the Philippines, c/o Goethe-Institut Philippinen, G/4-5/F Adamson Centre, 121 Leviste St., Salcedo Village, 1227 Makati City. Tel. 2-740-9625, e-mail aslpboard@yahoo.com.ph, World Wide Web http://aslpwiki.wikispaces.com. *Pres.* Joseph M. Yap.
Philippine Libns. Assn., P.O. Box 2926, 1000 Ermita, Manila. Tel./fax 2-525-9401, World Wide Web http://plainational.blogspot.com. *Pres.* Elizabeth R. Peralejo.

Poland

Stowarzyszenie Bibliotekarzy Polskich (Polish Libns. Assn.), al Niepodleglosci 213, 02-086 Warsaw. Tel. 22-825-83-74, fax 22-825-53-49, e-mail biuro@sbp.pl, World Wide Web http://www.sbp.pl. *Chair* Elizabeth Stefanczyk, e.stefanczyk@bn.org.pl; *Secy. Gen.* Marzena Przybysz.

Portugal

Associação Portuguesa de Bibliotecários, Arquivistas e Documentalistas (Portuguese Assn. of Libns., Archivists, and Documentalists), Rua Morais Soares, 43C, 1 Dto e Frte, 1900-341 Lisbon. Tel. 21-816-19-80, fax 21-815-45-08, e-mail apbad@apbad.pt, World Wide Web http://www.apbad.pt. *Pres.* Maria Paula Santos.

Puerto Rico

Sociedad de Bibliotecarios de Puerto Rico (Society of Libns. of Puerto Rico), Apdo 22898, San Juan 00931-2898. Tel./fax 787-764-0000, World Wide Web http://www.

sociedadbibliotecarios.org. *Pres.* Snejanka Penkova. E-mail snejanka.penkova@uprrp.edu.

Russia

Rossiiskaya Bibliotechnaya Assotsiatsiya (Russian Lib. Assn.), 18 Sadovaya St., St. Petersburg 191069. Tel./fax 812-110-58-61, e-mail rba@nlr.ru, World Wide Web http://www.rba.ru. *Exec. Secy.* Elena Tikhonova.

Senegal

Association Sénégalaise des Bibliothécaires, Archivistes et Documentalistes (Senegalese Assn. of Libns., Archivists, and Documentalists), BP 2006, Dakar. Tel. 77-651-00-33, fax 33-824-23-79, e-mail asbad200@hotmail.com, World Wide Web http://www.asbad.org. *Pres.* Lawrence Gomis Baaya; *Secy. Gen.* Alassane Ndiath.

Serbia and Montenegro

Jugoslovenski Bibliografsko Informacijski Institut, Terazije 26, 11000 Belgrade. Tel. 11-2687-836, fax 11-2687-760.

Sierra Leone

Sierra Leone Assn. of Archivists, Libns., and Info. Scientists, c/o Sierra Leone Lib. Board, P.O. Box 326, Freetown. Tel. 22-223-848.

Singapore

Lib. Assn. of Singapore, National Lib. Board, 100 Victoria St., No. 14-01, Singapore 188064. Tel. 6332-3255, fax 6332-3248, e-mail lassec@las.org.sg, World Wide Web http://www.las.org.sg. *Pres.* Gene Tan. E-mail president@las.org.sg.

Slovenia

Zveza Bibliotekarskih Druötev Slovenije (Union of Assns. of Slovene Libns.), Turjaöka 1, 1000 Ljubljana. Tel. 1-20-01-176, fax 1-42-57-293, e-mail info@zbds-zveza.si, World Wide Web http://www.zbds-zveza.si. *Pres.* Sabina Fras Popovic. E-mail sabina.fras-popovic@mb.sik.si.

South Africa

Lib. and Info. Assn. of South Africa, P.O. Box 1598, Pretoria 0001. Tel. 12-328-2010, fax 12-323-1033, e-mail liasa@liasa.org.za, World Wide Web http://www.liasa.org.za. *Pres.* Naomi Haasbroek. E-mail president@liasa.org.za.

Spain

Federación Española de Archiveros, Bibliotecarios, Museólogos y Documentalistas (ANABAD) (Spanish Federation of Assns. of Archivists, Libns., Archaeologists, Museum Curators, and Documentalists), de las Huertas, 37, 28014 Madrid. Tel. 34-91-575-1727, fax 34-91-578-1615, e-mail anabad@anabad.org, World Wide Web http://www.anabad.org. *Pres.* Gacho Miguel Angel Santamaría.

Sri Lanka

Sri Lanka Lib. Assn., 275/75 Sri Lanka Professional Centre, Stanley Wijesundara Mawatha, Colombo 7. Tel./fax 11-258-9103, e-mail slla@slltnet.lk, World Wide Web http://www.slla.org.lk. *Pres.* Upali Amarasiri. E-mail amarasiriupali@gmail.com; *Gen. Secy.* Indrani Ponnamperuma. E-mail indrani.ponnamperuma@gmail.com.

Swaziland

Swaziland Lib. Assn., P.O. Box 2309, Mbabane H100. Tel. 404-2633, fax 404-3863, World Wide Web http://www.swala.sz.

Sweden

Svensk Biblioteksförening Kansli (Swedish Lib. Assn.), World Trade Center, D5, Box 70380, 107 24 S-Stockholm. Tel. 8-545-132-30, fax 8-545-132-31, e-mail info@biblioteksforeningen.org, World Wide Web http://www.biblioteksforeningen.org. *Secy. Gen.* Niclas Lindberg. E-mail nl@biblioteksforeningen.org.

Svensk Förening för Informationsspecialister (Swedish Assn. for Info. Specialists), Box 2001, 135 02 Tyreso. E-mail kansliet@sfis.nu, World Wide Web http://www.sfis.nu.

Pres. Peter Almerud. E-mail peter.almerud@gmail.com.

Svenska Arkivsamfundet (Swedish Assn. of Archivists), c/o Stockholms stadsarkiv, Box 22063, 104 22 Stockholm. E-mail info@arkivsamfundet.se, World Wide Web http://www.arkivsamfundet.se.

Switzerland

Association des Bibliothèques et Bibliothécaires Suisses/Vereinigung Schweizerischer Bibliothekare/Associazione dei Bibliotecari Svizzeri (Assn. of Swiss Libs. and Libns.), Hallestr. 58, CH-3012 Bern. Tel. 31-382-42-40, fax 31-382-46-48, e-mail bbs@bbs.ch, World Wide Web http://www.bbs.ch.

Schweizerische Vereinigung für Dokumentation/Association Suisse de Documentation (Swiss Assn. of Documentation), Hallestr. 58, CH-3012 Bern. Tel. 31-382-42-40, fax 31-382-46-48, e-mail bbs@bbs.ch.

Verein Schweizer Archivarinnen und Archivare (Assn. of Swiss Archivists), Schweizerisches Bundesarchiv, Office Pontri GmbH, Solohurnstr. 13, CH-3322, Urtenen Schönbühl. Tel. 31-312-26-66, fax 31-312-26-68, e-mail info@vsa-aas.org, World Wide Web http://www.vsa-aas.org. *Pres.* Anna Pia Maissen, Zurich City Archives. E-mail annapia.maissen@zuerich.ch.

Taiwan

Lib. Assn. of the Republic of China (LAROC), 20 Zhongshan South Rd., Taipei 100. Tel. 2-2331-9132, fax 2-2370-0899, e-mail lac@msg.ncl.edu.tw, World Wide Web http://www.lac.org.tw.

Tanzania

Tanzania Lib. Assn., P.O. Box 33433, Dar es Salaam. Tel./fax 744-296-134, e-mail tla_tanzania@yahoo.com, World Wide Web http://www.tla.or.tz.

Thailand

Thai Lib. Assn., 1346 Akarnsongkrau Rd. 5, Klongchan, Bangkapi, 10240 Bangkok. Tel. 02-734-9022, fax 02-734-9021, e-mail tla2497@yahoo.com, World Wide Web http://tla.or.th. *Contact* Suwadee Vichetpan.

Trinidad and Tobago

Lib. Assn. of Trinidad and Tobago, P.O. Box 1275, Port of Spain. Tel. 868-687-0194, e-mail info@latt.org.tt, World Wide Web http://www.latt.org.tt. *Pres.* Karen P. Campbell.

Tunisia

Association Tunisienne des Documentalistes, Bibliothécaires et Archivistes (Tunisian Assn. of Documentalists, Libns., and Archivists), BP 380, 1000 Tunis RP. Tel. 895-450.

Turkey

Türk Kütüphaneciler Dernegi (Turkish Libns. Assn.), Necatibey Cad Elgun Sok 8/8, 06440 Kizilay, Ankara. Tel. 312-230-13-25, fax 312-232-04-53, e-mail tkd.dernek@gmail.com, World Wide Web http://www.kutuphaneci.org.tr. *Pres.* Ali Fuat Kartal.

Uganda

Uganda Lib. and Info. Assn., P.O. Box 8147, Kampala. Tel. 141-256-77-467698.

Ukraine

Ukrainian Lib. Assn., Vasylkovska 12, office 5, code 5, 01004, Kyiv. Tel. 380-44-239-74-87, fax 380-44-35-45-47, e-mail u_b_a@ukr.net, World Wide Web http://www.uba.org.ua. *Exec. Dir.* Soshynska Yaroslav.

United Kingdom

Archives and Records Assn., UK and Ireland (formerly the Society of Archivists), Prioryfield House, 20 Canon St., Taunton TA1 1SW, England. Tel. 1823-327-030, fax 1823-271-719, e-mail societyofarchivists@archives.org.uk, World Wide Web http://www.archives.org.uk. *Chair* Martin Taylor; *Chief Exec.* John Chambers.

ASLIB, the Assn. for Info. Management, 207 Howard House, Wagon Lane, Bingley BD16 1WA, England. Tel. 01274-777-700, fax 01274-785-201, e-mail support@aslib.com, World Wide Web http://www.aslib.com. *Manager* Diane Heath. E-mail dheath@aslib.com.

Bibliographical Society, Institute of English Studies, Rm. 306, Senate House, Malet St., London WC1E 7HU, England. World Wide Web http://www.bibsoc.org.uk. *Pres.* David Pearson.

Chartered Institute of Lib. and Info. Professionals (CILIP) (formerly the Lib. Assn.), 7 Ridgmount St., London WC1E 7AE, England. Tel. 20-7255-0500, fax 20-7255-0501, e-mail info@cilip.org.uk, World Wide Web http://www.cilip.org.uk. *Chief Exec.* Annie Mauger. E-mail annie.mauger@cilip.org.uk.

School Lib. Assn., 1 Pine Court, Kembrey Park, Swindon SN2 8AD, England. Tel. 1793-530-166, fax 1793-481-182, e-mail info@sla.org.uk, World Wide Web http://www.sla.org.uk. *Pres.* Kevin Crossley-Holland.

Scottish Lib. and Info. Council, 151 W. George St., Glasgow G2 2JJ, Scotland. Tel. 141-228-4790, e-mail slic@slainte.org.uk, World Wide Web http://www.slainte.org.uk/slic/slicindex.htm. *Chair* Fiona MacLeod.

Society of College, National, and Univ. Libs (SCONUL) (formerly Standing Conference of National and Univ. Libs.), 94 Euston St., London NW1 2HA, England. Tel. 20-7387-0317, fax 20-7383-3197, e-mail info@sconul.ac.uk, World Wide Web http://www.sconul.ac.uk. *Chair* Sara Marsh.

Uruguay

Agrupación Bibliotecológica del Uruguay (Uruguayan Lib. and Archive Science Assn.), Cerro Largo 1666, 11200 Montevideo. Tel. 2-400-57-40, e-mail lama@adinet.com.uy. *Pres.* Luis Alberto Musso.

Asociación de Bibliotecólogos del Uruguay, Eduardo V. Haedo 2255, 11200 Montevideo. Tel./fax 2409-9989, e-mail abu@adinet.com.uy, World Wide Web http://www.abu.net.uy. *Pres.* Ruth Santestevan. E-mail rsantestevan@yahoo.es.

Venezuela

Colegio de Bibliotecólogos y Archivólogos de Venezuela (Venezuelan Lib. and Archives Assn.), Foro Libertador, Edif. Biblioteca Nacional, Final Av. Panteón, Caracas. Tel./

fax 58-212-564-1203, e-mail cbav2001@ cantv.net, World Wide Web http://www. documentalistas.com/web/cbav.

Vietnam

Hôi Thu-Vien Viet Nam (Vietnamese Lib. Assn.), National Lib. of Vietnam, 31 Trang Thi, Hoan Kiem, 10000 Hanoi. Tel. 4-8254-938, fax 4-8253-357, e-mail info@nlv.gov. vn, World Wide Web http://www.nlv.gov.vn.

Zambia

Zambia Lib. Assn., P.O. Box 38636, 10101 Lusaka. *Chair* Benson Njobvu. E-mail benson njobvu@hotmail.com.

Zimbabwe

Zimbabwe Lib. Assn., P.O. Box 3133, Harare. Tel. 4-692-741, e-mail zimlanec@gmail. com, World Wide Web http://zimbabwe reads.org/zimla. *Chair* T. G. Bohwa.

Directory of Book Trade and Related Organizations

Book Trade Associations, United States and Canada

For more extensive information on the associations listed in this section, see the annual edition of *Literary Market Place* (Information Today, Inc.).

AIGA—The Professional Assn. for Design (formerly American Institute of Graphic Arts), 164 Fifth Ave., New York, NY 10010. Tel. 212-807-1990, fax 212-807-1799, e-mail aiga@aiga.org, World Wide Web http://www.aiga.org. *Pres.* Doug Powell, Schwartz Powell, 330 Elmwood Place W., Minneapolis, MN 55419. Tel. 612-875-6702, e-mail doug@schwartzpowell.com; *Exec. Dir.* Richard Grefé. E-mail grefe@aiga.org.

American Book Producers Assn. (ABPA), 151 W. 19 St., Third fl., New York, NY10011. Tel. 212-675-1363, fax 212-675-1364, e-mail office@ABPAonline.org, World Wide Web http://www.abpaonline.org. *Pres.* Richard Rothschild; *V.P.* Nancy Hall.

American Booksellers Assn., 200 White Plains Rd., Tarrytown, NY 10591. Tel. 800-637-0037, 914-591-2665, fax 914-591-2720, World Wide Web http://www.bookweb.org. *Fres.* Becky Anderson, Anderson's Bookshops, 123 W. Jefferson Ave., Naperville, IL 60540. Tel. 630-355-2665, fax 630-355-3470, e-mail becky@andersonsbookshop. com; *V.P./Secy.* Steve Bercu, BookPeople, 603 N. Lamar, Austin, TX 78703. Tel. 512-472-5050, e-mail steve@bookpeople.com; *CEO* Oren Teicher. E-mail oren@bookweb. org.

American Literary Translators Assn. (ALTA), Univ. of Texas at Dallas, 800 W. Campbell Rd., Mail Sta. JO51, Richardson, TX 75080. Tel. 972-883-2092, fax 972-883-6303, World Wide Web http://www.utdallas.edu/

alta. *Pres.* Gary Racz; *V.P.* Elizabeth Lowe; *Secy./Treas.* Matt Rowe.

American Printing History Assn., Box 4519, Grand Central Sta., New York, NY 10163-4519. World Wide Web http://www.printing history.org. *Pres.* Robert McCamant; *Exec. Secy.* Lyndsi Barnes. E-mail secretary@ printinghistory.org.

American Society for Indexing, 10200 W. 44 Ave., Suite 304, Wheat Ridge, CO 80033. Tel. 303-463-2887, fax 303-422-8894, e-mail info@asindexing.org, World Wide Web http://www.asindexing.org. *Pres.* Pilar Wyman. E-mail president@asindexing.org; *V.P./Pres.-Elect* Ina Gravitz. E-mail president elect@asindexing.org; *Exec. Dir.* David Stumph. E-mail dstumph@resourcenter.com.

American Society of Journalists and Authors, 1501 Broadway, Suite 403, New York, NY 10036. Tel. 212-997-0947, fax 212-937-2315, e-mail director@asja.org, World Wide Web http://www.asja.org. *Pres.* Minda Zetlin. E-mail president@asja.org; *Exec. Dir.* Alexandra Owens.

American Society of Media Photographers, 150 N. 2 St., Philadelphia, PA 19106. Tel. 215-451-2767, fax 215-451-0880, e-mail mopsik@asmp.org, World Wide Web http:// www.asmp.org. *Pres.* Shawn Henry; *Exec. Dir.* Eugene Mopsik.

American Society of Picture Professionals, 217 Palos Verdes Blvd., No. 700, Redondo Beach, CA 90277. Tel. 424-247-9944, fax 424-247-9844, e-mail director@aspp.com, World Wide Web http://www.aspp.com.

Pres. Michael Masterson; *Exec. Dir.* Jain Lemos.

American Translators Assn., 225 Reinekers Lane, Suite 590, Alexandria, VA 22314. Tel. 703-683-6100, fax 703-683-6122, e-mail ata@atanet.org, World Wide Web http://www.atanet.org. *Pres.* Dorothee Racette; *Pres.-Elect* Caitilin Walsh; *Secy.* Boris Silversteyn; *Treas.* Gabe Bokor; *Exec. Dir.* Walter W. Bacak, Jr. E-mail walter@atanet.org.

Antiquarian Booksellers Assn. of America, 20 W. 44 St., No. 507, New York, NY 10036-6604. Tel. 212-944-8291, fax 212-944-8293, e-mail inquiries@abaa.org, World Wide Web http://www.abaa.org. *Pres.* John Thomson; *V.P./Secy.* Thomas Goldwasser; *Treas.* Sam Hessel; *Exec. Dir.* Susan Benne. E-mail sbenne@abaa.org.

Assn. Media and Publishing (formerly Society of National Assn. Publications, or SNAP), 12100 Sunset Hills Rd., Suite 130, Reston, VA 20190. Tel. 703-234-4063, fax 703-435-4390, e-mail info@associationmedia andpublishing.org, World Wide Web http://www.associationmediaandpublishing.org. *Pres.* Gary Rubin; *V.P.* Kim Howard; *Exec. Dir.* Sarah Patterson. Tel. 703-234-4107, e-mail spatterson@associationmediaand publishing.org.

Assn. of American Publishers, 71 Fifth Ave., New York, NY 10003. Tel. 212-255-0200, fax 212-255-7007. Washington Office 455 Massachusetts Ave. N.W., Suite 700, Washington, DC 20001. Tel. 202-347-3375, fax 202-347-3690. *Pres./CEO* Tom Allen; *V.P.s* Allan R. Adler, Tina Jordan, Andi Sporkin, John Tagler; *Dir., Free Expression Advocacy* Judith Platt; *Exec. Dir., School Div.* Jay Diskey; *Exec. Dir., Higher Education* J. Bruce Hildebrand; *Exec. Dir., International Copyright Enforcement and Trade Policy* M. Lui Simpson; *Exec. Dir., Digital, Environmental, and Accessibility Affairs* Ed McCoyd; *Dir., Membership Marketing* Gail Kump.

Assn. of American University Presses, 28 W. 36 St., Suite 602, New York, NY 10018. Tel. 212-989-1010, fax 212-989-0275, e-mail info@aaupnet.org, World Wide Web http://aaupnet.org. *Pres.* Peter Dougherty, Princeton Univ. Press; *Pres.-Elect* Philip Cercone, McGill-Queen's Univ. Press; *Past Pres.* MaryKatherine Callaway, Louisiana State Univ. Press; *Exec. Dir.* Peter Berkery. Tel. 212-989-1010 ext. 29, e-mail pberkery@aaupnet.org.

Assn. of Canadian Publishers, 174 Spadina Ave., Suite 306, Toronto, ON M5T 2C2. Tel. 416-487-6116, fax 416-487-8815, World Wide Web http://www.publishers.ca. *Pres.* Bill Harnum, Pontifical Institute of Mediaeval Studies, Univ. of Toronto, 59 Queen's Park Crescent E., Toronto, ON M5S 2C4. Tel. 416-926-7126, fax 416-926-7258, e-mail bill.harnum@gmail.com; *V.P.* Erin Creasy, ECW Press, 2120 Queen Street E., Suite 200 Toronto, ON M4E 1E2. Tel. 416-694-3348, fax 416-698-9906, e-mail erin@ecwpress.com; *Exec. Dir.* Carolyn Wood. Tel. 416-487-6116 ext. 222, e-mail carolyn_wood@canbook.org.

Assn. of Educational Publishers (AEP), 300 Martin Luther King Blvd., Suite 200, Wilmington, DE 19801. Tel. 302-295-8350, Fax 302-656-2918, e-mail mail@aepweb.org, World Wide Web http://www.aepweb.org. *Pres.* Lee Wilson; *Pres.-Elect* Greg Worrell; *V.P.* David Beacom; *Treas.* Randy Wilhelm; *Past Pres.* Neal Goff; *CEO* Charlene F. Gaynor. E-mail cgaynor@aepweb.org.

Audio Publishers Assn., 191 Clarksville Rd., Princeton Junction, NJ 08550. Tel. 609-799-6327, fax 609-799-7032, e-mail info@audiopub.org; World Wide Web http://www.audiopub.org.

Authors Guild, 31 E. 32 St., Seventh fl., New York, NY 10016. Tel. 212-563-5904, fax 212-564-5363, e-mail staff@authorsguild.org, World Wide Web http://www.authors guild.org. *Pres.* Scott Turow; *V.P.s* Judy Blume, James Shapiro; *Secy.* Pat Cummings; *Treas.* Peter Petre.

Book Industry Study Group, 145 W. 45 St., Suite 601, New York, NY 10017. Tel. 646-336-7141, fax 646-336-6214, e-mail info@bisg.org, World Wide Web http://www.bisg.org. *Chair* Kenneth Michaels, Hachette; *V.* *Chair* Tara Catogge, ReaderLink Distribution Services; *Exec. Dir.* Len Vlahos. E-mail len@bisg.org; *Deputy Exec. Dir.* Angela Bole. E-mail angela@bisg.org.

Book Manufacturers' Institute, 2 Armand Beach Drive, Suite 1B, Palm Coast, FL 32137. Tel. 386-986-4552, fax 386-986-4553, e-mail info@bmibook.com, World Wide Web http://www.bmibook.org. *Pres.*

Mike Collinge; *V.P./Pres.-Elect* Jac B. Garner; *Exec. V.P./Secy.* Daniel N. Bach. Address correspondence to the executive vice president.

Bookbuilders of Boston, 44 Vinal Rd., Scituate, MA 02066. Tel. 781-378-1361, fax 419-821-2171, e-mail office@bbboston.org, World Wide Web http://www.bbboston.org. *Pres.* Tom Plain. E-mail tomp@hpcbook.com; *1st V.P.* Michael Mozina. E-mail mmozina@brillusa.com; *Treas.* Scott Payne. E-mail scott_payne@malloy.com; *Clerk* Anny DiCiccio. E-mail anny.diciccio@yahoo.com.

Bookbuilders West. See Publishing Professionals Network.

Canadian Booksellers Assn. As of January 2013, part of Retail Council of Canada. Toronto office: 1255 Bay St., Suite 902, Toronto, ON M5R 2A9.

Canadian International Standard Numbers (ISN) Agency, c/o Published Heritage, Lib. and Archives Canada, 395 Wellington St., Ottawa, ON K1A 0N4. Tel. 866-578-7777 (toll-free) or 613-996-5115, World Wide Web http://www.collectionscanada.ca/isn/index-e.html.

Canadian Printing Industries Assn., 221 Remic Ave., Ottawa, ON K1Z 5W6. Tel. 613-236-7208, fax 613-232-1334, toll free (Canada and USA) 800-267-7280, e-mail blinklater@cpia-aci.ca, World Wide Web http://www.cpia-aci.ca. *Pres.* Bob Elliott.

Chicago Book Clinic. See Midwest Publishing Assn.

Children's Book Council, 54 W. 39 St., 14th fl., New York, NY 10018. Tel. 212-966-1990, fax 212-966-2073, e-mail cbc.info@cbcbooks.org, World Wide Web http://www.cbcbooks.org. *Chair* Nancy Feresten; *V. Chair* Betsy Groban; *Secy.* Susan Van Metre; *Treas.* Simon Tasker; *Exec. Dir.* Robin Adelson. E-mail robin.adelson@cbcbooks.org.

Christian Booksellers Association, P.O. Box 62000, Colorado Springs, CO 80962-2000. Tel. 719-265-9895, fax 719-272-3510, info@cbaonline.org, World Wide Web http://www.cbaonline.org.

Copyright Society of the USA, 352 Seventh Ave., Suite 739, New York, NY 10001. World Wide Web http://www.csusa.org. *Pres.* Joseph Salvo; *V.P./Pres.-Elect* Eric Schwartz; *Secy.* Rose Auslander; *Treas.*

Nancy Wolff; *Dir. Operations* Amy Nickerson. E-mail amy@csusa.org.

Council of Literary Magazines and Presses, 154 Christopher St., Suite 3C, New York, NY 10014. Tel. 212-741-9110, fax 212-741-9112, e-mail info@clmp.org, World Wide Web http://www.clmp.org. *Co-chairs* Gerald Howard, Nicole Dewey; *Exec. Dir.* Jeffrey Lependorf. E-mail jlependorf@clmp.org.

Educational Book and Media Assn. (formerly Educational Paperback Assn.), P.O. Box 3363, Warrenton, VA 20188. Tel. 540-318-7770, e-mail info@edupaperback.org, World Wide Web http://www.edupaperback.org. *Pres.* Gene Bahlman; *V.P.* Jennifer Allen; *Treas.* Michael Raymond; *Past Pres.* Neil Jaffe.

Evangelical Christian Publishers Assn., 9633 S. 48 St., Suite 140, Phoenix, AZ 85044. Tel. 480-966-3998, fax 480-966-1944, e-mail info@ecpa.org, World Wide Web http://www.ecpa.org.

Graphic Artists Guild, 32 Broadway, Suite 1114, New York, NY 10004. Tel. 212-791-3400, fax 212-792-0333, e-mail admin@gag.org, World Wide Web http://www.graphicartistsguild.org. *Pres.* Haydn S. Adams. E-mail president@gag.org; *V.P.* Lara Kisielewska; *Exec. Dir.* Patricia McKiernan. E-mail admin@gag.org.

Great Lakes Independent Booksellers Assn., c/o Exec. Dir. Deb Leonard, 2113 Roosevelt, Ypsilanti, MI 48197. Tel. 888-736-3096, fax 734-879-11291, e-mail deb@gliba.org, World Wide Web http://www.gliba.org. *Pres.* Robin Allen, Forever Books, St. Joseph, MI 49085. E-mail foreverbooks@qtm.net.

Guild of Book Workers, 521 Fifth Ave., New York, NY 10175. Tel. 212-292-4444, e-mail communications@guildofbookworkers.org, World Wide Web http://www.guildofbookworkers.org. *Pres.* Mark Andersson. E-mail president@guildofbookworkers.org; *V.P.* Anna Embree. E-mail vicepresident@guildofbookworkers.org.

Horror Writers Assn., 244 Fifth Ave., Suite 2767, New York, NY 10001. E-mail hwa@horror.org, World Wide Web http://www.horror.org. *Pres.* Rocky Wood. E-mail president@horror.org; *V.P.* Lisa Morton. E-mail vp@horror.org; *Secy.* Joe McKinney.

E-mail secretary@horror.org; *Treas.* Les Klinger. E-mail treasurer@horror.org.

IAPHC—The Graphic Professionals Resource Network (formerly the International Assn. of Printing House Craftsmen), P.O. Box 2549, Maple Grove, MN 55311-7549. Tel. 800-466-4274 (toll-free) or 763-560-1620, fax 763-560-1350, e-mail headquarters@ iaphc.org, World Wide Web http://www. iaphc.org. *Pres./CEO* Kevin P. Keane. E-mail headquarters@iaphc.com.

Independent Book Publishers Assn. (formerly PMA), 1020 Manhattan Beach Blvd., Suite 204, Manhattan Beach, CA 90266. Tel. 310-546-1818, fax 310-546-3939, e-mail info@ ibpa-online.org, World Wide Web http:// www.ibpa-online.org. *Chair* Steve Mettee, The Write Thought, 1254 Commerce Ave., Sanger, CA 93657. Tel. 559-876-2170, fax 559-876-2180, e-mail mettee@ thewritethought.com; *Exec. Dir.* Florrie Binford Kichler, Patria Press, P.O. Box 752, Carmel. IN 46082. Tel. 317-577-1321; *COO/Secy.* Terry Nathan. E-mail Terry@ ibpa-online.org.

International Standard Book Numbering U.S. Agency, 630 Central Ave., New Providence, NJ 07974. Tel. 888-269-5372, fax 908-219-0188, e-mail isbn-san@bowker.com, World Wide Web http://www.isbn.org. *Dir., Identifier Services* Beat Barblan.

Jewish Book Council, 520 Eighth Ave., Fourth fl., New York, NY 10018. Tel. 212-201-2920, fax 212-532-4952, e-mail jbc@jewish books.org, World Wide Web http://www. jewishbookcouncil.org. *Pres.* Lawrence J. Krule; *V.P.* Judith Lieberman; *Secy.* Mimi S. Frank; *Dir.* Carolyn Starman Hessel.

Library Binding Institute/Hardcover Binders International, 4400 PGA Blvd., Suite 600, Palm Beach Gardens, FL 33410. Tel. 561-745-6821, fax 561-775-0089, e-mail info@ lbibinders.org, World Wide Web http://www. lbibinders.org. *Pres.* Jack Tolbert, National Lib. Bindery Co. of Georgia. E-mail nlbga@ mindspring.com; *V.P.* Duncan Campbell, Campbell-Logan Bindery. E-mail duncan@ campbell-logan.com; *Exec. Dir.* Debra Nolan. E-mail dnolan@lbibinders.org.

Midwest Independent Publishers Assn. (MIPA), P.O. Box 18536, St. Paul, MN 55118-0536. Tel. 651-917-0021 or 651-917-0021, World Wide Web http://www.mipa.org. *Pres.* Sher-

ry Roberts, Roberts Group. Tel. 952-322-4005, e-mail sherry@editorialservice.com; *V.P.* to be announced; *Secy.* Judith Palmateer, Amber Skye Publishing. Tel. 651-452-0463, e-mail jpalmateer0463@comcast. net; *Treas.* Dorie McClelland, Spring Book Design. Tel. 651-457-0258, e-mail dorie@ springbookdesign.com.

Miniature Book Society. *Pres.* Mark Palkovic. E-mail mark.palkovic@uc.edu; *V.P.* Stephen Byrne. E-mail sb@finalscore.demon.co.uk; *Secy.* Edward Hoyenski. E-mail ehoyensk@ library.unt.edu; *Treas.* Karen Nyman. E-mail karennyman@cox.net; *Past Pres.* Julian I. Edison. E-mail jiestl@mac.com. World Wide Web http://www.mbs.org.

Minnesota Book Publishers' Roundtable. E-mail information@publishersroundtable.org, World Wide Web http://www.publishers roundtable.org. *Secy.* Andrew Karre, Lerner Publishing Group.

Mountains and Plains Independent Booksellers Assn., 3278 Big Spruce Way, Park City, UT 84098. Tel. 435-649-6079, fax 435-649-6105, e-mail laura@mountainsplains.org, World Wide Web http://www.mountains plains.org. *Pres.* Andrea Avantaggio, Maria's Bookshop, 960 Main Ave., Durango, CO 81301. Tel. 970-247-1438, fax 970-247-5916, e-mail andrea@mariasbookshop.com; *V.P./Secy.* Liesl Freudenstein, Boulder Book Store, 1107 Pearl St., Boulder, CO 80302. Tel. 303-447-2074, fax 303-447-3946, e-mail childrens@boulderbookstore.com; *Exec. Dir.* Laura Ayrey.

MPA—The Assn. of Magazine Media (formerly Magazine Publishers of America), 810 Seventh Ave., 24th fl., New York, NY 10019. Tel. 212-872-3700, e-mail mpa@ magazine.org, World Wide Web http://www. magazine.org. *Pres.* Mary Berner. Tel. 212-872-3710, e-mail president@magazine.org; *Chair* Michael A. Clinton, Hearst Magazines; *V. Chair* Efrem Zimbalist III, Active Interest Media.

NAPL (formerly National Assn. for Printing Leadership), 1 Meadowlands Plaza, Suite 1511, East Rutherford, NJ 07073. Tel. 800-642-6275, 201-634-9600, fax 201-634-0324, e-mail info@napl.org, World Wide Web http://www.napl.org. *Pres./CEO* Joseph P. Truncale. E-mail jtruncale@napl. org.

National Assn. of College Stores, 500 E. Lorain St., Oberlin, OH 44074-1294. Tel. 800-622-7498, 440-775-7777, fax 440-775-4769, e-mail info@nacs.org, World Wide Web http://www.nacs.org. *Pres.* George Masforroll; *Pres.-Elect* Todd Summer; *CEO* Brian Cartier. E-mail bcartier@nacs.org.

National Book Foundation, 95 Madison Ave., Suite 709, New York, NY 10016. Tel. 212-685-0261, fax 212-213-6570, e-mail national book@nationalbook.org, World Wide Web http://www.nationalbook.org.

National Coalition Against Censorship (NCAC), 19 Fulton St., Suite 407, New York, NY 10038. Tel. 212-807-6222, fax 212-807-6245, e-mail ncac@ncac.org, World Wide Web http://www.ncac.org. *Exec. Dir.* Joan E. Bertin; *Dirs.* Michael Bamberger, Chris Csikszentmihalyi, Judy Blume, Susan Clare, Chris Finan, Eric M. Freedman, Robie Harris, Michael Jacobs, Chris Peterson, Larry Siems, Emily Whitfield.

New Atlantic Independent Booksellers Assn. (NAIBA), 2667 Hyacinth St., Westbury, NY 11590. Tel. 516-333-0681, fax 516-333-0689, e-mail info@naiba.com, World Wide Web http://www.newatlanticbooks. com. *Pres.* Margot Sage-El, Watchung Booksellers, Watchung Plaza, 54 Fairfield St., Montclair, NJ 07042. Tel. 973-744-7177, fax 973-783-5899, e-mail margot@watchungbooksellers.com; *Exec. Dir.* Eileen Dengler.

New England Independent Booksellers Assn., 1955 Massachusetts Ave., Cambridge, MA 02140-1405, e-mail steve@neba.org, World Wide Web http://www.newenglandbooks. crg. *Pres.* Annie Philbrick, Bank Square Books, Mystic, Connecticut. E-mail bank squarebks@msn.com; *V.P.* Lisa Sullivan, Bartleby's Books, Wilmington, Vermont. E-mail lisa@bookcellarvt.com; *Treas.* Michael Hermann, Gibson's Bookstore, Concord, New Hampshire. E-mail gibsons@totalnetnh.net; *Exec. Dir.* Steve Fischer.

New York Center for Independent Publishing (formerly the Small Press Center), c/o General Society Lib., 20 W. 44 St., New York, NY 10036. Tel. 212-764-7021, e-mail info@nycip.org.

North American Bookdealers Exchange (NABE), Box 606, Cottage Grove, OR 97424. Tel./fax 541-942-7455, e-mail nabe@bookmarketingprofits.com, World Wide Web http://bookmarketingprofits.com. *Dir.* Al Galasso.

Northern California Independent Booksellers Assn., Presidio National Park, 1007 General Kennedy Ave., P.O. Box 29169, San Francisco, CA 94129. Tel. 415-561-7686, fax 415-561-7685, e-mail office@nciba.com, World Wide Web http://www.nciba.com. *Pres.* Michael Barnard; *V.P.* Calvin Crosby; *Exec. Dir.* Hut Landon.

Pacific Northwest Booksellers Assn., 338 W. 11 Ave., Eugene, OR 97401-3062. Tel. 541-683-4363, fax 541-683-3910, e-mail info@pnba.org, World Wide Web http://www.pnba.org, blog Northwest Book Lovers (http://www.nwbooklovers.org). *Pres.* Karla Nelson, Time Enough Books. E-mail tebooks@willapabay.org; *Exec. Dir.* Thom Chambliss.

PEN American Center, Div. of International PEN, 588 Broadway, Suite 303, New York, NY 10012. Tel. 212-334-1660, fax 212-334-2181, e-mail pen@pen.org, World Wide Web http://www.pen.org. *Pres.* Peter Godwin; *Exec. V.P.* John Troubh; *V.P.s* Ron Chernow, Victoria Redel; *Secy.* Elinor Lipman; *Exec. Dir.* Steven L. Isenberg. E-mail sisenberg@pen.org.

Periodical and Book Assn. of America, 481 Eighth Ave., Suite 526, New York, NY 10001. Tel. 212-563-6502, fax 212-563-4098, World Wide Web http://www.pbaa. net. *Pres.* Jay Annis. E-mail jannis@taunton.com; *Chair* Will Michalopoulos. E-mail wmichalopoulos@hearst.com; *Exec. Dir.* Lisa W. Scott. E-mail lisawscott@hotmail.com; *Assoc. Dir.* Jose Cancio. E-mail jcancio@@pbaa.net.

Publishers Marketing Assn. (PMA). See Independent Book Publishers Assn.

Publishing Professionals Network (formerly Bookbuilders West), 9328 Elk Grove Blvd., Suite 105, Elk Grove, CA 95624. Tel. 415-670-9564, e-mail operations@bookbuilders. org, World Wide Web http://www.book builders.org. *Pres.* David Zielonka; *V.P.* Tona Pearce Myers.

Romance Writers of America, 14615 Benfer Rd., Houston, TX 77069. Tel. 832-717-5200, fax 832-717-5201, e-mail info@rwa. org, World Wide Web http://www.rwa.org. *Pres.* Sylvia Day. E-mail sylvia@sylviaday.

com; *Pres.-Elect* Terry McLaughlin. E-mail terry@terrymclaughlin.com; *Past Pres.* Linda Winstead Jones; *Exec. Dir.* Allison Kelley. E-mail allison.kelley@rwa.org.

Science Fiction and Fantasy Writers of America, P.O. Box 3238, Enfield, CT 06083-3238. World Wide Web http://www.sfwa.org. *Pres.* John Scalzi. E-mail president@sfwa.org; *V.P.* Rachel Swirsky. E-mail vp@sfwa.org; *Secy.* Ann Leckie. E-mail secretary@sfwa.org; *Treas.* Bud Sparhawk. E-mail treasurer@sfwa.org.

Small Publishers Assn. of North America (SPAN), P.O. Box 9725, Colorado Springs, CO 80932. Tel. 719-924-5534, fax 719-213-2602, e-mail info@spannet.org, World Wide Web http://www.spannet.org. *Pres.* Scott Flora; *Exec. Dir.* Brian Jud.

Society of Children's Book Writers and Illustrators (SCBWI), 8271 Beverly Blvd., Los Angeles, CA 90048. Tel. 323-782-1010, fax 323-782-1892, e-mail scbwi@scbwi.org, World Wide Web http://www.scbwi.org. *Pres.* Stephen Mooser. E-mail stephen mooser@scbwi.org; *Exec. Dir.* Lin Oliver.

Society of Illustrators (SI), 128 E. 63 St., New York, NY 10065. Tel. 212-838-2560, fax 212-838-2561, e-mail info@societyillustrators.org, World Wide Web http://www.society illustrators.org. *Pres.* Dennis Dittrich; *Exec. V.P.* Tim O'Brien; *V.P.* Victor Juhasz; *Secy.* Joan Chiverton; *Exec. Dir.* Anelle Miller. E-mail anelle@societyillustrators.org.

Southern Independent Booksellers Alliance (SIBA), 3806 Yale Ave., Columbia, SC 29205. Tel. 803-994-9530, fax 309-410-0211, e-mail info@sibaweb.com, World Wide Web http://www.sibaweb.com. *Pres.* Jamie Fiocco; *Exec. Dir.* Wanda Jewell.

Technical Assn. of the Pulp and Paper Industry, 15 Technology Pkwy. S., Norcross, GA 30092 (P.O. Box 105113, Atlanta, GA 30348). Tel. 770-446-1400, fax 770-446-6947, World Wide Web http://www.tappi.org. *Pres./CEO* Larry N. Montague. E-mail lmontague@tappi.org; *Chair* Norman F. Marsolan; *V. Chair* Thomas J. Garland.

Western Writers of America, c/o Candy Moulton, 271 CR 219, Encampment, WY 82325 Tel. 307-329-8942, e-mail wwa.moulton@gmail.com, World Wide Web http://www.westernwriters.org. *Pres.* Dusty Richards; *V.P.* Sherry Monahan; *Exec. Dir./Secy.-Treas.* Candy Moulton.

Women's National Book Assn., P.O. Box 237, FDR Sta., New York, NY 10150. Tel./fax 212-208-4629, e-mail info@wnba-books.org, World Wide Web http://www.wnba-books.org. *Pres.* Valerie Tomaselli; *V.P./Pres.-Elect* Carin Siegfried; *Secy.* Annette Marie Haley; *Treas.* Gloria Toler.

International and Foreign Book Trade Associations

For Canadian book trade associations, see the preceding section, "Book Trade Associations, United States and Canada." For a more extensive list of book trade organizations outside the United States and Canada, with more detailed information, consult *International Literary Market Place* (Information Today, Inc.), which also provides extensive lists of major bookstores and publishers in each country.

International

African Publishers' Network, 2 Lynton Ave., Marlborough, Harare, Zimbabwe. Tel./fax 4-300790, e-mail apnet@zol.co.zw, World Wide Web http://www.african-publishers. net. *Chair* Samuel Kolawole.

Afro-Asian Book Council, 4835/24 Ansari Rd., New Delhi 110002, India. Tel. 11-2325-8865, fax 11-2326-7437, e-mail afro@aab council.org, World Wide Web http://www. aabcouncil.org. *Secy.-Gen.* Sukumar Das; *Dir.* Saumya Gupta.

Centro Régional para el Fomento del Libro en América Latina y el Caribe (CERLALC) (Regional Center for Book Promotion in Latin America and the Caribbean), Calle 70, No. 9-52, Bogotá DC, Colombia. Tel. 1-540-2071, fax 1-541-6398, e-mail libro@ cerlalc.com, World Wide Web http://www. cerlalc.org. *Dir.* Fernando Zapata Lopez.

Federation of European Publishers, rue Montoyer 31, Boîte 8, 1000 Brussels, Belgium. Tel. 2-770-11-10, fax 2-771-20-71, e-mail info@fep-fee.eu, World Wide Web http:// www.fep-fee.be. *Pres.* Fergal Tobin; *Dir.-Gen.* Anne Bergman-Tahon.

International Assn. of Scientific, Technical, and Medical Publishers (STM), Prama House, 267 Banbury Rd., Oxford OX2 7HT, England. Tel. 44-1865-339-321, fax 44-1865-339-325, e-mail info@stm-assoc.org, World Wide Web http://www.stm-assoc.org. *Chair* Eric Merkel-Sobotta; *CEO* Michael Mabe.

International Board on Books for Young People (IBBY), Nonnenweg 12, 4003 Basel, Switzerland. Tel. 61-272-29-17, fax 61-272-27-57, e-mail ibby@ibby.org, World Wide Web http://www.ibby.org. *Exec. Dir.* Elizabeth Page.

International League of Antiquarian Booksellers (ILAB), c/o Cornstalk Bookshop, 112 Glebe Point Rd., Sydney, NSW 2037, Australia. Tel. 2-9660-4889, fax 2-9552-2670, e-mail secretary@ilab.org, World Wide Web http://www.ilab.org. *Pres.* Arnoud Gerits; *Gen. Secy.* Paul Feain.

International Publishers Assn. (Union Internationale des Editeurs), ave. de Miremont 3, CH-1206 Geneva, Switzerland. Tel. 22-704-1820, fax 22-704-1821, e-mail secretariat@ internationalpublishers.org, World Wide Web http://www.internationalpublishers.org. *Pres.* Youngsuk Chi; *Secy.-Gen.* Jens Bammel.

National

Argentina

Cámara Argentina del Libro (Argentine Book Assn.), Av. Belgrano 1580, 4 piso, C1093AAQ Buenos Aires. Tel. 11-4381-8383, fax 11-4381-9253, e-mail cal@ editores.org.ar, World Wide Web http:// www.editores.org.ar. *Pres.* Isaac Rubizal.

Fundación El Libro (Book Foundation), Hipolito Yrigoyen 1628, 5 piso, C1089AAF Buenos Aires. Tel. 11-4370-0600, fax 11-4370-0607, e-mail fundacion@el-libro.com. ar, World Wide Web http://www.el-libro.org. ar. *Pres.* Gustavo G. Canevaro; *Dir.* Gabriela Adamo.

Australia

Australian and New Zealand Assn. of Antiquarian Booksellers, P.O. Box 1610, Carindale, Qld. 4152. Tel./fax 07-3843-0556, e-mail admin@anzaab.com, World Wide Web http://www.anzaab.com. *Pres.* Sally Burdon.

Australian Booksellers Assn., 828 High St., Unit 9, Kew East, Vic. 3102. Tel. 3-9859-7322, fax 3-9859-7344, e-mail mail@aba. org.au, World Wide Web http://www.aba. org.au. *Pres.* Jon Page; *CEO* Joel Becker.

Australian Publishers Assn., 60/89 Jones St., Ultimo, NSW 2007. Tel. 2-9281-9788, fax 2-9281-1073, e-mail apa@publishers.asn. au, World Wide Web http://www.publishers. asn.au. *CEO* Maree McCaskill.

Austria

Hauptverband des Österreichischen Buchhandels (Austrian Publishers and Booksellers Assn.), Grünangergasse 4, A-1010 Vienna. Tel. 1-512-15-35, fax 1-512-84-82, e-mail sekretariat@hvb.at, World Wide Web http://www.buecher.at. *Mgr.* Inge Kralupper.

Verband der Antiquare Österreichs (Austrian Antiquarian Booksellers Assn.), Grünangergasse 4, A-1010 Vienna. Tel. 1-512-1535-14, e-mail sekretariat@hvb.at, World Wide Web http://www.antiquare.at.

Belarus

National Book Chamber of Belarus, 31a V Khoruzhei Str., Rm. 707, 220002 Minsk. Tel. 17-289-33-96, fax 17-334-78-47, World Wide Web http://www.natbook.org.by. *Dir.* Elena V. Ivanova. E-mail elvit@natbook. org.by.

Belgium

Vlaamse Boekverkopersbond (Flemish Booksellers Assn.), Te Buelaerlei 37, 2140 Borgerhout. Tel. 03-230-89-23, fax 3-281-22-40, World Wide Web http://www.boek.be. *CEO* Geert Joris; *Contact* Patricia De Laet. E-mail patricia.delaet@boek.be.

Vlaamse Uitgevers Vereniging (Flemish Publishers Assn.), Huis van het Boek, Te Boelaerlei 37, 2140 Borgerhout. Tel. 03-287-66-92, fax 03-281-22-40, e-mail vuv@boek.be, World Wide Web http://www.boekenvak.be/voor-uitgevers/vlaamse-uitgeversvereniging. *Contact* Geert Van den Bossche.

Bolivia

Cámara Boliviana del Libro (Bolivian Booksellers Assn.), Calle Capitan Ravelo No. 2116, 682 La Paz. Tel. 2-211-3264, e-mail cabolib@entelnet.bo, World Wide Web http://www.cabolib.org.bo. *Gen. Mgr.* Ana Patricia Navarro.

Brazil

Cámara Brasileira do Livro (Brazilian Book Assn.), Rua Cristiano Viana 91, Jardim Paulista, 05411-000 Sao Paulo-SP. Tel./fax 11-3069-1300, e-mail cbl@cbl.org.br, World Wide Web http://www.cbl.org.br. *Pres.* Karine Goncalves Pansa.

Sindicato Nacional dos Editores de Livros (Brazilian Publishers Assn.), Rue da Ajuda 35-18 andar, 20040-000 Rio de Janeiro-RJ. Tel. 21-2533-0399, fax 21-2533-0422, e-mail snel@snel.org.br, World Wide Web http://www.snel.org.br. *Pres.* Sonia Machado Jardim.

Chile

Cámara Chilena del Libro AG (Chilean Assn. of Publishers, Distributors, and Booksellers), Av. Libertador Bernardo O'Higgins 1370, Oficina 501, Santiago. Tel. 2-672-0348, fax 2-687-4271, e-mail prolibro@tie. cl, World Wide Web http://www.camlibro.cl. *Pres.* Arturo Infante.

Colombia

Cámara Colombiana del Libro (Colombian Book Assn.), Calle 35, No. 5A 05, Bogotá. Tel. 1-323-01-11, fax 1-285-10-82, e-mail camlibro@camlibro.com.co, World Wide Web http://www.camlibro.com.co. *Pres.* Enrique Gonzalez Villa; *Secy.-Gen.* Jose Manuel Ramirez Sarmiento.

Czech Republic

Svaz ceských knihkupcu a nakladatelu (Czech Publishers and Booksellers Assn.), P.O. Box 177, 110 01 Prague. Tel. 224-219-944, fax 224-219-942, e-mail sckn@sckn.cz, World Wide Web http://www.sckn.cz. *Chair* Vladimir Pistorius.

Denmark

Danske Boghandlerforening (Danish Booksellers Assn.), Langebrogade 6 opgang J, 1 sal, 1411 Copenhagen K. Tel. 3254-2255, fax 3254-0041, e-mail ddb@bogpost.dk, World WideWebhttp://www.boghandlerforeningen. dk.

Danske Forlæggerforening (Danish Publishers Assn.), Publishers Assn. Exchange, 1217 Copenhagen K. Tel. 45-33-15-66-88, e-mail danishpublishers@danishpublishers.dk, World Wide Web http://www.danskeforlag.dk. *Dir.* Christine Bødtcher-Hansen.

Ecuador

Cámara Ecuatoriana del Libro, Avda. Eloy Alfaro, N29-61 e Inglaterra, Edif. Eloy Alfaro, 9 no. piso, Quito. Tel. 2-5533-11, fax 2-222-150, e-mail celnp@uio.satnet.net, World Wide Web http://celibro.org.ec. *Pres.* Fabian Luzuriaga.

Egypt

General Egyptian Book Organization (GEBO), P.O. Box 235, Cairo 11511. Tel. 2-257-7531, fax 2-257-54213, e-mail info@gebo.gov.eg, World Wide Web http://www.gebo.gov.eg. *Chair* Nasser Al-Ansary.

Estonia

Estonian Publishers Assn., Roosikrantsi 6-207, 10119 Tallinn. Tel. 372-644-9866, fax 372-617-7550, e-mail kirjastusteliit@eki.ee, World Wide Web http://www.estbook.com. *Managing Dir.* Kaidi Urmet.

Finland

Kirjakauppaliitto Ry (Booksellers Assn. of Finland), Urho Kekkosen Katu 8 C 34b, 00100 Helsinki. Tel. 9-6859-9110, fax 9-6859-9119, e-mail toimisto@kirjakauppaliitto.fi, World Wide Web http://www.kirjakauppaliitto.fi. *Pres.* Tuula Korte; *Managing Dir.* Katriina Jaakkola.

Suomen Kustannusyhdistys (Finnish Book Publishers Assn.), P.O. Box 177, Lönnro-tinkatu 11 A, 00121, Helsinki. Tel. 358-9-228-77-250, fax 358-9-612-1226, World Wide Web http://www.kustantajat.fi/en. *Dir.* Sakari Laiho.

France

Bureau International de l'Edition Française (BIEF) (International Bureau of French Publishing), 115 blvd. Saint-Germain, F-75006 Paris. Tel. 01-44-41-13-13, fax 01-46-34-63-83, e-mail info@bief.org, World Wide Web http://www.bief.org. *Dir.* Jean-Guy Boin. *New York Branch* French Publishers Agency, 853 Broadway, Suite 1509, New York, NY 10003-4703. Tel./fax 212-254-4540, World Wide Web http://french pubagency.com.

Cercle de la Librairie (Circle of Professionals of the Book Trade), 35 rue Grégoire-de-Tours, F-75006 Paris. Tel. 01-44-41-28-00, fax 01-44-41-28-65, e-mail commercial@electre.com, World Wide Web http://www.electre.com.

Syndicat de la Librairie Française, Hotel de Massa, 38 rue du Faubourg Saint-Jacques, F-75014 Paris. Tel. 01-53-62-23-10, fax 01-53-62-10-45, e-mail contact@union-librarie.fr, World Wide Web http://www.syndicat-librairie.fr. *Delegate Gen.* Guillaume Husson.

Syndicat National de la Librairie Ancienne et Moderne (SLAM) (National Assn. of Antiquarian and Modern Booksellers), 4 rue Gît-le-Coeur, F-75006 Paris. Tel. 01-43-29-46-38, fax 01-43-25-41-63, e-mail slam-livre@wanadoo.fr, World Wide Web http://www.slam-livre.fr. *Pres.* Frederic Castaing.

Syndicat National de l'Edition (SNE) (National Union of Publishers), 115 blvd. Saint-Germain, F-75006 Paris. Tel. 01-44-41-40-50, fax 01-44-41-40-77, World Wide Web http://www.sne.fr. *Pres.* Antoine Gallimard.

Germany

Börsenverein des Deutschen Buchhandels e.V. (Stock Exchange of German Booksellers), Braubachstr. 16, 60311 Frankfurt-am-Main. Tel. 49-69-1306-0, fax 49-69-1306-201, e-mail info@boev.de, World Wide Web http://www.boersenverein.de. *CEO* Alexander Skipis.

Verband Deutscher Antiquare e.V. (German Antiquarian Booksellers Assn.), Geschäfts-stelle, Seeblick 1, 56459 Elbingen. Tel. 6435-90-91-47, fax 6435-90-91-48, e-mail buch@antiquare.de, World Wide Web http://www.antiquare.de. *Chair* Christian Hesse.

Greece

Hellenic Federation of Publishers and Booksellers, 73 Themistocleous St., 106 83 Athens. Tel. 2103-300-924, fax 2133-301-617, e-mail secretary@poev.gr, World Wide Web http://www.poev.gr. *Pres.* Annie Ragia.

Hungary

Magyar Könyvkiadók és Könyvterjesztök Egyesülése (Assn. of Hungarian Publishers and Booksellers), Postfach 130, 1367 Budapest. Tel. 1-343-2540, fax 1-343-2541, e-mail mkke@mkke.hu, World Wide Web http://www.mkke.hu. *Pres.* Tamas Kolosi.

Iceland

Félag Islenskra Bókaútgefenda (Icelandic Publishers Assn.), Baronsstig 5, 101 Reykjavik. Tel. 511-8020, fax 511-5020, e-mail baekur@simnet.is, World Wide Web http://www.bokautgafa.is. *Chair* Kristjan B. Jonasson.

India

Federation of Indian Publishers, Federation House, 18/1C Institutional Area, Aruna Asaf Ali Marg, New Delhi 110067. Tel. 11-2696-4847, fax 11-2686-4054, e-mail fip1@sify.com, World Wide Web http://www.fipindia.org. *Pres.* Anand Bhushan.

Indonesia

Ikatan Penerbit Indonesia (Assn. of Indonesian Book Publishers), Jl. Kalipasir 32, Jakarta 10330. Tel. 21-314-1907, fax 21-314-6050, e-mail sekretariat@ikapi.org, World Wide Web http://www.ikapi.org. *Pres.* Lucya Andam Dewi; *Secy.-Gen.* Husni Syawie.

Ireland

Publishing Ireland/Foilsiu Eireann (formerly CLÉ: The Irish Book Publishers' Assn.), 25 Denzille Lane, Dublin 2. Tel. 639-4868, e-mail info@publishingireland.com, World Wide Web http://www.publishingireland.com. *Pres.* Frank Scott-Lennon.

Israel

Book Publishers' Assn. of Israel, 29 Carlebach St., 67132 Tel Aviv. Tel. 3-561-4121, fax 3-561-1996, e-mail info@tbpai.co.il, World Wide Web http://www.tbpai.co.il. *Chair* Yaron Sadan.

Italy

Associazione Italiana Editori (Italian Publishers Assn.), Corso di Porta Romana 108, 20122 Milan. Tel. 2-89-28-0800, fax 2-89-28-0860, e-mail aie@aie.it, World Wide Web http://www.aie.it. *Dir.* Alfieri Lorenzon.

Associazione Librai Antiquari d'Italia (Antiquarian Booksellers Assn. of Italy), Via Cassia 1020, Rome. Tel. 39-347-646-9147, fax 39-06-2332-8979, e-mail alai@alai.it, World Wide Web http://www.alai.it. *Pres.* Fabrizio Govi.

Japan

Antiquarian Booksellers Assn. of Japan, 27 Sakamachi, Shinjuku-ku, Tokyo 160-0002. Tel. 81-03-3357-1417, fax 81-03-3356-8730, e-mail abaj@abaj.gr.jp, World Wide Web http://www.abaj.gr.jp. *Pres.* Takao Nakao.

Japan Assn. of International Publications (formerly Japan Book Importers Assn.), c/o UPS, 1-32-5 Higashi-shinagawa, Shinagawa-ku, Toyko 140-0002. Tel. 3-5479-7269, fax 3-5479-7307, e-mail office@jaip.jp, World Wide Web http://www.jaip.jp. *Exec. Dir.* Takashi Yamakawa.

Japan Book Publishers Assn., 6 Fukuro-machi, Shinjuku-ku, Tokyo 162-0828. Tel. 3-3268-1302, fax 3-3268-1196, e-mail research@jbpa.or.jp, World Wide Web http://www.jbpa.or.jp. *Pres.* Masahiro Oga.

Kenya

Kenya Publishers Assn., P.O. Box 42767, Nairobi 00100. Tel. 20-375-2344, fax 20-375-4076, e-mail info@kenyapublishers.org, World Wide Web http://www.kenyapublishers.org. *Chair* Lawrence Njagi; *Exec. Officer* James Odhiambo.

Korea (Republic of)

Korean Publishers Assn., 105-2 Sagan-dong, Jongro-gu, Seoul 110-190. Tel. 70-7126-4720, fax 2-738-5414, e-mail webmaster@

kpa21.or.kr, World Wide Web http://www.
kpa21.or.kr. *Pres.* Sok-Ghee Baek.

Latvia

Latvian Publishers' Assn., Baznicas 37, LV-
1010 Riga. Tel./fax 67-217-730, e-mail
lga@gramatizdeveji.lv, World Wide Web
http://www.gramatizdeveji.lv. *Pres.* Janis
Leja; *Exec. Dir.* Dace Pugaca.

Lithuania

Lithuanian Publishers Assn., Lukiskes g 5-317,
LT-01108 Vilnius. Tel./fax 5-261-77-40, e-
mail info@lla.lt, World Wide Web http://
www.lla.lt. *Pres.* Lolita Varanaviciene; *Exec.
Dir.* Aida Dobkeviciute-Dzioveniene.

Malaysia

Malaysian Book Publishers' Assn., No. 7-6,
Block E2, Jl PJU 1/42A, Dataran Prima 47301
Petaling Jaya, Selangor. Tel. 3-7880-5840,
fax 3-7880-5841, e-mail info@mabopa.
com.my, World Wide Web http://www.
mabopa.com.my. *Pres.* Husammuddin Yaa-
cub.

Mexico

Cámara Nacional de la Industria Editorial Mexicana (Mexican Publishers' Assn.), Holanda
No 13, Col San Diego Churubusco, Deleg
Coyoacan, 04120 Mexico DF. Tel. 155-
55-88-20-11, fax 155-56-04-31-47, e-mail
contacto@caniem.com, World Wide Web
http://www.caniem.com. *Pres.* Victorico Al-
bores Santiago.

The Netherlands

KVB—Koninklijke Vereeniging van het Boek-
envak (Royal Society for the Book Trade),
Herengracht 166, 1016 BP Amsterdam. Tel.
20-624-02-12, fax 20-620-88-71, e-mail
info@kvb.nl, World Wide Web http://www.
kvb.nl. *Dir.* Marty Langeler.
Nederlands Uitgeversverbond (Royal Dutch
Publishers Assn.), Postbus 12040, 1100 AA
Amsterdam. Tel. 20-430-9150, fax 20-430-
9199, e-mail info@nuv.nl, World Wide Web
http://www.nuv.nl. *Pres.* Loek Hermans.
Nederlandsche Vereeniging van Antiquaren
(Netherlands Assn. of Antiquarian Booksell-

ers), Singel 319, 1012 WJ Amsterdam. Tel.
70-364-98-40, fax 70-364-33-40, e-mail
info@nvva.nl, World Wide Web http://www.
nvva.nl. *Pres.* Ton Kok.
Nederlandse Boekverkopersbond (Dutch
Booksellers Assn.), Postbus 32, 3720 AA
Bilthoven. Tel. 30-22-87-956, fax 030-22-
84-566, e-mail info@boekbond.nl, World
Wide Web http://www.boekbond.nl. *Pres.*
Dick Anbeek.

New Zealand

Booksellers New Zealand, P.O. Box 25033,
Wellington 6146. Tel. 4-472-1908, fax
4-472-1912, e-mail info@booksellers.co.nz,
World Wide Web http://www.booksellers.
co.nz. *CEO* Lincoln Gould.

Nigeria

Nigerian Publishers Assn., GPO Box 2541,
Ibadan. Tel. 2-751-5352, e-mail info@
nigerianpublishers.org, World Wide Web
http://www.nigerianpublishers.org. *Pres.*
Samuel Kolawole.

Norway

Norske Bokhandlerforening (Norwegian
Booksellers Assn.), Øvre Vollgate 15, 0158
Oslo. Tel. 22-40-45-40, fax 22-41-12-89, e-
mail post@bokogsamfunn.no, World Wide
Web http://www.bokogsamfunn.no. *Editor*
Dag H. Nestegard.
Norske Forleggerforening (Norwegian Pub-
lishers Assn.), Øvre Vollgate 15, 0158 Oslo.
Tel. 22-00-75-80, fax 22-33-38-30, e-mail
dnf@forleggerforeningen.no, World Wide
Web http://www.forleggerforeningen.no.
Managing Dir. Kristen Einarsson.

Peru

Cámara Peruana del Libro (Peruvian Publishers Assn.), Av. Cuba 427, Jesús María,
Apdo. 10253, Lima 11. Tel. 1-472-9516,
fax 1-265-0735, e-mail cp-libro@cpl.org.
pe, World Wide Web http://www.cpl.org.pe.
Pres. Jaime Carbajal Perez.

Philippines

Philippine Educational Publishers Assn., 84P
Florentino St. Sta., Mesa Heights, Quezon

City. Tel. 63-2-711-7169, fax 63-2-559-1586, e-mail sasantiago@rexpublishing.com.ph. *Mgr.* Sonia Santiago.

Poland

Polskie Towarzystwo Wydawców Książek (Polish Society of Book Editors), ul. Swieto krzyska 30, lok 156, 00-116 Warsaw. Tel. 22-407-77-30, fax 22-850-34-76, e-mail ptwk@wp.pl, World Wide Web http://www.wydawca.com.pl. *Dir.* Maria Kuisz.

Władze Stowarzyszenia Księgarzy Polskich (Assn. of Polish Booksellers), ul. Mazowiecka 6/8 def. 414, 00-048 Warsaw. Tel./fax 0-22-827-93-81, e-mail skp@ksiegarze.org.pl, World Wide Web http://www.ksiegarze.org.pl. *Chair* Waldemar Janaszkiewicz.

Portugal

Associação Portuguesa de Editores e Livreiros (Portuguese Assn. of Publishers and Booksellers), Av. dos Estados Unidas da America 97, 6 Esq., 1700-167 Lisbon. Tel. 21-843-51-80, fax 21-848-93-77, e-mail geral@apel.pt, World Wide Web http://www.apel.pt. *Pres.* Pedro Moura Bessa.

Russia

Assn. of Book Publishers of Russia, ul. B. Nikitskaya 44, 121069 Moscow. Tel. 495-202-1174, fax 495-202-3989, e-mail askibook@gmail.com, World Wide Web http://www.aski.ru. *Pres.* Konstantin V. Chechenev.

Rossiiskaya Knizhnaya Palata (Russian Book Chamber), Kremlin Embankment, 1/9, 119019 Moscow. Tel. 495-688-96-89, fax 495-688-99-91, e-mail info@bookchamber.ru, World Wide Web http://www.bookchamber.ru. *Dir. Gen.* Elena Nogina.

Serbia and Montenegro

Assn. of Yugoslav Publishers and Booksellers, Kneza Milosa 25/I, 11000 Belgrade. Tel. 11-642-533, fax 11-646-339.

Singapore

Singapore Book Publishers Assn., 86 Marine Parade Central No. 03-213, Singapore 440086. Tel. 6344-7801, fax 6344-0897, e-mail info@singaporebookpublishers.sg, World Wide Web http://www.singaporebook publishers.sg. *Pres.* Triena Noeline Ong.

Slovenia

Zdruzenie Zaloznikov in Knjigotrzcev Slovenije Gospodarska Zbornica Slovenije (Assn. of Publishers and Booksellers of Slovenia), Dimiceva 13, SI 1000 Ljubljana. Tel. 1-5898-000, fax 1-5898-100, e-mail info@gzs.si, World Wide Web http://www.gzs.si/slo.

South Africa

Publishers Assn. of South Africa (PASA), P.O. Box 18223, Wynberg 7824. Tel. 21-762-9083, fax 21-762-2763, e-mail pasa@publishsa.co.za, World Wide Web http://www.publishsa.co.za. *Exec. Dir.* Brian Wafawarowa.

South African Booksellers Assn. (formerly Associated Booksellers of Southern Africa), P.O. Box 870, Bellville 7535. Tel. 21-945-1572, fax 21-245-1361, e-mail saba@sabooksellers.com, World Wide Web http://sabooksellers.com. *Chair and Pres.* Sydwell Molosi.

Spain

Federación de Gremios de Editores de España (Federation of Spanish Publishers Assns.), Cea Bermúdez 44-2, 28003 Madrid. Tel. 91-534-51-95, fax 91-535-26-25, e-mail fgee@fge.es, World Wide Web http://www.federacioneditores.org. *Pres.* Antoni Comas; *Exec. Dir.* Antonio María Avila.

Sri Lanka

Sri Lanka Book Publishers Assn., 53 Maligakanda Rd., Colombo 10. Tel./fax 112-696-821, e-mail bookpub@sltnet.lk, World Wide Web http://www.bookpublishers.lk. *Pres.* Ariyadasa Weeraman; *Gen. Secy.* Upali Wanigasooriya.

Sudan

Sudanese Publishers' Assn., c/o Institute of African and Asian Studies, Khartoum Univ.,

F.O. Box 321, Khartoum 11115. Tel. 11-77-0022. *Dir.* Al-Amin Abu Manga Mohamed.

Sweden

Svenska Förläggareföreningen (Swedish Publishers Assn.), Drottninggatan 97, S-11360 Stockholm. Tel. 8-736-19-40, fax 8-736-19-44, e-mail info@forlaggare.se, World Wide Web http://www.forlaggare.se. *Pres. and Dir.* Kristina Ahlinder.

Switzerland

Swiss Booksellers and Publishers Association (SBVV), Alder Strasse 40, P.O. Box CH-8034, Zurich. Tel. 44-421-36-00, fax 44-421-36-18, e-mail info@sbvv.ch, World Wide Web http://www.swissbooks.ch. *CEO* Dani Landolf.

Thailand

Publishers and Booksellers Assn. of Thailand, 83/159 Moo Chinnakhet 2, Ngam Wong Wan Rd., Thung Song Hong, Lak Si, Bangkok 10210. Tel. 2-954-9560-4, fax 2-954-9565-6, e-mail info@pubat.or.th, World Wide Web http://www.pubat.or.th. *Pres.* Worapan Lokitsatapo.

Uganda

Uganda Publishers Assn., P.O. Box 7732, Kampala. Tel. 414-286-093, fax 414-286-397. *Chair* David Kibuuka; *Gen. Secy.* Martin Okia.

United Kingdom

Antiquarian Booksellers Assn., Sackville House, 40 Piccadilly, London W1J 0DR, England. Tel. 20-7439-3118, fax 20-7439-3119, e-mail admin@aba.org.uk, World Wide Web http://www.aba.org.uk. *Admin.* Clare Pedder; *Secy.* John Critchley.

Assn. of Learned and Professional Society Publishers, 1-3 Ship St., Shoreham-by-Sea, West Sussex BN43 5DH, England. Tel. 1275-858-837, World Wide Web http://www.alpsp.org. *Chief Exec.* Audrey McCulloch.

Booktrust, Book House, 45 East Hill, Wandsworth, London SW18 2QZ, England. Tel.

20-8516-2977, fax 20-8516-2978, e-mail query@booktrust.org.uk, World Wide Web http://www.booktrust.org.uk. *CEO* Viv Bird.

Publishers Assn., 29B Montague St., London WC1B 5BW, England. Tel. 20-7691-9191, fax 20-7691-9199, e-mail mail@publishers.org.uk, World Wide Web http://www.publishers.org.uk. *Chief Exec.* Richard Mollet.

Scottish Book Trust, Sandeman House, Trunk's Close, 55 High St., Edinburgh EH1 1SR, Scotland. Tel. 131-524-0160, fax 131-524-0161, e-mail info@scottishbooktrust.com, World Wide Web http://www.scottishbooktrust.com. *CEO* Marc Lambert.

Welsh Books Council (Cyngor Llyfrau Cymru), Castell Brychan, Aberystwyth, Ceredigion SY23 2JB, Wales. Tel. 1970-624-151, fax 1970-625-385, e-mail info@wbc.org.uk, World Wide Web http://www.cllc.org.uk. *Chief Exec.* Elwyn Jones.

Uruguay

Cámara Uruguaya del Libro (Uruguayan Publishers Assn.), Colon 1476, Apdo. 102, 11000 Montevideo. Tel. 2-916-93-74, fax 2-916-76-28, e-mail gerencia@camaradellibro.com.uy, World Wide Web http://www.camaradellibro.com.uy. *Pres.* Alicia Guglielmo.

Venezuela

Cámara Venezolana del Libro (Venezuelan Publishers Assn.), Av. Andrés Bello, Centro Andrés Bello, Torre Oeste 11, piso 11, of. 112-0, Caracas 1050. Tel. 212-793-1347, fax 212-793-1368, e-mail cavelibrocgeneral@gmail.com, World Wide Web http://www.cavelibro.org. *Pres.* Leonardo Ramos.

Zambia

Booksellers Assn. of Zambia, P.O. Box 51109, 10101 Lusaka. Tel./fax 211-255-166, e-mail bpaz@zamtel.zm.

Zimbabwe

Zimbabwe Book Publishers Assn., P.O. Box 3041, Harare. Tel. 4-773-236, fax 4-754-256.

National Information Standards Organization (NISO) Standards

Content and Collection Management

Z39.2-1994 (R2009) Information Interchange Format
ISBN 978-1-880124-08-6

Z39.9-1992 (R2001) International Standard Serial Numbering (ISSN)
ISBN 978-1-880124-12-3

Z39.14-1997 (R2009) Guidelines for Abstracts
ISBN 978-1-880124-31-4

Z39 18-2005 (R2010) Scientific and Technical Reports—Preparation,
Presentation, and Preservation
ISBN 978-1-880124-66-6

Z39.19-2005 (R2010) Guidelines for the Construction, Format, and
Management of Monolingual Controlled Vocabularies
ISBN 978-1-880124-65-9

Z39.23-1997 (R2009) Standard Technical Report Number Format and Creation
ISBN 978-1-880124-30-7

Z39.29-2005 (R2010) Bibliographic References
ISBN 978-1-880124-58-1

Z39.41-1997 (R2009) Printed Information on Spines
ISBN 978-1-880124-32-1

Z39.43-1993 (R2011) Standard Address Number (SAN) for the Publishing
Industry
ISBN 978-1-880124-14-7

Z39.32-1996 (R2012) Information on Microfiche Headers
ISBN 978-1-880124-25-3

Z39.48-1992 (R2009) Permanence of Paper for Publications and Documents in
Libraries and Archives
ISBN 978-1-880124-00-0

Z39.71-2006 (R2011) Holdings Statements for Bibliographic Items
ISBN 978-1-880-124-69-7

Z39.73-1994 (R2012) Single-Tier Steel Bracket Library Shelving
ISBN 978-1-880124-09-3

Z39.78-2000 (R2010) Library Binding
ISBN 978-1-880124-43-7

Z39.84-2005 (R2010) Syntax for the Digital Object Identifier
ISBN 978-1-880124-68-0

Z39.85-2007	Dublin Core Metadata Element Set ISBN 978-1-880124-73-4
Z39.86-2005 (R2012)	Specifications for the Digital Talking Book ISBN 978-1-880124-63-5
Z39.96-2012	Standardized Markup for Journal Articles (JATS) ISBN 978-1-937522-10-0
Z39.98-2012	Authoring and Interchange Framework for Adaptive XML Publishing Specification ISBN 978-1-937522-07-0
ANSI/NISO/ISO 12083-1995 (R2009)	Electronic Manuscript Preparation and Markup ISBN 978-1-880124-20-8

Standards for Discovery to Delivery

Z39.9-2005 (R2010)	Guidelines for the Construction, Format, and Management of Monolingual Controlled Vocabularies ISBN 978-1-880124-65-9
Z39.50-2003 (R2009)	Information Retrieval (Z39.50) Application Service Definition and Protocol Specification ISBN 978-1-880124-55-0
Z39.83-1-2012	NISO Circulation Interchange Part 1: Protocol (NCIP) version 2.02 ISBN 978-1-937522-03-2
Z39.83-2-2012	NISO Circulation Interchange Protocol (NCIP) Part 2: Implementation Profile 1, version 2.02 ISBN 978-1-937522-04-9
Z39.85-2007	Dublin Core Metadata Element Set ISBN 978-1-880124-73-4
Z39.87-2006 (R2011)	Data Dictionary—Technical Metadata for Digital Still Images ISBN 978-1-880124-67-3
Z39.88-2004 (R2010)	The OpenURL Framework for Context-Sensitive Services ISBN 978-1-880124-61-1
Z39.89-2003 (R2009)	The U.S. National Z39.50 Profile for Library Applications ISBN 978-1-880124-60-4

Business Information

Z39.7-2004	Information Services and Use: Metrics and Statistics for Libraries and Information Providers—Data Dictionary ISBN 978-1-880124-72-7
Z39.93-2007	The Standardized Usage Statistics Harvesting Initiative (SUSHI) Protocol ISBN 978-1-880124-70-3

Preservation and Storage

Z39.32-1996 (R2012) Information on Microfiche Headers
ISBN 978-1-880124-25-3
Z39.48-1992 (R2009) Permanence of Paper for Publications and Documents in
Libraries and Archives
ISBN 978-1-880124-00-0
Z39.78-2000 (R2010) Library Binding
ISBN 978-1-880124-43-7

In Development/NISO Initiatives

NISO develops new standards, reports, and best practices on a continuing basis
to support its ongoing standards development program. NISO working groups are
currently developing or exploring the following:

- Digital Bookmarking and Annotation Sharing (NISO Z39.97-201x)
- E-book Accessibility, Discovery Tools and Linking, Distribution, and
Metadata
- Improving OpenURLs Through Analytics (IOTA) (NISO RP-21-201x)
- Institutional Identifiers (I2) (NISO RP-17-201x)
- Knowledge Base and Related Tools (KBART) Phase II (NISO RP-18-201x)
- Open Discovery Initiative (NISO RP-19-201x)
- Presentation and Identification of E-Journals (PIE-J) (NISO RP-16-201x)
- Providing a Test Mode for SUSHI Servers (NISO RP-13-201x)
- Web Resource Synchronization (NISO Z39.99-201x)

NISO Recommended Practices

Best Practices for Designing Web Services in the Library Context (NISO RP-
2006-01)
ISBN 978-1-880124-86-4
Cost of Resource Exchange (CORE) Protocol (NISO RP-10-2010)
ISBN 978-1-880124-84-0
ESPReSSO: Establishing Suggested Practices Regarding Single Sign-On (NISO
RP-11-2011)
ISBN 978-1-880124-98-7
A Framework of Guidance for Building Good Digital Collections, 3rd ed., 2007
ISBN 978-1-880124-74-1
Journal Article Versions (JAV) (NISO RP-8-2008)
ISBN 978-1-880124-79-6
KBART: Knowledge Bases and Related Tools (NISO RP-9-2010)
ISBN 978-1-880124-83-3

NISO Metasearch XML Gateway Implementers Guide (NISO RP-2006-02)
ISBN 978-1-880124-85-7

NISO SUSHI Protocol: COUNTER-SUSHI Implementation Profile (NISO RP-14-2012)
ISBN 978-1-880124-99-4

Online Supplemental Journal Article Materials (NISO RP-15-2013)
ISBN 978-1-937522-12-4

Physical Delivery of Library Resources (NISO RP-12-2012)
ISBN 978-1-937522-01-8

Ranking of Authentication and Access Methods Available to the Metasearch Environment (NISO RP-2005-01)
ISBN 978-1-880124-89-5

RFID in U.S. Libraries (NISO RP-6-2012)
ISBN 978-1-937522-02-5

Search and Retrieval Citation Level Data Elements (NISO RP-2005-03)
ISBN 978-1-880124-87-1

Search and Retrieval Results Set Metadata (NISO RP-2005-02)
ISBN 978-1-880124-88-8

SERU: A Shared Electronic Resource Understanding (NISO RP-7-2012)
ISBN 978-1-937522-08-7

NISO Technical Reports

Environmental Guidelines for the Storage of Paper Records (NISO TR01-1995) by William K. Wilson
ISBN 1-880124-21-1

Guidelines for Indexes and Related Information Retrieval Devices (NISO TR02-1997) by James D. Anderson
ISBN 1-880124-36-X

Guidelines for Alphabetical Arrangement of Letters and Sorting of Numerals and Other Symbols (NISO TR03-1999) by Hans H. Wellisch
ISBN 1-880124-41-6

Networked Reference Services: Question/Answer Transaction Protocol (NISO TR04-2006)
ISBN 978-1-880124-71-0

Other NISO Publications

The Case for New Economic Models to Support Standardization by Clifford Lynch
ISBN 978-1-880124-90-1

The Exchange of Serials Subscription Information by Ed Jones
ISBN 978-1-880124-91-8

Information Standards Quarterly (*ISQ*) (NISO quarterly open access magazine)
ISSN 1041-0031

Internet, Interoperability and Standards—Filling the Gaps by Janifer Gatenby
ISBN 978-1-880124-92-5

Issues in Crosswalking Content Metadata Standards by Margaret St. Pierre and
William P. LaPlant
ISBN 978-1-880124-93-2

*Making Good on the Promise of ERM: A Standards and Best Practices Discus-
sion Paper* by the ERM Data Standards and Best Practices Review Steering
Committee
ISBN 978-1-9357522-00-1

Metadata Demystified: A Guide for Publishers by Amy Brand, Frank Daly, and
Barbara Meyers
ISBN 978-1-880124-59-8

The Myth of Free Standards: Giving Away the Farm by Andrew N. Bank
ISBN 978-1-880124-94-9

NISO Newsline (free monthly e-newsletter)
ISSN 1559-2774

NISO Working Group Connection (free quarterly supplement to Newsline)
Patents and Open Standards by Priscilla Caplan
ISBN 978-1-880124-95-6

The RFP Writer's Guide to Standards for Library Systems by Cynthia Hodgson
ISBN 978-1-880124-57-4

Streamlining Book Metadata Workflow by Judy Luther
ISBN 978-1-880124-82-6

Understanding Metadata
ISBN 978-1-880124-62-8

*Up and Running: Implementing Z39.50: Proceedings of a Symposium Sponsored
by the State Library of Iowa,* edited by Sara L. Randall
ISBN 978-1-880124-33-8

Z39.50: A Primer on the Protocol
ISBN 978-1-880124-35-2

Z39.50 Implementation Experiences
ISBN 978-1-880124-51-2

NISO standards are available online at http://www.niso.org/standards. Recommended Practices, Technical Reports, White Papers, and other publications are
available on the NISO website at http://www.niso.org/publications.

For more information, contact NISO, 3600 Clipper Mill Rd., Suite 302, Baltimore, MD 21211. Tel. 301-654-2512, fax 410-685-5278, e-mail nisohq@niso.org,
World Wide Web http://www.niso.org.

Calendar, 2013–2022

The list below contains information on association meetings or promotional events that are, for the most part, national or international in scope. State and regional library association meetings are also included. To confirm the starting or ending date of a meeting, which may change after the *Library and Book Trade Almanac* has gone to press, contact the association directly. Addresses of library and book trade associations are listed in Part 6 of this volume. For information on additional book trade and promotional events, see *Literary Market Place* and *International Literary Market Place,* published by Information Today, Inc., and other library and book trade publications such as *Library Journal, School Library Journal,* and *Publishers Weekly. American Libraries,* published by the American Library Association (ALA), maintains an online calendar at http://americanlibrariesmagazine.org/calendar, and ALA keeps a separate calendar at http://www.ala.org/ala/conferences events/afficalendar/index.cfm. An Information Today events calendar can be found at http://www.infotoday.com/calendar.shtml.

2013

June

2–5	Semantic Technology and Business Conference (SemTechBiz)	San Francisco
3–5	New Jersey Library Assn.	Atlantic City
4–7	International Conference on Qualitative and Quantitative Methods in Libraries	Rome, Italy
5–7	Society for Scholarly Publishing	San Francisco
5–7	Specialized Information Publishers Assn. (SIPA)	Washington, DC
6–8	Canadian Assn. for Information Science	Victoria, BC
9–11	Special Libraries Assn.	San Diego
10–13	Assn. of Christian Librarians	San Diego
12–14	Assn. of Canadian Publishers	Toronto
13–14	International Symposium on Library Services for Children and Young Adults	Seoul, Korea
16–19	Assn. of Jewish Libraries	Houston
18–19	Streaming Forum 2013	London, England
19–22	American Theological Library Assn.	Charlotte, NC
19–23	Seoul International Book Fair	Seoul, Korea

June 2013 *(cont.)*

21–23	Cape Town Book Fair	Cape Town, South Africa
27–7/2	American Library Assn. Annual Conference	Chicago

July

2–3	CILIP (Chartered Institute of Library and Information Professionals)	Manchester, England
4–7	Tokyo International Book Fair	Tokyo, Japan
10–13	National Association for Government Archives and Records Administrators (NAGARA)	Indianapolis
13–16	American Assn. of Law Libraries	Seattle
17–23	Hong Kong Book Fair	Hong Kong
21–24	American Assn. of Law Libraries	Boston
22–26	Joint Conference on Digital Libraries	Indianapolis
28–30	Arkansas Assn. of School Librarians	Little Rock

August

11–17	Society of American Archivists	New Orleans
14–16	Pacific Northwest Library Assn.	Boise
15–17	Americas Conference on Information Systems (AMCIS)	Chicago
17–23	IFLA World Library and Information Congress (WLIC)	Singapore
28–9/1	Beijing International Book Fair	Beijing, China
29–9/8	Rio Book Fair	Rio de Janeiro, Brazil

September

2–5	International Conference on Preservation of Digital Objects	Lisbon, Portugal
5–10	Moscow International Book Fair	Moscow, Russia
9–11	IEEE International Conference on Healthcare Informatics	Philadelphia
10–11	WebSearch University 2013	Washington, DC
11–13	Assn. of Learned and Professional Society Publishers International Conference	Birmingham, England
11–14	Kentucky Library Assn./Kentucky School Library Assn.	Louisville
25–27	Mountain Plains Library Assn./North Dakota Library Assn./South Dakota Library Assn.	Sioux Falls
25–27	Virginia Library Assn.	Williamsburg
25–28	New York Library Assn.	Niagara Falls

| 26–29 | Göteborg Book Fair—Bok & Bibliotek | Gothenburg, Sweden |

October

2–4	Madrid International Book Fair	Madrid, Spain
2–4	Missouri Library Assn.	St. Louis
6–8	Arkansas Library Assn.	Hot Springs
8	STM Frankfurt Conference	Frankfurt, Germany
9–11	Assn. of Bookmobile and Outreach Services	Baton Rouge
9–11	Ohio Library Council	Sandusky
9–11	West Virginia Library Assn.	Shepherdstown
9–11	Kansas Library Assn.	Topeka
9–11	Nebraska Library Assn./Nebraska School Library Assn.	Kearney
9–13	Frankfurt Book Fair	Frankfurt, Germany
15–16	Internet Librarian International	London, England
15–17	Illinois Library Assn.	Chicago
15–18	North Carolina Library Assn.	Winston-Salem
16–18	Iowa Library Assn.	Coralville
16–18	Michigan Library Assn.	Lansing
17–18	Nevada Library Assn.	Reno
17–19	Colorado Assn. of Libraries	Loveland
20–22	New England Library Assn./Maine Library Assn.	Portland
20–23	Indiana Federation of Libraries	Indianapolis
20–23	Pennsylvania Library Assn.	Seven Springs
22–25	European Conference on Information Literacy (ECIL 2013)	Istanbul, Turkey
22–25	Wisconsin Library Assn.	Green Bay
28–30	Internet Librarian 2013	Monterey, CA
30–11/3	Helsinki Book Fair	Helsinki, Finland

November

1–6	American Society for Information Science & Technology (ASIS&T)	Montreal
3–5	California Library Assn.	Long Beach
6–8	KMWorld 2013	Washington, DC
7–10	Library and Information Technology Association (LITA) Forum	Louisville
13–15	Southeastern Library Assn./South Carolina Library Assn.	Greenville
13–17	American Assn. of School Librarians	Hartford, CT

November 2013 *(cont.)*

19–20	Streaming Media West	Huntington Beach, CA
21–24	Buch Wien International Book Fair	Vienna, Austria
30–12/8	Guadalajara International Book Fair	Guadalajara, Mexico

December

9–11	International Conference on Asia-Pacific Digital Libraries	Bangalore, India

2014

January

24–28	American Library Assn. Midwinter Meeting	Philadelphia

March

11–15	Public Library Assn.	Indianapolis

April

8–11	Texas Library Assn.	San Antonio
30–5/2	Tennessee Library Assn.	Murfreesboro
30–5/2	Washington Library Assn.	Wenatchee

May

7–9	Maryland Library Assn.	Ocean City
29–31	BookExpo America (BEA)	New York

June

26–7/1	American Library Assn. Annual Conference	Las Vegas

September

28–10/1	Pennsylvania Library Assn.	Lancaster

October

1–3	South Dakota Library Assn.	Pierre
7–10	Missouri Library Assn.	Columbia
8–10	Nebraska Library Assn.	South Sioux City
15–17	Iowa Library Assn.	Cedar Rapids
16–18	Mississippi Library Assn.	Biloxi

| 19–21 | New England Library Assn. | Boxborough, MA |
| 29–31 | Kansas Library Assn. | Wichita |

November

| 4–7 | Wisconsin Library Assn. | Wisconsin Dells |
| 6–9 | New York Library Assn. | Saratoga Springs |

2015

January

| 23–27 | American Library Assn. Midwinter Meeting | Chicago |

March

| 25–28 | Assn. of College and Research Libraries | Portland, Oregon |

April

| 14–17 | Texas Library Assn. | Austin |

May

| 6–8 | Maryland Library Assn. | Ocean City |
| 28–30 | BookExpo America (BEA) | New York |

June

| 25–30 | American Library Assn. Annual Conference | San Francisco |

October

| 14–16 | Iowa Library Assn. | Council Bluffs |
| 20–23 | North Carolina Library Assn. | Greensboro |

2016

January

| 22–26 | American Library Assn. Midwinter Meeting | Boston |

April

| 19–22 | Texas Library Assn. | Houston |

May

| | BookExpo America (BEA) | Chicago |

June 2016

23–28   American Library Assn. Annual Conference   Orlando

October

12–14   Iowa Library Assn.   Dubuque

2017

January

20–24   American Library Assn. Midwinter Meeting   Atlanta

March

29–4/1   Assn. of College and Research Libraries   Nashville

April

19-22   Texas Library Assn.   San Antonio

June

22–27   American Library Assn. Annual Conference   Chicago

2018

January

19–23   American Library Assn. Midwinter Meeting   Los Angeles

March

20–24   Public Library Assn.   Philadelphia

April

10–13   Texas Library Assn.   Dallas

June

21–26   American Library Assn. Annual Conference   New Orleans

2019

January

25–29   American Library Assn. Midwinter Meeting   Seattle

April

2–5   Texas Library Assn.   Austin

June

27–7/2   American Library Assn. Annual Conference   New York

2020
January

24–27   American Library Assn. Midwinter Meeting   Philadelphia

March

31–4/3   Texas Library Assn.   Houston

June

27–7/2   American Library Assn. Annual Conference   To be announced

2021
January

22–26   American Library Assn. Midwinter Meeting   Indianapolis

April

13–16   Texas Library Assn.   San Antonio

June

24–29   American Library Assn. Annual Conference   San Francisco

2022
January

           American Library Assn. Midwinter Meeting   To be announced

April

13–16   Texas Library Assn.   San Antonio

June

23–28   American Library Assn. Annual Conference   To be announced

Acronyms

A

AALL. American Association of Law
Libraries

AAP. Association of American Publishers

AASL. American Association of School
Librarians

ABA. American Booksellers Association

ABOS. Association of Bookmobile and
Outreach Services

ACRL. Association of College and Research
Libraries

AIIP. Association of Independent
Information Professionals

AILA. American Indian Library Association

AJL. Association of Jewish Libraries

ALA. American Library Association

ALCTS. Association for Library Collections
and Technical Services

ALIC. National Archives and Records
Administration, Archives Library
Information Center

ALISE. Association for Library and
Information Science Education

ALNs. Networks and networking,
asynchronous learning networks

ALS. National Center for Education
Statistics, Academic Library Survey

ALSC. Association for Library Service to
Children

ALTAFF. Association of Library Trustees,
Advocates, Friends, and Foundations

AMMLA. American Merchant Marine
Library Association

APALA. Asian/Pacific American Librarians
Association

ARL. Association of Research Libraries

ARLIS/NA. Art Libraries Society of North
America

ARSL. Association for Rural and Small
Libraries

ASCLA. Association of Specialized and
Cooperative Library Agencies

ATLA. American Theological Library
Association

B

BARD. Internet, Braille and Audio Reading
Download

BCALA. Black Caucus of the American
Library Association

BiB. Conferences and seminars, Books in
Browsers

BLC. Brody Learning Commons

BSA. Bibliographical Society of America

C

CACUL. Canadian Association of College
and University Libraries

CAIS. Canadian Association for Information
Science

CALA. Chinese American Librarians
Association

CAPL. Canadian Association of Public
Libraries

CARL. Canadian Association of Research
Libraries

CASLIS. Canadian Association of Special
Libraries and Information Services

CLA. Canadian Library Association

CLIR. Council on Library and Information
Resources

CLTA. Canadian Library Trustees
Association

CNI. Coalition for Networked Information

COSLA. Chief Officers of State Library
Agencies

CSLA. Church and Synagogue Library
Association

CWA. Crime Writers' Association

D

DICE. Software, Digital Image
　　Conformance Environment software
DLF. Digital Library Federation
DPLA. Digital Public Library of America
DRM. Digital rights management
DTIC. Defense Technical Information
　　Center

E

EAR. National Technical Information
　　Service, Export Administration
　　Regulations
EDB. National Technical Information
　　Service, Energy Science and
　　Technology Database
EMIERT. American Library Association,
　　Ethnic and Multicultural Information
　　and Exchange Round Table
ESEA. Elementary and Secondary Education
　　Act

F

FAA. FISA Amendments Act
FAFLRT. American Library Association,
　　Federal and Armed Forces Librarians
　　Round Table
FDLP. Government Printing Office, Federal
　　Depository Library Program
FDsys. FDsys (Federal Digital System)
FEDRIP. National Technical Information
　　Service, FEDRIP (Federal Research
　　in Progress Database)
FIAF. International Federation of Film
　　Archives
FRPAA. Federal Research Public Access Act

G

GLBT. American Library Association, Gay,
　　Lesbian, Bisexual, and Transgender
　　Round Table
GLIN. Global Legal Information Network
GODORT. American Library Association,
　　Government Documents Round Table

GPO. Government Printing Office
GSU. Georgia State University

I

IAALD. International Association of
　　Agricultural Information Specialists
IACs. Defense Technical Information
　　Center, Information Analysis Centers
IALL. International Association of Law
　　Libraries
IAML. International Association of
　　Music Libraries, Archives, and
　　Documentation Centres
IASL. International Association of School
　　Librarians
ICA. International Council on Archives
ICBS. International Committee of the Blue
　　Shield
IFLA. International Federation of Library
　　Associations and Institutions
ILS. Government Printing Office, Integrated
　　Library System
IMLS. Institute of Museum and Library
　　Services
ISBN. International Standard Book Number
ISO. International Organization for
　　Standardization
ISOO. National Archives and Records
　　Administration, Information Security
　　Oversight Office
ISSN. International Standard Serial Number

L

LCA. Library Copyright Alliance
LCDP. Association of Research Libraries,
　　Leadership and Career Development
　　Program
LCI. Leading Change Institute
LEED. Library buildings, LEED (Leadership
　　in Energy and Environmental Design)
　　certification
LHRT. American Library Association,
　　Library History Round Table
LIS. Library and information science
LITA. Library and Information Technology
　　Association
LJ. Library Journal
LLAMA. Library Leadership and
　　Management Association

LRRT. American Library Association, Library Research Round Table

LSCM. Government Printing Office, Library Services and Content Management

LSP National Center for Education Statistics, Library Statistics Program

LSTA. Library Services and Technology Act

M

MLA. Medical Library Association; Music Library Association

MOOCs. E-learning, MOOCs (massively open online courses)

N

NAGARA. National Association of Government Archives and Records Administrators

NAL. National Agricultural Library

NARA. National Archives and Records Administration

NCBI. National Center for Biotechnology Information

NCES. National Center for Education Statistics

NDC. National Archives and Records Administration, National Declassification Center

NDIIPP. National Digital Information Infrastructure and Preservation Program

NDNP. Newspapers, National Digital Newspaper Program

NEH. National Endowment for the Humanities

NFAIS. National Federation of Advanced Information Services

NISO. National Information Standards Organization

NLE. National Library of Education

NLM. National Library of Medicine

NMRT. American Library Association, New Members Round Table

NTIS. National Technical Information Service

NTRL. National Technical Information Service, National Technical Reports Library

O

ORI. Owners' Rights Initiative

OWF. Operation Warfighter

P

PLA. Public Library Association

PTDLA. Patent and Trademark Depository Library Association

R

RDA. Library of Congress, Resource Description and Access

RL/RC. National Library of Education, Research Library/Reference Center

RUSA. Reference and User Services Association

S

SAA. Society of American Archivists

SAN. Standard Address Number

SIIA. Software and Information Industry Association

SLA. Special Libraries Association

SPARC. SPARC (Scholarly Publishing and Academic Resources Coalition)

SRRT. American Library Association, Social Responsibilities Round Table

SRS. National Technical Information Service, Selected Research Service

SSP. Society for Scholarly Publishing

STEM. Education, STEM (science, technology, engineering, and mathematics)

StLA. State libraries and library agencies, IMLS State Library Agencies

T

TLA. Theatre Library Association

U

ULC. Urban Libraries Council

V

VHP. History, Veterans History Project

W

WDL. World Digital Library
WIPO. World Intellectual Property
  Organization

WISE. Web-based Information Science
  Education Consortium
WNC. World News Connection
WRP. Workforce Recruitment Program

Y

YALSA. Young Adult Library Services
  Association

Index of Organizations

Please note that many cross-references refer to entries in the Subject Index.

Subject Index

Please note that many cross-references refer to entries in the Index of Organizations.

G

H

I